Project Finance, BOT Projects and Risk

PROJECT FINANCE, BOT PROJECTS AND RISK

By Jeffrey Delmon

KLUWER LAW
INTERNATIONAL

A C.I.P. Catalogue record for this book is available from the Library of Congress.

ISBN 90 411 23652

Published by Kluwer Law International,
P.O. Box 85889, 2508 CN The Hague, The Netherlands.
sales@kluwerlaw.com
http://www.kluwerlaw.com

Sold and distributed in North, Central and South America
by Aspen Publishers, Inc.
7201 McKinney Circle, Frederick, MD 21704, USA

Sold and distributed in all other countries by
Extenza-Turpin
Stratton Business Park
Pegasus Drive, Biggleswade, Bedfordshire
SG18 8 TQ, United Kingdom

Printed on acid-free paper

Printed in The Netherlands

Ad majorem dei gloriam

Acknowledgments

I would like to thank Fred Ottavy of the Agence Française de Développement, Victoria Rigby of Veolia Environment, Falko Sellner, Trevor Taylor of Biwater and Richard Drummond of ECGD for their review of this text. I am also grateful to my colleagues at Allen & Overy for their support and advice, in particular Graham Vinter, Tom Levine (Telecommunications and Outsourcing), Steven Blanch (Power) and Fahad Doha (Oil and Gas).

Leah Horstmann made the whole thing beautiful and orderly; Philippa Smart did a stellar job organising the index and the glossary; and Roy Freke and Helen Sonnenthal kept a watch over my grammar.

Chapters 1 and 2 of this text form part of a PhD thesis that the author is currently pursuing at King's College, London.

And, as always, to Piglet and Roo …

Table of Contents

Detailed Table of Contents

Preface

The state of infrastructure, and public access to essential services, particularly in developing countries, is unacceptably poor. The world's population is growing faster than the provision of new infrastructure, resulting in an aggregate reduction of the proportion of the population receiving services in real terms.[1] We are putting unnecessary pressure on precious natural resources at a rate that seems unsustainable.

Our modern world has failed to reduce poverty to the extent anticipated. One critical cause of poverty is lack of access to infrastructure. Without transport, the poor are without the mobility needed to access jobs; goods and services are more difficult to ship and are therefore more expensive. Without electricity, medical facilities are limited and industry cannot grow to its full potential. Without water and sanitation the poor are often sick, are unable to hold down jobs or get an education, and die young.

The international community is increasingly aware of the importance of sustainable development. In 2000, the UN set the Millennium Development Goals, and reconfirmed them in 2002 at the World Summit on Sustainable Development in Johannesburg.[2]

However, public treasuries are short of resources, and are unable or unwilling to make the investment necessary to bring infrastructure up to necessary levels of efficiency and coverage. In the midst of this growing need, we have witnessed a reduction in overseas development assistance over the last 20 years, and though private investment grew from $50 billion in 1990 to over $300 billion in 1997, it has been in a steady state of decline over the past few years.

One of the solutions available to provide and improve infrastructure and its management is private sector participation. The private sector has many of the project management skills that can improve the efficiency of procurement, construction and operation of infrastructure. The private sector also has access to funds in addition to those available to national treasuries. One of the key issues limiting the extent to which the private sector has to date provided a comprehensive solution to the shortage of infrastructure and utilities is the assessment and allocation of risk.

Risk is the probability of an event occurring and the consequences of its occurrence.[3] Where infrastructure is concerned, the event in question will

---

[1] For an example from the water sector, see Guerquin, Ahmed, Hua, Ikeda, Ozbilen and Schuttelaar, World Water Actions: Making Water Flow for All (March 2003).

[2] www.un.org/millenniumgoals

[3] Megens, "Construction Risk and Project Finance – Risk Allocation as Viewed by Contractors and Financiers" [1997] ICLR 5 at 7.

generally have a negative effect on the project, either increasing cost, delaying completion, reducing performance or possibly rendering the project itself impracticable.   Where the construction and long-term management of infrastructure is at stake, risk becomes an even more important commodity. Probably one of the best examples of this phenomenon is a project financed Build-Operate-Transfer ("BOT") project, where risk allocation is very closely analysed and essential to the success of the project.

This text will examine risk and infrastructure, and how risk is managed in BOT projects. It will also look at how projects in different industrial sectors (e.g. water, electricity and transportation) address risk in different ways.

BOT projects are large and complex undertakings, usually involving major infrastructure such as roadways and power plants. Each project will be different. The title of this book makes reference to BOT. For ease of reference, the term "BOT" will be used as a generic term for all of its variants such as Build-Own-Operate, Build-Own-Operate-Transfer, Design-Construct-Manage-Finance and Design-Build-Finance-Operate.

BOT projects have had a relatively chequered experience over the last few years. The failure of Enron raised concerns about on/off balance sheet accounting (one of the key benefits of BOT projects). There have been suggestions that off balance sheet accounting shall be made more difficult or should disappear entirely. The electricity sector has also had serious problems with mounting debt burdens of most of the key investors, loss of confidence, reductions in electricity prices and lack of capital to invest in major projects. Private Finance Initiative ("PFI") and Public Private Partnership ("PPP") projects in the United Kingdom have continued in strength, though deal size appears to be dropping. There have been particular voices of discontent among labour unions and certain politicians about cost and distortion caused by PFI. They too have challenged whether PFI in the United Kingdom should be counted in the Public Sector Borrowing Requirement to take account of the liabilities and obligations undertaken by the public sector.

This book provides an introduction to the contractual structure which underlies a BOT project and how that structure allocates risk amongst the participants in the project; a description of man's relationship with risk assessment; various aspects of a BOT project (e.g. tendering procedures) that influence risk allocation; and a review of some of the key risk issues that arise in different sectors. It represents personal experience in the field and collective shared wisdom from other practitioners. The market for project financing and the risks which parties will accept vary from day to day, from place to place and from project to project. This text is not a definitive guide to risk allocation and market practice, but rather an introduction to the issues which arise in such contractual structures.

For the sake of consistency, I have made the following assumptions.

  ➢ The concession is issued by a public sector grantor.

  ➢ The project uses a separate concession agreement, offtake purchase agreement and input supply agreement.

> ➤ The lenders provide project financing.

Due to the nature of the subject matter of this text, a number of terms of art will be used throughout. These terms are defined in the glossary, which may be found at the end of the text.

This book will look first at the subject of risk, an often misunderstood subject. To this extent, chapter 1 introduces risk, how it is assessed and allocated, and chapter 2 discusses theories on the efficient allocation of risk. In order to address the broad range of issues encountered in a BOT project, general issues will be addressed first, followed by more specific issues consistent with particular sectors. The relationship between the parties in a BOT project and the relevant documents is discussed in chapter 3. Chapter 4 discusses issues specific to financing a project. The demands of bankability are discussed in chapter 5. Chapter 6 sets out risk allocation in a project, with interface risk discussed in chapter 7. Chapters 8-10 and 12-14 analyse the project agreements, addressing key issues and provisions. Issues common across these various project contracts are set out in chapter 15, while issues specific to splitting turnkey construction contracts are addressed in chapter 11. Tendering procedures are reviewed in chapter 16, while chapters 17-22 review issues specific to projects in the power, transport, oil and gas, telecommunications and water and sanitation sectors and outsourcing projects. These final chapters review some of the key technical and commercial issues specific to these different sectors and the associated risks that will need to be assessed, allocated and managed.

Chapter 1

Risk, Risk Assessment and Risk Allocation

He who doesn't take risks, doesn't drink champagne.

Alexander Lebed (1950-2000),
Russian General and politician

Risk is an essential part of life. It pervades everything we do, every decision we make and every path we choose. Each choice involves a consideration of risk, from what to wear in the morning to whom to marry and whether or not to wear your seat belt. Risk is both a hazard and an opportunity.

When considering an act, an individual first assesses the risk involved through the information provided via his senses. This initial assessment is then tempered by the individual's sensory and intellectual filter, leading him to his final choice between avoiding the risk, accepting it or allocating it elsewhere.

One might say that risk is the likelihood of the occurrence of an event or circumstance which will have an impact on a transaction. But this definition may lead one to think that risk is a simple process of cause and effect. Risk is:

> ➤ borne of change and uncertainty. If we lived in a static world, or if we had all knowledge and all understanding, there would be no risk;

> ➤ an essential aspect of decision-making and the structure of a commercial transaction;

> ➤ in a constant state of change. The riskiness of a set of circumstances can only truly be measured at any one instant in time. Once that instant in time has passed, the riskiness of that set of circumstances will need to be revised, since the relevant circumstances will have changed. Either the moment for the risk to arise has passed and the risk has arisen or it has not arisen, as the case may be. Or, more information has been obtained or more uncertainty has arisen in relation to that risk. The individual assessing the risk may also have changed his attitude towards the risk;

> ➤ an extremely difficult thing to define but, as with obscenity, we know it when we see it.[4] Certain people see it more often than others – "there is no activity, process or product that is free of risk";[5] and

> ➤ personal assessment, "perception", rather than an absolutely objective measure. Human reaction is an integral and inextricable element of risk assessment. "[Risk] is not a thing, it is a way of thinking, and a highly artificial contrivance at that."[6]

Risk assessment and allocation is a critical focus of any BOT project. Bankability (as discussed in chapter 5) is a question of risk allocation that provides the lenders with sufficient comfort and security. This book looks at risk allocation in BOT projects generally (chapters 6 and 7). Given the importance of risk in a BOT project, this chapter will analyse risk, how we understand and assess risk and why we react differently to risks. Later discussions of risk and risk allocation should be read in the context of this chapter. Theories and mechanisms in pursuit of the efficient allocation of risk are discussed in chapter 2, and will need to be considered in the context of this chapter.[7]

1.1   Risk Assessment

We can isolate two basic influences on how risk is measured and perceived. One is the quantitative measure of risk: the assessment of the probability of its occurrence and the likely impact it will have. The other is the qualitative measure, or the perception of the risk, based on an individual's past experiences, personal bias and intuition. Each is a valid part of risk assessment and will be described separately in this text, although in practice it may not be possible to truly separate these two aspects of risk assessment. To a certain extent, it is not relevant to ask, when analysing risk assessment, whether the assessment is accurate.[8] Even if no risk exists, the assessment affects the individual's actions and is therefore an important consideration. The assessment of a risk is more relevant than the risk itself.

1.1.1   Quantitative risk assessment

Quantitative risk assessment is comprised of two components. First, it is the likelihood of the occurrence of an adverse event measured in terms of its probability, often mathematically derived from its past frequency of occurrence: for example, the risk that an earthquake will occur in a given area over a specified period. Secondly, risk is the probable consequence of the occurrence of the event

---

4   Miller v California 413 U.S.15.
5   National Academy of Sciences, Risk Assessment in the Federal Government: Managing the Process (1983).
6   Douglas, Risk and Blame: Essays in Cultural Theory at 46 (1992).
7   The analysis set out in chapters 1 and 2 forms part of a PhD thesis that the author is currently pursuing at King's College, London; see also Delmon, "Tis a Risky World We Live In" [2004] ICLR.
8   Brehmer, "The Psychology of Risk" in Singleton and Hovden (eds), Risk and Decisions at 25 (1987).

measured in terms of its potential magnitude: for example, the effect an earthquake would have on a given property. Risk can therefore be measured as the probability of a cost incurred: not just monetary cost, but also the allocation of resources, reputation, management time, overhead costs and the emotional or physiological impact of the occurrence of a risk.

The variety of costs and consequences that must be measured make it difficult to weigh these consequences. For practical purposes, a common denominator should be identified to help calculate a single measure of consequences and compare those consequences with other risks. It is usually helpful to monetise risk (given the quasi-universal appreciation of money as an indicator of value), allocating a monetary value to the impact a risk will have and the likelihood of its occurrence. The monetary valuation of risk is often achieved by applying two measures: the willingness to pay (what the person would be willing to pay for the benefit) and the willingness to accept the potential losses (what the loser would be prepared to accept as compensation). This measure (the cost-benefit analysis) is, however, extremely difficult to make.

1.1.2   Qualitative risk assessment

Our experiences are based on cognition of single events. Those events are not necessarily related one to another, yet we extrapolate from a singular experience and create an abstraction which we connect with or relate to future experiences. We take an isolated concept from a single event or experience and universalise that concept for application in other circumstances or situations. In most cases, the associated event or circumstance is somehow related (or at least we perceive it to be related) to the original single event or experience in order to justify this abstraction. However, the method of association of the new event with the original event is subject entirely to the perception of the individual.

Once the concept is universalised and a related event is identified, that concept must be applied to the related event. The difficulty in this process revolves around the application of an abstraction to an entirely separate and independent event. This application will require an adjustment of the abstraction to compensate for contextual and factual differences between the original event and the related event. This adjustment will rely heavily on assessment of the related event, understanding of the original event and the ability to identify the differences between the two.

Various philosophers have struggled with these issues. The associationalists, for example Hume, Bain, Mill, Reid and Spencer, consider knowledge to be subject to sensory perception and experience. There is a very direct relationship between assessment of information, perception and experience. Though this view takes into consideration the filter applied by each individual to a given perception, it is limited to direct experience, without taking into consideration the creative aspect of association of an experience with unrelated circumstances.

Plato, and later St Augustine, viewed thought and ideas as independent of intellectual knowledge or experience. Ideas are drawn independently from the soul. This view diverges significantly from that of the associationalists and sees knowledge as external to an individual's perception or experiences. It places emphasis on the particular characteristics of an individual by associating them with external/spiritual influences but ignoring the contribution of learning.

Thomas Aquinas saw perception as both receptive and creative. The individual appreciates an object or occurrence as it is seen but also understands that object or occurrence through the individual's aggregate experience or education. This represents a mid-point between the associationalists and Plato by acknowledging inspiration as well as some of the external influences that contribute to the creative interpretation of information by an individual.

The distinction between the perception of a single event or piece of information and the extrapolation of this perception to an interpretation (knowledge) falls within the Thomistic identification of on the one hand a simple perception and on the other a compensational and divisional judgement or reasoning. It is the process of judgement that allows an individual to assess a risk based on its perceived merits, and to categorise that risk amongst all the other risks perceived by that individual and related to the same event or circumstances. This allows for the filter that is applied by an individual to an assessment and the construct of that filter to flow from the characteristics of the individual perceiving the event.

This chapter discusses separately the two principal characteristics of risk assessment: quantitative (mathematically/scientifically measurable risk) and qualitative (the application by an individual of his specific biases that create an individualised filter when assessing risk). This qualitative assessment is borne out of our human condition, and limitations on the information available to make an objective quantitative assessment of risk affect an individual rather like static affects a radio frequency or background noise interrupts a phone conversation, and will therefore be referred to here as "risk noise".

1.2   Quantitative Assessment

Risk can be measured. The mathematical or scientific approach to risk assessment involves the calculation of the likelihood of a given event and the possible impact of that event. These elements of risk are often subject to measurement, given a complete understanding of all potential causes of the event, the probability of their occurrence and the probable impact of the event if it were to happen.

As the old joke goes, a doctor tells a patient that he has good news and bad news. The patient asks for the bad news first. "Well, you have a fatal disease, we can operate, but nine out of ten people die from the operation." "Wow, that's bad," says the patient, "what is the good news?" "Well, I have done the operation nine times and all nine people died, so you have nothing to worry about!"

The very fact that man can contemplate the quantification of risk through mathematical theory of probability is in itself a revolution. The following is a short history of the quantitative analysis of risk as a mathematical and scientific field of study.[9]

1.2.1 Probability and standard mean variation

The measure of probability, the likelihood of the occurrence of an event based on past frequency of occurrence, is something we take for granted. We use statistics to prove and disprove odds for gambling and forecasts for investing. But it was not always so. Some of the earliest evidence of reliance on the use of probability was the Hebrew practice of casting lots to make decisions, as evidenced in the Old Testament. In ancient Athens the selection of rulers was made by drawing lots amongst a group of individuals who satisfied the requisite qualifications. For the Greeks, the use of the lot was probably not a reflection of their trust in some higher power that would guide their choice, but rather to avoid political intrigue in relation to the elections.[10] However, these examples do not give evidence of any understanding or measure of probability.

One of the first examples of the manipulation of the concept of probability was for more spiritual purposes. Arnobius the Elder, in the 4th century, wrote "Against the Pagans" as evidence of his new-found Christian faith.[11] Arnobius set forth what is likely the first effort at using probability theory (although he would not have defined it as such) to argue for adherence to the Christian faith. The individual's risk choice was whether to become a Christian or to remain a pagan. The risk to be managed by the individual related to whether or not God exists and whether that individual would end up in a less desirable position in the afterlife.

Amongst the earliest thinkers to address specifically the subject of probability was Cardano (1501-1576) in his book "Games of Chance". He identified the concept of probability as "weighted possibility", but never addressed risk nor identified the concept of "probability".[12]

This section examines some of the earliest developments in probability and the quantitative analysis of risk from some of the greatest mathematical minds the world has known.

1.2.1.1 Pascal

Possibly the grandfather of the study of risk, Blaise Pascal, a 17th century monk and sometime mathematician, was born in 1623. A child prodigy, Pascal mastered Euclidean geometry by the age of 13 and was attending weekly meetings of

---

[9] For a more exhaustive discussion of this issue, Bernstein, Against the Gods: The Remarkable Story of Risk (1998) provides an interesting and very readable account of the history of quantitative risk assessment. See also Royal Society, Risk: Analysis, Perception and Management (1992).

[10] Cohen, Behaviour in Uncertainty and its Social Implications at 148 (1964).

[11] Covello and Mumpower, "Risk Analysis and Risk Management: A Historical Perspective" in Covello, Menks and Mumpower (eds), Risk Evaluation and Management at 519 (1986).

[12] Cohen (1964) supra note 10 at 150.

France's top mathematicians by age 14. As a teenager, he wrote an essay on conics, the study of the curvature of cones, and at 18 he invented the world's first mechanical calculating machine, to help his father who was a tax collector. Pascal, however, followed a higher calling and struggled throughout his life with the choice between the worldly passion of mathematics and the calling of his order, the Jansenists, to the abandonment of all worldly pleasure. Pascal eventually abandoned mathematics, but not before addressing some of the most challenging mathematical issues of his day.

Pascal applied his considerable talent to the issue of probability when Chevalier de Mere, a brilliant mathematician, arrogant nobleman and gambling addict, proposed a centuries-old brain-teaser – the "problem of the points". Two players are in the middle of a game of balla, winner-takes-all, and one of them is winning. However, the game is interrupted. How can the prize-money be divided equally between the two? An even split would be inequitable for the winning player, but a winner-takes-all solution would deny the loser the opportunity to come back and win the match. The question is one of probability. What are the odds of one person winning the game?

In a society with little concept of risk, much less probability, Pascal's challenge was enormous. To put Pascal's quandary in context, Ross notes that William Shakespeare, an approximate contemporary of Pascal, never once uses the word "risk" in his writings. The closest concept he uses is the term "hazard". In the Merchant of Venice (Act 2, Scene VII), the Prince of Morocco notes: "Men that hazard all, do it in hope of fair advantages." The term "hazard" makes reference to a source of danger that poses a threat to humans. "Risk" as contemplated by Pascal is a wholly more complex concept that refers to the possibility or probability of that hazard occurring.[13]

Pascal contacted Pierre de Fermat, a lawyer in Toulouse and a fellow mathematical genius. Out of that collaboration, Pascal developed Pascal's Triangle and identified that the probability of an outcome could be established mathematically. Pascal later used this same revelation in his writings, proving the value of his Christian faith by probability theory: a classic example of risk-decision. What is the risk of unbelief? Is unbelief worth the potential consequences of eternal damnation?

1.2.1.2   Graunt

In 1660, in England, John Graunt began gathering data and identifying patterns in past events. Since William the Conqueror and the Domesday Book, the English had gathered information about the population of and property in England. Graunt used this data to identify distributions of events, mortality rates, causes of death and other aspects of life in England.[14] His studies were later used by insurers to

---

[13]   Ross, Living Dangerously: Navigating the Risks of Everyday Life (1999).
[14]   Observations on the Bills of Mortality (1662).

manage their risk exposure. Though not aware of it at the time, Graunt was the innovator of sampling theory and laid the foundations for the science of statistics.

1.2.1.3 Gauss

Late in the 18th century, during the Enlightenment, the search for knowledge was considered to be the highest form of human activity. Philosophers were encouraged to part with the metaphysical, and approach risk from a scientific and mathematical point of view. One of the greatest of the mathematicians to advance the concept of risk during this period was Carl Friedrich Gauss (1777-1855).

Gauss was a childhood genius, with an enormous capacity to memorise numbers. He committed the logarithmic tables to memory. His father, an uncouth labourer, despised his intelligence. Despite these challenges, at the age of 18 he made a discovery about the geometry of a 17-sided polygon, and his doctoral thesis, "A new proof that every rational integer function of one variable can be resolved into real factors of the first or second degree", is the original proof of the fundamental theorem of algebra. Gauss's fame was such that in 1807, when Napoleon's army approached Gauss's home town of Göttingen, it was ordered to spare the city because "the greatest mathematician of all times is living there".[15]

Gauss began to study the correlation between the likelihood of the occurrence of an event and natural distribution. He was driven by his passions for mathematics and for gambling. His early theories revolved around the probability of thrown dice resulting in a given number.

1.2.1.4 Galton

A later pioneer in the field of risk, though he would not have used this term, was Francis Galton (1822-1911), a social snob who never had to work to earn a living. He was typical of the Victorian bourgeoisie, travelling and studying the world with selfish detachment. Galton's motivation in his studies was a passion for both measurement and counting. A grandson of Erasmus Darwin and a cousin of Charles Darwin, Galton sought to identify "natures pre-eminently noble": in other words, those possessing elements of humanity which were "perfect" in his eyes. Galton's studies, which he labelled "Eugenics", required the marshalling of much data concerning human characteristics and led him to consider methods of statistical analysis. He found that whenever a large sample of chaotic elements are taken in hand, an unsuspected and most beautiful form of regularity proves to have been latent all along. Or, more conventionally, while no two human beings are the same, when we look at a cross-section of humanity by taking a distributive sample, we find a normal distribution pattern.[16]

Galton's work on eugenics proved to be far more sinister than a rich man's idle attempt to apply to humanity practices that apparently work with thoroughbred

---

[15] Bernstein (1998) supra note 9 at 136.
[16] *Ibid* at 141.

horses or pedigree dogs; half a century later it was adopted by the Nazis and used as justification for the extermination of millions of human beings. Ironically, Galton himself abandoned his views when he realised that "noble" parents would sometimes give birth to "ignoble" children. The transfer of characteristics was not so easily controlled.

Less controversially, Galton also identified the "risk factor", where there is a connection between a factor and a risk, but there is not necessarily a direct causal connection. For example, a proven causal connection exists between a high fat diet and heart disease. However, obesity is only a risk factor, since no direct causal connection between obesity and heart disease has been established.[17]   There is, therefore, correlation but not necessarily causation.

1.2.1.5   Quetelet

It was also in the mid-19th century that Lambert Adolphe Jacques Quetelet (1796-1874) made great advances in the study of statistics and the concept of a "standard deviation". He proposed the concept of the "average man" (1835) and that mathematics could be used to measure both the cause and the effect of a given event. Quetelet studied anything from the rates of conviction amongst people accused of crimes to the chest measurements of Scottish soldiers. In each case he found a pattern of standard deviation, obediently distributed in a bell curve, where in each case deviations from the standard fall symmetrically on both sides as the deviation increases.

As an example of the importance of accurate information, one of Quetelet's studies concerned the height of French conscripts. Oddly, he found that, from a sample of 100,000, the average height was shorter than the national average. After further research, he discovered that conscripts could be exempted from military service if they were too short. The measurements were probably distorted in order to help draft dodgers.

1.2.1.6   Probability

The classical or "frequentist" view of probability indicates that an event, the likelihood of the occurrence of the event and the impact of an event can be identified based on similar occurrences in the past. Therefore, the probability of a coin turning up heads can be assessed based on the number of other flips of that coin and therefore the frequency of the result of heads in that series.

Under the personalistic, subjectivist or Bayesian view, probability is a function both of the event and the degree of belief of an individual that that event will occur. Each individual has a different amount of information about an event, and that information will change over time. There is no such thing as "the" probability

---

[17]   Ross (1999) supra note 13 at 31.

of an event. Hence, the assertion by some experts that "probability does not exist".[18]

Bernstein supports this view, noting that the standard mean is of only limited usefulness: "The trick is to be flexible enough to recognise that regression to the mean is only a tool; it is not a religion with immutable dogma and ceremonies ... Never depend upon it to come into play without constantly questioning the relevance of the assumptions that support the procedure."[19] The ability to analyse standard mean deviation enables analysis of what is and what was, but does not permit the forecast of future events. Due to the vagaries of human interaction, the mean coefficient for the past will not necessarily apply to the future – tomorrow's normalcy may be different from that of today.

1.2.2   Utility and cost-benefit analysis

Daniel Bernoulli (1700-1782), in his "Papers of the Imperial Academy of Sciences in St. Petersburg" in 1738, was the first to look at "utility" when measuring risk. "The world is full of desirable things," he said, "but the amount that people are willing to pay for them differs from one person to another."[20] His view of utility was very one-dimensional; however, he successfully identified one of the basic characteristics that underlie an individual's approach to risk: when analysing the acceptable cost of managing a given risk, each individual will assess a different level of acceptable cost.

In its most simplified form, utility theory states that "performance will be best if the attractiveness of an option is summarised as the sum of the probability plus discounted utility corresponding to its potential pay-offs and if the decision-maker chooses the option that offers the greatest sum".[21] Prescriptive decision theory assumes that any risk decision that falls short of this measure is by definition faulty. The difference between what the decision-maker should do and what he actually does represents inefficient risk allocation by the decision-maker.

Utility theory has been criticised as not considering individual differences and contexts, by trying to identify a common criterion.[22] There is an interpersonal comparability of utility. Edgeworth pointed out that utility is ordinal (classified by ranking, where utility can be compared within a ranking but not between rankings) rather than cardinal (classified by a numerical value which can be compared in a direct and linear manner with any other measure of utility). This could be demonstrated through indifference curves.[23] Pareto then, using purely ordinal measures of utility, measured individual preference for one set of goods for

---

[18]   Morgan and Henrion, Uncertainty: A Guide to Dealing with Uncertainty in Quantitative Risk and Policy Analysis at 50 and 51 (1990).

[19]   Bernstein (1998) supra note 9 at 185 and 186.

[20]   Bernstein (1998) supra note 9 at 188.

[21]   Beach, The Psychology of Decision Making: People in Organisations at 13 (1997).

[22]   Schoemaker, Experiments on Decisions Under Risk: The Expected Utility Hypothesis (1980).

[23]   Edgeworth, Mathematical Psychics (1881).

another. He believed that it was not possible to compare utility measures. He also proposed Pareto optimality, where a good or risk should be shared amongst two individuals to the extent that the reallocation provides an advantage to one party but does not disadvantage the other. This allows management of individual utilities without the need to compare those utilities.[24]

Savage pointed out that concepts of utility are always subjective.[25] This subjectivity must be considered alongside ambiguous situations; therefore, Edgeworth's indifference curves become indifference regions. This makes a rational comparison of measures of utility difficult to achieve.[26] Add this subjectivity to the subjective measure of probability and Edwards calls this "subjective expected utility" – where an individual will maximise the product of utility and subjective probability.[27]

Tversky points out the combined influence of utility and subjective probability: the more probable a positive outcome is perceived the more valuable the utility.[28] But the subjective nature of this measure makes it impossible to prove or disprove (since both "positive perception" and "value" are subjective measures). This has lead to efforts to limit the scope of subjectivity by looking at preference models and learning theories to study the evolution of the subjective aspect of utility.[29]

Adams argues that the cost-benefit or utility analysis is in itself meaningless. It is based on an effort to create an objective measure for an entirely subjective question. It is also only ever used to justify decisions that have been taken, and not to help make risk decisions.[30]

For example, someone betting on a football match will often not bet based on the probability of winning the bet but rather to support his favourite team. Even though the bet does not in any way materially benefit his team, an individual will gain satisfaction by supporting his team. An individual, therefore, may place a higher utility value against this moral support than he does against the increased probability of winning the bet.

Simon and Fishburn challenge the assumption that risk decisions are made in order to maximise utility. They claim that in certain cases an individual will only take risk to a reasonable or rational level in search of satisfaction rather than optimisation of utility or return. In particular, investors may seek to manage a risk "well enough" but not to push the limit of the riskiness of their investments to

---

[24]   Pareto, Manual of Political Economy (1927).
[25]   Savage, The Foundations of Statistics (1954) reprinted in Edwards and Tversky (eds), Decision Making: Selected Readings (1967).
[26]   Edwards, "The Theory of Decision Making" Psychology Bulletin 51 at 380 (1954) reprinted in Edwards and Tversky (1967) supra note 25.
[27]   Edwards, "Behavioural Decision Theory" Annual Review of Psychology 12 at 473 (1961) reprinted in Edwards and Tversky (1967) supra note 25.
[28]   Tversky, "Additivity, Utility and Probability" in Edwards and Tversky (1967) supra note 25.
[29]   Luce, "Psychological Studies of Risk Decision Making" in Edwards and Tversky (1967) supra note 25.
[30]   Adams, Risk at 107 (1995).

maximise utility.[31] In the same way, when crossing the street, a pedestrian will usually choose a location for crossing that represents a balance between safety and accessibility consistent with his mood, and not in order to maximise utility.

The measure of utility or usefulness will depend entirely on the perception of the individual as to what is useful and what is consistent with his goals and interests. Therefore, utility theory cannot be analysed except through the individual's filter. For example, the cost or value of a risk is often measured against the perception of third parties. If the risk (either the risk itself or its impact) can be concealed from third parties, the individual may be able to ignore the risk: "Out of sight, out of mind." Similarly if the individual can justify bearing that risk or the impact within his own social or commercial circles, the cost of that risk may be perceived by that individual to be lower.

A vast literature has developed around utility theory and its evolution to take into consideration the number of different stimuli that influence perception of utility and probability. In particular, Kahneman and Tversky propose a perceptual framework for the coding, editing and framing of these stimuli, in an effort to create an overarching theoretical framework for this evolved utility theory.[32]

Fischhoff *et al* deny any easy answer to whether it is possible to identify the nature of the benefit that will encourage an individual to take a risk. They opt for the term "acceptable risk" to describe the very uncertain and ever-changing nature of utility.[33]

The measure of utility or usefulness will depend primarily on the perception of the individual as to what is useful and what is consistent with his goals and interests.[34] Tversky identifies availability as a key to an individual's measure of utility: the more available the utility, the more probable it seems.[35] Therefore, any concept of utility cannot be analysed except through the individual's filter.

Different methods have been used to assess an individual's preference. One theory identifies "revealed preference" as based on revelations of the individual's context, analysing the costs and benefits based on the individual's surrounding social and economic context. "Expressed preference" is based on asking the individuals what they prefer, but is limited by the individuals' awareness of their own preferences.

---

[31] Fishburn, "Mean-Risk Analysis with Risk Associated with Below-Target Returns" American Economic Review 67 at 116-126 (1977); Simon, "Rational Decision Making in Business Organisations" American Economic Review 69 at 493-513 (1979).

[32] Kahneman and Tversky, "Prospect Theory: An Analysis of Decision Under Risk" Econometria 47 at 263 to 291 (1979) reprinted in Kahneman, Slovic and Tversky (eds), Judgement and Uncertainty: Heuristics and Biases (1982).

[33] Fischhoff, Lichtenstein, Slovic, Derby and Keeney, Acceptable Risk (1981).

[34] For a survey of the evolution of utility theory, see Goldstein and Hogarth, "Judgement and Decision Research: Some Historical Context" in Goldstein and Hogarth (eds), Research on Judgement and Decision Making: Currents, Connections and Controversies (1997).

[35] Tversky, "Additivity, Utility and Subjective Probability" Journal of Math and Psychology 4 at 175 (1967) reprinted in Edwards and Tversky (1967) supra note 25.

"Natural preference" looks to the risk the individual has accepted in the past as a basis for preferences in the future.[36]

A complication in measuring the cost of a risk is time-discounting. The value of a risk in the future is discounted to present-day values by using a discount rate. That discount rate is normally based on interest rates, cost of money or some other measure appropriate to the risk in question and the method of valuation. Risk financing involves the evaluation of the potential cost of a risk by identifying a source of funding for such risk and the cost of securing such funding while making preparations to secure such funding where the risk arises.[37] Examples might include standby credit facilities for cost over-runs for construction work. However, a strictly financial measure may mask important moral ingredients of the cost of risk.[38]

1.2.3   Causation

It is often difficult to identify retrospectively the exact cause for a given event. It is even more difficult to assess how a future event could be caused. A certain school of great mathematicians, including the likes of Jules-Henri Poincaré (1854-1912), believe that every event has a cause.

The evolution of this view is "chaos theory". Chaos theory does not allow for accident. It states that much of what looks like chaos is actually produced by an underlying order, wherein the most apparently insignificant event can have an effect on an entirely separate event. Luck, or fortune, is just a word for unavailable or misinterpreted information, or the unidentified causal connection. The classic example is the movement of a butterfly's wings in South America which causes a hurricane in Asia.

Chaos theory rejects the bell curve and sees the world as being in a state of vitality, characterised by turbulence and volatility. Its adherents believe that poor results have a cause; however those causes may be non-linear, e.g. the results may not be proportionate to the cause. This makes identification of causation all the more difficult. Given the tenuous link between the cause and effect and the absence of rules of causation, chaos theory is extremely difficult to prove or refute.

1.2.4   Game theory

Game theory was first proposed by John von Neumann (1903-1957). The premise underlying game theory is that life is a game of strategy played by individuals, and risk is its currency. An individual chooses the level of risk he is willing to bear against the level of pay-off that he expects to receive. The highest potential pay-off usually involves the highest amount of risk. Game theory examines the

---

[36]   Douglas and Wildavsky, Risk and Culture: An Essay on the Selection of Technical and Environmental Dangers (1982).

[37]   Gordon, Risk Financing (1992).

[38]   Douglas and Wildavsky (1982) supra note 36.

balance of negotiating positions, assuming that most arrangements, in particular in the commercial realm, involve compromise alternatives.

Von Neumann argued that statistical methods in economics are useless except for descriptive purposes since, once the predictions are made, consumers, business managers and policy-makers act on them, causing the forecasters to change their predictions, prompting yet further reaction and the cycle begins again. Game theory looks at choices, potential rewards and the probability that actors will receive rewards. An individual following game theory will analyse other individuals' actions and reactions to elements of the game, examining both competitive and co-operative ways to change the game to his benefit.[39]

The original formulation of game theory assumes rational behaviour by individuals. Modern evolution of game theory addresses the need to take account of the social, cultural and commercial contexts of the individuals making risk decisions. Thinking therefore turned to how decisions are actually made, rather than how they "should" be made.[40] Even in competitive, commercial circumstances, individuals will react to circumstances under the influence of a number of conscious and subconscious attitudes and responses. Luce and Raiffa raise the difficult example of the prisoner's dilemma, where an individual pursuing a personal optimal strategy will gain more than if he pursues a "win-win" solution.[41]

1.2.5 Diversification

A related approach to analysis of risk is that used by investors in constructing portfolios of securities, balancing the risks to be taken and the return to be obtained. Diversification is used to spread out the amount of risk taken against more or less certain return, thus reducing volatility. This balance of risk to maximise return while reducing volatility follows the basic premises set out in game theory, and assumes the ability to measure risks accurately and compare them on a like basis.

Harry Markowitz (b. 1927), when still an unknown 25-year-old graduate student, wrote the seminal paper on portfolio diversification, "Portfolio Selection".[42] From Markowitz's point of view, the rational investor will use gut instinct to assess the appropriate level of aggressive investment appropriate for his portfolio. The effectiveness of the theory of portfolio diversification assumes that the investor has sufficient information about each investment to assess the variance of its return. Markowitz took a very narrow view of what creates volatility in investments. As a warning to those implementing his theory, he relates a story whereby a group of hikers in the wilderness came upon a bridge, the crossing of which would shorten

---

[39]   Brandenburger and Nalebuff, "The Right Game" Harvard Business Review on Managing Uncertainty (1999).
[40]   For a good description of game theory, see Goldstein and Hogarth (1997) supra note 34.
[41]   Luce and Raiffa, Games and Decisions: Introduction and Critical Survey (1957).
[42]   Journal of Finance (June 1952).

their journey. Noting that the bridge was high and rickety, they fashioned harnesses and other safeguards before crossing the bridge. Once they reached the other side, they found a hungry mountain-lion patiently awaiting their arrival. The risks we perceive will seldom be the only risks involved, and diversification can only help manage those risks which we have identified.

1.2.6   Information

To quote from Sun Tzu: "Unless you know the mountains and forests, the defiles and impasses, and the lay of the marshes and swamps, you cannot manoeuvre with an armed force. Unless you use local quirks, you cannot get the advantages of the land".[43]

One of the most difficult aspects of quantitative risk assessment is the lack of information available against which to measure risk. A mathematical quantification of risk is only as good as the mathematician making the quantification, and is limited by the quantity and quality of the information available to that mathematician.[44] Historical information is often incomplete and inaccurate and can be a poor basis upon which to measure the future. Even well-educated individuals may misunderstand the quantification process, and therefore misuse the available information.[45] An example would be the tendency for individuals to rely on small samples of information when making risk decisions, or to assume that the general characteristics of a large process are also located in each of that large process's component parts. This results in the well-known "gambler's fallacy", also known as the "Monte Carlo effect", and the law of small numbers.[46]

In the face of inadequate information and the perceived shortcomings of quantitative risk assessment, either doubting the expert or his tools, individuals turn to intuitive or predictive judgements.

An individual's judgement is bounded by his context: the information available to the individual within the context of the individual's condition. Simon calls this "bounded rationality".[47] It is impossible for that individual to assess every bit of information, therefore he will define the scope of information that he will assess in relation to that perception and will make his risk decision accordingly. Intuitive decision-making is a bit more difficult to define, but involves a gut instinct that is probably based on past experience, education and the emotional condition of the

---

[43]   Sun Tzu, The Art of War at 116 and 177 (translated by Thomas Cleary, 1988).

[44]   Janis and Mann point to the importance of "vigilant information processing" which includes the availability and assessment of information. Decision Making: A Psychological Analysis of Conflict, Choice and Commitment (1977).

[45]   Abercrombie, The Anatomy of Judgement: An Investigation into the Process of Perception and Reasoning (1960); Phillips and Edwards, "Conservation in a Simple Probability Inference Task" Journal of Experimental Psychology 72 at 346 (1966) reprinted in Edwards and Tversky (1967) supra note 25; Fischhoff, Lichtenstein, Slovic, Derby and Keeney (1981) supra note 33.

[46]   Tversky and Kahneman, "Introduction" in Kahneman, Slovic and Tversky (1982) supra note 32.

[47]   Simon, Models of Man (1957).

individual. Before a decision can be made in relation to the assessment of a risk, the risk must be identified. The understanding of that risk to the individual will depend on the various characteristics set out in this chapter.

The difficulty is that the relevant information:

> ➤ may not exist;

> ➤ may exist but it may be too expensive to obtain;

> ➤ may exist but it may take too long to obtain;

> ➤ may exist and may have been obtained, but may not be accurate;

> ➤ may exist and may have been obtained, but the individual believes incorrectly that the information is inaccurate and discounts it; or

> ➤ may exist and may have been obtained, but the individual incorrectly interprets it.

The amount of information needed (i.e. the level of acceptable uncertainty in relation to a risk) will vary significantly depending on the nature of, and the circumstances surrounding, a transaction. For example, the amount of information needed about the risk involved in throwing dice in a game of craps in order to undertake a reasonable assessment of the risk of losing is limited. The individual applying probability theory[48] only needs to know the nature of the dice, the number of sides on each die and the rules of the game. Where the transaction involves the construction of a large industrial plant, the level of uncertainty is significantly higher and hence the amount of information necessary to assess the risk accurately increases exponentially.

Certain risks require a significant amount of technical sophistication to be understood and analysed. One example is ground risk in a construction project. The nature of the soil on the site on which the building is to be constructed will have a direct influence on the cost of construction, the time required and the sophistication of the design. The technical sophistication necessary to assess samples and identify the risk involved in ground conditions is normally beyond the expertise of the owner wishing to procure the construction of the building. The owner will look to consultants or the contractor to assess the information.

Inaccurate or misinterpreted information is more misleading than missing information, since the individual who erroneously believes that the available information is accurate may not look to extrapolate further information or verify the information he has. *It's not what we don't know that gives us trouble, it's what we know that ain't so.*[49]

Commenting on the irony of the unavailability of information, and expressing the frustration of many a mathematician endeavouring to measure and demonstrate

---

[48] This issue is discussed further in section 1.2.
[49] Will Rogers (1879-1935).

probability and risk, Bernstein says, "The information you have is not the information you want. The information you want is not the information you need. The information you need is not the information you can obtain. The information you can obtain costs more than you want to pay."[50] This applies to any human venture. Lack of information is an unavoidable part of risk assessment. "Ignorance is both inescapable and an intrinsic element in social organisation generally, although there are marked differences in specific forms, degrees and functions of ignorance in known social organisations."[51]

Probability theory does not assume to create absolutes. It is quite comfortable with the fact that there is no absolute knowledge and no certainty, therefore it creates an average probability. "Regardless of which position one takes, that is, determinism versus indeterminism, we are forced to use probabilistic models in the real world because we do not know, cannot calculate or cannot measure all the forces contributing to an effect." The forces may be too complicated, too numerous or too faint, or as McCormick puts it "probability is nothing more than a measure of uncertainty about the likelihood of an event".[52]

1.3   Qualitative Assessment

The question of risk assessment goes to the basic premise of the nature of man. Is man a reasonable being, with measurable and reasonable approaches to life, or, as John Maynard Keynes (1883-1946) stated in an essay written in 1938, subject to "deeper and blinder passions"? Keynes referred to the "insane and irrational springs of wickedness in most men".[53] In 1921 he completed a book entitled "A Treatise on Probability" in which he discussed definable and undefinable events. Keynes had little patience with decisions based on the frequency of past occurrences. He felt that Galton's views on mean distribution would apply to nature but not to mankind, the fact that similar events have been observed repeatedly in the past being a poor excuse for believing that they will occur in the future.

Keynes highlighted the importance of an individual's qualitative assessment of a risk, stating that "[p]erception of probability, weight, and risk are all highly dependent on judgement" and "the basis of our degrees of belief is part of our human outfit".[54] The mathematical/scientific appreciation of a risk (however accurate that assessment might be) is subject always to the overriding influence of perception and the qualitative assessment of that risk. Once human reasoning touches risk decisions, the quantitative analysis is no longer sufficient. As one noted behavioural researcher concluded, "God gave all the easy problems to the

---

[50]   Bernstein (1998) supra note 9 at 202.
[51]   Moore and Tumin, "Some Social Functions of Ignorance" American Sociological Review 14 at 788 (1949) as cited in Aubert, "Chance in Social Affairs" in Dowie and Lefrere (eds), Risk and Chance (1980).
[52]   McCormick, Reliability and Risk Analysis: Methods and Nuclear Power Applications (1981).
[53]   Bernstein (1998) supra note 9 at 223.
[54]   *Ibid* at 227.

physicists",[55] the fortunate practitioners of a science theoretically untainted by human emotion.

"Risk, like beauty, lies in the eye of the beholder."[56] An individual will assess a risk in accordance with his own filter. This aspect of risk assessment is often unrelated to the information at hand or objective quantitative analysis. Risk by its nature is subjective and personal. Risk assessment cannot be de-contextualised or de-socialised.[57] Scientific rationality without social sensitivity is empty, social sensitivity without scientific rationality is blind.[58]

The filter used by individuals to assess a risk is multifaceted. It is made up of a large number of different aspects of an individual and that individual's environment. For this reason, an individual will have to struggle to reconcile conflicting identities within that filter created by its overlapping and sometimes contradictory elements, for example social networks, cultural influences, personal traits and organisational demands.

Filters that we apply to risk assessment are not created by a desire to ignore "the facts" but rather by an inability to obtain "the facts". It will be a rare occasion in which an individual has all of the facts and information in relation to a risk. In almost every risk assessment situation, the individual making the risk decision must apply his own filter in order to fill the gaps in his knowledge and the information available. In a commercial context, the market changes so dramatically and the nature of most technological issues are so far out of the ambit of the individual's knowledge or understanding that the filter plays an important role in risk assessment.

1.3.1   Basic needs

An individual's view of a risk may be biased by his perception of the necessity of that risk. An individual will justify a risk-taking act or continuously ignore the risk involved in the act in order to create the perception of certainty and safety; and to satisfy that individual's basic needs. The obvious example is an automobile. Automobiles are extremely risky instruments and are the cause of deaths and injuries in significant numbers. However, modern society views the automobile as so very necessary that it is willing to bear that risk.

Maslow's hierarchy of needs[59] provides for five different levels of basic human motivation.

> ➤ Physiological – including satiation of hunger, satiation of thirst and shelter.

> ➤ Safety – including security and protection.

---

55   Robbins, Organisational Behaviour at 12 (9th edition 2001).
56   Andrews, Upside, Downside: How to Take the Stress out of Business Risk at 1 (1987).
57   Douglas and Wildavsky (1982) supra note 36.
58   Beck, Risk Society: Towards a New Modernity at 30 (1992).
59   Maslow, Motivation and Personality (1954).

> Social – including affection and acceptance.

> Esteem – including internal and external esteem factors.

> Self actualisation – including growth and achieving potential.

Physiological and safety needs are low order needs while social, esteem and self actualisation needs are high order needs. Once low order needs are satisfied, the individual will attempt to fulfil high order needs.

Clayton Alderfer has proposed an amended version of Maslow's hierarchy of needs in his Existence, Relatedness and Growth ("ERG") theory. Existence relates to basic material requirements which equate with Maslow's physiological and safety needs. The second group is relatedness, which includes maintaining important interpersonal relationships, which is similar to Maslow's social needs and the external component of Maslow's esteem classification. Growth relates to the intrinsic desire for personal development, which equates with the intrinsic component of Maslow's esteem category.[60]

The ERG theory includes a frustration/regression dimension whereby the frustration of a high order need will increase the individual's desire to focus on a low order need. For example, where an individual experiences rejection on a professional level he may focus on social reinforcement or physiological needs. There is nothing like a hug when things aren't going well at the office.

1.3.2   Control and the search for certainty

One of the drivers for risk assessment is the importance for an individual to feel mastery or control over a situation, the search for security. Security ranks just below food, warmth and shelter in Maslow's hierarchy of needs.[61] Individuals will therefore act as if they know the outcome or understand the likelihood of an outcome in order to provide themselves with more certainty.[62]

Individuals seek certainty and to that end tend to ignore uncertainty or believe that chance events are a result of skill and the individual's control of the situation. The same assumption of control can also result in the individual taking more blame for failures than is necessarily appropriate.

To submit to this human tendency to seek certainty and security is to divert resources and effort from other more appropriate pursuits. In our effort to wrap ourselves in certainty, we tend to apply resources to things that improve our perception of security, rather than things that increase our security. An example might be the development of nuclear arsenals in an effort to dissuade other nations from attacking. A nuclear arsenal is probably more effective at creating a

---

[60]   Alderfer, "An Empirical Test of a New Theory of Human Needs" Organisational Behaviour and Human Performance at 142-75 (May 1969); Robbins (2001).

[61]   Maslow (1954) supra note 59.

[62]   Langer, "The Psychology of Chance" in Dowie and Lefrere (1980) supra note 51.

perception of security than improving actual security from attack, but maybe that perception is more useful than actual security.

1.3.2.1   Voluntary risk-taking

Human beings seek control.   Brehm and his colleagues used the term "psychological reactance" to describe the motivation to reaffirm an individual's power and control over a situation.[63]   Where he controls a situation or believes he controls a situation, an individual may permit more risky behaviour.   The sense of control in relation to taking a risk enables the individual to bear a risk that in other circumstances would be considered unacceptable.[64]   This is probably one of the reasons that individuals allow themselves to smoke or to engage in dangerous activities such as skydiving or skiing, despite the fact that they are fully aware of the risks involved.[65]   Whereas, if the individual is forced to bear a risk, he may assess that risk as more likely to occur or having a more serious impact.

More recent research questions whether activities such as smoking are indeed voluntary risk-taking, or more of an unconscious impulse undertaking.[66]   This corresponds with Kahneman's theory that decision utility (the perception of utility at the time of decision, how bad smoking would really be) is very different than experience utility (the perception after the risk is taken, the realisation that smoking is actually a bad idea), in that voluntary risk-taking is based on the perception of the risk at the time and may be based on inaccurate information.[67]

Another line of research on voluntary risk-taking shows that individuals tend to discount the potential harm of their activities on themselves, but recognise associated risks to others.[68]   This may be part of an individual's optimistic bias or an effort to defend his own internal accommodation to risk decisions (and therefore expressions of individual power and position) that he has made.

1.3.2.2   Loss aversion

Tversky and Kahneman note that individuals tend to make probability assessments based on probabilistic reasoning, a qualitative assessment of probability.   This is a practical, conservative approach to risk decisions, which they have called "prospect theory", whereby individuals are more risk averse when analysing loss and more risk prone when analysing gain.[69]

---

[63]   Brehm, A Theory of Psychological Reactance (1966) as cited in Langer (1980) supra note 62.
[64]   Starr, "Social Benefit Versus Technological Risk" Science 165 at 1232-1238 (1969) as cited by Slovic and Fischhoff, "How Safe is Safe Enough?" in Dowie and Lefrere (1980) supra note 51.
[65]   Yeomans, "Risks to Consumers" in Jouhar (ed), Risk in Society (1984).
[66]   Slovic, "Cigarette Smokers: Rational Actors or Rational Fools?" in Slovic (ed), Smoking: Risk, Perception and Policy (2001).
[67]   Kahneman, "New Challenges to the Rationality Assumption" Journal of Institutional and Theoretical Economics 150 at 18 to 36 (1994).
[68]   Romer and Jamieson, "The Role of Perceived Risk in Starting and Stopping Smoking" in Slovic (2001) supra note 66.
[69]   Kahneman and Tversky (1979) supra note 32 at 263-291.

Tversky asserts that one of the driving forces for human beings is "loss aversion"; people hate losing.[70] People respond better to negative than to positive stimuli.[71] Tversky uses the example of gambling, where people who start out with money in their pockets will generally choose to gamble while people who start out with empty pockets will generally elect not to gamble. Similarly, individuals tend toward a stubborn optimism (an optimistic bias); they perceive the likelihood of their own loss much lower than someone else's loss in the same circumstances.[72]

1.3.2.3   Ambiguity aversion

Ambiguity aversion is resistance to taking risks on the basis of unknown probabilities. Individuals prefer probabilities about which they have an acceptable amount of information. This may stem from the desire to make an educated decision, or from a lack of self-confidence. Individuals tend to take risks in situations where they feel confident or knowledgeable, even where they do not have much information. Ambiguity aversion may be related more to a lack of confidence in the situation than understanding of and control over the situation.

Where the individual believes that he can conceive the ways in which the risk might arise, his assessment will change. On the other hand, where the individual does not understand the risk, he may not be able to appreciate the safety functions or the certainty involved in the surrounding circumstances or situation. An airplane is an extremely complex machine and the cause of significant anxiety for many passengers. Few of those passengers truly understand the mechanism of flight or the safety mechanisms available for an airplane (or the lack thereof).

Being bombarded with too much risk information can cause the psyche to seek refuge from information which it cannot manage or completely understand, causing the individual to react to risk overload. An individual may obtain so much information about the number of different risks that confront him each day that he becomes less sensitive to risks generally. Another potential reaction to risk overload is risk focus. This involves an individual taking an exaggerated interest in one particular risk and focusing all his energies on managing that one particular risk to the detriment of the management of others, in order to achieve certainty.

1.3.2.4   Decision regret

Another related element of risk assessment is "decision regret" whereby it is difficult to accept or discover that the decision you have made was not the best, for example selling a stock too early.[73] Even though an early sale makes a profit, the

---

[70]   Tversky, "The Psychology of Risk" in Sharpe (ed), Quantifying the Market Risk Premium Phenomenon for Investment Decision-Making (1990).

[71]   Yates and Stone, "Risk Appraisal" in Yates (ed), Risk-Taking Behaviour (1992).

[72]   Weinstein, "Optimistic Biases About Personal Risk" Lofstedt and Frewer (eds), Risk and Modern Society (1998).

[73]   Shafir, Simonson and Tversky, "Reason-based Choice" Cognition 49 at 11 (1993); Slovic, "Choice Between Equally Valued Alternatives" Journal of Experimental Psychology: Human Perception and Performance 1 at 280 (1975).

loss of potential profit by not holding the stock can be painful. Decision regret creates an incentive for investors to trust their trading portfolio to professional managers, insulating the investor from potential regret, but also distancing the investor from the investment decision and causing him to incur the cost of the professional manager's fee.

1.3.2.5   Ambient risk

"Ambient risk" is the contemporaneous or associated risk run by the individual at the time of the risk decision.[74]   A high level of "ambient risk" reduces the subjective impact of a new risk, since the individual is already in a very risky situation. Lighting up a cigarette will be perceived as less of a risk by a soldier on the eve of a very dangerous battle.

The individual will also consider the risk balance. The individual may have chosen to limit the amount of a specific risk to a maximum aggregate level. Where the individual attains the maximum aggregate of any one type of risk that the individual is willing to bear, even a small amount of additional risk within that same type may be rejected. This decision will not be related to the gravity of that specific risk but instead to the total amount of risk borne by the individual.

1.3.2.6   Accommodation

An individual may "re-normalise" to a new status quo. Therefore, once a risk decision has been taken or once risks have been experienced, the individual may become more risk-seeking than before, having accepted the risk and therefore will readjust the status quo to include the accepted risk. Where the individual has "re-normalised", ambient risk falls away and new risks are considered *de novo*. This may be the case of an individual bungee jumping. After the first jump, he has conquered his fear and is more willing to do a second jump. The riskiness of bungee jumping has not changed, but the individual has accommodated for the risk. Over time, risk may also become more familiar (see section 1.3.6) and therefore less "risky". This is also known as "anchoring".[75]

1.3.2.7   Commitment escalation

Individuals and groups tend to value a risk based on the investment that they have put into the risk. The more they have invested, the more they are willing to invest in order to attempt to resolve the problem.[76]   "The decision-maker may, in the face of negative feedback, feel the need to reaffirm the wisdom of time and money

---

[74]   Philipson, "Risk Evaluation: A Review of the Literature" in Covello, Menks and Mumpower (1986) supra note 11 at 319.

[75]   Crouch and Wilson, Risk Benefit Analysis (1982).

[76]   See generally Bazerman, Judgement in Managerial Decision Making at chapter 4 (3rd edition 1994).

already sunk in the project",[77] and fall into the non-rational escalation of commitment.

Hence, when gambling, an individual may set a limit, an amount that he is willing to bet. However, once the gaming has begun, that amount may lose its relevance as the losses accumulate and risk-taking escalates, and the individual may become more prone to take risks. This results in the largest bets being placed on the last horse-race, in order to win back losses.[78] This is also indicative of the circumstances surrounding the fall of Barings Bank. In order to cover up significant accumulated losses, Nick Leeson was willing to take huge risks, since the quantum of loss far exceeded his relative risk threshold.

1.3.2.8   Compensation

Risk assessment is not generally about minimising risk, but rather taking risk only to the extent the individual receives a commensurate benefit (also known as the "risk premium").[79] Of course, risk is not subject to universally accepted methods of valuation, each risk must be analysed individually in accordance with its context and that of the individual perceiving the risk. The benefit may include enjoyment, personal improvement and financial gain. However, as noted by Viscusi, the best paying jobs are rarely the most risky: in fact, they are often the most attractive.[80]

Fischhoff *et al* therefore propose the concept of "acceptable risk" to mean that which satisfies this very inaccurate balance of risk-taking and benefit. In the context of acceptable risk, they note that compensation, or cost-effectiveness, is often an oversimplification of a very complex series of risk issues, in particular associated and interconnected cost issues. Cost-effectiveness is also often sought through the pursuit of Pareto optimality, which itself fails to address more complex issues of the impact of cost reductions and equity.[81]

1.3.2.9   Anchoring

Familiarity may be achieved vicariously, by the experiences of others or by association with some other experience;[82] this is also known as "anchoring".[83] Anchoring is subject to certain conditions, in particular the individual's perception as to the awareness of other people and their assessment of the relevant risk. Rowe

---

[77]   Northcraft and Wolf, "Dollars, Cents, and Sunk Costs: A Life Cycle Model of Resource Allocation Decisions" Academy of Management Review 9 at 225-234 (1984).

[78]   Levy, "An Introduction to Prospect Theory" in Farnham (ed), Avoiding Losses/Taking Risks: Prospect Theory and International Conflict at 7 (1994).

[79]   Viscusi, Risk by Choice: Regulating Health and Safety in the Workplace (1983).

[80]   *Ibid.*

[81]   Fischhoff, Lichtenstein, Slovic, Derby and Keeney (1981) supra note 33.

[82]   It is argued that this experience need not be factual. It may never have happened but the individual believes that it happened or that, if it had happened or if it were to happen, it would happen in a given way. Kahneman and Varey, "Propensities and Counterfactuals: The Loser that Almost Won" Journal of Personality and Social Psychology 59 at 1101 (1990).

[83]   Crouch and Wilson (1982) supra note 75.

calls this "mutual self-awareness".[84] We assume that individuals make risk decisions based on their independent assessment. We may trust the source of that assessment. The truth is that most people respond to risk based on what they have seen others do. An individual anchors on the risk decision of another individual, who anchors on another individual, who anchors on another individual ... the basis of the perceived certainty, being that other person's reliability, is falsely based on the assumption that the other individual made his own risk decision.

1.3.3 Magnitude

Every risk has a certain "signal of potential" that sends a message to individuals as to the value that should be attributed to that risk. This signal may not be direct, but often has a very high impact on risk assessment.[85] Magnitude is an important element of the "signal of potential" and will often be caught up in cultural biases that inflate or decrease magnitude. An example would be the risk of being attacked by a shark. The likelihood is small, but the "dread factor" is enormous given the potential impact. Equally, a large number of people affected by a risk creates a greater impression on an individual than does a series of risks affecting the same aggregate number of people. An airplane crash affects a large number of people and creates a large "dread factor", while isolated automobile accidents kill more people but are not considered with the same dread.

1.3.4 Immediacy

Bjorkman notes that where the consequence of the risk is not likely, in the individual's opinion, to arise for some time, that individual may be more comfortable making more aggressive risk decisions.[86] The eventual cost of the risk is discounted against the value to the individual in order to arrive at a present value for that future cost. The impact on the individual, and possibly those penalties attaching to the risk, will have a diminishing marginal impact on the individual risk assessment.

1.3.5 Focus

Individuals look for simplicity. By applying rules (whether or not such rules are reasonable or appropriate) an individual can simplify his analysis of a risk. This is known as "selection". Selection may facilitate the task of risk analysis due to the short time or small amount of resources available for the assessment of a large amount of information, or may simply be a matter of that individual not wishing to invest time and effort in the assessment process. An individual will tend to choose the easiest element of risk to understand or measure or the most familiar to him in order to ensure "successful" assessment of that risk or that facet of a risk.

---

[84]   Rowe, "Mutual Self-Awareness and Fat Tails" Risk at 79 (January 2004).
[85]   Slovic, Fischhoff and Lichtenstein, "The Psychometric Study of Risk Perception" in Covello, Menks and Mumpower (1986) supra note 11 at 3.
[86]   Bjorkman, "Time and Risk in Cognitive Space" in Sjoberg (ed), Risk and Society (1987).

Focus is recognised by a number of different names. Kahneman describes it as the ability of an individual to "switch off analysers", gate specific attributes or give selective attention to certain inputs[87]. This is often the case where an individual receives a number of inputs too large for him to analyse with the resources and time available. The individual will select the most dominant or important inputs to assess. This focusing process may fail to identify the most relevant inputs to an accurate assessment of the relevant risk, leaving the individual with little basis on which to make the risk decision, or a false sense of having understood the relevant issues.

An important element of focus is framing.[88] Framing of the issue should be carefully managed to avoid the adoption of the assumptions inherent in the way the issue is framed. Inaccurate framing can reduce the efficiency of the exercise, or even render it useless, where entrenched biases are adopted into the framing exercise, or where the chosen focus is not central to or representative of the risk scenario in question.

An individual may consciously ignore the potential of a risk and therefore endeavour not to make a risk decision.[89] This is often the case where a risk is too significant to consider or where the individual suffers from risk overload. However, the decision not to make a decision is still a risk decision.

1.3.6   Past personal experience/familiarity

Risk assessment is normally based on past experience with similar risks or similar issues. We rely on the past to understand the future. This results in extrapolated or "imagined" knowledge. However, this reliance tends to be exaggerated since the past is only a partial indication of the future.[90] Past experience does not allow for change, learning or innovation. The past is a very unreliable template for the future. Further, the context of past experience will normally differ from that of future projects and therefore the extrapolation will rarely be exact.

"Sampling" means judging the whole of a risk by one small sample, while the "mathematical man" looks to probability over a large representative sample. "There seems to be an inability to regard an independent event as separate and detached from a series of similar events in which it occurs."[91] One example is flipping a coin. No two flips of the coin are related; however, an individual will believe that if the coin lands on heads the first time, the likelihood of it landing on heads the second time is lower than the likelihood of it landing on tails (this is known as the "Monte Carlo effect"). The next toss of the coin is always 50/50. Where a game of roulette gives nine red numbers in a row, an individual will be

---

[87]   Kahneman, Attention and Effort (1973).
[88]   A term used extensively by Sigmund Freud to identify the framing of issues in daily life, and how people frame issues differently, based on their psychological context.
[89]   Luhmann, Risk: A Sociological Theory (1993).
[90]   Bjorkman (1987) supra note 86.
[91]   Cohen and Hensel, Risk and Gambling at 10 (1956).

tempted to bet that the next game of roulette will result in a black number. However, for each throw, the likelihood of a black number resulting is still always 50/50.[92]

1.3.6.1   Familiarity

A familiar risk becomes less risky. Those living near an active fault are less concerned about earthquakes than those living in less shaky areas. Familiarity (also known as "habituation"[93]) can also arise from the speed at which the risk crystallises. The old story goes that a frog thrown into boiling water will immediately jump out but a frog put in cold water that is slowly heated to boiling will become soup. A corollary could be: necessity or perceived necessity breeds familiarity. Necessary risks are generally assessed as less significant, or the inevitability of the risk causes the individual to accept the risk as a defence mechanism.

"Availability" occurs when a risk is more memorable or imaginable, and therefore the individual is more likely to believe that that risk will arise.[94] The obvious example would be a shark attack. Though actual shark attacks are rare, the number of movies and documentaries involving shark attacks and the dramatic images that most people see in relation to sharks and shark attacks cause that particular risk to increase in perceived likelihood and impact.

1.3.6.2   Cognitive dissonance

Individuals seek stability and therefore try to minimise the dissonance between their various behaviours and attitudes. Dissonance can create stress and a fundamental dissonance will create high levels of stress. Individuals therefore justify their activities in order to avoid this dissonance.[95] They tend to seek information that confirms their pre-judgement, rather than that which disproves it.

The individual's reactions to cognitive dissonance help the individual construct or achieve consistency and thereby security, by adjusting his perception of the circumstances to improve security. For example, someone who finds a well-paid job working in a nuclear power plant may justify the risk of being in close proximity to nuclear power production in view of the benefits available. The large salary is a sufficient driver to justify the risk. The individual may also justify the additional risk of close proximity to nuclear power generation by acknowledging that there is more risk in other normal, necessary daily experiences, such as in crossing the street, than living close to a nuclear power plant.

---

[92]   Ayer, "Chance" in Dowie and Lefrere (1980) supra note 51 at 33.
[93]   The Royal Society Study Group on Risk, the Assessment and Perception of Risk at 14 (1981).
[94]   Tversky and Kahneman, "Judgement Under Uncertainty" Science 185 at 1,124 (1974); see also Bannister and Mair, The Evaluation of Personal Constructs (1968).
[95]   Festinger, A Theory of Cognitive Dissonance (1957).

1.3.6.3   Proximity

Proximity breeds familiarity. A limited number of deaths occurring near to an individual or to someone similar to that individual will cause more anxiety, and therefore more risk consciousness, than many deaths far away from the individual or to people entirely dissimilar from that individual. An example would be the relative effect on the average English person of the Paddington rail disaster in London and the genocide committed in Rwanda. The average English person can identify with the people on the train in Paddington, but may not be able to identify with the victims in Rwanda. This is not generally a racist or culturalist issue, but rather a perception of the likelihood of a similar fate involving the individual.

Another element of proximity is "representativeness", whereby single events that an individual experiences are more persuasive, and are therefore considered more probable, than events about which that individual only has information.[96]

1.3.6.4   Commonality

Where a community or group is confronting a risk and the rest of that community has accepted, or has to bear, that risk, the individual may be more willing to bear that risk. An obvious example is cigarette smoking. Even though an individual may have a great amount of knowledge of the dangers of cigarette smoking, that individual may accept those dangers given the number of people surrounding that individual who smoke and therefore bear that risk.

1.3.6.5   Recency

The more recent the risk and the more recent the memory that the individual has of the occurrence of a risk and of its effect, the more the individual can imagine its occurrence and appreciate the potential impact of its occurrence. Recency includes ease of recall, retrievability (whether you can remember a series of past events that would indicate higher frequency) and presumed association (where you can remember two events coinciding and therefore the relationship between those two events appears to represent greater frequency). Barbara Kenworthy, manager of a portfolio at Prudential Investment Advisers, noted that "we are all creatures of what burned us most recently".[97]

1.3.7   Physical condition and preparedness

An individual's physical condition and preparedness can have a fundamental impact on his approach to a given risk. Even minor and temporary discomfort or inability can cause an individual to become more or less risk averse. The aspects of physical discomfort that can have an impact on risk assessment may include hunger, fatigue or disease. One theory of negotiation states that a hungry or tired opponent will accept risks more readily. Fatigue can break down resistance, and

---

[96]   Kahneman and Tversky (1979) supra note 32 at 263 to 291.
[97]   Bernstein (1998) supra note 9 at 286, citing an article in the Wall Street Journal of May 1995.

impair focus, concentration or objective decision-making. However, the opposite may be true. Fatigue can cause resentment and increase resistance to compromise. It may also render an individual more resistant to rational argument.[98]

1.3.8   Personal, genetic or natural propensity to take risk

Risk assessment will depend to a large extent on the personal traits of the individual assessing the risk. They may not be cognitive but can be significant. Certain risks can be emotive, raising feelings related to an object or a specific risk or set of circumstances.

Some argue that risk-taking, from currency trading to gambling to extreme sports, arises from an individual's gender make-up. Others point to the chemical reactions within the body, the adrenaline rush, that drives us to seek risk, to pursue risky situations, in order to heighten experience. It is very difficult to assess an individual's personality traits accurately given the large number of variables and influences that affect those traits.[99] For example:

> ➢ Complacency: A tendency to be non-confrontational or to avoid conflict can result in a specific reaction to the elements of risk. An individual who is complacent may also fail to appreciate certain subtleties of a risk, which would otherwise cause concern or, alternatively, provide comfort to the individual.

> ➢ Ambition: A person driven primarily by ambition will often have a greater appetite for risk.

> ➢ Sloth: While a complacent person may avoid confrontation, a slothful person will avoid any effort or activity.

> ➢ Greed: Like ambition, greed can cause an individual to take an aggressive approach to risk management against the potential gains. The impact of greed differs significantly from ambition in its linear agenda focused on wealth, where ambition creates often complex and overlapping agendas.

> ➢ Fear: Fear can drive an individual to take more or less risk as a reaction to an often imagined or exaggerated assessment of circumstances. Fear can flow from past experiences, lack of information, misinterpretation of information or other elements of an individual's context.

> ➢ Pride: The sense of invincibility and that, though risk may exist, it only applies to others, can cause an individual to accept higher levels of risk. Pride can cause an individual to believe, or pretend that, his negotiating position is better than it is, and to take an untenable stance.

---

[98]   Fisher and Ury, Getting to Yes (1991).
[99]   Bromiley and Curley, "Individual Differences in Risk Taking" in Yates (1992) supra note 71 at 88-126.

> Ignorance: Lack of education, intelligence or information can have a significant impact on risk assessment. The individual will not have the ability to analyse information necessary to understand the risk or manage it appropriately.

> Emotion: The euphoria at the beginning of a project often causes individuals to ignore certain risks. Apter considers the impact of the telic and paratelic state of the individual.[100] The telic is a serious frame of mind focused on a purposeful activity or task, such as work. The paratelic state is playful, focused on an activity undertaken for its own sake, such as leisure or sporting activities.

> Fatalism: The belief that the individual will probably fail anyway is wrapped up in nihilism and a feeling of general impotence. Part of fatalism or nihilism is "learned helplessness", the belief that you have no power and therefore you do nothing to change the circumstances or situation, avoiding any effort at empowerment or risk management; avoidance without first assessing whether this is the most efficient method of managing the risk.[101]

> Superstition: Often linked to cultural and sociological influences, an individual's risk assessment can be heavily influenced by superstitions. This involves an objectively unreasonable or unfounded characterisation of an object or event.

1.3.9   Cultural

Culture, in the broader sense, exists whenever two or more people have in common a set of beliefs and values that induce similar interpretations of events.[102]   These influences are cultural whether they are associated with institutional, organisational or sociological groupings.   By using behaviours that worked successfully in previous experiences, the individual is attempting to increase efficiency by applying a known successful solution. This boot-strapping exercise also benefits from a sense of community and belonging, or may be mandated by the group in an effort to improve conformity and efficiency within the group.

The adoption of behaviour used in past experiences in new situations is known in psychology as "policies", in the psychology of learning as "habits" and in social psychology as "scripts".

These external or organisational policies and scripts are validated by their acceptance by the group or community. They are generally built up over time creating validation as being built upon past experiences and known success. However, these past behaviours will need to be adjusted in order to meet the requirements of the new situation.

---

[100]   Waring and Glendon, Managing Risk: Critical Issues for Survival and Success into the 21st Century at 164 (1998).
[101]   Langer (1980) supra note 62.
[102]   Beach (1997) supra note 21 at 25.

Cultural context cannot be limited to the effects of a national or regional culture, and should not be permitted to create a stereotype of any particular people. Culture also exists on a local level, including the culture within a company, a family or even a couple or circle of friends. These different layers of culture, and how the individual fits into them, will form part of the cultural filter.

1.3.10   Sociological

Each individual's attitude towards risk is moulded by his society, the way those around him approach risk and the attitude encouraged or intimated by that society. "The perception of risk is a social process."[103] An example is the approach to risk advocated by certain religious societies. These societies encourage a specific view of risk consistent with their philosophy of life, and the attitudes and acts they find most valuable or repugnant in human activity. As Douglas argues, rituals of purity and impurity and attitudes toward hygiene and order bring a society unity in experience.[104]

Society, however, is a multifaceted and complex animal. It is not simply the influence of immediate community, but rather the combination of societies and social influences that make up an individual's life experience. It is the individual's relationship with that society, and not just the society itself.

An extreme approach to the socialisation of risk is supported by social constructionists such as Ewald who states that "nothing is a risk in itself; there is no risk in reality. Anything can be a risk; it all depends on how one analyses the danger, considers the event."[105] He argues that reality is merely the reproduction of meanings defined through socialisation and social interaction.

1.3.11   Justice, equity and law

Individuals tend to prefer an outcome which is "fair". Unequal distribution is often acceptable where one individual has "earned" that increased pay-off or where the disproportionate pay-off reverts to "need" rather than merely to "want".[106] Concepts of equity and justice can also be fed into the utility model. The individual assessing the risk will use equity as one of his interests and will therefore be willing to incur "cost" in pursuit of justice, co-operation, the common good, equity, or the values of the individual's society or community.

1.3.12   Political context

The political element of an individual's bias includes the larger political context that influences and drives the individual's country or region as well as that dominating the organisational structure of the workplace, community or home.

---

[103]   Douglas and Wildavsky (1982) supra note 36 at 6.

[104]   Douglas, Purity and Danger: An Analysis of the Concepts of Pollution and Taboo at 2 (1966).

[105]   Ewald, "Insurance and Risks" in Burchell, Gordon and Miller (eds), The Foucault Effect: Studies in Governmentality at 199 (1991).

[106]   Beach (1997) supra note 21 at 115.

The individual's view of his political position, his ability to make decisions, the need to confirm decisions with, or justify decisions to, other individuals and any internal political decision-making that needs to occur can have a significant effect on risk-taking and risk assessment.

The individual will have a specific view of hierarchy based on his view of the importance of hierarchical standing, of belonging to a group.[107] The political context may complicate the validation of a risk decision through the political structure of the individual's company or organisation. A risk decision may have to be presented to a committee or person in authority for confirmation. Therefore, the risk decision will be influenced by political considerations, including organisational requirements, standards and practices.

1.3.13   Power

Power is the ability of an individual to carry out his own will despite resistance.[108] It is contextual, specific to a set of circumstances and the individuals involved. An individual has power in relation to an objective or part of an objective. There are several different elements of power, which may act in concert or independently. By identifying these elements we get a better view of the nature of power.

Theories of power generally divide their perspectives into an analysis of types of power and how that power is obtained. Galbraith sees three forms of power: condign (which involves punishment), compensatory (which involves reward) and conditioned (which is based on belief, persuasion, education or social commitment). He also sees three sources of power: personality, property and organisation.[109]

Russell identifies three sources of power: direct physical power over one's body, rewards and punishments, and influence on opinion. He sees naked power being disassociated with tradition or assent.[110] This view focuses on the individual, and his ability to influence his own acts and his immediate surroundings. It ignores, however, the sources of power created through society, culture and organisations and other resources available to an individual, such as time and information. There is also the important and essential resource of self-realisation; an individual must know or believe that he has power before he can act on that power in any but an accidental way.

It should be noted that the context of power does not require action. An individual can have power without using it. However, given the contextual nature of power, it is probably fair to say that it will never be clear what power an individual holds until that power is exercised and the influence of that power is manifest.

---

[107]   Waring and Glendon (1998) supra note 100 at 80-81.
[108]   This definition was given by Weber (1947) and Bacharach and Lawler (1980) as reported by Waring and Glendon (1998) supra note 100 at 89.
[109]   Galbraith, "Power and Organisation" in Lukes (ed), Power (1986).
[110]   Russell, "The Forms of Power" in Lukes (1986) supra note 109.

An individual's power is also independent of the perception of others. There is no need for the common perception of an individual as having power before that individual is able to assert that power. However, common perception that an individual has power often gives the individual power, even if he would not have had that power in the absence of the common perception.

Over time, the source of power can change. Power is not an absolute, and in certain circumstances individuals will perceive power, and who holds power, in different ways. Power may be gained or lost through the legitimacy of a mandate from other individuals. However, power is not necessarily tied to legitimate structure or hierarchy. It is often purely a creature of perception.

1.3.14 Institutional approaches or policy

Our society seeks certainty and it is for this reason that it puts so much faith in certain organisations, such as science and the government. This may also be influenced by organised irresponsibility, where individuals divest responsibility on to some larger organisation only to blame that organisation when they find that their trust has been misplaced. "We need to be certain, partly because there are so few points of certainty in our lives, and partly because we relish the ritual slaughter when they are found out."[111]

Any institution will have a more or less developed set of policies or approaches to decision-making and risk management in order to promote conformity. An institutional policy can improve efficiency by co-ordinating risk management and facilitating affirmation of decisions. These policies and approaches may be formal, set out in writing and part of the training regime within the institution, or may be passed down within the institution by rote or not at all. Some institutions may only apply policies and approaches retrospectively, when reviewing a project after negotiation and before affirmation, leaving the negotiation team in a very uncomfortable position.

Institutional learning can be a complex and long-term process. It is often based on hindsight, on risks that have arisen, rather than future risks which have been identified and need to be managed. Unless it is carefully managed, institutional learning tends to be reactive rather than proactive.

Turner views organisational learning as a cultural activity, rather than a process of instructing individuals or an informational process.[112] Structural adjustment of the organisation following change is often slow and difficult to implement. The learning process must transcend the culture of the organisation and become part of that culture. The larger and more complex the organisational structure, the more difficult it usually is to implement changes, in particular where such changes might alter the political power structure of the organisation. This static tendency

---

111 Coote, "Risk and Public Policy: Toward a High-Trust Democracy" in Franklin (ed), The Politics of Risk Society at 125 (1998).
112 Turner (ed), Risk Management at 84 and 85 (1992).

normally continues until a crisis is perceived, at which point individual interests may submit to the global concern of the continued survival and profitability of the organisation.

1.3.15   Team structure

Groups are generally seen to improve decision-making by permitting the allocation of greater and more diverse resources to task performance and benefiting from social value enhancement (from a socio-political point of view) for those members of the group. The group can also offer risk diffusion, and therefore allow more aggressive risk-taking decisions.

Group decision-making also has its drawbacks, including time consumption, conformity pressure within the group or the desire for acceptance, allowing one or a few members of the group to dominate, creating ambiguity in relation to responsibility for the final decision.[113] "Group-think" is when members of a group focus on seeking consensus rather than looking to alternative opportunities or ideas. This denies the group the creative energy and variety of experiences available in the context of the group. Members of the group will put pressure on individuals to conform to the group's approach, although there may only be an illusion of consensus. "Group shift" is the phenomenon of group decisions differing from individual decisions. The shift tends to be towards one extreme or another. In some cases, the group will be more conservative, where in others the group will drift toward greater risk-taking.

As the group size increases, members must wait longer in order to voice their opinions and may forget their idea or become entangled by other ideas being mentioned by the group rather than focusing on their new idea. This is known as "production blocking".[114] A partial solution to these limitations is brainstorming, isolating the participants from criticism or judgement and sharing the new ideas by alternative methods of communication. As an example, an electronic brainstorming system has been developed in order to avoid the perceived limitations of face-to-face group brainstorming sessions.

Decisions in relation to risk are substantially influenced by the make-up of the project team. The behaviour of a person in an organisation is constrained by the position he or she holds in that organisation, such that an individual will not entertain the full array of options that an outsider might consider available to him.[115] The seniority of the team members within the organisation will have an important impact on risk management. Senior people may have more flexibility in making risk decisions. However, their decision-making may be more politically motivated.

---

[113]   Robbins (9th edition 2001) supra note 55 at 240.
[114]   Diehl and Stroebe, "Productivity Loss in Brain Storming Groups: Toward the Solution of a Riddle" Journal of Personality and Social Psychology 53 at 497-509 (1987).
[115]   Simon, Administrative Behaviour (1945); Beach (1997) supra note 21.

Decision-makers tend to forego the ideal solution in favour of the first acceptable or reasonable solution that they identify. This is known as decision-maker's "satisfice".[116] Decision-makers tend not to examine all possible alternatives, but rather to adopt the first reasonable solution identified.

Within the team there may not be a lone decision-maker ("the myth of the decision maker"[117]), but rather risk decisions may be made by some form of consensus. This raises associated issues of power, hierarchy, group-think and decision trade-off. The concessions made within the team in an effort to achieve consensus can alter significantly risk assessment and the collective approach to risk management.

1.3.16   Education and training

An individual's education and training can have an impact on risk assessment similar to technical expertise, allowing an individual to identify risks that other less educated individuals might not identify, or to appreciate the context of a risk and take a more objective view of the risk. Another theory argues that individuals with superior education adopt a "superman" complex which might motivate them to accept higher levels of risk under the impression that they are less vulnerable to risk than other individuals.

It is worth noting that education and training must not be limited to formal processes. As Mark Twain is reputed to have said: "I have never let my schooling interfere with my education."

1.3.17   Technical

An individual's technical bias will affect how that individual interprets information and the risk perceived in existing or new technology.[118] Recent experience with a technology may have a disproportionate impact on risk assessment. Recent bad experience, in particular with a certain type of technology, will often result in extreme sensitivity to risks related to that technology. A very technically experienced individual will identify and appreciate technical risks more readily, either permitting the taking of a realistic view of a risk, therefore reducing the impact of the risk on the individual's assessment, or resulting in the individual identifying risks that an individual with less technical acumen might not perceive.

---

[116]   March and Simon, Organisations (1958).

[117]   Chapman, Phillips, Cooper and Lightfoot, "Selecting an Appraisal to Project Time and Cost Planning" International Journal of Project Management 3 (1985).

[118]   Fischhoff, Slovic and Lichtenstein, "Weighing the Risks: Which Risks are Acceptable?" Environment 2 at 17 (1979) reprinted in Slovic (ed), The Perception of Risk (2000).

In order for experts to influence risk decisions there must be a perception of expertise, they must be trusted.[119] Slovic found that trust is easier to lose than it is to win.[120] This trust is hard to come by. Some studies found that experts are less accurate in their assessments than simple statistical models, or in some cases less accurate even than novices. They believe that this failing of experts is due to a lack of feedback. When experts learn inaccurate rules, no-one dares to correct them.[121] Also, experts appear to be less cognisant of their own cognitive limitations.[122] This research underlines the modern trend to distrust experts.

1.3.18   Financial

Finance is an important element of any commercial enterprise, from finding necessary funding and investment to arranging finance for a specific enterprise. Issues such as the nature of the funding or investment provided, the provider's financial status and the level of the provider's commitment to the enterprise will form part of the individual's assessment of risk. The nature of financing and the individual's perception of that financing will affect the way risks are perceived. Therefore, an individual's financial context will have a direct effect on risk assessment.

An individual will expend transaction resources in order to identify the parameters of a risk decision. These transaction resources will include:

> search costs (to gain more information about the decision);

> bargaining and decision costs (in order to further identify the parameters of the bargain being offered and to ascertain whether some other bargain or decision may be available that would be of more benefit to that individual); and

> monitoring costs (where the individual is uncertain about the enforceability of the alternative outcomes or, indeed, to learn more about the risk decision where that information might change over time).[123]

Money spent early buys more than money spent late. However, money spent early is also money at risk until the transaction is agreed and implemented.

---

[119]   See, for example, the review of regulatory regimes in Europe and the United States, and the relationship between consultative processes, adversarial relationships and trust. Lofstedt and Vogel, "The Changing Character of Regulation: A Comparison of Europe and the United States" Risk Analysis 21 at 399 (2001).

[120]   Slovic, "Perceived Risk, Trust and Democracy" Risk Analysis 13 at 675 (1993) reprinted in Slovic (2000) supra note 118.

[121]   See, for example, Camerer and Johnson, "The Process-Performance Paradox in Expert Judgement: How Can Experts Know so Much and Predict so Badly?" in Ericsson and Smith (eds), Toward a General Theory of Expertise: Prospects and Limits (1991).

[122]   Slovic, Fischhoff and Lichtenstein, "Rating the Risk" Environment 2 at 14 (1979) reprinted in Slovic (2000) supra note 118.

[123]   Coleman, Risks and Wrongs (1992).

The financial climate, cost of money and availability of finance that predominates in the relevant market can have a significant and immediate impact on risk assessment. Where money is more expensive, risk is more expensive to manage and the attitude of lenders toward risk will become more conservative. The converse is true. Risk attitudes become far more generous where markets are buoyant and hopes high.

1.3.19   Commercial

Individuals react to market forces. These forces create the context surrounding any transaction and risk assessment, and affect all of the parties to a project, though often in different ways. The nature of an individual's commercial context, his experience, technical expertise, the market with which he is familiar and the risk he is accustomed to bearing will form part of that individual's filter. As an example, an engineering firm will be comfortable with designing a technical solution for a project and warranting the performance of that technical solution, but may not be comfortable warranting the future market value of the product produced by the technical solution.

Risk assessment will often follow not only the reactions of the individual to market forces but also the approach adopted by other companies in the market. This may partially result from the desire of that individual to ensure a deal no worse than that obtained by other parties in the market. But, the market can be a fickle source of information. It influences risk decisions by creating expectations of the terms to be obtained, the costs to be incurred and the outcome to be achieved. The acceptance of certain risks by the market does not necessarily result from a demonstrable increase in efficiency. This attitude may stem from group-think or mob rule, where an individual adopts the risk perception of a group, with no logical or rational basis for adopting that perception. It may also result in the belief that the market would only accept reasonable and workable risk allocation. This is, of course, not always the case.

1.3.20   Risk Communication

In addition to the different factors influencing our personal filter and creating risk noise, an individual's assessment of risk will be influenced by the manner in which risk information (including an assessment of the risk) is provided to the public and to the individual ("risk communication").[124] The provision of risk information provides the individual part of the information upon which the individual will make a risk decision. Equally, the management of risk information shapes the

---

[124]   Slovic, "Informing and Educating the Public About Risk" Risk Analysis 6 at 403 (1986) reprinted in Slovic (2000) supra note 118; Covello, Slovic and von Winterfeldt, "Risk Communication – a Review of the Literature" Risk Abstracts 3 at 172 (1986); Jungermann, Kasperson and Wiedemann (eds), Risk Communication (1988); Kasperson and Stallen (eds), Communicating Risk to the Public (1991).

context against which an individual assesses risk.[125] Risk communication provides an important part of an individual's ability to assess a risk.[126]

Risk communication can be used to provide information, enable the receiver to understand that information, persuade the receiver of the appropriate assessment of the risk and/or provide the opportunity to discuss and debate the appropriate assessment of a risk.[127] There is some debate as to whether risk communication should be persuasive or just informative, whether information can ever be provided free of any bias or context, and how much information should be provided (e.g. simple statements, full descriptions or weighing-up of pros and cons).[128]

Risk issues are communicated to an individual and to the public via a number of media and processes. The use of messaging mechanisms that are understood differently by different individuals can have a significant impact on risk assessment.[129]

Individuals assign levels of trustworthiness and likelihood of accuracy to each source of information.[130] They tend to want information from a variety of sources, and will prefer certain sources to provide certain types of information.[131] As Slovic points out, "whoever controls the definition of risk controls the rational solution to the problem at hand". This corresponds with Flyvbjerg's view that rationality is context dependent, and that power defines what counts as rationality. Those in power are able to rationalise their chosen solution and thereby make it rationality.[132] Therefore risk decisions need more public participation to "make the decision process more democratic".[133]

1.3.21   Nature versus nurture

Certain schools of thought argue that risk assessment is partially or wholly genetic by nature. They see human beings as the victims or beneficiaries of genetic make-up, able to make only slight alterations to their genetic predispositions or indeed predestination. At the base of this view is the argument that an individual is driven by his nature, rather than the manner by which that individual is nurtured.

---

[125]   Wilkinson, Elahi and Eidinow, "Background and Dynamics of the Scenarios" Journal of Risk Research 6 at 365 (2003).

[126]   For an overview of risk communication see Lofstedt, "Risk Communication: Pitfalls and Promises" European Review 11 at 417 (2003).

[127]   Zimmerman, "A Process Framework for Risk Communication" Science, Technology and Human Values 12 (1987).

[128]   Jaeger, Renn, Rosa and Webler, Risk, Uncertainty and Rational Action (2001).

[129]   Jardine and Hrudey, "Mixed Messages in Risk Communication" Risk Analysis 17 at 489 (1997).

[130]   NRC, Improving Risk Communication (1989); Slovic (1986) supra note 124 at 401; Slovic, (1993) supra note 120.

[131]   Jungermann, Pfister and Fischer, "Credibility, Information Preferences, and Information Interests" Risk Analysis 16 at 251 (1996).

[132]   Flyvbjerg, Rationality and Power: Democracy in Practice (1998).

[133]   Slovic, "Trust, Emotion, Sex, Politics, and Science: Surveying the Risk-Assessment Battlefield" Risk Analysis 19 at 689 (1999).

The "nature versus nurture" controversy has plagued philosophers for centuries. Those advocating the nurture theory include Hippocrates, John Locke and Jean-Jacques Rousseau. These philosophers regard the newborn child as a blank page on which are to be inscribed his personality and character. This led to the belief that socialisation and education could change an individual's character. Those supporting the "nature" view include Thomas Hobbes and Herbert Spencer following on from certain of Darwin's theories. This school of thought sees genetic make-up as determinative to a large extent of the essential nature of a person. Francis Galton[134] believed that the "nature" view explained social stratification. Professor Dublos demonstrated the same conflict in the theories of Freud and Jung.[135] More recent studies appear to indicate that the "nature versus nurture" controversy is far too simplistic, that man is actually a complex combination of a variety of factors.

---

[134] See section 1.2.1.4 for further discussion of Galton.
[135] Thorpe, Animal Nature and Human Nature at 213 (1974).

Chapter 2

Traditional Theory of Risk Allocation

Not being able to make that which is just strong, man
has made that which is strong just.

Pascal

Allocation of risk is a key aspect of infrastructure projects, and misallocation of risk is one of the leading causes of disputes.[136] Such misallocation also increases the total cost of construction for both the employer and the contractor. Due to the importance of risk allocation and the desire to improve efficiency in infrastructure projects, a significant body of knowledge has grown up around the analysis of risk in infrastructure projects to help parties assess the most efficient method of allocating risk within a project.[137] For ease of reference, I will use "traditional approach" to describe the approach adopted in this body of knowledge.[138]

The traditional approach to risk allocation involves isolating each risk and finding the most efficient method of allocating that risk. Efficient risk allocation should lead to enhanced project performance evidenced by reduced costs, reduced time to build and/or improved quality of the completed works.[139]

This traditional approach is widely accepted in the construction industry and is described by Abrahamson as follows: "Risk should be placed on insurers or other professional gamblers where practicable; otherwise it should be placed on whoever gains the main economic benefit of running it; that is, on to one who carelessly or

---

[136] Smith, "Risk Identification and Allocation: Saving Money by Improving Contracts and Contracting Practices" [1995] ICLR at 40.

[137] Barnes, "How to Allocate Risks in Construction Contracts" International Journal of Project Management 1 at 24 (1983); Barnes, "Effective Project Organisation" Building Technology and Management (December 1984); Abrahamson, "Risk Management" [1984] ICLR at 241.

[138] The analysis in chapters 1 and 2 forms part of a PhD thesis that the author is currently pursuing at King's College, London; see also Delmon (2004) supra note 7.

[139] Chapman, Ward and Curtis, "Risk Theory for Contracting" in Uff and Capper (eds), Construction Contract Policy: Improved Procedures and Practice (1989).

wilfully creates it, or can best control the events that may lead to it occurring or best manage it when it does occur."[140]

It is believed that a project that follows the traditional approach to efficient risk allocation will have fewer significant problems and be more cost effective overall.[141] The proper allocation of risk between parties (where risk is assigned to the party best equipped to manage and minimise that risk) should reduce the overall cost of the project and promote a more positive working relationship between the parties. Where risk is unnecessarily assigned to one party, at best the project will be more dispute-prone, at worst the parties face the complete failure of the project.[142]

This traditional view of risk allocation uses the absolute measure of efficiency in pursuit of the maximisation of the effect of the investment of available resources. This chapter provides a discussion of the background to the traditional approach (section 2.1), analyses the elements that make up the traditional approach to efficient risk allocation (section 2.2) and identifies certain aspects of the literature that hint at the existence and importance of risk noise (section 2.3).[143]

2.1   Elements of the Traditional Approach

In order to describe the traditional approach to efficient risk allocation in more detail, this section will analyse the questions commonly asked in the context of the traditional approach to efficient risk allocation as follows:[144]

> ➤ who can control the occurrence of a risk? (2.1.1);

> ➤ who wants to be in a position of control over the circumstances related to the risk? (2.1.2);

> ➤ who can manage the risk for the least cost? (2.1.3);

> ➤ is the relevant party able to manage the risk, does it have the relevant resources and is it in a position to manage the risk? (2.1.4);

---

[140]   Abrahamson, "Risk Problems Relating to Construction" in Uff and Capper (1989) supra note 139. This viewpoint is supported by a number of other authors in the sector, in particular by Alan Muir Wood in his work "Tunnelling: Management by Design" (2000) where he attacks the concept of a zero-sum mode of operation, the theory that placing further risk on one party will have no effect or a beneficial effect on the other party. This, Muir Wood argues, is incorrect since inappropriate or inefficient management of risk will cause a project to become vulnerable and unstable, to the detriment of all.

[141]   Nunn, "Managing Risk in Construction: Should Contractors Have Legislative Protection to Ensure Prompt Payment?" [2001] ICLR at 469.

[142]   Muir Wood (2000) supra note 140.

[143]   Risk noise is described further in chapter 1.

[144]   Ashley, Dunlop and Parker, "Impact of Risk Allocation and Equity in Construction Contracts" in Uff and Odams (eds), Risk, Management and Procurement in Construction (1995); Jones, Savage and Westgate, Partnering and Collaborative Working: Law and Industry Practice at 217 (2003); Bower, "Contractor Selection, Contractor Work and Contractor Law in the UK" in Bower (ed), Management of Procurement (2003); Bunni, Risk and Insurance in Construction at 37 (2003).

> ➤ can the relevant party bear the consequences of the risk? (2.1.5);

> ➤ is there an interrelationship between the relevant risk and other project risks? (2.1.6); and

> ➤ will that party be motivated to manage the risk in the most efficient and effective manner possible? (2.1.7)

2.1.1 Who can control the occurrence of a risk?

The efficient allocation of risk will assign risk to the party best able to control it.[145] The party able to control whether or not the risk arises, or to what extent it can arise, can have a significant, advantageous influence on the potential effect of the risk on the project. Bearing the risk will motivate that party to use its control to reduce the likelihood of the occurrence of the risk or the impact of that risk and therefore protect the project from the potential effect of its occurrence. Abrahamson notes that this is in the interest of efficiency, including planning, incentive and innovation, which is key to the health of the construction industry.[146]

For example, in the construction industry, the party able to manage the design and construction of the works is most often best able to manage the risk of the performance of the completed works, the level of operation achieved and the output attained. The contractor who provides both design and construction services for an employer is generally best placed to manage the risk of implementation of the design and interfaces between the design and the construction methods used.[147] This rationale has resulted in the development of the turnkey construction contract, wherein the construction contractor designs and constructs the works and bears much of the risk associated with construction.[148] These contracts generally place the majority of the risk of the performance of the completed works on the contractor, under the premise that the contractor can control the occurrence of performance risk.[149]

This does not advocate an absolute allocation of risk to the party that can bear the risk at the lowest cost (least-cost risk bearer), because that party may not have the incentives necessary to properly bear that risk and it may not have the trust of the other parties. Responsible allocation of risk involves assigning a risk to a party

---

[145] Sweet, "Defects: A Summary and Analysis of American Law" in Selected Problems of Construction Law: International Approach (1982); Abrahamson (1984) supra note 137 at 241.

[146] Abrahamson (1984) supra note 137 at 241.

[147] Wallace, Construction Contracts: Principles and Policies in Tort and Contract at 407 (1986).

[148] Scriven, "Design Risk and Liability under Design and Build Contracts" Construction Law Journal 12 at 226. Scriven notes that this allocation of design risk is additional to those risks borne by the contractor in a traditional form of contract. He also notes that there is no legal definition of "design" and therefore specific consideration will need to be given to the extent of this risk allocation.

[149] Brown, "Opportunities and Risks of Design Build Projects" The Construction Superconference, San Francisco, USA (7 and 8 December 1995).

that has a comparative advantage in regard to risk-bearing ability and has control over the risk.[150]

2.1.2   Who wants to be in a position of control over the circumstances related to the risk?

The process of managing or avoiding a risk will require some control over the circumstances surrounding that risk. The party bearing the risk should have a desire to control the circumstances that surround the risk in order to avoid or manage its occurrence. For example, one party may want to be awarded the subcontract for the works associated with the risk, or those circumstances may relate to some other aspect of the party's business that would provide that party with some other benefit. Without the desire to control the circumstances related to the risk, the party bearing the risk may not avoid or manage the potential occurrence of the risk as efficiently or with as much expediency as a party that wants to control those circumstances. The party in control or wanting to control those circumstances may, therefore, be best placed to bear the relevant risk.

The reason for a party's desire to manage a risk can vary. One party may want the recognition or publicity related to the control of the circumstances surrounding a risk. The control of such circumstances may provide that party with other benefits. In poor urban areas in certain parts of the United States, parks and open areas have been handed over to local residents. They receive no compensation, but the ability to improve the neighbourhood (and some say to improve the value of their properties) provides sufficient motivation to invest the effort in managing and maintaining these areas. The party bearing the risk may also be paid a fee for bearing that risk. "The life-blood of business is to make money by dealing with the risks which other people do not want to bear."[151]

Capper notes that one of the keys to efficient allocation of risk is the creation of incentives. Unless a party is incentivised to manage a risk efficiently and properly, will the risk allocation mechanism ever be successful? Further, as noted above, this incentive must be practical, the party must be able to bear the risk if it arises, and the incentive must entice that party to commit the resources necessary to ensure that the risk is managed.[152]

2.1.3   Who can manage the risk for the least cost?

There is a cost associated with the management of any risk, including the allocation of resources, capital investment and technical expertise. Each party will be able to identify how much it will cost for it to manage a risk. The party that can

---

[150]   Jones, "Philosophies of Risk Allocation – The Case for Foreseeability" [1996] ICLR at 570.
[151]   Murdoch and Hughes, Construction Contracts: Law and Management (1992).
[152]   Capper, "Basic Choices in the Allocation and Management of Risk" [2001] ICLR at 324.

manage that risk at the least cost should bear the risk. This approach will result in a less expensive project and should benefit all parties involved.[153]

Least-cost risk management is an oft-adopted approach to risk allocation, even in organisations otherwise inexperienced in risk allocation methodologies. Cost is a simple and practical measure of the impact of risk and its efficient management. It is generally easy to measure, apply and compare risk management amongst different parts of the organisation using cost measurement.

2.1.4 Is the relevant party able to manage the risk, does it have the relevant resources and is it in a position to manage the risk?

Even if a party can control the occurrence of a risk at the least cost and is prepared to assume it, that party must have also the physical ability and the necessary resources, and must be in a position, to manage the risk.[154] An understanding of the risk and a command of the know-how and technology needed to manage the risk are insufficient in and of themselves: the party bearing the risk should have available to it sufficient information[155] and be able to commit the necessary resources to the project and the management of the risk. The party managing the risk will also be limited by the amount of information available on the relevant risk and its organisation's internal policy, cultural biases and other guiding factors in relation to risk management. Each of these elements will contribute to the party's "ability" to manage the risk.

2.1.5 Can the relevant party bear the consequences of the risk?

Risk should be allocated to the party which is best able to evaluate and control it. However, one must also consider that party's ability to bear the risk.[156] If the risk materialises and has an impact that the responsible party cannot sustain, or forces

---

[153] Head, "Risk and Reality in Private Infrastructure Development" in Uff and Odams (eds), New Horizons in Construction Law (1998); Chapman, Ward and Curtis adopt this logic by stating: "How should project risks be allocated, or what amounts to the same thing, what method of payment should be adopted for a given contract?" Chapman, Ward and Curtis (1989) supra note 139. Where uncertainty arises from a project, that uncertainty can be calculated through a cumulative probability distribution analysis, and where the contractual parties are not the rational, risk-averse decision-makers desired, then risk aversion and indifference can also be mapped and measured within the context of the analysis. Once these variables have been calculated, they translate into changes in the pricing of the project.

[154] Barber, "Risks in the Method of Construction" in Uff and Capper (1989) supra note 139; Abrahamson (1984) supra note 137 at 241.

[155] Placing risk on a party that is presumed to have sufficient information, when everyone knows it does not, is ultimately inefficient and renders the project more vulnerable to the detriment of all. Abrahamson (1984) supra note 137 at 241.

[156] Bishop, "Legal Obligation in Construction: Responsibility, Liability and Redress: Is There Anybody There?" in Uff and Lavers (eds), Legal Obligations in Construction: Revised Conference Proceedings (1992).

that party to turn to indiscriminate claims or other desperate measures in order to protect itself, this allocation is inefficient.[157]

In construction, for example, certain parties contend that any risk can be given to the construction contractor. The contractor will then put a contingency element for that risk in its price for that contract. Abrahamson points out that this kind of risk allocation can result in either the failure of the construction contractor, putting it out of business, or forcing the construction contractor to add the full amount of contingency to its price in relation to each contract because the event of that risk in one contract could put the construction contractor out of business. Therefore the construction contractor cannot diversify in order to manage the relevant risk.[158]

This aspect of the traditional approach also, for some, includes fundamental notions of fairness.[159] The concept of fairness, though it should not be allowed to dominate the question of the allocation of risk, is an essential element in such considerations. The contract should not be allowed to be blatantly one-sided or trap the unwary. This fairness is interpreted in accordance with the presumed approach of a prudent businessman or responsible government department.[160]

2.1.6   Is there an interrelationship between the relevant risk and other project risks?

The allocation of a risk must be seen in the context of other project risks. Risks within a project may be interrelated with other project risks, requiring joint management or at least management in co-ordination to achieve efficient and coherent risk management.[161] Certain risks can be managed more efficiently in parallel, therefore the different parties managing these risks may need to agree how to manage these risks together, or it may be more efficient for one party to manage all related risks. In a construction context, ground condition risk may be relevant to several contractors, e.g. those laying foundations, performing other civil and tunnelling works and those laying utility cables or pipes to and from the site. In such circumstances, it would be inefficient for each of these contractors to perform duplicate subsurface surveys; it may be more efficient for one contractor to bear all associated subsurface risk.

---

157   Barnes (December 1984) supra note 137. Barnes sees this inefficiency as the stimulus for the growth of the claims industry. Abrahamson (1984) supra note 137 at 241. Abrahamson sees it as discouragement to the growth and improved quality of the construction industry. See also Ashley, Dunlop and Parker (1995) supra note 144.

158   Abrahamson (1984) supra note 137 at 241.

159   This concept of fairness is probably inconsistent with the turnkey approach to contracting that has dominated the industry over the last 10 years. See also Sweet (1982) supra note 145.

160   Barber (1989) supra note 154.

161   Kerzner supports this statement, and also notes that risks should be prioritised in order to assist in their co-ordinated management, where one risk must be preferred over another or the management of one risk is inherently inconsistent with the management of another. Kerzner, Project Management: A Systems Approach to Planning, Scheduling and Controlling (8th edition 2003). Wirba, Tah and Howes, "Risk Interdependencies and Natural Language Complications" Engineering, Construction and Architectural Management 3 at 251 (1996).

2.1.7 Will that party be motivated to manage the risk in the most efficient and effective manner possible?

The party bearing a risk must be motivated to manage that risk efficiently and effectively in the context of the project as a whole.[162] In the above example of the construction contractor performing both design and construction services, the contractor may be motivated to under-design the works in order to decrease construction costs. Therefore, the allocation of risk to the contractor will need to ensure that it has an incentive to design the works to the level desired and to ensure that the finished product meets the requirements of the employer.

2.2 The Background to the Traditional Approach

The following is a discussion of the implementation of the traditional approach into recent reviews of the construction industry, some of the mechanisms used to help implement quantitative assessment and the use of the traditional approach in other disciplines.[163]

2.2.1 Latham, Egan, Grove and on[164]

The traditional approach has been adopted by several recent formal reviews within the construction industry.[165] It was adopted by the 1994 report of Sir Michael Latham in his review of the construction industry in the United Kingdom entitled "Constructing the Team", and by the report of the Construction Task Force led by Sir John Egan entitled "Rethinking Construction" in July 1998. These two reports formed the basis of a comprehensive review of the perceived shortcomings in the United Kingdom construction industry, with an eye to addressing criticisms and weaknesses within it. This review resulted in the introduction of the United Kingdom Housing Grants, Construction and Regeneration Act (2000) and significant changes in the industry.

In September 1998, Jesse Grove published his report for the Hong Kong Works Bureau reviewing the risk allocation approach adopted in the standard form contracts used for Hong Kong Government procurement. Grove based his analysis of construction contracting practice in Hong Kong on the traditional approach to efficient risk allocation.[166]

---

[162] Abrahamson (1989) supra note 140.
[163] Thompson and Perry, Engineering Construction Risk (1992); Lloyd, Humphrey, "The Grove Report: The Background to the Conference on Whose Risk?" [2001] ICLR at 302.
[164] Abrahamson (1984) supra note 137 at 241.
[165] This approach has been adopted in the United States by the American Society of Civil Engineers and the Construction Industry Institute, see Smith (1995) supra note 136 at 40; and in Australia, see Megens (1997) supra note 3 at 5.
[166] Lloyd (2001) supra note 163 at 302.

2.2.2 Mechanisms to assist in implementing the traditional approach

There is an inherent amount of uncertainty associated with such risks.[167] The parties should consider the extent to which these risks are calculable and quantifiable. As O'Reilly notes, the traditional approach is simply a set of baseline principles, ones that need to be applied to the project and the parties. It is for this reason that they tend to be very difficult to apply in their purest form.[168] For example, the very concept of measuring the probability of a risk arising is far more complicated than it may appear. Whyte divides the methods for risk analysis into deterministic risk analysis (which looks at each risk independently), probabilistic risk analysis (which looks at probabilities and interdependence of risk), and more complex mechanisms (which look at the interaction between the probability of various events).[169] In order to assess risk properly and take risk decisions, risk must be expressed in a quantifiable and comparable manner.[170]

In order to assist parties in applying the traditional approach, a number of methods and processes have been developed to quantify risk and assess its likelihood and potential. Mechanisms and techniques for risk analysis under the traditional approach include the following:[171]

> - life-cycles cost analysis – looks at the impact of risk on life-cycle and associated costs;

> - As Low As Reasonably Practicable (ALARP);

> - Best Available Techniques Not Entailing Excessive Cost (BATNEEC);

> - Total Risk Assessing Cost Analysis (TRACE);

> - decision tree analysis – analyses the frequency of prior events to identify the probability of the occurrence of a key event;

> - controlled interval methods – calculates a range of potential outcomes and the probability of the occurrence of a combination of events; and

---

[167]   Bishop (1992) supra note 156. Bishop identifies some of the technical, management and control uncertainties that plague even the most well-planned construction projects.

[168]   O'Reilly, "Risk, Construction Contracts and Construction Disputes" in Uff and Odams (1995) supra note 144.

[169]   Whyte, "Ground Uncertainty Effects on Project Finance" in Uff and Odams (1995) supra note 144.

[170]   This rate is extremely difficult to apply to all of the different risks that may be encountered. For example, a few of the methods used include death per unit measure, loss of life expectancy and frequency against consequence. None of these apply absolutely to every type of risk that may be encountered. A more common approach is to monetise risks, which again raises its own issues of accuracy and applicability. Royal Society (1992) supra note 9.

[171]   Marshall, "Risk Analysis in Dispute Resolution" [1995] ICLR at 600; Kerzner (8th edition 2003) supra note 161; Waring and Glendon, Managing Risk: Critical Issues for Survival and Success into the 21st Century (1998).

> ➢ Monte Carlo simulation – much like a game of roulette, this technique identifies the likely duration and probability of the occurrence of certain events for each individual activity. By combining these random probability measures, the technique enables the party to identify a combination of probabilities with respect to the actual duration and output of the project.

Computer-based techniques provide a probability analysis for an infrastructure project using these techniques, including Program Evaluation and Review Techniques (PERT) and Claims, Litigation and Arbitration Risk Assessment Technique (CLARAT), which uses a Monte Carlo simulation to achieve some 20,000 simulations calculated and graphed in less than 100 seconds.[172] Most of the popular specialist computer programs, for example @Risk™ and Predict™, used to calculate values for risk and combination of risks, employee the Monte Carlo simulation. These packages tend to use only a three-point triangular distribution, rather than the vastly more complicated distribution that would be necessary to measure the potential interdependence of variables.[173]

The traditional approach has also been adopted in project management and the mechanisms often used by project managers to manage risk, for example the Computer Aided Simulation for Project Appraisal and Review (CASPAR), which is used to calculate the probability of cost and duration of a project with only limited information.[174]

2.2.3   The traditional approach in other disciplines

This traditional approach to risk allocation does not belong solely to the construction industry nor to the hard sciences, but is also shared by various soft sciences. For example, in sociology and psychology literature, Doderlein notes that all risks can be reduced by the application of sufficient resources while the amount of available resources is limited. According to these soft sciences, an approach to risk reduction should deploy available risk-reduction resources to obtain maximum risk-reduction per dollar invested.[175]

2.3   The Traditional Theory and Risk Noise

The traditional approach to risk allocation focuses on the efficiency gains available in risk management, and the balance between the cost of taking a risk and the potential return or benefit to be obtained by the party taking the risk. The traditional approach uses quantitative risk assessment to make its calculations, in order to make a reasonable comparison between the cost efficiencies, time implications and comparable value that risk decisions represent for different parties. This quantification is generally based on mathematical mechanisms and, more recently, computerised methodologies, in order to achieve this quantification.

---

[172]   O'Reilly (1995) supra note 168.
[173]   Smith, Appraisal, Risk and Uncertainty at 28 (2003).
[174]   Uff, "Contract Documents and the Division of Risk" in Uff and Odams (1995) supra note 144.
[175]   Doderlein, "Introduction" in Singleton and Hovden (1987) supra note 8 at 1.

The traditional approach assumes that the parties are rational, risk-averse decision-makers.[176] It assumes a quantifiable analysis of risk[177] without providing for the human nature of those individuals performing the risk assessment and quantification necessary to its success.[178] Risk noise reduces this quantifiability and will therefore reduce the efficiency of risk management.[179]

2.3.1   Numeric quantification of linguistic quantitative assessment

In many cases the quantification of risk is extremely difficult as it is based on an individual's qualitative assessment, for example where an individual perceives that a risk is "very likely" to arise and its impact will be "high". These linguistic expressions of quantitative assessment of the likelihood and impact of a risk are not expressed as numbers and are therefore of limited use for mathematical calculations. However, by using fuzzy logic, these linguistic analyses, possessed of qualitative elements, can be quantified and given numerical values, which can then be processed by mathematical mechanisms. The use of fuzzy logic does not change the fact that the focus of the assessment is quantitative risk analysis; however it extends the otherwise quantitative analysis to include certain elements of qualitative analysis. The usefulness of fuzzy logic is limited to situations in which an element of quantitative assessment is available not in numerical form but only in a linguistic assessment of quantity, a subjective view of risk.[180]

---

[176]   Chapman, Ward and Curtis (1989) supra note 139.

[177]   See generally, Cooper and Chapman, Risk Analysis for Large Projects: Models, Methods and Cases (1987).

[178]   The Institution of Civil Engineers and the Faculty and Institute of Actuaries, Risk Analysis and Management for Projects (1998).

[179]   Risk noise is described further in chapter 1.

[180]   The conflict between qualitative and quantitative risk assessment and the inability of traditional mathematical models to address qualitative issues has been identified by certain academics. Fuzzy sets translate linguistic expressions such as "likely" or "low impact" into numerical membership functions, enabling mathematical mechanisms to analyse the impact of such linguistic expressions. This allows the personal and individual nature of quantitative risk assessment to be expressed in a numerical manner. (Mak, "Risk Analysis in Construction: A Paradigm Shift from a Hard to Soft Approach" Construction Management and Economics 13 at 385 (1995).) Tah and Carr also use fuzzy logic mechanisms in order to assess the qualitative influence on quantitative assessment. This is intended to resolve the problem of the inability to provide an exact value to the quantitative analysis of risk, since by definition risk is uncertain. Similar to Mak, Tah and Carr propose a method to quantify the qualitative nature of the quantitative analysis of risk, by applying a value to the concepts of the likelihood and severity which the relevant risk is perceived to embody. This proposal is a significant step forward from pure quantitative analysis that assumes all knowledge and an accurate calculation of risk; however, it does not provide for the effects of risk noise or the other concerns raised in this chapter. ("A Proposal for Construction Project Risk Assessment using Fuzzy Logic" Construction Management and Economics 18 at 491 (2000).) Lam, So, Hu, Ng, Yuen, Lo, Chung and Yang endeavour to establish a mathematical mechanism to address both qualitative and quantitative concepts. They used the fuzzy multiple-objective technique, inputting the decision-maker's stated preferences. ("An Integration of the Fuzzy Reasoning Technique and the Fuzzy Optimisation Method in Construction Project Management Decision-making" Construction Management and Economics 19 at 63 (2001).) It should be noted, however, that this mechanism takes only a very limited view of the qualitative variables that affect risk decision-making and will therefore not address all of the different elements associated with risk

2.3.2 Hints at risk noise and its effects in the traditional approach literature

The traditional approach does not allow for other drivers that influence risk.[181] Chapman, Ward and Curtis hint at this possibility when they note that there may be "situations where client and contractor do not have a shared view of cost uncertainties and the associated effects of optimism and pessimism about project costs" and the way they price risks.[182] Capper, concurring with Thompson and Perry, notes that parties should guard against differences in perceptions of risk.[183]

Jardine and Johnson note that any effort to assess risk is hampered by lack of information and the human tendency to perceive risk in accordance with individual attitudes. These challenges to effective risk assessment are further limited by the perception that the majority of the best engineers able to assess risk are not busy assessing risk, but are instead assessing claims and disputes: much energy is focused on resolving disputes once the parties' minds are focused on the problem, rather than focusing attention on properly managing the risk in the first place.[184]

Some authors challenge these basic concepts of a traditional approach, for example Smith who argues that although risk allocation is an essential task that must be undertaken with every project, it cannot be accomplished by a theoretical, intellectual exercise. Any risk allocation philosophy must be cost-effective and enlightened.[185] Jones argues that any assessment of an ability to control risk may be inconsistent with commercial reality. He argues that the foreseeability model, where the contractor only bears risks that could be reasonably foreseen by an experienced contractor, is a method more consistent with commercial reality providing an objective and flexible approach to the question of risk allocation.[186]

The very assessment as to who controls a risk or who is motivated to manage it, which is essential to the traditional approach, is rendered difficult to make in an abstract manner by the influence of individual bias and perception of risk.[187] O'Reilly, while assessing the view that risk should be allocated to the party best able to manage it, notes that "it seems to me, however, that this pre-supposes,

---

noise. It also only considers the qualitative influences of a single risk decision-maker, rather than the number of different decision-makers that will be involved in a normal project.

[181] Edwards and Bowen point to this movement in the study of risk in construction projects in "Risk and Risk Management in Construction: A Review and the Future Directions for Research" Engineering, Construction and Architectural Management 5 at 339 (1998); Rahman and Kumaraswany, in their article "Risk Management Trends in the Construction Industry: Moving Towards Joint Risk Management" Engineering, Construction and Architectural Management 9 at 101 (2002) note that the effort to agree on the traditional approach is itself inhibited by different parties' perceptions of risk and therefore their interpretation of the traditional approach.

[182] Chapman, Ward and Curtis (1989) supra note 139.

[183] Capper, "Overview of Risk in Construction" in Uff and Odams (1995) supra note 144.

[184] Jardine and Johnson, "Risk in Ground Engineering: A Framework for Assessment" in Uff and Odams (1995) supra note 144.

[185] Smith, Robert, "Allocation of Risk – the Case for Manageability" [1996] ICLR at 549.

[186] Jones (1996) supra note 150 at 570.

[187] Chicken and Posner, The Philosophy of Risk (1998).

wrongly in my view, that risks have an independent existence". He sees actual risk allocation based on concepts of self-interest, as that self-interest is perceived by each party.[188] Kerzner admits that "the ultimate decision on how to deal with risk is based in part upon the project manager's tolerance for risk".[189] Humphrey Lloyd identifies the importance of human nature in the analysis of risk, highlighting the effect of preconceptions that plague any effort at risk assessment. He notes that "I am not convinced whether such standards [the moral or ethical standards identifying who "ought" to bear a risk] can be defined or treated as universally accepted throughout the international construction industry".[190]

In 1992, the Royal Society published its "Risk: Analysis, Perception and Management", which provides a review of the study of risk over a variety of different industries and specialisms. Throughout its review, the Royal Society notes that quantification of risk is a serious academic subject and requires further attention through improved data availability and control procedures. However, quantifiable risk assessment should not be treated rigidly, as flexibility will allow it to be most effectively adapted to real situations. Risk, the Royal Society notes, is an essentially human and social phenomenon. The quantitative and qualitative aspects of risk assessment cannot be separated so simply; it is not helpful to try to devalue public attitudes and beliefs in favour of an abstract statistical rationality.[191]

2.4   Conclusion

One key difficulty in the application of the traditional approach to efficient risk allocation is that the traditional approach assumes that each individual will approach risk in an entirely objective manner, that each individual has all the information that it could need and interprets that information correctly, and that every individual assesses risk in the same way. This, unfortunately, is not the case.

Hatfield and Hipel point to the importance of "problem formation" in any effort at quantitative risk assessment. Implicit or undocumented assumptions or ambiguities in problem formulation can influence even the most thorough quantitative assessment.[192] Baldwin notes that purely quantitative or technical approaches to risk assessment fail to consider its qualitative aspects, which has eroded the idea of objectivity in risk assessment.[193] Risk noise is this eroding

---

[188]   O'Reilly, "Are Construction Contracts too Risky?" Construction Law: Looking to the Future, Conference at King's College, University of London (1998).

[189]   Kerzner (8th edition 2003) supra note 161 at 654.

[190]   Lloyd, "Prevalent Philosophies of Risk Allocation – An Overview" [1996] ICLR at 502.

[191]   The Royal Society (1992) supra note 9.

[192]   Hatfield and Hipel, "Risk and Systems Theory" Risk Analysis 22 at 1043 (2002).

[193]   Baldwin, "Introduction – Risk: The Legal Contribution" Baldwin (ed), Law and Uncertainty: Risks and Legal Processes (1997). Marshall blames this on the fact that even the most complex computer functions cannot properly analyse a risk if the information that is fed into the computer is inaccurate or insufficient. A party using such a mechanism to analyse risk without taking care to properly analyse the information supplied is at risk of being misled as to the true assessment of that risk. Marshall (1995) supra note 171 at 600.

factor, the combination of personal and societal influences that move us away from objective, quantitative assessment of risk.

Since we cannot separate the quantification of risk from the process of identifying, estimating and evaluating risks, something needs to be added to the traditional approach to efficient risk allocation in order to understand all of the different dimensions of risk when making risk decisions. The traditional approach is not enough. Consideration needs to be given to risk noise.

Risk noise influences parties to the project distracting them from the management of risk in accordance with the traditional approach. There are certain aspects of complex international infrastructure projects that will cause risk noise to play an even more important role in risk assessment. A certain amount of this "inefficiency" may be necessary to attract financing, satisfy political exigencies and otherwise promote the success of the project. This section addresses two such aspects:

> the political pressures and the need for political justification of the commercial transaction, which follows the demands made by political, legal and administrative authorities which have jurisdiction over the relevant transaction (2.4.1); and

> the requirements of investors and financiers specific to the provision of funding for the transaction and for management of the funders' involvement in that transaction that must be satisfied before the transaction can attract any funding or support. (2.4.2)

Finally, this section will propose a few conclusions from this review of the traditional approach to efficient risk allocation and risk noise and discuss the possibility of filtering out risk noise. (2.4.3)

2.4.1   Political Drivers

Every commercial transaction involves a political context, and will be influenced by the relevant political context of the parties and the regions where the commercial transaction will take place. Political context is not limited to legislative or governmental entities. It covers a variety of influences and organisations, including a country, region, religion, organisation, social grouping or company. Assessing risk by anchoring on the rules and *mores* of the relevant cultural, political or organisational structure represents the key source of popular political power and therefore carries a much greater relevance to politically driven risk decisions.

Public sector parties often have limited time and resources available to assess risk and encounter heightened public scrutiny, vulnerability to political agendas and requirements specific to concerns for public services and accountability, increasing their vulnerability to risk noise. These political imperatives are not addressed in the traditional approach, and therefore compliance with political requirements rarely satisfies the traditional approach to efficient risk allocation.

However, political requirements are often essential to the project's success. These overriding political concerns will be of particular interest to investors and lenders. A project is often only as successful as its relationship with the community and the political powers that be. Failure to comply with political concerns can undermine those relationships.

2.4.2   Finance Drivers

Those investing in or financing a project (in this section, the "financiers") will have a particular influence on risk allocation. Their view of risk is often different than those parties providing commercial or technical expertise to the project. The financiers will not be as comfortable with commercial and technical risks as will other of the project parties. This is particularly relevant in project financing where the lenders provide the majority of the funding for the project and take a significant portion of the project risk.

Where the financiers are unwilling to permit the company to bear a particular project risk, they will generally require the company to allocate such risks to more financially significant entities, even if this allocation is expensive and generally "inefficient". The bankability of the project (risk allocation that provides sufficient comfort to the lenders to permit them to lend to the project)[194] revolves around market practice, anchoring against the risk allocation structure accepted by other actors in the financing world. What one lender is willing to accept in relation to risk allocation in a given project, other lenders will be expected to accept. This involves the direct application of risk noise.

2.4.3   Risk noise

Risk analysis is therefore subject to the limitations inherent in the realities of the commercial world and the human condition, it is burdened by the distractions that are risk noise. Risk noise affects risk assessment in a number of ways. It alters:

> ➢ the way an individual will perceive whether a risk exists;

> ➢ the assessment of that risk, the perception of its likelihood and potential impact;

> ➢ an individual's willingness to bear a risk;

> ➢ risk decisions related to risk allocation; and

> ➢ the chosen approach to risk management.

This does not mean that the traditional approach to risk allocation and the pursuit of efficiency should be abandoned. Rather, our definition of efficiency must of necessity contemplate and accommodate for risk noise and include the overriding importance of the context of the commercial transaction, including the source of finance and the political context. However, any accepted inefficiency in the

---

[194]   This concept is discussed further in chapter 5.

method of allocating risk should not be permitted to threaten the stability of the project itself by increasing the likelihood of claims or reducing the likelihood that the company will be able successfully to perform its obligations.

The failure to pursue efficiency and maximise value for money may impinge on the ability to undertake certain projects and may reduce the number of projects that can be undertaken, due to the associated cost implications. These limitations must be acknowledged and appreciated in order to encourage each party to avoid any inefficiency that is not strictly necessary to the success of the process. Risk noise must not be permitted unnecessarily to restrain infrastructure development. Where it represents value for money, parties should endeavour to reduce risk noise, the earlier the better.

Risk noise can be filtered.[195] Though this issue is beyond the scope of this book, risk noise can be addressed, to a certain extent, to enable an individual to avoid its influence. Filtering risk noise requires the commitment of resources to adjust attitudes, perceptions and prejudices, to diminish or remove the impact of a risk noise.

---

[195] The filtering of risk noise, and assessing whether a given filter would represent value for money for the project, are two of the subjects of the author's PhD thesis at King's College, London, which, it is hoped, will be published in due course. The concept of filtering risk is consistent with Chauncey Starr's suggestion that an analysis be made of the social cost of fear reduction when decisions about resource allocation are made, "Hypothetical Fears and Quantitative Risk Analysis" Risk Analysis 21 at 803 (2001). See also, the Risk Analysis and Management for Projects (RAMP) approach for risk analysis which gives specific consideration to the difference between perceived and real risk, and makes reference to a concept that approaches the filtering of risk noise by saying that "we can sometimes improve our knowledge of risks by carrying out further research in an endeavour to make our perception of the risks more closely match reality". The Institution of Civil Engineers and the Faculty and Institute of Actuaries (1998) supra note 178 at 67.

Chapter 3

Introduction to BOT Projects

When you ain't got nothin', you've got nothin' to lose.

Bob Dylan (b. 1941),
singer, songwriter

The "concession" that developed in France from the Middle Ages and the Renaissance provides an early example of private investment in public services. After a pause during the French Revolution, the majority of infrastructure projects of the 19th century were developed through concessions, including railways, gas and electricity.[196]

The building of the Suez Canal was achieved through such a concession. In 1854, the private Compagnie Universelle du Canal Maritime Suez received a 99-year concession for the construction and operation of a canal connecting the Mediterranean and Red Sea. Although the costs of, and time for, construction far outstripped all forecasts, the project was a commercial success.[197] However, concessions did not truly attain independence from the public sector until the end of the 19th century, when they were recognised as private service contracts with the public sector. Modern concessions in France are subject to French administrative law.[198]

As the colonial hold vanished and governments provided financing directly as reparations resulting from the World Wars, private initiative in the public sector decreased[199] (with the exception of certain countries such as France).[200] This has

---

[196] Sokoloff, Marchés Publics et Délégations de Services Publics des Collectivités Locales at 17 (1998).
[197] Levy, Build, Operate, Transfer: Paving the Way for Tomorrow's Infrastructure at 19 (1996).
[198] Raymundie, Gestion Déléguée des Services Publics en France et en Europe at 38 (1995).
[199] Obvious exceptions include the railway industry in the United Kingdom and the United States where private funds were used with incentives and subsidies provided by the public sector.
[200] Payne, An Analysis of the Risks Inherent in the Build-Own/Operate-Transfer ("BOT") Method of Infrastructure Procurement (1994).

changed in recent years with countries and international financial institutions now seeking input from the private sector. This is a result of a combination of decreased funds being available owing to debt crises in many countries, and increased need for new infrastructure as technological advances and populations grow.

Private sector participation in infrastructure has had a tumultuous past. But the last 30 years have brought this occasionally popular option for infrastructure development into its own, from the oil fields of Texas and the North Sea to the Private Finance Initiative and Public Private Partnership in the United Kingdom, substantial projects in China and throughout Asia, the Middle East to Australia, South America and the ends of the earth. One of the most popular approaches to private sector participation in utility infrastructure development is BOT.

"BOT" means Build-Operate-Transfer, a term said to have been coined by Turgat Ozal, prime minister of Turkey in the 1980s.[201] A BOT project involves a grantor providing a private company with a concession to build and operate a project (often to support a public service). The private company operates the project for the term of the concession (the "concession period"), receiving revenues in exchange for operation of the project. The revenues are obtained from a single offtake purchaser, who purchases project output from the project company (this is different from a pure concession where output is sold directly to consumers and end users).

Although critics in a number of developed countries have begun to question whether the BOT project presents significant advantages in comparison to more traditional forms of procurement, this technique is being used in an increasing number of major infrastructure projects worldwide. The United Kingdom has adopted BOO as a solution to its infrastructure needs and public sector borrowing restrictions through the implementation of PFI. PFI projects have included the construction (or refurbishment) and operation of projects as diverse as railways and prisons, hospitals and military facilities.

This chapter will introduce BOT projects, their advantages and disadvantages (section 3.1), the commercial agreements involved and the general contractual structure used (section 3.2) including direct agreements between certain project parties (section 3.3). It will then discuss the parties involved in a project, their positions in the project and some of the mechanisms available to them (section 3.4). Finally, section 3.5 will discuss the stages of negotiation and development of a typical project.

3.1   Private Investment in Public Infrastructure

Potable water and electricity supplies are intermittent or non-existent in certain parts of the world. In many places only a privileged few in urban areas enjoy such services. In order to promote economic development, curtail the spread of disease

---

[201]   Levy (1996) supra note 197 at 310.

and raise standards of living, the financing and construction of infrastructure in developing countries must be our highest priority.

3.1.1   Public sector projects

Insufficient infrastructure is a problem for any country, although it is most prevalent and of greater significance in developing nations.   This lack is exacerbated by the paucity of funds available in the public coffers, and monetary and political policies which require public sector borrowing requirements to be restricted to a certain level. Such nations may not have a credit history which is sufficiently solid to elicit favourable financing conditions, they may not want the financing of infrastructure projects to affect their credit status or they may be restricted from undertaking further indebtedness by financial organisations, such as the IMF.   Gone are the days of Cold War politics and large-scale economic investment in exchange for political alignment and location of military bases. Governments are turning, therefore, with greater frequency to the private sector for such investment.

Private investment in public infrastructure development is also driven by the preference of international financial institutions, other lenders and some governments for projects built and operated by the private sector. Private sector management and risk-taking is perceived as being able to provide the public sector with greater efficiency, cost-effectiveness and transfer of know-how. Construction and operation of infrastructure projects, therefore, are contracted increasingly to private entities.

When bringing a project to the private sector, a government will have a variety of options as to the structure of the project to be let. The structures available for such projects are ultimately flexible, and should be adapted to the requirements of the project.   The categories commonly applied to the methods of private sector involvement include management contracting, privatisation and BOT.

Management contracting involves the public sector appointing a private sector entity to provide services to the public sector for a fee. Thus the public sector may, for example, hire a private company to run a water treatment system or operate a hospital facility or a school. Little of the project risk is passed to the private sector, but the public sector will benefit from the organisation, efficiency and technology of the private sector.

Where the public sector wants to pass project risk to the private sector, the project may be transferred to the private sector through divestment or a concession. This involves the public sector either selling all or part of the public entity that operates a public service to the private sector (divestment), or contracting with a private company to operate (and possibly build) a facility which provides a service directly to the end users or consumers (concession). Concessions raise issues similar to outsourcing arrangements, which are discussed further in chapter 22.

A popular middle ground between management contracting and divestment is the BOT structure. Under this structure the private sector builds, finances and operates a facility which delivers a service to the public sector or some public/private operator who will then distribute the benefit of the service to the end user or consumer.

3.1.2   Financing

Financing for a project can be obtained from public or private sources, or a combination thereof. Public sources of finance include grants or loans from the government, foreign aid, export credit agencies or multilateral agencies such as the World Bank. Privately financed projects can be bilateral or undertaken directly by private companies with strong balance sheets, either by self-financing or through corporate borrowing. However, these sources of finance can be expensive or otherwise undesirable, therefore the private company may prefer to use project finance techniques.   By using such techniques, the investors can reduce substantially both their financial investment (through debt injection) and exposure to project liability by creating a special purpose vehicle, called the project company, which finances, designs, builds and operates the project.

Project financing involves the financing of an infrastructure project through this special purpose vehicle to which non- or limited recourse loans are made. The lenders rely on the cash flow of the project for repayment of the debt, security for the debt is primarily limited to the project assets; therefore the lenders will bear some portion of the project risk.[202]   This book will assume the use of project financing in the context of a BOT project.

The BOT project places the responsibility for financing, constructing and operating the project on the private sector. The host country grants a concession to the private company to build and operate the facility over a period of time. The private company then uses the revenue from the operation of the facility to service debt and provide the investors with a return. Where the host country is also the offtake purchaser, the project is likely to be treated as payment for a service rather than financing of infrastructure. This can keep the project off the host country's books, and therefore not burden the country's debt ratios or public sector borrowing requirements.

The project company may obtain financing from a combination of private banks, multilateral or bilateral organisations, export credit agencies, bond financing, international financial organisations and other such entities, collectively known as the "lenders". Though referred to here by a single name, each lender will have its own interests and requirements and therefore lender issues will need to be managed carefully.

Lenders are careful to manage risk and are concerned to restrict the type of risks they take. Where risk is high, shareholders generally stand to gain high rates of return on their investment where the project performs well. Not so with lenders, who generally receive a fixed margin irrespective of the actual rate of return of the

---

[202]   *Ibid.*

project. Any risk that remains with the borrower and is not otherwise managed through shareholder support is borne by the lenders. Therefore, the lenders will be keen to take only a certain amount and type of risk.[203]

BOT projects are highly complex, commercially driven projects, requiring extensive documentation and negotiation. A BOT project represents a serious investment of money and time by everyone involved. The project company, and in turn the lenders, will undertake extensive and expensive technical, financial and legal due diligence exercises to analyse risk allocation for a project. A reasonable and efficient contractual structure with commercially appropriate risk allocation will be a deciding factor in the bankability of the project and whether the lenders will wish to go forward with the project financing of infrastructure development.

3.1.3   Progression of financing

Financing arrangements for BOT projects follow a rough two step progression. First, funding is provided by the lenders and the shareholders during the construction phase, which will include up-front fees, development costs, design and construction.

The lenders will advance funding progressively during the construction phase, putting procedures in place before drawdowns of financing are permitted, to ensure that the funds will be spent in an effective and efficient manner so as to encourage timely completion. Progress payments will usually be linked to milestones and verified by an independent expert acting for the lenders and possibly the grantor. During this first step, the lenders will insist on a careful balance of equity and debt funding and may require recourse beyond project assets, to the shareholders or some other guarantor, to cover the risk of any delays or cost overruns which have not otherwise been transferred to the construction contractor.

The second step is final completion of construction followed by operation. Completion of construction includes performance tests to ensure that the project is capable of achieving the necessary revenue stream. Approval of final completion will release the construction contractor from certain liabilities and will therefore be carefully controlled by the lenders. During operation, once the project has begun to produce output, the debt is serviced solely by the project revenue stream.

3.1.4   Benefits and disadvantages

A BOT project provides certain benefits to the project company. These can include:

> ➤ off balance sheet financing;

> ➤ non- or limited recourse financing;

---

[203]   The amount of risk the lenders will be willing to take is heavily market driven and is commonly considered within the concept of "bankability", which is discussed in further detail in chapter 5.

> higher leverage owing to the number and strength of the shareholders;

> effective risk allocation due to the BOT structure; and

> potential tax benefits through leasing and other structures.

Potential benefits for the grantor of the concession include:

> improved efficiency, closely managed costs and faster completion through private sector involvement;

> lower cost of offtake owing to improved technology and efficient operation from the private sector;

> infrastructure at no direct cost, owing to private sector financing, therefore no need for any other source of financing and no or little effect on the grantor's credit;

> earlier completion, since the project will not have to compete for scarce public sector funds;

> lower risk burden owing to allocation to the private sector and, possibly, guarantees provided by the project participants;

> involvement of experienced industry professionals and private financing organisations, ensuring exhaustive review of project feasibility;

> involvement of international financiers, including multilateral organisations such as the International Finance Corporation ("IFC");

> attraction of further foreign investment;

> maintenance of public sector strategic control over the project (as compared to privatisation) and transfer at the end of the concession period (where relevant);

> the interests of the project company in long-term facility operation, generally resulting in high quality construction;

> transfer of the most up-to-date technology and know-how, including training of local personnel;[204]

> indirect development of related industries;

> development of local capital markets (if bond financing is used); and

> involvement of local financiers, subcontractors, suppliers and shareholders.

---

[204]   For further discussion of transfer of know-how, see United Nations Industrial Development Organisation, Guidelines for Infrastructure Development through Build-Operate-Transfer at 75-90 (1996).

However, BOT projects may also involve certain disadvantages for the grantor, including:[205]

> ➢ distortion of development priorities, as the host government is more likely to favour projects which are financially viable rather than those which are necessarily appropriate for the economic and infrastructure needs of the country;

> ➢ increased financing costs, assuming that the host government would have available to it more beneficial financing terms and costs than would the private entity and considering the complexity of the project, the need for supervision, the cost of the due diligence exercise and the cost of risk management;[206]

> ➢ possible public or political resistance, in particular from labour unions and those unwilling to sacrifice any government control over infrastructure;

> ➢ some loss of control of an otherwise public sector operation; and

> ➢ possible loss of income stream from the sector in question.

The sponsors may also bear certain risks, including:[207]

> ➢ condition of the local market;

> ➢ failure or degradation of local infrastructure;

> ➢ project cost overruns;

> ➢ technological advances rendering the project inefficient or unusable;

> ➢ regulation by local authorities, for example regulation of pricing;

> ➢ failure or withdrawal of local partners;

> ➢ failure or withdrawal of shareholders;

> ➢ possible expropriation by the site country government, either direct or creeping, of project assets;

> ➢ loss of power by the political elements supporting the project;

> ➢ requirement for use of untested technologies;

> ➢ repeal of host government support or refusal by the host government to go through with the project;

> ➢ competition from parallel or alternative infrastructure;

---

[205]   Haley, A-Z of BOOT at 23 (1996).

[206]   Crozer and Miller, "BOT – The Host Country Perspective" at 7, presented at the 10th Biennial Conference of the IBA Section on Business Law, Hong Kong (September/October 1991).

[207]   Levy (1996) supra note 197 at 398-402.

> political or popular resistance to the project, its development, its developers or host government support thereof;

> increase in financing costs;

> currency convertibility, transferability and exchange risk;

> changes in law or taxation that affect the cost or viability of the project; and

> government bankruptcy or collapse of the local economic system.

3.2   Description of a BOT Project

In a typical BOT project the public sector grantor grants a concession to a private company to develop and operate what would traditionally be a public sector project. This private company, or project company, obtains financing for the project, and procures the design and construction of the works and operates the facility during the concession period. Thus the project company must have, or obtain access to, resources sufficient to satisfy these obligations.

Project company shareholders will often include companies with construction and/or operation experience, and with input supply and offtake purchase capabilities. It is also essential to include shareholders with experience in the management of the appropriate type of projects, such as working with diverse and multicultural partners, given the particular risks specific to these aspects of a BOT project. The project company will then co-ordinate the construction and operation of the project in accordance with the requirements of the concession agreement.

The operation of the facility will generate revenues from an offtake purchaser who compensates the project company for delivery of the project output or provision of the project service.[208] The revenues generated from the operation phase are intended to cover operating costs, maintenance, repayment of debt principal (which represents a significant portion of development and construction costs), financing costs (including interest and fees), and a return for the shareholders.

The lenders will be providing non-recourse or limited recourse financing and will, therefore, bear any residual risk along with the project company and its shareholders. In order to minimise such residual risk (as the lenders will only want, as far as possible, to bear a limited portion of the commercial risk of the project) the lenders will insist on passing the project company risk to the other project participants.[209]

The chart below shows the contractual structure of a typical BOT project.

---

[208]   As discussed in the preface, other approaches to revenue generation are possible, for example, from individual consumers in a concession or from an established market arrangement in the New Electricity Trading Arrangements in the electricity sector in the United Kingdom. See generally chapter 13.

[209]   The level of commercial risk the lenders will be willing to bear depends on the bankability of the project – a very fluid concept which is discussed further in chapter 5.

CONTRACTUAL STRUCTURE FOR A BOT PROJECT

```
                          Shareholders
                         (Shareholders'
                           Agreement)

      Lenders                                         Authority

             Lending      Shareholding    Concession
            Agreements                     Agreement

                          Offtake
   Operation and         Project           Offtake
   Operator  Maintenance  Company  Purchase  Offtake
            Agreement               Agreement  Purchaser

              Construction          Input
               Contract            Supply
                                  Agreement

          Construction                      Input Supplier
           Contractor
```

Each project will involve some variation of this contractual structure depending on its particular requirements. For example, not all BOT projects will require a guaranteed supply of input, therefore an input supply agreement may not be necessary. Similarly, the payment stream may not be guaranteed by an offtake purchaser, but rather by the grantor through the concession agreement, or possibly the project company may bear the market risk of offtake demand. The structure demonstrated above and discussed in this book should therefore be considered as a template to be adapted to the needs of each particular project. Chapters 17-22 discuss specific issues that will influence the variants used in certain industries.

3.2.1   Financing agreement

The financing agreement (this term normally covers several separate agreements) contains the terms and conditions pursuant to which the lenders agree to lend funds to the project company. The lenders to the project may include commercial banks, export credit agencies, bondholders, and multilateral and bilateral lending institutions. This relationship is of particular importance in the BOT context as the lenders will generally be responsible for the financing of a substantial portion of the project. As a result of this funding, the lenders will often have a substantial influence (directly or indirectly) on the drafting of the agreements involved in the BOT project, in order to ensure that the project is bankable.

The risk management mechanisms commonly found in the financing agreement will usually include security and account arrangements. Where more than one lender is involved, there will be intercreditor arrangements amongst the lenders to manage sharing of security and setting out priority and decision-making.

3.2.2   Shareholders' agreement

The shareholders' agreement governs the relationship between the shareholders within the project company. The shareholders' agreement may involve several documents, for example a sponsor's agreement for the pre-financial close phase of the project, a joint venture agreement and articles of association or incorporation or whatever constitutional documents exist for the project company. The shareholders' agreement will cover topics such as the business of the project company, conditions precedent to its creation, the issue of new shares, the transfer of shares, the allocation of project costs and the management of the project company including decision-making and voting. Such an agreement will often also include a non-competition clause, providing that the shareholders may not enter into activities directly or indirectly in competition with the project company.

3.2.3   Concession agreement

Under the concession agreement (also known as the "implementation agreement"), the grantor grants a concession (a series of rights) to the project company to build and operate infrastructure for a predetermined period; the concession period. The concession agreement may also set out the legal and tax regimes applicable to the project, including the environmental obligations of the project company. The terms of the concession will need to satisfy the requirements of all of the project participants, including the lenders. In practice, the concession agreement, the offtake purchase agreement and/or the input supply agreement will be combined in one agreement.

3.2.4   Offtake purchase agreement

The offtake purchase agreement secures the project payment stream. It obliges the offtake purchaser to procure a certain amount of project output or pay for an amount of project service (to a certain extent, whether or not it is used) over a given time.

The offtake purchaser will be looking for a guaranteed long-term output from the project. The offtake purchase agreement may provide sanctions if the project company fails to deliver output as promised; in particular if the construction of the project is not finished within the time for completion or does not perform as required when completed.

The obligation to purchase output may require that the offtake purchaser maintains sufficient facilities to receive the output delivered or use the service provided. The credit risk associated with the offtake purchaser will be of particular concern to the project company and the lenders. The offtake purchaser may be required to provide credit enhancement such as escrow accounts, revolving bank guarantees or state/federal guarantees for its payment obligations.

An offtake purchase agreement may, of course, be unnecessary in some projects, such as hospitals, tunnels, roadways and bridges, where no physical offtake is produced. In such cases it is often the grantor of the concession who will pay the project company for use of the project or the project company may collect tariffs directly from consumers. Therefore, the offtake purchase agreement may be one and the same as the concession agreement.

3.2.5 Input supply agreement

The input supply agreement obliges an input supplier to deliver to the project company a specified quantity of input necessary to the operation of the project, at a certain level of quality. This agreement allocates certain elements of the market risk associated with the price and availability of the input. The input supply agreement will only be needed where some supply of input is necessary for operation of the facility.

Input may be a misnomer for certain projects where the required service is effectively an offtake arrangement. For example, in waste water treatment projects the project company will need to subcontract for the removal and disposal of sludge or in hospital projects for the removal of medical waste. This type of agreement will require many of the same conditions and raise similar issues to other input supply agreements.

3.2.6 Construction contract

The construction phase of the BOT project is generally governed by a turnkey construction contract, sometimes also known as a "design and build" or an "EPC" (engineering, procurement and construction) contract. The lenders, who are seeking certainty of exposure, require a construction contract that establishes a fixed lump-sum price and a set time for completion and places the majority (and in some cases substantially all) of the construction risk on the construction contractor.

3.2.7 Operation and maintenance agreement

The project company will want to ensure proper operation of the works during the concession period and will therefore enter into an operation and maintenance agreement with the operator of the facility. The operator's obligations should mirror those set out in the concession agreement, the offtake purchase agreement, and those required to ensure continued and efficient operation of the project.

3.3 Direct Agreements

The lenders and the grantor may enter into direct agreements with the project participants to cover issues such as security over project assets, secondment of personnel, accommodation and costs. Similarly, these direct agreements may consider the management of know-how between the project participants and the project company including transfer, duration, licensing rights, exclusivity, distributorship, and the supply of spare parts, goods or raw materials. Direct agreements may contain collateral warranties in favour of the lenders and the grantor and will set out step-in rights, notice requirements, cure periods and other issues intended to maintain the continuity of the project where the project company defaults and/or falls away.[210] The following diagram identifies some of the large number of direct agreements that may exist in a BOT project.

DIRECT AGREEMENTS

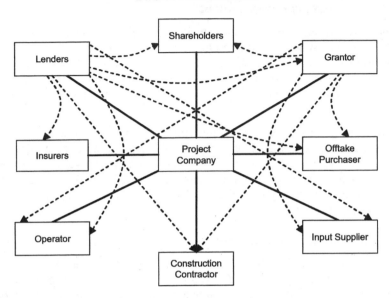

3.4 Parties Involved in a BOT Project

A number of parties will be involved in a BOT project. Each may have different interests, levels of sophistication and available resources.

3.4.1 Lenders

The profile of a lender group can range from project to project, and may include a combination of private sector commercial lenders together with export credit agencies, and bilateral and multilateral finance organisations.   Funding is sometimes provided by project bonds, sold on the capital markets.

As a general premise, the lenders will only want to take those risks which are measurable and measured.[211] The lenders will not be in the operation, construction or insurance business and therefore will not want to bear risks with which they are unfamiliar and which are more appropriately borne by other parties. The lenders will also want to have certainty as to financial exposure.

The lenders may be involved in most of the important phases of the works, including the drafting of the project documents and certification of completion.

---

210 For further discussion of direct agreements and collateral warranties, see chapter 29 of Scriven, Pritchard and Delmon (eds), A Contractual Guide to Major Construction Projects (1999).
211 Vinter, Project Finance: A Legal Guide (2nd edition 1998).

They will generally maintain their review powers over the project with the assistance of an independent engineer.[212] The lenders may require that direct agreements be entered into between themselves and each of the project participants.[213]

3.4.2   Grantor and host government

The BOT project discussed here is based on the provision of a concession by a national or local government, a government agency or some regulatory authority (referred to here as the "grantor"). The grantor will generally be responsible for the interface between the project and the government authorities of the host country. This may include:

> ➢ rights of access;

> ➢ protection from nationalisation or expropriation;

> ➢ protection from changes in law, regulations and tax; and

> ➢ foreign exchange and convertibility issues.

The grantor will need to have the authority to provide the concession. *Ultra vires* activities (those acts which are outside the scope of the grantor's legal mandate) by a government authority can render the concession void and available legal remedies are not likely to compensate the sponsors satisfactorily. It may be necessary to pass legislation or even a constitutional amendment before the concession as let by the grantor can be considered valid.

The host government and the national and/or local government (to the extent they are not party to the concession agreement) may also play an important role in providing guarantees and generally ensuring that the project commences and is completed successfully through its more or less active support. The host government will also play an important role during project operation, in relation to regulatory requirements and taxation/tariff restrictions.

Where the host government is not a party to, and is therefore not legally bound by, the concession agreement, the project participants will need to ensure continued support from the host government, which generally involves taking into consideration the interests of the host government. For its part, the host government may prefer to limit its involvement in the project and minimise any risk it may have to bear. As far as possible, the project participants should ensure that the project and any project activities continue to be consistent with the host government's interests.[214]

---

[212]   For further discussion, see section 10.7.3.

[213]   For further discussion, see sections 3.3 and 15.9; and chapter 29 of Scriven, Pritchard and Delmon (1999) supra note 210.

[214]   This issue is discussed further in chapters 5 and 6.

3.4.2.1   Host government interests

Project sponsors will need to be acutely aware of the interests of the host government in relation to the infrastructure project in particular and foreign investment generally.[215] Host government interests will include:

> ➤ perceived public or national interest;

> ➤ public control of the project during the concession to ensure protection of public interests and improved public perception of the host government;

> ➤ public safety including environmental and social impact;

> ➤ response of the relevant constituency (often related to tariff restrictions and levels of environmental impact and public nuisance);

> ➤ attracting benefits for political personalities or parties in power;

> ➤ minimising the need for injection of public funds, investment, guarantees and assistance;

> ➤ attracting foreign investment;

> ➤ minimising public risk while maximising public control; and

> ➤ smooth and efficient transfer of the project (if applicable) at the end of the concession period in good mechanical condition with no need for replacement of major parts or equipment.

3.4.2.2   Host government involvement

The host government will often be involved in the aspects of the project described below. These issues may be defined in the legal framework provided for BOT projects under local law. Any existing framework will define to some extent the grantor's approach to the project and the risks/obligations the grantor can undertake.[216] The host government's role will also depend largely on the position of the government in the project and the need for relevant support in order to attract the necessary private investment in infrastructure development.

(a)   *Invitation to tender*

The grantor may involve the host government, or be instructed by the host government, in the original promotion of the project, identifying the need for the project and defining its requirements. The host government may also be instrumental in choosing the successful bidders.

---

215   See generally, Tinsley, Practical Introduction to Project Finance: Introduction and Glossary at 10 (1996).

216   For further discussion of host government legal regimes, see United Nations Industrial Development Organisation (1996) supra note 204 at 41-72.

(b)   *Risk sharing*

The project company will ask the grantor to bear certain risks. In many cases the intention is not so much for the grantor to compensate the project company for the occurrence of the risk, but rather for the grantor to place pressure on the host government to avoid such risks, or for the host government, through its relationship with the grantor, to be a primary obligor in relation to such risks. The host government may therefore be called on where such risks arise or are likely to arise.

(c)   *Attracting investment*

Once the host government has decided to go forward with a project it will want to attract the necessary foreign investment. In order to attract the best quality at the least direct cost, the host country may provide some incentives to the project company, such as tax benefits (including tax holidays, the use of tax havens or creative use of tax credits), assistance in procuring land, relaxation of legal requirements (such as licensing and other administrative procedures), grants, debt financing, improved tariffs on utilities and other services or fuel, new or improved infrastructure, use of project resources for non-project related purposes, or involvement in bids for further projects in the host country.

(d)   *Political marketing*

The project company may need assistance in "selling" the project to the public and to any relevant government organisations. The host government is generally in a good position to advise or assist in conveying to the relevant parties the benefits of the project.

(e)   *Setting of government policy*

As the project will involve a traditionally public sector service, government policy will have a direct relation to the success of the project, including issues such as the setting of tariff requirements, environmental and discharge restrictions, and exchange and convertibility of currency matters and taxation. This may include passing legislation to facilitate the implementation of BOT projects.

(f)   *Provision of information basic to the feasibility of the project*

The site will be located within the territory of the host government and will often involve land either within the host country or provided by the host government. In either case, the host government might have a certain amount of information about the site; geographical, archaeological, hydrological and meteorological information useful for the development phase of the project.

(g)   *Documentation*

The host government may provide draft documentation for use in the project, in particular concession agreements and offtake purchase agreements.

(h)   *Assistance with finance*

The host government will often provide some finance and/or assist in obtaining financing, insurance and guarantees from local lenders, multilateral agencies, international organisations or export credit agencies.

(i)   *Guarantees*

The project company may need guarantees from the host government concerning various aspects of the project, possibly including:

> ➤ the offtake purchaser's and the input supplier's obligations;

> ➤ availability, transferability and convertibility of local currency; and

> ➤ other such risks that the project company and grantor cannot manage efficiently.

3.4.3   Multilateral, bilateral and export credit agencies

These international, largely political, entities are often involved in BOT projects and can have an important impact on the risk allocation and financing used in a project.[217]   Although each of these entities can play different roles and have differing requirements for getting involved in project financing, they have been grouped together for ease of reference.

When involved in such projects, these agencies will place strict requirements on the project structure and lending arrangements. Lenders anxious to benefit from such involvement will make it a priority to ensure that these requirements are satisfied. An example would be the procurement process required by the World Bank group and adopted by a number of other organisations. The World Bank group requires public tender, prefers the use of a pre-qualification mechanism and publishes a series of guidance documents outlining in relative detail its requirements for project bidding.[218]

3.4.3.1   Multilateral agencies ("MLAs") and bilateral agencies ("BLAs")

MLAs represent a grouping of nations, and are owned and funded by their members. Their purpose will often be set out in charter documentation and may include fostering transition to market economies, alleviating poverty, supporting the development of new markets, and providing commercial banks and companies with support and incentives to enter certain markets. Some MLAs are mandated to finance projects in specific geographical regions, such as the Inter-American Development Bank ("IADB") and the African Development Bank ("AfDB"). Each MLA will have its own slightly different approach to projects. MLAs can participate in projects through equity investments (usually quite small), by providing guarantees or insurance or by providing loans. An MLA can provide

---

[217]   For further discussion see Vinter (2nd edition 1998) supra note 211 at 187.
[218]   www.worldbank.org

financing from its own funds or act as a conduit for funding from commercial banks.

It is commonly believed that governments make greater effort to ensure that such loans are repaid, even in difficult times. Participation of the International Finance Corporation ("IFC") of the World Bank is often referred to as the "IFC umbrella" due to the probability of preferential treatment given to repayment of obligations to the IFC by governments looking to restructure indebtedness in hard times.[219] For example, EBRD's loans were not rescheduled during the Russian crisis in late 1998/1999.

As a representative of several countries, the MLA will want to encourage equality of treatment, transparency and free trade between its member countries. Therefore, MLAs will often require that tenders for the project contracts be on an internationally competitive basis.

Some of the more active MLAs in international project finance are the IFC, the Asian Development Bank ("ADB"), the European Bank for Reconstruction and Development ("EBRD") and the European Investment Bank ("EIB"). The IFC, the EBRD and certain other such organisations generally refer to themselves as "International Finance Institutions" ("IFIs") rather than MLAs.

Certain international organisations specialise in providing political risk coverage for projects, such as the Multilateral Investment Guarantee Agency ("MIGA") of the World Bank. Unlike the above-mentioned MLAs, these organisations will not provide funding for the project.

BLAs (sometimes described as development finance institutions) are similar to MLAs in purpose and approach, but are funded by only one nation. They are generally mandated to provide support to specific developing countries, in the form of debt or equity investment. They are politically oriented, in that they carry out the political will of their member nation. Although usually BLA involvement is not limited to projects involving investment by member country nationals, some BLAs have an origins clause requiring that projects funded by the BLA may not be in direct competition with member country nationals.

An example of a BLA is PROPARCO (Société de Promotion et de Participation pour la Coopération Economique S.A.) of France. PROPARCO is a development finance institution which specialises in providing long-term finance, by way of equity and debt funding (including mezzanine finance) to the private sector in specific countries, including notably the African, Caribbean and Pacific zones. It was incorporated as a *société anonyme* of which the Agence Française de Développement (an agency of the French Government) is a majority shareholder (with a 67 per cent. stake) along with 35 private minority shareholders.

---

[219]   See generally Fernandes-Duque, "Co-financing with IFC: Preferred Creditor Status and Inter-Creditor Agreements" International Business Lawyer 300 (1988).

3.4.3.2   Export credit agencies ("ECAs")

An ECA is an agency attached to a given country and can be an arm or a department of the government of that country. Its general role is to encourage and assist foreign investment and the export of goods and services by its nationals. Although traditionally government-run, certain of these agencies have been privatised.

The ECA can provide financing, insurance or guarantees for the goods and services exported by its source-country nationals. This financing is often extensive, up to 85 per cent. of the total price of the export. The more active ECAs in BOT projects include the Export-Import Bank of the United States, ECGD of the United Kingdom, COFACE of France, Hermes of Germany, SACE of Italy and the Japan Bank for International Cooperation ("JBIC").

ECAs may provide direct lending, or guarantee or insure repayment of commercial lender financing in case of political risk and/or commercial risk. The political risk borne by ECAs will generally include political violence, war, hostilities, expropriation and currency transfer risk.[220]   In certain cases, ECAs provide extended risk cover such as change in law, changes in taxation or breach of a government guarantee.

3.4.4   Project company

The sponsors will identify a project and put together a bid in an effort to be awarded the project. Once selected, they will create a special purpose vehicle ("SPV") which will contract with the grantor to design, construct, operate, maintain and transfer the project. The use of an SPV is likely to enable the sponsors to finance the project on a limited recourse basis. The project company will generally include shareholder companies which specialise in one or several of the tasks which need to be performed under the concession agreement. The project company should also include a party with experience in managing major international infrastructure development projects. The grantor may require that the project company includes local investors in order to improve transfer of technology, and provide jobs and training to local personnel.

The project company will need to decide how to distribute revenues to its members. The shareholders will want to distribute revenues as early as possible, while the lenders will want to delay revenue sharing to ensure that the shareholders remain committed to the operation of the project for the longest possible time and to retain control over amounts otherwise available for distribution.

Shareholders may also include specialist investment vehicles which provide equity financing to projects, for example mezzanine financing and venture capital. Such investors often wish to perform their own due diligence exercise before providing financing.

---

220   Vinter (2nd edition 1998) supra note 211.

3.4.5   Construction contractor

The project company will enter into a construction contract with the construction contractor in order to divest its obligation to the grantor to design, build, test and commission the project. This task is generally undertaken on a turnkey basis, placing completion and performance risk on the construction contractor. The construction contract will be, as far as possible, back-to-back with the concession agreement, and therefore any construction risk placed on the project company by the concession agreement will, through the construction contract, flow through to the construction contractor. The construction contractor will generally subcontract certain or all of its construction obligations to other entities in order to share risk and revenues, subject to any restrictions imposed by the concession agreement or the construction contract.

3.4.6   Operator

The operator will operate and maintain the project over an extended period, often from completion of construction, or the first completed section, until the end of the concession period. It will need to manage the input supply and offtake purchase, monitor testing of the project and ensure proper operation and maintenance. The operator will also need to manage interfaces:

> ➢ with the construction contractor, when the tests on completion are performed and when the project is handed over to the operator after completion; and

> ➢ with the grantor for confirmation of performance levels and confirming proper maintenance and testing of the works at the end of the concession period, if the project is to be transferred back to the grantor.

These stages in the project are some of the most difficult to manage and will require particular attention from the operator. A further point of interest for the operator will be payment. The project company will want to tie the operator's payment to the operator's performance of the project. The operator may not want to bear the risk of operation cost or actual output, and may prefer to be reimbursed for its costs and paid a fee for its services. In any case, the payment scheme should include penalty fees and incentive bonuses to encourage efficient operation of the project.

3.4.7   Offtake purchaser

In order to divert market risk away from the project company and the lenders, an agreement may be made with a purchaser for the use of the project or the purchase of any output produced. This offtake purchase agreement will require the offtake purchaser to pay for a minimum amount of the project output, and thereby create a secure payment stream which will be an important basis for financing. The offtake purchaser may also be the grantor, or a government entity such as a public utility, in which case the offtake purchase agreement and the concession agreement may be one and the same document. The entity driving the BOT project will often be the offtake purchaser.

The offtake purchaser may need to manage the connection of the project to transmission or transportation facilities. Often the project company will be responsible for connection to or building part of such facilities. The risks associated with interconnection and offtake purchase/project company interfaces will need to be managed sensibly to ensure the commercial and technical viability of the project.

The offtake purchaser will want to obtain a certain minimum output at a given level of quality and at a reasonable price. Therefore, the offtake purchaser will maintain a strict testing schedule, imposing sanctions where output or quality is insufficient. The offtake purchaser may also want to monitor maintenance of the project to ensure continued and efficient supply. The standards and testing may be imposed by a third party, such as a regulator. The costs associated with standards raised after the completion of construction or any change in the testing regime will need to be addressed.

Extensive reporting and communication protocols may need to be defined to allow the offtake purchaser to monitor and control the operation of the project in accordance with its needs, including periodicity of maintenance and scheduled shutdown of the project.

3.4.8   Input supplier

The input supplier assumes the supply risk for an input necessary for operation of the project. Thus the project company is protected from the risk that the project will not reach its intended production level for lack of an essential input, such as fuel or raw materials. The input supplier ensures a minimum quantity of input is delivered, at a minimum standard of quality and at a set price. The mechanism used to calculate this price can be extremely complex. The input supplier may also need to provide infrastructure to permit delivery of input, such as pipelines, ports or railways.

Only certain types of projects will require a form of input supply. Others will rely on market availability of input or may not need input at all. Still others will require a service rather than an input, such as the removal of sludge from a water treatment facility.

3.4.9   Interfaces

As can be noted from the discussion above and the chart that follows, a BOT project requires the various project participants to work together to discharge their obligations and ensure the success of the project. The following chart shows how the various parties involved will need to work together. The solid lines indicate periods during which the project participants may be involved concurrently on site activities and may be sharing project risk. The project documents will need to allocate risk appropriately in order to avoid disruption of the project.

PROJECT PARTICIPANT INTERFACES

| | = Defects liability period | | = Commissioning period | | = Preliminary deliveries |

3.5 Stages of Development and Negotiation of a BOT Project

A BOT project is generally preparation intensive, requiring careful analysis and negotiation before the project is performed. The most time-consuming elements include negotiating documentation and structuring the financing.

However, given the amount of money and risk involved, it behoves the project company to allow sufficient time for this important development stage. Similarly, appropriate specialist advice should be obtained from legal, insurance and financial advisers, technical and operational experts, and parties experienced in operations in the host country, its customs, politics and market.

The following chart gives an indication of the time commitment necessary to put together a BOT project and how that time is divided between several of the primary tasks.[221] This chart is only indicative, as each project will be different, and the nature of the financing and the site country will have a substantial impact on the time investment required for project development.

Feasibility reviews will be undertaken in the early bid process for the project to assess feasibility, availability of finance and profitability. They should be performed roughly in parallel, although each project will have different requirements. The commitment letter is an undertaking by the lenders concerning the proposed structure and financial feasibility. As indicated by this chart, project documentation can involve a substantial investment of time.

---

[221] Modified from Tinsley (1996) supra note 215 at 13-15.

STAGES OF A BOT PROJECT

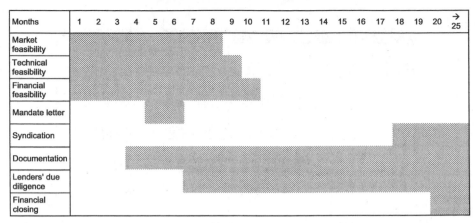

Months	1	2	3	4	5	6	7	8	9	10	11	12	13	14	15	16	17	18	19	20	→ 25
Market feasibility																					
Technical feasibility																					
Financial feasibility																					
Mandate letter																					
Syndication																					
Documentation																					
Lenders' due diligence																					
Financial closing																					

The table below shows the phases of a BOT project and the tasks to be performed during each of these phases.[222] The following chapters of this book will discuss in detail the commercial documents which create the contractual structure of the project. However, a BOT project will involve many other essential elements, including a bid-tendering procedure and financing (discussed in chapters 4 and 16). The following table outlines a roughly chronological list of the tasks to be performed in a BOT project, from identification of the project by the grantor (or the project company) to the transfer procedure (if any). It describes the whole project whereas the chart above is limited to the preparatory stages.

The identification phase (1) involves the grantor or a promoter identifying the need for, and the possibility of using, a BOT project structure. Once this need is identified, the grantor will review the proposal and make a decision as to its appropriateness. The grantor will then prepare for the tendering of the project and receiving bids (2). This will require preparing a tendering procedure, often involving pre-qualification of bidders, drafting preliminary provisions for the project documents, and preparing the tendering procedures including bid evaluation criteria.[223] The sponsors then prepare a bid based on the tender documents (3), and the grantor evaluates the bids received against its criteria, negotiates with those bidders which exemplify best the criteria required, and awards the project to the preferred bidder (4).

Based on the successful bid, the project is then developed (5), i.e. financing is put in place, insurance is arranged and the project documents are negotiated and drafted in final form. During the implementation phase the facilities are designed and built in accordance with the project documents (6). Once appropriate

---

222   Modified from United Nations Industrial Development Organisation (1996) supra note 204 at 22.
223   See generally United Nations Industrial Development Organisation (1996) supra note 204 at 93-149; www.worldbank.org; Fédération Internationale des Ingénieurs-Conseil, Tendering Procedures (1994).

performance levels are reached the operation phase will begin (7), during which the facilities are operated and maintained as agreed. It is during the operation phase that the project payment stream is produced, project debt is repaid and the shareholders earn a return on their investment. At the end of the concession period the facilities are either transferred to the grantor or re-let to another operator (8).

PHASES OF A BOT PROJECT

Phase	Task
(1) Identification (grantor)	Identify project Define possible forms of financing Perform preliminary feasibility study Assign project manager and team Decision to proceed to tender process
(2) Preparation for tendering (grantor)	Establish procurement procedure Prequalification of bidders Produce tender documents (including project documents) Define bid evaluation criteria
(3) Preparation of bid (bidders)	Perform feasibility study Identify potential project participants Submit bid
(4) Selection (grantor/bidders)	Perform bid evaluation Negotiations: clarification and modification Project award
(5) Development (grantor/project company/ lenders/project participants)	Form project company Arrange financing Perform due diligence exercise Negotiate project documents e.g.: • financing agreements • construction contract • operation and maintenance agreement • offtake purchase agreement • input supply agreement • insurance contracts Commitment of equity funding Financial closing

Phase		Task
(6)	Implementation (project company/lenders)	Equity contributions Design and construct facility Implement construction insurance Perform commissioning and tests on completion Takeover of project Training Carry out performance testing
(7)	Operation (project company)	Operation and maintenance during the concession period Implement operation insurance Inspections and testing Repayment of debt Distribution of return on equity Training of grantor personnel
(8)	End of concession (project company/grantor)	Transfer or re-tender procedure

Chapter 4

Project Finance

A banker is a fellow who lends you his umbrella when the sun is shining, but wants it back the minute it begins to rain.

Mark Twain

The financing arrangements are essential to the success of a BOT project. However, a detailed discussion of these arrangements is beyond the scope of this book. This chapter will discuss financing generally, lender recourse, financing agreement issues and other issues relevant to financing which affect the contractual structure and project documents.[224]

4.1   Project Financing

Project financing normally takes the form of limited recourse lending to a specially created project vehicle which holds a concession from the grantor to carry out the construction and operation of the project. One of the primary advantages of project financing is that it provides for off balance sheet financing of the project, which will not affect the credit of the shareholders or the grantor, and shifts some of the project risk to the lenders in exchange for which the lenders obtain a higher margin than for normal corporate lending.

There are two basic stages of project financing in the context of a BOT project. During the first stage, the construction stage, the lenders provide financing progressively as the project is designed, built and commissioned. The drawdowns of debt will be keyed to payment events or milestones, dividing this process into identifiable stages in order to provide incentives to complete in a timely fashion and so that the lenders can verify the completion of each stage before releasing more funds. These payment events or milestones will be structured to require a

---

[224]   For a more detailed discussion of project finance issues, see generally Vinter (2nd edition 1998) supra note 211.

few large drawdowns, so as to avoid the cost of administration of more numerous advances. An independent expert will often be used to verify the satisfaction of payment conditions for drawdowns.

Financing and refinancing on the capital markets may also be available for project financing. The capital markets are often used as a refinancing tool after completion of the project, since the bondholders prefer not to bear project completion risk although the capital markets have demonstrated an increasing willingness to take project risk, in particular in developed markets such as PFI projects in the United Kingdom.

After construction, completion will need to be verified by the lenders before the final drawdown can be made. This final drawdown should be of sufficient size to provide an incentive for the construction contractor to ensure proper completion of the project. Part of the contract price may also be retained until the end of the defects liability period and the carrying out of the performance tests. In certain cases final drawdown may occur before completion where final payments are to be made by equity infusion or where the lenders agree to allow drawdown against a completion guarantee. The lenders will still want to maintain the construction contractor's incentive to complete the works in a timely manner.

Completion represents the end of certain guarantees provided by the construction contractor, including liquidated damages for late completion. It may also signal the end of any lender recourse to the shareholders' assets that may have been available to the lenders (such limited recourse may be required until completion of construction or the end of the first year of operation, particularly when using untested technology). Therefore, the lenders will want to ensure that risks specific to the completion phase, and for which such guarantees were obtained, have been properly managed and fulfilled. Extensive testing of the works will therefore be required.

The second stage, the operation stage, finds the project on stream and operating at appropriate levels. It is during this phase that the lenders are repaid from the project revenues. The project company will normally be given a grace period of three to 12 months before repayments begin providing the project company with a period for "ramp-up" of the newly completed project.

Repayment can be calculated in many ways. By far the most common method of repayment is in accordance with a repayment schedule. The amount paid can be based on equal monthly rates, a percentage of the project's cash flow, a percentage of the project's revenue for output or a rate per unit of output. Repayment can also be made in unequal amounts, based on calculations of projected income and maintenance needs, such as replacement of parts, maintenance periods (during which income may be decreased) and peak/off-peak periods.

The flow of funding for a BOT project will look something like this:

FUNDING FOR A BOT PROJECT

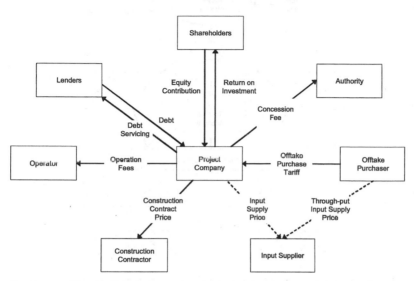

The lenders will require the revenue stream into the project company to be funnelled through accounts which provide the lenders with security over such funds and allow the lenders to control the cash flow waterfall.

The chart below sets out a typical cash flow waterfall and the associated account structure. Gross revenues (being principally the tariff from the offtake purchase agreement and any delay liquidated damages from the construction contractor) will be placed first into the proceeds account, for permitted payments (such as operating costs and tax liability) and debt service. The balance will flow into reserve accounts before ending up in a distribution account, from which funds can be made available for repayment of shareholder subordinated loans and distribution to shareholders.

REVENUE FLOW AND PROJECT ACCOUNTS

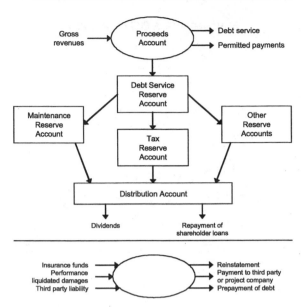

The reserve accounts are meant to protect the lenders from cash flow shortages, for example:[225]

> ➤ debt service reserve – an amount set aside, either funded up-front by the project debt or by project revenues during the operation period, to protect against future inability to repay debt where the project payment stream is insufficient;

> ➤ maintenance reserve – an amount set aside during the operation period for major maintenance and replacement costs. For example, major maintenance costs will generally occur every five to six years for thermal power projects;

> ➤ capital expenditures reserve – an amount set aside based on a percentage of the next year's capital expenditure forecast (where such amounts are particularly large or the project might be short of funds);

> ➤ rehabilitation reserve – an amount set aside in case of catastrophic damages;

> ➤ tax reserve – an amount set aside to satisfy project tax liability when it comes due; and

> ➤ standby reserve – which may also take the form of a loan facility, for any changes to be made to the project, not foreseen at the time of financial close. Standby reserves are sometimes used to cover specific project

---

[225]   On the subject of reserve accounts, see also Vinter (2nd edition 1998) supra note 211.

liabilities, such as where the project company bears the risk of some part of the cost of changes in law, grantor variations or changes in environmental regulations.

Other funds received by the project company, including insurance funds, performance liquidated damages from the construction contractor and third party liability, are paid into a compensation account. Restrictions on the use of these funds will be heavily negotiated and may depend on limitations placed on the funds received (in particular funds received from insurance cover). Generally speaking, funds in the compensation account will be allocated between reinstatement of any damage caused to the project, payments out to third parties, prepayment of debt and payment to the project company.[226] The lenders may require any payment from the compensation account which is to be made to the project company to be funnelled into the proceeds account.

It is often preferable for the sponsors to involve the lenders prior to bid submission so that any reserves can be included in the financial model and the bid tariff. However, early lender involvement can increase development costs.[227]

4.2 Types of Contributions

A BOT project will involve financing from various sources, in some combination of equity and debt. The ratios of these different contributions will depend on negotiations between the lenders and the shareholders.

4.2.1 Equity contributions

Equity contributions are funds invested in the project company which comprise its share capital and other shareholder funds. Equity holds the lowest priority of the contributions, therefore the other contributors will have the right to project assets and revenues before the equity contributors can obtain any return; or, on termination or insolvency, any repayment. Equity contributions bear the highest risk and therefore potentially receive the highest returns.

Equity contributors might include the project participants, local investors, the host government, the grantor, other interested governments, institutional investors and bilateral or multilateral organisations.

4.2.2 Debt contributions

Debt can be obtained from many sources, including commercial lenders, institutional investors, export credit agencies, bilateral or multilateral organisations, bondholders and sometimes the host country government.

---

[226] For further discussion of the allocation of performance liquidated damages, see chapter 11, and insurance funds through "head for the hills" clauses, see chapter 15.
[227] For further discussions of this issue, see chapter 16.

Repayment of debt is generally tied to a fixed or floating rate of interest and a programme of periodic payments. Given the lower risk, forecast return on debt is less than forecast return on equity.

Contrary to equity contributions, debt contributions have the highest priority amongst the invested funds (e.g. senior debt must be serviced before any other payments are made). In addition, senior lenders will want any further financing or investment to be subordinated to their interests.

Where multilateral organisations and export credit agencies number amongst the lenders, the debt package may benefit from certain insulation from political risk and preferential treatment by the host government in relation to repayment, although such lending may be more difficult to obtain due to restrictions and requirements of multilateral organisations and export credit agencies. Some of these multilateral organisations also benefit from preferred creditor status, providing greater comfort to the lender group. Commercial banks are desirable as long-term debt providers, given their flexibility in renegotiating loans and reacting to new or unforeseen conditions. This flexibility may not be available, for example, from bondholders.[228]

Bond financing generally provides lower borrowing costs, if the credit rating for the project is sufficiently strong. Rating agencies will be consulted to maximise the credit rating for the project. The project company may also wish to obtain an "insurance wrap". This instrument provides credit support to the project and therefore increases dramatically the project credit rating, often to AAA standards. A better credit rating will attract less expensive finance, justifying the cost of the insurance wrap.

4.2.3   Mezzanine contributions

Located somewhere between equity and debt, mezzanine contributions are accorded lower priority than senior debt but higher priority than equity. Examples of mezzanine contributions are subordinated loans and preference shares.[229] Use of mezzanine contributions (which can also be characterised as quasi-equity) will allow the project company to maintain greater levels of debt to equity ratio in the project, although at a higher cost than senior debt.

Mezzanine contributors will be compensated for the added risk they take either by receiving higher interest rates on loans than the senior debt contributors or by receiving partial participation in the project profits or the capital gains achieved by project equity. Sharing in capital gains may be provided by way of a share option or convertible right or some other "equity kicker" given to the mezzanine contributor. It should be noted, however, that the risk borne by mezzanine contributors is still less than that borne by equity providers; therefore their share in capital gains will be less than that of the equity contributors.

---

[228]   United Nations Industrial Development Organisation (1996) supra note 204 at 186, 192.
[229]   United Nations Industrial Development Organisation (1996) supra note 204 at 184.

Mezzanine contributions can be obtained from shareholders, commercial lenders, institutional investors and bilateral and multilateral organisations.

4.2.4   Debt-to-equity ratios

The lenders will prefer a lower debt-to-equity ratio in order to obtain a greater investment from the shareholders, ensure shareholder commitment to the project and protect lender debt contributions with the additional capital injection into the project thus increasing the net value of project assets. Shareholders will want an increased debt-to-equity ratio, decreasing the amount of investment they will need to supply and, since the return on debt contributions is fixed, increasing the potential return they can obtain from their equity contributions.

The actual level of debt-to-equity ratio will be the result of a compromise between the project company and the lenders, based on the overall risk to be borne by the lenders, the project risk generally, the nature of the project, the identity of the sponsors, the industrial sector and technology involved, the value of the project and the nature of the financial markets. For example, debt-to-equity ratios for power projects in developing countries tend to be in the order of 80:20 to 70:30, while other projects with higher market risks tend not to exceed 60-65 per cent. debt.[230]

4.3   Lender Recourse

One of the advantages to the shareholders of a BOT project is the absence, or limitation, of recourse by the lenders against the project shareholders. The project company is generally a limited liability special purpose project vehicle, therefore the lenders' recourse will be limited primarily or entirely to the project assets (including completion and performance guarantees and bonds).

4.3.1   Recourse, limited recourse and non-recourse financing

Recourse financing provides the lenders with full recourse to the assets or cash flow of the shareholders for repayment of the loan in the case of default by the project company. Where the project otherwise fails to provide the lenders with the repayments required, the lenders will have recourse to the assets and revenue of the shareholders, with no limitation.

Non-recourse (sometimes, confusingly, called "limited recourse") financing limits the lenders' recourse to the assets of the project at hand in case of default by the project company. Limited recourse financing may be structured in a variety of ways but will usually only provide the lenders with recourse to the assets of the shareholders in certain specified situations, up to a limited maximum amount and over a limited period. Thus, where some portion of the project involves more risk than another, recourse may be provided to the lenders to the extent of that risk or until that high risk period has passed. Alternatively, the amount of recourse allowed to the lenders may be limited in value. For example, the lenders may have

---

230   *Ibid.*

recourse to the assets of the shareholders but only to a limit of 10 per cent. of the project value or some percentage of the amount of the loan until completion of construction or perhaps during the first year of operation.

In a BOT project financing, the construction phase involves particular risks for the lenders. The value of the project against which the lenders provide financing is usually in the operation and the payment stream supported by the concession agreement and not in the equipment and materials, the physical assets of the project. Since the lenders will bear more risk until construction is complete, limited recourse is sometimes provided for the period up to completion of the works, which will generally be defined in the concession agreement and marked by the issue of a certificate or the passing of specified tests. It may also be limited to the period until certain financial ratios are achieved, or until the works have achieved a period of operation at a certain level. Another approach is to provide the lenders with limited recourse to sponsor assets in the event of certain breaches of the financing agreements by the project company or the shareholders.

The project company will want to limit the type of breaches resulting in full recourse to the shareholders, such as egregious or intentional breaches of essential covenants or representations which may alter the lenders' risk matrix. Limited recourse may involve the establishment of a fund, normally pledged or secured, which can be used, for example, where there is a deficiency of funds or an increase in costs during the period of limited recourse.[231]

The principal lender issues in relation to non-recourse financing in an effort to secure their lending against all of the project assets are:

> share pledge or retention;

> security over all (or substantially all) of the project assets and project agreements;

> security over insurance proceeds (as permitted), bonds, guarantees and liquidated damages obligations of the project participants;

> collateral agreements and direct undertakings between the lenders and the parties to the more significant project agreements;

> standby equity or debt; and

> limited shareholder support (i.e. limited recourse).

The nature of the security taken over project assets will depend on the provisions of the applicable law and negotiations between the lenders and the project company (see section 4.4.2).

Because BOT projects are typically financed on a non-recourse basis with the cash flow generated by the project and the project assets constituting the principal

---

[231]   Tinsley, Richard C, *Practical Introduction to Project Finance: Structuring and Funding* at 16 (1996).

project security, the lenders (and consequently the other project participants) in BOT projects have become particularly sensitive to the need to identify and allocate security over project assets and provide other comfort for the lenders.

4.3.2 Rights against other persons

The lenders may want to have rights, through the project company, against persons other than the project company and the project sponsors, such as:

> ➢ the offtake purchasers or project users, through for example "take-or-pay" arrangements, or "through-put" agreements in the case of a pipeline or similar project, to guarantee the purchase of a given amount of production or a given amount of use of the project;

> ➢ the input suppliers, through for example "put or pay" agreements, to supply a given amount of input, such as fuel or raw materials, at a set price;

> ➢ the operator, to guarantee proper operation of the project, for example so as to produce a set output per unit of input;

> ➢ the construction contractor, to provide completion guarantees and performance securities ensuring the project meets the performance criteria specified in the construction contract; and

> ➢ the insurers, to provide compensation for certain events which might have an impact on the performance and production of the project.

4.3.3 Loss of non-recourse treatment

A key question in any non-recourse financing is whether there will be circumstances in which the non-recourse nature of the borrower's liability is to fall away and the lenders are to have recourse to part or all of the shareholders' assets. Generally, the type of breach of covenant or representation which gives rise to this consequence is a deliberate breach on the part of the shareholders, and, in particular, the shareholders not using appropriate efforts to ensure that the project is successful by, for example, committing a breach of the operating or joint venture agreement which governs the running of the project. It should also be noted that applicable law will restrict the extent to which liability can be limited, for example liability for personal injury or death.

Difficult questions arise in relation to the obligations of the shareholders to take up the participation of joint venturers who drop out or default on their obligations, and, in particular, the question of when the shareholders are to be entitled to abandon the project in the event of catastrophe or in the event that the project no longer proves economic. These issues will either be resolved in the drafting of the financing agreement or at law (generally through the law of tort).

4.4   Issues Specific to Financing Agreement

Certain selected issues in relation to the financing agreement are discussed below.[232]

4.4.1   Conditions precedent

Conditions will be set against certain events to prevent the lenders from being committed to providing funds before the project structure and risk allocation matrix are consistent with the lenders' requirements. The events for which conditions precedent will be required will include the following.

4.4.1.1   Financial close

Before the financing arrangements become effective, the lenders will want evidence that the various project documents and security arrangements are in place. Conditions precedent may include effectiveness of project documents and issue of all permits, guarantees and letters of comfort required by the lenders.

4.4.1.2   Drawdown

Before any distribution, the lenders will want to confirm that the borrower is not in default of the financing obligations. Conditions precedent may include compliance with the debt-to-equity cover ratio, and that funds available to the project company at the time of drawdown are sufficient for completion.

4.4.2   Security issues

The lenders will want to put in place as much security for the financing as possible. Security is both "offensive" and "defensive": offensive to the extent the lenders can enforce the security to dispose of assets and repay debt where the project fails; defensive to the extent that senior security can protect the lenders from actions by unsecured or junior creditors.[233] Security rights may also allow the lenders to take over the project rather than just sell the project assets, since the value of the project lies in its operation and not in completed assets.[234] Creating a security package for the lenders may include security arrangements in relation to:

> physical assets;

> legal rights and revenue stream of the project company;

> share pledges;

---

[232]   For further discussion of negotiating and drafting the financing agreement, see chapter 5 of Vinter (2nd edition 1998) supra note 211.

[233]   *Ibid* at 149-150.

[234]   Lender rights to run the project rather than just sell off the assets will require consideration of the applicable legal system and its treatment of security and insolvency. Rights over project company shares may achieve the desired security, but may also involve the lenders taking on project risk, see *Ibid* at 150.

> ➢ bank accounts including retention and reserve accounts;

> ➢ sponsor support undertakings;

> ➢ guarantees from parent companies for their subsidiaries;

> ➢ government guarantees;

> ➢ bonds from project participants, including performance bonds;

> ➢ liquidated damages obligations from project participants, in particular the construction contractor;

> ➢ default, cross-default and step-in rights so as to give the lenders maximum control over the possible termination, and cure, of any default related to any of the project documents;

> ➢ take-or-pay or other arrangements in the offtake purchase agreement; and

> ➢ comprehensive insurances either as co-insureds or assignable to the lenders.

Security provided by the project company for the financing of the project may run into certain difficulties, primarily related to the site country's legal system. Since the types of security provided will often relate to either real property in the host country or moveable property found within the territory of the host country, the host country's legal system will generally apply to the ownership, seizure and security over such property. Insolvency and bankruptcy laws may also restrict the enforceability of security rights.

The most immediate issue is whether the type of security provided is recognised or even legal in the site country. Matters of priority of rights and registration of security must be considered, as well as the levels of fees, stamp duty, administrative costs and any subsequent delays which are commonly incurred. For example, in many countries there is no concept of the general floating charge, an instrument used often for United Kingdom-based project financings.[235]

4.4.3   Repayment

Repayment of the loan will need to be compatible with the project payment profile, either under the concession agreement or the offtake purchase agreement. The lenders will want to ensure that sufficient amounts to service the debt are set aside in the project cash flow and that where the cash flow is insufficient the insurances and project participant liability regimes (such as levels of liquidated damages) ensure payment of debt service in the event of default and acts or occurrences which might interrupt the project payment stream.

---

[235]   Rushton and McNair, "Proceed with Caution" ICL 29 at 34 (May 1994).

4.4.4   Shareholder support

The lenders may want access to non-project assets to protect their interests, where the project does not provide sufficient protection to the lenders. Shareholder support can take many forms. Its purpose is to provide the lenders with a guarantee or undertaking from the shareholders (which may need to be supported by bank guarantee, parent company guarantee or otherwise) giving the lenders either access to further security or comfort that the shareholders are committed to the project. The shareholders, however, have entered into a project financing in order to benefit from limited liability and recourse. They will not want to provide further support or increase their liability for the project.

4.4.5   Step-in

In the case of termination of the concession agreement, the lenders will have security over the project assets. However, the project assets are likely not to be worth the value of the outstanding debt. Therefore, the lenders often require some form of right to take over the project where the project company has failed in its obligations and the grantor intends to terminate the concession agreement or the offtake purchase agreement. Step-in provisions give the lenders the right to step in to the project company's rights and obligations under the project documents. The lenders will want to ensure that the grantor is in a position to continue with the project after step-in. However, the lenders themselves will not want to be involved in the actual step-in. They will generally mandate a "substitute entity" to step in for them. This entity will not necessarily act as a substitute for the project company, but rather will act for the lenders in the step-in procedure.

The step-in regime is usually included in direct agreements between the lenders, the grantor and the project participants. It can involve three different levels of lender intervention in the project: cure rights, step-in rights and novation or substitution.

4.4.5.1   Cure rights

Cure rights allow the lenders to cure a breach of an obligation by the project company under one of the project documents, including in particular the concession agreement. Each of the project participants will be required to inform the lenders of a relevant breach and allow the lenders to cure that breach. Where the lenders do not exercise their right to cure within an established cure period, the relevant project participant may proceed under its contractual remedies. Lenders will generally be hesitant to involve themselves in the cure of a project company breach unless the cure is limited to the payment of amounts due. The lenders may want the opportunity to cure before having to decide whether to step in.

4.4.5.2   Step-in rights

Step-in rights arise where the project company breaches one of the project documents and the relevant project participant chooses to terminate. The lenders are given a chance to step in with the project company, cure the relevant breach and put the project back on track. The other project participants will be required to continue their contractual relationships with the substitute entity in lieu of the project company, although the project company will not be released from its obligations under the project documents. The lenders will also be permitted to step out where they choose to do so, without incurring any continuing liabilities. The project company would remain liable both during step-in and after step-out. Step-in rights will also be available for each of the project documents.

4.4.5.3   Novation

A third level of step-in involves novation of all of the project company's rights and obligations to a substitute entity, in which case the substitute entity, for the purposes of the project, takes over the project company's role. The concession agreement, each of the other project documents and any licences or permits will need to provide for novation or be renegotiated before the lenders can successfully novate the project to the substitute entity. The various project participants may require the right to approve the substitute entity, although they should not be permitted to delay or withhold such approval unreasonably.

As noted above, step-in rights in project financing are generally considered to play a defensive, rather than an offensive, role.

4.4.6   Warranties, undertakings and representations

The lenders will want the project company to provide warranties and representations concerning the financial, legal and commercial status of the project company, and the construction, operation and performance of the works. The warranties and representations will be used by the lenders not so much as a basis for claiming damages but rather as potential events of default which permit the lenders to suspend drawdown, terminate, demand repayment and enforce security. The lenders will want the project company to repeat certain warranties and representations with each drawdown and periodically throughout the life of the loan, to ensure continued compliance.

The lenders will also want the project company to provide a series of undertakings in relation to the project documents and the project company's compliance with its obligations. These will include "reserve discretions" whereby the project company undertakes not to act on certain of its rights and discretions under the project documents without lender approval or to act on rights and discretions at the instruction of the lenders.

4.4.7   Use of insurance

Although the project participants may each provide insurance for the project, it is generally more efficient for the project company to provide or ensure provision of comprehensive insurance coverage for the entire project. In this way the interfaces between different insurance packages, the coverage provided by different insurance providers and the overlapping of the tasks performed by the various project participants will not result in overlapping insurance or gaps in insurance coverage.

The lenders may require that insurance proceeds received by the project company, in certain circumstances or over certain amounts and at their discretion, must be paid to the lenders for repayment of debt. The grantor and the project company will want insurance proceeds always to be used for reinstatement of the works. This is contrary to the interests of the lenders and will be a heavily negotiated issue. Restrictions imposed by insurers will need to be considered in this context.

4.5 Other Issues Relevant to Financing

A number of other important issues will be key to the successful financing of the project.

4.5.1 Completion

Completion represents the end of the construction phase of the project. The construction contractor will be liable for liquidated damages for late completion, therefore the definition of "completion" will have a large impact on the construction contractor's risk. The lenders will want to ensure that completion requires the works to be in a condition sufficient to merit release of the construction contractor from delay liquidated damages liability. The works will therefore be subject to certain technical tests and demonstration of performance capacity before completion is achieved.

The project company will want to ensure that the criteria placed on completion can be measured objectively as set out in the construction contract, and that the lenders do not have the right to refuse completion owing to their own subjective evaluation of the works. This may involve technical testing effectuated by independent experts, or by standard measures or tests with clearly ascertainable results, not unreasonably subject to dispute.

4.5.2 Host government support

The host government will have an important influence over the project throughout the concession period. Further, many of the project risks may be best managed or mitigated by the host government. Therefore, both the sponsors and the lenders may want to ensure that the project and project participants have host government support.

The project company will want to ensure that the grantor has the right and power to grant the concession and has the ability to fulfil its obligations and transfer the rights identified under the concession agreement, in order to prevent later claims that the concession was granted *ultra vires*. This may be difficult in times of change, for example during the break-up of the USSR where certain government entities changed form and function drastically. It may not be easy to identify the nature and capacity of a given government entity in such a situation.

The project participants should also ensure that the project has received all necessary approvals from the host government and any local authorities, and that the government will not change its regulation of the project's operation in such a way as to inhibit the project development and production plans. This risk is often difficult to manage in particular in countries with developing or highly volatile legal and regulatory structures. Legal opinions will be sought to confirm that the project approval structure is comprehensive and in compliance with legal requirements.

The lenders may want the host government to provide support for the grantor, the input supplier and/or the offtake purchaser, if they are public utilities or operators and where they are not safe credit risks. This support might be expressed through written guarantees, direct lender-grantor agreements, comfort letters, legislation or through some other contractual or moral obligation. Both the project company and the lenders will want to be covered by any such expression of support. This requirement may be difficult for developing countries which are seeking to decrease their national debt in order to improve their credit rating. Certain countries refuse to provide government guarantees for project financing. Various solutions have been suggested to replace a government guarantee where the lenders are not satisfied with the credit risk of a public entity and the central government refuses to provide a guarantee. These generally involve another entity providing a guarantee or other support, for example a local bank, a development bank, a multilateral organisation or the shareholders.

Grantor undertakings can cover a range of issues important to the success of the project and, to some extent, within the sphere of control of the host government. As an example, the following are undertakings received from the Philippine Government for power projects in the late 1990s:[236]

> ➤ repatriation of capital;

> ➤ timely and reasonable adjustment of tariffs;

> ➤ the fulfilment by the local utility of its obligations under the take-or-pay agreement;

> ➤ availability of fuel; and

> ➤ buy-out of the project by the utility in certain specified situations.

There have been a variety of difficulties related to these undertakings, in particular as governments change, but their presence has been critical to project viability.

4.5.3   Force majeure and change in law

It is important to note that the financing agreements will not include *force majeure* or change in law provisions. The obligation to repay the loans will continue in the event of *force majeure* or change in law.

---

[236]   Salcedo, "The Future of Financing Power Projects in the Philippines" PFI at 124 (2 July 1997).

The lenders will want to review the *force majeure* and change in law provisions in the project documents and ensure that they are back-to-back (as far as possible) with the concession agreement.[237]

4.5.4   Political risk

As the market for project finance transactions has expanded into developing countries, concerns about political risk have grown. Commercial lenders may be prepared to take a degree of political risk, but in some countries the perceived political risk inhibits or even prevents the financing of projects which otherwise might be viable. Since the commercial insurance market can only absorb a limited degree of true political risk, many project sponsors have turned to multilateral or export credit agencies to shoulder some or all of this burden. Issues which commonly arise in relation to such cover include:

> ➤ the definition of "political risk";

> ➤ whether or not political risk includes events in more than one country or different states of the host country;

> ➤ the relationship between political risk and other more "normal" project risks (for example completion risk);

> ➤ the extent to which a shareholder (particularly a local shareholder) can influence events which comprise political risk; and

> ➤ the consequences of a political risk event occurring and how it affects, for example, shareholder obligations to achieve completion, liability of shareholders under indemnities provided to export credit agencies or the basic liability of the borrower.

4.5.5   Environmental risk

The identification and management of environmental risk are key elements in infrastructure development and management. Environmental due diligence in respect of such projects and in respect of the legal regime within which they are being constructed, and an appreciation of the environmental requirements of public agencies which will be involved with the project, are crucial if the project company and lenders are to make a proper assessment of the risks involved.[238]

4.5.6   Currency exchange risk

Though a more detailed discussion of currency risk is provided in chapter 15, it is worth mentioning here that the lenders will be particularly concerned to review the management of currency risk. Where revenues are to be earned in some currency other than that in which the debt is denominated, the lenders will want to see the

---

[237]   *Force majeure* and change in law are discussed in further detail in chapter 15.
[238]   This issue is discussed in further detail in chapters 6 and 15.

revenue stream adjusted to compensate for any relevant change in exchange rate or devaluation. If this is not available, the lenders will want to see appropriately robust hedging arrangements or some other mechanism to manage currency exchange risk.

4.5.7 Lenders' technical adviser

The lenders normally will wish to engage a technical adviser in order to review the project and the project documentation in the pre-financial close phase. Then during the concession period, particularly during construction, the lenders may want their technical adviser to advise the lenders on the progress of the project, and in particular on technical issues. The lenders' technical adviser will usually certify completion of the works and milestones or progress preceding drawdowns under the financing agreements.

4.5.8 Intercreditor issues

As noted in section 3.1, financing for the project is likely to come from several sources, such as banks, multilateral organisations, international financial organisations and possibly the capital markets, including different levels and classes of debt and equity. An intercreditor agreement will often be entered into by the lenders in order to address issues of subordination; rights to security; management of drawdowns, insurance funds and technical advisers; exercise of discretion; and other intercreditor issues.

Chapter 5

Project Bankability

Most people think dramatically, not quantitatively.

Oliver Wendell Holmes

Since the lenders' recourse for repayment of debt will be limited primarily to the revenue flow from the project, the lenders will bear a substantial burden if the project fails. Therefore, before committing themselves to a project, the lenders will perform an in-depth review of the project structure, those involved in the project and the viability of the project. Effectively, a BOT project will be subject to the project finance market, including lender appetite for investment and risk and whether the lenders will be able to go to the market to syndicate the lending or access the bond market. The lenders will review the project documents and the project participants in light of the terms they will require for the financing to be "bankable".[239]

The lenders will want to ensure that the risks borne by the project company which are relative to the proper operation of the project are limited and properly managed. Therefore a bankable project will involve a solid financial, economic and technical plan, with a risk allocation scheme appropriate for the nature of the project, the risks involved and the interests of the lenders, i.e. whether the project is an acceptable credit risk.

This chapter considers bankability issues with a view to the practical requirements of the lenders when reviewing a project. Given the nature of projects and the variety of potential site locations and technical and financing issues involved, there is no commonly defined conception of the project structure necessary to achieve bankability. Each site country, each project and each group of shareholders will have its own particular needs, risks, technical requirements and sensitive issues in relation to the success of the project and the bankability of the project. The lenders will, however, be restricted by time, market and financial constraints, and may not

---

[239] For further discussion of bankability, see Vinter (2nd edition 1998) supra note 211.

perform an exhaustive review of bankability. In fact, the lenders may agree to consider a project based primarily on their perception of the site country market and the standing of the project sponsors.

Bankability will also vary based on the identity of the lenders. Different lenders will have different interests and concerns and different risk aversion. For example, where the lenders are public entities, they may be less averse to certain political risk than would private sector lenders. Public sector lenders may also have greater latitude in negotiations with the project company given the added benefits provided by public sector involvement, including political risk management.

Given the differences between markets and how rapidly markets change, this chapter will not attempt to define what it takes to make a project bankable but rather will review the risks which will be of primary importance to the lenders in assessing bankability. These issues will assess the viability of the project: economic, financial and technical viability (section 5.1); issues relative to project risk allocation including site issues (section 5.2); source country issues (section 5.3); project structure issues (section 5.4); and contractual structure issues (section 5.5). Many of these issues have been discussed in some detail in earlier chapters, but will be repeated here to provide a comprehensive analysis of bankability.

5.1   Project Viability

Lender review of project viability will concentrate primarily on four areas: financial, legal, economic and technical. The financial review will look at financial health and solidity of the project, represented in the financial model on which the project is based, to ensure that the revenues received will be sufficient for the various needs of the project and that all relevant costs have been calculated in the model. A legal review will consider the legal and tax system in the site country and identify the effect of this system on the project. The economic review will be sector and country based, analysing whether the local economy can support the project and whether the economic stress of the project will undermine the host country support of the project. The technical review will look at the design and equipment to be used in the works, and whether this has in the past demonstrated sufficient reliability and performance capacity to satisfy the requirements of a project of the size and type proposed, in the time, to the cost and over the period required, given the nature of the site and the site country.

5.1.1   Economic/political viability

When reviewing bankability, the lenders will wish to review the effect of the local economy on the project and the effect that the project may have on the local economy. Although it is the grantor and not the lenders who should be verifying that the project will have an overall beneficial impact on the site country and the local economy, the lenders will need to assess the net political and socio-economic benefit the project can have on the site country generally.[240] Multilateral and export credit agencies may have a particular interest or even a mandate related to the impact of the project on the site country.

Analysis of project impact on the site country should be made in real terms, with allowances for inflation, exchange rates, and other real rates and their impact. This evaluation will review, generally, the project objectives and how they relate to the host government's policy toward infrastructure development. The effect of the project on the national economy should be reviewed, including the political and economic sensitivities specific to the host country and the region in which the project will be located.

The benefit to the site country can be identified by the impact that the project will have, including:

> the nature of the infrastructure to be constructed;

> tangential improvements to infrastructure;

> development of national industry;

> transfer of technology and know-how;

> foreign exchange;

> development of local stock exchanges;

> procurement of local equipment and materials;

> imports;

> exports;

> job creation;

> use of local services;

> training; and

> reinvestment of profits in the local economy.

The detailed cost-benefit analysis should be reduced to an economic common denominator as far as possible in order to permit realistic comparisons, although this analysis will remain largely subjective.

While the lenders will need to consider the effect the project has on the economic wellbeing of the host country, they will also need to review the effect of the economic position and commercial sophistication of the site country on the project. In particular, the lenders will want to look at:[241]

---

[240] For further discussion of this issue, see Haley (1996) supra note 205 at 27.
[241] As modified from United Nations Industrial Development Organisation (1996) supra note 204 at 130.

> identification and location of the offtaker purchaser, end users and other customers;

> identification and location of the input supplier and other suppliers and service providers;

> flexibility, sophistication, skill and depth of the labour market;

> historical trends in prices, costs, production, availability, quality, competition, demand and the nature of the demand;

> administrative burden placed on imports, in particular specialised labour and equipment;

> tax/tariff policies, the history of such policies and indications of what changes might be made to those policies;

> trends which might indicate future government positions and attitude towards foreign investment and the project in particular;

> sophistication and stability of the legal system, for example protection of intellectual property rights, land rights, taking of security and dispute resolution;

> regulatory framework specific to the project, the history of such framework and indications of what changes might be implemented into the framework over the period of the concession;

> technical sophistication, cost and availability of local subcontractors, designers and operators;

> competition in the host country market; and

> other aspects of the market which might affect the project's construction, cost-effectiveness, production efficiency and competitiveness.

5.1.2   Legal viability

The lenders will wish to review the legal system of the host country and any other legal system which will apply to any substantial element of the project. This review will concentrate on several basic aspects of the applicable legal system.

5.1.2.1   Stability

The lenders will want to consider the legal system applicable to the project in view of a long-term commercial arrangement based on certain undertakings by the public sector and certain assumptions in respect of property rights, taking of security, asset management and corporate structures. Instability will increase lender risk and require further protections from either the host government, the grantor or the shareholders. The lenders will be particularly interested in the host government's record with foreign investors and protection of their interests.

5.1.2.2 Availability of justice

This review will also consider whether and to what extent the legal system is accessible to the project company and the lenders, including considerations of access to judicial review of legal issues and the time and resources required to access such review. Can a foreign investor get to an independent court? How long does it take, how much does it cost and will the court demonstrate a bias against foreigners? Reference to arbitration may be helpful, although the treatment of arbitration awards by local courts will need to be reviewed.

5.1.2.3 Enforceability

A legal decision or arbitration award is less effective if it is difficult or impossible to enforce either in the host country or abroad. The New York Convention[242] can be of assistance for execution of arbitral awards in foreign jurisdictions. The enforcement of court orders or judgements may also be complicated or impractical for foreign parties.

5.1.2.4 Security

Security will be one of the primary interests of the lenders given that their remedy in the event of project failure may depend largely on the effectiveness of the security created on behalf of the lenders over project assets. Civil code legal systems may have an extremely limited view of the taking of security. For example, in certain civil law systems the concept of "future assets" does not exist, therefore taking security over assets such as insurable proceeds may be impossible. These considerations can lead to rather complex legal structures in order to provide the lenders with the security they will require.[243]

5.1.2.5 Implied terms

Any legal system will imply certain terms in a contractual agreement. Implied terms create rights and obligations as between the parties at law. These terms may be limited to concepts of "reasonableness" and "equity", or may include more extreme terms. The lenders will need to review the relevant implied terms under the applicable law in view of the potential effect on the project's financial viability and risk allocation structure.

5.1.2.6 Stability of the tax regime

Just as the legal system must be stable for the lenders to be able to forecast their financial exposure, the tax regime applicable to the project must be sufficiently stable. The lenders will want some kind of reasonable forecast of exposure to tax liability to plug into the financial model and to allocate to the project participants.

---

[242] The United Nations Convention on the Enforcement of Arbitral Awards (1958) (the "New York Convention").

[243] The issue of security has been discussed in more detail in chapter 4.

5.1.3   Financial viability

The actual assets which make up a project will not be the basis for the lenders' financing, unlike other financing where it is the value and rate of depreciation of the underlying assets which defines the lenders' security and willingness to finance a project.   In project financing, it is the health of the project structure, the commercial plan and the forecast revenue stream that will convince the lenders to provide financing. This is because the project assets will be under construction and may be insufficient in value once completed to satisfy the outstanding project debt.

The lenders will wish to review the financial model upon which the project is based. This model will define the various financial inputs and outflows that make up the project cash flow. By calculating project risk into the financial model, the lenders will be able to assess project sensitivities and their costs, and how far the project can absorb the occurrence of a given risk.

A project is financially viable where the project payment stream less costs, expenses and fees leaves an appropriate rate of return on investment for the shareholders and debt service coverage for the lenders. The financial evaluation of a project may be simplified by the presence of an offtake purchase agreement. By pre-defining the project revenues the lenders will have a better picture of the financial viability of the project.   This certainty of revenue will be measured against the possibility of revenue failure or cost increases.   Although the shareholders will also review these issues carefully, they are generally less risk averse than the lenders given the potential upside of return on equity.

5.1.3.1   Debt-to-equity ratio

The debt-to-equity ratio compares the amount of debt in the project against the amount of equity invested. It is possible for a project to go forward financed entirely by debt; however, this is rare. Higher debt-to-equity ratios can mean increased lender exposure to project risk.[244] Higher equity investment will result in a greater "ownership" of the project by the shareholders, increasing their incentive to ensure that the project is a success. For example, power projects tend to attract debt-to-equity ratios of 90:10 to 70:30, while projects with higher market risk can require 55-60 per cent. equity.[245]

5.1.3.2   Debt service cover ratio

The debt service cover ratio (or "DSCR") measures the cash flowing into the project and available to meet debt service after deducting operating expenses against the amount of debt service due in the same period. This ratio can be either backward or forward looking. The DSCR should attain a target ratio of at least 1.2 to 1.6, although the ratio required by the lenders will depend on the site country, the commercial sector of the project and the lenders involved.

---

[244]   Haley (1996) supra note 205 at 33.
[245]   United Nations Industrial Development Organisation (1996) supra note 204 at 184.

Assuming a rather large DSCR of 1.6, the following diagram provides a very simplified indication of how project net income will be allocated between debt service requirements and cash flow available for distribution. The lenders will often restrict use of the latter, for example by requiring the funding of reserve accounts, in order to provide additional security for outstanding debt.

DEBT SERVICE COVER RATIO

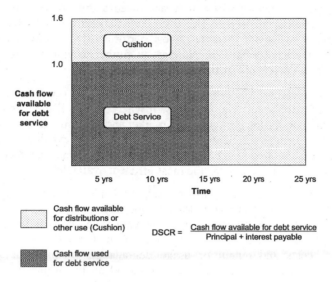

5.1.3.3   Loan life cover ratio

The lenders will want to review the net present value of future project income over the maturity of the loan against the amount of debt plus interest, often known as the "loan life cover ratio" (or "LLCR"). This calculation is forward looking and will be made periodically (generally every six months) during the project until the debt is repaid in order to verify that the LLCR meets the requirements of the lending agreements throughout the life of the debt.

5.1.3.4   Rate of return

The equity rate of return indicates the value of project return on equity over time and against other cost considerations. The shareholders may also be receiving benefit from other areas of the project such as the construction and operation tasks which will not appear in the equity rate of return.

5.1.4   Technical viability

The review of the project carried out by the lenders will also focus on the technical merits of the design, or intended design, and the technology to be used in the project. The lenders will prefer not to finance projects using cutting edge or untested technology. They will want to have relatively accurate performance forecasts, including operation, maintenance and life-cycle costs, and will therefore prefer tried and tested technology used in similar projects with well documented performance.

The lenders will wish to review the capacity of the technology to be used and its appropriateness for the site and the type of performance required from the project. This same review will have been undertaken by the project company at the early stages of feasibility studies of the project. The lenders may be satisfied with the project company's reviews where they are owed a duty of care by the project company's technical advisers. However, international financing organisations generally prefer to have a separate review performed by an independent expert. The lenders may have a particular interest in further technical review where the technology to be used is not sufficiently tested or tried.

The review of technical viability will be connected to the economic and financial viability discussed above. The lenders will wish to know if the technology to be used is appropriate for the host country's market and systemic needs. Will the new project provide gains in efficiency in comparison with the existing system or other projects being developed in the region? Is the operation and maintenance of the project, including life-cycle costs, the most efficient available?

When analysing the technology to be used, the lenders will perform a financial review of the use of the technology looking not only at output per unit of input but also at capital and operating costs, life of the equipment, the need for maintenance, durability, training requirements, and long-term forecasts of operation and maintenance costs and output or usage degradation. This technical/financial analysis will be central to the final financial model for the project and the lenders' review.

At the time the project company first contacts the lenders, the existing technical analysis will generally cover only preliminary capital cost forecasts, for example with an accuracy range of +15 to -10 per cent., which will be insufficient for the needs of the lenders. The lenders will want to review, in particular, the commercial assumptions and risk allocation used in this initial technical model.

The technology to be used will need to be reviewed in connection with output, environmental risks and the effect it will have on the surrounding community. Again, even where the host country does not at the time of negotiation impose strict environmental regulations, the lenders will prefer the project to be at least consistent with the technology used in other projects and in other countries in relation to environmental issues.

Site issues relevant to the review of technical viability will include:

> the nature of the proposed site, including access rights, ground conditions and setting out of the works;

> local consent and licence requirements;

> local climate conditions;

> local and associated infrastructure, including utilities, transportation, communication and offtake capabilities;

> environmental standards applied by national and local authorities and other government and non-government organisations, such as environmental pressure groups;

> cost and delay involved in the importation of equipment and materials;

> availability of local personnel, including suitable management staff, skilled labour, local subcontractors and the need for training of project personnel; and

> cost and availability of equipment, materials and spare parts for construction and operation.

5.2 Site Issues

Once the project viability has been assessed, the lenders will wish to review the risk allocation structure for the project. The risk allocation of the project documentation will define the relative "cost" of the project to the lenders by the risk they will bear. Each project is different, therefore lenders may be willing to bear risks in one project that they will not bear in another. Lenders will sometimes take risks:

> in order to gain entrance into a particular market;

> owing to the relationship they have with certain shareholders;

> following pressure from the source country government; or

> further to internal decisions about bankability, cash flow and risk management.

Risk issues relevant to the bankability of the project can be broken down into three general topics: site issues, source country issues and project structure issues. The following review is meant as a brief overview of risk issues in order to provide insight into the approach the lenders may adopt. A risk analysis of bankability is entirely subjective, based on the lenders' interests, the global market for financing, the local market for investment and lender appetite for risk.

The lenders will need to consider the location of the project. For example, infrastructure projects are often located in developing countries, while the shareholders in such projects are generally from developed countries. In such cases the shareholders will need to be aware of the different risks involved in owning, building and operating a project in the host country.

5.2.1 Political issues

A BOT project will require some involvement of the host government and many of its various entities. The lenders will wish to verify the underlying support of the host country and the protections put in place for the project against the host government's discretionary powers.

5.2.1.1   Host country guarantees

The host country government, while wanting the infrastructure provided by a BOT project, will wish to distance itself from the financial burden and risk of the project. The reason the host country grants the private sector a concession for the project is to pass on the cost and burden of the development of such a project. However, the lenders may want host government or local state government guarantees or possibly substantial letters of comfort for the project, in particular for the performance of the obligations (generally payment) of the offtake purchaser and possibly the input supplier where such parties represent inappropriate credit risks. Host government guarantees are increasingly difficult to obtain from more developed economies, such as India and China. The host government will often support the proliferation of BOT projects as a method of releasing itself from such obligations.

5.2.1.2   Host country policy

The lenders will want to ensure a supportive host country, and will review the host country government's policy both for clarity and long-term viability.[246] The host country government's policy must be consistent with the best interests of the project and sufficiently well defined to avoid misinterpretation or misunderstanding. Finally, the host country policy must be stable, couched in sufficiently immutable sources of law and not subject to the discretion of the host country government. The lenders will wish to know to what extent the project company will bear the risk of the host country government changing policy and interfering with the success of the project.

5.2.1.3   Change in political atmosphere

The project will probably be licensed and regulated by the public sector, therefore the host government and its entities may have the right to intervene frequently in the construction and operation of the project. Government intervention may occur through the permits and licences which are necessary for the project company and its subcontractors to be able to operate or through the regulations used to monitor and control the operation of such projects, including health and safety regimes. The successful project will need the support, or at least the disinterest, of local and national governments. The lenders will want to make sure that if the project does not have at least the active support of the host government, based on lasting shared interests which will survive changes in the host government and the political climate, that the host government will at least not oppose the project at some later date nor modify the applicable regulations and consents so as to threaten project

---

[246]   For further discussion of the host country legal regime and its relationship to the BOT project, see United Nations Industrial Development Organisation (1996) supra note 204 at 41-72.

profitability and viability. This is generally achieved by creating liabilities on the host government or one of its emanations if the project viability is so affected.

When reviewing the bankability of a project, the lenders will assess the host country's support, and the probability of continued support, by studying the host government's interests, how the project has been received by the political establishment and opposition groups, and the volatility of the host country's political structure.

5.2.1.4 Nationalisation and expropriation

The host country will generally have the right to nationalise any commercial entity and expropriate any property registered or located in its territory, provided that just and timely compensation is paid.[247] The parties may be able to agree by contract the nature, quantum and timing of such compensation. The lenders will want to review generally the protections provided to the project company in the case of such expropriation or nationalisation.

Similarly, the host government may be going through or planning a series of privatisations. Where the host government intends to privatise the public entity which happens to be the offtake purchaser or the input supplier, then the lenders may wish to consider the potential impact of such events on the project. Similarly, if the project company does not benefit from exclusivity, the lenders will wish to understand the impact of private sector competition where the entire sector is privatised or deregulated.

5.2.1.5 Change In law

The host government will change its laws, regulations, ordinances or the application or interpretation thereof during the period of the concession. The lenders will want to review what impact the allocation of the risk of such changes might have on the project, and particularly its commercial or financial viability. One of the important elements of change in law risk is the modification of performance requirements, including output and environmental requirements, during the concession period, increasing the cost of output and possibly decreasing production. Such changes may have a substantial impact on the profitability of the project.

The lenders will not want to bear the risk of a change in law. However, the grantor will want to place this risk on the project company. Although as a general proposition it is probably still correct to say that the lenders should not bear this risk,[248] it is becoming more common to see the grantor force some of this risk on the project company, up to a specified monetary limit or subject to limitations.

---

[247] Brownlie, Principles of Public International Law at 123 (4th edition 1990); Maryan, "Negotiating with the Monarch; Special Problems when the Sovereign is your Partner" Project Financing in Emerging Markets 1996; Successful Development of Power, Mining, Oil and Gas, Telecommunications and Transportation Projects at 122 (1996).

[248] Vinter (2nd edition 1998) supra note 211 at 86.

Examples of this shift can be as diverse as power projects in Pakistan (although recent political events may reverse this shift) and PFI projects in the United Kingdom. Where the project company is required to bear change in law risk the lenders will want the risk of these changes to be placed on the project participants, although they may require a substantial fee before bearing such a risk. Alternatively, and as far as the project company's change in law risk is measurable, the lenders may require the project company to maintain a reserve account in an amount sufficient to cover the potential cost of this risk.

Change in law risk will also include the risk of change in taxation. Increased taxation, or a change in the way taxation is calculated, can have a substantial effect on the financial viability of the project. Further, the authority defining the tax system and the grantor may be entirely separate entities, increasing the risk of retaliatory or discriminatory changes even where host government support is maintained.

The lenders will not want the project company to bear the risk of change in taxation. Often this risk will be isolated from the change in law risk and will be dealt with separately and specifically. The lenders may be willing to bear the risk of change in general taxation (those taxes applying to the whole of the business sector) but will desire protection from discriminatory taxation which is directed at the project or the project company.

5.2.2   Administrative issues

Not entirely within the political sphere, although closely related to it, the administrative functions of local and national authorities will be of specific interest to the lenders. Two aspects of the administration will be important: first, how clearly the administrative system is defined, and secondly, how stable is that definition.

The clarity of definition of the administrative system allows precise identification of administrative risk. But the system, no matter how clear, may change. Therefore, the stability of the system and its definition will provide the project company and the lenders with some security of its continued efficient functioning.

5.2.2.1   *Licences, permits and authorisations*

As part of the administrative procedure, licences, permits and authorisations will need to be obtained. The host government may change the requirements or costs of licences and permits required for the construction and the operation of the project during the concession period. The lenders will want to ensure that protections are provided to the project company for any changes in the licences and permits required, the cost of such licences and permits and the difficulties or delays involved in their obtention or renewal.

The preferred position of the lenders will be that:[249]

> ➤ licences and permits are sufficient for the construction and operation of the project in accordance with the concession agreement for the duration of the concession period;

> ➤ the project company will not be responsible for delay or cost resulting from any modification of the terms of the licences and permits; and

> ➤ the licences and permits shall run with the project, so that the lenders or the grantor or any other entity taking over the project from the project company will be able to construct and operate the project under the same terms and conditions for the duration of the concession period. This will be essential as the lenders will have an interest in the project succeeding where the project company has fallen away and has been replaced by a substitute entity.

The same will be true for import and export restrictions. A project's technical viability will often hinge on the importation of special equipment. Its financial viability may require the importation of fuel or other materials and equipment from other countries. Permissions to import and export will be vulnerable to changes of requirements, costs and availability. This is of particular relevance in the case of politically or militarily sensitive technology, for example in nuclear power plants where both the fuel and waste will be highly regulated and particularly sensitive to political pressures.

The host government will also often provide the land on which the project is to be developed. The lenders will need to review the project company's rights to this land, and any warranties provided, in case the land is no longer made available, access is refused or the right to use the land for the purposes of the project is lost.

5.2.2.2 Regulation

The regulatory structure intended to monitor and manage certain sectors or utilities provides a particularly salient example of an administrative function that will be key to the viability of a project. This entity will have significant power over the project and authority over its operation. An efficient and effective regulator can make every difference in the success of the project company and realisation of the project's potential. Water and sanitation projects tend to be highly regulated. Tariff structures, performance standards and additional obligations are often set by the regulator. Failure by the regulator to manage these issues in accordance with the concession agreement can undermine the entire project. In addition, the legal principle of fettering discretion may mean that the regulator cannot be bound by contract to set tariffs in a particular manner. The project company may need some other contractual or financial remedy to address regulatory risk.

---

[249] *Ibid* at 94.

5.2.2.3   Administrative policy

The administration that regulates the commercial sector of the project will generally be distinct from the grantor and may be completely independent. The lenders will want to review the administration's policy, whether that policy is consistent with the project and to what extent the project company bears the risk of a change in that policy which might have an impact on the success of the project. The project is more likely to succeed in a stable regulatory environment.

5.2.3   Currency issues

Although currency issues often overlap with political issues they are treated separately in this book, given their importance and specific nature. The currencies used in the project may undergo some change in availability, convertibility, or transferability. The lenders will need to ensure that these risks are either allocated to a party other than the project company or mitigated by some other means, such as hedging. Certain currency issues will be specific to the project structure, and will be discussed further below.[250]

5.2.4   Market issues

Lenders will look for a contractual structure that allocates the market risks associated with the project away from the project company. The lenders will need to verify that such risks are successfully allocated.

5.2.4.1   Local market for offtake

The price of offtake will be affected by the local market. In most BOT projects, the risk of change in the price of offtake will be allocated to the offtake purchaser. The project company may want to obtain part of the project financing in local currency. This will partly avoid the expense of linking the tariff scheme with the exchange rate of the foreign currency in which the debt is denominated to satisfy foreign currency debt servicing.

However, the market may have some effect on the revenues received by the project company where the offtake purchase agreement payment stream is index linked or otherwise based on actual market price, such as where the project company specifically accepts some element of the usage risk or where a merchant plant approach has been adopted. A merchant plant does not involve an offtake purchaser, therefore the project company and the lenders bear the offtake market price and demand risk. The merchant plant approach is generally limited to projects in sectors with a flexible, fluid market with consistent demand and free access to that market, or where the project company collects tariffs from individual consumers (in which case these tariffs are normally regulated or agreed in advance).

---

[250]   For further discussion of currency risk, see chapters 4 and 15.

Even where the offtake market price is not a factor in the market risk associated with the project payment stream, the lenders will be interested in its fluctuation since the cost of offtake on the national market may be a sensitive political issue. The public may not be prepared to see infrastructure cost rise, particularly where such increased cost will be seen to affect the competitiveness of local products. For example, toll roads are particularly sensitive to the political risk of tariff increases. The local population may not be willing to pay higher tolls for roads which they may consider to be a public service. As an example, the government in the United Kingdom has been very hesitant to introduce a system of toll roads for fear of political backlash.

5.2.4.2   Local market for input

The risk of change in the cost of input will be largely allocated to the input supplier. However, such contracts often include break clauses or allow for modification of the fixed price where the market price for the input exceeds the contract price by a given percentage. The same will be true for the cost of transporting the input to the site. For these reasons, although the fluctuation of the input cost will not be of concern, the lenders will want to ensure a reasonably flexible market for necessary input, such as fuel, raw materials and spare parts. The lenders will also be concerned if market fluctuations result in the failure of the input supplier.

5.2.4.3   Infrastructure issues

The state of the local infrastructure, including transportation systems, roadways, electricity, water and other utilities, will affect the bankability of the project. The lenders will want to ensure that the local infrastructure is sufficient to meet the needs of the project for managing output produced, transporting inputs to the site and waste to disposal areas; housing and transportation of personnel; and functioning of the facilities necessary for administrative functions. Where available infrastructure is insufficient, the lenders will want to ensure that the project participants are required to provide any additional infrastructure needed, or that reasonable undertakings to provide the same are obtained from the local or national authorities.

5.2.4.4   Legal issues

In line with the political issues discussed above, the lenders will want to review the legal system of the host country and ensure that it is sufficient to protect their interests in the project assets. The legal culture of the site country will have a direct impact on the local commercial market. The project will need to operate within the local market, efficiently and profitably. The review of applicable law has been discussed in greater detail above.

5.2.5   Force majeure

Force majeure is an event, act or circumstance which arises during the project, and which affects the project obligations and is beyond the control of either of the parties. It is often specific to the site country, although it may include events in neighbouring countries, source countries or countries through which materials and equipment must be shipped in order to reach the site. *Force majeure* will generally include political, natural and administrative events.

The intent of the *force majeure* provision is to allocate, partially or entirely, the risk of the occurrence of an event not contemplated by the parties at the time of contracting, outside their power to control or prevent, and which impedes the progress of the project.[251]

5.3   Source Country Issues

The lenders will wish to review project risks in relation to source countries. Source country issues will be similar to site country issues, only in relation to the countries from which equipment, materials, plant, labour, funding and necessary inputs are sourced. Sourcing of capital will be an important issue, as source country economic and political conditions may affect the cost and availability of funding.

Certain countries have established public or private agencies which provide financing, insurance cover and guarantees in order to promote national exports and industry. Further, bilateral and multilateral agencies may provide financing, guarantees and insurances for projects; however, their assistance will be restricted to products sourced from their member countries.[252] The identity of the source country and that country's willingness to support the project will be of particular interest to the lenders where the associated bilateral, export credit or multilateral agency support may be lost if the relevant content cannot be sourced from that country.

5.4   Project Structure Issues

The lenders will want to review the identity and nature of the shareholders, the financing plan and the contractual structure (including risk allocation and liability limitations) to be adopted by the project, in order to assess bankability.

5.4.1   Shareholders

The lenders will want to ensure that the shareholders have sufficient commercial experience, financial standing and technical acumen to implement the project and thereby protect the lenders' interests. The strength of the shareholders will be measured not only by their financial standing but also by their commitment to the

---

[251]   *Force majeure* is discussed in more detail in chapter 15.
[252]   For more information on these agencies, see chapter 3.

project. This may be measured by the equity invested in the project (be it monetary or in-kind), the period during which they are bound to the project (before they are able to transfer their interests in the project company or receive distributions) and the period during which the lenders may have some recourse to shareholder assets. The lenders will take particular interest in the creditworthiness of the shareholders where they provide stand-by facilities or other sponsor support.

The shareholders will also often be project participants, which creates potential conflicts of interest. The lenders will need to ensure that any such conflict does not have a negative effect on the structure of the project, including the pricing structure for the project documents and the transfer of risk from the project company.

The lenders will want to review the technical expertise of those shareholders providing services, particularly where they are local partners involved in the project as a result of site country regulations requiring a percentage of local involvement or ownership. Strong local support can do much to improve relations with local authorities and labour groups. However, local involvement may result in the use of less technically adept labour or materials of lesser quality.

5.4.2   Financing structure

The lenders will need to verify that the intended project structure has access to adequate funding, including:

> ➢ equity investment in appropriate amounts in relation to project risk;

> ➢ certainty of revenue flow from the project to satisfy coverage ratios with no interference;

> ➢ sufficient reserves created during the early stages of the project; and

> ➢ priority of debt repayment from project revenues.

The lenders will want to ensure that the special purpose vehicle, created by the shareholders, is sufficiently capitalised. The lenders will prefer to have all equity investment up-front. However, making equity contributions at the back-end of the construction period or over time may be allowed where the financial stability of the shareholder in question is sufficient to protect the lenders. The lenders may also require guarantees, letters of credit or other security where equity is to be provided progressively or at the end of the construction period.

The lenders will also want to ensure that distributions are not made to any of the shareholders until payments of the debt servicing have been made. The lenders will want to receive a priority share of the revenues of the project company and will also want to maintain a maximum of shareholder interest in the project. This may involve requiring shareholders to come up with added funds for cost overruns. The shareholders may also be required to cover gaps in insurance, which will often be the case for new technology, gaps in *force majeure* provisions, or maritime transport of equipment.[253] These shareholder obligations may need to be supported by parent company guarantees or other credit enhancement where the relevant shareholder is not sufficiently creditworthy.

5.4.3 Third party risk allocation

Certain risk issues can be managed through the involvement of third parties, either reviewing the project and affirming that a particular risk does not exist or quantifying that risk, or by bearing the risk themselves. The following are examples of such issues which the lenders will want to explore in some detail.

5.4.3.1 *Insurance*

The project must have in place a comprehensive insurance scheme, which should have no gaps or overlapping coverage. This may involve a complex weave of individual policies, often with several insurers, or (and this is often preferable) the project company will provide an overall insurance programme covering all risks.[254] It should be noted that insurance is not risk management and should not be relied upon as a primary element of the project risk allocation scheme.

The lenders will want to be co-insured on every insurance policy which covers project assets, to ensure that their interests are protected. This will include the waiver of subrogation rights against the lenders and other project participants and of any rights of contribution by the lenders' other insurances. Just as the lenders may step in to the project documents, they will want to be able to step in to the insurance policies in order to maintain coverage if they, or their substitute entity, take over the project.

The lenders will want any payments from insurance to be used either to remedy any damage to the project or to pay off the debt, before any other damages are paid. Generally, the parties will agree to use payments over a set amount to repay debt. The lenders will prefer that any insurance payments should be made directly to themselves or a party of their choosing in order to control such disbursements and their use. They will also want to be notified before any change in the insurance policy or coverage is made, or where any party to the insurance policy fails to perform its obligations thereunder. While the lenders will want the discretion to use insurance funds to pay off any remaining debt, the project company and the grantor will want to use such proceeds to reinstate the works or replace equipment as necessary. For this reason, the lenders will often seek to include "head for the hills" provisions to establish a regime which will allocate insurance proceeds in specific circumstances to repayment of debt.[255] The relevant insurance policy should be reviewed to ensure that repayment of debt with insurance proceeds is permitted.

---

[253] Vinter (2nd edition 1998) supra note 211 at 95.
[254] See chapter 15 for further discussion of insurance.
[255] See chapters 3 and 22 of Scriven, Pritchard and Delmon (1999) supra note 210.

5.4.3.2   *Environmental and other legal/regulatory issues*

Sanctions for breach of environmental regulations and compensation for environmental damage is a risk that the lenders will want allocated from the project company to the project participants or the grantor. The lenders will want to ensure that this risk is completely transferred away from the project company. Similarly, other legal and regulatory risks can threaten the construction and operation of the project. Equally, the lenders will want these risks to be passed to project participants.

Multilateral and export credit agencies are particularly concerned with environmental compliance and risk. They will look for the project to comply not only with local environmental requirements, but also those espoused by the World Bank and possibly the European Union or other national standards. They may also mandate environmental impact assessments ("EIAs") to establish the nature of the project and the environmental risks involved.

The lenders will often prefer to establish the existence and/or extent of these risks, rather than simply rely on the credit risk of the responsible party. They will, therefore, perform or ensure performance of legal and environmental reviews, with extensive performance of site surveys, obtaining the assurances of legal and technical experts in their respective domains.

5.5   Contractual Structure Issues

The lenders will review in detail the project documents, insurances, and other contractual arrangements that make up the project in an effort to ensure proper risk allocation and margins of financial cover.[256] The following discussion of the concession agreement sets out general project obligations which will need to be passed through to the project participants. The discussion of the other project documents will identify only issues specific to those documents and not risks passed through from the concession agreement.

5.5.1   Concession agreement

The concession agreement represents some of the most critical issues for lenders. It will often be combined with the offtake purchase agreement and will therefore contemplate the project revenue stream. The lenders will want the concession agreement to include the issues discussed below.

5.5.1.1   *Terms*

The key for the lenders reviewing a concession agreement is that risks passed down to the project company can then be passed on to the project participants. The lenders will want to review the concession agreement for unreasonable terms, risks

---

[256]   See generally Vinter (2nd edition 1998) supra note 211 at 96; The World Bank, Toolkits for Private Participation in Water and Sanitation at part 3 (1997).

or burdens placed on the project company; for example, the level of damages applied for late completion, late on-stream connection or insufficient performance. The project company will need to pass these obligations on to the project participants. The more unreasonable the terms of the obligations applied, the more expensive the underlying contracts and the less profitable the project generally.

5.5.1.2   Duration

The duration of the concession period will need to meet the requirements of the financial model for the whole of the project. Where one of the grantor's risks has occurred and the project company requires some compensation, the grantor may prefer that compensation to be in the form of an extension of the concession period. By lengthening the concession period the grantor provides the project company with greater income without having to invest its own funds in the project. The lenders may be willing to consider this approach, though it will generally result in the lengthening of the tenor of the debt. The financing agreements may need to provide for a modification of debt servicing requirements where the concession period is extended owing to grantor default. Such an extension would indicate some deficiency in the revenue stream and the project company's subsequent ability to satisfy debt servicing on an as-modelled basis.

5.5.1.3   Termination

The lenders will wish to review opportunities for termination of the concession period and they will want to limit the grantor's opportunity to terminate the concession. The lenders may also require cure rights as well as the right to step in to the concession agreement in order to cure any default before the grantor has the right to terminate the concession. In addition, the lenders will want termination to result in sufficient compensation to repay the debt, regardless of the cause for termination. The grantor will want to restrict termination compensation, possibly to actual value added, in particular where the project is terminated for project company default.

5.5.1.4   Grantor

The lenders will want to review the identity of the grantor to ensure that the proper party is issuing the concession with the legal rights over the public sector service and site. It may be necessary to have multiple grantors to assemble the necessary property and other rights and legal authority. The lenders will also want to know that the project will not suffer if the grantor becomes insolvent or is privatised.

5.5.1.5   Exclusivity

Where the project involves an offtake purchase agreement that guarantees a price for output, the lenders will be protected against market risk for sale of project offtake. However, where the project company is to take usage risk, the lenders will want to ensure that the concession agreement provides some level of exclusivity for the project company, providing a captive market for offtake. Where no offtake purchase agreement is envisaged, the lenders will also want to ensure that the project payment stream is secure to a minimum debt service ratio, possibly through a flexible approach to the area to be served by the project (and therefore the number of end users) or by the grantor ensuring a minimum level of return for the project.

5.5.1.6 Change in law/regulations

The project company will probably be required to operate the project in compliance with applicable laws and regulations. The grantor will want the project company to bear the risk of changes in law and regulations as the normal cost of doing business in the site country. The lenders will want the grantor to bear any added costs due to changes in law or regulations, in particular where those changes are discriminatory against the project.

5.5.1.7 Licences and permits

Where further licences and permits must be obtained, the lenders will want to ensure that they are obtained before financial close and that the fees charged or the requirements imposed for renewal will not be discriminatorily increased. The lenders may be satisfied with an undertaking from the grantor to assist in applying for and procuring such licences and permits.

5.5.1.8 Assignment and security

The lenders will require that the project company is able to assign its rights to the lenders and that the lenders will be able to take security over project assets. These rights will normally be reinforced by provisions of the direct agreements.

5.5.2 Construction contract

The lenders will look to the construction contractor to bear completion and performance obligations placed on the project company by the concession agreement. The lenders will also look to the general issues discussed below.

5.5.2.1 Turnkey contract

The lenders will want the whole of the completion risk to be allocated to the construction contractor, which means a tightly drafted turnkey construction contract with a fixed price and a fixed time for completion. Time will be of the essence, therefore the construction contractor will be entitled to an extension of the time for completion only to the extent such entitlement mirrors the project company's rights under the concession agreement or is owing to some default by the project company. Whereas the operator may be replaced during the concession period by another operator without significant loss of revenues, the replacement of the construction contractor will often result in significantly increased cost of and delay in completion.

5.5.2.2   Performance risk

From the lenders' perspective, the construction contractor should bear all design and construction risk, including performance of the completed works. Liquidated damages will be applied for late completion and insufficient performance. The level of liquidated damages should be sufficient to compensate the project company for any payments that must be made to the grantor under the concession agreement and any other costs the project company will incur, including debt servicing, administrative costs and other fixed costs. The works should not be considered complete until the construction contractor can demonstrate that the project has attained sufficient levels of performance to satisfy the obligations set out under the concession agreement and operation levels necessary to elicit payment of at least the fixed project costs.

5.5.2.3   Liability limitations

The construction contractor's liability will generally be capped to some percentage of the contract price, and the liability for liquidated damages resulting from delay or insufficient performance may also be individually capped. The lenders will want to review the construction contractor's liability to ensure that it is sufficient to satisfy its risks. The lenders will also want to consider carefully the level of liability available at termination for construction contractor default and the potential cost of a substitute construction contractor.

Further, the construction contractor will want to limit the period during which it will be liable for defects in the works. The period during which the construction contractor remains liable for the works should be of sufficient duration (for example, two years for mechanical works and five years for civil works, although these levels will vary substantially) given the type of project and the technology used.[257]

5.5.2.4   Payment

Drawdowns on the project financing should only be made against proven progress, to ensure added project value. The construction contractor should therefore only be paid for progress made, generally against a schedule of milestones.

5.5.2.5   Completion risk

As the construction phase bears a disproportionate amount of risk, the lenders will also want substantial guarantees and undertakings from the construction contractor, its parent company, substantial subcontractors, suppliers and possibly a third party guarantor for the completion of the works. These guarantees will include performance guarantees and retention money, or a retention bond, from the construction contractor. The lenders may also require guarantees from the

---

[257]   Vinter (2nd edition 1998) supra note 211 at 99.

shareholders, in spite of the limited liability protection sought through the use of a special purpose vehicle.

5.5.2.6 Warranties

The lenders will want to see the construction contractor providing appropriate warranties for the works, for example fitness for purpose of both the design and the construction of the works, compliance with the specification provided under the concession agreement and a guarantee of the life-cycle of major pieces of equipment.

5.5.2.7 Site risk

The construction contractor should bear site risk, including setting out the works, ground conditions, environmental contamination, project surrounds and access requirements, unless the grantor is better able to manage this risk. The lenders will also want risk specific to the discovery of fossils and antiquities to be allocated either to the grantor or the construction contractor.

5.5.3 Operation and maintenance agreement

The lenders will want the operator to bear the operation risks and obligations placed on the project company under the concession agreement. They will, in particular, want the operator to bear the risks described below.

5.5.3.1 Performance risk

The lenders will want the operator to bear the majority of the operation risk for the project and to maintain the project within the performance requirements as set out in the offtake purchase agreement, so as to ensure sufficient revenues to meet the cost of debt servicing. Failure to achieve these performance levels will result in the application of strict penalties, including liquidated damages. These penalties will need to be applied to the extent that the level of revenues necessary for debt servicing is threatened.

The operator will be given incentives to maintain performance at the required levels and efficiency of both operation and maintenance. Project efficiency should correlate to the project company's profitability and should therefore trigger some form of compensation or bonus scheme consistent with the resultant benefits to the project company. This scheme may mirror that used to calculate liquidated damages, rewarding the operator for every added level of performance or decrease in input use or other cost saving achieved. However, the operator's bonus should be based solely on the operator's performance and not the project company's ability to actually benefit from that performance for any reason not attributable to the operator.

5.5.3.2   Operating costs

The forecast costs of operation will need to be reviewed, ensuring that they give an accurate portrayal of actual future operation costs. The project company should not run the risk of the failure of the operator as a result of higher than expected costs, nor will the lenders nor the grantor wish to take control of a project which costs substantially more to operate than forecast. The process of transfer can be difficult enough without concerns about operation costs and possible requirements to modify the project in order to achieve forecast cost ratios.

5.5.3.3   Replacement of operator

Where the operator is unable to achieve its promised levels of performance or is otherwise chronically unable to meet its obligations under the operation and maintenance agreement, the lenders will want to have the power to replace the operator during the concession period. This may need to be done with the consent of the grantor and possibly the offtake purchaser. Although the project company may not be comfortable allowing the lenders this power, it will be difficult to deny them some influence over such decisions.[258]

5.5.3.4   Major maintenance

The lenders will want to see a comprehensive procedure for budgeting and minimising costs of major maintenance, either by creating a budget for the operator to perform or subcontract such works or by entering into a contract for performance of major maintenance works (often with the construction contractor).

5.5.4   Offtake purchase agreement

The offtake purchase agreement allocates the market risk involved in the sale of the project output or use to the offtake purchaser. This agreement will provide the project with the revenue stream necessary to satisfy debt servicing requirements and will therefore be of capital interest to the lenders. The most important issues in the offtake purchase agreement will be pricing, buy-out requirements, step-in rights and termination. As noted earlier, the offtake purchase obligation may be set out in a separate agreement, it may be rolled into one of the other agreements, such as the concession agreement, or it may not exist at all, in which case the project company and the lenders will bear market demand risk for project output.

5.5.4.1   Offtake price

The lenders will want to ensure that the offtake purchased is priced in such a way as to ensure a base revenue sufficient to satisfy debt servicing, generally against availability of the project (and not use). The conditions placed on the availability payment will directly affect the lenders' ability to obtain debt servicing. The higher or more subjective the standard availability of the project required (relative to the

---

[258]   Vinter (2nd edition 1998) supra note 211 at 101.

technical capacity of the project) before availability payments are made, the greater the risk borne by the lenders. The availability payments should compensate for all fixed costs, including working capital and operation costs.

5.5.4.2   Currency risk

The lenders will want the offtake pricing to be calculated in a currency matching that required by the project company for debt servicing and equity distributions. The lenders will not wish to bear any of the exchange risk on payments for offtake. Where this is not the case, the lenders may want to implement a currency risk management scheme, for example by hedging arrangements, or to review the forecast impact of currency exchange risk on the economic viability of the project. The events surrounding the difficulties encountered in the Dhabol power project in India, the water concessions in Manila and various Indonesian power projects in the late 1990s may cause greater attention to be given to this issue.

5.5.4.3   Termination

Termination of the offtake purchase agreement will obviously impede the revenue flow from the project unless an alternative purchaser or a readily accessible market for the output is available. The offtake purchaser should only have the right to terminate the agreement in very specific and extreme circumstances. Where the offtake purchaser has the right to terminate, the lenders should be given step-in rights to cure the project company's breach and avoid any termination. This right should extend to replacing the project company with another entity, where the lenders so desire. The lenders will want to receive compensation for termination, even in the case of termination for project company default, to cover the amount of project debt outstanding. The grantor will want to limit compensation for project company default to the value of project assets taken over by the grantor or offtake purchaser.

On the other hand, where the offtake purchase agreement is terminated for default by the offtake purchaser or the grantor, in circumstances such as failure to pay by the offtake purchaser, the privatisation of the offtake purchaser, the failure by the grantor to provide promised support or some other such breach, the offtake purchaser or the grantor should be required to buy out the project for at least the value of the remaining debt, the unpaid equity and the cost of termination. The lenders will want the termination compensation calculation to be set out specifically to avoid the complication of calculation of residual or market value. This may not be acceptable to the grantor or the offtake purchaser.

5.5.5   Input supply agreement

The risk of supply of fuel, raw materials and other inputs, and the cost thereof, can be allocated to the input supplier. The criteria for a bankable input supply agreement will vary with the type of input used and its source. The lenders will need to consider each input supply agreement as *sui generis*, reviewing the quality requirements, the sources available, alternatives available, cost and risk of transportation and any restriction on the method of transportation.

5.5.5.1   Failure to deliver

The lenders will want to ensure that this document places the risk of failure to deliver, as completely as possible, on the input supplier. The lenders will be concerned to ensure a secure supply of inputs. Therefore, appropriate sanctions should be placed on the input supplier where the supply of inputs is interrupted. Excusable interruptions will be limited, to the extent possible, to those situations in which the project company receives compensation from the grantor or one of the other project participants.

5.5.5.2   Failure to take

The input supply agreement may include take-or-pay provisions which require the project company to pay for a minimum amount of input, whether or not it orders and/or takes delivery of that amount of input. The lenders will want to be able to pass any such risk on to the grantor or one of the other project participants. Generally, the lenders will look to a corresponding minimum offtake requirement to be placed on the offtake purchaser to absorb any impact the take-or-pay provisions may have on the project company.

5.5.5.3   Duration

The duration of the input supply agreement should be sufficient to cover the length of the concession period plus a provision for extension where the concession period is extended or a margin of some length (such as two years) after the end of the forecast concession period. This is often very difficult to obtain from input suppliers, given the changing nature of markets and the limitation of supply sources. The lenders will require the debt to be repaid before the end of the concession period, therefore the lenders may only be concerned that the duration of the input supply agreement exceeds the repayment period. Further, certain inputs have a sufficiently fluid market to provide comfort about future availability, reducing the need for a long-term input supply agreement.

5.5.5.4   Supplier infrastructure

The input supplier is sometimes required to provide infrastructure to assist either in the preparation of the input for use or the transportation of the input to the site. The lenders will want the design and construction of this infrastructure to be performed on a turnkey basis, similar to the works under the construction contract. The lenders will not want to bear any of the risk of completion or performance of this infrastructure.

5.5.5.5   Transportation

The lenders will want the input supplier to bear the risk of transportation of the input, providing a delivery point at the project site or at the on-site storage facilities. In this scenario, failure in transportation should result in the same sanctions being applied to the input supplier as failure to deliver input. The concern here is that, where multiple counterparties are involved in supply and transportation of input, the liability levels of these counterparties may be insufficient and it is generally more difficult to allocate risk effectively to multiple counterparties than to a single counterparty.

Chapter 6

Allocation of Risk in Project Finance

EVERYBODY has won and all must have prizes.

The Dodo in Alice's Adventures in Wonderland,
Lewis Carroll

A successful project must incorporate a financial structure and security package that will satisfy both the lenders and the shareholders, while maintaining commercial flexibility and profitability of the project company. The successful project must also benefit from workable, commercially viable and cost-effective risk sharing. Given the differing interests and objectives of the parties involved, effective risk allocation will be an essential part of the drafting of the project documents and an integral part of the project's success.

Risks must be managed in a reasonable manner. The issue of efficient allocation of risk is discussed in further detail in chapter 2.

Risk management based on efficiency is, of course, an ideal, a goal. In practice, risk tends to be allocated on the basis of commercial and negotiating strength. The stronger party will allocate risk that it does not want to bear to the weaker party. This scenario does not necessarily provide the most effective and efficient risk management.[259] Improperly allocated risk will have an impact on the entire project and may affect the stronger party as well as the weaker. Efficient allocation of risk will generally result in a more successful and profitable project and will benefit each of the parties involved.

Financing for a project is provided by lending institutions, banks, bondholders or other entities which are not generally in the business of construction or operation of such projects. Further, lending institutions are generally heavily leveraged in

---

[259] This advice is corroborated by the Business Roundtable in "Contractual Arrangements" A Construction Industry Cost Effectiveness Project Report, The Business Roundtable, New York (October 1982).

the range of eight or ten to one.[260] These lenders will not be in a position, and therefore will not want, to take many of the risks commonly associated with such projects.

In order to avoid bearing project risk, the lenders will insist in the context of their review of the project documents that, as far as possible, the project risks are allocated to the project participants, such as the construction contractor and the operator, and away from the project company, their debtor.   The project participants will charge higher fees (a risk premium) for bearing such project risks, which will be included in the contract price, increasing the financial exposure of the lenders.   But such increased sums will represent value for money for the lenders, since the project participants are better placed to manage such risks and the lenders will be able to evaluate their exposure and cost the risk.

6.1   Allocation of Risk

In most conventionally financed projects, it is accepted that certain risks (such as market risk, certain political risks and completion risk) will be allocated by the grantor to the project company in relation to the role the project company plays in the project. For bearing such risks, the project company is compensated by return on its investment.

However, in a project financed BOT project, financing is obtained primarily through the lenders, rather than the investment or liability of the shareholders. The project company, as a special purpose vehicle, must avoid taking on risks which the lenders are not prepared to assume. The lenders will be compensated for their financing of the project in the form of a rate of interest appropriate to structured lending and will not benefit from project revenues which are higher than forecast. Residual risk will be borne in the first instance by the project company and therefore by the lenders. The lenders will attempt to limit their assumption of project risk by allocating to the project participants the risk placed on the project company through the concession agreement.

Ascertaining which parties will be affected by a particular element of risk can be quite complicated since project participants may assume several project roles (for example, the construction contractor may also be one of the shareholders and/or the operator).

The effort to transfer all project risk to the project participants is known as "back-to-back" risk allocation. The concession agreement will define what risk the grantor will take. All other project risk is borne by the project company. The other project documents will transfer the risk allocated to the project company by the concession agreement "back-to-back" to the other project participants. Complete back-to-back risk allocation will result in the transfer of all project risk assumed by the project company to the other project participants, as shown on the chart below. Rarely, if ever, will a BOT project achieve complete back-to-back allocation.

---

[260]   Nevitt and Fabozzi, Project Financing at 10 (6th edition 1995).

BACK-TO-BACK RISK ALLOCATION

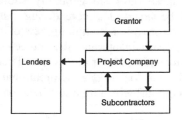

When drafting the project documents, one or more of the following mechanisms may be used to achieve back-to-back risk allocation.

> ➢ Provisions dealing with risk allocation can be drafted using terms and language mirroring that of the concession agreement and other relevant project documents. For example, identical descriptions of *force majeure*, or descriptions of events entitling the project company under the concession agreement, or the construction contractor under the construction contract, to extensions of time, will reduce ambiguity and gaps as between the two agreements. However, in order for this back-to-back allocation to function properly, the governing law clauses should be identical and the dispute resolution clauses should be linked (for example, through joined multi-party arbitration).

> ➢ One practical solution to avoid difficulties of matching cost and time risk is to include "if and when" language (also known as "pay-when-paid" and "time-when-time") in the project documents. For example, the construction contract can state that the construction contractor is entitled to time extensions under certain circumstances, if and when such extensions are granted to the project company under the concession agreement. Similarly, the project documents may include pay-when-paid provisions which specify that project company obligations under the construction contract to pay extra costs to the construction contractor are conditional upon the prior recovery of such costs by the project company under correlative provisions of the concession agreement. Such provisions may be restricted at law.[261]

> ➢ Finally, it is also possible to include in the project agreements an overriding provision that imposes on the project participants an obligation to perform so that the project company will not be in breach of its obligations under the concession agreement or which requires the construction contractor to undertake obligations placed on the project company by the concession agreement or other agreements.

---

[261] In the United Kingdom these provisions are regulated by the Housing Grants, Construction and Regeneration Act 1996. See also chapter 25 of Scriven, Pritchard and Delmon (1999) supra note 210.

The following is a discussion of certain basic project risks encountered in a typical BOT project, and how those risks are generally allocated among the project participants. It should be noted that considering risks in isolation is often unsatisfactory and does not provide a complete view of the project requirements. The nature of the project participants and the project will have a fundamental impact on the risks encountered and their allocation. Therefore, the following risk allocation analysis should only be used as a preliminary review. Each project should be considered as a one-off with a unique allocation regime.

6.2   Development Risk

The development phase involves the preparation of the project before financial close, including invitation to tender and bidding; negotiation of the various project documents; and obtaining debt and equity funding.[262] Given the nature of the BOT project, its complexity and the length of negotiations, risk borne during the development phase can be considerable.

Usually a large proportion of the development phase of a project is carried out by the project company before the lenders or some of the other project participants have been brought on board. This means that the project company, and more particularly the sponsors, will bear the majority of the development risk.

The early phase of development will generally be undertaken within the auspices of a procurement process, wherein the grantor defines the parameters of the project and goes to the market, or to parties with which he is familiar, to identify potential sponsors. This process is often regulated by local law and may be influenced by the rules set out by multilateral organisations. The grantor will put together a procurement package, including a call to tender, setting out the project requirements. The tender package will be sent to all interested bidders. The process may include a pre-qualification phase and extensive diplomatic missions by each of the interested sponsors' representatives in order to secure a preferential place among the several bidders. The project company will probably not exist at this stage, therefore the sponsors will undertake the early development tasks directly. The sponsors will need to undertake planning and feasibility studies and testing and review of technical, environmental and other requirements of the grantor. The cost of such reviews, including preliminary design and creating an appropriate consortium of project participants, will involve a reasonably heavy outlay of funds by the sponsors.

Further, development risk will include the cost incurred due to delays or errors in the procurement process. This risk can be managed by the grantor making efforts to organise the procurement process effectively and carry out its own reviews before embarking on the bidding procedure. However, the sponsors will generally bear development risk if the project does not proceed or if the sponsors' bid is not

---

[262]   For further discussion of procurement and public procurement, see *Ibid* at chapters 3, 15 and 16.

selected, placing little incentive on the grantor to manage such risk and reduce development costs.

Once the project company is formed and funded the sponsors will want to recuperate their costs. This can be accomplished by selling the project to the project company[263] or treating the investment in the development costs as in-kind equity investment. However, the lenders may want additional capital invested in the project company and will therefore want the sponsors' compensation for development costs to be treated as subordinated project company debt, to be repaid only where sufficient cash is available to the project company after the project ratios have been satisfied.

6.3 Completion Risk

The construction phase involves potentially the most costly project risk. The nature of BOT projects is such that an incomplete project will be of limited value. Therefore, both the grantor and the lenders will have a significant interest in ensuring that the works are completed in accordance with the project specifications. Completion risk includes construction, testing and commissioning of the project. This risk is then allocated to the construction contractor by the project company. Completion risk is discussed in more detail below.

6.3.1 Construction

The project must be built in accordance with the requirements set out in the concession agreement. These requirements will describe the performance to be obtained from the finished works, other requirements of the offtake purchaser and the characteristics of the project, including the requirements of the operator and, in particular, the grantor for operation, maintenance and the life-cycle of the project.

Construction risk includes:

> the adequacy of the design of the works;

> the nature of the technology to be used and the risk of defects in equipment or materials;

> unforeseen events or conditions, such as extreme weather or unforeseen subsurface conditions;

> environmental risks arising during construction;

> the availability of labour and materials, whether skilled labour can be procured locally, to what extent both labour and materials will need to be imported, visas and licences for such importation and restrictions imposed by local labour laws (including working hours and holiday entitlement);

---

[263] It should be noted that "selling" the project to the project company may involve tax liabilities or other unwanted legal consequences.

> the availability of experienced management, committed to the project;

> the availability of associated infrastructure and services, such as access roads, the provision of services to the site (including water, electricity and other utilities) and transportation to the site for labour and materials;

> the programme for completion, whether the time for completion is realistic in view of the labour and materials required for the project, the technology in question, the limitations of the host country infrastructure, climate and market, design requirements, and testing and commissioning;

> the cost of completion, changes in the market for labour and materials, services necessary for construction, financing costs, administrative costs and other costs subject to change over the period of the construction contract; and

> political and natural *force majeure*.

Construction risk will generally be allocated to the construction contractor, as it is the construction contractor who designs and builds the project. In order to ensure proper back-to-back apportionment of the construction obligations, the requirements for the project should be defined very specifically and completely in the construction contract based on the requirements and the specifications for the concession agreement. Any gap or inconsistency may defeat the back-to-back allocation of risk and leave additional residual risk with the project company.

The project company may want to impose a fitness for purpose standard on the construction contractor. A fitness for purpose obligation will help maintain the fixed price, by placing on the construction contractor the obligation to ensure the design is sufficient for the purpose intended for the project, and therefore decrease the need for variations in the scope of works.[264]

6.3.2   Commissioning

After the construction contractor has finished construction of the project, it must satisfy certain tests and inspections in order to demonstrate compliance with the project specifications; successful connections with any external network, such as a power grid or a water system; and proper management of interfaces between different equipment and technologies used in the project. The responsibility for commissioning the project is generally allocated to the construction contractor. The commissioning may be carried out in part, or verified, by the operator and possibly an independent engineer, but the responsibility for successful completion of commissioning will remain primarily that of the construction contractor.

The commissioning required by the project company to ensure compliance of the constructed project will need to be specifically defined. The independent engineer will probably be involved, or at least present, during this testing. The operator and

---

[264]   For further discussion of the "fitness for purpose" standard, see chapter 10.

possibly the offtake purchaser may also want to play a role in the commissioning of the project in order to ensure that the project as completed is in compliance with their requirements. The project documents will need to define a procedure for the performance of these tests and the involvement of the various interested project participants.

Commissioning will often involve a performance component to ensure that minimum levels of performance are achieved before taking-over by the project company. For this reason the construction risk and the performance risk, discussed below, will overlap to some extent. Completion, as evidenced by successful commissioning, generally involves a substantial transfer of risk away from the construction contractor, through taking-over, and a sizeable payment to the construction contractor as an incentive to complete the project successfully. By adding a performance element into completion, the project company increases the risk allocated to the construction contractor.

Given the construction contractor's need to ensure performance of the finished project, new or innovative technology is seldom utilised in project financing.[265] The construction contractor will not wish to warrant the performance of new technology, nor that design and construction will meet the projected time and cost commitments. Further, the lenders are not normally prepared to bear the project risks involved in new or untested technology. Guarantees may, however, be available from suppliers of equipment involving new technology, the benefit of which will be given to the project company.

6.3.3   Time for completion

The time for completion will be of great importance for the project company, the grantor and the offtake purchaser. The project company will want to commence operation of the project as soon as possible in order to earn maximum revenue and improve return on investment. The grantor and the offtake purchaser will have put the project out to tender owing to a pressing need for the service to be rendered and will therefore want the construction completed in the least possible time. The government may have given political undertakings to complete the project within a specific time frame or before the next election.

As the construction and commissioning risks are placed on the construction contractor, so too will be the risk of timely completion. If the construction contractor fails to complete the works on time, sanctions will be imposed, to reflect the losses the project company will incur, which may include debt servicing requirements, input supply agreement penalties, offtake purchase agreement penalties and concession agreement penalties.

---

[265]   Tinsley, Practical Introduction to Project Finance: Risk Analysis and Allocation at 5 (1996).

6.4   Cost Increase Risk

The risk that the amount allocated for construction and operation of the project in the financial model will, for some reason, be surpassed will need to be allocated. As this risk is basic to the interests of the lenders (who want to maintain a strict definition of their financial exposure, the project cover ratios and the net benefit anticipated from the revenue stream), the risk of cost increase allocated to the project company will be passed very carefully on to the project participants, as far as possible, and away from the project company.

Certain of the elements of cost increase risk are discussed below. Change in law and other similar events which can increase the project cost will be discussed later.

6.4.1   Currency risk

There will often be interplay between currencies within the context of the project. The project participants may have revenues in one or more currencies, but costs in several others. As an example, one proposed BOT project in Southeast Asia was to be built in Laos, the offtake purchaser was to be located in Thailand, the construction contractor and operator were from Europe, and the shareholders and the lenders were to be from various developing and developed countries. Such diversity among the project participants can create complex currency exchange interfaces.

Movement of funds between currencies can render the project vulnerable to changes in exchange rates. Such changes can often alter markedly the relevant revenue stream of the venture. The power project developed by Enron in Dhabol, India, suffered from extreme exchange rate shifts (revenues in rupees and lending costs in US dollars) defeating its economic and commercial viability. The Asian crisis in the late 1990s resulted in similar problems in power and water projects in Indonesia, Thailand and the Philippines. Devaluation can have the same effect. Where a currency is pegged against another currency (usually the US dollar), the government may choose to alter the relationship between those currencies or allow the currency to float. This happened in Argentina. The peso was pegged against the US dollar, but due to the associated stress on the economy the peso was allowed to float in the market. This had a significant effect on the rate of exchange between the peso and the US dollar. Any US dollar dominated debt was affected accordingly. As an example, the Buenos Aires Water Concession was financed using foreign denominated debt. The cost of that debt in pesos (in which the revenue stream was denominated) increased significantly with the devaluation.

This risk can be managed by matching currency of funding to cost and repayment requirements, by allocating it to the project participants (for example, by requiring the construction contractor to denominate a portion of the contract price in local currency or by borrowing in local currency) and/or by hedging the risk directly on the currency market. Each of these solutions will be subject to market restrictions. Hedging may be impossible or prohibitively expensive (especially over the long-term). Local lending markets may not have sufficient capacity to source the whole of the debt.

Another possibility is for the project company to allocate exchange rate risk to the offtake purchaser by requiring payment to be made either in the currency of the project company's expenses (i.e. the currency of operating costs, capital costs, input costs and/or debt servicing) or in a basket of currencies (where the project company has expenses in several currencies).

Further difficulties relating to project currencies are convertibility and transferability. As the offtake purchaser will generally be compensated by the end user in local currency, whether that currency can be converted and the transferability of such currency is of great importance.[266]

6.4.2   Inflation

Inflation will affect project costs. The project agreements will be fixed price, as far as possible, in order to place the commercial risk of cost increase, including inflation risk, on the project participants and away from the project company. Another approach is for the lenders to provide projections for inflation and feed these into the financial model for the project.[267]

6.4.3   Taxes

The project company may wish the grantor or the offtake purchaser to bear the risk of increased taxes. However, the authority acting as the grantor in the project may not be the same entity that regulates taxation; in fact, the grantor may be politically or legally segregated from the national tax authority. Even so, the grantor will generally be considered to be better placed to manage the tax risk, particularly where the grantor is funded by tax revenues, the reasoning being that the tax risk should come out of the same pocket that holds tax receipts.

Where the project company must bear the risk of increased taxation, which could in turn increase the cost of project tasks, the project participants (through fixed price project agreements) will have to take a portion of the risk of these added costs while the shareholders will bear the cost of additional taxes on project revenues. Even where the grantor will not take the whole of the risk of change in tax, it may bear the risk of discriminatory taxation (taxation aimed at the project or the project company) as the only party capable of managing such a risk. By allocating this risk to the grantor, an incentive is created, on the part of the host government, not to impose additional taxes on the project.

6.4.4   Input price increase

In order to manage the risk that the price of inputs might increase, and therefore increase the cost of operation and decrease project revenues, the project company will enter into an input supply agreement to ensure that the price paid for inputs is consistent with the revenue of the project. The cost of inputs under the input

---

[266]   For further discussion of currency risk, see section 15.3.
[267]   Nevitt and Fabozzi (6th edition 1995) supra note 260 at 36.

supply agreement is often fixed (although indexed), with only limited opportunity for modification (for example, where market prices are significantly different from the negotiated prices). Transportation of input to the project site may be more difficult to obtain at a fixed price. Also, where there is a free and liquid market for the input, the project company may have to pay market price or may choose not to have an input supply agreement and instead purchase input from the spot market.

6.4.5   Construction cost increase

Given the time frames involved in BOT projects and the construction period, costs specific to construction, such as the cost of labour and materials, are likely to change. The project company and the lenders will want the construction contract to be let for a fixed price with extremely limited opportunities for the construction contractor to increase the contract price. As far as possible, the responsibility for causing any increase to the cost of construction will be allocated to the construction contractor or the other project participants. For example, where the works must be varied to take into consideration changes in the offtake purchaser's requirements, the increased cost of construction will be allocated to the offtake purchaser.

6.4.6   Operation cost increase

The project company will need to manage its operating costs in relation to the revenues it receives from the project. Ideally for the project company, the operator will be paid a fee based on the output the project achieves (although the operator will be insulated from any reduction of output caused by construction defects, market risks or other risks not attributable to the operator). However, particularly in developing countries, the operator may not be willing to bear this long-term risk and may only be willing to fix a profit fee and identify a budget for operating costs which are then paid by the project company. Certain specific risks may be borne by the offtake purchaser (such as damage due to failure of the offtake purchaser's infrastructure or increases in the underlying cost of operation, possibly index linked) and the input supplier (such as damage caused by improper input quality). The construction contractor will usually be responsible for the cost of repair of any defect discovered during the defects liability period. The project company will then bear all residual operation cost increase risk. The project company's share of this risk is generally larger than other cost increase risks.

6.4.7   Cost of spare and replacement parts

The construction contractor will generally be required to provide the operator with a certain supply of spare parts upon completion of the project. The project company may in turn be required to provide the grantor with spare parts at the end of the concession period. The cost of these spare parts will be affected by market forces. The project company may also need to provide for replacement parts, either as part of the operation and maintenance agreement fee, or separately. The risk involved in changes in such costs will generally be managed by either applying a market price or fixed price or including the price of the parts into the fixed price of the construction contract or providing for a separate contract with a supplier, fixing the cost of parts for the duration of the concession period or some part thereof.

The issue of the cost of spare and replacement parts corresponds necessarily with projected life-cycles for plant and equipment and other indications of the type and quantity of such parts which will be needed for the project. Some or all of the risk of the accuracy of such projections could be allocated to the party providing the projections, which is often the construction contractor. Replacement parts may also be needed where technology updates are necessary for the continued performance of the project. This will be particularly relevant in information technology and telecommunications projects, where software and, in some cases, hardware, updates will be key to competitiveness and output pricing of the project.

6.4.8 Decrease in output price

Increases in project cost are measured against the income made by the operation of the project. Therefore, where the project produces a stream of output which is to be sold and the price received for the output of the project decreases, the gross margin will decrease. In order to provide a secure payment stream, the project company will enter into an offtake purchase agreement to ensure the amount of revenue the project company will receive from output. Where output is reduced owing to risks not allocated to the project company, the offtake purchaser will still pay the tariff under a take-or-pay obligation. Offtake purchase agreements are not appropriate for every BOT project, in particular where the payment stream is provided by the grantor.

6.4.9 Coverage of cost overrun risk

As noted above, cost increase risk is substantially allocated to the project participants through the project documents. However, the lenders may want additional facilities put in place to protect against failure of the project from cost overruns.[268] These facilities will generally involve funds being made available to the project, as follows.

6.4.9.1 *Additional capital provided by shareholders*

Provision may be made for the shareholders to advance the funds needed to complete the project when cost overruns have occurred. This additional capital may be provided in the form of a stand-by subordinated loan or as a stand-by capital contribution. Provision for such capital will need to be made in the shareholders' agreement, direct agreements and/or the lending agreement, and will usually be subject to caps of total amounts to be provided and conditions that must be satisfied before the obligation arises.

---

[268] *Ibid* at 19.

6.4.9.2   Standby credit facility

Lenders may provide standby credit facilities for cost overruns. Either the lending agreement or a separate agreement with the lenders will provide for such a facility. The project company will generally need to pay an additional availability fee for stand-by facilities.

6.5   Performance Risk

In order for the project to maintain sufficient revenues to satisfy debt servicing and to provide a return for the shareholders, the project must perform to specified levels. Therefore, performance requirements are provided in the concession agreement and the offtake purchase agreement which requirements are then passed on to the project participants (in particular, the construction contractor and the operator). The nature of the performance element will depend on the type of project. For example, a roadway will only necessitate limited performance requirements for construction, related to the effect of bad weather, lighting, drainage, and wear and tear.

6.5.1   Design and construction

The construction contractor will be responsible for designing and building a project capable of performing in accordance with the specified standards. However, this aspect of the performance risk will not be borne entirely by the construction contractor, whose liability will generally be limited, often to the contract price or some portion thereof. Residual risk will be borne by the project company, and therefore the lenders.

The lenders will generally be willing to bear some portion of the performance risk to the extent that it is based on proven technology, that the technology is projected to remain competitive with the relevant industry and the project life is significantly longer, often at least twice as long, as the life of the debt.[269] The technology used in the project will be warranted by the construction contractor to a certain extent; for example, by it providing performance-related damages, an appropriate defects liability period and possibly a latent defects liability period.

The project company may also wish to obtain further guarantees from suppliers and designers where relevant. These other entities may be best able to cure any defect in technology or to update technology, as necessary. Such arrangements can give the project company the opportunity to utilise the latest technology with the best output available while allowing the equipment supplier or construction contractor to ensure a return on its research and development investment. Insurance can also be obtained for the technology used in a project, including, for example, business interruption insurance for failed technology. The project company will want to assess the nature of the risk, the cost of such insurance and

---

[269]   Tinsley (1996) supra note 265 at 5.

whether the resultant decrease in lending costs or actual increase in security merits the cost of insurance.

6.5.2 Operation

The operator will be responsible for maintaining the project and operating it so that the required performance levels are attained. The operator will therefore bear performance risk other than that related to the design and construction of the project, the quality of the input used or the manner of offtake or use of services from the project. However, it should be noted that the operator, particularly if it is a non-shareholder operator, may not be willing to bear such a large part of the operation risk, especially where it relates to cost of asset replacement, by accepting compensation based entirely on performance of the works. The operator will probably limit its overall liability to the profit fee it is to earn on operation costs.

6.5.3 Input supply

In order for the project to reach the required performance levels, the input provided must be of a quality sufficient for efficient operation. The input supplier will be responsible for ensuring that the input provided is of such amount and quality that the project can achieve the performance levels required. Therefore, the input supplied will be tested before its acceptance and the input supplier responsible for damages incurred if it is not of the agreed quality.

6.5.4 Offtake purchaser infrastructure

The construction contractor may be responsible for the construction of some portion of the transportation system for project offtake from the project, generally to the edge of the site. Or the construction contractor will be responsible for providing some portion of the works needed for the offtake purchaser and/or project company to use the facilities provided by the project. The operator will be responsible for the operation of the project. Any shortfall in the performance of the project will be the responsibility of the construction contractor for defects, and of the operator for failure to operate and maintain such infrastructure in accordance with the specification. Testing of offtake is likely to occur at some point before delivery to or use by the offtake purchaser so that the risk of any defect caused by any subsequent transportation is placed on the offtake purchaser.

This last point is of particular interest in the case of BOT power projects, where the project company will not want the testing to be affected by any default in the offtake purchaser's transmission lines or the grid. For instance, the frequency of the grid will affect the output of the plant. Any such knock-on impact would be the responsibility of the offtake purchaser, to the extent that the cause of the defect in the transmission system or grid does not have its origins in the operation of the plant itself.

6.6   Operation Risk

The operation of the project involves certain risks of operation, performance and maintenance.   Generally this risk is shared by the operator and the project company, after takeover of the project from the construction contractor until the end of the concession period.

Operation risk will include:

> the risk of defects in design, equipment or materials beyond the construction contractor's defects liability period;

> the availability of labour and materials, the cost thereof, whether skilled labour can be procured locally, to what extent both labour and materials will need to be imported, visas and licences for such importation and restrictions imposed by local labour laws;

> changes in operating requirements, owing to changes in law, regulations or other circumstances;

> the cost of asset replacement and major maintenance;

> the availability of experienced management, committed to the project for the duration of the concession period;

> the availability of working capital financing to cover short-term financing needs;

> the availability of locally sourced/cost-effective supplies and services;

> the availability of associated infrastructure and services, such as access roads, the provision of electricity and other utilities to the site and transportation to the site for labour and materials;

> the programme for operation and maintenance and whether that programme follows a logical regime, correlated with the offtake purchaser's needs, and a realistic approach given the nature of the site country, government regulations on labour and operation and the technical requirements of the project; and

> other costs subject to change over the period of the concession.

In addition to its responsibility to operate the project to given performance levels, the operator will be required to operate the project in a proper and careful manner, so as to comply with applicable law, permits and consents; and to avoid damage to the project, the site, local or related infrastructure facilities and neighbouring properties. Therefore, any costs or damages that might arise from the operation of the project, except those damages which are attributable to one of the project participants or some third party, shall be to the account of the operator. The extent of this responsibility will be carefully defined and limited. The project company will bear residual costs and risks.

Often in projects involving advanced or complex technology, one of the selling points for the grantor is the transfer of know-how to either its own personnel or local partners or subcontractors. The grantor will often require the construction contractor or the operator to train personnel for the operation and maintenance of the project. This training must be considered carefully in its detail, including the number of people to be trained. Follow-up training may be required. Intellectual property rights should also be considered within the context of the project. The project company should have a clear incentive to provide such training, in the form of compensation or penalties, to ensure that training is provided in the manner and to the extent agreed. Breach of contract remedies will often be insufficient to protect the grantor against the failure to receive training.

The operator will also be responsible for the proper maintenance of the project until transfer to the grantor. Towards the end of the concession period it will be less important to the operator to continue to maintain the project as before, since the operator will soon be transferring the project, and its revenues will no longer be as closely dependent on the proper and efficient operation of the project. It may therefore be important to the grantor to require that the operator continues maintenance of the project to ensure that the project does not require substantial investment in replacement parts. The creation of an incentive for continued maintenance may also require some withholding of revenues until satisfactory transfer of the works in a condition consistent with the handover standards.

6.7   Market Risk

The lenders will not want to bear market risk in relation to the project, and will therefore require that the contractual structure of the project allocates market risk away from the project company and to the project participants.

The following are a few of the primary market risks which are likely to be encountered in a BOT project.

6.7.1   Output price

The most important market risk is the price obtained for project output. Given the importance of the project's payment stream in relation to repayment of debt, the lenders will require that market risk either be reasonable, foreseeable and manageable, or that market risk for the price of output be passed to an offtake purchaser. The former is relatively rare in BOT projects, and will be limited to projects with output for which a very strong and fluid market is available. This, for example, may be the case in the electricity sector in developed countries or in the oil and gas industries globally. Even in these cases, the lenders may require contracts for differences or futures contracts to hedge the risk of output price fluctuation. More commonly, the offtake purchase agreement will establish the price to be paid for output and will ensure a project payment stream, subject to the proper operation of the project.

6.7.2   Input cost risk

The cost of necessary inputs represents another area of substantial market risk. Where the project requires input for operation, and where the market for such inputs is not sufficiently flexible or there is some concern as to its future viability, the lenders may require that the project company enters into an input supply agreement. This "input" may involve a service, for example the transportation of coal for a coal-fired power plant or the disposal of sludge for a waste water treatment plant. The input supply agreement will fix the cost of input supply, often over the period of the concession. The cost of input will often form part of the calculation of the price paid for output by the offtake purchaser. In this way, the market risk for cost of input is allocated away from the project company and therefore the lenders.

6.8   Political Risk

Political risk, such as events of war, rebellion, default or failure of public sector entities, change in law and delays by authorities, can be a contentious issue. The project company will not generally be able to avoid or manage this risk, and conventional insurance coverage may not be a practicable alternative. The project company will attempt to allocate as much of this risk as possible to the grantor through the concession agreement. The grantor may accept such risk as the sole party who may be able to influence its advent and mitigate its effects. However, host governments may not be willing to bear all political risk, and may require the project company to bear certain aspects or the majority of this risk as part of the risk borne by anyone investing in that country.

6.8.1   Authority and enabling legislation

The first question to be asked when a government entity is involved in a project is whether that entity has the right or the power (*vires*) to enter into the obligations involved in the project and what administrative or legal requirements must be satisfied before the obligations can become binding. Often, major infrastructure projects require the permission of a governing body, either the state or the relevant local authority. However, the identity of this authority may be different from the grantor which will grant the concession agreement. Separate enabling legislation may be required before the construction of the project can begin. Obtaining such enabling legislation should generally be a condition precedent to the effectiveness of the project documents. The continued effectiveness of such permission or legislation would be the responsibility of the grantor.

6.8.2   Change in budget, government or political atmosphere

When faced with a government entity in a project it is important to ascertain whether the obligations once undertaken will continue where that entity's make-up changes. The membership of the government may change, budget restrictions may be altered, or the political atmosphere may simply become such that foreign involvement in infrastructure development is no longer desired. Where a government takes on such obligations, will they be adopted, or must they be adopted, by subsequent governments or governing bodies where the identity of its members or even its political colour changes?

The risk of a change in political climate can have a greater effect on BOT projects than most others, particularly in developing countries. As an example, a hydroelectric project in Southeast Asia was significantly delayed following disagreements between the governments involved and uncertainties over the new government's willingness to work with the World Bank, one of the primary lenders. The experiences of Enron in India should provide an effective warning of the dangers of this risk.[270]

The grantor is the only project participant with the ability to manage the risk of change in political climate. For this reason, this risk is often the responsibility of the grantor. However, simply placing the risk on the grantor will not necessarily protect the project company and the other project participants, as the fact that the political change has affected the project will probably adversely affect the project participants regardless of the grantor's responsibilities.

Three methods of mitigating this risk are:

> the consideration of the host government's interests, and their implementation in the project. Thus, the host government should have an interest in the success of the project, and should receive benefit from it;

> the involvement of local lenders and local shareholders or subcontractors; and

> the involvement of some other government body, or possibly an international or multilateral organisation.

Where the host government has an interest in maintaining the project's viability, the risk of political change is decreased. This may involve providing benefits to local communities such as employment, housing, reinvestment in the community, making use of local supplies, services and financing, or providing some valuable service or investment. Project participants can also fulfil host government interests by providing a benefit to individuals who hold political power or by supporting local politics. However, it is difficult to ensure that the interests of one government or individual will be the same as the interests of subsequent governments and individuals.

An effective method of mitigating the risk of political change may be to involve a multilateral organisation, such as the European Bank for Reconstruction and Development, the Asian Development Bank or the World Bank, or an export credit

---

[270] The Houston, Texas-based firm of Enron invested in the US$2.5 billion Dhabol power project in the state of Maharashtra, India. After a change in government of the state, the victorious right-wing nationalist alliance cancelled the project, rather than restructure it through arbitration. The Dhabol project has since been renegotiated, at a lower price, and expanded. "Enron and On and On" The Economist at 92 (14 June 1997).

agency in the project. Grantors will not generally ignore the interests of a multilateral organisation which provides them with financing for other projects. Further, a common precondition to the involvement of such an organisation will be the membership of the national government in that organisation. Host governments will generally not violate the interests of an export credit agency because that agency, although it might be private in nature, will have an explicit mandate from its government. For these reasons the involvement of such organisations can be an efficient method of mitigating the risk of change in host government interests.

6.8.3   Expropriations

It is a basic principle of international law that a sovereign government has the right to expropriate property within its territory for public purposes.[271] The project company will need to put in place guarantees and undertakings to protect against this risk. Where the grantor involved in the project is the same authority that would expropriate property, the concession agreement can act as a specific undertaking to restrict the grantor's right to expropriate the project assets. This may not, however, be effective under applicable law, nor indeed be enforceable against the grantor. A more efficient protection is to establish a regime for compensation for such expropriation. Assurances can also be obtained from other government entities or by way of constitutional reform or enactment of legislation.

As noted above, the involvement of an international or multilateral organisation in the financing of the project can put international political pressure on the host government. Often such pressure can provide a more effective protection for the project company than most other forms of guarantee.

Where the host government does expropriate project property, international law states that the injured party must be compensated promptly, adequately and effectively. This position is often supported by national law.[272] The project company may want to identify in the concession agreement that adequate compensation must be paid and how adequate compensation will be calculated. This provision is sometimes known as a "compensation clause".

As an example of export credit agency assistance, ECGD of the United Kingdom, through the United Kingdom's Foreign Office, has negotiated various Insurance Investment Agreements with countries around the world. These agreements arrange for suitable compensation payments in the event of any expropriation or creeping expropriation by a foreign country of assets owned by Her Majesty's Government or British companies.

---

[271]   A sovereign state holds the power of disposition over its territory as a consequence of title. Brownlie (4th edition 1990) supra note 247 at 123.

[272]   Maryan (1996) supra note 247 at 122.

6.8.4 Change of law or taxation

A project will be subject to the risk of a change in the laws (or taxation) of the host country or some other country. The risk of change in law will generally be borne by the grantor, or apportioned between the grantor and the project company. The concession agreement may use one or a combination of the following approaches.

6.8.4.1 Grantor risk

In certain cases, in particular in host countries whose political systems tend to be less stable, the grantor may need to bear the risk of change in law before a project can be considered bankable. This is often the case in projects located in developing countries whose political history may include hostility to foreign investors.

6.8.4.2 Apportionment of cost

The change in law risk can be shared between the parties by apportionment. For example, the project company may be required to bear the risk of minor changes in law, where the cost of compliance does not exceed a specified amount (generally based on a percentage of the contract price), or the cost of changes in law up to a maximum percentage of the construction cost over the first few years of the project (used in certain PFI projects). The latter may be an effective solution where the project company is able to pass this risk to the construction contractor. The grantor will need to be aware of the cost to the project company of bearing change in law risk, which is generally prohibitively expensive to insure and difficult to pass on (to the extent it has an impact on capital works) to any of the project participants.

6.8.4.3 Apportionment of risk

Another method of allocating change in law risk is to isolate risk for different types of change in law. The grantor may deem that the host country's legal system is sufficiently stable so that the project company should accept that the risk of trading in that country will include changes in law. However, the project company will not want to bear the risk of changes in law which target the project, in particular, or the sector in which the project is involved (which can amount to creeping expropriation). Therefore, the grantor may retain the risk of discriminatory changes in law, i.e. those changes which are specific to the sector involved, private financing of public projects generally or the project itself.

6.8.5 Change in technical requirements

Change in law can include a number of different aspects of legislative, legal, judicial and administrative obligations such as changes in the administrative requirements placed on the project: for example, permits, consents or import licences. However, technical requirements imposed by professional associations, or groups with a mandate which falls short of bringing them within the concept of administrative institutions, may not fall within the definition of "change in law": examples would include certain environmental or safety requirements.

Consideration should be given to the risk of change in such technical requirements, and how such risk is to be apportioned.

6.8.6   Immunities

Sovereign entities have certain immunities before their own and foreign courts. The immunities most commonly attributed to sovereigns by national courts are jurisdiction and execution;[273] however, each national legal system will use a different approach to sovereign immunity. Therefore, no hard and fast rule can be offered other than caution.

Sovereign immunity results both from the nature of the actor and the nature of the act. The actor must be a sovereign because a creature of sovereignty cannot be subject to the jurisdiction of another without specifically submitting to such jurisdiction.[274] However, the characterisation of an actor as sovereign or not can be difficult as public bodies become involved in very private/commercial acts, and those same public bodies may be wholly or partially privatised. One must then look to the nature of the act. Is it a governmental act (*jure imperii*) or a private/commercial act (*jure gestionis*)? Again, each legal system will characterise an act differently, even diametrically so.[275]

6.8.6.1   Jurisdiction

It is a principle of international law that state courts do not generally have jurisdiction over foreign government entities, in order to protect the independence of foreign sovereigns.[276] Therefore, where there is a dispute concerning the project, the project company may be denied the right to bring suit against a government entity in a foreign state court. Similar protection may be provided by national courts. In order to manage this risk, where a sovereign entity is a party, the relevant project document will generally include a waiver of sovereign immunity and a dispute resolution provision either submitting disputes to the jurisdiction of a court or submitting them to arbitration. It should be verified that the government entity in question has the right under local law to submit to such jurisdiction and to waive its sovereign immunity.

6.8.6.2   Execution

Just as courts do not have jurisdiction over foreign sovereigns under international law, they also may not seize the property of such sovereigns. A similar protection may exist under national law. This immunity is meant to protect the independence of a sovereign state.[277] A state's immunity to execution of judgements or awards can render any legal or arbitral decision ineffectual as seizure of assets may be

---

[273]   *Ibid* at 117.
[274]   O'Connell, International Law at 842 (2nd edition 1970).
[275]   *Ibid* at 845.
[276]   Maryan (1996) supra note 247 at 124.
[277]   O'Connell (2nd edition 1970) supra note 264 at 864.

impossible. Waiver of immunity to jurisdiction may not result automatically in waiver of immunity to execution. Further, characterisation of the actor or the act may be different for execution, and will often depend on the nature of the asset to be seized. For example, national courts will generally not seize military craft of a foreign sovereign. This may extend to other vessels otherwise linked to a sovereign.

6.8.6.3   Act of state

A further aspect of sovereign immunity before state courts is justiciability, whether the subject of the legal action is appropriate for resolution by a court.[278] This principle protects governments from having strictly political decisions reviewed by the courts of a foreign state. As above, one possible way to mitigate the risk of such immunity is to obtain from the government a submission to arbitration or waiver of its immunities.

6.8.6.4   ICSID

Where issues of sovereignty are a concern and no method of waiver or other resolution is available, parties may wish to consider the services of the International Centre for Settlement of Investment Disputes ("ICSID"), a body created under the auspices of the World Bank but wholly independent. It provides dispute resolution services for private sector investors with public sector partners. The services of ICSID are available only in relation to its signatory states. The treaty which established ICSID requires its signatory states to recognise ICSID awards as if they were final judgements rendered by their own national courts. As a precondition, the contract must make reference to ICSID dispute resolution or the parties must consent to ICSID jurisdiction.

6.8.7   Public perception

Where the grantor is a political entity, it takes on a further political risk in that the project is placed in the hands of a private sector entity not necessarily affected by the political repercussions of its actions. The public may not understand that the grantor is removed from the day-to-day operations of the public service which is the subject of the project and thus any mismanagement or politically unpopular decision made by the project company may be imputed to the grantor. Although the contract may provide for grantor influence in the selection of personnel to achieve a desirable image, the effectiveness of such influence may be practically minimal. Thus, the grantor will want to consider the independent status of the project company and the potential effect the project company's actions may have on the grantor's political position and public perception.

---

[278]   Maryan (1996) supra note 247 at 126.

6.8.8   Political risk insurance

Political risk insurance or guarantees may be available for the project. Certain government or private organisations (such as export credit agencies) provide such a service. They are generally supported by national governments and provide insurance for certain political risks. The purpose of such agencies is to support national commercial interests (for example, the supply of goods and services from that country), therefore the nature of the project and project participants will influence which organisations can be involved in the project and to what extent they will provide political insurance or other services.

An example of such a national agency is the Overseas Private Investment Corporation ("OPIC") of the United States Government. It was established to support the United States' private sector investment in developing free markets by providing financing, equity capital, pre-investment assistance and political risk insurance. The insurance available from OPIC is generally limited to the risks of currency convertibility, expropriation and violence of a political origin.[279]

For a project to be eligible for OPIC involvement, it must demonstrate a positive effect on the United States' economy. The project must also contribute significantly to the economic and social development of the host country.[280] Restrictions on the identity of the party able to obtain such insurance may have an impact on the decision about which of the project participants will bear which political risks.

A detailed discussion of these multilateral and international organisations is beyond the scope of this book; however, a brief review of the activities of one such multilateral organisation in a specific BOT project may be of some assistance as an example of the role such an organisation can play.

The Hub Power Project was a BOT project developed in Pakistan in the mid- to late 1990s at a forecast total project cost of US$1.8 billion, involving US$372 million in equity and US$1.46 billion in debt financing. Various guarantees were provided by the World Bank, the Export-Import Bank of Japan (now JBIC), COFACE of France, MITI of Japan and SACE of Italy. The Private Sector Energy Development Fund of Pakistan, which is in turn financed in part by the World Bank, also provided subordinated loans.[281]

For the Hub project, the World Bank provided partial risk guarantees for the following project risks:[282]

---

279   Betancourt, "OPIC Political Risk Insurance for Infrastructure Projects in Emerging Markets" Project Financing in Emerging Markets 1996: Successful Development of Power, Mining, Oil and Gas, Telecommunications and Transportation Projects at 179 (1996).

280   *Ibid* at 184.

281   Duvall, "World Bank Support for Private Sector Projects" Project Financing in Emerging Markets 1996: Successful Development of Power, Mining, Oil and Gas, Telecommunications and Transportation Projects at 72 (1996).

282   *Ibid.*

> ➢ where the project company is no longer able to convert local currency to foreign currency;

> ➢ where a change in Pakistani law alters the economics of the transaction;

> ➢ where a government entity fails to perform its obligations to the project company under certain of the project agreements;

> ➢ where the government revokes or fails to provide government consents required for the operation of the project or servicing of debt;

> ➢ where the government expropriates project company assets; and

> ➢ where the project company is unable to generate sufficient revenues due to war or civil disturbance in Pakistan.

The availability of political risk insurance may be a linchpin to a successful project. Lenders may not be willing to bear political risk and such insurance may simplify the provision of commercial funding. Certain countries continue to struggle with the implementation of project financing structures due to intransigence on these issues.

6.8.9　Source country political risks

The above-mentioned risks will also apply to the countries from which the plant, equipment, materials and specialised labour to be used in the project are sourced. Thus, where an embargo, change in tax regime, change in or refusal of export licensing or other such political risk occurs in the source country, the project could be affected. For this reason, the parties will need to consider such risks in respect of source countries, their application to the project and how best to allocate and manage them.

6.8.10　Choice of law

Although this does not result in a purely political risk, it should be noted that the project documents may be subject to the influence of different legal systems. Each contract will normally include a choice of law clause, and parties will want to apply a legal system with which they are comfortable and whose laws and contractual implied terms support that party's intentions. Therefore, a public sector grantor may not be willing to submit to any legal system but his own, while the lenders will want the lending agreements and possibly the construction contract and the operation and maintenance agreements to be subject to a familiar legal system (generally English law or the laws of the State of New York). This is particularly important in relation to taking security, though conflict of law principles will apply to many security issues. Having the project documents subject to more than one legal system increases the likelihood that gaps will appear in back-to-back risk allocation. However, the commercial reality is that mismatches in choice of law will often occur.

6.9   Environmental Risk

Although environmental risk has been discussed above in section 6.5, it deserves individual consideration. Environmental risk has become a far more central consideration over recent years, particularly in developed nations. International conventions and the pressure applied by developed nations have encouraged developing nations to follow suit. For this reason sponsors and governments alike will want to consider carefully possible changes in environmental regimes and the potential consequential effects on the project.

The extent of environmental risk will depend to some degree on the parties involved in the financing of the project. For example, where OPIC is involved in a project it will require an environmental assessment of the project. OPIC will apply the stricter of the local environmental regulations and those applied by the World Bank.[283] The World Bank follows a concept known as "sustainable development" which broadly means "development that meets the needs of the present without compromising the ability of future generations to meet their own needs".[284] Similar environmental assessment is required by many of the primary multilateral financing organisations, such as the ADB and the EBRD. International environmental management standards have also been developed by the International Organisation for Standardisation ("ISO") in its ISO 14000 series.[285]

The definition of "environmental damage" will change rapidly as our awareness of the effects of our actions on our surroundings increases. International organisations such as the World Bank have also permitted increasing involvement of Non-Governmental Organisations ("NGOs") in defining and analysing environmental requirements.   This represents a potentially unlimited and undefinable risk. Environmental assessment for World Bank regulation of major projects can take as much as six to 28 months and account for 5-10 per cent. of project preparation cost.[286]

The primary aspects of a BOT project relevant to environmental risk include:

> ➤ building the project (including the design and construction of the works);

> ➤ the maintenance and operation of the project; and

> ➤ the quality of input provided.

---

[283]   Betancourt (1996) supra note 279 at 185.

[284]   "Our Common Future, World Commission on Environment and Development" (1988) as cited in Korvis, "Environmental Issues in International Project Finance" Project Financing in Emerging Markets 1996: Successful Development of Power, Mining, Oil and Gas, Telecommunications and Transportation Projects at 250, 256 (1996). The heightened importance of environmental issues is partially the result of the restructuring of the World Bank after 1987.

[285]   See generally *Ibid* at 294.

[286]   *Ibid* at 261-262.

The performance requirements linked with environmental issues will be defined by existing applicable law, the requirements of the grantor and any requirement imposed by international lending agencies such as the World Bank.

An environmental impact assessment ("EIA") and statement ("EIS") will generally be required either by the host country before a major project can be let or by the successful project company. The assessment will identify and help to allocate environmental risk. Environmental risk will be allocated between the grantor and the project company and then passed by the project company to the construction contractor, the operator and the input supplier. Allocating the responsibility between these entities for such risk may not be straightforward. The cause of environmental damage may be difficult to identify and the potential level of damages such that project participants will not wish to bear such risk.

An important element of environmental risk relating to environmental regulation is the liability placed by law on the project company for environmental damages. Many countries apply a higher standard of liability on the owners of property where activities on that property may cause environmental damage. It may prove difficult, if not impossible, for the project company to allocate this liability to other project participants owing to the nature of the applicable legal liability.[287]

The project participants may be advised to undertake preventative measures to avoid disputes on environmental issues, such as by:[288]

> meeting representatives of the local population and NGOs early regarding any potential environmental impact of the project and available mitigation measures;

> enlisting the assistance of local experts, with credibility among the local population and the host government;

> using the assistance of local partners for project development;

> using project investment and project revenues to feed back into the local community, both economically and socially;

> creating appropriate lines of communication and contacts with host government authorities and agencies;

> ensuring appropriate due diligence on local, national and international environmental requirements;

> ensuring sharing of information with appropriate authorities in order to obtain feedback and early approval; and

> developing an environmental management procedure for those involved in the project.

---

[287] For further discussion of environmental liability, see chapter 21 of Scriven, Pritchard and Delmon (1999) supra note 210.

[288] Modified from Korvis (1996) supra note 284 at 308.

The lenders will wish to pay special attention to environmental risk, particularly where they are entitled to step in to the project. The lenders will not want to take on increased environmental risk if they step in. Export credit agencies are particularly sensitive to environmental risk, as are multilateral agencies, as discussed above. These entities will have their own particular environmental policies. They may not want to be party to the mortgage documents, in the event that the presence of a governmental body might encourage the host country or the relevant regulatory agency to pursue large claims against the lenders for environmental damage.

6.10   Credit Risk

The project company and the lenders must be comfortable that the project participants are able to assume their project obligations, in order to ensure the financial viability of the project. The project company and the lenders will need to take a view on the credit risk of the various project participants.

Where the project company or the lenders are not comfortable with the credit risk of a project participant, various methods are available to the lenders in order to enhance a party's credit, including bonds and guarantees. These may be limited to the most sensitive obligation of the relevant party. For example, the most important credit risk relates to the project payment stream, either from the grantor or the offtake purchaser. If this entity is a bad credit risk, the project company or the lenders may require a guarantee from the host government or some other creditworthy third party, letters or credit, an escrow arrangement over the entity's income or a combination thereof. The chart below provides a rough guide to the impact these risks can have on the various phases of a project.

PROJECT RISKS

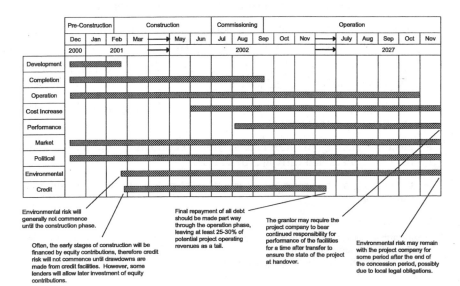

The above chart is merely a rough generalisation since BOT projects will differ in scope, content and risk structure. The period termed "pre-construction" on the chart indicates the site investigation, testing and basic design phase, before the commencement of work on the site.

The chart below shows generally the risks shared by project participants, assuming the project company, and therefore the lenders, will bear a portion of each of these risks. Again, this is only meant as a rough guide and should not be considered to be exhaustive or exclusive, since each project will have its own unique circumstances, requirements, relationships and parties.

The chart is complicated by the broad definitions of the risk categories; a necessity given the number of actual risks to be encountered as well as the individual nature of a BOT project and therefore the risks involved. It is also complicated by so much of the project risk being shared between several of the project participants. For example, the operation risk is shared by the grantor where a change in law, a *force majeure* event or other government risk occurs; the construction contractor bears the risk for construction defects which might affect operation, while the offtake purchaser and the input supplier will be responsible for their interfaces with the operator and the operator will be responsible for operating and maintaining the project in accordance with the operation requirements, leaving the balance of the operation risk for the project company.

RISK SHARING

	Political Risk	Cost Increase	Environmental	Market	Development	Operation	Performance	Completion
Project Company	X	X	X	X	X	X	X	X
Grantor	X		X		X			
Construction Contractor		X	X	X	X	X		X
Operator		X	X	X	X	X	X	
Offtake Purchaser				X			X	X
Input Supplier			X	X		X	X	X

Chapter 7

Project Participant Interface Risk[*]

A little neglect may breed mischief ... for want of a nail, the shoe was lost, for want of a shoe, the horse was lost, and for want of a horse, the rider was lost.

Benjamin Franklin (1706-1790),
Maxims ... Prefixed to Poor Richards Almanack (1758)

The obligations of the project company and the project tasks it must perform will be allocated to a series of third parties, the project participants. The project company will want the project participants to undertake most of the project company's obligations set out in the concession agreement, the offtake purchase agreement and local law, as well as any other obligations the project company is not equipped to undertake. The lenders will seek maximum divestment of project company obligations to the other project participants.

Project task sharing will result in areas of overlap called task "interfaces", where the project participants must act together or share together some action or obligation within the context of the performance of the project. As an example, where the project involves two or more sections, those sections may be taken over separately. In such a case where one section has been taken over by the operator and another neighbouring section is still in the hands of the construction contractor then certain tasks in relation to the site, such as site security, will be shared by these two project participants thus creating a task interface between the operator and the construction contractor.

A project may involve risk interfaces, a sharing of a risk between project participants which may involve an interface in the management of the risk. For example, the input supplier, the operator and the construction contractor may share

---

[*] While I acknowledge that the word "interface" is not necessarily grammatically correct, nor is it necessarily pleasing to the ear, it is a very useful Americanism that has been adopted by the market and is therefore used throughout this text. My apologies to the purists.

the performance risk.   Where the performance is not meeting the project specifications during the early period of operation, the project participants sharing this risk can either spend their energies placing blame on the other risk-bearing project participants or make concerted efforts to resolve the performance problem.

Each interface between the different project participants carrying out their project obligations involves a risk, either that the interface will not occur smoothly or that the works packages will not interface properly.   This has been termed an "organisational risk" by Kris Nielsen.[289]   It will be dealt with in this chapter separately from the other project risks as an organisational issue to be considered whenever undertaking a BOT project.

Interfaces come in many forms.   Those commonly identified in a project are interfaces between technologies or between construction or operation methods. Other interfaces may be social, cultural and ideological.   This chapter discusses a sampling of interface types and how they may affect the project (section 7.1) and then identifies particular project interfaces that should be considered when drafting the project documentation (sections 7.2-7.6).

7.1   Project Interfaces

Interfaces will exist between the various technologies and methodologies used by the project participants.   Management of these interfaces will be key to the efficiency of the project.

7.1.1   Technology interfaces

Anything from materials used, to electrical interfacing, to construction methods may have an appreciable impact on the progress and performance of the works. Interfaces between technologies in BOT projects are primarily allocated to the construction contractor, assuming a fully turnkey construction contract.   For example, the construction contractor will be responsible for completion of the project.   Therefore, it will be responsible for interfaces between differing technologies or differing construction methods used in the construction of the works and by its subcontractors.   The edges of such risk will blur where, for instance, the construction contractor must build infrastructure to connect with the offtake purchaser's facilities.   The offtake purchase agreement and construction contract should provide clarity to define responsibility for this interface.

7.1.2   Methodology interfaces

Interfaces can be complicated by the diversity of the project participants.   The project participants may be from different social, cultural or technical backgrounds, resulting in commercial and cultural diversity.

---

[289]   Nielsen, "Trends and Evolving Risks in Design-Build, BOT and BOOT Projects" [1997] ICLR at
        188.

7.1.2.1 Commercial diversity

The project company will include project participants such as the construction contractor, the operator and the input supplier, each with potentially a very diverse commercial culture, identity and approach.

The most important aspect of commercial diversity is differing interests. Each of these actors will be interested in a different part or aspect of the project and its success. Therefore, their personal bias, or knowledge base, will be relatively focused. The construction contractor, for example, will not have its primary attention focused on the most practical positioning of the works from the point of view of the operator, but will concentrate on the ease and efficiency of construction, and the cost thereof.

Another difference which lies somewhere between the commercial and cultural is business terminology and accounting practices.[290] The project documents will include business terminology and be based on accounting practices which may not be entirely familiar to all of the project participants, or which may be defined or approached from different perspectives by those involved. This form of diversity can cause a great deal of trouble as it affects the very basis of understanding between the two parties as to the project financials.

7.1.2.2 Cultural diversity

The project participants will often originate from different cultural backgrounds: western and eastern; developed and developing. These differences are a natural part of international commercial reality. They also involve certain risks to the project.

The following table provides an example of different approaches that may exist between parties from the corporate cultural biases of Europe, the United States and Japan.[291] Tables such as this, and the stereotypes they identify, do not provide a working method for analysis but merely demonstrate not only the existence of cultural diversity but also the variety of approaches to such diversity, and the understanding thereof. Managing cultural interfaces does not require categorisation, but rather flexibility, sensitivity and understanding.

Each project will need to be examined individually, although a general approach of cultural sensitivity can avoid unnecessary conflict where interfaces are concerned. It should be noted that this table compares three cultures whose commercial approaches are relatively similar. Cultural differences between more diverse parties can be even more significant.

---

[290] Rushton and McNair (May 1994) supra note 235 at 33.
[291] Modified from Nielsen (1997) supra note 289 (as modified from Kunishima and Shoji, "The Principles of Construction Management" Sankaido at 24 (1996)).

CULTURAL DIVERSITY

Cultural Trait	Europe	United States	Japan
Objectives	Continuity and social values	Profitability	Continuity
Characteristic features	Reliability	Self-assertion, individuality	Harmony
Business style	Client first policy	Short-term competitive relationships with long-term focus	Long-term credible relationships
Working conditions	Individual within team	Individual often within a team	Teamwork
Employment	Long-term; improvement of position by changing jobs	Improvement of position by changing jobs	Lifetime employment
Basis for wages	Ability, achievement and rank	Ability and achievement	Seniority and achievement
Measure of achievement	Short-term profits	Short-term profits	Contracts awarded and long-term profits
Change	Slow to medium	Rapid	Slow
Decision-making process	Moving from top-down to flat team	Discussion between superiors and subordinates	Top-down and mutual agreement
Working environment	Individual offices	Individual spaces	Large, shared offices
Loyalty	Medium	Little	Great
Relations between colleagues	Friendship	Individual with movement to teams	Sense of commonalilty
Perception of work	Responsibility	Responsibility	Lifetime employment

Cultural Trait	Europe	United States	Japan
Decision criteria	Ideas, philosophy and processes	Results oriented	Ideas, philosophy and processes
Punishment	Relocation or dismissal	Dismissal	Relocation
Salary difference between junior and senior	Medium	Big	Small

7.1.3 Management and allocation of interface risk

To some extent interfaces are a natural offshoot of human interaction and cannot be completely avoided. However, it is essential that the project company identifies such interfaces as far as possible and allocates responsibility for them in the early stages of the project. Sharing of such risks will often be necessary. Clear definition of the parameters and the nature of risk can avoid disputes later in the project.

The primary interfaces encountered in a BOT project are outlined below. Further discussion of project interfaces can be found in subsequent chapters. The chart at the end of this chapter shows the overlap of responsibilities and interests throughout the concession period which results in the basic interfaces between the project participants.

7.2 Grantor Interfaces

The interfaces between the grantor and the project company will be defined in the concession agreement. The project company will want to place the risk of most of these interfaces on the project participants.

7.2.1 Interfaces with construction contractor

The construction phase of the project involves the greatest concentration of project risk. The risk of completion of construction of the works is central to the success of the project and is the most difficult to manage. Given the weight of this risk, the grantor may take an intense interest in the progress of the construction works and the construction contractor's methods. Grantor involvement at this stage can result in grantor interference unless this interface is managed properly.

The most basic interface with the grantor in the early stages of construction is the provision of information regarding the site. The accuracy of this information may or may not be guaranteed by the grantor. The construction contractor will want to use and rely on this information as far as possible to avoid the cost and delay of providing its own information and undertaking further site tests and investigations. Where the grantor opts not to warrant the site information provided, in an attempt to place more of the project risk on the project company, the construction contractor will need to co-ordinate with the grantor's experts in an effort to establish for itself the accuracy of the information provided.

The next interface may be the provision of access to and possession of the site. This obligation may belong to the grantor and may involve the grantor in expropriation of property, resulting in displacement of persons, removal of movable and real property, and possible protests or delays for administrative or legal procedures.

The grantor will also co-ordinate with the construction contractor in relation to the issuance of licences and permits relating to the right to build on the site and the nature of the facilities being built. The construction contractor may need to satisfy the government agency responsible for such licences and permissions of the safety and environmental compliance of the construction, its impact on the surrounding area and populace as well as certain financial concerns regarding local suppliers and subcontractors. The government agency will define the fees to be paid, the procedures to be followed and the requirements to be satisfied when applying for these licences and permits. The grantor may be involved in providing assistance, information or even the goodwill of certain government agencies.

The grantor may also require the assistance of an independent engineer to oversee the construction of the works, including inspections and testing. The independent engineer will require some amount of access to the works during construction and at testing, particularly at the time of completion. The independent engineer may have some say in certifying the works as complete. Access for, and involvement of, the independent engineer will require consideration from the construction contractor in the programming of the works.

7.2.2   Interfaces with operator

The grantor will have very similar interfaces with the operator, although less frequent and over a longer period of time than with the construction contractor. Where it provides the site, the grantor may continue to ensure access to and possession of the site and necessary infrastructure, such as transport routes, water, telecommunications and other utilities.

Government agencies will require the operator to obtain licences and permits, defining the requirements, the procedures to be followed and eventually assessing the operator's application. Certain of these licences and permits will need to be maintained throughout the concession period and may be added to or modified during the concession period. The grantor may provide the operator with assistance, for example in obtaining such licences and permits, through direct contact with the relevant government agency and provision to the operator of information and documentation. The risk of change in the requirements for obtaining or renewing licences and permits will also need to be allocated between the grantor and the operator.

The independent engineer, or some other representative of the grantor and/or the lenders, may also be involved in the operation of the facility, to the extent that it will supervise, test and inspect the operation and maintenance of the works in order to ensure compliance with the concession agreement and applicable law. Provision will need to be made for the independent engineer to have access to the works, and inspect and perform periodic testing on the works during operation. The independent engineer is likely to become more involved during the final phases of operation, just before transfer or at the end of the concession period, in order to ensure that the works transferred to the grantor have received an appropriate amount of care and maintenance and satisfied the requirements set out in the concession agreement.

The operator may be required to accept the transfer of grantor employees from existing facilities which are being replaced or refurbished by the BOT project. The operator may also be required to employ a certain number of employees selected by the grantor in order to train local staff or train grantor staff for operation after the end of the concession period. The grantor and operator will need to allocate responsibility for employment issues such as rights of termination, redundancy, employment benefits and liability for employees and their negligent acts.

The interface between the grantor and the operator will be of particular importance during the transfer procedure, as this procedure will often receive little attention from the project company, unless some amount of revenue is retained, or some compensation paid, by the grantor to ensure compliance.

7.2.3 Interfaces with offtake purchaser

The grantor may co-ordinate with the offtake purchaser in relation to licences and permits, as described above.

The grantor will frequently intervene in the testing and inspection of the facilities provided by the offtake purchaser, such as transmission services from the plant; testing facilities for the output received; and verifying the availability of the project during operation. The grantor may also supervise construction, maintenance and testing of such facilities to ensure compliance with contractual and legal obligations.

The grantor may choose to continue operation of the project after the end of the concession period and may want to maintain not only the relationship with the offtake purchaser but also the equipment and procedures used during operation.

The interfaces between the grantor and the offtake purchaser are often illusory, as the grantor and the offtake purchaser may represent one and the same interest or may, in fact, be one and the same entity.[292]

---

[292] In certain types of project it is the grantor who takes on the obligation to provide a stream of revenue against the output of the project. For example, in a BOT road project, the grantor may provide all or part of the project revenue stream through shadow tolls or availability payments. For further discussion, see section 3.4.

7.2.4   Interfaces with input supplier

The supply of inputs to the site may require licences and permits from the host country government, including import licences, particularly where the input is dangerous in nature or potentially harmful, environmentally or otherwise. Transportation of the input across the host country and the handling and storage thereof may require licences and permits from the national and local governments and government agencies.

The grantor may want to maintain the relationship with the input supplier after the end of the concession period, in order to facilitate continued operation of the project after transfer. This will be of particular interest where the input supplier has built or has in place extensive infrastructure necessary for input supply such as rail links, processing plants and testing facilities.

The input supplier may also be closely related to the grantor, such as where the input supplier is a public utility or a publicly owned company. This close relationship can alter the nature of certain aspects of input supply risk and may reduce or remove it entirely.

7.3   Construction Contractor and Operator

Construction projects may be split into sections, completed in succession allowing specialised teams to work first on one section, completing their construction tasks on that section, and then to move on to the next section. The following chart shows a project with two sections, with a three-month time-lag between completion of each section.

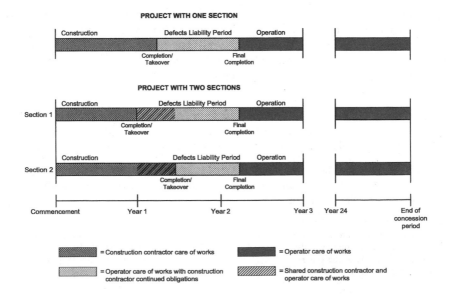

SECTIONAL COMPLETION

During the period between completion of the different sections, the interfaces between the construction contractor and the operator will be compounded since on one section of the work the construction contractor will be carrying out commissioning and testing while the other section will have been completed and will be in the hands of the operator, resulting in two project participants with responsibility for the site at the same time. Tasks such as security, fencing, signposting and waste disposal will need to be undertaken for the whole of the works, and shared between the construction contractor and the operator. These two parties will also need to manage together the use of and payment for utilities, provision of access to the site, inspections by third parties and special measures in emergency situations. The chart below demonstrates the risk of such an overlap period where care for the works is shared between the construction contractor and the operator.

TRANSFER OF RISK

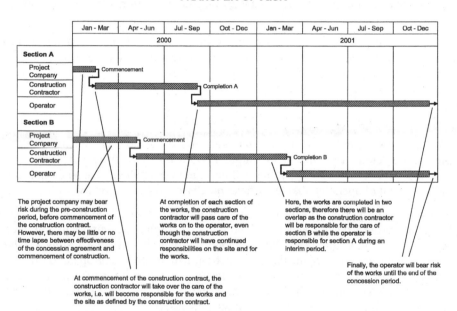

At the end of the construction phase, the construction contractor may be required to provide training for the operator. The construction contractor and the operator will need to discuss responsibility for such training, its extent, the number of personnel to be trained, liability for those personnel, the cost of training and what manuals or materials will be provided by the construction contractor to the operator. These are relatively straightforward issues, but should be decided early in the project to avoid dispute at later stages.

Performance testing may also need to be carried out, including possible re-testing. The operator may provide staff for testing. The operator will need to manage the construction contractor's activities to ensure that the operation of the works is not impeded.

The operator and the construction contractor are likely to be involved in extensive interfaces during taking-over and the defects liability period. These periods represent the transfer of responsibility for the site and the works from the construction contractor to the operator.

However, at takeover, the construction contractor maintains certain responsibilities for the site and the works for a period during the operation of the plant. This period will therefore involve shared tasks, responsibilities and management between the construction contractor and the operator.

The construction contractor's obligations after takeover will include a period of defects liability, during which the construction contractor will require access to the site and to the works to remedy any defects which may arise. The construction contractor and the operator may want to negotiate a regime for responsibilities during this period.

Throughout the period of taking-over of the works and defects liability, the management of the stock of spare parts, where required, will be shared by the contractor and operator, both using the spare parts as needed and both replenishing supplies of such parts as required.

7.4   Operator and Offtake Purchaser

The operator will liaise with the offtake purchaser throughout the operation of the project to identify the amount of output needed by the offtake purchaser, any additional services required by the offtake purchaser (where relevant) and any other element of operation that the offtake purchaser wishes to control.

The price paid by the offtake purchaser for the operation of the project will be based on tested capacity and actual output. Therefore, an important interface between the offtake purchaser and the operator will involve the testing of the project's capacity and output; the construction, maintenance and operation of the equipment needed for testing; and the testing or repair of any aspect of the transportation system for the output from the project to the offtake purchaser (which may itself be provided by the offtake purchaser).

During the operation of the project, both the operator and the offtake purchaser will need to shut down certain aspects of the project or the transportation/transmission system for maintenance and repair purposes. As far as possible these shutdowns will need to be co-ordinated between the operator and the offtake purchaser in order to minimise lost production time. The development of a programme for the operation of the project will involve consistent co-ordination between the operator and the offtake purchaser.

7.5   Operator and Input Supplier

The input supplier will also liaise with the operator repeatedly throughout the concession period, although not as extensively as will the offtake purchaser. The interfaces between the operator and the input supplier will relate primarily to the delivery of input, how much is needed, when deliveries should be made and whether the service provided by the input supplier is consistent with the input supply agreement. Further co-ordination may be necessary where the price agreed for inputs can be modified by reference to changes in market prices or where the relevant market for input is somehow significantly altered or distorted.

The operator and input supplier may also need to co-ordinate regarding licences and permissions for the transportation and import of the input. Depending on the nature of the required inputs, the government of the country of origin or the host country may regulate import, export and transportation of such inputs. For example, where necessary inputs involve dangerous materials such as nuclear fuels or highly sensitive materials such as advanced technology computer equipment, the administrative requirements of requisite licences and permissions can be burdensome.

Finally, the input will be tested at either, or some combination of, the point of extraction or production; the point of treatment, packaging, processing or refinement; when loaded for transportation; at arrival near the site, such as at the port of disembarkation; on arrival at the site; or on insertion into the works. Where testing is to be performed, the input supplier and the operator will need to co-ordinate the timing and location of tests, the carrying out of tests and the analysis of the test results. Further liaison may have to take place concerning the need for and undertaking of re-testing.

7.6   Intra-project Company Interfaces

One of the most important interfaces, particularly in the early stages of planning and implementation of the project, will be the one between the shareholders of the project company. The shareholders may have multiple roles in the project, including as sponsor, investor, lender, manager and project participant. This variety of roles will result in different, and conflicts of, interests between the various shareholders, rendering an otherwise challenging relationship (that of partners in a business venture) all the more difficult. The combination of roles can be beneficial. The relevant shareholder may be able to manage interfaces between these roles more effectively and possibly reduce project risk.

Interfaces between shareholders will generally be managed through the provisions of the shareholders' agreement. The shareholders' agreement is drafted during the early, and optimistic, days of bidding for a project and succeeding in the bid. Therefore, it is sometimes difficult to foresee the potential problems within the shareholders' relationship. However, it is an error not to take advantage of the positive atmosphere present in the early stages of a project in order to establish a reasonable and efficient regime for management of the project company's decisions. The day a dispute arises is a day too late.[293]

The following chart shows periods during which project participants will be active on site, and therefore the potential interfaces between them.

PROJECT PARTICIPANT INTERFACES

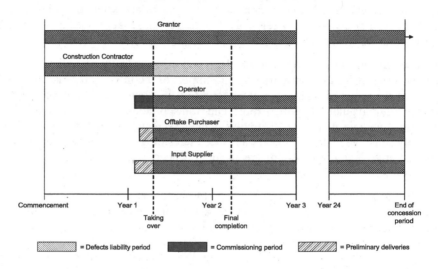

---

[293]   See chapter 9 for further discussion of the shareholders' agreement and conflicts of interest.

Chapter 8

Concession Agreement

It's a little Anxious to be a Very Small Animal Entirely
Surrounded by Water.

Piglet,
Winnie-the-Pooh

The backbone of a BOT project is the concession agreement. The grantor grants a concession to the project company over what traditionally would otherwise be a public sector project for a given period, during which the project company must build and operate the facility. The terms of that concession are set out in the concession agreement. The concession agreement sits in the BOT project structure as indicated in the chart below.

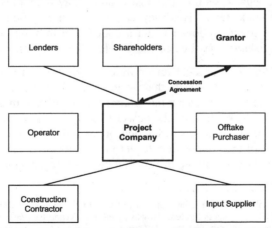

The concession agreement allows the grantor to allocate project risk to the project company. The grantor will identify those risks which it is prepared to bear and allocate the remaining risks to the project company. The grantor may also wish to define to some extent the sharing of risk among the project participants through the concession agreement. Therefore, it is not uncommon to find the primary

165

constituent documents defined and described in some detail in the concession agreement.

In certain cases, the grantor may append to the concession agreement drafts of the constituent documents, to ensure that the terms it wants to include are properly set out and form part of the concession itself. The sponsors will strongly resist this as it interferes with their commercial relationships with the other project participants and it increases development cost, particularly where the sponsors are required to negotiate these issues during the tender phase and before they have been selected as preferred bidder.

BOT projects will rarely involve all of the agreements indicated in chapter 3. In certain projects, the concession agreement may be combined with the offtake purchase agreement or the grant of the concession may be made by way of a licence or legislation. In many projects, the offtake provisions will be an element of the concession agreement. For example, in a BOT hospital project, it is likely that the grantor will be the purchaser of the use of the project, and therefore the concession agreement will include concepts discussed in chapter 13 of this book in relation to offtake purchase.

Care should be taken in relation to the legal regime in the host country which will apply to concessions for infrastructure projects and BOT projects in particular. Many countries modify their legal systems in order to allow greater freedom for government agencies to let concessions for the development of such projects. Certain jurisdictions have passed legislation specific to BOT projects, in order to manage better the growth of such projects.[294] However, the extent, effect and application of such legislation should be reviewed carefully.

In other cases the legal system of the host country may be defined very poorly or may be nearly non-existent. This may cause particular difficulties because the legal basis for the grantor's power to let a concession may be unclear. For this reason specific legislation may be necessary to legalise and protect the project.

Thus, in the context of the legal and political regime of the host country, the project company will need to ensure that the grantor has the legal right to enter into the concession agreement. Each act the grantor intends to take must be *intra vires*. Acts which are *ultra vires* (beyond the power of the party performing the act) may be unenforceable or subsequently rescinded or invalidated under applicable law. As noted, the right of the grantor to enter into the concession agreement and carry out its project obligations may require special enabling legislation, an extension of

---

[294]   A specific example would be the laws passed in China on the subject of BOT projects. China's experience in BOT projects is limited. However, the last decade has seen an explosion of such projects being proposed in several states in China, in particular power and water/waste treatment. In order to manage such projects more efficiently the Chinese Government passed legislation imposing a national approach to such projects and to improve and render consistent national government review of the project although the projects themselves are let by local authorities. For further discussion, see United Nations Industrial Development Organisation (1996) supra note 204 at 41-72.

authority from some other government body or even a change to the host country's constitution.

Two methods of granting a concession include by contract and by authorisation. The contract style involves the grantor entering into a contract with the private sector project company which contains the mutual project obligations. Sometimes applicable legislation will prescribe the form of contract. Authorisation (or licence) involves creation of the concession at law and may be more susceptible to revocation or modification. Therefore, it is probably safer for the project company to obtain a contractual concession agreement.[295] In certain countries, such as Greece, a concession contract is negotiated which is then submitted to the parliament and ratified as a law. This book will assume the use of a contractual concession.

During the concession, the primary interests of the grantor will generally be as follows:

> Completion date. The grantor's need for the infrastructure in question is generally immediate (often as much for political as practical reasons). Further, the grantor may be procuring other infrastructure or other investments closely related to the completion of the project, such as the building of roads or public housing in proximity to the works. Therefore, the success and revenue generation of several projects may be at risk where completion is not achieved by the identified completion date.

> Performance of the project. Since the grantor needs to receive sufficient output from the project for the duration of the concession to meet its needs as well as to ensure a project which performs in accordance with its requirements at the end of the concession period, the grantor will want to establish performance standards and requirements. The grantor's requirements will cover issues such as output, consumption, efficiency of operation, maintenance needs and costs, life-cycle, quality of the output generated and cost of operation. Performance will apply to any project, although projects involving primarily civil works will have a different approach to measuring performance. For example, a tunnelling project will involve performance requirements related to life-cycle issues, drainage, ventilation, lighting and emergency access.

> Maintenance regime. The project will have depreciated both in value and in operating capacity by the time for transfer back to the grantor (where applicable). In order to mitigate the detrimental effect of operation on the project during the concession period the grantor will want to ensure that the maintenance regime (including replacement of parts and materials) implemented by the project company during the concession is sufficient given the nature of the works involved. Further, the incentive for the project company to invest funds in maintenance during the final phase of

---

[295]   *Ibid* at 224.

the concession period may be diminished, as proper maintenance programmes will no longer result in greater revenue for the project company owing to the imminent transfer of the project to the grantor.

> Construction and operation. The concession may be of a public nature: for example, the service rendered by the project company may be one identified as being traditionally provided by the state. Therefore, the residents of the area surrounding the project or those affected by operation of the project may assume that its operation is somehow directly under the responsibility of the state. For this reason, the project company's acts and omissions may be directly imputed to the grantor by the public.

This chapter discusses risks (section 8.1), interfaces (section 8.2), and other issues specific to the concession agreement (sections 8.3-8.5). Further reference should be made to chapter 15 which analyses issues common to the project documents.

8.1   Risks

As noted previously, BOT projects are *sui generis* by nature, i.e. no two projects are exactly alike. No definitive risk allocation regime can be produced for all projects. The following section will consider project risks and risk allocation generally.

8.1.1   Political risk

Risk should be allocated to the party best able to manage it. It is for this reason that the grantor generally carries the greater burden of political risk. The risk of events such as wars, nationwide strikes or other political instability or events which might have an impact on the project are usually borne by the grantor.

If the grantor is an arm of the central government, the political risk which the grantor is willing to bear will normally include acts of its own authority or acts of government which might otherwise, as between private companies, be treated as *force majeure*. For this reason the grantor should be prepared to protect the project company from any act or omission of its own authority, of local governments or of administrative authorities under its authority.

The grantor may argue that political risk is one commonly borne by the private sector in everyday business transactions. As the BOT project should be considered a normal commercial transaction in the host country, the grantor may, therefore, contend that the project company should bear such risk. This argument is common in developed countries and more stable economies, such as in the United Kingdom where, in the case of PFI/PPP projects, the Treasury has very strict views as to what political risk will be borne by the grantor. This issue can be very market-specific and will often depend on what insurances or guarantees are available to the project company, such as from the host country government, export credit agencies or other international financial organisations.

8.1.2 Completion risk

Completion risk is generally wholly allocated to the project company (except, of course, any delay caused by the grantor or a grantor risk). However, in certain circumstances, the grantor may be convinced to share a portion of this risk. For example, as a general rule the project company will be required to take the risk associated with the site which will be passed through to the construction contractor. However, if the cost of certain aspects of site risk is disproportionate and the grantor can be persuaded of this, the grantor may also be willing to take certain risks which are specific to the site. The grantor may be the best placed to identify certain risks involved with the ground conditions, such as antiquities which might be found during construction. Where antiquities are discovered, they will generally belong to the host country. There may also be strict legislation in effect regulating how such antiquities must be handled.

8.1.3 Operation risk

The grantor will bear the part of the operation risk relating to the responsibilities it is taking on in the project. For example, in certain cases, the operation of the project may be based on the characteristics of existing infrastructure or the ability to connect to such infrastructure, as in the construction of a water treatment plant which treats water provided by the grantor and delivers it to the existing water systems. In such case, where the grantor maintains responsibility for the existing infrastructure, the grantor may bear the risk of availability of raw water or the proper functioning of the existing abstraction and offtake infrastructure. Without sufficient raw water and offtake, the plant will not operate, tests cannot be performed and commissioning cannot occur.

Further, where other facilities are necessary for operation, such as transportation by national roads, bridges or tunnels; use of national railways; utilities connected to the site providing electricity, water, gas or other fuel; obtaining and maintaining licences and consents; or the operation and maintenance of any associated facility which falls within the public domain, any such risk might be allocated to the grantor, as it can generally manage such risks most efficiently.

8.1.4 Permits and licences

The construction contractor and operator will need to go to the grantor, or some other related authority, to make requests for permits and licences to do the work necessary to carry out the project. These permissions will range from construction permits to operating licences to visas for imported labour. The permits will need to be renewed regularly, requiring further interfaces with the grantor, or some government agency, throughout the period of construction and operation of the works. The project company will also need to co-ordinate with the grantor, or some other related authority, to maintain and renew these permits and licences.

8.1.5   Transfer and re-tendering

An important interface for the grantor occurs at the end of the concession period, when the project will either transfer back to the grantor (in a BOT project) or the grantor will re-let the project to the same or a new project company (in a BOO project).

The grantor will want to ensure that transfer occurs properly and with the appropriate amount of assistance by the grantor's personnel. During this period the project company may be required to train and otherwise prepare the grantor's personnel to manage the operation of the project. The grantor will also want to make sure that the project has been appropriately maintained and managed during the period immediately preceding the transfer of the project.

Where the grantor intends to re-tender at the end of the concession period, the project company may be required to provide information and assist generally in the process of re-tendering. This may include providing accounting for the project, details on project assets, employment records, life-cycle projections and information on existing subcontracts.

8.2   Interfaces

Interfaces between the project participants can be key to the successful implementation of the project. Comprehensive and efficient management of the project will require careful consideration of each of these interfaces and their management.

8.2.1   Construction contractor

The grantor will co-ordinate with the construction contractor on many levels, not least of which will be access to and possession of the site. Often, the grantor will be providing the site to the project company. The project company will want to make sure that free access to and possession of the site is provided within a reasonable delay from commencement. The grantor may even want such access and possession to be a condition precedent to the effectiveness of the construction contract.

The grantor may also warrant the state of the site. The contractor may not have available to it the information, site surveys, hydrological or climatic information for the site. The grantor, on the other hand, may have developed detailed information during feasibility testing on the site, or during its use of the site for other purposes. Therefore, the grantor may give some warranty as to the nature of the site, the subsoil and its appropriateness for the construction to be undertaken. On the other hand, as noted above, the grantor may not have such information or may not be willing to invest in assembling such information or taking the associated risks, in which case the site condition and subsurface risks may be placed entirely on the construction contractor.

In the same vein, access to the site may depend on local infrastructure and the capacity and availability of transportation: roadways, railways and waterways. The grantor will often bear the risk for the upkeep, modification and maintenance of these routes.

The construction contractor will also need to go to the grantor, or some other related authority, to make requests for permits and licences to do the work necessary to carry out the project. These permissions will range from construction permits to operating licences to visas for imported labour. The permissions will need to be renewed regularly, requiring further interfaces with the grantor, or some government agency, throughout the period for construction of the works.

The grantor will also interface with the construction contractor throughout the execution of the works owing to the grantor's interest in verifying that the construction is carried out in accordance with the construction contract and the concession agreement. The grantor may want to monitor certain stages of the construction and testing of the works. Often the grantor may require access to testing when it occurs, or may want to have some say in the assessment of test results, in order to protect its interests.

Such testing may be reviewed by an independent expert or engineer, hired by the grantor to represent its interests on site, or by a combination of the grantor and the lenders. In such a case, the interface between the grantor and the construction contractor may, in respect of construction and commissioning of the works, be defined by the role of the independent engineer.

8.2.2   Operator

The interface between the grantor and the operator will be similar to that between the grantor and the contractor, although the issue of original possession of the site will not be as important. The operator will also need to apply to the grantor or some related authority for permits and licences concerning the operation of the project. These may include permission to operate, environmental assessments, permission to remove waste, or permits relating to housing and other labour related issues. The operator will also need to co-ordinate with the grantor, or some other related authority, to maintain and renew these permits and licences.

The operator may need to co-ordinate with the grantor in connection with the testing and the operation of the project. The grantor may want to ensure that the operator is maintaining the project and running it in accordance with the concession agreement, and therefore may put in place a testing regime wherein it performs tests or is present at testing performed by other entities.

An important interface for the grantor occurs at the end of the concession period. The grantor will want to ensure that transfer occurs properly and with the appropriate amount of assistance from the grantor's personnel. During this period the operator may be required to train and otherwise prepare the grantor's personnel to manage the operation of the project. The grantor may also want to make sure that the project has been appropriately maintained and managed during the period immediately preceding transfer.

8.2.3 Offtake purchaser

The relationship between the grantor and the offtake purchaser is often already close, if they are not indeed the same entity. Therefore, identifying interfaces between these two entities may be a non-issue. However, it is worth noting that the grantor may want to continue the relationship with the offtake purchaser after the end of the concession period. This will hold particular importance for the grantor where the offtake purchaser is legally or technically separate from the grantor or where internal political issues might complicate the relationship and the offtake purchaser is important to the continued benefit of the rest of the project.

In an interesting example from a power project in Southeast Asia, the government of one country was to provide a concession to a private company. The power produced was then to be sold to an offtake purchaser in a neighbouring country. Although not typical of power purchase regimes, this project demonstrates the potential interfaces between an offtake purchaser and the grantor.

8.2.4 Input supplier

The input supplier may be a government entity or a private entity sponsored by the grantor. However, the input supplier is just as likely to be a private company. In the latter case, the interface between the private input supplier and the grantor may involve a relationship that must extend beyond the concession period.

8.3 Payment and Guarantees

8.3.1 Tolls and tariffs

As noted above, concession agreements often regulate tolls and/or tariffs to be paid to the project company for the project. However, because of the number of different structures possible, tariffs and payment will be discussed in relation to a separate document, the offtake purchase agreement, in chapter 13.

8.3.2 Guarantees

The grantor may require guarantees from the project company or from the sponsors, primarily where the grantor has transferred to the project company existing infrastructure or other assets.

In the same way the project company and the lenders may want to receive guarantees from the host government for public sector bodies taking part in the project whose credit risk is otherwise insufficient. This may be the case where the offtake purchaser or input supplier is a public body. Host governments, however, will be reluctant to provide such guarantees, since one of the reasons they enter into concessions is to avoid the project being classified as a borrowing by the government or relevant public sector entity particularly in connection with reviews by the national government, the World Bank, the International Monetary Fund and other organisations.[296] Where government guarantees are not available, some other form of credit enhancement may be required to make the project bankable.

8.3.3   Non-competition/exclusivity

The grantor may supply the project company with some form of monopoly rights over the service to be provided. Where the project payment stream is based on actual use by end users, this monopolistic position may be an important element in ensuring a bankable project payment stream. Thus the project company may obtain from the grantor an undertaking to ensure that no other licence to perform the concession service or some related service will be given to a third party, within a specific area or otherwise in competition with the project company, during the concession period. The grantor will need to ensure that allowing exclusivity will meet its needs over the long-term, in particular in the face of demographic changes and the needs of poor communities. Exclusivity may be a very difficult proposition in certain essential sectors, such as water and sanitation.

8.3.4   Foreign currency exchange and transfer of funds

The project company may receive, manage and dispose of a variety of currencies received from the project, subjecting it to any host government restrictions on currency flow. The project company will need the right to open bank accounts in the country and deposit currency of the types to be used.

Convertibility is another issue essential to the financial management of the project. The project company will need to have the ability to convert currencies, either from foreign to local or local to foreign, at local rates, even where such exchange is not available through local banks. The shareholders, and especially the lenders, will not want funds tied up in the country any longer than necessary and will therefore want free transferability, and possibly repatriation, of project income.[297]

8.3.5   Taxation

Just as the project company will want protection from changes in law by the host government, so too it may be able to convince the grantor to provide some assurance about the host country's fiscal policies and the taxation to which the project will be subject. The concession agreement may specify a maximum amount of taxes, fees, levies, duties, royalties or other such charges which may be imposed on the project company. This maximum may be calculated per unit of production, as a total or annual amount or based on the total revenues after costs, debt servicing or other operation costs.

Any assurances by the grantor may require parliamentary and/or government approval. Placing a tax indemnification responsibility on the grantor where the

---

[296]   Recent changes in the way the IMF treats borrowing for essential infrastructure projects may change this.

[297]   Project currency issues generally have been discussed in more detail in chapters 6 and 15.

taxation exceeds that contemplated in the concession agreement is a viable option, although it may not be possible under local law and it will be strongly resisted by the grantor. Another option is to increase tolls and tariffs where tax burdens change.

8.3.6   Compensation events

Where an event, such as a risk assumed by the grantor under the concession agreement, results in some financial burden on the project company, the grantor may be required to compensate the project company for any costs, damages or loss incurred. This can be done either by a cash payment directly to the project company or by the grantor extending the concession period or increasing the level of tolls and tariffs allowed under the concession agreement. Such a provision is also known as a "financial balance clause".[298]

8.3.7   Compensation on termination

The grantor will generally provide the project company with a payment in the case of termination of the concession agreement for grantor default or extended *force majeure*. This payment is intended to compensate the project company for the value of the project assets (which on termination will generally revert to the grantor upon payment of this amount) and for loss of project income. The amount of the payment will generally equal the total amount due to the lenders plus equity invested plus the net present value of the forecast return on equity, generally calculated by reference to the financial model for the project.

The grantor may also be willing to compensate the project company where the concession agreement is terminated for project company default. In such cases, the payment is normally limited to the outstanding amounts due to the lenders, subject to certain reductions such as excluding any penalties charged to the project company.

8.4   Completion and Operation

The grantor will want to impose completion and operation requirements on the project company to ensure receipt of services consistent with grantor and consumer needs.

8.4.1   Design, construction and technical requirements

The project will often be a part of a larger development scheme, or may need to be able to interface with existing infrastructure. Therefore, the grantor will want to define design and construction obligations in the concession agreement. In particular, technical specifications will set out in some detail the technical requirements of the grantor for the project.

---

[298]   Vinter (2nd edition 1998) supra note 211 at 40-41.

The grantor will need to ensure that the project meets quality and life-cycle requirements. One way of doing so is to specify the key materials and equipment to be used in the works, or to set out a basic design for the project. However, the grantor will not want to relieve the project company of any of its design responsibilities and will therefore want to avoid taking over any of the design responsibility or will want the project company to undertake the risk for any errors, defects or shortcomings in grantor-provided design.

8.4.2 Modification of technical requirements

The grantor will not wish for the technical requirements to be modified by the construction contractor or the project company without its consent. Some provision for their modification without grantor consent may be made where the changes are necessary for the safety and integrity of the project, or owing to changes in the offtake purchase agreement. The latter will, of course, depend on the relationship between the offtake purchaser and the grantor.

The grantor will want the right to change the technical requirements of the project. This may prove to be a substantial difficulty for the project company as assessing the impact of any change on the project can be extremely difficult, if possible at all. The project company should at least protect its own interests by requiring that any such changes should not materially decrease performance of the project, increase the cost of the project (either in construction or operation and maintenance) or cause the construction or operation of the project to breach any environmental requirements.

The project company will want compensation from the grantor for any grantor-implemented change that affects the project, such as delay in completion, increased cost or decreased performance. However, it should be noted that the actual or long-term effect of any such change is generally very difficult to quantify accurately at the time the change is made. This is particularly true of increased cost of maintenance of the works and long-term degradation.

8.4.3 Time for completion and the project programme

Given the importance of time in any large infrastructure project, the construction contractor will be required to complete the works in accordance with the project programme. This programme will take into consideration the needs of the grantor for a completed project within a given period. The grantor may also impose on the project company penalties where the construction is not completed by the agreed date. These sanctions are likely to be in the form of liquidated damages, and will depend on the length of delay. The completion date will only be extended for specific reasons set out in the concession agreement. These will generally involve breaches by the grantor or events falling within the grantor's risks and possibly *force majeure* events.

8.4.4   Method of operation

The grantor will want to ensure that the project company runs the project in a manner consistent with proper maintenance of the equipment, applicable environmental standards, the requirements of the offtake purchaser and the input supplier, the regulations of government authorities, legal requirements and any other constraints necessary to ensure the proper and continued operation of the project. Unless the grantor is also the regulatory authority, it may be difficult to control the actions of the project company directly and the grantor must therefore establish the standards by which the project must be operated in the concession agreement. The grantor may endeavour to use legal or regulatory mechanisms to establish operating standards. This may not satisfy the project company, which will want certainty as to the standards to be applied to the project and any restriction that may be applied to the revenue stream.

The grantor will also want to restrict the scope of activities to be performed by the project company on the site, in particular as concerns non-project activities. This will ensure that the project company does not undertake activities on the site inconsistent with the grantor's interests or inconsistent with the better interests of the project, for example using project revenues to finance or guarantee other, more risky, investments. The grantor may wish to limit the project company from performing activities or using its funds to undertake any activities beyond the project purposes unless the grantor specifically consents to such use. Such limitations may not be appropriate in certain types of project, such as telecoms or airports, where flexibility in the manner of services performed may allow the project company to improve the payment stream and therefore reduce costs to the grantor and the offtake purchaser.

8.4.5   Maintenance manuals, records and as-built drawings

The project company will maintain certain records, manuals and as-built drawings, many originally drafted by the construction contractor. The maintaining and updating of such documentation is of particular importance for the grantor if the project is to be transferred at the end of the concession period. The grantor will want to have access to specific records and documents to educate its personnel about the operation and maintenance of the works and to ensure that the works are being maintained by the project company to standards sufficient for the grantor's needs.

8.4.6   Update of project technology

In order to ensure the transfer of know-how and technology to the host country, the concession agreement may require the project company to acquire any technical innovations which become available during the concession period or which are developed by the operator, either during the operation of the project or otherwise, and then transfer such technology to the grantor at the end of the concession period. Where the technology originates from a third party, this obligation may be limited by the project company's ability to obtain the technology at commercially reasonable rates. New technology may be the subject of a grantor change, for which the project company will be compensated by the grantor.

This is of particular concern in IT projects, or projects with a particularly high technology element. The grantor will obtain limited benefit from the project over a lengthy concession period if the technology used is superseded or no longer compatible. However, the project company will need to protect itself from increased costs which would affect overall profitability of the project. It may be necessary to impose value-for-money obligations to ensure efficient continued investment.

8.4.7 Training

A BOT project can provide the host government with an important transfer of technology and know-how to the site country.[299] Therefore the grantor may want to maximise the interaction between the project company and local partners or the grantor's personnel in order to ensure the proper transfer of such know-how.

During the period preceding transfer to the grantor or re-tendering, a training regime will often be implemented wherein the project company will train the grantor's personnel in the operation and maintenance of the project. This may involve the operator employing certain of the grantor's personnel for a time or the grantor hiring certain of the operator's personnel to operate and maintain the project after the transfer has taken place.

8.4.8 No discriminatory action by government or government entity

It is essential for the project company to obtain the goodwill of the host government; however, goodwill may not be enough. As noted above, the project company may want to obtain the grantor's undertaking that the host government will not act against the interests of the lenders, the shareholders, the project company, the performance of the project company's obligations or the project itself. This may include expropriation, compulsory acquisition or nationalisation of any or all of the project assets and any action that would have a material and adverse effect on the project or the rights and benefits granted to the parties.

Of course, these requirements may prove to be of little worth where the country involved experiences a dramatic change in political make-up or where the organic law of the country allows it some avenue of escape from its obligations. This risk is notoriously difficult to manage. Any discrimination is often indirect or difficult to prove, for example government influence on the judiciary. Some security may be obtained through political risk insurance or the participation of an export credit agency or international financial organisation which will be able to bring political

---

[299] For further discussion of the transfer of technology and know-how, see United Nations Industrial Development Organisation (1996) supra note 204 at 75-90.

pressure to bear.[300]   Express submission to the jurisdiction of the International Centre for Settlement of Investment Disputes may provide the project company with further ability to obtain and enforce a decision in relation to any claims or disputes.[301]

8.5   Procedures and Mechanisms

The following are general procedures and mechanisms often found in concession agreements.

8.5.1   Approval, appointment and replacement

The grantor will want to ensure that the project participants are experienced and reputable parties to large infrastructure projects. The grantor may prefer to provide appointment criteria, such as "of international repute and experience adequate for participation", or it may want an approval power over the identity of the project participants and their replacements (often a political as well as a practical issue). The project company, on the other hand, will not want to give up control over the management of its operations, nor will the lenders want to lose control over the identity of the project participants.

8.5.2   Granting the concession

The procedure for the actual grant of the concession should be included in the concession agreement.   The concession may be linked to enabling or issuing legislation. Therefore, organic law should be reviewed to verify whether and under what conditions the grantor has the power to grant a concession.   Further legislative or constitutional acts may be necessary in order to affirm or validate the concession.

8.5.3   Concession fees

The project company may be required to pay concession fees for the privilege of obtaining a concession. Such fees will generally be payable to the grantor before commencement and possibly periodically during the concession period.   The amount of the fees will provide the grantor with some early cash flow for its obligations in the early period of the project and will also provide the project company with the added incentive to continue and complete the project in order to recuperate those fees.

8.5.4   Independent expert

An independent expert may be appointed by the grantor and/or the lenders to ascertain whether the project is being performed in accordance with the project requirements. The independent expert will need to be given a right of access to the

---

[300]   See chapter 3 for further discussion of multilateral organisations and export credit agencies.
[301]   See chapter 15 for further discussion of ICSID.

site and the operation of the project. This may involve occasional visits to the site, or a discretionary right of access to any and all parts of the site at any time. The expert may also be allowed to perform tests, inspect the project or review the documentation and records kept for the project by disrupting progress of the works and distracting the project company management team from these other responsibilities. The access of the expert should be limited to that necessary to carry out its role, given that the expert may be an impediment to the construction or operation of the project. The project company may want to specify the role of the independent expert, ensuring that it remains strictly technical rather than commercial or legal.

8.5.5 Restrictions on transfer of shares of the project company

Because of the importance of the identity of the shareholders, owing to their financial and technical capacities, the grantor may want to place certain restrictions on the transfer or change of shareholding in the project company. The grantor may want a right of approval over the identity of any transferee, or to maintain some guarantee from the original shareholders. These restrictions will normally apply during the construction phase, and may apply during some portion of the operation phase of the project or indeed throughout the concession period.

8.5.6 Step-in and continuous operation provisions

Where the project company breaches the concession agreement in such a way as to entitle the grantor to terminate the concession agreement, and where the grantor intends to act on its rights, the lenders will want the right to step in to the project company's place, complete the project and avoid the termination of the concession agreement. The concession agreement, or a direct agreement, will therefore grant the lenders step-in rights.[302]

In the same way, the project is only of use to the grantor when it operates. The grantor may therefore want the right to continue operation of the project where it terminates the concession agreement. This is sometimes referred to as the "right to continuous operation", as it allows the grantor to ensure continuous operation of the project even in the event of termination. The grantor itself will often not undertake such operation, but rather pass such responsibilities on to some other party, such as the offtake purchaser.

8.5.7 Transfer or re-tender

At the end of the concession period, the grantor will either put the project out for re-tender or it will require the project company to transfer the project assets to the grantor or to a replacement operator.

The process of re-tender will usually begin six months to a year before the end of the concession period, at which point the grantor will obtain specified information

---

[302] For further discussion of step-in rights, see chapter 4.

from the project company. The grantor will issue tender information to potential bidders and may want the project company's assistance in compiling information and generally assisting with the re-tendering process. This may be complicated where the project company itself intends to bid for the new concession.

The grantor may wish to take over the project at the end of the concession period. The issues involved in the transfer of the project will include the transfer of project assets, land rights, testing of the works, training of personnel and treatment of the shares in the project company.

The required state of the project on re-tender or transfer will need to be defined as exactly as possible. This may include a testing regime and review by an independent expert. Failure to meet the requirements for transfer will result in sanctions, either in the form of liquidated damages for delay of transfer or possibly liquidated damages based on the extent to which the project does not meet the transfer requirements. There may also be some bonus payment to the project company based on residual value where the project, as transferred, exceeds the transfer requirements. This will provide the project company with an incentive to maintain and upgrade the project during and towards the end of the concession period.

The grantor may want to include some form of retention of payments to provide some security in case the project company does not deliver the project in the state intended and sanctions are imposed. This retention can either be made from funds due to the project company from the grantor or possibly from payments by the offtake purchaser to the project company. The grantor may accept an on-demand bond in lieu of retention money to allow the project company to maintain its cash flow.

Chapter 9

Shareholders' Agreement

He who walks with the wise grows wise, but a companion of fools suffers harm.

The Bible, Book of Proverbs,
chapter 13, verse 20

The shareholders' agreement establishes the rights and obligations of the shareholders with respect to the project company. It will define how the project company will be managed, how costs and revenues will be allocated and how intervening events encountered during the concession period will be handled. The form of the project company will be reflected in the shareholders' agreement and determine certain of its provisions. The shareholders' agreement sits in the BOT project structure as indicated in the chart below.

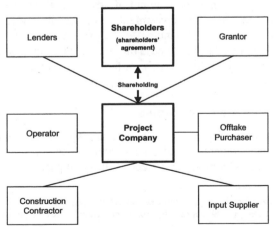

The project company will be governed by its constituent documents and the rights and obligations they create. The corporate form of the project company will determine to some extent how it will be organised internally but primarily how it will be perceived legally and what restrictions or rights it will be given. The term "shareholders' agreement" will be used to described the combination of these documents. The location of the provisions discussed below will depend on local practice and whether the obligations should apply only to the signatories or whether they should run with the shares and restrict ownership of the shares.

The shareholders' agreement, along with the provisions of law applicable to the special purpose vehicle, will define the relationship between the shareholders, their rights, obligations and role in management of the project. The shareholders' agreement will dictate how decisions are to be made within the project company, how profits and costs are to be shared, whether and how shares can be purchased or sold and other such issues basic to the internal organisation of the project company.

This chapter will not discuss shareholder agreements generally.[303] The difficulties encountered in generating a BOT shareholders' agreement are not dissimilar to those found in other such agreements. This chapter will concentrate on those issues specific to shareholder agreements in BOT projects. Reference should also be made to chapter 15, which discusses issues common to the project documents.

9.1   Form of the Project Company

Typically, as noted above, the project company will be a limited liability special purpose vehicle whose shares are owned by a number of investors. The benefits of choosing such a jointly owned vehicle include the following.[304]

9.1.1   Added source of equity capital

The grantor and the lenders will require a minimum level of equity investment in the project company. The level of equity required by them will depend on the security available, the creditworthiness of participants and the nature of the project, including country risk and the involvement of government entities. Although they will be required to provide equity investment, in cash or in kind, shareholders may also provide subordinated debt financing to the project company. Such financing may be used as a stand-by facility in case the project company incurs cost overruns or delays. Third party subordinated debt in the form of mezzanine financing may also be available.

9.1.2   Special project expertise

The project will require very diverse expertise and knowledge of the technologies to be used. The shareholders may also have complementary skills or host country expertise or presence. Operating experience will be of particular importance in an

---

[303]   For a general discussion of joint ventures and shareholder agreements, see chapter 26 of Scriven, Pritchard and Delmon (1999) supra note 210; Joint Ventures: Key Legal Issues (Allen & Overy 1997).

[304]   Nevitt and Fabozzi (6th edition 1995) supra note 260 at 225; Warner, "Some Key Considerations in Structuring International Project Joint Ventures" Project Financing in Emerging Markets 1996: Successful Development of Power, Mining, Oil and Gas, Telecommunications and Transportation Projects at 171 (1996).

international BOT project, given the limited number of operators with extensive international experience.

The project may involve captive infrastructure (specific to the project) such as the construction and operation of a port or pipeline in order to transport input; the provision of extensive transmission facilities to connect with a power grid; or permanent housing facilities for use by the operating personnel. Shareholders with expertise in such tangential services may be desirable, particularly where certain project tasks are beyond the experience and capabilities of the project sponsors.

9.1.3 Shareholder interest

A prospective contractor may need to invest in the equity of the project in order to obtain the contract. Although this can result in reluctant equity subscribers, it will provide the grantor and lenders with greater security, tying the contractors in to the long-term interests of the project. For this reason, certain strategic shareholders may be required to maintain a minimum shareholding in the project company over the term of the debt, and possibly over the term of the project.

9.1.4 Diversity of ownership

The host country may require that domestic equity should be invested in the project. The restrictions on foreign shareholding may even require that local shareholders have a majority interest. The intent of the host government is generally to ensure that a reasonable transfer of know-how and technology occurs and that certain of the project revenues will be reinvested in the host country. Local shareholders may not have the financial wherewithal to satisfy the level of equity investment required, and may therefore provide equity in kind.

Even where there is no requirement for local ownership, it may be preferable (where the project is located in an unfamiliar or commercially challenging country) to involve a local partner in the project. Such a partner may be well connected politically and commercially, and can ease administrative burdens and potentially alleviate some of the project's commercial and political risk.

9.1.5 Risk management

In a BOT project, because of the long-term nature of the project, and the fact that the project company is responsible for the whole of the design, construction and operation of the project, the risks encountered will be more diverse than those encountered in other projects. However, where the project is a joint venture, the risks of the project can be shared. Further, each risk can be allocated in a more efficient manner, to the shareholder best able to manage it.

9.1.6 Off balance sheet treatment

The ability of a shareholder to finance a project off balance sheet may be curtailed where a parent company owns more than a certain percentage of a joint venture. The accounting rules for many countries would in such cases require line-by-line consolidation of assets and liabilities.[305] By sharing the control of the joint venture with other shareholders, the parent company can avoid such consolidation. The project would therefore have a lesser impact, or no impact at all, on other corporate borrowing.

9.1.7   Availability of funding

The presence of several shareholders can allow easier access to financing. It may provide the project company with greater leverage to convince the lenders to accept terms more beneficial to the project company than they would have accepted for an individual shareholder.   The influence and commercial relationships of several shareholders with the lenders may be co-ordinated to maximum effect.

Often, lenders will be reluctant to provide financing to certain shareholders for political or financial reasons. One or more of the shareholders alone may not have sufficient access to funds or a sufficiently robust credit rating.   However, a consortium of such shareholders may provide sufficient security or assurances (although not necessarily financial), enabling the lenders to provide the necessary financing.

9.1.8   Control over a resource or market position

Shareholders may be willing to invest in and be bound to the project company in order to attain or maintain a market position or a commercial contract. BOT projects are often substantial undertakings involving construction, operation and input supply obligations of significant size. This fact will attract contractors willing to provide equity investment in order to obtain the relevant subcontracts. Further, the involvement of the host country government in the project may motivate shareholders to pursue a relationship with the host country government (particularly in a field not yet open to private investment) in the hopes of obtaining further work.

9.2   Investment, Return, Costs and Cash Flow

The shareholders' agreement will address issues of revenues and contributions, how the company receives money and what it does with that money.

9.2.1   Shareholder contributions

The shareholders will be required to provide equity contributions to the project company. The form of such investment can vary.

---

[305]   Nevitt and Fabozzi (6th edition 1995) supra note 260.

9.2.1.1 Pure equity

In a pure equity investment, the shareholder is subject to the risks and benefits of the project. The lenders often require that the project should first exhaust its equity before making drawdowns from debt, thereby obliging shareholders to make equity contributions early rather than late in the construction phase. However, increasingly, lenders are willing to consider contingent capital contributions (wherein the shareholders' equity contributions are implemented gradually throughout the construction period), at given times or in relation to the level of costs incurred, or possibly at the end of the construction phase, which is known as "back-ended equity". Such an equity injection scheme is beneficial to shareholders' return on equity when computing IRR.

The timing of contributions may be influenced by tax or transfer duty considerations. Contingent or back-ended equity contributions may also need to be supported by bank guarantees or stand-by letters of credit in order to ensure the credit risk of the shareholder to provide the equity promised.

9.2.1.2 Subordinated debt

Investment can also take the form of subordinated debt financing, with some equity benefit. The provider of subordinated debt will generally receive a defined rate of interest, denying the provider of any equity up-side from better than anticipated project performance. Subordinated debt will rank junior to the senior debt, but ahead of pure equity investment. Therefore, while subordinated debt does not benefit from potential up-side, it is also less vulnerable than pure equity to potential down-side, where the project does not perform as well as expected.

9.2.1.3 Contributions in kind

Shareholder contributions may also take the form of contributions in kind, whereby a shareholder provides materials, equipment or services rather than cash as its contribution. This is often the case in developing countries where a local shareholder may not have the liquidity to make a cash contribution but may have the ability to provide the site for construction, certain raw materials or some other valuable asset or service.[306] The shareholders will need to agree an appropriate valuation of any in-kind contribution.

9.2.2 New equity infusions

The shareholders' agreement will need to address funding for unanticipated costs. This may, for example, require the shareholders to inject new equity in proportion to cost overruns. The shareholders' agreement will need to define how minority shareholders will be affected by such new equity infusions. If no provision is

---

[306] Vinter (2nd edition 1998) supra note 211 at 35.

made, shareholders may have their shareholding diluted by the new equity injection.[307]

9.2.3   Application of cash flow

The shareholders' agreement will provide a procedure to decide how the cash flow received from the project is distributed. Contractual obligations to third parties, such as to the input supplier, the operator or other contractors, will generally be paid first. Then, debt servicing will be paid. The balance will be divided between reserve funds within the project company, for various contingencies such as debt service, major maintenance and asset replacement, and disbursements to the shareholders. The reserve accounts may be pre-funded by debt, but will be replenished by cash flow where reserve funds have been withdrawn. The management of project cash flow will be governed primarily by the financing agreement.[308]

9.2.4   Costs

The shareholders' agreement must specify how different costs incurred by the shareholders in the context of the project are to be treated. For example, the shareholders' agreement will need to specify whether the project company will bear the shareholders' individual costs incurred while fulfilling their obligations under the shareholders' agreement, the costs of negotiating and drawing up the project agreements or any other costs incurred due to the activities of the shareholders in the interest of the project.

This will generally involve the categorisation of costs as project costs, for which the project company is responsible, or individual costs, for which each shareholder is individually responsible. The allocation of project related costs will also depend on what role each shareholder plays. It may be preferable for the project company to hire external accountants to assume responsibility for the project company accounts and the characterisation of the costs incurred. This may be mandatory under local law, e.g. where the project company is required to publish audited accounts.

9.2.5   Contribution clause

As a general rule, assuming the project company is a limited liability vehicle, the shareholders will only be responsible for project company liability up to the amount of their investment in the project company. However, grantors and lenders may require further sponsor support. Where sponsor support is provided and in order to allocate the risk of further liabilities amongst the shareholders, the shareholders' agreement may include a contribution clause which will specify how liability will be shared.

---

[307]   Warner (1996) supra note 304 at 176.
[308]   For further discussion of cash flow and project accounts, see section 4.1.

The shareholders may allow some preference to certain members. This may be the case for less financially substantial members of the project company who are brought in for particular skills or technology. In such cases the project company may allow that partner to bear less liability than the other shareholders, in an effort to ensure his participation. Similarly, where the host country law requires the participation of local partners, these local companies may not be willing or able to bear the full additional liability for the project.

9.3 Shareholder Rights and Obligations

Shareholders will have certain rights and obligations under the shareholders' agreement. This section addresses certain of the most important rights and obligations.

9.3.1 Shareholder undertakings

The shareholders will want to maintain a non-recourse structure for the financing for the project as far as possible. As noted above, the lenders may want to extend this non-recourse status to limited or full recourse during the construction phase, or perhaps during the early part of the operating phase, in certain cases due to the amount of risk involved in this part of the project.

The shareholders may be required to give guarantees within the context of the project. These guarantees and their scope should be described in detail in the shareholders' agreement or a separate sponsor support agreement, setting out in particular who will provide them, who will pay for them and how the procedure will be managed. Such guarantees and undertakings will be strongly resisted by the shareholders.

9.3.2 Conflicts of interest

Owing to the inter-relationship between the parties to a BOT project, the shareholders may find themselves in situations involving a conflict of interests. For this reason, the shareholders may want to require a shareholder to withdraw from certain decision-making or other roles within the project where a conflict of interest may affect his judgement or his ability to carry out a task in the best interests of the project company. A difficulty when drafting such provisions is how to define a conflict of interest that is considered to be severe enough to force a shareholder to withdraw from some act or deliberation. If the bar is set too low then only the non-participant shareholders will make decisions or act for the project company, yet if the bar is set too high then the exercise will not achieve its purpose.

The shareholders' agreement may need to provide for the creation of "Chinese walls" where the shareholders are discussing matters relevant to one of their number in its capacity as a project participant rather than a shareholder. In such a case the relevant project participant shareholder should be excluded from any vote on the issue, including counting its presence or vote towards the creation of a quorum necessary to vote or the majority vote needed to take an action on the issue. This may also involve keeping certain information confidential from the relevant shareholder and limiting its management responsibilities either altogether or in relation to those issues relevant to the matter at hand. For example, where the project company is negotiating the terms and price of the operation and maintenance agreement, the operator may be a shareholder in the project company. Therefore, the shareholders may want to provide that where the operator finds itself in such a position of conflict of interest, it may not take part in the decision-making process of the project company relating to that issue.

Where a project participant shareholder is in serious breach of its obligations as a project participant (e.g. construction contractor or input supplier), the other shareholders may wish to restrict that project participant's voting rights on any issue to avoid any disruptive behaviour on its part in an attempt to influence project company activities in relation to its breach.

9.3.3   Confidentiality

Depending on the nature of the project and the technology to be used, the shareholders may wish to include a confidentiality clause in the shareholders' agreement. This clause will protect information gained within the context of the project and may also avoid publicity of the financial health, difficulties or disputes of and within the project company before the project company shareholders have had an opportunity to manage the situation and/or protect their interests.

Information obtained by the shareholders is likely to be of a sensitive nature, particularly the commercial practices and technical information contributed by the various shareholders. The shareholders in the project company may also be competitors in other projects or in other markets. This competition should not be permitted to motivate the parties to engage in the non-disclosure of information or other concealment of know-how or skills that might be beneficial for the purposes of the project company's activities. Secure confidentiality obligations will allow the shareholders to participate fully in the project without sacrificing their competitive edge on future projects.

9.3.4   Transfer to grantor

The shareholders' agreement may also need to provide for the transfer of the project to the grantor at the end of the concession period. This may involve the grantor paying for a certain portion of the residual value of the facilities, spare parts or other project assets. A single purpose project company will then generally be wound up, liquidating all remaining assets, distributing what funds remain and terminating the obligations of the shareholders.

9.3.5   Transfer of shares

Shareholders will want to avoid the transfer of shares to any third party or to any unauthorised third party without their prior consent. This restriction may be a blanket restriction on transfer, it may define the type of third party to which shares may be transferred or it may identify a list of the third parties to which a shareholder may transfer its shares. The purpose of such restriction is to maintain a tight control on who or what may be a shareholder: for example, restricting the national origin of the shareholders, the type and amount of experience a given shareholder must have or the financial solidity of a given shareholder. Often, the shareholders will not want shares to be transferred to competitors.

Where a shareholder intends to sell its shares or a portion thereof to a third party, pre-emption rights allow the other shareholders to purchase such shares at a pre-agreed price, at a "market price" (which may be very hard to define) or at the price the third party is willing to pay (first right of refusal). The other shareholders will then decide whether to exercise their right of pre-emption.

Any transfer to a third party purchaser should also cover the obligatory undertaking of that third party of the obligations of the transferor including, possibly, guarantees, parent company guarantees and provision of debt contributions. Such requirements will need to be expressed specifically in the shareholders' agreement. They should include an agreement to be bound by any obligation undertaken by the seller in the context of the project and the shareholders' agreement, including any project company indemnities or borrowings and guarantees or cross-indebtedness to third parties in relation to the business of the project company. The shareholders may wish to provide for referral to an expert for any dispute involving the transfer of shares, the right to transfer and the price to be paid by other shareholders for such shares, either through pre-emption or other share purchase rights, in order to obtain resolution quickly and from an expert on the relevant issue.

Although requirements for and restrictions on share transfers will be set out in the shareholders' agreement, in certain jurisdictions (for example, the United Kingdom and South Africa) the shareholders' agreement is a contractual undertaking. Any breach of such requirements or restrictions will entitle the non-breaching parties to contractual remedies against the breaching party, but such remedies will not alter the actual ownership of the shares. For this reason, in such jurisdictions, the requirements and restrictions are repeated in the articles of association of the project company, which bind shares and shareholders, and will effectively restrict ownership of the shares.

It should be noted that the financing agreements will restrict share transfer and may create a pledge over the shares to the benefit of the lenders. Therefore any share transfer will be subject to prior lender approval. This approval, usually, must not be unreasonably delayed or withheld.

9.4 Management and Administration

An essential aspect of the role of the project company is its ability to manage a large international project over an extended period. To this end the shareholders' agreement will also define the management of the project company and thereby the management of the project. This management power will be defined primarily through the voting rights, the appointment of project company directors and the resolution of any disputes which may arise between the shareholders.

9.4.1   Management

Management rights are not necessarily based on the corresponding number of shares in the project company that a shareholder owns. They may be allocated based on other capabilities that a shareholder brings into the project company. For example, the shareholder which acts as sponsor and makes the first contact with the grantor may be accorded a more prominent management role in the project company. Similarly, a shareholder which has a good reputation in the area of large infrastructure projects may be the key to the grantor granting the concession to the project company and the lenders providing finance and therefore may be given greater latitude to manage the project company.

9.4.2   Dispute resolution

Even where a reasonable system of voting rights and administration is put in place, with appropriate deadlock breaking mechanisms, disputes may still arise. The shareholders will need to define the method of dispute resolution to be used between themselves. This dispute resolution mechanism should be very flexible, as the disputes that arise between the shareholders will often range in nature from technical issues to commercial decisions relating to the management of the project company. Specialist experts are generally more efficient with technically based issues, while it may be preferable to refer business related and legal decisions to arbitration.[309]

---

[309]   Warner (1996) supra note 304 at 176.

Chapter 10

Construction Contract

The wise man builds his house on the Rock.

Jesus, Sermon on the Mount,
Matthew's Gospel, chapter 7, verses 24-27

The project company will allocate the task of designing and building the project to a construction contractor. Banks and other financing institutions will generally condition their financing of a BOT project on the implementation of a contractual scheme that provides them with protection against construction risks and some certainty as to financial exposure during the construction phase.

The value of the project assets will be the lenders' primary form of security. However, until completion, the project assets may be worth very little. It is during the construction period that delays and cost increases most often arise. Therefore construction risk, in particular completion and performance risk, will have an important impact on the bankability of the project.

The construction contract will define the responsibilities of the construction contractor and the project company and their relationship during the period of construction.[310] It will sit in the BOT project structure as indicated in the chart below.

Tasks to be allocated by the construction contract include design, supply of materials and equipment, construction of civil works, erection and commissioning. Risk to be allocated includes site conditions, access, permits and licences, warranty of equipment and materials, cost, timely completion and performance of the finished works.

---

[310] For further discussion of construction contracts, see generally Scriven, Pritchard and Delmon (1999) supra note 210.

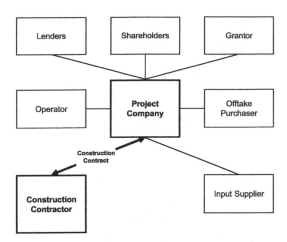

To allocate the construction risk efficiently, and provide greater certainty of total financial exposure for the project, the lenders will want the construction contractor to bear as much of the construction risk as possible. In order to place the majority of the construction risk on the construction contractor and ensure a fixed price, lenders generally insist on using a turnkey construction contract.

This chapter discusses issues specific to the construction contract. Reference should also be made to chapter 15 for issues common to the project documents.

10.1   Turnkey Construction Contracts

A construction contract can take a number of forms, requiring one or several contractors to take on certain risks and responsibilities in relation to the construction of the works. The form of construction contract chosen by the employer will define the allocation of construction risk.

Lenders in a BOT project generally require the use of a turnkey construction contract. The turnkey construction contract, also known as a "design and build" ("D&B") or an "engineering, procurement and construction" ("EPC") contract, is a contractual arrangement placing the whole of the responsibility for design and construction of the works on one contractor. The term "turnkey" suggests that after completion one need only "turn the key" to commence operation of the constructed facility. This concept is, of course, over-simplified.

There is no accepted definition in the construction industry of an archetypal turnkey construction contract. Model form contracts, such as FIDIC, ICE and ENAA, are often used as a basis for the construction contract to ease the task of drafting.[311] The following are a few of the more important characteristics of a turnkey construction contract.

---

[311]   References here are to the Fédération Internationale des Ingénieurs-Conseil ("FIDIC"), the Institute of Civil Engineers ("ICE") and the Engineering Advancement Association of Japan ("ENAA").

It should be noted that in certain cases a turnkey construction contract may not be practicable or desirable. This is often the case in industries where construction works are historically separated into several packages and no single contractor could undertake a "turnkey" role. Procurement exigencies may also lead to the use of several contractors, for example where long-lead items (those which require significant time to manufacture and/or transport) must be contracted very early in the process. Where a single turnkey construction contract is not available, the lenders will want the several contracts to work together as a turnkey contract, or will want a completion guarantee from the sponsors to cover any gaps in risk allocation.

10.1.1 Single point responsibility

The turnkey construction contract places single point responsibility for both the design and the construction of the works on one party, the construction contractor. Single point responsibility simply means that the construction contractor is bound to provide to the project company a completed project in accordance with the contract specifications, and will be held accountable to ensure that the performance and the quality of the works comply with all of the contractual requirements, so that where there is a problem, the project company has a single point of liability.

Single point responsibility will require several important obligations to be placed on the construction contractor. The construction contractor will be required to design the whole of the works, co-ordinate design and construction interfaces and complete the works to satisfy the completion and performance targets, all in accordance with a specified contractual standard of care. Thus, where the project company wishes to make a claim concerning a defect in the works, it need not specify whether the defect was caused by inadequate design or faulty workmanship since responsibility for both of these elements of the work falls on the construction contractor.

10.1.1.1 Design

In the construction industry, there tends to be a distinct division between contractors who are expert builders and expert designers. Therefore, in traditional construction contracts it is common for separate parties to provide design and construction services for a project, thereby creating an essential interface between the "designer" and the "builder". Since the construction contractor under a turnkey construction contract both designs and builds the works, the construction contractor will not need to take the time to study and understand designs provided by a third party. The design will be developed in co-ordination with the builder, by the construction contractor. The co-ordinated input of both entities can accelerate understanding and facilitate construction, since the designer will have the builder's input during early preparation of the design.

The control given to the construction contractor facilitates implementation during construction of new and better approaches to design, developed through its experience and expertise. The construction contractor will have an incentive to implement changes under the turnkey structure (such as new technology or time saving methods), which may not be true under more traditional, segregated contracting methods.

The design under a turnkey construction contract will also take into consideration the construction contractor's methods of construction, providing more efficient and timely completion.[312] The designer will be familiar with the builder's construction methods, the technology it uses, its experience and the interfaces between the various subcontractors to be used. This familiarity is likely to help to identify critical flaws in the design at an early stage, facilitating avoidance or mitigation of such flaws during construction when such action is more effective.[313]

10.1.1.2   Co-ordination

Under traditional contractual approaches, design and construction tasks are performed by separate entities or at least pursuant to separate contracts. The employer divides the construction works into packages, representing separate construction and design tasks. This leaves the risk of interfaces between the construction packages and the possibility of delays or cost overruns with the employer (i.e. the project company, a situation the lenders would find undesirable in a BOT project).

For example, the works may have been divided into a civil works package (the building of a dam) and a mechanical/engineering package (the installation of turbines and a generator). The ability of the civil works to house the turbines and sustain the vibrations emitted from the generator would be a project interface. Project interfaces will include ascertaining whether materials can be combined, equipment can be interconnected, construction methods work well together and technologies are compatible. These interfaces represent significant project risks unless they are allocated and otherwise managed appropriately.

The turnkey construction contract seeks to overcome these difficulties by placing all of these responsibilities and interfaces on the construction contractor, who must guarantee the interfaces between subcontractors, materials, technologies and working procedures used, as well as ensuring the performance of the project as a whole.

10.1.1.3   Completion

Single point responsibility will place completion and performance requirements on the construction contractor for the finished works. The construction contractor must warrant that the finished works will comply with the completion and performance criteria set out in the construction contract. The completion criteria, including the technical specifications, must be satisfied before the works can be considered complete. The works will also need to perform in accordance with

---

[312]   Wallace (1986) supra note 147 at 407.
[313]   Brown (7 and 8 December 1995) supra note 149.

performance criteria, placing on the construction contractor the obligation to ensure that the completed works achieve the performance targets imposed by the project company. These criteria generally flow down from the concession agreement and the offtake purchase agreement.

The performance criteria may specify output requirements, input requirements, environmental impact, waste output, operating costs and any other performance that the project company may require of the finished works. For instance, for the construction of a thermal power plant the project company will want to ensure that the plant produces sufficient power per unit of fuel to satisfy its commercial needs, in particular in relation to the input supply and offtake purchase agreements. The duty to ensure production of power may also include, to some extent, its transmission, where the project involves transmission lines to connect with the offtake purchaser's facilities.

Completion will be confirmed by the project company's representative. Under traditional methods of procurement, the employer is represented by the engineer, who plays an important role in the design and co-ordination of construction. The project company's representative under a turnkey contract will be limited to supervision of compliance with the construction contract, and confirmation that milestones and completion are accomplished satisfactorily.

10.1.1.4   Contractual standard of care

A further element relevant to single point responsibility is the standard of care placed on the construction contractor, i.e. with what level of care the construction contractor must perform the works. The standard of care is often defined by the relevant legal system and in accordance with industry practice. However, for clarity, a contractual standard of care will often be imposed in the construction contract.

In standard procurement, the builder is held to a standard of "good workmanship" while the designer will be held to "reasonable skill and care", thus focusing on the method of carrying out the construction ("*garantie de moyens*" in French law). Construction contractors under a turnkey construction contract are generally required to guarantee results rather than method. They are held to have sufficient competence and ability to complete the design and construction so as to meet the needs of the project company. The result-oriented standard often applied to the performance of a turnkey construction contract is known as "fitness for purpose" ("*garantie de résultats*" in French law).

The fitness for purpose standard requires the construction contractor to complete the works so that they are fit for their intended purpose as described in the construction contract.[314] For example, in the construction of a refinery, the project company will set out the project's "purpose" in the construction contract requirements, such as the size and nature of the plant desired as well as its

---

[314]   May, Keating on Building Contracts at 57-60 (6th edition 1995).

operational output and the consumption necessary to reach such output. Therefore, if the project company's original conception of the works lacked some element necessary for it to be fit for the purpose intended, the construction contractor would be responsible for ensuring that the finished works contained the missing element.

As a general proposition, where the construction contract in question applies fitness for purpose and single point responsibility, the construction contractor guarantees the outcome of the finished works with no exception for design defects apart from an error in the project company's requirements. Since the construction contractor must deliver works that are fully operational to the specifications of the project company, any defect or default is necessarily the responsibility of the construction contractor, except where the construction contract specifically provides otherwise.

10.1.1.5   Contractor's claims

Single point responsibility can also reduce the opportunity for claims by the construction contractor. Claims can result in inefficiency, causing delay in construction and increase in the cost of the project. Under more traditional contracting arrangements, these claims are often based on directions given by the employer's engineer or interfaces between the design and construction packages. Since the project company's engineer is not a central co-ordinating figure in the turnkey construction contract and the construction contractor has taken on the whole of the responsibility for the design and construction of the project, the turnkey construction contract can reduce the opportunity for claims and disruption.

10.1.2   Time for completion

In BOT projects, timely completion is essential, as penalties may apply under the input supply, offtake purchase and concession agreements for late completion. Further, debt servicing obligations will arise at the end of the forecast construction period. Therefore, the project company will need to ensure a fixed time for completion and commencement of operating revenues. Turnkey construction contracts are conducive to a fixed time for completion since they combine all design and construction tasks under the responsibility of one construction contractor.

Traditional contracting contemplates separate and distinct design and construction phases. Therefore a time-lag exists between the design and the construction of the works. Further, these two tasks will be undertaken by entirely separate contractors.

The turnkey method combines these two phases and allows construction to proceed "fast-track", whereby the construction contractor can start construction prior to the completion of the design. The construction contractor will complete basic design, then begin construction while performing detailed design. By overlapping construction tasks, completion can be accelerated, as demonstrated in the chart below. Further, the interface between the design and construction can be managed during the design process, avoiding complications. Consequently, the turnkey method of contracting may result in earlier project completion.

FAST-TRACK NATURE OF TURNKEY CONSTRUCTION

Months													
	3	6	9	12	15	18	21	24	27	30	33	36	39
Traditional													
Tender of design	▓												
Design		▓											
Tender of construction				▓									
Construction					▓	▓	▓	▓	▓	▓	▓	▓	▓
Turnkey													
Tender of project	▓												
Design		▓	▓										
Construction			▓	▓	▓	▓	▓	▓	▓	▓	▓		

10.1.3   Fixed price

Turnkey construction contracts generally use a fixed price lump-sum structure, wherein the contractor is paid one lump sum for the design and construction of the works, with limited opportunity for price increases, so providing greater price certainty for the project company and the lenders.   Lenders often insist on lump-sum pricing for construction projects, in order to reduce their completion risk and obtain greater certainty of overall financial exposure.

The lump-sum pricing method used for turnkey construction contracts also facilitates the use of fixed payments by stages of completion (for example, milestones).   Where the total price is fixed, it can be more easily divided into fixed payments, based on completion of construction tasks or phases, allowing the lenders to predict the timing of drawdowns and manage better the outflow of funds.[315]

The use of a lump-sum price combined with payments on the completion of stages of construction (for example, milestone payments) can result in an increased rate of progress.[316]   To get paid under milestone payments the construction contractor must complete certain specified construction tasks to the satisfaction of the project company's representative.   If the milestones are well defined, the construction contractor will be encouraged to complete the works efficiently and at an increased speed in order to obtain payment.   With other payment methods, the construction contractor may be motivated to complete only the tasks which result in large payments and leave less profitable tasks idle, potentially delaying completion.

---

[315]   Wallace (1986) supra note 147 at 408.
[316]   *Ibid* at 331.

10.1.4   Disadvantages

The employer's role of supervision of design and construction, which is found in traditional construction contracts, is absent from the turnkey construction contract. Where the construction contractor takes responsibility for the design of the works, the project company's advisers find their involvement limited primarily to the tender process, supervision of the construction contractor's work and confirmation of completion. The definition of "supervision" will be heavily negotiated by the parties, as the project company, the grantor and the lenders will want to maintain control over the construction process while the construction contractor will want to avoid outside intervention.

As the responsibility for co-ordination of the project passes to the construction contractor, so does some of the control over the project. The project company will have less day-to-day control of the construction of the works, and its decreased role of supervision and management may result in certain disadvantages.

10.1.4.1   Control of design

The project company will be distanced from the design under a turnkey construction contract, reducing its understanding of the processes used in the works. For this reason, where the construction contractor suggests a variation of the works, the project company may have a difficult time verifying whether a proposed variation is the responsibility of the construction contractor, whether it will affect the performance of the finished works and whether it is necessary for the works. The lenders will therefore often employ an independent engineer to test the works during construction and oversee the construction contractor's performance.

The construction contractor, receiving a lump-sum price, will be given an incentive to provide less sophisticated designs in order to save on costs and increase profit. In many situations, the construction contractor will be at liberty to decide what elements will go into the design and construction of the works. Since the project company is removed from the dominant position in the design and co-ordination of the project it will need to find some other method of monitoring the construction contractor's performance. This often requires hiring private consultants to follow the preparation of the designs and perform tests, which can increase the costs to the project company and possibly to the construction contractor.

10.1.4.2   Risk premium

The construction contractor bears an increased amount of project risk under a turnkey construction contract. Further, in a BOT project, the construction contractor will bear increased risk of late completion as liquidated damages will need to correspond with the project company's exposure to damages, lost income and debt servicing. Depending upon market forces, a construction contractor will attempt to increase the contract price in accordance with the risk it undertakes. Thus the project company may end up paying a higher overall price for the construction of the project due to the cost of such increased risk.

10.2　Risk Allocation

The construction contract is used to allocate obligations and risks between the construction contractor and the project company. The following discusses the primary risks which should be addressed by the construction contract.

10.2.1　Completion risk

The project company will be responsible to the grantor for completion of the works in accordance with the requirements (in relation to scope, method, time and quality) specified in the concession agreement, the offtake purchase agreement and the input supply agreement. The operation and maintenance agreement will generally set out requirements applicable to the construction works. The project company will therefore pass these risks on to the construction contractor. The project company will also wish to add requirements to the construction contract to promote the efficiency and minimise the costs of operation and maintenance in order to maximise the profitability of the project. For example, the project company may require the construction contractor to warrant fitness for purpose of the completed works and/or life-cycles for important equipment, even though the other project documents do not impose such requirements on the project company.

10.2.1.1　Concept of completion

The construction contractor will be required to complete the works in accordance with the specification and performance criteria set out in the construction contract. An added difficulty of a BOT project is the number of parties wishing to ensure the compliance of the works with the contract requirements, including the project company, the grantor and the lenders. The compliance of the works with the requirements set out in the construction contract will be verified through testing and inspection, generally confirmed by the project company's representative. In order to satisfy the interests of the other project participants, the assistance of an independent engineer is often solicited to verify the passing of tests and compliance with the construction contract requirements.

10.2.1.2　Time for completion

The construction contractor, through the construction contract, should be responsible for completion of the construction of the project within the time frame supplied in the concession, offtake purchase and input supply agreements, subject to certain exceptions which are discussed later in this chapter. Where the works are not completed within the time for completion due to failure by the construction contractor, liquidated damages, based on a pre-estimate of the damages and losses to be incurred by the project company, will be imposed on the construction contractor.[317] The pre-estimate of damages and losses should include any penalties

---

[317]　As further discussed in section 10.5.2.2, the applicable law may place restrictions on the level of liquidated damages which may be imposed.

imposed by the concession, input supply and offtake purchase agreements, unavoidable operating expenditures and lost income. The definition of "completion" should be considered carefully as it will have an important impact on the risk borne by the construction contractor in relation to the timing of completion.

10.2.2   Performance risk

The completed facility must perform to a certain standard to achieve the revenue stream required to satisfy the debt servicing, provide a return on investment and cover any other costs. The risk of failure to achieve the levels of performance required is basic to the success of the project. The construction contractor will bear a part of the performance risk for the project: it will be responsible for constructing works capable of attaining the performance levels required under standard operating conditions, taking into consideration the site conditions, and any other project-specific limitations.

The performance capacity of the project will generally be measured by performance tests, possibly separate from those carried out to verify completion. Such performance tests will involve the operation of the project during a given period under normal operating conditions. The lenders will wish to be involved in the supervision of the performance tests.

Performance of the works is not limited to availability for use or output. The performance tests can monitor, for example, input requirements, heat rate, waste output, climate variations, lighting, accessibility, ventilation, consumption of input, temperature and environmental impact. The performance demanded from the project will be specific to the nature of the project and the needs of the offtake purchaser.

Liquidated damages are often imposed to sanction the construction contractor where the works fail to meet the performance levels mandated, particularly where the works include a process plant. Some minimum performance level may be included in the definition of "completion". Once completion is achieved and within a period thereafter, the construction contractor will be required to achieve the target levels of performance. The project company will be entitled to impose sanctions on the construction contractor to the extent of any failure to achieve the target performance level before a given date. The lenders may mandate that any liquidated damages paid by the construction contractor for failure to achieve the performance targets be used to prepay debt in order to maintain financial cover ratios for the project company over the life of the concession in view of the lesser performance, and therefore lower revenues, obtained from the defective project.

Once the performance of the completed works has been verified as compliant with the contract requirements, the construction contractor will generally remain liable to cure any defects that may arise, over an agreed period (usually one to five years, depending on the technology used and market standards). This defects liability period may also act as a delimitation of the construction contractor's liability for the works, except for any additional liability period provided for latent defects.

Once the works are in operation, the performance risk will be shared with the operator, who will be responsible for any failure to perform to the prescribed limits owing to improper operation or maintenance.

10.2.3   Increase of cost risk

The lenders will want a clear understanding of their financial exposure, so the construction contractor will be asked to bear a large part of the risk of increased cost of construction. The construction contract is likely to be turnkey by nature (as discussed above), placing responsibility for the completion of the works on the construction contractor for a fixed lump-sum contract price. Therefore, as a general proposition, any increase in the cost of construction will be for the account of the construction contractor, subject to specified exceptions which are discussed in section 10.5.1.

10.3   Interfaces between Construction Contractor and Other Project Participants

Interfaces during the construction phase of the project may have an effect on the timely completion of the works. The most important interfaces specific to construction and covered under the construction contract will be those between the technologies used in the works, the construction methods adopted and the presence of multiple subcontractors on the site, each needing access to site facilities and the works. However, the project interfaces between the construction contractor and the other project participants are not caught by the normal risk allocation of a turnkey construction contract. These interfaces must be managed by the project company either through its own intervention or through the project documents.

10.3.1   Operator

An important relationship which will need to be managed very carefully is that between the construction contractor and the operator. Problems arise particularly during the commissioning of the works and the performance testing.

The construction contractor is responsible for the care of the works during the construction period. Generally, after the works have achieved completion, they are handed over, in this case to the operator. Once the works are handed over, the operator takes responsibility for the care of the works, although the construction contractor will remain on site to carry out the performance tests and to fulfil its obligations during the defects liability period. Therefore the operator, although it is responsible for care of the works after completion, must allow for the construction contractor's presence on the site and its intervention in the works in order to fulfil its various responsibilities. This may involve extensive contact between the operator and the construction contractor, meriting a separate regime for management and sharing of risk.

Furthermore, projects often involve several sections, each to be completed at a different time. This is done to permit staggered and fast-track project completion, enabling, for example, the testing and commissioning team to complete its work on one unit and then begin immediately on the next. In such cases, the first section to be completed will be handed over to the operator before the second section has been completed, leaving a period during which the construction contractor will bear the risk for one section and the operator will bear the risk for the other. During this overlap period, the respective responsibilities of the operator and the construction contractor will need to be defined in detail, for example site security or waste removal responsibilities. To avoid duplication or impediment, these responsibilities should be considered carefully in both the construction contract and the operation and maintenance agreement.

10.3.2   Offtake purchaser

The construction contractor may also have certain dealings with the offtake purchaser. Although the primary intervention of the offtake purchaser in the project will not occur until operation begins, certain interfaces will take place earlier. The first such interface involves the connection of the project by the construction contractor to the offtake purchaser's transmission or transportation facilities (where relevant).

The responsibility for equipment to connect the project to the offtake purchaser's facilities will generally be divided between the offtake purchaser and the construction contractor. The point of connection between the two will involve a technical interface, although preferably a relatively minor one. The construction contractor may also be asked to provide the equipment that will be used to test and measure the output of the project during operation. This equipment will be of great interest to the offtake purchaser, as it will measure the quantity and quality of the offtake for which it will have to pay.

While the commissioning and performance testing is being carried out by the construction contractor, it may be necessary for the offtake purchaser's facilities to be available before such testing can occur. For example, performance tests on a power plant cannot be carried out unless the grid and the offtake purchaser's facilities are available and sufficient to receive the energy generated. Output may be produced during testing which the offtake purchaser can purchase. However, the output produced will be of an indeterminable amount, therefore a special purchasing regime, where appropriate, may need to be developed. The performance tests may also include testing of the connection of the project with the offtake purchaser's facilities.

The offtake purchaser will share a portion of the performance risk with the construction contractor. The offtake purchaser will be responsible for any defect in its facilities which impedes the performance of the project or where its instructions to the project company in relation to operation of the project and the output required have a negative effect on performance. This latter is the case in power or water projects where sustained or repeated shut-downs are required. Start-up of the plant will generally be costly and may impede efficient performance of the project.

During operation, the offtake purchaser will periodically schedule for its facilities to be shut down for maintenance and repairs. Where, during the defects liability period, the construction contractor needs to perform repairs or replacements which might interrupt the performance of the project, the project company will want to co-ordinate such repairs with the scheduled shut-down periods mandated by the offtake purchaser in order to reduce impact on the operation of the project.

10.3.3   Input supplier

The construction contractor will liaise with the input supplier during the carrying out of the completion and performance tests, as the construction contractor will need to have delivered to the site the correct quantities and quality of input. Any failure on the part of the input supplier will delay and disrupt the tests to be carried out and may therefore affect the completion or performance of the project.

Further interfaces may arise where input supplier infrastructure is to be built, possibly as part of the works. The construction contractor and the input supplier may need to co-ordinate on design, construction and management.

10.4   Completion and Performance

There are a number of issues to be considered in relation to completion of the works and performance of the construction contractor's obligations when drafting a construction contract in the context of a BOT project.

10.4.1   Scope of works

The work which the construction contractor is obliged to perform under the contract will be defined by the contractual scope of works. The scope of works generally involves a detailed description of the works, their properties, and the equipment and materials to be used in construction. In certain cases this may also include a description of the type of equipment the construction contractor is to use in performing the works. As noted earlier, the turnkey approach may give the construction contractor an incentive to under-design the works and use cheaper materials in construction. The scope of works is one place where the project company can define added quality into the works.

The project company will develop the scope of the works in accordance with its need for a project that will be easy to maintain and operate and one that will last without extensive reworking through to the end of the concession period. The grantor, on the other hand, will also have some say in the scope of works and may place requirements on the project company under the concession agreement to use certain equipment or materials in an attempt to ensure that the project's life is sufficient to satisfy the grantor's needs. The grantor's needs may be more onerous than those of the project company, as the grantor may want to use the works well beyond the end of the concession period. The grantor may also be more interested in locally sourced goods. Such grantor requirements will need to be passed through back-to-back into the construction contract.

10.4.2   Design

The project design will be developed in accordance with the project company's requirements, as specified in the construction contract. The construction contract will also specify, as part of the project company's requirements, any special technical requirements imposed by the grantor in the concession agreement, or by any of the other project participants, for example the environmental standards to be applied to the project.

Neither the grantor nor the lenders will be willing to bear any of the design risk for the project, which will include any design contained in the project company's requirements. Therefore, design risk will be passed on to the construction contractor, which is considered a reasonable allocation of risk given the construction contractor's expertise in design and its knowledge of the technology to be used.

It is essential that the construction contract set out responsibility for the documentation, design and requirements provided by the project company. The project company may provide some information basic to the design of the project and the lenders will be anxious to avoid the risk for this information. There may be some third party against which the project company has recourse for this information or design, such as a design consultant or the provider of a process licence.[318] The lenders will then need to verify that the liability and the financial viability of the third party are sufficient to cover the risk involved. Alternatively, and more commonly, the lenders may require the construction contractor to bear the whole of the risk for the design, including that provided by the project company.

10.4.3   Quality assurance

The parties will need to establish a quality assurance regime; providing systems, processes and procedures which work together in order to provide a customer with products and services consistent with defined quality standards. The International Organisation for Standardisation has produced a series of model form quality standards. The ISO 9000 series is an internationally adopted quality assurance specification which contains five distinct but complementary standards: ISO 9000, ISO 9001, ISO 9002, ISO 9003 and ISO 9004.[319] ISO 9000 was developed in 1987 and revised in 1994. The series of standards includes 20 conformance areas covering issues such as design and management procedures, document and data control, and inspection and testing.[320]

---

[318]   Scriven, "A Banking Perspective on Construction Risks in BOT Schemes" [1994] ICLR 313 at 324.

[319]   Klafter and Huntley Walker, Legal Practice Management and Quality Standards at 20 (1995).

[320]   Gibbons and Moser, Quality Assurance: ISO 9000 Standards (presentation 23 November 1997 at www.cs.unr.edu).

The quality assurance system will place requirements on the construction contractor to ensure the quality of the works and the finished product. The applicable system will generally be appended to the construction contract.

10.4.4   Site risk

The allocation of site risk will depend on the nature of the parties and their expertise. Site conditions, such as geographical, geological and hydrological conditions, are difficult to define with great accuracy, even after extensive site investigations. Manmade obstructions or conditions may be dealt with separately when allocating this risk, because they are even more difficult to assess accurately by site investigations. As a general rule, the party with the greatest knowledge and best ability to verify and test the site conditions should be responsible for them. This knowledge must also include an understanding of the needs and particularities of the design of the works.

Site condition risk allocation is often based on the foreseeability of the risk at the time of contract. As noted, however, site conditions are extremely difficult to anticipate with any accuracy. One option, in an effort to allocate site risk reasonably, is for the parties to define the anticipated ground conditions, based on previous tests and other relevant information. Where actual conditions are different from those anticipated, the project company bears the risk of any increase in cost or delay. This method is often used for tunnelling work, given its particular sensitivity to ground conditions.

In practice, the grantor will generally allocate this risk to the project company who will pass it on to the construction contractor. At the end of the day, this approach may be the most reasonable. The grantor is not usually in a position to judge site conditions against the needs of the technology to be used by the construction contractor. The construction contractor is therefore given the site "as is". Any losses incurred due to site conditions will be to the charge of the construction contractor, who can gather information with the knowledge of the specific needs of the project design and its own construction techniques. An exception to this practice is where the grantor provides the site and has particular knowledge of site conditions or is best placed to obtain such knowledge.

Generally, the construction contractor bears the responsibility for any damage that may occur to the site, to neighbouring property or to equipment, materials and persons on or near the site in relation to the performance of its obligations (in particular, its obligation for care of the works).

10.4.5   Completion and takeover

The construction contract will define when the project is sufficiently complete to pass the care for the works (responsibility for the site and the works) to the operator and to relieve the construction contractor of its liability for liquidated damages for late completion. Therefore, the definition of "completion" will often include a certain level of minimum performance capacity. This is done to ensure compliance with the minimum requirements of the offtake purchaser and to generate sufficient revenues to satisfy fixed costs, including debt servicing. Until this level of performance is reached to the satisfaction of the project company's representative, the project company will not want to lose its right to claim liquidated damages from the construction contractor for late completion.

As a general rule, the financing for a BOT project is non-recourse.[321] The lenders may require further sponsor support, in particular during the construction phase of the works (for example, where the shareholders provide guarantees of completion) as the construction phase generally involves the greatest amount of project risk. For this reason the recourse available to the lenders may decrease after completion. The lenders will therefore want to ensure that the requirements for completion are sufficiently extensive to protect their interests.

The lenders will be interested in the allocation of responsibility for the works during the period of transfer between the construction contractor and the operator. This transfer may cover an extended period, where the works are taken over section by section. The lenders will want to ensure that there is no gap in responsibility for the works, and that overlapping responsibilities do not inhibit efficient operation of the project.

Where the parties choose to allow taking-over of sections, the project company should consider the relationship between the sections and their interdependency. For example, under a combined cycle turbine power plant, the completion of the first unit, the gas turbine and any common facilities should be made provisional until it can be tested together with the second unit, the steam turbine and any common facilities, as the two must function together properly. Completion would, therefore, require completion and operation of both sections together to ensure that any interfaces between the sections have been properly constructed.

10.4.6   Tests on completion

Tests on completion are those tests to be performed on the works to demonstrate their completion. The construction contract must establish when the tests are performed, what the tests entail, who carries out the tests, who analyses the data obtained, what is required to pass the tests, and how and when tests may be repeated. Tests on completion will often be combined with, or closely linked to, performance tests. The lenders may want to oversee the carrying out of tests on completion and review the data obtained from such tests.

The construction contract is likely to impose a minimum performance level, which may be part of completion. In this way, the construction contractor will need to satisfy the minimum performance level before being relieved of liability for delay liquidated damages and any other completion related liabilities. Performance tests are then carried out to test whether the works achieve target performance levels.

---

[321]   See section 4.3.

10.4.7 Performance tests

The construction contractor will often bear the majority of the risk that the works will not perform to the target levels required. This risk is generally allocated by placing performance criteria in the construction contract and requiring the works to pass specified performance tests to ensure the performance of the works in accordance with the performance criteria. If the works fail such tests, the construction contractor will be exposed to performance liquidated damages up to an amount relative to any costs and damages incurred by the project company due to poor performance. The project company will want these liquidated damages to cover back-to-back any damages that would be incurred through other agreements, such as the offtake purchase agreement, and to compensate the project company for lost income. The amounts paid to the project company for shortfalls in performance may need to be used to prepay debt due to the long-term effect poor performance may have on the project payment stream and cover ratios.

Just as for tests on completion, the construction contract will need to define when the performance tests are to be performed, who will perform them and what the tests will entail. The construction contract will also need to specify how the tests are to be performed, who will analyse the data obtained, what is required to pass the tests, and whether and how such tests can be repeated. The project company will generally want its representative to be involved in any testing and confirmation that tests have been passed.

10.4.8 Language

The parties will want to identify the language of the agreement, and how that language will be applied. For example, it will be necessary to establish a language for communications between the construction contractor and the project company, the language of documents to be provided to the project company and the language for day-to-day communications.

Once such language has been established, the obligation and cost of translation (where necessary) will need to be allocated. This issue may be heavily negotiated given that the resulting cost can represent a substantial sum, particularly in projects where a large number of communications or documents will be exchanged. Documents to be handed over to the project company, such as operation and maintenance manuals which may have been drafted originally in several languages by various suppliers and subcontractors, may also have to be translated. Such translations will require the assistance of highly skilled technical translators, further increasing the cost of such an undertaking.

10.5 Time

Timely completion is important for any construction project; and in particular for BOT projects where multiple parties depend on completion of the works. The construction contract needs to manage time carefully.

10.5.1   Time for completion and project programme

The project programme will be of increased importance in a BOT project when compared with a typical construction project. This is due primarily to the number of other agreements which rely on the programme. For example, in a BOT power project, if completion of a given unit of the plant is not achieved within the period set out in the project programme, the following aspects of the project may be delayed:

> ➤ commencement of the operation and maintenance agreement;

> ➤ deliveries of input from the input supplier;

> ➤ receipt of energy by the offtake purchaser, affecting its grid programme;

> ➤ payments from the offtake purchaser;

> ➤ payments of debt servicing, as well as drawdowns scheduled from the lenders and possibly injections of equity contributions from the shareholders; and

> ➤ the project programme which may result in damages payable under the concession agreement.

Because of the potential substantial impact of failure to satisfy the project programme, the project company will prefer to place this risk squarely on the shoulders of the construction contractor. This allocation of risk is based on the lenders' unwillingness to bear risk over which it has little direct control and the construction contractor's experience and skill in this area which will allow it to manage best the timing of the construction work and co-ordinate construction programmes to meet the project programme, and therefore the contractual time for completion.

It is commonly accepted that the construction contractor will not be responsible for delays caused by certain types of events outside its control. This risk allocation is generally set out in the *force majeure* clause and the series of risks placed on the project company specific to its project obligations. Potential causes of delay which will frequently entitle the construction contractor to an extension of the time for completion include:

> ➤ a variation order issued by the project company which leads to a delay in the completion of the works;

> ➤ a suspension order issued by the project company (other than when the project company issues such an order owing to the construction contractor's default);

> ➤ a delay, impediment or prevention by the project company;

> ➤ failure by the project company to provide access to or possession of the site;

> ➤ an event of *force majeure* as defined by the construction contract;

> ➤ failure of the local government authorities to issue building, import or other permits and licences on a timely basis where the obligation to provide such permissions belongs to the project company; and

> ➤ the discovery of fossils or antiquities on the site.

The circumstances which entitle the construction contractor to an extension of time will depend entirely on the risk and task allocation established in the construction contract. These same issues will be relevant to the construction contractor's entitlement to an increase in the contract price as discussed in section 10.6 below. As a general rule, the construction contractor will receive an extension of time for any delay caused by a breach by the project company of its contractual obligations.[322]

10.5.2 Late completion

The project company will be extremely sensitive to the risk of late completion of the works as the lost revenues caused by late completion can be extensive. Further, the other obligations taken on by the project company, such as the offtake purchase and the input supply agreements, may provide for some penalty relative to late completion of the works. Timely completion may also be of importance to the grantor, therefore the concession agreement may include penalties for late completion.

To protect itself from these and other liabilities the project company can use a variety of tools to penalise the construction contractor and create an incentive for timely completion. The methods used will apply either during the construction period, when the construction contractor falls behind its projected programme, or at the end of the contractual time for completion, once the construction contractor is late in completion. Two of the more common methods are outlined below.

10.5.2.1 Holdbacks

The project company may choose to hold back certain payments where the progress of the construction contractor is insufficient to satisfy the programme set out in the construction contract. These holdbacks will be consistent with the value of the work which has not been completed as scheduled or the potential damage which the project company is likely to incur owing to a delay. Holdbacks may be measured either by a set periodic penalty, similar to the type of calculation used for liquidated damages (see below), or at the discretion of the project company, the project company's representative or an independent engineer.

Holdbacks may be inconsistent with the interests of both the construction contractor and the project company. Where the construction contractor is delayed

---

[322] Failure to provide for this in the construction contract may release the construction contractor from the specified dates for completion, and require the construction contractor to complete the works in a "reasonable" time, also known as "time at large". This is the case under English law. Supply of Goods and Services Act 1982.

in completion of the works, it may need all of its resources either to accelerate progress or avoid further delays. If payments are held back, the construction contractor's resources may be adversely affected, causing further delays, further holdbacks and a cash flow spiral ending in the complete failure of the construction contract.

10.5.2.2   Liquidated damages and bonuses

The project company may provide for liquidated damages to sanction late completion. The applicable law may place limits on the level of liquidated damages which can be imposed. Under English law, these sums must be the exclusive liability for the delay and represent a reasonable pre-estimate of the amount of damages that the party will incur.[323] A similar standard applies in the United States.[324] In other jurisdictions the courts may have the power to open up and revise contractual levels of liquidated damages where they are not reasonable.[325]

Liquidated damages allow the injured party to receive the relevant amounts without having to make reference to an arbitrator or a national court (although this may not be true in every jurisdiction). For example, construction contracts often provide that for each day completion is delayed beyond the time for completion, or a specific construction task has not been completed in accordance with the project programme, the construction contractor must pay a given sum. This amount can then either be set off against sums due to the construction contractor or treated as a debt due.

If properly drafted, the liquidated damages provision of a construction contract will provide the construction contractor with a powerful incentive to complete the project on time and will clearly apportion the financial responsibility for late completion.

From the perspective of the project company, in the event of late completion due to construction contractor default, the construction contractor should be obliged to pay liquidated damages in an amount equal to or greater than the amount of the delay payments the project company will be required to make, including liability for debt servicing.

The construction contract will generally apply a cap to the amount of liquidated damages chargeable to the construction contractor. This cap generally ranges from 10-50 per cent. of the contract price. The project company should have the right to terminate for construction contractor breach once the cap has been reached and if the delay continues.

---

[323]   Chitty on Contracts at 26-061 (27th edition 1994).

[324]   For example, 36 N.Y. Jur. 2d Damages §154 (2002); Consolidated Rail Corp. v MASP Equip. Corp. (1986) 67 NY2d 35, 499 NYS2d 657, 490 NE2d 514.

[325]   For example, article 1152 of the French Civil Code as amended by law no. 75-597 of 9 July 1975.

The construction contractor may also receive bonuses for early completion. This will only be appropriate where and to the extent that early completion provides a benefit to the project company, for example where the offtake purchase agreement provides for the early purchase of output where the project is completed ahead of schedule. Bonus provisions often work in the same way as liquidated damages, providing bonus payments for each day completion is achieved ahead of the time for completion.

10.5.3   Defects liability period

After completion of the construction of the works, the operator will take over care of the works (the responsibility to secure and protect the site and for any event on site unless otherwise stipulated). For a period (usually at least one year, in order to verify that seasonal changes do not affect the works) after completion the construction contractor will remain responsible for the remedy of defects in the works. The period during which the construction contractor is liable for defects is generally called the "defects liability period" although it may also go under the name of "maintenance period" or "warranty period".

This responsibility may be limited to defects for which the construction contractor is responsible or may include any defect which might arise. Under the former, the construction contractor only remedies those defects which are specifically its responsibility and will do so at its cost. Under the latter, the construction contractor must remedy any and every defect which arises and at its own cost. For all remedial work performed for which the construction contractor is not responsible, the project company must compensate the construction contractor for the cost of remedy. The project company may prefer the latter regime, as the construction contractor will know the project and therefore will be able to provide the most cost and time effective remedy.

The length of the defects liability period will depend on the nature of the works and commercial practice in the site country, but will generally last from one to five years (possibly longer for civil works). It is in the project company's and the lenders' interests to keep this duty with the construction contractor for the longest period possible, although an unreasonably long defects liability period may add substantially to the price of the construction contract. The construction contractor should be required to maintain equipment on the site sufficient to comply with its defects liability obligations.

10.5.4   Latent defects

Besides those defects which arise during the defects liability period, the project company may want the construction contractor to be responsible for hidden or latent defects which do not become apparent until after the end of the defects liability period. These latent defects will often be covered for a set period after completion. The construction contractor will then have the option of remedying the defect itself, having another contractor remedy the defect or having the project company remedy the defect to the construction contractor's account. Liability periods will be set by the applicable law or by the parties under the construction contract. It should be noted that in certain circumstances, the liability period may be mandated under the applicable law, even where alternative arrangements have been made under the construction contract.[326]

10.6   Price and Payment

To provide certainty of financial exposure during the risk laden construction phase of the project, the project company will need a fixed price construction contract, with only limited opportunity to open up that price.

10.6.1   Contract price

As noted above, the lenders will want a fixed price for the construction contract, which will be important for the development of an accurate financial model for the project. In general, the risk of an increase in construction costs will be borne by the construction contractor. However, there are a number of situations in which the risk of a price increase may be borne by one of the other project participants.

To ensure that the construction contract reflects the principle of a fixed price contract and to define clearly the circumstances in which the contract price can be changed, the lenders may require that each event allowing the construction contractor to request an increase in the contract price be specifically identified in the contract. These events are generally similar or identical to those entitling the construction contractor to an extension of time for completion.[327]

10.6.2   Payment

Payments of the contract price to the construction contractor will generally be based on the completion of milestone events. As noted above, the use of milestones allows the project company to motivate the construction contractor to complete in a timely and reasonable fashion. Milestones enable the lenders to ensure that drawdowns are used in a reasonable manner and that they are made only against completed work which benefits and adds value to the project. It should be noted that certain export credit agencies (for example, ECGD) require that payment be made to their national supplier once that supplier has performed its obligations. This may be inconsistent with the milestone payment schedule that is imposed on the construction contractor, and therefore an exceptional payment may be needed.

To provide the construction contractor with the necessary liquidity during the early phases of construction, when costs for services such as basic design and site investigations can be considerable, the construction contract may provide for an advance payment soon after commencement. The project company may require the construction contractor to provide a bond against repayment of the advance

---

[326]   For example, decennial liability in France, see article 1792 of the French Civil Code.
[327]   See section 10.5.1, above.

payment. The lenders may prefer this advance payment to come from an equity contribution by the shareholders.

As added security, the project company will retain a certain percentage of each payment as retention monies, in order to provide security for completion and incentive for the construction contractor to complete on time. This security is generally provided as a percentage of all payments, for example 5 or 10 per cent., with half released to the construction contractor on completion and the other half at the end of the defects liability period. The construction contractor may prefer to provide a retention bond in place of the retention monies in order to support the construction contractor's liquidity and encourage cash neutrality.

The payment regime for a typical BOT project will resemble the chart below. For ease of reference, this chart is a simplification of an otherwise complex regime. During the construction phase, contributions towards the cost of construction are made to the project company by a combination of equity and debt injections, generally made against milestones or other demonstration of progress. The construction contractor is similarly paid through milestone payments.

During operation, once the payment stream has begun, project operation costs and inputs will be paid out of fixed and variable payments from the offtake purchaser. Debt servicing will be paid out of the fixed charge while equity return will be paid out of a combination of the fixed and variable charges.

CONTRIBUTION AND REVENUE STREAM
CONSTRUCTION PHASE

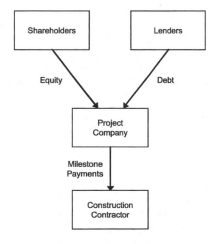

OPERATION PHASE

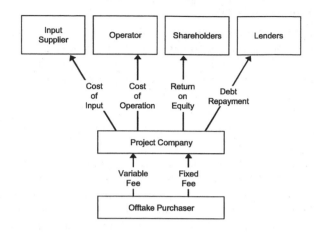

10.6.3   Bonds, guarantees and retention

When passing the project risk on to the construction contractor, the lenders will want to obtain guarantees and bonds from other parties in order to protect their interests. As noted earlier, these guarantees and bonds are generally more defensive than offensive, used to encourage the parties to perform and protect the lenders' interests against the acts of other creditors.

These guarantees and bonds can take several forms.

10.6.3.1   Advance payment bond

The lenders will generally condition drawdowns of loans during the construction period to proof of successful progress of the project. However, an advance payment may be made in a sum sufficient to cover part or all of the construction contractor's costs during the early stages of preparation and construction. Generally the project company will require the construction contractor to provide a bond in the amount of any advance payment it is to receive as security for the eventual recuperation of the advance payment.

10.6.3.2   Performance bond

The construction contractor is generally obligated to provide a performance bond. The amount of the performance bond, often relative to the amount of risk borne by the lenders and the financial status of the construction contractor, will generally fall within a range of 5-50 per cent. of the overall contract price. A performance bond of 10-25 per cent. of the contract price is average.

10.6.3.3   Retention monies

The project company may also retain a certain percentage (often in the region of five per cent.) of each payment made to the construction contractor, which is generally released half after completion and half after the end of the defects liability period. These funds are known as "retention monies". The project company may allow the construction contractor to provide a bond in lieu of the retention monies, known as a "retention bond". This will improve the construction contractor's cash flow without reducing the security available to the project company.

10.6.3.4 Parent company guarantee

Where a subsidiary acts as the construction contractor (frequently desirable to avoid withholding tax in certain jurisdictions), the project company may want to have a guarantee from the parent company for the subsidiary's obligations under the construction contract. This guarantee will normally cover both payment and performance obligations and will create a primary obligation on behalf of the parent company.[328]

10.6.3.5 Form of bond

Where bonds are provided as guarantees, the project company will generally require on-demand bonds to ensure its ability to call the amount of the bond without interference from the construction contractor. On-demand bonds allow the beneficiary to draw on the bond on demand without the guarantor of the bond verifying that the amounts claimed are due.[329]

10.6.4   Limitation of liability

Construction contractors will often seek to limit their liability under the construction contract. This limit may take the form of a provision relieving either party from responsibility for consequential or economic loss that may result from any breach, such as loss of profit or lost market share. Any such waiver should exclude liquidated damages, third party loss indemnities and other provisions specifically intended to protect the project company against loss of profit (its own, or a third party's). The contract may also place a cap on the maximum aggregate liability of the construction contractor under the contract and/or at law (as far as possible).

The lenders may want the cap of the construction contractor's liability to be increased in line with any increase in the contract price. They may apply different considerations to any liability for termination of the construction contract for construction contractor default or for breach of the construction contract owing to wilful or gross misconduct (which will be defined either by law or in the construction contract) on the part of the construction contractor.

---

[328]   For further discussion of key issues in relation to parent company guarantees, see Wood, Comparative Law of Security Guarantees (1995).

[329]   For further discussion of bonds and guarantees, see chapter 24 of Scriven, Pritchard and Delmon (1999) supra note 210.

10.6.5   Joint and several liability

Where the construction contractor is a group of contractors acting through a joint venture, the project company may require that the joint venture partners be jointly and severally liable. This means that where any liability arises among the joint venture partners, the project company will be able to claim compensation of the whole of the construction contractor's liability from any one of the joint venture partners.[330] This structure may have to be implemented through joint and several parent company guarantees where the consortium operates through a joint venture vehicle.

10.7   Additional Considerations

Further provisions with specific relevance to BOT projects may need to be included in the construction contract.

10.7.1   Procurement restrictions

The construction contractor will need to be conscious of procurement restrictions imposed by the lenders (such as the IFC and the EBRD), the grantor or the host country government on projects undertaken within its jurisdiction. This will generally involve some effort to use local subcontractors or suppliers, or possibly a direct restriction requiring the use of a certain percentage of locally sourced materials and labour where possible or reasonable. The concession agreement will often include such restrictions because part of the grantor's interest in the project is the opportunity to transfer technology and know-how to its local businesses and nationals. The grantor may be very strict about such procurement arrangements and may wish to oversee the local involvement in the construction of the works.

10.7.2   Subcontracting

It is common for the construction contractor to subcontract certain of the works. The project company and the grantor will want to ensure that the quality of work to be obtained from the subcontractor is in compliance with the project requirements and up to the standards expected of the construction contractor. The project company and the grantor will not wish to lose security of quality through the subcontracting of the works. The project company will also want to ensure that any proposed subcontractor complies with any requirements under the concession agreement.

The lenders and project company may restrict the construction contractor's right to subcontract the works or may list works which may not be subcontracted. The project company is likely to require any proposed subcontract over a maximum value to be submitted for its approval.

---

[330]   Chitty (27th edition 1994) supra note 323 at 17-001.

10.7.3 Independent engineer

As noted above, the lenders or the grantor may wish to enrol the assistance of an independent engineer. Rather than allow this independent engineer discretionary access to the works for inspection and testing purposes, it may be less intrusive to involve the engineer in supervision of the testing procedures or in inspection and testing of the works (either on a pre-defined schedule or with some reasonable notice period). The role of the independent engineer may provide an acceptable compromise for the lenders and the grantor to provide oversight while making an effort to reduce the chance of interference in and delay of the performance of the works.

10.7.4 Training and operation manuals

It is sometimes the case in BOT projects that the operator is not entirely familiar with the technology used by the construction contractor. This is generally the case where the operator is required to employ grantor personnel, who may not have relevant experience. For this reason a training regime is often required from the construction contractor to instruct the operator's personnel about the operation and maintenance of the facility. This training will be more or less comprehensive depending on the knowledge and the experience of the operator.

The extent of the training required, as well as the responsibility of the parties for the personnel during training, and damage such personnel may cause or injury they may sustain during such time, must be set out in detail to avoid disputes about the nature of the training and liability at later stages of completion. Training will generally occur either during or shortly before commissioning, in order to take advantage of the near complete state of the project.

The construction contractor will also need to provide the operator with manuals explaining the operation of the project and the maintenance requirements. These are commonly known as "operation and maintenance manuals" and are generally required to be provided by the construction contractor to the operator at or shortly after completion.

10.7.5 Transfer of title and risk

The construction contract will need to define at what point title in the equipment and materials brought on site for use in the works transfers to the project company. In general, title will transfer once the construction contractor has received payment for equipment and materials or where such equipment and materials have been delivered to the site.

A related, although distinctly separate, question is when risk of the works transfers from the construction contractor to the operator. As noted above, the risk of the works transfers from the project company to the construction contractor at commencement of the construction contract. At completion, ideally, risk transfers to the operator until transfer to the grantor or another operator at the end of the concession period. At no time should risk of the works revert to the project company, subject to certain specific project company risks or termination for project company breach or suspension of the construction contract or operation and maintenance agreement.

Chapter 11

Splitting Turnkey Construction Contracts

United we stand, divided we fall.

Motto of the Commonwealth of Kentucky,
adapted from "The Liberty Song"
by John Dickinson

As discussed in chapter 10, turnkey construction contracts provide an effective method of managing risk within a construction project and imposing construction risks on the construction contractor. They place on one contractor responsibility for the design, procurement, installation, construction and commissioning of the whole of the works. The project company benefits from the single point responsibility of one contractor for the whole of the works, at a more or less fixed price and within a more or less fixed time for completion.

However, in some jurisdictions, turnkey contracts performed in that country have the unfortunate habit of increasing the tax liabilities of the construction contractor and consequently increasing the overall cost of construction.[331] Also, the performance of one turnkey construction contract on works that straddle several jurisdictions can have unfortunate tax implications, exposing the construction contractor to tax liability on the combined value of works in different jurisdictions and causing problems in the taxation of asset management.

In such circumstances, the parties may wish to consider splitting the single turnkey construction contract into a number of separate construction contracts, with work performed by separate companies in the various jurisdictions rather than by branches of a single construction contractor.[332] This split would be implemented

---

[331]   See also, chapter 9 of Scriven, Pritchard and Delmon (1999) supra note 210.

[332]   The performance of works by branches located in different jurisdictions or subcontracted to companies in those jurisdictions will not achieve the desired effect. It is the use of a single contract for these different works that attracts the adverse tax treatment.

so as to manage the risks related to tax exposure and other costs while maintaining the "turnkey" nature of the construction arrangements. The split structure is not simple to formulate and can require a significant amount of time and effort to implement.

This chapter discusses some of the most important issues which arise in relation to splitting turnkey construction contracts, introducing the types of contracts which may need to be split, the advantages of a turnkey contract which can be lost in the process of a split, the mechanics of splitting turnkey construction contracts, those areas where the project company's contractual position would be weakened by a split contract structure and the mechanisms available to manage the consequent risks while maintaining the benefits of a single turnkey construction contract.[333]

11.1   Domestic Contracts

Some tax authorities treat materials and engineering services sourced within their own jurisdiction differently from materials and engineering services sourced "offshore". Different tax rates may apply or, in many cases, additional taxes (for example, business taxes, stamp duty, works taxes, or service taxes) may apply to one or the other. The tax authorities in these jurisdictions may also treat certain activities, onshore or offshore, differently. For example, different tax rates (in particular sales tax) may apply to the various engineering, procurement and construction services to be performed.

These same tax authorities may view a turnkey construction contract which combines different services, from onshore and/or offshore sources, as one single commercial activity. In such circumstances it may be very difficult to identify which tax rates apply to which parts of the turnkey contract, and they may therefore apply higher tax rates to the value of the whole of the turnkey contract. This tax treatment can result in an increase of 5 per cent. or more to the contract price.

In addition, the contractor may not wish to create a permanent establishment in the jurisdiction. The contractor may be deemed or required to create such an establishment as the result of performing works that exceed a certain value or duration in that jurisdiction. This could subject the contractor to additional corporate tax in the jurisdiction and withholding and other taxes on any profits repatriated from that jurisdiction. The foreign jurisdiction would generally be entitled to tax the permanent establishment on the part of the contractor's profits attributable to that permanent establishment. There may also be uncertainty about apportionment methods with an element of double taxation of profits where only part of the works performed under a single contract would justify a permanent establishment. The tax authority may tax the whole of the works as if they were performed by the permanent establishment even where part of the works are

---

[333]   This chapter is adapted from an article published in the International Construction Law Review in 2003, Delmon, "Splitting Up Is Hard To Do: How to Manage Fiscally Challenged Turnkey Contracts".

performed offshore. This problem is particularly acute where there is no double taxation agreement between the jurisdictions in which the head office and permanent establishment are situated, but can also occur where a double taxation agreement exists if the mutual agreement or reciprocity provisions between the contracting states do not work effectively.

Thus, onshore work is performed by existing permanent establishments while offshore works remain with foreign companies to avoid such tax liabilities. Use of local companies is less likely to result in excess apportionment of profits to overseas operations although many jurisdictions with sophisticated tax systems can use transfer-pricing provisions to protect their tax base. Further, the foreign contractor may not have sufficient nexus with the jurisdiction to become VAT registerable, and therefore would be unable to claim any input tax credit for VAT paid on purchases. For ease of reference, the projects described in this section will be called "Domestic Contracts" in this chapter.

The approach used for the split of Domestic Contracts will depend primarily on the relevant tax regime and how division of the works will result in the most advantageous tax treatment. Moving works, and therefore part of the contract price, between the different split contracts, can make a significant difference in total tax exposure, justifying careful consideration of the options available for the split structure. Also, however, the parties will want to avoid liabilities, sometimes criminal, for tax evasion due to a split structure that is unreasonable or overly aggressive.

It should also be noted that, particularly in the case of Domestic Contracts, the project company may be subject to procurement restrictions, such as public procurement regimes. The splitting of the Domestic Contract may require multiple public tenders to comply with those restrictions, complicating the procurement process and increasing costs for the project company and the contractor. These procurement restrictions need to be managed from commencement of the procurement process.

An example of a split Domestic Contract would be the construction of a power plant in a country whose tax treatment of turnkey contracts justifies a split contract structure. The construction of the power plant would involve a combination of civil and mechanical/electrical engineering, design and construction performed onshore and offshore which, in our example, each attracts a different rate of taxation. The high value of materials and equipment sourced offshore – such as boilers and turbines – will make this project particularly vulnerable to differing tax rates and the aggregation of the contract prices for tax purposes.

In this example, the turnkey contract might be split between five different contracts:

> an offshore equipment procurement contract – for sourcing the equipment to be obtained outside the jurisdiction;

> an offshore engineering contract – for design and engineering work performed outside the jurisdiction, where taxation tends to be lower;

> ➢ an offshore project management contract – for head office, management and other overheads, possibly including management performed in the jurisdiction but only to the extent that such onshore activities will not affect the tax treatment of the contract;

> ➢ an onshore civil works contract – for all construction work to be performed in the jurisdiction, possibly including receipt, assembly and installation of equipment sourced offshore; and

> ➢ an onshore engineering contract – for any design work that must be performed onshore, for example local planning and zoning issues.

These contracts would need to work together to deliver to the project company, on a turnkey basis, the power plant in the time allotted, at the agreed price and performing in accordance with the project specification. From their descriptions it is quite clear that the interfaces between these contracts are significant. They do not contemplate isolated or separable sections of the works, but instead represent interdependent and interrelated elements of an integrated system. The potential for gaps between or loopholes in these contracts is substantial.

11.2   International Contracts

In other cases, a turnkey construction project may involve works located in several jurisdictions, such as a pipeline, power transmission cable or fibre optic cable. An example would be the construction of a fibre optic telecommunications network that stretches across several countries, including submarine fibre-rings crossing significant bodies of water, with backhaul to a number of terrestrial landing stations in different countries. The construction of the works would involve civil works for the construction of stations and the installation of ducts, the procurement and installation of network operating centres, maintenance facilities, terrestrial fibre optic cables and associated electronics, and the procurement, armouring and laying of submarine fibre optic cable. The whole would be tested and would operate as a single unit. For ease of reference, these multi-jurisdictional projects will be called "International Contracts" in this chapter.

One single turnkey construction contract for a project like this with works located in several jurisdictions can raise a number of practical and tax issues. Each tax authority will need to assess a value for the part of the works to be performed in its jurisdiction. It may assign that value to the relevant part of the turnkey contract price that corresponds to the work to be performed in that jurisdiction. However, that assessment may be difficult to make, and may not maximise tax receipts for the tax authority in the relevant jurisdiction. Therefore, the relevant tax authority may assign a value far higher through use of its own assessment criteria. For this reason, a single turnkey contract for an International Contract can be tax inefficient.

Further, once the works are complete, the project company may wish the assets to be owned by a local company. This will satisfy legal requirements in that jurisdiction, for example, where only a local company can obtain necessary licences, or where withholding or additional taxation on revenues earned on the assets in that jurisdiction are applied to foreign project companies or profit centres. However, transferring the completed assets from the foreign holding company (who would normally enter into the single turnkey construction contract) to the local asset company may attract transfer taxes and costs, reducing commercial efficiency.

In the above example, in order to manage the potential tax exposure of an International Contract, the parties may choose to split the works between one contract for those works located in international waters,[334] and different contracts for the works to be performed in each jurisdiction. The contract for works in international waters (the wet contract) can be located in a tax-friendly jurisdiction. Those contracts located in each jurisdiction (the dry contracts) will be limited to those assets in that jurisdiction, given that those jurisdictions will be likely to impose taxes at a higher rate than the tax-friendly jurisdiction of the wet contract.

SAMPLE OWNERSHIP/CONTRACT STRUCTURE FOR AN INTERNATIONAL CONTRACT

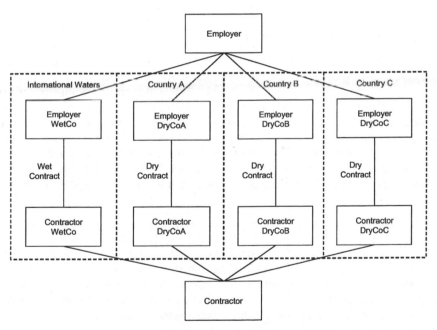

The project company will contract for dry services through its local subsidiaries, in order to avoid the need to transfer the completed work between subsidiaries with the resultant costs. The contractor will normally act through its local subsidiary, or

---

[334] The definition of "territorial waters" and "international waters" will depend on local law; however, international law provides guidance, in particular establishing the 12 nautical mile limit on "territorial waters". (UN Convention on Law of the Sea (1994))

may wish to endeavour to avoid having a local establishment by subcontracting most of the onshore work to local contractors and providing design and project management services sourced from offshore.

The contractor will provide construction services for assets located offshore through a single company, and the project company will similarly act through a single offshore vehicle. The companies used for wet services can be located in a tax-friendly jurisdiction, in particular where project revenues flow through that vehicle.

The dry and wet services provided by the contractor may also be subject to an umbrella contract (which may take the form of a guarantee). This umbrella contract would ensure that the several wet and dry contracts act together to provide the project company with a turnkey construction package, including single point responsibility, fixed price and a fixed time for completion.

Some of the dry contracts, to be performed in the individual jurisdictions, will need themselves to be split owing to that jurisdiction's tax treatment. This would arise where the relevant jurisdiction characterises the dry contract as a Domestic Contract.

11.3   Splitting Contracts

In order to manage the tax exposure inefficiencies inherent in Domestic and International Contracts, turnkey construction contracts and the relevant works are often split between two or more contracts. While the project company will be happy to take the benefit of the reduction in project costs resulting from the avoidance of the higher taxes and costs, it needs to appreciate that the division of the works between several contracts can, unless carefully managed, create additional risks for itself. These additional risks arise from the fact that a split contract structure results in separate scopes of work, with the contractors and the project company faced with separate rights and obligations in respect of different contracts.

These complexities can leave the project company exposed to a series of risks and liabilities that are inconsistent with the turnkey arrangements originally negotiated. As an example, any failure by one contractor to comply with its obligations could result in a non-defaulting contractor being entitled to raise claims for costs and/or an extension of time for completion in excess of that provided for under his contract. It could also provide the non-defaulting contractor with defences against claims brought by the project company in relation to its contract.

The goal of the project company is to ensure that the split contract structure imposes a seamless set of obligations on the split contractors in order to provide the finished works on a turnkey basis.

11.4　　　Setting the Terms

Splitting is usually an afterthought. In the normal course of events, the parties negotiate a single turnkey construction contract. It is generally only after negotiation of the single contract that the parties realise or address the potential benefit of splitting. The split is therefore usually done on a very tight timetable to avoid any delay to the construction programme. This places unfortunate time constraints on a process that will require significant thought and effort.

There may be some adjustment to the contract price for the split contract, to share the benefit of the resultant lower costs of the project between the project company and the contractor. Negotiating power will often lie with the party that has the least incentive to perform the splitting exercise, the one that will receive the least benefit from the split. The party receiving benefit from the split may be forced to share the benefit of the split in order to encourage the other parties to undertake a costly and time-consuming splitting process.

It may not be clear whether a split contract will achieve the desired effect in any given jurisdiction. There will generally be limited experience with split contracts that have been tested before the local courts or tax authority and therefore no precedent to support arguments as to the proper structure to adopt. Further, even where the works are split, the tax authorities may seek to levy duty on split works under the premise that those works are inextricably linked by nature. For example, services provided in relation to goods before importation into the relevant jurisdiction, like engineering and design, may be taxed at the rate of the imported goods even where those services are performed under a separate contract. Therefore much care and close attention by tax advisers will be important to the success of the tax structure and to protect against the risk that the structure will not protect the project against the potential tax liabilities. The contractor may also be required to provide certificates confirming compliance with withholding obligations and other such tax specific requirements (in particular to the extent any under-valuation would create liability in the project company as importer or owner of the goods or beneficiary of the services).

Regardless of legal theory, one commercial issue, which is often contentious in such arrangements, is the question of who should bear the risk of whether the split contract approach achieves the desired effect of insulating the project against additional tax exposure. The split contract structure is usually proposed by the contractor, given the potential reduction in the contractor's tax exposure. This suggests that the contractor should bear the risk associated with the structure he is proposing. The contractor has agreed and is paid for providing turnkey construction risk allocation. Any alteration to the contractual structure for tax purposes should not prejudice the turnkey nature of the construction arrangements.

11.5　　　Fixed Time for Completion

The project company will want the contractor to deliver all of the completed works by the completion date. The imposition of a single date is complicated by splitting the obligations between numerous separate contracts, each with a different time for completion and different specific circumstances which entitle the contractor to request an extension of that time. The split structure will need to knit these contracts together to maintain the fixed time for completion and the limited opportunities for extension of that time.

The contracts may also be subject to different legal systems and local dispute resolution forums. This is particularly true in International Contracts where each split contract may be subject to a different legal system. There is a risk that the contractor could be entitled under one of the contracts to an extension of time under the applicable law for circumstances that would not have entitled the contractor to an extension of time under the original single turnkey construction contract. It would not be appropriate for the time for completion of the project to be extended due to such a delay, or indeed due to a delay caused by the breach of one of the contractors.

One option is to place the obligation to deliver the works by the completion date on one of the contracts (the "Principal Contract"). The choice of the Principal Contract will depend on a number of legal and practical issues, for example the Principal Contract should be subject to a legal system familiar to the parties that places emphasis on the intention of the parties. The parties may prefer that the Principal Contract be subject to the most beneficial tax regime available, since a significant portion of the aggregate contract price may be allocated to that contract. The Principal Contractor should receive an extension of time only for delay under the Principal Contract, but not for any circumstances caused by the failure or breach of one of the other contractors. Any delay on the part of the other contractors in meeting their obligations would then not entitle the Principal Contractor to claim an extension of time in relation to the scheduled project completion date.

The Principal Contractor would therefore be required to deliver the completed works by a fixed date. The Principal Contractor would also be responsible to co-ordinate and receive delivery of the completed works from the other contractors and ensure that they interface properly with the works performed by him, and will therefore bear the risk of any delay of completion or delivery by any other contractor.

11.5.1   Co-ordination of work programmes

The plan of work for the single turnkey construction contract will need to be split to identify the scope of work for each of the contracts. The plan of work, in particular in relation to the construction programme, milestones and required permits, will need to be sufficiently detailed to identify the various time limitations which will apply to each of the contracts. Each of the contractors must have the obligation to deliver the required materials and equipment in such time as will enable the Principal Contractor to comply with its installation and completion obligations. Unfortunately, it will almost certainly be impossible, at the time the contracts are executed, to specify precise delivery dates for each shipment of plant, materials and equipment.

Which particular plant, equipment and materials will be required, and when, are clearly dependent upon the detailed design of the relevant project, including construction methodology and interfaces between construction packages. This design is likely still to be in the course of preparation at the date of contract signature. For this reason, a comprehensive and accurate delineation of the programme for delivery across the several contracts can be difficult if not impossible.

Even if it were possible to identify work packages and specific delivery dates, this information may not adequately protect the project company. It is difficult to manage time obligations under a series of contracts, in particular where those obligations are interdependent. In the end, gaps between work packages are almost inevitable.

11.5.2   Testing and completion

Completion is a key concept in construction contracts. It is the date on which the project company accepts that the whole (or some section) of the works is complete. Upon completion of the works, the contractor is released from liability for delay liquidated damages, passes care of the works and responsibility for the site to the project company and ceases to provide certain insurance for the works. Therefore, completion will not normally be certified by the project company until it is satisfied that the works are complete in accordance with the construction contract and have passed a certain series of tests. The testing regime may need to be followed by retesting where the completed works do not pass the relevant tests. There will normally be an element of performance testing when assessing completion.

The contractors should be required to provide any support and assistance required by the Principal Contractor in the performance of completion testing. In particular, in International Contracts, this may require the involvement of a particular contractor long after it has completed the works under its contract. In our example of the fibre optic project, one of the dry contracts may be complete long before the relevant part of the submarine backbone or network operating centre, and therefore before comprehensive testing of the system, is complete. That dry contractor may need to return to the site during testing to monitor equipment on-site. This may have specific cost and logistical implications that would need to be managed by the Principal Contractor.

11.5.3   Timing of completion

The project company will only want to accept the completed works where all of the works under all of the contracts are complete. This "big bang" approach to completion allows the project company to implement a comprehensive operation, maintenance and insurance programme, without concern for interfaces between different parts of the works and timing of the implementation of such programme for each section. The contractors continue to bear the risk of care and the obligation to provide insurance over all of the works until acceptance of the whole.

The "big bang" approach also helps to protect the project company from the risks arising from imperfect interfacing between the different contracts. These interfaces will often not be tested until the final testing of the whole of the works together. For example, in a power project, where the coal delivery plant is to be accepted separately from the boilers, any defect in the delivery system for coal into the boilers may not be identified until both the coal delivery and boiler systems can be tested together. If the works under one contract are accepted separately, there will be less opportunity to identify problems in this regard. Equally, under a fibre optic International Contract, a terrestrial link may be completed before the submarine rings or the network operating centre. The project company will want to confirm that the hardware and software for the network operating centre and the submarine network will "talk" to the terrestrial landing station and point-of-presence in the relevant jurisdiction.

The split contracts will need to address the timing and cohesive nature of the defects liability period. This period will normally run from the completion of the works under a contract until the end of a fixed period. Under a split contract, the project company may not want the risk of multiple defects liability periods for different sections of the works. By using the "big bang" approach, the defects liability period should run from provisional acceptance of each of the contracts until a fixed period of years after acceptance of the whole of the works under the Principal Contract.

For many of the reasons discussed above, the contractor will want to deliver the works in sections. The project company will normally only agree to split the works into sections where taking over one or more of these sections will permit the project company to earn revenues on the accepted sections. For example, in our fibre optic project, delay of one terrestrial segment may not have a significant effect on the revenue stream obtained from commercial operation of the whole system. In this case, the project company may accept the risk of multiple sectional completion against the benefits to be obtained from early commercial operation of part of the project.

The project company may also find that each contractor assigns a high price to bearing the risk of care of his part of the works until completion of the whole. Again, in relation to the fibre optic project, the terrestrial links may be completed long before the submarine backbone (which will be subject to the risk of delays for availability of cable-laying ships and inclement weather) and may result in the contractor insuring and caring for those completed works for an extended period of time. Therefore, the project company may prefer to bear the additional risk associated with sectional completion in exchange for a lower aggregate price.

11.5.4   Liquidated damages for delay

Where the contractor fails to complete the works within the time for completion, the project company will normally look for liquidated damages for delay. These liquidated damages may have to be divided amongst the split contracts to ensure that the amount of liquidated damages corresponds to the value of the relevant contract. However, from the project company's perspective, aggregate delay damages need to cover the whole of the project. Delay in completion of any part of the works may have a serious impact on the revenue stream of the project. The project company needs to be protected from the damages it will incur due to such loss of revenue. The use of limited recourse financing will make this requirement all the more critical as lenders seek protection for the project company's debt service obligations during any period of delay.

It could be argued that the aggregate liquidated damages should be based on the (presumably lower) cost of accelerating some of the other works packages to take account of the delayed delivery, or should be limited to those damages relating solely to the delayed package or contract rather than the losses suffered by the project company owing to the resultant delay to the completion of the project as a whole. The contractor may also argue that assessment of an aggregate level of liquidated damages is inappropriate given the commercial value to the project company of the completed parts of the works if the project company agrees to accept them separately (as discussed above). For example, in a fibre optic cable project, where one terrestrial landing is not available, revenues may be obtained from connectivity to the remaining terrestrial landings.

Domestic Contracts are less likely to be segregated into commercially viable sections. The different elements of a Domestic Contract are normally interdependent to the extent that no one section can attract sufficient reviews to justify its separate acceptance. Exceptions might include an LNG plant with several trains or a power plant with multiple generating units, where each train or unit is sufficiently independent to earn revenues. However, even in these cases, the project company will need to ensure that all common facilities – such as fuel handling and employee facilities – have been completed and will be tested with the whole of the works.

Despite these arguments, the project company will look to the contractor to deliver a completed facility. Any effort by the contractor to dilute its liabilities and therefore provide partial remedies will not provide the project company with the security it seeks and will not protect the project company from the likely damages arising from such delay. Further, any lenders to the project will measure the available damages against the total cost of the project. The project company may not be able to convince the lenders that lower levels of liquidated damages will provide sufficient security, even in the face of evidence of the quantum of potential revenues from the completed part of the works, or the reasonableness or "fairness" of less extensive liabilities.

Liquidated damages may, under applicable law, be subject to restrictions. Certain civil law systems give the courts discretion to revisit liquidated damages levels, and adjust those levels if they consider them to be manifestly excessive or derisory.[335] While in others, the parties are free to set levels of liquidated damages at their discretion.[336] Common law systems tend to assess whether the levels of liquidated damages at the time of contract signature represent a reasonable forecast of the damages likely to be incurred. For example, under English law, there needs to be a genuine pre-estimate of the loss to be suffered by the project company under the relevant contract.[337] Under principles of United States law, while liquidated damages benefit from a presumption of validity, they must be difficult to compute at the time of contract and must bear a reasonable relationship to anticipated damages at the time of contract.[338]

Given the difficulties identified above, it may be advisable to draft the split contracts on the basis that one of the contracts (possibly the Principal Contract) contains the project company's remedies for delayed completion, regardless of which of the contractors may be at fault. The liquidated damages imposed on the Principal Contractor could be extremely large in comparison to the Principal Contract price, as they will represent the whole of the liquidated damages which would have been applied under a single turnkey contract. In order to manage the risk that the level of liquidated damages might seem excessive or penal in nature, the Principal Contractor should be deemed expressly to have taken into account in its programme the possibility of delays, and should assume responsibility for recovering any delay to the construction programme, caused by any late deliveries under the other split contracts. This express acceptance of liability should establish the link with the rest of the project and help justify the reasonableness of the liquidated damages and delivery obligations placed on the Principal Contractor, though this will need to be reviewed under the applicable law.

Where it is the intention that the project company will look to the Principal Contractor for compensation for damages related to delay in delivery of the works, the contractor may argue that the other split contracts should not provide for liquidated damages. On the other hand, the project company will want to incentivise each of the contractors. Spreading liability among all of the contractors for delay may improve the likelihood of recovery of any liquidated damages that may fall due.

However, the imposition of liquidated damages under the other contracts might threaten the viability of the liquidated damages under the Principal Contract, giving an appearance of unreasonableness. The liquidated damages under the Principal Contract may also be required by law to represent the contractor's exclusive liability for the relevant delay (in order to justify their status as liquidated damages – as discussed above). For these reasons, it may be necessary to count payment of

---

[335] For example, article 1152 of the French Civil Code as amended by law no. 75-597 of 9 July 1975.

[336] For example, South Africa.

[337] Dunlop Pneumatic Tyre Co Ltd v New Garage and Motor Co Ltd [1915] AC 79, HL.

[338] See for example New York law, 36 N.Y. Jur. 2d Damages §154 (2002); Consolidated Rail Corp. v MASP Equipment Corp. (1986) 67 NY2d 35, 499 NYS2d 657, 490 NE2d 514.

liquidated damages under the other split contracts against any liability to pay liquidated damages under the Principal Contract.

11.5.5 Duration of performance security

Each contract will provide for performance security to protect the project company against default by, and payment risk of, the contractor. The performance security provided by the contractor under each contract will normally fall away at a specified point in time. Under a normal construction contract, that point in time would be the completion of the works to be performed under that contract. Under a split contract, the project company will want this point in time to be the completion of the Principal Contract works, rather than completion of the relevant contractor's obligations. In this way the aggregate performance securities will be available to the project company until completion of the whole of the works. However, it should be noted that each performance security will probably only make reference to works performed under that contract and will therefore probably not be available to compensate the project company for damages or costs under other contracts. Therefore, the project company may not benefit from sufficient performance securities in the event of a significant defect in one part of the project that has an effect on the works far exceeding the relative value of the relevant contract. For this reason, the project company may want to receive a performance guarantee for the whole of the works from the Principle Contractor.

11.6 Fixed Cost of Completion

The fixed price agreed for the single turnkey construction contract will need to be divided amongst the split contracts. A note of caution needs to be sounded here. The allocation of the contract price between the contracts must be reasonable. If the parties weight the contract price unjustifiably in favour of one contract in order to maximise the tax savings, this could leave the project company and contractors open to the imposition of tax penalties and possibly criminal liability.

Each contract will have a contract price, but the project company will want assurances that there is a fixed overall cost of completion, subject to any valid claim for increase in cost that the contractors may have. Any claims for price increase will be made under the relevant contract and in accordance with the relevant dispute resolution mechanism. A split contract price could result in claims not contemplated in the single turnkey construction contract and could put in jeopardy the fixed nature of the aggregate contract price. This is a particular problem under an International Contract where applicable law may be different for each contract and may give the contractor different rights to claim for cost increases. In addition, local law (no matter the choice of law made under the relevant contract) may create obligations or rights which cannot be waived or modified by contract (mandatory laws) that will change the pricing structure created under the construction contract.

The project company will want to ensure that any entitlement to an increase in cost under a split structure does not exceed the amount of increase that would have arisen under a single contract. Further, the existence of a series of contracts with different dispute resolution mechanisms, possibly under differing local laws, increases the risk that the award or judgement rendered in resolution of a claim in one jurisdiction may be inconsistent with that or contradict the award or judgement rendered in another jurisdiction. Each award or judgement will be enforceable, possibly in parallel in several jurisdictions, with the resultant confusion and inefficiencies.

Claims for additional cost under the several contracts must be managed in the same way as claims for extensions of time. For example, the project company's desire to ensure a fixed price, further to the expectations created under turnkey construction arrangements, can be managed by the Principal Contractor providing an indemnity to the project company for any change in price claimed by a contractor that would not have been awarded under the single turnkey construction contract. This raises evidentiary issues, as it will be difficult to argue what increase in price would or would not have been awarded under the single turnkey construction contract.

11.7   Single Point Responsibility

An important element of turnkey construction arrangements is the provision to the project company of a single point of responsibility for the completion of the works in accordance with the specification and the performance standards. Under single point responsibility, where a default occurs or some defect is identified, it is not necessary for the project company to establish which of the contractor's many subcontractors is at fault in order for the project company to be able to succeed in a contractual claim against the contractor. With a split contract structure, the project company runs the risk of being caught in the middle of an argument between the different contractors as to whether the defect in question is caused by, for example, one contractor's defective design, a different contractor's supply of defective equipment or yet another contractor's defective installation of the equipment.

The project company will want to have one single point of reference for claims and communications. Ideally, the split contract structure should be drafted in such a way that the project company avoids becoming embroiled in such arguments and only needs to bring proceedings against the Principal Contractor. In order to achieve this, the Principal Contractor should be obliged to check, and assume responsibility for, all work performed by the other contractors and should be deemed to have accepted full responsibility for all of the works and therefore not be entitled to raise as a defence in respect of any claim brought by the project company that the reason for any failure in the final work is defective design, plant, materials, equipment, testing or commissioning by the other contractors.

This single point of contact can also be of assistance to the contractor. The split contracts will require notice of certain events, reports, approvals and documentation. The contractor will want a central, comprehensive means for providing the same despite the splitting of the contract. This may be of particular relevance for payment mechanisms to avoid the need to issue invoices from or to several different companies.

11.7.1 Quality of the works

The contractors will be individually responsible for the design of the works to be performed under their contracts. It is unlikely in practice that the Principal Contractor will perform all of the design. The Principal Contractor will usually prepare the overall design, with each other contractor then being responsible for the detailed design applicable to its own part of the work. To avoid the possibility of each contractor arguing that any failure in the completed work is caused by a defect in the design prepared by another, each contractor should be obliged to check and assume responsibility for any design on which its own design will be based. Ideally, the Principal Contractor will be ultimately responsible for the design of all of the works.

In a Domestic Contract, it is easier for one contractor to provide the designs for the whole of the works. The offshore engineering contract, in the power plant example, will often include the majority of the project design. Only detailed design and fit-out will usually be performed by the onshore contractors. This may differ for an International Contract where each element of the design may need to be specific to local requirements and may need to be managed by a locally licensed or registered designer. In the fibre optic cable project example, the contractors may all be involved in the preparation and design of the cable route, since each landing, network operating centre, substation and terrestrial and submarine route will have requirements specific to their location.

11.7.2 Defects

Under a turnkey construction contract, the contractor is liable during the defects liability period for defects that may arise in the works. As discussed above, the project company will want to have similar comprehensive coverage in the case of split contracts. Each contractor will be responsible for any defect in the works provided under its contract, but this may leave gaps in the liability for defects with resultant disputes arising among the contractors as to who is responsible for a given defect.

This is particularly true for Domestic Contracts, where interfaces between the different works packages are significant. Therefore, the project company may want the Principal Contractor to be responsible for any defect which arises in the work performed under the Principal Contract and to be responsible for the remedy of any defect in the other works. The Principal Contractor would therefore act as the single point of responsibility for defects liability. This will need to be managed carefully with relevant tax advice to ensure that remedy of defects under the Principal Contract does not result in the Principal Contractor being deemed to be performing tasks onshore or in a jurisdiction other than that intended, and therefore a less efficient tax treatment.

11.7.3 Interfaces between the contracts

Care will need to be taken in drawing up each contract to ensure that the procedures for responsibility for and management of any plant, materials and equipment are all covered in a consistent and logical manner. These interfaces will include technical, commercial and legal issues, such as:

> shipment;

> physical transfer;

> transfer of risk and responsibility;

> provision of insurance cover;

> testing and inspection ex-works and on delivery;

> procuring of all import/export approvals and documentation; and

> the associated transfer of legal ownership from one contractor to another.

However, despite care in managing the interfaces between contracts, the Principal Contractor should be responsible for the co-ordination and interfacing between all of the different works packages and contractors. The Principal Contractor should be responsible for the delivery of the whole of the works, so the project company will want the Principal Contractor to co-ordinate communications amongst the contractors. It would also be sensible to provide that a notice given to one contractor is treated as being given also to the other contractors, to avoid gaps in notice provided or mismatches in timing requirements from the giving of notice.

11.7.4   Dispute resolution

Each contract will have its own dispute resolution procedure. There may be some desire to select a dispute resolution mechanism for each contract that is specifically appropriate for the context and requirements of that contract, however, there are certain advantages to the project company in ensuring that all disputes can be heard in a common set of dispute proceedings. The project company will not want to risk inconsistent solutions rising from differences in procedure. The dispute resolution procedure chosen for the project contracts must be consistent in each of the split contracts. In an ideal dispute resolution mechanism, the parties will be able to reference specific disputes to one single mechanism in order to join all related or associated disputes, to ensure consistent resolution. If arbitration is the chosen procedure, the project company should be entitled to join proceedings with different contractors in respect of a related dispute or event, or all of the contractors could enter into a separate agreement to manage the resolution of any dispute that may arise.

11.7.5   Choice of law

The single turnkey construction contract will usually apply a choice of law that is familiar to the project company, perceived as being responsive to the intentions of the parties and flexible in its application. Similarly, each split contract will include its own choice of law. However, it may not be desirable or possible for all of the contracts to be subject to the same choice of law. Certain legal systems require that contracts apply local law unless they meet conditions intended to identify truly

International Contracts. Even if all of the contracts apply the same choice of law, local courts may interpret them differently to the manner in which the terms of the Principal Contract would be interpreted by an arbitrator under its choice of law.

No matter which law is selected, it will be necessary to review the application of local law. Certain provisions of local law can be waived by contract, but the waiver included in the contract may need to take a certain form. Other provisions may be mandatory – not subject to waiver. The parties will need to be aware of such provisions and draft their contracts accordingly.

11.7.6   Limits of liability

The single turnkey construction contract will inevitably contain caps on the contractor's liability whether in relation to that contractor's liability for delay or performance liquidated damages or in relation to its overall liability. These limits are generally expressed as, or calculated by reference to, a percentage of the contract price. A split contract structure requires the contract price to be divided up between the various contracts. This division needs to be reflected in the drafting of any liability limits.

The contracts can each provide for an overall limit of liability calculated by reference to the combined contract price. Separate liability caps determined by reference to each individual contract price would prejudice the project company's interest to ensure the overall cap rather than to be limited by separate caps under each contract: clearly, the project company will not want to have to act against each contractor under its respective contract to achieve the total aggregate cap. But, to protect the contractors' overall combined exposure, these limits of liability can be reduced to take account of any damages paid out under any of the contracts.

11.7.7   Insurance

A turnkey construction contract will provide for a comprehensive insurance package for the whole of the works. Under a split contract, the project company will want to ensure that seamless insurance cover is in place for the duration of the works and during the defects liability period. The easiest way to ensure a comprehensive, seamless insurance package is by the project company taking out the majority of the project insurances. However, where it is envisioned that the contractor will be responsible for providing such insurance cover, the project company will want to ensure that no gaps exist in the insurance coverage and so the responsibility should be imposed upon one of the contractors to take out the required insurances on behalf of the other contractors, the project company and the lenders.

11.8   Splitting Terms

The project company will need to implement a contractual structure that sets apart services performed and assets delivered in each tax jurisdiction, while maintaining the turnkey, single point nature of the contractor's obligations. Under normal circumstances, the parties will agree upon the terms for a single turnkey construction contract before embarking on the splitting exercise. Drafting of split contracts will normally follow the terms agreed under the single turnkey construction contract to avoid prolonged renegotiation of terms. Some terms will only apply to certain of the contracts. Although not always easy to draft, contractual provisions can be inserted into a split contract structure in order to provide the project company with similar rights and remedies as would be available to it under a turnkey contract arrangement. In the alternative, the project company may prefer to enter into an umbrella contract with the contractor that will implement such provisions and protect the project company from the implications of a split contractual structure.

In some jurisdictions there is a further complication in drafting a split contract structure in that there would be a difficulty from a tax perspective in referring directly between the contracts. In which case, it is necessary in each contract to make oblique references to the other contracts, for example, by referring to "any other contract entered into between the project company and the contractor or any affiliate of the contractor".

This section will discuss certain issues that will assist in the practical exercise of splitting.

11.8.1   Effective date

The project company will not want one split contract becoming effective until each component of the split contract structure becomes effective. Generally, the split contracts individually are of limited use to the project company. The structure must work together as a comprehensive package before its value can be extracted. This issue is particularly complicated where the contracts cannot cross-refer to each other. In such case, some central reference point will need to be used as an all-encompassing condition precedent. Financial close in the case of a project-specific loan might operate as an appropriate reference point.

11.8.2   Payment

The payment provisions for the single turnkey construction contract will need to be split into the several contracts. This can provide the contractor with additional benefits such as the ability to make and receive payments in hard currency to avoid currency risks and hedging costs. Payments may also be permitted offshore to avoid repatriation complications, withholding taxes and other associated costs.

Milestones and other mechanisms intended to encourage timely completion and to place specific risks on the contractor will need to be fitted to the split structure. For example, under the single turnkey construction contract, the contractor is not paid until he supplies the parent company guarantee and the performance guarantee to the project company. These restrictions should apply to payments under any of the contracts. This drafting may need to go in the umbrella contract. The single turnkey construction contract may also provide for an advance payment, to fund the design performed and long-lead items ordered during the early phase of construction. This payment may need to be divided amongst the split contracts, and the mechanism to repay that amount and guarantee its repayment will need to be co-ordinated amongst those contracts.

11.8.3 Cross-indemnities

Under a single contract, the contractor's and project company's scopes of work are clear. Under a split contract, the application of local law may create liability in the project company for acts or omissions of the contractors under the other contracts. A general provision should be added to each contract to the effect that nothing in that contract obliges the project company to procure the carrying out of any work or services under any other contract. Further, in the event that, owing to the default of one contractor, the project company is liable to pay any damages to one of the other contractors, whether under the other contract or otherwise, then the project company should be indemnified by the defaulting contractor for this loss.

Given the split nature of the contracts, local law or even the interpretation of the contract within the context of the dispute resolution mechanism (possibly a court or arbitrator that does not have knowledge of the whole of the split structure) may give the contractor the right to an increase in its price or an extension in the time for completion that would be inconsistent with the split structure agreed by the parties. For example, the need for changes in one contract resulting from the performance of one of the other contractors could be interpreted as a project company change, permitting the contractor to claim extra cost and an increase in time for completion.

The project company will not want the contractor to have any rights additional to those that would otherwise have been granted by the single turnkey construction contract. The contractors should not be entitled to submit a change order entitling it to additional time and money as a result of a default of any of the other contractors and, similarly, no contractor should be entitled to be relieved of any of its obligations under the *force majeure* provisions of its contract in the event that the *force majeure* in question is triggered by a breach by one of the other contractors.

11.8.4 Termination

The consequences of one of the split contracts being terminated needs to be addressed. The split contracts should act as one single contract and so there should logically be no termination of one of the contracts while the others remain in place. The project company should be automatically entitled to terminate all of the contracts if it is entitled to terminate one of the contracts. Equally, the contractors may not wish to continue to perform their obligations under their contracts if one of the other contractors has already terminated its contract because of project company default.

This said, in an International Contract, it may be of interest for the project company to continue with the remaining contracts, even where one of the other contracts is terminated. In the fibre optic project example, where one of the terrestrial contracts is terminated, the balance of the works may still be commercially viable. Even where one or more of the contracts is terminated, the project company may want to maintain the other contracts. It may not be possible for the project company to assess the viability of the remaining contracts at the time of contract signature, therefore the project company may want a discretionary right to maintain the contracts.

11.8.5   Umbrella contracts

The purpose of the split contracts is to achieve the greatest tax efficiency while maintaining the rights, obligations, duties and risk allocation set out in the single turnkey construction contract. Therefore, the project company will look to this split structure to provide the appropriate single point responsibility, fixed price, fixed time for delivery, joint and several liability and the other warranties and guarantees provided by, and agreed with, the contractor under the single turnkey construction contract.

Often the drafting of the split contracts will not provide sufficient comfort to the project company that all of the above issues have been managed and that the split structure provides turnkey protection for the project company. The project company may require an umbrella contract from the contractors and their parent companies to guarantee and indemnify the project company against the breach of payment and performance obligations, management of claims and interfaces, the fitness for purpose of the finished works and the other issues necessary to ensure that the split structure works together as a turnkey construction contract. An umbrella contract may not be available for use in all jurisdictions, since in some jurisdictions such a contract would negate the tax benefits which the split contract structure is intended to achieve, since it clearly indicates the intention of the parties to combine the works under one contract. These protections may also form part of a parent company guarantee, which may prove a more familiar mechanism for tax authorities and therefore attract less unwanted attention.

In order to avoid delays during dispute resolution under each contract or in the local court, the project company will want the right to make claims under this umbrella contract (without first claiming under the relevant contract) making it the first point of reference when anything goes wrong with the contractual structure and providing the project company with a single point of reference – possibly in a country where enforcement of the agreement may be easier. The umbrella contract will also specify liability limitations, mitigation obligations, restrictions on double counting and aggregation of claims under one single dispute resolution procedure.

The form of umbrella contract would include an acknowledgement from the contractor that there is intended to be one single scope of work and that the obligations of the contractors under the contracts are, when taken together, intended to constitute a single, integrated, turnkey project. Such an acknowledgement would then be backed up by an undertaking from the contractor to ensure that each of the contractors performs its obligations in a manner consistent with that acknowledgement, and that none of the contractors will make or submit any claim or rely on any defence which would be inconsistent with that acknowledgement. A concern with this arrangement is that in the absence of an actual turnkey contract, an obligation on a party to procure that claims will not be made which are inconsistent with that contract may give rise to evidentiary difficulties.

The original single turnkey construction contract could be appended to the umbrella contract in order to ensure that the provisions of any agreement, reached before the decision to split the works between several contracts was taken, are preserved. The use of a turnkey contract as an appendix to the umbrella contract should always be considered carefully to avoid compromising the intended tax structure.

The project company may need to show actual loss under the umbrella contract before making a claim. In certain jurisdictions, a party to a contract may only be permitted to recover damages for losses which it has himself suffered; hence a party who has suffered no loss cannot recover substantial damages for breach.[339] Therefore, an umbrella contract between the project company and a contractor may not suit the project company's purposes where it may be difficult to show actual losses of the project company for breaches under that umbrella contract, in particular where subsidiaries of the project company are the parties to certain of the split contracts and therefore the parties actually incurring loss. This is particularly true in International Contracts where the project company will often contract through local asset companies to manage withholding and other tax and cost issues.

A variety of mechanisms are available to overcome this particular restriction, for example the third party may be included as a third party beneficiary under the umbrella contract or the project company may be entitled to act as agent for those third parties and therefore collect damages and losses on their behalf. Another approach is to include every party in the split structure as signatories to the umbrella contract in order to bring all parties that might suffer loss under the protection of the umbrella contract. This same analysis will need to be made in relation to liquidated damages under the umbrella contract. If those damages (delay or performance) are incurred by a third party, could those liquidated damages be considered a penalty or otherwise unreasonable since the project company is not incurring such damages directly?

11.9 Splitting the Works

The scope of work to be performed by the contractor will be divided between the split contracts, resulting in multiple scopes of work, one for each contract. This will be done for practical purposes, to co-ordinate responsibilities amongst the contractors and provide clarity as to roles and requirements. This split of the works will also endeavour to satisfy the requirements of tax authorities, to demonstrate the nature of works to be performed and the characterisation that

---

[339] For a discussion of this issue under English law, see Alfred McAlpine Construction Limited v Panatown Limited, House of Lords, 27 July 2000.

should be applied to the relevant contract by the tax authority. While, as explained below, the creation of multiple scopes may in many cases not wholly reflect the commercial reality of the project, if separate work scopes are produced, then these scopes will need to be thoroughly reviewed to ensure that they are consistent with one another and, when combined together, cover the whole of the works. It is imperative that the sum of the parts equals the whole. This includes not only the sum of the materials and equipment to be provided, but more importantly the interfaces between the different elements of the works and the performance requirements for the end product.

Rather than go through the mechanical exercise of dividing up the project specification between the contracts, one possible short-cut is to keep one project specification, but define the work under each contract making reference to that one project specification. The scope of work for the Principal Contract would then cover any work not performed by the other contractors. Providing the full specification to each of the contractors will also ensure that each of the split contractors will perform its part of the works with full knowledge of the whole project and its requirements. This approach has a potential drawback in that it may be used by the tax authority to justify aggregating certain or all of the split contracts due to the appearance of consortium that a single specification might portray.

11.10   Conclusion

Splitting of turnkey construction contracts can be a financially rewarding proposition, managing tax exposure and improving financial efficiency. However, the process of splitting a contract is time and resource intensive, requiring significant involvement of legal and tax advisers. A split contract will not necessarily provide the protections and risk allocation of a single turnkey construction contract. The split structure must therefore be carefully crafted in an effort to retain the turnkey benefits sought by the project company, in particular single point responsibility, fixed price and fixed time for completion, while achieving the desired tax and cost efficiencies.

Chapter 12

Operation and Maintenance Agreement

> *It is, after all, the responsibility of the expert to operate the familiar and that of the leader to transcend it.*
>
> *Henry Kissinger (b. 1923)*

After completion of construction of the works, the project company will need to operate and maintain the project during the concession period. This will involve managing the operation of the project, providing maintenance for and replacing materials and equipment, receiving and managing inputs and developing the relationship with the offtake purchaser. In order to allocate the risks involved in operation and maintenance, the project company may contract with an operation and maintenance contractor, also known as the "operator". The following chart indicates the position of the operation and maintenance agreement in a typical BOT project structure.

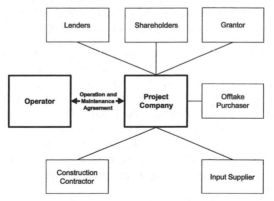

A number of contractual structures are available to the project company in relation to operation. For example, the project company may let the operation and maintenance agreement to an arm's length third party, to one of the shareholders (or one of its subsidiaries), or may (though rarely) undertake the obligations itself.

The project company may also enter into a technical services agreement for the provision of skilled labour, or may split the operation and maintenance obligations between multiple contractors. Whatever the structure of contractual arrangements, the whole will be referred to here as the "operation and maintenance agreement".

The role of the operator is of particular importance to the project company in view of the long duration of the concession agreement and the fact that the payment stream flows during the operating phase. Further, as BOT projects are often located in developing countries, the operation of the project will require an understanding of the local market; the demands on operation in developing countries, such as availability of materials and labour for maintenance and repairs; as well as the importance of relationships with local authorities. The operator will need to have experience of operating major infrastructure projects in political and commercial climates similar to that of the host country, and preferably in the host country.

The project company will want to transfer the majority of the operating and maintenance task and risk to the operator, including the operating requirements and the interfaces between the grantor and the operator and those involved in the testing of the works and transfer of the project at the end of the concession period in accordance with the concession agreement. The operator will often be responsible for interfaces with the offtake purchaser and the input supplier.

Risk allocation under an operation and maintenance agreement is generally not as clear cut as under the construction contract or the input supply agreement where a more substantial transfer of project company risk may be possible. This is often explained by the fact that the construction contractor and the input supplier provide products, while the operator provides a service. Operation and maintenance agreements for projects located in developed markets with well-defined scopes of work, for example a PFI or PPP project in the United Kingdom, may provide a more exhaustive transfer of risk from the project company to the operator. This may not be the case in international projects located in developing markets, where the relevant scope of works is not normally as well defined.

The project company and the lenders will want the price for operation and maintenance of the project to be fixed or its method of calculation defined. This would provide them with some certainty of financial exposure, and ensure a substantial transfer of the operation cost risk to the operator and of the operation costs to the offtake purchaser (through the fixed offtake revenue stream). The operator, on the other hand, may want to be paid on a cost-plus basis (the costs incurred in providing the services plus a margin for profit) with no limitation or restriction. The operator would be liable for penalty payments where the project does not perform as required and the performance failure is not related to a construction defect.

Provision will be made for the replacement of the operator where it does not satisfy its obligations under the operation and maintenance agreement. Although this is true generally of the agreements entered into in the context of a BOT project, it is particularly important for the operation and maintenance agreement given its long duration and the importance of the operator in the contractual scheme of the project. The grantor and the lenders may require a right of approval over the identity of any such substitute operator, and the terms of appointment.

This chapter will discuss first the risk allocation to be found in the operation and maintenance agreement (section 12.1), then the interfaces between the operator and the other project participants (section 12.2). The final sections (12.3 to 12.5) will review certain of the provisions that are specific to the operation and maintenance agreement. As is the case with the other project documents, a complete coherence should be sought between this document and the other constituent documents, in particular the concession agreement. Issues common to the project documents are set out in chapter 15.

12.1   Risk Allocation

Owing to the importance of the operation risk, back-to-back transfer of the project company's operating tasks to the operator will be of particular importance to the lenders. The operator will generally be allocated the following risks, together with a transfer of the operating tasks from the concession agreement.

12.1.1   Performance risk

The operator will share the risk of proper performance of the works with the other project participants, pursuant to the requirements of the concession agreement and the offtake purchase agreement. This risk sharing will typically allocate responsibility to:

> the input supplier for the quantity and quality of input delivered, and the impact any non-compliant input has on project performance;

> the offtake purchaser for any effect that the offtake purchaser-supplied infrastructure and transmission facilities may have on the performance of the works;

> the construction contractor for delivering a project capable of operation at the required levels and for any defect which might arise during the defects liability period; and

> the operator for the proper operation and maintenance of the works to achieve the required levels of output or availability.

Where the works do not operate at the levels required, the offtake purchaser will, unless it is at fault, have some right to withhold payments or collect damages from the project company in relation to the amount of the damages incurred, or (subject to certain requirements) terminate the offtake purchase agreement. The project company will want to place this risk, as far as possible, on the responsible project participant.

12.1.2   Increase of cost risk

The operator may provide a fixed price for operation and will therefore bear the risk of increased cost of operation. In certain cases the project company will bear the risk for increased cost against controls placed on the operator to ensure mitigation of cost and efficient use of resources.

An alternative would be the use of short periods (possibly three to seven years) during which the operator's fee is fixed. At the end of the period, market testing is carried out and the operator's fee is modified accordingly or a new operator is selected. This approach requires a flexible market of potential operators and, as a result, is generally restricted to developed markets.

Increased cost will generally only be allocated to the grantor where the cause of the increased cost is somehow linked to a grantor risk, such as changes of law, *force majeure* or some other such event. The grantor will generally not be liable for the effects of inflation, increases in the market price of materials or labour or increases in the cost of other required services, such as insurance. The offtake purchaser, on the other hand, must pay a price for the offtake delivered.[340] This price will generally be tied to the fixed and variable costs of the project. The offtake purchaser may be allocated some portion of the risk of change in price through the pricing mechanism of the offtake purchase agreement, which will take into consideration some portion of changes in market prices, inflation or other factors that can affect the price of generation of output.

12.1.3   Operation risk

The operator will be allocated the majority of the operation risk of the project. To some extent this risk will correspond with the performance risk, as discussed above, whereby the operator will be responsible for operating the project in accordance with the standards and performance levels set out in the concession and the offtake purchase agreements, which will be incorporated into the operation and maintenance agreement.

12.1.4   Political risk

The operator is in a very sensitive position as the operator of a public service in the host country. Therefore, the operator's methods of operation and its relationship with its employees and the local and national communities will be under close observation by both the local population and the host government to ensure that the services rendered by the operator are consistent with public expectations. This can be an extremely subjective set of criteria, and therefore difficult to measure or set out in the operation and maintenance agreement.

---

[340]   Please note that the grantor may also be the offtake purchaser, and that both roles may dovetail into a single agreement. This concept is discussed further in chapters 3 and 8.

The operator's services can have an impact on the popular perception of the grantor, which can cause conflict between the operator, the project company and the grantor. Although the risk of grantor intervention should be covered by the concession agreement, the risk involved in interfaces with local and national governments should not be underestimated. The operator will need to make an effort to work in accordance with the political interests of the grantor and its local representatives.

Similarly, as the entity which will be present on site for the majority of the concession period, and long after the excitement and international attention involved in the early period of the project have faded, the operator will, whether it likes it or not, bear a portion of the risk of change in the political climate of the host country. Although the risk for changes in law and other such events may be placed on the grantor through the concession agreement, the political climate in the host country, and locally, represents an important risk for the operator. It is in the operator's interest to link the interests of the local and national governments closely with the profitable operation of the project.

The best method for linking government interest with the proper operation of the project will depend on the nature of the host country's political system and the interests of its political leaders. For example, in certain situations the operator may find that the need for jobs in the host country is such that employing local labour will create a bond between the operator and the host government which in turn is sufficient to create the mutual interest desired. In other situations, the operator may need to create a mutual interest with a particular individual or group. This mutual interest may evolve as the political atmosphere of the host country changes. For this reason alone the operator will need to be experienced at working in the host country and will need sufficient contact in the host country to understand the changing needs of the local and national governments.

12.2   Interfaces

During the operating phase of the project, it is essential that one of the project participants undertakes a strong management role. Where the operator plays this central role in the management of the project, it will need to liaise with all of the project participants, manage the input and output needs of the project, and manage the transfer of care for the project from the construction contractor at completion of construction and to the grantor at the end of the concession period.

12.2.1   Construction contractor

The operator will interface with the construction contractor during and after completion of the works. The obligation to ensure that the construction design meets the operator's requirements can either be placed on the operator or the construction contractor. The operator may be required to agree the project design, which will necessitate relatively extensive liaison between the operator and construction contractor during the design phase. This approach runs the risk of delaying the design process as a result of operator intervention. Neither the operator nor the construction contractor will want to be responsible for any such delay in design.

Another approach is to require the operator to produce operating requirements which are then included in the construction contractor's design requirements. The construction contractor will bear the risk of designing to the operator's requirements and the operator will be required to show non-compliance with these requirements before being allowed to claim any relief of its obligations or added cost for defective design which impedes the operator's ability to operate the project. The project company will need to manage carefully the operator's requirements, since the project company will be responsible for any error in the operator's requirements under the construction contract.

The operator will need to co-ordinate with the construction contractor about the operation of the works. The construction contractor will be providing the operation and maintenance manuals and may need to train the operator's personnel. As the operator will be responsible for the proper operation of the works during the concession period, it is essential that this transfer of information between the construction contractor and the operator occurs as efficiently and effectively as possible.

At completion and handing-over, the care of the works will often pass from the construction contractor to the operator. Where the works are split into sections, and therefore taken over in sections, a procedure will need to be established as to how the operator and the construction contractor will manage the taking-over process, particularly in relation to the temporary parallel management of the site by the two entities. Common responsibilities, such as security, safety, access and removal of waste, will need to be carefully allocated between these two project participants.

During the defects liability period, although the works will be under the care of the operator, the construction contractor will need to have the right of access to the works in order to satisfy its obligation to remedy any defects in the works discovered during the defects liability period. Further, it may be during the defects liability period, while the operator has control of the site and the works, that the construction contractor is required to carry out further performance tests. The operator will need to manage the site so as to provide the construction contractor with the necessary access to the site to carry out tests and repairs without unnecessarily impeding the operation of the project.

The construction contractor may also be responsible for major maintenance such as replacement of materials and equipment during the operation phase. The operator is likely to be required to manage the construction contractor's intervention in relation to major maintenance to ensure that operation of the project is not impeded.

12.2.2   Offtake purchaser

The operator may be required to co-ordinate with the offtake purchaser throughout the concession period. It is the offtake purchaser, in many cases, who will direct the operator as to the operation of the project. Where the offtake purchaser requires more output, the operator will need to generate this within the time frame of, and in accordance with the output requirements set out in, the operation and maintenance agreement. The output requirements will variously cover quality, quantity, timing, transportation, and other output specific issues. In the case of power projects, for example, the offtake purchaser will need to consider issues such as backing-down, blackstart and frequency responsive generation. For this reason the relationship between the operator and the offtake purchaser will need to be well defined, providing a clear yet flexible procedure for operation and communication.

Testing equipment will be installed into the offtake system to measure the quality and quantity of output required. Output may simply involve availability, for example of a hospital or educational facility, or may involve quality intensive products, such as a clean water treatment plant or a processing facility for a raw material. The operator and offtake purchaser may need to work together to operate and maintain the testing regime and any associated equipment.

As far as possible, scheduled shutdowns and periods of maintenance or repairs should be carried out in parallel to limit the impact on project output. The offtake purchaser may need to carry out system and localised shutdowns, in response to system needs and repairs and in accordance with scheduled maintenance and system upgrades. For example, a water treatment plant may need to be shut down for the purchasing utility to carry out necessary inspections or repairs. Because of the interruption of output caused by shutdowns, the operator and offtake purchaser will need to co-operate in order to manage shutdowns to their mutual benefit.

12.2.3   Input supplier

The operator may need to liaise with the input supplier throughout the concession period to communicate its input needs. The input supply agreement may specify different points for delivery, or different types of input based on the needs of the operator. Further, where the input supplier must make reference to another supplier or otherwise subcontract its supply obligations owing to its inability to obtain the input required, the input supplier and operator may need to co-ordinate the management of third party suppliers. The operator will have to establish an effective means of communication to manage these interfaces.

The input supplied may need to be tested, to ensure conformity with quantity and quality requirements. This testing will often be carried out in conjunction by the input supplier and the operator.

12.2.4   Grantor

The grantor will have an interest in the proper operation and maintenance of the project, to ensure that the assets it receives at the end of the concession period are in an appropriate condition and will not require extensive replacement or repair. Therefore, during operation, the grantor may wish to review to some extent the testing carried out, and to perform testing of its own, on the works to confirm the general operating condition of the project; although it will probably not want to be involved in the more detailed testing. This testing will be most important toward the end of the concession period.

Where the project is to be transferred to the grantor at the end of the concession period, the operator may need to liaise extensively with the grantor in relation to the implementation of the transfer. The transfer to the grantor may involve the operator in training the grantor's personnel, or providing other services connected with the grantor's operation of the project. The grantor may wish for the operator to continue to provide services for a time after the end of the concession period, to ensure that the grantor's personnel are completely trained in the operation, maintenance and repair of the works.

12.3   Operator's Obligations

The operator's primary obligations include ensuring the availability and efficient operation of the project. Project availability is the capacity of the project to operate to certain performance levels, i.e. level of availability of the capacity of the project to the offtake purchaser. Availability will be of great importance to the lenders, as the capacity charge is generally linked to availability and it is the capacity charge that ensures payment of fixed costs such as debt servicing. The operating regime will flow primarily from the requirements of the concession agreement and the offtake purchase agreement.

The operator will be responsible for the operation of the project in accordance with operating requirements. It will be required to ensure that the project uses inputs as efficiently as possible. The levels of efficiency achieved will need to be sufficient to satisfy the levels required in the projected financial model and the project output specifications.

12.3.1   Scope of services

The scope of services for the operation and maintenance agreement will need to be carefully drafted to include all of the services and works necessary to provide the operation and maintenance of the project and to specify which are to be allocated to the operator. The project company will bear any residual obligations.

The scope of services will need to be drafted specifically, as far as possible, to include the work and services necessary to satisfy the purpose for which the operation and maintenance agreement is let; however, it will not be able to identify all the services or work to be provided over the period of the concession. To include less specific obligations, the scope of services provisions will include standards of performance and performance criteria which will measure the work and services to be provided by the operator. The operation and maintenance agreement will also often include provision for the operator to perform "additional services" to those set out in the scope of services. Additional services will often follow a separate regime with separate pricing.

12.3.2   Standards of performance

The operator will be required to work to a standard of performance generally based on the performance standard or operating requirements set out in the concession agreement and the offtake purchase agreement. The operator will also need to comply with the construction contractor's operation and maintenance manuals and any other supplier instruction in order to maintain relevant warranties. The operator may be obliged to indemnify the project company for warranties voided by the operator's failure to comply with such requirements.

In relation to the operator's obligations, ideally the operator will accept an absolute obligation to ensure performance of the project company's obligations under the concession agreement and the offtake purchase agreement. The operator will need to carve out of his liability the effects of construction defects in the works and any default by the input supplier or the offtake purchaser.

The operation and maintenance agreement will often oblige the operator to comply with "Good Industry Practice", which definition might be:

"the practices, methods, techniques and standards that are generally accepted internationally from time to time and commonly used in the international [   ] industry for the operation and maintenance of equipment of the size and having the other characteristics of the Project in a safe, prudent and reliable manner, consistent with the parameters for such operation and maintenance set forth in this Agreement. These practices, methods, techniques and standards shall be adjusted as necessary to take account of the requirements of Law, physical conditions at the site on which the Project is located and operation and maintenance guidelines of the manufacturers of plant and equipment incorporated in the Project which the Operator is required to follow in order to maintain in effect any warranties, guarantees or insurance policies relating thereto."

The definition of "Good Industry Practice" will be modified to the specific concerns of the industry in question and may make reference to the industry standard of a particular country or group of countries, where the industry standards of the host country are not appropriate or sufficiently developed.

12.3.3   Remedy of defects

As discussed above, the operation and maintenance agreement will need to provide for management of the interfaces between the operator and the construction contractor during the defects liability period. During this period the operator will be in control of the works that have been taken over and will be responsible for the care of those works. The operator will also be responsible for operating the project to the required levels during this period. At the same time the construction contractor will be on site to repair any defects that may arise.

Defects in the works and the remedy thereof may have an impact on the operation of the project. The operator, in respect of the construction contractor intervening on the site in order to remedy defects, will need to monitor:

> identification of defects and communication thereof to the project company and the construction contractor;

> management and co-ordination of the construction contractor's activities on the site during the defects liability period;

> losses, costs and damages incurred, including both direct and indirect damages, such as loss of profit or loss of sales, owing to the construction contractor's intervention on the site in order to repair defects in the works;

> inability of the operator to operate the project to the levels required due to the construction contractor's intervention; and

> liquidated or other damages to be incurred due to failure to meet performance criteria which are attributable to the construction contractor's intervention.

12.3.4   Emergency situations

In certain emergency situations, the project company, the grantor and/or the lenders may wish to have the ability to intervene. This may involve a *force majeure* event, economic emergency or hardship, such as the failure of the input supplier or the bankruptcy of the operator or some partner of the operator. These rights are often called step-in rights or rights of intervention.[341]

12.3.5   Procurement restrictions

The host country government may apply certain procurement restrictions to foreign entities operating in its territory.[342] These requirements may be placed on the operator by local law or contractually through the concession agreement and the operation and maintenance agreement. The operator will therefore need to consider the cost and delay which it is likely to incur because of such requirements as well as the possibility that sufficient stocks of materials or necessary labour may not be available at all in the host country and the risk of breaching local content or preference obligations.

12.3.6   Spare parts

The construction contract will often require the construction contractor to provide a store of spare parts at completion. These spare parts may be available to the

---

[341]   Step-in rights are discussed in more detail in chapter 4.
[342]   Further discussion of this issue can be found in section 15.2.

construction contractor for use during the defects liability period, although they should be replenished by the construction contractor. These parts will then be put to use by the operator.

The operation and maintenance agreement may provide that the operator itself replenish the stock of spare parts to ensure their availability and that any defect or breakdown will have a limited effect on the operation of the project in accordance with the project requirements. This is of critical importance in pipeline and fibre optic cable projects, where the loss for any time that the project is unavailable is very high, and therefore the relative cost of maintaining stocks of spare parts at a variety of locations is low. Further, the grantor may wish to receive the project with the store of spare parts intact, for its own use, at the end of the concession period.

12.3.7   Asset removal/replacement

More substantial pieces of equipment and materials will need to be replaced during the concession period. The timing of asset replacement can have a direct and substantial impact on the cost of the project. Early asset replacement will generally increase the project cost and decrease the cost of operation.

The removal and/or replacement of certain parts or elements of the project during the operating period will need to be forecast, allowing the operator to notify the offtake purchaser of any need to shut down or limit operation of the project so that the removal and/or replacement can be carried out, and to notify the project company in order to budget for cost (where relevant). In some circumstances, a failure can occur requiring removal or replacement without such advanced notice.

The decision to undertake asset replacement should be made by the project company based on need, timing (including other planned maintenance procedures and shutdowns), performance goals of the project, performance demands of the offtake purchaser (including forecasts of peak demand periods) and cost. Where the project company is responsible for the cost of asset replacement, a fund will normally have been created within the project company, and provided for in the financial model, for the project to finance major maintenance operations. The project company will want to provide the operator with an incentive to manage removal and replacement of assets responsibly and reasonably, in view of the needs of the offtake purchaser, in an effort to minimise any impact on project performance and operation revenues.

12.4   Payment

The BOT project involves non-recourse lending to the project company whose primary asset is the project payment stream. The lenders will seek comfort from the financial modelling of the project which will demonstrate that the project payment stream is sufficient to satisfy debt servicing with an appropriate level of cover. Therefore, the calculation of the cost of operation, including fees paid to the operator and its relationship to the project revenues, will be essential to the lenders' cover and the viability of the project.

12.4.1   Cost of operation and payment

The financial model for the project will apply forecast operating and maintenance costs supplied by the operator. These forecasts will then be used in the pricing mechanism for the offtake purchase agreement. For this reason the lenders will want to tie the operator's payment to the figures provided in the financial model. However, in certain markets it may be difficult to obtain a fixed price, especially where the operator is not linked to the project company, the construction contractor or the equipment supplier. Therefore, another option is to tie in an escalation clause to the offtake purchase agreement, allowing for modification of the projected cost of operation which is then carried over to the price to be paid by the offtake purchaser. This will generally involve an escalation of the capacity or availability charge based on market indices specific to the cost of labour and materials.

The parties may also want to provide for a bonus scheme for the operator where the operation results in higher revenues from the offtake purchaser. In the same way, penalties can be levied on the operator for failure to perform within the offtake purchase agreement requirements. Such penalties should be sufficient to cover the project company's liability under the offtake purchase agreement and any other costs incurred by the project company owing to default by the operator, for example debt servicing and any penalties to be levied by the input supplier. It should be noted that the penalties will only cover the project company's liabilities up to the operator's liability cap.

A few of the more common options for the pricing of the operation and maintenance agreement include the following.

12.4.1.1   Fixed cost

The project company may wish to provide for a fixed price for operation and maintenance of the project, either over the concession period or for a fixed period of time. This fixed price will usually escalate with inflation and may include a variable element for certain costs.

12.4.1.2   Cost-plus

The payment stream may be based on the actual costs of the operation plus a fee or a pre-defined margin of profit. The margin will often be on a graduated scale to encourage the operator to decrease the cost of operation. By implementing target or guaranteed maximum costs, the project company provides the operator with a higher total profit margin if it keeps the overall costs below the target costs.

12.4.1.3   Unit cost

The operator may be paid based on the cost of defined tasks to be performed. The project company will then identify the tasks to be performed and set out an amount of compensation in a schedule of costs. This approach requires a very detailed schedule of costs, forecasting all tasks to be performed by the operator. It does not provide the operator with an incentive to manage the cost of operation and, in fact, could motivate the operator to do as many of the more profitable tasks in the schedule as possible early in the process to maximise its profit.

12.4.1.4 Performance-based

This payment regime provides increased income for better-than-expected results without damage to the works. This method provides an incentive to operate the project to maximum capacity but does not promote careful operation and maintenance of the facility and may result in decreased life span of the project.

12.4.1.5 "Back-to-back" or "pay-when-paid"

The most efficient mechanism to protect the project company is achieved where the operator is only paid when and to the extent that the project company is paid by the grantor or the offtake purchaser. The operator's compensation is therefore directly affected by any shortfall in output or any sanction imposed on the project company. The effectiveness of these provisions will depend on their treatment under local law.[343]

12.4.2 Budgeting for spare parts, major maintenance and asset renewal

Over the life of the concession, as discussed above, the project will require replacement of spare parts used during operation, asset renewal and major maintenance performed on the works. The operator may be required to manage such operations, in particular where the project company is lightly staffed, but may not necessarily be required to carry them out directly. Where this is the case, the operation and maintenance agreement will need to provide for budgeting approved by the project company for the purchase of spare parts, the installation of renewed assets and the performance of major maintenance. The operator would then have the budgeted funds made available by the project company to carry out the various procurement exercises.

12.4.3 Operator as agent

The project company may prefer the operator to act as its agent for some or all of the procurement exercises discussed above. The operator acting as agent can improve tax efficiency, and will result in supplier warranties provided directly to the project company. However, it may be more advantageous to the project company for the operator to be the purchaser, as the operator may have connections among regular suppliers resulting in larger discounts. Further, under applicable sale of goods laws, a warranty of the merchantability of the goods from the operator may be more interesting than a warranty provided by its suppliers.[344]

---

[343] For example, in England, Scotland and Wales, the Housing Grants, Construction and Regeneration Act 1996, see chapter 25 of Scriven, Pritchard and Delmon (1999) supra note 210.

[344] Vinter (2nd edition 1998) supra note 211 at 64.

12.4.4   Liability

The operator may be liable for liquidated and other damages in respect of failure to achieve the performance requirements and time restrictions placed on the operator for start-up of operations after completion of the construction of the works. However, the operator's liability for such damages will generally be limited for each type of damage incurred and the operator's overall liability will be limited to one aggregate maximum amount, generally per annum. The operator's liability will need to be sufficiently high to protect the project company and the lenders from inadequate performance eating into the fixed cost element of the project payment stream.

12.4.5   Foreign exchange and convertibility

The operator may have costs in both foreign and local currencies, as its personnel and equipment are likely to be sourced in both foreign and local jurisdictions, and may therefore need both a foreign and a local currency element in its fee structure. The project company will want to be paid by the offtake purchaser in multiple currencies in proportion to its costs. Where the offtake purchaser does not agree, the project company will not want to bear the risk of currency exchange rates nor the convertibility of such currencies and will therefore try to limit the cases in which it must pay out in a currency different to that in which it is paid by the offtake purchaser. Some currency risk can be shifted to the grantor or the operator; for example, the operator may have other uses for local currency and may be able to take receipt of the whole of its fee in local currency. Other aspects of currency risks can be managed by the project company, perhaps by entering into hedging or swap arrangements.

12.5   Procedures

The operation and maintenance agreement will establish a series of procedures allowing the project company to monitor the performance of the project and the compliance by the operator with his obligations.

12.5.1   Transfer of risk

The operation and maintenance agreement should specify the point at which care of the works will transfer from the construction contractor to the operator, at completion, and then from the operator to the grantor, at the end of the concession period. This transfer of risk should be defined by the passage of specified tests and the issuance of a certificate, in order to avoid disputes over the exact time of transfer.

Closely related to the transfer of risk is the definition of "completion". Although completion will play a primary role in the construction contract, it will also help to define the moment at which the operator takes on the risk for part or all of the project. Completion should require a sufficient level of performance for the project to begin commercially viable operation.

12.5.2 Independent engineer

The grantor and/or the lenders may wish to use an independent engineer to supervise the operation of the facilities to ensure the project requirements are met and that their respective interests in the project assets and revenue stream are protected. Provision should be made for the rights of access of the independent engineer to the site and the project, the tests or inspections it may attend or perform and what notice will be provided to the operator. The independent engineer should be given some latitude of access without impeding the proper and efficient operation of the project.

12.5.3 Access to books and records

The project company will wish to monitor the records of the operator which are specific to the project to ensure proper operation, response to project requirements, outages and compliance with the operation programme developed with the offtake purchaser. The grantor may also want to have access to the operator's books and records to provide a detailed picture of the operation of the project to ensure that operation and maintenance has been carried out in accordance with relevant requirements and to provide information to future operators or personnel who will be involved after the end of the concession period.

The operator will want to limit access to its books and records so as to protect confidential information and restrict the scope of audit to manage the administrative cost of such reviews and the potential impact on the proper functioning of the project.

12.5.4 Training of the grantor's personnel

The grantor may require the project company to provide for the training of the grantor's personnel before transfer at the end of the concession period. The project company will generally allocate this obligation to the operator. The training will usually be carried out at the end of the concession period, just before transfer of the project to the grantor. The grantor's personnel will be trained in operation, maintenance and basic repair, where feasible. The training obligation will also permit a greater transfer of know-how to the host country through the education of local staff in the operation and maintenance of the project.

A regime will need to be developed for the timing of training sessions, the selection of the personnel to be trained, the training methods to be used, the extent of the training to be given and the allocation of responsibility for the personnel to be trained. As it is the grantor who will select the candidates for training, the operator may be hesitant to take on the responsibility for such personnel during the training period, including, for example, accidents, damage to the works owing to trainee negligence, sickness, workers' compensation and other employment liabilities. However, the grantor will not want to bear the risk of employing personnel who are under the direction and tutelage of the operator. This issue may be further complicated where training must take place at a location far from the trainees' homes and where lodging, transportation and other necessities must be provided on or to the site.

The training obligations may be partially or wholly obviated where the operator merely transfers its own personnel responsible for the project to the grantor, at least for an agreed time. This would involve the creation of a direct relationship between the relevant personnel and the grantor, and will provide the grantor with on-site, experienced assistance for the operation and maintenance of the project.

12.5.5   Transfer

At the end of the concession period, the project will be transferred back to the grantor or to another operator. The regime for such transfer will need to be defined in the operation and maintenance agreement. This regime will need to include any tests to be performed, the levels of spare parts to be provided, the shifting of responsibility to the grantor's personnel and the transfer of risk to the grantor. The transfer arrangements will need to be co-ordinated with similar arrangements in the input supply and the offtake purchase agreements in order to provide a seamless transfer to the grantor.

Chapter 13

Offtake Purchase Agreement

A human being has a natural desire to have more of a
good thing than he needs.

Mark Twain

The offtake purchase agreement allocates the market risk of demand and the price for project output to an offtake purchaser. The offtake purchaser, although there may be more than one, is generally a local utility, public service provider or operator which will purchase the output from the project company and then sell the output on the market, either directly to end users or to other offtake purchasers. The offtake purchase agreement sits in the BOT project structure as indicated in the chart below.

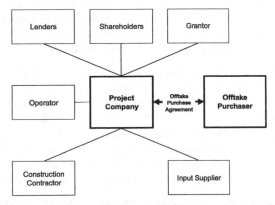

The offtake purchase agreement defines and delimits the revenue stream to be received by the project company, and therefore the lenders and shareholders, over the life (usually 15 to 30 years) of the project. It will define not only the amount of the revenue stream but also when it can be interrupted, modified or terminated. Although in theory the offtake purchase agreement is intended merely to allocate the market risks involved in distribution of the project output to end users, the offtake purchaser frequently plays a much more central role in the development of the project. Generally, the offtake purchaser is one of the driving forces behind the project. It is often the offtake purchaser itself which has identified the need for the output and initiated or influenced the putting of the project out to tender.

The provisions of the offtake purchase agreement must reflect the nature of the output and the specific market of the project. This chapter assumes an offtake purchase agreement for a project whose output is an asset produced by the project and sold on to the offtake purchaser. Where the project involves an output which is a facility or service, such as a road or bridge, or possibly a hospital or prison whose facilities will be made available to the offtake purchaser, the provisions of the offtake purchase agreement described below will need to be modified accordingly. Chapters 17-22 provide further information on the requirements of different outputs and products.

Offtake purchase agreements will only be appropriate to certain types of BOT projects. They are common to power projects, the so-called "power purchase agreement", and may be used in water projects, often called "water purchase agreements", or other production projects, such as industrial plant (for example, aluminium smelters and oil refineries). However, BOT projects will often be structured without an offtake purchase agreement. For example (and by definition), merchant plants will not secure purchase of offtake, placing demand and price risk on the project company and therefore the lenders. Where the grantor benefits from the offtake of the project a more common approach is to include the elements of the offtake purchase agreement (set out below) in the concession agreement. In such cases, this chapter should be read together with chapter 8.

The amount of output required by the offtake purchaser will fluctuate based on market demand, and the project company will often want to allocate to the offtake purchaser both the risk of generation cost and market demand. The offtake purchase agreement will generally provide, in one form or another, for the offtake purchaser to bear a substantial portion of both of these risks.

A common method of defining the amount due by the offtake purchaser to the project company is by way of a dual payment system, commonly including a capacity (or availability) charge and a usage (or offtake) charge. The capacity charge is that amount paid by the offtake purchaser to the project company for making the project available to the offtake purchaser and on the amount of capacity the project places at the disposal of the offtake purchaser. For example, a BOT hospital project would include a capacity payment based on the availability of hospital facilities to the offtake purchaser irrespective of actual usage.

The capacity charge will compensate the project company for the fixed costs it incurs in running the project including, for example, financing charges, labour and insurance. Therefore, no matter what amount of output the offtake purchaser decides to draw from the system, it must pay for the fixed costs of the project company in consideration of the project company making the project available to the offtake purchaser. Where the project does not perform sufficiently well and does not make available the capacity required, then the capacity charge can be reduced.

The usage charge is that paid for the amount of project output actually taken, or used, by the offtake purchaser during the payment period. This payment will cover the variable costs of operation, such as the cost of input, some or all of the equity return and variable maintenance costs. The input cost may simply flow through to the offtake purchaser; however, care should be taken in case the cost of input increases owing to inefficiency of the project, such as high heat rate in the case of a power plant (where the power plant requires more fuel per unit of energy than was intended, or where the fuel is of an insufficient quality requiring more fuel to be burned).

The input may also be directly provided by the offtake purchaser, in particular where the offtake purchaser is vertically integrated, i.e. where a company owns or controls an upstream and downstream network allowing it to control a product from raw materials through to the end user. This may be the case, for example, for a:

> ➢ water project, where the water utility offtake purchaser also provides the raw water; or

> ➢ pipeline, which will use a through-put agreement where the offtake purchaser puts a product in one end and takes it out at the other; or

> ➢ power project, where the power purchaser provides gas and through a tolling agreement the project company is paid to convert gas into electricity.

The validity and applicability of the offtake purchase agreement and its payment provisions need to be reviewed under local law. Where, under English or United States law, the concept of the offtake purchaser paying a price several times that of the market price because of a take-or-pay agreement would not cause any problems, this may not be the case in other jurisdictions.[345]

This chapter will review the project risk allocation generally encountered (section 13.1), the interfaces between the parties involved (section 13.2), the major obligations placed on the offtake purchaser (section 13.3), the payment provisions (section 13.4), and the mechanisms and procedures to be included in an offtake purchase agreement (section 13.5). Further issues which are common to the project documents are discussed in chapter 15.

13.1   Risk Allocation

The project company will allocate to the offtake purchaser the majority of the demand risk related to project output and other related market and operation risks.

---

[345]   Rushton and McNair, "Public Projects: Private Finance" [December 1994] PLC 21 at 24; this said, care will need to be taken in relation to the formulation of that take-or-pay payment to avoid it being considered a penalty and therefore unenforceable.

13.1.1   Market risk

During the concession period it is likely that the price of output will fluctuate. The lenders, not wanting to bear the risk of volatility, will want such risk allocated away from the project company. The project company will use the offtake purchase agreement to allocate a part of the project market risk to the offtake purchaser. Market risks will include price, cost and demand. The offtake purchaser will generally pay the project company for the output produced in accordance with a fixed formula defined in the offtake purchase agreement.

Similarly, during the concession period the cost of transmission or transportation of output to the offtake purchaser may increase, due to increased cost of structural improvements, new mechanisms or other costs such as higher taxation. The risk of increased cost of transmission will generally be allocated to the offtake purchaser. The price for capacity or usage will, therefore, not take into consideration any increased costs of transmission, nor will the offtake purchaser be allowed to levy such charges against the project company or the operator during the concession period.

Further, the lenders will not wish to bear the risk of demand for output. Where popular demand for output decreases, the offtake purchaser will be required to bear a large portion of this risk. This would potentially cover the risk that government regulation might limit use of the output or reduce its attractiveness, for example by increasing the associated tax burden. This allocation is accomplished through mechanisms such as take-or-pay and capacity charge/usage charge discussed later in this chapter.[346]

13.1.2   Operation risk

The project company may require the offtake purchaser to bear any risk in connection with the operation of the project which is related to the transportation/transmission system or the offtake purchaser's acts or omissions. This allocation of risk should follow reasonable lines, including the responsibility for those aspects of the project which are in the control of the offtake purchaser; for example, in a power project, the grid and other aspects of the transmission system. Where the offtake purchaser fails to take the output as required or where the offtake purchaser's improper management of any offtake infrastructure results in failure of the project, the offtake purchaser should be responsible.

13.2   Interfaces

Interfaces between the project participants can be crucial to the successful implementation of the project. Comprehensive and efficient management of the project will require careful consideration of each of these interfaces and their management.

---

[346]   See section 13.4.1.

13.2.1 Operator

The offtake purchaser and the operator will need to maintain a constant relationship throughout the concession period. They will need to develop an efficient mechanism to facilitate the communication to the operator of the offtake purchaser's needs. The parties will then have to organise the delivery and receipt of the output provided, including inspections and testing. The parties will want to decide how testing of the output will occur, who will analyse the results and decide who will maintain or replace the equipment as needed.

The offtake purchaser and the operator will need to shut down part or all of the project from time to time in order to perform maintenance or repairs to the project or to some aspect of the offtake purchaser's system. These outages should be carried out in parallel where possible. Certain outages will be planned and therefore easy to co-ordinate. Provision will need to be made for emergency maintenance or repairs.

An additional interface between the operator and the offtake purchaser is their shared liability for operation failures. The operator will be responsible for operation failures generally, while the offtake purchaser will be responsible for failures related to that part of the facilities provided by and/or under the care of the offtake purchaser and any defect in the offtake purchaser's methods for lifting or benefiting from the project output.

13.2.2 Construction contractor

The offtake purchaser will liaise with the construction contractor, primarily during the construction phase. The construction contractor's works will need to interface properly with the offtake purchaser's system and any infrastructure the offtake purchaser may provide. The offtake purchaser will need to provide the necessary technical information to the construction contractor for the design of such interfaces and may want to be present for the testing of works which will interface with its facilities.

During the testing and commissioning phase of construction, the completion and performance tests carried out on the works will generate a certain amount of output. The offtake purchaser may need to take this output in order to enable the construction contractor to finish commissioning the works and perform tests. The output generated may be of an appreciable quantity, in which case the construction contractor or the project company should be credited with the value of the output generated. This will, of course, only apply to projects such as power, water and industrial plants, but will not generally apply to facility projects such as hospitals, offices and prisons where no actual use of the works can occur during testing.

13.3 Primary Obligations

The offtake purchase agreement will set out a series of important obligations to be placed on each of the parties. These obligations will be set out both in the body of the offtake purchase agreement and in the schedules, in particular the scope of services.

13.3.1   Scope of services

The services to be performed by the project company will focus primarily on operation of the project in accordance with the requirements of the offtake purchaser, and proper communication with the offtake purchaser concerning the programme of operation of the project. The majority of these obligations will be passed down to the operator and mirrored in the operation and maintenance agreement.

The offtake purchaser will provide services related generally to the efficiency of transmission or transportation of offtake or enjoyment of the services to be rendered by the project company (through the operator). The scope of offtake purchaser services may include development of infrastructure, provision of equipment or connection with existing infrastructure. The offtake purchaser may be required to provide services during operation, such as maintenance of its own or specified common facilities, performance of tests, assistance to the project company during operation, obtaining permits and licences, access to and possession of land, and providing input necessary for the proper and effective operation of the project.

13.3.2   Quantity

The project company will generally contract to sell the entire product of the project, assuming an appropriate offtake purchaser can be found. Alternatively, the project company may find several separate offtake purchasers for the output produced. The project company may contract with the local utility or other offtake purchasers for the purchase of any remaining capacity.

The offtake purchaser may also be required to take a minimum amount of output, or be restricted to the extent to which it can reduce the amount of output taken. This will be particularly important to the project company where it is required to take a minimum amount of input. Breach of this minimum take requirement could result in termination of the input supply agreement.

13.3.3   Technical and performance specifications

The offtake purchaser will want to define closely the technical parameters of operation in order to satisfy performance and other technical requirements. The simplest method of ensuring such technical parameters is for the offtake purchaser to specify minimum levels of performance and capacity. These will include levels of secure, clean and safe operation within certain ranges of technical, climatic and other operating parameters and other important requirements, such as the time necessary to alter project output to meet a variation in the offtake purchaser's requirements. The project company will then be penalised where the project does not satisfy these basic requirements.

The project's technical requirements will often be set out in a code of operation used by the offtake purchaser, particularly where the offtake purchaser is a utility or where local law applies specific standards. This code will describe the operation parameters of the offtake purchaser and may also provide the requirements placed on the project in order for it to operate within the applicable technical standards and any special requirements of the offtake purchaser's system. For example, a rail project will be required to match the technical code set out for the relevant railway system, including track gauge, signalling, fouling points and OHLE mast positioning. The code will generally be attached to the technical specifications to ensure fitness of the project for operation with the offtake purchaser's system. Failure by the project to operate within the parameters of the code may render the output useless to the offtake purchaser, therefore appropriate sanctions are likely to be included in the offtake purchase agreement.

13.3.4   Modifications to the project

The offtake purchaser will want to ensure that the project is not modified where such modifications might contravene industry practice, or render the project incompatible, in any way, with the offtake purchaser's system or the transmission system. Further, the offtake purchaser will want to receive a detailed description of any modifications proposed. The offtake purchaser's concerns may translate into either a restriction of changes to the project which might affect the offtake purchaser, or a restriction on any change without offtake purchaser approval.

13.3.5   Facilities provided by offtake purchaser

The offtake purchaser may be required to provide certain assistance to the project company to enable it to construct and operate the project. For example, the offtake purchaser may be required to connect the project to its facilities, provide equipment and personnel for the services to be rendered or possibly ensure operation of the necessary infrastructure. This may involve extensive construction of interconnection facilities or associated infrastructure.

In order to procure less expensive land, the project may be constructed at a distance from other facilities. The offtake purchaser may therefore be required to provide necessary access, such as pipelines, ports, roads and bridges. The project company may also want the offtake purchaser, in particular where it is also a local utility, to provide supplies, such as electricity, water or other utilities.

Where the offtake purchaser does not complete the facilities required by the date for completion, then the offtake purchase agreement may provide that, unless the failure is caused by some excepted event or circumstance, the offtake purchaser will be liable for payment of the whole of the capacity charge during the delay period.

13.3.6   Ancillary services

The offtake purchaser may require certain ancillary services from the project company. A cost regime should be provided for any such services, including a payment for making available to the offtake purchaser such ancillary services and the actual provision of the services. Examples of ancillary services which may be required by the offtake purchaser for power projects are discussed further in chapter 17.

13.3.7 Completion and transition

The offtake purchaser will require commencement of output production, and therefore completion of the construction works, by a specified date. The transition from the construction period to the operation period, completion and commencement of output production, should be identified by the passing of defined tests or the issue of a certificate. Completion under the offtake purchase agreement should correspond to completion under the construction contract.

The offtake purchaser will want to ensure that, on completion, the project is sufficient to satisfy its performance needs. Therefore, the offtake purchaser will probably wish for the concept of completion to include a minimum performance requirement, sufficient for its basic needs.

13.3.8 Transfer to grantor

The offtake purchase agreement may need to provide for the eventual transfer of the project to the grantor, and to define how the offtake purchaser is to be involved in that transfer. The transfer regime may involve extensive testing of the project, including the interfaces with the offtake purchaser and other facilities provided and maintained by the offtake purchaser. The grantor may also wish to continue the relationship with the offtake purchaser after the end of the concession period. Such an agreement would generally be contained in a direct agreement between the offtake purchaser and the grantor.

13.4 Price and Payment

The offtake purchase agreement provides the project cash flow. For the project to be bankable, the lenders must be comfortable that the output produced will be purchased at a price sufficient to sustain the required debt service and loan life cover ratios.

The payment provisions of the offtake purchase agreement will need to be co-ordinated with the financing agreement and its debt service requirements as well as the input supply agreement, the operation and maintenance agreement and, possibly, payments due to the construction contractor.

The offtake purchase agreement will provide a procedure for the calculation of the amount to be paid by the offtake purchaser to the project company, which should be objective, sensible and either easy to calculate or self-policing.[347] The pricing mechanism should be efficient with a view to avoiding or managing disputes.

The pricing mechanism will need to take into consideration inflationary pressures on the market in question. This concern can be addressed by either providing for a fixed method of calculating price (without consideration of inflation), or by calculating the rate of inflation into the price to be paid. The rate of inflation will usually be identified by indices defined by a reliable source, such as the host country's central bank. Where the risk of inflation is placed on the project company, this risk can be hedged or allocated to other project participants.

The pricing mechanism should also focus on encouraging the project company to maximise efficiency. This will require a flexible mechanism, sensitive to the performance of the project and managed by the grantor. Where the pricing mechanism is managed by some other government agency not bound by the concession agreement and which has discretion in the setting of tariffs, the project company may bear substantial political and pricing risk which may render the project unbankable.

Certain rudimentary methods of pricing are sometimes used in developing countries where the respective governments have not yet developed a sophisticated approach to BOT projects. For example, early independent power projects in China used a simple cost-plus pricing method compensating the project company for operating costs, taxes and a "reasonable profit" (in an effort to fix the project company's margin).[348] Since the only negotiable aspect of this formula is the amount of profit allowed, it does not provide a benefit for more efficient production, therefore no emphasis is given to competitive pricing and lower cost of production.

More sophisticated approaches include, for example, charging a straight per unit output fee with a minimum offtake requirement to cover fixed costs. However, this method will need to be adjusted in consideration of the project company's variable costs. The project could also use a tolling arrangement where the offtake purchaser provides the input at no charge. The project company is then paid a fixed amount per unit of input processed with some minimum toll per payment period imposed to cover fixed costs. The project company is effectively paid for processing each unit of input.

The most common method of payment in BOT projects splits the cost paid into a charge for capacity/availability and a charge for the actual use of the facility. By splitting the charge between these two elements, the project company is given an incentive to ensure that the project is available to the offtake purchaser and provides sufficient capacity, as required. The offtake purchaser will also compensate the project company for actual use of the project. The basic approach

---

[347] Private Finance Panel, Practical Guidance to the Private Finance Initiative: Further Contractual Issues at 4 (1997).
[348] Boykin, "Financing Progress" First Magazine 1 at 11 (1997).

to this particular payment scheme is described further in sections 13.4.1 and 13.4.2. This is a very simplified illustration which in practice may be complicated by the particular nature of the project and the relationship between the project participants.

13.4.1   Capacity charge

Capacity means that the project has been designed and built to comply with the requirements under the project documents. But, capacity by itself is of no use to the offtake purchaser if output is not available to the offtake purchaser as and when required. This issue will arise only where capacity and availability are separable. For example, on a toll road project capacity may be defined as the ability to accommodate a certain traffic flow; availability would merely be how much traffic had access measured on an hourly basis. For a water treatment project, capacity may be the technical wherewithal to treat a certain volume of water per hour, and availability the ability to process a given volume of water during a given period.

The project company is paid a set amount based on the level of capacity and availability achieved by the project, called the "capacity charge" (or the "availability charge"). The capacity charge provides the whole of the project's fixed costs, including debt servicing, and will therefore be of particular interest to the lenders.

The capacity charge is usually calculated per unit, based on the intended capacity of the project. For example, a water treatment facility with an intended capacity of 250 megalitres per day will receive the whole of the capacity fee only where the project makes the required level of capacity available to the offtake purchaser. Any capacity shortage will result in a reduction of the capacity charge. The offtake purchaser should decide whether the charge will be capped at 100 per cent. of the intended capacity of the project or whether the project company should be rewarded for extra capacity. The extent to which the project company is rewarded should be based on the value of extra capacity to the offtake purchaser. In developing countries, where infrastructure supply is generally at a premium, the offtake purchaser will often prefer to provide for such a bonus.

The offtake purchaser may provide that a minimum level of capacity must be reached before it will pay any of the capacity charge. The liability for the project failing to reach the minimum capacity required should be specifically allocated to the project company, and then passed through to the responsible project participants.

The parties must decide when the project will be tested for capacity and whether planned tests can be delayed or repeated. Where the test results are not satisfactory, the project company will want the opportunity to re-test the works. The project company may also want to delay testing where there are temporary problems or where the conditions are inappropriate for reasonable testing. However, the parties should establish how any deficiency found after delayed tests should be treated. The offtake purchaser will want to apply the penalty for insufficient capacity retroactively to the date on which the tests were to have taken place. The offtake purchaser may also insist on re-testing after any serious event, such as a forced closure or outage.

Where project availability does not meet the requirements of the offtake purchase agreement, the capacity charge may be affected. The project company will generally be penalised in accordance with the difference between the availability provided and that required, either scaled or per percentage point of difference; although the parties may prefer to use lump-sum liquidated damages. This calculation may also take into consideration the offtake purchaser's need for output at the time the availability falls below the required level. For example, during peak demand periods the penalty for lack of availability may be greater.

The project company may be required to issue availability notices periodically; often hourly or daily. Monitoring the project company's availability declarations may be difficult. The offtake purchaser will need to put in place a procedure for policing the project company's claims of availability as well as imposing penalties for incorrect declarations. Consideration should be made for sudden project breakdown, or other causes not within the project company's responsibility.

The difficulty in verifying the project company's declaration may necessitate imposing a penalty for inaccurate declaration which is sufficiently severe to dissuade the project company from further inaccurate declarations. Some agreements decrease the penalty where the project company has provided 100 per cent. availability during an immediately preceding period to compensate for sudden and short-term breakdown; however, such a provision could result in abuse by the project company.

Obviously, these issues will only be relevant for projects in which demand cycles change rapidly, for example power generation, telecommunications and hospitals.

13.4.2   Usage charge

The usage charge is based on the variable costs to be incurred by the project company, such as input costs and variable operation and maintenance costs. The input costs will either be factored into the calculation of the usage charge, or they may simply flow through to the offtake purchaser. The usage charge is often the principal source of return on equity.

The usage charge is generally calculated per unit of output. The charge per unit is calculated by project efficiency, the input needed per unit. For example, in thermal power projects, fuel is often purchased according to its energy content. Fuel energy content is measured in Joules in the metric system and BTUs (British Thermal Units) in the British system. Project efficiency will provide a certain kJ/kWh. Thus, where the project company pays US$.00001 per kJ of fuel and the project produces 5,000kJ/kWh, then the cost of fuel in relation to output will be US$.05 per kWh.

13.4.3   Input efficiency

The offtake purchase agreement will require an efficiency of input use (known in thermal power projects as a "heat rate") which identifies the number of units of input needed for each unit of output. A large margin between required and actual efficiency can provide the project company with a substantial source of profit. The inverse is also true in that a negative margin will represent a project risk. Input efficiency will form part of the performance requirements placed on the construction contractor and verified through the performance tests. Failure to achieve the required input efficiency will result in the construction contractor being liable for performance liquidated damages, which will compensate for increased cost of input over time.

The project company holds all of the information on the anticipated input efficiency of the project; this is particularly true when the offtake purchaser is not familiar with the technology being used. Therefore the offtake purchaser may be advised to obtain the services of an independent engineer in order to establish a reasonable input efficiency to be implemented into the offtake purchase agreement.

The operation and maintenance of the project will have an important impact on the efficiency of input use. Input efficiency may also be a function of the demands made by the offtake purchaser. The project may be less efficient at lower levels of output or where the output requirements are frequently altered.

Input efficiency forecasts will need to take into consideration the depreciation of the project assets over time. Some modification of the usage charge may need to be made as a function of normal deterioration of materials and equipment.

13.4.4   Input supply

The project company may be bound to a certain minimum take requirement under the input supply agreement. This requirement can be passed through to the offtake purchaser by passing the input costs directly to the offtake purchaser as part of the usage charge. This may not be possible in certain more regulated economies where utility prices are subject to central controls.[349]

Project sites are often located in remote areas where facilities are limited. For this reason input suppliers are often required to provide special facilities, such as port facilities, pipeline access, or transportation and storage facilities for the input. Project input requirements may mean that the project company needs the input supplier to provide a dedicated input source. The minimum amount of input which must be purchased by the project company may be extremely high, such as 90-95 per cent. of total project requirements, to compensate for the high cost of dedication of resources to the project company's needs and the construction of infrastructure.

---

[349]   Rushton and McNair (May 1994) supra note 235 at 30.

13.4.5 Metering of output

The parties will need to allocate the responsibility to measure the output produced. Certain types of output require meters to be installed to measure offtake. Because of the potential cost and complexity of metering equipment, its provision will generally fall to the project company. Multiple meters should be installed, with one set being the primary meters and the others acting as reserve units in case of failure of the primary units. An operation and maintenance procedure should be established for the metering facilities.

The nature of the meters should also be established in the offtake purchase agreement. Metering for roadways may be limited to toll booths or, particularly where shadow tolls are to be paid, sensors may be installed in the road to measure the number and type of vehicles that use the road, as larger and heavier vehicles will elicit a higher per-unit payment. The meters in power, water and other such projects may need to monitor both production and consumption. In power projects, for example, the project company will need to use energy from the grid in certain circumstances, such as for start-up of the plant. Therefore, some agreement must be achieved as to how to treat the energy used by the project company from the grid. Where that energy will merely be deducted from the energy produced, then bi-directional meters will provide such information. However, where the cost of energy taken from the grid is different from energy produced by the project company, separate unidirectional units must be installed (one for each direction).

The location of the metering equipment must also be established. Some amount of output may be lost during transmission (for example from leaks in pipes from a water treatment plant). The party responsible for the transmission should be responsible for the loss incurred. Offtake purchase agreements generally use the commercial boundary of the project as the place at which metering occurs. In this way the project company is responsible for any loss within the works, as far as those works may extend. Where the project company is also responsible for providing transmission facilities, the offtake purchaser may want to place the responsibility for any loss during the relevant transmission on the project company. Therefore, the definition of the point of delivery of output is of great importance.

13.4.6 Other offtake

The project may produce other valuable and saleable services besides the primary output. Two examples of projects which produce multiple offtake in the power generation sector are combined heat and power plants and co-generation plants. These examples are discussed in further detail in chapter 17. Where other offtake or services are to be provided, a parallel revenue stream may need to be provided. The several services may be mutually exclusive. For example, steam drawn from a co-generation plant can reduce electrical generation. Therefore the offtake purchaser will want to control what is generated and when. The project company will need to ensure that the offtake purchaser's choice of output does not unacceptably reduce revenues.

13.4.7   Other pricing schemes

The above describes pricing schemes commonly used for projects which produce some physical product which will be sold to an end user or possibly distributed by the grantor. Other types of project include those offering a facility to the grantor or some other end user. The grantor will generally pay the project company for availability and use of the project over the period of the concession. This would be the case for a hospital project or educational facility. The project company might provide the infrastructure and maintain it over the concession period, while the grantor uses the facility and provides services (for example, medical or educational) from the facility to end users.

The payment schemes for such facility projects follow similar logic to production projects. The project company's fixed costs and possibly some equity return will be compensated for against the provision of the capacity and availability of the infrastructure. Payments for variable costs and the balance of the equity return would then be made against actual use of the facility.

13.4.8   Bonuses

The offtake purchase agreement may provide for bonuses where the target availability is surpassed and such added availability will provide the grantor with a benefit. These bonuses will generally be proportional to the amount by which actual availability differs from the target availability and the extent to which the additional availability benefits the project company. The timing and procedure for measuring and calculating these variations from target availability must be defined in the offtake purchase agreement.

13.4.9   Guarantees

The project company may require guarantees of the offtake purchaser's obligations, based on the creditworthiness of the offtake purchaser. In the case of a public utility, this may involve a government guarantee. However, in some situations, the host government may refuse to provide such a guarantee. This has been a problem recently in projects in India, where the government has refused to provide government guarantees except for certain "fast track" power projects. In order to protect the lenders and enable the project to go forward, certain alternative mechanisms have been considered; for example, in some cases, multilateral agencies have been asked to provide such guarantees. Although this represents a departure from previous practice, it may become more commonplace, as developing countries are increasingly less willing to guarantee their public utilities or are prevented from doing so by financing bodies such as the International Monetary Fund (the "IMF").

13.4.10   Foreign exchange risk

International projects will often involve currency risks. Generally, the financing for the project will be partially denominated in a foreign currency. Project participants may be foreign entities, requiring partial payment in foreign currencies, and the shareholders often include foreign entities amongst their number, who may prefer to obtain a return on their investment in foreign currency. Yet, the income from the sale of the output produced will generally be denominated in local currency (this may not be the case where, for example, the output is to be exported). Therefore, some exchange of currency will need to occur, and the risk that the exchange rates between the relevant currencies will vary during the concession period is high. There is also a risk that the currency may not be transferable or convertible when needed, or may only be partially convertible.[350]

13.5 Mechanisms and Procedures

As noted in chapter 7, an essential risk to be managed through the project documents is the practical interface between the project participants. Certain of these have been noted above. The following section gives a general overview of two aspects of this risk related to the offtake purchaser.

13.5.1 Operation regime

The offtake purchaser may have periodic input into the operation of the project in view of its own offtake requirements. The offtake purchaser may want to have access to the project's capacity at the times and in the amounts it requires. The decision to draw on the project's capacity may depend on the demand from end users, the transmission or transportation facilities available to the offtake purchaser, the relative cost of the output provided, the output or facilities available from other sources, the cost of starting up and shutting down the project facilities, ancillary services available from various other facilities, and a multitude of other technical, commercial and financial variables. Therefore, for certain projects, for example power generation, telecommunications, and hospitals, only the offtake purchaser is able to decide when and to what extent output should be taken or usage should be made available from the project.

To permit efficient and effective management of the project the parties will need to share information. This sharing of information will start with the project company's reports to the offtake purchaser on the capacity and availability of the project. With this information in hand the offtake purchaser will be able to calculate what part of its needs it will source from the project. The offtake purchaser will then provide the project company with additional output instructions for the operation of the project.

13.5.2 Maintenance regime

Maintenance of the project facilities may involve shutting down part or all of the facility for certain periods of time. For this reason the offtake purchaser will want to influence the decision as to when such maintenance is performed, so that such

---

[350] For further discussion of currency issues, see section 15.3.2.

decisions correspond either with the offtake purchaser's maintenance of associated and mutually dependent facilities or with periods of decreased demand, to ensure that the offtake purchaser's needs are met or can be fulfilled by other sources of supply.

A detailed programme of the maintenance procedure should be submitted by the project company to the offtake purchaser in order to permit appropriate management of scheduled shutdowns or outages. New maintenance schedules can be negotiated periodically. A procedure for negotiations should be set out as well as the right of one party, or possibly a third party expert, to resolve any disputes that may arise. Further provision will need to be made for scheduling unforeseen outages, as far as possible, and otherwise managing such shutdowns so they will have the least possible impact on both the offtake purchaser and the project company.

Chapter 14

Input Supply Agreement

Garbage in, garbage out.

My Mom and Saint Paul,
The Bible, Epistle to the Philippians

The BOT project may need some form of input in order for it to operate. The project company will not want to bear the risk that required input will not be available when it is needed and at an appropriate price in view of the project's financial model. Therefore, the project company will often contract with an input supplier to provide the necessary input to the extent of the project's needs or to the minimum level necessary for the project's operation. This contract is known as the input supply agreement. It sits in the BOT project structure as indicated below.

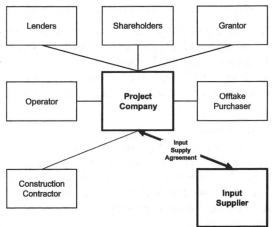

The input supply agreement involves an input supplier contracting to provide a certain amount of input of a given quality at a given price. Only certain input suppliers will be willing to sign up to such a commitment over the entire term of the concession. For example, coal suppliers will have long-term capacity, using

273

the income from an input supply agreement to finance the development of new coal fields or infrastructure. The supply of fuel oil, on the other hand, may be more difficult to commit to over the concession period owing to fluctuations in the market. LNG or natural gas will suffer from other constraints, such as transportation and storage limitations; however, a local utility may be in a position to supply gas to the plant, which may satisfy the grantor's preference for locally sourced (and therefore priced) fuel.

The necessary input may be provided by the grantor and/or the offtake purchaser. In such cases the input supply provisions discussed below may be incorporated in the concession agreement or the offtake purchase agreement.[351]

Input suppliers willing to commit to long-term obligations to provide input at a given price are often protected by back-to-back long-term sales agreements with other suppliers, or by a monopoly position. The latter is often the case where the input supplier is a local or national utility. Relying on the monopoly position of the input supplier may result in difficulties where the host government decides to privatise the utility or liberalise the industry, removing the monopolistic position of the input supplier and throwing confusion into the future of the take-or-pay agreement. The parties to the input supply agreement should provide a remedy for such a situation to avoid the potential delay and expense of a resolution provided by the courts.[352]

Not all projects will require such agreements. Input supply agreements are less common in projects which provide a facility, such as a hospital or roadway, than those which produce an output or refine or process raw materials, such as a refinery or a power project. The project company and the lenders may also be willing to take market risk on input supply. This will be the case where the relevant input has a very flexible market with abundant supply.

The issue of transportation will also need to be addressed. The project company may need to enter into a long-term contract for transportation of the input, even where the project company and the lenders are willing to take market risk on procurement of the input itself. The mode of transportation will depend on site location, the nature of the input, the state of local infrastructure and also licensing availability and restrictions.

The input needed for operation of the project can vary in form and nature. The most common form of input supply agreement is that used for the supply of fuel for a fossil fuel power project. These agreements are known as "fuel supply", "coal supply" or "gas supply" agreements. Other forms of input for which an input supply agreement may be needed include raw materials or electricity for industrial plants, or raw water for water treatment projects.

---

[351] This chapter may therefore need to be read in conjunction with chapters 8 and 13.
[352] Griffin, Take or Pay Contracts in Liberalised Gas and Electricity Markets, PFI 120 at 39.

In some BOT projects, the project company may need to pay for certain types of offtake. For instance in a sewage treatment project, the project company may need to pay a third party to remove sludge from the project for landfill, incineration, processing or dumping. These services may require a long-term contract, in order to secure financing. This chapter will cover issues relevant to most types of input supply agreement, but the specific requirements of such alternative supply contracts will need to be considered carefully.

In discussing the input supply agreement, this chapter will review first the risks generally allocated to the input supplier (section 14.1), the interfaces of the input supplier with the other project participants (section 14.2), principal obligations (section 14.3), payment (section 14.4), and the mechanisms and procedures commonly used (section 14.5). For ease of reference, this chapter will assume an input supply agreement for the supply, transportation and delivery to the site of the input required for the duration of the project. Further issues, which are common to the project documents, are discussed in chapter 15.

14.1 Risk Allocation

14.1.1 Market risk

The project company and the lenders may not want to bear the risk of the cost of input rising during the concession period. Therefore, they will often pass this risk to the input supplier by agreeing to a fixed (though generally index linked) price equation in the input supply agreement. The cost of input will include the cost of export from the source country, import into the host country, and transport to the site. The input supplier will generally be responsible for obtaining the proper permits and licences for importing the input into the host country.

The input supplier will also bear the risk of providing the full amount of input required. Any failure on the part of the input supplier to provide the amount required will result in liquidated damages or a decrease in the price paid for the input delivered. Where shortages occur, the input supplier will be responsible for obtaining the necessary amount of input from other suppliers or other locations.

14.1.2 Operation risk

The input supplier will also be allocated some of the performance risk for the project, in as much as it is required to provide a given quantity of input at a given quality and at a given time. Where the input is provided late or in insufficient quantity, the performance of the project will suffer. The input supplier will be responsible for the risk associated with this failure.

The quality of the input provided can be a more complex issue. Inputs will have different measures of quality and there will be different results from the use of input which does not meet the quality standards set. The quality of the input may be measured by the amount of foreign substances present in the input. This is the case for coal which may contain a certain measure of ash, moisture or other contaminants. Other input may be measured by purity or possibly by the effort required to use, refine or process the relevant input. In any case, a testing regime will identify the quality of the input delivered. The risk of failed performance may be allocated to the input supplier where it is caused by the provision of input which does not meet the established quality requirements.

14.2   Interfaces

The input supplier will be involved during the operation phase of the project, therefore it will liaise primarily with the operator. However, the input supplier will also liaise with the construction contractor during testing, commissioning and performance testing of the works.

14.2.1   Operator

The input supplier will need to co-ordinate with the operator to identify the quantity of input needed and manage delivery of input to the site. Delivery to the site may be complicated; for example, where the input used is considered to be a potentially dangerous item and therefore heavily regulated, or where transportation and storage are complicated. Where the project in question uses quantities of highly toxic or volatile materials, the host government will control carefully the importation and transportation of such inputs. The project company may need to enter into agreements for disposal of used fuel, lubricants and other substances necessary for operation that require special or costly disposal processes. Disposal services may be provided by the input supplier or alternatively by another contractor better placed to effectuate such disposal.

The input supplier will also liaise with the operator about the testing of the input supplied. The input will need to be tested to ensure that it satisfies the input supply agreement quality requirements, and the input supplier may want to be involved in this testing. Another option is to appoint a testing authority; a third party who will intervene to perform any testing necessary and ensure the validity of test results. This independent entity will be chosen for its neutrality and its specific technical acumen in the area in question.

14.2.2   Construction contractor

The input supplier will also have to interface with the construction contractor. The input supplier will need to provide the construction contractor with sufficient input to perform testing (including commissioning and performance tests) during the construction phase. The construction contractor will wish to verify the quantity and quality of the input provided, probably pursuant to a procedure similar to that used by the project company as discussed above, to ensure that the tests performed are not in any way compromised by the input provided.

14.3   Principal Obligations

The input supply agreement will address the principal obligations to be borne by the parties related to the supply of input, its transportation, storage and quality.

14.3.1 Quantity

The quantity of input needed for the commissioning and operation of the project must be carefully calculated. Input needs for operation will generally follow a cyclical demand curve of production. For example, fuel requirements for power stations in warmer climates will be greater during the summer months for operation by end users of air-conditioning and other cooling mechanisms, whereas in colder climates, energy demand will increase in the winter months for the operation of heating units. Electricity demand for water treatment or desalination may be higher during the summer months, when water demand increases for personal consumption, watering lawns and gardening.

The input supply agreement may be a supply contract or a depletion contract. A supply contract is a covenant to provide up to a certain amount of input within a certain period. The depletion contract, on the other hand, involves a more exclusive relationship wherein the project company has the right to purchase up to the entire output of one source of input, for instance the entire output of a given mine or well.

The project company must be able to modify the amount of input to be supplied under the input supply agreement in accordance with its output needs. One option is to use a take-or-pay scheme, where the project company pays for a given amount of input per period. The project company will then order input as it is required. Thus, the project company will not need to store input, but rather take delivery up to the specified amount. This also provides the input supplier with a guaranteed minimum income. However, because of storage demands, and possibly the nature of the input in question, the input supplier may want to impose a minimum and maximum amount of input which the project company can order during a given period.

The parties may want to include some provision to modify the input supply figures, in case of modification of the project company's needs, a change in the amount of input available to the input supplier or a fundamental change in the market price of the input. Once such a fundamental change to the input market occurs, these provisions will open the input supply agreement to market pressures in a manner not dissimilar to a hardship clause.

The input supply agreement can also provide the input supplier with a guaranteed source of sales, by requiring that the project company either takes, or pays for, a certain minimum amount of input. This amount can run to large figures, such as 90-95 per cent. of the total amount to be made available. By inserting such take-or-pay provisions, the input supplier is protected to some extent from the risk of decreased demand. The project company will want to pass the risk of insufficient demand for project output, and therefore increased input cost due to take-or-pay requirements, to the offtake purchaser.

Where the input supply agreement is being used to finance development of a new input source or where the input supplier is not a sufficiently robust credit risk, the project company may be advised to seek advice from independent experts and obtain guarantees from the grantor or a parent company of the input supplier.

The amount to be supplied may be tied to reserves available to the input supplier from a given source, such as a specific mine or well. An accurate measure of possible and potential reserves can be difficult to identify. In identifying available reserves the parties should consider:[353]

> the amount of input found on the site;

> the amount of input that is technically recoverable; and

> the amount of input that is economically recoverable under current or future economic conditions.

It is extremely difficult to measure existing reserves and their recoverability with any certainty. The exercise will necessarily involve a degree of uncertainty and in the end the parties will need to work, to some extent, from estimates. Estimates will need to take into consideration technical and atmospheric conditions, such as the effect of drought or a surplus of rain. The parties may prefer to appoint an independent expert to provide these estimates.

Where the supply of input is tied to identified reserves the lenders and the project company will want to be protected from the possibility that the reserves tied to the input supply agreement are not sufficient to satisfy the needs of the project. Therefore, the project company will need to ensure that the input needs of the project can be satisfied by a portion of the identifiable reserves, leaving a comfortable amount, possibly 25-30 per cent., as a cushion, or "tail".

14.3.2   Procurement restrictions

The input supplier may be restricted by procurement regulations of the host country or those set out in the concession agreement, which should be mirrored in the input supply agreement.[354] Such restrictions may include a requirement that a percentage of the personnel or materials used in a project be sourced in the host country. More often the concession agreement will mandate a procurement preference for locally sourced labour and materials, often using standards such as "where reasonable" and "as far as economically feasible". The project company and input supplier will need to establish between them what the actual effect of such requirements will be and how best to satisfy them.

14.3.3   Source of input

The grantor or the project company may wish to place restrictions on the project company in order to mandate a source of input. This may result from a concern to

---

[353]   George and Stanbury, "Financing Energy Projects – The Technical Advisor's Role" in Hornbrook (ed), Project Finance Yearbook 1995/96 at 15 (1996).

[354]   Procurement requirements have been discussed in greater detail in chapter 15; see also chapters 4 and 5 of Scriven, Pritchard and Delmon (1999) supra note 210.

obtain input from a specific source for example to encourage locally sourced input. It may also result from a desire to ensure consistency of quantity and quality of input.

14.3.3.1   Locally sourced

It may be important for the project company to specify where input is to be sourced. This may involve preference for local sourcing or legal restrictions requiring such local sourcing. Where legal restrictions are involved, the project company will want to assess the nature of the restrictions, the extent to which foreign ownership of local sources is allowed, and what, if any, pricing restrictions are included in the relevant legal restrictions.

The host government will want to use the project to benefit the local economy where possible. By using locally sourced input the project company can benefit from political and national goodwill which may translate into practical benefits such as protection against changes in law, administrative requirements and any potential backlash against foreign investment.

Locally sourced input can also help the project company manage many of the political risks involved in import and export licences, war and expropriation risks during transportation, insurance costs and cross-border administration. Local input will generally be priced in local currency. Since the project company will usually receive payments from the offtake purchaser in local currency, use of locally sourced input can avoid certain exchange and convertibility costs and risks. However, the project company will need to review the sufficiency of local infrastructure affecting the supply and transportation of locally sourced input, as well as the quality of input available.

Domestic suppliers may be closely related to, if not controlled by, the host government. The grantor, or the host government, may therefore be convinced to provide guarantees for the input supplier and bear a larger portion of the credit risk. Where the offtake purchaser is also a government entity, the risk allocation matrix can then be tightly drawn between the grantor and the project company.

14.3.3.2   Consistency of source

The project company may also want to ensure that input comes from a specific place or region, for example where the technology of the project requires a specific type of input. Often, ensuring the same source of input will provide consistent quality of input, allowing for more efficient operation. When the reserves of a given source are either wholly or substantially dedicated to the project company's needs, the project company will want to define clearly how the source will be managed. For example, the project company may want to ensure that the input supplier will extract the maximum amount of economically recoverable input in the most efficient manner.

14.3.4   Shipment and storage

Responsibility for the various aspects of shipment and storage of the input must be allocated in the input supply agreement. The issues specific to shipment will depend largely on the nature of the input in question. The parties will need to decide who will provide and pay for the transportation of the input, including the manner of carriage, the protective measures to be taken and the method of shipping to be used.

In India, for example, in the case of coal-fuelled power projects, there has been an historic shortage of rail wagons for transportation. For this reason, projects located at the mouths of coal mines, called "mine mouth" projects, became increasingly popular.[355]   Another option is the Indian Railway's "Own Your Own Wagons" programme, which permits private parties to purchase wagons and lease them to the railway for use in transporting the owners' goods. Such innovative responses to country risks and limitations require special consideration, such as interfaces with the transporter, necessary permits and licences, government regulation, limitation of transporter liability and residual transportation risk borne by the project company.

The parties will need to establish transfer of care and title as well as responsibility for storage of the input until its use in the project. Transfer of care will be based generally on the point of delivery of the input. At point of delivery, the input supplier's obligation to deliver will be satisfied and the duty of care will pass to the project company.

The obligation to store input may include storage at the site of production, refinement or extraction, providing the project company with security of availability of input. The project may also require storage of input at the site. The task and risk of storage, protection, maintenance and management of the input stock must be allocated between the input supplier and the project company.

Insurance will need to be provided for the input, from its production or extraction, during storage at the input supplier's facility, shipment to the site country, domestic transportation to the site, storage at the site, and, possibly, insertion into the project. Often, insurance for the whole project is procured by the project company to allow the greatest continuity possible. Ideally one provider will insure the project to ensure no gap exists in the coverage. However, some part of the project insurance will need to be provided by the project participants. This is particularly true of the input supplier's obligation in relation to transportation and storage, where the project company's business interruption insurance will not cover delays caused by damage to a third party's property unless supplier's extension cover is available.[356]

---

[355]   Shroff, "Financing Private Power Projects in India" in Hornbrook (1996) supra note 353 at 65.
[356]   For further discussion of insurance, see chapter 15 of this book and Scriven, Pritchard and Delmon (1999) supra note 210 at chapter 22.

14.3.5 Quality

The project will often lose efficiency and suffer a decrease in output where the input is of insufficient quality. For this reason, the project company may require that the input provided be of a certain minimum quality, measured in purity, concentration, energy content, or otherwise. The project company should specify in detail the quality of input needed for operation and specify appropriate tests, as well as what results are expected from such tests.

The penalty for delivery of input which does not achieve the quality requirements should be set out in detail in the input supply agreement. Possible sanctions include:

> ➤ rejection of any input delivered which does not meet the minimum quality requirements;

> ➤ liquidated damages, including decrease in input price, in relation to the extent to which the input does not meet the quality requirements and in accordance with the extent to which the lesser quality affects the performance of the project; and/or

> ➤ damages relating to costs incurred by use of non-conforming input including cleaning, repairs, the cost of decreased performance, increased operation and maintenance costs, and any sanctions applied by the offtake purchaser.

The input supplier may not, however, accept a level of liability which would be sufficient to compensate fully the project company and the lenders for all costs, damages and lost profit caused by the delivery of substandard input. The grantor and/or the lenders may wish to review the decision to use lesser quality input as it may have an effect on the residual value of the project and therefore affect the value of the project at the end of the concession period.

Where possible, the input supplier may also be given the opportunity to cure any defect discovered in the quality of the input. A specific timescale for cure should be provided, which will generally allow for cure up to the date the input was meant to be delivered in order to avoid any impact on the performance of the project due to lack of input.

14.3.6 Completion and transition

Completion will be an important step in the fulfilment of certain of the construction contractor's obligations and it will mark the beginning of the operator's obligations.[357] Completion will also affect the input supplier in that deliveries of input will need to be made during the commissioning and testing periods, as well as during performance tests and when the project comes on line.

---

[357] For further discussion of completion, see chapters 6, 8 and 10.

Completion may also require delivery of input supplier-provided infrastructure, which may include transportation and storage facilities.

14.4   Payment

The availability of input in accordance with the project company's requirements will be one of the keys to the successful operation of the project. Payment for input supply will need to provide built-in incentives to ensure sufficient quantity and quality of supply.

The cost of input and timing of payment for input must protect the project cash flow and financial ratios. Input price will need to correspond with the project company's payment stream. Any indexation or escalation of input process should result in a corresponding increase in project revenue. The timing of payment for input will need to be scheduled to follow payments through the concession agreement and/or offtake purchase agreement, as far as possible, in order to maintain the lenders' cover ratios.

14.4.1   Price

It is essential that the price for the input delivered is calculated in a reasonable manner to ensure continued delivery of the input. A base price should be set per unit, possibly in accordance with the quality of the input provided. Depending on the nature of the input, the parties may wish to make provision for recalculation of the price, in which case a timetable and procedure for recalculation should be established.

There are many ways to recalculate the base price to take into consideration any changes in the market. For example:

- ➢ The parties could refer to reputable indicia, such as market prices or indices provided by certain organisations, federations or government publications. The parties could also refer directly to changes in the fixed costs of the input supplier. Where these fixed costs have increased by a given amount, the base price could be modified accordingly.

- ➢ An independent expert could also be consulted who would review the base price in relation to market prices and rule whether the base price is reasonable. The expert should be given guidelines in order to understand the parties' intentions, including permissible variations of the market price. For example, the input supply agreement may specify a percentage amount by which the base price must differ from the market price before modification should occur. Alternatively, the expert could be instructed to modify the base price only where that price is considered unreasonable or unconscionable in the face of market prices.

- ➢ The parties may prefer to provide for renegotiation of the input price in the input supply agreement, either periodically or where the circumstances encountered by the input supplier or the project company are extreme. The parties would then be required to negotiate in good faith, possibly based on the preliminary opinion of an expert or given indicia.

> The parties may decide to place the entire market risk on the input supplier and simply provide for a pre-defined escalation of the base price over the period of supply. This approach will also allow the lenders greater certainty as to the financial exposure for market changes over the life of the concession.

An exchange rate risk specific to the input supply agreement may arise where the offtake purchaser is a local utility or company and prefers to pay for offtake in the local currency. Where the input is supplied locally the input supplier will probably accept payment for input in local currency. However, where input must be imported, a foreign supplier is less likely to want local currency. The project company will need to consider any mismatch in currencies and the resultant exchange rate risk when establishing the price for input.[358]

Where the input provided does not achieve the quality requirements set, the sanction applied by the input supply agreement may include a decrease in the price paid. This change in the price will generally correspond to the impact that a lower quality input will have on the functioning and performance of the project. The parties may also wish to provide the input supplier with a bonus for the supply of input of a higher quality than required. The amount of such a bonus will depend on the benefit such higher quality of input will provide to the project company.

The input supply agreement may allow either of the parties to alter the fixed nature of the input price where the effect of the market is such as to render the fixed price unreasonable. For instance, where the market for the relevant input is liberalised or privatised the market price may change radically, the input supply agreement may allow either party to repudiate the input supply agreement or negotiate a modification of the pricing provision.

14.4.2   Failure to deliver

If the input supplier does not have available to it the quantity of input contracted for delivery from its own resources, it is generally required to procure the required input on the open market. The input supplier is then responsible for any extra cost incurred in purchasing input. The project company may want to specify that if the input supplier does not provide the input as contracted then the project company may procure the missing input. Any extra cost, including that of sourcing the input, will be for the input supplier. Costs incurred will need to be reasonable; the project company may need to pay for part of the cost of provision from unreasonably expensive sources. The project company may also be required to share the cost of alternatively sourced input with the input supplier where some minimum required amount has been delivered.

---

[358] This and other currency issues are discussed further in chapter 15.

Where the project company is not able to procure the input needed, and particularly where the input supplier was to have dedicated certain of its resources to the needs of the project company, then provision of liquidated damages or other sanctions may be appropriate. These damages would represent the cost to the project company of diminished or failed performance owing to lack of input.

14.4.3   Testing quality

To ensure proper operation and requisite performance levels, the input quality must match the input supply agreement specification. Lesser quality may have an effect on project output, payment stream, cost of operation and maintenance, life-cycle of materials and equipment, and the nature of exhaust, effluent and other waste characteristics. A procedure must be laid out for inspection and testing of the quality of the input provided. This procedure will set out the tests to be performed, who will perform them, the type and amount of testing equipment to be used and where testing will take place. The input supplier will want testing to take place at the source. The project company will want to measure the quality of the input once it has been delivered to the site or to the project storage facilities. The choice of testing equipment will involve issues such as who will procure the equipment and who will be responsible for its cost, the cost of its maintenance and operation and its accuracy.

The testing procedure will also describe who will do the testing and who will be present at the time of testing. The parties may wish to use an independent expert to do the actual testing to avoid disputes. No matter who does the testing, some mechanism for resolution of disputes should be provided, generally using an independent expert and further testing to expedite the dispute resolution process. The cost of the dispute resolution procedure should also be allocated.

14.4.4   Measuring quantity

After the quality of the delivered input has been established, a procedure will need to be implemented to measure the quantity delivered. Just as in testing of input quality, as discussed above, issues specific to provision, maintenance, replacement and operation of measurement equipment will need to be addressed. The input supplier, the project company, the lenders and, possibly, the offtake purchaser may wish to be involved in the measurement process.

14.4.5   Payment

The input supply agreement and the offtake purchase agreement will be closely linked in that the project company will rely on the usage payment from the offtake purchaser to pay the input supplier. For this reason, the project company may want to pay the input supplier only if and when payment is received from the offtake purchaser.

Where take-or-pay provisions are used in the input supply agreement, some minimum annual payment may be required from the project company regardless of the amount of input used. Such provisions may also need to be integrated into the payment mechanism of the offtake purchase agreement. Another option is to pass the input cost directly through to the offtake purchaser. The offtake purchaser can make payment directly to the input supplier or the price paid for offtake can include an element for supply, transportation and any other costs related to input supply. The offtake purchaser will then effectively pay the project company a fee for processing or through-put of the input, based on the availability and efficiency of processing.

14.4.6 Guarantees

The project company may want the input supplier to provide performance guarantees, parent company guarantees, government guarantees or possibly retention monies to guard against input supplier non-performance or credit risk. However, money alone will not solve the project company's problems if it is without input. Therefore, the provision of some alternative source of input may be a more appropriate guarantee, possibly from a local stockpile, a named additional source, or a performance bond from another supplier (or a parent company) able to guarantee delivery.

14.5 Mechanisms and Procedures

Certain mechanisms and procedures are specific to the input supply agreement. These are key to the success of the project, its management, efficiency and funding.

14.5.1 Independent engineer

The lenders and/or the grantor may wish to involve an independent engineer in the project to verify the delivery of input in accordance with the input supply and concession agreement requirements, in amount, quality and timing. Therefore, provision will need to be made in the input supply agreement for the intervention of this independent engineer in such a way as to provide sufficient inspection and testing rights, without interfering in the input supplier's performance of its obligations and the operation of the project.

14.5.2 Transfer to grantor

At the end of the concession period, the project may be transferred to the grantor. The input supplier's role in this transfer will need to be established in the input supply agreement. It is common for the input supplier's role to end on the termination or expiration of the concession period. However, the input supplier may need to ensure a certain level of input in the site storage facility, or may need to ensure delivery of input for a period after transfer in order to assist the grantor in continuous operation of the project. Alternatively, the grantor may wish to continue its relationship with the input supplier after the end of the concession period.

Chapter 15

Issues Common to the Project Documents

Creditors have better memories than debtors.

Benjamin Franklin

As discussed in chapter 6, the lenders and the shareholders will want to ensure that risk placed on the project company under the concession agreement is then passed on to the project participants under the project documents. Chapters 6-14 of this book identify issues specific to each of the project documents.

This chapter discusses issues common to all the project documents. Different treatment of these issues could result in unallocated risks, costs or contingencies which will disrupt the balance of the project and increase the residual risk borne by the project company and therefore the lenders. It is important that the concession agreement obligations are transposed faithfully into each of the other documents to avoid overlap or gaps in the risk allocation structure for the project. Several of the more important of these issues will be discussed below.

15.1   The Site

Risk related to the site will need to be allocated within the project. Risk allocation will generally follow the party that provides the site. Where the grantor provides the property for the site, possession, access and possibly a part of site risk will be borne by the grantor. However, where the project company must procure the site commercially, or already owns it, the grantor's responsibility for the site, if any, will be substantially reduced.

15.1.1   Possession of and access to the site

The site may be provided by the grantor or the project company, preferably before financial close of the project, or possibly within a short period after closing, to avoid any delay in the project programme. Early and timely access will be essential to prompt completion of the works, therefore the responsible party will generally be liable for any delay or added cost incurred owing to late provision of the site. Certain permissions to use the site in the manner intended will also be required, for example zoning ordinances.

Site possession may be based on a lease or a licence by the grantor, in which case third party rights to the site and access thereto, such as covenants and easements, will need to be reviewed or the grantor will need to ensure that no such third party rights exist. The project company may also need to register the lease in order to protect itself against third party rights arising over the site. The party providing the site should, in any case, provide vacant possession.

The party responsible for providing the site may have further obligations related to the site. For example, it may be responsible for delivering the site in a certain specified condition, levelled to a certain specification, connected to necessary services (such as water and electricity) or with access to sewage and industrial drainage.

This possession may or may not be exclusive. Where the grantor plans to allow other parties on the site, provision should be made for sharing of risk, indemnification for damages and dispute resolution where a third party impedes the project. In particular, the offtake purchaser may need access to the site for the construction of certain facilities necessary for transport of the offtake, including substations, transmission lines, pipelines or transportation systems for testing and maintenance of the equipment and possibly later for their repair and replacement. The input supplier will need access to the site for delivery of input and may be required to provide support facilities for the provision of input; this may range from the construction of a roadway, port, railway line, pipeline or storage container to the processing equipment necessary for the use of the input, for example LNG (liquid natural gas).

One of the parties must be responsible for providing the project company with access to the site, including easements across neighbouring land, building roads, bridges or any other necessary infrastructure. Site access should be specific to the needs of the project. Major works, and the use of specialist equipment, may involve reinforcing access routes, permits and approvals from local authorities and neighbouring landowners and possibly the construction of new access routes. This can be a costly and time-consuming exercise. For example, the construction contractor may need access routes capable of withstanding the weight of certain of the plant and equipment to be transported to the site; rail transport may be necessary to provide input supplies in sufficient quantities; and overpasses and bridges may need to be reinforced sufficiently to avoid accidents and damage to the access route itself. The responsibility to provide sufficient access routes may be best allocated to the project company (and therefore the construction contractor), as the party most aware of the type of access necessary and best able to modify its methods in view of access restrictions.

The provision of land for the site can often be a lengthy process, particularly in developing countries. Where land is provided by the project company, the cost of the site may increase owing to speculation by local investors (where news of the project is released to the public) which can also result in substantial delay of the project. Where inhabitants must be relocated, the grantor or the host government will need to be responsible for, or assist in, expropriation and relocation. This should be done carefully and appropriately. Projects can fail where relocation is mismanaged.

Where the project company bears the obligation to obtain proper access to the site, it will generally pass this responsibility on to the construction contractor. However, the situation may be quite different during the operation phase. The operator will want to place the risk that access to, or possession of, the site rests firmly with the project company. This may include basic licences or permits provided by the grantor, leases of the land, rights of access over neighbouring property or public access routes, or the ability to operate the project on the site.

15.1.2   Site conditions

Risk for site conditions, in particular subsurface conditions, will need to be allocated in the project. Generally, the grantor will want to allocate this risk to the project company. The grantor may provide any information it has available, but will not want to warrant its accuracy and often will not have the expertise necessary to verify ground conditions or ensure that the design, and subsequent operation, of the project will work in the context of the site conditions.

The project company will then pass this risk on to the project participants, primarily the construction contractor. The construction contractor has specific knowledge of the design to be implemented, its construction methods and the requirements of the finished project and is therefore an appropriate party to bear this risk. The construction contractor will also have the technical expertise necessary to assess the ground conditions and their potential impact on the project.

Nonetheless, where the grantor provides the site it may be more time and cost-effective for the grantor to bear this risk, in particular risks related to site conditions or fossils and antiquities that are not reasonably foreseeable by an experienced contractor or those not reasonably discoverable during the time available for due diligence. The construction risk premium for site risk can be substantial and the grantor may be in possession of the information or technical capacity needed to manage site risk in order to maximise value-for-money.

15.2   The Works

The project company will allocate most of the responsibility for the works to the construction contractor. However, certain issues specific to the works will cut across the obligations of the other project participants.

15.2.1   Procurement restrictions

Certain host governments place procurement restrictions on the project company to ensure that local industry benefits from the project. This may involve restrictions ranging from a preference for domestic subcontractors and suppliers to a requirement that a certain percentage of goods and services is procured from local industry. These restrictions will be defined either by the concession agreement or by applicable law.

The level of domestic preference required will also be imposed by the financial institutions involved. Certain organisations, such as the World Bank group, suggest consideration of locally sourced materials, although only as an encouragement of local industry. The World Bank group does not permit any strict limitation of sources of plant, materials or contractor's equipment.[359]

However, restrictions applied by local law on sourcing of materials or services used in international construction contracts are not uncommon. Local law may require that contracts prefer products or services of local origin if they satisfy the purpose intended, even if their specifications are inferior to their foreign origin counterparts.

15.2.2   Transfer of title and risk

Title and risk of the works will transfer at different times and for different reasons during the life of the project. It is most likely that the title of material and equipment to be used in the works will pass directly to the project company when such materials and equipment are either paid for or brought on to the site for the purposes of the project. Risk of care of the works, on the other hand, will transfer from the project company at commencement of the construction contract to the construction contractor. After completion of construction, risk should pass to the operator. Therefore, the project company will endeavour to draft the project documents so that the risk of care of the works, in the normal course of the project, will not transfer back to the project company. The more exact and definable the procedure which identifies transfer, the less likely disputes about who is responsible for care of the works.

The following chart provides a simplified view of how risk will pass between project participants for two specific sets of equipment to be used in the project. Sections A and B will be carefully defined in the project documentation, probably in the main schedules. The time of risk transfer will also be defined identically in all of the relevant project documents. Thus, in the example set out in the chart, "commencement", "completion" and "transfer" will be defined and easily identified through procedures set out in the project, such as by the passing of tests or the issue of a certificate.

---

[359]   The World Bank, "Standard Bidding Documents: Procurement of Works" at 106 (January 1995).

TRANSFER OF RISK

	Jan - Mar	Apr - Jun	Jul - Sep	Oct - Dec	Jan - Mar	Apr - Jun	Jul - Sep	Oct - Dec
		2000				2001		

Section A
- Project Company — Commencement
- Construction Contractor — Completion A
- Operator

Section B
- Project Company — Commencement
- Construction Contractor — Completion B
- Operator

The project company may bear risk during the pre-construction period, before commencement of the construction contract. However, there may be little or no time lapse between effectiveness of the concession agreement and commencement of construction.

At commencement of the construction contract, the construction contractor will take over the care of the works, i.e. will become responsible for the works and the site as defined by the construction contract.

At completion of each section of the works, the construction contractor will pass care of the works on to the operator, even though the construction contractor will have continued responsibilities on the site and for the works.

Here, the works are completed in two sections, therefore there will be an overlap as the construction contractor will be responsible for the care of section B while the operator is responsible for section A during an interim period.

Finally, the operator will bear risk of the works until the end of the concession period.

15.2.3 Completion

Completion occurs when the construction contractor substantially completes the works, less any minor outstanding items (usually identified on a punch-list) which do not affect the proper operation or performance of the works. Completion is often established when the project has successfully passed a series of tests. These tests, particularly in process plants, will generally include the verification of a minimum level of performance. Completion establishes an essential point in the progress of a project: the transition from the construction phase to the operation phase.

The completion of the works does not relieve the construction contractor of all of its project obligations, but will signify a substantial modification of the construction contractor's risk profile and its role in the project. For example, the completion of the project by the construction contractor will result in the transfer of the care of the works from the construction contractor to the operator and will also indicate an end to certain project liabilities, for example the construction contractor's liability for liquidated damages for late completion.

The lenders may also be given some level of recourse to the shareholders' assets or to guarantees during the construction period. Therefore, completion will represent the end of this period of increased liability for the shareholders and any guarantees provided for during the construction period.

For the lenders, completion also represents a movement from the construction phase, when advances of debt are paid out, to the operation period, during which debt is repaid. It also represents a decrease in the lenders' risk profile, since it is during the construction period that the lenders bear the most risk and after completion that the lenders' security in the project assets approaches the amount of the debt. Therefore, completion must properly identify the moment at which the construction risk has entirely or substantially passed and the project is able to come on-stream and begin creating revenue. The project company may also consider refinancing after completion, since financing should be less expensive given the change in risk profile.

15.2.4   Spare parts

The construction contractor will often be required to supply spare parts to the project company. These spare parts are generally intended to satisfy the needs of the operator for an agreed period, usually one or two years. The construction contractor may be allowed to use such spare parts during the defects liability period, although such spare parts as are used must then be replaced immediately at the cost of the construction contractor.

The construction contractor may be involved in the future supply of spare parts to the project. It may also have an exclusive or priority right of supply of spare parts for the project. The price for spare parts will normally follow market values or the best price offered to a competitor. Or, the construction contractor may provide the project company with a guaranteed price for any additional spare parts.

15.3   Payment

Payment mechanisms in each of the project documents will share certain characteristics. The lenders will prefer that the different payment regimes work in close co-ordination, to avoid any negative cash flow of the company or other delay in revenues to cover costs incurred.

15.3.1   Price, payment and revenues

The payment scheme chosen for each of the project tasks must correspond to the project revenue stream. The project company will have limited funds available. Therefore, any outgoings, including operating costs, debt servicing, taxes and fees, will need to be scheduled to follow revenue payments.

The project will usually not receive any revenue payments during the construction phase, thus development and construction will need to be financed by a mixture of debt and equity contributions. The lenders generally prefer to have equity contributions injected first, to ensure that the interests of the shareholders remain firmly entrenched in the success of the project and to decrease their own costs. However, the lenders may agree to later injections of equity contributions for the sake of the shareholders. In such cases the lenders often require some payment security (such as a letter of credit) for the deferred equity contribution, unless the medium-term credit of the relevant shareholder is sufficiently robust and the obligation of that shareholder sufficiently firm.

Debt contributions will generally be provided by periodic drawdowns. The size of each drawdown will be relatively large, as smaller and therefore more numerous drawdowns increase the administrative cost of financing. The lenders will want to ensure value for money, and provide the project company and the construction contractor with an added incentive to progress the works in a timely manner. Therefore, drawdowns will be linked to milestone payments based on work completed which has a concrete benefit to the project. As an exception to the pay-as-you-perform rule, the lenders may provide an advance payment to assist the construction contractor with liquidity in the early stages of construction.

The revenue stream in a BOT project generally commences during the operation phase. Revenues will be allocated to project costs, servicing of debt and then distributions. Costs and debt servicing obligations will take priority, often delaying any payment of return on equity investment until later in the project once debt servicing has been satisfied. In the early stages of operation, contingency funds will be set aside out of project revenues by the project company, to satisfy future or potential costs such as maintenance and major repairs or to cover specific risks which might impede the flow of debt servicing.

In the early stages of construction, commissioning, testing and start-up, funding will flow into the project from the lenders (debt contributions) and the shareholders (equity contributions). During operation, the offtake purchaser typically provides a payment stream based on a capacity payment for the output capacity made available to it (which covers the fixed costs of the project) and the usage payment for the actual offtake (which covers the variable costs of the project).[360]

15.3.2   Foreign currency exchange

BOT projects usually involve multiple currencies for payment, including those of the sale of the output, purchase of the input, purchase of other materials and supplies, the construction and operation of the project and the currencies in which the lenders and shareholders wish to be paid. The host government may place some restrictions on the payment for goods or services within its territory in currencies other than the local currency. However, debt may be denominated partially or wholly in one or several foreign currencies, as may debt servicing. Thus, exchange and convertibility risks will need either to be allocated to the grantor, as a public sector risk, to other project participants, or to the project company and managed, possibly, through financial mechanisms such as hedging.

Exchange risk has caused serious complications in a number of projects, including the Dhabol power project in India, power projects in Indonesia and water concessions in Manila, the Philippines. In each case the cost of the project for the grantor and the end users became extremely expensive due to the relative decrease in value of many Asian currencies in the late 1990s.

---

[360]   For further discussion of capacity and usage payment, see chapter 13.

Convertibility is another issue essential to the financial management of the project. The project company will want the right to convert currencies, either from foreign to local or vice versa, at local rates, even where such exchange is not available through local banks. The country may have an artificial local bank exchange rate and the project company will not want to be restricted to this rate. Owing to the political changes experienced worldwide over the past 10 years, convertibility concerns have decreased; however, this risk remains an issue in certain developing countries, particularly in times of economic crisis.

Certain countries also restrict the ability to transfer funds out of the country. These restrictions are meant to encourage reinvestment in the local economy. However, the shareholders, and especially the lenders, may not be prepared to have their funds tied up in the site country any longer than necessary. For this reason, the project company will want the ability to repatriate funds freely.

15.3.3   Guarantees

The lenders and the project company will want to maintain a comprehensive regime of guarantees. Common guarantees obtained in the course of a project include parent company guarantees; performance guarantees and retention monies for project contractors; government guarantees for performance by the offtake purchaser and/or the input supplier; and guarantees from export credit agencies and others concerning certain project risk, such as political risk. The project company may also wish to receive an assignment of warranties and guarantees or collateral warranties from major suppliers and subcontractors, as far as possible. In this way, where the construction contractor or the operator falls away, the guarantees provided by the suppliers and subcontractors will continue to protect the project company.

15.4   Changes

The concession covers an extended period. Much will change over that period, in particular changes in circumstances or conditions which affect the operator, the input supplier, and/or the offtake purchaser, and the parties should prepare for such change as far as possible.[361] Preparation for change requires provisions in the project documents allowing modification of party obligations in view of changes encountered. This may include a reset mechanism.[362] At the same time the consideration of change should not defeat the purpose of the project documents; that is to allocate to the project participants, and away from the project company, a certain number of risks.

---

[361]   Private Finance Panel (1997) supra note 347 at 28.
[362]   The World Bank, Toolkit for Water and Sanitation Projects (2005).

15.4.1 Assignment

The concession agreement and the other project documents will need to provide the project company with the ability to assign its rights and obligations to a third party both for financing purposes and to provide step-in and buy-out rights to the lenders and possibly the grantor/offtake purchaser. In such case, the grantor and the project participants may wish to limit the project company's right to assign the project by specifying the acceptable assignees and requiring their consent for any assignee other than those nominated. In particular, the project participants, and possibly the grantor, will want to ensure that the project company cannot assign its rights to a competitor. This may involve imposing a reasonable discretion over acceptable assignees.

The project documents will each need to provide for such assignment. Assignment in relation to step-in rights may be rather complex, providing the project participants with protection in the course of step-in while allowing the lenders sufficient flexibility to step in smoothly and effectuate any remedy necessary to put the project back on track.[363]

15.4.2 Change in law

During the concession period, the laws of the host country will change. Any change may have an impact on the project. The grantor is often asked to bear the risk of a change in the legal or political climate of the site country, where such change is contrary to the interests of the project, resulting in the project company being in a less advantageous position than at the time of signature of the concession agreement.

This said, the project company may be required to bear some part of the change in law risk, particularly where the site country is politically and legally stable or where the project company is local to the site country (and therefore change in law could be considered a normal risk of doing business). Where the project company is asked to share change in law risk, the grantor will still generally bear the risk for discriminatory change in law, changes which are specific to the project, the industry sector or specific to foreign investment.

The project company will want the concession agreement to define the concept of "law" broadly so as to include any law or rule or regulation (be it legal or administrative) that could directly or indirectly affect the project or its execution. This would include any standard applied to the project, by official, semi-official or other regulatory bodies. The concept of "change in law" should also include a change in the interpretation of an existing law.

---

[363] Step-in is discussed in more detail in section 4.4.

15.4.3   Change in pricing mechanism

The pricing mechanisms for each of the project documents will need to take into consideration the possibility of change. For example, the price of fuel may collapse owing to the discovery of enormous reserves or of a replacement fuel. To avoid the need to refer to the courts or an arbitrator to resolve this difficult situation, the parties should provide for such cases, possibly through renegotiations or re-pricing using an appropriate index or market prices.

The method of payment can be negotiated at the time of the change in accordance with the nature of the change and the needs of the parties. Payment can be used as a financing tool or project management tool, therefore the method to be used should be devised at the time of change rather than artificially in the concession agreement. However, as the project payment mechanisms will necessarily be interrelated, and substantially back-to-back, renegotiation of one payment mechanism may require renegotiation of the payment mechanisms of related agreements.

15.4.4   Change in requirements

The offtake purchaser or the grantor may need to modify the requirements originally placed on the project during either the construction or operation period. For example, where environmental legislation is modified over time, the grantor may need to make changes to the project in order to meet such regulations. These changes may have a positive or negative effect on the revenue stream and operation costs of the project company. Provision should be made for such changes by the party requesting the change.

15.4.5   Dispute

Because of the sensitivity of the issue, and the different interests involved, negotiation of changes to party obligations may be very difficult. The assistance of an arbitrator or an independent expert/mediator may be preferable to prolonged or fruitless negotiations and disputes.[364] Such dispute resolution provisions will need to be consistent in each of the project documents as change may affect the whole of the project or multiple project tasks or risks.

15.4.6   Lenders' interests

Clearly any change may have an impact on the revenue stream of the project. The cost of any change may require an increase in project debt. For these reasons, the lenders will want to be involved in the change procedure, either directly or through their reserve discretions over the project company as set out in the lending agreement.

---

[364]   Delmon, "Mediation and Major International Projects: a Proposal" PFI 169 at 59 (19 May 1999); Kendall, Expert Determination (3rd edition 2000).

15.5 Political and Natural Events

Any project will be subject to political risk and the possibility of natural events which may have an impact on the parties or the project. These risks will need to be allocated amongst the parties.

15.5.1 Licences and permits

A variety of consents, licences and permits (referred to collectively in this section as "consents") must be obtained in order to construct and operate the project. The importance of such consents will depend on the type of project and local requirements. For example, road projects may require more in the way of construction consents than water projects, which may require more in the way of operation consents.

The risk of obtaining the appropriate consents must be allocated. Ideally, this will involve listing the necessary consents and specifically allocating each to one or the other party. The project company will argue that the grantor should bear the majority of the consent risk since the grantor is the most likely party to be able to put pressure on the relevant administrative body. However, the grantor has an interest in ensuring that the project company satisfies the relevant local regulations when constructing the works. There may also be serious political tension between the grantor and the administrative body that grants consents. Further, the project may require consents from other jurisdictions.

The consents obtained should be assignable, where possible, in the case of a buy-out by the grantor or the offtake purchaser or step-in by the lenders or the grantor. The risk of refusal to assign, the increase of requirements on renewal of consents, or the refusal of consents by the relevant authority, must be managed and/or allocated.

The project company will need to ensure that no influence by the grantor can make obtaining consents more difficult or add requirements to any application procedures. The project company will not want to be penalised where the relevant authority unreasonably withholds such consents. The same should be true for renewal applications. The project company will want to place the risk of delayed or refused consents on the grantor, where the project company has complied with the administrative procedures, as defined in advance.

The project company will want to allocate the risk that the requirements for consents become stricter, causing the project company increased cost or delay. The renewed consents may have a diminished scope, their terms limiting the permitted activities of the project company. The project company will argue that the project risk involved in renewing consents is best borne by the grantor, who will generally be in a better position to manage this risk and better able to mitigate any impact on the success of the project. The project company may therefore want to provide that the application for the renewal of consents may not contain terms and conditions less favourable than those of the original application.

In developing countries, the offtake purchaser is often the local public utility or a public company, therefore it may not be as heavily affected by consents. However, the offtake purchaser may be required to bear the risk of loss of consents where it is in a better position to ensure the continuity of such consents. On the other hand, where the offtake purchaser is a private entity, the project company will want to ensure that the offtake purchaser maintains the consents necessary to operate the facilities and take delivery of output from the project.

The operator will be requested to comply with all consents and to obtain all consents necessary to comply with his obligations. The project company will want to place further obligations on the operator to ensure that the operator makes all reasonable efforts to monitor any changes in the nature or number of consents and to renew them as appropriate for the proper and legal operation and maintenance of the project.

Consents will generally be required to produce, transport, ship and deliver input provided by the input supplier. For example, where nuclear fuel is involved, the obtaining of consents will involve an extremely political and often burdensome administrative process involving review by both political and administrative bodies, private oversight committees and probably a combined effort by both parties. The risk involved in the application for such consents as well as the cost involved is often allocated to the input supplier as the expert on the subject of the input to be delivered.

The construction contract will need to allocate carefully the responsibility to obtain project consents. The consents necessary to carry out the construction of the works will range from visas for foreign personnel, permissions for construction on the site, and environmental assessments to operating licences for the commissioning of the works. The consents in question and the responsible party should be listed by title or detailed description to avoid disputes at a later date. Where the identity or nature of such consents is not known at the time of contracting, reference may be made to the general nature of consents to be obtained by each of the parties. It will always be important to allocate the risk of obtaining consents that the parties failed to list, were not aware of, or were not required at the time of the contract.

Certain standard form construction contracts use the identity of the party that is required by law to obtain such consents as the criterion for allocating responsibility.[365] For example, where local law requires that consents must be obtained by the construction contractor, then it is the construction contractor's responsibility to obtain them. However, where the local law is not clear as to who must obtain the consents, or where a third party is obliged to do so, then the construction contract must allocate the responsibility for obtaining such consents to one of the parties.

---

[365]   For example, the Engineering Advancement Association of Japan (ENAA), Model Form International Contract for Process Plant Construction (1992).

The issue of consents can be particularly complex in developing countries where requirements may not be well defined and may change from day to day. Where the project company does not have sufficient experience in the host country it may wish to require the construction contractor to bear the whole of the risk to obtain consents.

15.5.2   Force majeure

Certain events, beyond the control of the parties, may inhibit the parties from fulfilling their duties and obligations under the project agreements. To avoid the resultant breach of contract, the parties will prefer to excuse contractual obligations which have been so inhibited. Theories of law have developed in response to this need, including the doctrines of impossibility and frustration under English and United States law[366] and *force majeure* under French law.[367] Under French law *force majeure* is an event that is unforeseeable, unavoidable and external that makes execution impossible.[368]

Similarly the legal systems applicable to the project documents will often provide for an allocation of risk in similar situations, usually suspending all performance requirements, where performance is prevented by such an event. However, each legal system will define *force majeure* events in a different fashion. In order to avoid the potential vagaries and uncertainties as well as the delays involved under applicable law, contracts often provide for a specific regime for *force majeure*, along with a definition of which events shall qualify for special treatment. The term *force majeure* used in drafting project documents comes originally from the *Code Napoléon* of France, but should not be confused with the French doctrine. Generally, *force majeure* means what the contract says it means.

The risk of *force majeure* is generally allocated to the grantor. The theory goes that the grantor is best able to manage *force majeure* risk, as such risk relates partially to the activities of the host country government and its relations with other countries and/or its populace, and that the grantor is the only party able to bear such risk, given its size and the difficulty of obtaining adequate insurance. However, in certain markets, the grantor may require the project company to bear a portion, or all, of the *force majeure* risk.[369]

The parties will need to discuss how a *force majeure* event will be treated in the context of the project. The *force majeure* regime may include issues of release from project obligations during the duration of the *force majeure* event, continued or commercial payment by the grantor or the offtake purchaser during such period, extension of the concession period or release from penalties otherwise imposed by

---

[366]   May (6th edition 1995) supra note 314 at 143-150.

[367]   Liet-Veaux and Thuillier, Droit de la Construction at 270 (10th edition 1991).

[368]   "Impossibilité absolue de remplir ses obligations due à un événement imprévisible, irrésistible et extérieur" French Civil Code, arts 1147 and 11248 (30 August 1816, reprinted 1991).

[369]   Miller and Harlan, "Force Majeure Provisions in Emerging Market PPAs" in Hornbrook (1996) supra note 353 at 23.

the grantor for failure to perform in accordance with the requirements of the concession agreement.

The parties may also wish to provide for termination in case of extended *force majeure* events. They may wish to identify a maximum period during which one single event or an aggregate duration of *force majeure* events over the period of the concession may last before one or both of the parties can act to either remove itself from the project or obtain compensation for damages incurred.

The definition of *"force majeure"* will vary from project to project and in relation to the country in which the project is to be located. The definition of *"force majeure"* generally includes "risks beyond the reasonable control of a party, incurred not as a product or result of the negligence of the afflicted party, which have a materially adverse effect on the ability of such party to perform its obligations".[370]

The parties will generally provide in the *force majeure* provision a list, which may or may not be exhaustive, of examples of *force majeure* events. *Force majeure* events generally can be divided into two basic groups, natural events and political events.

15.5.2.1   Natural events

Although these events form an important part of the *force majeure* concept, they are not automatically attributable or allocable to the grantor. The parties will need to look at the availability and cost of insurance, the likelihood of the occurrence of such events and any mitigation measures which can be undertaken. For example, although the grantor will be best placed to appreciate the ramifications of national weather patterns and common natural disasters, the project company should be able to obtain insurance for the majority of this risk.

Natural *force majeure* events may include:

> ➤ unusually severe weather conditions;

> ➤ fire;

> ➤ adverse natural phenomena, including, but not limited to, lightning, subsidence, mudslide, landslip, heave, collapse, earthquake, hurricane, tornado, typhoon, storm, flood, drought, unusual accumulation of snow or ice, meteorites, volcanic eruption and tidal waves;

> ➤ plague; and

> ➤ Acts of God (based on either a definition of this concept in the contract or under the applicable law).

---

[370]   *Ibid.*

15.5.2.2   *Political and special events*

The grantor's willingness to protect the project company from political risk will go a long way to reassure the project company and the lenders that the project has host government support. In many developing countries, the risk of political upheaval or interference is of great concern. As a general proposition the grantor in a developing country should be willing to bear a certain amount of political *force majeure* risk. Special risks included in this list generally represent those risks which are uninsurable under normal commercial conditions, such as nuclear contamination. These risks are generally considered to be beyond the control of the project company.

The host government may be in such a dominant negotiating position, that it can require the project company to bear some or all of the political project risk. Further, political risk insurances may be available, either through private insurances, multilateral organisations or export credit agencies. Political *force majeure* events often include:

> ➤ terrorism;

> ➤ riots or civil disturbances;

> ➤ war, whether declared or not;

> ➤ hostilities, including, but not limited to, sabotage, vandalism and riot;

> ➤ blockade or embargo;

> ➤ strikes (usually excluding strikes which are specific to the site or the project company or any of its subcontractors);

> ➤ change of law or regulation;

> ➤ nuclear or chemical contamination;

> ➤ failure of public infrastructure; and

> ➤ pressure waves from devices travelling at supersonic speeds.

15.5.3   Sovereign immunity

It should be noted that certain of the project participants will be government entities, especially in developing countries where many of the project roles have not yet been privatised. In such cases, the project company may want to require that any government entity waive its sovereign immunity.

States generally benefit from two forms of immunity: jurisdiction and execution. A state's immunity to jurisdiction results from the belief that it would be inappropriate for one state's courts to call another state under its jurisdiction. Therefore, state entities are immune from the jurisdiction of the courts of another state. However, this immunity can generally be waived by the state entity. The state will also have immunity from execution, as it would be improper for the courts of one state to seize the property of another state. Immunity from execution may also generally be waived.

Reference to arbitration is in many legal systems sufficient to demonstrate a waiver of immunity to jurisdiction by the state. However, certain developing countries may be hesitant to submit themselves to international arbitration, believing that arbitration is dominated by Western principles and would not give a developing country a fair hearing. These same developing countries may feel more secure submitting to arbitration under the UNCITRAL rules, which are often considered more culturally neutral than those of the ICC or other Western tribunals.[371]

The issue of waiver of immunity of execution may be more difficult for a government to address. As a general proposition under most legal systems, certain assets belonging to the state should not be available for satisfaction of the execution of an arbitral award; for example, the country's foreign embassies, or consular possessions. Therefore, some method may have to be made available for the private party to seize certain state assets, possibly through careful definition of those possessions available for seizure.[372]

15.5.4   Types of insurance

Given that the project will generally be financed on a non-recourse basis during the operation phase, using project revenues for servicing of debt, it will be of great importance to the lenders and to the grantor to ensure that proper insurance is obtained. Insufficient insurance, resulting in lack of funding to repair the works or recommence operation after an insurable event, may seriously compromise the success of the project. Further, as the lenders will require back-to-back risk allocation, and the project participants may be unwilling to bear certain of the project risks, insurance can be used to close any gap in risk allocation and ensure protection of the lenders' and the grantor's interests.

Some generalisations can be made about the insurance necessary for BOT projects, although each project will require specific insurance coverage, based on the risks inherent to a particular project.[373] Generally, the following insurances will be required.

15.5.4.1   *Insurance during transportation*

Every element of materials and equipment to be used for the project should be insured during shipment to the site, including equipment to be integrated into the works, temporary plant and the construction contractor's equipment. This coverage may include marine cargo insurance. Transportation insurance must be correlated with the all-risk policy on the site. A "fifty-fifty claims funding" clause can help

---

[371]   Craig, Park and Paulsson, International Chamber of Commerce Arbitration (3rd edition 2000).

[372]   For further discussion of sovereign immunity, see section 6.8.

[373]   For further discussion of insurance, see Scriven, Pritchard and Delmon (1999) supra note 210.

clarify liability for damage that may occur at or shortly after delivery, by stipulating that each insurer will pay 50 per cent. of the claim if it cannot be established whether it occurred during transit or after delivery.

15.5.4.2 Insurance of project assets

Equipment and materials will first need to be insured up to delivery to the site. This project asset coverage may include the construction contractor's equipment brought onto the site where such equipment is essential to progress and/or very expensive, for example, tunnel boring machinery. The loss of such equipment can seriously hamper the construction contractor and therefore the progress of the works. Project assets should be insured ex-works to delivery at the site either into the hands of the construction contractor or into the construction contractor's storage facilities.

15.5.4.3 Construction all-risk policy

Construction all-risk ("CAR") or construction and erection all-risk ("CEAR") insurance will cover all operations and assets on the site during the construction of the works. This policy generally excludes war-risk. Parties may include a war-risk endorsement to cover risks generally considered political in nature. The construction contractor may prefer to leave the grantor to provide the political aspect of the project asset insurance, to reduce costs and in an effort to maximise value-for-money in its insurance arrangements.

15.5.4.4 Professional indemnity ("PI")

This form of insurance is available under certain CAR or CEAR policies, or it may be provided separately. PI insurance covers design faults or other such professional services provided by the construction contractor or its designers. Such insurance is generally carried by a designer as a part of its normal business.

15.5.4.5 Operational damage

The final major aspect of project insurance will cover all-risk insurance during operation, including, in particular, insurance of property damage during operations.

15.5.4.6 Third party liability insurance

The project should be covered from commencement of construction to the end of the concession period by liability insurance for any claim by third parties for the acts or omissions of the project company, and any of the contractors, subcontractors or other persons for whom it may be responsible, during construction and operation of the project. The grantor and the lenders may also want to be covered by this policy. This policy should cover, as far as practicable, any environmental effects of construction and operation.

15.5.4.7   Consequential loss

Insurance cover will generally exclude consequential losses or damages incurred by the project company. Therefore, the project company or the lenders may require that the project company obtain insurance coverage for consequential losses. These include delayed start-up, advance loss of profit and business interruption insurance. The amount of such insurance obtained will generally be calculated to compensate for the fixed costs of the project. A separate consequential loss policy must be taken out for each form of insurance obtained. For example, where the construction contractor obtains a CAR policy and a marine cargo policy, it will need a consequential damage policy for each of them.

15.5.4.8   Mechanical or electrical failure

The operational policy may not cover events of mechanical or electrical breakdown, therefore separate insurance must be obtained. The nature of, and need for, this insurance cover will depend on the works in question and the cost of replacement of key equipment.

15.5.4.9   Automobile liability insurance

This policy should cover all vehicles to be used on site, and will often be mandatory under local law. The vehicles in use during construction and operation may extend beyond motor vehicles, to aeroplanes, helicopters, boats and ships or possibly more expensive machinery requiring specialist local and/or international insurance.

15.5.4.10   Workers' compensation, employer's liability

The construction contractor and the operator will be obligated either to the host government or to its staff for some form of statutory compensation or other form of benefits or other liability, which should be covered by an insurance policy. The coverage of this policy will depend on the provisions of local law concerning such liability, and local and international practice.

15.5.4.11   Directors' and officers' liability insurance

The project company will want to be protected from the possibility that a director's or officer's act or omission may have an impact on the project. Generally, the director or officer in question will not have the financial wherewithal to compensate the project company for such damages.

15.5.4.12   Political risk

A range of political and war risks will not be covered by the above insurances. Therefore, the project company may need to obtain special insurance to cover these risks. This coverage usually involves a multilateral agency or an export credit agency.

15.5.5 Insurance issues

It is beyond the scope of this book to discuss insurance in detail, however the following is a general discussion of issues specific to BOT project insurance.

It should be noted that insurance may not provide an entirely satisfactory solution. The exclusions and conditions included in any insurance policy may limit the effectiveness of coverage, and insurance will generally not cover all effects of an event, such as loss of reputation or loss of market share.[374] Therefore, it may be more efficient, in addition to provision of insurance, for the risk to be allocated to a project participant who can manage and take steps to mitigate the risk in question.

15.5.5.1 Sufficiency of insurance cover

The lenders may prefer insurances to be provided by the project company rather than by one of the project participants, since the lenders have more influence over decisions and acts of the project company.[375] This also works well with the concept of global insurance coverage for the entire project, since the project company will probably be best placed to provide insurance for the whole of the works and for the duration of the concession period. Global insurance provided by one party and one provider will also help to avoid gaps or overlaps of coverage. Further, insurance from one single source for the entire project may be more commercially efficient. Reinsurance may also provide an element of global coverage.

When reviewing insurance coverage, the creditworthiness of the insurer is as important as the coverage and cost of the policy required.[376] The risks to be covered by insurance are generally costly. Further, given the length of time involved in BOT projects, the insurer will need to be of sufficient standing to ensure complete insurance coverage throughout the concession period. The insurer will often be asked to cover the whole of the project insurances to avoid gaps or overlap in the project's insurance coverage; therefore, insurers should be sufficiently diverse to be able to provide all of the different types of insurance needed. This risk can often be managed by re-insurance cover.

Further, the lenders and the project company will need to bear in mind that insurance payouts may be slow in coming; even where the claim is not disputed, the delay in payment can take up to two years.[377] Such delays will have an effect on the financial model and the extent of security to be provided. Interim financing for necessary repairs to permit renewed operation and reinstatement of the payment stream should be considered, possibly as a stand-by facility.

---

[374] Pey, "The Application of Insurance to Project Finance" in Hornbrook (1996) supra note 353 at 15.

[375] Scriven (1994) supra note 318 at 326.

[376] Tinsley, Practical Introduction to Project Finance: Legal and Documentation Issues at 7 (1990).

[377] See Tinsley (1990) supra note 376.

15.5.5.2   Co-insureds

The project insurances should name each of the parties as co-insureds,[378] including the project company, the lenders, the construction contractor, the operator, and the subcontractors.   When it comes to the management of insurance monies, the grantor, the project company and the lenders will each have different interests. The grantor will want to use insurance monies to ensure completion or repair and rehabilitation of the project in order to meet the requirements of the concession agreement. The project company will have varied interests including, possibly, the payment of the construction contractor and the operator. The lenders will want to ensure payment of debt servicing. Where the insurance payment relates to serious damage to the project, the lenders may wish to use the insurance monies to pay off project debt rather than reinstate the project assets. Therefore, provisions may be included allowing the project company to manage insurance payments under a specified amount and the lenders to manage greater amounts.

15.5.5.3   Subrogation

Project insurances should also include a waiver by the insurer of its rights to subrogation (the right to pursue the party at fault in respect of amounts paid out under the insurance contract). These rights may be inconsistent with the intention of the project company. The project company will not want the project to fail because the insurers used their rights of subrogation against one of the project participants or subcontractors, rendering them unable to perform their obligations. The insurers may therefore be asked to waive certain of their rights of subrogation.

15.5.5.4   Vitiation

A further issue to be considered is vitiation. Insurance policies will generally require full disclosure, allowing insurers to avoid coverage for reasons such as non-disclosure of material information, misrepresentation or breach of warranty. Where the project insurance involves several insured parties (with varying interests in the insured risk), there is a risk that the insurance will fail due to a breach of one of those obligations by one of the insureds. For this reason, the project company may need to obtain "non-vitiation" coverage. Other options to cover off the risk of vitiation include non-vitiation clauses or endorsements, parallel policies for interested parties, and indemnities from the joint insureds.[379]

---

[378]   A discussion of the difference between joint insured and co-insureds is beyond the scope of this book. Reference should be made to Hordingham and Connell, "Project Insurance: Diverse Risks and Multiple Interests" Oil and Gas Law and Taxation Review at 159 (April 1998); Connell, "Insurance and Latent Defects Insurance" in Scriven, Pritchard and Delmon (1999) supra note 210; Vinter (2nd edition 1998) supra note 211 at chapter 7.

[379]   On the issue of vitiation and insurance generally see *Ibid.*

15.5.5.5   *Gaps in insurance cover*

These insurances will each include exclusions and exceptions which need to be carefully considered by the parties in relation to the risks covered. It would be inefficient for the coverage of the various policies to overlap. The project company will need to undertake an exercise similar to the verification of back-to-back risk allocation in the project for the establishment of a comprehensive insurance programme, to ensure that no gap is left between coverage of different aspects of the project and that the levels of deductibles and exceptions/exclusions fit properly with those provided in other aspects of the project.

In relation to the construction phase, care should be taken that the provision of all-risk insurance continues through the construction phase to the commencement of the operation phase, with no gap in between. If there is sectional completion, special arrangements may need to be made to cover the handover phase; for example extending the construction policy to insure the entire project until the all-risk insurance for operation begins, or correlate the insurance for both phases of the project to ensure continuity.

Insurance coverage will need to be provided for the input supplier, including marine cargo insurance for the transportation of the input, workers' compensation, third party injury and all-risk for the delivery of the input to the site and transportation to and on the site. A portion of this risk may be included in the global insurance coverage. However, because of the separate nature of some of the input supplier's tasks, such as transportation of input to the site, it may be more reasonable for the input supplier to provide appropriate insurance for such tasks, particularly as the input supplier will be comfortable with the insurance involved and may already have appropriate policies in place as a part of its ordinary course of business.

15.6   Termination and Step-in

The project documents will need to co-ordinate termination, the right to terminate, events of default, consequences of termination and step-in rights.

15.6.1   Termination

To avoid the need to refer to national legal systems in order to terminate a given project document, the parties will define situations which may result in termination, and will specify the consequences of such termination by contract, in the project documents and in direct agreements.

Each of the project documents will have its own particular termination regime, with events of default defined in accordance with the obligations of each party. Other default events will be common to the parties such as liquidation or bankruptcy of the other party or extended *force majeure*. However, the project documents will need to be co-ordinated to follow closely the termination provisions found in the concession agreement. The project company will usually be able to terminate the concession agreement for:

> fundamental breach of the concession agreement by the grantor;

> failure to provide access and possession of the site within a certain period from the effective date;

> failure to provide specified permits and licences;

> extended *force majeure*;

> extended suspension;

> extended failure to make payments due;

> bankruptcy of the grantor; or

> grantor inability to continue with the project.

The following is a list of grantor termination events which might be found in a concession agreement:

> breach of a material provision of the concession agreement;

> failure to commence the works within a certain period from the effective date of the concession agreement;

> failure to achieve completion within a certain period;

> abandonment of a portion of the project without consent;

> bankruptcy;

> replacement of the operator other than in accordance with the concession agreement;

> replacement of the construction contractor other than in accordance with the concession agreement;

> calling of loans above a certain threshold related to the project;

> failure to achieve a certain level of performance over time; or

> fundamental breach of any of the project documents.

Each project document will need to include a procedure for termination, including notification requirements and remedy periods before a party is entitled to terminate, and set out the consequences of termination, such as compensation, buy-out of the project and other damages. Consistency between the procedures used in the project documents will help manage termination between the various documents. Such provisions will need to take into consideration notice to the lenders and the lenders' right to step in. The grantor may also want the right to step in to or buy out the project.

15.6.2   Step-in and continuous operation provisions

The lenders are interested in the success of the project throughout the term of their financing. Where the project company breaches the concession agreement in such a way as to permit the grantor to terminate the concession agreement, the lenders will want the right to step-in, continue the project and avoid the termination of the concession agreement. The grantor will therefore grant the lenders step-in rights.[380]

In the same way, the project is only of use to the grantor when it is in operation. The grantor may therefore want the right to continue operation of the project where it terminates the concession agreement. This is often called the right to continuous operation, as it allows the grantor to ensure continuous operation of the project even in the event of termination. The grantor itself will often not undertake such operation, but rather pass such responsibilities on to the operator, the offtake purchaser or some other third party.

The grantor may also wish to have a right to step in to operate the project where, during operation, the project company is temporarily unable to continue operation.[381] Given the urgent need of the host country for the project, the grantor may need the right to step in during the temporary disability and ensure continuous operation. The grantor will not want to act on such a right if it is not technically and physically capable of undertaking operation. Generally:

> temporary step-in should not involve any reversion of risk to the grantor or the offtake purchaser except in cases of negligence; and

> neither party should benefit from temporary step-in; e.g. the grantor should be compensated for its reasonable costs of operation.

The lenders and/or the grantor may also want step-in rights in relation to the other project documents to ensure the continuity of the project structure and continuity of operation of the project. Thus, each project document, either in the project document itself[382] or in a direct agreement with the lenders and/or the grantor, is likely to provide for step-in rights. The project participants may want to receive guarantees from the party stepping in at least as good as those given by the project company.

15.6.3   Transfer to grantor

The concession agreement will need to include a comprehensive strategy for the transfer of the project and its assets to the grantor at the end of the concession period (this procedure may also apply, to some extent, on the termination of the concession). The project documents may then need to allocate some role in the

---

[380]   See chapter 4 for a further discussion of step-in rights.

[381]   Private Finance Panel (1997) supra note 347 at 19.

[382]   Provision of the step-in rights in a project document is only effective under legal systems which do not require privity of contract before entitling a non-signatory to rights and obligations under a contract. England is an example of a jurisdiction which will require privity, therefore necessitating a separate contract to create such rights and obligations in relation to the lenders and/or grantor, unless the lenders and/or grantor are parties to the project documents in question. However, this has changed in England following the passage of the Contracts (Rights of Third Parties) Act 2000.

transfer to the project participants, for example, to the offtake purchaser and the input supplier; particularly where either or both have contributed additional facilities to the project, such as storage facilities, or transportation facilities that either form part of the works or are merely connected to the works.

At the time of transfer the grantor may provide the project company with compensation for the residual value of the project assets. This retention of equity return for the end of the project motivates the shareholders to ensure proper operation and maintenance in order to maintain the residual value of the project through to the end of the concession period.

Issues to be considered in establishing a transfer regime are:

> maintenance schedule prior to the transfer;

> supervision by the grantor of the final phase of operation;

> training of grantor personnel;

> scope of the transfer, including project assets, intellectual property rights, spare parts, warranties, insurances and other know-how;

> timing of the transfer, including any conditions which must be satisfied at the end of the concession period and any opportunity for extension of the concession period;

> passing of risk to the grantor;

> termination of project documents;

> testing before the transfer, including operation, environmental impact and life-cycle forecasts;

> guarantees provided by the project company to the grantor in respect of the status of the works;

> termination of all remaining project bonds and guarantees; and

> cost of transfer, taxes, fees, repatriation, testing, inspections, and allocation thereof.

15.7   Supervision and Disputes

Different project participants will require rights of inspection of the construction of the works or operation of the project. Similarly, interim and final dispute resolution will need to be co-ordinated as between the project participants.

15.7.1   Grantor/lender access and inspection

The grantor and/or the lenders may wish to have access to the site during construction and the opportunity to inspect and/or test the works before completion. They may also want the right to test for compliance with local requirements, the concession agreement, the lending agreements and the interests of the grantor in maintaining the maximum residual value of the works for their use after transfer. An access regime could include a programme of scheduled visits to the site, the storage sites, and other project locations or a notice requirement before access would be allowed. The discretion each project participant will have to refuse or limit such access should also be defined.

15.7.2   Independent engineer

The lenders and the grantor will have an interest in the successful completion and operation of the project in compliance with the requirements set out in the concession agreement. They may not be satisfied with the compliance regimes established by the project company, the construction contractor and the operator. For this reason they may wish to appoint their own representative or, possibly, an independent engineer to oversee construction and operation, attend testing and possibly issue certain certificates. These certificates are generally used as the basis for drawdowns or satisfying concession agreement milestones. The independent engineer can also play a dispute resolution role, in particular where issues arise requiring immediate resolution through technical assessment.

The construction contractor and the operator will need to allow for the presence of this supervision during the performance of their obligations under the project. Further, the offtake purchaser and the input supplier will need to allow the independent engineer to be present or to be involved in testing and inspection of part or all of the facilities, input and offtake.

15.7.3   Dispute resolution

Large infrastructure projects are ripe for complex and often debilitating disputes. For this reason it may be worth the effort to develop dispute resolution procedures specific to the project requirements. BOT projects often involve parties from a variety of legal, social and cultural backgrounds. Identifying a national court capable of meeting the needs of such a diverse collection of parties, and acceptable to each of these parties, may be difficult. It is for this reason that parties to a BOT project generally prefer to submit any disputes that may arise to a private form of dispute resolution rather than to state courts.

The parties will have available to them a range of options for public and private forms of dispute resolution. The private forms will range from the most non-contentious, non-binding forms of facilitated negotiation, to formal, contentious and binding arbitration. A comprehensive dispute resolution mechanism in the concession agreement will generally involve a mixture of such systems. The parties will start with less contentious forms of dispute resolution in an effort to resolve their differences with the least detriment to their working relationships. However, this soft approach should be backed-up by final and binding resolution, such as arbitration.

It is important that the dispute resolution regime in all of the project documents is similar, if not identical, in order to facilitate the resolution of complex issues involving large parts or all of the project and multi-party resolution before a single forum.

15.7.3.1   Interim resolution

The parties may wish to refer disputes in the first instance to less formal dispute resolution mechanisms. Two types of third party facilitators are commonly used in BOT projects: the expert and the mediator.

The parties may submit their dispute to expert resolution which generally involves review of the dispute by an independent expert (or adjudicator), who monitors the progress of the works and their compliance with the project requirements. The expert then gives an opinion as to the appropriate remedy to the dispute or on some factual aspect of the dispute. The decision of the expert may either bind the parties unless or until the decision is overturned by an arbitrator, or merely serve as a basis for negotiation between the parties.

Mediation does not involve a decision or factual interpretation, but rather the assistance of an independent third party who facilitates negotiation between the parties. The mediator, through discussions with the parties, attempts to work with them to identify a mutually satisfactory resolution of the dispute. The mediator may be called upon to give a suggested resolution, but will not normally issue a decision nor in any way bind the parties.[383]

15.7.3.2   Final resolution

The parties will want to include a method of obtaining a final and binding resolution to their dispute. This may involve expert decision, arbitration or reference to national courts. The expert decision is similar to the expert opinion discussed above, but imposes a decision on the parties.

The method most often used, because of its flexibility and greater ease of award execution, is arbitration. The subject of arbitration is beyond the scope of this book,[384] but two different arbitration forums will be discussed briefly.

Some of the best known of the international arbitration bodies include the International Chamber of Commerce ("ICC") in Paris, the London Court of International Arbitration ("LCIA"), the Arbitration Institute of the Stockholm Chamber of Commerce, and the Singapore International Arbitration Centre. By making reference to one of these private forums in a contract, the parties submit their dispute to resolution by arbitration in accordance with the rules of that forum, under the administration of the representative organisation. The assistance of an administrative body is of considerable benefit once a dispute has arisen as the parties may have difficulty agreeing on a procedure once their relationship has become contentious. Most private forums for international arbitration have

---

[383]   Mackie, Miles and Marsh, Commercial Dispute Resolution: an ADR Practice Guide (1995); Delmon (19 May 1999) supra note 364 at 59.

[384]   See generally Kendall, Sutton and Gill (eds), Russell on Arbitration (1998).

administrative bodies to assist the parties in identifying arbitrators and defining the procedure to be used in the arbitration. The notable exception is the United Nations Commission on International Trade Law ("UNCITRAL") rules for arbitration. Many of the private administrative bodies, the ICC and LCIA included, will administer UNCITRAL arbitration if asked.

Where the parties to the contract include a foreign government, or a government entity, the private contracting party must take into consideration the risks of immunity of the government entity and the difficulty of executing arbitral decisions against government assets. A separate arbitral body has been developed for this purpose under the International Centre for Settlement of Investment Disputes ("ICSID"). This body has greater powers of enforcement over its member states and has been successful in the resolution of investment disputes between private parties and sovereign entities. A strict procedure must be followed in order to submit disputes arising under a contract to ICSID.

15.8 Miscellaneous

Certain other issues will be common to the project documents and will need to be considered by the parties.

15.8.1 Definitions

The parties will want to create maximum coherence between the project documents. The choice of terms to be defined and the drafting of their definitions in each of the project documents are essential to contract interpretation. In this way, where interpretations of the contractual provisions are to be made, the project document terminology will be consistent, reducing the risk of gaps between the documents which would leave risks or obligations uncovered.

15.8.2 Conditions precedent

Certain issues should be resolved and tasks fulfilled before the parties will be prepared to be bound by the project documents. Therefore, the project documents may impede conditions which must be satisfied before the project becomes effective, also known as "conditions precedent". Conditions precedent may include:

> ➢ achieving financial close to ensure that the project company does not take on the obligation to complete the project unless financing has first been obtained. Therefore, the project will first need to meet the relevant conditions precedent in the financing agreements;

> ➢ entering into and effectiveness of ancillary agreements, which should include all other project documents and direct agreements, and therefore all conditions precedent of these other agreements are satisfied;

> ➢ the acquisition of rights over and access to property, which are often amongst the most important obligations of the grantor in the early days of the project;

> obtaining necessary consents (which may involve the consent of neighbouring landholders or occupiers), import licences, building permits, environmental or other administrative permits or other such necessary preliminary consents and permits which must be obtained by one or both parties;

> ratifying of laws in the country approving the concession agreement, where the legislative body of the host country needs to ratify legislation or the constitution allowing the creation of the concession or possibly of the legal vehicle which is to be the project company;

> obtaining insurances either prior to commencement of the concession period or shortly thereafter (in which case the obligation may be framed as a condition subsequent);

> execution of guarantees and security documents, including completion guarantees and parent guarantees; and

> obtaining tax clearances (where appropriate).

Once satisfied or waived, and upon notice thereof to the parties, the relevant project documents become effective.

The parties may also wish to specify a long-stop date. If the conditions precedent have not been satisfied by this date then the project documents are open for renegotiation. Provision will need to be made for cost allocation in the case of such failure.

15.8.3   Duration

The duration of each of the project documents and the rights and obligations contained therein will need to be carefully co-ordinated. Any gaps should be identified and analysed. Where the periods are to run in parallel, identical wording or cross-referencing may be preferable. The financial drawdowns and revenue allocation will be based on these periods and durations. The structure of the project and programme for completion will need to remain consistent for each of the project documents.

The concession agreement will define the length of the concession period. This period should be calculated based on the length of time the grantor is willing to give the concession, the life span of materials and equipment (the residual value of the project) and the period of operation necessary for the project company to accumulate sufficient revenues to satisfy the lenders and the shareholders. Concession periods generally run from 15 to 30 years, possibly longer for projects with a high infrastructure cost-to-revenue flow ratio.

The concession agreement may provide for modification of the concession period in certain circumstances. Generally, the concession period will be extended where one of the grantor's risks has arisen and the project company is entitled to compensation. The grantor may be hesitant to commit its own funds to compensate the project company, but by extending the concession period the grantor provides the project company with increased income without having to invest capital funds in the project. Given the resultant delay before such compensation is received, the project company may not accept this solution.

The concession agreement may also offer an option to extend the concession period, although this option will generally belong to the grantor. In this way, where the concession period is coming to an end and the grantor is not prepared to take over operation, the project company will continue with operation and maintenance and supply the output needed. Alternatively, the project company may be willing to pay a fee in order to extend the concession period.

Where the duration of an agreement or an obligation can be modified, that modification will necessarily affect the duration of other project agreements and obligations contained therein. Cross-referencing between different project agreements may need to be used to ensure consistency of duration.

15.8.4   Language

The parties will want to identify the languages to be used in the project. For example, it will be necessary to establish a language for communications between the project participants, the language of documents to be provided to the grantor, the lenders and the project company, and the language for day-to-day communications. The parties should also indicate language requirements for the interfaces between the operator, the input supplier and the offtake purchaser, allocating responsibility for translation and the language for communications. This will avoid confusion and disorganisation during the operation of the project.

Once such language, or languages, have been established, the obligation and cost of translation will need to be allocated to include those documents to be handed over to the grantor, the lenders or the project company, such as operation and maintenance manuals, which may have been drafted originally in several languages by various suppliers and subcontractors. Such translations require the assistance of highly skilled technical translators, increasing further the cost of such an enterprise.

15.8.5   Confidentiality

The performance of the project will involve the sharing of information, often technically sensitive information. The parties will want to provide that such information remains confidential and is not disseminated to third parties, except as necessary for the performance of the project and on a need-to-know basis. The duty of confidentiality should continue throughout the concession period and beyond, as long as the information remains confidential and proprietary. Therefore, confidentiality provisions will need to be included in each of the project agreements, as well as subcontracts to restrict the use and sharing of information provided within the context of the project. However, confidentiality provisions may be difficult to enforce. Once the information is disclosed, there may not be an appropriate remedy to make the injured party whole.

15.8.6   Training

The operator may require its personnel to be trained in the operation and maintenance of the project, particularly where the project uses some new technology or methodology or where the operator is required to take on grantor personnel who may not be trained in the relevant technologies. The construction contractor will generally provide such training towards the end of the construction period. The training required will need to be specifically defined in order to avoid misunderstandings and disputes at later stages of construction.

Similarly, the grantor will generally require the project company to provide some form of training for its personnel in the operation and maintenance, and possibly repair, of the project. This training will often take place immediately prior to the end of the concession period, in order to provide the most up-to-date education possible. However other arrangements can be made; for example, the operator may be required to employ a certain number of grantor personnel throughout the operation period to provide proper experience and training.

The project company will need to arrange for such training in the most efficient manner possible so as not to interrupt construction and operation of the project. A regime for responsibility for trainees will need to be established including allocation of costs, resources and facilities, liability for damages and injuries, and indemnities.

15.8.7   Choice of law

The governing law of a contract will to some extent define the obligations of the parties, and provide the basis for interpretation of the intent of the parties as expressed in the contract. Therefore, governing law is of primary importance to the parties and should be considered carefully.

The concession agreement will generally be governed by the law of the host country. It would be difficult for the grantor to justify entering into an agreement which regulates an important public service, under a foreign law. The host country law may have important implications to the concession. Certain civil law countries have a very developed concept of concessions and public law contracts. Legal review may be required before termination of a public law contract is allowed and more sanctions may be available to the grantor for termination than are specified in the concession agreement.

The effect of local law on the dispute resolution clause should also be considered. Arbitration is not welcomed in every jurisdiction, and local law may make referral to arbitration or enforcement of an arbitral award very difficult. Certain jurisdictions will not recognise foreign arbitral awards.

An example of the potential effect of local law is the concession in France, which has a long history and a comprehensive body of law that has developed over the last 450 years. French law treats concession contracts as administrative contracts, which are therefore subject to public law. Public law gives the grantor the right to scrutinise the project company's performance, the right to make unilateral changes in certain situations, and the right to special sanctions against the project company for certain breaches.[385] Rights such as these, which may contrast with the structure set up by the parties, should be considered carefully when choosing and reviewing the applicable law.

The relationship between the governing laws used in the various project documents should be considered. Some practitioners believe that conformity is essential, using the same governing law for each of the project documents. However, the project company may not wish all of the project documents to be subject to local law, particularly where that local law is not sufficiently familiar to the parties. The lenders will generally insist on the financing agreements being subject to their own local law. Where there is a different applicable law for two or more of the project documents, the project company and the lenders will need to consider the differences between the legal systems, how the local courts will treat each document and how this might affect the risks involved, and how those risks are allocated within the project.

15.8.8 Schedules

Schedules and appendices will be included in each of the project documents, often the same documents will be appended to each of the project documents or modified versions of the basic documents will be appended to each, adjusted to take into consideration the specific needs of the project document in question.

The schedules will include:

- description of the project;
- site description;
- site conditions;
- access to, possession of and rights of way over the site;
- setting out;
- preliminary design;
- design approval and modification;
- technical specifications;
- performance requirements;
- operating requirements;
- maintenance requirements;
- selection and approval of subcontractors;
- supervision rights of the grantor;

---

[385]   Frillet, "BOT Contracts – The Critical Ingredients of the French Model" 74 PFI 33 at 35.

> supervision rights of the lenders;

> role of the independent engineer;

> quality assurance;

> environmental requirements, testing and assessment;

> necessary licences and permits and who must obtain them;

> milestone payment schedule;

> payment schedule for operation;

> insurances;

> programme for testing and commissioning;

> programme for performance testing;

> programme and requirements for training; and

> forms of bonds and guarantees, potentially including an advance payment guarantee, performance guarantee, retention guarantee, and parent company guarantee.

Care should be taken that changes in the schedules appended to different project documents do not affect the project risk allocation regime. This concern is particularly relevant in connection with the technical specification and performance requirements set out in the concession agreement which must be faithfully adopted into the other project documents.

15.9   Direct Agreements

Several different direct and other agreements may be necessary to manage the relationships between the project participants, the lenders and the grantor. A project may not require direct agreements where provisions can be included in the relevant project document or where some other solution is available (see section 15.6.2 above).

The lenders will have a vested interest in the success of the project. Direct agreements allow the lenders, among other things, to step in to the relevant agreement where one of the parties intends to terminate.[386] Collateral warranties may be included in each direct agreement, although the lenders may prefer to have separate collateral warranties from certain project participants.[387]

---

[386] Further discussion of step-in rights is found in chapter 4.

[387] Scriven, "A Funder's View of Risk in Construction" in Uff and Odams (1995) supra note 144 at 93.

The chart below indicates with broken lines certain of the principal direct agreements found in BOT projects.[388]

DIRECT AGREEMENTS

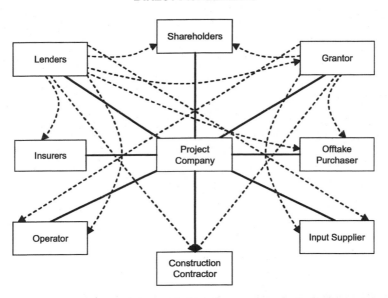

---

388   Further direct agreements may be required, in particular parties with step-in rights (possibly both the lenders and the grantor) may want to receive either direct agreements or assurances from appropriate authorities that licences and permits basic to operation of the project will not be cancelled or renegotiated in the event of step-in. Further direct agreements may also be entered into with certain construction subcontractors and suppliers, transporters and possibly key personnel.

Chapter 16

Tendering Procedures

Man should put as much effort into simplifying life as he does in complicating it.

Henri Bergson,
French philosopher 1859-1941

Once the grantor has selected the commercial approach he wishes to take towards the BOT project, he may choose to use tendering procedures to select the sponsors who will implement the project. Tendering procedures are meant to achieve efficiency, manage costs, maintain quality, uphold expediency and maximise value-for-money. Yet the tendering procedures that we currently use often lack elements of dynamism and flexibility. This is due at least partially to the application of legal and organisational restrictions in an effort to maintain the fundamental purposes for tendering. Inefficient tendering procedures, no matter how well-intentioned, are not meeting the needs of the grantor, the prospective bidders, or the general public.

One particular difficulty encountered in major projects is the cost of tendering.[389] Bidders are sometimes expected to undertake a very complex, lengthy and costly exercise of project analysis, due diligence, design development, cost analysis and negotiation of the underlying commercial deal before being selected as preferred bidder. This results in wasteful duplication and a substantial increase in the costs incurred for each bid attempted. These costs will inevitably be passed on by unsuccessful bidders through their margins for future projects and may also dissuade potential bidders from submitting bids. In turn, infrastructure projects as a whole become more expensive and more difficult to procure, reducing the amount of infrastructure available.

---

[389] For further discussion of tendering procedures, see Scriven, Pritchard and Delmon (1999) supra note 210 at chapter 4.

Formulating tendering procedures is a question of balance between control, flexibility and efficiency. The grantor will want to protect its own negotiating position vis-à-vis the bidders and obtain the best price from the bidders. However, other forces influence tendering procedures. The grantor will want to maintain sufficient flexibility to adapt the procedure and the project in accordance with changing circumstances. It will also want to manage the entry costs for bidders, or possibly compensate bidders, in an effort to attract a number of serious, highly qualified bidders to improve competition and the likelihood of finding the right bidder at the best price.

Lack of sophistication on the part of the grantor can reduce the efficiency of tendering procedures. Often the grantor will not have significant experience in the type of procurement in question, whether the project is a one-off or if the nature of the procurement is different than that normally encountered by the grantor. The grantor may not be sufficiently familiar with the market to know market standards in prices, terms, technology and methodology.

This lack of sophistication may also limit the grantor's ability to design the works and select the most advantageous commercial structure for the project. The grantor may not appreciate the most recent innovations in design and construction, or may not have available financial and commercial advisers aware of the different commercial options available. The grantor may therefore want to use the tendering procedure to obtain proposals on these matters from the bidders as part of their bids.

This chapter discusses the current approaches used for tendering and identifies various weaknesses and inefficiencies.[390] First, it will describe a typical contractual tendering process, and the steps normally taken by grantors when letting a project but without the procedures required by any specific legal or institutional context. It will then consider the purposes of tendering procedures and the goals that should drive these processes. The advantages and disadvantages of tendering procedures are discussed by examining two opposing examples, the fixed approach and the negotiated approach, as it is easier to compare extreme examples, bearing in mind that there are an infinite number of variations of tendering procedures. The involvement of the financiers will be discussed as a separate issue. Finally, this chapter will propose some solutions to the complexity and cost of tendering for projects and consider how these solutions can maximise efficiency.

16.1   The Procedures

In its most basic form, the tender process involves a party offering a project to the market and asking for bids from parties interested in performing the project, or some part of the project. The party wanting the project performed in this scenario

---

[390]   This chapter is adapted from Delmon, "Tendering for the Future – You Get What You Pay For" [2002] ICLR at 446; see also Delmon, "Streamlining Tendering Procedures for Major Projects" PFI 186 at 52-58 (2000).

is the "grantor", while the parties interested in performing the project and offering to do so under certain terms are the "bidders".

The procedure used for putting a project out to tender will depend largely on the applicable legal system and the parties involved in the project.[391] Certain public law entities or private entities that fulfil a public service or interest may be subject to procurement restrictions and requirements under their own national legal systems or under other law, such as the EU procurement regulations.[392] Certain financial institutions also impose their own procurement restrictions, such as the World Bank[393] and the EBRD.[394] Where these institutions are involved in the financing of the project, they may require use of their standard procurement rules or some variation thereof. Legal systems will apply specific rules to tendering procedures such as the concept of good faith or the interpretation of tendering as an administrative rather than a contractual exercise. These legal and institutional requirements are varied and complex and therefore will not be addressed in any detail in this book.

The following describes the steps involved in a typical tendering process. Not all tendering procedures will follow this format, particularly where the nature of the project or the nature or number of bidders requires some divergence from common practice. Furthermore, specific countries or industries may apply some variation from this procedure. However the concepts discussed below will be relevant to most tendering situations.

16.1.1   Pre-qualification

The first stage of the tender will often involve the pre-qualification of bidders. This means that potential bidders will be asked to provide information about themselves, allowing the grantor to select a core group of bidders, generally six to eight in number, who will be allowed to bid for the project. When judging the bidders for pre-qualification, the grantor will not consider the detailed requirements of the project, but will rather assess the minimum requirements to be met in terms of the bidders' technical ability, capacity, financial position and experience in similar projects. The grantor should specify the standards to be applied in assessing pre-qualification when it issues its invitation to bid. That invitation may be sent to specific parties, or may be publicised in some mass media, such as an official journal, popular newspaper or magazine.

---

[391]   For a more detailed review of procurement mechanisms, see the United Nations Commission on International Trade Law Model Law on Procurement of Goods, Construction and Services with Guide to Enactment at www.uncitral.org ("UNCITRAL").

[392]   For further discussion of public procurement restrictions, see Vinter (2nd edition 1998) supra note 211; Scriven, Pritchard and Delmon (1999) supra note 210 at chapter 4; and Lindrup (ed), Butterworths Public Procurement and CCT Handbook (1997).

[393]   The World Bank publishes a series of Standard Bidding Documents for projects of various types and sizes, available through its publications departments in Washington DC and around the world. See also www.worldbank.com

[394]   The EBRD publications are available through www.ebrd.com

16.1.2   Tender documentation

Those bidders who pre-qualify will then be invited to bid for the project. The grantor will provide tender documentation to the pre-qualified bidders, often at a cost.[395] The tender documentation will set out a more detailed description of the project and the basis of the bid. Applicable law will set restrictions on tendering documentation and establish its legal standing.

16.1.2.1   Bid criteria

The tender documentation should set out the basis upon which bids will be reviewed, including the criteria for bid evaluation. The grantor should in the interest of clarity, and in some jurisdictions may be required to, indicate the weighting of different criteria. In this way, the bidders will be able to focus their bids in accordance with the grantor's interests. For example, the bid may have technical, financial and environmental elements. The tender documentation would indicate the relative weight of these elements, say 25 per cent. technical, 60 per cent. financial and 15 per cent. environmental. The cheapest bid is not always the best, and the grantor will want to measure the true value-for-money represented by each bid, the technical and financial standing of the bidder and the likelihood that the project will be a success if that bidder is selected at the price bid.

The public sector comparator is a calculation made by the grantor to identify how much the relevant project would cost for the public sector to perform. It is used to assess the bid against the cost and benefit of the project to the public sector. This requires significant honesty on the part of the individual representatives of the public sector, acknowledging any inefficiency that might be inherent in the relevant bureaucratic structure. Though often not politically palatable, the public sector comparator provides public sector grantors with a useful and practical standard of measurement for assessing bids and the ultimate value-for-money obtained from any tendering procedure.

This assumes that relative cost and value-for-money are relevant considerations. In certain cases, as has been argued for PFI and PPP in the United Kingdom, the grantor is not concerned with cost efficiencies or value-for-money, it is primarily interested in obtaining financing for new infrastructure. Therefore, the fundamental measure is affordability and not value-for-money.

16.1.2.2   Variant bids

The grantor may wish to allow variant bids. These are bids that the bidder believes satisfy the grantor's needs but do not comply specifically with the requirements set out in the tender documentation. A variant bid may involve a technical innovation or some other change in approach which will reduce costs or improve efficiency such as, for example, a different tariff structure.

---

[395]   UNCITRAL at Article 25.

The grantor may want to require bidders to submit a compliant bid with any variant bid. In this way, the grantor is able to consider the compliant bid instead of the variant bid, where the variant bid does not in fact meet its needs. Failure to require compliance may invalidate the variant bid and open the process to legal challenge from an unsuccessful bidder, and will in any case make a proper comparison between bids extremely difficult to perform. The grantor may also wish to restrict the extent to which a bid may be variant, by specifying those elements of the bid which are fixed or otherwise not subject to variation.

16.1.2.3   Procedure for submission

The grantor should describe the procedure to be used for bid submission, time requirements, format restrictions, procedure for questions to be asked and issues raised by the bidders and any other aspects of the tender procedure with which the grantor wishes the bidders to comply. For example, the grantor may wish to limit the period during which questions may be asked by bidders, the manner in which questions will be answered, the time frame in which bids must be submitted and the amount of time allowed for the grantor to evaluate the bids and select a preferred bidder. Responses to questions will generally be provided to all bidders (subject to the confidentiality of commercially sensitive information), putting each bidder on the same footing.

It is important for the grantor to allow for flexibility in the bidding procedures. Any number of circumstances may arise requiring change. The grantor will want to allow itself such flexibility without exposing itself to liability or unnecessarily disadvantaging the bidders. Under English law and many other legal systems, these documents can be treated as contractual in nature,[396] and therefore the grantor will want to consider them carefully before issuing them to bidders. For example, the grantor will want to reserve the right to modify the tender procedure and the information provided under certain conditions and the right not to choose any of the bidders and proceed with the project in some other way. Failure to provide for these and other protections may result in the tendering process being vulnerable to legal challenge and the grantor being responsible for the costs and lost opportunity of unsuccessful bidders.

16.1.2.4   Bid bonds

The tender documentation may also require bidders to provide bid bonds, which give the grantor security that the bidders are serious about their bid and the project. The grantor will be allowed to call on such a bond if the bidder is selected as preferred bidder but then refuses to continue with the project. The amount secured from the bond will cover the cost of pursuing negotiations with other bidders once the preferred bidder drops out. Bid bonds will remain valid until either the selection of the preferred bidder or until the award of the project.

---

[396]   Blackpool and Fylde Aero Club Ltd. v Blackpool Borough Council [1990] 1 WLR 1195, CA.

16.1.3   Bid evaluation

Once bids have been received and the relevant time limits have lapsed, the grantor will consider each of the bids against the criteria they set out in the tender documents. Evaluation of a bid should consider the whole of the bid, not only cost and finance issues.[397] The bid evaluators should select the most economically advantageous bid, meaning the bid which embodies the most beneficial combination of characteristics, including technical performance, cost-effectiveness, flexibility, environmental impact, investment in the local community, social responsibility and consideration of any particular interests of the grantor. The evaluation should follow the regime and criteria set out in the tender documentation to avoid any challenge of the propriety or legality of the award.

16.1.4   Preferred bidder

The grantor will elect one or two of the bidders as the preferred bidder (the singular will be used for ease of reference and as the more common scenario). It will then undertake detailed negotiations with the preferred bidder, agreeing and signing project contracts, finance agreements and any other documentation required for the project. Where the grantor is not able to agree compliant documentation with the preferred bidder, he will be replaced with the second place bidder. However, replacement of the preferred bidder is not common as it is time-consuming and expensive.

The bid bonds mentioned above may be retained until the grantor has signed the project contracts with the preferred bidder, thereby tying the other bidders to the project in case the preferred bidder drops out. The preferred bidder may be required to pay a fee or provide a further bond when it accepts this mandate. This fee or bond may be sacrificed if the preferred bidder withdraws from the project or if financial close is not achieved before a certain date.

16.2   The Purpose

Tendering procedures, when properly managed, can provide the grantor, the bidders and the public generally with security regarding the transparency of the process of selecting bidders, competition amongst bidders to obtain the best price, and overall value for money. They ensure that every aspect of the contract (price, quality, time and risk) is subject to competition and equal and fair consideration of each of the bidders for the project. Tendering procedures can also improve efficiency by providing more information, creating avenues of communication and reducing the time required for procurement and the cost of the procedure for all involved.

---

[397]   UNCITRAL at Article 34.

16.2.1   Efficiency

Tendering procedures are meant to provide greater certainty to all the parties involved, setting out a clear view of the scope of the project, the criteria upon which tenders will be judged and defining the key information that the grantor will need to obtain from the bidders in order to judge the different bids. By providing certainty, the procedures are intended to improve the efficiency of the project and reduce the need for the grantor to provide repeated clarification of the process and its requirements. Greater efficiency is achieved where the grantor obtains the information it needs to make a proper decision. Pricing and technical terms are then judged on a consistent basis and each bidder is allowed to use its creativity and its particular experience and skills to provide the grantor with the most efficient method of performing and implementing the project, with particular focus on value for money.

Efficient tendering procedures can provide bidders with a clearer view of the resource commitment and costs associated with the bid. The procedures implemented should help to contain those costs and encourage more bidders to submit a bid. Bidders will calculate the likelihood of success against the cost of bidding before deciding to submit a bid. The grantor will benefit if this ratio encourages more bidders to pursue the project. An example would be the proposed private sector participation in Nepal's water sector in the late 1990s. The Government of Nepal went out to tender without providing the clarity and commercial considerations sought by the bidders. This, along with political insurgency in Nepal and the demise of Azurix (one of the proposed bidders and a subsidiary of Enron) resulted in only one bidder willing to submit a formal bid.

16.2.2   Competition

Tendering procedures allow market forces and competition to impact upon the procurement strategy of the grantor. Competition amongst the bidders is intended to reduce the ultimate price to be paid for the procurement and to bring the variety of technical and financial expertise of the various bidders to bear on the procurement strategy. This helps to ensure that anti-competitive practices do not reduce the efficiency of the procurement process, increasing price and delay.

The impact of competition on the bidding process is in its essence quite simple. The bidders know that there are other bidders in contention. They are made aware of the presence of those bidders and in certain cases are provided with information about those other bidders. Each bidder will reduce its price as much as possible and improve the technical and financial basis of its bid in an effort to win the project.

In certain tendering procedures, the bidders are made aware of the types of pricing and technical solutions being proposed by the other bidders. A more extreme example of this approach is the procedure that was used to auction 3G telecoms licences in the United States and the United Kingdom at the turn of the century (21st century, that is). By using game theory, the grantor was able to play each of the bidders off against the others. Through a very long and complex bidding process, each bidder was aware of the price offered by the other bidders. If they wanted to continue to the next stage of the process they had to improve their bid against the competition. This resulted in a frenzied competition situation, with bids perhaps going far beyond what was a reasonable price for the relevant licences. The telecoms market was very buoyant at the time; financing for these inflated bids was readily available.

Competition is not only focused on price. It can also motivate bidders to seek more efficient technical and commercial solutions, apply other resources available to them to improve their bid and the project, and propose new solutions to the grantor's requirements. Innovation can be encouraged and rewarded through greater competition.

Increased, open competition can also provide new market entrants with opportunities, helping to develop local markets. Strong competitors often dominate markets with their superior experience, financial wherewithal and political connections. Fair competition allows new competitors to use their technical expertise and innovative creativity to gain entry into new markets. It also reduces the ability of established operators to use their dominant position to eliminate new market entrants from competing for new opportunities.

Ironically, the pursuit of fairness and open competition can eliminate the more reasonable and cost-effective bid. Where a bidder has more information about the project and surrounding circumstances, that bidder may be disqualified as having an unfair advantage, under certain legal systems. An example is the concession for the Périphérique Nord of Lyon.[398] The bidder that submitted the best price was also the concessionaire for another nearby road, linked to the one to be built. That bidder had a better understanding of ground conditions and local requirements, so its bid was the most advantageous, but it was considered to have an unfair advantage and was therefore disqualified.

16.2.3   Transparency

Traditional procurement processes award projects to those with the best connections or the most influence with the representative selecting the successful bidder. Transparency in tendering procedures is intended to improve competition and reduce the unseen costs associated with unequal treatment amongst bidders. Transparency can also reduce corruption and influence-peddling within the context of a bidding situation. It is hard to act in a manner contrary to legal and social standards when those acts and their effects are visible to everyone.

Implementing transparency into the tendering process introduces competitive forces that tend to push prices down.[399] It also supports the development of new

---

[398]   Conseil d'Etat, Assemblée, 6 février 1998, L'actualité juridique – Droit administratif at 458 (20 May 1998).

[399]   It should be reiterated that a low price is not a panacea. Squeezing margins means less money available to perform work, with the associated temptation to use lower quality materials and personnel, and to save money on management, safety and quality assurance resources.

players in the market. New entrants are able to compete on a level playing field, aware of the criteria applied to bids and the requirements of the grantor. Requirements to win the bid, the cost of bidding and the likelihood of success become more calculable, encouraging a larger number of bidders to participate, increasing opportunities for new market entrants and improving the competitive pressures that drive prices down.

Increased transparency can also attract new forms of investment, potentially reducing the cost of the project. By providing financiers with the information available from the transparency of the process, bidders may be able to obtain financing from new sources such as the capital markets, commercial banks, private pension funds, export credit agencies and international finance institutions (for example, the EBRD and the World Bank) which must satisfy transparency restrictions set by their own management, shareholders or stakeholders, or as set by law. These forms of funding may provide additional benefits to the project. For example, encouraging investment by local capital markets can provide stimulus for the local economy and increase the capital available to other local ventures.

16.3 The Approaches

Two methods often used for tendering for a project are the negotiated approach and the fixed approach. These two approaches to tendering procedures are discussed here as examples to identify the weaknesses encountered in the search for efficiency. Tendering procedures will most often adopt some combination of these approaches in an effort to obtain their respective benefits and avoid their disadvantages.

The negotiated procedure involves the selection of a preferred bidder based on pricing, financial, contractual and technical terms. The grantor and the preferred bidder then negotiate the terms of the contract based on the concepts already agreed. Under the fixed procedure, the grantor issues a set of contractual terms and outlines the scope of work to be allocated to the project company. Each bidder bids a fixed price for that contract. The grantor then chooses the best price against the terms and technology required. There is little if any scope for the bidders to negotiate the terms of the project, unless variant bids are permitted.

16.3.1 Bidder response

When bidding, bidders have the option of submitting an aggressive bid with a very low price. In this context, the bidder, in its desire to win the project, may agree to strictly uncommercial or unreasonable terms. This could be termed the "Trojan Horse" approach[400] – the bidder gets through the gate with an attractive bid, only later to emerge from an opening in the bid to ambush the enemy and throw open the gates of the city to the waiting army. This approach relies on the assumption that the bidder, once it has been selected as preferred bidder, will be able to

---

[400] Or the Trojan Rabbit approach, for those with a penchant for Monty Python.

renegotiate any unreasonable risks that the grantor is asking it to bear. One cannot help but think of the very aggressive bids and unrealistic forecasts used for one of the water concessions in Manila and the Azurix bid for one of the Buenos Aires water projects.

This is a dangerous gamble. The bidder may be stuck with its very aggressive bid if the grantor refuses to negotiate. The bidder will then attempt to extricate itself from the bid and possibly abandon the project. This is a costly process and a waste of time for the bidder and the grantor.

The bidder adopting this approach may also rely on the fact that when the financiers are brought into the deal they will raise issues in the context of their due diligence process and assessment of project bankability.[401] The bidder may hope that any outstanding difficult issues will be brought up by the financiers in the context of the financing. The preferred bidder would then appear to be compliant with the grantor's requirements, while blaming the need for further negotiation of issues on the needs of the financiers.

Another option is for the bidder to submit a reasonable bid, compliant with the tender documents. In an effort to provide further value-for-money, the bidder may choose to submit a variant bid or specific pricing for different aspects of the project in order to demonstrate to the grantor that the risk specified in the tendering documentation may not be reasonable and may not provide value for money. By stripping away the excessive risk, the bidder can remove much of the contingency element in the price and thereby provide a more competitive price. Though more honest and reasonable, this approach carries with it the risk that the grantor will not bother looking at the variant bid or will not bother considering the detail of the bid and will simply select the lowest-priced bid.

The choice between these two approaches is an uncomfortable one. The more reasonable approach is to submit a considered bid focused on value-for-money drivers. However, if one of the other bidders uses an aggressive approach seeking renegotiation, a reasonable bid may not be competitive and therefore may not afford the bidder the opportunity to advance to the next bid round. This leaves the reasonable bidder with a disadvantage and the more aggressive bidder an opportunity to renegotiate in search of a deal that works.

Rarely is it entirely clear what approach the grantor will take when reviewing bids. It would be nice to think that the grantor will appreciate the merits of a reasoned bid, and will not be convinced solely by the best price. However, even if it is sufficiently sophisticated and diligent, the grantor will have its own responsibilities toward public officials, corporate boards, shareholders or elected officials, who may not understand the subtleties of a reasoned bid versus a low price tag. Azurix's bid in the Buenos Aires water concession was so far removed from the fundamental assumptions adopted by the other bids, it is difficult to imagine that

---

[401]   For a discussion of "bankability", see chapter 5.

the relevant grantor did not struggle with this issue. This inherent uncertainty can reduce significantly the efficiency of tendering procedures.

The following is a simplified discussion of the fixed and negotiated approaches. These extremes in approach have been chosen to highlight the various disadvantages of tendering and to give an understanding of the potential characteristics of the full spectrum of approaches available for tendering procedures.

16.3.2   Fixed approach

The grantor may want the detailed contractual structure for the project to be agreed and fixed at the time the preferred bidder is selected. This will require comprehensive specifications and documentation to be included in the invitation to tender. The bidders then review the documentation and submit their proposed price. There is little if any scope for negotiation or modification of the grantor's terms and requirements.

16.3.2.1   The benefits

The grantor maintains its negotiating position by fixing the terms of the bid and not allowing bidders to negotiate those terms. The grantor's requirements as set out in the tender documentation are therefore fixed. This can place significant risk on the bidders to the extent that they must accept terms with limited opportunity to discuss and negotiate them with the grantor. However, it can also expedite the tender and selection processes, since the grantor need only compare bid prices with no consideration of alternative proposals, conditions, qualifications or other changes to the grantor's terms. The cost of this fixed approach for the grantor should also be reduced, given the limited scope for negotiation. This must be weighed against the cost of developing detailed grantor requirements before issuing tender documentation.

For their part, the bidders have clarity as to the basis on which the bid will be awarded and on which competitors will be judged. This can reduce the opportunity for corruption and abuse. Any inappropriate activities or preference will normally be visible to the other bidders. The bidders in a fixed procedure have increased certainty that clarifications, discussions of alternate approaches and other such variables will not delay the procurement timetable, nor cause an increase in the resource commitment required of them. The fixed approach can also offer a greater opportunity for new competitors to enter the market. Bids will not be selected based on relationships, influence or past experience, but on the ability to provide a better price and service.

The fixed approach appears to be ideal from the grantor's point of view, increasing grantor control, managing loss of negotiating position and reducing cost. It is for this reason that legal structures and systems tend to impose a fixed approach for most projects. This is true, for example, of the proposed EU procurement directive.[402]   However, the fixed approach fails to allow the bidders to provide ideas, input and objectivity, denying the grantor of so many of the opportunities that are available through tendering procedures.

16.3.2.2   Grantor requirements

The tender process has the potential to provide a fertile forum for suggesting new approaches, challenging assumptions, reassessing requirements and modifying methodologies in the search for efficiency. Given the resources available to the bidders and their combined experience and creative energy driven by competitive forces, the tender process should refine and improve the project generally. However, the fixed approach does not allow for this efficiency and instead establishes the grantor's original requirements as the final terms for the project. Any change in the original terms could be a breach of the tender procedure and result in rejection of the bid or legal challenges from the unsuccessful bidders. Therefore, the fixed approach may be appropriate for projects with little scope for variation or innovation but does not facilitate the sharing of information, technology, know-how and ideas between the grantor and the bidders.

Another advantage gained from allowing bidder input into the project requirements is value for money.   The bidders will be able to identify aspects of the risk-allocation assumptions in the project requirements that would be expensive for the bidders to manage. The grantor then has the option of retaining certain risks in exchange for a cheaper bid. Since the bidders do not have this luxury in the fixed approach, their bid prices will include contingency elements. In its extreme, the bidder may not be able to price for specific risks, resulting in significant uncertainty and potentially the need for the eventual renegotiation of the project, or its ultimate failure, due to the inefficient risk allocation regime.

16.3.2.3   The nature of the bid

The grantor may require each of the pre-qualified bidders to review the detailed commercial documentation in the bid submission. This documentation can include technical, financial and legal terms drafted in full detail that will require extensive due diligence to properly consider a bid and its ramifications. This can involve a substantial outlay of resources at the bidding stage.

By taking such a strict approach to tendering, the grantor intends to reduce scope for renegotiation of the deal after the preferred bidder has been selected, at which point the grantor loses much of its negotiating power.

However, a bidder will assess the desirability of bidding for a project based on a number of factors, including the cost of bidding against the likelihood of success and the rewards available from a successful bid. The increased cost of bidding may drive potential bidders away, reducing competition and potentially increasing

---

[402]   2000/0115 (COD), which can be found at www.europa.eu.int/abc/doc/off/bull/en/200201

the price. A smaller number of bidders decreases competition and reduces the market forces that help to drive down price.

16.3.2.4 Information

The bidders will often only have available to them the information provided by the grantor. This information will often not be warranted and therefore will be at the risk of the bidders. Further, bidders may assume that this information has been "packaged" in an overly optimistic manner in order to sell the project to them to obtain a better price. Without the opportunity to manage the risk of inaccurate information through the project documentation, bidders will need to add contingencies into their prices to protect against these risks and costs, increasing costs to the grantor.

16.3.2.5 The result

The grantor may place the substantial demands of a fixed approach on the bidders in an effort to maintain negotiating power and obtain a bid compliant with its requirements. The grantor runs the risk that by selecting the more complacent and compliant bidder it is obtaining an illusory benefit. That same bidder is likely to raise, or ensure that another party raises, the same type of issues after its selection as preferred bidder, once the grantor's negotiating position is weakened.

The disadvantages associated with the fixed approach can be summarised as follows:

> ➢ a tendency toward unreasonable tenders and therefore expensive risk allocation;

> ➢ the inability of the grantor to explore with the bidders options for innovation, added efficiency and value-for-money; and

> ➢ the need for early investment of significant resources by the grantor.

16.3.3 Negotiated approach

Another approach is to identify basic terms during the bidding process, including some basic guidelines for pricing, but to allow negotiation of the project terms in order to implement bidder ideas and concerns. After the preferred bidder is selected, the grantor negotiates the contractual structure for the project with the preferred bidder and its financiers.

16.3.3.1 The benefits

The negotiated approach can permit a full and frank discussion between the bidders and the grantor. The bidders are encouraged to raise issues, explore the grantor's needs and requirements, identify priority of interests, focus their resources on satisfying the most important requirements and develop ideas specific to the project and the grantor's needs.

In order to benefit from the new ideas raised by the bidders, the grantor will need to remain flexible and open-minded. It is common for the grantor to feel defensive about any suggestions or proposals different to those it has put forth and therefore to become positional, refusing to consider new ideas. However, the grantor will need to acknowledge that the bidders may well have valid and even better ideas.

The grantor will want to adopt new ideas that it considers to be more efficient and better value for money. It will then want to issue these ideas to all the bidders in order to reduce the price of the new ideas through competitive pressure. However, new ideas will constitute a competitive currency for the bidders, a costly and valuable advantage that they will not want to lose. If those new ideas are to be disclosed to the other bidders and indeed used by them, the creative bidder will not be motivated to share its ideas. The creative bidder should be allowed to benefit from its innovative ideas by keeping them confidential.

The grantor will not need to have developed its requirements in great detail in order to follow the negotiated approach to tendering. The specific requirements of the grantor can be developed during the due diligence and negotiation phase, once input and innovation from the bidders has been received. By evolving the grantor's requirements in parallel with the tendering procedure the project timetable can be accelerated or "fast-tracked" and associated costs reduced. The grantor will have additional information and a more complete understanding of the project once the tendering procedure has developed.

16.3.3.2   Disadvantages

The negotiation process can be long and costly. The grantor will need to negotiate with each bidder, provide clarification of any queries raised and discuss variant proposals and possibly negotiate the drafting of detailed and often lengthy technical and legal documentation. This may also result in a loss of competition, since the basis of the project and therefore each bid will change as new ideas and approaches are proposed. The original bidders may only be aware of the terms set out in the grantor's preliminary documentation. As discussions progress, the different bidders may have separate dealings with the grantor. The preferred bidder's arrangements with the grantor, often without external consultation or transparency, may be significantly different from those proposed to bidders at the beginning of the tender process.

The grantor may also lose negotiating power by allowing the bidders to open up and challenge its requirements. The bidders, when submitting their proposals, will generally make reservations or subject the bid to caveats where they have assumed a specific risk allocation or certain circumstances which may be encountered when constructing the works or operating the facility. This may jeopardise the benefit that the grantor can obtain from applying competitive and market forces to the bidders. That benefit may be lost where the preferred bidder is able to revert to a previous position during negotiations.

The bidders will therefore make great efforts to advance to later bid stages and eventually preferred bidder status, without raising many of their issues. The selection of the preferred bidder is particularly sensitive since it represents a significant reduction in any competition. At its worst, the negotiated approach can result in the dilution of the grantor's requirements. The grantor will always have the ability to revert to one of the previous bidders, but that can be a costly and time-consuming proposition and can constitute a loss of face and further loss of negotiating power for the grantor.

16.3.3.3   The nature of the bid

The bid submitted by the various bidders will be simplified. Rather than a detailed review and negotiation of the project documentation, the bidders will provide only basic responses that assess the risk structure proposed. Bidders will not need to invest resources in detailed due diligence until later in the bid process, when the likelihood of success has improved as other bidders are dropped from the process. The delay in investment of resources should improve the ratio of bid cost to likelihood of success, and should attract more bidders, improving competition and driving down the ultimate price.

16.3.3.4   The result

The negotiated approach reduces the amount of effort and resources required of the grantor before the project can be put out to tender. It represents a form of collaboration between the grantor and the preferred bidder in developing the scope and structure of the project. The bidders are able to make proposals and suggest innovative ideas to increase the efficiency of the project.

The primary risk run when opting for a negotiated approach is the loss of negotiating position by the grantor. In particular, where the project is a one-off and the grantor has no other influence over the project company, there is a risk that the project company will attempt to modify the project significantly once it has been selected as preferred bidder. There is also a significant potential loss of transparency when the negotiation of substantive issues is left to the preferred bidder.

16.4   Project Finance and Involving the Financiers

Once selected, the bidder must structure the commercial deal according to the specific nature of the project, the requirements of the grantor, and any other cost, time, technical or financial constraints placed on the project. In particular, when structuring its bid, the bidder will need to consider the requirements of financiers.

Where the bidders intend to procure limited recourse financing, the financiers bear a portion of the commercial risk for the deal. Before committing funding, the financiers will want to ensure that the amount of risk borne by the preferred bidder is appropriate for the relevant market (i.e. that the project is bankable).

Bankability reviews often raise issues of particular substance and impact on the project and the grantor. In certain cases, bidders will use the presence of lenders to bring further pressure to bear in relation to outstanding bidder issues or introduce new issues. For this reason, the grantor will pay close attention to the involvement of financiers and their ability to raise issues.

Each bidder will generally provide its own financing proposal, including its own set of financiers. These financiers may be involved from the very beginning of the tender process or may be selected once the bidder has achieved some later level of success. The timing of involvement of the financiers can have an important effect on the total cost to the bidders, the due diligence the financiers are able to perform and the ability of the financiers to be involved in the negotiation of the project contracts.

16.4.1   Bankability

The financiers' review analyses the underlying bankability of the project.[403] This is the measure of the risk allocation structure used for the project, and the extent to which the financiers will be protected if any risk arises. A market approach to bankable risk allocation has developed in relation to each form of financing, and will be applied to the project.

To the extent the project is not bankable, the financiers will require changes in the project structure. Therefore, even once the preferred bidder has negotiated a deal with the grantor and various subcontractors, the financiers may have further requirements to impose on the project. The introduction of the financiers, unless the timing and the financiers' expectations can be managed, can have a serious impact on the limitation of exposure to project risk that the grantor is hoping to obtain through the tender process. This "second bite of the cherry", allowing the bidder to revisit issues previously agreed, may cause some resentment from the grantor, in particular where the result of the negotiations with the bidder were publicised or politicised.

16.4.2   Introduction of the financiers post-bid

The financiers are often not involved in reviewing the project until after the relevant bidder is selected as preferred bidder. Common practice is for bidders to conclude negotiations with the grantor and possibly begin or even conclude negotiations with subcontractors before getting the financiers involved in performing detailed due diligence on the project documentation.

The involvement of the financiers can be a time-consuming and expensive process. Popular wisdom indicates that the less time the financiers have available to review the project, the less costs will be incurred by the financiers' advisers and the less the financiers will want to amend the underlying documentation. Restricting time and resources available to the financiers to perform their review can be used as a blunt instrument in order to restrict financier input. However, it may prove to be an inefficient mechanism. Financiers will not normally approve funding for a project until they are comfortable with the risk allocation and commercial viability

---

[403]   For further discussion of "bankability", see chapter 5.

of that project. It is in the grantor's interests to obtain funding on the most reasonable terms possible. Restricting the financiers' ability to raise issues may only create a feeling of increased insecurity and reduce the availability of funding.

By waiting until after the bidder has been selected as a preferred bidder to involve the financiers, the bidder and the grantor run the risk that the project as structured is not bankable. As an example in a project in Africa, the construction arrangements were finalised and partially implemented before consulting the financiers. The selection of construction contractor was made on price, rather than experience and creditworthiness. This choice made the financier's task more difficult, prolonged the due diligence process and threatened the bankability of the project.

16.4.3 Introduction of the financiers pre-bid

Another approach is for the grantor to require the financiers to perform some element or even all of their due diligence exercise before selection of the preferred bidder. By requesting early involvement of the financiers, the grantor can benefit from its strong negotiating position during this early period and try to force the financiers to raise any issues before the grantor selects the relevant consortium.

The grantor may require from the financiers a binding undertaking to underwrite the financing of the project on the terms of the bid. However, financiers will rarely bind themselves to a project without first completing a thorough due diligence review of the project documentation and the security available over project assets, negotiating finance agreements with the borrower and submitting the whole for approval to a credit committee or some other internal review procedure. In most cases, this approval process must be complete before a financier can provide any undertaking or assurances.

Therefore, where it is not possible for the financiers to bind themselves to fund the project, requiring the financiers to perform their due diligence before selection of the preferred bidder, or possibly before development of a more complete commercial deal, may be an inefficient use of resources for potentially limited benefit. That said, it may be possible to obtain a letter of comfort or other indication from the financiers as to their willingness to finance the project on its terms, subject to due diligence. Though this letter of comfort may not be legally binding, it does provide some moral leverage to press the financiers to take a proactive approach to financing the project.

16.4.4 Managing financiers

There are few satisfactory methods of managing the involvement of financiers, and their ability to influence the structure of the project agreed between the grantor and the relevant bidder. The project negotiated with the bidder must be bankable. The grantor can reduce the ability of the financiers to demand further changes or comments if it can demonstrate that the project is indeed bankable.

One method of managing financier involvement that could be available to very strong bidders and grantors is for the preferred bidder to pay for a due diligence review of the project by legal, technical and insurance advisers familiar to and respected by the lending market. This due diligence review would then be issued to each of the financiers who are interested in the project. The financiers then bid for the project by proposing the margin and terms that they would offer to the preferred bidder. This creates a form of second tendering procedure in relation to the financing of the project. This approach has had very limited exposure to date.

Realistically, the financiers will not legally bind themselves to provide financing for a project until such time as their credit committee has received an exhaustive due diligence report and has reviewed the whole of the project. The position of the preferred bidder and the status of negotiations between the grantor and the preferred bidder will have only limited influence on the decision of the credit committee. Involving the financiers early in the process may provide some limited moral incentive to restrict them from raising further issues, reducing the associated costs and time required.

16.5   Solutions to Efficient Tendering

Tendering is a complex and highly contextual task, and one of significant importance. An efficient tendering procedure takes thought, preparation and time. In the search for efficiency in procurement, there are no easy answers. A variety of approaches to tendering procedures are available. The selection of the appropriate procedure will depend on the nature of the project, the complexity of the technical and commercial issues involved, the sophistication of the grantor, the resources available to it, and its experience with similar projects and tendering procedures, and the source of financing for the project. Each project requires a bespoke solution.

The fixed procedure is becoming increasingly popular. This is principally due to changes in legal and administrative regimes requiring the use of the fixed procedure on anything but the most complicated projects. The intention of these requirements is to maintain consistency of approach and conformity of terms used in different projects, to reduce the level of corrupt practices and maintain general control over the procurement process. As discussed above, these intentions are laudable, but the effect has been to increase the use of the fixed procedure without remedying many of its disadvantages.

Structuring an appropriate tendering procedure is a question of balance. The solution must secure for the grantor the benefit of its negotiating position while reducing the cost to bidders of preparing a careful, reasoned bid. It should be as time and cost-effective as possible. From the grantor's point of view, the bidding process must establish at least the critical terms of the project before the selection of one preferred bidder, or empower the grantor to manage negotiations with the preferred bidder and motivate a reasonable and practical approach to these negotiations. For example, where the grantor has a series of further projects planned, or works with the parties to the project in other contexts, it may have greater leverage to motivate the preferred bidder to act reasonably.

This section discusses the process of resolving the disadvantages of the fixed approach and suggests some solutions that might prove beneficial when developing tendering procedures.

16.5.1 Availability of resources to the grantor

The grantor may be hampered by a lack of familiarity with tendering procedures and the contractual structure to be implemented. An increase in the resources available to the grantor, in particular in relation to the standard and experience of the grantor's advisers, can make a significant difference in the efficiency and effectiveness of the tendering procedures and the contractual structure adopted by the grantor. The grantor's advisers should have a scope of work large enough to review the entire project and to provide advice. The advisers, for their part, must not focus on an idealised approach to risk allocation, or "risk cramming", but rather a sensible and commercial approach to keep the cost of tendering down and to keep the level of competition up by attracting numerous bidders and new competitors.

16.5.1.1 *Source of funding for grantor resources*

An obvious solution is to improve the availability of resources to the grantor. Several mechanisms are available in order to fund additional grantor resources.

> The bidders may be asked to pay a certain fee for the opportunity to submit a bid.

> The preferred bidder may be charged a fee for achieving that status.

> The bidder who finally wins the project could be required to pay a fixed fee, or to reimburse the grantor for its tender costs.

> In the United Kingdom, Partnerships UK ("PUK")[404] assists the grantor in structuring the tender procedure, in adopting a contractual structure for the project and in selecting professional advisers and funding their advice. In consideration for this advice and funding, PUK receives a fee from the successful bidder and a portion of the equity in the project vehicle. A similar structure could be implemented in the relevant country or region.

> Funding may also be available, in particular for public sector grantors, from international bodies such as the World Bank or the EBRD. However, some consider that the World Bank and other such entities have their own

---

[404] PUK grew out of the Treasury Taskforce, a body organised within the auspices of the United Kingdom Treasury to help encourage and develop the Private Finance Initiative in the United Kingdom. Following from its success in the public sector, it became a public private partnership to provide the Government and the public sector with private sector expertise. See www.partnershipsuk.org.uk

agendas, and local and public sector grantors may therefore resist the use of these sources of funding.

16.5.1.2   Advisers

It is essential that the grantor receive the best advice available from experienced and professional advisers. In certain cases, the grantor has available to it capable and experienced advisers, but out of lack of experience or the understandable desire to reduce costs, the grantor limits its advisers' ability to provide advice by restricting their scope of work or permitting political or other interests to dictate policy rather than a reasonable and commercial consideration of the issues. The grantor must be free to manage the cost of its advisers, but it must allow its advisers to give comprehensive and complete advice.

On the subject of professional advisers, it should be noted that often these advisers are guilty of over-zealous defence of their clients' interests. Professional advisers must give counsel to the grantor not only on the best method of achieving the strongest negotiating position, but also the importance of value-for-money and the need to allocate risk in the manner that best meets the needs of the project. This means a practical, commercial analysis, rather than just unilaterally advantageous risk allocation.

16.5.2   Reducing terms

The grantor may wish to improve efficiency by reducing or prioritising the amount of commercial, legal and contractual information which must be reviewed and negotiated by the bidders. The delay and cost associated with the fixed approach to tendering results partly from the volume of information and documentation that must be reviewed and negotiated by each of several bidders. In certain cases, when constructing tendering procedures, less is more.

The grantor may also succumb to the temptation to take an overly optimistic approach to the risks and obligations that bidders will accept. Although the possibility exists that bidders will not identify such risks and obligations, a more likely result would be their renegotiation or the bidder placing a contingency amount in his financial bid to cover the risks and costs involved. The grantor may therefore prefer to follow a reasonable/market-driven risk allocation regime when drafting the tender documentation. However, grantors may not have available to them a clear view of market standards. Precedents from previous projects may be too context-specific to provide a reasonable view of the market. Nevertheless, sophisticated external advisers can provide insight into a reasonable allocation of risk.

16.5.2.1   Document rationalisation

Clear and concise documentation that is easy to follow will generally reduce the time needed for review, the number of questions to which the grantor will need to respond and the resources required to negotiate such provisions. This approach will require investment of resources by the grantor when preparing the tender documentation.

The current trend is to include all possible contingencies in drafting the documentation with little consideration for the implementation of the project. The complex and seemingly unnecessarily voluminous documentation of projects such as Aquatrine (the outsourcing of the Ministry of Defence's water services in the United Kingdom) and London Underground give pause.[405] Too much detail can restrict flexibility and the ability to apply a structure in a sensible and commercial manner. Once agreed, it may be difficult for the people on the ground – the project and line managers, engineers and operations personnel – to implement these detailed, complex and heavily documented projects. All the hard work and thought that goes into developing such documentation may not yield much practical benefit to the management of the project if the documentation is too unwieldy and not implementation-friendly.

16.5.2.2   Standard form documentation

Familiarity with a set of documentation can facilitate the review process. There is less need to commit resources to review of project documentation that follows a standardised risk allocation and drafting model. This has been accomplished, to some extent, in Private Finance Initiative and Public Private Partnership projects in the United Kingdom. Parties are aware, when they first receive bid documentation, what the basic approach will be, with a sufficiently strong market standard to facilitate negotiation of many difficult issues.

Standard form documentation is helpful, but it will never eliminate the need for professional and experienced advice and the commitment of significant resources to project development. Further, standard form documentation only seems to work where there will be:

> ➤ multiple projects, in order to develop the standard form and create acceptance within the relevant market;

> ➤ the same or similar legal, commercial, political and financial environment, to ensure consistency of context and interpretation of the documentation; and

> ➤ either a consensus to use, or a single grantor or central administrative power that can mandate the use of, the documentation throughout the market.

These characteristics may not be present from commencement of the use of the standardised documentation, but can emerge as the market develops.

---

[405]   Aquatrine is a very complex outsourcing of water and sanitation services for the MOD involving services on some 3,000 sites across the United Kingdom. London Underground is the Public Private Partnership project for the subway system in London. It is meant to have one of the most complex performance indicator structures in the industry (even measuring the size of each piece of trash that is collected from the platforms).

16.5.2.3   Term sheets

Another potential method of reducing the complexity of the tender documentation, and the investment of resources required to prepare, review and negotiate them, is the use of term sheets[406] to set out the grantor's requirements. Projects are unique structures, each taking a different form and different structure for technical, social and cultural reasons. Standard form documents lack flexibility, and therefore may not meet the needs of a varied and diverse portfolio of projects. Term sheets are, by nature, flexible and conceptual, allowing easier adaptation for project-specific considerations. They allow the grantor to set certain parameters, improving efficiency without reducing flexibility unnecessarily. Term sheets focus on the major issues permitting a simplified review and negotiation procedure.

The grantor could also use the term sheet to manage the introduction of the financiers. The financiers would be required to agree to the term sheet at the time of the bid (though whether this agreement would be legally binding as not sufficiently certain or as an agreement to agree will depend on applicable law). Detailed due diligence would be carried out after selection of the preferred bidder, adding detail to the term sheet or addressing specific issues not already set out in the term sheet. The financiers may not bind themselves to the term sheet, but if they agree in principle to its terms, it will be more difficult for them to seek to alter the agreed terms.

The creation of standard form term sheets would permit further efficiency and could simplify the tender procedure. It would be familiar to those professionals involved in the industry, thereby reducing the time and effort necessary for review. The grantor could show changes on the term sheet provided in the tender documentation against the standard form, to help bidders identify project specific issues.

In order to achieve the level of standardisation desired, the term sheet could be drafted and issued by an independent, neutral and widely respected organisation, for example by the World Bank, UNCITRAL or some other international body. The key would be to convince grantors (in particular from the public sector) that the issuing body did not have some hidden agenda and was indeed neutral in its drafting of the term sheet.

16.5.3   Variant bids

Even with the most reasonable and commercial of professional advice, the grantor may not attract the desired level of financing, may not obtain value for money, or may misunderstand market structures and may demand a risk allocation structure that is not commercially viable. In order to provide the flexibility within the

---

[406]   A term sheet is a document, not generally meant to be legally binding, that sets out the main terms and conditions to a transaction. It is the precursor to, and the template for, the detailed drafting of the contract.

context of a fixed procedure, it may be possible to allow the bidders to submit variant bids (as discussed in section 16.1.2.2).

A variation on this flexible approach is for the variant bid that the grantor finds particularly attractive to be circulated to the other bidders, who then submit a price for the variant bid. This permits a sharing of ideas and allows the grantor to create competition and to apply market forces to those ideas. Also, if one proposal is preferred to all others, it might be inefficient or it may create an unfair advantage not to permit all bidders to bid on that basis. If the grantor has decided that one of the variant bids is its chosen procurement route, it would be inefficient and unfair to leave the other bidders to submit bids on any other basis.

The difficulty in this approach is the reaction of the bidders. They will want to use their best ideas for competitive advantage. The grantor will want to encourage this competitive advantage and may, therefore, prefer to maintain confidentiality in relation to certain aspects of the variant bids. Bidders may not submit their best ideas or be innovative where those ideas and innovations will be disclosed to others. Worse, they will be concerned that those ideas and innovations will be used against them by the other bidders in the tender process.

When considering instructions for variant bids, the grantor will need to review applicable law. Many legal systems limit the abuse of any dominant position or unfair advantage where one of the bidders has more information than, or a preferential position to, the other bidders.[407] The tendering procedure, and the indication of a preferred variant approach, will need to be implemented carefully to avoid breaching these restrictions.

16.5.4 Reducing numbers

One of the main difficulties involved in using the fixed approach is the large number of bidders who must review in detail the proposed documentation and with whom the grantor must negotiate this documentation. Reducing the number of bidders involved in such negotiations can decrease the time required for, and cost of, this phase of the tendering procedure. It also provides the remaining bidders with an improved opportunity cost, increasing their willingness to invest resources in the tender process.

A reduction of the number of bidders reviewing and negotiating the proposed documentation could be achieved by adding further phases to the tendering procedure. For example, where the grantor has prequalified six bidders, it could require those bidders to provide a technical and financial bid based on the information available on the project. The six bidders can then be reduced to two "final bidders" following an evaluation of their technical and financial bids. The two final bidders would review and negotiate the detailed project documentation with the grantor. Thus, the grantor maintains its bargaining position by negotiating with two prospective bidders.

---

[407]   This example and that of the Périphérique Nord of Lyon is discussed further in section 16.2.2.

The grantor will want the option to bring one or more of the remaining pre-qualified bidders into the negotiation if proceeding with one or both of the final bidders is not progressing as intended or where one of the final bidders must withdraw or is disqualified. The process of involving the other pre-qualified bidders should be as trouble-free as possible, keeping costs and complications to a minimum. This may not be possible in all jurisdictions, for example under EU procurement rules, where the selection procedure may not be sufficiently flexible.

The reduced number of bidders may not provide the grantor with sufficient comfort that it will be able to conclude an agreement on the terms it desires. In most cases, for example the water concession for Dar-es-Salaam in Tanzania,[408] too few bidders is unacceptable. Fewer bidders reduces the competitive pressure and, in turn, the incentive to submit a low price. The reduction in numbers should only be attempted once the grantor has made satisfactory progress tying the remaining bidders to its requirements, objectives and interests. These key terms should be agreed before any reduction in the grantor's position is permitted.

16.5.5   Three-stage bidding

The grantor may want to use a three-stage bidding process. This would involve a preliminary stage of pre-qualification, reducing the number of bidders based on certain technical, financial and experiential factors for pre-qualification. The second bidding stage would involve discussion of value and efficiency, proposing solutions and structures intended to satisfy the grantor's requirements, as expressed. The bidders would propose these solutions and indicate how they represent value for money, improved life-cycle, reduced maintenance and operating costs, as well as any improvements in the grantor's requirements.

The second stage should be considered by the grantor and the bidders as an opportunity to share ideas with a partnering attitude. This is not a challenge of the grantor's assumptions nor is it an attack on the grantor's position. It is an opportunity to consider new ideas and search for efficiency. It is also an opportunity for all sides to clarify their needs and assumptions. The key to the success of this three-stage bidding is the grantor's willingness to consider new solutions and to listen to and understand the bidders' concerns. A grantor taking a very narrow-minded or restricted approach to the tender structure would achieve only limited benefit from a three-stage bidding process.

The third stage would involve the grantor issuing its final documentation, using a fixed approach. This documentation would take into consideration the proposals and concerns raised by the bidders during the second stage. The third stage would require each bidder to submit a bid compliant with the grantor's final position, and provide an appropriate price. This third bidding stage may also allow the bidders to submit variant bids, or possibly variants only on certain aspects of the tender documentation.

---

[408]   In each case, at an early stage of the project, only two bidders showed interest.

16.5.6 Consolidation of technical information

The bidders may not have available to them sufficient technical information to provide a reasoned bid without investing substantial resources in technical due diligence. The bidders will need information on the site, site conditions, property rights, the nature and condition of existing assets (many of which may be buried or otherwise covered up), facilities available on site, and a myriad of other technical considerations. The common approach is for the grantor to require the bidders to bear the risk of the unavailability or inaccuracy of technical information.

However, this requires each bidder to perform technical due diligence or include a contingency element in their bid price to cover this risk. This may not be cost-effective or efficient. Three potentially more efficient uses of resources are:

> ➢ grantor provided information – where the grantor provides and warrants the accuracy of information;

> ➢ assumed technical parameters – where the grantor sets technical parameters against which the bidders formulate their bids – the successful bidder is then protected from any cost or delay where the assumed parameters are incorrect; and

> ➢ a single technical review provided by an independent expert for the benefit of each of the bidders – where the bidder's sole recourse for inadequate or inaccurate information is against the independent expert.

16.5.6.1 Grantor provided information

One obvious solution is for the grantor to provide information on the site, the existing equipment and any technical parameters. The grantor will be in the best position to supply this information, particularly where it has owned the site for a long time.

However, the grantor may also only have limited information about the site and existing equipment. Thus it may not want to warrant the accuracy or completeness of information provided. Such a warranty could lead to grantor liability for design or construction faults, costs or delays owing to the insufficiency or inaccuracy of the information provided.

16.5.6.2 Assumed technical parameters

The grantor may prefer to provide a set of technical assumptions against which the bidders prepare their bids. This approach is used in tunnelling projects, where the type of soil to be excavated is closely related to the cost of excavation. During implementation, if actual conditions exceed those technical assumptions and the preferred bidder incurs delays or increases in cost, it would have a claim against the grantor. If the grantor wishes to restrict such claims, it may specify that the cost incurred must exceed a certain level before a claim arises.

This approach provides the bidders with a basis of technical information against which to bid, without having to perform expensive technical due diligence. However, for the grantor, any actual condition that differs from the technical assumptions will entitle the bidder to an increase in price and extension of time for any cost and delay incurred. The preferred bidder receives the upside. If the actual situation is not as bad as the technical assumptions indicated, the preferred bidder gets the benefit of any savings or unnecessary contingency included in its bid. This can reduce bidder cost and encourage lower bid prices, but increase potential grantor exposure to increased costs and delay without the potential benefit of upside.

16.5.6.3   Common technical review

The grantor may prefer to provide for a single technical review by an independent technical adviser of the issues essential to preparation of a bid. This review would be made available to each of the bidders to help them develop their bids. The grantor would not be liable for the information provided. The bidders' sole remedy would be against the independent technical adviser.

The independent technical adviser would be of international repute and carry sufficient insurance to give comfort to the bidders as to his liability for the accuracy of the information provided. His report could be issued to the bidders directly to create liability on the part of the independent technical adviser to the benefit of the bidders. The bidders would look to the technical adviser's liability for the accuracy of information provided in this manner.

The cost of the independent technical adviser's report could be managed in several different ways. It could:

> ➢ be borne by the grantor;

> ➢ form part of the concession fee charged to the preferred bidder or on award of the contract;

> ➢ be charged proportionally to the bidders who request a report be issued to them. This would permit bidders to share the cost of technical review or choose to undertake their own review; or

> ➢ be charged to each bidder that pre-qualifies.

The bidders could also be entitled to request clarification or meet with the independent technical adviser to discuss findings and interpretation of information and charged individually on an hourly or man-day basis for any additional time spent by the independent technical adviser in clarifying information or meeting with a bidder.

The common technical review can reduce the total costs incurred by the bidders, create a level playing field (permitting more competition and the opportunity for new competitors to enter into the market) and attract additional bidders and a better price (given the lower cost of bidding).

Chapter 17

Power Projects

Increase of power begets increase of wealth.

William Cowper

The power sector has been one of the greatest beneficiaries of BOT projects and project financing structures. The levels of investment necessary for the construction of major power generation facilities is prohibitive to most private companies, even the most substantial private sector power companies. Eventually, as national treasuries diminish and debt levels rise, they become too expensive for the public sector, too. Project financing provides a way to fund generation and transmission infrastructure without the consequential burden on corporate and public balance sheets.

BOT projects have been particularly successful in providing new generating capacity. Generation facilities are large and very expensive and therefore fit well into the project financing structure. They also involve completely new build and a separate isolated asset over which security can be provided to the lenders and whose revenue stream is easily identifiable. Far less common are transmission and distribution projects within the power sector. Unlike generation capacity, transmission and distribution may not fit well within the BOT model. An exception to this is the large transmission line or interconnector. Examples include the interconnectors between Tasmania and Australia, England and the Isle of Man, and Ireland and Scotland. These interconnection projects involve a single separate asset constructed to provide a definable service with an isolated revenue stream.

This chapter will address the two key issues for any power generation project: what to do with the electricity generated and how to manage the fuel needed to generate the electricity. Sections 17.1-17.5 discuss, respectively, BOO structures; merchant plants; tolling agreements; and grid requirements. Section 17.6 addresses currency risk, while section 17.7 describes the development and implementation of NETA in the United Kingdom. Sections 17.8 and 17.9 discuss some of the other forms of offtake that can be produced by, and characteristics of, power generation facilities.

The fuel used in power generation is described in sections 17.10-17.13, from nuclear fuel to renewables and energy from waste.

17.1   BOT to BOO

Power generation projects are often structured as BOT projects. The power purchase agreement creates a revenue stream sufficient to repay the high, up-front capital expenditure over the period before transfer.

But other structures may be more efficient. As an example, Turkey's first BOO power deal is a 1,210mW bituminous coal-fired plant. The Government opted for this particular structure because the BOO does not need to pay for itself within the concession period. It is able to provide a downward trending tariff profile in contrast to BOT projects, which must extract the total amount of debt repayment and equity return within the concession period. The BOO approach also supports the Government's intention to ultimately privatise energy generation and distribution, by leaving the completed plant in the hands of the private sector. This US$1.37 billion deal achieved a 75:25 debt-to-equity split, sourced from a blend of bank debt and ECA financing. The project will use South African coal and has therefore benefited from South African ECA financing. The payment stream is fully supported by a Turkish Treasury guarantee, which is unconditional.[409]

17.2   Merchant Power

The merchant power industry involves a more or less regulated electricity distribution market wherein generators are able to sell the energy that they generate. The financial basis of merchant projects is their ability to sell energy into this market, and not against a long-term offtake purchase agreement that will guarantee a revenue stream. When times are good the merchant power market can result in security of revenues and profitability levels beyond that expected at the time of signing the deal. However, when times are bad, the merchant power market can be a painful experience.[410]

Experience with merchant power has been successful, though recent years have raised some serious issues and identified critical risks. A certain number of relationships are key to understanding the financial trends within that market:[411]

> ➤ when looking at revenue forecasts, the forecast price of power is less important than the relationship between power and fuel prices (the "spark spread");

> ➤ when analysing supply and demand, comparing "reserve margins" is less useful than checking weather forecasts, seasonality and the dominance of hydroelectric power in the relevant areas; and

---

[409]   "Turkey: Inkenderun – Birth of the BOO" Project Finance (September 2000).

[410]   Poirier, "The Demise of Good Old Times of US Merchant Power" Project Finance International 240 at 48 (1 May 2002).

[411]   Juidera, Gal and Damas, "Different Angle" Project Finance (September/October 2001).

> the "volatility value" of a merchant power plant is observable in the position of spot and forward markets. This measure is more valid than attempting to analyse the project's "commodity value".

The energy trading industry has a lot to do during the next two to five years. It must first replace the important role that Enron played in the market and adjust its trading patterns in order to compensate for the lack of liquidity over the short-term. The current political attitude in the United States is also likely to change the regulatory framework on which the global market is based. New rules in relation to corporate governance and risk management in financing and managing utilities are likely to be one of the key influences on the energy trading market for the foreseeable future. This may mean an increase in on-balance sheet treatment of investment and financing and the consequential requirement for additional equity investment.

17.3 Merchant Power in the United States

The United States merchant power market at the beginning of 2002 experienced an increase in project cancellations and a decrease in demand. Even with suspensions and cancellations of generation projects in the range of 30 GW to 90 GW, there is still currently a perception of over-capacity in the market, possibly 30-50 GW. Forward prices have also tumbled, by up to 40 per cent. Those traditional utilities, which control generation and distribution, will be able to prioritise their own generation facilities and avoid a certain amount of the impact of this painful situation. Other generators may suffer.

The upshot of this bear market is that US$5-6 billion of previously forecasted EBIT was wiped from the top 20 merchant power groups in 2001-2002. Given current construction programmes, over-capacity in the United States is predicted to remain at the level of 42-45 GW through 2005.[412]

Even the outstanding performance of the spark spread in the United States could not compensate for the unexpected low rainfall in the Pacific North West and the insistence in California of following "NIMBY" (not in my back yard) and effectively "BANANA" (build absolutely nothing anywhere near anything) policies. The power crisis in California provides an excellent example of some of the things that can go wrong. The California market seemed to have many characteristics that merchant generators would find attractive. California suffered from:[413]

> a fundamental imbalance between demand and capacity;

> a drought which removed much of the hydro capacity (normally up to 25 per cent.);

> a very hot summer which increased demand;

---

[412] *Ibid.*
[413] *Ibid.*

> increasing gas prices; and

> market regulation which forced the three major utilities to purchase the whole of their electricity requirements from the spot market.

With the crisis in California and the situation generally in the Western States, merchant power producers began investing heavily in plant construction. But as soon as these companies began investing heavily, mild weather, reduced economic activity from the burst of the internet bubble and the supplier-side response to the energy crisis pushed power prices back down. Suddenly the merchant power generators' share prices dropped dramatically, and the market was talking about a power surplus.[414]

17.4   Tolling Agreements

Under a tolling agreement, the power purchaser delivers fuel to the project company and pays the project company for turning that fuel into electricity. The tolling agreement therefore treats the generation project as if it were a process plant. The sponsor of the generation project provides the fuel and takes the electricity. The generating plant simply turns the fuel into electricity. The sponsor pays for the processing of fuel assuming a certain level of efficiency.

The structure is very similar to the through-put agreement that is often used to fund the construction of pipelines. In effect, the sponsor, which is both fuel supplier and power purchaser, uses project financing to fund the cost of building the power generation facility, undertakes the offtake purchase obligation and provides the fuel in order to isolate the project from market risks, while benefiting from the off-balance sheet financing for the generating asset. Such tolling agreements can be used for any type of generating asset or indeed for transmission assets, such as the construction of transmission facilities.

17.5   Grid Requirements

Generally, power generation projects fall into one of three categories: baseload, peak or mid-merit. Baseload generators provide energy continuously, operating on a daily basis. Peak generators operate only where demand exceeds the output of other generation facilities. Peak generators are commonly either combined-cycle or open-cycle gas generators because of the need for quick start-up. Mid-merit generators fill requirements somewhere between those of the baseload and peak generators. A mid-merit generator will be used as a base generator during the day, or during periods of high demand, and will then be used as a peak generator at night or in times of lesser demand. Mid-merit generators are often older baseload plants removed from continuous use.

The electricity generated must be delivered to end users. Unless the plant is captive or otherwise serves a limited number of consumers, the energy generated

---

414   Morash, "The Next Wave" Project Finance (September/October 2001).

will need to be delivered to the local grid. The local grid will place requirements on anyone wanting to interconnect with it.

Interconnection with the local grid will generally be on a fixed set of terms that will be applied to anyone connecting to that grid. It will place significant obligations on the generator to comply with the grid's requirements, and give little protection to the generator in the event of failure of the grid. Connection to the grid will be very important not only during operation when revenues are earned from electricity generated, but also during construction when in order to properly test the facility the electricity must be offtaken from the generating unit. If the grid is not available, the facility may not be able to be tested and therefore commissioning and completion of the construction may not be possible.

The interconnection agreement will generally establish a comprehensive mechanism for communication and identification of any defects or defaults in the grid or the transmission of electricity by the generator. It will also set out the grid requirements. The grid requirements will include any number of different issues that are important to the proper management and operation of the grid. These will include the frequency of electricity delivered into the grid, the timing of delivery of electricity to the grid, levels of reactive energy generated by the plant and emergency mechanisms to be implemented where necessary.

Certain assets will be necessary in order to connect the generator to the grid, such as transmission cables and substations. These assets are generally provided by the generator. The interconnection agreement will set out the requirements for such interconnection assets and will give the grid company the right to oversee and approve any such interconnection with the grid to ensure that no damage is caused to the grid. The agreement will also address metering of electricity generated and delivered.

17.6   Currency Mismatch

BOT power projects in developing countries are particularly vulnerable to currency exchange rate risk. The high construction cost of the facility and the number of elements that must be purchased from developed countries, result in a large portion of financing that must be sourced in foreign currency. Revenues, however, come principally from local domestic and industrial use and are therefore likely to be denominated in local currency. Any exchange rate shift can make the energy particularly expensive.

Currency risk has been the downfall of many BOT power projects. Examples would include Enron's Dhabol project. This naptha powered generating plant was built at great expense to provide electricity to the state of Maharashtra in India. The cost of construction was financed in US dollars, while the revenues obtained from the local electricity board were denominated in Indian rupees. A dramatic variation in the rate of exchange between US dollars and rupees resulted in the actual cost to Indian consumers of electricity from the Dhabol plant becoming extremely expensive. Enron had little choice but to try to recover its money from the electricity generated in order to repay debt and recover its own investment.

The state of Maharashtra had little choice but to stop taking electricity from the plant and endeavour to avoid its obligations under the contract given the cost of electricity and the political implications if the cost of electricity rose to the levels necessary. Similar situations occurred in Indonesia and the Philippines where the Asian currencies have been particularly weak, in particular in the 1990s, electricity revenues have not been sufficient to pay the high tariffs demanded from BOT power projects financed in US dollars and British sterling.

Some of the rare exceptions to this currency mismatch risk are those projects which can be funded locally, where the local market has sufficient finance capacity to support a large scale power project and therefore the currency exchange risk is limited to the need to purchase plant and materials in foreign currencies. Another possibility is to generate revenues in the country of currency of finance, for example, power projects built in Mexico exporting electricity, or at least part of their generating capacity, to the United States. In that way revenues and financing can be sourced in US dollars.[415]

17.7   New Electricity Trading Arrangements

The United Kingdom has developed a particularly sophisticated and free market approach to electricity generation and distribution, regulated by the Office of Gas and Electricity Markets ("OFGEM"). The industry has been divided into generators, Transco (the national electricity transmission company) and distributors. The arrangements entered into by these different parties must follow structured procedures.

In March 2001, the United Kingdom launched the new electricity trading arrangements ("NETA").[416] The aim of NETA is to reduce electricity prices and improve efficiency by avoiding inflexible governance arrangements. The old pool system created a facility for generators to bid their capacity into an electricity pool in half-hourly segments. NETA replaced the pool and instituted a wholesale electricity trading market under a series of bilateral contracts between generators and purchasers. NETA is meant to work like any other commodity trading system, while allowing the grid to maintain balance between supply and demand. The balancing mechanism allows demand to meet with supply and penalises suppliers where they do not meet their delivery obligations. This financial reconciliation is known as an "imbalance settlement".

Since the introduction of NETA, electricity prices have indeed fallen, by some accounts by as much as 21 per cent. NETA has also faced a few problems. The first was technical, where the default pricing mechanism caused erratic price spikes during the first few days of operation. This was due to the software that was being used by the independent operator managing the balancing system website. Certain industry experts believe that electricity companies lost around £20 million during

---

[415]   Currency risk is discussed in further detail in chapter 15.
[416]   Bowman, "Competition Killer" Project Finance (September/October 2001).

the early days of NETA due to mismanaged trades, software bugs and other problems.[417]

Some criticise NETA for being overly market driven. NETA rewards those generators who can accurately predict future levels of generation. This can have an unfortunate impact on renewable energy sources and co-generation, where other factors can have a direct impact on the amount of electricity that can be generated from hour to hour. Certain United Kingdom power generators have claimed that NETA has caused their efficiency to drop and reduced the amount of output they are able to achieve. Powergen points to a fall in electricity output from 2.25tWh to 1.72tWh between calendar years 2001 and 2002 despite an increase in co-generation capacity from 78.6mW to 94.3mW in the same period. Indicatively, steam output rose from 2.25 to 5.24tWh/therm. Scottish and Southern Energy saw the efficiency of its 78mW co-generation portfolio fall from 87.1 per cent. to 62.8 per cent., year on year. The efficiency of its entire thermal generation portfolio fell from 51.9 per cent. to 50.8 per cent. The company claims that this is largely due to the flexible way in which it is required to run its generating plants under NETA. Scottish and Southern Energy also points to an increase in the number of breaches of environmental regulations, up by 160 per cent. from 2001.[418]

One of the more serious criticisms of NETA in its current form is its lack of liquidity.[419] Where there is a small number of bids, those bids may be extremely diverse, resulting in price volatility. The large operators are able to manage their risk of outage and plant failure by hedging their bids. This aspect of the system makes it very risky for small operators. A single plant failure can be extremely costly for that operator given the difficulty of altering bids once they have been made.

As an example of a smaller generator, Slough Estates runs a small power plant in one of it business parks. It announced in early September 2001 that NETA had cost the company £4.6 million in the first half of 2001. OFGEM had hoped that the smaller generators would group together to create pools and sell capacity as one block; however this did not happen, probably due to the complicated nature of the facilities in place. This may well lead to a reduction in the number of smaller power generators and domination by a few larger players. One option would be for the insurance industry to provide cover against such contracts. This would allow generators to protect themselves; however, it would also add to the cost of electricity.[420]

17.8 Other Offtake

Power projects may generate other offtake. For example, a hydroelectric project may also provide a reservoir for raw water that can be used for irrigation or treated

---

[417]   *Ibid.*
[418]   "NETA has hit CHP output and efficiencies Companies" Power UK 102 at 1 (August 2002).
[419]   Bowman (September/October 2001) supra note 416.
[420]   *Ibid.*

and used as potable water. Multiple offtake requires consideration of issues of resource management, operation effectiveness and revenue flows where the various offtakes are compensated differently. Two common examples of power projects with multiple offtakes are combined heat and power ("CHP") and co-generation plants.

A CHP plant provides for the sale of the heat generated while producing energy. The project company may therefore want to enter into a second offtake agreement in order to allocate the market risk for the sale of the heat produced. This demand risk may be more difficult to allocate over the concession period, since the buildings near to the site, which are most likely to purchase such heat, may change ownership and function repeatedly during the period of the concession.

A similar regime will be needed for co-generation plants, which involve two offtake purchasers, one purchasing the electricity generated and the other purchasing steam bled off from the steam turbine during certain hours of operation.[421] The steam purchaser will need to satisfy the requirements of its facility, usually a refinery or other industrial plant. There is, therefore, an inconsistency between the needs of the steam purchaser, the consistent supply of steam for its plant, and the power purchaser, since bleeding off steam decreases electricity output. Also, the steam purchaser may not have the technical experience of the power purchaser to run the power plant in the case of default by the operator. Co-generation plants require careful management of these competing interests, including setting out schedules for priority of offtake (i.e. which of the purchasers has priority when ordering output).

17.9   Special Characteristics

Beyond the basic characteristics of generating output, a power generation facility may have other qualities essential to the power purchaser's needs. These characteristics are not strictly speaking offtake, but they are often services that are provided to the offtake purchaser or the grantor for compensation. For example, black start capacity, reactive power generation, frequency-responsive generation and load shedding.

17.9.1   Black start

This service requires a power plant to have the ability to start-up operations from complete shutdown without using an outside source of electrical energy, generally through the use of a separate diesel generator. This may be of use to the offtake purchaser where its entire system of power plants shuts down. The grid will not have the energy necessary to start up the power plants, therefore the offtake purchaser must have the ability to energise the grid without the assistance of energy from the grid.

---

[421]   Vinter, "Legal Issues Involved in Co-Generation Projects" in Hornbrook (1996) supra note 353 at 32.

17.9.2 Reactive power

The grid can also be affected by the reactive power generated by a power plant. Reactive power is present wherever active power is transmitted, and is an essential part of that transmission. An imbalance of reactive power can cause disruption and damage to the grid. Certain power plants can be operated to generate more reactive power in order to stabilise the grid; however, the power plant will generate less active power if it does so. Reactive power cannot be metered in the same way as active power. Therefore a special regime must provide for the generation of reactive power and compensation for the project company.

17.9.3 Frequency responsive generation

Frequency is alternating current, cycles per second (measured in Hertz). The system will need to be within 5 or 10 per cent. of the grid frequency. The frequency of the electricity transmitted within the system (generally 50 or 60 Hertz) is extremely important to the efficiency of that system.[422] An increase in demand can modify the frequency of the energy produced. Therefore, the offtake purchaser may want the power plant to have frequency-responsive generating capacity, which ensures consistent frequency in generation and can be used to correct frequency imbalance in the system. Where the frequency of the grid drops below a certain level, the plant will automatically increase generation in order to re-establish the frequency of the grid.

17.9.4 Load shedding

Where the offtake purchaser experiences an increase in demand so that even fast start generation and frequency responsive generation cannot compensate, the offtake purchaser may need to use demand shedding, or load shedding, by switching off demand centres or decreasing provision as necessary to avoid the failure of other power plants. This would require extremely rapid response by the project to offtake purchaser requirements and the ability to modify output accordingly.

17.10 Fuel

The fuel used in a traditional power generation plant will generally be gas, coal, oil, hydro, wind or nuclear. Each fuel type will have its own special requirements. For example, the treatment of fuel and waste in a nuclear plant will be of particular concern and will be closely regulated. The risk of drought or reduced spring run-off will be paramount for hydroelectric projects.

In certain cases, there is little or no opportunity to guarantee sufficient availability of fuel, for example hydroelectric generation or wind power. In other cases, the fuel required is available from a fluid market with sufficient availability of volumes, for example oil or gas. Where fuel is not as fungible or available, the

---

[422] Thompson, *Technical Aspects of Power Station Project Financing* at 18 (1994).

project company may need to enter into a long-term fuel supply agreement, with appropriate contingency arrangements, to ensure the availability of sufficient amounts of fuel at the appropriate time.

17.11   Nuclear Fuel

The arguments for and against nuclear power run from the political to the environmental and emotional. No matter the policy chosen, the economics of nuclear power require careful consideration. Using the United Kingdom nuclear power industry as an example, the United Kingdom Government has had to mount a rescue operation for British Energy. The country's privatised nuclear power generator claims to be a victim of the Government's ill-formed energy policy.[423] Management faces serious criticism as well, however.

Privatisation in the electricity sector in the United Kingdom occurred in the 1990s, in an effort to make the industry more efficient. Recent changes in the regulation of the electricity sector (as discussed in section 17.7) have pushed electricity prices down. Wholesale prices, current as of mid-2003, of £16 per megawatt hour are about £3 shy of the level required to make British Energy's nuclear generation profitable.

Electricity generators that burn gas, oil and coal get off relatively lightly on tax and environmental burdens as compared to the nuclear industry. Nuclear generators must pay £200 million annually for the processing of their waste at Sellafield, the state-owned nuclear processing plant. Most other countries simply store spent nuclear fuel, which is a great deal cheaper. Even though nuclear generation does not emit carbon, British Energy is still required to pay the government's special tax aimed at reducing CO_2 emissions. This costs British Energy an additional £80 million annually. Further, nuclear power plants pay higher local taxes and must provide retention for future decommissioning costs. The nuclear industry has never been extremely competitive compared with more conventional thermal-powered generators, but this series of politically-oriented disadvantages puts British Energy in an extremely difficult position.[424]

17.12   Renewables

Power generation may use renewable forms of fuel, for example energy from waste, landfill gas, sewage gas, agricultural and forestry residues, wind, water and the sun. Renewable energy is energy that can be generated naturally and repeatedly in the natural environment. This is a difficult concept to define accurately. In many cases, legislation will use a more simplified approach identifying not only the concept of renewable energy but also the political position on how this energy market should be managed and encouraged. In the United Kingdom, the Utilities Act 2000 defines renewable energy as that which comes

---

[423]   "Nuclear Industry: Fallout" The Economist at 29 (14 September 2002).
[424]   *Ibid.*

from a renewable source. Renewable sources are defined as "sources of energy other than fossil fuel or nuclear fuel ...".

The underlying assumption is that renewable energy sources produce lower levels of pollutants, including greenhouse gases, than other sources of energy. They also do not deplete the natural resources available in the environment in the same manner or to the same extent. Certain such sources of energy may divert the use of natural resources, for example hydroelectric energy generation diverts the use of water, and alters the way that the resource is otherwise managed. Renewable energy is also perceived to help encourage sustainable energy supply and developing new technologies in consideration of the long-term needs of society.

Renewable sources of energy can involve any number of different fuel sources, from biomass to solar. Biomass is derived from plant or animal matter such as forestry or wood waste or residues. Certain crops can be used which have a short rotation period and thereby provide a renewable source for the generation of electricity. Waste can be used as an alternative fuel, a flexible and plentiful resource. Wind is another source, but is inflexible and less reliable. Electricity can also be generated from wave and tidal power, though this technology is still in development.

Solar power has fallen in price significantly over the last 25 years. There are hopes and expectations that solar power will be a viable source of electricity in the medium- to long-term. Fuel cells provide a more promising short-term solution. They produce electricity from hydrogen and air. The only by-product of the generation process is water. Fuel cells are also extremely portable.

17.12.1   The drive for renewable energy sources

The fear of climate change and rising temperatures on the earth have fuelled a particular focus on renewable energy. Concerns about climatic changes such as El Niño, the thinning of icecaps and potential weather-related economic losses have raised demands for the reduction of the generation of greenhouse gases. The power generation industry is one of the largest producers of greenhouse gases.

Renewable energy sources also reduce reliance and dependency on foreign imports of fuels. Many developed countries, the United States and United Kingdom included, do not have sufficient indigenous fuel supplies to meet their needs over the medium- to long-term. Creating a dependency on foreign sourced fuels is often contrary to political interests and national defence concerns.

One of the driving forces behind the use of renewable sources of energy is the series of international agreements entered into by many of the world's nations. The Kyoto Protocol sets out targets to reduce greenhouse gas emissions. It uses the basis of 1990 levels of greenhouse gas emissions and aims to reduce those levels by around 5 per cent. in the period between 2008 and 2012. Though the United States and Australia have withdrawn from the Kyoto Protocol, this still forms the basis of policy development in many countries. One of the underlying questions will be the total cost to the economy and the consumer of implementation of renewable energy sources. Implementation should be measured in order to ensure that the impact on the economy is not inconsistent with the benefit to be obtained from both the short- and long-term goals of the increased use of renewable sources of energy.

17.12.2   Other available solutions

The demand for increasing volumes of available electricity may also be satisfied by the increase in efficiency of use of currently available sources of electricity. This may include improved insulation of buildings and control of heating, ventilation, air-conditioning and lighting. Energy saving devices, including heaters, boilers, air-conditioning, kitchen appliances and light bulbs, can also reduce total energy use.

This current lack of efficiency can often be resolved by improving building standards and higher standards applied to home appliances. This will gradually remove the most inefficient projects from the market and improve electricity management in households and new buildings. These saving mechanisms can be implemented in the private sector and the public sector, in business, industry and in the home.

Efficiency gains are also available from generation. Combined heat and power plants achieve a fuel efficiency of around 70-90 per cent., much better than most thermal power stations which only achieve around 40-50 per cent.[425] New technology in water treatment, boilers and turbines can also improve generation efficiency.

17.12.3   Government incentives

Generally speaking, renewable energy is not as yet commercially viable. The most common methods of encouraging and achieving the objectives of renewable energy include setting limits, placing liability on producers and providing economic incentives. Governments may provide incentive packages in order to encourage the development of renewable energy technology and the operation of renewable energy facilities. The level of these incentives will depend on the cost of renewable energy and the desire of the government to encourage its use. Some generation technology may be considered renewable in nature, but may be sufficiently commercially viable to discourage the government from providing any additional incentives. In the United Kingdom, for example, energy from waste and large-scale hydroelectric generation is considered to be sufficiently commercially viable that it does not attract direct government subsidies.[426]

---

[425]   Department of Trade and Industry, Energy White Paper: Our Energy Future – Creating a Low Carbon Economy at 47 (February 2003).

[426]   Department of Trade and Industry, New and Renewable Energy Prospects for the 21st Century: The Renewables Obligation Preliminary Consultation (October 2000).

Given the speed with which such incentive programmes change as policies in governments change, lenders and generators will be concerned where they rely on such subsidies for the commercial viability of any renewable energy project.

The government may wish to support early projects with incentives such as additional subsidies. This will offset the early market risk of the first mover, to encourage firms to seek first mover status.

17.12.3.1 Command and control

The most obvious way for governments to achieve their objectives is for them to introduce regulations applicable to both the public and private sectors which, for example, set emission limits. This approach requires careful monitoring by the government, efficient and sophisticated enforcement mechanisms which identify those who fail to comply, and robust sanctions which are sufficient to motivate appropriate behaviour. The resources necessary for monitoring and enforcement can be expensive.

17.12.3.2 Producer responsibility

This initiative requires that a producer be responsible for what he produces. This approach can be less costly to the government than the command and control, since the producer will be required to implement the programme and demonstrate to the government's satisfaction that it has complied with its obligations. However, this approach will increase costs for the producer, and, in turn, the consumer. It may also be more difficult to enforce such obligations on foreign producers. Further, it is only a partial solution to the problems of waste disposal, landfill demands and emission control.

In England, the solution selected by the government is to require all licensed electricity suppliers to supply a specified portion of electricity from renewable sources. OFGEM will issue renewable obligation certificates ("ROCs") which indicate the amount of electricity generated using renewable sources. The generating company will also have the option of purchasing the satisfaction of such obligation by making payments to OFGEM. Those with extra ROCs can sell them to those who need them. It is anticipated that this will create a dynamic market for ROCs. (ROCs are also known as "Green Certificates".)

By placing an obligation on generators to ensure that a certain percentage of energy distributed within the United Kingdom is generated from renewable sources, the cost of using such renewable sources is placed on electricity generators, who then pass this cost on to their consumers. Due to market forces through competition, the generators will look for the cheapest source of electricity from renewable sources, increasing the efficient use of renewable sources but decreasing the incentive to develop new sources of renewable energy or improve existing technology that might be more expensive to develop in the short-term.

17.12.3.3   Economic measures

The government may choose to make use of taxes and other financial measures in order to achieve its environmental objectives. Economic measures can include both negative and positive incentives, imposing an economic cost where the party does not comply or providing a benefit where it does comply. As an example of an economic measure, the government may levy taxes on those who do not comply with certain environmental goals or who perform activities which the government wishes to discourage such as the landfill tax.

The use of subsidies for renewable energy places the cost of renewable energy on the taxpayer generally. One important issue to be addressed, in particular in the European Union, is the characterisation as state aid of any subsidies provided for the generation of electricity using renewable sources. State aid is heavily regulated by the EU and must be approved by the European Commission.

The government may prefer to offer an incentive for compliance with relevant government programmes, in the form of tax breaks or other subsidies for the companies concerned. In the United Kingdom, generators using renewable energy sources are given a preferable tariff rate and greater certainty as to tariff levels over the long-term than are available for generators using conventional fuels.

The use of economic instruments to benefit parties using renewable energy sources is the most efficient and the easiest to implement of the methods of control for the government. However, such economic instruments also involve a financial investment by the government in encouraging the use of alternative forms of energy production. The creation of economic incentives may be politically more difficult to implement for the government. They also create an increased opportunity for abuse, at the expense of the limited resources committed to such environmental concerns, where the government is not able to supervise the implementation of financial benefits and police those receiving such benefits.

17.12.4   Wind projects

One of the most common forms of renewable energy currently in use is wind. As an example of a recent programme, the United Kingdom Government granted consent for 38 2mW wind turbines in 2002, which should generate enough electricity to power about 52,000 homes.[427] The figures for 2003 and 2004 will be significantly higher. New generation turbines are able to use more economic sources of electricity. In addition, incentives provided by local governments in an effort to reduce greenhouse gases and other environmental impacts of thermal power generation, as well as the increased reliance on fossil fuels and the political implications of such reliance has led to wind power becoming financially viable.

Wind-farms may be land (onshore) or sea (offshore) based. Key issues for wind-farms (combining offshore and onshore issues) include the following.

---

[427]   Project Finance International 241 at 48 (15 May 2002).

17.12.4.1 Environmental specificities

Wind-farms involve a variety of specific environmental issues that arise in relation to their construction and operation, and the selection of their location. Wind-farms require a relatively high wind speed over the relevant area, but not so much wind as would damage the equipment. This wind speed should also be consistent, to avoid the starting and stopping of the turbine. It is also preferable if wind speed is consistent over time, avoiding seasonal generation of electricity. In certain areas, wind-farms may require special lightning protection (in particular on offshore installations, where lightning strikes are more frequent).

Where the wind-farm is to be located offshore, where the water is deep, the cost of foundations can increase as can the cost of supports and superstructure in order to maintain the stability of the windmill and the turbine generator. Wave forces can have a significant impact on the stress levels incurred by the supports, the transmission cable leading from the generator and other infrastructure involved in the support of the windmill and the turbine.

The infrastructure that supports the facility will be anchored in solid subsoil or sub-seabed strata. Sediment build-up can cause particular complications and therefore tidal influences will need to be considered carefully. The facility may require a certain amount of dredging, before construction and/or periodically during operation. To this extent tidal action will need to be considered as well as wave action, currents, sandbank movements, sediment deposited by rivers and streams, underground waterflow and springs and any other accumulation of sediment.

The location of the wind-farm will also need to consider existing oil and gas pipelines, electricity transmission cables, telecommunication cables and other infrastructure that may already exist on the site. The wind-farm will need its own infrastructure, for example it will need to be connected with the local grid via a transmission cable.

The location of the wind-farm must also be accessible, either by land or sea, to facilitate construction and the requirements of maintenance during the operating period. Wind-farms are generally located far from major population centres, and therefore accessibility may be a particular concern. This is of course a special issue in relation to offshore wind-farms.

17.12.4.2 Environmental impact

Wind-farms are subject to, or may have a particular impact on, specific environmental vulnerabilities. The noise generated by certain types of turbines and the windmills themselves can be disruptive.

Noise pollution is often closely associated with wind-farms, in particular onshore developments, where local communities may resist planning permission and other consents necessary in order to construct such facilities. As a general comment, any construction project may have an impact on existing flora and fauna, including migratory animals. But wind-farms raise particular issues that will need consideration. Wind-farms will also raise issues and concerns in relation to climate and air quality, and the visual intrusion caused by the size of the windmills. Many areas where the conditions are ideal for wind-farms are also areas of natural beauty and therefore generally considered to be inappropriate for wind-farms.

The size of the infrastructure used for wind-farms can cause disruption to television, radio and radar facilities or may create an aviation obstruction. Offshore facilities may cause damage to fisheries or may otherwise cause navigation obstruction. They can also affect water quality due to the disruption during construction or possibly the vibrations during operation.

17.12.4.3   Legal requirements

The location and installation of wind-farms will need to satisfy a variety of legal requirements, including environmental and zoning restrictions. Planning permission for wind-farm installation can often be a challenging issue. Local communities are often very supportive of the concept of renewable energy, but generally suffer from the "NIMBY" (not in my back yard) attitude that is common for local communities. Where the site or coastline has been officially designated with regard to its specific landscape or special physical features, this may cause particular complication for planning and zoning requirements.

As a practical issue, access to the site for construction may be limited by seasonal restrictions, for purposes of tourism, due to environmental issues, such as migratory animals, or due to other local requirements. There is often a "weather window" during which construction can be performed. This is in particular the case for offshore construction, where weather patterns may restrict construction during seasons where ships may not be able to access the relevant area or where the sea freezes during a certain part of the year.

17.12.4.4   Commercial specificities

Certain commercial restrictions will also apply to the implementation of wind-farms. Though wind-farms are generally located far from populated areas, the electricity generated will need to be transmitted to the grid network. Where transmission cables must be connected between the wind-farm and the nearest grid, those transmission cables may need to be protected or located in a manner so as not to breach planning or zoning restrictions or environmental requirements. Subsea transmission cables will need to be armoured in a manner sufficient to protect them from currents, shifts in the seabed and anchors from ships that can cause significant damage to cables.

Wind-farms can provide a certain amount of flexibility for construction and development of the facility in that they can easily be phased as demand increases. With all of the supporting infrastructure in place, including the necessary transmission cable, new windmills and turbines can be added to the facility as and when demand grows.

As an example of a wind-farm that will be rolled out as demand grows, the Irish Government has approved a 200-turbine wind power development which should generate 10 per cent. of the country's power demand when completed. The whole development will be rolled out gradually, with documentation agreed from the outset on a template basis during the course of the first year. The sponsor of the project, Eirtricity, is also the offtake purchaser.[428]

17.13   Energy from Waste

Waste management is a substantial global market and a major focus for those seeking to improve land use and the management of resources and the environment. Concepts of sustainable development indicate that new thinking be applied to the management of waste. The most common methods of waste disposal are disposal at sea and landfill. Disposal at sea can result in damage to animal and plant life, often essential parts of the cycle on which coastal or riparian communities depend for economic survival, and to beaches which attract tourism and foreign investment. Landfill is a limited resource. Economic concepts of land use may dictate that landfill be restricted as far as is economically feasible.

Governments therefore seek alternative methods of reducing the need for landfill or place strict requirements on the waste which can be disposed of at sea. Recycling is one useful tool to reduce the waste which requires disposal; however it is not a commercially effective operation: substantial subsidies are required, along with the support of the local community. Successful recycling programmes have been undertaken for example in Japan, in Germany and in California (which have strong Green lobbies and an environmentally conscious community).

Another method of dealing with waste more efficiently is to incinerate it and use the heat produced to generate electricity. This process is commonly known as "energy from waste". Although the cost of per-unit generation exceeds that of conventional thermal power plants, energy from waste provides an efficient method of incineration with a valuable product.

17.13.1   The call for energy from waste

The market for generating energy from waste has expanded substantially in recent years and in certain countries it stands to increase further and more rapidly. In 1997, 145 million tonnes of waste were produced in the United Kingdom, of which 2 per cent. was incinerated in order to produce energy. The amount of waste produced increases by about 3 per cent. each year. In England and Wales, waste is about 50 per cent. industrial and about 25 per cent. each of commercial and municipal. As of 2001, the commercial and industrial waste was 60 per cent. landfilled, 35 per cent. recycled and 5 per cent. incinerated; while municipal waste was 83 per cent. landfilled, 9 per cent. recycled and 8 per cent. incinerated.[429]

---

[428]   Project Finance International 233 at 36 (23 January 2002).

[429]   "Burying to Burn: The Move from Landfill to Incineration", a presentation given at Allen & Overy (2001).

In an effort to encourage responsible waste management and the development of new sources of energy, governments and international bodies have focused on creating obligations and incentives for the private sector to implement such schemes. In the EU, the Kyoto Protocol[430] and the European Directive on the Landfill of Waste[431] in particular will have a significant impact in bringing about the expansion of the market for energy from waste.

17.13.1.1   Reduction in landfill

The recent European Directive on the Landfill of Waste sets stringent targets for diverting waste away from landfill to more sustainable recovery options such as recycling, composting and energy recovery. By prescribing a reduction in the amount of waste which is disposed of to landfill, the Directive will have a profound impact on waste management practices in Europe, requiring heavy investment in non-landfill options, including incineration facilities.

17.13.1.2   Reduction of emissions and efficiency of energy production

Further to the Kyoto Protocol and other international pressure, focus has moved to the reduction of greenhouse gas emissions. One method of reducing greenhouse gas emissions is by utilising less polluting forms of energy generation. Energy from waste plants (primarily incinerators, but also gasification and pyrolysis plants) release carbon dioxide from burning fossil carbon (e.g. waste oils and plastics) and biogenic carbon (from wood, paper, food and green wastes) and reduce the need to use more polluting fossil fuels.

Governments are also looking to diversify the sources used for supply of energy. As part of this effort, the use of renewable energy has become central to new energy policies. Renewable energy sources include hydroelectric, solar and wind. The Government of the United Kingdom, for example, has set a target for renewable energy of 10 per cent. of total United Kingdom energy supplies by 2010. However, neither the United Kingdom nor the EU consider energy from waste as a renewable energy source; yet strangely, wood burning generators (with their negative impact on the environment through deforestation) are considered to be renewable energy.

17.13.2   Project issues

Reviewing the structuring of, or bidding for, an energy from waste project raises several issues specific to energy from waste projects.

---

[430]   The Koyoto Protocol is an international agreement between countries of the UN signed in 1998 to reduce the emissions of greenhouse gases. It sets out a number of policies aimed at addressing climate change. The European Community promised to reduce emissions of greenhouse gases by eight per cent. during 2008-2012.

[431]   1999/31/EC.

17.13.2.1 Quantity of waste

The technical requirements of the energy from waste plant and the expected energy generation will depend partly on the volume of waste which the plant is intended to process. The grantor and the project company will need to review historic data on the volume of waste generated in the area to be serviced by the project as well as information necessary to forecast future demand, including demographic change and residential/industrial sourcing of waste produced. In particular, energy from waste projects obtains a large proportion of revenues from the "gate fees" for taking waste. Without sufficient quantity of waste, the gate fees and electricity generated will not create the level of revenues needed.

The project company may be required to bear the risk of the accuracy of forecasts provided. Often, in order to attract private sector investment, the grantor may need to guarantee the minimum amount of waste to be received. An alternative approach may be for the grantor to provide the project company with an exclusive right to treat waste from a certain geographical area. When structuring exclusivity, the grantor will need to consider future recycling requirements and changes in local requirements. The grantor may want to grant an exclusive right to receive a fixed quantity of waste per year (possibly an amount equal to the guaranteed amount on which the project company is basing its financial calculations).

17.13.2.2 Calorific value

Along with quantity of waste to be received, the nature of the waste to be received will be important in determining the type of plant to be built and the energy to be generated. The type of plant used and the amount of energy to be produced will be driven in particular by the calorific value of the waste processed. As discussed below, recycling exercises may have a substantial impact on the calorific value of the waste delivered to the plant.

The grantor may guarantee a minimum calorific value for the waste to be delivered. On the other hand, the project company may be comfortable with an exclusive right to receive a certain quantity of the waste produced by certain consumers (possibly municipal rather than industrial waste).

Where the calorific value of the underlying waste is insufficient, the project company may need to use a secondary fuel to increase calorific value to a level sufficient to produce the required amounts of energy. The added fuel may well defeat the benefits of reducing emissions and may breach requirements for any subsidised tariff for energy generated from renewable sources or low emission generation, where relevant.

17.13.2.3 Electricity generation

The electricity generated by the plant will normally be sold either to bulk purchasers or to a utility. This long-term purchase agreement will need to be set out in a contract. The importance of the long-term sales contract will increase where limited recourse financing is provided for the project. The sales agreement will need to be sufficiently flexible to support the potential changes to be encountered in the project and the variable amount of energy to be delivered based on the amount of waste delivered and the calorific value of that waste. The termination provisions in the sale agreement will need to coincide with the termination provisions in the underlying concession agreement, to make sure that the sale agreement will not fall away except where the rest of the project will also fall away.

In certain countries, part of the benefit of using an energy from waste solution is the sale of energy at a tariff that is subsidised either by the purchasing utility or by the government. This subsidy is intended to encourage the use of renewable energy and low emission generation. The project company will base its financial model on the subsidised tariff, and will therefore want to review carefully the requirements for receiving such subsidy and the possibility of losing the subsidy where elements of the project change over time or owing to breach by the grantor.

17.13.2.4   Recycling

Another method of responsible waste disposal and reduction of landfill is to implement a recycling programme, reusing certain waste materials such as paper, aluminium, glass, plastic and rubber. Recycling is generally not a financially viable venture unless prescribed by law or subsidised. Recycling will have a direct effect on the viability of an energy from waste solution since it reduces the quantity of waste available for incineration and it removes the waste which is highest in calorific value, such as paper, wood and plastic. The project company will therefore need to consider the potential implementation of a recycling programme and the resultant impact on the viability of the energy from waste project.

17.13.2.5   Landfill and storage

Whilst energy from waste reduces the need for landfill by incinerating waste, the incineration process will have certain by-products, such as metals, carbon and ash. These materials will need to be disposed of in a proper manner, often by landfill. Certain processes, for example tyre pyrolysis, endeavour to utilise the majority of the materials produced by the incineration of the relevant waste, such as carbon black, but no absolutely efficient process has yet become commercially viable.

The nature of the landfill required may change as the type of waste delivered to the project changes, particularly where local land use changes from a residential to industrial base. For this reason, the project company will need to consider the cost of landfill or disposal and the potential for alternative disposal facilities.

The plant will also require adequate storage facilities. Waste will arrive at the site in varying amounts at different times of the day, week or year. It will need to be stored during peak delivery times for incineration during periods of low demand. Also, where a certain amount of waste at a substantially lower or higher calorific value is delivered to the site, this waste will need to be stored until it can be mixed with other waste that will result in waste of the required calorific value.

17.13.2.6   Emissions requirements

Local law may apply emissions requirements to the energy from waste plant. These emission requirements may be particularly strict where the project receives subsidies or other benefits as a low-emission or renewable source of energy. Higher emissions will generally indicate the use of large amounts of secondary fuel, therefore failing to achieve the demands placed on renewable or low-emission generation.

The effect of failure to achieve emission requirements may therefore include both normal sanctions under the applicable law and loss of the subsidy or other benefit. This latter benefit will often be an essential part of the financial structure of the project and therefore emission failures may threaten the financial viability of the project. The project company will want to consider the emission standards to be applied and consider the guarantees that it will need from the grantor to ensure that these emission standards can be satisfied.

17.13.2.7   Government incentives

As mentioned above, the government may provide incentives to the project company or the grantor to encourage the use of alternative waste disposal and energy generation methods, such as energy from waste solutions. The grantor and project company will want to consider carefully the requirements of such incentives and structure the project so as to ensure that such incentives are not reduced or lost during the project.

Chapter 18

Transportation

*I may not have gone where I intended to go, but I think
I have ended up where I intended to be.*

Douglas Adams

Transportation projects, including airports, roads, railways, tunnels and bridges, have traditionally been financed by a combination of private and public funding. The early days of railways in the United States involved private companies building railway networks with land provided by the public sector. Bridges have seen a similar combination of public and private involvement, benefiting from a toll from those wishing to use the bridge. Airports and roads, however, have historically been financed using public funds. It is only over the last 20-30 years that private sector involvement has become common in these areas.

Governments are looking increasingly to the private sector for input in the development of new transportation schemes and the privatisation of those already existing. This trend has developed largely as a result of the tremendous expense the public sector has incurred in subsidising transportation operations and the less than admirable efficiency of certain publicly funded operations. The cost concern in the public sector is multiplied by the need to increase capacity in the near future. Developing economies have a particular need for increased capacity in their transportation services, yet the costs of such increases are prohibitive.

18.1   Roads and Bridges

Roads and bridges are historically considered to be within the public domain, their construction financed with public money and their operation subsidised by local or national taxation. However, private sector investment in roads and bridges is increasing significantly, in particular in Europe.

18.1.1   Operating costs

BOT projects often relate to developing transportation infrastructure, such as roads and bridges. The primary difference between a BOT power project and a BOT toll road project is the cost of operation. A road will not require high operation and maintenance costs, nor fuel nor any other input. Therefore, the revenue stream will be devoted primarily to debt servicing; around 80 per cent. of revenue is allocated to debt servicing (during the period of repayment of the financing) and return to the investors.[432]

18.1.2   Revenues

The principal issue in relation to road and bridge projects is viable offtake purchase. Whereas demand for power is relatively calculable, the offtake purchasers in a transportation project are generally individuals. Therefore demand risk is more difficult to quantify and harder to allocate in a toll road project.[433] An example of demand risk gone wrong would be a toll road project in Southeast Asia where the project company replaced an old national roadway (which was considered insufficient for the traffic needs of the region) with a new toll road. The project company planned to recuperate the cost of building and maintaining this roadway through charging tolls to users over the period of the concession. However, the locals were not happy with the idea of paying tolls on a road which they and their ancestors had used for free for hundreds of years. Therefore, they opted to use alternative routes, avoiding the toll road. With the diminished traffic, the project company will never be able to satisfy debt servicing, much less obtain a sufficient return on its investment. This risk is incumbent on any BOT project where an offtake purchase agreement is not available and the project does not enjoy monopoly status.

Even where offtake purchase arrangements are not feasible, the project company will still have several options available. The project company can require a guarantee from the grantor of a certain level of demand (with compensation paid where demand does not meet that forecast[434]). The project company could also obtain shadow tolls from the grantor to ensure the income stream (by grossing up the tolls received or replacing them entirely). For example, the users may not be required to pay a toll, but rather the project company is paid directly by the grantor for each motorist who uses the motorway. In many countries, where charging tolls is deemed politically unacceptable, shadow tolls may be a viable option.

It is essential that the toll regime for a transportation project be based on reliable economic, technical and financial assumptions. The applicable calculations for shifts in the underlying assumptions should be flexible. However, it should be

---

432   Macquarie Corporate Finance Limited, "Project Finance: The Guide to Financing Transport Projects" at 12 (1996).
433   Macquarie Corporate Finance Limited (1996) supra note 432; for further discussion of traffic forecasts, their use and complexities, see page 23.
434   For further discussion of forecasts, see sections 18.2.5 and 18.3.6.

noted that renegotiation of the tariff regime after commencement of the project may be very difficult.[435] Therefore, lenders will generally undertake their own traffic forecasting exercises to verify those provided by the grantor and the project company. Unfortunately, many traffic forecasts suffer from political orientation, where they are undertaken with the intent to show the need of the local economy for state investment in infrastructure rather than to provide an objective analysis of demand.[436]

18.1.3   Existing facilities

The construction of toll roads and bridges can often interrupt the operation of existing transportation routes, either roadway or maritime. For this reason, the programme of works executed by the project company will have to correspond with the need for uninterrupted access routes and any additional requirements from the host government. For example, the host government will want work to be completed to co-ordinate with existing transportation systems during off-peak hours or seasons. Further, where the existing route will need to be closed for other reasons, such as maintenance, then the project company's work should be carried out in parallel with such scheduled closures.

18.1.4   Land and environmental risks

The construction of roads requires a significant amount of land. For this reason, the government will generally be involved in expropriation or procurement of that land and its provision to the project company for construction and use of the road. The time required to complete the procurement of the land necessary for a road project will depend largely on the local legal system and the extent of consultation and legal challenge available to the public in relation to the location of the proposed road and the procurement of the land. This public procurement of land also has a knock-on effect on the willingness of the private sector to bear ground condition risk, as the project company may not have an opportunity to do a proper subsurface analysis or geological survey.

A risk that arises frequently in toll road and bridge projects is environmental impact and, in particular, the knock-on sensitivities in the political arena. Nuclear and hydroelectric plants aside, roads elicit a disproportionate amount of media attention and public anguish. This is owing to their visibility and their impact on a multitude of people. The project company will not want to take the risk of protestor action (direct or indirect) or any political interference, where public opinion moves the government or local politicians to act against the project. However, the grantor will want the project company's assistance in managing the political image of the project and avoiding any aggravation of public sentiment.

---

[435]   Mates, "Financing Private Infrastructure Projects in the Transportation Sector" Project Financing in Emerging Markets 1996: Successful Development of Power, Mining, Oil and Gas, Telecommunications and Transportation Projects at 164 (1996).

[436]   Macquarie Corporate Finance Limited (1996) supra note 432.

18.2   Railways

Private investment in and financing of railways has a long and illustrious history. The development of railways in Europe and the United States has been key to demographic and industrial development. In the United Kingdom, the railway network was developed during the 19th century by the private sector, in exchange for certain benefits, including an increase in land values.[437] As the government's interests in such forms of infrastructure increased, it nationalised the railways, only for them to be re-privatised in 1995. This privatisation has involved separating the assets between train operating companies ("TOCs") and rolling stock leasing companies ("ROSCOs"). The TOCs lease rolling stock from the ROSCOs. Freight services are managed separately. The whole of the infrastructure (the tracks, signalling system and stations) was, until recently, owned by Railtrack.

Similarly, governments throughout the world are discovering the potential benefits of having the private sector finance and often operate railway services. The Channel Tunnel rail link is an example of a BOT approach to development of railways.

18.2.1   Revenues

Taking over existing rail services can be a challenge for project finance models, as they are often unprofitable. This is particularly true of routes which are primarily passenger service oriented. Recovering operating costs alone can be difficult. It is often the intervention of the public sector to support such projects for the benefit of the community that makes rail project finance possible.[438] This said, there has been some success in project financed light rail systems and a few high-speed rail systems in recent years.

One of the primary differences between a BOT railway project and a BOT power project is the absence of a universal offtake agreement. Although commercial carriers may make contracts with the railway operator for long-term rail access, such contracts will, generally, not cover the entire period of the concession. Further, just as with roadway and bridge projects, there is no guarantee that once the project has been completed private passengers will use the service. Even with market testing and traffic forecasts, the project company can be left holding the majority of the market risk for the project. For this reason the lenders will seek to allocate this risk to another party. Certain methods have been developed to allocate part of this risk to the grantor, such as through shadow tolls as discussed above under section 18.1.

The revenue stream for a rail project is usually based on track access charges. Operators pay track access charges to run their rolling stock on the network. Track access charges are usually based on a fixed track charge (set against fixed costs), a

---

437   Elliott, "Transportation Infrastructure: Recent Experience and Lessons for the Future" Project
       Lending at 137 (1992).
438   Macquarie Corporate Finance Limited (1996) supra note 432 at 24.

variable track usage charge based on the number of vehicle miles travelled, and a variable traction electricity charge. This payment structure works well with project financing where the lenders will want a fixed part of the payment stream to cover debt service. One difficulty with track access payments is the credit risk of the counterparty. Train operating companies often have a limited balance sheet. The lenders may want to obtain comfort directly from the relevant rail authority.[439]

18.2.2   Interface with existing facilities

BOT railway projects often need to be linked to existing transport services, particularly where such services are to be operated by the government or by a third party. Railway projects may not involve the construction of new lines or systems, but will often or generally involve the enhancement of an existing system. The infrastructure enhancements that might be required for a rail project can include car parks, platform extensions, station upgrades, depots, track doubling, improved timetable/performance, improved signalling for safety and/or performance purposes, new rolling stock, addition of new lines, removal of redundant lines, management of customer services and replacement of existing track.

Where a railway project must connect to the national railway service (which may suffer from operation and maintenance failures, inefficient scheduling or high cost for users) the project company's eventual revenues, or efficient operation of the rail project itself, may be inhibited. Specific undertakings from both the grantor and the national railway should be obtained, as well as practical and practicable sanctions sufficient to provide incentive to operate the railway effectively and to compensate the project company for the damages it could potentially incur.

18.2.3   Land and the environment

Access to land is extremely important for railway projects. The land required involves large strips, sometimes passing through highly populated and industrialised areas. These large tracts of land are generally procured by expropriation, and therefore significant involvement of the relevant government authority will be essential to the success of procuring the land as necessary. Many of the early railways were developed by the public sector using its powers to appropriate land as necessary for the public good. In the United States, the first cross-country railways were built by private railway companies which made a large part of their revenues from the land provided by the government for building the railways. In particular, the railway company obtained rights to land contiguous to the railway and developed it.

Where the railway company will need access to land in order to construct a railway, it will also need to restrict access to that land in order to ensure health and safety and avoid injury to third parties. This can be a particularly expensive aspect of the construction of a railway line given the large amount of land that must be

---

[439]   Pritchard, "Project Financing the UK Rail Industry" PFI 246 at 29 (24 July 2002).

protected and the difficulty of monitoring such large tracts of land. The construction of bridges and tunnels to manage the geographical features encountered in constructing a railway also raises issues of environmental damage, planning and other necessary legal requirements in relation to environmental impact and management of potential environmental damage.

18.2.4   Capital cost and subsidies

Rail projects involve quite significant capital costs where a system must be extended or where significant parts of its infrastructure must be replaced. This amount of capital may exceed the appetite of the private sector finance market. In particular, the cost of financing needed for capital improvements may exceed the willingness of passengers to incur fare increases and may therefore require a long-term subsidy from the Government. Even where public money is used to build the track and install signalling for a rail system, private money can be used to purchase equipment like rolling stock. That is the plan for the Madrid to Barcelona high-speed rail link. The previous Madrid-Seville high-speed rail link was entirely publicly funded.[440]

The significant level of government subsidy provides the lenders with improved cover ratios, which therefore encourages them to take usage risk. However, farebox risk is extremely unattractive (see the discussion of usage forecasts in section 18.2.5 below). Another approach is to implement the subsidy as an availability payment. This was done in the United Kingdom for the Nottingham Express Transit, which received approval in 2000. However, the Government may assume other forms of risk. For example, in the Barcelona Metro light rail system, the Government assumed 50 per cent. of the risk of usage where it fell below a certain agreed level.[441]

18.2.5   Forecasts

One of the major weaknesses of transport projects, be they roads, bridges or rail, is traffic forecasts. Wherever the private sector must take volume risk, they must rely on traffic forecasts. These forecasts have proven historically unreliable, often failing to be sensitive to demographic changes, demand shift, competition, cost increase and willingness to pay.

The first tram link project to be built with private money in the United Kingdom was the Croydon tram link. This project was formally approved in 1994, and a DBFO concession was eventually awarded for 99 years. The scheme was predicted to cost around £200 million, £95 million of that coming from the private sector and the balance from central government. The 28 km line was finally opened in May 2000. The original forecasts expected 20 million passengers per

---

[440]   Gelinas, "Private and Public Road Business Now a Two Way Street in US" Project Finance International 225 (19 September 2001).
[441]   *Ibid.*

year and a saving of two million car journeys, hence the justification for the public sector subsidy.

The private sector took usage risk, in fact there were no availability payments made for provision of the service. The private sector relied on traffic forecasts to identify the anticipated revenue stream and the amount and ratio of debt obtained and equity investment made. However, the forecasts turned out to be significantly optimistic. One important element of a tram link is speed. Where the tram travels a significant part of the journey off-street (which is faster) and has green light priority to the extent that it travels on-street, speed can be improved, justifying higher costs. The inaccuracy of the revenue forecasts was partially due to the fact that there was a competing bus route that charged lower fares and therefore reduced patronage of the tram link.

18.2.6   Extension or refurbishment of existing railways

The key to projects involving existing rail systems is the number of extra train paths that have been created.[442] Additional train paths allow the carriage of additional passengers and cargo. However, various factors will affect the number of train paths created such as the type of signalling systems on the relevant section of track, rolling stock characteristics (for example, line speed and acceleration) and timetabling. Timetables will change with seasonal variation and demand.

Rail projects raise particular issues in relation to construction. Where work is to be done on an existing rail system, access to that rail system will be extremely limited. The time available for access for construction or improvements will be limited to those times when the track can be cleared (i.e. when it is not in use or when it can be closed down for such work). The less time available each day for access to the track, the more time the contractor will require to complete the works. Given health and safety restrictions, access to track must follow and be followed by time required to set up safety checks and ensure that none of the line is encumbered and none of the equipment has been rendered useless during the works. For example, working on signalling boxes can disable the relevant signalling box, particularly where the electronics within that signalling box are particularly old or fragile.

Construction works will need to take into consideration the specific requirements of existing signalling systems, rolling stock and other issues associated with the management of services for the railway. As an example, signalling will be reliant on measurements of the existing railway. Where the existing railway is to be modified, the signalling system design will need to be amended to take into consideration changes in the physical infrastructure. The works will be measured and managed, often based on the positioning of OHLE masts which support the electrical wires and equipment to power the track system and often the trains. Moving these masts without considering the implication of any displacement can have a serious effect on the safety mechanisms provided for the railway.

---

[442]   Pritchard (24 July 2002) supra note 439 at 29.

18.2.7 Regulation and safety

Given the various safety risks and heightened public perception, rail is a highly regulated industry. Any construction or improvements will need to comply with regulatory restrictions and may need regulatory approval. These regulatory matters will form an important part of the timetable for project implementation and should be anticipated at the beginning of the process.

Given the sensitivity to safety and other issues, termination rights of a rail authority are often more strict in a railway franchise agreement than they would be in a typical BOT project. Any event that might give rise to concerns over the continued ability of the operator to perform its obligations could result in immediate termination, including the termination of any funding arrangements, the insolvency of the operator or its parent and the termination of any other franchise agreement with the same operator. In order to manage these increased risks, the lenders will generally enter into a direct agreement with the railway authority ensuring that even if the operator is removed, the same franchise assets will be used by the replacement operator and therefore the lender's security will be maintained.

18.2.8 BOT and DBT models

A number of different structures and models are available for private sector involvement in rail projects. The most common of these is the BOT model, where the project company finances and constructs new infrastructure and operates that infrastructure over the long-term. Revenues are obtained from the availability of the system and usage by either freight, passenger or other operating arrangements. The BOT model is most often used for the provision of the entire railway service (for example, constructing a new line or a new branch line) or just one part of that service (for example, the track or the rolling stock).

Another model proposed for use in rail development is the DBT model – design, build and transfer. This in effect creates a turnkey arrangement whereby the special purpose vehicle builds the enhancements and transfers those enhancements to the operator at a predetermined price. The special purpose vehicle must demonstrate engineering and safety criteria in the performance of those enhancements. This arrangement can either be restricted to the transfer and delivery of those physical enhancements or, instead, the special purpose vehicle may be required to ensure outputs, for example, in the form of train paths or other increased performance. If the special purpose vehicle is required to provide performance, then it will need to protect itself against matters outside its control which might restrict or reduce that performance.

The potential drawbacks of the DBT approach include the need for the operator to monitor carefully the performance by the special purpose vehicle to ensure that no defects arise or damage occurs due to the special purpose vehicle's involvement. This will be a particularly sensitive issue where the special purpose vehicle is working on an existing and operating network, where access is limited and safety is critical. Further, this DBT model will require two sets of financing, one in the short-term for the special purpose vehicle during construction and thereafter to finance the purchase price for the enhancements.

18.3   Airports

The need for expansion of airport facilities, particularly in the Asia-Pacific region, has led to the increased use of project financing for this sector. Airports benefit from a relatively stable minimum business baseload and a diversity of revenue sources, such as air traffic fees, car parking, concessions and property rentals. They also generally have a strong monopoly position, limiting possible competition.[443]

Airport privatisation can either involve a new facility, for example under a BOT scheme, or the sale of an existing operation to the private sector. The privatisation may involve one or more airports or indeed the privatisation of the national airports authority. Privatisation may also be limited to certain operations within the airport. The privatisation of an airport is often accomplished in two separate stages. The first stage involves the commercialisation of the operation, possibly through the corporatisation of the government entity owning and operating the airport, or the partial flotation of that entity. The second stage then sees the private sector acquiring the whole of the operation. This approach was used in the major British airports, which were first commercialised under the British Airport Authority ("BAA"). BAA was then privatised in 1987 by means of a public share issue.[444]

The BOT approach to airport development is exemplified by the third terminal at Toronto International Airport in Canada. Development of an entirely new airport is less common due to the massive capital investment required. The Athens Spata International Airport is one such example. It is being developed under a 25-year BOT concession. The new Berlin-Brandenburg airport is intended to be developed under a BOT arrangement.[445]

18.3.1   Revenue

Airport projects involve a multiplicity of commercial arrangements. Terminal facilities, fuelling facilities, cargo warehouses and handling, catering, parking, hotels, commercial businesses and a variety of other support services must be provided by the operator or a series of different operators. Each of these functions must be co-ordinated in order for the entire airport to work efficiently as a single unit. Given the diversity of airport activities, the project company will need to enlist the assistance of operators experienced in such areas.

---

[443]   Macquarie Corporate Finance Limited (1996) supra note 432 at 12.

[444]   Craig, "Risk and Due Diligence in Airport Privatisation" International Civil Aviation Authority, Airport Privatisation Seminar (13-16 December 1999) www.icao.int/icao/en/ro/nacc/aps

[445]   Haarmeyer and Coy, "Struggling for Capital in the US and Global Water Sector" Project Finance International 232 at 47 (9 January 2002).

The grantor and the shareholders will also need to allow the project company sufficient flexibility in the businesses it can undertake. In most other BOT projects, the grantor and the lenders generally limit the nature of the business that can be performed by the project company and on the site. In the case of an airport, the grantor and the lenders may be best served by broadening the nature of the businesses which can be operated in order to improve revenue flow and investment in infrastructure on the site.

Airport charges are often based on taxes that can be imposed on the use of airport services or other such fees and charges. The willingness of the airport's various clients to pay such charges will need to be considered in relation to the economic viability of the project. By some calculations, 46 per cent. of airport revenue comes from non-airspace sources. For example, when airports were no longer able to benefit from duty-free standing in relation to goods purchased by passengers flying within the EU, there was a significant fear amongst airports that revenue would fall significantly.[446]

Airport projects are viewed as an opportunity to encourage the economy, and to provide infrastructure for commercial and industrial growth. Even in the face of the continuing downturn in Asia, airport projects seem to be immune to such economic ills. A US$400 million airport in Malaysia, a US$5.8 billion airport in Korea and a US$5.3 billion airport in Japan are just a few of the airport projects planned over the first 10 years of this century. In Asia, airports tend to be funded by public money, and therefore the budgeting process will commence a long time before the actual project is begun.

The nature of funding available for airport projects helps to explain their tendency to resist economic cycles. In Asia, airports tend to be built with public money while ancillary projects may be financed with private funds. In Europe, airports are more likely to be funded with private money. However, even then, the public sector will provide significant support. Stansted Airport in the United Kingdom is one of the few projects financed entirely by private funds.[447]

18.3.2   Regulation

Just as the purchase price for electricity or the toll charges available to the project company will be regulated by the host government in respect of power stations and toll roads, so too will the number of landing slots, noise regulation, hours of operation, landing fees and passenger fees in airport projects be restricted by host government regulation. Therefore, similar considerations will need to be made in airport projects as are made concerning regulated fees in other BOT projects. Airport projects are also far more sensitive to safety issues than any other transport project. This will include the safety procedures used within the airport, any relevant interfaces with air traffic control, the natural features surrounding the

---

446   Bennett, "A New Thrust of Energy" Project Finance (August 1999).
447   *Ibid.*

airport and the way the airport is designed to deal with such features. As an example, the airport at Wellington, New Zealand has a serious lack of runway-end safety areas. The airport runway-end lies along a narrow neck of land with the sea at both sides, a steep drop from the runway at one end and a rocky shore at the other. This represents a serious risk in overrun or undershoot situations and would require either rectification or living with the risk of an accident and the significant resulting costs of capital and possibly loss of life.[448]

The Government will not want the private sector to use a minimalist approach to airport design in an effort to maximise return. Careful examination and regulation of private sector involvement in an airport is necessary to avoid substandard design and development as well as appropriate safety levels.

Where changes occur to government policy or regulatory requirements, the private sector's opportunities for revenue may be reduced. Other institutional influences may also have an impact on the airport. For example, express or tacit government subsidies may be changed or withdrawn. Government decisions in relation to management of air traffic can also have a significant impact on a project. As an example, the concessionaire for Manila's new international Terminal 3 discovered during construction that the Filipino Government was thinking about relocating all of Manila's international air traffic to a different airport, some 100 km north of the city. This would have had a serious impact on the viability of the new Terminal 3.[449]

18.3.3 Design and long-term planning

Given the specific demands of airports and the importance of aesthetics, privatisation bids often focus on attractive or innovative architectural designs for the airport. Less attention is given to practical issues such as air side or terminal design. Congestion issues for passengers and personnel within the terminal as well as aircraft moving to and from the gates will be critical to the efficient operation of the airport. Design will also need to take into consideration total capacity of the chosen site and the ability to expand. Yet, these issues are often ignored in the short time frame available during the privatisation process.[450] In the case of the Taipei Chiang Kai Chek International Airport, the Taiwanese Government has decided to provide the concept and layout of the airport to the bidders for the BOT scheme in order to ensure the design for the 14 million passenger terminal complies with the Government's requirements.[451]

An airport project will need to consider changes in aircraft mix. Capital expenditure will be specific to a certain mix of size and type of aircraft. Where the expected mix of aircraft is inaccurate, further capital expenditure may be required. Issues such as airline alliances and modifications in operating procedures among

---

[448]   Haarmeyer and Coy (9 January 2002) supra note 445 at 47.
[449]   Craig (13-16 December 1999) supra note 444.
[450]   *Ibid.*
[451]   *Ibid.*

airlines can have a significant impact on the way the airport must be managed, and how the traffic and management issues are dealt with within the design elements of the infrastructure provided. For example, airlines have recently debated whether long haul flights should use smaller, faster planes or larger, slower planes. These types of operational decisions can affect airport infrastructure requirements significantly.

Rolling capital expenditure plans for airports are sensitive to change in demand over time. Where there is a planned capital build-out of the airport over time, this may not be appropriate due to insufficient passenger numbers or because the nature of the service required in the future may change dramatically, resulting in variations in the original capital expenditure plan. The government will want sufficient flexibility in this capital expenditure plan to permit it to satisfy the needs of the local population. At the same time, the private sector will want to be protected from any loss of revenue or increased costs arising from such variations.

18.3.4   Land and environment

An airport requires a significant amount of land. This difficulty was encountered in particular in construction of the new airport for Hong Kong (Chek Lap Kok). Due to a lack of vacant land in or near Hong Kong, large amounts of land had to be reclaimed from the sea. A number of issues arise in relation to the reclamation of land from the sea or previously uninhabitable swamp and/or open space. These issues relate primarily to the environmental damage associated with such reclamation and development and the planning issues related to land for which the legal ownership may not be entirely clear.

Airport construction also raises significant environmental issues surrounding noise and air pollution. Local residential populations may not react positively to the possibility of construction of a new airport in their region given the potential for noise pollution and the reduction of property value, the prolonged consultation process surrounding the proposed Heathrow Terminal 5 in London being a prime example. At the same time, it should be noted that the location of a new airport can significantly improve land values, in particular in developing countries where the location of jobs and transportation may involve more complex, socio-political issues.

18.3.5   Financing

In the United States, there is no private funding of airports. Municipal bonds have been used to finance infrastructure for some time. Their tax-free status and the lending capability of the investing public have made these bonds an extremely attractive mechanism for funding new infrastructure. There are Internal Revenue Service restrictions on the use of tax-exempt bonds that would restrict their use for purely privately owned infrastructure or privatisation models. This has left little space for private sector funding. The private sector has used the design and build contract to make a bit more room in the project for its own investment and involvement. However, many municipalities are limited in their ability to use design and build contracts due to legislative requirements to choose the lowest responsible bid. Private sector involvement can smooth out funding requirements and the immediate large capital expenditure of a typical infrastructure project. However, selection processes that are based entirely on lowest cost will inevitably mitigate away from the design and build model.[452]

Further, the domination of United States airports by individual airlines under the current system results in an extremely inefficient business model. Infrastructure could be shared by different airlines and used efficiently as each airline's time slots demand. Instead, a single airline dominates a certain amount of infrastructure but will not use it continuously and effectively throughout the day. In contrast, South America has caught on to the privatisation process far more quickly.[453]

Airports, like many other utilities with a consistent revenue stream, have also turned to securitisation for funding. The London City airport's £100 million securitisation closed in November 1999. Most airports have not had to use this mechanism. Large airports can usually obtain corporate debt or issue corporate bonds, while very small airports would not have enough critical mass to guarantee the revenue stream necessary for securisation. In Europe, airports are generally government owned and therefore benefit from inexpensive financing and the issue of bonds with a state guarantee.[454]

18.3.6   Traffic forecasts

As in other transport projects, traffic forecasts are critical for airport privatisation. They will depend on economic and demographic indicators as well as views as to methods of transport and available competition in the future. For airports, competition means alternative methods of transportation (for example, high-speed trains), the construction of new airports or the development of a whole new method of transportation. In addition, investors need to consider traffic forecasts in relation to air passengers and cargo traffic, consumption forecasts, the purchase of goods in the airport, the use of parking facilities, the use of other facilities within the airport and the special services, for example business lounges, that can be provided to consumers and to the airlines.

Air traffic forecasts provide two different services:[455]

> ➤ a forecast of the number of passengers and cargo passing through the airport, thereby providing an estimate of annual revenues; and

> ➤ forecasts of daily and hourly passengers, cargo and aircraft characteristics in order to measure the airport capacity and performance requirements for services and infrastructure.

---

452   Gelinas (19 September 2001) supra note 440.
453   Bennett (August 1999) supra note 446.
454   "This Year's Model" Project Finance (March 2000).
455   Craig (13-16 December 1999) supra note 444.

The first measure is indicative of revenues while the second measure shows capital costs requirements and operating expenditure.

Where demand exceeds the forecast, there will be pressure to invest further capital in order to expand services. Where the original business model does not contemplate expansion, then it may not be possible to attract additional investment or debt. This may lead to further public involvement and funding.

Forecasts are often provided by the bidders themselves, meaning that there will be as many forecasts as bidders. This is inherently inefficient since an error in the forecasts can result in serious problems in the project. The grantor will want to review those forecasts and how they have been applied to the bidders' business models when reviewing the bid, to avoid the complication of forecasting errors.

Chapter 19

Oil and Gas

Black gold, Texas tea.

The theme song to the "Beverly Hillbillies"

From the political power of OPEC, to the importance of politics in the Middle East and the constant increase in the number of petrol-powered automobiles in the world, our addiction to oil and gas and their derivatives has had significant influence on our international political structures, the global economy and our daily lives. Despite efforts to focus on more diverse, sustainable and environmentally friendly sources of energy and industrial materials, this critical reliance continues and shows no serious likelihood of abating in the short- to medium-term.

Oil provides 40 per cent. of the world's energy supply. By 2020, oil production should achieve 115 million barrels per day. Gas, however, is increasingly becoming the thermal fuel of choice due to its high efficiency and environmental benefits. Its share of world energy use is currently 20 per cent., and is predicted to rise to 30 per cent. by 2020. We are currently aware of 170 to 200 years' of supply of gas available globally. Our proven gas reserves have doubled in the last 20 years due to improved extraction methods and efficiency of use.[456]

The oil and gas industry includes some of the largest companies in the world amongst its number (grouped by size):

➢ ExxonMobil;

➢ Shell;

➢ BP;

➢ ChevronTexaco; and

➢ Total.

---

[456] Oil and Gas Journal (online story) 14 June 2000.

The nature of oil and gas products differs significantly from projects found in other sectors. The companies involved in oil and gas projects are often of significant financial standing, with robust balance sheets. Further, the revenues available from oil and gas projects offer margins well in excess of projects in most other sectors. The fact that there are higher returns on investment available, and therefore the lenders have more cushion, in the oil and gas sector allows more flexibility in choosing a financing structure for a project than would be available for projects in most other sectors.

Section 19.1 reviews the nature of oil and gas projects. Section 19.2 will discuss extractive projects generally, discussing how the BOT structure must be modified in order to deal with specific issues related to extractive projects. Pipelines and refineries will then be discussed in section 19.3. Given the importance of the developing markets in natural gas and LNG, this chapter will discuss the LNG market in section 19.4, its rapid development and specific aspects of LNG projects.

19.1   Oil and Gas Projects

From extraction to refinement and transportation, oil and gas projects involve the exploitation of a natural resource. This process is dissimilar from most of the other utilities and industrial processes discussed in this book. Its closest cousin among the projects discussed here would be the extraction, treatment and transportation of water. However, water does not benefit from the margins available in the oil and gas industries, and therefore even if the market exists regionally or internationally for the export of water, the cost of transportation as a function of revenues is normally far too high to justify its exploitation for any but the local market.

19.1.1   Oil and gas industries

The oil industry is highly vertically integrated. Oil companies tend to provide services covering most aspects of the oil industry, including the exploration of potential fields, to the extraction of oil, its refinement and finally retail sales to consumers. This process involves several major steps outlined below:

- exploration;
- extraction;
- refinement;
- transportation;
- storage;
- distribution; and
- retail sales.

Gas on the other hand involves exploration and extraction, but generally refinement is less of an issue. Gas is distributed through a network of pipes to the eventual retail purchaser. The transportation of gas through pipelines is most common, when in its gaseous state, but it is more difficult and costly to transport long distances. In certain countries, such as the United States and the United Kingdom, a fluid domestic gas market has developed. Natural gas is uneconomic to transfer by sea or by rail in its gaseous state.

The use of natural gas has increased significantly since the development of technology enabling the liquificaton of natural gas for its transport. Liquefied natural gas ("LNG") is much more practical and efficient to transport. After extraction, natural gas is liquefied, stored and transported to the relevant user or to the relevant pipeline or transmission system. On delivery it is vaporised or "regasified" for use or transportation to appropriate customers.[457]

19.1.2   Operational issues

The operation of an oil and gas project is managed quite differently from other traditional infrastructure projects. Reserves of oil or gas may be exploited by a number of different operating arrangements, licences or production-sharing contracts. Where several licences or permits relate to the same reserves, there may be some agreement amongst the various parties to allocate interests in those reserves to avoid one party extracting a disproportionate amount of those reserves. Given the continued improvements in the ability to identify reserves, this allocation may be based on technical characteristics and calculations which may be rebased from time to time.

Pipeline, gasification and regasification, and other treatment and/or transportation projects are normally sponsored by the company that plans to use its services. Where several companies intend to use the facility, they may club together to share capacity. Such projects are not usually undertaken for speculative purposes.

19.2   Extractive Projects

The BOT structure is used not only for public services, but also for the extraction of raw materials, for example minerals, oil and gas, and lumber. These are known as "upstream" projects. The concept of BOT in extractive projects allows the owner of a site rich in raw materials, often publicly owned resources, to attract investment (both financial and technical) from specialists to allow the owner to exploit these resources. Thus the grantor will want to receive financing for the extraction to be made, and benefit from the technology and operating knowledge of the specialists holding shares in the project company. It should be noted that, given the substantial nature of many of the companies that develop upstream capacity, limited recourse financing is less common for upstream projects.

---

[457]   Weems, "Overview of Issues Common to Structuring, Negotiation and Documenting LNG Projects" The International Energy Law and Taxation Review 8 (2000).

19.2.1   Regulation

One of the challenges of extractive projects is the variety of regulatory restrictions found in many countries, in particular in those developing nations which rely on natural resources for a substantial portion of their domestic wealth. Local law will often govern environmental safety, use of resources and utilisation or joint development with local entities. Investors will therefore wish to verify the requirements for gaining title to the resources and the methods of access and extraction available. The host country may also raise export restrictions or tariffs to regulate extractive activities.

Extractive projects are particularly vulnerable to environmental regulation. Such regulation may exist on an international, national and local level and may impose increased liability for any environmental damage resulting from the project, or otherwise discovered on the site.

For a long time, oil and gas projects were put together with little consideration of the life-cycle of the underlying assets and the need to decommission those assets once they were no longer economically useful or desired. This has changed with modern concepts of "polluter pays" liability and the public reaction to the irresponsibility associated with the disposal of assets without provision to protect the environment. These projects may therefore contemplate funds or reserve accounts set aside for the cost of decommissioning and the clean-up operations surrounding such decommissioning.

19.2.2   Reserves

A central part of any extractive BOT project will be the analysis of data to establish the amount of reserves available on the site and their accessibility. This measure is not exact and will therefore give rise to substantial project risk. The recent announcement by Shell that it overstated its reserves has caused particular concern in the industry. The limitation of available reserves will often result in a shorter time for repayment of debt as compared to other infrastructure projects, which tend to have longer repayment periods.[458]

Geological conditions will be extremely important for oil and gas projects, affecting the cost of extraction and the nature of the equipment needed to extract the resource efficiently. As discussed in chapter 10, subsurface conditions are difficult to assess in advance with any accuracy in the absence of expensive and time-consuming subsurface investigations.

Extractive projects are not limited to the exploration and extraction of the raw commodity. They also include the services to be provided thereafter, such as its transportation or refinement. These issues will be discussed in further detail in section 19.3 below.

---

[458]   Appia, "Infrastructure Projects: BOT Developed Country Structuring" [1998] IBL at 206.

19.2.3   Oil and gas rights

The rights to oil and gas are almost always held by the local government, whether they be onshore or offshore (this is not the case in certain jurisdictions such as the United States).   Offshore oil and gas may also be found in international (as opposed to territorial) waters, in which case the legal ownership of that oil and gas may be less clear.   These rights are generally the subject of multinational treaty.

Where title to the resource remains with the state, the project company will often obtain rights to develop a certain field under a licence or a production-sharing agreement ("PSA").   PSAs are more common in developing countries.

PSAs are often a contract between the national oil company and the project company.   Performance or production obligations or expenditure requirements are placed on the project company, and it is paid compensation either in kind or calculated by reference to actual production.   The project company may not have any direct property right in the oil extracted or produced; this allows the developing country to avoid political sensitivity surrounding ownership of natural resources.   It is often a very detailed contractual mechanism to compensate for the lack of statutory framework in most oil-rich countries.   The grantor generally maintains approval rights over development plans, and the project company incurs all associated costs.   The grantor will also play a supervisory role and will maintain certain decision-making rights.

Licences are usually a statutory instrument providing some amount of exclusivity and giving the holder of the licence ownership of the resource extracted and produced.   The government will then receive a royalty, either a fixed annual amount or an amount based on the total volume of oil or gas extracted.   The holder of the licence may also have certain obligations, e.g. to drill a certain number of wells or provide specific infrastructure.   The licence may expire if it is not "used".

The parties may enter into arrangements jointly to manage resources under multiple licences or PSAs.   This is often known as a "unit operating agreement" ("UOA").   A UOA may allocate rights by "tract participation", divided by different areas or blocks.   Farm-in or farm-out agreements provide for risk sharing where one party explores or extracts under another party's licence or PSA.

19.2.4   Commercial arrangements and equipment

Oil and gas equipment is often financed on a limited recourse basis where a special purpose vehicle or possibly the contractor himself purchases the equipment and finances that purchase against long-term agreements for the use of that equipment. Examples might be floating production, storage and off-loading vessels ("FPSOs"), and floating drilling rigs (including semi-submersible and drilling ships).

In oil and gas projects, similar to any BOT project, the contractor procures the equipment from the fabrication yard, leases the equipment and provides services to the oil company, obtaining financing from a lender.   The construction contract is assigned to the lender and the lender receives part of the lease payments for debt service.[459]

The contract between the contractor and the oil company is usually based on a fixed day-rate. It is not connected with the volume of oil recovered, which is often a concern for lenders. The lenders will prefer a payment stream closely associated with the performance of the project, and therefore the revenues available for servicing debt. This, they reason, places a greater incentive on the contractor to maximise performance.

The minimum contract period can vary from a couple of months for a drilling rig, to five to 10 years for an FPSO. The tenure of these contracts depends on the need of the oil company and the task at hand. FPSOs are generally used for the forecast economic life of a field while drilling rigs are only used in the early exploitation of the field. Long-term contracts for drilling rigs may be available where oil companies have a concern about short supply of drilling rigs. They may also wish to "sponsor" drilling rigs which have specific characteristics that they may require or are specially fitted to a given form of exploration that the oil company intends to undertake.[460]

The lease payments are generally performance-based. Where the equipment does not perform to specification, those lease payments may be reduced or not paid at all. In the case of equipment failure (also known as "down time") the contractor will normally be given reasonable cure periods in relation to specific equipment, given the difficulty in the replacement of that equipment. FPSOs in particular are tailored to a specific field, and are therefore very expensive to replace. Drilling rigs are less tailored and therefore easier to replace.[461]

19.2.5   Credit risk and security

Another obvious challenge is the credit risk of the offtaker. Major oil companies are significant, credit-worthy entities. Smaller highly leveraged oil companies may be vulnerable to changes in oil prices or poor performance in the relevant field. The lenders may look to the underlying economics of the field for comfort as to the credit worthiness of the counterparty. Lenders may also take comfort in the ability to shift the relevant equipment to some other offtaker and therefore reinstate the revenue stream. This will depend on market conditions and also the extent of specificity of the relevant equipment. Where the equipment is specifically designed for a given field, it may be difficult to find a suitable alternative offtaker.

The reservoir report will be critical to financing. The report will indicate proven, probable or possible reserves. It will give an indication of the feasibility of extraction, the total revenues and incremental revenues to be expected from the project and an indication of the cost of refinement or treatment necessary to

---

[459]   Borghans, "Structured Service" Project Finance (December/January 2001).

[460]   *Ibid.*

[461]   *Ibid.*

produce marketable products. Given the margins available for most oil and gas projects, once the lenders have reviewed the reservoir report they may be willing to bear reservoir risk and not require full guarantees from the sponsors, but only to the extent the report indicates proven reserves in developed fields and the lenders are otherwise comfortable with their exposure in the project. Recent revelations from the likes of Shell on its overestimation of reserves are rapidly eroding this willingness of lenders.

The lenders may also take comfort in the residual value of the relevant equipment.[462] FPSOs typically have an economic life of 15 years or more. However, as noted above, they are normally specifically tailored to the characteristics of an oil field, and therefore their residual value may be limited. Drilling rigs have an economic life of 15 to 30 years and are not normally tailored to a specific field, and therefore are easily moved from one user to another. This said, the lenders will need to examine the residual value of a drilling rig to a much greater extent than in the financing of an FPSO, given the very short-term offtake contracts available for drilling rigs.

19.2.6 Market liquidity

Oil can be transferred either by tankers or pipeline. Due to this ease of transport and universal demand, a vibrant spot market exists for oil. Gas, on the other hand, is still subject to long-term contracts. Gas can be transferred by pipeline, but is not practicably transferable by truck or ship in its gaseous state. However, it can be liquefied and carried by tanker. Though the potential of LNG to create a spot market is promising, it is still a relatively rigid market.

The rigidity of the LNG market can be seen in the high level of dedication of LNG ships to specific projects. This restricts the amount of capacity in the transportation sector for the development of a more fluid market. In particular, the capital expenditure invested in shipping generally amounts to approximately 30 per cent. of the total cost of an LNG project. However, this dedication of ships to specific LNG projects may be in the process of change. Of the 30 LNG ships on order in the middle of 2002, only about half were tied to any particular project.[463] This is partly due to suppliers wanting to control the market into which their gas is sold and thereby manage price and market stability risk.

19.2.7 Investment structures

The typical oil and gas project is quite different to any other BOT project. Rather than a limited liability project company, oil and gas projects generally use an unincorporated joint venture as the ownership vehicle. The sponsor companies will be able to book reserves as their assets to the extent a direct ownership can be demonstrated, which is facilitated by an unincorporated joint venture. The use of

---

[462] *Ibid.*
[463] Wright, "Asian LNG: Moving Towards a Short Term Market" Project Finance International 248 at 42 (4 September 2002).

unincorporated joint ventures is also tax driven. The sponsors may wish to use tax deductions immediately.

The typical unincorporated joint venture, at least in upstream projects, does not result in a partnership under English law since the parties obtain a share of the petroleum, rather than sharing a common profit pool. Parties are subject to "cash calls" where, when the unincorporated joint venture requires cash injection, each party is required to provide such cash in accordance with its share. The right to take its share of oil is called "lifting rights". Where a party fails to comply with its cash call obligations, its lifting rights may be prejudiced. Parties will also need to consider abandonment of the project, the associated costs and how those costs would be shared.

Project security is limited to partial and indirect security, rather than direct security over all project assets as one would expect in a project financing. Financing for oil and gas tends to be provided to each separate joint participant, relying on the credit and performance of each participant. For, in relation to the joint venture, the banks will only lend to each party individually. They will therefore not have the usual controls over the joint venture, but only over the borrower's participating interest in that joint venture, their voting rights and their rights to the oil or gas produced. The revenue cascade will be specific to that borrower, and will not cover the whole of the project. This structure is slightly different where the gas is to be liquefied, where tolling arrangements may be used or a co-ordinated approach to marketing and commercialising the product may be preferred.

Upstream oil and gas projects have a risk profile somewhat different to other infrastructure projects using limited recourse financing. These differences in risk profile include:

> capital expenditure demands are more commonly at the risk of the project company and the sponsors. There may not be the type of EPC contract typical in other BOT projects to fix the construction price for the project possibly relying on completion guarantees from sponsors;

> lenders may be more willing to take reservoir risks (where other projects would use fixed supply contracts) although, as noted above recent revelations about Shell's reserves have changed this attitude;

> the revenue stream market risk (where other projects would use a fixed offtake agreement);

> lenders may take a certain level of political risk (where normal BOT projects would look to a government termination payment); and

> the project scope may be unclear until such time as geological requirements are assessed (where a normal BOT project will have a fixed project scope).

These are fundamental differences in project structures that can be explained partially by the significant up-side available in an oil and gas project and the margins that the lenders can look to as part of their security package. As an example of the difference in leverage expected from an oil and gas project, the average power project financing will look for a loan life cover ratio of 1.1 to 1.6, while the average oil project financing will look to a loan life cover ratio well in excess of 2.0.

19.3 Pipelines to Refineries

Another form of BOT oil and gas project is the construction of oil and gas facilities such as pipelines and refineries. This type of BOT project closely follows the structure set out for power projects. The entity which will be introducing a product into service is the input supplier. This entity may be the grantor, a private entity or a third party government entity. The input supplier may also be the offtake purchaser. In fact, as a general rule, the project developer for a pipeline project will be the entity who needs the pipeline. Pipelines are rarely developed by independent investors for speculative purposes.[464]

19.3.1 Revenues

Payment may be required at one or both ends of the pipeline; the project company charging for introduction of the product into its system and/or for receipt from its system. The availability charge for a pipeline is often called a demand or "on-call" element, while the usage charge is also known as a "commodity" element. As in other structures these elements cover the fixed and variable costs, respectively, of the project company. Other options also exist, such as payments to the project company for access to the pipeline over an agreed period or per unit of input sent through the pipeline, also known as a "through-put arrangement".

Oil and gas projects also often involve a large amount of market-related risk. Oil and gas prices can fluctuate rather dramatically. Repayment of debt is often triggered by market price, therefore the lenders will take a certain element of market risk. Where through-put arrangements are envisaged, the through-put charge can be calculated to satisfy debt servicing requirements and associated cover ratios, protecting the lenders from some or all market risk associated with oil and gas prices or demand for use of the infrastructure.

19.3.2 Political/cross-border issues

Pipelines may cross national boundaries, therefore host government issues may be more complex and require greater preventative measures by the project company. Further, concessions may be received from several countries, requiring that extension and takeover regimes in relation to assets located in different jurisdictions work in parallel, no matter what events intervene. These issues may be subject to protection under Bilateral Trade Agreements, by export credit agencies, or under local laws which protect investors from expropriators and other government acts. Pipelines are also more vulnerable to security threats such as

---

[464] Smith, "Project Finance in the Utility Industries" Project Finance at 154 (1992).

terrorism and misappropriation, requiring special undertakings by the grantors involved and more complex insurance structures to protect the pipeline.

19.4   Gas and LNG

The market in natural gas is growing dramatically. Though historically considered to be nothing but a nuisance, natural gas is now becoming the fuel of choice. The chart below shows forecast growth in the natural gas market over the next 15 years.

GAS DEMAND
WORLD NATURAL GAS CONSUMPTION

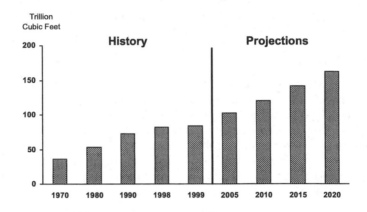

Source: History: EIA, Office of Energy Markets and End Use, International Statistics Database and International Energy Annual 1999. Projections: EIA, World Energy Projection System (2001)

The availability of pipelines is the major constraint on the transport of gas, but the ability to liquefy natural gas into LNG has made transportation viable and practicable.[465] Liquefaction reduces the volume of natural gas to some 1/600th of its volume in gaseous form.

While natural gas currently fuels only 16 per cent. of the United States power plants, 90 per cent. of plants to be built in the United States by 2020 are expected to be gas fuelled. This corresponds with the development of gas fuel capacity in Mexico of at least 6,600mW, an enormous increase in this market. More than 50 per cent. of the growth in gas demands is being met by imports of LNG. The popularity of natural gas has therefore resulted in construction of significant new pipeline capacity and investment in the capital intensive process of liquification, shipping and regasification of LNG.[466]

---

465   Gelinas, "Hyping in the LNG" Project Finance International 225 at 57 (19 September 2001).
466   *Ibid.*

Another reason for the popularity of LNG is the fact that known reserves of natural gas are not generally located near potential customers. The table below shows the location of the largest known reserves of natural gas. Building pipelines from these reserves of natural gas to customers may be financially, technically or geographically impossible. Further, since pipelines are subject to a point-to-point rigidity, they are vulnerable to changes in customer make-up. Where the location or demand changes significantly, new pipelines or extensions of existing pipelines will need to be built.

GAS RESERVES BY COUNTRY
1 JANUARY 2001

Country	Reserves (trillion cubic feet)	Percentage of World Total
Russia	1,700	32.20
Iran	812	15.40
Qatar	394	7.50
Saudi Arabia	213	4.00
UAE	212	4.00
United States	167	3.20
Algeria	160	3.00
Venezuela	147	2.80
Nigeria	124	2.30
Iraq	110	2.10

Source: EIA, International Energy Outlook 2001

LNG is ultimately flexible. Once the gas has been liquefied it can be shipped to any corner of the planet – as long as a regasification facility is available. LNG can reach customers wherever they may be found.

One of the levels of security for lenders in an LNG project is the protection of the chain between liquification, shipping and regasification. Lenders do not like to see that any of the supply chain is vulnerable. Given the volume of LNG projects, this secure chain may become less common, in particular where existing plants and chains are being expanded or extended.

At the moment, demand outstrips capacity and spot sales can be lucrative. As capacity increases, this gap between capacity and demand will diminish and the attractive nature of spot sales will decrease. Further, as energy markets are being deregulated, the large state utilities, whose primary concern is a stable supply of gas, are being broken up. Therefore, customers are no longer as large or as dependable. We may also find the development of LNG swap trading in order to reduce the cost and delay involved in transporting gas.

19.4.1   The LNG chain

LNG projects involve a complex chain of interdependent elements. The LNG cost chain looks something like this (with the approximate share of cost indicated in brackets):[467]

> ➢ field development (10-20 per cent.);
>
> ➢ liquification (25-35 per cent.);
>
> ➢ shipping (15-25 per cent.);
>
> ➢ receiving terminal (5-15 per cent.); and
>
> ➢ gas distribution and marketing (25-35 per cent.).

As of 2000, only about 25 per cent. of the internationally traded natural gas moved as LNG. However, vast investments in LNG facilities at the beginning of this decade will continue to increase LNG's part of this market.[468] Another issue that has constrained the growth of the LNG market is the cost of liquification and receiving terminals. Shipping can also be a challenge, given the specialist ships required.

19.4.2   Revenues

The LNG market has grown dramatically over the past quarter of a century. Its capital costs have fallen and its customer needs have become more diversified. The traditional model of an LNG project included a single or relatively small number of buyers wanting long-term stability of LNG deliveries. This market is moving toward a more fluid market for LNG. In theory, if this market does increase in fluidity, without some form of mitigation or hedge against the resultant market risks, uncertainty in sales volumes is likely to increase credit risk for LNG projects as the market becomes more flexible.[469]

In LNG projects, the project company typically purchases gas upstream, liquefies it, transports it, gasifies it and sells it to purchasers. This approach is very conducive to financing given the isolated revenue stream and the secure long-term arrangements with sellers of gas and purchasers of gas at either end. However, this approach has certain limitations. For example, it may be difficult to provide for its future expansion when all assets and revenues are controlled by the lenders to the original project. Given the growth of the market, this may be an unfortunate limitation.

---

[467]   Mace, Presentation on LNG Projects at Allen & Overy (2002).
[468]   *Ibid.*
[469]   Rigby, "After Burn?" Project Finance (December/January 2001).

Where strict arrangements for gas sale are made, the parties will need to consider how to manage excess capacity. The project company should be able to sell excess capacity to third parties, where there is sufficient demand. The parties will want to share the benefit of such excess capacity and identify any right of first refusal that any of them may have to such excess gas or transport capacity. For example, Japanese buyers, more by custom than by contract, have a right of first refusal on any excess capacity.

Another option is to use an unincorporated joint venture whereby each of the participants holds one share of the LNG plant, supplies one part of the gas and is entitled to one part of the revenues typically known as a "tolling structure". However, this structure may not permit the limited recourse financing sought by many investors.

LNG can also provide revenues from associated products. Condensate is produced from certain condensate-rich reservoirs (for example, those located in Qatar that are being used by the Ras Gas and Qatar Gas projects).[470] However, condensate is a difficult liquid to transport. Therefore, revenues from the sale of condensate are only available where the project benefits from an appropriate geographic location near to purchasers of condensate.

Where natural gas is not "sweet", the sulphur will need to be removed from the gas before it is liquefied. This sulphur may be saleable, which can offset some of the cost of removing the sulphur. Ideally, however, natural gas will be naturally free of sulphur.

An LNG project can also act as the anchor project to finance an upstream development to exploit sources of natural gas. The local gas company will thus benefit from the sale of natural gas into the local market and the development of a market that, without the LNG project, would not be economically viable.[471]

19.4.3 Transport

Maritime risk should be considered carefully, in particular in relation to liability for delivery of the LNG, be it ex-ship or FOB or otherwise. Even the condition of the relevant ships will be important. The party shipping LNG or receiving shipment of LNG may be liable where they knowingly hire or use ships which are in a less than operable condition, in particular in the event of an accident or spillage.

Issues associated with shipping risk will also include availability of the port, sharing of port facilities and the costs that the project company can claim for resultant delay and inability to meet delivery requirements. Where there are

---

[470] *Ibid.* It should be noted that the development of a spot market in LNG is likely to take some time. Violent energy price volatility in the United States underlines the major market risk borne by any LNG project that does not have a long-term purchase agreement from a creditworthy purchaser.

[471] *Ibid.*

several offtakers looking to share one port facility, competing access demands will take on an increased relevance. The parties will need to agree priority and rules for sharing access, which is one of the most important issues in LNG projects currently.

The project company may or may not choose to own the ships used for transport. It may prefer to charter ships to avoid ownership interest or it may prefer to own the ships in order to reduce costs and control offtake patterns. It should be noted that the key driver to an integrated project, where the project company owns the ships, is to control the market into which the LNG is sold and therefore manage market risk.

The gas may also need to be transported from the wells to the gasification facility or from the regasification facility to the offtake purchaser. The parties will need to allocate risk of availability of these transmission systems and any losses during transmission.

Traditionally, buyers have insisted on owning and controlling the tankers. This has restricted the development of an LNG spot market. However, although the buyers still want to control the tankers, the sellers too want to control shipping to manage their market risk and control the markets into which the gas is to be sold, with a certain number of suppliers purchasing or restoring LNG tankers to service the developing market.

19.4.4   Regulation

Local regulatory and political issues will be of particular interest in the country of extraction. Natural resources are often regulated and that regulation will tend to follow the interests of any political power. Contractual arrangements may or may not protect the relevant project company, depending on the availability of justice and the status of the rule of law.

Local community issues will be important at extraction and delivery points. Extraction, onshore or offshore, will involve some impact on and possible resistance from local communities and the environment. Similarly, construction of ports designed to receive shipments of LNG and the availability of regasification facilities may meet similar resistance. Regasification is also regulated in many countries, including the United States, the United Kingdom and Spain. The rest of the EU plans to follow suit.

19.4.5   Taxation and the project structure

Taxation issues often have a significant influence on the final structure to be adopted for the project company. Tax holidays and other forms of government subsidies may be available in certain countries. However, it will be important to consider the likely longevity of such arrangements and the enforceability of any promises provided by the government. Transfer of legal ownership of the gas during transport, and its sales tax implications, will need to be considered.

19.4.6   The future of LNG

LNG is becoming the fuel of choice due to three principal characteristics. Firstly, traditional sources of natural gas are insufficient to meet increasing demand (e.g. Canada's supply of gas to the United States) and therefore buyers are looking to new sources. Secondly, natural gas used to generate electricity emits fewer pollutants and waste products. Ash and radioactive waste are not concerns for natural gas users. Thirdly, gas-fired electricity generation capacity is relatively cheaper and quicker to build.[472] This cost-effectiveness has, in the past, been offset by high transmission costs and inflexibility of availability. Lower tanker prices, which have dropped nearly 50 per cent. during the last decade, have helped certain sellers to develop shipping capacity and therefore the ability to satisfy spot market requirements.[473]

From a construction point of view, it is difficult to find contractors large enough with the appropriate experience to be able to guarantee completion dates for the whole of an LNG project, especially where the price tag is in multi-billions of dollars. The need to split the construction packages for an LNG project among a number of contractors can have a detrimental impact on the level of completion guarantee obtainable from the contractors. Sponsors of LNG projects, therefore, must generally be substantial market players, willing to provide guarantees of completion to the lenders, with the associated benefit of cheaper construction than if the contractor were required to provide a completion guarantee. This has limited project uptake and market development.

Japan and Korea continue to be large consumers of LNG, while the United States is planning to increase its consumption significantly over the next 25 years and is seen as the largest potential consumer over the medium-term. New markets for the purchase of LNG have developed in India and China. The potential demand from these countries is enormous, as neither of them have indigenous natural gas supplies in any significant quantities.[474] The ever-increasing market opportunities and maturation of the sector should ensure a long and profitable future for LNG.

---

[472]   This said, combined cycle gas turbine generators are a little more expensive to operate; see generally *Ibid.*

[473]   *Ibid.*

[474]   *Ibid.* It should be noted that the development of a spot market in LNG is likely to take some time. Violent energy price volatility in the United States underlines the major market risk borne by any LNG project that does not have a long-term purchase agreement from a creditworthy purchaser.

Chapter 20

Telecommunications

*The Americans have need of the telephone, but we do
not. We have plenty of messenger boys.*

> Sir William Preece,
> Chief Engineer of the
> British Post Office, 1876

Another traditional public sector service increasingly offered by the private sector is telecommunications. Increased demand and changes in technology have exceeded the funding available from the public sector. BOT projects provide an opportunity for development of telecommunications infrastructure without placing the burden of the ultimate financial demands on the sponsor's balance sheet. They also allow the operator to spread the cost of infrastructure over time, rather than requiring a considerable up-front capital expenditure.

Together with power and transportation, telecommunications is one of the primary growth areas in BOT projects in developing countries. However, telecommunications projects are often difficult to fit into the BOT model. This is not to say that telecommunications projects are incompatible with the BOT model, but rather issues specific to telecommunications play a more important role and will need to be considered carefully.

BOT projects in telecommunications have historically involved a significant level of vendor financing. This is an additional level of financing provided by suppliers of equipment as an incentive for the project company to procure from them. The level of funding provided by vendors soon became a weakness of many of these projects given the subsequent, often critical, financial troubles of many of the vendors, and their financing arms.

20.1   Telecommunications

Projects that one would find appropriate for a BOT structure in telecommunications might include the development of fibre optic networks, satellite systems, mobile phone mast networks and local loop unbundling (also known as "last-mile" services). Where new-build residential or business developments are contemplated, BOT projects can provide the full range of audio, video and telecommunication services from fixed line telephone services to broadband video streaming. Alternatively, the provider of telecommunications services may treat directly with individual end users, resulting in an adjustment to the classic BOT structure. A recent example is the need for full telecommunications infrastructure at the Dubai marina development which includes residential facilities, hotels and business. The promoters of the Dubai marina preferred to outsource the provision of these services, to obtain greatest value for money from experienced operators.

Securitisation has also been used in the area of telecommunications to realise value from future debts due from customers. In the current market this would be limited to secure revenues from existing customers, probably in a monopoly situation.

Telecommunications operators over the last two to five years have invested heavily in fibre optic infrastructure. The broadband capacity developed during this period has created a glut in the market in certain regions. The same companies then found it very difficult to achieve levels of revenue sufficient to justify their investment or to satisfy their lenders, as the demand forecasts for broadband proved overly optimistic.

The corresponding development of third generation ("3G") mobile phone technology, and the prices paid at auctions for 3G licences, created huge holes in these companies' balance sheets. Astronomical figures were paid for licences in the United States, the United Kingdom and Germany. An equivalent amount would be required for capital investment in order to implement the infrastructure and network capacity to satisfy the number of 3G customers that would need to be attracted in order to justify the levels of investment made. Unfortunately, to date, these customers have not appeared. Some of these large operators are experiencing corporate finance difficulties, some of them have become insolvent and others remain in critical financial situations.

20.1.1   Market risk

The market risk associated with telecommunications projects is more difficult to manage than that of power projects or even transportation projects. It generally relies on services provided to a number of individual consumers, with demand subject to the changes in a very competitive market. The competitive nature of the telecommunications market makes it generally impossible for the lenders to obtain the revenue certainty required in other projects.

In the past, lenders and investors relied on buoyant and optimistic forecasts of market demand to justify taking market risk. The market tribulations of 2001 and 2002 experienced in the telecommunications sector have deflated lender confidence in the market. Some methods of ensuring a revenue flow may include intervention by the government to purchase unused capacity for its own or others' use, or making an agreement with a particular user, such as a corporate subscriber, for the commitment of a substantial portion of the available capacity.

The difficulties of the 3G market provide a good example of the challenges faced in the telecommunications market. Second generation ("2G") mobile phone technology provides digital voice and limited data technology over a mobile telecommunications platform. 3G technology can support enhanced services such as e-mail, fast internet access, video (in some cases) and a diverse range of further entertainment and corporate applications. In the United Kingdom, 3G licences were auctioned to five different licence holders at a total price of Euro 38.475 billion. In Germany, six licences went for Euro 50.8 billion at auction. However, the licence alone is insufficient, 3G services cannot be delivered to customers on 2G infrastructure. Those operators investing in 3G technology must install additional infrastructure.

As an example, in the United Kingdom 2G carriers require approximately 3,000 base stations for nationwide coverage. 3G carriers will require 10 to 15,000 3G base stations for nationwide coverage. With five carriers this could mean a total of 50 to 75,000 masts, although in many cases operators have agreed to share mast sites. The construction of 3G telecoms infrastructure requires the installation of a mast on land, either leased or owned, plus connection of that mast to the local fibre optic backbone by way of fibre optic connection and backhaul, as well as connection to the local electricity grid for a power supply. Therefore, in addition to the leased or owned land on which the tower is installed, the operator will need a right of way over adjoining land, between the mast and the local electricity grid and the fibre optic backbone. The estimated cost of rolling out these 3G infrastructure networks is Euros 2.4-3.25 billion per carrier in the United Kingdom and from Euros 4.5-6.5 billion per carrier in Germany.

Market risk in telecommunications projects is largely managed on a project-by-project basis. For example, where the project in question is a telecommunications network for use by the primary carrier or the host government itself, such as the construction and installation of submarine fibre optic cable between two countries, the capacity of the system could be sold to various carriers. If the project company wishes to avoid the market risk of demand for broadband, it could enter into a contract with one or several of the major carriers for use of the cable capacity over the period of the concession, similar to the system developed for pipeline projects.

If, however, the project involves providing infrastructure for use directly by end users, such as providing new technology to a municipal telephone system, the host government may need to guarantee that the sale of capacity will provide sufficient revenue before the lenders and shareholders are willing to invest in the project.

20.1.2 Technology

Other difficulties encountered when financing telecommunications projects on a limited recourse basis result from the rapidly changing nature of the sector, the new technology being produced, combined with the need to interconnect, in certain cases, with other providers or with public infrastructure.

The grantor will need to consider how it will manage upgrades of technology and to what extent it will allow the project company discretion in how it implements such upgrades. Intellectual property rights will also play an important role in telecommunications projects. The project itself must benefit from all associated intellectual property rights in order to avoid any interruption in service provision. Where royalty payments must be made for any intellectual property rights and those payments increase significantly or the relevant rights are no longer available, the project itself may cease to be commercially viable.

As new technology is implemented, the specification for the project will change. Interfaces between different technologies and the need for a flexible platform for the implementation of such new technology will be essential to the ongoing viability of the project. Unlike most other infrastructure projects, a telecommunications project will not be governed by the same specification over its life. The specification will evolve significantly as technology changes and its flexibility must be considered from the earliest days of structuring the project.

20.1.3   Regulation

During the operation phase, the project company will need the support of a regulatory system sufficiently stable to protect the integrity of the project and yet flexible enough to offer a reasonably commercial approach to the operation of the facility. The telecommunications industry is a dynamic growth sector. It may be difficult for national legislation or even regulatory authorities to keep pace.

The legislative framework should provide for an independent regulatory body with a mandate to develop a commercial, competitive system and with the power to set standards and enforce them. This system should preferably be implemented before the signing of any commercial arrangements and financing. The project company will look to be protected from the risk of changes in regulatory requirements, or actions inconsistent with the expectations of the parties as set out under the concession agreement.

Finally, the project company will want to ensure that a reasonable system of administrative review is available for any decision imposed by the regulatory body, with appropriate notice and eventual judicial review at the request of the project company or the operator.

20.2   Fibre Optic Projects

Telecommunications projects focus on transmitting the maximum amount of data or voice traffic to market quality standards as quickly and inexpensively as possible. One of the best ways of achieving this is the installation of fibre optic cables. These glass fibres are able to carry information by transmitting laser light from one end to the other. They provide one of the most effective methods of transmitting telecommunications.

Where these fibre optic cables are laid on land, property rights must be obtained, trenches must be dug and ducts installed in order to house the fibre optic cable. Where the cable is to be laid under the sea, that cable must be armoured and laid properly in order to protect it from ship anchors and other hazards at sea.

As an example of the issues that arise in relation to a telecommunications project, this section will discuss fibre optic infrastructure projects and the issues that arise therewith.

20.2.1   What is a fibre network?

The chart below shows a typical fibre optic network, either terrestrial or submarine. The cable is laid in a ring in order to improve redundancy. Where the cable is cut at any point information can be transmitted from one point to another by going in the other direction around the circle. Where the software that drives the fibre optic system makes this change in direction automatically, it is known as a "self-healing" system. Out of this fibre optic ring or backbone radiate a number of "backhaul" circuits that connect the fibre optic ring to each point of presence ("POP"). At the POP, information is passed to another network. These POPs are often located in exchanges, where the fibre optic network is connected to multiple networks. The "last mile", which passes information from the exchange to individual consumers, is often across copper wires, unless the consumer has a "broadband" connection, which is either a fibre optic connection direct to the consumer or a coaxial cable (e.g. in a cable-TV network).

The equipment that sends signals from one part of the fibre optic network to another is not sufficiently powerful to send that signal an infinite distance. Therefore, where the distances are very large, repeater or amplifier sites will need to be installed in order to strengthen the signal and enable it to cover the distance required. In addition, where two cables are connected together or jointed this joint reduces the strength of the signal and the distance which that signal can travel. Faulty jointing can reduce the intended amplification of the signal and therefore the efficacy of the network.

FIBRE OPTIC RING

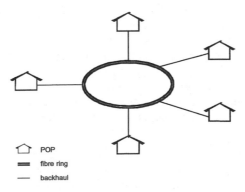

POP

fibre ring

backhaul

20.2.2   Property

For terrestrial fibre optic networks, access to long strips of land will be essential for installation. The project company will need the right to dig a trench in this strip of land, install ducts and the fibre cable and have periodic access to jointing chambers or the fibre optic cable itself for maintenance and the repair of defects. In order to find land available for the installation of fibre optic cables, the project company will often look to local authorities to allow it to install cables underneath the street or the pavement or alongside the highways. This raises the concern of traffic congestion and disruption during installation and whenever any access is necessary for maintenance or repair.

Where the project company is laying large amounts of fibre optic cable, property owners may be able to hold that project company hostage by requiring large payments for access to land. However, it is in the interest of the public generally to allow the installation of such telecommunications networks in order to improve services and connections provided to consumers. In order to facilitate this, most governments will provide specific legal regimes to allow telecommunications companies to have access to property for the installation of such infrastructure.

In the United Kingdom, the Communications Act 2003 provides for "electronic communications code powers" that give telecommunications operators and other registered providers the right to access public land and highways for the installation and operation of their infrastructure. This right to access is limited only by important overriding considerations raised by local authorities. In practice, it protects the telecommunications undertakers from excessive pricing of any such access, but it does not protect them from the demands of local authorities. For example, in 1999 and 2000, when a significant amount of fibre optic infrastructure was being installed, local authorities were requiring telecommunications undertakers to share trenches in order to reduce the disruption caused by digging up the roads. In addition, in certain popular holiday destinations, telecommunications undertakers were required to delay implementing such works until low season when less disruption would be caused.

Other more innovative methods have been used for obtaining access to property. British Waterways, the entity that controls the canal network in England, entered into commercial arrangements with a subsidiary of Marconi to provide access for fibre optic cables along the canal footpaths, where disruption to the public would be limited and environmental damage minimal. Some operators entered into agreements with water and sewage companies in order to obtain access to sewerage systems within large cities. They were able to run fibre optic cable through the existing sewer network without disruption of above-ground traffic. Others obtained access from Eurotunnel in order to cross the English Channel without taking the risk of laying submarine cables in one of the busiest shipping lanes in the world.

Even if access to land is obtained, the project company will need to consider whether or not it maintains property rights in the fibre optic cable once it is installed in the land. In many countries, this legal regime is unclear. Although the project company has a right to install, operate and maintain such cable networks in and through public land, in many cases the company does not have an ownership right in the asset that is the fibre optic cable.

20.2.3   Construction contracts

Construction contracts for the implementation of fibre optic telecommunications infrastructure must address a number of issues that are specific to this sector and the nature of the associated works.   The works for a fibre optic project will generally involve digging a trench and installing ducts into that trench. The ducts will connect onto jointing chambers where different lengths of fibre optic cable are spliced together, and regeneration sites, where repeater or amplification equipment is installed. The ducts will also lead to nodes, where the fibre optic cable connects onto different cables within the same system, and POPs where the fibre optic network connects onto other networks.   These nodes and POPs allow the fibre optic cable to transmit voice and data onto different systems or to different users such that all of the different telecommunications systems are in fact one large complex telecommunications system with enormous interconnectivity.

20.2.3.1   *Installing cable*

The fibre optic cable is installed into the ducts either by pulling or blowing. When the ducts are installed, the contractor may leave a wire in each of the ducts. That wire will travel from one end of the duct to the other and allow the contractor to tie one end of the wire onto the fibre optic cable and then physically pull the cable through the duct. There is obviously a limit as to the weight of cable that can be pulled through the duct, and therefore limitations as to the length of duct between two jointing chambers. The other method is to ensure that the duct when installed is airtight. A disc is placed at the end of the cable and placed into the duct. Air-pressure is applied to the duct and the cable is "blown" through the duct. Again, there are physical limitations as to how much weight and length of fibre optic cable can be blown through the duct, and therefore the distance between jointing chambers.

The POPs constructed by the contractor may involve co-location facilities. Co-location facilities house the equipment for several different telecommunications operators. Each will have a network connection into that co-location facility that connects onto its system. Installation of cables and equipment into a third party's facility to interface with equipment belonging to other third parties raises a number of interface issues.

20.2.3.2   *Site selection*

For terrestrial fibre optic networks, access to land for installation of the ducts and the cable, and rights of way over jointing chambers, repeater stations and other facilities is essential to the ongoing operation and maintenance of the infrastructure.

Part of the risk relating to rights of way and the access to land is the route selection. The fibre optic network will follow a footprint. The cable route will follow the land access that fits most easily with the legal rights available to the project company and the engineering methods necessary to install the ducts and cable on that site. Site conditions will have a significant influence on the cost of installing a fibre optic cable route. The contractor will need to install ducts and cable into carriageways, footways and verges. The condition of the site will include the nature of subsurface soil, the presence of manmade obstructions and crossing, or sharing infrastructure with, other pipes, cables or conduits.

Where the cable route can follow a road, railway, canal, transmission line or pipeline, the installation may be easier. In more difficult site conditions, where non-standard trenching methods are necessary, the construction costs can increase exponentially. Difficult conditions include the need to tunnel under obstructions, install cable along bridges and aqueducts and avoid subsurface impediments.

Also, the longer the total length of the cable, the more expensive the project becomes. Given the importance of the cost of the cable as an element of the total cost of construction, cable length may form an important part of the selection of the cable route. Where the cable length increases significantly, the project company may need to install additional repeater sites in order to enable the signal to traverse the length of the cable. Where additional cable length will increase the number of repeater sites necessary, this can have a significant influence on the total cost of construction.

20.2.3.3   Completion

Specific arrangements will need to be established to verify completion of the works. Completion testing will consider not only the nature of the individual pieces of equipment, but also the testing of their interdependencies and of the performance of the network as a whole. Each bit of equipment will need to be able to "talk" to each other bit of equipment. This testing can normally only be performed once the whole of the system has been installed.

In some cases, the project company may permit sectional completion. This means that the contractor does not have to complete the whole of the works before achieving completion. It will be entitled to complete just part of the works, and achieve completion for that section. This is normally only acceptable where that section is sufficiently "stand alone" that it has an inherent value. Where revenue can be obtained from that single section, then it makes sense for the project company to permit acceptance of that section before acceptance of the whole. The risk for the project company is that normally as the contractor achieves acceptance of a section the earlier its liabilities for the remaining parts of the system will be reduced. In addition, it is difficult to identify defaults in the accepted section where difficulties arise when testing later sections. Comprehensive provisions will need to be implemented in order to allow the project company to "claw-back" the earlier acceptance of a section where testing of later sections identifies difficulties in the accepted section.

20.2.4   Operation issues

During the operation phase of a fibre optic project, a variety of specific issues require consideration. Fibre optic products are less employee-intensive than many projects. Besides the ability to react quickly to defects that may arise in the infrastructure, the operation of fibre optic projects is very centralised, focused on self-healing systems running sophisticated software to match capacity with demand.

20.2.4.1   Operation and maintenance

Fibre optic networks may involve operation and maintenance contracts. These contracts will include many of the conditions typical of other operation and maintenance arrangements, but with far more focus on technology. The responsiveness of the operation and maintenance contractor to the requirements of consumers and the project company is far more important in a telecommunications project. In a fibre optic infrastructure project, the operator will need to monitor the operation of the network and move information through the network in the manner most efficient for consumers. This is normally performed automatically by specialist software.

The operator will need to be in a position to remedy any defect or replace any faulty equipment as quickly as possible. The redundancy available in most networks will facilitate this task, making it possible to continue operation even though a major piece of equipment has a default. But once that redundancy has been lost, it is important to return the system to its full availability and functionality as quickly as possible. Therefore the operator will need to respond quickly to any such defect, and performance will be measured against response and repair times as well as routine maintenance.

Technology will change very rapidly during the period of the project. The operator will generally be required to implement new technology and refresh any obsolete technology or equipment. In some cases this technology refresh will require the replacement of certain parts of the hardware or software platforms, in particular where that platform is no longer compatible with the latest technology. In addition, the lenders or the project company may be uncomfortable with technology that has not yet been proven.

20.2.4.2   Network operation centres

An important part of the operation of a fibre optic network is the network operation centre ("NOC"). This centre holds all of the important equipment that manages the system and implements the software that manages transmission of information across the system and identifies faults as soon as possible. It can also be used to manage consumer needs, pricing and market information in relation to available capacity.

The project company may enter into a network management contract in order to appoint an operator to manage the NOC. The project company may also want to have a back-up NOC, in the event that a major failure affects its primary NOC. A NOC can also be leased, on a short- or long-term basis, either as the principal NOC or a back-up NOC. The reliability and cost of these arrangements will be extremely important to the revenue to be received by the project company and therefore the protection of the interests of lenders and equity investors alike.

20.2.4.3   Lease and sale of ducts

The amount of construction and installation of ducts and fibre optic cable in Western Europe and the United States in the late 1990s and early 2000s resulted in a market for the sale or swap of ducts. Where one operator has ducts in one area but wants ducts in another, that operator may choose to swap ducts with another operator. Different accounting treatment opportunities can make this duct swap more attractive than purchases or installation. This accounting treatment will need to be considered carefully given some unfortunate results in the United States with accounting irregularities following on from such swaps, and consequent changes in the accountancy treatment of asset swaps.

An alternative approach may be the sale of existing ducts or fibre optic cable. This is of particular interest for telecommunications companies that have become insolvent or must otherwise reduce their debt and therefore sell assets. As noted above, the legal ownership of ducts and fibre optic cable that have been installed into public land may be unclear. This generally results in different contractual and legal solutions. The sale of the "indefeasible right of use" (an "IRU"), whereby the operating company sells all the rights that it has in the duct or fibre optic cable without claiming to transfer title, which it may not own, may avoid some of the difficulties regarding ownership of the installed ducts and cables.

20.2.5   Offtake contracts

Offtake arrangements in relation to fibre optic infrastructure projects can cover a range of different variations. In certain cases, the operator installs fibre optic infrastructure for its own use in order to sell capacity directly to end users. The revenues obtained from such capacity follow market pricing and will depend largely on the nature of consumers served by the operator, the location of the operator and the type of services that the operator can provide.

In some cases, in addition to building for themselves, operators build additional capacity, e.g. ducts or sub-ducts which are empty or with cables installed, which can then be sold or traded with competitors. In this way, the operator offsets the total cost of construction, obtaining lower cost capacity of ducts or fibre optic cables for its own use. Installed fibre optic cable can also be leased as "dark fibre", where repeater stations and other equipment have not been installed, but only dark cable is made available, already installed in ducts, but not connected to any network, and not lit. The fibres within a cable or the cable itself can either be leased, sold or provided through an IRU.

The operator may also offer to competitors managed bandwidth services, whereby the project company owns, maintains and operates the installed cable and equipment in order to provide a large-scale user with large amounts of bandwidth between specific points. The sale of bandwidth can take the form of a forward purchase of services or capacity, before the infrastructure in installed, in order to ensure a sufficient revenue stream to obtain financing and attract investment.

The provision of services by the operator may also be provided in the form of the outsourcing of telecommunications services within the context of a given company. Where a company has, or needs, significant communication infrastructure between different locations, that company may hire a telecommunications operator to manage those facilities, or install and provide such facilities, at a lesser price than the company may be able to provide such services for itself. This service management, known as outsourcing, is discussed further in chapter 22.

20.2.6   Lenders' security

Lenders to a fibre optic infrastructure project may encounter certain challenges in relation to the security package that will be available to them. The individual pieces of equipment may be available as security for the lenders. However, given the rate and pace of technology improvements in the telecommunications sector, these assets and equipment over which the lenders have security may not be worth much within a short period of their installation. In addition, given the differences in technical requirements of different systems, that equipment may not be wanted by other operators or usable for other projects.

Security over underlying assets such as ducts or fibre optic cables may not be available to the lenders where those ducts and cables have been installed in public land. The ownership regime for such ducts and cables may not be sufficiently clear to provide the lenders with comfort that they have appropriate security rights.

Given the importance of the role of service providers to the project company, such as maintenance and operation, network management services and technology refresh, the lenders may take a certain amount of comfort from the existence of direct agreements with those subcontractors. The services provided by these subcontractors focus on essential technology, equipment and software. Rights over these contracts may be even more important than the operation and maintenance agreements under projects in most other sectors.

In many cases, the lenders may have to satisfy themselves with security over shares in the various companies involved in the project. This may include asset management companies, operating companies and revenue producing companies. Fibre optic telecommunications projects often cross several different jurisdictions. In these cases, arrangements may need to be made with companies in a variety of jurisdictions, and therefore the available security may differ significantly between these jurisdictions. The potential benefits of splitting the construction contract in such a large, multi-jurisdictional fibre optic infrastructure project should be considered carefully. The splitting of construction contracts is discussed further in chapter 11.

Chapter 21

Water and Sanitation

Water, water, everywhere
And all the boards did shrink
Water, water, everywhere
Nor any drop to drink.

Samuel Taylor Coleridge 1772-1834,
The Rime of the Ancient Mariner (1798) pt. 2

Water is a finite resource. Although the earth and its atmosphere contain large amounts of water, 90 per cent. of this water is saline in the form of sea water. A majority of the remaining fresh water is trapped in the polar icecaps. Only 0.7 per cent. of the earth's water is contained in freshwater lakes, rivers, accessible aquifers and the atmosphere in a constant cycle of movement from the sea to the atmosphere to the land and back to the sea.

Not everyone has access to clean water or sewerage facilities. As the world population grows and congregates in small areas in search of urban opportunity, limited water resources are being continually stretched. Developing countries are particularly vulnerable to the lack of access to safe water supplies and adequate sanitation. In 1980, approximately 44 per cent. of people in developing countries had access to safe water supplies. This number had risen to only 61 per cent. by 1998. Similarly, in 1980, only 46 per cent. of people in developing countries had access to adequate sanitation. This figure had risen to 56 per cent. by 1998.

The need for private sector involvement in water and sanitation is critical.[475] The World Bank has estimated that over the coming decade some US$800 billion will need to be invested in the water sector. With some US$100 billion coming from international financial institutions and a further US$200 billion from government

---

[475] For further discussion of water and sanitation projects and private sector investment, see Delmon, Water Projects: A Commercial and Contractual Guide (2001).

financing, the private sector will need to provide the remaining US$500 billion.[476] The acceleration of demographic growth and urbanisation creates an increasing need for advanced technologies and management in the water sector, which is largely sourced from the private sector.

The opportunities for private sector investment in the water and sanitation sector are vast. As focus turns to the standards and scope of existing water and sanitation services, private sector investment stands out as one of the principal vehicles available for improving these services. Currently, only approximately five per cent. of the world's population receives water services from the private sector. Global consumption of water doubles every 20 years, at twice the rate of human population growth.[477] However, the number of private sector water companies active internationally is relatively small. The majority of the global players are based in France, Germany, Spain, the United States and the United Kingdom.

The following charts indicate the number of public private partnership ("PPP") water projects undertaken in middle and low income countries ("MLIC") from 1989 to 1999. The first chart shows the number of water projects commenced; and the second shows global distribution of water projects by region. They do not weigh projects based on investment value or population size.[478]

NUMBER OF MAJOR PPP MLIC WATER CONTRACTS STARTING IN YEAR

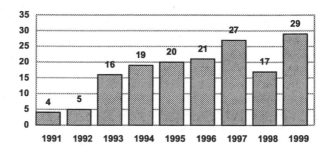

---

[476]   Owen, Masons Water Yearbook (1999-2000), from the preface by David Neil-Gallacher.

[477]   Barlow, "The Global Water Crisis and the Commodification of the World's Water Supply" International Forum on Globalisation (1999).

[478]   This data is derived from published sources and a questionnaire, and is taken from a paper presented at the Hague Forum on Public Private Partnerships by Richard Franceys, Associate Professor, Sector and Utility Management, at IHE Delft and a member of the United Kingdom's Ofwat Central Customer Service Committee, cited in Global Water Report 92 at 16-17 (31 March 2000).

PPP WATER CONTRACTS BY REGION

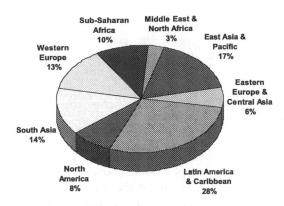

A number of factors have come together over the past two decades to motivate the public sector to turn its attention to private sector involvement in the water sector. These factors include:

> investment demands exceeding government and utility resources;

> underperformance of public sector utilities;

> inadequate technical and management resources in the public sector;

> lack of international competitiveness owing to the poor state of infrastructure; and

> success of early private sector investments.[479]

This chapter addresses a few of the issues that arise specific to projects in the water and sanitation sector. For ease of reading, reference to water projects and the water sector include sanitation and waste management.

21.1   Structures for Private Sector Participation in Water Projects

The water sector knows the greatest variety of structures and approaches used given the great diversity of needs to be resolved by private sector participation and the sensitivity of the water sector as critical to health and life. Although the commercial arrangements and contractual structures available for use in private sector involvement in public sector water projects are entirely flexible, three common approaches are used in the water sector: management contracts, BOT projects and concessions. These approaches are discussed here not as a restrictive

---

[479]   *Ibid* at 33.

exercise, limiting the public sector to certain approaches, but rather as examples of methods by which a project company can be involved in a water project.

21.1.1   Management contracts

The management contract involves the grantor contracting with the project company (which may or may not be a special purpose vehicle) as management contractor to undertake certain tasks. These tasks can range from training to operation; construction management to engineering. The grantor will define these terms according to its requirements and will generally maintain control over the ambit of the task and how it is carried out.

The intention of a management contract is that the grantor retain control and ultimate decision-making power over the project. The project company, for its part, will not want to accept risk for a situation over which it does not have control. The grantor will therefore generally retain the majority of the project risk. Where more risk is passed to the project company through the management contract, the project company will generally require a payment scheme which provides it with a benefit proportionate to the level of risk that it accepts and possibly some limitation on the decision-making powers of the grantor.

Under a management contract, the project company is paid for services rendered. It is also the grantor which generally bears the risk of increased cost if the scope of the project is different from that forecast, or possibly if costs increase.

The payment mechanism can be a very effective instrument for placing project risk on the project company. For example, where the price paid is partially based on performance, the project company will bear part of the risk of non-performance of the project. The payment scheme may include performance-specific portions, possibly structured as bonuses and penalties based on the achieved performance of the facility or system involved.

Management contracts are often used by multilateral agencies in order to inject special management skills into local water companies (for example, the incentive-based management contracts promoted by the EBRD). They allow the grantor to maintain substantial control of the services rendered and they do not require extensive resources to be invested before commencement. Management contracts may also be performed in stages; so that as each stage is completed and further information is obtained, the scope of the project can be changed in line with that new information.

Vivendi (now called Veolia Environnement) is a company that has focused on operating capabilities as the most effective private sector investment in water services. For example in Kazakhstan, a Vivendi project company entered into an operating agreement for the city of Almaty that involves the supply, purification and distribution of drinking water, the collection and treatment of waste water, and the billing and payment collection for the city. In this way, the grantor keeps ownership of the assets and the private sector provides its expertise in improving management and increasing the efficiency of billing and payment collection. It also permits the grantor to make the important decisions in relation to financing any needed capital investment, on the basis of information from the private sector on the need for such investment.[480]

21.1.2   BOT projects

Water and sewage treatment projects are increasingly let through BOT schemes.[481] As discussed in chapter 3, in a typical BOT project the grantor grants the right to a private company to develop and operate what would traditionally be a public sector project. The project company obtains financing for the project, procures the design and construction of the works and operates the facility during the specified period in return for a revenue stream provided by sale of its services. At the end of the specified period, the facility or system is transferred back to the grantor.

The project company will be remunerated during the operation of the facility by a single bulk purchaser (possibly the grantor or a utility) or a group of purchasers (such as industrial, corporate or public bodies) for providing services (such as sewage treatment or disposal). The capital cost is generally project financed.[482] The revenues generated from the operation phase are intended to cover operating costs, maintenance, repayment of debt principal (which represents a significant portion of development and construction costs), financing costs (including interest and fees), and a return for the shareholders.

21.1.2.1   Water purchase (or sewage treatment) agreement

The water purchase agreement secures the project payment stream. It obliges the water purchaser to procure a certain amount of project output or pay for an amount of project service (whether or not it is used) over a given time. A similar agreement will govern the discharge and treatment of sewage for a sewage treatment plant. The purpose of this agreement is to insulate the project company's revenue stream from market risk, and place a signification portion of this risk on the purchaser.

A water purchase agreement may not be necessary in some projects, such as the upgrade and operation of a water distribution system or a reservoir where no water or sewage treatment is involved. In such cases it is often the grantor who will pay the project company for use of the facilities concerned. The revenue stream and performance requirements will therefore be set out in the concession agreement.

21.1.2.2   Raw water supply agreement

For clean water treatment projects, the raw water supply agreement obliges a raw water supplier to deliver to the project company a specified quantity of raw water necessary for the operation of the project, at a certain level of quality for a set

---

[480]   Global Water Report 91 at 10 (17 March 2000).
[481]   For further discussion, see The World Bank (1997) supra note 256.
[482]   See chapter 4 for further discussion of project finance.

price. This is the input supply agreement for a water project, and allocates the risks associated with the price and availability of raw water away from the project company and to the supplier. In many jurisdictions no such agreement can be obtained and the project company must rely on water abstraction licences and the local authority's management of its water resources.

Different types of water projects may require other forms of supply or service agreements, for example in a sewage treatment project the project company will need to arrange for the removal and disposal of sludge or treated waste water. This type of agreement will require many of the same conditions and raise similar issues to those of the raw water supply agreement.

21.1.3   Concessions

The grantor may wish to transfer responsibility for water services in a specific area, such as collection, treatment or distribution, to the private sector. This can be accomplished by granting a full concession to a project company. It should be noted that there is no commonly agreed definition of a "concession" despite the existence of a French legal concept bearing this same name. However, for lack of more precise terminology, this chapter will use the term concession to describe the type of project discussed in this section.

21.1.3.1   Transfer of assets

A concession can involve the transfer of possession to the project company of all existing assets, including facilities or systems which are located in the area of the concession or which service that area. The project company will then maintain and operate the facility or system for a given period or it may be required to improve or build onto that facility or system and then provide the services over a specific period.

The concession is generally structured as a contractual arrangement between the grantor and the project company. The project company will often undertake to improve or refurbish existing assets and/or provide new capital assets. The grantor may prefer not to transfer ownership of assets, but rather grant to the project company a lease or licence over the assets. This will allow the grantor to repossess project assets immediately on termination, in order to ensure continued provision of services to consumers.

21.1.3.2   Delivery of services to consumers

The project company will generally be granted the right to undertake all specified services within an exclusive area and then to deliver services to consumers. The project company may bear the risk of non-payment by consumers and possibly also by public sector entities.

The primary difference in structure between a concession and a BOT project will be the origin and security of the revenue stream. The concession will not benefit from a single bulk purchaser, therefore the revenue stream will be subject, to some extent, to the market risk of actual use, the collection of tariffs from consumers and the level of tariffs that the project company is permitted to charge.

The project company will look to the consumer for payment, and will need the right to collect revenues directly from consumers and impose sanctions, such as penalty fees or (ultimately) disconnection, where consumers fail to pay.[483] This can be a difficult proposition for the grantor, owing to political and cultural attitudes towards private sector parties having such powers. The grantor may also need to restrict the rights it provides to the project company where it is illegal or politically impractical for the grantor to transfer to the project company rights or powers considered to be strictly public sector or "police" powers.

However, private involvement may necessitate government subsidies or financing, particularly where the government is not willing to put tariffs up to profitable levels or where substantial investment in capital works over the short-term is needed or desired. The level at which tariffs are set for water services can be an extremely political issue. Increasing and/or collecting tariffs may be difficult where a concordant culture has not been developed in the host country.

This point was illustrated in Cochabamba, Bolivia, where farmers were used to receiving water for free. The country was brought to a standstill by six days of rioting, during which nine people died, when the government proposed to increase water tariffs and force farmers to pay for water in order to fund significant capital works, including a dam. Although this uprising was the result of a combination of several different factors, including the government's attempts to restrict coca farming, it provides an unfortunate example of political and social tensions and sensitivities revolving around paying for the supply of water.[484]

21.1.4 Share or asset sale privatisation

Another method of introducing the private sector into water services is to privatise an existing public water company, either by selling shares in the company or selling its assets. The project company will be required to undertake certain work or provide services to a certain level as part of its entitlement to purchase the shares of a public company and therefore a share sale transaction often involves a concession agreement or some licensing or regulatory obligations. The transfer of the public company to the private sector may also be accomplished by a public offering of shares. Privatisation may be politically sensitive since it may be difficult to charge investors the actual cost of project assets, yet any undervaluation may appear to be "giving away" public assets.

In some circumstances complete divestiture of the public water company will be the most efficient option for the grantor. This will be the case in particular where the public water company is technically sound, and therefore a sale of shares or

---

[483]   These issues are discussed further in chapter 8.
[484]   Global Water Report 93 at 1 (14 April 2000).

management buyout can result in the desired improvements in management, consumer service and profitability.

However, the fact that the water company to be privatised is financially and technically healthy will not be enough to protect the grantor and the consumers. The grantor will need to ensure that the legal/regulatory regime that monitors and regulates the water sector is sufficiently robust, has the experience and resources, and the political will necessary to manage private sector involvement. Where this legal/regulatory regime does not exist or is insufficient, the grantor should consider implementing a contractual regime to compensate for these shortcomings, if only over the short-term, until the legal/regulatory regime can be adjusted as necessary.

21.2 Water Projects, BOTs and Concessions

The water sector does not always fit within the traditional project finance models developed for other sectors. The power sector has historically sought investment in generation capacity or large transmission projects with bulk purchasers of the generated energy or transmission capacity. Similarly, the transport sector has sought investment in new highways, bridges and railways with a forecast body of users from whom tolls, or for whom shadow tolls, may be collected, often with government guarantees of traffic forecasts. The water sector, on the other hand, needs private sector investors to provide services directly to consumers, to improve aspects of the water system which may not have a fixed or definable scope of work and to take the risk of the condition of existing assets. The classic BOT approach does not necessarily provide the flexibility and range of services sought from private sector investment in the water sector.

For this reason, water concessions have become more common, permitting the grantor to involve the private sector in a water project in a way which satisfies the grantor's requirements. Water concessions can provide the lenders with increased opportunities for lending, in particular over the long-term. However, lenders must take a flexible view of their financing requirements, setting aside the assumptions that they have built up through financing BOT projects, and permitting themselves to apply the basic concepts of financing to the needs and requirements of concessions.[485]

21.2.1 Why water projects often require concessions

In the water sector it is often not sufficient for private sector involvement to be limited to the provision of a new treatment plant under a BOT structure. Increases in treatment capacity may not provide the required benefits where leakages in the distribution system or inability to collect tariffs persist at chronic levels. Although private involvement may include development of water and sewage treatment plants, the water sector is also in need of private sector investment in areas such as distribution and customer services, which do not normally fit into the BOT

---

[485] This section is based on Delmon, "The Trouble with Water Projects" PFI 195 at 56-60 (2000).

structure. Water projects will therefore require high levels of creativity from those responsible for developing project structures.

The needs and nature of the water sector are therefore different from those sectors which have historically benefited from private sector investment and project finance, for example the power sector. It is often difficult for investors and financiers to appreciate the fundamental differences in the water sector. Particular investment needs in the water sector which are better suited to the concession structure are set out below.

21.2.1.1   Investment in distribution

Where one of the difficulties encountered by the water authority is the rate of leakage of the distribution system, adding further water treatment capacity will not provide the equivalent benefit of additional delivered treated water. The grantor may therefore look to the private sector to improve distribution capacity, reduce leakages and provide long-term maintenance to ensure that the condition of the distribution system is consistently monitored and improved. Where BOT projects are an effective method of increasing treatment capacity, a management contract or a concession may be the most efficient method of improving distribution and reducing leakage.

21.2.1.2   Improving management of the sector

The relevant water company may need to implement modern management approaches, particularly where the company's historic operating methods are unnecessarily labour intensive and not orientated towards the needs of consumers. Currently, the water sector is the domain of the public sector, with limited involvement of the private sector and only partially influenced by commercial forces. A concession involves the private sector in every aspect of the supply of water, and is therefore seen as providing the best method of improving management of the sector, reducing labour costs and improving service standards for consumers through the introduction of market forces and the technological and management capabilities of the private sector.

21.2.1.3   Relationships with consumers

The water authority may seek assistance from the private sector in its relationship with its consumers. Introducing commercial, and possibly competitive, pressures into the water sector can improve focus on consumer services, such as billing procedures, complaints procedures and emergency services provided to consumers. The private sector may also have superior technology or methodology, developed with a focus on consumer needs.

21.2.1.4   Political insulation

The involvement of the private sector through a concession arrangement may also provide some insulation for the grantor from the political powers wishing to make unpopular changes in the water system. For example, it may be a way of ensuring that future improvements to the system required by such political powers or by law will result in an increase in the tariffs which can be charged to consumers in an amount sufficient to provide at least some of the cost necessary to compensate the private sector investor. The increase in tariffs may also be a political issue, often unpopular with voters. The commercial necessity of increased tariffs where a private sector operator is involved may provide the water authority with the justification needed to make such a politically sensitive decision. A solemn lesson should be learned, however, from the experiences in Cochabamba where tariffs were increased before consumers could see any appreciable improvement in the services, resulting in violent public uprisings.

Concessions may be more politically acceptable than privatisation. An example would be Hungary, where the government has been hesitant to follow the path of privatisation because of the lack of political support for such an approach. Municipalities mistrust foreign companies, while the population at large may not understand the role of a foreign partner in the ownership of a utility.[486]

21.2.1.5   Comprehensive solution

The grantor may look to the private sector to fulfil a number of needs, to improve relations with consumers (making the company more commercial in its outlook and reputation) and to improve the system (reducing leakages and adding new connections or increased capacity). As discussed above, this comprehensive approach cannot normally be fulfilled by a BOT structure. The water authority will effectively need to transfer to the private sector the whole of the system in order for the project company to provide a comprehensive solution to these many needs. Although BOT water projects have in the past represented the vanguard of project financing, water projects often need to focus on the private sector providing an "abstraction-to-end-user" service via concessions.

21.2.2   Problems with concessions

Organisations looking to structure, or bid for, a concession, will encounter certain issues which are not commonly encountered in BOT projects. The following is a discussion of a few of these issues.

21.2.2.1   Future expansion

Rather than being bound to a strict scope of works to be built or improvements to be made, the project company will be bound to more general obligations to improve the quality of water delivered, the level of leakage of the distribution system or the quality of service rendered to consumers. The need for capital expenditure will not usually be clear at commencement of the project. The concession must be flexible to allow the project company to manage the

---

[486]   Global Water Report at 13 (14 April 2000).

circumstances encountered on site. The project company must have the right and the resources to respond to the needs of the project, as they arise.

For example, the best way to manage levels of leakage may not be identified until later in the period of the concession, possibly after the project company has taken over the project and has had the time to perform a series of tests and due diligence on the existing facilities. This may necessitate the project company agreeing with the grantor on rolling programmes for capital investment against an investment programme or budget based on the amount of income obtained by the project company or as required to satisfy the performance criteria placed on the project company. The permitted level of tariffs charged to consumers is also likely to have an important impact on the value and nature of capital works undertaken by the project company.

21.2.2.2 *Existing assets*

The grantor will usually transfer ownership, or use, of existing assets to the project company for the purpose of performance of the project company's obligations. These assets may not be identified and categorised before the project company takes over control. Further, the condition of those assets and need for replacement or refurbishment may not be clear until well into the concession. The condition of existing assets represents a serious risk for the project company and one which it will be difficult to pass on to any construction contractor or operator. The grantor's requirements will need to allow the project company sufficient flexibility to manage these conditions.

21.2.2.3 *Existing business*

Unlike BOT projects, concessions generally involve an existing business, which may be taken over by the project company (another option is to transfer the assets of the company only, the liabilities of the company remaining with the government). The transfer of an existing business generally requires extensive due diligence by the project company to ascertain the extent of the risks inherent in such an existing business. Where this business is run by an existing company, that company may be transferred in whole or in part to the project company. Often, the personnel of the existing water company will be transferred to the project company in order to provide training and continuity and to satisfy the requirements of public sector labour unions, which are generally hostile to any form of privatisation which might threaten their members' employment or benefits.

The transfer of an existing business and, in particular, the transfer of public sector employees will need to be managed carefully by the project company. To some extent these risks can be managed more efficiently by the public sector prior to the entry into the concession agreement rather than during the period of the concession. However, some residual risks may nevertheless remain with the private sector. Consideration may also need to be given to the transfer of existing liabilities, unidentified liabilities and contractual or other obligations which may bind the project company's activities in the future.

21.2.2.4   *Tariff levels and payments*

The level at which tariffs are set for water services can be an extremely political issue. Historically, water tariffs may have been used to subsidise certain elements of society, specific industries or public sector entities. More often, public water companies are subsidised and tariffs are not charged, charged at very low rates or not collected. Private sector involvement may necessitate formal arrangements with the project company for government subsidies or financing, particularly where the government is not willing to put tariffs up to profitable levels or where substantial investment in capital works is needed or desired.

Many countries suffer from a culture of non-payment of water bills. In certain cases, consumers are not charged for water, or non-payment of water bills rarely (if ever) results in sanctions imposed on the defaulting consumer. Overcoming a culture of non-payment often requires a concerted effort between the project company and the grantor. In many cases this will be a very sensitive political issue, that will require careful management. High profile public relations and advertising campaigns may be required.

The water authority will often look to the private sector to help improve rates of collection. The project company may therefore need the right to impose sanctions on consumers who do not pay. It may want to launch a campaign in order to raise awareness of the water sector and publicise the fact that water is a commodity like electricity and equally worth the cost of an increased tariff.

21.2.3   Challenges in financing concessions

Limited recourse financing permits the project company to obtain financing against the future revenue stream of the project, isolating project risk and liabilities in a special purpose vehicle. This type of financing has achieved a high level of sophistication in the development of IPPs and in the oil and gas industry.

This sophisticated market has established concepts of bankability based on BOT projects, with a fixed scope of works and secure or commercially viable offtake arrangements, which in some cases may involve an element of market risk. Water concessions exhibit characteristics quite different from those of a BOT project. Although lenders have shown a level of flexibility in providing financing for structures involving offtake market risks, such as merchant power plants, an additional level of creativity and flexibility will be required of lenders to develop a fluid market for financing water concessions.[487]

21.2.3.1   *Existing income stream*

Most concessions will involve an existing water system which is to be taken over by the project company and improved. This will provide the lenders with the

---

[487]   No pun intended ...

security of an existing revenue stream, a captive pool of consumers, an existing financial structure and a technical/management structure that is already mobilised.

An existing income stream can provide some security for the repayment of debt. It may also permit debt repayment to commence before the major capital works have been completed, unlike in a BOT project where the revenue stream generally does not commence until shortly after the end of the construction period. Sponsors may endeavour to replace equity investment in cash with the expected cash flow of the existing business. However, as a general premise, the grantor will involve the private sector in a concession either because the existing revenue stream is insufficient to finance capital expenditure needs and/or to meet costs, or because the condition of existing assets is so poor that the revenue stream is not sufficiently certain to continue. The existing income may therefore only be of limited comfort to the lenders.

21.2.3.2   Existing assets

A typical concession arrangement will involve the transfer of existing assets, or the right to use them, to the project company. Depending on the nature of the rights transferred by the public sector, the presence of existing assets can provide the lenders with additional security. This contrasts with a BOT project where the lenders will not normally have available to them any substantial project assets against which to secure their lending until the works have been completed at the end of the construction period. The lenders therefore lend to a BOT project during the construction period and delay servicing of the debt until some time after the end of the construction period. The lenders have very little security during the construction period, which is the period during which they bear the greatest amount of project risk.

In a concession, the lenders will have security over existing assets from the date of commencement. Thus, this initial construction period will not represent the same level of project risk for the lenders in a concession as it does in a BOT project. However, the exact nature of these existing assets may not have been identified in detail before signature of the concession. Similarly, the condition of these assets may not be clear since many of the assets will be buried and therefore may be difficult to survey.

21.2.3.3   Scope of works

The scope of works for a concession will not be defined to the same extent as would be possible in a BOT project. The concession will normally provide for a rolling programme of works, to be developed as the project company is able to perform further review of the state of the existing assets, and as it is able to assess the best way to improve project performance. This rolling programme of works will usually be agreed with the grantor (or, failing such agreement, determined by dispute resolution mechanisms), subject to defined parameters. The preliminary programme of works, typically between three and six years, may be agreed by the date of commencement of the project. This means that the lenders may only be committed to lend for the first programme period.

The lenders often use the construction programme as a trigger event for a default by the project company. However, in a concession, the lenders will need to take a more flexible view of the approach to construction of the works. The absence of a specified scope of works means that the construction programme will not provide an appropriate time frame for default events under the credit agreement.

21.2.3.4   Future works financing and shared security

The scope of works for a concession will evolve over time. The financing needs of the project company will therefore change as the project evolves. This can either provide the lenders with an opportunity or a disadvantage.

Two possible scenarios arise. Firstly, the scope of works may be defined, but separated into phases to be undertaken once a set of conditions are satisfied. Second, the scope of works may depend on decisions made during the concession period, and only a preliminary programme of works will be identified at commencement. Each of these two scenarios will require flexibility from the lenders.

In the first scenario, where all the financing required is not committed at the outset, the capital works programme will provide a clear picture of the financing needs of the project over the period of the concession, and therefore the lenders will have a reasonable forecast of the future financing needs of the project. However, there may be a need for the lenders to share project security in order to permit the project company to obtain financing from other sources, should the initial lenders be unwilling to lend to further phases of the works.

21.3   Water and Sewage Treatment

The following provides a basic description of water and sewage treatment, to explain how these processes work and some of the challenges that arise from a technical perspective. This is meant to assist in identifying and understanding some of the key risks associated with the water sector.

21.3.1   Sewage treatment

Sewage treatment usually involves a series of phases, each designed to reduce progressively the environmental and health impact of the effluent. Sewage is carried in the effluent either as solid matter or in dilute, suspended solids. While several performance criteria are used to assess the performance of a sewage treatment works (mainly, the removal of silts, BOD and ammonia), each level of treatment can be judged by its success in removing these solids from the effluent stream prior to its final discharge. There is a fairly close relationship between ultimate solids removal and the lowering of an effluent stream's BOD. The stages of sewage treatment are described below.

21.3.1.1   Preliminary/screening

This simple screening procedure is intended to remove solids from waste water. It does not reduce the environmental impact of the resulting sludge.

21.3.1.2   Primary

The first stage of the treatment process involves physical treatment, where the effluent is placed in a settlement tank. After a period of settlement, solids are left behind and the liquid effluent is then discharged.

21.3.1.3   Secondary

The first effort at biological treatment to remove suspended solids begins during secondary treatment. The effluent trickles through inert materials, so that it comes into contact with micro-organisms, which oxidise and clarify the effluent. Examples of such processes include granular activated carbon absorption, where water is passed through granules of activated carbon. Contaminants such as volatile organic compounds ("VOCs") adhere to the carbon and are thus removed from the water. Air stripping uses oxygen to remove dissolved gases and volatile substances from water, accomplished by bubbling air through the water. Packed tower aeration is a variation of the air stripping treatment process. Water flows down through packing material, while air flows upward to "strip" VOCs from the water.

21.3.1.4   Tertiary

This catch-all term covers the further nutrient removal from the remaining effluent by filtration. Tertiary treatment usually refers to chemical treatment in order to achieve the removal of nutrients such as nitrogen and phosphorous from the effluent.

21.3.1.5   Advanced treatment and disinfection

Reverse osmosis membranes are adopted where space is at a premium. Treatment can be extended to include further disinfection by exposing the effluent to ultra-violet light or ozone prior to its final discharge.

21.3.1.6   Sludge treatment

Sludge treatment involves the reduction of sludge volume and rendering of the sludge suitable for disposal/reuse.

Digestion is a process for stabilising sewage sludge before application to land. It involves heating the sludge to 40°C to reduce the number of bacteria and pathogens. Anaerobic digestion (or pasteurisation) generates methane, which can be extracted for energy recovery.

In the process of pasteurisation, sewage sludge is more extensively treated than digested sludge. By heating the sludge to 60°C for several days, all pathogens and bacteria are removed, making it satisfactory for a wide range of agricultural applications. The main techniques are known as "anaerobic digestion" and "composting".

Sludge can be used for a number of purposes, from fertiliser to building materials to animal feed. These uses can encounter political resistance due to public reaction and cultural taboos.

21.3.2   Water treatment

Available raw water will be of varying quality, which can be classified. EU classifications range from "Very Good" (1A) quality waters that have no appreciable indicators of human activities, to "Poor" (III) quality waters that support a significantly degraded community of plant and animal species, and "Bad" (IV) quality waters that (with the exception of some fungi and algae) are usually incapable of supporting life.

Where raw water must be treated before distribution to consumers, the nature and extent of treatment will depend on the quality of the raw water and the requirements placed on water that can be delivered to consumers. The following describes a typical water treatment facility, whose main source of raw water is a river, by providing an explanation of the diagram of this system provided at the back of this chapter.[488] The numbered description corresponds to the numbered images on the diagram.

21.3.2.1   *Sources of water and abstraction (number 1)*

Water from abstraction (from boreholes, reservoirs, rivers or the like) flows through screens to remove large pieces of debris. A sophisticated water quality monitoring system checks the water for traces of pollution and other chemicals such as nitrates. Turbidity (how "cloudy" or dirty water is owing to suspended solids or silt borne along by the river) is measured, and the amount of oxygen in the water is checked (low oxygen content can be caused by pollution).

21.3.2.2   *Main and standby pumps (numbers 2 & 3)*

The main pumping station lifts the raw water from the bottom of the supply shaft into the concrete pre-ozonation tanks. From this point the water flows round the site by gravity.

21.3.2.3   *Pre-ozonation tanks (number 4)*

This building houses tanks fitted with turbines, generally two per tank. Ozonised air produced in the ozone generation plant is pumped to the pre-ozonation tanks. The ozone is mixed and dissolved into the raw water using high-speed turbines.

---

[488]   This section was adapted from a description of the Iver treatment works, owned by Three Valleys Water plc in the United Kingdom.

The tank may have a system to remove the floating debris where the raw water has a high algae concentration. Thermal destructors eliminate any excess ozone, which ensures that any ozone not dissolved into the water does not escape into the atmosphere.

Ozone, acting as a powerful oxidant and disinfectant, kills some of the algae and bacteria present in the raw river water. Ozone breaks back down to oxygen, giving a higher oxygen content to the water, and helping to give it a "fresher" taste. The dead algae forms a film on the top of the water which is removed before the water flows to the next process.

The advantages of pre-ozonation include the following:

> oxidation of free and combined iron and manganese, which generally avoids pH reduction at later stages;

> colour and taste are removed by oxidation of the unsaturated compounds;

> improvement of the clarifier stage, which alters surface charges on particles encouraging them to join together resulting in better removal of dissolved organic carbon;

> algae destruction or growth control; and

> replacement of pre-chlorination, especially on highly turbid water, avoids production of trihalo methanes and heavy halogen organic compounds.

21.3.2.4   Pulsator clarifiers (number 5)

The next stage of treatment, the pulsator clarifiers removes the suspended solids from the raw water to reduce the turbidity. This is done by adding strictly controlled amounts of coagulants which help bind the solids together to make them heavier. Sulphuric acid is occasionally added to adjust the pH balance – the acidity or alkalinity of the water. It may also help coagulation.

The raw water with the coagulant flows into the bottom of a large chamber. As the water flows upwards the solid particles join together and reach a point where they start to move downwards under their combined weight against the flow of incoming water. A balance is reached and the fresh solids coming in add to the combined solids already present and form what is called a "sludge blanket". A vacuum pulsator creates shock waves which help to form the blanket.

The clarified, cleaner water is carried away to the next stage. The sludge is collected at the base of the chamber and pumped away to the sludge pumping station. The sludge thickening tanks concentrate the sludge produced by the pulsator clarifiers. The thickened sludge is pumped to lagoons. The water recovered is returned to one of the shafts just before the main pumping station.

21.3.2.5   Intermediate ozonation tanks (number 6)

Water flows under gravity into the intermediate ozonation tanks. Reaction tanks, each divided into four compartments, allow a maximum contact time of three minutes at maximum flow rate. The advantages of intermediate ozonation include improving the final (biological) filter run. Ozone splits organic molecules into more biologically active products and increases the dissolved oxygen content, so that treatment through granulated activated carbon ("GAC") filters is much improved. The organoleptic (colour, taste and odour) qualities are improved and micro-pollutants, e.g. phenols and certain detergents and pesticides, are partially oxidised, making them easier to treat.

21.3.2.6   Ozone generator house (number 7)

Ozone is produced by tubular generators. Air, or oxygen, is compressed, dried and passed through an ozonator where a high voltage discharge changes part of the oxygen into ozone. Ozone is usually added at two stages in the water treatment process (see numbers 4 and 6).

The whole ozone generation and distribution to pre-ozonation and inter-ozonation tanks is controlled by a computer based in the ozone building. The computer monitors water flow rates and makes adjustments, controlling the amount of ozone sent to each set of tanks.

The pre-ozonation treatment rate will be set and adjusted by plant operators. The inter-ozonation treatment rate will be set by the plant operator or automatically adjusted to maintain the correct residual ozone level at the outlet of the third compartment.

21.3.2.7   Final stage filtration (number 8)

After passing through intermediate ozonation, water then flows to filters packed with GAC. Water flows from the top of the filter through the GAC bed which traps the remaining solids and organic matter.

Filters are backwashed, to maintain their efficiency. First the GAC is air-scoured, which makes its grains rub together to loosen attached material. Then clean water, flowing in the opposite direction to normal, washes the filter clean. Material which has been retained by the filter floats to the surface and is removed to wash water tanks. The "activated" carbon slowly becomes exhausted and is monitored to see if regeneration is needed or if new carbon is required.

21.3.2.8   Disinfection – the final stage (number 9)

Chlorine is added to the water as it enters a contact tank where the flow is slowed by a series of baffles or obstacles to a constant speed to ensure good mixing and contact between the chlorine and water. Orthophosphoric acid is dosed at the contact tank. The addition of orthophosphoric acid reduces the lead level in the water where water is provided via lead pipes. The alkalinity of the water may be adjusted by the addition of caustic soda before flowing into the treated water reservoir tanks.

HOW RAW WATER IS ABSTRACTED AND TREATED

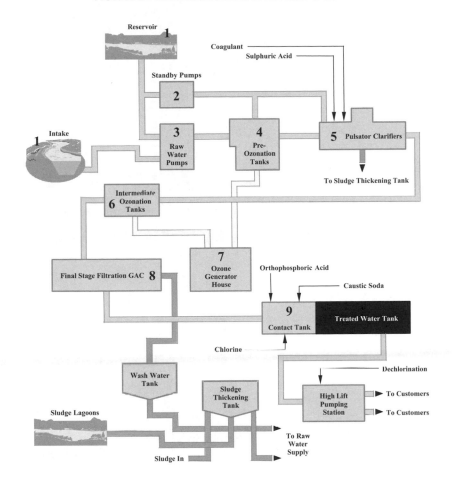

Chapter 22

Outsourcing

It's so much more friendly with two.

Piglet,
Pooh's Little Instruction Book

Another approach to managing infrastructure and sharing the risks associated with infrastructure is outsourcing. This involves a public or private sector entity appointing a company to take over a given service currently provided internally by the entity. This usually involves a specialist service provider taking over that service from the grantor where the grantor does not have special expertise in this area. An example would be the management of water treatment infrastructure for refineries, power plants or other industrial plant. The company running the relevant plant does not have specialist expertise in managing water infrastructure, nor can it benefit from economies of scale in relation to personnel, replacement parts and new infrastructure. For this reason, the entity running the plant will outsource the water treatment facility and services to a specialist company. Outsourcing is particularly popular with information technology ("IT"), where specialist expertise is key to managing IT efficiently and continuous updating of infrastructure through a specialist's understanding of the sector and economies of scale in purchasing technology can be key to the continued success of the enterprise.

This chapter will address a number of the most important issues and risks which arise in relation to outsourcing. The intention here is to address outsourcing in any number of sectors. It will not focus on any specific sector; however, sector issues will apply to outsourcing as with any other project, as discussed in earlier chapters in this book.

Many of the issues to be discussed in this chapter may also be relevant to concession arrangements. In both outsourcing and concessions, a service is handed over to a project company, and that project company will be responsible for certain internal processes and interfaces with the grantor's customers. Outsourcing may or may not involve collecting revenue directly from the grantor's customers, as would a concession. For further discussion of concessions see chapter 3.

22.1   Risk Allocation

The key to outsourcing is to pass to the expert project company the risks and responsibilities associated with the sector in which the project company is expert. The grantor, on the other hand, should retain commercial risks and control over its other operations.

Transfer of risk does not necessarily correspond with transfer of control. Though the project company will want to have control over issues associated with the risks that it is taking, the grantor will be very hesitant to relinquish control over very visible and sensitive operations. This will be of particular importance where the outsourced services involve a direct interface with the grantor's other infrastructure or services. Indeed, in certain regulated industries the operator may be restricted from contracting out control over (as opposed to daily operation of) its core activities.

At the same time, the retention of control by the grantor should not inhibit the project company's ability to perform its service. The project company will not want to find itself in a position where it is required to continue to provide services even though payments are not being made or the grantor is otherwise preventing the project company from operating efficiently.

22.2   Governance

Outsourcing structures require a certain amount of governance by the grantor. The grantor will need to obtain sufficient information and have the resources necessary to understand the operation of the services and whether the project company has complied with its different obligations. Proper governance may also require the grantor to have certain controls over decision-making and notification of specified events. When making the decision to outsource a service, the grantor will need to maintain sufficient commercial and technical expertise to manage this flow of information and ensure proper governance, and may also wish to retain sufficient capacity to take back operations, or re-tender operations to another contractor, in the event the project company fails.

The grantor may retain certain audit rights over information gathered by the project company. This may be full transparency, with a right to view the project company's books and the records of its operational services. It may also involve the provision of detailed information by the project company to the grantor, in the form of unaudited accounts, audited accounts, quarterly accounts, personnel records, operational reports, construction reports, programme and progress reports and specific information about the continued performance of the project. This information may be provided on an open book basis, where the grantor can see all of the project company's current books, or on a more restricted basis. These audit rights may also need to limit the sites on which the grantor can perform its investigations, the nature of its access to project company and subcontractor personnel and the frequency of access by the grantor.

Independent auditors may be used where there is any concern about confidentiality, interference by the grantor's personnel or concerns that the grantor's personnel may misinterpret the information provided. For example, in the water industry in the United Kingdom, an independent expert "reporter" is used to verify the information provided by the water operators to OFWAT. The cost of such an expert will need to be allocated between the parties.

The cost of information gathering will also need to be allocated between the parties. This may depend on the nature of the information provided and whether further information requirements from the grantor, in addition to those set out in the contract, identify information that is inconsistent with that of those given by the project company or indicative of a breach of other misdeed by the project company. Often the grantor is required to pay for the cost of information audits, unless that audit uncovers some failure by the project company or inaccuracy in the information provided by the project company.

In order to improve interface management and encourage efficient governance, the parties may wish to appoint relationship managers, whose job will be to manage the interface between the project company and the grantor. These parties can manage the flow of information, communications, invoices and materials between the project company and the grantor. They will also be required to meet on a frequent basis and issue to the parties reports pertaining to their meetings and the functioning of the project.

These relationship representatives will need to be appointed by each party, and possibly reviewed or approved by the other party. There may also be provision for the removal of a representative. The grantor will generally require a right to remove the project company's representative where it is not happy with that representative's activity within the context of the meeting or reporting function or the character or abilities of that representative.

22.3   Exclusivity

The project company will seek to have exclusivity of the provision of the services, to avoid the grantor obtaining all or part of the services from another provider. The grantor will wish to resist granting exclusivity since it would deny the potential for market competition and the influence of market forces on pricing and the standard of services provided. The grantor may instead provide a minimum revenue or volume of service commitment to the project company in order to ensure a minimum revenue stream to protect the project company's investment. This would then protect the project company while maintaining the flexibility of the grantor to implement competition from other service providers.

The project company will generally be required to work with other service providers. This would be particularly important where the service provided by the project is integrated within the grantor's other activities and therefore the project company will be working alongside the grantor and third party employees. This interface will need to be carefully managed, with programmes for access to certain facilities, joint management of working processes and practices and a constant flow of information to ensure that no contractor is preventing another from performing its obligations.

22.4   Scope of Services

The grantor will need to set out carefully those services which the project company is to provide. Part of the assessment of the scope of services to be allocated to the project company is the critical or non-critical nature of those services. It will be important to provide appropriate incentives to the project company to provide those services which are deemed to be critical as a priority.

22.4.1   Nature of services

When the project company takes over the services, there are likely to be issues associated with existing infrastructure, personnel and services. The project company will need to consider existing liabilities, the discovery of defects and the ability to comply with performance standards in view of existing infrastructure, personnel and services. This is normally achieved during a controlled due diligence process before contracts are signed. The scope of services will need to respond to the demands of these issues.

The project company may be required to provide transitional services in the process of taking over the existing services. This may involve additional time or relief from certain obligations or remedies during a transition or mobilisation period. It is during this time that the project company will be able to assess conditions of staff and equipment to be transferred from the grantor to the project company and identify any constraints that had not been identified at the time of contract. In the event that the project company has not had the opportunity pre-contract to perform sufficient due diligence, the project company will generally require the opportunity to perform such due diligence after contract signature with the right to re-open contract terms where conditions encountered are not as anticipated. The grantor will want to establish the basis on which such contract re-openers might arise.

It will generally not be possible to give an exhaustive definition of the scope of services. For this reason the grantor will generally require that the project company provides the enumerated services as well as all services which are necessary and incidental to those specifically indicated. The grantor will want to ensure that the services as a whole are fit for their purpose, as described in the contract.

The scope of services may also evolve over time. At first it will normally mirror those services currently being provided to the grantor by its own internal functions. However, the project company may be required to provide additional services and functionality (as discussed in section 22.6). Further, the grantor may not have a detailed description, or an in-depth understanding, of current service demands.

The project company may be responsible for providing further infrastructure or technology refresh, providing continuous improvements to the services to be supplied and the state of the underlying infrastructure. The risk and cost associated with these updating and upgrading responsibilities need to be set out clearly. They may be paid for separately or rolled up in unit pricing. In addition, it will be important to identify who owns the new infrastructure and whether the grantor will have the exclusive benefit of that infrastructure.

In certain cases, the services may be provided from a common platform, where the project company provides similar services to a number of different clients. This will allow the project company to provide services at a lower cost through economies of scale, but may also cause concern for the grantor where it requires exclusivity of attention to its requirements or where there are specific security or confidentiality concerns that might be jeopardised by common services being provided to a number of different clients.

In certain cases, the grantor will have intricate and detailed business continuity and contingency plans to ensure that no failure by the project company or external event will threaten the continuity of the business of the grantor. In certain industries, this continuity plan will involve split-second reactions due to events that might otherwise threaten the grantor's business or continued provision of services to its clients. In some cases this will be a more important decision than others where the outsourced service is a core dependency of the grantor's business, for example in telecommunications where redundancy and the ability to respond immediately to any loss of services can be a question of thousands of dollars for each minute of interrupted services. These continuity plans may need to be tested periodically, and the results of those tests reported to the grantor and possibly to other service providers.

22.4.2   Nature of provision of services

The method for providing services will generally be set out in an operations or business process manual. The project company will be required to comply with this manual. The grantor may want to provide the conditions upon which this manual can be amended over time. The parties will need to ensure that such manuals and/or schedules are consistent with the terms of the underlying contractual arrangements between the grantor and the project company, to avoid confusion.

In the event of the presence of existing infrastructure, the project company will need to obtain significant information about that infrastructure and may require a continuous data and information interface between the grantor and the project company. The services provided by the project company may also need to reflect the changing nature of the grantor's business and requirements, necessitating further evolutionary characteristics to the services provided.

The grantor will also need to decide to what extent the project company will be allowed to subcontract the provision of services, and whether the grantor will want the right to approve any subcontractors. Whether or not the services are so contracted, the grantor will want to know that the project company is responsible for the delivery of those services, despite the presence of the subcontractor. Such subcontractors will also be required to comply with the same standards, policies, procedures and requirements placed on the project company.

The services provided by the project company will need to comply with the grantor's security requirements and existing security arrangements. Where the project company is responsible for providing security, the grantor will want significant flow of information in relation to supervision of those security arrangements and any breaches of security and the remedy of any such breaches. The extent of the grantor's control over such information will depend on the sensitivity of the security arrangements and the ability of the grantor to manage this flow of information.

The grantor may wish to require that the project company provides "most favoured customer" treatment, in particular where the project company is awarded the project due to its ability to provide economy of scale. This means that the grantor gets the best service and/or price that the project company provides to any other customer. This arrangement can be difficult to police and measure given the variety of different customers to whom the project company may be providing services. The project company will normally be unwilling to give to the grantor the confidential information on other customers that would be needed to verify "most favoured customer" status.

The grantor and project company will need to assess the implementation of cost saving initiatives. Cost savings should benefit the grantor, but the grantor will need to appreciate the need for an incentive for the project company to implement such initiatives, and more importantly to propose further cost saving initiatives. Where the potential benefit can be shared between the grantor and the project company, the project company will have the incentive to research and propose new potential cost savings.

The outsourcing arrangements will need to provide for remedies in the event that the project company breaches its service requirements. These remedies may include financial remedies compensating the grantor for poor performance, direct indemnities, liquidated damages for specific breaches (where a value can be placed against a specific breach), the ability of the grantor to step in to take over the services at the project company's cost, and termination of the outsourcing arrangements due to such breach.

22.5   Service Levels

Once the scope of services is defined, as discussed above, the level to which the services are to be provided must be clearly defined. This should involve objective test criteria as to whether or not the services have been provided to the level required. It will be easier for measurement and management if service levels can be categorised and defined in such a way as to allow the grantor to monitor them efficiently and for the project company to manage them effectively.

In certain cases, it will be possible to identify graduated or variable service level requirements, providing for improved services over time. However, in other cases, the extent of the project company's ability to improve services may not be clear. The project company and the grantor will need to work together to identify appropriate potential service level improvements, the costs associated with achieving such improvements and the benefit that the project company will receive for achieving such improvements.

The original service levels set will generally correspond to the existing service levels achieved by the grantor. This assumes the grantor is able to identify accurately the level of services that it is currently achieving. To the extent that it cannot give the project company comfort as to the level of those services, there may need to be an initial post-contract verification period during which this service level is tested to set a base line against which the project company's performance can be measured. The current service levels may then need to be improved over time by the project company.

The service level mechanism may identify penalties to be imposed where the services are provided incorrectly, and reduced to the extent that services are provided correctly or exceed requirements. Where additional or improved services will provide a financial or other benefit to the grantor, the grantor may wish to implement a bonus structure where the project company exceeds the level of service guaranteed under the outsourcing arrangements. The project company will not generally have the incentive to improve services, or adapt with change. The mechanism for testing service levels will need to provide such an incentive.

There may be a certain tolerance before service credits are applied to allow for minimum performance levels and cure of poor performance. The more grievous the poor performance, the more significant the service credits that will be applied. There may also be a special period of tolerance (often known as a "holiday") at the beginning of the outsourcing arrangements to allow for ramping up of services.

The service levels may need to change as the grantor's business requirements change. The overall impact on the project company should not change, but the grantor should be allowed to modify service credits to create incentives in the areas most important to the grantor. This should be achieved through the change mechanism discussed in section 22.6.

The project company will generally be required to use qualified and trained personnel with all due skill, care and diligence. It must avoid infringing any third party intellectual property rights and comply with such rights to the extent they apply to software, hardware or other intellectual property used by the project company to provide the services. As discussed above, security and confidentiality obligations may be applied to the services and, generally, the project company will need to comply with law, regulations and industry standards that may apply to the services or the contract.

22.6   Change of Requirements and Additional Services

Change procedures generally involve placing greater obligations, or different obligations, on the project company against changes in the remuneration structure. An outsourcing arrangement usually covers a period of many years and must be flexible enough to respond to changes in business requirements. It must also change as technology and know-how in relation to the services change. Because business change is common and often significant, a successful outsourcing arrangement must implement the flexibility necessary to provide for such changes. This flexibility may involve certain specific dates for re-negotiation, where specific business events may occur or technology life-cycles provide an appropriate moment to reconsider the entire arrangement.

The grantor will need the right to require changes to services or functionality. There will need to be a mechanism for investigating proposed changes and identifying the impact of such changes including their cost.   This is often performed by the project company, although the task and the cost of that task may need to be shared. The cost of such change must then be shared, often based on the purpose for the change and the party requesting the change.

To the extent the project company is permitted to refuse to make any such changes, the basis on which the project company can so refuse must be identified. A special provision may be necessary for urgent or emergency changes, often for legal or regulatory reasons or to remedy a defect in the existing infrastructure.

The grantor is often concerned that once the contract with the project company has been signed, the project company has a significant amount of influence as the only provider of critical services.   Providing for a reasonable and rational change procedure should not place more power in the project company's hands, but instead create a practical platform on which the parties can build, rebuild or modify their existing relationship.

22.7   Compensation

Where the compensation structure is reliant on actual costs incurred, the grantor may need special audit powers to ensure the costs being paid are not in some way exaggerated or inflated. The project company may also benefit from increases in business associated with the services it is providing. If that is the case, the project company may need similar audit powers.

In some cases, services being provided will be compensated in different ways. Services which involve a significant portion of initial capital expenditure and investment in infrastructure may result in fixed charges to compensate for the infrastructure and variable charges against the provision of services.   In other cases, services will be more reliant on variable costs and therefore compensation can be based on actual services provided and the actual costs incurred by the project company in providing those services.

22.8 Grantor Obligations

In addition to the payment obligations discussed above, the grantor will provide information, access to the site and certain infrastructure and potentially access to other services. The grantor may have special obligations during the transitional period, when the project company first takes over operation of the services and mobilises its personnel and its equipment. Those obligations may relate to licences and permits necessary for the project company's access, and the availability for consultation of the grantor's personnel and other information in relation to the site and the grantor's operations.

22.9 Benchmarking

As part of the ability of the outsourcing arrangement to respond to changes in market demands, the grantor will often demand a benchmarking exercise. This involves the periodic testing of the outsourcing arrangements (in particular, the compensation arrangements and service levels) against market standards, and is usually performed every five to eight years to allow the project company sufficient time to make improvements in services and to be compensated for the initial outlay of funds in running the project (in the event that the project company loses out to a competitor in the benchmarking process).

Benchmarking is a relatively blunt instrument. The project company bidding for a project which has early or frequent benchmarking may not be able to give as robust a price for services, as the project company will not have the full length of the contract to recover the amounts it might invest in the early period of providing the services. The project company will also have a certain amount of costs and investment sunk into winning the actual contract and mobilising its services. The period before the first benchmarking exercise will need to provide the project company with the opportunity to recover those costs through the compensation scheme.

Further, benchmarking may not provide the grantor with the protections it seeks. The incumbent is generally in a better position to provide the cheapest prices during benchmarking due to its improved information and the fact that its personnel and equipment are already on site. Therefore benchmarking may not avail the grantor of the market and competitive forces that it may desire.

A benchmarking exercise can be carried out by a third party expert, to ensure it is an objective measure. However, this increases the cost of benchmarking, which is generally relatively high, in particular for the project company. It may be necessary to provide some incentive for bidders, to encourage competition.

The parties will also need to agree the focus of the benchmarking analysis, what characteristics will be judged, what information will be made available and which services will be benchmarked. The project company will want services to be benchmarked as a whole and on a like-for-like basis. The incumbent project company is usually given the option of matching the best benchmark bid or losing the project to that lowest bidder. The parties will need to decide how long the project company will have to implement any improvements which may be required by the benchmarking exercise.

22.10   Intellectual Property Rights

A variety of intellectual property rights ("IPRs") will be involved in most outsourcing projects. The first will be those associated with the existing infrastructure and services. The grantor will need to give the project company the right to act under these IPRs to provide the initial services and to make such changes as are necessary to improve the services in line with the requirements of the outsourcing arrangements.

IPRs may also be developed specifically by the project company for the project. The parties will need to agree who will own these IPRs and whether the grantor will be given a perpetual royalty-free licence to use (and to assign the right to use) those IPRs for the purpose of the project. The grantor will also need the right to make changes in the infrastructure or the services over time, even after the project company is no longer involved in the services, to enable it to meet the needs of its business.

IPRs will be associated with new infrastructure or services provided by the project company. Where the project company does not own these IPRs, arrangements will need to be made as to what rights the grantor will have in those IPRs. In certain cases the IPRs developed for the project will be considered commercially sensitive and proprietary for the grantor. The grantor may wish to mandate that those IPRs are used exclusively for the project and restrict their use by any competitor.

The grantor will need to ensure that it and any replacement supplier have the right to use any and all IPRs associated with the services.

The requirements of and protections provided by the local jurisdiction will need to be considered carefully when looking at protection of IPRs. In some cases, the local jurisdiction will not provide sufficient protection and offshore vehicles may need to be developed in order to provide appropriate protection for such rights.

22.11   Employees

In outsourcing arrangements, there will be particular focus on the transfer of employees and the importance of continuity of personnel. The grantor will want to avoid complications with those of its employees that are to be transferred to the project company. Those employees will want to see their benefits protected and their position in the company unaltered further to such changes.

In addition, in each jurisdiction, employees will be provided certain protections at law, or possibly under their relevant contracts and collective bargaining arrangements. These rights may include job security, the terms and conditions of their employment, information to be provided or consultation before and during transfer, limitations on the right to dismiss employees, and the right of employees to resist being transferred to the new employer. The approach to such employee protections will differ significantly between jurisdictions and should be considered carefully. In particular, the employees may be transferred by operation of law (with their rights and benefits intact) to the extent that business or assets are transferred to a new owner. Data protection and privacy laws may restrict access to certain information by the project company, and therefore make identifying the scope of liabilities and the cost of the transfer of employees difficult to ascertain.

The grantor will also want to ensure that the key employees, often the basis on which the grantor awarded the project to the project company, remain in place over time. The grantor will not want to see those employees stripped out of the project company as soon as the project is won. In some cases the project company may have similar concerns, where the management by the grantor is reliant on the key personnel appointed by the grantor to manage the project. The project company may not be comfortable that those key employees could be changed over time, potentially preventing the project company from performing the services at the levels required.

To this extent the grantor and the project company may require consent before certain key personnel are changed, removed or replaced. They may also require information about the use of such employees to ensure that they are fully involved in the relevant project; this may include the provision of time sheets and audit rights over the relevant employees.

Key personnel will be valuable commodities. Parties to the project may be tempted to head-hunt such personnel for their own needs. The parties may agree to a restriction on the ability of one party to offer employment to the other parties' employees.

22.12 Legal and Regulatory Compliance

The grantor and the project company will need to ensure that the services comply with legal and regulatory requirements. This will include compliance with any changes in legal and regulatory requirements. The parties will need to agree how the project company will be compensated where its costs increase due to such changes.

The grantor may want to place specific requirements on any personnel or subcontractors that will be involved in specific aspects of the services where legal or regulatory compliance is particularly sensitive. For example, special security clearance may need to be obtained before such personnel or subcontractors can become involved in the project. The grantor may want to have some input on the personnel or subcontractor to be used where the project company will need to have direct contact with the relevant regulator.

The parties will also need to agree allocation of the risk of breach of such legal and regulatory requirements or where penalties have been imposed by the regulators. This will be particularly sensitive for the project company following a change to the regulatory or legal requirements and the time and cost involved in compliance.

22.13   Termination

Because the project company has taken over the grantor's current services, the grantor will generally not have another source of such services in the event of termination. Therefore, the grantor may need the right immediately to take over the relevant infrastructure and services in order to ensure continued performance. This is quite common in public services, such as water and sanitation.

Where there are difficulties in the project and the grantor does not want to terminate, it may want the right to step-in and manage the services over the short-term until the relevant breach can be cured. The lenders will want to ensure that they are protected during this time, and that the project company will not incur any undue penalty for a failure by the grantor to properly manage the services during this time. This becomes more complicated where there are multiple customers of the project company.

Where the project company provides services to multiple grantors or customers, the parties will need to consider carefully what happens to the infrastructure on termination. The other customers will not want their services interrupted by the actions of the grantor or assets essential to the provision of their services transferred to the ownership of the grantor.

In addition, the parties will need to agree whether the grantor is entitled to terminate for convenience, for example, where some other service provider has offered to provide the services at a lower price. Such termination can provide economic efficiency, allowing the grantor to maximise value-for-money. However, it will not give the project company the exclusivity and security of tenure that it might otherwise desire. The project company would then need to recover its development and mobilisation costs either early in the project period or as termination compensation.

As under BOT projects, the project company will need to ensure that in the event of termination it recovers the initial capital cost that it has invested in the project. This cost will often be financed and the lenders will normally require an undertaking to repay outstanding debt on termination if the relevant assets will become the property of the grantor on termination.

22.14   Joint Venture Arrangements

In certain cases, rather than handing the services over to the project company, the grantor will want to enter into a joint venture with the project company, possibly owning part of the project company, in order to manage the service provision. In this case, the issues relevant to the shareholders' agreement as discussed in chapter 9 will be relevant to the structure of the joint venture. In particular, the parties will need to discuss who controls the decision-making process within the joint venture, how voting for specific issues will be managed, how profits from the joint ventures are shared, how the management and various board members are appointed, and how decisions will be taken. The parties will probably want to reserve certain matters for agreement for all parties to the joint venture with some deadlock procedure where unanimous decision is not achieved.

The specific challenges associated with a joint venture between the project company and the grantor relate primarily to conflicts of interest. Where there is to be a formal agreement between the grantor and the joint venture company, the grantor may need to be removed from decision-making in relation to claims that the joint venturer may have against the grantor. Similarly, many of the tasks to be performed are likely to be subcontracted to the project company's or sponsors' subsidiaries. These parties will then have a conflict of interest in relation to any management of those contractual relations from the project company's or joint venturer's point of view, and therefore may need to be removed from that decision-making process. There will also be concerns that one of the shareholders in the joint venture could frustrate the joint venture or prevent its activities where disputes have arisen between the joint venturer and the relevant shareholder. These other interests of the members of the joint venture should not be permitted to prevent the proper and efficient functioning of the joint venture or the performance of its contractual obligations and may therefore need to be contemplated within the management and voting structure of the joint venture.

22.15 Multi-jurisdictional Arrangements

Some outsourcing arrangements are multi-jurisdictional. This arises where services are provided to the grantor in a number of different countries. The contractual structure will need to contemplate the legal requirements and cultural specifications in each different country. In order to achieve this, there is generally a master services agreement (including transfer arrangements) which brings together multiple local service agreements intended to comply with local requirements and laws. The intention is to provide consistency of the services to be supplied and the terms on which those services are to be supplied between the different jurisdictions while at the same time complying with the specific legal and regulatory requirements, and possibly the cultural and commercial specificities, of each jurisdiction.

Local requirements will have particular effect on the transfer of assets, the assignment of contracts, the ownership of IPR and the transfer of employees from the grantor to the project company and from the project company to any replacement supplier. The relevant warranties and indemnities will need to be structured accordingly. A template local services agreement can be set out which will then be amended following due diligence on each country's circumstances, the status of assets and employees in that country, and the nature of any transfer. For example, in some countries, the sale of assets and transfer of employees may result in the transfer of part or all of the relevant business. This could include associated debts and obligations. In many cases the transfer of employees will involve the employees maintaining the rights that they had under their contracts with the grantor, including accumulated benefits. The process for novation of contracts will differ between countries, and may require some special procedure to achieve the desired results.

22.16   Offshore Outsourcing

In an effort to create economies of scale, certain outsourcing exercises have involved outsourcing to offshore locations. An example in the United Kingdom is the growing fashion for outsourcing call centres or document management services to India. Advances in information technology have enabled the movement of communication and information between the United Kingdom and India at a low cost and with high efficiency. This has allowed businesses in the United Kingdom to benefit from the lower labour costs to be found in India. These lower labour costs are combined with higher levels of education, proficiency in English and lower turnover, enabling Indian outsourcing companies to provide more consistency of service; but offshore outsourcing raises issues not encountered in other approaches to outsourcing.

Offshore outsourcing has grown out of improvements in infrastructure and the ability to communicate over long distances with greater efficiency. It will be important to review the stability of the relevant infrastructure. Where that infrastructure fails, it is often difficult to implement alternative methods of communication which might otherwise be available were the outsourcing not offshore.

The difference in political situation between the country in which outsourcing is performed and the country where the outsourcing is sourced may cause difficulties in consistency of service. Many of these popular offshore locations may be in countries that experience a higher level of political instability.

Where communication or other failures interrupt the services, the grantor will need to find an alternative source for the services. In certain cases, this alternative source will need to be implemented immediately. The damages payable by the project company may not be sufficient to compensate the grantor from the damages associated with such an interruption in the services. Where possible, contingency plans should be implemented and back-up or other service provision alternatives made available.

Consideration will need to be given to the level of service to be provided. Appropriate due diligence will need to be performed in relation to the customs and practices of companies operating in that jurisdiction as well as cultural attitudes that might impede effective communication and management of the services. To the extent that global standards can be implemented, this may be an effective way to cut through the cultural expectations of a grantor and the cultural attitudes of the project company. However, it is important for both parties to address such cultural differences by improving awareness and training in how to manage these expectations.

Language proficiency will be a consideration in the choice of project company. Offshore outsourcing will either initially or eventually be provided by local personnel, and language proficiency will be important for all parties.

The project company will need to consider issues of compliance with laws in the country in which it is providing the services and in the country from which the services are being sourced. Export controls may need to be considered in relation to the transfer of assets and the movement of information or technology between countries. Similarly, data protection rules in different countries may limit the ability to transfer information or the amount of information that can be provided across national boundaries.

Intellectual property rights will differ, requiring careful consideration of the laws in both countries to ensure that intellectual property is protected accordingly both in the country where the services are to performed as well as the country in which the services are sourced. In certain of the countries where information technology outsourcing is most likely to occur (e.g. China and India), careful consideration should be given to the protection provided for intellectual property that may be associated with or may arise from that outsourcing relationship.

Glossary

"When I use a word" Humpty Dumpty said in a rather scornful tone, "it means just what I choose it to mean – neither more nor less."[489]

This glossary of terms, abbreviations and acronyms is included exclusively for use as a reference aid and therefore should not be considered an exhaustive or complete discussion of any of the terms set out below.[490] Definitions are generally given under their spelt-out form, and the abbreviation refers to the spelt-out form. Terms within the definition which are themselves defined are indicated in bold face. The list is fully cross-referenced.

2p Proved and probable (reserves of oil or gas).

3p Proved and possible (reserves of oil or gas).

abandon To cease work on a **well** which is non-productive, to plug off the well with cement plugs and salvage all recoverable equipment.

abandonment Used in the context of terminating field operations, abandonment refers to abandoning a **well** (as above) together with the decommissioning of the installation and structures surrounding it. This may involve plugging the well, cleaning and/or removing and/or disposing of the structures, and applies to pipelines and subsea equipment as well as **platforms**.

absorption A process for separating mixtures into their constituents, by taking advantage of the fact that some components are more readily absorbed than others. An example is the extraction of the heavier components from **natural gas**.

abstraction The taking of water from surface water (rivers, lakes and reservoirs) and groundwater (boreholes and springs from water-bearing rocks such as chalk, limestone and sandstone).

acceleration After a default, the right of the lenders to make the loan immediately and fully due and payable. Repayments are accelerated to the present.

---

[489] Carroll, Lewis, Through the Looking Glass at chapter 6.

[490] Terms in this glossary have been adopted and modified from several sources: Private Finance Panel (1996) supra note 347; Tinsley (1996) supra note 215; Black's Law Dictionary (6th edition 1990); Haley (1996) supra note 205; Nevitt and Fabozzi (6th edition 1997) supra note 260; Levy (1996) supra note 197; United Nations Industrial Development Organisation (1996) supra note 204; Merrett, Introduction to the Economics of Water Resources: An International Perspective (1997); Biwater Plc, the Perfect Water Company (1996); and the website of the Shell corporation (www.shell.com).

acidising The technique of pumping a form of hydrochloric acid down the **well** hole to enlarge the pore space in oil bearing rocks, thus increasing oil flow and recovery. See also **enhanced oil recovery**; **primary recovery**; **secondary recovery**; **tertiary recovery**.

acreage The area covered by a lease granted for oil and gas exploration and for possible future production.

acre-foot The volume of water that covers an area of one acre to a depth of one foot. Equivalent to 43,560 cubic feet or 325,829 US gallons.

ADB Asian Development Bank. A multilateral agency with headquarters in Manila, the Philippines.

additive A chemical added to a product to improve its properties.

administration order A court order made in relation to an insolvent company, or one that is likely to become insolvent. The purpose of such an order is to preserve the company's business, allow reorganisation, or to ensure the most profitable realisation of the company's assets by placing it under the control of an administrator and protecting it from action by its creditors.

administrative receiver A person appointed by the holder of a **floating charge** covering the whole (or substantially the whole) of an insolvent company's assets, in order to recover the money due to the secured creditor. An administrative receiver can carry on the company's business and sell the business and other assets secured by the charge (an **administration order**).

advance payment A payment made by a project company to the construction contractor at or around commencement in order to offset preliminary costs, including purchase of equipment and organisational expenses.

AFD Agence Française de Développement of France.

AfDB African Development Bank. A multilateral agency with headquarters in Abidjan, Côte d'Ivoire.

AFE See **authority for expenditure**.

agent A person that executes orders for or otherwise acts on behalf of another party (the **principal**) and is subject to its control and authority. The agent may receive a fee or a commission for his services.

aggregate The mineral matter used together with bitumen to create asphalt for road construction.

all-in cost Total costs, explicit and other.

API A measure of the density of oil (higher index indicates less density, range 14-60, average 40) established by the American Petroleum Institute. See also **API gravity**.

amortisation Reduction of capital or up-front expenses (capitalised) over time to reflect life-cycle depreciation and obsolescence, often an equal amount per annum. Sometimes describes repayments. See also **depreciation**.

anhydrous Without water or dried.

annuity Repayment of debt where the sum of **principal** and **interest** is equal for each period.

API gravity The gravity of crude oil or other liquid hydrocarbon as measured by a system recommended by the American Petroleum Institute. Gravity is the weight per unit of volume of a compound.

appraisal well A **well** drilled as part of a programme to determine the size and likely yield of an oil or gas field.

aqueduct An artificial channel for conveying water.

aquifer An underground formation of rock or sediment which is saturated and sufficiently permeable to transmit suitable quantities of water to a well or spring. Water-bearing strata.

aquifer recharge Restoration of water to an aquifer such that water can be extracted in useable quantities.

ARR See **average rate of return**.

arrangement fee The fee paid to an arranger of financing for its work in relation to a transaction.

arranger The senior tier of a syndication. Implies the entity that agreed and negotiated the project finance structure. Also refers to the bank/underwriter entitled to syndicate the loan/bond issue. The arranger may not necessarily also be the **agent** and may not even participate in the transaction.

artificial lift The application of power to lift oil mechanically or otherwise to surface from a producing **well**.

asset All tangible and intangible property of a company including real property, chattels money, and debts owing to such company.

assignment The transfer of a right or interest to another. See also **novation**.

associated gas Natural gas found in association with oil in a reservoir, either dissolved in the oil or as a cap above the oil.

atmospheric pressure The weight of the atmosphere on the earth's surface. At sea level this is approximately 1,013 bars, 101,300 newtons per square metre, 14.7 pounds per square inch or 30 inches of mercury.

audit An independent examination of the financial statements or project studies/projections.

authentication The physical signing of a security by the issuing and paying agent in order to give it legal effect.

authority for expenditure (AFE) A form used to list proposed expenses and includes such items as department number, division, AFE numbers, description of an oil or gas field and its location. Very similar (in theory) to the common purchase requisition used in the traditional office.

availability Where the financing is available for drawdown.

availability charge See **capacity charge**.

available cash flow Total cash sources less total cash used before payment of debt service.

average life Average for all repayments of a debt, usually weighted by amounts outstanding.

average rate of return (ARR) The ratio of average net earnings to average investment.

balance sheet The accounts that show **assets**, **liabilities** and net worth/shareholders' **equity**.

balancing mechanism The mechanism used in the United Kingdom by the national grid company to balance the supply and demand of electricity.

bankruptcy A legal condition in which an individual's or a company's **assets** are assumed by a court official and the company is operated and/or its assets are used to pay off creditors.

barrel (BBL) A unit of measure for crude oil and oil products equal to approximately 160 litres.

barrels of oil equivalent (BOE) A term frequently used to compare gas with oil and to provide a common measure for different quality gases. It is the number of barrels of stabilised crude oil, which contains approximately the same amount of energy as the gas: for example, 5.8 trillion cubic feet (of lean gas) approximates to one billion BOE.

barrels of oil per day (BOPD, BPD or B/D) In production terms, the number of barrels of oil produced from a **well** over a 24-hour period, normally an average figure from a longer period of time. (In refining terms, the number of barrels input or production of a refinery during a year, divided by 365 less the downtime needed for maintenance. World production is 30 million BPD.) See also **BOEPD**.

base rate The rate of **interest** used as a basis by banks for the rates they charge their customers. In the United Kingdom, the base rate refers to the rate at which the Bank of England lends to discount houses, which largely governs the lending rate throughout the banking system.

basis point (BP) One hundred basis points equal one percentage point.

BBL See **barrel (BBL)**.

BBO Buy-Build-Operate (similar to BOO).

BCF See **billion cubic feet**.

BCM or BN CM Billion cubic metres, unit of measurement.

BCPD Barrels of **condensate** per day.

beach price Price applying to gas at landfall, when water and liquid hydrocarbons have been removed.

benchmark A reference point to measure performances of financial or other instruments of a given kind or in a given market. Also the standard specification of a commodity or financial instrument used as a basis for pricing other specifications, e.g. North Sea Brent or Saudi Light in the case of crude oil.

best efforts or best endeavours A high standard to which a duty must be performed, obliging the party concerned to use its best endeavours to meet the specified obligation. This term will have a legal meaning under the relevant legal system.

best management practices Techniques and practices that are accepted as the most effective and practical means of controlling pollutants or conserving water resources.

bid bond A **bond** of a fixed amount, usually one per cent. to three per cent. of the tender contract price, deposited by bidders with the tendering authority at the time of submission of their tenders as a form of **guarantee** that the bidder will submit a tender. Once the contract is awarded, bid bonds are refunded to the losers. The bid bond is generally returned to the successful bidder on effectiveness of the relevant contract or on financial close. Also known as a **tender bond**.

bid price The price offered.

bilateral agencies An agency of one country, either public or private, which funds development in other countries. See also **export credit agencies**; **multilateral lending agencies**.

billion cubic feet (BCF) Unit to measure size of gas field (medium is 400 BCF); 6 BCF = 1 **MMBOE**.

biochemical oxygen demand/chemical oxygen demand (BOD/COD) Biochemical/chemical determinants of water quality. Biochemical oxygen demand (BOD) measures the amount of oxygen consumed in water, usually by organic pollution, and so lower values indicate better quality. Chemical oxygen demand (COD), unlike BOD, includes all the oxygen consumed by effluents. See also **sewage treatment**.

biodegradable Material that can be decomposed or rotted by bacteria or other natural agents.

biogas A medium **British thermal unit (BTU)** gas containing methane and carbon dioxide, produced from the anaerobic decomposition of organic material in a landfill. Also called "biomass gas".

biomass conversion The conversion of biochemically derived material for the production of energy.

bit The cutting or pulverising tool attached to the lower end of the **drill string** boring a hole in underground formations. See also **drill bit**.

bitumen A naturally occurring viscous mixture, mainly of hydrocarbons heavier than pentane, that may contain sulphur compounds and that, in its naturally occurring viscous state, is not recoverable at a commercial rate through a well.

black products Diesel oils and fuels oils, i.e. products from the low or heavy end of the distillation process. See also **white products**.

BLO(T) Build, Lease, Own (Transfer). The grantor builds the project, then leases it to the project company which operates it for the duration of the concession period.

block The subdivision of a nation's exploration and production acreage. Blocks are generally defined in terms of latitude and longitude, at one-degree intervals.

block valve A large heavy-duty valve on a crude oil or products trunk line installed usually at intervals of from 8 to 32 kilometres. These valves can be used to isolate sections of the pipeline in an emergency and are called "block valves". The block valve and its fenced compound are known together as a "block valve station".

blocked accounts In a foreign exchange context, deposits maintained in a country which does not allow exchange into another currency or removal of the deposits from the country.

blocked currency A currency whose convertibility or transferability is restricted, in part or whole, by government regulations. There are generally considered to be three categories of currency: convertible, semi-convertible and non-convertible. A blocked currency belongs in one of the last two categories.

blowdown A method of producing a gas/**condensate** reservoir by letting the reservoir depressure over time without re-injecting any gas. With this method of production some condensate may condense within the reservoir, where its recovery is no longer a practical proposition.

blowout The uncontrolled escape of oil, gas or water from a **well** due to the release of pressure in a **reservoir** or the failure of containment systems.

blowout preventer A stack or assembly of heavy duty valves to the top of the casing to control well pressure.

BOD/COD See **biochemical oxygen demand/chemical oxygen demand (BOD/COD)**.

BOE See **barrels of oil equivalent** (comparison of gas and oil quantities).

BOEPD Barrels of oil equivalent per day.

bond The paper evidence of a legal promise by the issuer to pay the investor on the declared terms. Bonds are usually negotiable and customarily long-term, e.g. five to 25 years. Short-term bonds are usually referred to as **notes**. See also **bid bond; maintenance or retention bond; performance bond; straight debt**.

BOO Build-Own-Operate. The private entity will build, own and operate the project just as in a **BOT** project, but there is no transfer back to the government. This method is often used where there will be no residual value in the project after the concession period or accounting standards do not permit the **assets** to revert to the grantor if the grantor wishes to benefit from off-balance sheet treatment.

BOOS Build-Own-Operate-Sell. Same as a **BOT** except that the grantor pays the project company for the residual value of the project at transfer.

BOOST Build-Own-Operate-Subsidise-Transfer (similar to BOT).

booster station A **platform** on a section of subsea gas **pipeline**, designed to boost the flow of gas.

BOOT Build-Own-Operate-Transfer (similar to BOT).

BOPD Barrels of oil per day.

BOR Build-Operate-Renewal of concession (similar to **BOO**).

borehole (oil/gas) The hole as drilled by the **drill bit**.

borehole (water) A means of abstracting water from **aquifers**.

borrower An institution or individual that raises funds in return for contracting into an obligation to repay those funds together with payment of **interest** either as **capital appreciation** (as in a discount security) or as a **coupon** payment or at determinable periods over the life of a loan facility.

BOT Build-Operate-Transfer. In this, the project is transferred back to the party granting the concession. The transfer may be for value or at no cost. See also **constituent documents**.

bottom-hole pressure The reservoir or formation pressure at the bottom of the hole.

BPD See **barrels of oil per day**.

break clause A clause giving a party the right to terminate the contract at a particular point, often called the "break point".

brent blend A blend of North Sea crudes, used as an international marker for crude oil pricing.

bridge financing Interim financing, before a long-term financing is put in place.

British electricity trading & transmission arrangements (BETTA) Arrangements to create a single wholesale electricity market for Great Britain.

British thermal unit (BTU) The amount of heat needed to raise the temperature of one pound of water one degree Fahrenheit.

BRT Build-Rent-Transfer (similar to **BOT**).

BS&W Bottom sediment and water.

BT Build-Transfer. The project company builds the facilities and transfers them to the grantor (similar to BOT).

BTO Build-Transfer-Operate (similar to BOT). This often involves the grantor paying for construction of the facility, separate from operations, at or before transfer.

builders' or contractors' all-risks The standard insurance package during construction projects which is nominally intended to cover "all" construction risks.

bulk cargo Any liquid or solid cargo loaded onto a vessel without packaging (e.g. oil or grain).

bullet A one-time repayment, often after no/little **amortisation** of the loan. A balloon.

bunker fuel Any diesel or fuel oil supplied to fuel a ship's engines; i.e. to run the ship rather than as cargo to be transported for sale. The "bunkers" are the place where it is stored on the ship.

business risk See **commercial risk**.

buy-back A promise to repurchase unsold production. Alternatively, a promise to repay a financial obligation.

buyer credit Financing provided to a buyer to pay for the supply of goods or services, usually by an exporting country or the supplier company.

BWPD Barrels of water per day.

call option A contract sold for a price that gives the holder the right to buy from the writer of the option, over a specified period, a specified property or amount of securities at a specified price. Also known as a "call". In a **bond** or loan, the call option gives the borrower a refinancing option if **interest rates** fall below the call option interest rate. The borrower will pay a higher **coupon** for this right.

calorific value The quantity of heat produced by the complete combustion of a fuel. This can be measured dry or saturated with water vapour; and net or gross.

cap A ceiling on an interest or foreign exchange rate created through a **swap** or an **option** or by agreement.

capacity allocation The allocation of **ullage** amongst the pipeline owners.

capacity charge Payment by the purchaser to the project company for the available capacity of the project. This charge will cover fixed costs, including **debt service**, operating costs and service fees. Also known as **availability charge**.

capex See **capital expenditure**.

capital The amount invested in a venture, i.e. capitalisation.

capital appreciation The increase in the value of an asset over time.

capital costs Costs of financing construction and equipment. Capital costs are usually fixed, one-off expenses.

capital expenditure (capex) Long-term expenditure on fixed assets such as land, buildings, plant and equipment.

capital markets A term that includes tradable debt, **securities** and **equity**, as distinct from private markets or banks.

capital productivity index The present value of cash as per the present value but excluding the initial capital cost divided by that initial capital cost.

capitalised interest Accrued **interest** (and **margin**) which is not paid but added ("rolled up") to the **principal** amount lent at the end of an interest period.

carbon black A carbon product obtained from liquefied carbon feedstock and used mainly in the rubber industry (e.g. in tyres).

carbon capture Removal of CO_2 from fossil fuels either before or after combustion. In the latter, the CO_2 is extracted from the fluegas.

carbon credits A credit or permit arising from a **greenhouse gas** emissions reduction scheme, such as emissions trading.

carbon emissions trading scheme/ carbon trading A scheme in which greenhouse emissions are controlled by setting a **cap** on total emissions and allowing the market sector(s) to reach an economically balanced response via trading of emissions allowances. Allowances are allocated initially, perhaps through a free distribution or through an auction, and the total allocation is adjusted (capped) periodically.

carbon storage The long-term storage of CO_2 (as at **carbon capture**) in forests, soils, ocean or underground in depleted oil and gas **reservoirs**, coal seams and saline **aquifers**. Also referred to as **engineered carbon sequestration**.

cash flow See **revenue flow**.

cash return $ Trading cash flow less economic **depreciation**.

cash return percentage Cash return percentage as a proportion of the gross investment base (being depreciating assets at historic cost inflated by **capital productivity index** plus net monetary assets).

cash return spread The difference between cash return percentage and **weighted average cost of capital (WACC)**.

casing Steel pipe run into a **well** to line the hole and protect it from caving and invasion from other formation waters.

casing point The objective depth in a drilling contract, either a specified depth or the depth at which a specific zero is penetrated.

cat. cracking See **cracking**.

catalyst A substance which aids or promotes a chemical reaction without forming part of the final product. It enables the reaction to take place faster or at a lower temperature, and remains unchanged at the end of the reaction. In industrial processes, nevertheless, the catalyst must be changed periodically to maintain economic production.

catchment (area) The land area from which all rainfall eventually flows into a specified river.

cathodic protection A method employed to minimise the rate of electrochemical corrosion of structures such as oil drilling and production **platforms, pipelines** and storage tanks.

CCGT See **combined cycle gas turbine**.

CDC Commonwealth Development Corporation – the British development finance institution. A bilateral agency.

cementing To fix the casing firmly in the hole with cement, which is pumped through the **drill pipe** to the bottom of the **casing** and up into the space between the hold and the casing.

central bank The official government-owned bank of a given country.

cetane number A measure of the ignition quality of diesel fuels. See also **octane rating**.

CF/D See **cubic feet per day**.

change (or variation) A technical term in construction contracts referring to a change of the client's requirements at the instance of the client and potentially entitling the construction contractor to a change in the contract price, the time for completion and any other obligation affected by the change ordered.

change (or variation) mechanism The contractual procedure set out for making a **change**, specifically how a change can be made and how to calculate the resulting change in contract price and time for completion.

change in law The situation in which the law of the **host country** changes after the date of contract and in such a way as to have an impact on the project.

charge Security rights over an asset. Under United States or English law, a **fixed charge** refers to a defined set of assets and is usually registered, while a **floating**

charge refers to other assets that change from time to time – e.g. cash at bank, inventory, and so on – which become a fixed charge (crystallise) after a default.

Christmas tree The assemblage of valves and fittings at the top of a **well** used in the control of production.

CHP See **combined heat and power**.

circulate To cycle drilling fluids down through the **drill pipe** and up between the drill pipe and the wall of the hole to the surface.

city gate The point at which gas passes from a main transmission system to a local distribution system. There is not necessarily a change of ownership.

clawback The ability (e.g. on the part of the grantor) to recover prior project cash flow that may have been distributed/paid away, e.g. as dividends to the sponsors.

clean letter of credit A letter of credit payable upon presentation of a draft, not requiring the presentation of documents.

CNG See **compressed natural gas**.

CO_2 Carbon dioxide. A **greenhouse gas**.

coal gas Manufactured gas made by the destructive distillation of bituminous coal. The chief components are methane (20-30 per cent.) and hydrogen (about 50 per cent.). See also **gas**.

COFACE Compagnie Française d'Assurance pour le Commerce Extérieur – the trade finance agency for France.

co-financing Lending by different lenders under the same documentation and security packages, but where there may still be different **interest rates**, repayment profiles and terms, perhaps via multiple tranches.

co-generation The production in a single power facility of another output besides electricity, from the waste heat, e.g. steam, hot air, refrigeration.

coking A thermal **cracking** process to break up large molecules into smaller ones with the generation of quantities of petroleum coke.

collar A combination of a ceiling and a floor to an **interest** or **foreign exchange rate**, structured through **swaps, options, hedging** or by agreement. Also known as a **tunnel**.

collateral Assets pledged as **security** under a loan, to assure repayment.

combined carrier Ship that can carry oil or dry bulk cargoes.

combined cycle Waste heat from an electricity generation unit is recovered as steam, and used to generate more electricity through a steam turbine.

combined cycle gas turbine (CCGT) A gas-fired electricity generation plant.

combined heat and power (CHP) The simultaneous generation of usable heat and power (usually electricity) in a single process, thereby discarding less wasted heat.

combined sewer A sewer that carries both sewage and storm water run-off. See also **storm sewer**.

commercial bank A bank that both accepts deposits and grants loans and, under certain stipulations in some countries, such as the United States, pays interest on current accounts.

commercial paper A short-term unsecured promise to repay a **debt** on a certain future date. Invariably written as a promissory note and generally sold at a discount. The most active commercial paper market is in the United States.

commercial risk Risk due to uncertainty about investment outlays, operating cash flows, supply, demand and asset values. Also known as **business risk**.

commitment fee A per annum fee applied to the portion of the unused financing (the amount not yet drawn down) until the end of the availability period.

common carriage The transport of gas or water through a pipeline system on behalf of a third party. The obligation on transmission or distribution companies to allocate transport of utilities to customers on a pro rata basis, without discrimination between new and existing clients.

complementary financing Funding by different lenders under similar, yet parallel, documentation and a related **security** package.

completion In a **project financing**, the stage at which the project's cash flows become the primary method of repayment. It occurs after a **completion test**. Prior to completion, the primary source of repayment is usually from the sponsors or from the construction contractor. See also **multiple completion; substantial, physical or mechanical completion**.

completion (oil/gas) The installation of permanent wellhead equipment for the production of oil and gas.

completion risk The risk that a project will not be able to pass its **completion test** within the time for **completion**.

completion tests Tests of the project's ability to satisfy the contract requirements, perform to a specified minimum standard and generate the expected cash flows.

compound interest Interest resulting from the periodic addition of simple interest to **principal**, the new base thus established being the principal for the computation of interest for the following period.

compressed natural gas (CNG) This is a fuel. **Natural gas** is compressed to a high pressure of up to 3,000 pounds per square inch and stored in high-pressure cylinders. See also **liquefied natural gas**.

compressor station A place in which gas is compressed or re-compressed for pipeline transmission. A compressor station is used to boost the gas pressure in gas transmission systems in much the same way that pumps are used on liquids pipelines. An impeller shaft studded with hundreds of short, fixed blades rotates at speeds of 3,000-6,000 rpm, moving up to 300,000 cubic feet per minute.

concentration In banking terms, the centralisation of a cash pool.

concession The right granted by the **host government** for a private company to undertake an otherwise public sector project and operate that project over a period of time.

concession agreement The agreement with a government body that entitles a private entity to undertake an otherwise public service. See also **constituent documents; project documents**.

condensate A light crude oil recovered during the production of **natural gas**, generally water-white, straw or bluish in colour.

conditions precedent Conditions which must be satisfied before a right or obligation accrues. The matters which have to be dealt with before a borrower will be allowed to borrow under a facility agreement. These will be listed in the agreement.

confirmation well A second test **well** drilled to "prove" that the formation or producing zone encountered by an initial **exploratory well** extends beyond the limit of the initial drill and spacing unit.

confirmed letter of credit A **letter of credit** in which the issuing bank's obligation to pay is backed by a second bank. The confirming bank agrees to pay if the terms of the letter of credit are met, regardless of whether the opening bank pays.

conjunctive use A programme that co-ordinates the storage of surface water supplies in local groundwater basins for future withdrawal and use.

connate water Salt water occurring with oil and gas in the reservoir.

consortium Two or more parties acting together as a partnership or joint venture.

constant dollar Prices and costs are de-escalated or re-escalated to a single point in time. Inflation or escalation is not applicable.

constituent documents The commercial documents involved in a BOT project, which generally include a **concession agreement**, a **construction contract**, an **input supply agreement**, an **offtake purchase agreement** and an **operation and maintenance agreement**.

construction contract The contract between the project company and the construction contractor for the design, construction and commissioning of the works. See also **constituent documents; project documents**.

construction contractor The project participant bearing the obligation to design, construct and commission the works.

consumptive use A use of water in which water is removed from available supplies without direct return to a water resource system.

contaminant Any physical, chemical, biological or radiological substance or matter that pollutes, infects or otherwise harms air, water or soil when it mixes with, or comes into contact with, such substances.

contingency An additional amount/percentage set aside against a cash flow item, e.g. **capital expenditure**. For liabilities, those that do not appear on the **balance sheet** until they crystallise, e.g. guarantees, supports and dispute settlements.

contractual structure The series of contracts comprising the project.

convertible A financial instrument that can be exchanged for another **security** or equity interest at a pre-agreed time and **exchange rate**.

convertible currency A currency which can be freely exchanged into foreign currency or gold without government central bank restrictions or authorisation.

core A cylindrical column of rock cut by using a special diamond **bit**, to sample an underground formation.

corporatised utility A utility that is in public ownership while being run in a manner similar to that of a private sector entity. A corporatised utility may be structured as a limited liability company, with its share capital controlled by the public, while publishing the equivalent of an annual report containing a profit and loss account, balance sheet and cash flow data.

cost of debt Yield to maturity on debt; frequently after tax, in which event it is one minus the tax rate times the yield to maturity.

counterparty An adverse party usually in a **swap** or contract, and includes intermediaries.

country risk Risk specific to a particular country, including **political risk** and economic risk. See also **sovereign risk**.

coupon The interest amount or rate payable on a **bond**. A coupon may be physically attached to the bond certificate.

covenant An agreed action to be undertaken (positive) or not done (negative). A breach of a covenant will generally constitute a **default**.

cover The amount above unity of a cover ratio. See also **cushion**.

cover ratio The ratio of income to **debt service** requirements used as an indicator of the safety margin for servicing debt. Sometimes known as **debt service cover ratio**.

CPI Consumer Price Index.

cracking The process of breaking down large molecules of oil into smaller ones. When this process is achieved by the application of heat only, it is known as **thermal cracking**. If a catalyst is used as well it is known as "catalytic (cat.) cracking". It is known as **hydrocracking** if the catalytic process is conducted in a hydrogen atmosphere. See also **coking**.

crane barge A large barge, capable of lifting heavy equipment onto offshore **platforms**. Also known as a **derrick barge**. See also **laybarge**.

credit risk The risk that a counterparty to a financial transaction will fail to perform according to the terms and conditions of the contract (default), either because of bankruptcy or any other reason, thus causing the asset holder to suffer a financial loss. Sometimes known as **default risk**.

creditworthy An entity which is "creditworthy" is deemed to have a low risk of default on a debt obligation.

critical pressure The minimum pressure required to liquefy a gas at its **critical temperature**.

critical temperature The temperature above which a gas cannot be liquefied whatever the pressure.

cross-collateral A pool of collateral of two or more project sponsors, from which the sponsors agree to allow recourse to each other's collateral.

cross-default An event of default triggered by a default in the payment of, or the actual or potential acceleration of the repayment of, other indebtedness of the same borrower or group.

crude oil A fossil fuel in liquid form which can be refined to produce various oil products – unrefined petroleum. See also **equity crude; light crude; syncrude**.

cryogenics The process of producing, maintaining and utilising very low temperatures (below -46°C).

cubic feet per day (CF/D) The number of cubic feet delivered in a 24-hour period.

cure Make good a default. See also **defects liability**.

currency basket The situation in which a selection of currencies (the basket) is combined to create a common unit. In such cases, the value of each currency is usually weighted according to various economic criteria, such as the foreign component of a country's total trade, its gross national product and its importance in world trade.

currency option A currency option entitles the holder to buy or sell an agreed amount of foreign currency at an agreed price until or on an agreed date.

currency risk The risk associated with changes in the exchange rate for a currency. See also **transfer risk**.

currency swap A **swap** in which the parties sell currencies to each other subject to an agreement to repurchase the same currency in the same amount, at the same exchange rate, and at a fixed date in the future. The exchange ensures that neither party is subject to **currency risk** because **exchange rates** are predetermined.

cushion The extra amount of net cash flow remaining after expected debt service. See also **cover**; **residual cushion**.

cuttings Rock chippings cut from the formation by the **drill bit**, and brought to the surface with the mud. Used by geologists to obtain formation data.

cyclic storage Storage of supplemental water in a groundwater basin for subsequent recovery and use.

D:E ratio See **debt-equity ratio**.

daily average send-out Total volume of gas delivered during a period of time, divided by the total number of days in the period.

daily contracted quantity (DCQ) The average daily quantity of gas which is contracted to be supplied and taken.

daisy chain The process by which a cargo of oil or oil products is sold many times before being delivered to the customer.

DBFO Design-Build-Finance-Operate. The grantor retains title to the site and leases the project back to the project company for the period of the concession. Similar to **BOO**.

DCMF Design-Construct-Manage-Finance, similar to BOO.

DCQ See **daily contracted quantity**.

dead weight tonnage (DWT) The weight of cargo, stores and fuel which a vessel carries when fully loaded.

debenture A document evidencing actual indebtedness. Often also used to refer to a document creating a charge, **mortgage** or other security interest. (It should be noted that the exact legal meaning of the term "debenture" is uncertain and there are differing views on whether or not documents such as loan agreements constitute debentures.) A legal security over the issuer's general credit/**balance sheet**.

debt An obligation to pay cash or other goods or to provide services to another. See also **liability**; **straight debt**; **subordinated debt**.

debt capacity The total amount of debt a company can prudently support, given its earnings expectations and equity base.

debt-capitalisation ratio The proportion of a firm's debt to its capitalisation. The higher this ratio, the greater the financial leverage and the risk.

debt-equity ratio The proportion of debt to equity, often expressed as a percentage. The higher this ratio, the greater the financial leverage of the firm. Also known as **D:E ratio**. See also **gearing**.

debt leverage The amplification in the return earned on equity funds when an investment is financed partly with borrowed money.

debt rescheduling Adjusting the tenor, interest rate or other terms and conditions of a debt agreement.

debt service Payments of **principal** and **interest** on a loan.

debt service cover ratio (DSCR) The ratio of income to debt service requirements for a period. Also known as the **cover ratio**.

debt service reserve An amount set aside either before completion or during the early operation period for debt-servicing where insufficient revenue is achieved.

deductible Amount or period which must be deducted before an insurance payout or settlement is calculated.

default The breach of a covenant by one of the parties. A default may be involuntary. See also **cross-default; event of default; latent default**.

default interest A higher **interest rate** payable after default.

default risk See **credit risk**.

defects liability The construction contractor's obligation to cure defects which may arise after completion.

defects liability period The period during which the construction contractor is liable for defects after completion.

deficiency The amount by which project cash flow is not adequate to cover **debt service**.

deficiency agreement The situation in which cash flow, working capital or revenues are below agreed levels or are insufficient to meet **debt service**; a deficiency or make-up agreement provides the shortfall to be met by the sponsor or another party, sometimes to a cumulative limit.

degradation Chemical or biological breakdown of a complex compound into simpler compounds.

demand line of credit A bank line of credit that enables a customer to borrow on a daily or an on-demand basis.

depletion The removal of a non-renewable resource from a known deposit that may be sold.

depreciation Amortisation for accounting (book), tax calculations or income calculations. A regular reduction in asset value over time. See also **straight-line depreciation**.

derrick A tapered mast of open steel framework used in drilling to support the **drill string** and other equipment.

derrick barge See **crane barge**.

derv See **diesel fuel (oil)**.

desalination The removal of dissolved salts, such as sodium chloride, from water.

despatch instructions The instructions given to the operator by the bulk purchaser as to how much output is required. These instructions will often include specific requirements for offtake and how the operator is to fulfil these requirements.

devaluation A formal government action which has the effect of decreasing the value of its own national currency by reducing the equivalent value in gold, special drawing rights, US dollars or other currencies. However, devaluation is only possible where fixed **exchange rates** exist.

development bank A lending agency that provides assistance to encourage economic and commercial development in different countries.

development well A **well** drilled in a productive **reservoir** underlying a geographical area of known oil or gas accumulation and within a definable trap. A development well is a well that is drilled after an **exploratory well** has confirmed the presence of petroleum in the formation. Usually, it takes several development wells to produce hydrocarbons efficiently from a formation.

deviation well A **well** drilled at an angle to the vertical (deviated drilling), to cover the maximum area of an oil or gas reservoir or to avoid abandoned equipment in the original hole.

DFID Department for International Development of the United Kingdom.

diesel fuel (oil) A general term covering light fuel oil derived from gas oil used in diesel engines. Sometimes called "diesel engine road vehicle (derv)" fuel.

diffusion The movement of suspended or dissolved particles from an area of higher concentration to an area of lower concentration as the result of random movement of individual particles.

digital network analysis Computer-based model providing mathematical representation of a supply/distribution network.

direct agreement An agreement made in parallel with one of the main **project documents**, often with the lenders or the grantor. **Step-in rights** and other lender rights are often reinforced or established through direct agreements between the lenders and the project participants.

disbursement A term used in accounting and finance to indicate the actual paying out of cash.

discovery well An exploration test **well** that encounters a new and previously untapped oil or gas **reservoir**.

disposal In this book, the process of getting rid of waste water and sludge.

distillation See **fractional distillation**.

distributed generation Electricity generation usually on a relatively small scale that is connected to the distribution networks rather than directly to the national transmission systems. See also **embedded generation**.

distribution In this book, the delivery of fresh water to users.

distribution mains See **mains**.

distribution network operators Companies that are responsible for operating the networks that connect electricity consumers to the national transmission system and provide interconnection with **embedded generation**.

diurnal storage Literally, daily storage. Refers to short-term or peak storage in pipelines or gas holders, as opposed to seasonal storage.

dividend A return on an investment in stock, usually in the form of cash or stock.

DOT Develop-Operate-Transfer (similar to **BOT**).

double bottom tanker A tanker in which the bottom of the cargo tanks is separated from the bottom of the ship by a space of up to 2 to 3 metres. The space is empty when the tanker carries cargo, but full of sea water on the ballast voyage. See also **double hull tanker**.

double hull tanker A tanker in which the bottom and sides of the cargo tanks are separated from the bottom and sides of the hull by spaces of up to 1 to 3 metres' width or depth. These spaces are empty when the tanker carries cargo but full of sea water on the ballast voyage. See also **double bottom tanker**.

downstream Those activities which take place between the loading of crude oil at the export terminal and the use of the oil by the end user. This encompasses the ocean transportation of **crude oil**, supply and trading, refining, and the distribution and marketing of the oil products. See also **upstream**.

drawdown The obtaining by the borrower of some of the funds available under a credit facility.

drill bit The part of a drilling tool that actually cuts through the rock. See also **cuttings; spud; whipstock**.

drill collar A heavy wall component of the **drill string** placed between the **bit** and the drilling pipe to maintain vertical penetration of the bit and supply the weight necessary for drilling.

drill pipe High strength pipe, usually in 30-foot lengths, with threaded connections on each end.

drill stem The entire drilling assembly; composed of the **kelly, drill pipe** and **drill collars**, used to rotate the bit and to carry the mud or circulating fluid to the bit.

drill stem test A method of obtaining a sample of fluid from a formation via a formation-tester tool attached to the **drill stem**. If the pressure is sufficient, fluid flows into the tester and up the drill pipe to the surface.

drill string Steel pipes roughly 10 metres long joined together to form a pipe from the drill bit to the drilling **platform**. It is rotated to carry out the drilling operation, and also is the conduit for the **drilling mud**.

drilling mud A mixture of clay, water and chemicals pumped downhole through the drill pipe and drill bit, used in drilling operations to lubricate and cool the drill bit, carry drilling wastes to the surface, prevent the walls of the **well** from collapsing and to keep the upward flow of oil or gas under control. It is circulated continuously down the drill string and up to the surface between the drill pipe and the wall of the hole. See also **lost circulation**; **oil-cut mud**.

drilling rig A drilling unit that is not permanently fixed to the seabed (e.g. a drill ship, a semi-submersible or a jack-up unit). This term also means the **derrick** and its associated machinery.

dry gas A mixture of **methane**, ethane and **liquefied petroleum gas** and up to three per cent. of carbon dioxide. See also **natural gas**.

dry gasfield The production from such a reservoir will yield dry/lean gas and very small quantities of **condensate**; typically less than 10 barrels per million cubic feet.

dry hole An unsuccessful well that has been drilled to a certain depth without finding oil or gas. The well may flow water, gas or even oil but not in sufficient quantities for production; a duster.

dry tonne The standard measure of sewage sludge or industrial effluent after most of the water has been removed. It is used for comparing sewage sludge generation and disposal statistics. See also **wet tonne**.

DST See **drill stem test**.

dual completion The completion of a **well** in two separate reservoirs which are producing at the same time.

dual supply The supply of water of different qualities to different categories of user.

due date Date on which payment of interest or principal becomes due and payable.

due diligence The detailed review of the borrower's/issuer's overall position, which is supposed to be undertaken by the lead manager of a new financing in conjunction with the preparation of legal documentation.

DWT See **dead weight tonnage**.

E&P, E/D&P Exploration (development) and production.

earnings The excess of revenues over all related expenses for a given time. Sometimes used to describe income, net income, profit or net profit.

EBRD European Bank for Reconstruction and Development, a multilateral lending agency that targets certain member countries in Eastern Europe and the former Soviet Union.

ECA See **export credit agencies**.

ECGD Export Credits Guarantee Department – the ECA for the United Kingdom.

ECIC Exports Credit Insurance Corporation – the ECA for Singapore.

ECO Extended co-financing facility of the World Bank.

economic rate of return The project's rate of return after taking into account economic costs and benefits, including monetary costs and benefits.

economies of scale Lower average total cost achieved as a result of higher output levels.

ecosystem A unit consisting of a community of organisms and their environment.

EDC Export Development Corporation – the ECA for Canada.

effluent Liquid wastes typically discharged into a body of water, e.g. the liquid discharged from a waste water treatment plant into a body of water, which is often subject to various quality criteria.

EFIC Export Finance Insurance Corporation – the ECA for Australia.

EIA See **environmental impact assessment**.

EIB European Investment Bank.

EIS See **environmental impact statement**.

EKN Exportkreditnamden – the ECA for Sweden.

electric log Survey of an uncased hole which measures the resistivity and spontaneous potential of the rock formations penetrated. See also **log**.

elevation Elevation above sea level of the **derrick** floor or rotary table.

embedded generation Generation for a specific area (such as an industrial park or zone) or for a specific requirement (such as a refinery or a desalination plant – also known as a "captive" power plant). See also **distributed generation**.

end user The final consumer of the output produced by a project.

Energy Charter Treaty (ECT) A treaty signed by 45 governments and the EU in Lisbon, Portugal on 17 December 1994.

energy intensity Energy consumed per unit contribution to gross domestic product. For business sectors it is the energy per unit of gross value added. The equivalent for the domestic sector is the energy consumed per household or per person.

engineered carbon sequestration See **carbon storage**.

enhanced oil recovery (EOR) The recovery of oil from a reservoir other than by the use of natural reservoir pressure. This can involve increasing the pressure (secondary recovery) brought about by injecting gas (e.g. CO_2) or water or heating or increasing the pore size of the reservoir (tertiary recovery). See also **acidising**.

environmental costs Negative ecological consequences.

environmental impact assessment (EIA) An assessment of the potential impact of a project on the environment that results in an environmental impact statement.

environmental impact statement (EIS) A statement of the potential impact of a project on the environment. The result of an **environmental impact assessment**, which may have been subject to public comment.

environmental risk The economic or administrative consequences of slow or catastrophic environmental pollution.

EPC contract Engineering, procurement and construction contract (i.e. turnkey construction contract).

equity The cash or assets contributed by the sponsors in a project financing. A company's paid-up share capital and other shareholders' funds. For accounting purposes, it is the net worth or total assets minus liabilities.

equity crude The proportion of **crude oil** to which a producing company is entitled as a result of its financial contribution to the project.

equity kicker A share of ownership interest in a company, project or property, or a potential ownership interest in a company, project or property, in consideration for making a loan. The kicker may take the form of stock, stock warrants, purchase options, a percentage of profits or a percentage of ultimate ownership.

ERG ERG Geschaftsstelle für die Exportrisikogarantie – the ECA for Switzerland.

ERR Economically recoverable reserves.

escrow A deed that has been signed and sealed but is delivered on the condition that it will not become operative until some stated event happens. It will become effective as soon as that event occurs and it cannot be revoked in the meantime. Banks often hold escrow accounts, in which funds accumulate to pay taxes, insurance on mortgaged property, etc.

event of default One of a list of events which would entitle the lenders, under the terms of the relevant credit facility or debt instrument, to cancel the facility and/or declare all amounts owing by the debtor to be immediately due and payable. Events of default typically include non-payment of amounts owing to the lenders, breach of covenant, **cross-default**, insolvency and **material adverse change**. See also **default**.

evergreen A contract that rolls over after each agreed (short-term) period until cancelled by one party.

exchange controls Restrictions that are applied by a country's monetary authority, or central bank, to limit the convertibility of the local currency into other specific foreign currencies.

exchange rate The price at which one currency trades for another. Also known as **foreign exchange rate**. See also **floating currency**.

expected NPV (ENPV) Weighted by probability of outcome.

exploratory well A **well** drilled either in search of a new undiscovered pool of oil or gas, or to extend greatly the limits of a known pool.

export credit agencies (ECA) An agency established by a country to finance its national goods, investment and services. They often offer political risk insurance. Also known as a **trade finance agency**. See also **bilateral agencies; multilateral lending agencies**.

export credit incentive programmes The governments of most of the world's industrial and trading nations sponsor trade support programmes that are designed to promote the **host country**'s exports. The programmes usually include a variety of short-, medium- and long-term financing, guarantees, or insurance programmes in which governments share commercial and political risks ranging from currency inconvertibility and bankruptcy to war, riot and revolution. Also known as **trade financing programmes**.

Export-Import Bank of the United States (US Eximbank) The ECA of the United States of America.

expropriation The taking over by the state of a company or project, with compensation usually being paid. Creeping expropriation occurs when a government gradually takes over an asset by taxation, regulation, access or **change in law**.

facility fee An annual percentage fee payable to a bank providing a credit facility on the full amount of the facility, whether or not utilised. See also **front-end fee**.

farm-in An arrangement whereby one oil operator buys into a lease owned by another operator where oil or gas has been discovered or is being produced. Farm-ins are often negotiated to assist the original owner with development costs or to secure a source of crude or natural gas for the buyer.

farm-out The agreement made between oil operators whereby the owner of a lease not interested in drilling at the present time agrees to assign the lease or part of it to another operator who wants to drill the **acreage**.

fault A break or fracture zone in the rock in which adjacent rocks have moved relative to one another.

fault trap A trap for oil or gas in which the closure, forming the trap, results from the presence of one or more faults.

FCIA See **Foreign Credit Insurance Association**.

featherweight floating charge A **floating charge** whose purpose is only to defeat the appointment of an administrator in relation to a company.

Federal Energy Regulatory Commission (FERC) The Government organisation in the United States whose responsibilities include regulating the gas industry.

feedstock Raw material for a processing unit.

field A test well or group of test wells defining the limit of an oil or gas pool.

field appraisal The process of quantifying reserve levels and production potential of a newly-discovered petroleum reservoir, usually by drilling a delineation **well**.

filtration The process of removing particulate matter from water by passing it through a porous medium.

financial close In a financing, the point at which the documentation has been executed and conditions precedent have been satisfied or waived. **Drawdowns** become permissible after this point.

financial model A method of analysing the revenues and costs of the project, identifying the need for contingencies, and allocating revenue to costs in accordance with the needs of the project and the project company's obligations towards the project participants and other contractors.

fishing The effort to recover tools, pipe or other objects from the **well** bore that may have become detached while in the well.

fixed charge A charge usually contained in a debenture over a company's assets which prevents the company from dealing in any way with the property covered by the fixed charge without the consent of the chargee. See also **floating charge**.

fixed cost Any cost which does not vary over the observation period.

fixed currency A currency where the official exchange value in terms of gold or other currencies is maintained by the central bank or monetary authority of the concerned country and which does not vary.

fixed rate An **interest rate** that is fixed for a defined period.

fixed rate loan A loan for which the rate paid by the borrower is fixed for the life of the loan.

flaring The burning of unwanted gas as a means of disposing of it during completion operations.

flash point The temperature at which a given substance will ignite.

floating charge A form of security taken by a creditor over the whole or substantially the whole of a company's assets. The company can continue to use the assets in its business until an **event of default** occurs and the charge crystallises. The holder of the floating charge can then appoint an **administrative receiver** (although under English law, see the implications of the Enterprise Act 2002). See also **featherweight floating charge**; **fixed charge**.

floating currency A currency whose rate of exchange (**exchange rate**) is allowed to fluctuate according to the forces of supply and demand. All currencies are subject to some degree of central bank intervention to soften the effects of market forces.

floating interest rate An interest rate that fluctuates during the term of a loan in accordance with some external index. See also **interest rate**.

floating storage unit (FSU) A large moored chamber in which oil produced from an offshore production platform is stored before being transferred to a tanker. See also **single buoy mooring**.

floor The level below which an interest rate or currency is ordained not to fall.

flotel The floating accommodation used as quarters for offshore personnel.

fluid injection The injection, down the **borehole** or a single test **well** or a group of test wells, of gas, water or other liquid to force oil toward adjacent producing wells.

force majeure Events outside the control of the parties and which prevent one or both of the parties from performing their contractual obligations.

Foreign Credit Insurance Association (FCIA) An unincorporated consortium of more than 50 leading United States insurance companies that co-operate with **Export-Import Bank (US)** to cover commercial and political risks for short-term and medium-term export credit transactions.

foreign exchange rate (FX rate) The price at which the currency of one country can be bought with the currency of another country. Also known as the **exchange rate**.

foreign exchange risk The effect on project cash flow or debt service of a movement in the FX rate for revenue, costs or **debt service**.

forex (FX) Foreign exchange.

formation An individual bed or group of beds distinctive in character and persisting over a fairly large area.

formation pressure The pressure at the bottom of a well when it is shut in at the **wellhead**.

formation water Salt water underlying gas and oil in the formation.

forward contract (forwards) An agreement to exchange currency or interest obligations in the future. For tradable commodities or securities, an agreement to buy or sell at a future date. See also **futures contract**.

forward market A market in which participants agree to trade some commodity, security or foreign exchange at a fixed price at some future date. Unlike futures and options, trading in forward markets does not occur on organised exchanges but through the forex traders of financial institutions. Forward currency contracts are not transferable instruments and settlement is usually expected to be through actual delivery of currencies. See also **futures market**.

forward rate The rate at which forward transactions of some specific maturity are being made; e.g. the US dollar price at which Euros can be bought for delivery three months hence.

fossil fuel Energy derived from coal, crude oil, natural gas – combustible hydrocarbon formed from organic matter in the earth over millions of years.

FPSO Floating production storage offloading facility.

fractional distillation A process based on the difference in boiling points of liquids in a mixture to be separated. Successive vaporisation and condensation of crude oil in a fractionating column will separate out the lighter products, leaving a residue of fuel oil or bitumen. Distillation is carried out in such a way as to avoid any **cracking**. It is the basic process that takes place in an oil refinery.

fractionating column See **fractional distillation**.

fractionation The general name for the process of separating a mixture into its constituents or fractions. See also **absorption; fractional distillation**.

fracturing Application of hydraulic pressure to a reservoir to create or enlarge fractures through which oil and gas may be produced.

fresh water Water that contains less than 1,000 milligrams per litre of dissolved solids such as metals and nutrients.

front-end fee A fee, calculated as a percentage of the principal value of an issue of securities, which is payable once at issue (front-end), as opposed to a percentage fee payable each year. See also **facility fee**.

FSU See **floating storage unit**.

fuel cell An electric cell used to generate electrical energy from the reaction of a number of chemicals, without the need for combustion and without producing noise or pollution. Can use **natural gas** as a **feedstock**. Potential applications include stationary power generation, transport (replacing the internal combustion engine) and portable power (replacing batteries in mobile phones).

fuel gas Refers to gaseous fuels, capable of being distributed by pipeline, such as **natural gas, liquefied petroleum gas, coal gas** and refinery gas.

fuel oils The heavy oils from the refining process; used as fuel for power stations, industry, ships, etc. See also **heavy fractions**.

fuel poverty The common definition of a fuel poor household is one needing to spend in excess of 10 per cent. of household income to achieve a satisfactory heating regime (21°C in the living room and 18°C in the other occupied rooms).

full recourse No matter what risk event occurs, the borrower's or its guarantor's guarantee to repay the debt.

funding risk The impact that higher funding costs or lack of availability of funds can have on project **revenue flow**.

future value The value of an initial investment after a specified period at a certain rate of interest (**interest rate**).

futures (oil) The sale and purchase of oil at a price agreed upon in advance for delivery at a future date. The seller may not yet have the oil, and both buyer and seller are speculating on how prices will change in the future.

futures contract A legal agreement between a buyer/seller and an established exchange or its clearing house in which the buyer/seller agrees to take/make delivery of something at a specified price at the end of a designated period. The price at which the parties agree to transact in the future is called the "futures price". The designated date at which the parties must transact is called the "settlement" or "delivery" date. Futures contracts are usually tradable on exchanges or computer trading screens. See also **forwards contract**.

futures market A market in which contracts for future delivery of a commodity or a security are bought and sold. Different exchanges specialise in particular kinds of contracts. The exchange generally acts as a middleman, guaranteeing payment in case either buyer or seller defaults. See also **forward market**.

futures option The right of a buyer to buy from or sell to a writer a designated **futures contract** at a designated price at any time during the period stated.

FX Foreign exchange. Sometimes abbreviated to forex.

FX rate See **foreign exchange rate**.

FX risk See **foreign exchange risk**.

gas A combustible or non-combustible fluid produced in a natural state from the earth and which maintains a gaseous or rarefied state at ordinary temperature and pressure conditions. See also **associated gas; coal gas; inert gas; interruptible gas; lean gas; natural gas; rich gas; sour gas; synthetic gas; town gas**.

gas cap The portion of an oil reservoir occupied by free gas.

gas-cap drive A type of primary reservoir drive, in which expansion of a gas cap forces oil out of the reservoir and into the **well** bore.

gas/condensate field A **reservoir** containing both **natural gas** and oil, with a greater proportion of gas. **Condensate** appears when the gas is drawn from the well, and its temperature and pressure change sufficiently for some of it to become liquid petroleum.

gas/condensate ratio (a) For a gas/condensate reservoir this is the ratio of the **condensate** to the **gas**. As for oil, it can be measured in **SCF** per **BBL**. Alternatively, the inverse is used and the typical units are BBL per **MMSCF**. (b) For a **dry gasfield**, only the inverse is normally used. Typical units are again BBL per MMSCF, but grammes per cubic metre may well be used.

gas/condensate reservoir A reservoir in which neither **natural gas** nor **crude oil** is the predominant production stream. To increase the recovery of the **condensate**, the gas may be recycled for the early years and produced at a later date.

gas cut Adjective applied to oil or mud which is mixed with some gas on a **drill stem test** or **completion test**.

gas cycling or recycling A process in which produced gas is re-injected into the reservoir after removal of the **condensate**. This is to maintain the reservoir pressure and prevent condensate from "condensing" in the reservoir and then becoming difficult to recover. This is called **retrograde condensation**.

gas detector An instrument to detect the pressure of various gases, often as a safety precaution to guard against flammable or toxic gases.

gasfield A field or group of reservoirs of hydrocarbons, containing **natural gas** but insignificant quantities of oil.

gas gathering system A central collection point for offshore **gasfields**, with **pipelines** from a number of fields, often owned by a number of different companies. From there, the gas is transported to a central processing system onshore.

gas grid The term used for the network of gas transmission and distribution pipelines in a region or country, through which gas is transported to industrial, commercial and domestic users.

gasification The production of gaseous fuel from solid or liquid fuel.

gas lift One of several methods of artificial lift. A mechanical process using the continuous or intermittent injection of a gas into the production conduit (tubing or casing) to aerate or displace the produced fluids. This creates a reduction of the bottom hole pressure of the **well**, increasing or sustaining the flow rate of the well.

gas liquefaction The process of cooling **natural gas** to a temperature of -162°C, thereby reducing its volume by a factor of 600 and making it liquid. The resulting **liquefied natural gas** (LNG) is then transportable by purpose-designed ships (**LNG carriers**) or may be stored in tanks.

gas oil The medium oil from the refining process; used as a fuel in **diesel** engines, burned in central heating systems and also used as a **feedstock** for the chemical industry.

gas/oil ratio (GOR) The number of cubic feet of **natural gas** produced with a barrel of oil.

gas processing The separation of oil and gas, and the removal of impurities and natural gas liquids from **natural gas**.

gas treatment Removal of impurities, **condensate**, hydrogen sulphide and any liquids from the **raw natural gas** contained in a **gasfield**.

gas turbine A turbine propelled by the combustion of a compressed mixture of **natural gas** and air, used for power generation.

gas well A **borehole** sunk into the ground with the objective of bringing natural gas to the surface.

gauge pressure The pressure which a normal measuring device would register. Such devices measure the pressure which is in excess of the atmospheric pressure.

gearing The level of **debt** to **equity**. Interest-bearing debt divided by shareholders' equity.

general partner The partner with unlimited liability.

general partnership A partnership in which all partners have unlimited liability.

geographical information system (GIS) A computer system used to record spatial data as an overlay on a digital map.

geological log A detailed description of all underground features discovered during the drilling of a **well**, including types of formations encountered and their physical characteristics.

gigajoule (gJ) One billion joules, or 109, the unit of measure for gas equivalent to barrel.

gigawatt One thousand megawatts.

GIS See **geographical information system**.

gJ See **gigajoule**.

GOR See **gas/oil ratio**.

GPD Gallons per day, a measure of flow.

grantor The party which grants a concession, a licence or some other right.

greenfield Often used to refer to a planned facility which must be built from scratch, without existing infrastructure.

greenhouse gases Gases that contribute to global warming. See also **Kyoto protocol**.

grid The transmission system that brings energy to the end users.

grid codes The industry codes that govern the technical interface between the users of the electricity transmission systems and the transmission licence holders.

gross-up Additional payments made by a borrower or issuer of debt instruments to compensate its creditors for withholding taxes or similar levies which reduce the amounts actually received by the creditors.

groundwater Water found beneath the earth's surface (usually in **aquifers**).

groundwater basin Interconnected permeable geologic material capable of storing a significant groundwater supply surrounded by less permeable material.

guarantee An undertaking to repay in the event of a **default**. It may be limited in time and amount. See also **subrogation**.

guarantor A party which will guarantee repayment or performance of a covenant.

gun perforation A **well** completion method in which holes are made through casing and cement into the adjoining formation by the firing of steel bullets from a perforating gun. See also **jet perforation**.

hard currency A currency considered by the market to be likely to maintain its value against other currencies over a period and not likely to be eroded by inflation. Hard currencies are usually freely convertible. See also **soft currency**.

hard water Alkaline water containing dissolved salts that interfere with some industrial processes and impede the ability of soap to lather.

heat rate The amount of fuel required to generate a **kilowatt hour** (kWh) of electricity, usually expressed as an energy value such as **kilojoules** (kJ).

heavy fractions Also known as "heavy ends", these are the oils made up of the large molecules that emerge from the bottom part of the **fractionating column** during oil refining. See also **fuel oils**.

hedge A method whereby currency exposure (the risk of possible loss due to currency fluctuations) or commodity exposure is covered or offset for a fixed period of time. This is accomplished by taking a position in futures equal and opposite to an existing or anticipated cash or commodity position, or by shorting a security similar to one in which a long position has been established. For example, a manufacturer may contract to sell a large quantity of a product for delivery over the next six months. If the product depends on a raw material that fluctuates in price, and if the manufacturer does not have sufficient raw material in stock, an open position will result. This open position can be hedged by buying the raw material required on a **futures contract**; if it has to be paid for in a foreign currency the manufacturer's currency needs can be hedged by buying that foreign currency forward or on an **option**.

hell-or-high-water An absolute commitment, under English law, with no contractual defence.

HERMES HERMES Kreditversicherungs AG – the ECA for Germany.

host country The country of the site of the project, which is considered to be hosting the project.

hurdle rate Minimum acceptable rate of return on investment.

hydrocarbons Organic chemical compounds of hydrogen and carbon atoms forming the basis of all petroleum products. They may exist as gases, liquids or solids. An example of each is methane, hexane and asphalt.

hydrocracking See **cracking**.

hydrogeneration Electricity generation involving the use of water to turn a turbine.

hydroskimming refinery A refinery with a configuration including only distillation, reforming and some **hydrotreating**.

hydrotreating Usually refers to the hydrodesulphurisation process, but may also be applied to other treating processes using hydrogen.

IBRD International Bank for Reconstruction and Development, a multilateral agency based in Washington D.C. Also known as the **World Bank**.

ICC The International Chamber of Commerce, an organisation based in Paris that represents the interests of the global business community. For example, it provides a variety of international dispute resolution services through its International Court of Arbitration.

ICSID International Centre for Settlement of Investment Disputes, a body created under the auspices of the World Bank but wholly independent. It provides dispute resolution services for investment disputes.

IDC See **interest during construction**.

IEA See **International Energy Agency**.

IFC See **International Finance Corporation**.

IFI International Finance Institution, for example the **IFC** or the **EBRD**.

IGCC See **integrated gasification combined cycle**.

IMF International Monetary Fund.

IMOH Imperfect market opportunity hypothesis.

in situ **treatment** Water treatment conducted where the source of **raw water** is located, without moving it to another location for treatment.

income statement A report of a company's revenues, associated expenses and resulting income for a period. The profit and loss statement.

inconvertibility A local currency that cannot be exchanged for another currency.

incremental borrowing rate The **interest rate** that a person would expect to pay for a certain loan at a certain time.

indemnity A legal obligation to cover the liability of another.

indexed loan A loan with debt service repayment tied to some standard that is calculated to protect the lenders against inflation and/or currency exchange risk.

indexed rate An interest rate linked to an index.

indigenous energy Energy produced from local resources.

inert gas A chemically inert **gas**, resistant to chemical reactions with other substances.

infiltration Water or other liquid flowing into a pipe or system, usually through some defect in that pipe or system.

influent Water or other liquid flowing into a reservoir, basin or treatment plant.

information memorandum A document detailing a project and its financing, usually in connection with a syndication. See also **project documents**.

initial public offering (IPO) An initial public offering of shares; a float.

injection well Well used for the injection of gas or water under pressure into a subsurface zone.

input supplier The project participant that will bear the market risk of purchase and transportation of the input necessary for operation of the project.

input supply agreement The agreement entered into by the project company and the input supplier which defines the rights and obligations in relation to the supply of input for the project. It will be used to allocate the market risk of input cost and provision. This agreement will often be on either a **take-or-pay** or a **take-and-pay** basis. See also **constituent documents**; **project documents**.

institutional investors Investors such as banks, insurance companies, trusts, pension funds and foundations, and educational, charitable and religious institutions.

instrument A financial tool. Sometimes a discrete type of funding or a security.

intangible assets Assets that are not tangible, such as goodwill, patents and trade marks, deferred charges and share/bond premiums.

integrated gasification combined cycle (IGCC) IGCC plants initially gasify the raw fuel input, before passing the so-called "synthesis gas" through a conventional combined cycle set-up. IGCCs can be designed to use a range of raw fuel inputs, including coal, oil products and wastes.

integrated pollution prevention and control (IPPC) Integrated pollution prevention and control regulates the discharges from industrial processes into the air, land and water.

intercreditor agreement An agreement between lenders as to the rights of creditors in the event of default, covering such topics as collateral, waiver, security and set-offs.

interest Cash amounts paid by borrowers to lenders for the use of their money. Normally expressed as a percentage. See also **capitalised interest**; **compound interest**; **simple interest**.

interest during construction (IDC) This interest usually equals **capitalised interest**.

interest rate The percentage payable to a lender calculated at an annual rate on the **principal**.

intermediary An entity standing between parties to a funding or a **swap**.

internal rate of return (IRR) The discount rate that equates the present value of a future stream of payments to the initial investment.

International Energy Agency (IEA) Established in 1974 to monitor the world energy situation, promote good relations between producer and consumer countries and develop strategies for energy supplies during times of emergency.

International Finance Corporation (IFC) This is the private sector arm, and a subsidiary, of the International Bank for Reconstruction and Development (**IBRD**) (the World Bank).

interruptible gas Gas made available under agreements permitting the termination or interruption of delivery by the suppliers, usually for a limited number of days in a specific period. The opposite is "firm gas".

intra vires An act within the scope of one's authority. See also *ultra vires*.

investment bank A financial institution specialising in the original sale and subsequent trading of company securities.

investor One of the shareholders in the project company.

IPIECA International Petroleum Industry Environmental and Conservation Association.

IPO See **initial public offering**.

IPP Independent power project.

IPPC See **integrated pollution prevention and control**.

IRR See **internal rate of return**.

irrigation The **abstraction**, distribution and use of water in agriculture.

jacket The structure used to support an offshore steel production **platform**.

jet perforation A well completion method in which holes are cut through the casing and cement by means of a shaped charge of high pressure, high temperature gas. See also **gun perforation**.

JICA Japan International Cooperation Agency.

JOA See **joint operating agreement**.

joint and several liability In the context of a **guarantee** for which there is more than one guarantor, liability that gives rise to one joint obligation and to as many several obligations as there are joint and several promisors. The co-promisors are not cumulatively liable, so that performance by one discharges all. See also **liability**.

joint liability Liability that is owed to a beneficiary by two or more obligors. Each joint obligor has the right to insist that any co-obligor be joined to a dispute as co-defendant. See also **liability**.

joint operating agreement (JOA) An agreement governing the manner in which the parties to the agreement will manage a **block**, and entered into following award of the licence. See also **licence block**.

joint venture Often used to describe any jointly owned corporation or partnership which owns, operates or constructs a facility, project or enterprise. More specifically, an arrangement between two or more parties for the joint management or operation of a facility, project enterprise or company under an operating agreement which is not a partnership.

joule Unit of measurement equal to 1/3600 of a kilowatt hour, or approximately 0.7375 foot-pounds. The work done when a force of 1 newton is applied to an object, displacing it through a distance of 1 metre in the direction of the force.

kelly The heavy square or hexagonal shaped steel pipe used to transfer a rotary drive from the rotary table to the **drill stem**.

KFF/KSF Key failure (success) factor.

kick A surge in gas or mud pressure at the top of a well while drilling.

kilocalorie One thousand calories. A unit of heat used in the chemical processing industry.

kilojoule (kJ) A measure of energy.

kilowatt hour (kWh) Unit of measurement in electric power. One thousand watts delivered for one hour. One kilowatt hour is equivalent to 0.0949 cubic metres of gas.

know-how Knowledge, experience and skills, including technical, management, scientific and financial.

Kyoto protocol A protocol to the UN framework convention on climate change (UNFCCC) agreed in 1997. Developed nations are required to cut overall **greenhouse gas** emissions by an average of 5.2 per cent. below 1990 levels during the period 2008-2012.

landfill A facility in which solid waste from municipal or industrial sources is disposed of by burial.

landward areas The land down to the low water mark together with inland waters (i.e. waters on the landward side of base from which the territorial sea is measured). See also **seaward areas**.

latent default A potential **default** that may have always been present but unidentified.

laybarge A barge that is specially equipped to lay submarine pipelines. See also **crane barge**.

LDO Lease-Develop-Operate (similar to BOO).

LDs See **liquidated damages**.

lead arranger The senior tier of arranger.

lead bank The bank which negotiates a large loan with a borrower and solicits other lenders to join the syndicate making the loan.

lead manager A ranking of lenders and advisers according to the underwriting, final take, or number of project finance loans or advisory mandates.

lean gas Gas with relatively few hydrocarbons other than methane. The calorific value is typically around 1,000 **BTU** per **SCF**, unless there is a significant proportion of non-hydrocarbon gases present.

legal risk A risk that a defect in the documentation or legal structure will affect cash flow or **debt service**.

lenders The entities providing debt contributions to the project company.

lending agreements The documents that provide the terms of financing.

lessee A user who pays lease rentals to the owner/lessor against rights to use the underlying **assets**.

lessor An owner who offers use of the asset to the lessee for a time and for a price.

letter of credit A **guarantee** limited in time and amount. A letter of credit is a written undertaking by a bank (issuing bank) given to the seller (beneficiary) at the request and in accordance with the instructions of the buyer (applicant) to effect payment up to a stated sum of money within a prescribed time limit and against stipulated documents. See also **confirmed letter of credit; revocable letter of credit; stand-by letter of credit**.

liability An obligation to pay an amount or perform a service. See also **joint and several liability; joint liability; off-balance sheet liabilities; several liability**.

LIBOR London interbank offered rate, the quoted rate of interest on money lent between financial institutions, often quoted as a one-, three- or six-month rate. See also **NIBOR**.

licence block A section of continental shelf area bounded by latitude and longitude lines, generally at one degree intervals, and subdivided into smaller areas. The "licences" are sold to companies giving them oil exploration rights. See also **joint operating agreement (JOA)**.

licence round A period during which a state offers and then allocates a number of specified areas within its national boundaries to oil companies.

lien A legal security interest in an asset.

light crude Crude oil with relatively high proportions of light fractions and low specific gravity. See also **syncrude**.

light fractions The low molecular weight, low boiling point fractions that emerge from the upper part of **fractionating distillation** during oil refining. See also **black products**; **white products**.

lightening See **lightering**.

lightering A ship-to-ship cargo transfer operation to enable a vessel to enter a draft-restricted port. Sometimes known as **lightening**.

limited partnership A partnership consisting of one or more general partners, jointly and severally responsible as ordinary partners, by whom a business is conducted; and one or more limited partners, contributing in cash payments a specific sum as capital and which are not liable for the debts of the partnership beyond the funds so contributed.

limited recourse Under certain conditions (legal or financial), there is access to the sponsors' credit or other legal security for repayment (besides the project's cash flows). There is usually recourse in the event of fraud or misrepresentation/ non-disclosure – thus "non-recourse" is better described as "limited recourse". See also **recourse**.

line of credit A commitment of a bank to a borrower to extend a series of credits to the borrower under certain terms and conditions up to an agreed maximum amount for a specified period.

line pack The ability to increase the amount of gas in a **pipeline** by increasing the pressure above the normal pressure of the system, but still within a safe limit. Used as a method of peak or **diurnal storage**.

liquefied natural gas (LNG) When **natural gas** is cooled to a temperature of approximately -160°C at atmospheric pressure it condenses to a liquid called "liquefied natural gas (LNG)". Natural gas is composed primarily of methane (typically, at least 90 per cent.), but may also contain ethane, propane and heavier hydrocarbons. Liquefaction reduces its volume to a fraction of the original gas. See also **compressed natural gas**; **gas liquefaction**; **natural gas liquids**.

liquefied petroleum gas (LPG) Gas, usually propane or butane, derived from oil and put under pressure so that it is in liquid form. Often used to power portable cooking stoves or heaters and to fuel some types of vehicle, e.g. some specially adapted road vehicles and forklift trucks. These gases can be extracted from **natural gas** and liquefied by compression to a pressure of up to 200 pounds per square inch and when stored in pressure cylinders its volume is reduced to a fraction of the original gas, as is the case with LNG.

liquidated damages (LDS) A fixed periodic amount payable as a sanction for delays or substandard performance under a contract. Also known as a **penalty clause**.

liquidation The process of closing down a company, selling its assets, paying off its creditors and distributing any remaining cash to owners.

liquidity The ability to service debt and redeem or reschedule liabilities when they mature, and the ability to exchange other assets for cash.

LNG carrier A tanker specifically designed to carry **liquefied natural gas**, fitted with insulated pressure tanks made of stainless steel or aluminium. The load is refrigerated to -162°C.

LNG terminal A receiving station for LNG shipments, typically with storage and regasification facilities.

LNG train An LNG plant comprises one or more LNG trains, each of which is an independent unit for **gas liquefaction**. It is more cost-effective to add a train to an existing LNG plant than to build a new LNG facility (known as a **greenfield** project), because infrastructure, such as ship terminals, does not have to be built for a new LNG train.

load factor The ratio of the average load to the peak load during any particular period.

load-on-top A system of clearing tanks in an oil tanker by collecting washings in one "slop" tank, allowing the water to separate from the oil, then discharging the clean water overboard, leaving the oil residues in the tank and minimising pollution at sea.

local currency The official domestic currency (currency of issue) of any particular country.

log A record of activity or results of plans or surveys. In drilling a well there are a number of different kinds of logs, such as downhole density log, driller's log, **electric log**, **geological log**, **mud log** and **well log**.

long-term debt A borrowing over a long period, usually through bank loans or the sale of **bonds**. On **balance sheet**, any debt due for more than one year is classified as "long-term".

lost circulation An interruption in the circulation of **drilling mud** caused by the mud entering a porous zone, fracture or cavity, such that the mud fails to return to the surface.

lost time injury (LTI) A measure of safety performance.

LROT Lease-Refurbish-Operate-Transfer. The project company leases the project, refurbishes it, operates it for a period and then transfers it back to the grantor. Similar to **BOT**.

LTI See **lost time injury**.

luboil Lubricating oil used to grease and ease the working of mechanical joints and moving parts.

mains Pipes that carry treated drinking water to the customer's supply pipe via a connection pipe. Also called the **distribution mains**.

maintenance or retention bond A **bond** to provide funds for maintenance and repair of equipment or a facility. Maintenance bonds are used in connection with construction contracts to ensure that a construction contractor will repair mistakes and defects after completion of construction. The retention bond may be used in lieu of the construction contractor, leaving a portion of the contract price on deposit with the project company to ensure performance.

maintenance reserves Reserves set aside to make up for any lack of funds available to the project company when maintenance costs exceed forecasts or where, periodically, maintenance costs will be higher than during other periods of the project.

majors The world's largest privately/publicly owned oil companies (Shell, ExxonMobil, ChevronTexaco and BP). National oil companies can be much larger.

management contracting A structure whereby a private company takes on the management of the project, selecting contractors, setting prices, and overseeing construction and other services for the benefit of the grantor for a fee, generally based on performance or total cost.

mandate The authorisation from a borrower to a **lead manager** to arrange a transaction on agreed (usually outline) terms.

margin The amount expressed as a percentage per annum above the **interest rate** basis or cost of funds. For **hedging** and **futures contracts**, the cash collateral which is deposited with a trader or exchange as insurance against default. See also **spread**.

marginal cost of capital The incremental cost of financing.

marginal tax rate The tax rate that would have to be paid per additional dollar of taxable income earned.

marine riser A pipe that connects an offshore **platform** to a subsea wellhead or pipeline for drilling or production purposes.

market risk Changes to the amounts sold or the price received which would have an impact on gross revenue. Sometimes known as **sales risk**.

market value The price at which an item can be sold at arm's length on the open market.

material adverse change clause A general **event of default** designed to pick up any change in circumstances which might affect the likelihood of a borrower paying its debts or performing its covenants. The clause is couched in general language and is used to supplement more specific events of default.

maturity The date upon which a given **debt** falls due for repayment.

MCF One thousand cubic feet of gas at a specified temperature and pressure.

MD See **millidarcy**.

medium-term Generally from two to six years.

megajoule (MJ or mmJ) Equivalent to one million watts.

megalitres per day (ml/day) This equals 100m^3 per day. A measure of the availability of water or some other liquid.

mega watt (mW) One million watts, a measure of power.

mega watt hour (mWh) One thousand kWh. A 1mW power-generating unit running for one hour produces 1mWh of electrical energy.

merchant bank A bank which, besides lending and deposit taking (usually not from the public), engages in trading and advisory services, and acts as an underwriter and fund manager of securities.

methane (CH$_4$) This is the chief constituent of **natural gas**, but also occurs in coal beds, and is produced by animals and the decay of vegetable material. It is a light, colourless, odourless flammable gas under normal conditions.

mezzanine financing A mixture of financing instruments, with characteristics of both debt and equity, providing further debt contributions through higher-risk, higher-return instruments, sometimes treated as equity.

mg/l See **milligrammes per litre**.

MGAL One thousand cubic feet of gas at a specified temperature and pressure.

MGD One million gallons per day. A measure of flow.

micro-chp Combined heat and power, but in very small scale applications, typically below 5kW electrical output (e.g. in the residential and commercial sectors). It is likely to operate in place of a domestic central heating boiler.

MIGA Multilateral Investment Guaranty Agency, the political risk insurance (PRI) arm of the **IBRD**.

milliard Synonymous with billion (10^9).

millidarcy (MD) Unit of measure of **permeability** (flow property) of rocks.

milligrammes per litre (mg/l) A measure of concentration of a dissolved substance. A concentration of 1 mg/l means that one milligramme of a substance is dissolved in each litre of water. For practical purposes, this unit of measurement is equivalent to parts per million, or PPM.

MITI The Japanese Ministry of International Trade and Industry.

MJ/mmJ See **megajoule**.

ml/day See **megalitres per day**.

MLA Multilateral lending agency.

MMBBL One million barrels.

MMBO One million barrels of oil.

MMBOE One million barrels of oil equivalent.

MMBTU One million British thermal units.

MMCFD One million cubic feet of gas per day.

MMCFG One million cubic feet of gas.

MMSCF One million standard cubic feet.

MMSCF/D One million standard cubic feet per day.

modelling Use of mathematical equations to simulate and predict real events and processes.

module A package of plant and equipment for installation, or installed, on an offshore **platform**.

monoline Specialist insurers, whose business is the provision of financial guarantee insurance.

monomer A single molecule which can be chemically joined into long chains known as "polymers".

mortgage A pledge or assignment of **security** of particular property for payment of debt or performance of some other obligation. Also an indenture of trust or a security agreement.

MSCF One thousand standard cubic feet.

MTC One million tonnes of carbon.

MTOE One million tonnes of oil equivalent.

mud A mixture of base substance and additives used to lubricate the **drill bit** and to counteract the natural pressure of the formation. See also **drilling mud**.

mud log A progressive analysis of the well bore cuttings and mud circulated up from the bottom of the hole. See also **log**.

multicurrency loan A loan in which the borrower has the option to choose to make borrowings in more than one currency. See also **export credit agency**.

multilateral lending agencies Organisations jointly owned by a group of countries and designed to promote international and regional economic co-operation. In particular, these lending agencies have such goals as aiding development and furthering social and economic growth in member countries. Also known as "multilateral agencies". See also **bilateral agencies; export credit agencies**.

multiple completion The completion of a single **well** in more than one producing horizon.

municipal waste Waste originating from a community, which may be composed of domestic (sewage) and industrial waste water.

mW See **mega watt**.

mWh See **mega watt hour**.

naphtha A range of distillates lighter than kerosene; used as **feedstock** for motor gasoline production and the chemical industry (e.g. ethylene manufacture).

natural gas (NG) Gaseous forms of petroleum consisting of mixtures of hydrocarbon gases and vapours, the more important of which are methane, ethane, propane, butane, pentane and hexane; gas produced from a **gas well**. Natural gas is usually classified as "wet" or "dry" depending on whether the proportions of gasoline constituents that it contains are large or small. See also **gas; associated gas; compressed natural gas; dry gas; liquefied natural gas; liquefied petroleum gas; non-associated gas; raw natural gas; sales gas; solution gas; sweet gas; wet gas**.

natural gas liquids (NGL) Gas liquids such as propane, butane or pentane or a combination of them obtained from the processing of raw gas or **condensate**.

natural monopoly A monopoly exists where consumers are limited to one supplier for a specific service. A natural monopoly occurs where it is only feasible for one supplier to supply the services in question, perhaps because the service is dependent upon an existing infrastructure which would be prohibitively expensive to duplicate. A natural monopoly makes it impossible for a competing supplier to provide the services desired at a lesser or equal cost.

NCM Nederlandsche Credietverzekering Maatschappij NV – the ECA for the Netherlands.

negative pledge The borrower agrees not to pledge any of its assets as security and/or not to incur further indebtedness.

negotiable A financial instrument which can be bought or sold by another investor, privately or via a stock exchange and/or computer trading.

netback The value of gas sold to the customer at the burner-tip less the cost of transportation through the **pipeline** system and cost of production.

net income Operating cash flows less overheads and depreciation, either before tax (BT) or after tax (AT) earnings.

net pay That portion of a formation considered to have enough permeability and oil and gas saturation to produce in sufficient paying quantities.

network analysis model Digital model of a distribution network.

net worth Equity, total assets less liabilities.

New Electricity Trading Arrangements (NETA) In England and Wales these arrangements replaced the "pool" from 27 March 2001. The arrangements are based on bilateral trading between generators, suppliers, traders and customers, and are designed to be more efficient and to provide greater choice for market participants.

NG See **natural gas**.

NIBOR New York Interbank Offered Rate, which a few bankers promote as a standard equivalent to **LIBOR**.

NOC National oil company or network operating centre, in the case of telecommunications.

non-associated gas Sometimes called **unassociated gas**. **Dry gas** that is not associated with oil in a productive reservoir, or where only **gas** can be produced economically. See also **natural gas**.

non-convertible currency Those currencies whose circulation is restricted by the local authorities and where the exchange rate is artificially set by those authorities (usually well above the inevitable local black market rate).

non-point source A source (of pollution) that does not have a single point of origin.

non-potable Water that may contain objectionable pollution, contamination, minerals or infective agents and is considered unsafe or unsuitable for drinking. Applicable law will generally establish the standard at which water is considered to be **potable**.

non-recourse The lenders rely on the project's cash flows and collateral security over the project as the only means to repay **debt service**, and therefore the lenders do not have recourse to other sources, for example shareholder assets. See also **recourse**.

non-revenue water Water which is put into supply but which is not paid for as a result of, for example, illegal access or loss through leakage.

note An instrument recognised as a legal evidence of a **debt** that is signed by the maker, promising to pay a certain sum of money, on a specified date, at a certain place of business, to the payee or other holder of the note. The difference, if any, between notes and **bonds** is normally that of maturity, notes having a shorter life.

novation The transfer of rights and obligations from one entity to another, e.g. following the substitution of a new debtor for an old debtor or one bank for another under a loan facility by way of transfer certificate. Under a novation the transferor is released from all obligations to the creditor. Also known as **assignment**.

O&M Operation and maintenance.

OAPEC Organisation of Arab Petroleum Exporting Countries.

octane rating A performance rating of gasoline in terms of antiknock qualities. The higher the octane number, the greater the antiknock quality; e.g. 94 octane gasoline is superior in antiknock qualities to a gasoline of 84 octane. See also **cetane number**.

ODA Official Development Assistance. A general term for assistance provided by developed countries to developing countries, whether in the form of grants, loans or other assistance. Japanese government agency providing loans for feasibility studies and the development of infrastructure projects in neighbouring Asian countries.

OECD Organisation for Economic Cooperation and Development, based in Paris.

off-balance sheet liabilities Corporate obligations which do not need to appear as liabilities on a balance sheet, e.g. lease obligations, project finance and take-or-pay contracts.

off-peak The period during a day, week, month or year when the load being delivered by a gas system is not at its maximum volume.

Office of Gas Supply (OFGAS) The United Kingdom gas industry regulator.

offset well A well drilled on the next closest location to the original well.

offshore entity An entity operating outside the restrictions of the legal and tax regimes of a given country.

offtake The product produced by a project.

offtake purchase agreement The agreement whereby the offtake purchaser undertakes to purchase an amount of some or all of the project output, e.g. the **power purchase agreement** in the context of a power project and a water purchase agreement in the context of a water treatment project. See also **constituent documents; project documents**.

offtake purchaser The purchaser of the product produced by a project. The term is often used in connection with **take-or-pay** contracts.

OFGAS See **Office of Gas Supply**.

OIIP See **oil initially in place**.

oil gasification The conversion of petroleum into gas to be used as a fuel.

oil in place (OIP) The amount of crude oil estimated to exist in a reservoir underlying a pool or field area.

oil initially in place (OIIP) The total amount of oil identified in a given reservoir. Normally, not all the oil initially in place is recoverable.

oil string The string of casing set on top of, or through, the producing formation.

oil-cut mud Term used to describe a mixture of oil and **drilling mud**.

OKB Österreichische Kontrollbank AD – the ECA for Austria.

O&M Operation and Maintenance.

OPEC Organisation of Petroleum Exporting Countries, formed in 1960.

open cycle The waste energy/exhaust from a power plant which is not recycled to produce more energy.

open flow The maximum flow rate of a well with no restriction.

open hole An uncased well bore.

operating cash flow Project revenues accruing from operation.

operating risk Risk related to cost, technology and management components, including inflation, that have an impact on **opex** and project output/throughput.

operation and maintenance agreement The agreement allocating to the operator the obligation to operate and maintain the project in accordance with its requirements. See also **constituent documents; project documents**.

operation and maintenance costs (O&M costs) The costs of operating a system such as a treatment plant. O&M costs are ongoing expenses, such as for repair or for employee salaries.

operator The project participant which undertakes the operation and maintenance obligations.

opex Operating expenditures, always expressed as cash.

OPIC Overseas Private Investment Corporation. A self-supporting United States Government corporation providing insurance and, in some cases, partial financing to United States private investment in developing countries.

option A contract under which the writer of the option grants the buyer of the option the right, but not the obligation, to purchase from or sell to the writer something at a specified price within a specified period (or at a specified date). See also **purchase option; put option**.

overriding royalty interest (ORRI) An interest in oil and gas produced at the surface free of any cost of production.

PAH See **polyaromatic hydrates**.

par Principal amount at which an issuer agrees to redeem its notes or bonds at maturity.

pari passu Of instruments, ranking equally in right of payment with each other and with other instruments of the same issuer. From Latin: with equal step.

partnership An arrangement in which two or more persons place their money, efforts, labour and skill in lawful commerce or business with the understanding that there shall be a proportional sharing of profits and losses between them.

parts per million (PPM) A measure of concentration of a dissolved substance.

pay zone The rock strata which constitutes the oil and gas reservoir.

payback The period in years to recover an investment or loan. It may be calculated on a discounted, non-discounted, leveraged or unleveraged basis.

payback period The amount of time required to recover the initial investment.

payment mechanism The mechanism in a contract for calculating the amount of payment due from one party to the other.

pdc bit Polycrystalline diamond compact drill.

peak lopping See **peak shaving**.

peak shaving Increasing the normal supply of gas from another source during emergency or peak periods.

penalty clause See **liquidated damages**.

PEP See **petroleum exploration permit**.

perforating A method of shooting holes in a casing to allow fluids into the well.

perforations Holes made in the casing, cement and formation through which formation fluids may blow into the well bore. See also **gun perforation**; **jet perforation**.

performance bond A **bond** payable if a project is not completed as specified. Some performance bonds require satisfactory completion of the contract while other performance bonds provide for payment of a sum of money for failure of the contractor to perform under a contract.

permanent works A technical term in the construction industry referring to works performed by the construction contractor which are to form part of the completed works and therefore stay at the site. See also **temporary works**.

permeability A measure of the ability of a rock to transmit fluids, usually measured in **millidarcies (MD)**.

PEST Political, environmental, social and technological analysis.

petajoule (pJ) A unit of measure for gas reserves market. A petajoule = 1,015 Joules.

petrochemicals Chemicals derived from petroleum; **feedstocks** for manufacturing a variety of plastics and synthetic rubbers.

petroleum exploration permit (PEP) An exclusive right to explore for petroleum within the licence area, usually for a five-year period.

petroleum mining licence (PML) An exclusive right to mine for petroleum within the licence area. This is generally a long-term licence to enable field development.

petroleum prospecting licence (PPL) An exclusive right to prospect for petroleum within a licence area. This is generally short-term, approximately five years, and is renewable for a second five-year term.

PFI See **private finance initiative**.

pH A measure of acidity or alkalinity. Acids have a pH of less than 7 and alkali have a pH of greater than 7.

photovoltaics (PV) The direct conversion of solar radiation into electricity by the interaction of light with the electrons in a semiconductor device or cell.

physical or mechanical completion The project is substantially complete with only minor elements, usually identified on a punch-list, left outstanding.

pigs "Pigs" is the industry nickname for devices that can be sent down gas or liquids pipelines for a variety of purposes, e.g. cleaning pigs have wire brushes or scrapers to clean the inside of the pipeline, batching pigs are used on liquids pipelines to separate different products being pumped. Pigs are launched and received in "pig" (or "scraper") launches and "traps" (or "receivers") respectively. "Intelligent" pigs are used to inspect pipelines. See also **swab**; **wire line**.

pip One hundredth of one per cent. of the market value of a security. It is used to express price differentials.

pipeline A tube for the transportation of **crude oil** or **natural gas** between two points, either offshore or onshore.

pipeline capacity The amount of oil or gas required to keep a pipeline full, or the amount that can be passed through a pipeline over a given period of time.

pJ See **petajoule**.

plant A technical term in the construction industry referring to the major pieces of equipment used in the construction of the works, which are to become a part of the finished works. See also **permanent works**.

platform A fixed or floating offshore structure from which **wells** are drilled. Drilling platforms can become production platforms once the wells are producing oil. See also **module**; **single buoy mooring (SBM)**; **topsides**.

platforming A catalytic reforming process using a platinum catalyst.

plug a well To fill the borehole of an abandoned well with mud and cement to prevent the flow of water or oil from one strata to another to the surface.

PML See **petroleum mining licence**.

POCS Probability of commercial success.

POCV Probability of creating value.

POGS Probability of geological success.

point source A stationary source or fixed facility from which pollutants are discharged.

political risk Risks usually comprising currency inconvertibility, expropriation, war and insurrection, terrorism, non-government activists, and legal and administrative approvals. The first three are normally insurable. It often overlaps with the political component of *force majeure* risk. See also **country risk**; **sovereign risk**.

polyaromatic hydrates (PAH) A toxic industrial pollutant of increasing concern in EU and WHO water quality assessment criteria.

possible reserves An estimate of possible oil and/or gas **reserves** based on geological and engineering data from undrilled or untested areas.

potable Water that is safe and satisfactory for drinking and cooking. Water that is suitable for human consumption, as defined by WHO, EU or national standards. See also **non-potable**.

pour point The temperature below which an oil tends to solidify and will no longer flow freely.

pour point depressant (PPD) A chemical agent added to oil to keep it flowing to low temperatures.

power purchase agreement (PPA) An **offtake purchase agreement** in relation to a power project, for the purchase of electricity generated.

PPD See **pour point depressant**.

PPI Producer Price Index.

PPM Parts per million.

PPP See **public private partnership**.

pre-emptive rights Shareholder rights to maintain their proportional share of the entity by subscribing proportionally to any new stock issue or attempted sale of shares by a shareholder to a third party.

prepayment A payment made ahead of the scheduled payment date.

pre-qualification The process whereby the number of qualified bidders is limited by reviewing each bidder's qualifications against a set of criteria, generally involving experience in the relevant field, capitalisation, site country experience, identity of local partners and international reputation.

present value The value today of a future payment, calculated by discounting at a specified discounting rate.

PRI Political risk insurance.

pricing base The mutually agreed-upon basis for setting a rate of interest, such as the prime rate, or **LIBOR**.

primary recovery The recovery of oil and gas from a **reservoir** using only the natural pressure of the reservoir itself to force the oil or gas out. See also **acidising; enhanced oil recovery; secondary recovery; tertiary recovery; ultimate recovery**.

prime rate The rate at which banks lend to their best (prime) customers. The all-in cost of a bank loan to a prime credit equals the prime rate plus the cost of holding compensating balances.

principal A sum on which **interest** accrues. It is capital, as distinguished from income or the **par** value of a loan, exclusive of any premium or interest which is the basis for interest computations. Also, a person on whose behalf an **agent** or broker acts.

private finance initiative (PFI) The United Kingdom private finance initiative is a specific mechanism for funding infrastructure with standard form terms and conditions set out by the United Kingdom Treasury. It follows a **BOO** structure. This term has been replaced in the United Kingdom by "public private partnerships"; however, the term "public private partnerships" is also used internationally as a general term. Therefore, this text will refer to PFI when discussing the United Kingdom structure. See also **public private partnership (PPP)**.

pro rata Shared or divided in proportion or according to a ratio.

probable reserves An estimate of oil and/or gas **reserves** based on penetrated structures, but needing more advanced confirmation to be classified as proven reserves.

profitability index The ratio of the present value of future cash flows from a project to the initial investment in the project.

project The asset constructed with, or owned via, a **project financing**, which is expected to produce cash flow at a **debt service cover ratio** sufficient to repay the project financing.

project documents or project agreements The commercial agreements that are the subject of this book, including the **concession agreement**, the **construction contract**, the **input supply agreement**, the **offtake purchase agreement** and the **operation and maintenance agreement**. See also **constituent documents**.

project financing A loan structure that relies for its repayment primarily on the project's cash flow, with the project's assets, rights and interests held as secondary security or collateral.

PROPARCO Société de Promotion et de Participation pour la Coopération Economique S.A., the French development finance institution. A **bilateral agency**.

prospect Leases or other rights over a particular geographical area believed to include specific geologic structural or stratigraphic traps believed to contain oil or gas or both.

proved developed reserves Reserves that can be expected to be recovered through existing **wells** with existing equipment and operating methods. Additional oil and gas expected to be obtained through the application of fluid injection or other improved recovery techniques for supplementing the natural forces and mechanisms of **primary recovery** are included as "proved developed reserves" only after a testing by a pilot programme or after the operation of an installed programme has confirmed through production response that increased recovery will be achieved.

proved reserves Those quantities of **crude oil**, **natural gas** and **natural gas liquids** which, upon analysis of geologic and engineering data, appear with reasonable certainty to be recoverable in the future from known oil and gas reservoirs under existing economic and operating conditions.

proved undeveloped reserves Reserves that are expected to be recovered from new wells on undrilled **acreage** or from existing **wells** where a relatively major expenditure is required for recompletion.

public private partnership (PPP) An initiative of the United Kingdom government to pass the risk and expense of infrastructure development to the hands of the private sector through **DCMF** and **DBFO** projects. Formerly known as **private finance initiative**. Also, a generic term indicating any public sector service provided partially or wholly by the private sector.

pumping well A **well** produced by artificial lift by a subsurface pump.

purchase option The right to buy or sell property during a certain period or on the happening of certain events at a particular price (the "exercise price"). See also **option**.

put or put option An **option** whereby one person has to sell an asset to another person at a set price at some established point in the future (European). A contract allowing the holder to sell some property to some person at a fixed price at any time within a given period (United States).

put-or-pay contract See **supply-or-pay contract**.

PV See **photovoltaics**.

qualitative risk assessment The emotional, reactive assessment of risk, resulting from an individual's social, cultural, educational, commercial and emotional context.

quantitative risk assessment The mathematical assessment of the likelihood and gravity of a given risk, for example by probability analysis. An accurate quantitative risk assessment is rarely, if ever, possible due to **risk noise**.

raw natural gas Natural gas containing impurities and unwanted substances such as water, nitrogen, carbon dioxide, hydrogen sulphide gas and helium. These are removed before the gas is marketed.

raw water Water from surface or ground sources prior to treatment.

reactor The reactor is the central part of the petrochemical plant. It is in this part of the plant that the **feedstock** materials are chemically reacted and transformed into the desired end products. Catalytic crackers, regenerators and fractionators are, broadly speaking, reactor vessels.

receiver A person/entity appointed under the legal security documents to administer **security** on behalf of the project financiers.

recourse In the event that the project (and its associated **escrows**, sinking funds or cash reserves/stand-by facilities) cannot service the financing or the project completion cannot be achieved, then the financiers have recourse either to cash from other sponsors and/or corporate sources or other non-project security. See also **non-recourse**.

recoverable reserves The proportion of hydrocarbons that can be recovered from a reservoir using existing techniques.

reef effect The increase in marine life on and around an offshore structure.

reference banks In relation to **interest rates** calculated by reference to a particular basis rate, the bank or banks whose quote, or the average of whose quotes, for the basis rate is taken as being the basis rate for the purposes of calculating interest payable.

refinancing Repaying existing **debt** by obtaining a new loan, typically to meet some corporate objective such as the lengthening of maturity or lowering the **interest rate**. See also **rescheduling**; **restructuring**.

refining The manufacturing process that turns **crude oil** into different petroleum products.

reforming A process that improves the antiknock quality of gasoline fractions by modifying the molecular structure. The process is known as **thermal reforming** when achieved by heat and pressure, and as "catalytic reforming" when aided by a catalyst.

regulator A governmental or independent body setting standards or striking a balance between the interests of consumers and the service provider.

remedial action plan A formal plan of action for clean-up of a contaminated site.

renewable energy Energy resources that are continually available or can be replenished (e.g. solar, wind, wave, biomass, hydroelectric, geothermal).

renewables obligation certificate (ROC) In the United Kingdom, eligible renewable generators receive renewables obligation certificates (ROCs) for each **mWh** of electricity generated. These certificates can then be sold to suppliers. In order to fulfil their obligation, suppliers can either present enough certificates to cover the required percentage of their output, or they can pay a "buy-out" price.

representations A series of statements, e.g. about a project, a party or obligations.

required rate of return The minimum future receipts an investor will accept in choosing an investment.

requirements contract A contract whereby a user of a product agrees to buy its requirements for a plant or operation from a supplier. There is no requirement to take a minimum amount or to pay if not delivered, as in a **take-or-pay** contract.

rescheduling In relation to **debt** obligations, the renegotiation and agreement of revised terms of a loan facility (usually involving the spreading of interest and capital repayments over a longer period) as a result of the borrower being unable to comply with the original terms. See also **refinancing; restructuring**.

reserve account A separate amount of cash or a **letter of credit** to service a payment requirement such as **debt service** or maintenance.

reserves The unproduced oil or gas in place in a formation that remains but is still recoverable. See also **possible reserves; probable reserves; proved developed reserves; proved reserves; proved undeveloped reserves**.

reserves risk See **supply risk**.

reserves-to-production ratio For any given well, field or country, the length of time that reserves would last if production continued at its current rate, at the current level of technology.

reservoir (oil/gas) An accumulation of oil and/or gas in a porous rock such as sandstone. A petroleum reservoir normally contains three fluids (oil, gas and water) which separate into distinct sections, owing to their varying gravities. Gas occupies the upper part of the reservoir as it is the lightest, oil the middle section, while water and rocks occupy the lower section.

reservoir (water) A body of water, usually artificially impounded, for maintaining controllable supplies of **raw water**. Prior to distribution, water is usually sent to a treatment works to be made **potable** and is then held in a service reservoir.

residual The assumed value of an asset at the end of a loan, lease or pro forma cash flow. It is sometimes insured. See also **tail**.

residual cushion The amount of net cash flow from the project after the **project financing** has been repaid. If it is expressed as a percentage of the original loan amount, it is the "residual cover". See also **cushion**.

residual value Sometimes used to indicate the value of the assets associated with a project at the expiry of the concession period, for example the value of the assets transferred to the grantor at the end of the life of a BOT project.

residual value risk The **residual value** is not known at the time of entering into a BOT project. The residual value risk relates to this uncertainty and to the fact that the project as transferred to the grantor will be worth more or less than projected.

residue The heavy, non-volatile components of **crude oil** that flow from the bottom of the fractionating column during **fractional distillation**.

restructuring An arrangement by a borrower to replace debt of one maturity with debt of another (longer) maturity – and perhaps of a different type. See also **refinancing; rescheduling**.

retention An amount held back from construction contract payments until the construction contractor fulfils certain obligations, generally 5-15 per cent. of the contract price.

retention bond See **maintenance or retention bond**.

reticulation Sewage collection pipework.

retrograde condensation See **gas cycling**.

return flow The water that returns to the surface or ground water system and thus becomes available for re-use.

return on assets (ROA) Net profits after taxes divided by assets. This ratio helps a firm determine how effectively it generates profits from available assets.

return on equity (ROE) Net profits after taxes divided by equity investment.

return on investment (ROI) Net profits after taxes divided by investment.

revaluation A formal and official increase in the **exchange rate** of a currency that is made unilaterally by a country or through the International Monetary Fund.

revenue flow Net income, depreciation and amortisation during a given period. A measure of a company's liquidity. Also known as **cash flow** or "revenue stream".

revenues Sales or royalty proceeds.

reverse osmosis Liquid desalination or treatment using pressure across a semi-permeable membrane.

revocable letter of credit A **letter of credit** that can be changed or cancelled by the issuing bank or by any party involved until the time payment is made.

revolving credit agreement or revolving line of credit A legal commitment on the part of a bank to extend credit up to a maximum amount for a definite term. The **notes** evidencing debt are short-term, such as 90 days. As notes become due, the borrower can renew the notes, borrow a smaller amount or borrow amounts up to the specified maximum throughout the term of commitment.

rich gas Gas which is predominantly methane but with a relatively high proportion of other hydrocarbons. Many of these other hydrocarbons would normally be separated out as **natural gas liquids (NGL)**.

riser (drilling) A pipe between a seabed blow-out preventer and a floating **drilling rig**.

riser (production) The section of pipework that joins a seabed wellhead to the **Christmas tree**.

risk Instability or uncertainty about the future; more specifically, the degree of uncertainty involved with a loan or investment.

risk aversion An unwillingness either to bear any **risk** or to bear risk without compensation of some form.

risk premium An additional **required rate of return** that must be paid to investors who invest in risky investments to compensate for the risk.

risk noise The combination of **qualitative risk assessment** and insufficiency of information that influence an individual's assessment of a risk and distract from an accurate **quantitative risk assessment**.

RLT Refurbish-Lease-Transfer (similar to BOT).

ROA See **return on assets**.

ROE See **return on equity**.

ROI See **return on investment**.

ROO Rehabilitate-Own-Operate (similar to BOO).

ROT Rehabilitate-Operate-Transfer (similar to BOT).

rotary drilling The common method of well drilling involving the cutting of a hole by rotating a bit at the bottom of a column of **drill pipe**.

roughneck A driller's helper and worker on a drilling rig.

royalty A share of revenue or cash flow or a fee paid to the government or grantor of the concession or licence.

Rule 144a A regulation allowing sophisticated investors in the United States to take up project financing debt, bypassing some of the more burdensome Securities and Exchange Commission requirements. This rule has significantly opened up **project financing** to the capital markets in the United States.

SACE Servizi Assicurativi del Commercio Estero S.p.A. – the ECA for Italy.

safe yield The annual quantity of water that can be taken from a source of supply without depleting the source beyond its ability to be replenished.

sale and leaseback A transaction in which an investor purchases assets from the owner and then leases such assets back to the same person. The lessee receives the sale price (and can return it to capital) and continues to enjoy the use of the assets.

sales gas Raw gas is **natural gas** that has been processed to remove **liquefied petroleum gas, condensate** and carbon dioxide. Sales gas consists of methane and ethane. **Dry gas** is raw gas after deducting own use and flared gas.

sales risk See **market risk**.

salvage value The estimated selling price of an asset once it has been fully depreciated.

sample Cuttings of a rock formation broken up by the **drill bit** and brought to the surface by the **drilling mud**.

sanitary sewer Underground pipes that carry off only domestic or industrial water, not storm water. See also **storm sewer**.

SBM See **single buoy mooring**.

SCF Standard cubic feet.

scrubbing The process of purifying a gas or liquid by washing it in a contact vessel.

SDG Strategic Decisions Group.

seaward areas The remainder of the territorial sea which is not included within **landward areas**.

SEC Securities Exchange Commission (United States).

secondary humus/sludge Sludge produced during biological treatment.

secondary market After the initial distribution of bonds or securities, secondary market trading begins. New issue houses usually make a market in **bonds** or **securities** which they have co-managed.

secondary recovery Any method of increasing **ultimate recovery** of oil or condensate by the application of outside energy. See also **acidising; enhanced oil recovery; primary recovery; tertiary recovery; waterflooding**.

secondary treatment Stage of waste water treatment wherein bacteria are used to break down organic materials and significantly reduce biochemical oxygen.

secured creditor A creditor whose obligation is backed by the pledge of some asset and is therefore secured debt. In liquidation, the secured creditor receives the cash from the sale of the pledged asset to the extent of its loan.

securitisation A process that changes bank loans or other non-tradable financial transactions into tradable securities.

security A legal right of access to value through **mortgages**, contracts, cash accounts, **guarantees**, insurances, pledges or cash flow, including licences, concessions and other assets. A negotiable certificate evidencing a debt or equity obligation/shareholding.

security agreement An agreement in which title to property is held as collateral under a financing agreement, usually by a trustee.

seismic survey Geophysical information on subsurface rock formations using a seismograph; the investigation of underground strata by recording and analysing shock waves artificially produced and reflected from subsurface bodies of rock.

semi-convertible currency Semi-convertible currencies can only be bought or sold through a central bank at specific fixed rates of exchange.

send-out The quantity of gas delivered by a plant or system during a specified period of time.

separator An apparatus for separating well fluids into gaseous and liquid components. Separators segregate oil, gas and water with the aid, at times, of chemical treatment and the application of heat.

septic tank Tank used to hold domestic waste where a sewerage system is not available to carry it to a treatment plant; part of a rural on-site sewage treatment system.

set-off An agreement between the parties involved to set off one **debt** against another or one loss against a gain. A banker is empowered to set off a credit balance on one account against a debit balance on another if the accounts are in the same name and in the same currency.

several liability In the context of a guarantee, for which there is more than one guarantor, each guarantor's liability to pay the whole of the debt guaranteed. The promises of the co-guarantors are cumulative and payment by one does not discharge the other. See also **liability**.

sewage treatment This usually involves a series of phases, each designed to reduce progressively the environmental and health impact of the effluent. Sewage is carried in the effluent either as solid matter or in dilute, suspended solids. While several performance criteria are used to assess the performance of a sewage treatment works (mainly, the removal of silts, **biochemical oxygen demand** (BOD) and ammonia), each level of treatment can be judged by its success in removing these solids from the effluent stream prior to its final discharge. There is a fairly close relationship between ultimate solids removal and the lowering of an effluent stream's BOD. There are four principal stages of sewage treatment:

> Preliminary/Screening

> Primary

> Secondary

> Tertiary/Advanced.

shareholder An equity holder in the project company.

shareholders' agreement The agreement entered into by the shareholders of the project company which governs their relationship and their collective approach to the project. See also **constituent documents**; **project documents**.

shareholders' equity The book value of the net assets (total assets less total liabilities). Also known as **net worth**.

ship-to-ship transfer (STS) The transfer of **crude oil** or products from one ship to another while both are at sea.

short-term debt An obligation maturing in less than one year.

show of oil A small amount of oil in a **well** or rock sample.

shut-in pressure Pressure measured after a well has been shut in for a period.

simple interest The charge for the loan of money or for a deferment of the collection of an account, computed by applying a rate of interest against only the amount of the loan or account. Contrasts with **compound interest** in that interest is only charged on the **principal** for the entire life of the transaction and no interest is charged on any interest already accrued. See also **interest rate**.

single buoy mooring (SBM) A single floating chamber moored near an offshore production platform to serve as a connection to a tanker. It has no storage capacity. Also known as "single point mooring (SPM)". See also **floating storage unit**.

sinking fund A reserve fund established or set aside for the purpose of payment of a **liability** anticipated to become due at a later date.

sludge Residue left after treating **raw water** or foul water.

slug catcher Plant installed in a gas pipeline system to catch unwanted "slugs" of liquid.

SOFC Solid oxide fuel cell.

soft currency A currency perceived by the market to be reasonably unlikely to maintain its value against other currencies over a period. The convertibility of soft currencies is usually, or may become, restricted. See also **hard currency**.

solution gas Natural gas which is dissolved in the **crude oil** within the reservoir.

solvency The state of being able to pay **debts** as they become due.

solvent Common name for a liquid which is capable of dissolving or dispersing other substances.

sour gas Gas containing acid gases, principally hydrogen sulphide and carbon dioxide. See also **sweet gas**.

sour oil Oil containing high levels of hydrogen sulphide or mercaptans. Treatment of such oils to convert them to marketable products is known as "sweetening". See also **sweet oil**.

source country The country from which important materials, equipment or one of the project participants originates. This country may provide financing or insurance to the project to promote exportation of materials, equipment or services and thus assist its national economy.

sovereign immunity A historical doctrine of law in certain jurisdictions under which sovereign governments may not be sued or their assets seized.

sovereign risk Political risk caused by the fact that one of the parties is a sovereign entity. See also **country risk**.

sovereignty The complete independence and right to self-government which entitles a nation to certain immunities and special rights and privileges.

special purpose vehicle An entity created to undertake a project in order to protect the shareholders with limited liability and limited or non-recourse financing.

specific gravity The ratio of the density of a substance at a particular temperature to the density of water.

SPM Single point mooring. See **single buoy mooring**.

sponsor A party wishing to develop/undertake a project. A developer. A party providing financial support.

spot market An international market in which oil or oil products are traded for immediate delivery at the current price (the "spot price").

spread In the trading or quotation of a security's price, the difference between the bid and the offered price. Also used in loans as a synonym for **margin**.

spud To begin the actual drilling of a **well**.

stanching The process whereby odourless **natural gas** is given a smell for safety reasons by injecting small quantities of organic sulphur compounds, typically at the rate of 30 **PPM**.

standard deviation The volatility of returns, or the average deviation from an expected value or mean.

stand-by credit An arrangement to lend money on demand, usually at market rates and sometimes with a commitment fee. Overdraft facilities are sometimes used for stand-by credit by corporate borrowers.

stand-by letter of credit A **letter of credit** that provides payment to the beneficiary when it presents a certification that certain obligations have not been fulfilled.

step-in rights The right of a third party to "step in" to the place of one contractual party where that party fails in its obligations under the contract and the other party to the contract has the right to terminate the contract.

step-out well A **well** in an unproved or semi-proved area in an attempt to extend the productive limits of a field.

stimulation The technique of getting more production from a formation, by the use of **acidising**, hydraulic fracturing or other method.

storm sewer A system of pipes (separate from **sanitary sewer**) that carry only water run-off from building and land surfaces. See also **combined sewer**.

straddle A strategy comprising an equal number of **put options** and **call options** on the same underlying stock, stock index or commodity future at the same strike price and maturity date. Each option may be exercised separately, although the combination of options is usually bought and sold as a unit.

straight debt A standard **bond** issue or loan without the right to convert into the common shares of the issuer.

straight-line depreciation Depreciation of an asset by equal amounts each year over the life of the asset. See also **depreciation**.

straight-run A description applied to a product of **crude oil** that has been made by distillation with no chemical conversion.

STS See **ship-to-ship transfer**.

subordinated creditor A creditor holding a debenture having a lower priority of payment than other liabilities of the project.

subordinated debt Debt which, by agreement, is subordinated to senior debt. It does not include reserve accounts or deferred credits.

subrogation The acquisition of another person's rights, usually as a result of assuming or discharging that person's **liabilities**, particularly in connection with **guarantees** and insurance.

substantial, physical or mechanical completion The stage at which a project is virtually complete with only minor elements, usually identified on a punch-list, left outstanding. See also **completion**.

sunk costs Capital already spent.

super-turnkey contract Based on a **turnkey construction** contract, the contractor is required to contribute to the financing of the construction, often by agreeing to the deferral of the payment due to it until after **completion** or during operation.

supply risk The risk that the availability of raw materials or input to a project (for example, raw water) will change from those assumed/projected. In the case of a resources extraction project, this is called **reserves risk**.

supply-or-pay contract A contract under which a party agrees to supply a raw material, product or service for a certain price during a stated period and agrees to pay for an alternative supply if it cannot perform. Also known as a **put-or-pay contract**.

sustainable development The meeting of present needs without compromising the ability of future generations to meet their own needs.

swab Cleaning out the borehole of a **well** with a special tool attached to a **wire line**, and attempting to start the well producing. The tool is called a "rabbit". See also **pigs**.

swap The exchanging of one security, debt, currency or interest rate for another. Also known as a **switch**. See also **currency swap**.

sweep All available cash flow used for debt service.

sweet gas Natural gas containing very small amounts of hydrogen sulphide gas and carbon dioxide. Sweet gas reduces sulphur dioxide emissions into the atmosphere. See also **sour gas**.

sweet oil Crude oil that contains virtually no sulphur or hydrogen sulphide and has a good colour. See also **sour oil**.

swing The amount by which the rate of gas to be supplied under a contract at any one time may differ from the daily contracted quantity at the buyer's choice.

switch Sometimes used as a synonym for a swap; for example, buying a currency spot and selling it forward.

syncrude A **crude oil** made from coal or gas. See also **light crude**.

syndicate A group of banks making a syndicated loan. A group of bond houses which act together in underwriting and distributing a new securities issue.

syndicated credit facility A credit facility in which a number of banks undertake to provide a loan or other support facility to a customer on a pro rata basis under identical terms and conditions evidenced by a single credit agreement.

syngas Petrol made from coal or gas.

synthetic gas Methane-rich gas manufactured from oil or coal that has the same basic characteristics and chemical composition as **natural gas**. After treatment to remove carbon dioxide, it is suitable as low-calorific **town gas**.

T/D Tonnes per day.

T/Y Tonnes per year.

tail The remaining reserves after the **project financing** has been repaid. Sometimes means the **residual**.

take-and-pay If the project's output is deliverable and can be taken, it will be paid for.

take-or-pay In the event the project's output is not taken, payment must be made whether or not the output is deliverable. Also known as **through-put contract** or **use-or-pay con tract**. See also **requirements contract**.

TCF Trillion cubic feet.

temporary works Works performed by the construction contractor which are designed to assist in the construction of the **permanent works** but do not form part of the completed works and will therefore be removed from the site before completion.

tender bond See **bid bond**.

tenor The number of years a loan is outstanding; the **term** or maturity.

terajoule (tJ) One trillion joules.

term The loan life or **tenor**; the period to a loan's maturity. "Term" also means a condition attached.

term loan A fixed-period loan, usually for one to 10 years, that is paid back by the borrower in regular (often monthly) instalments with interest. This is the most common form of business loan; it may be secured or unsecured.

term sheet A document, not generally intended to be legally binding, setting out the main agreed terms and conditions to a transaction between the borrower and arranger.

terminal An onshore transit installation that receives and stores **crude oil** and products from offshore production facilities via pipeline and/or tankers.

termination The act of bringing the contract to an end by one of the parties in accordance with a right to do so granted by the applicable law or the contract.

tertiary recovery Recovery of hydrocarbons from a reservoir over and above what can be recovered using **primary recovery** and **secondary recovery**. It usually means employing a sophisticated method such as heating the reservoir or enlarging the pore spaces using chemicals. See also **acidising; enhanced oil recovery; ultimate recovery**.

tertiary treatment An advanced stage of **waste water** treatment designed to remove nutrients or other constituents remaining after **secondary treatment**.

thermal cracking See **cracking**.

thermal reforming See **reforming**.

third-party access (TPA) A TPA regime obliges companies operating gas transmission or distribution networks to offer terms for the carriage of gas on their system by other gas distribution companies or particular consumers.

through-put contract An agreement by the parties to ship certain minimum quantities of oil, refined products or gas at a fixed rate through a **pipeline**. Certain quantities have to be shipped in each period, such as a month or a year, to provide the cash flow to meet operating expenses and debt service of the pipeline company. Usually in the form of a **hell-or-high-water** contract. Also known as a **use-or-pay contract**.

TCE See **tonnes of coal equivalent**.

tight hole A drilling **well** in which all information is kept secret by the operator.

tJ See **terajoule**.

TOE See **tonnes of oil equivalent**.

tonne (ton) A metric tonne is 1,000 kg (2,205 pounds). In the United States, "ton" is a different measure; a long ton is 2,240 pounds, a short ton is 2,000 pounds. See also **dry tonne; wet tonne**.

tonnes of coal equivalent (TCE) A method of assessing the work or calorific value of different sources of energy in terms pertaining to one tonne of coal.

tonnes of oil equivalent (TOE) A method of assessing the work or calorific value of different sources of energy in terms pertaining to one tonne of oil.

topsides The superstructure of a **platform**.

town gas Gas piped to consumers from a gas plant. It can comprise manufactured gas as well as **natural gas** for enrichment.

trade finance agency Another term for **export credit agency**.

trade financing programmes Another term for **export credit incentive programmes**.

tranche A separate portion of a **project financing**, perhaps with different financiers, **margins** and **term**.

transfer risk The risk that a given currency will not be allowed to be sent out of the country, usually due to central bank restrictions or a national debt-rescheduling. See also **currency risk**.

translation risk A type of **foreign exchange risk** arising from the need to translate the assets and liabilities of a foreign subsidiary into the currency of the home country.

transmissible pipeline A network of pipelines distributing **natural gas** from an onshore station, via **compressor stations**, to storage centres or distribution points

transmissivity The rate at which water is transmitted through the total thickness of an **aquifer** under a unity hydraulic gradient.

trust deed The deed in which an issuer of **notes** or **bonds**, any guarantor and the trustee set out the obligations of the issuer and guarantor and appoint a trustee to represent the interests of the bond or note holders.

tubing A string of pipe, usually 2-2½ inches in diameter, run inside casing and through which oil and gas are produced.

tunnel See **collar**.

turnkey construction The design and construction of a project to completion, so that it is ready to produce cash flow.

ullage The space in a tank not occupied by its contents. Used as a measure of storage space still available.

ultimate recovery The complete expected recovery of oil or gas from a well, pool or lease. See also **primary recovery; secondary recovery; tertiary recovery**.

ultra-large crude carrier (ULCC) An extremely large ocean-going tanker, more than 300,000 metric tonnes **DWT**, used to transport crude oil. See also **very large crude carrier**.

ultra vires An act outside the scope of one's authority. See also ***intra vires***.

unassociated gas See **non-associated gas**.

unbundling The separation of the gas transport, storage and merchandising functions.

undivided interest A property interest held by two or more parties whereby each share in profits, expenses and enjoyment, according to its respective interest, and whereby ownership of the respective interest of each may be transferred but physical partition of the asset is prohibited.

UNIDO United Nations Industrial Development Organisation.

unitisation Agreement by the owners of a single oil field which extends into more than one licence area to develop the field as a single unit.

unsaturated zone The area between the land surface and the water table in which pore spaces are not completely filled with water. Also known as the **vadose zone**.

unsecured The financier has no **security**, merely the obligation/undertaking from the borrower to repay.

unsecured loan A loan made on the general credit of a borrower. The lenders rely upon the borrower's **balance sheet** and the capability of the borrower's management to manage its assets and produce sufficient cash flows to repay the debt. No assets are pledged.

upstream Those activities relating to the exploration, production and delivery to an export terminal of **crude oil**. See also **downstream**.

useful life The period during which an asset will have economic value and be usable. The useful life of an asset is sometimes called the "economic" life of the asset.

use-or-pay contract Another name for a **take-or-pay contract** or **through-put contract**.

vacant possession Property which has been abandoned, vacated and forsaken by any tenant or third party.

vadose zone See **unsaturated zone**.

variable duration notes At the coupon payment date of a note, the holder elects either to receive payment or an additional note with identical terms.

variable rate loan A loan made at an interest rate that fluctuates with the prime rate, the **LIBOR** or some other index.

variation or change A technical term in construction contracts referring to a variation of the client's requirements ordered by the client, generally entitling the contractor to a change in the contract price, the time for completion and any other obligation affected by the variation ordered.

very large crude carrier (VLCC) A large ocean-going tanker, more than 200,000 metric tonnes **DWT**, used to transport crude oil. See also **ultra-large crude carrier**.

viscosity Stickiness, i.e. the resistance that a liquid has to motion or flow; it normally falls as the temperature rises.

viscosity index A measure of the relationship between temperature and viscosity of an oil.

volatile Term used to describe substances with low molecular weight that will evaporate at normal atmospheric temperature and pressures.

volatile organic compound (VOC) One of several organic chemical compounds characterised by their ability to evaporate readily at normal temperatures.

volatility The degree of fluctuation that occurs away from a value, such as the mean, of a series of figures. The greater the volatility in returns, the higher the risk.

warrant An instrument allowing the holder to purchase a given **security** at a given price; for either a set period or into perpetuity (a **call option** on a security).

waste water Typically either sewage or an effluent. Water that carries waste from homes, businesses and industries. A mixture of water and dissolved or suspended solids. Includes municipal waste or sewage.

water purchase agreement (WPA) The offtake purchase agreement for a BOT water treatment project.

waterflooding A method of **secondary recovery** in which water is injected into an oil reservoir through which oil and gas are produced.

weighted average cost of capital (WACC) The total return required by both debt and equity investors expressed as a real post-tax percentage on funds usage.

well A hole drilled in rock from the surface to the reservoir in order to explore for, or extract, oil, gas or water. See also **appraisal well**; **confirmation well**; **development well**; **deviation well**; **discovery well**; **exploratory well**; **gas well**; **injection well**; **offset well**; **pumping well**; **spud**; **step-out well**; **tight hole**; **wildcat well**.

wellhead Surface control equipment for a well that includes the casinghead, control valves, testing equipment, take-off piping and the **Christmas tree**.

well log A record of geological formation penetrated during drilling, including technical details of the operation. See also **log**.

wet gas Gas containing recoverable liquid hydrocarbons. See also **natural gas**.

wet tonne Weight of measure for sewage, sludge or industrial effluent. In the case of sewage sludge, this usually refers to material removed from the sewage treatment process. Sewage sludge usually consists of 95-98 per cent. water, falling to 75-85 per cent. after basic drying. The variability of the water content makes

wet tonnes an inconsistent measure of sewage generation, hence the use of **dry tonnes** when comparing sewage data.

whipstock A special tool used at the bottom of the hole to change the direction of the **drill bit**.

white products Gasoline, naphtha, kerosene and gas oil, i.e. products from the high or light end of the distillation process. See also **black products**; **light fractions**.

wildcat well An **exploratory well** drilled some distance from known production. This distance from production determines whether the wildcat is low, medium or high risk. An exploratory well or "wildcat" is one that is drilled primarily for the purpose of determining that oil or gas actually exists in a subsurface rock formation.

wire line Wire that is run in the hole through production tubing with tools at the end of the wire that either open valves, pull plugs or obtain data. When this wire parts and becomes lodged in the tubing, "fishing" is required with fishing tools run on yet more wire. See also **pigs**; **swab**.

withholding tax A tax on interest, royalty or dividend payments – usually those paid overseas. It may be deducted at source.

Wobbe index Defined as calorific value divided by the square root of the specific gravity. This index is controlled to ensure satisfactory combustion of the gas in the burning appliance. If this specification is not met, the amount of air mixed with the gas will be incorrect.

working capital The part of the capital of a company that is employed in its day-to-day trading operations. It consists of current assets (mainly trading stock, debtors and cash) less current liabilities (mainly trade creditors).

working capital replenishment An undertaking by an industrial company sponsor and/or parent to make liquid funds available to a special purpose subsidiary or company to enable such a company to keep its **working capital** at sufficient levels to service debt and meet operating expenses.

workover Remedial work to the equipment within a **well** or the well pipework, in an attempt to increase the rate of flow.

works A technical term in construction identifying the entirety of the facilities and services to be provided by the construction contractor.

World Bank A multilateral agency based in Washington, D.C. Also known as the **International Bank for Reconstruction and Development (IBRD)**.

worldscale rates A schedule of nominal freight rates against which tanker rates for all voyages, at all market levels, can be compared and readily judged.

wraparound loan A long-term loan structured with a short-term loan in such a manner as to postpone payments of **principal** (and sometimes **interest**) on the long-term loan until the short-term and long-term wraparound may produce level debt service for both loans over the life of the long-term loan.

WTI West Texas Intermediate.

yield Rate of return, expressed as a percentage and annualised.

yield to maturity The rate of return yielded (for example, by a debt security held to maturity) when both interest payments and the investor's capital gain or loss on the security are taken into account.

Index

This index does not include definitions as these are listed in the glossary. It does not include footnotes either, as these can be accessed through the main text, via this index. Page numbers in italic indicate that the reference is to an illustration.

Introduction

O.L. LANGE, P.S. NOBEL, C.B. OSMOND, and H. ZIEGLER

In the original series of the Encyclopedia of Plant Physiology, plant water relations and photosynthesis were treated separately, and the connection between phenomena was only considered in special chapters. O. STOCKER edited Volume III, *Pflanze und Wasser/Water Relations of Plants* in 1956, and 4 years later, Volume V, Parts 1 and 2, *Die CO_2-Assimilation/The Assimilation of Carbon Dioxide* appeared, edited by A. PIRSON. Until recently, there has also been a tendency to cover these aspects of plant physiology separately in most textbooks. Without doubt, this separation is justifiable. If one is specifically interested, for example in photosynthetic electron transport, in details of photophosphorylation, or in carbon metabolism in the Calvin cycle, it is not necessary to ask how these processes relate to the water relations of the plant. Accordingly, this separate coverage has been maintained in the New Series of the Encyclopedia of Plant Physiology. The two volumes devoted exclusively to photosynthesis are Volume 5, *Photosynthesis I,* edited by A. TREBST and M. AVRON, and Volume 6, *Photosynthesis II,* edited by M. GIBBS and E. LATZKO. When considering carbon assimilation and plant water relations from an ecological point of view, however, we have to recognize that this separation is arbitrary. Since growth is essential to plant survival, the most crucial problem facing terrestrial plants is the balancing of the need to minimize plant water loss against the need to assimilate sufficient carbon for growth. In response to this dilemma, plants have evolved a close link between water status and the CO_2 assimilation processes. This linkage has to be taken into consideration in any ecological interpretation of these phenomena. Because a precise understanding of the manner in which the link is accomplished might lead to improvement in plant productivity, an integrative approach to photosynthesis and plant water relations is also of particular relevance in agronomy.

Until fairly recently, experimental approaches to water relations and photosynthetic processes in plants, respectively, were very different, making a combined analysis of the total water-photosynthesis syndrome difficult. Only during the last three decades have methods become available which allow adequate ecophysiological studies of both aspects of plant performance to be carried out. Whereas the discovery of the radioactive isotope carbon-14 permitted enormous advances in studies of carbon assimilation, the availability of tritium at about the same time had scarcely any impact on plant water relation investigations. Indeed, the combined tritium/carbon-14 porometer is a relatively recent invention; and it was only a few years earlier that the use of infrared gas analyzers in parallel with dewpoint hygrometers permitted rapid advances in the simultaneous measurement of CO_2 and H_2O exchange. The recognition among ecophysiologists of the need for a more unified approach to the study

of photosynthesis and plant water relations has increasingly led to the use
of the newer techniques for measuring gas exchange in conjunction with methods
for investigating plant water status, i.e., pressure chamber and psychrometric
methods. Such investigations have contributed immensely to our understanding
of plant photosynthetic response in relation to plant water economy, and have
made possible the concept of the present volume, namely, the integrated treatment of photosynthesis and water relations within an ecophysiological framework.

   With the exception of submerged freshwater plants which comprise a trivial
portion of plant biomass and production, photosynthetic activity shows marked
responses to the water potential of the plant environment. In terrestrial plants,
which comprise about 70% of plant biomass, water relations processes are
integrated to maintain leaf water potential within acceptable limits. Generally
speaking these limits are set by the requirements that living roots usually have
access to water in the soil at water potentials in the range of about 0 to
− 30 bar, while the living leaf is exposed to the atmosphere with an equivalent
water potential of − 500 to − 2000 bar. The dynamics of plant water relations
(Chap. 1, this Vol.) are such as to ensure water potentials of functional leaves
within the range of about − 2 to − 50 bar. However, photosynthesis and other
metabolic functions over this range of water potentials are only possible if
the osmotic potential of vacuolar sap is sufficient to maintain a positive turgor
pressure in the cytoplasm of about 1 to 5 bar (Chap. 2). Although direct methods
for the measurement of this important parameter in cell water relations have
been devised, its application and integration in complex tissues remains a problem.

   The principles of water uptake by roots and of water transport through
the plant are well established (Chaps. 3 and 5) but the study of key elements,
such as water transfer from soil to root, and across the root, remains difficult.
The complexity of the soil environment and the difficulty of differentiating
symplastic and apoplastic pathways in the root continue to try our ingenuity.
Maintenance of leaf water potential and turgor within acceptable limits is largely
due to the formation of cuticular layers at the plant-atmosphere interface
(Chap. 6) and consequently due to stomatal control of water fluxes across the
large water potential gradient between leaf mesophyll cell walls and the atmosphere. Since the physiological bases of stomatal function have been reviewed
in Volume 7 of this series, our treatment is confined to ecologically significant
stomatal responses (Chap. 8) and their function in photosynthesis and growth.

   Although stomatal closure to preserve leaf water status often occurs, it
is inevitably associated with a decrease in intercellular CO_2 partial pressure,
which often results in a reduction in photosynthesis and growth (Chap. 7).
Furthermore, if stomatal closure and cuticular resistance are insufficient to
prevent excess water loss, then photosynthetic and other processes are reduced
as a result of water stress, or even damaged due to serious dehydration (Chaps. 9
and 11). The significance of the compromise that stomata effect between the
hunger of photosynthesis and the thirst of transpiration has been highlighted
by comparative studies of plants with different pathways of CO_2 fixation
(Chap. 15). Among other things, the differences in the biochemistry of C_3

and C_4 plants allow C_4 plants to achieve equal or greater rates of CO_2 fixation than C_3 plants with more tightly closed stomata, at much lower intercellular CO_2 partial pressures, with consequent lower water costs of CO_2 fixation. In spite of this, both photosynthetic types display midday depression of photosynthesis due to stomatal closure in response to atmospheric and soil water stress. The possible ecological significance of these differences in photosynthetic pathway and water use pattern has been appreciated for some time, but only recently have we seen comparative evaluations of these processes in terms of plant performance (productivity) and survival (distribution).

In succulent plants with CAM the above compromise is extreme; extraordinarily low stomatal and cuticular conductance can sometimes prevent CO_2 exchange altogether, and confer drought avoidance at the expense of photosynthesis and growth. These plants endure drought as functional photosynthetic systems at high water potential. By contrast, some poikilohydric thallophytes and cormophytes endure drought as nonfunctional photosynthetic systems at low water potential, but these systems are readily reconstituted on rehydration (Chap. 10). Aside from their intrinsic ecological interest, it is likely that these systems will provide fundamental insights into the integration of CO_2 fixation and photochemistry in photosynthesis. In ecological terms they are fascinating mechanisms to preserve the advantages of autotrophy, and to avoid the hazards of seed or spore germination (Chaps. 12 and 13) and seedling establishment. There are interesting analogies between germination and the reconstitution of metabolism in poikilohydric plants, and there are virtues in establishing some principles of water transport in these nonvacuolated quiescent systems. Similar processes are presumably involved in water uptake by plant organs other than roots (Chap. 4). On the other hand, in some cases excessive water (e.g., flooding) has also led to functional adaptations of certain organs (roots) of terrestrial plants. Through special metabolic pathways they are able to avoid generation of poisonous products which might occur due to the anaerobic situation (Chap. 14).

An increasing body of evidence relating daily and seasonal patterns of transpiration and carbon uptake has stimulated the development of the theory that stomata function so as to minimize the water cost of carbon gain (Chap. 17). These notions lead to provocative interpretations of transpiration patterns and the biochemistry of photosynthetic carbon uptake (Chaps. 8 and 16). Extension of the concept of optimal stomatal behavior to embrace water use patterns during growth and development, will undoubtedly provide a framework within which long-held notions of plant form and function (Chap. 18) can be tested. Progress in these areas is likely to be limited more by our ability to digest and distil data than by the acquisition of data.

Although the infrared gas analyzer and the pressure chamber facilitated this explosion in ecological research, new technologies already promise integration. For example, the serendipitous observation that C_3 and C_4 plants differ in their discrimination against carbon-13 has made the ratio mass-spectrometer indispensable to studies of photosynthetic metabolism on a geographical scale. Measurements of $\delta^{13}C$ values also provide integrated historical accounts of composition and competition between C_3 and C_4 plants in communities, as

ensuring a supply of water to their shoots; the development of a cuticle punctured with stomata enabled them to conserve water when the supply from their roots was outstripped by the evaporative demand.

Van den Honert's (1948) classic analysis of the resistances in the transpiration stream showed the pivotal importance of the stomata in controlling water loss. Stomatal behaviour has consequently dominated the study of plant water relations. But a resistance analogue such as van den Honert's (1948) gives us an essentially instantaneous view of the behaviour of a plant. More sophisticated treatments add capacitors (e.g., Cowan 1972a) and thus allow us to study time-dependent behaviour, but even these rely on an instantaneous view of the main structure of a plant, and the phenomena dealt with have time scales no greater than one day. These short-term phenomena tell us a great deal about a plant, but if our interest is in photosynthetic productivity and its relationship to ecological processes, we must ultimately concern ourselves with phenomena occurring at an ontogenetic or even demographic time-scale. The behaviour of a plant in the short term may tell us little about its prospects for long-term productivity. For example, a plant that photosynthesizes rapidly and hence appears to be productive, will die if its concomitant prodigal transpiration exhausts a limited supply of water before the next rain; a conservative plant, in these circumstances, may be the more productive.

Water deficiency influences the behaviour of a plant at all levels of organization: metabolism, physiology and gross morphology are all affected. Of these three it is probably the physiology of the droughted plant that has received the most attention, particularly where it has been concerned with the behaviour of stomata. Yet it is the control of leaf area and morphology that is often the most powerful means a plant has of influencing its water economy, and ultimately its productivity, if it is subjected to drought in its natural environment: To control transpiration is to control the amount of incoming energy that is dissipated as latent heat. A plant that maintains a large leaf area index can control this amount by varying its stomatal conductance, and can conserve water during a drought by closing its stomata. But this may be an unsatisfactory solution if it means that the plant, though still respiring, spends a long time with a large area of hot leaves slowly losing water through their cuticles while

Table 1.1. Physiological processes affecting plant water relations

Process	Time scale
Root growth	Days, weeks
Leaf growth (area, thickness)	Days, weeks
Leaf shedding or senescing	Days, weeks
Changes in hairiness	Days
Conditioning (adaptation at cellular level)	Days
Changes in albedo	Hours, days
Leaf movement (photonasty, rolling)	Hours
Wilting	Hours
Changes in hydraulic resistance	Minutes, hours
Stomatal movement	Minutes, hours

Table 1.2. Environmental processes affecting plant water relations

Process	Time scale
Seasonal evaporative demand	Weeks, months
Run-down in soil water	Days, weeks
Diurnal evaporative demand	Hours
Rain, irrigation	Seconds, hours
Movement of clouds and other shadows	Seconds, hours

barely photosynthesizing. Such a plant is likely to be inefficient in its use of water. A better solution may be to control leaf area.

The point of this preamble is that, when considering photosynthetic productivity in relation to water use, it is necessary to consider processes occurring at a wide range of time scales, not only within the plant, but also within the plant's environment. Tables 1.1 and 1.2, adapted from PASSIOURA (1976), list processes occurring both in the plant and in its environment that affect plant water relations. This introductory chapter will deal with some of the interactions between these processes insofar as they affect photosynthetic productivity. It will firstly cover what is meant by the water status of a plant, then how the water status is influenced by short-term processes, i.e., those we normally think of in relation to the resistance analogue of transpiration, and finally how the long-term processes influence the water relations and photosynthetic productivity.

1.2 Water Status

1.2.1 Definitions

"Water status" is a vague though nevertheless useful term. It has no units, for it can refer to any measure of the general state of a plant in relation to water, and is therefore used only in a relative sense. It may refer to the plant's water potential, its relative water content, or its turgor. In general, it is perhaps best used to qualitatively describe turgor or relative water content rather than water potential, for a given plant could be wilting badly at a moderate leaf water potential while another could be turgid and growing well at a substantially lower water potential. One would normally think of the latter as having the higher water status.

In an attempt to avoid vagueness in describing the energy status of plant water, SLATYER and TAYLOR (1960) introduced thermodynamics to plant physiology, and provided a valuable service in removing many unsatisfactory features of the existing terminology. They showed how terms like "diffusion pressure deficit" were related to chemical potential, and they showed (TAYLOR and SLATYER 1962) how force fields, such as gravity, could be coherently taken into account. Their treatment, and especially the subsequent development of it (NOY-

this means that it maintains positive turgor, i.e., that P in the symplast be everywhere positive. Depending on the values of Π in the symplast, it is clear from Eq. (1.2) that positive turgor could be associated with a very wide range in Ψ. In practice, there is an upper limit to symplastic Π in natural conditions that is generally in the range of 1.0 to 2.5 MPa in mesophytes but may be more than double that in some xerophytes (LARCHER 1975). Positive turgor may not be essential to continued photosynthesis (RAWSON 1979) but is certainly associated with rapid photosynthesis; it is strongly associated with large stomatal conductance, at least in mesophytic crop plants (TURNER 1974), and also with leaf growth (HSIAO et al. 1976; BUNCE 1977; see also Chaps. 7 and 9, this Vol.).

Measurements of Ψ and of symplastic P and Π are therefore crucial to the understanding of the performance of a plant under water stress. How these may be made are discussed in the following chapter of this volume. Bulk measurements, such as those made on a leaf, provide insights into the control of short-term productivity and into how the tissue may have adapted to water stress, for example by increasing symplastic Π at full turgor so that turgor remains positive down to lower values of Ψ (JONES and TURNER 1978).

Of equal importance, but rather more difficult to make, are measurements of symplastic P and Π in small regions of tissue such as meristems, or groups of expanding cells, or pulvini. These tissues profoundly influence both the short- and long-term responses of a plant to water stress. Pulvini, where present, can alter the orientation of leaves so as to improve their water economy (BEGG 1980; SHACKEL and HALL 1979); the growth of meristems, and the expanding tissues they give rise to, affect the leaf area and hence the evaporative demand on a plant. These systems are particularly important because falling water status typically affects growth well before it affects photosynthesis (HSIAO et al. 1976; see also Chap. 9, this Vol.).

The most difficult measurements of all to make are those on single cells (HÜSKEN et al. 1978) especially those on stomatal cells (e.g., EDWARDS and MEIDNER 1975), which are particularly important because of the influence of turgor on stomatal conductance.

When the water status of a plant at or near full turgor does start to fall, which it will if the evaporative loss from the leaves exceeds the influx of water from the roots, the rate of fall of Ψ, and, in the short term, of symplastic P, depends not only on the net rate of water loss, but also on the bulk elastic modulus of the cells, ε, which is given by V dP/dV, where P is the turgor pressure, and V the symplastic volume. If ε is large, a small change in relative water content will bring about a large change in Ψ. If ε is small, Ψ is much more strongly buffered against changes in relative water content, and this may be an advantage if it means that positive turgor is maintained for longer, although not necessarily so if conservative behaviour is called for (see Sect. 1.4.2.2).

So far I have been largely concerned with "static" aspects of water status. In a transpiring plant, there are gradients in Ψ. It is these gradients that are the driving forces for the transport of water across perfect semi-permeable membranes. For transport across leaky membranes however, i.e., those having a reflection coefficient less than 1, the osmotic component of Ψ does not fully manifest itself, and it is necessary to consider the pressure-induced and osmoti-

cally induced flows separately, as discussed in detail by DAINTY (1976) and ZIMMERMANN and STEUDLE (1979). Where there are no membranes, as in soil, or within the apoplast, or perhaps even within the symplast, the driving force for the flow of water is the gradient in τ; since Π_D in the apoplast is usually small (TYREE 1976), gradients in τ within it are virtually identical with those in Ψ; the same is not necessarily true for the symplast.

The current water status of a plant depends largely on the recent history of the evaporative losses from it and the fluxes of water into and through it. These fluxes are discussed in the next section.

1.3 Transport of Water in the Soil-Plant-Atmosphere Continuum

The electrical analogue of VAN DEN HONERT (1948) and its theoretically sounder successors (e.g., COWAN 1965, 1972b; RICHTER 1973) have been of great help in providing a conceptual framework for thinking about the transpiration stream in general terms. When dealing with particular parts of the pathway, however, the faithful application of the electrical analogue is often more confusing than enlightening, particularly where there is a change of phase, or where the transport of water is non-linear, or where active transport of solutes is involved. It is often expedient to abandon the idea that the flux of water between two points is given by $\Delta\Psi/r$, where r is a resistance, and to use a formalism that is more appropriate.

The following discussion explores the factors influencing the movement of water through soil and plant to the atmosphere, assuming quasi-steady conditions, i.e., that the main structure of the plant remains essentially unchanged, and that changes in the plant's environment are slow compared with the rate at which disturbances in Ψ are propagated through the plant.

1.3.1 Through Soil to Root

The old controversy about whether or not soil water was equally "available" to plants all the way down to the "permanent wilting point" was defused during the 1950's and early 1960's when it was realised that availability had to be considered in terms of how fast water could move through the soil to a plant's roots rather than simply in terms of how firmly the water was held by the soil (see Chap. 3, this Vol.). This controversy has subsequently reemerged in a more sophisticated form; some have argued that the rate of flow of water through the soil may limit its uptake by roots even when the soil is quite moist (GARDNER 1960; COWAN 1965; CARBON 1973; GREACEN 1977); others have argued that in real situations, the rooting density is so high, and the rate of uptake of water per unit length of root is so low, that it is only when the soil is quite dry and τ approaches 1.5 MPa that the rate of movement becomes limiting (NEWMAN 1969; LAWLOR 1972; HANSEN 1974; TAYLOR and

would be proportional to θ, so that the hydraulic conductance of the root: soil system might depend more on θ than on D. This is an interesting suggestion, and implies that the major radial resistance within the root is at the epidermis, rather than at the endodermis as is usually assumed, but it does not explain why the uptake of water by roots can sometimes be satisfactorily explained in terms of Eq. (1.3) without the need to invoke a major interfacial resistance (PASSIOURA 1980a). If the conductance does depend on θ in some cases, why not in all?

Another, and perhaps more likely explanation is that the roots shrink as the soil starts to dry, and in so doing lose some of their hydraulic contact with the soil. If the major hydraulic resistance within the root is in the endodermis rather than in the bulk of the cortex or in the epidermis, the water potential in the cortex, Ψ^{cortex}, will be close to that of the soil, Ψ^{soil}, rather than to that of the xylem, Ψ^{xylem}. Since Ψ^{xylem} is typically much less than Ψ^{soil} (e.g., HERKELRATH et al. 1977a), any loss of contact due to shrinkage of the root will, as pointed out by FAIZ and WEATHERLEY (1978), be self-amplifying, for it will result in Ψ^{cortex} moving from Ψ^{soil} to the substantially lower Ψ^{xylem}, which will lead to further shrinkage. If hydraulic contact is important, and if it is influenced by shrinkage, then the rate of change of Ψ^{soil} may have a major influence on the hydraulic properties of the system; if Ψ^{soil} changes slowly enough for the roots to maintain turgor by osmoregulation, there may be no shrinkage; but if Ψ^{soil} changes rapidly, the roots may not be able to maintain turgor and may then shrink. The need to invoke an interfacial resistance in some cases (HERKELRATH et al. 1977a; FAIZ and WEATHERLEY 1978) but not in others (PASSIOURA 1980a), may have been due to the fairly large differences in $d\Psi^{soil}/dt$ that existed between the experiments.

Another possible explanation for a large apparent interfacial resistance is that there may be a major pile-up of solutes at the surface of the root (or perhaps at the endodermis; NULSEN and THURTELL 1978), owing to the solutes being carried to the root by convection at a faster rate than they are being taken up (TINKER 1976). Such a pile-up would manifest itself osmotically and would lead to a large difference between Ψ^{xylem} and Ψ^{soil} that would appear to be due to a large hydraulic resistance. This effect would be small in a moist soil, for the solutes can quickly diffuse away against the transpiration stream, but if the hydraulic connections between root and soil become scarce, they may remain adequate for the flow of solution into the cortex, but inadequate for the diffusion of the rejected solutes back into the soil. These and other aspects of behaviour at the root:soil interface are discussed in more detail by TINKER (1976) and PASSIOURA (1980a, 1981) and, in Chapter 3, this Volume.

1.3.3 Through the Root

The largest drop in Ψ within a plant usually occurs somewhere between the surface of the root and the xylem, and probably at the endodermis. There is considerable doubt about what is the main pathway for water through the cortex, although NEWMAN (1976) concludes that it is through the symplast

rather than the cell walls, for measured permeabilities of walls seem to be too low. If he is right it would imply that the major radial resistance is at the epidermis rather than at the endodermis, which would be compatible with the hypothesis of HERKELRATH et al. (1977a) discussed earlier. However, NEW-MAN's (1976) calculations of permeabilities refer to transverse flow across the walls; the permeabilities for tangential flow, which are much more important, may be much larger, especially if there is flow along irregularities in the surfaces of the walls and if fillets of water occupy the intercellular spaces, as seems likely (PASSIOURA 1981).

The nature of the radial hydraulic resistance in the root is even more mysterious than the pathway for the water. Some have found the resistance to be highly variable, and, within limits, inversely related to transpiration rate, so that $\Delta\Psi$ across the root is independent of transpiration rate (WEATHERLEY 1975). Others have found the resistance to be constant (HAILEY et al. 1973; NEUMANN et al. 1974; PASSIOURA 1980a). WEATHERLEY (Chap. 3, this Vol.) discusses this puzzle in detail. One possible explanation, which will be touched on again later, is that much of the variable hydraulic resistance within the plant which is usually assumed to be in the roots may well be in the leaves.

Axial flow in the roots usually suffers little hindrance, particularly in dicots, whose facility for secondary growth endows them with abundant xylem unless vascular disease or a physically constricting soil causes some disruption (TAYLOR and KLEPPER 1978). There are however several reports of large axial resistances in the roots of the Gramineae, whose lack of secondary growth sometimes results in a meagre vascular system. WILSON et al. (1976) for example showed that blue grama (*Bouteloua gracilis*) seedlings grew poorly if drought prevented the development of nodal roots. The large hydraulic resistance of the small xylem vessels of the seminal roots and the sub-coleoptile internode apparently prevented the leaves from getting an adequate supply of water. A similar problem can occur in droughted wheat plants, which may have to rely on a few seminal roots containing only one substantial xylem vessel each to extract water from a moist subsoil, although, in this case, the large resistance may be an advantage if it results in the plants conserving water when young for later use during the critical periods of flowering and grain filling (PASSIOURA 1977).

Axial resistance in the xylem is usually assumed to follow Poiseuille's equation, and, for smooth-walled vessels such as occur in grasses, this is a fair assumption (GREACEN et al. 1976). Where the walls are rough, however, which they typically are in dicots, Poiseuille's equation may grossly underestimate the resistance (GIORDANO et al. 1978; JEJE and ZIMMERMANN 1979), although there is little evidence that the actual resistance has a major influence on the water economy of the plant.

1.3.4 Through the Shoot

Resistance to the longitudinal flow of water in the shoot is generally small (JARVIS 1975), although there have been reports of large resistances in the stems and branches of Sitka spruce (HELLKVIST et al. 1974) and of hemlock (TYREE

1.4 Water Relations and Photosynthetic Productivity

We normally think of photosynthetic productivity as being the net increase in biomass of a plant, or a community of plants, during a growing season, or perhaps a year. This section is concerned with the connection between productivity, in this sense, and the quasi-steady or instantaneous behaviour of plants that was discussed in the previous section, given the constraint of a limited water supply. On a seasonal scale, it is useful to think of the productivity (B) of a plant as being the product of the amount of water transpired (W) and the efficiency with which that water is used to produce biomass, that is, $B = W \times WUE$, where WUE is the dry matter produced per unit water transpired, and typically refers to aboveground dry matter only. These two factors are to a first approximation independent of each other, and are sufficiently robust functions of major environmental and physiological variables, such as precipitation, pan evaporation, and photosynthetic pathway, to give us a crude but nevertheless useful understanding of variation in B due to drought (Fischer and Turner 1978). It is obvious that both the plant and its environment influence both W and WUE, but it is worth emphasizing that a plant's influence on W can be very large, even after allowing for the area of ground that it occupies; the vigour and extent of its root system, its ability to extract water from the topsoil before it evaporates directly, or its ability to channel rain down its stems so as to make it more accessible, all influence W and hence all affect B. The following discussion explores the ways in which a plant can influence both W and WUE during given periods of time, so as to maximize B in the face of a fluctuating environment. I will assume that this behaviour is evolutionarily advantageous (for detailed discussion of water use and optimization of carbon assimilation see Chap. 17, this Vol.).

1.4.1 Daily Production

I take as a starting point a single leaf. The connection between its evaporation rate per unit area, E, and its assimilation rate per unit area, A, has been discussed in detail by Cowan and Farquhar (1977) and by Cowan (1978). In general, when E and A change in response to stomatal conductance, g, E(A) is positively curved as shown in Fig. 1.1. Furthermore, since the environmental conditions experienced by a leaf change during the course of a day, E(A), though still remaining positively curved, will change its shape during the day.

Cowan and Farquhar (1977) have argued that the optimal stomatal behaviour of a leaf faced with a limited supply of water is that which allows maximal assimilation during a day of given evaporation, or its converse, that which allows minimal transpiration during a day of given assimilation. They point out that this behaviour ensures that any small deviations in stomatal conductance from its optimal function of time g(t) are such that the concomitant deviations, δE, in transpiration rate per unit leaf area satisfy the inequality $\int \delta E \, dt \geq 0$,

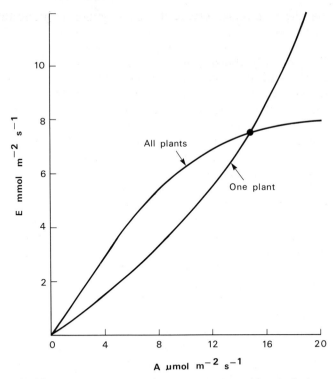

Fig. 1.1. Hypothetical relationships between rate of transpiration, E, and rate of assimilation, A, for an individual plant in an extensive community of plants. The plant is assumed to function normally at the point of intersection of the two lines, one of which represents the variation which would occur if stomatal aperture in the individual, only, were to vary and the other represents the variation which would occur if stomatal apertures in all the plants in the community were to vary in unison. (Reproduced from COWAN 1978)

given that the mean net assimilation rate, $\bar{A}$, is fixed for the day, i.e., that $\int \delta A dt = 0$. This inequality implies that behaviour is optimal if $\delta E/\delta A$ is a constant (λ) throughout the day, providing that $(\partial^2 E/\partial A^2)$ is positive. COWAN and FARQUHAR (1977) chose to concentrate their treatment on stomatal behaviour, but COWAN (1978) has pointed out that the criterion, $\partial E/\partial A = \lambda$, applies for any short-term reversible behaviour of the leaf that influences E, notably those listed here in Table 1.1 with time scales of hours or less; the influence of nastic leaf movement on improving leaf microclimate can be very large (SHACKEL and HALL 1979; BEGG 1980), as can the passive movement associated with wilting (RAWSON 1979). The criterion that $\partial E/\partial A$ be constant for a single leaf also applies to a whole plant and to every leaf on the plant.

Constancy in $\partial E/\partial A$ has some interesting consequences, the most important of which is that when evaporative demand is high, g may be reduced so much that E actually decreases, a phenomenon that has now been observed several times in natural environments and that is discussed in detail in Chap. 7, this Volume. FARQUHAR (1979) has pointed out that a decrease in E with increasing evaporative demand cannot be explained in terms of feedback based on some

sensing mechanism within the leaf, for the water status of the leaf is actually improved. The explanation must be in terms of feedforward, which implies that the sensing mechanism (which is perhaps related to peristomatal transpiration) is on the outside of the leaf.

COWAN and FARQUHAR's (1977) hypothesis is an extremely interesting and ingenious one, and FARQUHAR et al. (1980) have recently provided evidence verifying it for the leaves of two species exposed to a range of humidities in a controlled environment. But it is based on an implicit assumption that the water supply of the plant is not only limiting, but is also fixed. This assumption seems appropriate for isolated plants, such as commonly occur in arid environments, but where the plants are competing for water, optimal behaviour may be to maintain g as large as possible whenever A is positive, for water that is saved in the interests of improving $\bar{A}/\bar{E}$ (where the bars denote mean values) may become water that is lost to a competitor. In the context of the hypothesis that $\partial E/\partial A = \lambda$, this means making λ as large as possible, which brings us to a question that cannot be answered by studying diurnal behaviour alone, namely, what is the optimum size of λ? To answer this question requires us to extend our time scale and to adopt a criterion of optimal behaviour that includes the amount of water transpired during the period of time in which we are interested. This leads to considerable complications, for while it is worthwhile assuming, as we implicitly have done, that a plant does not grow during the course of our interest in it, this assumption is untenable when we consider behaviour during several days or weeks. The plant does grow, and its growth influences not only $\bar{A}$ and $\bar{E}$ but also the size of its potential water supply, through, for example, the growth of the root system. Furthermore, the way in which the growth is partitioned, especially between water-harvesting and water-using structures, profoundly influences both W and WUE. These issues are discussed in the next subsection.

1.4.2 Weekly or Monthly Production

The net rate of assimilation of a whole plant, A*, is substantially less than the net rate of assimilation of its leaves. Respiratory losses from heterotrophic tissues such as roots, stems, and possibly fruits, explain the difference. Let us assume for the moment that plants behave optimally if they maximize $\bar{A}$* over a given period of say several weeks, that is that they maximize the product of W (or $\bar{E}$*, the evaporation rate from the whole plant) and WUE (or $\bar{A}$*/$\bar{E}$*). What are the compromises that they must make? An obvious one is in the partitioning of assimilate. To keep $\bar{A}$*/$\bar{E}$* large requires that the proportion of heterotrophic tissue in the plant be kept small, especially that in the roots, for there is evidence that they respire (or at least consume assimilate) much more rapidly per unit weight than does the shoot (SAUERBECK and JOHNEN 1976). But sacrificing roots to improve $\bar{A}$*/$\bar{E}$* may result in a substantial drop in $\bar{E}$* and hence in $\bar{A}$*, owing to the roots being unable to extract as much water from the soil. Another obvious compromise is in the value of λ: a large λ may increase $\bar{E}$*; a small one will increase $\bar{A}$*/$\bar{E}$*.

There are many such compromises, the nature of which depends on a plethora of climatic and edaphic factors and on competition from neighbours. Their complexity suggests that elegant hypothetical generalizations, such as that achieved by COWAN and FARQUHAR (1977) for diurnal behaviour, may be unattainable. Nevertheless, there is much to be said of a qualitative nature, and the rest of the discussion will concentrate on this, exploring in turn (a) behaviour which primarily influences the water supply of a plant, and (b) behaviour which primarily influences the effectiveness with which that water is used.

1.4.2.1 Water Supply

There are several ways in which a plant can influence the amount of water accessible to its roots. The most obvious of these concerns the size of the root system, but other, less obvious, ways include (1) the channelling of rainfall down stems, so that it tends to concentrate close to the centre of the plant, (2) the improvement of the permeability of the soil so that there is less run-off during heavy rains, and (3) the shading of the soil surface (by leaves or by litter), which protects any surface water from rapid evaporation by the sun. The extent to which the roots can ultimately lower Ψ^{soil} will also influence the amount of available water, although the variation may not be great. Most plants that grow in drought-prone environments are capable of lowering Ψ^{soil} to less than -2.0 MPa and some can even lower it to -10 MPa (NOY-MEIR 1973). But the amount of water held by soil between Ψ^{soil} of -2.0 and -10 MPa is usually small unless the soil is very heavy, and its advantage to those plants that can extract it is probably in aiding their survival during severe drought rather than in improving their medium-term productivity.

Variation in the size of root systems is enormous, ranging from those of desert ephemerals and cacti that might tap a soil volume of only a few litres, to those of some trees that may penetrate tens of metres to deep water-tables. I am concerned here not so much with variation between species as with environmental influences on the growth of roots into previously untapped volumes of soil.

The major influences of temperature, aeration, mechanical resistance, and nutrition, have been recently and comprehensively discussed by RUSSELL (1977). Insofar as these adversely affect root growth and thereby limit a plant's water supply, the largest effects are usually in the subsoil.

Apart from riparian and deep-rooted perennial plants which can often tap a permanent supply of water from the subsoil, it is those plants that grow in climates having alternating long dry and long wet spells that particularly rely on subsoil water during much of their lives. Established perennial plants usually have their roots ramified through the subsoil in such circumstances, but annual plants, and establishing perennial ones, may not. There are several examples, particularly amongst cereal crops, in which the roots failed to extract substantial amounts of water from moist subsoils even though the plants were suffering from drought (e.g., SCHULTZ 1971; BLUM 1974; HURD 1974; WALTER and BARLEY 1974). These failures appear often to be due not so much to

the roots failing to penetrate the subsoil, as to their failure to develop adequate densities there (Jordan and Miller 1980).

Subsoils typically are dense and have a shear strength large enough to slow down root growth. Furthermore, the effect of a high shear strength is exacerbated at the low temperatures that often prevail in the subsoil in cold or temperate climates (Greacen 1977). In Mediterranean and steppe climates, for example, the temperature of the topsoil rises rapidly during the spring, thus encouraging root growth, but the temperature of the subsoil does not, at least at depths below about 50 cm, where the annual variation in temperature is small, and in any case lags well behind the mean air temperature. Nutritional problems are also rife in subsoils, which are generally poor in macronutrients such as N, P, and K, and are often poor in micronutrients as well; it is particularly important for Ca and B to be available locally because they travel so poorly in the phloem and are essential for root growth (Kramer 1969).

Surprisingly, soil water potential per se does not seem to have a major effect on root growth, except in quite dry soil or in soil with a high bulk density (Taylor and Gardner 1963). Newman (1966), Taylor and Ratliff (1969) and Portas and Taylor (1976) have all shown substantial root growth in soil having $\Psi < -1.0$ MPa, and Portas and Taylor (1976) even found that roots of maize and tomato grew with $\Psi^{soil} < -4$ MPa. This is remarkable behaviour and presumably means either that the roots are able to generate very large osmotic pressures, or that they are hydraulically isolated from dry soil and that there is a substantial flow of water to them from other roots in wetter parts of the soil. The amount of available water contained in such dry soil is so small that it may seem pointless for a plant to expend assimilate in growing its roots in this way, but the growth may be more a reflection of the continuing vigour of these roots, which seem to be able to respond rapidly if their dry soil is rewatered (Portas and Taylor 1976). Rapid responses of this sort may not be particularly important in the subsoil, but they may be crucial in the topsoil if the roots are to harvest a substantial proportion of a light fall of rain before it evaporates directly from the soil surface.

Since roots are heterotrophic, their growth ultimately depends on the supply of assimilate from the shoot. This supply does not seem to be diminished by mild water stress, and often seems to be even improved by it. It has often been observed that drought increases the ratio of root to shoot (Mooney 1972; Larcher 1975), and there are several reports of root growth actually increasing during drought (Bennett and Doss 1960; Hsiao and Acevedo 1974; Schultz 1974; Cutler and Rains 1977). The mechanism for this behaviour is unknown, but it may be due to water stress affecting shoot growth more than it does photosynthesis, so that increased assimilate becomes available to the roots (Hsiao and Acevedo 1974). An increase in the root-shoot ratio of a plant during drought has obvious advantages in helping the plant match its water supply to the evaporative demand on its leaves, but it is worth reemphasizing that such a response has a respiratory cost that may greatly reduce WUE.

While the growth of the roots has a large influence on the uptake of water already contained in the soil, the architecture of the shoot can have a large influence on the gain of usable water by the soil, through its effects both

on the interception of light falls of rain and on the partial channelling down the stem of heavy falls of rain. The interception capacity of foliage varies considerably and may exceed 2 mm (SLATYER 1967), so that a substantial proportion of light falls of rain may evaporate directly from the leaves and be of little use to the plant. On the other hand, the influence of the shoot on directing intercepted rain to the main stem can be very large. Most of the interest in "stem flow" has concerned that in trees, where it may account for up to 40% of heavy falls of rain. But stem flow can also be great in non-woody plants, for example, potato, for which SAFFIGNA et al. (1976) showed that stem flow could also be up to 40% of rainfall.

The direction of rainfall to the base of the main stem may be of little use in improving the accessibility of the water to the plant unless the permeability of the soil there is adequate to cope with the increased water flow. In general, this permeability is largely a property of the soil, but there are two effects that a plant can have on improving infiltration rate. The first is that it often provides litter under its canopy which slows down any run-off of water and allows more time for the water to sink in. The second is that it may actually improve the permeability of the soil in its vicinity. SLATYER (1962) found that the permeability of the soil near the base of a mulga tree was much greater than that of the soil some distance away, and what is more, the ponded infiltration rates near the tree became virtually constant after about 20 min, which suggests that the water was flowing predominantly down large pores and was not moving as a well-defined wetting front. The distribution of large pores is presumably influenced by the growth of roots, particularly those of perennial plants. The ability of a plant to harvest and sequester water in this way undoubtedly has a major influence on its performance during drought.

Channelling the rain to the base of the stem not only keeps the water within the rooting zone of the plant; it also ensures that it penetrates much more deeply into the soil than would be the case if the infiltration were uniform. The water is therefore much less likely to be lost by direct evaporation from the soil. Such evaporative losses can be a major part of light to medium falls of rain (FISCHER and TURNER 1978) particularly on heavy soils, where > 10 mm of rain may be needed to wet the top 50 mm of soil from air-dry to a water potential > -1.5 MPa. As mentioned earlier, the ability of the roots in dry soil to grow rapidly once the soil is re-wet is very important in such circumstances.

1.4.2.2 Water Use and Efficiency of Water Use

I have so far been discussing the amount of water potentially accessible to a plant's root system over a period of some weeks. The way in which the plant actually uses that water depends on both the size of its shoot and its stomatal conductance. RITCHIE (1974) has discussed the effect of the size of the shoot, expressed in terms of leaf area index (LAI), on the transpiration rate per unit ground area, E', of a community of like plants. Figure 1.2 shows, in schematic form, the behaviour of unstressed plants, i.e., ones having a large stomatal conductance. Little information is available about the behaviour of

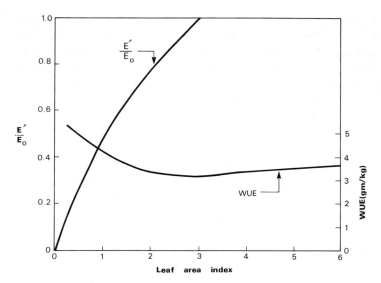

Fig. 1.2. The ratio of actual to potential transpiration rate per unit ground area (E′/E₀), and water use efficiency (WUE), as functions of leaf area index. (After Ritchie 1974)

stressed plants, but we can probably assume that E′ is scaled down by a factor that is approximately uniform over a wide range in LAI.

It is useful to think in terms of two contrasting strategies that plants may have evolved for dealing with a limited water supply (see also Chap. 18, this Vol.).

a) Conservative: This would be appropriate for plants with access to a supply of water that is unlikely to be diminished by competitive neighbours, i.e., plants growing essentially in isolation. Stomatal behaviour would be that discussed in Section 1.4.1, i.e., $\partial E/\partial A$ would be kept at a constant value λ, on a daily basis, and would presumably decline progressively as the water supply diminished. It is difficult to make precise statements about the time course of λ, but its optimal value at any given time will no doubt depend on the water status of the soil, and on the expected duration of the drought, the "expectation" having been built into the genome of the plant through evolution. This issue is dealt with at length in Chapter 17, this Volume. The optimal LAI of a conservative plant would tend to be small, and both the growth and the shedding of leaves would be sensitive to water stress.

b) Prodigal: This would be appropriate for plants that are competing for a limited water supply or that are subject to mild droughts of short duration. Stomatal conductance and growth rate are high, and the water supply is used rapidly until it is almost gone, at which point the plants eke out the remainder so as to survive until the next rain. This behaviour seems to be common in natural ecosystems (Fischer and Turner 1978). Many crop plants also appear to behave in this way (Ritchie 1973, 1974) even though with a crop, it is the behaviour of the community rather than of the individual that is important,

so that one might expect any selection for drought tolerance to have produced conservative plants. Actually, depending on the severity of the drought, there are two distinct, and indeed, contradictory strategies that may result in drought tolerance. If a drought is likely to be long, conservative behaviour is appropriate, for it will improve the WUE of the crop without prejudicing W, the amount of water ultimately transpired. But if early relief of drought is likely, or if there is a series of short droughts, prodigal behaviour will probably produce higher yields, for, although it may decrease WUE, it does not necessarily do so (as we shall see below) and it may substantially increase W, through, for example, a greater infiltration of rain into the drier soil, and a smaller evaporative loss of water directly from the soil surface.

Physiologically, the most important distinction between prodigal and conservative plants is that the former probably have a greater ability to maintain turgor when faced with a poor supply of soil water. Variation in this ability is discussed in detail in Chapter 9, this Volume, particularly the ability that some plants have to osmoregulate, i.e., to increase the number of osmoles in their cells in response to falling water status. Morphologically, the most important distinctions are in LAI and in rooting density, both of which must be large if soil water is to be extracted quickly.

So far this section has been primarily concerned with how the plant's behaviour may influence its cumulative transpiration, W. The following discussion concerns the efficiency with which the plant uses water in producing dry matter, and in particular returns to the issue of the influence of $\partial E/\partial A$ on $\bar{A}/\bar{E}$.

Cowan and Farquhar's (1977) hypothesis that $\partial E/\partial A$ should be constant if $\bar{A}/\bar{E}$ is to be maximized applies only if $E(A)$ is positively curved when stomatal conductance varies. As discussed in Section 1.4.1, positive curvature would be expected for a single plant whose stomatal conductance varies independently from that of the other plants in its community. Where the plant is part of a large community of similar plants, however, such as in a crop, the stomatal conductance of all plants may vary in unison, whereupon $E(A)$ may become negatively curved as shown in Fig. 1.1 (Cowan 1978). The reason for this is that there is an upper limit to the rate of evaporation from a community, so that when the actual evaporation rate is near this limit, as it is for a crop having a well-developed canopy and a high stomatal conductance, further opening of the stomata will have little influence on E but will still result in an increased A. In these circumstances, a maximal $\bar{A}/\bar{E}$ is achieved by having the stomata wide open whenever there is enough light for photosynthesis. This does not mean that Cowan and Farquhar's (1977) hypothesis is generally inapplicable to crop plants, for during a drought, when both g and LAI are small, the transpiration rate of the crop will be much less than the potential rate and $E(A)$ should be positively curved.

$\bar{A}/\bar{E}$ (or WUE) also increases with increasing LAI in a crop that is transpiring at or near potential rate (Fig. 1.2). When LAI > 3, further increase in LAI has a negligible influence on E', yet may still harvest more light for use in photosynthesis (Ritchie 1974). Thus the prodigal plant will be the more efficient under well-watered conditions. Where E'/E_o is small, however, the conservative plant will be the more efficient, not only by keeping $\partial E/\partial A$ constant, but

also by keeping LAI small (see Fig. 1,2), if we accept RITCHIE's (1974) argument that WUE increases with decreasing LAI when LAI < 1.5.

Finally, I reiterate the point touched on in previous sections that heterotrophic tissues, such as roots, necessarily lower WUE, especially if this is defined, as it usually is, in terms of the aboveground production of dry matter. Optimum behaviour would require that the extra water obtained by investing a parcel of assimilate in the roots must enable the plant to at least replace that parcel of assimilate. The compromises reached by wild plants in their allocation of assimilate have been discussed by MOONEY (1972) and in Chapter 18, this Volume. With crop plants, where it is the performance of the community rather than of the individual that is important, competition for water loses its meaning, and we might therefore expect that domestication has reduced the root/shoot ratio. Whether or not this has happened is hard to say, for no data appear to be available. But given the tremendous concentration of roots that some crops have in the topsoil (BARLEY 1970), with rooting densities perhaps ten times larger than that needed to extract all the available water at a reasonable rate, it would seem that there is much scope for reducing the root/shoot ratio without prejudicing the supply of water to the shoot.

1.4.3 Seasonal Productivity

The previous section is largely concerned with physiological and morphological behaviour that may maximize the photosynthetic productivity of a plant over a period of some weeks when it is faced with a limiting water supply. When one looks at the longer time scale of a complete growing season, it is necessary to consider additional factors, particularly where they influence the productivity over several generations.

With long-lived perennials such as shrubs and trees, persistence rather than short-term procreation is usually the key to the productivity of a species, and while different strategies have evolved for coping with the great variation in climate through the year that is common in drought-prone environments [e.g., see the discussion by FISCHER and TURNER (1978) on aridoactive and aridopassive plants], optimal behaviour can usually be discussed along the lines of the previous section. With annual plants, however, whose long-term productivity depends on the ability to produce an ample supply of seeds each year, it is appropriate to ask what behaviour maximizes seed production, rather than simply what maximizes the production of general dry matter. A thorough discussion of this question has been recently provided by FISCHER and TURNER (1978), and it is sufficient to point out here that the production of seed is often very sensitive to conditions at particular times during the life cycle, for example at around flowering or during grain filling, especially with plants of determinate habit. Phenology in relation to climate is therefore of great importance, as also is the way in which a plant meters out any large store of water that it may have access to in the soil; conservative behaviour may have a much profounder effect on seed production than on dry-matter production if it improves the supply of water to the plant during critical periods.

1.5 Conclusions

The theme of water in the soil-plant-atmosphere continuum is usually discussed at time scales short enough for any growth of the plant to be ignored. Photosynthetic productivity on the other hand is generally discussed in relation to a growing season. The object of this chapter has been to explore, in general terms, the connection between the two when the plant is subjected to a limiting water supply. The connection depends largely on the medium-term behaviour of the main physiological and morphological variables, namely stomatal conductance and leaf area, respectively, and these in turn depend on the pattern of allocation of assimilate within the plant, particularly as it affects the compromise that must be made between water-harvesting and water-using structures. The emphasis has been on adaptive responses that a plant of given genetic constitution may make during its life-span. The genetic responses to drought that have resulted in the evolution of a wide range of life-forms and different photosynthetic pathways have been largely ignored, but are discussed in detail later in this Volume (see for instance Chaps. 15 and 18).

1.6 Symbols and Abbreviations

Symbol	Description	Unit
a	radius of root	m
b	$(\pi L)^{-\frac{1}{2}}$, i.e., half the distance between adjacent roots	m
x	distance	m
A	assimilation rate	$mol\ m^{-2}\ s^{-1}$
$\bar{A}$	mean assimilation rate during a given period	$mol\ m^{-2}\ s^{-1}$
$\bar{A}^*$	mean assimilation rate per plant	$mol\ s^{-1}$
B	biomass produced	kg
E	transpiration rate	$mol\ m^{-2}\ s^{-1}$
$\bar{E}$	mean transpiration rate during a given period	$mol\ m^{-2}\ s^{-1}$
$\bar{E}^*$	mean transpiration rate per plant	$mol\ s^{-1}$
E'	transpiration rate per unit ground area	$mol\ m^{-2}\ s^{-1}$
E_o	potential transpiration rate per unit ground area	$mol\ m^{-2}\ s^{-1}$
F	flux density of water	ms^{-1}
I	rate of water uptake per unit length of root	$m^3\ m^{-1}\ s^{-1}$
K	hydraulic conductivity	$m^2\ s^{-1}\ Pa^{-1}$
L	rooting density, i.e., the length of root per unit volume of soil	$m\ m^{-3}$
LAI	leaf area index	$m^2\ m^{-2}$
P	pressure	Pa
Q	rate of change of soil water content	$m^3\ m^{-3}\ s^{-1}$
V_w	partial molar volume of water	$m^3\ mol^{-1}$
W	water transpired	kg
WUE	efficiency of water use $(=B/W)$	$kg\ kg^{-1}$
ε	volumetric elastic modulus	Pa
θ	soil water content	$m^3\ m^{-3}$
λ	$\partial E/\partial A$	
μ_w	chemical potential of water	$J\ mol^{-1}$
τ	matric suction	Pa
Ψ	water potential $(\Delta\mu_w)$	$J\ mol^{-1}$
	or water "potential" $(\Delta\mu_w/\bar{V}_w)$	Pa
Π	osmotic pressure	Pa

References

Barley KP (1970) The configuration of the root system in relation to nutrient uptake. Adv Agron 22:159–201

Begg JE (1980) Morphological adaptations of leaves to water stress. In: Turner NC, Kramer PJ (eds) Adaptation of plants to water and high temperature stress. Wiley-Interscience, New York, pp 33–42

Begg JE, Turner NC (1970) Water potential gradients in field tobacco. Plant Physiol 46:343–346

Bennett OL, Doss BD (1960) Effect of soil moisture level on root distribution of cool-season forage species. Agron J 52:204–207

Black CR (1979) The relationship between transpiration rate, water potential, and resistances to water movement in sunflower (*Helianthus annuus* L.). J Exp Bot 30:235–243

Blum A (1974) Genotypic responses in sorghum to drought stress I. Response to soil moisture stress. Crop Sci 14:361–364

Bolt GH, Iwata S, Peck AJ, Raats PAC, Rode AA, Vachaud G, Voronin AD (1976) Soil physics terminology. Bull Int Soc Soil Sci 49:26–35

Boyer JS (1974) Water transport in plants: mechanism of apparent changes in resistance during absorption. Planta 117:187–207

Boyer JS (1976) Water deficity and photosynthesis. In: Kozlowski TT (ed) Water deficits and plant growth, vol IV. Academic Press, London New York, pp 153–190

Boyer JS (1977) Regulation of water movement in whole plants. In: Jennings DH (ed) Integration of activity in the higher plant. Univ Press, Cambridge, pp 455–470

Bunce JA (1977) Leaf elongation in relation to leaf water potential in soybean. J Exp Bot 28:156–161

Burch GJ (1979) Soil and plant resistances to water absorption by plant root systems. Aust J Agric Res 30:279–292

Burch GJ, Smith RCG, Mason WK (1978) Agronomic and physiological responses of soybean and sorghum crops to water deficits. II. Crop evaporation, soil water depletion and root distribution. Aust J Plant Physiol 5:169–177

Caldwell MM (1976) Root extension and water absorption. In: Lange OL, Kappen I, Schulze E-D (eds) Water and plant life. Ecol Stud Vol 19. Springer, Berlin Heidelberg New York, pp 63–85

Carbon BA (1973) Diurnal water stress in plants grown on a coarse soil. Aust J Soil Res 11:33–42

Cowan IR (1965) Transport of water in the soil-plant-atmosphere system. J Appl Ecol 2:221–239

Cowan IR (1972a) An electrical analogue of evaporation from, and flow of water in plants. Planta 106:221–226

Cowan IR (1972b) Oscillations in stomatal conductance and plant functioning associated with stomatal conductance: observations and a model. Planta 106:185–219

Cowan IR (1977) Stomatal behaviour and environment. Adv Bot Res 4:117–228

Cowan IR (1978) Water use in higher plants. In: McIntyre AK (ed) Water: planets, plants and people. Aust Acad Sci, Canberra, pp 71–107

Cowan IR, Farquhar GD (1977) Stomatal function in relation to leaf metabolism and environment. In: Jennings DH (ed) Integration of activity in the higher plant. Univ Press, Cambridge, pp 471–505

Cowan IR, Milthorpe FL (1968) Plant factors influencing the water status of plant tissues. In: Kozlowski TT (ed) Water deficits and plant growth, vol I. Academic Press, London New York, pp 137–193

Cutler JM, Rains DW (1977) Effects of irrigation history on responses of cotton to subsequent water stress. Crop Sci 17:329–335

Dainty J (1976) Water relations of plant cells. In: Lüttge U, Pitman MG (eds) Transport in plants II Encyclopedia of plant physiology New Ser vol II, Part A. Springer, Berlin Heidelberg New York, pp 12–35

Denmead OT, Miller BD (1976) Water transport in wheat plants in the field. Agron J 68:297–303

Dunin FX, Aston AR, Reyenga W (1978) Evaporation from a *Themeda* grassland. II. Resistance model of plant evaporation. J Appl Ecol 15:847–858

Eavis BW, Taylor HM (1979) Transpiration of soybeans as related to leaf area, root length, and soil water content. Agron J 71:441–445

Edwards M, Meidner H (1975) Micromanipulation of stomatal guard cells. Nature 253:114–115

Faiz SMA, Weatherley PE (1978) Further investigations into the location and magnitude of the hydraulic resistances in the soil:plant system. New Phytol 81:19–28

Farquhar GD (1979) Feedforward responses of stomata to humidity. Aust J Plant Physiol 5:787–800

Farquhar GD, Schulze E-D, Küppers M (1980) Responses to humidity by stomata of *Nicotiana glauca* L. and *Corylus avellana* L. are consistent with the optimisation of carbon dioxide uptake with respect to water loss. Aust J Plant Physiol 7:315–327

Fischer RA, Turner NC (1978) Plant productivity in the arid and semiarid zones. Annu Rev Plant Physiol 29:277–317

Gardner WR (1960) Water availability to plants. Soil Sci 89:63–73

Giordano R, Salleo A, Salleo S, Wanderlingh F (1978) Flow in xylem vessels and Poiseuille's law. Can J Bot 56:333–338

Greacen EL (1977) Mechanisms and models of water transfer. In: Russell JS, Greacen EL (eds) Soil factors in crop production in a semi-arid environment. Univ Queensland Press, St Lucia, pp 163–196

Greacen EL, Ponsana P, Barley KP (1976) Resistance to water flow in the roots of cereals. In: Lange OL, Kappen L, Schulze E-D (eds) Water and plant life. Ecol Stud Vol 19. Springer, Berlin Heidelberg New York, pp 86–100

Hailey JL, Hiler EA, Jordan WR, Van Bavel CHM (1973) Resistance to water flow in *Vigna sinensis* L. (Endl.) at high rates of transpiration. Crop Sci 13:264–267

Hansen GK (1974) Resistance to water transport in soil and young wheat plants. Acta Agric Scand 24:37–48

Hellkvist J, Richards GP, Jarvis PG (1974) Vertical gradients of water potential and tissue water relations in sitka spruce trees measured with the pressure chamber. J Appl Ecol 11:637–668

Herkelrath WN, Miller EE, Gardner WR (1977a) Water uptake by plants: I. The divided root experiments. Soil Sci Soc Am J 41:1033–1038

Herkelrath WN, Miller EE, Gardner WR (1977b) Water uptake by plants: II. The root contact model. Soil Sci Soc Am J 41:1039–1043

Honert van der TH, (1948) Water transport in plants as a catenary process. Discuss Faraday Soc 3:146–153

Hsiao TC, Acevedo E (1974) Plant responses to water deficits, water-use efficiency, and drought resistance. Agric Meteorol 14:59–84

Hsiao TC, Fereres E, Acevedo E, Henderson DW (1976) Water stress and dynamics of growth and yield of crop plants. In: Lange OL, Kappen L, Schulze E-D (eds) Water and plant life. Ecol Stud Vol 19. Springer, Berlin Heidelberg New York, pp 281–305

Hurd EA (1974) Phenotype and drought tolerance in wheat. Agric Meteorol 14:39–55

Hüsken D, Steudle E, Zimmermann U (1978) Pressure probe technique for measuring water relations of cells in higher plants. Plant Physiol 61:158–163

Janes BE, Gee GW (1973) Changes in transpiration, net carbon dioxide assimilation and leaf water potential resulting from application of hydrostatic pressure to roots of intact pepper plants. Physiol Plant 28:201–208

Jarvis PG (1975) Water transfer in plants. In: Vries de Da, Afgan NH (eds) Heat and mass transfer in the biosphere I. Transfer processes in the plant environment. Halsted, Washington DC, pp 369–394

Jeje AA, Zimmermann MH (1979) Resistance to water flow in xylem vessels. J Exp Bot 30:817–827

Jones MM, Turner NC (1978) Osmotic adjustment in leaves of sorghum in response to water deficits. Plant Physiol 61:122–126

Jordan WR, Miller FR (1980) Genetic variability in sorghum root systems: implications for drought tolerance. In: Turner NC, Kramer PJ (eds) Adaptation of plants to water and high temperature stress. Wiley-Interscience, New York, pp 383–399

Kramer PJ (1969) Plant and soil water relationships: a modern synthesis. McGraw-Hill, New York

Larcher W (1975) Physiological plant ecology. Springer, Berlin Heidelberg New York

Lawlor DW (1972) Growth and water use of *Lolium perenne*. I. Water transport. J Appl Ecol 9:79–98

Legg BJ, Day W, Lawlor DW, Parkinson KJ (1979) The effect of drought on barley growth: models and measurements showing the relative importance of leaf area and photosynthetic rate. J Agric Sci 92:703–716

Meiri A, Plaut Z, Shimshi D (1975) The use of the pressure chamber technique for measurement of the water potential of transpiring plant organs. Physiol Plant 35:72–76

Monteith JL (1965) Evaporation and environment. In: Fogg GE (ed) The state and movement of water in living organisms. Univ Press, Cambridge, pp 205–234

Mooney HA (1972) The carbon balance of plants. Annu Rev Ecol Syst 3:315–346

Neumann HH, Thurtell GW, Stevenson KR (1974) In situ measurements of leaf water potential and resistance to water flow. Can J Plant Sci 54:175–184

Newman EI (1966) Relationship between root growth of flax (*Linum usitatissimum*) and soil water potential. New Phytol 65:273–283

Newman EI (1969) Resistance to water flow in soil and plant. I. Soil resistance in relation to amounts of root: theoretical estimates. J Appl Ecol 6:1–12

Newman EI (1976) Water movement through root systems. Philos Trans R Soc London Ser B 273:463–478

Noy-Meir I (1973) Desert ecosystems: environment and producers. Annu Rev Ecol Syst 4:25–51

Noy-Meir I, Ginzburg BZ (1967) An analysis of the water potential isotherm in plant tissue. I. The theory. Aust J Biol Sci 20:695–721

Nulsen RA, Thurtell GW (1978) Osmotically induced changes in the pressureflow relationship of maize root systems. Aust J Plant Physiol 5:469–476

Oertli JJ (1969) Terminology of plant-water energy relations. Z Pflanzenphysiol 61:264–265

Passioura JB (1976) The control of water movement through plants. In: Wardlaw IF, Passioura JB (eds) Transport and transfer processes in plants. Academic Press, London New York, pp 373–380

Passioura JB (1977) Grain yield, harvest index, and water use of wheat. J Aust Inst Agric Sci 43:117–121

Passioura JB (1980a) Transport of water from soil to shoot in wheat seedlings. J Exp Bot 31:333 345

Passioura JB (1980b) The meaning of matric potential. J Exp Bot 31:1161–1169

Passioura JB (1981) Water collection by roots. In: Paleg L, Aspinall D (eds) Physiology and biochemistry of drought resistance in plants. Academic Press, London New York, pp 39–53

Philip JR (1966) Plant water relations: some physical aspects. Annu Rev Plant Physiol 17:245–268

Pierce M, Raschke K (1980) Correlation between loss of turgor and accumulation of abscisic acid in detached leaves. Planta 148:174–182

Portas CAM, Taylor HM (1976) Growth and survival of young plant roots in dry soil. Soil Sci 121:170–175

Raschke K (1979) Movements of stomata. In: Haupt W, Feinleib ME (eds) Physiology of movements. Encyclopedia of plant physiology New Ser vol. VII. Springer, Berlin Heidelberg New York, pp 383–441

Rawson HM (1979) Vertical wilting and photosynthesis, transpiration, and water use efficiency of sunflower leaves. Aust J Plant Physiol 6:109–120

Reicosky DC, Ritchie JT (1976) Relative importance of soil resistance and plant resistance in root water absorption. Soil Sci Soc Am Proc 40:293–297

Richter H (1973) Frictional potential losses and total water potential in plants: a reevaluation. J Exp Bot 24:983–994

Ritchie JT (1973) Influence of soil water status and meteorological conditions on evaporation from a corn canopy. Agron J 65:893–897

Ritchie JT (1974) Atmospheric and soil water influences on the plant water balance. Agric Meteorol 14:183–198

Rose DA (1968) Water movement in porous materials. III. Evaporation of water from soil. Br J Appl Phys Ser 2, 1:1779–1791

Russell RS (1977) Plant root systems: their function and interaction with the soil. McGraw-Hill, London

Saffigna PG, Tanner CB, Keeney DR (1976) Non-uniform infiltration under potato canopies caused by interception, stemflow, and hilling. Agron J 68:337–342

Sauerbeck D, Johnen B (1976) Der Umsatz von Pflanzenwurzeln im Laufe der Vegetationsperiode und dessen Beitrag zur "Bodenatmung". Z Pflanzenernaehr Bodenkde 3:315–328

Schultz JE (1971) Soil water changes under fallow-crop treatments in relation to soil type, rainfall and yield of wheat. Aust J Exp Agric Anim Husb 11:236–242

Schultz JE (1974) Root development of wheat at the flowering stage under different cultural practices. Agric Rec 1:12–17

Shackel KA, Hall AE (1979) Reversible leaflet movements in relation to drought adaptation of cowpeas *Vigna unguiculata* (L.) Walp Aust J Plant Physiol 6:265–276

Sheriff DW (1979) Water vapour and heat transfer in leaves. Ann Bot (London) 43:157–171

Slatyer RO (1962) Methodology of a water balance study conducted on a desert woodland (*Acacia aneura* F. Muell.) community in central Australia. Arid Zone Res 16:15–26

Slatyer RO (1967) Plant-water relationships. Academic Press, London New York

Slatyer RO, Taylor SA (1960) Terminology in plant-soil-water relations. Nature London 187:922–924

Spanner DC (1973) The components of the water potential in plants and soils. J Exp Bot 24:816–819

Taylor HM, Gardner HR (1963) Penetration of cotton seedling taproots as influenced by bulk density, moisture content, and strength of soil. Soil Sci. 96:153–156

Taylor HM, Klepper B (1975) Water uptake by cotton root systems: an examination of assumptions in the single root model. Soil Sci 120:57–67

Taylor HM, Klepper B (1978) The role of rooting characteristics in the supply of water to plants. Adv Agron 30:99–128

Taylor HM, Ratcliff LF (1969) Root elongation rates of cotton and peanuts as a function of soil strength and soil water content. Soil Sci 108:113–119

Taylor SA, Slatyer RO (1962) Proposals for a unified terminology in studies of plant-soil-water relations. Arid Zone Res 16:339–349

Tinker PB (1976) Transport of water to plant roots in soil. Philos Trans R Soc London Ser B 273:445–461

Turner NC (1974) Stomatal response to light and water under field conditions. In: Bieleski RL, Ferguson AR, Creswell MM (eds) Mechanisms of regulation of plant growth. Roy Soc NZ Bull 12:423–432

Turner NC, Long MJ (1980) Errors arising from rapid water loss in the measurement of leaf water potential by the pressure chamber technique. Aust J Plant Physiol 7:527–537

Tyree MT (1976) Negative turgor pressure in plant cells: fact or fallacy? Can J Bot 54:2738–2746

Tyree MT, Caldwell C, Dainty J (1975) The water relations of hemlock (*Tsuga canadensis*). V. The localization of resistances to bulk water flow. Can J Bot 53:1078–1084

Walter CJ, Barley KP (1974) The depletion of soil water by wheat at low, intermediate and high rates of seeding. Proc 10th Int Congr Soil Sci Moscow 1:150–158

Weatherley PE (1970) Some aspects in water relations. Adv Bot Res 3:171–206

Weatherley PE (1975) Water relations of the root system. In: Torrey JG, Clarkson DT (eds) The development and function of roots. Academic Press, London New York, pp 397–413

Weatherley PE (1976) Introduction: water movement through plants. Philos Trans R Soc London Ser B 273:435–444

Wilson AM, Hyder DN, Briske DD (1976) Drought resistance characteristics of blue grama seedlings. Agron J 68:479–484

Zimmermann U, Steudle E (1979) Physical aspects of water relations of plant cells. Adv Bot Res 6:46–119

2 Water in Tissues and Cells

M.T. TYREE and P.G. JARVIS

CONTENTS

2.1 Introduction

As already explained in the previous chapter, generally the water potential, Ψ, of a plant cell is expressed as the sum of three components, as follows (Dainty 1976):

$$\Psi = P + \pi + \tau \qquad (2.1)$$

where P, π and τ are the pressure, osmotic and matric potentials, respectively. In a tissue or organ, Eq. (2.1) applies to each cell individually but if different cells have different solute concentrations, moduli of elasticity or volumes of apoplasmic water, then even at equilibrium the cellular values of P, π and τ may differ from cell to cell. Although measurements of π have frequently been made on individual cells using plasmolytic methods and measurements of P have recently been made on individual cells of higher plants using the pressure probe (Steudle et al. 1975; Hüsken et al. 1978, 1980), it is in general not practical to make a large number of such measurements in the tissues and organs of higher plants. In spite of this problem Tyree and Hammel (1972) have argued that it is meaningful to define bulk values of the water relations parameters to characterize the water relations properties of tissues and organs. They derived *volume-averaged,* or more precisely *weight-averaged,* values of pressure potential, $\bar{P}$, and osmotic potential $\bar{\pi}$, from analysis of the Ψ isotherms of individual cells, with the following specific meanings:

$$\bar{\pi} = \sum_{i}^{n} \frac{W_i}{W} \pi_i \qquad (2.2)$$

and

$$\bar{P} = \sum_{i}^{n} \frac{W_i}{W} P_i \qquad (2.3)$$

where W is the weight of water in the tissue symplasm, and W_i the weight of water in the ith cell of osmotic-potential π_i and pressure potential P_i. The bar represents weight-averaged values, the summation being made over all n cells in the tissue. Thus for a tissue at equilibrium, Eq. (2.1) should be replaced by the appropriate weight-averaged parameters, i.e.,

$$\Psi = \bar{P} + \bar{\pi} + \bar{\tau}, \qquad (2.4)$$

recognizing that the components of Ψ are averaged over each of the heterogeneous phases in the tissue, i.e., vacuole, cytoplasm *or* cell wall.

In principle, weight-averaging over heterogeneous phases is unsatisfactory because, strictly speaking, Ψ and its components are intensive variables which vary from point to point in a cell and tissue (Weatherley 1970). This always obtains when water flow occurs but even at equilibrium when Ψ is the same at all points the components can and do change with position as long as their recognizing that the components of Ψ are averaged over each of the heterogeneous phases in the tissue, i.e., vacuole, cytoplasm or cell wall.

sum, $(\bar{P}+\pi+\tau)$, is constant. For example, at equilibrium, values of $\bar{P}+\pi+\tau$ might be $(10)+(-20)+(-0)$ bar in the vacuole, $(12)+(-15)+(-7)$ bar at a particular point near a charged surface in the cell wall. However, since at the present time we are unable to measure such point potentials, weight-averaged values provide a practical means of characterization of average tissue properties. Nonetheless, their use should not be allowed to obscure the fundament definition of the component potentials. There is general agreement on the meaning of Ψ and how it should be measured for a tissue. However, much less agreement has been reached on the meaning and measurement of the components of Ψ, particularly of τ (e.g., PASSIOURA 1980).

2.2 The Components of Tissue Water Potential

2.2.1 Matric Potential, τ

Matric potentials in tissues were originally conceived as a component of the total potential resulting from interactions between the water and the matrix by analogy with the identification of a matric component in soils (TAYLOR and SLATYER 1961). Matric potentials in soils were considered to be largely the result of capillarity between the pores with "surface forces", especially in clays, important at low potentials (BOLT and FRISSEL 1960). It was assumed that similar potentials would exist in cell walls and possibly also in the cytoplasm where swelling phenomenon such as imbibition were well known. Since the original postulation, the physical meaning of $\bar{\tau}$ has been the subject of unresolved controversy. Some have defined it in terms of a measurement procedure without much regard to thermodynamic principles (e.g., WIEBE 1966; WARREN WILSON 1967a; ACOCK 1975): others have taken more cognizance of the thermodynamic restrictions imposed on definitions based on experimental procedures (e.g., NOY-MEIR and GINZBURG 1967). All such definitions are unsatisfactory because they are derived from tissue properties obtained by volume or weight-averaging over the heterogeneous phases of vacuole, cytoplasm, and cell wall. A satisfactory definition of matric potential must be based upon consideration of it as an intensive property acting at a point. To pursue this concept and consequences quantitatively, we must stray a little from purely thermodynamic theory into a mixture of thermodynamics and statistical mechanics. This approach has been taken with some success by TYREE and KARAMANOS (1980) for plant tissues. Some of the basic concepts were originally put forward for soil by BOLT and MILLER (1958), but unfortunately the merits of this earlier paper appear to have been largely unheeded by plant physiologists.

2.2.1.1 The Physical Origin of τ

Matric forces are interfacial forces, which occur between liquid and solid phases. The forces are short-range and therefore influence only a very small fraction

of the total water even in systems with large surface to volume ratios, e.g., clays and plant cell walls. At uncharged surfaces the force interactions are largely London-van der Waals forces or hydrogen bonds, and probably extend for only one or two diameters of the water molecule, 0.3 to 0.6 nm. At charged surfaces in contact with electrolytic solutions the longer range electrostatic forces extend a few nm. The surface charges are balanced by swarms of counterions that arrange themselves in a diffuse layer near the surface. Very high, localized concentrations of counterions can develop and contribute to low localized values of π. The impact of these counterions on π has been calculated according to the Gouy-Chapman theory by TYREE and KARAMANOS (1980) who showed that localized concentrations can exceed 2 molar resulting in values of π below -50 bar. However, it does not seem appropriate to identify τ with such osmotic effects of swarms of counterions because there is no sharp distinction between π within the diffuse layer and outside it; π declines gradually from the microregion where the electric effects are negligible to the sites where they are important.

Within the electric fields of the surface charge there is another effect that reduces the energy of water molecules. This is the interaction of the water dipole with the electric field. Plant cell wall surfaces and clay surfaces have a net negative charge. This causes the water dipole to orient itself with the positive (hydrogen) end a little nearer the surface than the negative (oxygen) end because like charges are repelled and opposite charges are attracted. The net effect is a lowering of the free energy of the water molecules within the electric field. In terms of water potential the magnitude of the effect is given by

$$\tau = -\left(\frac{N_0^2 P_0^2}{3V_w RT}\right) F^2,$$

(2.5)

where N_0 is Avogadro's number, R is the gas constant, T is the Kelvin temperature, V_w is the volume of a mole of water, P_0 is the dipole moment of water, and F is the electric field.

Figure 2.1 shows the magnitudes of the components of Ψ near a charged surface according to the Gouy-Chapman theory. In this case bulk water containing 10 mM NaCl at $\Psi = -15$ bar is at equilibrium with water near a surface with a net charge of -4×10^{-5} C cm^{-2}. The large positive pressure that develops near the charged surface can be identified as the swelling pressure of the gels. The pressure arises because of the force with which water molecules are drawn towards the charged surface. The molecules piling on top of each other produce a pressure in much the same way that gravity produces pressure under deep water. Given that π and τ are both very negative near charged surfaces, large positive values of P are necessary to balance Eq. (2.1) since at equilibrium Ψ is uniform over space.

2.2.1.2 The Effect of τ on Water Potential Isotherms

Since the forces contributing to τ are short-range (Fig. 2.1), they influence only a small fraction of the total water volume even in cell walls. Figure 2.2

Fig. 2.1. The components of water potential near a charged surface according to the Gouy-Chapman double layer theory with a surface charge of -4×10^{-5} C cm^{-2}. The univalent ion concentration outside the double layer is taken as 10 mM. π and τ are calculated at distances from the charged surface from the calculated electrical potential and electric field, respectively; $P = \Psi + \pi + \tau$. (TYREE and KARAMANOS 1980)

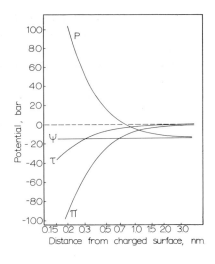

Fig. 2.2. A scale diagram of the air–water interface near a water-filled, charged pore. The pore is 20 nm in diameter and is filled with water at $\Psi = -15$ bar. The other parameters are as in Fig. 2.1. A is a thin layer of water on the charged surface held there by π and τ; B is the distance from the charged surface at which $\Psi_p = 0$; C is the distance at which Ψ is more than 90% attributable to negative P; D is the air–water interface with a radius of curvature of 96 nm. (TYREE and KARAMANOS 1980)

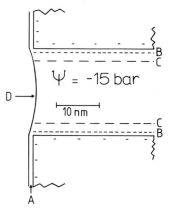

shows a scale diagram of the water in a cylindrical pore 20 nm in diameter in a plant cell wall based on the profiles in Fig. 2.1. The water in the pore and the water vapour above it are taken to have a Ψ of -15 bar. The water layer A close to the charged surface is held by both π and τ. The water layer between the surface and the boundary B is at P > 0 bar. However, beyond boundary C, P accounts for more than 90% of Ψ, i.e., P < -13.5 bar. Thus most of the water is outside the force effects of the charged surface. The negative pressure in the pore in Fig. 2.2 arises from the surface tension of the air–water interface which has a radius of curvature of 96 nm at -15 bar in this figure. In the xylem negative pressures are included in P and for consistency and clarity we feel that such surface tension effects in pores should also be included in P, rather than in τ, as suggested by WARREN WILSON (1967a) and others.

Only if the air–water interface intrudes into the pore as a result of evaporation of water from the cell walls, for example, will the thin layer of water remaining under the influence of τ become a substantial proportion of the water present.

A disadvantage of this method is that an hour or more of experimental time is required to evaluate $\bar{\pi}$, whereas the sap extraction and tissue killing methods can give results in minutes. In some cases speed may be important. In soybean (*Glycine max*) π is light-dependent and can change rapidly when irradiance changes (WENKERT 1980). WENKERT used the sap–extraction method and corrected for dilution effects by use of the pressure–volume method in darkness, when π was stable.

2.2.3 Analysis of Ψ Isotherms

As water is lost from the tissue, either by successive increments of pressure in a pressure bomb or by evaporation from the organ, $\bar{P}$ falls to zero at the turgor loss point. If negative turgor does not occur, then at lower potentials $\Psi = \bar{\pi}$ and, from Eq. (2.9)

$$\frac{1}{\Psi} = \frac{-W}{RTN_s\rho_w} = -\frac{(W_o - W_e)}{RTN_s\rho_w} = \frac{W_e}{RTN_s\rho_w} - \frac{W_o}{RTN_s\rho_w}, \tag{2.10}$$

where W_o is the weight of symplasmic water at full hydration and W_e is the weight of water lost from the whole sample. This equation is valid only if the amount of apoplasmic water, W_a, does not change during dehydration so that all the water lost comes from the symplasm. This assumption is discussed in more detail in Section 2.2.6. A plot of $1/\Psi$ versus W_e will yield a "straight" line with an intercept equal to $-W_o/RTN_s\rho_w = 1/\pi_o$ where π_o is the osmotic potential at full hydration, and a slope of $1/RTN_o\rho_w$. At any other state of hydration π can be calculated from

$$\bar{\pi} = \bar{\pi}_o\, W_o/W. \tag{2.11}$$

Thus this analysis yields π as a function of W over the whole range of water contents.

It is also possible to calculate $\bar{\pi}_o$ by plotting $1/\Psi$ against relative water content, R* (HELLKVIST et al. 1974; TYREE 1976b; RICHTER 1978). This is so because

$$R^* = \frac{W + W_a}{W_o + W_a} \tag{2.12}$$

and hence

$$W = (W_o + W_a)R^* - W_a. \tag{2.13}$$

Substituting for W in Eq. (2.10) gives

$$\frac{1}{\Psi} = \frac{-W}{RTN_s\rho_w} = \frac{W_a}{RTN_s\rho_w} - \frac{R^*(W_o + W_a)}{RTN_s\rho_w}. \tag{2.14}$$

Fig. 2.4. A contemporary Höfler diagram derived from analysis of the Ψ isotherm. The relationships between relative water content (R*) and the total potential (Ψ), the osmotic potential (π), the pressure potential ($\bar{P}$) and the bulk modulus of elasticity ($\bar{\varepsilon}$) of a shoot of Sitka spruce (*Picea sitchensis*) taken from a well-exposed position in forest canopy in midwinter. $\bar{P}$ was calculated from Eq. (2.17) and $\bar{\varepsilon}$ from Eq. (2.21). (From data given by HELLKVIST et al. 1974)

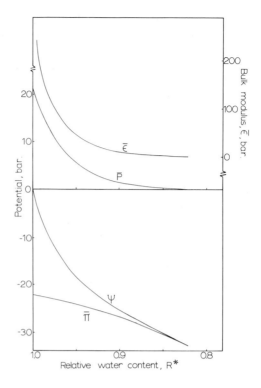

Thus a plot of $1/\Psi$ against R* also yields a straight line when $\bar{P}$ is zero provided that W_a is constant. π_o is found from extrapolation of the line to R* = 1 when $1/\Psi = -W_o/RTN_s\rho_w = 1/\pi_o$.

From Eq. (2.14) it is also clear that extrapolation of the relation between $1/\Psi$ and R* to $1/\Psi = 0$ yields an estimate of the relative water content of apoplasmic water,

$$R_a^* = W_a/(W_o + W_a), \tag{2.15}$$

as the intercept on the R* axis.

Thus a plot of $1/\Psi$ against R* provides a description of tissue water relations in terms of the relationships between Ψ and R*, and $\bar{\pi}$ and R* as well as an estimate of R_a^*. From these estimates of $\bar{\pi}$ and Ψ, $\bar{P}$ can be calculated as a function of R* and a Höfler diagram constructed showing how Ψ, $\bar{\pi}$ and $\bar{P}$ change with R* as shown in Fig. 2.4 (e.g., HELLKVIST et al. 1974; RICHTER 1978). Subsequently a quick measurement of Ψ on a *comparable* sample can immediately yield information on the probable value of $\bar{\pi}$ and $\bar{P}$ and R*. Seasonal and environmentally induced changes in these parameters can also be deduced by measuring the change in the Ψ-isotherms (see TYREE et al. 1978).

Recently, RICHTER (1978) proposed that there were certain advantages in the derivation of parameters from the inverse plot of Ψ against $1/R^*$ and this approach has been developed by RICHTER et al. (1980) and HINCKLEY et al.

to measure P in cells below 20 μm in diameter. Although many vascular plant cells are smaller than that, the technique has led to great advances in our understanding of the physiological role of P at the cellular level in osmoregulation, turgor-dependent ion fluxes (Zimmermann 1978) and the movements of guard cells (Edwards and Meidner 1979), and will permit a useful re-evaluation of our understanding of the physics of cell enlargement (Green et al. 1971).

At the tissue and organ levels, $\bar{P}$ can be deduced from the analysis of water potential isotherms. Once the relationship between water loss, W_e, or relative water content, R^*, and $\bar{\pi}$ has been established (Sect. 2.2.3.3) $\bar{P}$ is simply evaluated at any given value of R^* or W_e by

$$\bar{P} \simeq \Psi - \bar{\pi}. \qquad (2.17)$$

The $\bar{P}$ calculated in this way for an organ is a weight-averaged figure for all the cells because individual cells will have different values of P wherever their values of π differ. For example, values of π in the phloem in sugar beet are twice as negative as in the surrounding parenchyma (Geiger et al. 1973) and similarly large differences have been reported between the values of π in guard cells, subsidiary cells and epidermal cells of *Tradescantia virginiana* (Edwards and Meidner 1979). When such cells are at equilibrium with each other, so that each cell has the same value of Ψ, P will vary from cell to cell.

The theory for the analysis of Ψ isotherms (Sect. 2.2.3) assumes that negative pressure potentials (i.e., negative turgor) do not develop in living cells. Much of the contemporary evidence for negative turgor is based on a negative difference being obtained when Eq. (2.17) is applied to measurements of Ψ and π made on the same or parallel samples of a tissue, π being measured after destruction of the selective permeability of the cell membranes by heating or freezing the tissue sample (e.g., Warren Wilson 1967a; Beadle et al. 1978). At the present time, we have no independent means of knowing if negative turgor really exists. Tyree (1976a) has argued strongly that negative values are obtained from Eq. (2.17) because destruction of the cell membranes results in dilution of the cell sap by the apoplasmic water.

Negative turgor would produce curvature in the Ψ isotherm. The question, therefore, arises as to how much negative turgor could occur and escape notice, particularly in view of the other contributions to non-linearity discussed in Section 2.2.3. To answer this question Tyree and Richter (1982) have computed the theoretical isotherm of a hypothetical shoot having eight different cell types all capable of developing negative turgor. They conclude that curvature resulting from negative turgor will be detectable when it reaches about -2 bar at $\Psi = -20$ bar. Thus negative turgor could contribute up to 10% of the measured water potential without being detected. Whilst this would have little effect on the estimate of $\bar{\pi}_0$ it may affect the estimate of R^* by over 50%.

Recently there has been some discussion over the relative merits of the pressure probe and pressure bomb or psychrometer for the evaluation of water relations parameters of cells and tissues (e.g., Zimmermann and Steudle 1978). Although the pressure probe is of incomparable value for studying the related

physiology of single cells it is unlikely that it can easily give a representative picture of a complex tissue because the P-volume relationships of cells inside a tissue are probably strongly influenced by the "tissue-pressure" of surrounding cells, i.e., if the volume and P of one cell increases it will influence the P of surrounding cells in mechanical contact with it. Since a pressure probe cannot be inserted deeply into a tissue without considerable mechanical damage to surrounding cells or to the tip of the probe, it is difficult to assess the probable importance of "tissue-pressure". However, even if "tissue-pressure" is not important it is clearly impractical to build up a composite picture of the behaviour of a complex tissue by measuring and integrating the effects of the large number of individual cells in the tissue.

It is difficult to reach a useful comparison of the errors in measuring P of single cells and $\bar{P}$ of tissues and organs. Superficially, the error in determining $\bar{P}$ ought to be about the same as the error in measuring the balance pressure $(=-\Psi)$ with the pressure gauge. The mechanical pressure gauges commonly used can resolve the balance pressure to ± 0.07 bar (TYREE and HAMMEL 1972). With a better gauge or pressure transducer it is possible to resolve a balance pressure with an even greater accuracy (e.g., ± 0.02 bar) that compares favourably with the accuracy of the pressure probe of ± 0.03 to 0.05 bar.

Nevertheless, the assessment of the accuracy of $\bar{P}$ is complicated by the time scale of the measurement. In the time required to measure the complete Ψ-isotherm of a tissue by the pressure bomb or psychrometer the isotherm may become distorted because of: (1) plastic deformation of cell walls or growth, (2) gradual changes in π, and (3) small internal disequilibria causing small shifts in the apparent value of the balance pressure. The pressure probe, therefore, *appears* to be more accurate because of the short time scale required for the measurement of P of a cell. However, weight-averaged values of $\bar{P}$ for a tissue can be obtained much more rapidly from the measurement and analysis of Ψ-isotherms than would be possible by the integration of measurements made with the pressure probe on individual cells. Over a lengthy period of measurement pressure probe values are also likely to change for the reasons given above and, in addition, as a result of solute exchange with the bathing medium in which it is necessary to maintain the tissue during measurement. The presence of the bathing medium does, of course, make it difficult to reproduce tissue water contents similar to those which occur in the field.

For these reasons, and since the financial investment and technical expertise needed to make measurements of Ψ-isotherms with pressure bombs and psychrometers are less than for the pressure probe, bulk values of $\bar{\pi}$ and $\bar{P}$ made with these methods will continue to be preferred by many ecologists.

2.2.5 Cell Wall Elasticity and Plasticity

When a stress ($=$ a stretching force) is applied to material a strain ($=$ a deformation of shape) results. The strain that results from a stress can be elastic, plastic or both. A totally plastic strain or deformation is said to occur if the material retains completely its deformed state after the stress is released. A

totally elastic strain occurs when the material completely returns to its prestressed shape after the stress is released.

Many materials, including plant cell walls, have both plastic and elastic properties (HAUGHTON et al. 1968). A growing cell has a more plastic wall than a mature cell, but even mature cells retain measurable plasticity. Generally speaking elastic deformations arise sooner after the onset of strain than plastic deformations. Plastic strain is a slow "creep", taking minutes or hours to reach completion; the plastic "creep" stops when the material has "hardened" sufficiently so that the applied stress is completely taken up by a new arrangement of molecular bonds. In a weakly cross-linked polymer sometimes even elastic deformations can take a long time to reach completion because time is required for polymer coils to change shape governed by the time for cross-linking bonds to break and reform. This tends to blur the distinction between elastic and plastic strains, since the distinction is based primarily on their relative permanence after the stress is released or on their speed of formation when stress is applied.

In a living plant cell, it is the elastic property of the strained cell wall that applies the restoring force on the cell sap and thus produces the positive internal pressure, P. As the wall stretches to enclose a greater volume of cell sap, the internal pressure increases in much the same way as the pressure of air inside a rubber balloon must be increased to stretch it to enclose a larger volume. The plastic properties, on the other hand, allow a permanent increase of volume (=growth) without a permanent increase of P, although a high P is needed to produce plastic stretch. Since even the cell walls of mature plants retain some plasticity, the relationship between P and cell volume changes. If the cell volume increases by Δv_i the increase in P may be more than the decrease in P when the cell volume is decreased some hours later. Such hysteresis in the P-volume relationships will also cause hysteresis in the water potential isotherm (WENKERT et al. 1978b).

The bulk modulus of elasticity, ε, describes the amount by which a small change in volume brings about a change in P (e.g., ZIMMERMANN 1978):

$$\Delta P = \varepsilon \, \frac{\Delta v}{v} \qquad\qquad\qquad (2.18)$$

or

$$\varepsilon = \frac{dP}{dv} \cdot v \qquad\qquad\qquad (2.19)$$

The bulk modulus, ε, is thus the proportionality parameter between the observed change in P, ΔP, and the change in relative cell volume, $\Delta v/v$, where v is the cell volume. Since ε is not a constant, but varies with pressure, the formulation of Eq. (2.19) is more appropriate. The more elastic the cell wall, the smaller the value of ε.

Using the pressure probe, ε of a single cell can be measured directly by injecting a known small volume of Δv of oil rapidly into the cell and measuring

the resulting instantaneous increase in P, ΔP. So far only a few estimates of ε have been made with the pressure probe on single cells of higher plants. Such values of ε range from zero at $P \simeq 0$ to ca. 100 bar at $P \simeq 5$ bar in a selection of eight kinds of cell (ZIMMERMANN and STEUDLE 1980). The measurement is sufficiently sensitive to discriminate between the ranges of values of ε in the subsidiary, epidermal and mesophyll cells of *Tradescantia virginiana*. In the mesophyll cells of the CAM plant *Kalanchoë daigremontiana*, ε varied between 13 and 128 bar with a mean value of 42 bar in the range of P from 0 to 3.4 bar (STEUDLE et al. 1980). This relatively low value of ε allows substantial changes in cell volume and water storage as N_s increases as a result of malic acid synthesis during the dark period. The resulting changes in P may regulate the entire CAM syndrome including malic acid synthesis in the mesophyll and stomatal movements in the epidermis.

Pressure probe measurements of ε of single cells of algae and higher plants all reveal that ε is pressure dependent, i.e., ε is smaller at low P than at high P (Fig. 2.6). In addition ε is "volume-dependent", i.e., small growing cells have lower values of ε than large mature cells (ZIMMERMANN 1978). The pressure dependence may simply reflect non-linearity of the stress–strain relationship of cell walls; the volume dependence may indicate a correlation between elasticity and plasticity. Small growing cells must be plastic and it is possible that the structural peculiarities that make cell walls plastic may also make them more elastic. In the case of cells of *Nitella* and *Chara* species, pressure and volume dependence is clearly the result of large differences in ε of different regions of the internodal cells (ZIMMERMANN and STEUDLE 1975).

The walls of cells are subject to stresses and strains in several directions at once because of their geometry and attachment to other cells. In addition the cell wall is anisotropic, i.e., it is more "stretchable" in one direction than another and a stretch in one direction may cause a contraction in the perpendicular direction. If a perfectly spherical cell with isotropic walls did exist, then ε would depend in a simple way on the wall thickness, δ, cell radius, r, and Young's modulus of elasticity ε^*. Young's modulus relates stress to strain in one direction. In this hypothetical case

$$\varepsilon = \frac{2\delta\varepsilon^*}{3r} \qquad (2.20)$$

but in real plant cells ε depends on geometrical properties in a much more complicated way (see, for example, VINTERS et al. 1977). Nonetheless, it is probably safe to say qualitatively that small thick-walled cells have larger values of ε than large thin-walled cells, since for an isotropic spherical cell this is the case.

At the tissue level it is also possible to define a weight-averaged bulk elastic modulus, $\bar{\varepsilon}$.

$$\bar{\varepsilon} = \frac{d\bar{P}}{dW} \cdot W \qquad (2.21)$$

where $\bar{P}$ is as defined by Eq. (2.3) and W is the weight of water in the symplasm.

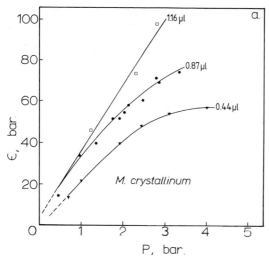

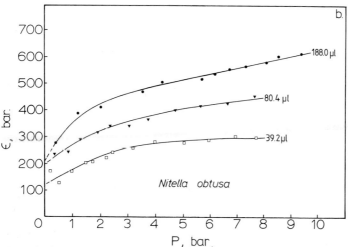

Fig. 2.6. The elastic modulus, ε, of **a** the giant epidermal bladder cells of *Mesembryanthemum crystallinum* and **b** the giant algal cells of *Nitella obtusa* in relation to the pressure (turgor) potential in the individual cells, P. The change in pressure in the cells was measured in response to changes in volume brought about by manipulating the position of the cell sap/oil interface in the pressure probe. The *figures beside the curves* are the volumes of the cells at full turgor, v_0. ε was calculated from $\varepsilon = V_0 \Delta P/\Delta V$. (Steudle et al. 1977)

To estimate $\bar{\varepsilon}$, $\bar{P}$ is measured as described in Section 2.2.4 and plotted against W ($=W_0 - W_e$). $\bar{\varepsilon}$ is then calculated as the slope of the line, $d\bar{P}/dW$, at particular values of W. Figure 2.7 shows that, as in single cells, $\bar{\varepsilon}$ for a tissue is also pressure-dependent (Hellkvist et al. 1974; Cheung et al. 1976), but reaches much lower values at low $\bar{P}$ than does ε at low P because of the effect of weight-averaging. In a population of cells at low $\bar{P}$ many of the cells may have no turgor at all, whereas at high $\bar{P}$ all the cells have some turgor. When Ψ decreases at already low $\bar{P}$ the cells with turgor will experience a decrease in both W and $\bar{P}$; the cells at zero turgor will also lose water and thus contribute to dW, but they will not contribute to $d\bar{P}$ because their pressure potential is already zero. This leads to low values of $d\bar{P}/dW$ and $\bar{\varepsilon}$ is correspondingly small. As with ε, $\bar{\varepsilon}$ is also volume-dependent, being less in growing leaves than in mature leaves (Tyree et al. 1978) (see Fig. 2.7).

Fig. 2.7. The bulk elastic modulus, $\bar{\varepsilon}$, of leaves of *Populus* in relation to pressure (turgor) potential in the tissue, $\bar{P}$. The *figures beside the curves* are the age of the leaves and the leaf number from the top of the plant. $\bar{\varepsilon}$ was calculated from Ψ-isotherms measured with the pressure bomb using Eq. (2.21). (Unpublished data of TYREE and MCGREGOR)

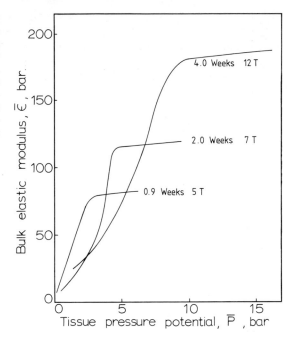

However, ε and $\bar{\varepsilon}$ are not exactly comparable quantities, so the comparison should not be pushed too far. In particular ε is defined in terms of cell volume [Eq. (2.19)] and $\bar{\varepsilon}$ in terms of the weight of symplasmic water [Eq. (2.21)]. Treating both in terms of the weight of water, TYREE (1981) has shown that

$$\bar{\varepsilon} = \sum^{n} \left(\frac{dw_i}{dW}\varepsilon_i\right) + \sum^{n}\left(\frac{dw_i}{dW}P_i\right) - \bar{P} \qquad (2.22)$$

where w_i is the amount of water in the ith cell of a population of cells and the summation is carried out over all n cells in the tissue or organ which contains an amount of water W $(=W_0 - W_e)$. Thus $\bar{\varepsilon}$ is not identical with ε but in practice is numerically very close to it. Using a model of a tissue containing nine cell types varying in π_0, W_0 and ε, TYREE (1981) has shown that generally ε lies within 2% of the first term on the right of Eq. (2.22).

Whilst such quantitative similarity can be demonstrated by simulation, qualitative comparison between ε and $\bar{\varepsilon}$ is rendered rather obscure because plastic hysteresis effects must affect their quantitative values as well as their heuristic meaning. Furthermore, when comparing values of ε or $\bar{\varepsilon}$ it is necessary to bear in mind that minor differences in the way in which they are measured can affect their values. For example, if the time scale over which ε is measured is long, then a much smaller value of ε may be computed than if the time scale of the measurement is short (ZIMMERMANN and HÜSKEN 1980; VINTERS et al. 1977).

The accuracy with which $\bar{\varepsilon}$ can be determined with the pressure bomb is about the same or better than the accuracy with which ε can be obtained using the pressure probe (TYREE 1981). With the pressure bomb $\Delta\bar{P}$ can be measured with an error of about ± 0.07 bar, although this can be improved

with the use of better pressure gauges, which can be compared with an error of ± 0.04 bar for the pressure probe. The larger error in measuring ΔP with the pressure bomb is offset by a higher accuracy in measuring W or W_0. With the pressure bomb W_0 is evaluated from the isotherm and probably has an error of about 5% of the fresh weight. In the pressure probe technique, however, v must be measured optically on cells which may not be of regular geometric shape; the resulting error can be 10% to 30% of the true value depending on the cell.

2.2.6 Apoplasmic Water

Apoplasmic water consists of all water in the plant not in the symplasm. In a tissue, such as the mesophyll, this is almost wholly water of hydration in the cell walls, but in an organ such as a leaf or shoot, apoplasmic water includes water in the lumens of the xylem vessels, tracheids and fibres, as well as water in the cell walls.

The Ψ-isotherm theory so far developed has assumed that the amount of apoplasmic water, W_a, remains constant as the tissue or organ is dehydrated and that it can be estimated as the intercept on the R^* axis by extrapolation of the straight line described by Eq. (2.14) to $1/\Psi = 0$ [see Eq. (2.15)]. Tyree and Richter (1982) point out that this procedure should be viewed with caution since constancy of W_a with change in Ψ is by no means certain. Whilst the pores in the cell walls are unlikely to drain at the negative pressure potentials obtaining ($\Psi > -30$ bar), in the much larger lumens of the xylem vessels and tracheids the water may cavitate or be withdrawn at these values of P. In addition, both cell walls and xylem vessels and tracheids will shrink as a result of the tensions which develop within them, the degree of shrinkage depending on their bulk compressive modulus.

Changes in W_a during dehydration result in curvature of the linear relationship expressed by Eq. (2.14). Using a model of a tissue containing eight different cell types, Tyree and Richter (1982) showed that the curvature induced has only a small effect on the estimation of $\bar{\pi}_0$ (an underestimation of 0.4 bar in 10 bar in an extreme case) but can result in a 50% underestimation of R_a^*.

Tyree and Richter (1982) also demonstrated that non-ideality of the cell sap solution can lead to curvature in the Ψ-isotherm which may result in error in the estimate of R_a^* of up to ± 0.05. Such errors could be significant when R_a^* is small (e.g., 0.1), and can also lead to apparent negative values of R_a^* when ϕ decreases with increasing solute concentration.

Cavitation of xylem vessels and tracheids (see Chap. 5, this Vol.) is a regular occurrence as a consequence of the relatively moderate, diurnal changes in xylem pressure potential (Milburn and McLaughlin 1974), and large seasonal changes in the water content of stem sapwood occur as a result (e.g., Waring and Running 1978). Loss of apoplasmic water as a result of cavitation would be most likely to occur during determination of Ψ-isotherms by vapor pressure methods. In the pressure bomb, on the other hand, the water potential at the balance point is zero and cavitation is unlikely. However, water may be

driven out from the lumens of the vessels and tracheids if the size of the pit pores is sufficient to allow the passage of the water–air interface. Ψ-isotherms for conifer sapwood measured with the pressure bomb show that about 15% of the water is removed by an applied pressure of 10 bar (EDWARDS and JARVIS 1982) in contrast to previously published Ψ-isotherms measured by vapor pressure equilibration which show a fall in R* of approximately 80% for a reduction in Ψ of 10 bar (WARING and RUNNING 1978; WARING et al. 1979). In sapwood most of the water is apoplasmic occurring in the dead conducting cells, the ray parenchyma occupying only a very small proportion of the volume (5%), whereas in a leaf or leafy shoot, the xylem contains a very much smaller proportion of the total water content. Nonetheless, some careful measurements of changes in xylem water content during the determination of Ψ-isotherms with the pressure bomb are desirable to establish the magnitude of the change in relation to the total organ water content.

The relationship between the tensions which develop in the apoplasmic water in association with changes in W_a can be expressed in terms of the bulk compressive modulus, $\bar{\varepsilon}_c$ as follows:

$$\bar{\varepsilon}_c = \frac{d\bar{P}_a}{dW_a} \cdot W_a$$

where $\bar{P}_a$ is the pressure potential in the apoplasmic structures and has a negative value almost equal to Ψ. In an incompressible structure $\bar{\varepsilon}$ is very large. Since cell walls are made up of closely cross-linked, dense polymers, we would expect to find the largest values of $\bar{\varepsilon}_c$ there, with smaller values, in decreasing order, in the lumens of sclerenchyma fibres, tracheids and vessels. However, since the walls of vessels are structurally modified to withstand substantial tensions, their values of $\bar{\varepsilon}_c$ are likely to be substantially larger than the values of the bulk elastic modulus of mesophyll cells experiencing positive turgor (see Sect. 2.2.5). Less than 5% of the diurnal swelling and shrinkage which occurs in the stem of a conifer is associated with swelling and shrinkage of the sapwood, the remainder occurring in the living cells of phloem and cambium. The values of $\bar{\varepsilon}_c$ for wood are of the order of 3,000 bar (SKAAR 1972) and probably largely reflect changes in lumen dimensions, values for cell walls being much larger. Consequently compressibility of cell walls can probably be regarded as a negligible source of change in W_a in leaves.

2.3 Ecological Implications of Tissue-Water-Potential Characteristics

2.3.1 Osmotic Potential

2.3.1.1 Origin of Changes in π

Decreases in π in response to water and salt stress have been widely reported over many years (e.g., WALTER 1955; KREEB 1963). In some cases the fall

in solute concentration as a result of dehydration according to Eq. (2.9), cannot be regarded as an osmotic adjustment to maintain a positive pressure potential in the cell: such a fall in π is accompanied by a decrease in $\bar{P}$. On the other hand, either an increase in N_s or a change in the distribution of water between symplasm and apoplasm leading to a decrease in π may represent adjustments to maintain turgor as W decreases.

2.3.1.2 Osmotic Adjustment

Recently considerable emphasis has been placed on demonstrating changes in π of plant tissues that can be ascribed to changes in N_s (see review by Turner and Jones 1980), and changes in π of this kind are summarized in the following paragraphs.

Diurnal changes in π with amplitudes ranging from 4 to 16 bar have been reported in higher plants. The amount of change resulting from diurnal fluctuation of N_s per cell is from 2 to 8 bar (Turner 1975; Hsiao et al. 1976; Powell and Blanchard 1976; Cutler et al. 1977; Davies and Lakso 1978, 1979; Wenkert et al. 1978b). It is not known how diurnal shifts in N_s per cell are induced. Diurnal fluctuations in water stress might affect metabolic pathways or ion pumps, change the balance between the PCO and PCR cycles or cause an imbalance between photosynthesis and translocation. In giant algal cells a reduction in P leads to stimulation of K^+ transport into the cell (see reviews by Zimmermann 1977, 1978) and a similar feedback system seems to exist in the guard cells of *Tradescantia virginiana* (Edwards and Meidner 1979).

Medium-term reductions in π have been induced in the leaves of stressed plants in comparison with unstressed controls by one or more cycles of soil drying or the application of polyethylene glycol or salt solutions to the rooting medium. Reductions in $\bar{\pi}$ of from 1 to 10 bar as a result of an increase in N_s have been found, the changes being completed in 3 days to 3 weeks (Jarvis and Jarvis 1963a; Lawlor 1969; Simmelsgaard 1976; Cutler and Rains 1978; Morgan 1977; Hanson et al. 1977; Hanson and Nelson 1978; Jones and Turner 1978, 1980; Turner et al. 1978; Storey and Wyn Jones 1978; Wyn Jones and Storey 1978; Munns et al. 1979; Cutler et al.; 1980a, b; Wilson et al. 1980). Similar osmotic adjustments have been observed in the floral apex of wheat (Munns et al. 1979) and in the root tips of *Zea mays* (Sharp and Davies 1979).

The decreases in π in these experiments are largely drought-induced but in some cases they may have ontogenetic (e.g., Tyree et al. 1978) or microenvironmental origins (e.g., Turner 1974). For example, osmotic adjustment of 2 to 5 bar has been found in the upper levels of canopies as compared with the lower levels (Turner 1974; Hellkvist et al. 1974; Hsiao et al. 1976; Kirkham and Smith 1978) although Wilson (1977) found no differences with respect to insertion level in leaves of a *Panicum maximum* cultivar.

Long-term or seasonal changes in π range from 2 to 18 bar. These changes occur over several weeks or months and it is difficult to know how much of the change results from increases in N_s per cell or from changes in water distribution between the symplasm and apoplasm. In some cases the decline

in π is a response to drought and is larger on unirrigated than irrigated plants (GOODE and HIGGS 1973; HSIAO et al. 1976; ELSTON et al. 1976; ROBERTS and KNOERR 1977; TURNER et al. 1978; FERERES et al. 1978; HINCKLEY et al. 1980). In other cases the decline in π may be ontogenetic in origin (CLINE and CAMPBELL 1976; TYREE et al. 1978; HINCKLEY et al. 1980), or in evergreens, a response to the onset of winter. In sugar maple (*Acer saccharum*), for example, π_0 declined during leaf development in May and June and then remained more or less constant until leaf fall in October. In *Tsuga canadensis,* in contrast $\bar{\pi}_0$ cycled seasonally in phase with air temperature reaching the lowest values (-27 bar) in mid winter and the highest (-15 bar) in late summer (TYREE et al. 1978).

The degree of diurnal, medium-term and seasonal osmotic adjustment apparently varies widely between species. There are some species which have on investigation shown little or no adjustment and these have not been referred to here. There have been too few studies that clearly demonstrate the presence or absence of osmotic adjustment to allow generalizations to be made. On the whole there is considerable evidence for osmotic adjustment in crop plants and halophytes, perhaps because they have been more intensively investigated, and some evidence that osmotic adjustment is less well developed in woody shrubs and trees (see TURNER 1979; WYN JONES 1981; HINCKLEY et al. 1980; TURNER and JONES 1980).

2.3.1.3 Advantages of N_s-Induced Osmotic Adjustment

Low values of $\bar{\pi}$ throughout the plant should enhance the ability of plants to take up soil water under dry or saline conditions (TYREE 1976 b). This advantage is probably marginal in sandy soils because the available water reserves at soil water potentials below -4 bar are very small and the plant's ability to grow deep roots is probably of greater advantage. In clay soils, however, there are considerable soil water reserves at water potentials below -4 bar, so that low leaf or root π may be as important as root growth in assisting water uptake. In salt marsh conditions and saline media reduction in $\bar{\pi}$ within the plant also assists water uptake (e.g., SLATYER 1961; WYN JONES 1981).

Low $\bar{\pi}$ in the leaf also enables turgor to be maintained above zero at higher values of $\bar{P}$ than would otherwise be the case as Ψ falls. This allows the maintenance of open stomata with larger apertures and higher stomatal conductances and rates of net photosynthesis down to lower values of Ψ than would be the case if π did not adjust (e.g., McCREE 1974; BROWN et al. 1976; FERERES et al. 1978; BEADLE et al. 1978; JONES and TURNER 1978; TURNER et al. 1978; DAVIES and LAKSO 1979; JONES and RAWSON 1979; HINCKLEY et al. 1980; LUDLOW 1980).

Finally N_s-induced lowering of π also enables maintenance of high turgor pressure for growth. This last possibility deserves special consideration and is discussed in Section (2.3.4).

There are apparently limits to the accumulation of osmotic solutes and the decline of $\bar{\pi}$ in tissues. Further osmotic adjustment does not occur once a certain level of $\bar{\pi}$ is reached in particular species and further environmental drought or osmotic stress may lead to loss of solutes and reversal of adjustment

(LAWLOR 1969; MORGAN 1977; JONES and RAWSON 1979; TURNER and JONES 1980; CUTLER et al. 1980a). In rice (*Oryza sativa*) for example, CUTLER et al. (1980a) found that $\bar{\pi}_0$ fell to ca. -18 bar with both rapid (4–6 days) or slow (20–22 days) drought treatment and would not decline further. The following three possible reasons for a limit to osmotic adjustment can be advanced.

At high concentrations even the so-called compatible solutes may become inhibitory to certain enzymes and processes. Glycinebetaine, for example, has been shown to be relatively nontoxic to mitochondria, chloroplasts, protein synthesis and a range of other enzymes up to concentrations of about 500 osmol m^{-3} but starts to inhibit significantly at higher concentrations (FLOWERS et al. 1977; POLLARD and WYN JONES 1978; LARKUM and WYN JONES 1979). Whilst K^+ is the main electrolyte which accumulates in the cytoplasm in higher plants (CRAM 1976) it too is probably not tolerated at concentrations above ca. 200 mol m^{-3}. Secondly, the production of organic solutes also requires a considerable expenditure of energy. According to WYN JONES (1981), the energy cost of producing one osmole of K_2^+ malate^{2-} from gaseous CO_2, via the PCR cycle and PEP-carboxylase, is 13 mol of ATP, and the cost of producing one osmole of glucose from gaseous CO_2, via the PCR cycle, is 54 mol of ATP, whereas the cost of accumulation of one osmole of NaCl is only 0.54 mol of ATP. Whilst accumulation of Na^+ and Cl^- in the vacuole is inexpensive with respect to both energy and carbon, accumulation of organic acids and sugars as osmotica is much more demanding of both energy and carbon. The energy and carbon costs of compatible solutes are likely to be of the same order. In addition, there is a substantial nitrogen cost in the accumulation of nitrogen dipoles such as proline and glycinebetaine which may contain up to 20% of the nitrogen in a leaf (STOREY et al. 1977; STEWART and HANSON 1980). Clearly, if growth is nitrogen-limited, the capability to adjust osmotically may also be restricted.

Thirdly, at high vacuolar and cytoplasmic concentrations of osmotica, there will be a strong tendency for leakage of both solutes and electrolytes across the cell membranes. To maintain high concentrations of osmotica within the cell and compartmentalization of electrolytes and compatible solutes between vacuole and cytoplasm, and possibly also between cytosol and organelles, requires the continuous expenditure of energy which could therefore add up to substantial amounts (RAVEN and SMITH 1977; JESCHKE 1979).

2.3.2 Bulk Modulus of Elasticity, $\bar{\varepsilon}$

The bulk modulus of elasticity, $\bar{\varepsilon}$, depends on structural properties of the tissue and walls of the individual cell and is also pressure and volume-dependent. Consequently, $\bar{\varepsilon}$ would be expected to vary widely between species and to change as a result of ontogeny and environmental stress.

Differences in $\bar{\varepsilon}$ are partly responsible for the extent to which turgor changes as a result of a change in R*; the slope of the relation between $\bar{P}$ and Ψ is largely dependent upon $\bar{\varepsilon}$. In an elastic tissue, i.e., one with small $\bar{\varepsilon}$, the cells and tissue shrink following loss of water. This results in a smaller decrease

in turgor for the loss of a given volume of water than in a more rigid tissue. Thus for a particular value of Ψ, a more elastic tissue has lower R*, lower π and higher $\bar{P}$ than a more rigid tissue (WEATHERLEY 1970). A small ε thus contributes to turgor maintenance in much the same way as osmotic adjustment (TURNER 1979). However, a proper appreciation of the value of R* or Ψ at which turgor is zero for a particular tissue depends upon full knowledge of the relationship between $\bar{\varepsilon}$ and $\bar{P}$ and cannot be derived from knowledge of a single value of $\bar{\varepsilon}$, since both the maximum value of $\bar{\varepsilon}$ and $d\bar{\varepsilon}/d\bar{P}$ vary from tissue to tissue (CHEUNG et al. 1976; TYREE et al. 1978).

Since the definition of a coefficient of enlargement by BROYER (1952), inferences regarding changes in ε have been made from variations in the relationships between Ψ versus R* and $\bar{P}$ versus R* in different species and treatments. These relationships differ widely amongst leaves of different species (e.g., JARVIS and JARVIS 1963b; GARDNER and EHLIG 1965; MAXWELL and REDMANN 1978) and show ontogenetic, seasonal and water stress-induced changes (e.g., JARVIS and JARVIS 1964; KNIPLING 1967; NOY-MEIR and GINZBURG 1969; KASSAM and ELSTON 1974; SHEPHERD 1976; FERERES et al. 1978). The coefficient of enlargement, e (variously defined — see GARDNER and EHLIG 1965; WARREN WILSON 1967c, for example), has shown substantial differences amongst species (e.g., JOHNSON and CALDWELL 1976; MAXWELL and REDMANN 1978) and it is likely that similar differences would emerge from calculation of $\bar{\varepsilon}$ as a function of $\bar{P}$. However, since the values of e available are not defined in relation to $\bar{P}$, we feel that not too much should be read into them. Nonetheless, the often determined relationship between Ψ and R* is informative and useful. We may define the capacitance of a tissue for water storage as $dW/d\Psi = W_0\, dR*/d\Psi$ and this can be shown to be equal to $W/(\bar{\varepsilon}+\bar{\pi})$ (see ZIMMERMANN and STEUDLE 1978). Thus the slope of the Ψ/R* relationship, which describes the amount of water exchanged per unit change in water potential, depends on both the amount of water in the tissue and on its bulk modulus.

Comparative measurements of $\bar{\varepsilon}$ are few and of the $\bar{\varepsilon}/\bar{P}$ relationship even fewer. CUTLER et al. (1980b) and JONES and TURNER (1980) found no changes in the $\bar{\varepsilon}/\bar{P}$ relation in rice and sunflower, respectively, as a result of drought pretreatment, whereas the pretreatment caused osmotic adjustment of 2 to 6 bar.

Indication of probable adjustment in $\bar{\varepsilon}/\bar{P}$ can be found in the data given by ELSTON et al. (1976) for beans (*Vicia faba*), JONES and TURNER (1978) for *Sorghum bicolor*, TYREE et al. (1978) for maple (*Acer saccharum*), DAVIES and LAKSO (1979) for apples (*Malus domestica*) and WILSON et al. (1980) for four tropical forage species. In the beans and apples, $\bar{\varepsilon}$ decreased during the spring and early summer before increasing again in late summer and autumn, the range of variation being ca. 20 to 40 bar, whereas in the sorghum $\bar{\varepsilon}$ increased as a result of drought preconditioning by 11 to 16 bar. In these cases $\bar{\varepsilon}$ varied not only as a result of season or treatment but also because of ontogenetic changes in cell size and seasonal stress-induced changes in $\bar{P}$. Thus, as in the case of changes in π in the presence of dehydration, it is not possible to evaluate the influence of changes in $\bar{\varepsilon}$ as an adjustment mechanism in the presence of changes in $\bar{P}$. However, TYREE et al. (1978) showed that in sugar maple the asymptotic, maximum value of $\bar{\varepsilon}$ changed from 50 bar in May to 180 bar

in July, declining again to about 70 bar in October. In this case adjustment in $\bar{\varepsilon}$ clearly contributed to shifts in the relationship between Ψ and R* and $\bar{P}$ and Ψ. Evaluation of the combined effects of adjustment of π and $\bar{\varepsilon}$ on these relationships must take into account their volume and pressure dependence and therefore requires a model such as used by TYREE (1981).

2.3.3 Turgor Maintenance

The maintenance of turgor as Ψ or R* falls can result from equivalent reduction in either π or in $\bar{\varepsilon}$. In the absence of information as to the response of $\bar{\varepsilon}$ in most studies, turgor maintenance has generally been explained in terms of the reductions in $\bar{\pi}$ as a result of increase in the cell content of N_s (see review by TURNER and JONES 1980).

Partial diurnal turgor maintenance was first described by HSIAO et al. (1976) who found variation in $\bar{P}$ restricted to 2 to 6 bar as Ψ varied between -3 and -12 bar during the course of a day. Similar observations of diurnal change in $\bar{\pi}$ leading to partial stabilization of $\bar{P}$ have been reported in one or two other cases (e.g., DAVIES and LAKSO 1979) but observations of diurnal turgor maintenance are few.

Partial, medium-term turgor maintenance has been observed in several cases (e.g., BEADLE et al. 1978; JONES and TURNER 1978). For example, TURNER et al. (1978) found that Ψ for stomatal closure fell from -17 to -27 bar in *Helianthus annuus* during a dry period in the growth of the crop, but as a result of reduction in $\bar{\pi}$ of 0.6 bar per bar reduction in Ψ the mean value of $\bar{P}$ at stomatal closure remained at 5 bar.

HSIAO et al. (1976) draw attention to full and medium-term turgor mainte-nance resulting from osmotic adjustment (i.e., $\Delta\pi/\Delta\Psi=1$) in *Sorghum bicolor* (see also FERERES et al. 1978). Since then a number of other cases have been identified (see for examples JONES and TURNER 1980; WILSON et al. 1980) and TURNER and JONES (1980) list 15 other examples of full turgor adjustment dating back to 1972.

Medium term turgor maintenance has been evaluated quantitatively in a number of cases as the relation between $\bar{P}$ and Ψ (TURNER 1974; JOHNSON and CALDWELL 1976; JOHNSON and BROWN 1977; JONES and TURNER 1978; JOHNSON 1978; CUTLER et al. 1980a, b). JONES and TURNER (1978) tried to separate the effects of π and ε in bringing about turgor maintenance in sorghum. Since drought pretreatment resulted in an increase in ε rather than a decrease, the substantial turgor maintenance observed was attributed solely to osmotic adjustment. In the experiments by JOHNSON and co-workers (see above), a range of values of leaf Ψ were obtained by withholding water for 6–10 days from potted plants of a number of species growing in controlled environments. The species able to maintain turgor to low values of Ψ were also the species assessed by more subjective criteria to be the most drought-resistant. *Zea mays*, for example, maintained $\bar{P}$ over a much smaller range of Ψ than a number of species of range grasses and *Agropyron* hybrids. The ability to maintain positive $\bar{P}$ to low Ψ was shown to depend on both the value of $\bar{P}$ at $\Psi=0$, i.e., on

$\bar{\pi}_0$, and on the slope of the straight line, $d\bar{P}/d\Psi$. The value of $\bar{\pi}_0$ depends on the degree of osmotic adjustment which has taken place whereas $d\bar{P}/d\Psi$ depends on several properties of the tissue, including the non-ideality of the osmotic solutes, but probably most strongly on $\bar{\varepsilon}$. Reductions in the slope $d\bar{P}/d\Psi$ at low turgor have been cited as evidence of reduction in $\bar{\varepsilon}$ (CUTLER et al. 1980a, b). Thus by inference from the variation in $d\bar{P}/d\Psi$ substantial variations in $\bar{\varepsilon}$ probably also exist amongst species and have considerable influence on the value of Ψ at zero turgor. Lower growth temperatures also change the values of both parameters but generally have a larger effect on $\bar{\pi}_0$, which was reduced in some species by up to 7 bar by a change in temperature regime to lower day and night temperatures (TURNER and JARVIS 1975; JOHNSON 1978).

Substantial long-term turgor maintenance has also been found over almost the whole growing season. FERERES et al. (1978) found that the decline in leaf $\bar{\pi}$ in *Sorghum bicolor* was sufficient to maintain $\bar{P}$ at an average value of 5 bar for 100 days of the growing season. In *Zea mays,* on the other hand, osmotic adjustment maintained $\bar{P}$ only partially in unirrigated plants. Similar partial turgor maintenance was found by GOODE and HIGGS (1973) in apple. The complete turgor maintenance in sorghum allowed stomata to remain open at values of leaf Ψ down to -20 bar.

2.3.4 Turgor Maintenance and Growth

2.3.4.1 The Growth Equations

The physics of growth of plant cells is best understood in *Nitella* (GREEN et al. 1971) but there is circumstantial evidence that similar relations hold in higher plant cells (HSIAO et al. 1976). In its simplest formulation, growth consists of two separable phenomena. The first is the plastic deformation of the cell walls to encompass a larger cell volume. With a slight modification of Green's original formulation this relation can be written:

$$r = \frac{dV}{dt} = m(P - Y), \tag{2.23}$$

where r, the growth rate, is equated to the rate of volume increase of the cells, dV/dt. The driving force for growth is the amount by which P exceeds the yielding point of the wall, Y. The rate at which the plastic deformation occurs is governed by m which incorporates the wall fluidity and some shape factors.

The second phenomenon is the permeation of water across the cell membrane which can be described by a water transport equation,

$$\frac{dV}{dt} = L \Delta\Psi = L(\Psi_e - P - \pi), \tag{2.24}$$

where L is the membrane hydraulic permeability times surface area and $\Delta\Psi$ is the driving force for water flow, equal to the external water potential, Ψ_e,

minus the internal water potential Ψ_i ($=\pi+P$). In considering growth at the whole plant level, $\Delta\Psi$ can be considered as the water potential difference between the soil and growing cell and L the corresponding conductivity of the hydraulic pathway. It is important to realize that the driving force for plastic deformation $(P-Y)$ is much smaller than Y and that Y is under metabolic control. Hence P, although it does partly control growth, is a very insensitive indicator of long-term growth, because metabolism can change the value of Y and can thus dominate the real driving force $(P-Y)$.

The value of Y can change with time at a rate given by

$$\frac{dY}{dt}=rh-s,$$

(2.25)

where s is the rate of wall softening, and is probably a complex function of temperature, light, water stress history, metabolism and plant hormones, and h is a mechanical hardening coefficient, which depends on the physical properties of the cell wall. Equation (2.25) shows that in the absence of metabolic softening r will cause Y to increase $\left(\frac{dY}{dt}>0\right)$ so that growth will eventually stop when $P-Y=0$ (Eq. 2.23). Growth depends on the long-term, integrated effects of a wide range of factors on the time integral of Eq. (2.25). Even in the steady state when Y does not change $\left(\frac{dY}{dt}=0\right)$, it can be argued that growth is totally controlled by s because then

$$r=s/h.$$

(2.26)

Thus we have three equations (2.23, 2.24 and 2.26) that describe growth in terms of three separate driving forces, i.e., $(P-Y)$, $\Delta\Psi$, and s or metabolism.

2.3.4.2 What Controls the Rate of Short-Term Growth?

Better insight into the overall rate control of short-term growth can be obtained by combining the above equations. Equating Eq. (2.23) to Eq. (2.24), solving for P and substituting into Eq. (2.23) gives

$$r=\frac{mL}{m+L}\,(\Psi_e-\pi-Y),$$

(2.27)

or

$$r=\frac{mL}{m+L}\,(\Delta\Psi+P-Y).$$

(2.28)

Equation (2.27) demonstrates the role of osmotic adjustment in controlling the ability of plants to grow at low external water potentials, Ψ_e: decreases in π lead to increases in r. Equation (2.28) emphasizes the control of $(P-Y)$ over plastic wall deformation and the influence of $\Delta\Psi$ on the flow of water

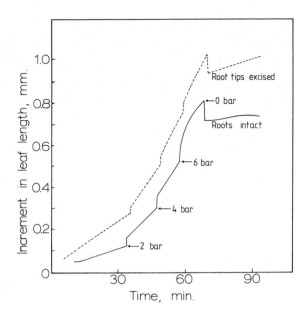

Fig. 2.8. The response of leaf elongation in *Oryza sativa* cv. Kinandang Patong to stepwise increase in pressure applied to the roots of plants in dilute nutrient solution. The *figures beside the curves* indicate the time at which the pressure was raised to the value indicated. The length of an expanding leaf on a seedling in the seven-leaf stage was measured with a linear displacement transducer. (CUTLER et al. 1980c)

from the source, for example, the soil to the cell. The fraction $mL/(m+L)$ can be regarded as a growth coefficient. If $m \gg L$, then $mL/(m+L)=L$, L dominates the magnitude of the growth coefficient and $\Delta\Psi$ is larger and more important than $(P-Y)$. At the other extreme if $L \gg m$ then $mL/(m+L) \simeq m$, m dominates the growth coefficient and $(P-Y)$ is larger and more important than $\Delta\Psi$.

In *Nitella* it is clear that m and $(P-Y)$ dominate short-term growth because $L > m$ (GREEN et al. 1971), but in this case L is determined only by the membrane hydraulic conductivity. In a whole plant L may be less than m because the water pathway includes the series-linked conductivities of the soil+root+ xylem+cell wall–membrane complex. In soybean hypocotyl, on the other hand, BOYER and WU (1978) found m and L to be approximately equal. Thus in this case wall extensibility and membrane hydraulic conductivity control cell enlargement about equally. Because of the comparatively low values of L, values of Ψ in the enlarging tissue were -1.7 to -2.5 bar during rapid growth. Similar values of Ψ were predicted with an appropriate water transport model (MOLZ and BOYER 1978).

CUTLER et al. (1980c) have argued that in whole rice plants m is larger than L so that growth is rate-limited by L, and $\Delta\Psi$ in Eq. (2.28) is larger than $(P-Y)$. In their experiments, the rooting medium of water-cultured rice plants was pressurized. This caused a rapid "elastic elongation" of the leaves followed by an increased growth rate (see Fig. 2.8). CUTLER et al. (1980c) suggest that the observed increase in growth rate after the "elastic elongation" is the result of increase in $\Delta\Psi$ as a consequence of the root pressurization. This seems unlikely, however. The increase in $\Delta\Psi$ will be transitory if transpiration does not also increase because of rehydration of the leaf cells. During the transitory increase in $\Delta\Psi$ the leaf will elongate more rapidly either because

of growth or because of rehydration of the cells. It is unlikely that the stepwise increase or decrease in leaf length after an increase or decrease in root pressure is the result of cell hydration or dehydration alone because the speed of the changes in length is too rapid. The kinetics of rehydration or dehydration of leaves in a pressure bomb indicate that several minutes are required to complete the process in *Fagus grandifolia* (TYREE and CHEUNG 1977), in *Helianthus annuus* (CRUIZIAT et al. 1980) and in *Populus* spp. (TYREE et al. 1978). Consequently, the increases in elongation rate after the stepwise changes in pressure are probably the result of both growth and rehydration of the leaf tissue. It is thus unclear exactly how much growth has been increased. If, on the other hand, it is argued that rice leaves do rehydrate in a matter of seconds as a result of root pressurization, then P will have increased and $\Delta\Psi$ will have been reduced almost to the prepressurization value. In this case the increased growth rate could have been the result of an increase in $(P-Y)$.

We think it is possible that L and $\Delta\Psi$ do limit short-term growth in whole plants. The problems involved in the interpretation of Fig. 2.8 serve to illustrate the difficulties in establishing the true limitation on short-term growth. More work will need to be done to answer the question and measurements of P during growth may be the only way to provide the answer.

2.3.4.3 What Controls the Rate of Long-Term Growth?

In some recent studies attempts have been made to find a simple correlation between maintenance of high $\bar{P}$ and long-term growth rate. JOHNSON and BROWN (1977) and JOHNSON (1978) compared the response of $\bar{P}$ to Ψ in the leaves of several grass species. They tested the hypothesis that the grasses in which zero $\bar{P}$ is reached at the lowest values of Ψ would grow better at lower Ψ than the others. When several grass species were grown at night/day temperatures of 10°/15 °C, this was the case. At other night/day temperatures, however, the ranking of the species changed, the suggestion being that temperature affected Y. BUNCE (1977) found linear relations between leaf elongation rate and $\bar{P}$ in soybean in three different environments. However, the relationship changed with environment and in drier conditions lower $\bar{P}$ was required to maintain the elongation rate, suggesting a lower value of Y. In contrast, CUTLER et al. (1980d) found that rice plants that had been conditioned by three previous drought cycles required higher values of $\bar{P}$ to maintain daily leaf elongation rates than did well-watered controls, although the maximum rate of elongation in drought-conditioned plants did not differ from that of controls. Thus maintenance of $\bar{P}$ by osmotic adjustment in the conditioned plants was not sufficient to ensure the same rates of leaf elongation as in the controls at the same values of Ψ; other factors were involved. They attributed this result to control of the growth rate by $\Delta\Psi$ rather than by $\bar{P}$ or by $(\bar{P}-Y)$ [see Eq. (2.28)], but proper account was not taken of possible shifts in Y between droughted and control plants so the interpretation remains unclear.

In grasses considerable problems arise in measuring growth-controlling variables at the right place — the meristem. WATTS (1972, 1974) showed that leaf growth in young maize plants was much more sensitive to variations in

soil temperature than in air temperature because of the location of the meristem close to the soil surface. CUTLER et al. (1980c) point out that Ψ of enclosed non-transpiring rice leaves was 8 to 10 bar higher than in the transpiring leaves, the implication being that Ψ at the meristem would be similarly different. Thus calculation of $\bar{P}$ from measurements of Ψ and π on transpiring leaves may lead to wholly irrelevant estimates for use in growth equations.

It is not surprising that little correlation has been found between $\bar{P}$ and long-term growth even though correlations can be found in the short term (e.g., WENKERT et al. 1978a). This is probably because of long-term shifts in Y which is under the influence of many different factors. Since the net driving force for plastic wall deformation $(\bar{P}-Y)$ may be 0.3 bar or less (GREEN et al. 1971), long-term shifts in Y of several bars would destroy a simple correlation between $\bar{P}$ and growth or drought hardiness. Thus failure to find simple correlations between parameters derived from Ψ-isotherms and drought hardiness (e.g., CUTLER and RAINS 1978; MAXWELL and REDMANN 1978) may be based on long-term changes in Y. Given our present state of knowledge, all we can say is that long-term growth patterns are controlled by wall softening. In terms of Eq. (2.26) this means that net growth is the time integral of r which in turn depends on s, i.e.,

$$\text{net growth} = \int r \, dt = \int \frac{s}{h} \, dt.$$

There is little doubt that water stress and the history of water stress a plant has experienced influence growth, but the mechanisms by which some plants either tolerate or avoid water stress are probably very important and influence growth via complex and unknown feedback mechanisms. That is not to say that turgor maintenance is unimportant, but that turgor maintenance is only one of several interdependent factors determining growth and drought hardiness.

2.3.5 Apoplasmic Water

CARR and GAFF (1961) and GAFF and CARR (1961) were the first to suggest in recent times that water in cell walls — apoplasmic water — could act as a reservoir protecting cells from water loss by acting as a buffer for the symplasmic water. Recently this suggestion has been taken up by CUTLER et al. (1977) who have suggested that a high apoplasmic water content is a common feature of drought-adapted plants.

A number of estimates of the apoplasmic water fraction, $R_a^* (= W_a/(W_0 + W_a))$ exist, but some (e.g., WARREN WILSON 1967b; ACOCK 1975) are based on dubious methods of analysis of water potential isotherms (see Sect. 2.2.4). Selected values of R_a^* ranging from 0.05 to 0.4 are shown in Table 2.1, but it is difficult from this table alone to draw any correlations between R_a^* and drought adaptation. It is very unlikely, however, that apoplasmic water *in the leaf* can act as much of a buffer against the loss of symplasmic water. In the middle of the day the amount of water transpired hourly can be a large fraction of

Table 2.1. Some relative apoplasmic water volumes

Species	Method of analysis	$R_a^* = (W_a/W_0 + W_a)$	Comments and references
Acer saccharum	P-B	0.2 (June) 0.4 (Sept.)	Single leaves (1)
Picea abies	P-B	0.4 (mature leaves) 0.3 (during leaf flush)	Shoots (1)
Picea sitchensis	P-B	0.2 (Sept.) 0.4 (Jan.)	Shoots (8)
Helianthus annuus	P-B		Single leaves (unpublished)
Populus spp	P-B	0.2 to 0.3	Single leaves (2) and unpublished
Fraxinus pennsylvanica	P-B	0.15	Single leaves (2)
Clematis ligustifolia	P-B	0.05	Single leaves (2)
Cornus stolonifera	P-B	0.05	Single leaves (2)
Acacia aneura	V-E	0.18	Phyllodes (3, 4)
Ceratonia siliqua	V-E	0.08	Single leaves (3, 5)
Pennisetum typhoides	T-S	0.05	Single leaves (3, 6)
Eucalyptus globulus	G	0.4	Leaf tissue (7)

(1) TYREE et al. (1978); (2) CHEUNG et al. (1975); (3) TYREE (1976a); (4) SLATYER (1960); (5) NOY-MEIR and GINZBURG (1967); (6) BEGG et al. (1964); (7) GAFF and CARR (1961); (8) HELLKVIST et al. (1974)

P-B   Pressure bomb isotherm analysis (xylem water included)
V-E   Vapor equilibrium isotherm analysis (note in this method the xylem conduits may be empty so xylem water does not contribute to W_a)
G   Removal of cell wall material and gravimetric analysis

the total leaf water content. For example, in *Eucalyptus* the hourly water loss amounts to 50% to 120% of the total leaf water content (GAFF and CARR 1961), and in cotton less than 5% of the total amount of water transpired comes from net water loss *from the leaf* during the day (WEATHERLEY 1970). JARVIS (1975) calculated for several different kinds of vegetation canopies and transpiration rates that the normal diurnal reduction in R* of leaves could wholly supply transpiration for only 15 to 70 min. Furthermore, since most of the apoplasmic water in the cell wall requires large tensions to remove it (see the earlier discussion in Sects. 2.2.1 and 2.2.4), this apoplasmic water must be regarded as unavailable, so that the daily reductions in leaf R* must be largely at the expense of symplasmic water: the apoplasmic water in the cell walls would be retained and only become available in extreme drought conditions (TEOH et al. 1967). In trees, however, the vastly larger water reservoirs in the stem and branches can act as a significant buffer against net water loss from the leaves (JARVIS 1975; LANDSBERG et al. 1976; POWELL and THORPE 1977; WARING and RUNNING 1978; WARING et al. 1979; WHITEHEAD and JARVIS 1981; Chap. 5, this Vol.). In wheat grown in a temperate climate, water stored

in the shoot may also act as a significant buffer to net water loss from leaves (JONES 1978). In these examples there is no evidence that apoplasmic water in the cell walls constitutes a significant fraction of the available water, and only in trees is there evidence of the continued importance of apoplasmic stored water under conditions of high evaporative demand. The significance of cell wall apoplasmic water must therefore lie elsewhere.

Table 1 shows large variations amongst species in R_a^* and more extensive lists are given by CHEUNG et al. (1975) and TYREE et al. (1978). At the present time, there seems to be little apparent discrimination amongst the species with 5% or 40% apoplasmic water with respect to habitat or environment. The only consistent difference between species is the larger values of R_a^* when Ψ-isotherms are determined for shoots rather than for individual leaves, as is usually the case with conifers.

In addition, large seasonal variations in R_a^* and the symplasmic water fraction, $= W_0/(W_0 + W_a)$, have been found, particularly in conifers (Table 2.1) (HELLKVIST et al. 1974; TYREE et al. 1978). Some of this variation is ontogenetic in origin, higher values of R_a^* being found in mature leaves than in young developing leaves (WENKERT et al. 1978b; TYREE et al. 1978), but, in the conifers in particular, the substantial increase in R_a^* in the autumn seems to be associated with cold hardening (HELLKVIST et al. 1974; TYREE et al. 1978). How this relates to changes in the symplasm or in cell wall structure is still completely unknown. However, there is no doubt that certain features of the Ψ-isotherms, including the proportion of apoplasmic water, can be related to the relative amount of dry matter or cell wall material present. Tissues with Ψ-isotherms indicating a large ε also contain a large proportion of dry matter, W_d, per unit saturated water content $(W_s - W_d)$, i.e., large $W_d/(W_s - W_d)$, as well as a large apoplasmic water fraction (P.G. JARVIS and M.S. JARVIS, unpublished, FERERES et al. 1978; RICHTER et al. 1980). The seasonal increase in R_a^* may therefore be the result of growth in cell wall thickness or changes in cell wall structure in "mature" leaves. Such shifts in water distribution could account for some of the observed decrease in $\bar{\pi}$ over the medium and long term, even if N_s/cell remains constant. However, the significance of secondary wall growth is unlikely to lie solely in its effect of decreasing $\bar{\pi}$, because this is an energetically wasteful way to lower $\bar{\pi}$.

2.3.6 Cell Size

Reduction in cell size has often been noted in plants which have developed under conditions of water stress (see HENCKEL 1964). Recently CUTLER et al. (1977) have restated the case for the importance of small cell size to drought adaptation. They measured N_s/cell, cell size and cell wall thickness in leaves of cotton plants (*Gossypium hirsutum*) grown under water stress and found statistically significant differences in cell size (32 versus 37 µm), in π (an increase of about 3 bar) and in cell wall thickness (0.76 versus 0.68 µm) between the stressed plants and the controls. Rather similar observations were made by WILSON et al. (1980) on *Panicum maximum, Heteropogon contortus* and the tropical legume *Macroptilium atropurpureum*.

Having observed that water stress caused a reduction in cell size in cotton leaves, Cutler et al. (1977) examined the consequences of *diminishing* cell size on $\bar{\pi}$ under the following three theoretical conditions (1) N_s/cell increases linearly with decreasing cell size, (2) N_s/cell is constant and (3) N_s/cell decreases linearly with decreasing cell size. In all three cases they calculated that N_s/cell will increase and hence that π will decrease with decreasing cell size and so lead to more effective turgor maintenance. However, their assumption of linear changes in N_s/cell with changing cell size leads to misleading results. If, during growth, N_s/cell, and hence $\bar{\pi}$, are to remain constant N_s/cell must change in proportion to the *cube* of the cell dimension rather than in linear proportion to the dimension, since to maintain a constant concentration N_s must be proportional to the volume of the cell. It is, therefore, not surprising that their analysis yields a remarkable but, in our view, wholly unconvincing result. We do not doubt the older literature they quote which indicates that drought-adapted plants tend to have smaller cells with thicker walls than mesic plants, or their observations on changes in cell size in cotton. However, we remain unconvinced that the adaptive advantage of small cells results from a decrease in $\bar{\pi}$ which is wholly consequent upon the small size of the cells.

The case relating cell size or structure to function is an interesting one but is still open to speculation, observation and experiment. More careful anatomical and physiological studies of the changes occurring in tissues during acclimation to water stress are required, especially in circumstances when Ψ and R_a^* are changing, coupled with more realistic models of cell water relations such as that of Cheung et al. (1976).

2.3.7 Resurrection Plants

A wide variety of plants appear to be able to survive extremely low water potentials for prolonged periods (see Chap. 10, this Vol.). Besides thallophytes such as many algae, lichens, and mosses about 50 species of angiosperms and 23 species of ferns can be dried to equilibrium with water vapor at 10% relative humidity or less ($\Psi < -3,000$ bar) for many months and are still viable and resume metabolism within a few hours or days after rehydration (Gaff and Hallam 1974; Gaff 1980). There appears to be no consistent pattern between structural features and desiccation tolerance. Although resurrection plants are usually pioneer xerophytes, they often lack the classical xeromorphic characteristics. Most Dicotyledons and ferns retain chlorophyll throughout the dehydration and rehydration cycle but chlorophyll is lost during dehydration in many Monocotyledones. About two days are required for the reappearance of chlorophyll after rehydration. Rapid drying of these angiosperms will preserve chlorophyll but not viability. The preservation of cellular fine structure after dehydration also varies from almost complete preservation to complete destruction in resurrection plants (Gaff and Hallam 1974; Gaff et al. 1976; Gaff 1977). Almost complete destruction of the fine structure also occurs in intolerant plants after desiccation (Fellows and Boyer 1978). One can only presume that tolerant plants undergo an orderly dismantlement. There must be very

subtle relationships between structure and survival of resurrection plants. Despite the considerable interest shown in these plants by GAFF and his colleagues (see above) in recent years, we are still far from understanding how the plants do it. In view of the extreme desiccation tolerance shown by resurrection plants, more detailed study of the cellular changes occurring during dehydration and rehydration could provide important leads to metabolic water stress parameters in more ordinary plants (GAFF 1980).

References

Acock B (1975) An equilibrium model of leaf water potentials which separates intra- and extracellular potentials. Aust J Plant Physiol 2:253–263

Aikman DP (1979) Movement of water trough membranes. In: Wierzchowski KL, Przestalski S (eds) Biophysics of Membrane Transport. Wroclaw, Poland pp 19–28

Barnett NM, Naylor AW (1966) Amino acid and protein metabolism in Bermuda grass during water stress. Plant Physiol 41:1222–1230

Beadle CL, Turner NC, Jarvis PG (1978) Critical water potential for stomatal closure in Sitka spruce. Physiol Plant 43:160–165

Begg JE, Bierhuizen JF, Lemon ER, Misra DK, Slatyer RO, Stern WR (1964) Diurnal water and energy exchanges in bullrush millet in an area of high solar radiation. Agric Meteorol 1:294–312

Bolt GH, Frissel MJ (1960) Thermodynamics of soil moisture. Neth J Agric Sci 8:57–78

Bolt GH, Miller RD (1958) Calculation of total and component potentials of water in soils. Trans Am Geophys Union 39:917–928

Boyer JS, Potter JR (1973) Chloroplast response to low leaf water potentials, I. Role of turgor. Plant Physiol 51:989–992

Boyer JS, Wu G (1978) Auxin increases the hydraulic conductivity of auxin-sensitive hypocotyl tissue. Planta 139:227–237

Brown KW, Jordan WR, Thomas JC (1976) Water stress induced alterations of the stomatal response to decreases in leaf water potential. Physiol Plant 37:1–5

Broyer TC (1952) On volume enlargement and work expenditure by an osmotic system in plants. Physiol Plant 5:459–469

Bunce JA (1977) Leaf elongation in relation to leaf water potential in soybean. J Exp Bot 28:156–161

Carr DJ, Gaff DF (1961) The role of the cell-wall in the water relations of leaves. Proceedings of the Madrid symposium on plant-water relationships in arid and semi-arid conditions. Arid Zone Res 16:117–125

Cheung YNS, Tyree MT, Dainty J (1975) Water relations parameters on single leaves obtained in a pressure bomb and some ecological interpretations. Can J Bot 3:1342–1346

Cheung YNS, Tyree MT, Dainty J (1976) Some possible sources of error in determining bulk elastic moduli and other parameters from pressure-volume curves of shoots and leaves. Can J Bot 54:758–765

Cline RG, Campbell GS (1976) Seasonal and diurnal water relations of selected forest species. Ecology 57:367–373

Cram WJ (1976) Negative feedback regulation of transport in cells. The maintenance of turgor, volume and nutrient supply. In: Lüttge U, Pitman MG (eds) Transport in plants IIA. Encyclopedia of plant physiology new ser Vol 2. Springer, Berlin Heidelberg New York, pp 284–316

Cruziat P, Tyree MT, Bodet C, LoGullo MA (1980) The kinetics of rehydration of detached sunflower leaves following substantial waterloss. New Phytol 84:293–306

Cutler JM, Rains DW (1978) Effects of water stress and hardening on the internal water relations and osmotic constituents of cotton leaves. Physiol Plant 42:261–268

Cutler JM Rains DW, Loomis RS (1977) The importance of cell size in the water relations of plants. Physiol Plant 40:255–260

Cutler JM, Shahan KW, Steponkus PL (1980a) Dynamics of osmotic adjustment in rice. Crop Sci 20:310–314

Cutler JM Shahan KW, Steponkus PL (1980b) Alteration of the internal water relations of rice in response to drought hardening. Crop Sci 20:307–310

Cutler JM, Steponkus PL, Wach MJ, Shahan KW (1980c) Dynamic aspects and enhancement of leaf elongation in rice. Plant Physiol 66:147–152

Cutler JM, Shahan KW, Steponkus PL (1980d) Influence of water deficits and osmotic adjustment on leaf elongation in rice. Crop Sci 20:314–318

Dainty J (1976) Water relations of plant cells. In: Lüttge U, Pitman MG (eds) Transport in plants II. Encyclopedia of plant physiology new ser Vol II A. Springer, Berlin Heidelberg New York, pp 12–35

Davies FS, Lakso AN (1978) Water relation in apple seedlings. Changes in water potential components, abscisic acid levels and stomatal conductances under irrigated and non-irrigated conditions. J Am Soc Hortic Sci 103:310–313

Davies FS, Lakso AN (1979) Diurnal and seasonal changes in leaf water potential components and elastic properties in response to water stress in apple trees. Physiol Plant 46:109–114

Edwards M, Meidner H (1979) Direct measurements of turgor pressure potentials, IV. Naturally occurring pressures in guard cells and their relation to solute and matric potentials in the epidermis. J Exp Bot 30:829–837

Edwards WRN, Jarvis PG (1982) Relations between water content, potential and permeability in stems of conifers. Plant Cell Environ (in press)

Elston J, Karamanos AJ, Kassam AH, Wadsworth RM (1976) The water relations of the field bean crop. Philos Trans R Soc London Ser B 273:581–591

Fellows RJ, Boyer JS (1978) Altered ultrastructure of cells of sunflower leaves having low water potentials. Protoplasma 93:381–395

Fereres E, Acevedo E, Henderson DW, Hsiao TC (1978) Seasonal changes in water potential and turgor maintenance in sorghum and maize under water stress. Physiol Plant 44:261–267

Flowers TJ, Ward ME, Hall JL (1976) Salt tolerance in the halophyte Suaeda maritima: some properties of malate dehydrogenase. Philos Trans R Soc London Ser B 273:523–540

Flowers TJ, Troke PF, Yeo AR (1977) The mechanism of salt tolerance in halophytes. Annu Rev Plant Physiol 28:89–121

Ford CW, Wilson JR (1981) Changes in levels of solutes during osmotic adjustment to water stress in leaves of four tropical pasture species. Aust J Plant Physiol 8:79–91

Gaff DF (1977) Desiccation tolerant vascular plants of Southern Africa. Oecologia 31:95–109

Gaff DF (1980) Protoplasmic tolerance of extreme water stress. In: Turner NC, Kramer PJ (eds) Adaptation of plants to water and high temperature stress. Wiley and Sons, New York, pp 207–230

Gaff DF, Carr DJ (1961) The quantity of water in the cell wall and its significance. Aust J Biol Sci 14:299–311

Gaff DF, Hallam ND (1974) Resurrecting desiccated plants. In: Bieleski RL, Ferguson AR, Creswell MM (eds) Mechanisms of regulation of plant growth. Roy Soc NZ Bull 12:389–393

Gaff DF, Zee S-Y, O'Brien TP (1976) The fine structure of dehydrated and reviving leaves of Borya nitida Labill. – a desiccation-tolerant plant. Aust J Bot 24:225–236

Gardner WR, Ehlig CF (1965) Physical aspects of the internal water relations of plant leaves. Plant Physiol 40:705–710

Geiger DR, Giaquinta RT, Sovonick SA, Fellows RJ (1973) Solute distribution in sugar beet leaves in relation to phloem loading and translocation. Plant Physiol 52:585–589

Goode JE, Higgs KH (1973) Water, osmotic and pressure potential relationships in apple leaves. J Hortic Sci 48:203–215

Green PB, Erickson RO, Buggy J (1971) Metabolic and physical control of cell elongation rate – in vivo studies in Nitella. Plant Physiol 47:423–430

Hanson AH, Nelson CE (1978) Betaine accumulation and ^{14}C formate metabolism in water stressed barley leaves. Plant Physiol 62:305–312

Hanson AD, Nelson CE, Everson EH (1977) Evaluation of free proline accumulation as an index of drought resistance using two contrasting cultivars. Crop Sci 17:720–726

Haughton PM, Sellen DB, Preston RD (1968) Dynamic mechanical properties of the cell wall of *Nitella opaca*. J Exp Bot 19:1–12

Hellebust JA (1976) Osmoregulation. Annu Rev Plant Physiol 27:485–505

Hellkvist J, Richards GP, Jarvis PG (1974) Vertical gradients of water potential and tissue water relations in Sitka spruce trees measured with the pressure chamber. J Appl Ecol 11:637–668

Henckel RA (1964) Physiology of plants under drought. Annu Rev Plant Physiol 15:386–408

Hinckley TM, Duhme F, Hinckley AR, Richter H (1980) Water relations of drought hardy shrubs: osmotic potential and stomatal reactivity. Plant Cell Environ 3:131–140

Hsiao TC, Acevedo E, Fereres E, Henderson DW (1976) Water stress, growth and osmotic adjustment. Philos Trans R Soc London Ser B 273:479–500

Hüsken D, Steudle E, Zimmermann U (1978) Pressure probe technique for measuring water relations of cells in higher plants. Plant Physiol 61:158–163

Hüsken D, Zimmermann U, Schulze E-D (1980) Water relations of leaves of *Tradescantia virginiana*: direct turgor pressure measurement. In: Spanswick RM, Lucas WJ, Dainty J (eds) Plant membrane transport: current conceptual issues. Elsevier/North-Holland Biomedical Press, Amsterdam New York, pp 469–470

Jäger H-J, Meyer HR (1977) Effect of water stress on growth and proline metabolism of *Phaseolus vulgaris* L. Oecologia 30:83–86

Jarvis PG (1975) Water transfer in plants. In: Vries de DA, Afgan NH (eds) Heat and mass transfer in the biosphere I. Transfer processes in plant environment. Scripta, Washington DC, pp 369–394

Jarvis PG, Jarvis MS (1963a) Effects of several osmotic substrates on the growth of *Lupinus albus* L. seedlings. Physiol Plant 16:485–500

Jarvis PG, Jarvis MS (1963b) The water relations of tree seedlings IV. Some aspects of the tissue water relations and dought resistance. Physiol Plant 16:501–516

Jarvis PG, Jarvis MS (1964) Presowing hardening of plants to drought. Phyton (Buenos Aires) 21:113–117

Jeschke WD (1979) Univalent cation selectivity and compartmentation in cereals. In: Laidman DL, Wyn Jones RG (eds) Recent advances in the biochemistry of cereals. Academic Press, London New York, pp 37–61

Johnson DA (1978) Environmental effects on turgor pressure response in range grasses. Crop Sci 18:945–948

Johnson DA, Brown RW (1977) Psychrometric analysis of turgor pressure response: a possible technique for evaluating plant water stress resistance. Crop Sci 17:507–510

Johnson DA, Caldwell MM (1976) Water potential components, stomatal function and liquid phase water transport resistances of four arctic and alpine species in relation to water stress. Physiol Plant 36:271–278

Jones HG (1978) Modelling diurnal trends of leaf water potential in transpiring wheat. J Appl Ecol 15:613–626

Jones MM, Rawson MM (1979) Influence of rate of development of leaf water deficits upon photosynthesis, leaf conductance, water use efficiency, osmotic potential in sorghum. Physiol Plant 45:103–111

Jones MM, Turner NC (1978) Osmotic adjustment in leaves of sorghum in response to water deficits. Plant Physiol 61:122–126

Jones MM, Turner NC (1980) Osmotic adjustment in expanding and fully expanded leaves of sunflower in response to water deficits. Aust J Plant Physiol 7:181–192

Jones MM, Osmond CB, Turner NC (1980) Accumulation of solutes in leaves of sorghum and sunflower in response to water deficits. Aust J Plant Physiol 7:193–205

Kassam AH, Elston JF (1974) Seasonal changes in the status of water and tissue characteristics of leaves of *Vicia faba*. L. Ann Bot (London) 38:419–429

Kirkham MM, Smith EL (1978) Water relations of tall and short cultivars of winter wheat. Crop Sci 18:227–230

3 Water Uptake and Flow in Roots

P.E. WEATHERLEY

CONTENTS

3.1 Introduction

The loss of water by evaporation from the leaves of plants (transpiration) is an inevitable accompaniment of the photosynthetic absorption of carbon dioxide from the atmosphere. Water is absorbed from the soil by the roots to make good this transpirational loss. There is thus a flow of water through the plant from the soil to the atmosphere — the so-called transpiration stream — and it is the purpose of this chapter to focus attention on one part of this stream, namely the flow of water from the soil into, and through the roots. However, to abstract this partial process from the whole root-plant-atmosphere system can be misleading and a note of caution is necessary.

In 1948 VAN DEN HONERT resuscitated and developed Gradmann's analysis of the transpiration stream in which he described the process as a catena of resistances which could be treated as an analogue of Ohm's Law (cf. Chap. 1, this Vol.). VAN DEN HONERT brought out the cardinal fact that in the soil-plant-

3.4.2 The Cell Wall Pathway

It has long been known that the cell walls of the root cortex are readily permeable to many solutes (RUFZ DE LAVISON 1910; STRUGGER 1938–9, TANTON and CROWDY 1972). Soluble dyes and readily detectable ions which cannot cross the plasmalemma are nevertheless taken up by the cell walls as far as the endodermis, whilst it has been demonstrated (CLARKSON and ROBARDS 1975) that colloidal lanthanum hydroxide can move across the cortex in the cell walls but is effectively stopped by the Casparian strips. Thus BERNSTEIN and NIEMANN (1960) were able to measure the apparent free space (cell wall space) of the root cortex by equilibrating the roots with standard solutions of mannitol or sodium chloride and then measuring the solute leached out in pure water. For barley, wheat, kidney bean and other species values ranging from 5% to 30% were obtained.

Clearly apoplastic space is available for flow, but its resistance is not easy to ascertain. If the spaces between the microfibrils of the cell wall cellulose are analogous to a bundle of capillary tubes, the Poiseuille law can be applied. RUSSELL and WOOLLEY (1961) in this way found the calculated conductance of an artificial cellulose cell wall was some 20 times that of the vacuolar pathway, whilst BRIGGS (1967) states that the diameter of the interfibrillar spaces in a cellulose wall ranges from 10^{-7} to 10^{-6} cm and with a pressure gradient of 1 bar cm^{-1} the rate of flow comes out as 1.56×10^{-6} cm s^{-1} which is at least ten times that expected through the vacuoles.

Of course the cell wall is not like a bundle of capillaries and the microfibrils in the primary wall do not run parallel, but form a criss-cross pattern. Perhaps the most realistic calculation is that of PRESTON (1974). This is based on the lamella hypothesis of cell wall structure in which water would move in effectively flattened tubes. The equivalent of the Poiseuille equation for such a lamella is:

$$Q = \Delta p \, (4b) \, a^3 / 12 \, l\eta, \tag{3.12}$$

where Q = rate of flow (cm^3 s^{-1}); b and l are the radial and tangential dimension of the cell (cm); a is the diameter of the lamella tube (cm); Δp the drop of pressure through the cell (dynes cm^{-2}); η = viscosity of water (10^{-2} poise).

Inserting as typical values $b = 20 \times 10^{-4}$ cm, $l = 20 \times 10^{-4}$ cm, $a = 4 \times 10^{-7}$ cm then for $\Delta p = 1$ bar, $Q = 2 \times 10^{-12}$ cm^3 s^{-1}. The equivalent flow through a plasmalemma of $Lp = 10^{-7}$ comes out as 4×10^{-13} cm^3 s^{-1}. Thus the conductance of the cell wall lamella is five times that of the plasma membrane. But there are about 50 lamellae per μm thickness of wall thus the conductance of such a wall could be 250 times greater than that of the membrane. On the other hand for a more permeable membrane with $Lp = 10^{-6}$ the wall would be no more than 25 times more conductive. But the conductance increases in proportion to the thickness of the wall, thus if the cortical cell walls were 2 μm thick and there were five cells across the cortex, the conductance of the whole cortex would be 10^{-5} cm s^{-1} bar^{-1}. 10^{-5} cm s^{-1} represents a high rate of flow through the root but this would evidently only need a pressure drop of 1 bar

across the cortex. A. PETTY (personal communication) has recently made a direct measurement of the conductance of the walls of spruce tracheids. Plugs of wood were completely dried out and the lumens of the tracheids filled with paraffin wax. The molten wax does not penetrate the cell walls. When the wax had solidified the walls were allowed to imbibe water and the flow of water through them measured on the application of a known pressure. A figure of 40×10^{-12} cm^3 s^{-1} b^{-1} was obtained which is of the same order of magnitude as that resulting from PRESTON's (1974) calculation. It would thus seem that the cell wall can provide a pathway for the transpiration stream of sufficiently high conductance to require only a modest drop of pressure between the outside of the root and the endodermis. It is the plasmalemmae of the endodermis which will present the greatest resistance in the apoplastic pathway.

3.4.3 The Symplast Pathway

In addition to the resistance of the plasmalemmae of the epidermal cells and the stelar cells surrounding the xylem tracheae, the main resistance to flow in the symplast will probably be in the plasmodesmata where the pathway is much restricted. Here, as with the apoplast, the only way of attempting to arrive at the conductance of the plasmodesmata is by the application of the Poiseuille equation. But lack of knowledge of the details of plasmodesmatal structure makes it difficult to assign reliable figures to some of the parameters. Two possible structures are shown in Fig. 3.7. Clearly flow is more restricted in A than B and the radius of the tube, to which the calculation is very sensitive (4th power), is not easy to measure precisely. Again the viscosity of the moving fluid is not known. The viscosity of pure water is 0.01 poise, but that of cytoplasm can be more than an order of magnitude greater than this. However, it is not suggested that it is the cytoplasm that is flowing, if it were, it would accumulate in the stele and would need to travel back by some form of cyclosis — an unlikely procedure. Somehow the water must flow through the cytoplasm, i.e., between more or less fixed structures which one would think would exert a considerable drag on the flow. Electron micrographs of plasmodesmata reveal them as containing stain and this suggests that they may be occluded and are thus rather poor candidates for bulk flow transport. Of course the occluding material may be an artefact resulting from fixation etc. Details of their structure cannot be seen in the living state. For a fundamental discussion of flow through plasmodesmata the reader is referred to TYREE (1970) and GUNNING (1976).

The rates of water flow through plasmodesmata have been measured by GRAHAM et al. (1973). Working with barley and marrow they fitted micropotometers along a single root so that water uptake could be measured for consecutive 3.5 mm segments. They found (Fig. 3.8) that the water uptake rose sharply behind the tip but at 8–10 cm it fell steeply to a steady rate which was maintained along the rest of the axis. Examination of the endodermis revealed that the steep fall coincided with the change from State 1 to State 2, i.e., to the suberization of the entire wall. Thus the slow steady rate represented uptake where the flow into and out of the endodermis was restricted to the plasmodesmata,

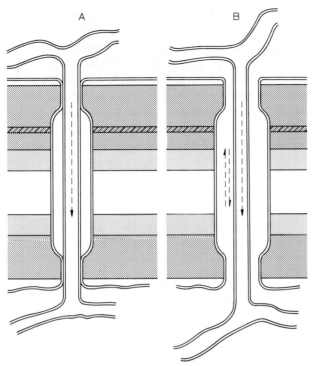

Fig. 3.7 A, B. Possible pathways through the wall cavity created by a plasmodesmos. **A** Situation envisaged by ROBARDS (1971) and seen frequently in electron micrographs of fixed tissue. **B** Hypothetical situation in vivo. (CLARKSON and ROBARDS 1975)

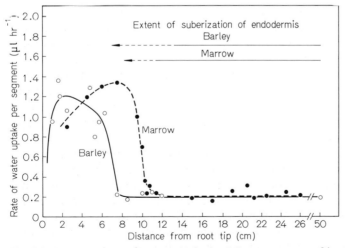

Fig. 3.8. A comparison of water uptake by 3.5 mm segments of intact root and suberization of the endodermis. Length of axis where the endodermis is only partly suberized is shown as *broken lines*. (GRAHAM et al. 1974)

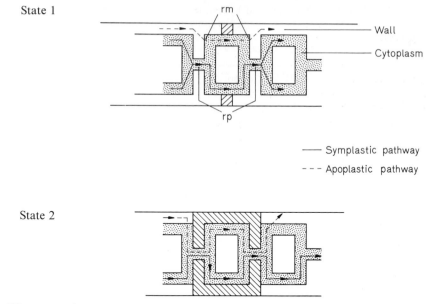

Fig. 3.9. Diagrammatic representation of apoplastic and symplastic pathways for water movement through the endodermis in State 1 and 2. In State 1 the suberization is confined to the Casparian Strip. In State 2 the walls of the endodermal cells are completely suberized

see Fig. 3.9. The frequency, length and radius of the plasmodesmata of the inner tangential wall were measured (CLARKSON et al. 1971; CLARKSON and RO-BARDS 1975). Two possible radii were measured, that of the desmotubule $(5 \times 10^{-6}$ mm) and that enclosed by the plasmalemma $(10^{-5}$ mm). Also two values for the viscosity of the moving solution were selected (2 and $50 \times$ the value for pure water). The rate of flow (J_v) was 2.5×10^{-6} cm s^{-1}. Application of the Poiseuille equation using these values gives the pressure differences (ΔP) through the plasmodesmata (see Table 3.1 column 4) necessary to produce this rate of flow. The two values for the radius and the two for viscosity are combined to give 4 possible pressure differences. Corresponding values for the hydraulic conductance of the inner tangential wall $(=J_v/P)$ are given in the last column. It will be seen that apart from the last figure (lower radius and higher viscosity) the values are within the range found for the plasmalemmae of plant cells. These figures suggest that the plasmodesmata are unlikely to provide an adequate pathway for water flow across the cortex of the root. From Table 3.1 it appears that the pressure drop would need to be about 1 bar at each cell layer. If the cortex consisted of 10 cell layers, the total drop of pressure would be about 10 bar — certainly more than would be expected. Also it must be borne in mind that in the application of the Poiseuille equation it is implicit that the tubes are free of obstruction — which they hardly appear to be judging from electron micrographs.

There is a further argument for the plasmodesmata not providing the major pathway across the cortex. In passing along the root from the region with

Table 3.1. Pressure differences and hydraulic conductance calculated for a measured rate of flow $(2.53 \times 10^{-6}$ cm s$^{-1})$ through the inner tangential wall of the suberized endodermis where flow is restricted to the plasmodesmata. Two values for pore diameter and viscosity were used. (CLARKSON and ROBARDS 1975)

Case	r(nm)	η (poise)	ΔP (bar)	Hydraulic Conductivity cm s^{-1} bar^{-1}
I	10	2×10^{-2}	6.06×10^{-2}	4.18×10^{-5}
II	10	5×10^{-1}	15.10×10^{-1}	1.68×10^{-6}
III	5	2×10^{-2}	9.69×10^{-1}	2.61×10^{-6}
IV	5	5×10^{-1}	2.42×10	1.05×10^{-7}

the endodermis at State 1 to that with the endodermis at State 2 the only change is the suberization of the walls. The frequency of the plasmodesmata is the same (CLARKSON and ROBARDS 1975), the cortical plasmodesmata are presumably similar and the tension in the xylem will be little different since the xylem has a high longitudinal conductance. Thus the plasmodesmatal flow should be the same in the State 1 and State 2 segments and if the plasmodesmatal pathway were the major one, there should be little change in rate along the root. Fig. 3.8 shows that in fact there was a 6:1 fall with barley and 7:1 fall with marrow. Clearly there was a six or sevenfold increase in hydraulic resistance concomitant with the suberization of the walls of the endodermis and this suggests that the major radial resistance resides in the endodermis. Reference to Fig. 3.9 shows that in State 2 as a result of suberization both the apoplastic and vacuolar pathways are blocked and flow is canalized through the plasmodesmata of the tangential walls of the endodermis.

Let us consider flow through one face of the endodermis. The ratio of the conductances of the plasmamembrane and the plasmodesmatal pathways can be found in the following way:
For State 1

$$J_m = \frac{\Delta \Psi}{r_m}, \quad J_p = \frac{\Delta P}{r_p} \quad \text{(see Fig. 3.9)}$$

where J_m is the flow through the plasmalemma in response to $\Delta \Psi$, the difference in water potential between the cytoplasm of the endodermis and the cell wall of the adjacent stelar cell. ΔP is the difference in turgor pressure between the endodermal cells and the cells of the outermost layer of the stele, i.e., the pressure drop through the plasmodesmata. It can be shown that if the osmotic potentials in the cytoplasm of the endodermal and adjacent stelar cells are the same, then $\Delta \Psi = \Delta P$. r_m and r_p are the resistances of the plasmalemma and plasmodesmatal pathway respectively.

Thus total flow in State 1:

$$J_{v_1} = J_m + J_p = \Delta P \left(\frac{1}{r_m} + \frac{1}{r_p} \right). \tag{3.13}$$

For State 2:

$$J_m = \frac{\varDelta P}{r_m + r_p} \quad \text{and} \quad J_p = \frac{\varDelta P}{r_p}.$$

Thus total flow in State 2:

$$J_{v_2} = \varDelta P \left(\frac{1}{r_m + r_p} + \frac{1}{r_p} \right). \tag{3.14}$$

Now $J_{v_1}/J_{v_2} = (13) \div (14) = 6/1$ for barley. Solving the resulting quadratic equation it is found that $r_p : r_m = 10.1$.

Thus to account for the 80% drop in rate of flow on passing from State 1 to State 2 manifest in Fig. 3.8, the hydraulic resistance of the plasmodesmata of the tangential walls must be ten times the resistance of the plasmalemmae encountered by the flow on leaving and entering the apoplast as it crosses the endodermis.

The above analysis assumes that the suberization of the endodermis causes a complete stoppage of the flow of water through the cell wall material. There is some evidence that this may not be so (CLARKSON et al. 1978). However, the argument is not weakened — for if there was a partial flow through the suberized wall which had been attributed to the plasmodesmata, then the flow through the latter would have been even less and their resistance correspondingly greater. A more questionable assumption is that the conductances of the plasmodesmata in State 1 and State 2 are the same. The 6:1 fall in rate could have been due to a fall in plasmodesmatal conductance related to the laying down of the suberin lamellae (see refs in GUNNING and ROBARDS 1976).

If the above conclusion is correct and the conductance of the cortical cell walls is high, the site of the main resistance might well reside in the endodermis. The work of GINSBURG and GINZBURG (1970), however, provides evidence to the contrary. They used root segments from which the steles had been pulled out leaving cortical sleeves in which the endodermis was ruptured and therefore played no part in the water movement. They measured the flux of water into or out of the sleeves in response to differences of osmotic pressure and obtained values of L of approximately 10^{-6} cm s^{-1} not dissimilar to an intact root. This suggests that the endodermis is not the site of the main resistance. Further in contrast to the intact root the cell walls in the sleeves could not have provided a pathway since there was no difference in hydrostatic pressure across the sleeves.

GINSBURG and GINZBURG (1970) concluded that the movement of water was in the symplast and regarded flow through the cell wall as inconsistent with their finding that the reflexion coefficient was unity (no leakage through the cell walls) and flow was sensitive to inhibition by DNP, KCN, and CCCP. Such inhibition they attributed to an effect on movement within the symplast, since the permeability of membranes to water is insensitive to inhibitors. A study of the flux of water across the sleeves in response to a difference of hydrostatic pressure would be interesting since this would induce a flow through

the cell walls if such could take place. However, the sleeves are too delicate to withstand the necessary pressure difference.

Meantime we are faced with a conflict of evidence both theoretical and experimental. The ranges of values attributable to the various parameters involved is so great that unequivocal discrimination between the possible pathways is not possible. In my view the balance of evidence is in favour of the cell wall. Its conductance seems to be greater than that of the alternative pathways and teleologically it fits in with the structure of the endodermis with its Casparian strips. Indeed, with the apoplastic pathway the endodermis assumes a central role. Here the flow of water must cross the plasmalemma twice and within the endodermis it must briefly travel in the symplast. The function of the symplastic pathway via the plasmodesmata is seen as the transport of solutes probably by diffusion (TYREE 1970). For a contrasting view on the pathway for water movement see NEWMAN (1976).

3.4.4 Additional Points Relevant to the Pathway

With this pathway before us we can return to certain topics considered earlier in this Chapter.

3.4.4.1 The Mechanism of the Variable Root Conductance

That this can lead to a constant leaf water potential over a wide range of transpiration rates was left unexplained. Recently POWELL (1978) has put forward a convincing hypothesis for this in terms of the endodermis of the root. It is suggested that the solute content of the endodermal cells is maintained by an active transfer process, but the transpirational flow of water, canalized through the endodermis, flushes out these solutes so that the greater the rate of transpiration the lower the osmotic value of the endodermal cells. This leads to a fall in turgor pressure in these cells. Now ZIMMERMANN and STEUDLE (1975) have found that the hydraulic conductance of the membranes of the internodal cells of spp. of *Nitella* and *Chara* rises with a fall in turgor pressure, thus if this applied to the root cells of higher plants there would be a rise in conductance with a rise in rate of transpiration. Combining the fundamental equations for these processes and applying realistic values for the various parameters involved, POWELL (1978) demonstrated that in terms of the hypothesis a constant leaf water potential over a wide range of rates of transpiration could be accounted for. Presumably any factor which leads to a fall in turgor of the endodermis should bring about an increased conductance. Thus lowering the water potential round the roots, e.g., by soil drying or flooding with a non-penetrating osmoticum, should lead to an increased conductance. It is interesting to note here that MACKLON and WEATHERLEY (1965) found that when the osmotic pressure of the root medium of transpiring *Ricinus* plants was raised by 3.5 bar by the addition of polyethylene glycol, there was no response in the leaf water potential which remained near to 5 bar. Could this have been due to the reduced difference in water potential through the plant being offset by an increased conductance? However, a completely opposite effect

— a reduction of conductance — was found by LAWLOR (1973) applying polyethylene glycol to wheat plants.

3.4.4.2 The Effect of Rapid Changes in the External Solution

It is implicit in the concept of flow in the apoplast that solutes in the medium round the roots can readily enter the cell wall system and indeed must be drawn in with the transpiration stream as far as the endodermis. If the cell membranes are permeable to a particular solute, it will be taken up by the cortical cells or pass through the endodermis to the stele. But if the plasmalemma is less permeable to the particular solute than it is to water, then the solute will accumulate at the endodermis and will diffuse back against the flow of water and a steady reverse gradient will arise. In view of this, how rapid will be the response in uptake of water on changing the osmotic pressure of the outside solution? If mannitol is added to the solution it might be expected that this will have little effect until it reaches the endodermis. However, it is evident from the experiments of ARISZ et al. described earlier in this chapter, that the response occurs in a matter of a few seconds (Fig. 3.1). The question arises how rapidly does water move through the cortex of the root? A rate of 10^{-5} cm^3 cm^{-2} s^{-1} (BROUWER 1953) can be taken for the root of a transpiring plant. If the distance across the cortex is 0.03 cm and the water were moving across the whole surface of the root, then allowing for the acceleration due to the diminishing surface with inward movement, it would take about 30 min to cross the cortex. If the water movement was confined to the cell walls and these occupied a tenth of the tangential surface, the time taken would be 3 min and if half the volume of the cell wall was occupied by the pathway the time would be 1.5 min. A lag of this duration might be expected before the sudden drop manifest in the experiments of ARISZ et al. (1951). No lag is apparent. Of course although the vacuolar pathway through the epidermal and cortical cells may be of relative high resistance, a sudden rise in osmotic pressure of the medium will draw water out of the epidermal cells and this reverse movement will spread through the cortex, endodermis and stele to the xylem tracheae. But this spread, involving a change in water content of all the cells might be expected to take a noticeable time before *exudation* was reversed. But the reversal (Fig. 3.1) appears to be virtually immediate. Perhaps this fact can be reconciled with apoplastic flow if the roots of the tomato plants as used by ARISZ were very fine and so presented a very short distance across the cortex. Alternatively perhaps the cell wall is differentially permeable with respect to water and mannitol, i.e., the reflection coefficient is greater than zero and so the surface of the epidermis acts osmotically and there would be no lag in change of rate of uptake in response to a sudden change in the medium.

3.4.4.3 The Significance of Endodermal Suberization

Reverting to the change in water uptake along the root, the data presented in Fig. 3.8 whilst showing a sharp reduction in rate of water uptake with the

suberization of the endodermis, do show as pointed out by GRAHAM et al. (1974) that the measured uptake by the suberized roots of barley and marrow was equal to about a sixth of that by the younger roots and in the whole root system there is probably a far greater amount of suberized relative to unsuberized root. However, the suberization does lead to a considerable increase in hydraulic resistance and one is led to speculate what advantage the suberization confers. One suggestion (D.T. CLARKSON personal communication) is that the older roots may often occupy the drier regions of the soil and this could lead to the partial desiccation of the cortex leaving the endodermis as a barrier to further drying out but possibly allowing uptake of water via the plasmodes-mata on rewetting. Another suggestion is in relation to the possible interfacial resistance between the soil and root surface to be discussed in the next section. It is possible that the interfacial resistance is a function of the rate of water movement across the interface. Now a high endodermal resistance will reduce the rate of uptake and so the interfacial resistance will be less or may not arise at all. Also the cortex being on the upstream side of the endodermal resistance will not suffer an additional water stress and will therefore not contract in volume and no interfacial gap will form (see next section) to exacerbate the interfacial resistance. On this hypothesis the development of an endodermal resistance is seen as a positive advantage.

3.5 The Soil-Rooted Plant

So far consideration has been restricted to the internal water relations of the root which has been regarded as immersed in free water. The water stress developing in the leaves (Ψ_l) under these circumstances is a function of the rate of transpiration (J) and the resistance of the plant (r_p). As pointed out above r_p is often found not to be a constant, but decreases with an increase in rate of flow through the plant. An additional factor arises if the roots are immersed in unsaturated soil. Now water is held by surface tension forces (τ) in the soil matrix and a lower water potential must be developed in the plant if water is to be abstracted from the soil. Furthermore movement of water through the soil to the surface of the root must be down gradients of τ, the magnitude of which is related to the rate of flow of the water (J) and the hydraulic conductance of the soil (K) in accordance with Darcy's Law:

$$J = -\frac{K\,d\tau}{dx} \qquad\qquad\qquad (3.15)$$

x being the distance between the source of water supply within the soil and the surface of the root. The question as to whether these gradients are significant or negligible is a matter of discussion and experiment and is dealt with in some detail by PASSIOURA in Chapter 1, this Volume. Here I shall merely illustrate the situation with reference to the data from a specific experiment (FAIZ and WEATHERLEY 1978) represented in Fig. 3.10.

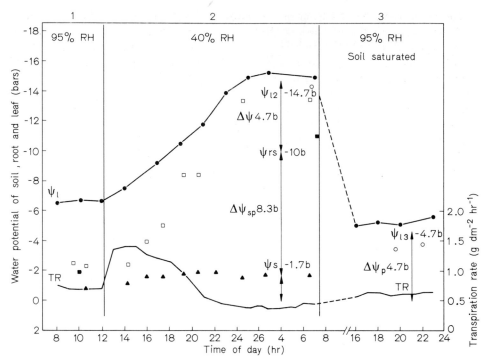

Fig. 3.10. Sunflower plants were grown in soil in pots with upper and lower compartments separated by fine nylon gauze which confined the roots to the upper compartment, but allowed upward capillary rise of water from a water-table maintained at 27 cm below the gauze. The *curves* show the effect of changing the humidity of the airstream on the rate of transpiration (*TR*) and the leaf water potential Ψ_l measured with the psychrometer (●) and with the pressure bomb (○). The water potential of the soil was measured from time to time at several locations within the rooting zone. Means of such values are shown (▲). In addition, the potential of the roots (Ψ_r) was measured: in situ (□) and from samples (■). For further information see text. (After FAIZ and WEATHERLEY 1978)

As was pointed out earlier it has been demonstrated that the leaves of plants in water culture manifest a water potential of -5 to -8 bar which remains constant over a wide range of rates of transpiration. Plants rooted in water-saturated soils behave similarly. In unsaturated soil Ψ_l remains at the steady value at low rates of transpiration (Fig. 3.10 period 1) but at high rates (period 2) there is a steep fall in Ψ_l to a value approaching -15 bar. That such a fall in Ψ_l is dynamic in origin can be demonstrated by the fact that there is complete "recovery" on returning to a slow rate of transpiration (not shown in Fig. 3.10).

This fall in Ψ_l (period 2) is accompanied by a rise in the hydraulic resistance (r) of the soil:plant system as can be seen in Table 3.2 in which the data refer to the end of periods 1, 2 and 3. There is clearly a three- to four-fold increase in resistance when there is high evaporative demand. The resistance of the soil:plant system (r_t) consists therefore of two resistance in series: the resistance of the soil (r_s) and the resistance within the plant (r_p).

Table 3.2. Showing the change in the resistance of the soil:plant system (r) in conditions of lesser (periods 1 and 3) and greater (period 2) stress (Data from Fig. 3.10)

Period	1	2	3
Ψ_l	−6.5	−15.0	−5.0
Ψ_s	−0.9	−1.7	0
Transp	0.55	0.4	0.6
$\Psi_s - \psi_l$	5.6	13.3	5.0
$r = \Psi_s - \Psi_l / \text{transp}$	10.2	33.3	8.3

Water potentials in bar. Transpiration: gm dm^{-2} leaf h^{-1}

$$r_t = r_s + r_p \tag{3.16}$$

Thus the question is: what is the relative magnitude of these resistances and how do they change? The difficulty is that there is no method of measuring the water potential at the root surface — answers can therefore only be inferred and certainty is not attainable. We will consider the two resistances in turn.

3.5.1 The Plant Resistance

The leaf water potential in Fig. 3.10, period 3 (Ψ_{l_3}) is a measure of the drop in water potential ($\Delta\Psi_p$) through the plant, since the water potential at the root surface is zero, the soil being saturated. The mean value of $\Delta\Psi_p$ is 4.7 bar. Does this figure also apply to the end of period 2 in Fig. 3.10? Certainly the rate of transpiration is nearly the same but Ψ_l is much lower at the end of period 2. There is no clear evidence whether this would alter the resistance, but the measurements of water potentials of the roots strongly suggest that the plant resistance did not change much during the experiment. The water potential of the root tissues was measured psychrometrically either in situ using capsules buried in the soil (Fiscus 1972) or from samples of roots obtained from soil borings. It will be seen in Fig. 3.10 that during period 1 the drop of water potential between the roots and the leaves was about 4.5 bar; whilst at the end of period 2 it was about 3 bar. Thus there was not a large change in potential drop through the plant between periods 1 and 2. The water potential of the roots (Ψ_r) was near to that of the soil in period 1 but a large gap (11 bar) between soil and roots opened up in period 2. This perirhizal drop in water potential, i.e., difference in water potential between the bulk soil and the root surface, can be calculated from the data in Fig. 3.10, the potential drop through the plant being taken to be equal to Ψ_{l_3} in period 3 when the roots were in saturated soil. The water potential of the leaves Ψ_{l_2} in period $2 = -14.7$ bar. Therefore the potential at the root surface, Ψ_{rs} is $4.7 - 14.7 = -10$ bar and this, less the water potential in the soil (Ψ_s) gives the perirhizal drop ($\Delta\Psi_{sp}$), i.e., $10 - 1.7 = 8.3$ bar. This is rather less than twice the drop in water potential through the plant. In a similar experiment with sand the perirhizal drop was rather greater than twice that of the plant.

It appears then with a fair degree of certainty that a low level of water potential can develop at the surface of the root. The question now arises how far is this a manifestation of a resistance in the soil?

3.5.2 The Soil Resistance

A model based on Darcy's Law has been developed by GARDNER (1960) which gives the drop in water potential $\Delta\Psi$ through the perirhizal soil as:

$$\Delta\Psi = \frac{Jv}{K \cdot 2\pi L_t} \ln \frac{b}{r}. \tag{3.17}$$

where Jv is the rate of flow, K the hydraulic conductivity coefficient, L_t the total length of the root, r the mean radius of the root and b the distance between the surface of the root and the soil supplying the water, is taken as half the distance between adjacent roots and is obtained from the identity $b = 1/(L_v)^{\frac{1}{2}}$, where L_v is the root density, i.e., the length of root/volume of soil (ANDREWS and NEWMAN 1969).

All the parameters required in Eq. (3.17) were measured for the plants used in Fig. 3.10. K was measured using the pressure plate technique (see CHOWDHURY 1979). Unfortunately the sample of soil used for this was not that actually used in the experiment, but it was garden soil taken from the same location.

$\Delta\Psi$ is found to be only 13 mm of water, a negligible value compared with the drop in Ψ found in Fig. 3.10, i.e., 8.3 bar (8,466 cm of water). Clearly under the conditions of this experiment detectable perirhizal gradients of water potential could not arise.

Before discussing the implication of this, a note of caution must be sounded. Firstly the measurement of the total length of the roots is subject to considerable error. The technique involves washing the roots before length measurement and inevitably there is a loss of very fine roots. Secondly uptake of water is not uniform over the total area of the roots. Uptake may not occur with the older roots so that the effective L_t may be smaller. However, it is unlikely that $\Delta\Psi$ is more than an order of magnitude out whilst it is several orders of magnitude too small to constitute a significant perirhizal gradient. This is in line with Newman's conclusion (NEWMAN 1969a, b) that under normal conditions appreciable perirhizal gradients will not arise.

If the perirhizal gradient is negligible, how can the drop in water potential of 7.8 bar (Table 3.3) be accounted for? It is suggested that a resistance arises at the interface between soil and root. There is no a priori reason for choosing this location, but it is difficult to see where else it could be and possible ways in which a resistance might arise at the interface can be visualized. It might for example simply be a matter of reduction of the area of contact between soil and root. Also it would be expected that the relative size of the roots and the soil particles would be important. The testing of such hypothesis is a matter of future work. If it is confirmed that the soil-root interface is a

major resistance in the soil-plant system, and therefore an important cause of water stress in plants, such work assumes a major importance. A further related occurrence is the contraction of the roots with increased stress in the plant. This would lead to gaps forming between the root and soil which would increase the interfacial resistance. Such gaps have been envisaged by Philip (1957, 1958); Bonner (1959); de Roo (1969) and Huck et al. (1970), the last authors finding that on a dry day the roots of cotton plants shrank by as much as 40%. Such a contraction would lead to a positive feedback increasing the stress in the plant which would be moderated by stomatal closure. This presumably was the cause of the fall in transpiration during period 2 of our experiments. For a further discussion of this subject see Tinker (1976) and Newman (1974).

3.6 Root Hairs

It is perhaps appropriate to discuss root hairs last, not as a measure of their unimportance, but because their possible functions may be related to several of the aspects of root water relations dealt with in previous sections. It has been assumed in the past that root hairs have an absorption function and that their importance lies in presenting a greater surface area than the epidermis alone. There is, however, little information about their function (Newman 1974).

Rosene (1943) showed, by fixing micro-potometers round individual root hairs, that they are capable of rapid uptake of water. But the root system was in a humid atmosphere and it is not certain how relevant this uptake is to normal submerged conditions. Cailloux (1972) used micro-potometers of special designs to measure the water uptake by localized areas of a single hair. He showed that uptake seemed to be restricted to regions where there was underlying cytoplasm. Here again it is difficult to relate the results to behaviour under natural conditions.

The occurrence of root hairs is hardly suggestive of their role. They are limited to a region just behind the elongating region of the root and are often short-lived but not always so. In water culture they are usually sparse or non-existent, whilst they are most prolific where the root passes through larger air filled gaps in the soil — but their function in such a situation would seem to be limited.

Where they occur, root hairs could increase the surface area for absorption. But the water they absorb still has to pass through the inner tangential wall of the epidermal cell. So there would be no advantage unless entry into the cell presents a greater resistance than passage from cell to cell within the root. This could be the case with the symplastic pathway if the plasmalemma were of higher resistance than the plasmodesmata. However, as shown above (Sect. 3.4.3), this did not appear to be true of the endodermis. Another point which argues against the root hair facilitating uptake of water is that the conductance of the soil surrounding the root is 10^5 times higher than the conductance of the pathway offered by the root hairs (Newman 1974). Thus water would move

more rapidly up to the epidermal surface through the soil than through the root hairs — the root hairs would indeed be a disadvantage!

Root hairs might, however, have an advantage over the epidermal surface in that their small dimensions permit them to penetrate and mould themselves into the irregular pores between the soil particles, thus making a much closer contact with the soil — a matter perhaps of importance if the soil-root interface has a high resistance. Also they might have an important mechanical function in connexion with the root contraction discussed in the previous section. When the root contracts the root hairs would presumably be dragged inwards pulling with them the soil particles to which they adhere. Thus a zone of small gaps would develop round the roots rather than large cylindrical gaps. Here the mucigel, the layer of mucilage with which the younger roots are invested, might play an important part. (For a further discussion on the role of the mucigel see RUSSEL 1977).

Lastly, the root hairs might have an anchorage function — not in the crude way of preventing the plant from being uprooted, but in forming a solid base for the tips of the growing root to thrust forward through the soil. All these possible functions of the root hair are speculative and will remain so until appropriate experiments can be done. Such experiments are however not easy to carry out.

3.7 Conclusions

In the above discussion of the movement of water through the soil-root system attention has been focussed on three features: (a) The hydraulic resistance of the root, (b) the pathway through the root, (c) the hydraulic resistance of the soil up to the root surface. Each of these present problems the answers to which are still by no means clear.

The exuding root system seems to behave like an osmometer. The rate of flow is a function of the difference in osmotic potential between the surrounding medium and the xylem tracheae. When, however, a difference of hydrostatic pressure is imposed either artificially with a pump or by increasing the rate of transpiration, the hydraulic resistance falls. Several hypotheses for this have been put forward, but as yet no convincing experimental confirmation for any of them has been achieved. The position is further obscured by the fact that even working with the same species contradictory results have been obtained by different workers. Some find a constant resistance, others a changing resistance with changing rate of transpiration.

Of the three possible pathways followed by the transpiration stream across the root cortex, endodermis and stele, there seems to be general agreement that the resistance of the root is not very different from that of a single layer of cells. Therefore flow through the membranes at each cell layer seems unlikely. There remain the apoplastic and symplastic pathways. These are not easy to differentiate since both pathways involve entering the symplast through one membrane and leaving it through another and this constitutes the major resis-

4 Water Uptake by Organs Other Than Roots

P.W. Rundel

CONTENTS

4.1 Introduction

The extensive early literature on foliar uptake of moisture, spanning nearly three centuries, has been reviewed by STONE (1957a, 1970) and GESSNER (1956a). Early field studies by a number of workers demonstrated water uptake by leaves or stems of intact plants (LLOYD 1905; WETZEL 1924; KRAUSE 1935). These and other laboratory experiments (see STONE 1957a, 1970) led to a unanimity of opinion on the ability of leaves to absorb water, but a strong divergence of views on the ecological and physiological significance of this uptake. Remarkably, however, the flow of papers on the subject over the past 50 years has done little to resolve the questions of significance, and foliar water uptake remains as controversial a subject as ever.

    There is no question of what the theoretical basis of foliar uptake of water should be. The physical requirements are a gradient of decreasing water potential from the atmosphere to a leaf and through a plant to the soil. Such conditions can be expected to occur in arid and semi-arid habitats where atmospheric vapor pressure deficits are low at night and soil water potentials may be -2 to -3 MPa or lower. In theory, neither saturated atmospheric conditions nor dew point temperatures on leaf surfaces are required for water uptake and

One of the most celebrated reports of foliar uptake among desert plants is the example of *Prosopis tamarugo,* a tree mesquite from the virtually rainless Atacama Desert of northern Chile. Studies of this species by SUDZUKI (1969), SUDZUKI et al. (1973) and WENT (1975) have all indicated that the major supply of moisture for this species came from atmospheric water vapor. Recent studies by MOONEY et al. (1980b), however, provide evidence to suggest ground water is the predominant and likely sole source of moisture for these trees.

4.2.2 Foliar Uptake of Water by Bromeliads

While the significance of foliar uptake of water by vascular plants may be controversial in many groups, there is no question of the critical importance of such absorption for many epiphytic Bromeliaceae. The mechanism of water uptake through the leaves of tillandsias and certain other bromeliads has been studied in considerable detail (HABERLANDT 1914; MEZ 1904; BENZING 1976; BENZING and BURT 1970; BENZING and DAHLE 1971; BENZING et al. 1976, 1978). The absorbing qualities of trichomes on the leaves of these bromeliads was first described nearly 100 years ago by SCHIMPER (1888). While most members of the Bromeliaceae possess foliar trichomes, tillandsioid trichome structures are the most highly evolved (BENZING 1976). These peltate trichomes are frequently referred to as scales or shields. The shield is composed of an orderly arrangement of flat cells arrayed only a single cell deep (Fig. 4.1). These arrangements of cells have been described in detail (MEZ 1904; STEINBRINCK 1905; BIEBL 1964; DOLZMANN 1964, 1965; BENZING 1976). At the center of the shield form equal-sized and thick-walled empty cells connect to a column of living stalk cells, usually three to five in number. While the morphology of the shield may vary considerably between species, it is thought to be quite constant within an individual species.

Both shield and stalk cells are cutinized on their exterior surfaces, producing a waterproof tube and valve system. As liquid water strikes the leaf surface of a *Tillandsia,* the wettable surface spreads out droplets to form a thin uniform film of water. The shield cells rapidly fill with water at this time. At this stage the central disc cells become turgid, forcing their upper walls outward, while simultaneously the wings of the shield are flexed downward against the leaf surface (Fig. 4.2). This combined action produces a small suction which draws liquid water in under the shield and down into the stalk cells through osmosis. From these cells water can diffuse throughout the leaf. DOLZMANN (1964, 1965) has suggested on the basis of electron micrographs that water uptake in *Tillandsia* involves a type of pinocytosis.

With subsequent drying and dehydration of the shield cells, the central disc cells shrink and lower to their former position, and the wings flex upward. In this configuration the shield is tightly sealed to prevent water loss from the thin-walled stalk cells. In effect the shields operate as efficient one-way valves.

Since the stomata of *Tillandsia* species are characteristically located flush on the leaf surface among the trichome shields, the presence of even a thin

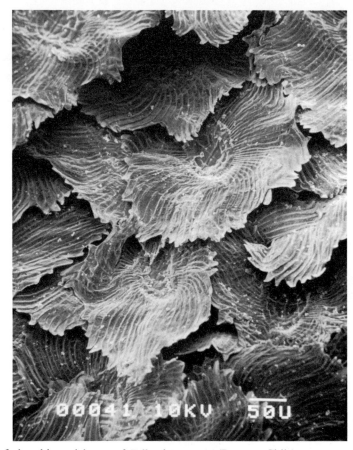

Fig. 4.1. Surface view of absorbing trichome of *Tillandsia geissei* (Paposo, Chile)

film of water on the leaf surface significantly reduces CO_2 exchange and thus restricts photosynthesis. For this reason regular wetting and drying cycles are necessary for *Tillandsia* survival. It is not surprising, therefore, to find that the stands of such species are generally lacking in regions subject to long moist periods.

While BENZING (1976) suggests that the genus *Tillandsia* is only able to absorb liquid water, a number of studies have found significant absorption of water vapor (PENFOUND and DEILER 1967; VIRZO DE SANTO et al. 1976; MARTIN 1980). The exact mechanism of water vapor uptake in *Tillandsia* is unknown, although it appears to be a physical process since dead plants behave similarly to live plants. MARTIN (1980) has hypothesized that water absorption by guard cells may enhance stomatal opening. Whatever the mechanism, nocturnal CO_2 uptake is decreased at low nighttime relative humidities (MARTIN 1980; LANGE and MEDINA 1979).

The water balance of one terrestrial bromeliad, *Tillandsia straminea* has been studied in the field in Peru (ALVIM and UZEDA: in WALTER 1971). The

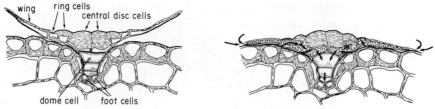

Fig. 4.2. Cross-section of a typical tillandsioid trichome in a dry condition (*left*) and in the process of water absorption (*right*). (Redrawn from Benzing et al. 1976)

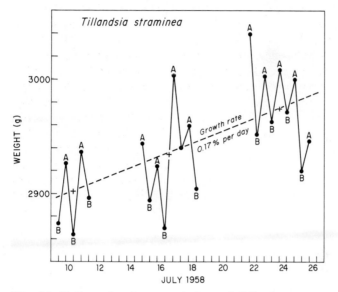

Fig. 4.3. Daily cycle of water relations of *Tillandsia straminea* in the coastal fog desert of Peru. Plant fresh weights were measured at 9 h (*A*) and 17 h (*B*) daily. (Redrawn from Alvim and Uzeda in Walter 1971)

water content of several plants was followed with morning and afternoon weighings over a two-week period during July 1958. Despite the lack of precipitation their results (Fig. 4.3) show a clear cyclical water uptake at night and loss through transpiration during the day. They calculated a mean growth increase of 0.17% per day. If sufficient fog was present to maintain this net growth rate for four months of the year, an annual growth in excess of 20% would be possible, without any water input from precipitation.

4.2.3 Foliar Uptake of Water by Orchids

Although epiphytic Orchidaceae are clearly able to utilize liquid water from fogs or mists, there has only recently been data to suggest that significant

foliar uptake of moisture takes place. Most orchid leaves have very heavy cuticles that would prevent any uptake.

The presence of absorbing trichomes, however, has now been established in the subtribe Pleurothallidinae (PRIDGEON 1981). These pleurothalloid trichomes are constructed in much the same way as the more elaborate tillandsioid trichomes. Stalk cells with heavily cutinized outer walls and noncutinized transverse walls through which water flows are present in both groups. Both draw water in using much the same mechanisms (PRIDGEON 1981). Absorbing trichomes similar to those of the Pleurothallidinae have been described for at least three other subtribes of the Orchidaceae (SOLEREDER and MEYER 1930). There appears to be a strong correlation between presence of absorbing trichomes and possession of some type of water-storage organ such as a pseudobulb or hypodermis (PRIDGEON 1981).

Some small amount of foliar moisture absorption is also possible in thin-leaved epiphytic orchids from very humid tropical environments (see WENT and SHEPS 1969), but the roots of such species are still thought to be the major route of water absorption (SANFORD 1974). Some controversy is present in the literature on the importance of water absorption by specialized aerial roots in orchids. DYCUS and KNUDSON (1957) found that the velamen (spongy outer tissue layer) of aerial roots was impermeable to water except in the apical region. They ascribed a mechanical function to the velamen to prevent loss of stored moisture, and suggested that water uptake occurs through root surfaces adpressed to a substrate. More recently, however, workers have questioned these results (BARTHLOTT 1976).

4.2.4 Foliar Uptake of Water by Poikilohydric Angiosperms

Poikilohydric angiosperms with leaves which are able to rehydrate from air-dry condition have been described from many arid and semi-arid habitats (cf. Chap. 10, this Vol.). These include both dicots and monocots, representing such families as the Scrophulariaceae, Gesneriaceae, Myrothamnaceae, Velloziaceae, Liliaceae, Cyperaceae, and Poaceae. A large number of poikilohydric angiosperms, many of which are thought to show significant foliar uptake of water, have been described from southern Africa (GAFF 1971, 1977; GAFF and ELLIS 1974). The water relations of poikilohydric angiosperms have been broadly reviewed by GESSNER (1956a, b) and ZIEGLER and VIEWEG (1970).

The most carefully studied of these species is *Myrothamnus flabellifolia*. CHILD (1960) concluded that rehydration of *Myrothamnus* leaves occurred through root uptake of water. GAFF (1977), however, disputed this contention and provided experimental data to indicate that foliar uptake of water was equally as important as uptake through the xylem system. Hydathodes have been described for *Myrothamnus* (GRUNDELL 1933) and these may in reality function as absorbing trichomes.

Air-dry leaves of *Craterostigma plantagineum* (Saxifragaceae) rehydrate more rapidly in water than air-dry roots. Leaf surfaces take up three times the water that cut petioles do following 8 h of rehydration (GAFF 1977). The drought

a ventral groove along the stalk between scales where tuberculate rhizoids are concentrated (BOWER 1935). This channelization supplies the majority of moisture to the reproductive areas on the thallus. Young sporophytes of *Pellia* (Metzgeriales) have also been shown to receive most of their water from external conduction (CLEE 1939).

In mosses and leafy liverworts the pattern of branching and leaf arrangement may strongly influence external water transport. Many mosses, for example, have closely imbricated leaves whose strongly decurrent bases form long narrow channels (HÉBANT 1977). Dry leaves of many arid zone species may be closely appressed but spread rapidly with wetting (RUNDEL and LANGE 1980). This movement strongly influences the level and efficiency of external conduction (MÄGDEFRAU 1935; BAYFIELD 1973). The morphological arrangement of leaves in leafy liverworts has also been shown to affect rates of external conduction of water (CLEE 1937). Morphological structures such as lamellae and filaments on bryophyte leaves may be important in this respect as well.

Although experimental data are very limited, a variety of stem structures in mosses may influence external water transport. These include specialized foliose or filamentous expansions of the stem and the frequent occurrence of rhizoids on the lower stem surface (HÉBANT 1977). Colony growth form is also important in determining rates of water uptake (GIMINGHAM and SMITH 1971; OECHEL and SVEINBJORNSSON 1979).

Since the major importance of external conduction of water in bryophytes is to serve to redistribute moisture, efficient absorption related to this conduction should be expected. While this phenomenon has been shown in many cases, there are many studies that have shown efficient water uptake by bryophyte leaves (ISAAC 1941; ANDERSON and BOURDEAU 1955; ZACHERL 1956). Uptake is particularly efficient in apical areas in comparison to thicker-walled tissues (BOWER 1931, 1933). It must be remembered, however, that bryophytes have motile sperm and require external films of water for fertilization.

4.3.3 Internal Conduction of Water

While internal water conduction may occur in tissues on the basis of simple diffusion between cells, many mosses have specialized water-conducting cells which are dead and hollow at maturity. These cells are most frequently termed hydroids, but have also been referred to as Begleiter, hadrom cells, or stenocysts. In mosses these water-conducting hydroids form central strands in the leafy stem or seta. Similar structures forming portions of the midribs of leaves do not typically interconnect with the axial strands of the stem. Numerous studies over the past 80 years have documented the preferential movement of internal water through these pathways (see HÉBANT 1977). Rates of water conduction through hydroids forming large central strands of bryophyte stems are comparable to rates of xylem flow in vascular plants (ZACHERL 1956). Despite their structural and functional similarity with vascular plant tracheids, a major difference of hydroids is their lack of lignified secondary thickenings on the conducting cell walls. Although a considerable body of literature exists on this subject,

no unambiguous reports of the presence of true lignin exist for bryophytes (HÉBANT 1977).

In mosses with both leafy aerial stems and creeping branches, the conducting cells of the upright stems are usually much more highly developed (LORCH 1931). In the Polytrichales, however, a high degree of structural complexity is present in all tissues. The subterranean branches of species of this group have an organization comparable to that of a vascular plant root in many ways (HÉBANT 1977). Large cells of the internal cortex of these have even been interpreted as an endodermis (TANSLEY and CHICK 1901; SCHEINER 1974), but HÉBANT (1977) questions this view. Despite these structures, little convincing evidence exists for uptake of water from these underground branches to the rest of the thallus.

The role of rhizoids in the uptake of water through internal conduction appears to be minor, but there is some disagreement in the literature (see CLEE 1943; BOPP and STEHLE 1957; RIFOT and BARRIERE 1974). Low rates of absorption may be explained in part by the presence of a cuticle on the rhizoids (TRACHTENBERG and ZAMSKI 1979). On the other hand, studies of rhizoids of young fern gametophytes have shown efficient uptake of water (SMITH 1972). In *Radula flaccida,* an epiphyllous leafy liverwort, rhizoids penetrate through the cuticle and epidermal cells of their leaf substrate, and take up water and nutrients from the host substrate (BERRIE and EZE 1975).

In addition to specialized water-conducting cells, living support cells (stereids) adjacent to the hydroids may also function in water conduction (TRACHTENBERG and ZAMSKI 1979). It has long been noted that many xerophytic mosses have unusually large masses of such supporting cells (GOEBEL 1905). These cells are far more than those necessary for mechanical support (LORCH 1931). Heavy masses of these supporting cells in the leaves and leaf bases of many mosses may serve important roles in water uptake and transfer to internal leaf cells and water-conducting cells of the stem (ZAMSKI and TRACHTENBERG 1976; TRACHTENBERG and ZAMSKI 1979).

It has been hypothesized that water held in the thick cell walls of xerophytic bryophytes acts as a buffering system for internal water content during periods of water stress (HÉBANT 1977). PATTERSON (1964), however, strongly doubts that there are any significant structural adaptations for drought in mosses. The significance of such apoplastic water is discussed in more detail in Chapter 2 of this Volume.

The rates of water uptake in bryophytes exposed to liquid water are rapid. Detailed measurements of rates of water uptake for stem and leaf tissue of tundra mosses have been made by GIMINGHAM and SMITH (1971) and OECHEL and SVEINBJORNSSON (1979).

A variety of morphological features of mosses may facilitate condensation and absorption of water under conditions of very light rain or dew (WATSON 1914). Architectural considerations of leaf arrangement may also influence rates of water uptake and loss (WATSON 1914; TOBIESSEN et al. 1977) but PATTERSON (1964) questions whether bryophytes possess special structures which influence rates of water uptake and loss. New experimental work in the significance of leaf arrangement on water relations is needed to resolve this question clearly.

A fundamental difference between mechanisms of water uptake by bryo-phytes and lichens is the apparent inability of most bryophytes to absorb suffi-cient water vapor under humid atmospheric conditions to allow significant levels of positive net photosynthesis to occur (Rundel and Lange 1980). A number of studies have documented the low levels of water absorption which do occur in equilibrium experiments in humid atmospheres (Müller 1909; Renner 1933; Clausen 1952; Patterson 1943; Anderson and Bourdeau 1955; Tallis 1959; Willis 1964). Contrary to this general pattern, however, Lange (1969) was able to show significant levels of photosynthesis in *Hypnum cupressi-forme* following equilibration at 96% ralative humidity.

4.4 Water Uptake by Lichens

The water relations of lichens have been an active area for research as evidenced in recent reviews (Blum 1973; Farrar 1973; Harris 1976). The majority of data on this subject, however, has concentrated on aspects of ecological and physiological responses to changes in thallus water content. The biophysical and biochemical consequences of water uptake in lichens is very poorly under-stood, particularly with respect to the absorption of water vapor.

Water uptake, as well as loss, is a rapid and purely physical process and there are no strong data to suggest any active metabolic control of the uptake process (cf. Blum 1973). Nevertheless, morphological and anatomical structure of lichen thalli may be very significant in determining the rates. In addition to uptake from precipitation, runoff, and dew, most lichens are able to hydrate beyond their moisture compensation point in humid atmospheres and this prop-erty sets them aside from most vascular plants and most bryophytes.

Uptake of liquid water by lichens is a rapid process which takes place over the entire thallus surface. For most species, full saturation is reached in 1–4 min or less (Stocker 1927; Smith 1962; Blum 1973). Comparative data for the thallus water content of several groups of lichens following immersion of air-dry thalli for 30 s is shown in Table 4.1. These contents are typically 70%–100% of saturation levels. The process of this rapid uptake is thought to occur by both absorption of water by the thick-walled fungal hyphae and capillary movement external to the hyphae. At this stage of saturation, the water content of most foliose and fructicose lichens is 100%–300% of the dry weight of the thallus. Limited data for crustose lichens suggest similar values (Ried 1960; Blum 1973). No significant differences occur in water con-tents of fructicose and foliose taxa. However, gelatinous lichens in the Collemata-ceae have structural characteristics which allow far greater saturation water contents.

Water storage within the lichen thallus appears to be very uneven. The majority of storage is certainly extracellular, with thick hyphal walls and algal sheaths the most important storage sites. Bachmann (1923) reported that water accumulation in *Umbilicaria* (*Gyrophora*) is concentrated in the medulla. Smith

Table 4.1. Comparative thallus water content (fresh wt/dry wt) of groups of air-dry lichens after a 30-s immersion in liquid water. (Adapted from BLUM 1973)

Fructicose thalli		Foliose thalli	
Cladonia rangiformis	118	Anaptychia ciliaris	120
C. crispata	133	Umbilicaria grisea	152
C. gracilis	125	U. hirsuta	157
C. furcata	126	U. pustulata	197
C. uncialis	129	Hypogymnia physodes	128
C. mitis	140	H. tubulosa	202
C. rangiferina	145	Parmelia ryssolea	122
Cetraria islandica	109	P. sulcata	151
Ramalina fastigiata	139	P. vagans	124
R. farinacea	141	P. prolixa	160
Bryoria implexus	162	Dermatocarpon miniatum	142
Bryoria jubatus	145	D. vellereum	149
Usnea hirta	154	Lobaria pulmonaria	150
Pseudevernia furfuracea	185	Evernia prunastri	149
Mean	139	Mean	152

Gelatinous lichens		Semi-gelatinous lichens	
Collema cristatum	394	Peltigera polydactyla	247
		P. rufescens	254
C. flaccidum	566	P. canina	275
Mean	480	Mean	259

(1960) found 25% more water per unit of dry weight in the medulla of *Peltigera* than in the upper cortex and algal layer. TOBLER (1925), however, described just the opposite pattern in saxicolous lichens with the cortex and algal layer more important than the medulla. Finally, SHOWMAN and RUDOLPH (1971) found water storage concentrated in the algal layer of *Umbilicaria*. The water storage significance of central cords in the medulla of *Usnea* and certain members of the Ramalinaceae has not been investigated.

Differential water storage within lichen thalli is clearly induced by wetting and drying cycles. As fungal hyphae in the upper cortex swell with water up-take, a stage is reached where gas exchange to the algal layer is restricted. Rates of photosynthetic assimilation for most lichens increase directly with thallus moisture content up to this stage, but commonly decline as moisture content approaches saturation. During a drying cycle water loss occurs rapidly from the outer cortex, thereby decreasing resistance to gas exchange. The result is a hysteresis effect with significantly different moisture contents for maximal rates of photosynthetic assimilation in wetting and drying cycles (Fig. 4.4).

Moisture uptake from water vapor and dew condensation are extremely important to many lichens. The ecological and physiological significance of these sources of water have been documented in considerable detail for lichens in the Negev Desert. LANGE et al. (1975) summarize these studies. Dew fall

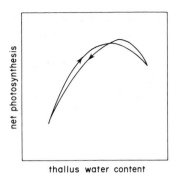

Fig. 4.4. Relationship of thallus moisture content to photosynthetic rate in typical lichens. Note the hysteresis effect differentiating wetting and drying cycles

in the Negev is frequently enough to cause sufficient hydration for several hours of active photosynthesis in the early morning. Over the course of a year, moisture input principally from dew can account for net production rates of 8%–15% of the original thallus biomass (LANGE et al. 1975; KAPPEN et al. 1975, 1979). This is a level equal to or greater than that of vascular plants in the same region.

Under conditions of high relative humidity, lichen thalli will slowly absorb moisture until they reach a level with an internal vapor pressure in equilibrium with the atmosphere. Most lichens will reach a water content of 40%–50% in a saturated atmosphere, but a number of days are required to reach this stage. Exposure for several hours to relative humidities above 90% is usually sufficient to bring thallus moisture contents up above the photosynthetic compensation point. It is not surprising, therefore, to observe that areas of the world with consistent patterns of high humidity but low precipitation support rich lichen floras. This diversity and associated ecological importance of lichens is particularly notable in desert fog zones (RUNDEL 1978a).

Despite the general suggestion in many reviews of lichen-water relations that water uptake and loss is very similar in most lichens, there is good evidence that morphological factors are very important in determining rates of these processes. LARSON and KERSHAW (1976) have shown how branch surface-to-weight ratio, surface water-holding capacity, and growth habit may all influence leaf resistance to water vapor transport in lichens. Patterns of very similar characteristics have been shown to be correlated with specific habitat types for several species of *Ramalina* (RUNDEL 1974, 1978b). The observation by BLUM (1973) that sorediate and isidiate forms of lichens characteristically have more rapid rates of uptake than forms without these structures may well be interpreted on the basis of increased surface area for absorption.

In addition to morphological characteristics, both organic and inorganic compounds deposited on the surface of lichen thalli may influence water uptake. GOEBEL (1926) suggested that the presence of nonwettable secondary lichen compounds on the outer surface of medullary hyphae may help maintain air chambers in an otherwise saturated thallus. Although there is no experimental data to support this suggestion, it would be interesting to look for such compounds in correlation with the presence of cyphellae, pseudocyphellae, and other structures which hypothetically serve as breathing pores (RUNDEL 1978c).

FOLLMANN (1967a, b) described heavy salt encrustations on coastal lichens in central Chile and speculated that hydrophilic salt crusts might provide a favorable water potential gradient for uptake of atmospheric water vapor. Although his published data are difficult to interpret because of unrealistic time axes, RUNDEL (1978a) has shown that such crusts do increase water vapor uptake considerably and that many coastal lichens are able to maintain high rates of photosynthesis under the accompanying levels of low osmotic potential.

4.5 Conclusions

Despite the large existing body of literature suggesting foliar uptake of water in vascular plants, many more studies are needed to assess the physiological significance and ecological importance of direct foliar uptake of dew, precipitation and/or water vapor. Existing data on water uptake by tillandsioid bromeliads are the best-documented examples of direct foliar uptake. All four of the criteria for critical acceptance of foliar absorption which were described in the introduction to this paper have clearly been met. Gradients of decreasing water potential from atmosphere to plant frequently exist, morphological specializations for water absorption are present. Significant amounts of water are absorbed and redistributed and plant water potentials are reduced. Although these criteria are not so clearly met for many epiphytic Orchidaceae and poikilohydric vascular plants, the existing evidence is very strong. For other vascular plants, however, the data are far less convincing. *Prosopis tamarugo,* frequently cited as the best-documented example of foliar uptake of water, almost certainly does not use this mechanism (MOONEY et al. 1980b). In virtually every case, reports of direct foliar uptake of water for other vascular plants lack sufficient data to meet the necessary criteria for critical acceptance unambiguously. While these comments are in no way meant to suggest that all such reports are in error, more rigorous experimental studies are badly needed to validate earlier work. Several areas of study are particularly important for future research. First, what is the potential significance of small amounts of foliar uptake in reducing transpiration loss? Consideration must be given not only to total transpirational loss but also to water-use efficiencies and maximizing total rates of photosynthetic production in water-limited ecosystems. Secondly, the direct effects of foliar uptake of water and the secondary effects of concentration and utilization of fog-drip by roots need to be more clearly differentiated. These effects are frequently blended. Finally, much more consideration must be given to anatomical and morphological adaptations in species for which foliar uptake has been suggested. Only when these new data are assembled will it be possible to present a clear overview of the occurrence of foliar uptake.

For bryophytes and lichens the situation is much less controversial but new research initiatives are nevertheless badly needed. A large part of the descriptive studies of thallus water relations in these groups is now more than half of century old, yet many current studies utilize fundamentally the same approach.

Fuller utilization of modern techniques of physiological ecology and cell physiology would do a great deal toward providing a better elucidation of mechanisms of water uptake. An evolutionary perspective of adaptive mechanisms is far too frequently ignored in current investigations.

References

Akhatar P, Shaukat SS (1976) Role of dew in the survival and phenology of *Gossypium hirsutum* L. cv. Qalandri. Pak J Bot 8:151–155

Akhatar P, Shaukat SS (1979) Drought endurance and dew utilization capacity of *Sorghum bicolor* (L.) Moench and *Ipomoea pes-caprae* (L.) Sweet. Pak J Bot 11:85–91

Anderson LE, Bourdeau PF (1955) Water relations in two species of terrestrial mosses. Ecology 36:206–212

Azevedo J, Morgan DL (1974) Fog precipitation in coastal California forests. Ecology 55:1135–1141

Babu VR, Went FW (1978) The effect of dew on plant water balance in desert shrubs. Annu Arid Zone 17:1–11

Bachmann E (1923) Untersuchungen über den Wasserhaushalt einiger Felsenflechten. Jahrb Wiss Bot 62:20–64

Barthlott W (1976) Struktur und Funktion des Velamen radicum der Orchideen. Dtsch Orchideen Ges Proc Eighth World Orchid Conf, Frankfurt, pp 438–443

Barthlott W, Capesius I (1974) Wasserabsorption durch Blatt- und Sprossorgane einiger Xerophyten. Z Pflanzenphysiol 72:443–455

Bayfield NG (1973) Notes on water relations of *Polytrichum commune* Hedw. J Bryol 7:607–617

Benzing DH (1976) Bromeliad trichomes: structure, function and ecological significance. Selbyana 1:330–348

Benzing DH, Burt KM (1970) Foliar permeability among twenty species of the Bromeliaceae. Bull Torrey Bot Club 97:269–279

Benzing DH, Dahle C (1971) The vegetative morphology, habitat preference and water balance mechanisms of the bromeliad *Tillandsia ionantha* Planch. Am Midl Nat 85:11–21

Benzing DH, Henderson K, Kessel B, Sulak J (1976) The absorptive capacities of bromeliad trichomes. Am J Bot 63:1009–1014

Benzing DH, Seemann J, Renfrow A (1978) The foliar epidermis in the Tillandsioideae (Bromeliaceae) and its role in habitat selection. Am J Bot 65:359–365

Bernick W (1938) Untersuchungen über den Taufall auf der Insel Hiddensee und seine Bedeutung als Pflanzenfaktor. Mitt Naturwiss Ver Neuvorpommern Rügen 65/66:67–127

Berrie GK, Eze JMO (1975) The relationship between an epiphyllous liverwort and host leaves. Ann Bot (London) 39:955–963

Biebl R (1964) Zum Wasserhaushalt von *Tillandsia recurvata* L. und *Tillandsia usneoides* L. auf Puerto Rico. Protoplasma 5:345–367

Blum OB (1973) Water relations. In: Ahmadjian V, Hale ME (eds) The lichens. Academic Press, London New York, pp 381–400

Bopp M, Stehle E (1957) Zur Frage der Wasserleitung in Gametophyten und Sporophyten der Laubmoose. Z Bot 45:161–174

Bornman CG, Botha CEJ, Nash CJ (1973) *Welwitschia mirabilis*: observations on movement of water and assimilates under foehn and fog conditions. Madoqua 2:25–31

Bower EJ (1931) Water conduction in *Polytrichum commune*. Ann Bot (London) 45:175–200

Bower EJ (1933) The mechanism of water conduction in the Musci considered in relation to habitat. Ann Bot (London) 47:401–422, 635–661

Bower EJ (1935) A note on the conduction of water in *Fimbriaria blumeana*. Ann Bot (London) 49:844–848

Breazeale EL, McGeorge WT (1953a) Exudation pressure in roots of tomato plants under humid conditions. Soil Sci 75:293–298

Breazeale EL, McGeorge WT (1953b) Influence of atmospheric humidity on root growth. Soil Sci 76:361–365

Breazeale EL, McGeorge WT, Breazeale JF (1950) Moisture absorption by plants growing in an atmosphere of high humidity. Plant Physiol 25:413–419

Breazeale EL, McGeorge WT, Breazeale JF (1959a) Movement of water vapor in soils. Soil Sci 71:181–185

Breazeale EL, McGeorge WT, Breazeale JF (1959b) Water absorption and transpiration by leaves. Soil Sci 72:239–244

Cannon WA (1906) The effects of high relative humidity on plants. Torreya 2:21–25

Carrodus BB, Specht RL (1965) Factors affecting the relative distribution of *Atriplex vesicaria* and *Kochia sedifolia* (Chenopodiaceae) in the arid zone of South Australia. Aust J Bot 13:413–434

Child GT (1960) Brief notes on the ecology of the resurrection plant (*Myrothamnus flabellifolia*). JS Afr Bot 26:1–8

Clausen E (1952) Hepatics and humidity. Dan Bot Ark 15:5–80

Clee DA (1937) Leaf arrangement in relation to water conduction in the foliose Hepaticae. Ann Bot (London) 1:325–328

Clee DA (1939) The morphology and anatomy of *Pellia epiphylla* considered in relation to the mechanism of absorption and conduction of water. Ann Bot (London) 3:105–111

Clee DA (1943) The morphology and anatomy of *Fegatella conica* in relation to the mechanism of absorption and conduction of water. Ann Bot (London) 7:185–193

Crafts AS (1933) Sulfuric acid as a penetrating agent in arsenical sprays for weed control. Hilgardia 8:125–142

Dolzmann P (1964) Elektronenmikroskopische Untersuchungen an den Saughaaren von *Tillandsia usneoides* (Bromeliaceae). I. Feinstruktur der Kuppelzelle. Planta 60:461–472

Dolzmann P (1965) Elektronenmikroskopische Untersuchungen an den Saughaaren von *Tillandsia usneoides* (Bromeliaceae). II. Eine Beobachtung zur Feinstruktur der Plasmodesmen. Planta 64:76–80

Drable E, Drable H (1907) The relation between the osmotic strength of cell-sap in plants and their physical environment. Biochem J 2:117–132

Duvdevani S (1957) Dew research in arid agriculture. Discovery 18:330–334

Dycus AM, Knudson L (1957) The role of the velamen of the aerial roots of orchids. Botan Gaz (Chicago) 119:78–87

Eickmeier WG (1979) Photosynthetic recovery in the resurrection plant *Selaginella lepidophylla* after wetting. Oecologia 39:93–106

Eisenzopf R (1952) Ionenwirkung auf die kutikulare Wasseraufnahme von Koniferen. Phyton (Horn Austria) 4:149–159

Farrar JF (1973) Lichen physiology: progress and pitfalls. In: Ferry BW, Braddeley MS, Hawksworth DL (eds) Lichens and air pollution. Univ Press, Toronto, pp 238–282

Follmann G (1967a) Zur Bedeutung der Salzbestäubung für die Krustenflechten. Ber Dtsch Bot Ges 80:206–208

Follmann G (1967b) Fördern Salzkrusten die Wasseraufnahme von Krustenflechten? Umsch Wiss Tech 13:420

Fraymouth J (1928) The moisture relations of terrestrial algae. III. The respiration of certain lower plants including terrestrial algae with special reference to the influence of drought. Ann Bot (London) 42:75–100

Gaff DF (1971) The desiccation tolerant higher plants of Southern Africa. Science 174:1033–1034

Gaff DF (1977) Desiccation tolerant vascular plants of Southern Africa. Oecologia 31:95–109

Gaff DF, Ellis RP (1974) Southern African grasses with foliage that revives after dehydration. Bothalia 11:305–308

Gallace A (1974) The fine structure and physiology of drought tolerant plants. B Sc Honors Thesis, Monash Univ Melbourne, Aust

Gessner F (1956a) Die Wasseraufnahme durch Blätter und Samen. In: Ruhland W (ed)

Encyclopedia of plant physiology Vol III. Springer, Berlin Göttingen Heidelberg, pp 215–246

Gessner F (1956b) Wasserspeicherung und Wasserverschiebung. In: Ruhland W (ed) Encyclopedia of plant physiology Vol III. Springer, Berlin Göttingen Heidelberg, pp 247–256

Gimingham C, Smith R (1971) Growth form and water relations of mosses in the maritime Antarctic. Br Antarct Surv Bull 25:1–21

Gindel I (1964) Attraction of atmospheric moisture by woody xerophytes in arid climates. Commonw For Rev 45:297–321

Goebel K (1900) Organography of plants. Hafner, New York (reprint 1969)

Goebel K (1926) Ein Beitrag zur Biologie der Flechten. Ann Jard Bot Buitenz 36:1

Grundell R (1933) Zur Anatomie von *Myrothamnus flabellifolia* Welw. Symb Bot Ups 2:1–17

Haberlandt GFJ (1914) Physiological Plant Anatomy. MacMillan, London

Haines FM (1952) The absorption of water by leaves in an atmosphere of high humidity. J Exp Bot 3:95–98

Haines FM (1953) The absorption of water by leaves in fogged air. J Exp Bot 4:106–107

Halket AC (1911) Some experiments on absorption by the aerial parts of certain salt-marsh plants. New Phytol 10:121–139

Harris GP (1976) Water content and productivity of lichens. In: Lange OL, Kappen L, Schulze E-D (eds) Water and Plant Life. Ecol Stud Vol. 19 Springer, Berlin Heidelberg New York, pp 452–468

Härtel O, Eisenzopf R (1953) Zur Physiologie und Ökologie der kutikularen Wasseraufnahme durch Koniferennadeln. Zentralbl Gesamte Forstwes 72:47–64

Hébant C (1977) The conducting tissues of bryophytes. Kramer, Vaduz

Heil H (1924) *Chamaegigas intrepidus* Dtr., eine neue Auferstehungspflanze. Beih Bot Zentralbl 41:41–50

Hickel B (1967) Zur Kenntnis einer xerophilen Wasserpflanze: *Chamaegigas intrepidus* Dtr. aus Südwestafrika. Int Rev gesamten Hydrobiol Hydrogr 52:361–400

Hiltner E (1930) Der Tau und seine Bedeutung für den Pflanzenbau. Wiss Arch Landwirtsch Abt A 3:1–70

Hiltner E (1932) Der Tau, ein vernachlässigter Lebensfaktor der Pflanzen. Mitt Dtsch Landwirtsch Ges 47:825–827

Höhn K (1954) Untersuchungen über das Wasserdampfaufnahme- und Wasserdampfabgabevermögen höherer Landpflanzen. Beitr Biol Pflanz 30:159–178

Hornby HE, Hornby RM (1964) The reaction of *Craterostigma plantagineum* Hochst. to desiccation. Kirkia 4:217–220

Isaac I (1941) The structure of *Anthoceros laevis* in relation to its water supply. Ann Bot (London) 5:339–351

Janes BE (1954) Absorption and loss of water by tomato leaves in a saturated atmosphere. Soil Sci 78:187–197

Johnston RD (1964) Water relations of *Pinus radiata* under plantation conditions. Aust J Bot 12:111–124

Jones RL (1957) The effect of surface wetting on the transpiration of leaves. Physiol Plant 10:281–288

Kappen L, Lange OL, Schulze E-D, Evenari M, Buschbom U (1975) Primary production of lower plants (lichens) in the desert and its physiological basis. In: Cooper PJ (ed) Photosynthesis and productivity in different environments. Univ Press, Cambridge, pp 133–143

Kappen L, Lange OL, Schulze E-D, Evenari M, Buschbom U (1979) Ecophysiological investigations on lichens of the Negev Desert. VI. Annual course of the photosynthetic production of *Ramalina maciformis* (Del) Bory. Flora (Jena) 168:85–108

Krause H (1935) Beiträge zur Kenntnis der Wasseraufnahme durch oberirdische Pflanzenorgane. Oesterr Bot Z 84:241–270

Lange OL (1969) CO_2-Gaswechsel von Moosen nach Wasserdampfaufnahme aus dem Luftraum. Planta 89:90–94

Lange OL, Medina E (1979) Stomata of the CAM plant *Tillandsia recurvata* respond directly to humidity. Oecologia 40:357–363

Lange OL, Schulze E-D, Kappen L, Buschbom U, Evenari M (1975) Adaptations of desert lichens to drought and extreme temperatures. In: Hadley NF (ed) Environmental physiology of desert organisms. Dowden, Hutchinson and Ross, Stroudsberg, pp 20–37

Larson DW, Kershaw KA (1976) Studies on lichen-dominated systems, XVIII. Morphological control of evaporation in lichens. Can J Bot 54:2061–2073

Lehman P, Schanderl H (1942) Tau und Reif, pflanzenwetterkundliche Untersuchungen. Springer, Berlin

Leyton L, Armitage IP (1968) Cuticle structure and water relations of the needles of *Pinus radiata* (D. Don) New Phytol 67:31–38

Lloyd FE (1905) The artifical induction of leaf formation in the ocotillo. Torreya 5:175–179

Lorch W (1931) Anatomie der Laubmoose. In: Linsbauer K (ed) Handbuch der Pflanzenanatomie, vol VII. Borntraeger, Berlin

Mägdefrau K (1935) Untersuchungen über die Wasserversorgung der Gametophyten und Sporophyten der Laubmoose. Z Bot 29:327–375

Marloth R (1907) Notes on the absorption of water by aerial organs of plants. Trans R Soc S Afr 1:429–433

Marloth R (1926) Weitere Beobachtungen über die Wasseraufnahme der Pflanzen durch oberirdische Organe. Ber Dtsch Bot Ges 44:448–455

Martin CE (1980) Field and laboratory studies of crassulacean acid metabolism in the epiphyte *Tillandsia usneoides* L. (Spanish moss). Ph D Dissertation, Duke Univ, Durham, NC

McConaha FA (1941) Ventral structures effecting capillarity in the Marchantiales. Am J Bot 28:301–306

McConaha M (1939) Ventral surface specializations of *Conocephalum conicum*. Am J Bot 28:301–306

Meidner H (1954) Measurements of water intake from the atmosphere by leaves. New Phytol 53:423–426

Mez C (1904) Physiologische Bromeliaceen-Studien. I. Die Wasser-Ökonomie der extrem atmosphärischen Tillandsien. Jahrb Wiss Bot 40:157–229

Monteith JL (1963) Dew: facts and fallacies. In: Rutter AJ, Whitehead FH (eds) The water relations of plants. Blackwell, London, pp 37–56

Mooney HA, Gulmon SL, Ehleringer JR, Rundel PW (1980a) Atmospheric water uptake by an Atacama Desert shrub. Science 209:693–694

Mooney HA, Gulmon SL, Rundel PW, Ehleringer JA (1980b) Further observations on the water relations of *Prosopis tamarugo* of the northern Atacama Desert. Oecologia 44:177–180

Müller K (1909) Untersuchungen über die Wasseraufnahme durch Moose und verschiedene andere Pflanzen und Pflanzenteile. Jahrb Wiss Botan 46:587–598

Nehler N (1977) Bromelienstudien. II. Neue Untersuchungen zur Entwicklung, Struktur und Funktion der Bromelien-Trichome. Akad Wiss Lit Mainz Trop Subtrop Pflanzenwelt 20:1–40

Nobel PS (1978) Microhabitat, water relations, and photosynthesis of a desert fern, *Notholaena parryi*. Oecologia 31:293–309

Oechel WC, Collins NJ (1976) Comparative CO_2 exchange patterns in mosses from two tundra habitats at Barrow, Alaska. Can J Bot 54:1355–1369

Oechel WC, Sveinbjornsson B (1979) Primary production processes in arctic bryophytes at Barrow, Alaska. In: Tieszen LL (ed) Vegetation and production ecology of an Alaskan arctic tundra. Ecol Stud Vol 29. Springer, Berlin Heidelberg New York pp 269–298

Oppenheimer HR, Halevy AH (1962) Anabiosis of *Ceterach officinarum* Lam. et DC. Bull Res Counc Isr Sect D 2:127–147

Patterson PM (1943) Some ecological observations on bryophytes. Bryologist 46:1–13

Patterson PM (1964) Problems presented by bryophytic xerophytism. Bryologist 67:390–396

Penfound WT, Deiler FG (1967) On the ecology of Spanish moss. Ecology 28:445–458

Pessin LJ (1924) A physiological and anatomical study of the leaves of *Polypodium polypodioides*. Am J Bot 11:370–381

Pisek A, Cartellieri E (1939) Zur Kenntnis des Wasserhaushaltes der Pflanzen. IV. Bäume und Sträucher. Jahrb Wiss Bot 88:22–68

Pridgeon AM (1981) Absorbing trichomes in the Pleurothallidinae (Orchidaceae). Am J Bot 68:64–71

Potts R, Penfound WT (1948) Water relations of the polypody fern *Polypodium polypodioi-des*. Ecology 29:43–53

Renner O (1933) Zur Kenntnis des Wasserhaushalts javanischer Kleinepiphyten. Mit einem Anhang zu den osmotischen Zustandgrößen. Planta 18:215–287

Ried A (1960) Stoffwechsel und Verbreitungsgrenzen von Flechten. II. Wasser- und Assimi-lationshaushalt, Entquellungs- und Submersionsresistenz von Krustenflechten benach-barter Standorte. Flora 149:345–385

Rifót M, Barriere G (1974) La conduction dans le thalle de l'hepatique *Conocephalum conicum* (L) Dum. I. Etude du transit de l'eau a l'aide d'une solution d'acetate de sodium ^{14}C. Rev Bryol Lichenol 40:45–52

Rouschal E (1938a) Eine physiologische Studie an *Ceterach officinarum* Willd. Flora 132:305–318

Rouschal E (1938b) Zur Ökologie der Macchien. I. Jahrb Wiss Bot 87:436–523

Rouschal E (1939) Beiträge zum winterlichen Waserhaushalt von *Cheiranthus cheiri* und anderer wintergrünen Gartenpflanzen. Oesterr Bot Z 88:148–154

Rundel PW (1974) Water relations and morphological variation in *Ramalina menziesii* Tayl. Bryologist 77:23–32

Rundel PW (1978a) Ecological relationships of desert fog zone lichens. Bryologist 81:277–293

Rundel PW (1978b) Evolutionary relationships in the *Ramalina usnea* complex. Lichenolo-gist 10:141–156

Rundel PW (1978c) The ecological role of secondary lichen substances. Biochem Syst Ecol 6:157–170

Rundel PW, Lange OL (1980) Water relations and photosynthetic response of a desert moss. Flora 169:329–335

Sanford WW (1974) The ecology of orchids. In: Withner CL (ed) The orchids: scientific studies. Wiley and Sons, New York, pp 1–100

Scheiner DC (1974) The anatomy, histochemistry and ultrastructure of the gametophore of *Dendrolignotrichum dendroides* (Hedw) Broth. (Bryopsida: Polytrichaceae). PhD Diss Penn State Univ

Schill R, Barthlott W (1973) Kakteendornen als wasserabsorbierende Organe. Naturwissen-schaften 60:202–203

Schimper AFW (1888) Die epiphytische Vegetation Amerikas. Bot Mitt Tropen 2:1–162

Schonland S (1909) On the absorption of water by the aerial organs of some succulents. Trans R Soc Afr 1:395–401

Seely MK (1979) Irregular fog as a water source for desert dune beetles. Oecologia 42:213–227

Seely MK Ecological importance of fog to Namib vegetation. In: Juvik JO (ed) The role of fog in ecosystem. Univ Press, Cambridge in press

Seely MK, Vos de MP, Louw GN (1977) Fog imbibition, satellite fauna and unusual leaf structure in a Namib Desert dune plant *Trianthema hereroensis*. S Afr J Sci 73:169–172

Showman RE, Rudolph EE (1971) Water relations in living, dead and cellulose models on the lichen *Umbilicaria papulosa*. Bryologist 74:444–450

Slatyer RO (1956) Absorption of water from atmospheres of different humidity and its transport through plants. Aust J Bot 9:552–558

Slatyer RO (1960) Absorption of water by plants. Bot Rev 26:331–392

Smith DC (1960) Studies in the physiology of lichens. Ann Bot (London) 24:186–199

Smith DC (1962) The biology of lichen thalli. Biol Rev (Cambridge) 37:537–570

Smith DL (1972) Localization of phosphatases in young gametophytes of *Polypodium vulgare* L. Protoplasma 74:133–148

Solereder H, Meyer FJ (1930) Systematische Anatomie der Monokotyledonen. VI. Micro-spermae. Borntraeger, Berlin

Spaulding VM (1906a) Biological relationships of desert shrubs. II. Absorption of water by leaves. Bot Gaz (Chicago) 41:262–282

Spaulding VM (1906b) Absorption on atmospheric moisture by desert shrubs. Bull Torrey Bot Club 33:367–375

Stark N, Love LD (1969) Water relations of three warm desert species. Isr J Bot 18:175–190

Steinbrinck D (1905) Einführende Versuche zur Cohäsionsmechanik von Pflanzenzellen nebst Bemerkungen über den Saugmechanismus der wasserabsorbierenden Haare von Bromeliaceen. Flora 94:464–477

Stocker O (1927) Physiologische und ökologische Untersuchungen an Laub- und Strauchflechten. Flora 121:334–415

Stocker O (1956) Wasseraufnahme und Wasserspeicherung bei Thallophyten. In: Ruhland W (ed) Handbuch der Pflanzenphysiologie Vol III, Springer, Berlin Göttingen Heidelnerg, pp 160–172

Stone EC (1957a) Dew as an ecological factor. I. A review of the literature. Ecology 38:407–413

Stone EC (1957b) Dew as an ecological factor. II. The effect of artificial dew on the survival of Pinus ponderosa and associated species. Ecology 38:414–422

Stone EC (1964) The role of dew in pine survival in soils below the wilting point and its measurement. In: Methodology in plant eco-physiology. UNESCO, Paris, pp 421–427

Stone EC (1970) The ecological importance of dew. Quart Rev Biol 38:328–341

Stone EC, Went FW, Young CL (1950) Water absorption from the atmosphere by plants growing in dry soil. Science 111:546–548

Stone EC, Fowells HA (1955) The survival value of dew as determined under laboratory conditions with Pinus ponderosa. For Sci 1:183–188

Stone EC, Shachori AY, Stanley RG (1956) Water absorption by needles of ponderosa pine seedlings and its internal redistribution. Plant Physiol 31:120–126

Stuart TS (1968) Revival of respiration and photosynthesis in dried leaves of Polypodium polypodioides. Planta 83:185–206

Sudzuki F (1969) Absorcion foliar de humedad atmosférica en tamarugo, Prosopis tamarugo Phil. Bol Tech Fac Agronomía Univ Chile 30:1–23

Sudzuki F, Bitti C, Acevedo E (1973) Relaciones hidricas del tamarugo (Prosopis tamarugo Phil.) en la localidad de Canchones. Bol Tech Fac Agronomía Univ Chile 37:1–23

Sveshnikova VM (1972) On the absorption of water vapor by the overground parts of the Kara-Kum Desert plants (Russian). Bot Zh (Leningrad) 57:880–886

Tallis JH (1959) Studies in the biology and ecology of Rhacomitrium lanuginosum Brid. II. Growth, reproduction and physiology. J Ecol 47:325–350

Tansley AG, Chick E (1901) Notes on the conducting tissue-system in Bryophyta. Ann Bot (London) 15:1–38

Tobiessen PL, Mott KA, Slack NG (1977) a comparative study of photosynthesis, respiration and water relation to their vertical distribution. Bryophytorum Bibliotheca 13:253–277

Tobiessen PL. Slack NG, Mott KA (1979) Carbon balance in relation to drying in four epiphytic mosses growing in different vertical ranges. Can J Bot 57:1994–1998

Tobler F (1925) Biologie der Flechten. Borntraeger Berlin

Trachtenberg S, Zamski E (1979) The apoplastic conduction of water in Polytrichum juniperinum Willd. gametophytes. New Phytol 83:49–52

Turrell FM (1947) Citrus leaf stomata structure, composition and pore size in relation to penetration of liquids. Bot Gaz (Chicago) 108:476–483

Vaadia Y, Waisel Y (1963) Water absorption by the aerial organs of plants. Physiol Plant 16:44–51

Virzo De Santo A, Alfani A, Luca De P (1976) Water vapor uptake from the atmosphere by some Tillandsia species. Ann Bot (London) 40:391–394

Volkens G (1887) Die Flora der ägyptisch-arabischen Wüste auf Grundlagen anatomisch-physiologischer Forschungen. Borntraeger, Berlin

Wahlin BJO (1943) Daggen dess betydelse for vaxternas vattenhushallning. Sven Vall Mosskulturforen Medd 5:348–367

Waisel Y (1958) Dew absorption by plants of arid zones. Bull Res Counc Isr Ser D 6:180–186

Walter H (1971) Ecology of tropical and subtropical vegetation. Van Nostrand, New York

Watson W (1914) Xerophytic adaptations of bryophytes in relation to habitat. New Phytol 13:149–169, 181–190

Went FW (1975) Water vapor absorption in *Prosopis*. In: Vernberg FJ (ed) Physiological adaptations to the environment. Intext Educational Publ, New York, pp 67–75

Went FW, Sheps LO (1969) Environmental factors in regulation and development: ecological factors. In: Plant physiology: a treatise, vol Va:299–406

Wetzel K (1924) Die Wasseraufnahme der höheren Pflanzen gemäßigter Klimate durch oberirdische Organe. Flora 117:221–269

Willis AJ (1964) Investigations on the physiological ecology of *Tortula ruraliformis*. Trans Br Bryol Soc 4:439–445

Wood JG (1925) The selective absorption of chlorine ions and the absorption of water by the leaves in the genus *Atriplex*. Aust J Exp Biol Med Sci 2:45–56

Zacherl H (1956) Physiologische und ökologische Untersuchungen über die innere Wasserleitung bei Laubmoosen. Z Bot 44:409–436

Zamifirescu N (1931) Cercetari asupra absorptiunii apei prin organele aeriene ale plantelor. Supl Bul Minst Agric Si Romeniilor 3(5–6), 1–105

Zamski E, Trachtenberg S (1976) Water movement through hydroids of a moss gametophyte. Isr J Bot 25:168–173

Zattler F (1932) Agrarmeteorologische Beiträge zum Tauproblem auf Grund von Messungen im Hopfgarten. Wiss Arch Landwirtsch Abt A Archiv Pflanzenbau 8:371–404

Ziegler H, Vieweg GH (1970) Poikilohydre Kormophyten. In: Walter H, Kreeb K (eds) Die Hydratation und Hydratur des Protoplasmas der Pflanzen und ihre ökophysiologische Bedeutung. Protoplasmatologia Vol II. Springer, Wien New York, pp 88–108

5 Transport and Storage of Water

M.H. Zimmermann and J.A. Milburn

CONTENTS

5.1 Introduction

This chapter consists of two parts, the first part (by M.H.Z.) describes the structural basis of water conduction from roots to leaves. Xylem anatomy has been known for a long time. However, those aspects which concern water movement through the plant as a whole have remained rather elusive and therefore neglected. The problem was partly that we are dealing here with microscopic structures spread throughout the whole plant body. We need the microscope to look at the structure, but it is too myopic to give us the information we seek.

which, together with diameter, gives us a measure of vessel volume, a likely measure of safety (in terms of cavitation). But vessel-length measurements are very time-consuming. We also need a precise expression of safety, as discussed in the preceding Section 5.2.4. At this point we can merely state that, in general, vessels are smaller in plants that are subject to greater water stress simply because smaller vessels are safer vessels. This is obviously a very crude statement, but it can nevertheless be illustrated very nicely by the genus *Quercus* whose temperate species have very large vessels, but evergreen species of dry areas have very small vessels.

5.2.6.2 Vessel-to-Vessel Pits

The greatest mechanical stress is not imposed upon vessel walls when vessels are functioning, but when one or a few are air- or vapor-blocked next to intact conducting vessels. Vessel-to-vessel pit membranes permit passage of water, but at the same time prevent the passage of a gas-water interface. When a vessel is embolized, the pressure in its lumen is anywhere between zero (vacuum) and +1 bar (atmospheric pressure) while the neighboring intact vessel is still under negative pressure. A considerable pressure gradient thus exists directly across the pit membranes. The smaller the pores in the pit membranes, the larger the pressure gradient necessary to cause failure to hold the gas-water interface confined to the damaged vessel. One would thus have to anticipate conspicuously small pores in the vessel-to-vessel pit membranes of desert plants. Pit-pore sizes have unfortunately never been measured. Pit membranes are primary walls. Pore sizes in primary walls have only been measured in leaves and found to be of the order of 20 nm. Pore sizes in vessel-to-vessel pit membranes are obviously of importance to plant pathology. Virus particles, for example, can only be distributed via xylem if they are smaller than the pores in the vessel-to-vessel pit membranes.

Vessel-to-vessel pit membranes must offer large surfaces to facilitate water flow from one vessel to the next. At the same time they must be mechanically strong in order not to collapse when one of the vessel embolizes. The bordered pits (secondary wall arching over the primary wall) are unique structures serving both purposes. Some dicotyledons have so-called "vestured" vessel-to-vessel pits (BAILEY 1933; OHTANI and ISHIDA 1976). Here, the tertiary wall of the bordered area develops projections (vestures) into the pit cavity. In the case of embolism, when the pit membrane is forced toward the water-filled element, the vestures support the membrane and prevent it from being torn (ZWEYPFENNIG 1978).

5.2.6.3 Quantity of Xylem

Some early German authors (see Table IV-I, p. 181 in ZIMMERMANN and BROWN 1971) noted that the transverse-sectional area of xylem, when expressed per supplied leaf quantity, increases as one goes from wet to dry habitats (excluding the special case of succulents). This may seem strange at first sight. However, if one considers that at the same time vessel lumen must decrease for reasons

of safety, the situation becomes understandable. Volume flow is proportional to the fourth power of capillary diameter. In order to achieve the same conductance the xylem with smaller vessels must have more transverse-sectional area (a second-power relationship). To compensate for this, small-vessel plants must have more xylem area (ZIMMERMANN 1978 b).

5.2.6.4 Scalariform Perforation Plates and Wall Sculptures

Features of wall structure such as scalariform perforation plates and spiral thickening may be of adaptive significance. Although scalariform perforation plates are evolutionary relics, the question arises whether they are, under certain circumstances, functionally useful. Remnants of perforation plates and other wall sculptures may be effective in keeping bubbles separated during the thawing of frozen xylem water, thus facilitating their redissolution (ZIMMERMANN 1978 b). It has been reported that the incidence of scalariform perforation plates and spiral wall thickenings increases as one moves from tropical lowlands to high altitudes, and from tropical and subtropical to temperate and cold latitudes (VAN DER GRAAF and BAAS 1974; BAAS 1976). Another interesting phenomenon is the fact that a capillary with smooth walls has more resistance to flow than one with spiral thickenings with equal inside diameters (JEJE and ZIMMER-MANN 1979). However, we have to be cautious when considering relatively small differences in resistance to flow, because so many other factors (transpiration rate, soil water availability, etc.) are more significant.

5.2.6.5 Adaptation in Aquatic Angiosperms

Although there are aquatic plants that lack roots, there is increasing evidence that hydrophyte roots are functionally similar to those of terrestrial plants: they take up mineral nutrients and synthesize cytokinins and other growth substances which are then transported via xylem to stem and leaves (BRISTOW 1975). In other words, roots are not mere holdfasts, but sources of essential growth factors (KURSANOV 1957). If the plant is entirely submerged, the structural requirements of the xylem are totally different from those of terrestrial plants, because xylem pressures are always positive. Such conduits do not need thick and lignified walls, but might resemble the resin ducts of conifers. While the large cavities in stems and petioles of aquatic plants are gas ducts, the smaller ones within vascular bundles seem to be xylem ducts. This is an interesting area for future investigations.

5.2.7 Patterns of Water Flow Through the Stem

Water rarely flows from a specific root to a specific branch. The flow path in the stem is usually such that an individual root can supply many parts of the crown. In herbaceous plants and arborescent monocotyledons this distribution pattern is based upon the three-dimensional primary vascular anatomy (for palms see p. 179 in ZIMMERMANN and BROWN 1971). In woody plants with

secondary xylem, the cambium must produce additional initials as the stem increases in diameter. This is usually accomplished by pseudotransverse divisions of the S or Z type, and the prevalence of one or the other causes the "grain" of the wood to follow a helical rather than an "axis-parallel" path. Spiral grain and its changing angle from year to year has been investigated in conifers with dye ascents by VITÉ and coworkers (e.g., VITÉ and RUDINSKY 1959). In dicotyledons, a spread of dye solution within each growth ring is prevalent, due to the vessel network described in Section 5.2.3 of this chapter. These complex flow patterns make water conduction in the stem amazingly safe (for a more detailed discussion see ZIMMERMANN and BROWN 1971).

5.2.8 The Hydraulic Architecture of Trees

It is of considerable interest to look at sap ascent in plants as a whole. We still know very little about this. There are few attempts to quantify the vascular tracks to specific points in the crown, although there are numerous literature reports on comparative xylem conductivities (e.g., TYREE et al. 1975) in different plant parts, and quantitative information on pressure gradients etc. in different parts of trees which reflect conductivities (e.g., HELLKVIST et al. 1974; RICHTER 1976).

An early attempt at studying what we like to refer to as the hydraulic architecture of trees was made by HUBER (1928), who measured xylem transverse-sectional areas in stems and branches and expressed them per fresh weight of supplied leaves. Huber restricted his measurements to reasonably small individuals of *Abies,* thus avoiding the problem of nonfunctional xylem (heartwood). This, as well as the fact that conductivity is enormously sensitive to conduit diameter, can be overcome by measuring conductance and expressing it per supplied leaf weight or leaf surface area. This has been called leaf-specific conductivity (ZIMMERMANN 1978c). Only a few such measurements are available thus far, concerning some diffuse-porous tree species. Stems have the highest, branches have lower, and twigs have still lower leaf-specific conductivities. One of the most interesting observations was the presence of hydraulic bottlenecks at branch and twig junctions (ZIMMERMANN 1978c). An even sharper constriction seems to be represented by the petiole insertion (LARSON and ISEBRANDS 1978). Flow causes a sharp pressure drop from twigs to leaves. Under conditions of stress the pressure in the petiole xylem may drop so much that cavitation takes place and the leaves are lost. During periods of continued stress lateral branches are often lost (even if the tree is standing in the open), because the resistance to flow from roots to lower lateral leaves may be as great or greater than the resistance to flow to the topmost leaves in the tree. This is an obvious adaptive advantage, because the stem and the top of the crown are the most important parts of the tree. Loss of leaves, twigs, and lower branches is comparable to the loss of the lizard's tail: by losing it the lizard can save its body and grow another tail later. By losing peripheral organs, the tree can save its stem and grow new leaves and branches later. This is particularly important for palms which cannot replace lost stem xylem because of the lack of a cambium.

Much work remains to be done in the area of hydraulic architecture of whole plants.

5.3 Storage and Adversity

Water storage is most evident in succulent plants. Over 5,000 kg of water can be stored by the giant saguaro cactus in its concertina-like stems. Though the physiology has been studied less thoroughly than crop plants and meso-phytes, it appears that they can utilize their water reserves extremely frugally when necessary. Three mechanisms facilitate water conservation during adversity. Their stomatal control is highly effective. The metabolism can be reduced and it can also shift from C_3 to CAM. The latter enables gas exchange to occur at night or even cease because it is recycled internally. These physiological adaptations allow succulents to persist at relatively high water potentials for long periods (see also Chap. 15, this Vol.). Water conservation mechanisms are triggered below −10 bar in succulents such as *Portulacaria* and *Peperomia* (HANSCOM and TING 1978).

In contrast, xerophytic plants such as the creosote bush (*Larrea* spp.) have no obvious stores of water and are adapted to tap external stores of water even at very low water potentials. *Larrea* can maintain high rates of transpiration, photosynthesis and cell division at internal water potentials from −8 to −26 bar but these functions are reduced below −45 bar (see BARBOUR et al. 1977). Similarly, mangroves (such as *Avicennia*) which normally desalinate sea-water (water potential ca. −25 bar) have large reserves of water available but must be capable of normal metabolism with internal water potentials ranging from −35 to −55 bar (SCHOLANDER 1968). PASSIOURA (1972) suggested that crop plants might be induced to leave water effectively stored in the soil profile at high water potentials through limited rates of utilization. This notion is interesting from the viewpoint of agricultural monoculture but provides no advantage to plants under normal competitive conditions. (For detailed discussion of water use and optimization of carbon assimilation see Chaps. 17 and 18, this Vol.).

Some mesophytic plants, when abundantly supplied with water and subjected to strong sunshine, can lose their own fresh weight as water daily or even hourly. Most mesophytes cannot reduce their diffusive resistance much below 10% of that of normal transpiration rates, so it is unlikely that the 10% to 20% of water available before severe wilting occurs provides a significant store during drought. Nevertheless, certain plants which are nominally mesophytes such as *Tradescantia* or *Pelargonium* (p. 156, MILBURN 1979) have the capacity to survive for long periods on water reserves in their fleshy stems especially when protected from strong light.

Tree trunks can store considerable quantities of water. A 60-m *Sequoia* tree was estimated by RUNNING et al. (1975) to contain 4,000 kg of water. However, the quantity of water in trunks seems to vary on a seasonal basis (WARING and RUNNING 1976, 1978). JARVIS (1975) estimated that water stored

in sapwood might support normal transpiration for 0.3 to 14 h. However, since the cells and conduits in wood are strongly lignified and relatively inelastic, it seems that this water can only become available at the expense of embolization following cavitation. The benefit of such a store, which if used must impair the conduction system itself, may legitimately be questioned.

5.3.1 Water Potentials of Stored Water in Plant Tissues

Many techniques can be used to measure the quantities of water held in plant tissues at a range of water potentials (see Chap. 2, this Vol., also RITCHIE and HINCKLEY 1975). All techniques suffer from some defects but the errors and discrepancies result from the different methods and are generally not serious. In addition to quantitative methods there are qualitative measurements such as dendrometry (see KOZLOWSKI 1972) and electrical probes (e.g., SPOMER 1968) which indicate changes in water content of bulky tissues.

5.3.2 Cavitation and Gas Emboli

During the period 1898 to 1914, DIXON (1914) steadily accumulated evidence that water must cohere more strongly than hitherto thought possible. Yet evidence indicating that sap columns did not always withstand severe tensions accumulated gradually from microscopic observation. It was known from gravimetric studies on wood that the moisture content of wood decreased progressively with age. The question then arises if water loss is always irreversible.

The technique of acoustic detection of cavitation by MILBURN and JOHNSON (1966) has been used with increasing effect to analyze the extent and occurrence of cavitation in plants. During its subjection to negative pressure the xylem conduit tends to become distorted mechanically. If the pressure drops low enough, a gas phase develops, either by drawing a gas bubble through the conduit wall or by expanding a microscopic bubble within the conduit. The moment this happens the walls of the conduit release their distortion energy in the form of a vibration which sounds like a "click". Evidence that "clicks" do in fact correspond to cavitation have built up gradually (MILBURN 1973a, b; MILBURN and McLAUGHLIN 1974; MILBURN and McLELLAN 1978; WEST and GAFF 1976).

A leaf hung on the detecting microphone in an acoustic chamber and illuminated with an incandescent bulb produces a succession of clicks which develop to a crescendo, then die away as the leaf becomes more wilted in a few hours. Clicks and weight of the leaf are recorded. The leaf is then supplied with water in a humid chamber and restored to maximum water content, and allowed to lose water under the same conditions a second time. At intervals the balancing pressure is measured using a pressure bomb and the dry weight is measured last. Finally, through the intermediary of weight, the tensions at which cavitation occurs can be computed (Fig. 5.2). Up to now only a few species have been studied extensively using this method. Table 5.1 shows striking similarities be-

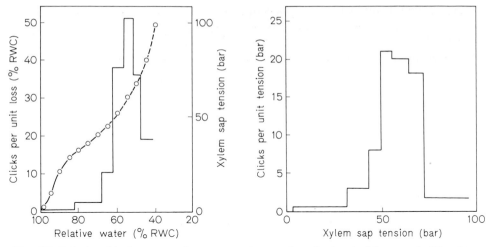

Fig. 5.2. Relationship between xylem sap tensions and cavitation in Manna ash (*Fraxinus ornus*) compound leaf with petiole. *Left Histogram* shows relationship between clicks produced per unit relative water content. *Curve* shows equivalent xylem tension inferred from pressure bomb extraction of water to give different relative water contents. (*Broken line* is extrapolated from the pressure-volume curve) (From MILBURN, TYREE, LO GULLO and SALLEO unpublished results). *Right* Numbers of the xylem conduits disrupted by cavitation (clicks) as xylem sap tensions increase. Most cavitation occurs from 30 to 70 bar tension

Table 5.1. Approximate ranges of xylem sap tensions encountered in a range of plants growing under relatively natural fluctuating water regimes. The ranges of sap tensions at which cavitation occurs in most conduits, as indicated by acoustic detection, are only slightly greater than those encountered naturally in most instances. The correlation between plant stature and cavitation susceptibility seems slight. All tensions were measured with a pressure bomb except two[a] measured by psychrometer. *Fraxinus ornus* grew in Sicily; *F. excelsior* in Scotland. (Unpublished results marked with an asterisk*)

Plant	Xylem Pressure (Approx. range) (bar)	Cavitation Pressure (Approx. range) (bar)	Source
Tomato (*Lycopersicum*)	0 to −5	−6 to −9	NONHEBEL and MILBURN*
Plantain (*Plantago*)	0 to −15	−5 to −15	MILBURN and McLAUGHLIN (1974)
Castor bean (*Ricinus*)	−2 to −10	−10 to −15	DODOO and MILBURN*
Coconut (*Cocos*)	−2 to −13	−13	MILBURN and DAVIS (1973)
Larch (*Larix*)	−2 to −14	−5 to −15	MILBURN and McLELLAN*
Apple (*Malus*)[a]	ca. −6	−12 to −25	WEST and GAFF (1976)
Gumtree (*Eucalyptus*)[a]	?	−28 to −40	CROMBIE and DOLEY*
Ash (*Fraxinus excelsior*)	ca. −9	−30 to −70	CROMBIE and MILBURN*
Ash (*Fraxinus ornus*)	−30 to −45	−30 to −70	MILBURN et al.*

5.4 Regulation of Water Flow

While the magnitude of water storage is not very great in most plants, its significance may be greater than immediately apparent. Plants function as hydraulic units in which the different stores are connected via hydraulic resistances which can have the effect of isolating water sources and sinks.

The mechanism of transport of water through living cell catenas, especially in roots and leaves, has been a controversial issue. The hydraulic conductance of cell protoplasts is most unlikely to remain constant because of the changes in solute composition and the well established changes in cytoplasmic viscosity. Cell walls are in some measure compressible, which affects the dimension of the matrix capillaries and hence also their hydraulic capacitance (e.g., Klemm 1956). Even the xylem, a seemingly simple physical transport tissue, is likely to change rapidly in hydraulic conductance if it becomes embolized through cavitation. Tylose formation introduces yet another factor which may decrease the hydraulic conductance of the tissue, although it normally follows embolism (Zimmermann 1979).

5.5 Conclusions

Xylem anatomy is of fundamental importance in the ascent of sap. Negative pressures can only survive in the xylem of plants for long periods of time because water is confined to millions or even billions of small compartments (tracheids and vessels). Tracheid-to-tracheid and vessel-to-vessel movement of water is facilitated by bordered pits in which large primary-wall areas are exposed so that resistance to flow from one compartment to the next is relatively low. The secondary wall arches over these pit areas in such a way that mechanical strength of the conducting channels is maintained, thus preventing them from collapse. The pores in pit membranes (primary walls) are small enough (probably of the order of 20 nm) that a gas-water interface cannot easily pass from an injured compartment to a functioning one. Water-conducting compartments thus become isolated as soon as they become nonfunctional by entry of air through an injury, or by appearance of water vapor by cavitation, and damage remains confined. The presence of many short vessels in xylem with long vessels (Fig. 5.1), the three-dimensional network of vessels and the varying "spiral grain" of the stem assures distribution of water along the stem. Water stored in plants in different specialized organs fulfils a number of roles. In only a few species does water in living cells serve as a significant reservoir of water during drought. Nevertheless, the smaller stores of readily available water are probably of great significance in cushioning the physiology of the plant from sudden environmental changes. These stores cause diurnal hysteresis in sap fluxes. Significant changes in water storage occur seasonally and also to a small extent diurnally, but their major role lies in maintaining xylem sap transport. Decreasing conductivities in peripheral plant parts, and conductivity con-

strictions at junctions to branches, twigs, and petioles assures survival of tensile water of the main stem in case of extreme stress.

References

Baas P (1976) Some functional and adaptive aspects of vessel member morphology. Leiden Bot Ser 3:157–181

Bailey IW (1933) The cambium and its derivative tissues. VIII. Structure, distribution and diagnostic significance of vestured pits in dicotyledons. J Arnold Arbor Harv Univ 14:259–283

Barbour MG, Cunningham G, Oechel WC, Bamberg SA (1977) Growth and development, form and function. In: Mabry TJ, Hunziker JH, DiFeo DR (Jr) (eds) Creosote bush, biology and chemistry of *Larrea* in New World deserts. Dowden, Hutchinson and Ross, Stroudsburg, pp 48–91

Bartholomew ET (1926) Internal decline of lemons III. Water deficit in lemon fruits caused by excessive leaf evaporation. Am J Bot 13:102–117

Braun HJ (1959) Die Vernetzung der Gefäße bei *Populus*. Z Bot 45:421–434

Bristow JM (1975) The structure and function of roots in aquatic vascular plants. In: Torrey JG, Clarkson DT (eds) The development and function of roots. Academic Press, London New York, pp 221–236

Carlquist S (1975) Ecological strategies of xylem evolution. Univ Cal Press. Berkeley Los Angeles London

Chaney WR, Kozlowski TT (1971) Water transport in relation to expansion and contraction of leaves and fruits of Calamondin orange. J Hortic Sci 46:71–78

Dixon HH (1914) Transpiration and the ascent of sap in plants. MacMillan, London

Dobbs RC, Scott DRM (1971) Distribution of diurnal fluctuations in stem circumference of Douglas fir. Can J For Res 1:80–83

Friedrich J (1897) Über den Einfluß der Witterung auf den Baumzuwachs. Zentralbl gesamte Forstwes 23:471–495

Gibbs RD (1958) Patterns of the seasonal water content of trees. In: Thimann KV (ed) The physiology of forest trees. Ronald, New York, pp 43–69

Graaf Van der NA, Baas P (1974) Wood anatomical variation in relation to latitude and altitude. Blumea 22:101–121

Hanscom Z, Ting IP (1978) Responses of succulents to plant water stress. Plant Physiol 61:327–330

Hellkvist J, Richards GP, Jarvis PG (1974) Vertical gradients of water potential and tissue water relations in Sitka spruce trees measured with the pressure chamber. J Appl Ecol 11:637–668

Hinckley TM, Chambers JL, Brukerhoff DN, Roberts JE, Turner J (1974) Effect of mid-day shading on net assimilation rate, leaf surface resistance, branch diameter, and xylem potential in a white oak sapling. Can J For Res 4:296–300

Huber B (1928) Weitere quantitative Untersuchungen über das Wasserleitungssystem der Pflanzen. Jahrb Wiss Bot 67:877–959

Huber B, Schmidt E (1936) Weitere thermo-elektrische Untersuchungen über den Transpirationsstrom der Bäume. (Further thermo-electric investigations on the transpiration stream in trees). Tharandter Forstl Jahrb 87:369–412 (1936) (Xerox copies of English translation available from National Translation Center, 35 West 33rd Street, Chicago, Illinois 60616)

Jarvis PG (1975) Water transfer in plants. In: Vries de DA, Alfen van NK (eds) Heat and mass transfer in the environment of vegetation. Scripta, Washington DC, pp 369–394

Jeje A, Zimmermann MH (1979) Resistance to water flow in xylem vessels. J Exp Bot 30:817–827

Klemm G (1956) Untersuchungen über den Transpirationswiderstand der Mesophyllmembranen und seine Bedeutung als Regulator für die stomatäre Transpiration. Planta 47:547–587

6.1 Introduction

The driving force of transpiration is the water potential gradient between leaf cells and the surrounding atmosphere. The water potential of the atmosphere decreases rapidly with decreasing humidity and may exceed $-2,000$ bar. This is a hostile environment for plant cells having a water potential of about -5 to -50 bar, and in adapting to terrestrial growing conditions, aerial parts of plants have evolved water-saving devices in the form of cuticle and periderm. All primary aerial parts of higher plants and ferns are covered by a cuticle, retained in submerged leaves and stems of the higher water plants (ARBER 1920), and there are indications that at least some mosses have a cuticle (PRIESTLY 1943). In secondary organs the cuticle is replaced by a periderm.

BRONGNIART (1830) was probably the first to observe and isolate plant cuticles. Since that time cuticles have been the subject of numerous investigations. The early literature on cuticular transpiration was reviewed by STÅLFELT (1956). An extensive and comprehensive review of chemistry, structure and function of cuticles and periderms is found in MARTIN and JUNIPER (1970). Penetration of cuticles by solutes applied to the foliage has been studied extensively and was reviewed by HULL (1970). There are a number of reviews on chemistry and biochemistry of cutin, suberin, and associated waxes, some of the most recent being by HOLLOWAY et al. (1972) and KOLATTUKUDY (1975, 1980). The present review focuses on the magnitude of permeability coefficients for water transport across cuticles and periderms and on the relationship between permeability of the membranes and their chemistry and structure. For this purpose unambiguous permeability coefficients are needed. These can be obtained only by working with isolated membranes, and this review is therefore restricted to these studies. The cuticular transpiration measured using whole leaves or plants is a complex function of different permeabilities and resistances which are affected by many variables. Some of them cannot be controlled adequately when using whole leaves and uncertainties arise due to the presence of stomata and trichomes.

6.2 Theory and Experimental Methods

6.2.1 Flux Equations

Permeation of liquids or vapors across polymer membranes is usually described and analyzed in terms of the following parameters: The diffusion coefficient (D) which reflects the mobility of the species in the membrane; the solubility or the distribution coefficient (S) which reflects the concentration of the species in the membrane; the permeability coefficient (P) which reflects both mobility and solubility (CRANK and PARK 1968).

The flux (J) of any species, as given by Fick's law, is proportional to D and the driving force dC/dx where C is the concentration and x is the space coordinate in direction of flow. In the steady state

$$J = \frac{-D\,(\bar{C}_i - \bar{C}_o)}{l} \tag{6.1}$$

where l is the membrane thickness and the $\bar{C}$'s are the concentrations of the species in the membrane just at the outer and inner membrane surfaces.

If the surface concentrations are not known Eq. (6.1) may be rewritten in terms of a permeability coefficient P:

$$J = \frac{P\,(p_i - p_o)}{l} \tag{6.2}$$

where $(p_i - p_o)$ is the driving force in terms of the partial pressures of the vapor at the opposite sides of the membrane and

$$P = DS, \tag{6.3}$$

provided the membrane is homogeneous and the diffusion coefficient is independent of the driving force. The permeability coefficient often includes the membrane thickness when it is unknown or difficult to measure (SCHÖNHERR 1976a, b).

The permeability coefficient is easily obtained by measuring the steady-state flux due to a given driving force and S may be obtained from the sorption isotherm. With P and S known, D can be calculated from Eq. (6.3). Alternatively, D may be obtained from the extrapolated time lag t_e, the intersection of the straight line portion of a plot total amount diffused vs. time (CRANK and PARK 1968):

$$t_e = \frac{l^2}{6D}. \tag{6.4}$$

Water permeation of porous membranes is often analyzed in terms of total pore area A^p or fractional pore area (A^p/A^m), where A^m is the membrane area. Equation (6.3) may than be written

$$P = \frac{D\,A^p/A^m}{l} \tag{6.5}$$

and water permeability can be analyzed in terms of number of pores (n), average pore radius (r^p), and average path length (l) (SOLOMON 1968; SCHÖNHERR 1976a).

6.2.2 Experimental Methods

6.2.2.1 Membranes

Since the relationship between membrane structure, membrane composition, and membrane permeability is to be studied, enzymatically isolated membranes that lack stomata and trichomes must be used. Isolation with pectinase and cellulase at 35 °C does not change membrane structure (HOCH 1975) or perme-

ability (Schönherr 1976b; Schönherr and Mérida 1981). High temperatures
cause irreversible changes in membrane permeability and structure (Schönherr
et al. 1979) and must be avoided.

Components of cuticles will operationally be classified according to their
solubility in lipid solvents such as chloroform. Nonextracted cuticles will be
called cuticular membranes (CM), the soluble components will be called soluble
lipids or soluble cuticular lipids (SCL) and the insoluble remainder will be
called polymer matrix (MX). Layers of periderms obtained by enzymatic isolation (potato tuber periderm) or by stripping (birch trunk) are called periderm
membranes (PM).

6.2.2.2 Types of Flux Measurements

Diffusion

Permeability coefficients for diffusion of water (P_d) are obtained using the system
water/membrane/water with identical solutions on both sides, such that no
gradient of water potential or water activity acts across the membrane. Under
these conditions the only possible mechanism of water transfer is diffusion.
Since there is no net water transport the diffusional flux is measured using
tritiated water (THO). Under steady-state conditions the permeability coefficient
is calculated from Eq. (6.6)

$$P_d = \frac{J^*}{\Delta[THO]} \tag{6.6}$$

where J^* is the tracer flux (in dpm m^{-2} s^{-1}) and $\Delta[THO]$ is the concentration
gradient of THO across the membrane (in dpm m^{-3}). Using these dimensions
P_d has the dimension m s^{-1} and contains implicitly the membrane thickness.

Volume Flow of Water

The volume flow of water (J_v in m^3 m^{-2} s^{-1}) caused by a gradient of osmotic
pressure (or more generally by a gradient of water potential) can be obtained
using the system water/membrane/water. Again, solutions on both sides are
identical, except that on one side a solute is added. In the steady state the
osmotic permeability coefficient (P_f) is calculated from Eq. (6.7)

$$P_f = \frac{J_v}{\bar{v}\Delta C_s} \tag{6.7}$$

where $\bar{v}$ is the partial molar volume of water (in m^3 mol^{-1}) and C_s (mol m^{-3})
is the concentration gradient of solute across the membrane. Using these dimensions P_f has the dimensions m s^{-1}. If a water potential gradient acts across
the membrane, the mechanism of transport may no longer be diffusion alone.
P_f is equal to P_d only if water molecules move individually across the membrane.
However, when liquid continuity exists across the membrane (porous membranes) a gradient of osmotic pressure or water potential causes a laminar
flow that increases with increasing pore size (Solomon 1968; Schönherr 1976a).
Thus, in porous membranes $P_f > P_d$.

Transpiration

Ordinarily, the inner surface of the cuticle is in contact with the water of the epidermal wall and the outer surface is exposed to the atmosphere. This situation is mimicked by measuring water permeability using the set-up water/ membrane/water vapor (SCHÖNHERR and SCHMIDT 1979; SCHÖNHERR and LENDZIAN 1981).

Permeability coefficients of transpiration (P_{tr}) have been measured using either THO (SCHÖNHERR and SCHMIDT 1979; SCHÖNHERR and MÉRIDA 1981) or by using a gravimetric method (SCHÖNHERR and LENDZIAN 1981).

Using THO as tracer J^* is measured in the steady state and P_{tr} is calculated from Eq. (6.6). It should be noted that the magnitude of P_{tr} usually depends on the relative humidity on the outer surface of the cuticle (SCHÖNHERR and SCHMIDT 1979). The maximum value of P_{tr} is measured when $a_{wv}=1$ (relative humidity 100%). The P_{tr} values usually decrease with decreasing a_{wv}. The cause for this phenomenon will be discussed later.

From P_{tr} the actual transpirational flux (J_{tr}) can be calculated for any gradient of water activity ($a_w - a_{wv}$) from Eq. (6.8)

$$J_{tr} = P_{tr} (a_w - a_{wv}) \tag{6.8}$$

provided P_{tr} is independent of a_{wv} or the dependence is known. In Eq. (6.8) a_w is the activity of the liquid phase (usually close to 1) and a_{wv} is the water activity of the vapor phase as defined by Eq. (6.9)

$$a_{wv} = \frac{p_{wv}}{p_{wv}^0} = \frac{RH}{100} \tag{6.9}$$

where p_{wv}^0 is the saturation vapor pressure at a given temperature, p_{wv} is the actual vapor pressure and RH is the relative humidity.

The gravimetric method gives J_{tr} (in $kg\ m^{-2}\ s^{-1}$) directly and P_{tr} is calculated from Eq. (6.10)

$$P_{tr} = \frac{J_{tr}}{\rho\ (a_w - a_{wv})} \tag{6.10}$$

where the specific gravity of water (ρ in $kg\ m^{-3}$) is needed to obtain P_{tr} in the usual dimension (ms^{-1}).

6.3 Water Permeability of Cuticular Membranes

6.3.1 Diffusion

Permeability coefficients for diffusion of water across CM are around $10^{-9}\ m\ s^{-1}$ (Table 6.1). One of the lowest values was found for CM from onion bulb scales (*Allium cepa*) which is also the thinnest membrane studied.

Table 6.1. Permeability coefficients for transport of water across isolated cuticular membranes from various species

Species	Organ	pH	Cation		Coefficient $(m\ s^{-1})$	CV	Membrane thickness (m)	Number of membranes
Citrus aurantium[c]	Leaf	6.0	Ca^{2+}	P_d	1.08×10^{-9}	(72)	2.5×10^{-6}	69
Citrus aurantium[a]	Leaf	3.0	Na^+	P_d	1.01×10^{-9}	(36)	2.5×10^{-6}	27
Citrus aurantium[a]	Leaf	9.0	Na^+	P_d	1.75×10^{-9}	(44)	2.5×10^{-6}	27
Pyrus communis[a]	Leaf	5.0	Na^+	P_d	0.86×10^{-9}	(37)	2.0×10^{-6}	3
Pyrus communis[e]	Leaf	6.0	Ca^{2+}	P_{tr}	0.49×10^{-9}	(22)	2.0×10^{-6}	10
Hedera helix[e]	Leaf	6.0	Ca^{2+}	P_{tr}	0.10×10^{-9}	(35)	1.5×10^{-6}	10
Lycopersicon esc.[e]	Fruit	6.0	Ca^{2+}	P_{tr}	1.89×10^{-9}	(40)	4.0×10^{-6}	10
Solanum melongena[b]	Fruit	6.0	Ca^{2+}	P_d	2.30×10^{-9}	(31)	2.0×10^{-6}	6
Clivia miniata[f]	Leaf	6.0	Ca^{2+}	P_{tr}	0.10×10^{-9}	(23)	6.0×10^{-6}	10
Allium cepa[d]	Bulb	6.0	Ca^{2+}	P_d	0.43×10^{-9}	(43)	0.8×10^{-6}	30
Potamogeton lucens[a]	Leaf	7.0	Na^+	P_d	2.55×10^{-6}	(13)	0.2×10^{-6}	3

Membrane thickness represents rough estimates obtained either from the weight per cm^2 of membrane or from electron micrographs. CV is the coefficient of variation. Number of membranes refers to the number of membranes studied individually.
[a] SCHÖNHERR 1976b;   [b] SCHÖNHERR and SCHMIDT 1979;   [c] HAAS and SCHÖNHERR 1979;   [d] SCHÖNHERR and MÉRIDA 1981;   [e] SCHÖNHERR and LENDZIAN 1981; [f] SCHÖNHERR unpublished

The large variability (compare standard deviations) of P_d values even if membranes are taken from the same leaf, fruit, or bulb scale is a typical characteristic of CM. It has been shown that this variability is due to the soluble cuticular lipids associated with cuticles (HAAS and SCHÖNHERR 1979). Due to this variability the effects of pH, counterion, or water activity on permeability can only be studied using the same membranes for all treatments. With CM no significant effects of pH and counterions were found (SCHÖNHERR 1976b). There is no obvious correlation between P_d and membrane thickness, as predicted by Fick's law [Eq. (6.1)]. Permeability of onion CM is just as low as that of *Clivia* CM, even though the latter is more than ten times as thick. Interestingly, the CM of *Potamogeton* leaves are orders of magnitude more permeable than the CM of terrestrial organs, as the submerged leaves of *Potamogeton* do not need protection against water loss.

6.3.2 Effect of Vapor Pressure on Permeability of Cuticular Membranes

Permeability of CM depends on the vapor pressure of the atmosphere in contact with the outer surface of the CM (Fig. 6.1). The effect is most pronounced with *Citrus* CM and egg plant fruit CM, while little effect is observed with onion bulb scale CM. In fact, many CM of onion did not respond at all to a_{wv} (SCHÖNHERR and SCHMIDT 1979). In view of the large variability between membranes it must be stressed that the effect of a_{wv} on P_{tr} was investigated

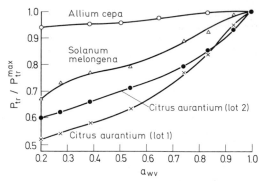

Fig. 6.1. Effect of water activity of the vapor phase (a_{wv}) on permeability coefficients of transpiration P_{tr} of cuticular membranes. P_{tr}^{max} was determined at $a_{wv}=1$. The maximum permeability coefficients were for *Citrus aurantium* 5.17×10^{-10} m s^{-1} (lot 1, Na$^+$-form pH 3) and 3.33×10^{-9} m s^{-1} (lot 2, Ca^{2+}-form, pH 6); *Allium cepa* 4.30×10^{-10} m s^{-1} (Ca^{2+}-form, pH 6); *Solanum melongena* 2.5×10^{-9} m s^{-1} (Ca^{2+}-form, pH 6). Values are averages of 5 to 30 membranes (SCHÖNHERR and SCHMIDT 1979, and unpublished results)

using the same membranes at all values of a_{wv}. Since experimental error was smaller than 3% the effect of a_{wv} on P_{tr} is highly significant.

6.3.3 Cuticular Resistances

The parameter most frequently used to characterize water permeability of cuticles is the resistance (r). The resistance is defined as driving force per unit flux, thus P^{-1} is a resistance, its dimension is s m^{-1}. Unfortunately, the driving force of transpiration which is used most frequently to calculate r is not the gradient of vapor pressure or the gradient of water activity used to calculate permeability coefficients. Instead, the gradient of absolute humidity (ΔC_{wv}) (kg water vapor per m^3 of air) is employed, and the resistance (r) is calculated from Eq. (6.11):

$$r = \frac{\Delta C_{wv}}{J_{tr}}. \tag{6.11}$$

Again, the dimension of (r) is s m^{-1} which may lead to confusion. If resistances are calculated according to Eq. (6.11) it is assumed that the gradient of water vapor concentration is the driving force of transpiration. It is further assumed that the inner side of the cuticle is in equilibrium with saturated vapor (SLATYER 1967). This implies that the liquid-vapor transition occurs prior to entry of water into the cuticle and that single individual water vapor molecules move across the cuticle.

Cuticular resistances quoted in the literature (COWAN and MILTHORPE 1968) range from 2,000 to 5,000 s m^{-1} for mesophytes and 5,000 to 40,000 for xerophytes. HOLMGREEN et al. (1965) reported cuticular resistances of 8,500 (*Acer platanoides*), 8,300 (*Betula verrucosa*) and 38,000 s m^{-1} (*Quercus robur*).

In order to compare these conventional resistances determined using whole leaves with permeability coefficients as defined by Eq. (6.6), (6.8) and (6.10),

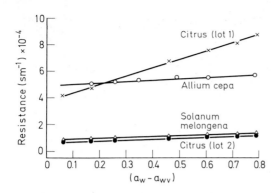

Fig. 6.2. Resistances of cuticular membranes as function of $a_w - a_{wv}$. Data taken from Fig. 6.1. See text for calculation

Table 6.2. Comparison of water permeability of cuticular membranes with permeability of artificial hydrophobic polymer membranes at 25 °C

Type of membrane			Permeability coefficient $m\ s^{-1}\ cm^{-1}$
Artificial membranes	Kel-F	(polychlorotrifluorinated ethylene)	4.12×10^{-14}
	Saran	(polyvinylidenechloride)	6.39×10^{-14}
	Manolene	(polyethylene)	8.33×10^{-14}
	Profax	(polypropylene)	24.20×10^{-14}
Cuticular membranes	*Hedera helix*	(leaf CM)	2.00×10^{-14}
	Allium cepa	(bulb scale CM)	3.44×10^{-14}
	Pyrus communis	(leaf CM)	9.80×10^{-14}
	Citrus aurantium	(leaf CM)	27.00×10^{-14}
	Solanum melongena	(fruit CM)	46.00×10^{-14}
	Lycopersicon esculentum	(fruit CM)	75.60×10^{-14}

Permeability coefficients are expressed per cm thickness of membrane. Data for artificial membranes taken from Sivadjian and Ribeiro (1964), data for cuticular membranes are taken from Table 6.1

the permeability coefficients must be converted to resistances by combinding Eq. (6.8) with Eq. (6.11) which yields:

$$r = \frac{\Delta C_{wv}}{P_{tr}\,(a_w - a_{wv})}. \tag{6.12}$$

Resistances range from approximately $10^4\ s\ m^{-1}$ to $6.8 \times 10^4\ s\ m^{-1}$ (Fig. 6.2) which is in fair agreement. However, all resistances are dependent on humidity. Between 94% and 21% humidity resistances increased by a factor of 1.87 (*Citrus*, Na^+-form), 1.73 (*Citrus* in Ca^{2+}-form), 1.59 (egg plant fruit) and 1.12 (onion). It has been argued that the dependence of r on a_{wv} shows that liquid continuity exists across the cuticles and therefore C_{wv} is not the proper driving force of transpiration (Schönherr and Schmidt 1979).

6.3.4 Water Permeability of Cuticular Membranes as Compared to Artificial Polymer Membranes

Before attempting to analyze the chemical and physical bases of cuticular resistance to water transfer it is interesting to compare them with artificial polymer membranes of low permeability and known composition. For this purpose permeability coefficients are expressed per cm thickness of membrane. This procedure is legitimate for homogeneous polymer membranes. With cuticles, however, the calculated values should be used only for purposes of comparison, as Fick's law is not obeyed, as was pointed out already.

Water permeability of plant cuticles is of the same order of magnitude as permeability of hydrophobic synthetic polymer membranes (Table 6.2). Interestingly, the thinnest CM (*Hedera* and *Allium*) proved to be the least permeable ones. The polymer membranes included in Table 6.2 are the least permeable to water manufactured so far. Given the fact that the building materials available to plants for making a hydrophobic barrier are simply carbon and hydrogen, it appears that evolution selected the optimum solution to the problem.

6.4 Water Permeability of Periderm Membranes

Limited information is available on water permeability of isolated periderm membranes. Permeability of periderm membranes stripped off the trunks of *Betula pendula* has been investigated by SCHÖNHERR and ZIEGLER (1980). Permeability of potato tuber periderm membranes (*Solanum tuberosum*) isolated enzymatically was studied by VOGT in this laboratory (unpublished results).

6.4.1 Water Permeability of *Betula* Periderm

Permeability coefficients are proportional to the reciprocal of membrane thickness or the reciprocal of membrane weight (Fig. 6.3) as predicted by Fick's law [Eq. (6.1)]. Thus the individual periderm layers act as resistances in series and the permeability of the periderm covering the trunk can be calculated from Fig. 6.3. This periderm layer is usually about 1 mm thick, which gives a P_d of 1.6×10^{-10} m s^{-1}. This is a very high level of protection if compared with cuticular membranes (Table 6.1). However, about 3% of the total periderm area is covered by lenticels that have a much higher permeability. The problem of lenticels has been discussed elsewhere (SCHÖNHERR and ZIEGLER 1980).

The permeability coefficient of a hypothetical periderm layer having 1 cm thickness would be 1.60×10^{-11} m s^{-1} which is about two orders of magnitude higher than the permeability of cuticles (cf. Table 6.2). Thus, on a unit thickness basis birch periderm is quite permeable. Permeability coefficients depend on humidity (Fig. 6.4). The effect of a_{wv} on P_{tr} is more pronounced than with cuticular membranes.

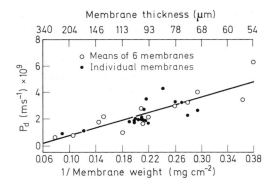

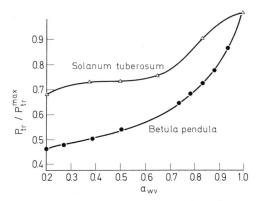

Fig. 6.3. Permeability of *Betula* periderm as affected by membrane thickness (SCHÖNHERR and ZIEGLER 1980)

Fig. 6.4. The effect of water activity of the vapor phase (a_{wv}) on permeability coefficients of transpiration of potato tuber and birch trunk periderm. P_{tr}^{max} (determined at $a_{wv}=1$) for potato periderm 2.5×10^{-9} m s^{-1} (SD 56%, means of six membranes) and for *Betula* periderm 9.55×10^{-9} m s^{-1} (SD=39%, means of six membranes) [SCHÖNHERR and ZIEGLER 1980, and unpublished results (potato)]

6.4.2 Permeability of Potato Tuber Periderm

Potato tuber periderm layers are only three to five cell layers thick, which amounts to about 30 to 50 μm. Permeability coefficients of these membranes range from 10^{-9} to 10^{-10} m s^{-1}, providing a level of protection comparable to that of cuticular membranes. There are indications that permeability decreases rapidly after harvesting and storage in dry air. Permeability coefficients decrease with decreasing humidity (Fig. 6.4) (unpublished results).

6.5 Interpretation of Permeability Coefficients

Plant cuticles and periderms have both been shown to have an extremely low water permeability. Permeability coefficients range from 10^{-9} to 10^{-10} m s^{-1} and it appears that this is the level of protection necessary for terrestrial plant growth in temperate zones. The challenge is now to relate permeability coefficients to chemistry and structure of cuticles and periderms.

The permeability to water of a polymer membrane is proportional to its water content and to the mobility of water in the membrane [Eq. (6.3)]. It

follows that the permeability coefficient for water should be higher for the more polar polymers than for the nonpolar ones. This prediction is generally observed (BARRIE 1968).

Permeability coefficients are simply proportionality coefficients that relate the fluxes to the driving forces. Information concerning the effects of structure and composition on cuticular permeability can be obtained on the basis of certain transport models. In developing these models I shall rely on studies with artificial polymer membranes, as these membranes have a lower degree of complexity, both in composition and in structure.

6.5.1 Membrane Models Based on Composition of Membranes

Polymers with low permeability to water have a number of properties in common: they consist of carbon chains with no hydrophilic substituents and there is lateral symmetry on each carbon atom in the chain (BARRIE 1968). Regularity of structure which enables close packing and the absence of polar groups are prerequisites for low water permeability. Even though crystallinity reduces water permeability, it is not essential, as amorphous polymers in the glass state can be excellent barriers (BENNET et al. 1962). High permeabilities are usually found for polar polymers and polymers having a high segmental mobility.

Polymers may be classified according to the effect of vapor pressure on permeability. Hydrophobic polymers such as polyethylene, polypropylene, and polyethylenetetraphthalate have permeability coefficients that are independent of water vapor pressure. Fluxes are proportional to the driving force, the vapor pressure gradient. Solubility is proportional to vapor pressure, that is a linear sorption isotherm is observed (YASUDA and STANNETT 1962). In these polymers solubility is extremely low. For example, in polyethylene only 2.8×10^{-5} g of water vapor are sorbed (at 25 °C and 100% humidity) per cm^3 of polymer. At all vapor pressures water permeates as individual molecules and water clusters do not form. Hence, over the entire range of p/p_o there is only water-polymer interaction and no water-water interaction in the polymer. Permeability coefficients are constant over the entire range of p/p_o (Fig. 6.5, polyethylene) and the system vapor/membrane/vapor yields the same values as the system water/membrane/water vapor (YASUDA and STANNETT 1962). These types of membranes will be referred to as solubility membranes (SCHÖNHERR and SCHMIDT 1979). If the membrane is exposed to water on one side all hydrogen bonds must be broken before the molecule can enter the membrane (Fig. 6.6). In this specific case it is permitted to use the gradient of water vapor concentration as driving force [Eq. (6.11)] in calculating permeability coefficients, as the phase transition liquid water–water vapor occurs prior to the entry of water molecules into the membrane.

In a membrane containing polar substituents Henry's law (sorption proportional to vapor pressure) is not obeyed and solubility is not directly proportional to vapor pressure. The sorption isotherm increases with vapor pressure (BARRIE 1968; YASUDA and STANNETT 1962), such that often a BET type isotherm is observed. With increasing vapor pressure the number of water molecules sur-

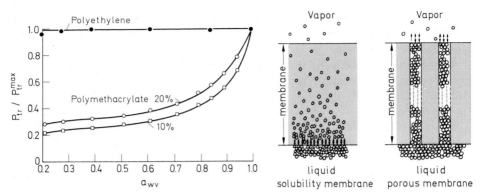

Fig. 6.5. The effect of the activity of water vapor (a_{wv}) on water permeability of polyethylene and polymethacrylate membranes in Ca^{2+}-form at pH 6. Maximum permeabilities (at $a_{wv} = 1$) were 6.2×10^{-11} m s^{-1} (polyethylene); 4.23×10^{-7} m s^{-1} (polymethacrylate, 20% cross-linking) and 4.30×10^{-7} m s^{-1} (10% cross-linking) (Schönherr and Ziegler 1980)

Fig. 6.6. Transport models for lipid membranes. *Model I* solubility membrane. *Model II* porous membrane. Liquid/vapor interface indicated by *double arrows* (Schönherr and Schmidt 1979)

rounding the polar groups increases and as a consequence both diffusion and permeability coefficients usually increase with increasing water content of the polymer (Barrie 1968).

In polar polymers water sorption leads to the formation of water clusters or to continuous water-filled channels, provided the polar groups are sufficiently close to each other. Membranes of this type, having permeability coefficients that depend on vapor pressure (such as polymethacrylate in Fig. 6.5) have been termed porous membranes (Schönherr 1976a; Schönherr and Schmidt 1979). In these membranes water continuity exists across the entire membrane when it is exposed to water on one side and vapor on the other and the liquid/vapor transition takes place at the membrane/vapor interphase. Therefore ΔC_{wv} is not the driving force of water across the membrane (Fig. 6.6).

6.5.2 Membrane Models Based on Structure of Membranes

The membrane matrix may be amorphous or crystalline. Within a given membrane both amorphous and crystalline regions may occur. The presence of crystallites reduces the cross-sectional area for diffusion and increases the effective path length.

Analysis of transport in heterogeneous membranes is difficult (Barrer 1968). In the simplest case water permeability of polymers containing crystalline regions (nylon, polyethylene-tetraphthalate) was analyzed using the equation

$$P = P_a v_a k \tag{6.13}$$

where P_a and v_a are the permeability coefficient and the volume fraction of the amorphous phase and k is a structure factor which is a function of v_a

(LASOSKI and COBBS 1959; KLUTE 1959a, b). In this case the crystalline phase is practically impermeable to water and is dispersed within a continuous amorphous phase.

A heterogeneous membrane may also consist of two (or more) interpenetrating phases which are continuous, or they may consist of laminates of the type AB, ABA, ABAB etc. when they consist of only two phases. For this latter case explicit relations between diffusion coefficients of the two phases and the hold-up time have been worked out for the special case of D being independent of vapor pressure and a linear sorption isotherm (BARRER 1968). For all other cases theory is incomplete and rather involved (see discussion by BARRER 1968).

In a heterogeneous membrane consisting of alternating layers of A and B normal to the direction of flux (resistances in series) the total permeability of a membrane P of thickness 1 is related to the permeabilities and thicknesses of the laminates by the equation

$$\frac{1}{P} = \frac{1_A}{P_A} + \frac{1_B}{P_B} + \cdots \tag{6.14}$$

provided D is independent of vapor pressure and the sorption isotherm is linear (BARRER 1968).

6.5.3 Chemistry and Structure of Cuticular Membranes

According to these models analysis of cuticular permeability to water must focus on the following points: (1) chemistry of cuticles and their structure, (2) arrangement of components of cuticles within the membrane, (3) mobility of water within the components and solubility of water in the components. A complete analysis of cuticular permeability cannot be given at the present time because water vapor sorption of cuticles (or periderms) has not been studied so far. Therefore D and S have not been studied independently and only the product of both, namely P, has been measured. The discussion can therefore only be a qualitative one.

6.5.3.1 Chemistry of Cuticles

The polymer matrix makes up the bulk of the CM. Unfortunately, little is known concerning the intact polymer matrix, as practically all investigations focused on the degradation products obtained by hydrolysis or hydrogenolysis (MARTIN and JUNIPER 1970; KOLATTUKUDY 1975, 1980). The insoluble fraction of cuticles is never pure cutin, it also contains various nonlipid components such as cellulose, polyuronic acids, proteins, and phenolic compounds (MEYER 1938; ROELOFSEN 1952; HUELIN 1959; MARTIN and JUNIPER 1970; KOLATTUKUDY 1975, 1980; SCHÖNHERR and HUBER 1977; HUNT and BAKER 1980). In isolated cuticles the cutin ranges from 20 to 1,030 µg cm^{-2} or from 20% to 84% by weight (HOLLOWAY et al. 1972; BAKER and PROCOPIOU 1975). According to HOLLOWAY et al. (1972) plant cutins may be classified depending on the major

monomer acid found after hydrolysis. They distinguish the hexadecanoic acid, the dihydroxyhexadecanoic, and the trihydroxyhexadecanoic acid type. Since cutin monomers are cross-linked by ester, peroxide, and ether bridges (Crisp 1965) the presence of high amounts of di- and trihydroxyfatty acid may affect the degree of cross-linking and therefore swelling in water. However, this relationship has not been investigated.

The soluble cuticular lipids (SCL or so-called waxes) are a very complex mixture, comprising from 6 to 380 $\mu g\,cm^{-2}$ or from 2% to 30% by weight (Norris 1974; Baker and Procopiou 1975; Baker et al. 1975; Haas and Schönherr 1979). Of the CM used in permeability studies only *Citrus* leaf CM has been quantitatively investigated so far (Haas and Schönherr 1979) and this contains fatty acids (C_{16} to C_{26}), fatty alcohols (C_{26} to C_{34}), esters (C_{38} to C_{44}) and paraffins (C_{16} to C_{33}). The total amount of SCL was about 10 $\mu g\,cm^{-2}$, or 3% by weight. With respect to water permeability it must be stressed that all SCL have long hydrophobic chains, the major homologs have no side chains, and some have a polar functional group.

Water permeability of lipids that form monolayers has been investigated (LaMer et al. 1964; Gaines 1968). The resistance to evaporation of a stearic acid or hexadecanol monolayer at high surface pressures is about 20 $s\,m^{-1}$. Interestingly the resistance is not a linear function of chain length. Rather, it is the logarithm of the resistance that increases linearly with chain length, such that for every 2 $-CH_2$ groups added resistance doubles (Archer and LaMer 1955; LaMer et al. 1964). For example, the resistance of monolayers of fatty alcohols 16, 18, 20, and 22 carbon atoms long is 20, 40, 80, and 160 $s\,m^{-1}$, respectively. Thus, a monolayer of a C_{22}-alcohol has the same resistance as eight monolayers of hexadecanol in series. To build the same resistance only 0.22 $\mu g\,cm^{-2}$ are needed in the first case and 13 $\mu g\,cm^{-2}$ in the second. This fact provides a very interesting hint as to the selective advantage of using long chain lipids in the cuticle to build a transpiration resistance. For the log relationship to be effective it is necessary that the SCL molecules are oriented parallel to the normal of the membrane. This type of arrangement has been proposed for CM from studies using polarized light (Meyer 1938; Roelofsen 1952).

6.5.3.2 Structure of Cuticular Membranes

Chemical analysis shows cuticles to be heterogeneous membranes. Studies into the fine structure of CM using polarized light or electron microscopy essentially confirm this. In describing the fine structure of cuticles the terminology proposed by Roelofsen (1952), Sitte and Rennier (1963) and Wattendorff and Holloway (1980) will be used. The outer epidermal wall consists of cuticular membrane and cell wall. In many plant species the CM is composed of a thin, outer cuticle proper (CP) and a thicker cuticular layer (CL). The CM of *Clivia* leaves (Figs. 6.7–6.8) and onion bulb scales (Fig. 6.9) belong to this class. In other species, however, such a distinction is not possible, for example in *Citrus* CM (Fig. 6.10), where a fine electron-dense reticulum or fibrillae extend throughout the entire CM.

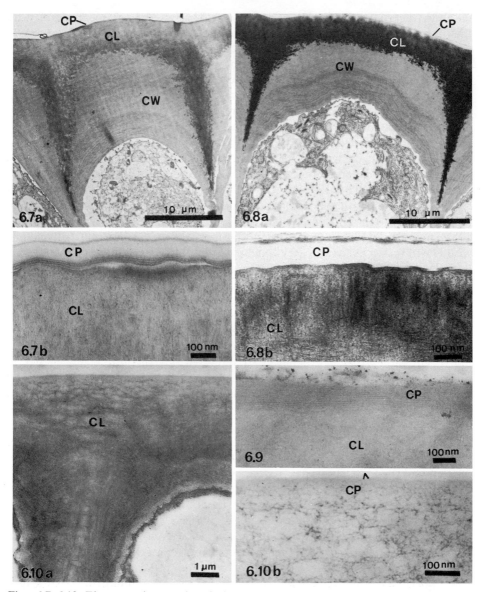

Figs. 6.7–6.10. Electron micrographs of plant cuticles. The upper cuticular membrane of *Clivia miniata* leaves fixed with glutaraldehyde and osmium tetroxide (**6.7**) and with glutaraldehyde and potassium permenganate (**6.8**); **6.7b** and **6.8b** are high magnification images of the cuticle proper. **6.9** Cuticular membrane of the inner bulb scale of *Allium cepa* fixed with glutaraldehyde and osmium tetroxide. **6.10** Cuticular membrane (**6.10a**) and the outer layer of the CM (**6.10b**) of the upper surface of *Citrus aurantium* leaves fixed with glutaraldehyde and osmium tetroxide. *CP* cuticle proper; *CL* cuticular layer; *CW* cell wall

With regard to permeability the key problem is the chemical identity of the fine structures observed. The stains commonly used (OsO_4, $KMnO_4$, uranyl-acetat, lead citrate) are not specific for any of the components of cuticles and the problem cannot be solved at the present time. Using a histochemical reaction, Wattendorff and Holloway (1980) demonstrated that the electron opaque layers of the CP of *Agave* leaves and most of the CL consist of cutin. The fibrils of the CL gave a polysaccharide reaction but it could not be precluded that other substances present in the cuticle may also contribute to the electron-dense fibrillae seen following osmium fixation and staining with other heavy metals. Indirect evidence was presented to the effect that the electron-lucent lamellae of the CP represent layers of SCL. However, it was pointed out that most of the SCL associated with the CM must be located elsewhere, as *Agave* leaves contain much more SCL than could be accommodated in the electron-lucent layers of the CP.

Mérida et al. (1981) demonstrated that the CP of *Clivia* leaves hardly stains with $KMnO_4$ (Fig. 6.8a) and they concluded that the CP is nonpolar. In contrast, the CL did stain heavily with $KMnO_4$, especially in young, expanding leaves, showing it to be more polar than the CP (Fig. 6.8). Following post-fixation with osmium and staining with heavy metals, the CP showed a lamellar appearance (Fig. 6.7b). More lamellae were observed if the specimen had been extracted with chloroform at room temperature prior to fixation with osmium, and it was suggested that the electron-lucent layers are not simply voids where SCL had been, rather they are believed to represent a structural element that is nonextractable; possibly a nonpolar type of cutin. The thickness of the electron-lucent layers is about 5 nm, which represents the length of chain with about 35 carbon atoms. Since many of the SCL are of this length, this nonpolar cutin layers would be ideally suited to serve as a matrix within which the SCL molecules could be packed in an orientation parallel to the normal of the membrane. According to Mérida et al. (1981) the CP represents the main barrier to water transport due to its nonpolar nature, even though the CL is much thicker. The electron-dense fibrillae in the CL were interpreted to represent channels of relatively high polarity due to the presence of polar functional groups from cutin, polyuronic acids, proteins, and cellulose. These polar channels are not incrusted by SCL, rather the SCL contained within the CL were assumed to be located within the electron-lucent globules of the CL.

This picture of the cuticle of *Clivia* tallies with earlier results of studies using polarized light (Meyer 1938; Roelofsen 1952). The CL of *Clivia* leaves is anisotropic and appears negatively birefringent when cross-sections are viewed with polarized light. Birefringence disappeared on heating to 90 °C and reappeared on cooling. Extraction with lipid solvent removed birefringence irreversibly. Meyer (1938) concluded that negative birefringence was due to SCL embedded in the CL. The CL exhibited form double refraction and it was suggested that the SCL are contained in tangentially oriented pores of the cutin, with the long axes of the molecules arranged parallel to the normal of the membrane. Meyer (1938) found the CP of *Clivia* to be isotropic, when cross-sections were viewed. However, using very thin sections and high magnification Roelofsen (1952) found the CP to be weakly negatively birefringent. After extraction

with chloroform or pyridine the CP was weakly positively birefringent. This positive double refraction could not be eliminated by heating or imbibition with solvents matching the refractive index of the CP. Hence, it cannot be form birefringence and was attributed to a nonextractable structural element of the CP. The CP does not contain cellulose and it is most likely that the positive double refraction is due to cutin. Birefringence due to embedded SCL has been observed with all CM investigated so far (FREY-WYSSLING 1959; ROELOFSEN 1959). SITTE and RENNIER (1963) investigated a wide variety of cuticles using polarized light, staining techniques, and electron microscopy. In most species the outermost layer of the CM was negatively birefringent and the innermost layer was positive. In thick CM (*Agave americana, Ficus elastica, Picea excelsa, Prunus laurocerasus*) more than two layers differing in optical properties were observed. The negative birefringence of the outer layer of the CM was attributed to embedded crystalline SCL, as it disappeared on heating and on extraction with hot pyridine. In many instances, a residual birefringence was found even in extracted cuticles imbibed with suitable solvents. This form birefringence was attributed to the presence of voids in the polymer matrix orientated parallel to the surface of the cuticles. In very young leaves of *Ficus elastica* form birefringence was found even in nonextracted cuticles which disappeared during development. Possibly, SCL are deposited in preformed voids in the cutin during leaf evelopment. Occasionally, the authors observed a weak birefringence due to cutin itself.

Lamellation of the CP has been observed in the CP of other species as well (CHAFE and WARDROP 1973; JARVIS and WARDROP 1974; SARGENT 1976; HEIDE JØRGENSEN 1978; WATTENDORFF and HOLLOWAY 1980). However, with many other species lamellae could not be found (see WATTENDORFF and HOLLOWAY 1980 for a discussion). Possibly not all cuticles have a lamellar CP, or standard procedures of sample preparation are not suited to reveal the lamellar character of some types of cuticles. Lamellae could not be detected in the CM of *Citrus aurantium* (Figs. 6.10a and b) by transmission electron microscopy. On the other hand, ECKL and GRULER (1980) found lamellae in *Citrus* leaves by a freeze fracturing technique. Freeze fracturing revealed lamellae in the CP of tobacco leaves, *Tilia* buds and hairs from ovules of cotton (WILSON 1980).

The lamellar structure of *Citrus* CM was confirmed by electron spin resonance (ESR) spectroscopy (ECKL and GRULER 1980). At ambient temperatures the hydrophobic SCL occur in distinct layers orientated parallel to the membrane surface and the long axis of the molecules is also parallel to the surface. The soluble lipids are in the solid state. The hydroxy fatty acid monomers of cutin are not randomly orientated, rather they have a preferred orientation normal to the surface below 16 °C, and between 16° and 38 °C they are slightly tilted.

This brief discussion shows that the fine structure of cuticles is not well understood at the present time. Polarized light microscopy clearly shows that SCL occur in a highly ordered state. This was confirmed by ESR-spectroscopy, which also demonstrates a considerable degree of order within cutin (ECKL and GRULER 1980). However, the exact location and orientation of the SCL within the cuticle is not yet known.

ingly, comparing permeability and composition of *Citrus* CM of different years, HAAS and SCHÖNHERR (1979) found permeability to be highest in years when "polar" SCL (fatty acids and alcohols) were highest and alkanes were lowest. They also pointed out the need to study both permeability and composition on the same membranes, otherwise differences will not be statistically significant.

In spite of these difficulties encountered in interpretation two facts have clearly emerged: (1) soluble cuticular lipids determine water permeability of CM. This can be attributed to their long hydrophobic chains which are unbranched and highly oriented. Future research must show to what extent the type of SCL and their amounts affect permeability. The interaction between cutin and SCL is another problem that must be solved. (2) There is no relationship between thickness of CM and permeability. There are a number of indications that the cuticle proper is the main barrier to water and that the cuticular layers are relatively permeable.

6.5.6 Transport Properties of Periderm Membranes

Periderm membranes are cellular membranes. Secondary walls of the individual cells are free of cellulose and consist of suberin, polyphenols, and soluble lipids (SITTE 1955, 1962, 1975; WATTENDORFF 1974; FALK and EL-HADIDI 1961; HOLLOWAY et al. 1972; KOLATTUKUDY 1975, 1980). The secondary walls are birefringent and show numerous light bands in the EM, believed to represent soluble lipids (SITTE 1975; FALK and EL-HADIDI 1961; SOLIDAY et al. 1979). Thus the secondary walls of phellem cells are the barriers to water transport and the role of the hydrophobic lamellae has been pointed out (SITTE 1975). Phellem cells are connected by their mutual middle lamellae and primary walls.

From the point of view of water permeability the key questions are: What is the composition of middle lamellae and primary walls? Are they polar or apolar?

In *Betula* periderm middle lamellae and primary walls are very polar, they stain readily with toluidine blue and if $AgNO_3$ is added as tracer of water flux, silver precipitates form abundantly in middle lamellae and primary walls but not in secondary walls (SCHÖNHERR and ZIEGLER 1980). It was concluded that in *Betula* periderm water flows across the network formed by middle lamellae and primary walls. Consistent with this view are the following observations: extraction with chloroform causes a weight loss of 50% but has little effect on water permeability; P_{tr} strongly depends on a_{wv} and this dependence is little altered by solvent extraction; no phase transition was found between 5° and 65 °C (SCHÖNHERR and ZIEGLER 1980). In *Betula* periderm tangential secondary walls contain numerous pores in radial direction believed to be the remains of plasmodesmata. They are accessible to water as they always contain silver precipitates (SCHÖNHERR and ZIEGLER 1980).

The lumina of phellem cells are probably filled with water when the membranes are submerged in water.

If subjected to dry air the lumina will drain (SCHÖNHERR and ZIEGLER 1980), the secondary hydrophobic walls will function as excluded volume [Eq. (6.13)]

and water will flow through the hydrophilic middle lamellae and primary walls. Since per unit length birch periderm is quite water-permeable, a relatively thick layer (1 mm) is needed to build a barrier that provides sufficient protection.

A similar analysis cannot be given for potato tuber periderm for lack of detailed information. It is clear, though, that potato tuber periderm differs in many respects from birch periderm. The effect of a_{wv} on P_{tr} is smaller and chloroform extraction increases water permeability markedly. This observation agrees with a recent report according to which water permeability of potato wound periderm depends on synthesis of alkanes and alcohols but not on synthesis of suberin (SOLIDAY et al. 1979). Attempts to trace the path of water across potato tuber periderm failed; no silver could be found anywhere, not even after 5 days of exposure at 40 °C. This shows that middle lamellae and primary walls differ markedly from those of *Betula* periderm. The secondary walls also differ in that no plasmodesmata could be found. In flowing across potato tuber periderm water must cross numerous laminated and hydrophobic barriers arranged in series. This agrees with a observed hold-up time of 6 to 12 h. A detailed analysis must await further experimentation.

6.6 Concluding Remarks

6.6.1 The Problem of Adaptation to Water Stress

Most xerophytic plant species have much thicker cuticles than mesophytic, hygrophytic, or even hydrophytic ones. This observation is probably responsible for the common belief that plants respond to water stress with the formation of thick cuticles that reduce passive water loss from the plant. Data do not support this belief. The thin CM of onion bulb scales, pear or ivy leaves are just as efficient water barriers as the thick *Clivia* CM. Water permeability coefficients for CM or periderm membranes all range from 10^{-9} to 10^{-10} m s^{-1}, and it appears that this is the level of protection necessary for terrestrial plant growth. Thus, water permeability coefficients do not differ greatly between species. The real difference lies in the way plants accomplish this goal. Some species build a very thin CM (*Allium, Pyrus, Hedera*), others a rather thick one (*Clivia, Lycopersicon*). By the same token, the thin potato tuber periderm is just as efficient a water barrier as the very heavy *Betula* trunk periderm. Why different plants have adopted such widely different strategies is not known. It is clear that SCL represent the major water barrier. However, the amounts and composition of SCL differ widely among species that differ only little in water permeability such as *Allium, Clivia,* and *Citrus.* Also, environmental conditions are known to affect composition of SCL but at the present time it is not known whether or not water permeability is also affected. Combined studies of lipid composition and water permeability have not been performed. At the present time there is insufficient evidence to show that there is an adaptation to water stress at the level of the cuticle.

7 Stomatal Responses, Water Loss and CO_2 Assimilation Rates of Plants in Contrasting Environments

E.-D. SCHULZE and A.E. HALL

CONTENTS

7.1 Introduction

Stomatal apertures are the major pathway for the movement of CO_2 from the atmosphere into the mesophyll of leaves. The presence of this pathway for the movement of gases also results in water loss from the hydrated surfaces within leaves to the atmosphere. Stomatal aperture appears to be controlled by complex mechanisms which operate to maintain a variable balance between allowing CO_2 uptake to proceed, while restricting the loss of water vapor, and preventing leaf desiccation. Recent reviews have examined the physiological

bases of stomatal function (Raschke 1979; Allaway and Milthorpe 1976) and stomatal responses to environment (Sheriff 1979; Burrows and Milthorpe 1976; Hall et al. 1976). Analyses which integrated stomatal effects on CO_2 exchange, transpiration, and energy balance were developed based upon theory (Cowan 1977), which have led to hypotheses concerning optimal stomatal function (see Chap. 17, this Vol.; Cowan and Farquhar 1977). However, information concerning the simultaneous responses of stomata, water loss, and CO_2 assimilation rates has not been reviewed for plants in natural environments.

The following chapter attempts a comparative analysis of the variation in the operational range of leaf conductance and CO_2 assimilation rate, and the regulation of these processes within the operational range, including an analysis of the relationships which exist between stomata, plant water loss and plant water status. Finally, consideration is given to the responses of plants in contrasting natural environments, and levels of leaf conductance, water loss, and CO_2 assimilation rate are examined in relation to maximal levels for natural conditions.

For this review, studies were analyzed in which simultaneous measurements of leaf conductance and CO_2 assimilation rate had been determined. Many studies of this type have been conducted in controlled environments but few data are available for naturally varying field conditions. Data obtained by micrometerological methods were not included because they usually lack precision and are difficult to interpret due to the complexity of plant canopies. When evaluating relationships between stomata and plant water status, data obtained with viscous flow porometers were generally not included because they tend to be inaccurate.

Leaf conductance was used rather than leaf resistance because conductance is more linearly related to transpiration, CO_2 assimilation, and stomatal aperture (Burrows and Milthorpe 1976; Hall et al. 1976). Leaf conductance values refer to water vapor and were calculated from the transpiration rate and the difference in vapor pressure between leaf and air. Conductances are presented — unless explicitly stated — on a projected leaf area basis and are expressed in the same units as the vapor and CO_2 fluxes using the definition of Cowan (1977) described in Chapter 8, this Volume. Leaf conductances refer to the combined effects of boundary layers, stomata, and cuticles on both sides of the leaf. Intercellular CO_2 concentrations were calculated from independent measurements of CO_2 flux and leaf conductance.

7.2 Operational Range of Leaf Conductance and CO_2 Assimilation Rate

Maximum leaf conductance for water vapor is mainly determined by the density and geometric properties of open stomata, and the boundary layer. Minimum leaf conductance for water vapor is determined by the conductance of the cuticle and the extent of stomatal closure. Körner et al. (1979) examined maximum leaf conductances of 13 groups of morphologically and/or ecologically comparable plant species and related these data to estimates of photosynthetic capacity mainly obtained from other sources. They proposed that, for a wide range of C_3 plants, photosynthetic capacity was linearly correlated with maximum leaf conductance and that C_4 grasses had greater photosynthetic capacity

than C_3 grasses, but similar maximum leaf conductances. The way in which CO_2 assimilation (A) and leaf conductance (g) are correlated appears to have great ecological significance. If during variations of environmental or plant internal conditions, A and g change proportionally in a straight line relationship which passes through the origin, the intercellular CO_2 concentration, c_i remains constant. To the extent that leaf temperature and atmospheric vapor pressure do not vary, water use efficiency also remains constant. In this case stomatal movements do not change the conditions of CO_2 fixation in the mesophyll. In contrast, curvilinear correlations between g and A and linear relations which do not pass through the origin indicate that either g or A responds more strongly than the other parameter to changes of environmental or plant internal conditions. In this case c_i and water use efficiency are not maintained constant; c_i decreases whenever g is more affected by changes of environmental or plant internal conditions than A. In the following section we shall examine this correlation between the range of leaf conductance and the photosynthetic capacity for plants subjected to different environments during growth.

In contrast to KÖRNER et al. (1979), in the following study leaf conductances (g) were examined for conditions where CO_2 assimilation rate was maximal, and with natural concentrations of CO_2 and O_2 (A_{max}), as suggested by HALL and SCHULZE (1980a). This upper reference level for the range of leaf conductance (g at A_{max}) is probably lower, in many circumstances, than the maximal leaf conductance which could have been achieved in a leaf by special experimental treatments. But, few data are available where maximum leaf conductances have been deliberately sought, and measurements of maximum leaf conductance may be difficult because stomata may not respond in a steady-state manner under such conditions, e.g. at high temperatures. Instead, leaf conductance at which CO_2 assimilation is maximal appears to have greater ecological significance for understanding plant adaptations to their environment.

Several data sets are available where correlations had been examined between A and g in attempts to explain stomatal effects on photosynthesis. These data are evaluated in an inverse manner to determine the extent to which the operational range of leaf conductance is linearly or curvilinearly correlated with photosynthetic capacity. Long-term effects of plant climate and effects of leaf age, plant conditioning, and genotype are investigated.

7.2.1 Long-Term Effects of the Level of Visible Radiation During Growth

Plants adapted to shaded habitats have a lower capacity for CO_2 assimilation than plants adapted to, and grown in, habitats where they are exposed to high levels of solar radiation. These differences in capacity are associated with many differences between sun and shade leaves in photosynthesis and respiration, in leaf anatomy, and in leaf conductance to water vapor (BJÖRKMAN 1973; see Chap. 3, Vol. 12 A). *Atriplex patula* normally grows in exposed habitats, but it exhibits shade-type responses when grown in the shade (Fig. 7.1). BJÖRKMAN (1973) calculated the dashed lines in Fig. 7.1 from CO_2 response curves

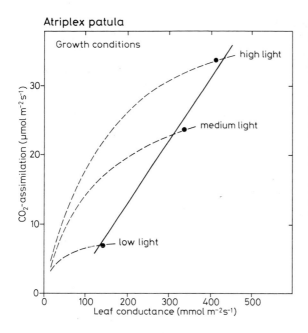

Fig. 7.1. CO_2 assimilation of *Atriplex patula* grown in different light climates as related to leaf conductance. The data points are CO_2 assimilation rates measured under saturating light, optimal temperature, and humidity, and natural concentrations of CO_2 and O_2, and leaf conductance to water vapor measured concurrently. The *dashed lines* are predicted effects of leaf conductance on CO_2 assimilation rate calculated using measured responses of assimilation to CO_2 concentration. (After Björkman 1973)

and used them to demonstrate that the lower CO_2 assimilation rates of the shade-grown plants were not solely due to their smaller leaf conductances. It is apparent that g (at A_{max}) was linearly correlated with A_{max}.

Comprehensive investigations of correlations between stomatal conductance and photosynthetic capacity were conducted by Wong (1979) and Wong et al. (1979). Also their data exhibit linear regression lines between g (at A_{max}) and A_{max} for plants of several species, as they varied due to several factors including long-term effects of the radiation environment during plant growth. For maize, the varying characteristics in leaves of both sun- or shade-grown plants are well approximated by one regression line passing through the origin (Fig. 7.2). Downes (1971) studied a wide range of C_4 genotypes within the genus *Sorghum*; and their characteristics of g (at A_{max}) and A_{max} yielded also a regression line with a slope similar to that of *Zea mays* (Fig. 7.2). In this and subsequent figures, it will be apparent that substantial differences exist between C_3 and C_4 plants in the slope of the regression line of g (at A_{max}) with A_{max}. This is a corollary of the fact that c_i is lower in C_4 than in C_3 plants. A smaller slope of the regression line indicates that higher CO_2 assimilation rates would be obtained at similar leaf conductances; and, therefore, small slopes are associated with high intrinsic water use efficiency.

Large differences are also apparent in the slopes of the regression lines obtained with different C_3 species. The study of Holmgren (1968) with sun and shade ecotypes of *Solidago virgaurea* grown in both sun and shade environments, exhibit a linear regression between g (at A_{max}) and A_{max} which had a much lower slope than the regression line of g (at A_{max}) and A_{max} in *Fagus silvatica*. Björkman (1968) demonstrated that substantial differences were present amongst ecotypes of *Solidago virgaurea* in their photosynthetic and respirato-

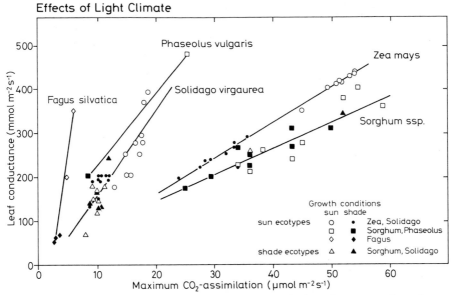

Fig. 7.2. The effects of light climate on the relation between leaf conductance and maximum CO_2 assimilation at optimal temperatures and humidity, and natural concentrations of CO_2 and O_2. The variation resulted from differences among leaves of plants grown under sun and shade conditions. *Fagus silvatica:* SCHULZE (1970), *Phaseolus vulgaris* and *Zea mays:* WONG (1979), *Solidago virgaurea:* HOLMGREN (1968), *Sorghum ssp.:* DOWNES (1971)

ry metabolism. Consequently, the linear regression in Fig. 7.2 is not simply due to stomatal effects on CO_2 uptake rate. The data on *Fagus silvatica* were obtained on the same tree and contain the long-term effects of different levels of radiation in the exposed and more shaded part of the forest canopy.

7.2.2 Influence of Inorganic Nutrition

In many habitats, the supply of plant nutrients, especially nitrogen, strongly limits plant growth and photosynthetic capacity. Linear regressions passing through the origin were observed between g (at A_{max}) and A_{max} by WONG (1979) for C_3 and C_4 plants subjected to variations in the supplies of nitrogen and phosphate (Fig. 7.3). Similar correlations are apparent in the data of GOUDRIAAN and VAN KEULEN (1979) for the effects of nitrogen deficiency on *Zea mays;* however, their data for *Helianthus annuus,* subjected to nitrogen deficiencies, exhibit only poor correlations between g (at A_{max}) and A_{max}. In addition, the data of MEDINA (1972) for *Atriplex patula* exhibit no association between g and A at two levels of nitrogen supply. The lack of correlation between g (at A_{max}) and A_{max} that has been observed on some occasions may indicate that conductance is not influenced by the metabolism of the leaf mesophyll.

    It is unlikely that the linear correlations described by WONG (1979) can be solely explained by nutrient deficiencies affecting g, and g affecting A. Defi-

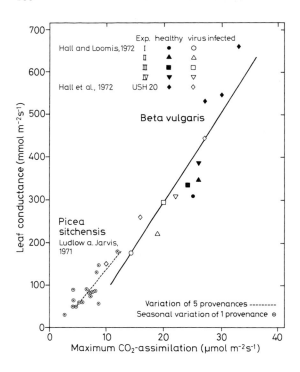

Fig. 7.5. The effects of genotype and virus infection on the relation between leaf conductance and maximum CO_2 assimilation, made under near optimal conditions for assimilation. The *data points* for *Picea sitchensis* indicate seasonal variation, whereas the *regression line* indicates genotypic variation. *Beta vulgaris:* Hall and Loomis (1972) and Hall et al. (1972), *Picea sitchensis:* Ludlow and Jarvis (1971)

clones of *Pinus radiata*. Apparently, genetic variation within a species can result in variation in the range of leaf conductance which exhibits the same relationship with photosynthetic capacity as may occur due to long-term environmental effects on one genotype. The studies with ecotypes of *Solidago virgaurea* (Fig. 7.2) also support this observation.

Interspecific effects on the relationship between g (at A_{max}) and A_{max} are evident in studies with *Citrus* species (Khairi and Hall 1976a, b). *Citrus limon,* which is thought to be native to a warm subhumid region, was compared with the hybrid between *Citrus limon* and *Eremocitrus glauca;* the latter species is thought to be native to a hot semi-arid region. The relationship between the curves of g (at A_{max}) versus A_{max} for the species and the hybrid (Fig. 7.6) is similar to that already described for C_3 versus C_4 species. A higher ratio of A_{max} to g, as exhibited by the hybrid, should result in higher water use efficiency and improved adaptation to arid habitats compared with *Citrus limon*. In another study, *Citropsis gabunensis,* which is thought to be native to shade environments in the humid tropics, was compared with *Citrus sinensis,* which is thought to be native to the subhumid subtropics. Compared with *Citrus sinensis,* the data for *Citropsis gabunensis* are displaced toward the origin as might be expected for a shade species, and are rotated away from the A axis, which is consistent with an environment which has lower evaporative demands (Fig. 7.6).

A schematic description of possible relationships between the operational range of leaf conductance and the capacity for photosynthesis which summarizes

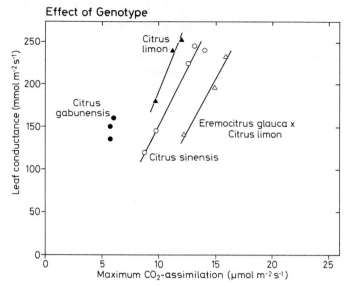

Fig. 7.6. The effects of genotype within the genus *Citrus* and related genera on the relation between leaf conductance and maximum CO_2 assimilation made under near-optimal conditions for assimilation. The variation resulted from day-to-day changes in conductance and capacity for CO_2 assimilation which may have been due to source-sink effects. (After KHAIRI and HALL 1976a, b)

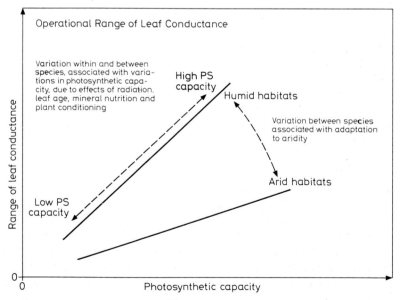

Fig. 7.7. Hypothetical relations between the operational range of leaf conductance and photosynthetic capacity as indicated by maximal CO_2 assimilation rate at near-optimal conditions for assimilation

also the previous figures is presented in Fig. 7.7. It is hypothesized that environmental and plant conditions which result in a lower photosynthetic capacity (and a lower investment) per unit leaf area, may result in a smaller range of leaf conductance. Farquhar (1978a) demonstrated that a linear association between g and the capacity for CO_2 assimilation is consistent with the concept of optimal stomatal function as proposed by Cowan and Farquhar (1977). The slopes of the regression line of g (at A_{max}) versus A_{max} varied substantially among C_3 species, although C_3 plants may not reach a slope as low as in C_4 plants. In the present study *Fagus silvatica* showed the steepest slope of all C_3 species and *Gossypium hirsutum* the lowest slope. Smaller slopes, as exhibited by some C_3 species and most C_4 species, signify higher intrinsic water use efficiency and lower c_i, and improved adaptation to arid habitats. It is hypothesized that genotypes within the same species will tend to exhibit relations between g (at A_{max}) and A_{max} which have similar regression lines, whereas substantial differences in slope of the regression line will normally require substantial differences in genotype.

7.3 Regulation of Leaf Conductance and CO_2 Assimilation Rate Within the Operational Range

During diurnal courses, stomatal conductance varies in response to short-term changes in the level of visible radiation, humidity, and temperature; and to a variable extent, these changes are influenced by effects on stomata of variations in CO_2 concentration inside the leaf. These stomatal responses are substantially reversible, except where plants are subjected to extreme variations in environment. In the following sections, the short-term reversible responses of stomata to radiation, humidity, and temperature are discussed; and the regulation of leaf conductance is examined in relation to the balance between water loss and CO_2 assimilation.

7.3.1 Short-Term Effects of Visible Radiation

Stomatal responses to light have been examined on many occasions in controlled environments. Leaf conductance usually exhibits a hyperbolic response to photon flux (Burrows and Milthorpe 1976), which is similar to the response of CO_2 assimilation rate, resulting on some, but not all, occasions in a linear regression between g and A (Wong 1979; Ramos 1981). Gain analyses based upon the methods developed by Cowan (1977) and Farquhar et al. (1978) have been used to determine the extent to which stomatal responses to light are indirect and mediated by internal CO_2 concentration. For some C_4 species, g response to internal CO_2 concentration may be an important factor in g response to light (Ramos 1981; Raschke et al. 1978). In contrast, the response of stomata in some C_3 species is either a direct response to photon flux or a response

to some product of photosynthesis in the mesophyll tissue (WONG et al. 1978, 1979), and stomatal response to internal CO_2 concentration is relatively insignificant.

The photon flux required for 95% of maximal conductance varies substantially (100 to 2,000 µmol photon $m^{-2} s^{-1}$) depending upon the species, leaf age, and preconditioning. On many occasions, greater photon fluxes are required for full stomatal opening in C_4 than in C_3 species. In addition, plants with grass-type stomata from the families Poaceae and Cyperaceae may respond differently to blue light than plants from other families (JOHNSSON et al. 1976). On occasions, plants have exhibited only small responses of leaf conductance to light; e.g., sunflower in the studies of GOUDRIAAN and VAN LAAR (1978), but not in the studies of RAMOS (1981). These variations in stomatal sensitivity to light have not been explained. Responses obtained with *Larix decidua* in natural conditions by BENECKE et al. (1981) are described in Fig. 7.8. Stomata of older leaves were less responsive to reductions in photon flux than younger leaves. These studies also demonstrated that there are cases where the short-term relations between A and g are different from the long-term relations between A_{max} and g (at A_{max}).

7.3.2 Responses to Humidity and Temperature

Stomatal responses to humidity may reflect a mechanism which prevents extreme rates of plant water loss and extreme plant water deficits when plants are subjected to high evaporative demands (HALL et al. 1976). The mechanism for stomatal response to humidity has not been clearly established (SHERIFF 1979). LANGE et al. (1971) proposed that stomatal response to humidity was mediated by cuticular transpiration of the outer epidermis, whereas SHERIFF and MEIDNER (1975) proposed that it may be a consequence of the evaporation from the inner walls of the guard and subsidiary cells. It should be recognized, however, that the latter mechanism could not result in steady-state decreases in transpiration with increases in evaporative demand (COWAN 1977; FARQUHAR 1978; TYREE and YIANOULIS 1980).

Stomatal responses to humidity have been observed with virtually all species that have been examined (some exceptions are discussed by LÖSCH 1980). Stomatal responses to humidity were first comprehensively described for plants in desert habitats (SCHULZE et al. 1972a), but they have also been observed with plants from less arid habitats (CAMACHO-B et al. 1974), arctic zones (JOHNSON and CALDWELL 1976), temperate zones (JARVIS 1980), and even humid tropical zones (KHAIRI and HALL 1976b). In addition, stomatal response to humidity has been observed at night with CAM plants (LANGE and MEDINA 1979; OSMOND et al. 1979).

The sensitivity of stomata to humidity has not been associated with either habitat conditions or leaf type. Generally, stomata of plants with larger maximal conductances are more sensitive to humidity, whether the differences in maximal conductance are genetic in origin (Fig. 7.9) or due to long-term drought (HALL and SCHULZE 1980a; LUDLOW 1980). However, on a relative scale, the responses

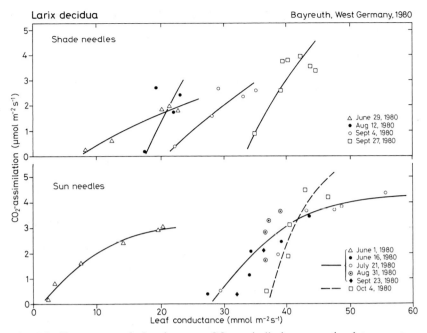

Fig. 7.8. Short-term relation between CO_2 assimilation at optimal temperature and high air humidity and leaf conductance of sun and shade needles of *Larix decidua* in different seasons. The *data points* show steady state conditions at different light intensities. All rates are related to total surface area (ratio of total/projected area is about 2.3). (After Benecke et al. 1981)

may be similar with an increase in vapor pressure difference from 10 to 20 mbar resulting in a 50% decrease in stomatal conductance. Pretreatment with dry air may inhibit stomatal response to humidity (Rawson et al. 1977).

Substantial regulation of transpiration by sensitive stomatal responses to humidity has been observed with several conifers (Bennett and Rook 1978; Jarvis 1980), and some herbaceous angiosperms (Drake et al. 1970; Hall and Kaufmann 1975; Hall and Schulze 1980b; Ludlow 1980). For *Macroptilium atropurpureum* and *Vigna unguiculata*, sensitive regulation of water loss was associated with extreme drought avoidance. However, studies with several woody angiosperms indicated that stomatal effects on transpiration during responses to humidity were smaller, and substantial increases in transpiration rate occurred with decreases in external humidity (Khairi and Hall 1976b; Osonubi and Davies 1980).

In natural environments, the regulation of transpiration is strongly dependent upon stomatal responses to both vapor pressure difference and temperature. When the vapor pressure deficit of the air decreases during the day time, it is usually due to increasing temperature because ambient vapor pressures frequently remain relatively constant during the day. Stomatal responses to temperature per se have often been confounded with responses to vapor pressure difference. When the effects of temperature and humidity are separated, leaf

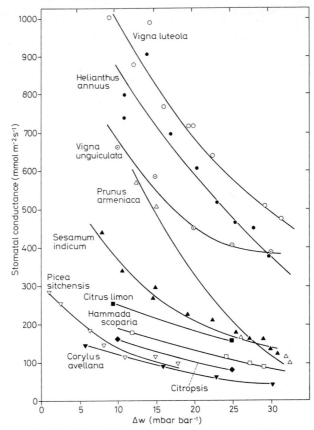

Fig. 7.9. Stomatal conductance as related to the relative leaf/air vapor pressure difference, Δw, with constant leaf temperature and radiation, *Hammada scoparia* (rates related to total surface area of the round twigs), *Helianthus annuus, Prunus armeniaca, Sesamum indicum, Vigna luteola:* after HALL et al. (1976), *Corylus avellana:* SCHULZE and KÜPPERS (1979), *Citrus limon, Citropsis gabunensis:* KHAIRI and HALL (1976b), *Picea sitchensis:* JARVIS (1980), *Vigna unguiculata:* HALL and SCHULZE (1980a)

conductance increases with temperature at temperatures above the optimum for photosynthesis (HALL et al. 1976).

Transpiration influences leaf energy balance; in plants adequately supplied with water, stomata may regulate temperature, either maintaining leaf temperature near the optimum for processes such as photosynthesis, or preventing high temperatures that would result in tissue necrosis.

7.3.3 The Balance Between Water Loss and Assimilation

A comprehensive and elegant hypothesis for the regulation of leaf conductance within the operational range has been developed by COWAN (1977) and COWAN and FARQUHAR (1977). Detailed discussions of this hypothesis have been pre-

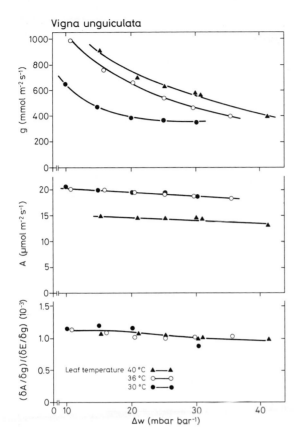

Fig. 7.10. Leaf conductance to water vapor, g, CO_2 assimilation, A, and the ratio for the sensitivity of assimilation and transpiration to changes in leaf conductance, $(\partial A/\partial g)/(\partial E/\partial g)$, as related to changes in relative leaf/air vapor pressure difference. The experiment was conducted with step decreases in humidity at three constant leaf temperatures on 3 days with the same attached leaflet and photon flux of 900 μmol m^{-2} s^{-1}, and external CO_2 relative partial pressure of 300 ± 5 μbar bar^{-1}. (After Hall and Schulze 1980a)

sented in Chapter 17, this Volume (see also Chap. 1, this Vol.). However, some discussion is warranted in this chapter because this hypothesis integrates stomatal effects on energy balance and the transport of H_2O and CO_2 between leaf and air.

If daily CO_2 assimilation is to be maximized at a given level of daily transpiration, stomatal conductance should vary during the day in a manner which keeps the gain ratio $\frac{\partial A}{\partial g} / \frac{\partial E}{\partial g}$ constant. These partial differentials describe the sensitivity of CO_2 assimilation rate (A) and transpiration rate (E) to changes in leaf conductance (g). Recent studies under steady-state conditions in controlled environments demonstrated that stomatal responses to humidity (Farquhar et al. 1980), and to humidity and temperature (Hall and Schulze 1980a) resulted in relatively constant gain ratios. The constancy of the gain ratio with different temperatures was quite remarkable (Fig. 7.10, also see Table 1 in Hall and Schulze 1980a). It is of interest to determine how well these data fit alternative hypotheses for stomatal function. Farquhar et al. (1980) demonstrated that their data for stomatal response to humidity by *Nicotiana glauca* did not exhibit sufficient feedback control of plant water relations to keep transpiration constant nor sufficient feedback control of internal CO_2 concentra-

Fig. 7.11. The ratio for the sensitivity of transpiration and assimilation to changes in leaf conductance, $\partial E/\partial A$, the rate of transpiration, E, and the intercellular mole fraction of CO_2, c_i, as related to the relative leaf/air vapor pressure difference, Δw. The *circles* represent the measured data. The relationships represented by the various lines were derived assuming constant $\partial E/\partial A$ (1,200 mol H_2O mol^{-1} CO_2 *drawn line*), constant E (2.36 mmol m^{-2} s^{-1} *dotted line*), and constant c_i (231 µbar bar^{-1} *dashed line*). (After FARQUHAR et al. 1980)

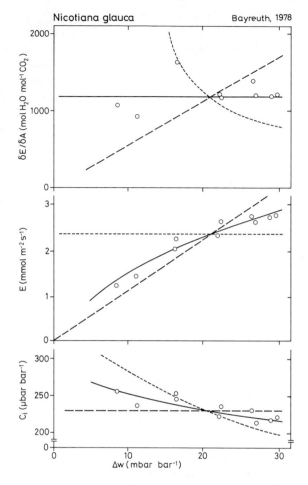

Nicotiana glauca   Bayreuth, 1978

tion to keep CO_2 assimilation rate constant (Fig. 7.11). The data in Fig. 7.10 are consistent with partial regulation of leaf temperature by stomata; but this is, also, an integral part of the hypothesis that $\partial A/\partial E$ is kept constant with diurnal variations in air temperature and humidity. At this time, it is not known how $\partial A/\partial E$ is influenced by short-term variations in photon flux or by the multiple variations in environment that occur during the day in natural conditions. If the daily assimilation of canopies is to be maximized at a given level of daily transpiration, all leaves must exhibit the same constant gain ratio during the day (COWAN and FARQUHAR 1977). The predictions of the model of FARQUHAR (1978a) may be interpreted as indicating that, where g (at A_{max}) and A_{max} vary in a proportional manner, $\partial A/\partial E$ may be relatively constant. This indicates that the long-term effects of radiation and mineral nutrition during leaf growth and of leaf age may result in only small variations in $\partial A/\partial E$ within the canopy (except where short-term variations in photon flux cause g and A to vary in a nonproportional manner). Higher values of $\partial A/\partial E$ are generally to be expected where the slope of g (at A_{max}) versus A_{max} is smaller.

Smaller slopes have been observed for C_4 versus C_3 species (Figs. 7.2, 7.3, and 7.4) and for some C_3 species which have been subjected to drought (Hall and Schulze 1980a and Fig. 7.16 in Sect. 7.4). In addition, correlation coefficients closer to one, for g (at A_{max}) versus A_{max}, may indicate more precise regulation of $\partial A/\partial E$. It is apparent that data concerning relationships between the ranges of leaf conductance and photosynthetic capacity may provide an approach toward defining the optimality of stomatal function, which may allow comparisons between species in different environments at a more general level than was previously possible.

7.4 Stomatal Responses and Plant Water Status

Leaf conductance responds to changes in plant water status but it also influences leaf water potential through effects on transpiration. Under natural conditions the effect of leaf conductance on transpiration and leaf water potential can often be detected. However, it is usually difficult to separate the effects on stomata of changes in plant water status from effects due to changing atmospheric conditions.

7.4.1 Leaf Conductance and the Control of Water Loss and Plant Water Status

The flow of water through the soil-plant-atmosphere continuum has been described as being proportional to the water potential gradient, and inversely proportional to the resistance to flow imposed by the soil, roots, vascular system, leaves, and canopy (Cowan and Milthorpe 1968; Cowan 1965; see Chap. 1, this Vol.). However, it can be demonstrated that this model is only approximately valid and it is not consistent with some experimental observations (Chap. 8, this Vol.).

The dominant resistance to flow is in the vapor phase. Consequently, leaf water potential should be regarded as the dependent variable, responding to changes in the flow rate of water (as determined by atmospheric conditions and leaf and canopy resistance), and upon the resistance to flow of liquid water in the soil plant system (Cowan and Milthorpe 1968; Elfving et al. 1972; Kaufmann 1976). When the flux of water through plants is much greater than the rate of change in plant water content, it is possible to describe diurnal changes in leaf water potential and water flux by a sequence of steady states even under variable natural conditions (Cowan 1965).

A schematic description of possible short-term and long-term relations between leaf water potential, Ψ, and transpiration, E, is presented in Fig. 7.12a. When transpiration rates are low, such as during the night, leaf water potentials approach a maximum value which is related to the soil water potential in the root zone. Leaf water potential usually decreases after sunrise and approaches

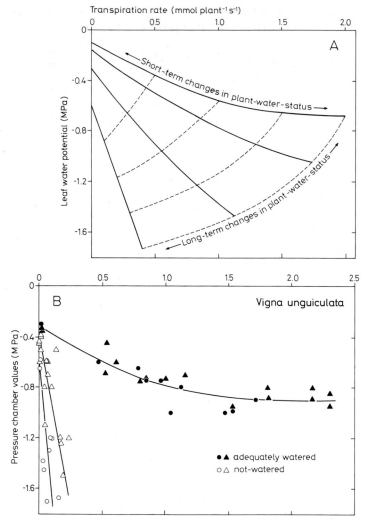

Fig. 7.12. A Schematic representation of short-term and long-term relations between leaf water potential and transpiration under different equal increments of evaporative demand. **B** Xylem pressure potential as a function of transpiration per plant of *Vigna unguiculata* in controlled environments. The plants in the dry treatments had not been supplied with water for 25 days, whereas the other plants had been irrigated on the evening prior to the day on which measurements were made. (After HALL and SCHULZE 1980b)

a minimum value at the time of maximum transpiration. In Fig. 7.12A this change of Ψ by variations in E is referred to as "short-term changes in plant-water-status". The plant may operate at different slopes for these short-term changes in plant-water-status depending on the conductance in the pathway of water from the soil into the leaf. Soil drought results in both a decrease in pre-dawn leaf water potential and increases in resistances to flow in the soil and plant (see Chaps. 1 and 3, this Vol.). In addition, other factors such

as dying of root tips, hardwood formation, or cavitation of xylem vessels will decrease the conductance of the pathway of water from the soil into the leaf (see Chap. 5, this Vol.). Only some of these factors, e.g., the flow of water from the surroundings of the root tip may be reversible in the short term. In Fig. 7.12A those factors which change the slope of the Ψ/E relationship are referred to as "long-term changes in plant-water status". The dependence of Ψ on changes in E has provided explanations for diurnal and seasonal variations in leaf water potential (ELFVING et al. 1972; KAUFMANN 1976; KAPPEN et al. 1975), and descriptions of species differences in the efficiency of the water transport system from soil to leaves (CAMACHO-B et al. 1974). This conceptual model demonstrates that the same level of leaf water potential may occur in dry and in well-watered plants but at different levels of transpirational water loss. However, plants subjected to drying soils usually exhibit lower leaf water potentials than well-watered, but genetically similar plants.

Substantial differences have been observed among plants in the extent to which leaf water potential decreases when plants are subjected to short-term changes in atmospheric conditions (e.g., CAMACHO-B et al. 1974; SÁNCHEZ-DÍAZ and MOONEY 1979; LUDLOW 1980). Several woody species have exhibited larger changes in leaf water potential with variations in atmospheric conditions than herbaceous species, possibly due to differences in resistances to flow within the conducting system between soil and leaves.

Seasonal changes in leaf water potential resulting from changes in soil water status have often been greater for xerophytes and woody species than for herbaceous mesophytes. Some herbaceous legumes and succulents have exhibited extremely small changes in leaf water potential under long-term drought. Differences between plants in leaf water potential under long-term drought are mainly due to differences in rooting density and depth and in the regulation of transpiration at the stomata and canopy level. Transpiration rates of the whole plant determine both the rapidity and extent to which soil water is depleted in the root zone, and the extent to which leaf water potential decreases during the day. The strong influence of the regulation of transpiration on the leaf water status of *Vigna unguiculata* is shown in Fig. 7.12B for both adequate soil water and soil drought. In this example, the differences in transpiration rates were due to differences in leaf area, leaf orientation, and average leaf conductance (HALL and SCHULZE 1980b).

In the schematic description of possible relations between leaf water potential and transpiration (Fig. 7.12A), the maximal transpiration rate which can be achieved in an individual plant is described as decreasing with long-term drought, and this is clearly apparent in Fig. 7.12B. Possible mechanisms for the relationship between stomatal conductance and plant water status are examined in the next section.

7.4.2 Effects of Short-Term and Long-Term Changes in Plant Water Status on Leaf Conductance and CO_2 Assimilation

When plants are subjected to constant atmospheric conditions and soil water is not replenished, plant water deficits develop and leaf conductance decreases.

However, the relationship between stomatal conductance and plant water deficits is not simple.

STÅLFELT (1929) described leaves as a hydraulic feedback system in which turgor pressure changes occur in guard cells and subsidiary cells, due to passive and active processes, and cause stomatal responses. This hypothesis is consistent with the transient stomatal opening and subsequent closing when leaves are excised, and the dynamic stomatal responses described for excised leaves by RASCHKE (1970), who proposed for these conditions that "stomatal aperture is controlled by the water potential in the water conducting system". Close coupling of stomatal aperture with leaf water potential is also apparent with intact plants during stomatal oscillations (COWAN 1972). In most studies with intact plants, however, close coupling between stomatal conductance and leaf water potential has not been observed.

In natural environments leaf water potential, temperature, and ambient humidity change in synchrony and it is not known which of these factors is responsible for the changes in stomatal conductance that also occur. SCHULZE and KÜPPERS (1979) separated these factors using a system in which attached leaves were maintained in constant temperature and humidity, while plant water potential was varied by changing the evaporative demand on the remaining part of the shoot. They established for adequately watered plants and for plants subjected to soil drought, that for *Corylus avellana* the changes in leaf water potential which occur in the natural environment (up to 8 bar) would have negligible influence on stomatal conductance of this plant even at -24 bar total water potential.

It has also been proposed that insensitivity to changes in leaf water potential only occurs up to a threshold level, beyond which stomata abruptly close (TURNER 1974; LUDLOW 1980). Threshold responses have been observed when the water supply to the leaves has been drastically changed by excision or by manipulating the root environment in an artificial manner (HALL and HOFFMAN 1976). Evidence for threshold responses under natural conditions is not strong. It is of two types. Firstly, correlations have been made between leaf resistance (mainly measured with transit-time porometers) and leaf water potential using data obtained during diurnal courses. These correlations may also be explained by reduced humidity causing both partial stomatal closure and decreases in leaf water potential (through effects on transpiration, see Fig. 7.12). Furthermore, when data are expressed as resistance rather than conductance a linear relation may appear curvilinear. Secondly, correlations have been made between leaf conductance and leaf water potential using the day-to-day changes in values which occur during a drying cycle. Some examples are presented in Fig. 7.13, and the correlations indicate progressive changes in leaf conductance over a range leaf water potentials. For example, leaf conductance of *Glycine max* decreased rapidly when leaf water potential was between -15 and -16 bar. However, these data were obtained at midday on different days, and diurnal courses for the same days show that the response was not a simple and direct reaction to changes in water potential. The diurnal courses of leaf conductance and leaf water potential of *Glycine max* on the 13th and 33rd days after irrigation are presented in Fig. 7.14. On both days leaf conductance

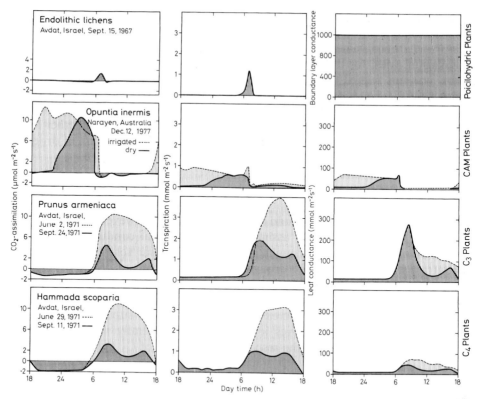

Fig. 7.17. Diurnal courses (dark and light shaded areas) of CO_2 assimilation, transpiration, and leaf or boundary layer conductance in different plant types in a desert environment: Poikilohydric plants (endolithic lichens: Lange et al. 1970b), CAM plants (*Opuntia inermis*: Osmond et al. 1979), C_3 plants (*Prunus armeniaca*: Schulze et al. 1980a, 1974, 1975), C_4 plants (*Hammada scoparia* with rates related to total surface area of the round assimilating leafless twigs: Schulze et al. 1980a; Kappen et al. 1976, and original data of the Israel 1971 investigation of O.L. Lange)

(Fig. 7.17). Many arid regions are characterized by the presence of poikilohydric lichens. Their water relations are completely different from homoiohydric plants since they have no stomata. Without regulation, water status is governed by the humidity of the surrounding air and by the boundary layer. In a dynamic equilibrium with their surrounding, lichens gain water at night with humid air and dew fall (see Chap. 4, this Vol.). This activates respiration at night and allows a short period of CO_2 uptake in the morning before the thallus dries out again due to evaporative water loss (Lange et al. 1970a, b). Water uptake from the atmosphere is generally restricted to poikilohydric plants, since the cuticle of homoiohydric plants which is effective in restricting water loss is also an effective barrier for water uptake. Hydration of vascular plants by dew may occur to a small extent, and it is still a controversial topic (e.g., Slatyer 1956; Kerr and Beardsell 1975), as discussed in Chapter 4, this Volume.

Different patterns of CO_2 and water vapor exchange are exhibited by succulents during Crassulacean acid metabolism (Chap. 15, this Vol.). CO_2 uptake occurs at night through open stomata when air humidity is high and the transpiration rate is low. During the day stomata are fully closed and transpiration is very low even though evaporative demands may be high. The result is a high intrinsic water use efficiency. Leaf conductance of CAM plants appears to be partially controlled at night by stomatal response to humidity (OSMOND et al. 1979; LANGE and MEDINA 1979). The rate of CO_2 exchange of CAM plants is highly dependent on night-time temperatures and on the water status of the plant (LANGE et al. 1975; VON WILLERT et al. 1980). CAM plants exhibit changes in the pattern of CO_2 uptake from day-time CO_2 uptake, to night-time CO_2 uptake, and even to internal recycling of CO_2 when stomata are permanently closed (SZAREK and TING 1974).

Figure 7.17 gives examples of one-peaked and two-peaked daily courses of CO_2 and water vapor exchange and leaf conductance for C_3 and C_4 plants as they have been observed depending on environmental conditions and on the long-term effects of drought. It should be made clear, however, that a distinction of various types of daily patterns is convenient, but that all these patterns are part of a continuum, in which gas exchange depends on a considerable number of factors.

One-peaked daily courses of C_3 and C_4 plants with high rates of CO_2 and water vapor exchange are frequently observed with well-watered plants. One-peaked diurnal courses of leaf conductance were found in *Phragmites communis,* growing in a moist habitat but under extremely high evaporative demands, and leaf temperatures were up to 8 °C below ambient air temperatures due to transpirational cooling (PEARCY et al. 1974a). Irrigated *Tidestromia oblongifolia* maintained one-peaked daily courses of CO_2 uptake even at temperatures close to 50 °C (BJÖRKMAN et al. 1972b). However, other species may show irregular one-peaked patterns even when adequately irrigated. *Prunus armeniaca* (Fig. 7.17) showed greater stomatal opening in the morning and a steady decline during the day. The pattern of CO_2 and water vapor exchange varies with increases in atmospheric and soil drought. But it appears that C_4 plants, e.g., *Hammada scoparia,* may maintain one-peaked courses of gas exchange under more extreme conditions of atmospheric and soil drought than C_3 plants growing in the same habitat, e.g., *Zygophyllum dumosum* or *Artemisia herba-alba* (SCHULZE et al. 1980b).

Plants sometimes exhibit one-peaked patterns of gas exchange at very low rates of CO_2 uptake and water vapor loss as a result of long-term drought (STOCKER 1956). *Atriplex hymenelytra* maintained daily leaf conductance and CO_2 uptake at almost constant but low levels in the dry season (PEARCY et al. 1974b). With more extreme conditions of soil drought a short morning peak of CO_2 uptake was observed followed by CO_2 losses in the light (SCHULZE et al. 1980). In this case transpiration rate was low and mainly due to cuticular water loss. Under natural environmental conditions one-peaked patterns of A at low rates of CO_2 uptake may be due to high day-time temperatures, and leaf conductance may be low due to the effects of low air humidity in addition to severe soil water stress. But even under conditions of constant

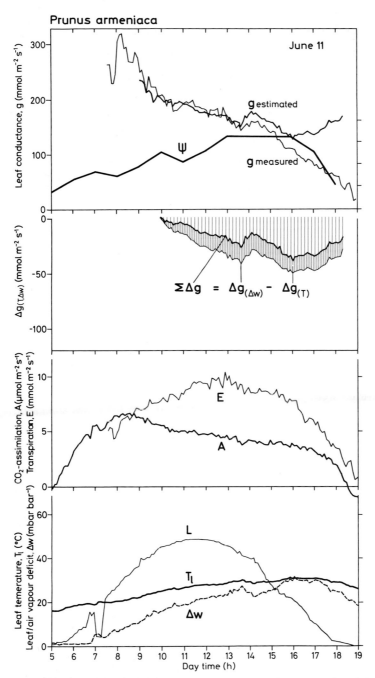

Fig. 7.18. Diurnal courses of leaf water potential (Ψ), measured and predicted leaf conductance for water vapor, g, change in leaf conductance caused by changes in the leaf/air vapor pressure concentration difference ($\Delta g_{(\Delta w)}$), change in leaf conductance caused by changes in leaf temperature ($\Delta g_{(T)}$), total change in leaf conductance caused by changes in humidity and leaf temperature ($\Sigma \Delta g$), CO_2 assimilation, A, transpiration, E, leaf tempera-

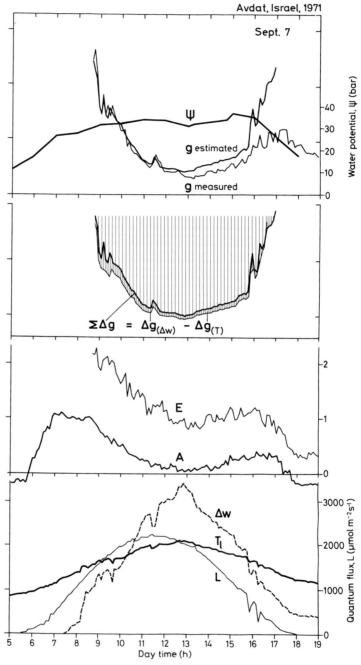

ture, T_l, leaf/air vapor concentration difference, Δw, and quantum flux, L. The changes in leaf conductance with temperature and humidity were calculated from independent steady-state experiments with only one factor variable. The calculations are based on the measured early morning leaf conductance and the measured changes in temperature and humidity from that time on. (After SCHULZE et al. 1972, 1973, 1974, 1975)

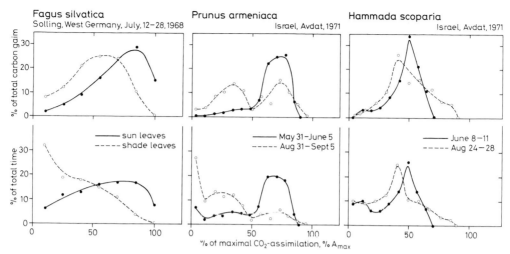

Fig. 7.26. The relative proportions of the total carbon gain which are assimilated at various rates of CO_2 assimilation, and the relative portion of the total daytime during which certain rates of assimilation were observed under natural conditions of *Fagus silvatica* sun and shade leaves, and *Prunus armeniaca* and *Hammada scoparia* leaves early and late in the dry season

the time of light saturation, but light was below saturation only during 30%–40% of the time for C_3 plants and 46%–50% for C_4 plants (Table 7.1).

Using an empirical model of CO_2 assimilation (Schulze et al. 1976), calculations were made keeping either light, temperature, or humidity at optimal levels throughout the daylight time while varying all the other factors as they occur in the natural environment. Thus interpolations were made between $\bar{A}$ and A_{max} for conditions which were partially optimal. In all simulations the effects of light, humidity, and temperature explained more than 90% of the measured variation in A. In *Fagus silvatica* light appears to be the single dominant factor reducing the rate of A below A_{max} in the natural environment. The conditions were similar for *Picea abies* (Fuchs et al. 1977) and for herbaceous plants on the forest floor (Schulze 1972b). It would be interesting to know the extent to which a high rate of A_{max} is adaptive in conditions of low average irradiance, recognizing the investment cost for maintaining a high level of A_{max}. Figure 7.26 shows that a relatively large proportion of carbon gain was assimilated during the short period of light saturation in sun leaves of *Fagus silvatica*. Therefore CO_2 uptake at A_{max} significantly contributed to the carbon balance. In contrast, however, in shade leaves the contribution of CO_2 assimilation rates at A_{max} to the daily carbon gain was negligible. Experiments with *Larix decidua* and various broad-leaved shrubs, such as *Acer, Crataegus,* and *Rosa* indicate that the results of *Fagus* may be representative for the temperate region.

In arid regions, the effect of nonsaturated light was predicted as being low but the effects of temperature (too cool or too hot for *Prunus* and too cool for *Hammada,* Lange et al. 1978) and air humidity were substantial (Table 7.1). For *Prunus armeniaca* the effect of air humidity was dominant, demonstrat-

ing the limitations to CO_2 assimilation of this species in a desert environment, where it can exist only under conditions of run-off farming (EVENARI et al. 1977). It is obvious from Fig. 7.26 for *Prunus armeniaca* that a relatively large proportion of the total carbon gain was assimilated during the cool and humid morning hours at low light at 75% of A_{max}. A second large proportion of the total carbon gain was assimilated at 25% of A_{max} during the time of stomatal closure at noon. This is in contrast to the desert species *Hammada scoparia* in which the largest portion of total carbon gain was assimilated at 50% of A_{max} and the short periods which allowed higher rates of CO_2 uptake did not contribute significantly to the carbon balance.

7.6 Conclusions

The environmental and plant factors that influence the range of stomatal conductance were examined. Linear correlations were apparent between maximal CO_2 assimilation rates (A_{max} was determined at optimal temperature, light and humidity, and natural concentrations of CO_2 and O_2), and concurrent levels of leaf conductance (g), as they both varied due to long-term effects of light, mineral nutrition, and leaf age. In some cases, however, g (at A_{max}) was not correlated with A_{max}; and it is likely that the linear correlations were not due to a close physiological coupling of these plant parameters. For C_3 species, the correlation is not simply due to environmental influences on g which, in turn, influence A through effects on the diffusion of CO_2 into leaves. Apparently, the range of stomatal conductance varies such that it matches the photosynthetic capacity as it is determined by the long-term effects of several environmental and plant factors.

The linear regression of g (at A_{max}) versus A_{max} was relatively constant for plants from the same species but varied among and between C_3 and C_4 plants from different species. Smaller regression slopes, indicating higher intrinsic water use efficiency, were apparent in C_4 species and some C_3 species that are adapted to more arid habitats.

The regulation of leaf conductance and CO_2 assimilation rate within the operational range is strongly dependent upon the short-term responses of stomata to light, humidity, and temperature. Stomatal responses to light may result from indirect effects of light on CO_2 assimilation rate which operate via stomatal response to internal CO_2 concentration or some product of CO_2 assimilation in the mesophyll tissue, or direct effects of light on guard cell metabolism. Stomatal response to internal CO_2 concentration is substantial in some C_4 species, whereas stomatal response to light by some C_3 species cannot be explained by their responses to internal CO_2 concentration.

Leaf conductance response to humidity is present in many species with contrasting adaptation, including species from humid habitats. Increases in temperature result in increases in leaf conductance over a substantial range of temperatures when the vapor pressure difference between leaf and air is kept constant. Evidence has been obtained which indicates that stomatal responses

to humidity and temperature may maximize daily water use efficiency as described by the optimization hypothesis of Cowan and Farquhar (1977). This
approach for defining and analyzing optimal function has general applicability
to many plant processes and should provide a useful conceptual base for future
research.

The effect of water stress is complicated by the interaction of effects of
transpiration on plant water potential due to stomatal opening and air humidity
and effects of plant water status on leaf conductance. It is useful from a conceptual and an experimental standpoint to separate the long-term and short-term
effects of plant water status on stomatal function. Evidence for the occurrence
of short-term effects under natural conditions is controversial. It is suggested
that stomata of intact plants, under natural conditions frequently do not respond
to changes in bulk leaf water status in either a coupled or a threshold manner
even with extreme soil drought. However, leaf water potential is strongly dependent upon the transpiration rate. The sensitivity with which leaf water potential
changes with transpiration is affected by resistances to liquid water flow from
the soil to the leaf, and is strongly influenced by water depletion in the root
zone. Long-term effects of water stress determine the maximum capacity of
the stomata to open and the sensitivity of their responses to atmospheric conditions, and this appears to be associated with long-term effects of drought on
the stomata themselves and possibly long-term effects of drought on the capacity
of the leaf for fixing CO_2. The relation between g (at A_{max}) and A_{max} during
water stress was not linear for some C_3 plants. This indicated that the effect
of long-term water stress on stomata was greater than on CO_2 assimilation.
Separate studies indicate that maximal leaf conductance was correlated with
pre-dawn leaf water potentials, whereas CO_2 assimilation was correlated with
the drought experience as expressed by cumulative pre-dawn water potentials.
The differential response of g and A causes a rotation of the g/A_{max} regression,
indicating greater intrinsic water use efficiency with progressive depletion of
soil water.

Although mechanisms of plant responses have been studied successfully in
the laboratory, the integrated effect of habitat conditions and the species-specific
adaptations of plants to certain environments can only be studied under natural
conditions. The diurnal courses of CO_2 assimilation rate and water vapor exchange provide fundamental information on plant responses and adaptations
to natural environments. But it is difficult to determine the mechanisms responsible for diurnal courses if several environmental factors change simultaneously.
In this case an interpretation appears to be only possible if measurements
under naturally variable conditions are supplemented by field experiments where
individual environmental factors are changed. The diurnal courses of CO_2 assimilation and leaf conductance describe the short-term effects of mainly atmospheric conditions on A and g within their operational range. The operational ranges
reflect the long-term effects of habitat conditions during growth. In humid
and arid, as well as in hot and cold climates, daily changes of stomatal response
and CO_2 assimilation appear to be closely associated with short-term changes
in light, humidity, and temperature. Even on the forest floor of a rain forest,
plants appear to adjust stomatal aperture at a level which is related to the

rate of CO_2 uptake. But this short-term relation is not unique, e.g., during the morning hours of a desert environment, or during light saturation with humid air in a temperate climate, g might increase more than the short-term association between A and g would suggest. Air humidity appears to be the next most important atmospheric parameter in humid, arid, and arctic environments, whereas some plants appear to be quite well adapted to the temperature regimes of their habitats. At the present time, the effects of plant water status during diurnal courses appear not to be adequately understood. A continual decrease of leaf conductance during the day, which was observed not only in diurnal courses at low rates of CO_2 and water vapor exchange, but also under constant environmental conditions, may be related to long-term effects of drought, which may partially operate through changes in the root which cause concurrent changes in photosynthetic capacity and leaf conductance.

During short-term changes in environment the association between A and g is modified by differential effects of light, humidity, and temperature on CO_2 uptake and leaf conductance. Average daily rates of CO_2 uptake were related to A_{max} for three species from humid temperate and arid regions. Ecologically it seems important that the highest rates of CO_2 assimilation which were measured under natural weather conditions were 15% to 40% below A_{max} in arid regions. The photon flux was too low in the morning and later in the day the air was too dry for maximal CO_2 uptake. The daily average rate of CO_2 assimilation was only 32% to 68% of A_{max} in humid temperate and arid regions. But the reasons for the depression of A below A_{max} were different for humid and arid environments. More than 95% of the depression was due to non-saturated light in the humid temperate region, whereas air humidity (39–63% of the depression) followed by light (15–42% of the depression) were the most significant factors in arid climates. Ecologically, it is not clear to what extent a higher rate of A_{max} is adaptive, when A is more than 50% below A_{max} recognizing the high investment costs of maintaining a high level of A_{max}.

It is quite obvious that the foregoing discussion on plant responses in contrasting environments is based on a relatively small number of species which have been studied thoroughly. Understanding plant adaptation to contrasting environments will require information on mechanisms obtained in the laboratory and in the field and descriptions of the responses of plants under natural conditions. A more balanced approach appears to be essential in future research. The large number of response curves for single variables, which have been obtained in laboratories, have not been adequately complemented by studies of plant responses under naturally varying conditions in the field, not even for agricultural plants. For understanding stomatal function and regulation it appears necessary to study the concomitant variations of leaf conductance and CO_2 assimilation rate. Investigations on plant responses under natural conditions should be given priority in which measurements are made of diurnal courses of CO_2 and water vapor exchange under naturally varying weather but over prolonged periods of time, as well as of response curves of single variables under experimentally controlled constant conditions in the field. In these latter experiments A_{max} and g (at A_{max}) should be determined. The extent

to which the daily average rates of CO_2 assimilation and leaf conductance fall below their maximal levels appear to provide quantitative information on the adaptation of plants in natural habitats, and on the factors which have a major influence on the performance of plants in contrasting environments.

Acknowledgements. The work was supported by the Deutsche Forschungsgemeinschaft SFB 137. We thank Prof. Dr. I.R. Cowan for reviewing the manuscript.

References

Allaway WG, Milthorpe FL (1976) Structure and functioning of stomata. In: Kozlowski TT (ed) Water deficits and plant growth Vol IV. Academic Press, London New York, pp 57–102

Bates LM, Hall AE (1981) Stomatal closure with soilwater depletion not associated with changes in bulk leaf water status. Oecologia 50:62–65

Bauer H (1978) Photosynthesis of ivy leaves (*Hedera helix*) after heat stress. I. CO_2 gas exchange and diffusion resistance. Physiol Plant 44:400–406

Benecke U (1980) Photosynthesis and transpiration of *Pinus radiata* D. Don under natural conditions in a forest stand. Oecologia 44:192–198

Benecke U, Havranek W, McCracken I (1976) Comparative study of water use by tree species in a mountain environment. Proc Soil Plant Water Symp, Palmerston North

Benecke U, Schulze E-D, Matyssek R, Havranek M (1981) Environmental control of CO_2 assimilation and leaf conductance in *Larix decidua* Mill. I. A comparison of contrasting natural environments. Oecologia 50:54–61

Bennett KJ, Rook DA (1978) Stomatal and mesophyll resistances in two clones of *Pinus radiata* D. Don known to differ in transpiration and survival rate. Aust J Plant Physiol 5:231–238

Björkman O (1968) Further studies on differentiation of photosynthetic properties in sun and shade ecotypes of *Solidago virgaurea*. Physiol Plant 21:84–99

Björkman O (1973) Comparative studies in photosynthesis in higher plants. In: Giese A (edd) Current topics in photobiology and photochemistry, Vol VIII. Academic Press, London New York, pp 1–63

Björkman O, Ludlow MM, Morrow PA (1972a) Photosynthetic performance of two rainforest species in their native habitat and analysis of their gas exchange. Carnegie Inst Washington Yearb 71/72:94–102

Björkman O, Pearcy RW, Harrison AT, Mooney HA (1972b) Photosynthetic adaptation to high temperatures: a field study in Death Valley, Calif. Science 175:786–789

Burrows FJ, Milthorpe FL (1976) Stomatal conductance in the control of gas exchange. In: Kozlowski TT (ed) Water deficits and plant growth, vol IV. Academic Press, London New York, pp 103–152

Caldwell MM, Johnson DA, Fareed M (1978) Constraints on tundra productivity: photosynthetic capacity in relation to solar radiation utilization and water stress in arctic and alpine tundras. In: Tieszen LL (ed) Vegetation and production ecology of an Alaskan arctic tundra. Ecol Stud, Vol 29. Springer, Berlin Heidelberg New York, pp 323–342

Camacho-B SE, Hall AE, Kaufmann MR (1974) Efficiency and regulation of water transport in some woody and herbaceous species. Plant Physiol 54:169–172

Collatz J, Ferrar PJ, Slatyer RO (1976) Effects of water stress and differential hardening treatments on photosynthetic characteristics of a xeromorphic shrub, *Eucalyptus socialis* F. Muell. Oecologia 23:95–105

Connor DJ, Tunstall BR, Driessche Van den (1971) An analysis of photosynthetic response in a Brigalow forest. Photosynthetica 5:218–225

Cowan IR (1965) Transport of water in the soil-plant-atmosphere system. J Appl Ecol 2:221–239

Cowan IR (1972) Oscillations in stomatal conductance and plant functioning associated with stomatal conductance: Observations and a model. Planta 106:185–219

Cowan IR (1977) Stomatal behaviour and environment. Adv Bot Res 4:117–228

Cowan IR, Farquhar GD (1977) Stomatal function in relation to leaf metabolism and environment. In: Integration of activity in the higher plant. Soc Exp Biol Symp 31. Univ Press, Cambridge, pp 471–505

Cowan IR, Milthorpe FL (1968) Plant factors influencing the water status of plant tissues. In: Kozlowski TT (ed) Water deficits and plant growth Vol I. Academic Press, London New York, pp 137–193

Davies WJ, Kozlowski TT (1977) Variations among woody plants in stomatal conductance and photosynthesis during and after drought. Plant Soil 46:435–444

Davis SD, McCree KJ (1978) Photosynthetic rate and diffusion conductance as a function of age in leaves of bean plants. Crop Sci 18:280–282

De Puit EJ, Caldwell MM (1973) Seasonal pattern of net photosynthesis of *Artemisia tridentata*. Am J Bot 60:426–435

Doley D, Trivett NBA (1974) Effects of low water potentials on transpiration and photosynthesis in Mitchell Grass (*Astrebla lappacea*) Aust J Plant Physiol 1:539–550

Downes RW (1971) Relationship between evolutionary adaptation and gas exchange characteristics of diverse sorghum taxa. Aust J Biol Sci 24:843–852

Drake BG, Raschke K, Salisbury FB (1970) Temperatures and transpiration resistance of *Xanthium* leaves as affected by air temperature, humidity and wind speed. Plant Physiol 46:324–330

Ehleringer JR, Miller PC (1975) Water relations of selected plant species in the alpine tundra, Colorado. Ecology 56:370–380

Ehleringer JR, Mooney HA (1978) Leaf hairs: effects on physiological activity and adaptive value to a desert shrub. Oecologia 37:183–201

Ehleringer JR, Björkman O, Mooney HA (1976) Leaf pubescence: Effects on absorptance and photosynthesis in a desert shrub. Science 192:376–377

Elfving DC, Kaufmann MR, Hall AE (1972) Interpreting leaf water potential measurements with a model of the soil plant atmosphere continuum. Physiol Plant 27:161–168

Evenari M, Lange OL, Schulze E-D, Kappen L, Buschbom U (1977) Net photosynthesis, dry matter production and phenological development of apricot trees (*Prunus armeniaca* L.) cultivated in the Negev highlands (Israel). Flora 166:383–414

Farquhar GD (1978a) Carbon assimilation in relation to transpiration and fluxes of ammonia. In: Marcelle R (ed) Internal control of photosynthesis. Junk, The Hague, pp 321–328

Farquhar GD (1978b) Feedforward responses of stomata to humidity. Aust J Plant Physiol 5:787–800

Farquhar GD, Dubbe DR, Raschke K (1978) Gain of the feedback loop involving carbon dioxide and stomata. Plant Physiol 62:406–412

Farquhar GD, Schulze E-D, Küppers M (1980) Responses to humidity by stomata of *Nicotiana glauca* L. and *Corylus avellana* L. are consistent with the optimization of carbon dioxide uptake with respect to water loss. Aust J Plant Physiol 7:315–327

Fuchs M, Schulze E-D, Fuchs MI (1977) Spatial distribution of photosynthetic capacity and performance in a montane spruce forest of Northern Germany. II. Climatic control of carbon dioxide uptake. Oecologia 29:329–340

Goudriaan J, Keulen van H (1979) The direct and indirect effects of nitrogen shortage on photosynthesis and transpiration in maize and sunflower. Neth J Agric Sci 27:227–234

Goudriaan J, Laar van HH (1978) Relations between leaf resistance, CO_2 concentration and CO_2 assimilation in maize, beans, Lalang grass and sunflower. Photosynthetica 12:241–249

Hall AE, Hoffman GJ (1976) Leaf conductance response to humidity and water transport. Agron J 68:876–881

Hall AE, Kaufmann MR (1975) Stomatal response to environment with *Sesamum indicum* L. Plant Physiol 55:455–459

Hall AE, Loomis RS (1972) An explanation for the difference in photosynthetic capabilities

of healthy and beet yellows virus infected sugar beets (*Beta vulgaris* L.) Plant Physiol 50:576–580

Hall AE, Schulze E-D (1980a) Stomatal responses to environment and a possible interrelation between stomatal effects on transpiration and CO_2 assimilation. Plant Cell Environ 3:467–474

Hall AE, Schulze E-D (1980b) Drought effects on transpiration and leaf water status of cowpea in controlled environments. Aust J Plant Physiol 7:141–147

Hall AE, Hunt WF, Loomis RS (1972) Variations in leaf resistance, net photosynthesis, and tolerance to the beet yellow virus among varieties of sugar beet (*Beta vulgaris* L.) Crop Sci 12:558–561

Hall AE, Schulze E-D, Lange OL (1976) Current perspectives of steady state stomatal responses to environment. In: Lange OL, Kappen L, Schulze E-D (eds) Water and plant life. Ecol Stud Vol 19. Springer, Berlin Heidelberg New York, pp 169–188

Hall AJ, Milthorpe FL (1978) Assimilate source-sink relationships in *Capsicum annuum* L. III. The effects of fruit excision on photosynthesis and leaf and stem carbohydrates. Aust J Plant Physiol 5:1–13

Havranek WM, Benecke U (1978) The influence of soil moisture on water potential, transpiration and photosynthesis of conifer seedlings. Plant Soil 49:91–103

Holmgren P (1968) Leaf factors affecting light saturated photosynthesis in ecotypes of *Solidago virgaurea* from exposed and shaded habitats. Physiol Plant 21:676–698

Jarvis PG (1980) Stomatal response to water stress in conifers. In: Turner NC, Kramer PJ (eds) Adaptation of plants to water and high temperature stress. Wiley and Sons, New York, pp 105–122

Jones MM (1979) Physiological responses of sorghum and sunflower to leaf water deficits. Ph D Thesis, Austr Natl Univ

Jones MM, Rawson HM (1979) Influence of rate of development of leaf water deficits upon photosynthesis, leaf conductance, water use efficiency, and osmotic potential in *Sorghum*. Physiol Plant 45:103–111

Jones MM, Turner NC (1978) Osmotic adjustment in leaves of *Sorghum* in response to water deficits. Plant Physiol 61:122–126

Johnson DA, Caldwell MM (1976) Water potential components, stomatal function, and liquid phase water transport resistances of four arctic and alpine species in relation to moisture stress. Physiol Plant 36:271–278

Johnsson M, Issaias S, Brogårdh T, Johnsson A (1976) Rapid blue-light-induced transpiration response restricted to plants with grass-like stomata. Physiol Plant 36:229–232

Kappen L, Oertli JJ, Lange OL, Schulze E-D, Evenari M, Buschbom U (1975) Seasonal and diurnal courses of water relations of the arido-active plant *Hammada scoparia* in the Negev desert. Oecologia 21:175–192

Kappen L, Lange OL, Schulze E-D, Evenari M, Buschbom U (1976) Distributional pattern of water relations and net photosynthesis of *Hammada scoparia* (Pomel) Iljin in a desert environment. Oecologia 23:323–334

Kaufmann MR (1976) Water transport through plants. Current perspectives. In: Wardlaw IF, Passioura JB (eds) Transport and transfer processes in plants. Academic Press, London New York, pp 313–327

Kerr JP, Beardsell MF (1975) Effect of dew on leaf water potentials and crop resistances in a paspalum pasture. Agron J 67:596–599

Khairi MMA, Hall AE (1976a) Temperature and humidity effects on net photosynthesis and transpiration of *Citrus*. Physiol Plant 36:29–34

Khairi MMA, Hall AE (1976b) Comparative studies of net photosynthesis and transpiration of some *Citrus* species and relatives. Physiol Plant 36:35–39

Körner CH, Scheel JA, Bauer H (1979) Maximum leaf diffusive conductance in vascular plants. Photosynthetica 13:45–82

Lange OL, Medina E (1979) Stomata of the CAM plant *Tillandsia recurvata* respond directly to humidity. Oecologia 40:357–363

Lange OL, Koch W, Schulze E-D (1969) CO_2-Gaswechsel und Wasserhaushalt von Pflanzen in der Negev-Wüste am Ende der Trockenzeit. Ber Dtsch Bot Ges 82:39–61

Lange OL, Schulze E-D, Koch W (1970a) Experimentell-ökologische Untersuchungen an Flechten der Negev-Wüste. CO_2-Gaswechsel und Wasserhaushalt von *Ramalina macifor-mis* (Del.) Bory am natürlichen Standort während der sommerlichen Trockenperiode. Flora 159:38–62

Lange OL, Schulze E-D, Koch W (1970b) Ecophysiological investigations on lichens of the Negev Desert. III. CO_2 gas exchange and water relations of crustose and foliose lichens in their natural habitat during the summer dry period. Flora 159:525–528

Lange OL, Lösch R, Schulze E-D, Kappen L (1971) Responses of stomata to changes in humidity. Planta 100:76–86

Lange OL, Schulze E-D, Kappen L, Evenari M, Buschbom U (1975) CO_2 exchange pattern under natural conditions of *Caralluna negevensis*, a CAM plant of the Negev Desert. Photosynthetica 9:318–326

Lange OL, Schulze E-D, Evenari M, Kappen L, Buschbom U (1978) The temperature-related photosynthetic capacity of plants under desert conditions. III. Ecological signifi-cance of the seasonal change of the photosynthetic response to temperature. Oecologia 34:89–100

Larcher W (1971) Ergebnisse des IBP-Projektes „Zwergstrauchheide Patscherkofel" Sit-zungsberichte Österr Akad Wiss Math Naturwiss K1 Abt I 186:301–371

Larcher W, Moares De JAPV, Bauer H (1981) Adaptive responses of leaf water potential, CO_2 gas exchange and water use efficiency of *Olea europaea* during drying and rewater-ing. Proc Saloniki Symp Productivity of Medit Ecosystems

Lawlor DW (1976) Water stress induced changes in photosynthesis, photorespiration, respi-ration and CO_2 compensation concentration of wheat. Photosynthetica 10:378–387

Lösch R (1980) Stomatal responses to changes in air humidity. In: Sen DN, Chawan DD, Bunsal RP (eds) Structure, function and ecology of stomata. Dehra Dun, pp 189–216

Ludlow MM (1980) Adaptive significance of stomatal responses to water stress. In: Turner NC, Kramer PJ (eds) Adaptation of plants to water and high temperature stress. Wiley and Sons, New York, pp 123–138

Ludlow MM, Jarvis PG (1971) Photosynthesis in sitka spruce (*Picea sitchensis* (Bong) Carr) I. General characteristics. J Appl Ecol 8:925–953

Ludlow MM, Wilson GL (1971) Photosynthesis of tropical pasture plants. I. Illuminance, carbon dioxide concentration, leaf temperature and leaf-air vapour pressure difference. Aust J Biol Sci 24:449–470

Medina E (1972) Photosynthetic capacity and carboxydismutase activity in *Atriplex patula* leaves as determined by nitrogen nutrition and light intensity during growth. In: Forti G, Buron M, Metzner H (eds) Proc 2nd int congr photosynthes res. Junk, The Hague, pp 2527–2536

Miller PC, Stoner MA, Ehleringer JR (1978) Some aspects of water relations of arctic and alpine regions. In: Tieszen LL (ed) Vegetation and production ecology of an Alaskan arctic tundra. Ecol Stud Vol 29. Springer, Berlin Heidelberg New Yrok, pp 343–358

Mooney HA, Ehleringer JR (1978) The carbon gain benefits of solar tracking in a desert annual. Plant Cell Environ 1:307–311

Mooney HA, Harrison AT, Morrow PA (1974) Environmental limitations of photosynthesis on a California evergreen shrub. Oecologia 19:293–301

Mooney HA, Björkman O, Collatz GJ (1976) Photosynthetic acclimation to temperature and water stress in the desert shrub *Larrea divaricata*. Carnegie Inst Washington 76:328–335

Nobel PS (1978) Microhabitat, water relations, and photosynthesis of a desert fern, *Notho-laena parryi*. Oecologia 31:293–309

Osmond CB, Ludlow MM, Davis R, Cowan IR, Powles SB, Winter K (1979) Stomatal responses to humidity in *Opuntia inermis* in relation to control of CO_2 and H_2O exchange patterns. Oecologia 41:65–76

Osonubi O, Davies WJ (1980) The influence of plant water stress on stomatal control of gas exchange at different levels of atmospheric humidity. Oecologia 46:1–6

Pearcy RW, Berry JA, Bartholomew B (1974a) Field photosynthetic performance and leaf temperature of *Phragmites communis* under summer conditions in Death Valley, California. Photosynthetica 8:104–108

Pearcy RW, Harrison AT, Mooney HA, Björkman O (1974b) Seasonal changes in net photosynthesis of *Atriplex hymenelytra* shrubs growing in Death Valley, Calif. Oecologia 17:111–121

Ramos C (1981) Relationship between leaf conductance, CO_2 partial pressure and CO_2 uptake rate in leaves, and a test of a portable instrument for its measurement in the field. Ph D Thesis, Univ Calif Riverside

Raschke K (1970) Stomatal response to pressure changes and interruptions in the water supply of detached leaves of *Zea mays* L. Plant Physiol 45:415–423

Raschke K (1979) Movements of stomata. In: Haupt W, Feinleib ME (eds) Physiology of movements. Encyclopedia of plant physiology new series Vol VII. Springer, Berlin Heidelberg New York, pp 383–441

Raschke K, Hanebuth WF, Farquhar GD (1978) Relationship between stomatal conductance and light intensity in leaves of *Zea mays* L. derived from experiments using the mesophyll as shade. Planta 139:73–78

Rawson HM, Gifford RM, Bremner PM (1976) Carbon dioxide exchange in relation to sink demand in wheat. Planta 132:19–23

Rawson HM, Beeg JE, Woodward RG (1977) The effects of atmospheric humidity on photosynthesis, transpiration and water use efficiency of leaves of several plant species. Planta 134:5–10

Roberts SW, Knoerr KR, Strain BR (1979) Comparative field water relations of four co-occurring tree species. Can J Bot 57:1876–1882

Running SW (1976) Environmental control of leaf water conductance in conifers. Can J For Res 6:104–112

Running SW (1980) Environmental and physiological control of water flux through *Pinus contorta*. Can J For Res 10:82–91

Sánchez-Díaz ÜF, Mooney HA (1979) Resistance to water transfer in desert shrubs native to Death Valley, Calif. Physiol Plant 46:139–146

Schulze E-D (1970) Der CO_2-Gaswechsel der Buche (*Fagus silvatica* L.) in Abhängigkeit von den Klimafaktoren im Freiland. Flora 159:177–232

Schulze E-D (1972a) A new type of climatized gas exchange chamber for net photosynthesis and transpiration measurements in the field. Oecologia 10:243–251

Schulze E-D (1972b) Die Wirkung von Licht und Temperatur auf den CO_2-Gaswechsel verschiedener Lebensformen aus der Krautschicht eines montanen Buchenwaldes. Oecologia 9:235–258

Schulze E-D, Küppers M (1979) Short-term and long-term effects of plant water deficits on stomatal responses to humidity in *Corylus avellana* L. Planta 146:319–326

Schulze E-D, Lange OL, Buschbom U, Kappen L, Evenari M (1972a) Stomatal responses to changes in humidity in plants growing in the desert. Planta 108:259–270

Schulze E-D, Lange OL, Koch W (1972b) Eco-physiological investigations on wild and cultivated plants in the Negev Desert. III. Daily courses of net photosynthesis and transpiration at the end of the dry period. Oecologia 9:317–340

Schulze E-D, Lange OL, Kappen L, Buschbom U, Evenari M (1973) Stomatal responses to changes in temperature at increasing water stress. Planta 110:20–42

Schulze E-D, Lange OL, Evenari M, Kappen L, Buschbom U (1974) The role of air humidity and leaf temperature in controlling stomatal resistance of *Prunus armeniaca* L. under desert conditions. I. A simulation of the daily course of stomatal resistance. Oecologia 17:159–170

Schulze E-D, Lange OL, Kappen L, Evenari M, Buschbom U (1975a) Physiological basis of primary production of perennial higher plants in the Negev desert. In: Cooper JP (ed) Photosynthesis and productivity in different environments, IBP Vol III. Univ Press, Cambridge, pp 107–119

Schulze E-D, Lange OL, Kappen L, Evenari M, Buschbom U (1975b) The role of air humidity and leaf temperature in controlling stomatal resistance of *Prunus armeniaca*

L. under desert conditions. II. The significance of leaf water status and internal carbon dioxide concentration. Oecologia 18:219–233

Schulze E-D, Lange OL, Evenari M, Kappen L, Buschbom U (1976) An empirical model of net photosynthesis for the desert plant *Hammada scoparia* (Pomel) Iljin. I. Description and test of the model. Oecologia 22:355–372

Schulze E-D, Hall AE, Lange OL, Evenari M, Kappen L, Buschbom U (1980a) Long-term effects of drought on wild and cultivated plants in the Negev desert. I. Maximal rates of net photosynthesis. Oecologia 45:11–18

Schulze E-D, Lange OL, Evenari M, Kappen L, Buschbom U (1980b) Long-term effects of drought on wild and cultivated plants in the Negev desert. II. Diurnal patterns of net photosynthesis and daily carbon gain. Oecologia 45:19–25

Shackel KA, Hall AE (1979) Reversible leaflet movements in relation to drought adaptation of cowpea, *Vigna unguiculata* (L.) Walp. Aust J Plant Physiol 6:265–276

Sheriff DM, Meidner H (1975) Water movement into and through *Tradescantia virginiana* L. leaves. J Exp Bot 26:897–902

Sheriff DW (1979) Stomatal aperture and the sensing of the environment by guard cells. Plant Cell Environ 2:15–22

Slatyer RO (1956) Absorption of water from atmospheres of different humidity and its transport through plants. Aust J Biol Sci 9:552–558

Stålfelt MG (1929) Die Abhängigkeit der Spaltöffnungsreaktionen von der Wasserbilanz. Planta 8:287–340

Stocker O (1956) Die Abhängigkeit der Transpiration von den Umweltfaktoren.In: Ruhland W (ed) Encyclopedia of plant physiology Vol III. Springer, Berlin Göttingen Heidelberg, pp 436–488

Szarek SR, Ting IP (1974) Seasonal patterns of acid metabolism and gas exchange in *Opuntia basilaris*. Plant Physiol 54:76–81

Tenhunen JD, Meyer A, Lange OL, Gates DM (1980) Development of a photosynthesis model with emphasis on ecological applications. V. Test of the applicability of a steady state model to description of net photosynthesis of *Prunus armeniaca* under field conditions. Oecologia 45:147–155

Tenhunen JD, Lange OL, Braun M, Meyer A, Lösch R, Pereira JS (1981) Midday stomatal closure in *Arbutus unedo* leaves in a natural macchia and under simulated habitat conditions in an environmental chamber. Oecologia 47:365–367

Thorpe MR, Warrit B, Landsberg JJ (1980) Responses of apple leaf stomata: A model for single leaves and a whole tree. Plant Cell Environ 3:23–28

Tieszen LL (1975) CO_2 exchange in the Alaskan arctic tundra: Seasonal changes in the rate of photosynthesis of four species. Photosynthetica 9:376–390

Tieszen LL (1978) Photosynthesis in the principal Barrow, Alaska, species: A summary of field and laboratory responses. In: Tieszen LL (ed) Vegetation and production ecology of an Alaskan arctic tundra. Ecol Stud Vol 29. Springer, Berlin Heidelberg New York, pp 241–268

Tranquillini W (1957) Standortklima, Wasserbilanz und CO_2-Gaswechsel junger Zirben (*Pinus cembra* L.) an der alpinen Waldgrenze. Planta 49:612–661

Turner NC (1974) Stomatal response to light and water under field conditions. In: Bieleski RL, Ferguson AR, Cresswell MM (eds) Mechanisms of regulation of plant growth. Roy Soc NZ Bull 12:423–432

Turner NC (1979) Drought resistance and adaptation to water deficits in crop plants. In: Mussell H, Staples R (eds) Stress physiology in crop plants. Wiley and Sons, New York, pp 344–372

Turner NC, Begg JE, Rawson HM, English SD, Hearn AB (1978) Agronomic and physiological responses of soybean and sorghum crops to water deficits. III. Components of leaf water potential, leaf conductance, $^{14}CO_2$ photosynthesis, and adaptation to water deficits. Aust J Plant Physiol 5:179–194

Tyree MT, Yianoulis P (1980) The site of water evaporation from substomatal cavities, liquid path resistance and hydroactive stomatal closure. Ann Bot (London) 46:175–193

Vowinkel T, Oechel WC, Boll WG (1975) The effect of climate on the photosynthesis of *Picea mariana* at the subarctic tree line. 1. Field measurements. Can J Bot 53:604–620

Walter H (1968) Die Vegetation der Erde. II. Die gemäßigten und arktischen Zonen. Fischer, Stuttgart

Willert von DJ, Brinckmann E, Scheitler B, Schulze ED, Thomas DA, Treichel S (1980) Ökophysiologische Untersuchungen an Pflanzen der Namib-Wüste. Naturwissenschaften 67:21–28

Wong SC (1979) Stomatal behaviour in relation to photosynthesis. Ph D Thesis, Aust Natl Univ, Canberra

Wong SC, Cowan IR, Farquhar GD (1978) Leaf conductance in relation to assimilation in *Eucalyptus pauciflora* Sieb. ex Spreng: influence of irradiance and partial pressure of carbon dioxide. Plant Physiol 62:670–764

Wong SC, Cowan IR, Farquhar GD (1979) Stomatal conductance correlates with photosynthetic capacity. Nature (London) 282:424–426

Woodward RG, Rawson HM (1976) Photosynthesis and transpiration in dicotyledonous plants. II. Expanding and senescing leaves of soybean. Aust J Plant Physiol 3:257–267

Zobel DB, Liu VT (1980) Effects of environment, seedling age, and seed source on leaf resistance of three species of *Chamaecyparis* and *Tsuga chinensis*. Oecologia 46:412–419

8 Mathematical Models of Plant Water Loss and Plant Water Relations

A.E. HALL

CONTENTS

8.1 Introduction

Quantitative descriptions of the functioning of individual organisms or plant communities in different environments are a major objective of physiological research. Mathematical models of plant water loss and plant water relations represent attempts to quantify these aspects of plant function. In addition, mathematical models can be objective and efficient systems for integrating and summarizing available information, and they are useful for expressing and testing hypotheses. However, the values and limitations of mathematical models of biological systems have been underestimated. The development and use of mathematical models should follow rational guidelines analogous to the conceptual constraints that are widely accepted as being appropriate in experimental studies. Unfortunately, guidelines for the development, evaluation, and use of mathemat-

ical models of ecological systems are only just beginning to emerge. Guidelines will be briefly discussed in the section on objectives and procedures of modeling to illustrate some of the limitations of mathematical models.

In this chapter the physiological and physical concepts on which models of plant water loss may be based will be examined. The transport of water in the soil-plant system is examined mainly in relation to models of water loss. More detailed treatments of water flow in the soil-plant-atmosphere continuum are provided in Chapters 1, 3, and 5, this Volume.

Mathematical models have been described as being mechanistical, phenomenological, or empirical (it should be recognized, however, that a model which is mechanistic at one level of organization, such as the cellular level, is not mechanistic at lower levels of organization, such as the organelle or enzyme levels). The development of phenomenological and empirical models that may be useful for pursuing objectives of physiological ecology will be discussed. Only *deterministic models* are considered. The other type of model, *stochastic,* is used where the objective is to predict the probability of specific outcomes, and where probabilities are assigned to input variables and parameters. The reader is referred to JONES (1980) for a description of a *stochastic model* of water relations, and a discussion of the importance and uses of stochastic modeling. However, few stochastic models of water relations have been developed, and difficult problems arise when attempting to develop stochastic models of biological systems, due to the presence of homeostatic mechanisms (refer to the review by LOOMIS et al. 1979).

This analysis is restricted to homeohydric plants (those having stomata), and does not consider plants having Crassulacean acid metabolism which are discussed in Chapter 15, this Volume. The intent is to provide a conceptual basis for the development of models that reliably predict water loss from plants. Current models are discussed in relation to this objective.

8.1.1 Objectives and Procedures of Modeling

Mathematical models of biological systems are works of art combining both fact and fiction, and they only occasionally and partially simulate reality (PASSIOURA 1973). These models are only gross representations of the elegantly complex systems that are called plants. It would be prudent to assume that we will *never* be able to develop mathematical models that *perfectly* mimic biological systems. *However, it is possible to usefully model, for specific purposes, mental constructs of the subsystems within plants and ecosystems* (LOOMIS et al. 1979, see also the discussion of general questions of modelling in Chap. 4, Vol. 12 D).

Consequently, the mandatory initial step in modeling is to define precisely the objectives of the intended study. As with experimental studies, this frequently involves testing hypotheses. Some examples of objectives of earlier models illustrate the diverse possibilities in modeling plant water relations.

Hypotheses concerning stomatal mechanics have been subjected to considerable analysis using mathematical models (COOKE et al. 1976; DEMICHELE and

SHARPE 1973; SHARPE and WU 1978; SHOEMAKER and SRIVASTAVA 1973) but the complexity of the analyses and paucity of experimental data precluded simple or general interpretation of the results that were obtained. Consequently, including submodels of stomatal mechanics in models of the regulation of water loss may not, at this time, improve predictions or explanations concerning the effects of environment on transpiration by leaves or canopies.

Models have been developed for evaluating stomatal responses to environment by applying differential calculus and classical feedback theory (FARQUHAR et al. 1978). This approach has been used to evaluate the extent to which stomatal responses to internal $[CO_2]$ are responsible for stomatal opening with increases in irradiance (WONG et al. 1978). An extension of this approach has been used to describe the contributions of stomatal water loss (feedback) and cuticular water loss (feedforward) to stomatal response to humidity (FARQUHAR 1978). This approach can be used in a general manner both to determine and quantify the effects of environment on stomata, and provides a fundamental basis for understanding and modeling the regulation of water loss by stomata.

Models have been used to explore relations between the regulation of water loss and plant water status (COWAN and MILTHORPE 1968; COWAN 1972), including the effects of water storage in plants (RUNNING et al. 1975; WARING and RUNNING 1978). These models have the potential capability of relating water transport to plant function as mediated by water stress.

Models of water and solute transport in plants (DALTON et al. 1975; FISCUS and KRAMER 1975) indicate the errors that may occur when water flow in the soil-plant system is treated without considering effects of solute transport. Consequently, when modeling water transport it is necessary to consider whether submodels of ion uptake and translocation should be included.

Relationships between stomatal regulation of transpiration and carbon dioxide assimilation have been modeled (COWAN and FARQUHAR 1977), and are examined in detail in Chapter 17, this Volume. Models of this type illustrate the need for considering both of these processes when relating stomata to plant function.

Another type of objective, that has significance for both agriculture and for understanding natural systems, is the prediction of plant water use (SLABBERS 1980) and seasonal balances of water (FITZPATRICK and NIX 1969; HALL and DANCETTE 1978; ROSENTHAL et al. 1977). For these objectives, models must describe the regulation of water loss at the canopy or community levels. Ultimately, predictions of water and carbon balances should provide information that explains certain aspects of plant adaptation and competition (EHLERINGER and MOONEY 1978; JONES 1980; MOONEY and EHLERINGER 1978).

It is unlikely that any single model could accomplish all of these objectives. However, when models are developed, consideration should be given to the possibility that they may also be useful as submodels of more comprehensive models. For example, LANDSBERG and BUTLER (1980) linked a model of stomatal response to environment, developed by THORPE et al. (1980), to the model of energy balance and aerodynamic transfer described by MONTEITH (1965), and examined the implications to transpiration of stomatal response to humidity. This example illustrates the hierarchic levels within ecosystems and the use

of models to predict or explain the function of upper levels (i.e., the canopy) by integrating information obtained at a lower level (i.e., the leaf).

Model development should include testing. A *predictive* model must provide reasonable predictions over the range of environmental and plant conditions that are relevant to the objectives for which the model was developed. *Explanatory* models, which are developed for analyzing hypotheses concerning the internal functioning or regulation of systems, must be tested with respect to both internal consistency and gross prediction. The extent of testing depends upon the quality of submodels. Certain aspects of mass transport and energy relations may be considered as being firmly based upon established laws of physics and require little additional testing. In contrast, submodels based upon biological assumptions will usually require at least some tests of their validity with the appropriate species and environmental conditions as determined by the objectives of the study. The quantitative and qualitative variations in results of experimental studies of soil-plant water relations and stomatal physiology indicate that for these systems specific tests are essential procedures in model development at this time. Plant water relations and stomatal responses are strongly dependent upon previous growth conditions, present environmental conditions, and the methods used for measurement, and in some cases the causal factors for major differences in response have not been adequately identified. Some of the contrasts and similarities that have been observed in stomatal responses to environment are discussed in Chapter 7, this Volume.

Lastly, it should be expected that all models will have deficiencies. Comprehensive analyses of model deficiencies should be conducted and reported, so that the constraints concerning model use and interpretation of model responses are obvious. Models, like interpretations from experimental studies, should be recognized as only occupying some position on a continuum between the states of general ignorance and partial understanding.

8.1.2 The Significance of the Linkage Between Plant Water Loss and Plant Water Relations

The boundaries of models normally should not exclude processes which strongly interact with the processes described by the model. In this context, when modeling plant regulation of water loss, it would appear necessary to consider possible relations with plant water status and liquid water transport in the plant. It may be anticipated that a coherent system would include interactions between the regulation of water loss and tissue water relations which act to prevent extreme dehydration of the protoplasm or to maintain plant turgor (COWAN 1977a; DAVIES et al. 1980). Differences do exist, however, among different plant life forms in the extent to which transpiration is regulated in response to changing environmental conditions (FISCHER and TURNER 1978).

Changes in plant water status influence plant water loss through effects on stomatal function and canopy characteristics. These interactions should be included in comprehensive models and are discussed in Sections 8.2.2.2 and 8.4. Additional linkages between plant water status and water loss, which may

be important in specific circumstances, are discussed in the remainder of this section.

Changes in water potential have small effects on the equilibrium vapor pressure. For example, vapor pressure would be decreased only 1%, 2%, and 10% by decreases in water potential from 0 to −14, −28 and −145 bar, respectively (SLATYER 1967). In addition, variation in water potential over this range would have little effect on the latent heat of vaporization (COWAN 1977a). Consequently, if the water potential of the solutions at the evaporating surfaces within leaves is similar to bulk leaf water potential, it may be assumed that decreases in leaf water potential have little *direct* effect on the rate of water loss from leaves (COWAN 1977a; WEATHERLEY 1970).

However, JARVIS and SLATYER (1970) proposed that the water potential at the sites of evaporation within the leaf may be substantially lower than the bulk leaf water potential at high rates of transpiration. The studies of FARQUHAR and RASCHKE (1978) did not confirm this observation and they concluded that "under conditions relevant to studies of stomatal behavior, the water vapor pressure at the sites of evaporation is equal to the saturation vapor pressure". At this time it is not known whether this conclusion is generally valid and further studies should be conducted, especially with xeromorphic plants, and plants subjected to drought.

Additional nonstomatal features which influence water loss include wax tubes in the stomatal antechamber of some conifers (JEFFREE et al. 1971), resinous layers over stomata, such as may be observed on the leaves of *Eriodictyon trichocalyx,* and the various leaf characteristics that influence boundary layer and cuticular resistances. Leaf-rolling (O'TOOLE and CRUZ 1980), leaf pubescence, and changes in leaf size, due to drought, influence boundary-layer resistance. In addition, drought-induced changes in leaf orientation (SHACKEL and HALL 1979) and leaf pubescence (EHLERINGER and MOONEY 1978) influence transpiration through effects on radiation balance and leaf temperature.

The linkages present between the regulation of plant water loss and plant water relations have implications for experimental approaches. It would appear prudent to study stomata as they function as integral parts in whole plant systems. Excised leaves and epidermal strips may have value, as simplified systems, for studying specific mechanisms but in some of these systems stomatal responses may have differed from their responses in intact plants. The following sections of this review mainly consider experimental evidence obtained with intact plants to avoid the possibility of artifacts of this type.

8.1.3 The Significance of the Linkage Between Regulation of Transpiration and Carbon Dioxide Assimilation

There are several reasons why it is useful to include submodels of carbon dioxide assimilation in some models of the regulation of transpiration. Photosynthesis and transpiration are intimately linked through mutual dependencies on gaseous exchanges between leaf and air, and on leaf energy balance. In addition, stomatal apertures of some species are strongly dependent upon the concentra-

tion of CO_2 inside the leaf (RASCHKE 1976). Modeling the CO_2 concentration inside leaves requires a submodel of carbon dioxide assimilation. Recently, it has been proposed that stomatal conductance may be influenced by a product from photosynthesis in the mesophyll tissue (WONG et al. 1979) or by the energy status of the mesophyll (WONG 1979; see also Chap. 7, this Vol.). If relations of this type are present between photosynthesis and stomata a more complex submodel of photosynthesis and respiration would be required to describe stomatal responses to the internal and external environment of the leaf. Alternatively, the regulation of water loss may be modeled based upon hypothetical relationships between transpiration and CO_2 assimilation (COWAN and FARQUHAR 1977; HALL and SCHULZE 1980a) as will be discussed in Section 8.2.2.3.

Where the objective of models of water loss is to predict plant performance or adaptation, it may be useful to incorporate a submodel of CO_2 assimilation, although more empirical models relating plant performance to plant water status (TURK and HALL 1980a, b) or relative water use (TURK and HALL 1980c) are more appropriate in some circumstances.

8.2 Models of Leaf Water Loss and Stomatal Response to Environment

Consideration is given to quantitative aspects of water loss at the leaf level of organization (Sect. 8.2.1). Detailed analyses of stomatal responses to environment are presented in Section 8.2.2. A brief analysis of canopy water loss is presented in Section 8.4 to illustrate approaches that may be used to relate leaf function to the functioning of isolated plants or plant communities.

8.2.1 Physical Aspects of the Influence of the Leaf and the Environment on Water Loss from Plants

This discussion is designed as a supplement to the comprehensive treatment of the transfer of H_2O and CO_2 between leaf and air by JARVIS (1971) which describes methods widely used at this time. However, these widely used methods can result in errors of interpretation in some circumstances, and mathematical treatments are available to overcome these problems.

Methods should clearly specify and differentiate between the effects of the leaf epidermis and the environment on the regulation of water loss. To facilitate explanation, but with no loss in rigor, it is assumed, at this stage, that the boundary layer resistance is negligible and the system is isothermal. The widely used approach considers

$$J_i = \Delta C_i / r_i \tag{8.1}$$

where J_i is the flux (mass area^{-1} time^{-1}) of a specific gas (i), ΔC_i is the difference in concentration (mass volume^{-1}) of the gas along the flow path,

and r_i (time length^{-1}) is a resistance to diffusion. The characteristics of this resistance may be ascertained by comparing Eq. (8.1) with Fick's law which shows that:

$$r_i = L/D' \tag{8.2}$$

where L is the effective path length, and D' is an effective diffusion coefficient. D' may be related to conventional diffusion coefficients (D_i) by the following equation:

$$D' = D_i/K^* \tag{8.3}$$

where K^* is a dimensionless coefficient describing the influences of stomatal densities, and aperture dimensions on gaseous diffusion. However, diffusion coefficients are dependent upon temperature and atmospheric pressure as described by the experimentally determined function of FULLER et al. (1966):

$$D_h = D_h^o \, (T/T_o)^{1.75} \, (P_o/P) \tag{8.4}$$

where D_h^o is the diffusion coefficient for water vapor in air at reference levels of absolute temperature (T_o) and atmospheric pressure (P_o). $D_h^o = 0.25$ cm^2 s^{-1} at 293 K and 1.01 bar. D_h is the same diffusion coefficient but at ambient temperature (T) and atmospheric pressure (P). The characteristics of the commonly used resistance to water vapor (r_h) may be specified by combining Eqs. (8.2), (8.3) and (8.4).

$$r_h = L \, K^*/[D_h^o \, (T/T_o)^{1.75} \, (P_o/P)] \tag{8.5}$$

Consequently, a leaf with constant epidermal properties, as specified by L and K^*, would have an apparent resistance to water vapor (r_h) that is 19% greater at 10 °C than at 40 °C, and 44% greater at sea level compared with r_h at 3,000 m elevation (atmospheric pressures are approximately 1.01 bar at sea level and 0.7 bar at 3,000 m elevation). Influences of pressure on gaseous fluxes that are similar to theoretical expectations have been demonstrated using physical models and leaves by GALE (1973). Fortunately, the errors due to variations in pressure and temperature are not large enough to invalidate the conclusions of most earlier studies of plant regulation of water loss based upon Eq. (8.1). However, the errors are large enough to justify development of an improved system, especially for studies along altitudinal gradients (GALE 1972; SMITH and GELLER 1979) or where a large range of temperature is encountered.

A method has been described by COWAN (1977b) which appears to overcome some of the error due to effects of temperature and pressure on diffusivities.

$$J_h = \frac{\Delta e}{r^t \, P} \tag{8.6}$$

In this method the flux of water vapor (J_h) is related to the difference in vapor pressure (Δe) divided by the atmospheric pressure (P), and the total

resistance to diffusion of water vapor (r^t) has the units 1/transpirational flux. The relation between r^t and the terms in the empirical Eq. (8.5) may be ascertained by assuming isothermal conditions and applying the ideal gas equation:

$$r^t = \frac{R\, T_o^{1.75}}{M\, D_h^o\, P_o\, T^{0.75}}\, L\, K^*,$$

(8.7)

r^t is a function of the geometric properties of the epidermis (L and K*) and several constants (R, T_o, M, D_h^o and P_o) where R is the universal gas constant and M is the molecular weight of water, but it also has a small dependence upon absolute temperature ($1/T^{.75}$). However, epidermises of leaves may not have this particular temperature dependence. The movement of water vapor through stomata involves additional complexities including incomplete molecular slip of diffusing molecules at surfaces and the effects of temperature gradients (COWAN 1977b). These complexities have not been adequately quantified for leaves but the definition proposed by COWAN (1977b) in Eq. (8.6) has advantages and should be used instead of the commonly used definition of resistance [Eq. (8.1)]. Resistances based upon the old system (r) may be converted to the system of COWAN using the following equation:

$$r^t = r\, V_o\, \frac{P_o\, T}{P\, T_o}$$

(8.8)

where V_o is the molar volume of an ideal gas at T_o and P_o ($V_o = 0.0224$ m^3 mol^{-1} at $T_o = 273$ K and $P_o = 1.01$ bar).

   Gaseous transport equations are also useful for estimating the carbon dioxide concentration inside the leaf as described by JARVIS (1971). It is appropriate to continue using concentrations that are on a volume basis because at low concentrations, volume fractions are equivalent to relative partial pressures (e.g., ppm is equivalent to µbar partial pressure/bar atmospheric pressure). Resistances to the diffusion of one gas are commonly converted to apply to another gas, by using the ratios of the diffusion coefficients as described by JARVIS (1971). One uncertainty in this approach is that at any time several gases are diffusing between leaf and air, and for a complete analysis all molecular collisions must be considered. JARMAN (1974) provided equations which describe the effects of these collisions, and concluded that estimates of the difference in CO_2 concentration between the external air and intercellular spaces based upon the old system (JARVIS 1971) may be in error by 0% to 80%. However, JARMAN (1974) pointed out that the large relative errors only occur at the light or CO_2 compensation points where the absolute gradients and absolute errors are small. Estimates of internal CO_2 concentration may be improved by assuming that CO_2 transfer in the cuticular pathway is negligible and basing the calculation on flow in the stomatal pathway.

   It is useful to separate the influence of the epidermis on gaseous transfer from the effects of the boundary layer which depend upon leaf dimensions, surface roughness, wind speed, and air-flow characteristics. A detailed analysis of the measurement and properties of boundary layer resistances has been presented by JARVIS (1971) and only supplementary information will be presented

here. Boundary layer effects on water vapor loss from a single leaf surface may be described as follows:

$$J_h = \frac{\Delta e}{(r^a + r^e)\, P} \tag{8.9}$$

where r^a is the boundary layer resistance, and r^e is the resistance of the leaf epidermis. When leaves are isolateral (equal resistances on both adaxial and abaxial surfaces) Eq. (8.9) is also appropriate for partitioning epidermal and boundary layer effects on both surfaces using a total flux measurement. However, leaves are often anisolateral and errors occur if r^e is estimated from total flux measurements using Eq. (8.9) (HALL, Appendix A 1970). The most straightforward approach is to measure gaseous fluxes separately at each surface of the leaf, but this increases the equipment and effort required for controlled environment studies, and may put serious constraints on cuvette design. An alternative approach was suggested by HALL (Appendix A 1970).

The level of anisolaterality (K) is defined as:

$$K = \frac{r^u}{r^l} \tag{8.10}$$

where r^u and r^l are the resistances of the upper and lower epidermises. The combined resistance of the two surfaces (r^*) may be obtained from

$$\frac{1}{r^*} = \frac{1}{r^u} + \frac{1}{r^l}. \tag{8.11}$$

It may be shown that the estimate of leaf resistance (r^e) obtained from whole leaf fluxes and Eq. (8.9) is related to r^* as determined from separate measurements on both leaf surfaces by

$$r^e = \frac{r^a\, r^* (K-1)^2}{r^* (K+1)^2 + 4\, r^a\, K} + r^*. \tag{8.12}$$

The error term is a function of r^a, K and r^*. The error approaches zero when r^a is small and does not exceed the magnitude of r^a. Consequently, epidermal and boundary layer effects on gaseous fluxes can be reasonably partitioned using measurements of whole leaf fluxes, providing the boundary layer resistance is maintained at a low level by using high wind speeds and turbulent air flow. In addition, it is easier to resolve changes in epidermal resistance when the boundary layer resistance is small, and the high wind speeds and turbulence result in only small gradients in gaseous concentrations within cuvettes.

When comparing the effects of phenomena that operate in a catenary sequence, such as epidermal and boundary layer effects, it is convenient to use resistances. However, conductance is generally more useful when evaluating plant responses to environment. Transpiration, leaf water potential, and net photosynthesis are more linearly related to leaf conductance than to leaf resis-

tance. Arithmetic means may be taken of multiple measurements of leaf conductance in canopies because the system consists of parallel pathways. In addition, the relationship between stomatal aperture and conductance is more linear than the relationship with resistance (BURROWS and MILTHORPE 1976). This preference for conductance is not trivial in that erroneous interpretations, including some of those supporting "threshold response hypotheses", have arisen because stomatal properties were expressed in terms of resistance.

8.2.2 Steady-State Models of Stomatal Function

A *mechanistic model* of stomatal responses to environment would require adequate descriptions of the following submodels: the mechanics of guard cell wall deformation and physical relations with adjacent cells; the biochemistry and biophysics of the control of osmotic potential within guard cells, and relations with other epidermal and mesophyll cells; and the characteristics of water, solute, and possibly hormonal transport within leaves and throughout plants. I consider that, given the present state of understanding of these systems, *mechanistic models* of stomatal response to environment would be cumbersome and highly unreliable, but ALLAWAY and MILTHORPE (1976) are more optimistic. However, *predictive models* capable of providing useful information could be developed for specific circumstances. Three types of *predictive models* are considered: multiple correlation models, phenomenological models, and models based upon hypothetical systems of stomatal regulation.

Substantial simplification may be achieved if the diurnal course of stomatal conductance may be treated as a sequence of steady states. It has been suggested that this assumption may be valid for the treatment of water flow in some plants (COWAN and MILTHORPE 1968), and steady-state analysis may provide adequate descriptions of a substantial proportion of stomatal responses in natural environments. The hysteresis observed on some occasions for stomatal responses to humidity and radiation may be approximately treated by steady-state models if the direction of change is included as a variable. Steady-state models would not be appropriate for strongly dynamic systems such as where stomatal oscillations occur.

8.2.2.1 Multiple Correlation Models

The simplest model of stomatal response to environment would include the independent variables: radiation, leaf temperature, some measure of plant water status, and possibly some aspect of atmospheric humidity and internal CO_2 concentration. Even with only four or five independent variables, it is likely that multiple correlation models, for which the definition and relations of variables have been determined empirically, will have little generality for treating different environments. HINCKLEY et al. (1975) developed multiple regression equations relating leaf resistance to solar irradiance, air temperature, vapor pressure deficit, and xylem pressure potential, but they concluded that these equations gave poor predictions. An intrinsically linear, logarithmic multiple

regression analysis was applied by PALLARDY and KOZLOWSKI (1979). They obtained empirical relationships between leaf resistance and solar radiation, vapor pressure deficit, temperature, and leaf water potential. Surprisingly, the partial correlation coefficient for leaf water potential implied stomatal opening with greater leaf water deficits.

It is apparent that caution should be exercised in using empirical models to estimate the contribution of individual factors to stomatal responses in natural environments. Generally, highly empirical models should only be used for predicting the outcome of complex processes, and not for analyzing the mechanisms involved. For example, multiple correlation models may be used to predict missing values in diurnal and seasonal courses so that improved estimates of daily and annual balances may be obtained. An important principle is that empirical models are more reliable when used to interpolate rather than to extrapolate outside of the range of values used in developing the model. Empirical approaches may be considerably strengthened by developing *phenomenological models* of the type described by JARVIS (1976), with subsequent use of least squares regression analysis to obtain input parameters.

8.2.2.2 Phenomenological Models

The reader is referred to the paper by JARVIS (1976) which provides an excellent description and example of a *phenomenological model* of stomatal responses to environment. In the development of phenomenological models of stomatal responses to environment there are six basic steps. First, the external and internal variables that substantially influence stomatal conductance must be determined. Second, the manner in which individual variables influence stomatal conductance must be established at appropriate levels of the other variables. Third, equations must be developed that describe the effects of individual variables and interactions with the other variables. Fourth, values for the input parameters in these equations must be ascertained. Fifth, the predictions of the model must be tested. Sixth, it is likely that the predictions will not be perfect and it will be necessary to analyze the model to search for the sources of error, and correct them by returning to previous steps and repeating the process.

A detailed analysis of information that is relevant to each of these steps is provided, beginning with an examination of the manner in which stomata responded to light, humidity, temperature, CO_2 concentration and plant water status (see the detailed discussion in Chap. 7, this Vol.).

1. *Light*. Variations in solar radiation or visible light below the levels required for maximal stomatal opening result in changes in stomatal conductance. Three hypotheses for the mechanism of stomatal response to radiation have been proposed: that the response is a direct response of the guard cells to radiation; or that the response is an indirect consequence of radiation effects on mesophyll photosynthesis, either via changes in internal CO_2 concentration or changes in leaf energy status. However, a submodel based only upon stomatal responses to internal CO_2 concentration would not adequately describe the stomatal responses to light of many species (WONG et al. 1978; WONG 1979; RAMOS 1981). Stomatal responses to light may be modeled as depending upon the photon

flux, but the action spectrum should be considered. For some species, blue light appears to have specific effects on stomata, and the action spectrum differs from that of photosynthesis (RASCHKE 1979). In cases where the major response to light of stomata is associated with photosynthesis, the appropriate variable for modeling this effect would be the photon flux between 400 and 700 nm.

The responses of stomatal conductance to photon flux approximate a rectangular hyperbola, although other functions may be more appropriate for some species (BURROWS and MILTHORPE 1976). The photon flux (between 400 to 700 nm) required for 95% of maximal conductance varies from low values to full sunlight (100 to 2,000 μmol photon m^{-2} s^{-1}) depending upon the species, leaf age, and environment (TURNER 1974; BURROWS and MILTHORPE 1976). These reviews demonstrate that the concept of stomata opening fully at a low light threshold applies to only a few species and conditions. The use of resistance, and transit-time porometers, which are imprecise when stomatal conductances are moderate to large were partially responsible for the threshold hypothesis. Stomatal responses to photon flux may vary for opening responses in the morning and closing responses in the evening with some species (HINCKLEY et al. 1975; RAMOS 1981). Larger stomatal conductances were observed in the morning than in the evening at the same intermediate photon fluxes. These data may be explained by either hysteresis in opening and closing responses or the effects of endogenous diurnal rhythms. In addition, hysteresis may be observed in the opposite direction if stomatal responses to photon flux are determined over a short period of time (JARVIS 1980). This indicates that in some circumstances different parameters for stomatal responses to photon flux may be needed with increasing and decreasing fluxes or at different times during the photoperiod. For environments with variable cloud cover or where sunflecking is present, the use of steady-state models may result in some error because the half-time for stomatal response to radiation is several minutes, and stomatal conductances may reflect an integrated, earlier experience and not prevailing light levels (JARVIS 1980).

2. *Humidity*. Variations in atmospheric humidity frequently result in changes in stomatal conductance independently of effects due to changes in bulk leaf water status (HALL et al. 1976; HALL and HOFFMAN 1976; SCHULZE and KÜPPERS 1979; LÖSCH 1979; OSONUBI and DAVIES 1980a). It has been hypothesized that the response is related to changes in the water status of the epidermis through influences of humidity on cuticular water loss (LANGE et al. 1971; LÖSCH 1977); consequently, the vapor pressure difference between leaf and air (or relative vapor pressure difference) appears to be the most appropriate characterization of "humidity".

Mechanisms for stomatal response to "humidity" have been discussed in relation to water transport within leaves by SHERIFF (1979) and LÖSCH (1979). A model of stomatal response to humidity has been developed which assumes that the response is related to water loss from the external surfaces of the stomatal apparatus and from inside the leaf (FARQUHAR 1978). This model provides an excellent basis for further studies, but it has not been rigorously tested due to present inability to measure cuticular water loss from surfaces containing stomata. Empirical, exponential (BURROWS and MILTHORPE 1976)

and linear (THORPE et al. 1980) models have been proposed for conductance response to vapor pressure difference, but these models only approximately predict observed responses. Stomatal conductance responses to the combined effects of vapor pressure difference and photon flux have been modeled by THORPE et al. (1980).

Some complexities of stomatal response to humidity warrant discussion. Stomatal opening responses to increasing humidity are slower than closing responses to decreasing humidity, and incomplete opening may occur after stomata are subjected to very low humidities (LANGE et al. 1971; LÖSCH 1977, 1979; SCHULZE and KÜPPERS 1979). In addition, at very high humidities, leaf conductance may decrease when humidity is increased (ASTON 1976). It is possible that part of leaf conductance response to humidity is nonstomatal, but much of the response is stomatal (ASTON 1976) and its significance to adaptation necessitates its inclusion in predictive models.

3. *Temperature*. Stomata respond to temperature, but until recently the characteristics of the responses have been varied and subject to dispute (HALL et al. 1976; LÖSCH 1979). It has been shown that much of the variation may have been due to measuring stomatal responses under unspecified, varying, and different levels of vapor pressure difference between leaf and air (HALL et al. 1976).

Measurements of stomatal conductance response to temperature, in which vapor pressure difference was kept constant, gave either the optimum-type response (JARVIS 1980) typical of many biological responses to temperature (SHARPE and DEMICHELLE 1977) or progressive increases in conductance over a substantial range of temperature (HALL et al. 1976). The shape of the curve relating stomatal conductance to temperature may change with drought (SCHULZE et al. 1973) or may remain the same (OSONUBI and DAVIES 1980b).

Irreversibility in stomatal responses to temperature causes difficulties for both measurement and modeling. Plants that were exposed for less than 1 h to extremely high (BAUER 1978) or extremely low (NEILSON and JARVIS 1975) temperatures had leaf conductances that remained low for several hours or days. SCHULZE et al. (1974) simulated the diurnal course of stomatal resistance of *Prunus armeniaca* with a model that assumes additive effects of leaf temperature and vapor pressure difference. The model reasonably predicted much of the diurnal variation in leaf resistance, but during the afternoons of hot dry days the observed stomatal resistances were larger than predicted values. The authors suggested that this partial stomatal closure in the afternoons may have been due to after-effects of high temperature or hysteresis in stomatal response to humidity.

4. CO_2 *Concentration*. Different regions of the stomatal apparatus are exposed to CO_2 concentrations varying between external ambient levels and the concentration within leaves. It is usually assumed that stomata only respond to the internal CO_2 concentration, which is defined as the average concentration at the evaporating surfaces within leaves, but this has not been rigorously established. Alternatively, stomata may respond to the gradient in CO_2 concentration between the external and internal walls of guard cells. In this case, they would respond differently to variations in internal concentration due to

changes in external concentration, than to those due to changes in internal processes such as photosynthesis. The only studies that I am aware of on this point are the unpublished observations of I.R. Cowan and G.D. Farquhar reported by Wong (1979, p 162), which do not support the hypothesis that stomata respond to the gradient in CO_2 concentration.

Models of stomatal responses to CO_2 concentration may contribute to predictions concerning the consequences to plants of the expected increases in global CO_2 concentration (Baes et al. 1977). However, the inclusion of submodels for describing stomatal responses to natural variations in internal CO_2 concentration may not be necessary in natural plant habitats. There are many experiments with intact, attached leaves in which external CO_2 concentrations were varied to simulate natural variations in internal CO_2 concentration, which only had small effects on leaf conductance (Burrows and Milthorpe 1976; Hall et al. 1976; Jarvis 1980). However, stomata of some species respond strongly to changes in CO_2 concentration (Raschke et al. 1978; Wong 1979; Ramos 1981). When evaluating and modeling stomatal responses to internal CO_2 concentration it is useful to apply gain analysis methodology as described by Wong et al. (1978) to separate the effects of different factors on stomatal conductance and internal CO_2 concentration.

Raschke (1976) has hypothesized that "stress" may sensitize stomata to internal CO_2 concentration. This hypothesis is particularly important as a possible conceptual basis for modeling stress effects on stomata, and for modeling and understanding the relationships between regulation of water loss and CO_2 assimilation. Unfortunately, few rigorous tests of this hypothesis (with intact plants) have been reported, and there are some indications that water stress does not influence stomata of certain conifers (Jarvis 1980) or *Zea mays* in this manner (Wong 1979).

Several models have included assumed relations between stomatal conductance and internal CO_2 concentration (Penning de Vries 1972; van Bavel et al. 1973; Waggoner 1969) or external CO_2 concentration (Jarvis 1976). Little evidence was provided to justify these submodels, but most authors stated that the effect of CO_2 was either small or unknown. It is apparent that further experimental studies are needed of stomatal responses to CO_2 with intact plants grown in different environments.

5. *Plant Water Status.* It is well known that stomatal conductances tend to decrease when plants are subjected to drought, but general relationships between stomatal conductance and plant water status have not been discovered. Present differences of opinion illustrate the controversy that prevails concerning relations between stomatal conductance and plant water status. Turner and Begg (1978) stated "It is now generally recognized that the stomata do not respond to changes in leaf water potential ⋯ until a critical threshold level ⋯ is reached, and then stomatal closure occurs over a narrow range of leaf water potential ⋯. ⋯ Many of the differences in the leaf water potential for stomatal closure can be accounted for by differences in the osmotic potential or osmotic adjustment of plants". In contrast, Jones and Rawson (1979) stated "in sorghum, leaf conductance declines continuously over a range of leaf water potential from −15 to −30 bar. The steepness of the initial decline was depen-

dent upon the rate of change of leaf water potential so that although at high rates of stress (7 and 12 bar/day) the response of leaf conductance to water potential resembles the threshold response reported elsewhere for sorghum (TURNER 1974), at lower rate of stress (1.5 bar/day) the response extends over an approximately 15 bar range of leaf water potential. ⋯ osmotic adjustment in sorghum is not responsible for the higher values of leaf conductance at low leaf water potentials in slowly stressed plants ⋯ it appears that in sorghum the relationship between leaf conductance and leaf turgor potential is not unique ⋯ ". They also suggested that the threshold concept "may be a result of combination of factors such as the use of diffusion porometry, the use of stomatal resistance units, and the imposition of very rapid rate of stress, rather than being a reflection of an inherent mechanism involved in guard cell movement". Evidence which supports both sets of statements is available in the literature.

I will present an analysis of the influence of plant water status on stomata that partially reconciles these apparently conflicting points of view, and provides a conceptual basis for the development of a general model. It should be recognized that a priori we should not expect stomatal conductance to be uniquely related to either bulk leaf water potential or bulk leaf pressure potential. Stomatal apertures are probably related to the turgor pressures of guard cells and adjacent cells, but it cannot be assumed that the osmotic potentials of these cells are either constant or uniquely related to bulk leaf osmotic potential (RASCHKE 1979; BEADLE et al. 1978). It is also useful to distinguish between effects on stomata of short-term (minutes) and long-term (days) changes in plant water status. When the water status of leaves of several species was rapidly disturbed by detaching them or manipulating the osmotic potential of the root zone, leaf conductance exhibited threshold responses to bulk leaf water potential (EHLIG and GARDNER 1964; HALL and HOFFMAN 1976). These responses resemble the threshold model of TURNER and BEGG (1978). In contrast, EHLIG and GARDNER (1964) observed progressive decreases in relative transpiration for whole plants with day-to-day decreases in leaf water potential as the water in the root zone was depleted which do not fit the threshold model. It should be noted that under field conditions, environmental factors and plant water status vary during the day, and leaf water potential depends upon the transpiration rate. Consequently, it is difficult under these conditions to determine separately the effects on stomata of leaf water status and the environmental factors that also influence the evaporative demand. In an ingenious experiment, SCHULZE and KÜPPERS (1979) modified the water status of individual attached leaves of *Corylus avellana* as much as 8 bar, during the day, without changing the environment of these leaves or the root zone environment (they varied the evaporative demand on the remaining part of the shoot). They established that the changes in leaf water potential that could occur during a diurnal course had negligible influence on stomatal conductance. ACKERSON et al. (1977) also observed little change in stomatal resistance of cotton with decreases in leaf water potential to as low as −25 bar under field conditions. Consequently, it is possible that progressive decreases in transpiration with progressive decreases in leaf water potential are not due to a close coupling between leaf conductance and leaf water potential.

It is hypothesized that short-term (minutes) changes in leaf water status have a threshold effect on stomatal conductance, but that in some natural conditions and with some species the threshold leaf water potential for stomatal closure may not be reached. The results of JONES and RAWSON (1979) and others which are not consistent with the threshold hypothesis may be partially explained by a hypothesis for long-term (days) effects of changes in plant water status on stomata. Long-term changes in plant water status influence maximum daily leaf conductance (HALL and SCHULZE 1980a) and may also modulate stomatal response to other environmental variables (HALL et al. 1976). Progressive decreases in leaf conductance were observed with decreases over 2 weeks in soil water potential in the root zone of a desert fern (NOBEL 1978). Pre-dawn plant water potential provides another measure of day-to-day changes in plant water status. Correlations have been reported between pre-dawn pressure chamber values and mean daily leaf conductance (RUNNING et al. 1975) or maximum morning conductance (RUNNING 1980a). It is also possible that plant water potential values integrated over time may provide a better measure of long-term changes in plant water status than pre-dawn water potential. SCHULZE et al. (1980) have shown that drought-induced changes in photosynthesis were related to cumulative daily plant water potential, but this type of analysis has not been applied to the effects of drought on leaf conductance. A model which includes a time-integrated measure of drought experience could also incorporate the effects of rate of drying described by JONES and RAWSON (1979) and possibly after-effects of water stress on stomatal opening potential of the type described by FISCHER et al. (1970).

A comprehensive model would include submodels for both the long-term effects of drought experience, and short-term, possibly threshold, relations with leaf water status. The only interpretation of leaf conductance data that I am aware of, which follows this scheme, is that of RUNNING (1976). He described leaf conductance responses of conifers as including both a relation between early-morning maximum leaf conductance and pre-dawn water potential, and threshold relations with leaf water potential during the rest of the day. It should be recognized, however, that it is difficult to determine from diurnal courses whether leaf conductance is responding to leaf water potential. The decreases in leaf conductance during the day, observed by RUNNING (1976), could have been due to the effects of one or more of several covarying factors, including the humidity difference between leaf and air (RUNNING 1980a).

Methods for quantifying the responses of stomata to environment are considered. Ideally the development of equations for stomatal responses would be based upon leaf conductance responses to individual variables in controlled environment cuvettes in the field (SCHULZE et al. 1974) or in growth chambers (THORPE et al. 1980). Next, the extent of interactions between variables must be determined so that the individual equations may be linked in a coherent general function. Individual functions may be combined by multiplication (JARVIS 1976), by addition (SCHULZE et al. 1974), or by using reciprocals (BURROWS and MILTHORPE 1976). The most effective method for combining functions is not known at this time.

A reference stomatal conductance may be included in models as a parameter which is influenced by the long-term effects of drought, temperature preconditioning, leaf age etc. (HALL and SCHULZE 1980a). The short-term effects of radiation, humidity, and temperature are then considered as having proportionate effects (multiplicative model) or additive effects in relation to the reference conductance. The reference conductance is defined as the stomatal conductance which occurs when the CO_2 assimilation rate is maximized by optimizing temperature and humidity, and using saturating photon flux and normal air (21% $[O_2]$ and 330 ppm $[CO_2]$). An alternative procedure would be to include maximum conductance as a parameter, but its measurement may require use of conditions which result in instability of the stomatal system such as high temperatures (and also moderately high humidity, saturating photon flux, and possibly low CO_2 concentration). The values of input parameters may be determined from studies where variables are individually changed in steps (SCHULZE et al. 1974; THORPE et al. 1980) or from field data, where several variables were changing at the same time, by simultaneous solution of equations using nonlinear least squares regression analysis (JARVIS 1976).

Ideally, model tests should be conducted with a set of field data which includes an adequate range of values for important variables, and which was not used for obtaining input parameters. If the tests indicate that the model is not adequate, investigations of the sources of error could include sensitivity tests using reasonable ranges of parameter values, but excessive juggling of parameter values in attempts to obtain a reasonable fit is not recommended. To improve the model it may be necessary to go back and determine whether the assumptions, environmental variables, and functions are appropriate for the system and objectives of the model.

8.2.2.3 Models Based Upon Hypothetical Systems of Stomatal Regulation

The complexity of stomatal responses to environment described in the previous section indicates that developing phenomenological models of this system will be a difficult task. An alternative approach has evolved from recent research that may contribute to the development of predictive models. In this approach it is assumed that the complex responses of stomata have certain end results, such as maintenance of leaf turgor (DAVIES et al. 1980) or internal CO_2 concentration (WONG 1979) or specific types of water-use optimization.

The elegant theory of COWAN and FARQUHAR (1977) provides a basis for modeling stomatal function in relation to the optimization of water-use (see also Chaps. 1, 7, and 17, this Vol.). They pointed out that, within the constraints set by the maximal and minimal stomatal conductances that are possible for a particular leaf: on any day, a specific diurnal course of stomatal conductance would result in maximum daily CO_2 assimilation for a specific level of daily water use. They hypothesized, based upon the calculus of variations, that this optimal function would be achieved if stomatal apertures varied so that $\partial A/\partial E$ remained constant during the day: where ∂A is the change in CO_2 assimilation rate and ∂E is the change in transpiration rate that would result from an

infinitesimal change in stomatal conductance (δg). $\partial A/\partial E$ may be more explicitly described by the ratio of partial derivatives $(\partial A/\partial g)/(\partial E/\partial g)$. For this hypothesis to provide a basis for effective predictive models of stomatal response to environment, two aspects must be evaluated. First, the extent to which $\partial A/\partial E$ is constant during the day must be determined for different species and environmental conditions. Second, the plant and environmental factors which cause short-term and long-term changes in the value of $\partial A/\partial E$ and the response functions for these effects must be determined.

It has been established that $\partial A/\partial E$ remained reasonably constant with variations in atmospheric humidity at constant leaf temperature for *Nicotiana glauca* and *Corylus avellana* (FARQUHAR et al. 1980), and with variations in both humidity and temperature for *Vigna unguiculata* (HALL and SCHULZE 1980a). However, $\partial A/\partial E$ was not constant when stomata did not fully recover with humidification after exposure to low humidities, and in one set of studies with a plant subjected to drought (HALL and SCHULZE 1980a). In addition, provisional studies indicated that $\partial A/\partial E$ was not constant when photon flux was varied, but stomatal conductance was linearly correlated with CO_2 assimilation rate (C. RAMOS personal communication). Linear associations between stomatal conductance and CO_2 assimilation rate, with short-term changes in photon flux, have been reported for several species (GOUDRIAAN and VAN LAAR 1978; LOUWERSE and ZWEERDE 1977; WONG et al. 1978, 1979; WONG 1979).

An approach for modeling diurnal courses of stomatal conductance is proposed based upon the observations described in the previous paragraph. It is assumed that the effects of light, at constant humidity and temperature, may be modeled by assuming a relation between stomatal conductance and CO_2 assimilation rate. Stomatal responses to humidity and temperature would be modeled by assuming that $\partial A/\partial E$ remains constant at a particular photon flux. Operationally, it would be necessary to determine the stomatal conductance that satisfies these constraints. Stomatal conductances that result in constant $\partial A/\partial E$ could be determined by computerized iteration procedures to simultaneously solve the equations in Appendix I of COWAN and FARQUHAR (1977), which were also presented by HALL and SCHULZE (1980a), and equations for modeling photosynthesis and respiration. A model of leaf photosynthesis and respiration was developed by HALL (1979) for applications of this type. Models of photosynthesis are discussed in Chapter 16, this Volume. The relation between stomatal conductance and CO_2 assimilation rate with changes in photon flux could be determined empirically.

For modeling long-term (day-to-day) changes in stomatal response to environment it would be necessary to understand and quantify the day-to-day changes in level of $\partial A/\partial E$ or reference stomatal conductance that may occur (as mentioned earlier the reference stomatal conductance is that which occurs when CO_2 assimilation rate is maximized but at normal $[O_2]$ and $[CO_2]$). The studies of HALL and SCHULZE (1980a) with *Vigna unguiculata* indicated that day-to-day values of $\partial A/\partial E$ increased and reference stomatal conductance decreased with progressive drought. However, for *Corylus avellana* there was a tendency for $\partial A/\partial E$ to decrease with progressive drought (FARQUHAR et al. 1980). Obviously, more studies are needed of the levels of $\partial A/\partial E$ that occur

especially in natural environments, but these measurement require sophisticated technology (HALL and SCHULZE 1980a). It is possible that the levels of $\partial A/\partial E$, the reference stomatal conductance, and the capacity for assimilation CO_2 are all interrelated (HALL and SCHULZE 1980a). As discussed in Chapter 7, this Volume, there is abundant evidence that day-to-day decreases in capacity for assimilating CO_2 are accompanied by decreases in the reference level of conductance irrespective of the factor responsible for the decreases in capacity for assimilating CO_2. The extent to which these associations between the reference conductance and capacity for assimilating CO_2 indicate a relatively constant $\partial A/\partial E$, as suggested by FARQUHAR (1979), is not known.

The advantages and disadvantages of modeling stomatal responses to environment based upon assumptions concerning the levels of $\partial A/\partial E$ and relations with reference stomatal conductance and CO_2 assimilation capacity are considered. Requiring an effective model of CO_2 assimilation is not a disadvantage for most applications because this model is also necessary for predicting the consequences of stomatal conductances to photosynthesis and adaptation. A major advantage of the $\partial A/\partial E$ hypothesis is that it integrates stomatal effects on the gaseous transfer of both water vapor and CO_2, the effects of energy balance on transpiration and leaf temperature, and the effects of internal CO_2 concentration and leaf temperature on internal leaf capacity for assimilating CO_2. The model does not include possible relations between leaf conductance and short-term effects of changes in leaf water status. However, for cases where short-term effects of leaf water status do occur, they could be modeled by assuming a threshold response of leaf conductance to bulk leaf water potential or that a system exists for maintaining bulk leaf pressure potential above a particular level. Modeling long-term effects by assuming that there is a relationship between reference stomatal conductance and CO_2 assimilation capacity would be extremely effective if the relationship is generally valid for specific genotypes or species and independent of the factor responsible for the long-term effects. The disadvantage of this approach is that it is constrained so that, if it does not work adequately, it will be difficult to modify.

8.2.3 Dynamic Models of Stomatal Function

Models which describe phenomena that continuously change with time and which contain time as an independent variable are defined as being dynamic. When steady-state models are applied in discrete-time-step simulations there is frequently the appearance but not the substance of dynamic modeling. Discrete-step simulation models which include dynamic submodels describing endogenous rhythms or the long-term effects of drought may be considered hybrids with both steady-state and dynamic characteristics.

Superficial evaluation would indicate that all biological processes are dynamic, and that dynamic models would be more powerful than steady-state or hybrid models. In practice, the type of model that would be more powerful would depend upon the objectives of the exercise, and a trade-off between the increased predictive and analytical capabilities of dynamic models, and

their increased complexity which approximates an order of magnitude greater than that of steady-state models of the same system.

A dynamic model has been developed for analyses of oscillations in stomatal conductance (COWAN 1972). At this time, it is not known whether stomatal oscillations occur in natural environments, and what their adaptive significance might be (COWAN 1977b), although the relevance of stomatal oscillations to water-use efficiency and plant growth has been discussed by COWAN and TROUGHTON (1971). A powerful quantitative method has been developed for predicting the environmental conditions that promote the occurrence of stomatal oscillations (FARQUHAR and COWAN 1974). This model predicts that the lack of oscillations in some controlled environment systems may be due to lack of control of external humidity or control of leaf temperature, both of which are artificial compared with natural environments and would tend to dampen oscillations. The study of stomatal oscillation may ultimately lead to insights into the mechanisms and regulation (CRAM 1976) of stomatal response to environment and water transport in plants. But the development of comprehensive, dynamic models of stomatal function requires a better understanding of the system than is available at this time.

8.3 Integrated Models of Plant Water Loss and Water Relations

The models of plant water loss which were discussed in Section 8.2 should be linked with models of liquid water transport in the soil-plant system and of plant water relations as suggested in Section 8.1.2. A major problem with this approach is that even though simple models are available of liquid water transport in the soil-plant system, there are indications that these models and current understanding have substantial flaws (as will be discussed in this section). Also, special problems arise when attempting to link certain threshold models for the response of leaf conductance to leaf water potential with models for liquid water transport in the soil-plant system. A threshold model which has only two states, open versus fully closed, cannot be linked to a steady-state model for liquid water transport if discontinuities are to be excluded. A threshold model of this type could be linked to a dynamic model of liquid water transport but, depending upon the time constants of the system, it would tend to predict oscillations of leaf conductance and these rarely occur in natural conditions. A threshold model which includes the possibility of progressive stomatal closure over a particular range of leaf water potentials would not necessarily exhibit these problems.

8.3.1 Steady-State Models of Plant Water Loss and Water Relations

Submodels describing the short-term (diurnal) changes and long-term (seasonal) changes in leaf water status are both necessary if a comprehensive model of plant water loss and water relations is to be developed. The diurnal course of leaf water potential may be modeled as mainly depending upon transpiration

(ELFVING et al. 1972; JARVIS 1976) and as a sequence of steady states (COWAN and MILTHORPE 1968), providing the rate of change in plant water content is small compared with the flow through the system. This approach may be valid for most herbaceous species and for some woody species (KAUFMANN 1976), but not for some succulents and many conifers where water loss from foliage may be sustained for several days or weeks by water stored in the plants (RUNNING et al. 1975; WARING and RUNNING 1978; RUNNING 1980b). A hydrologic balance model would also be needed to predict day-to-day changes in soil water conditions in the root zone (HALL and DANCETTE 1978).

However, relations between leaf water potential and transpiration rate frequently do not fit simple models. They have varied substantially depending upon the species, conditions of growth and measurement, and laboratory in which the studies were conducted (KAUFMANN 1976; COWAN 1977b). There are several areas where further research may resolve some of the controversy.

First, theoretical analyses indicate that liquid water transport may be intimately linked with solute transport (DALTON et al. 1975; FISCUS and KRAMER 1975). A cycling of solutes within plants, due to active pumping of ions into xylem tissue and active removal from xylem tissue, could provide the energy necessary for water to move against a water potential gradient in the whole-plant system (HALL and HOFFMAN 1976). The observation that roots excised from transpiring plants exuded sap (MEYER and RITCHIE 1980) supports this interpretation. However, the contribution of solute cycling to water transport may be small, especially at high transpiration rates.

Second, substantial interface resistance between roots and soil may occur in specific circumstances (COWAN and MILTHORPE 1968; FAIZ 1973; HERKELRATH 1975). This may resolve some of the controversy concerning whether the major resistance to water flow is in the root or the soil (ROSE et al. 1976). Under conditions where roots shrink away from soil particles, the major resistance would be neither in the soil nor in the root per se but between them.

Third, the liquid water pathway between soil and roots may exhibit irreversibility. Root systems frequently penetrate both dry and moist layers in the soil profile; yet they probably do not normally act as conduits cycling substantial quantities of water from the moist zone to the dry zone. An exceptional case of water cycling within root systems has been hypothesized for trees in an arid region of Chile where deep ground water is present (MOONEY et al. 1980). Adequate explanations for this irreversibility have not been provided, and this phenomenon has not been incorporated into models of the soil-plant continuum of water.

Fourth, the expected equilibrium between plant and soil water potentials, when transpiration is slow, has not been observed in some circumstances. Leaf water potential of some xerophytes and woody species have remained at low values (several bars negative) even after irrigation (SCHULZE et al. 1980; SYVERTSEN et al. 1975). Associations between lack of equilibrium at zero transpiration and rapid leaf enlargement have been described by BOYER (1974). But it is unlikely that the flow of water involved in growth, by itself, could account for the large deviations from equilibrium exhibited by some xerophytes and woody species. Lack of equilibrium also occurs when the liquid water continuum

between soil and plant is broken. This has been observed with certain CAM plants which maintained extremely high water potentials even though the soil was very dry. The plant-soil system becomes coupled soon after rain, due to the rapid growth of new roots. The extent to which uncoupling occurs among different species and environments is not known.

It should be apparent that current controversy and lack of understanding of water transport in the soil-plant system seriously constrains model development. Even the basis for evaluating components of water potential has been questioned (SPANNER 1973; PASSIOURA 1980).

8.3.2 Dynamic Models of Plant Water Loss and Water Relations

There are some plants which have low rates of water loss during certain seasons and sufficient water within the plant to sustain this water loss for several days or weeks, even though water uptake from the soil is negligible. Examples of this phenomenon are provided by evergreen conifers during winter, succulent CAM species in dry soils, and bottle trees (e.g., *Brachychiton australis*). By analogy with electrical circuits this phenomenon may be modeled as being dynamic and equivalent to capacitance (COWAN and MILTHORPE 1968). Charge and discharge of water stored in the plant could exhibit diurnal cycles superimposed upon seasonal cycles. The occurrence of substantial capacitance may partially explain hysteresis in relations between leaf water potential and transpiration with water potentials being lower in the afternoon than in the morning at a particular transpiration rate (JARVIS 1976; KAPPEN et al. 1975). A detailed discussion of the quantitative treatment of the capacitance of different plant tissues has been presented by JARVIS (1975). A dynamic model of water transport in plants has been developed by COWAN (1972), which incorporates effects due to capacitance, and which was used for analyzing oscillations in stomatal conductance. The influence of capacitance on the water balance of conifers has been examined using a discrete-step (daily increment) steady-state model (RUNNING et al. 1975).

Water flow in the soil-plant system as a whole may be influenced by the capacitance of specific tissues. The relationship between root water potential and root shrinkage would influence water flow through effects on the root-soil interface resistance. Stomatal apertures may be influenced by water flow and water deficits in the epidermal and mesophyll tissues (SHERIFF 1979; RUNNING 1980b), and consequently, by the capacitance of the epidermis or mesophyll. Limited information concerning values of parameters for these phenomena makes it difficult to model them at this time.

It is speculated that dynamic characteristics of water transport in plants may be due to linkages between oscillations in plant water status and stomatal apertures, and solute pumping across membranes. Evidence has been obtained indicating that ion pumping across membranes may be influenced by turgor pressure (CRAM 1976; COSTER et al. 1977). In an analogous manner increased tension in the xylem vessels of roots may cause increased ion pumping into the xylem. A mechanism of this type, if coupled with regulated removal of solutes from the xylem vessels in the shoot, could keep xylem pressure potential

and leaf water potential relatively constant with changes in transpirational flow (as was observed by HALL and SCHULZE 1980b; KAUFMANN 1976; WEATHERLEY 1970) or result in water flow in the direction of higher water potentials (HALL and HOFFMAN 1976; SHARP and DAVIES 1979). The development of realistic dynamic models of plant loss and water relations will require a more complete understanding of the water transport and water relations of the soil-plant system than is currently available.

8.4 Integrated Models of Canopy Water Loss and Water Relations

The water use of the dense populations of uniform plants commonly used in mechanized agriculture may be interpreted on a unit land area basis. In contrast, the water use of sparse populations may be interpreted on a unit plant basis. For dense communities containing different species it may be appropriate to determine the water-use of the community as a whole per unit land area, and attempt to quantify the contribution of each species in the community. A review of integrated models of canopy water loss has been presented by JURY (1979) and additional information has been presented by SLABBERS (1980).

Modeling canopies on a unit leaf area basis must be considered a monumental task because the structural and environmental characteristics of canopies are extremely complex. Canopies have been modeled as discrete strata containing leaves having a specific leaf area index and average angle (DUNCAN et al. 1967), but the substantial input requirements of models of this type preclude many uses, even with uniform populations of plants. Gaseous transfer characteristics within canopies are even more complex and may contain mesoscale mass flow of air (LEMON et al. 1973). Comprehensive models have been developed for simulating the soil-plant-atmosphere continuum of water, and CO_2 exchange of field crops (LEMON et al. 1973; VAN BAVEL 1974), but for input they require a detailed description of the canopy structure, and this is usually not available.

Some guidelines are presented for phenomenological models of canopy water loss and water relations which have modest input requirements. Evaporation from soil surfaces has been successfully modeled as being dependent upon the evaporative demand, until the surface dries, after which it is assumed to be dependent upon the water transfer properties of the soil (RITCHIE 1972). Soil evaporation may be considered as only occurring from the land surface that is not covered by the canopy (HALL and DANCETTE 1978) or as depending upon leaf area index (RITCHIE 1972) or the net radiation at the soil surface (TANNER and JURY 1976). Percent cover is by far the most convenient of these parameters for partitioning evaporation and transpiration. Transpiration per unit land area has been modeled as being proportional to the proportion of land area covered by the canopy (HALL and DANCETTE 1978), but this neglects micro-scale advection that may be important in some cases (HANKS et al. 1971). In addition a submodel for the canopy conductance to water vapor loss may be developed and incorporated into a model of canopy energy balance and gaseous transfer such as the model of MONTEITH (1965). In field studies, canopy conductances have been estimated by a model consisting of summing leaf con-

ductance × leaf area index for different strata in the canopy (BISCOE et al. 1976). They found that this model gave canopy conductances which were correlated with values obtained using micrometeorological data and the equation of MON-TEITH (1965).

Linking canopy resistance to soil water deficits is a major problem. First, it should be recognized that the development and maintenance of ground cover (and leaf area index) will be influenced by long-term drought (TURK and HALL 1980a, b). For canopies that completely cover the land surface, drought will mainly influence canopy water loss through effects on leaf conductances. A threshold hypothesis has been proposed for this phenomenon because changes in canopy conductance were not observed until more than 75% of the available water in the root zone was depleted (RITCHIE 1973). This hypothesis has been used in hydrologic balance models where the regulation of transpiration was linked to available soil water (ROSENTHAL et al. 1977). In addition, this threshold hypothesis for the regulation of canopy water loss has been linked to the threshold hypothesis for relations between stomatal conductance and leaf water potential in a model developed by SLABBERS (1980). In contrast, TURK and HALL (1980c) did not observe a threshold response, they observed an approximately linear relation between canopy conductance and the amount of available water in the root zone. By analogy with the hypothesis presented in Section 8.2.2.2 for relations between stomatal conductance and drought, it is proposed that long-term drought may have progressive effects on canopy conductance as observed by TURK and HALL (1980c), whereas more rapidly induced soil water deficits may result in threshold responses of the type described by RITCHIE (1973).

Submodels relating the development of ground cover (or leaf area index), and canopy conductance to soil water status in the root zone have the advantage that soil water status can be approximately modeled by hydrologic budget simulations (HALL and DANCETTE 1978). Linking the development of ground cover (or leaf area index), and canopy conductance to plant water status has the disadvantage that it would be necessary to develop a submodel of canopy water status. Models of canopy water status may have to include the effects of branched pathways (RICHTER 1973) and differential transpirational fluxes within the canopy.

It may be anticipated that developing models of water loss and water relations of canopies formed by communities of different species will be difficult. One approach to this complex system would involve a three-dimensional assemblage of unit cubes describing the root and shoot distribution and characteristics of component species in the community (personal communication by R.S. LOOMIS).

8.5 Conclusions:
Contributions of Mathematical Models to Research

Mathematical modeling of biological systems is a relatively new approach to obtaining improved understanding and it has been criticized. Some of the criti-

cism is warranted and may be partially due to the primitive state of ecological modeling and the fact that guidelines concerning procedures to be used in modeling ecological systems are only just evolving. I suggest, however, that much is to be gained from close integration between modeling and experimental studies.

The complexity of ecosystems requires integrated modeling and experimental approaches. Experimental studies can only provide limited quantities of information concerning the hydrologic budget of ecosystems because of the infinite number of soil-plant-atmosphere systems that are of interest to ecologists, agriculturalists, and others. Mathematical models can be used in an interpolative manner to reconstruct certain aspects of the functions of ecosystems over a period of days, months, or years using only isolated sets of experimental data (VAN BAVEL 1974).

Evaluating the effects of individual environmental variables on the soil-plant-atmosphere system represents another contribution of modeling. Individual response curves may be determined in controlled environments. Mathematical models based upon this information may then be used to predict, and are tested against, responses observed in natural environments in which many variables are changing over the same time period. In this way, mathematical models provide an important link between controlled environment studies and field studies (VAN BAVEL 1974). However, the quality of the link depends upon the adequacy of the controlled environment studies. Much of our present knowledge of water transport and plant response to water deficits has been obtained with plants in small pots of sterilized root media or even worse, with hydroponics or excised roots or shoots. It is likely that in many cases the responses may not be relevant to plant responses in most natural habitats.

Mathematical models coupled with controlled environment studies can provide information that cannot be obtained in the field at this time. For example, it is possible that atmospheric CO_2 concentrations may double during the next century (BAES et al. 1977). It would appear important for man to obtain some estimates of the consequences of this drastic disturbance to the ecosphere and to the habitats of man and the other biological organisms. These estimates could be obtained with controlled environment studies, to obtain isolated data sets describing plant responses to elevated CO_2 concentrations, and by using mathematical models to predict plant responses in hypothetical field environments. Another example is illustrated by the work of LANGE et al. (1978). They evaluated the adaptation of different plant species to the thermal regime of a location in the Negev desert by examining deviations between optimal temperatures for CO_2 assimilation and actual diurnal temperatures. Mathematical models are well suited to studies of this type. First, it is necessary to have a model that is able to predict the functions of a particular ecotype in its habit during the appropriate season. The model may then be used to predict ecotype performance in moderately different environments (e.g., warmer or cooler) to obtain information on the adaptation of the ecotype to its present habitat.

Plant breeders frequently attempt to develop genotypes of crop species with improved adaptation to specific habitats. A major problem with respect to water-limiting environments is that a priori it is not known whether it will

be necessary to select for increased or decreased rates of particular processes such as root growth (HALL et al. 1979). It is likely that some intermediate level will be optimal and this level will depend upon both the genetic background and the habitat. Mathematical models may be used to predict the consequences to plant performance of genetic manipulation of specific plant parameters. This may help plant breeders to establish priorities among the infinite possibilities open to them for genetic manipulation. Mathematical models of hydrologic balance have been used to predict optimal cycle lengths for annual crops in semiarid environments (DANCETTE and HALL 1979; HALL and DANCETTE 1978) which may be used to guide plant breeding programs.

Possibly the most important present and future applications of mathematical modeling of the systems described in this chapter concern water management including: water sheds, planning and operating water supply systems, and irrigated agriculture. Mathematical models have made major contributions in these areas but in one area it can only be assumed that modern science and human societies have failed. Irrespective of considerable research on soil-plant-atmosphere water relations, the timing of irrigations in much of the world is still based upon a combination of empirical experience and artistry. It is hoped that a combination of experimental studies, mathematical modeling, and development of new technologies will soon provide effective and practical scientific methods for determining when different crops should be irrigated in different environmental conditions.

I will conclude by pointing out a unique contribution that mathematical modeling can provide for ecology. Studies with mathematical models can, in principle, make contributions to understanding that are not possible at this time through experimental studies. The history of the physical sciences has many examples of predictions based upon mathematical models, some of which, with the passage of time and development of technology, have been supported or disproved by experimental studies. Mathematical models will probably play this same role in plant water relations and ecology as a whole.

Acknowledgements. I appreciate the comments provided by Professors C.B. OSMOND, O.L. LANGE and E.-D. SCHULZE, and Dr. J.B. PASSIOURA concerning earlier drafts of this review.

References

Ackerson RC, Krieg DR, Haring CL, Chang N (1977) Effects of plant water status on stomatal activity, photosynthesis, and nitrate reductase activity of field grown cotton. Crop Sci 17:81–84

Allway WG, Milthorpe FL (1976) Structure and functioning of stomata. In: Kozlowski TT (ed) Water deficits and plant growth Vol IV. Academic Press, London New York, pp 57–102

Aston MJ (1976) Variation of stomatal diffusive resistance with ambient humidity in sunflower (*Helianthus annuus*). Aust J Plant Physiol 3:489–502

Baes CF Jr, Goeller HE, Olson JS, Rotty RM (1977) Carbon dioxide and climate: the uncontrolled experiment. Am Sci 65:310–320

Bauer H (1978) Photosynthesis of ivy leaves (*Hedera helix*) after heat stress 1. CO_2-gas exchange and diffusion resistances. Physiol Plant 44:400–406

Bavel Van CHM (1974) Soil water potential and plant behavior: a case modeling study with sunflowers. Oecol Plant 9:89–109

Bavel Van CHM, DeMichele DW, Ahmed J (1973) A model of gas and energy exchange regulation by stomatal action in plant leaves. Tex Agric Exp Stn Publ MP-1078:28

Beadle CL, Turner NC, Jarvis PC (1978) Critical water potential for stomatal closure in sitka spruce. Physiol Plant 43:160–165

Biscoe PV, Cohen Y, Wallace JS (1976) Community water relations. Daily and seasonal changes of water potentials in cereals. Philos Trans R Soc London Ser B 273:565–580

Boyer JS (1974) Water transport in plants: mechanism of apparent changes in resistance during absorption. Planta 117:187–207

Burrows FJ, Milthorpe FL (1976) Stomatal conductance in the control of gas exchange. In: Kozlowski TT (ed) Water deficits and plant growth Vol IV. Academic Press, London New York, pp 103–152

Cooke JR, Debaerdemaeker JG, Rand RH, Mang HA (1976) A finite element shell analysis of guard cell deformation. Trans ASAE 19:1107–1121

Coster HGL, Steudle E, Zimmermann U (1977) Turgor pressure sensing in plant cell membranes. Plant Physiol 58:636–643

Cowan IR (1972) Oscillations in stomatal conductance and plant functioning associated with stomatal conductance: observations and a model. Planta 106:185–219

Cowan IR (1977a) Water use in high plants. In: McIntyre AK (ed) Water: planets, plants and people. Aust Acad Sci, Canberra, pp 71–107

Cowan IR (1977b) Stomatal behaviour and environment. Adv Bot Res 4:117–228

Cowan IR, Farquhar GD (1977) Stomatal function in relation to leaf metabolism and environment. In: Integration of activity in the higher plant. Soc Exp Biol Symp XXXI. Univ Press, Cambridge, pp 471–505

Cowan IR, Milthorpe FL (1968) Plant factors influencing the water status of plant tissues. In: Kozlowski TT (ed) Water deficits and plant growth Vol I. Academic Press, London New York, pp 137–193

Cowan IR. Troughton JH (1971) The relative role of stomata in transpiration and assimilation. Planta 97:325–336

Cram WJ (1976) Negative feedback regulation of transport in cells. The maintenance of turgor, volume and nutrient supply. In: Lüttge U, Pitman MG (eds) Transport in plants II. Part A. Cells. Encyclopedia of plant physiology new series Vol II. Springer, Berlin Heidelberg New York, pp 284–316

Dalton FN, Raats PAC, Gardner WR (1975) Simultaneous uptake of water and solutes by plant roots. Agron J 67:334–339

Dancette C, Hall AE (1979) Agroclimatology applied to water management in the Sudanian and Sahelian zones of Africa. In: Hall AE, Cannell GH, Lawton HW (eds) Agriculture in semi-arid environments. Ecol Stud Vol 34. Springer, Berlin Heidelberg New York, pp 97–118

Davies WJ, Wilson JA, Sharp RE, Osonubi O (1980) Control of stomatal behaviour in water-stressed plants. In: Jarvis PG, Mansfield TA (eds) Stomatal physiology. Univ Press, Cambridge

DeMichele DW, Sharpe PJH (1973) An analysis of the mechanics of guard cell motion. J Theor Biol 41:77–96

Duncan WG, Loomis RS, Williams WA, Hanau R (1967) A model for simulating photosynthesis in plant communities. Hilgardia 38:181–205

Ehleringer JR, Mooney HA (1978) Leaf hairs: effects on physiological activity and adaptive value to a desert shrub. Oecologia 37:183–200

Ehlig CF, Gardner WR (1964) Relationship between transpiration and the internal water relations of plants. Agron J 56:127–130

Elfving DC, Kaufmann MR, Hall AE (1972) Interpreting leaf water potential measurements with a model of the soil-plant-atmosphere continuum. Physiol Plant 27:161–168

Faiz SMA (1973) Soil-root water relations. Ph D Thesis, Univ Aberdeen

Farquhar GD (1978) Feed forward responses of stomata to humidity. Aust J Plant Physiol 5:787–800

Farquhar GD (1979) Carbon assimilation in relation to transpiration and fluxes of ammonia.

In: Marcelle R, Clijsters H, Poucke van M (eds) Photosynthesis and plant development. Junk, The Hague, pp 321–328

Farquhar GD, Cowan IR (1974) Oscillations in stomatal conductance the influence of environmental gain. Plant Physiol 54:769–772

Farquhar GD, Raschke K (1978) On the resistance to transpiration of the sites of evaporation within the leaf. Plant Physiol 61:1000–1005

Farquhar GD, Dubbe DR, Raschke K (1978) Gain of the feedback loop involving carbon dioxide and stomata. Plant Physiol 62:406–412

Farquhar GD, Schulze E-D, Küppers M (1980) Responses to humidity by stomata of *Nicotiana glauca* L. and *Corylus avellana* L. are consistent with the optimization of carbon dioxide uptake with respect to water loss. Aust J Plant Physiol 7:315–327

Fischer RA, Turner NC (1978) Plant productivity in the arid and semiarid zones. Annu Rev Plant Physiol 29:277–317

Fischer RA, Hsiao TC, Hagan RM (1970) After-effects of water stress on stomatal opening potential. I. Techniques and magnitudes. J Exp Bot 21:371–385

Fiscus EL, Kramer PJ (1975) General model for osmotic and pressure-induced flow in plant roots. Proc Natl Acad Sci USA 72:3114–3118

Fitzpatrick EA, Nix HA (1969) A model for simulating soil water regime in alternating fallow-crop systems. Agric Meteorol 6:303–319

Fuller EN, Schettler PD, Giddings JC (1966) A new method for prediction of binary gas-phase diffusion coefficients. Ind Eng Chem 58(5):19–27

Gale J (1972) Elevation and transpiration: some theoretical considerations with special reference to mediterranean-type climate. J Appl Ecol 9:691–702

Gale J (1973) Experiment evidence for the effect of barometric pressure on photosynthesis and transpiration. In: Plant response to climate factors. Proc Uppsala Symp, 1970 UNESCO, pp 289–294

Goudriaan J, Laar Van HH (1978) Relations between leaf resistance, CO_2-concentration and CO_2-assimilation in maize, beans, Lalang grass and sunflower. Photosynthetica 12:241–249

Hall AE (1970) Photosynthetic capabilities of healthy and beet yellows virus-infected sugar beets (*Beta vulgaris* L.). Ph D Thesis, Univ California, Davis

Hall AE (1979) A model of leaf photosynthesis and respiration for predicting carbon dioxide assimilation in different environments. Oecologia 143:299–316

Hall AE, Dancette C (1978) Analysis of fallow-farming systems in semi-arid Africa using a model to simulate the hydrologic budget. Agron J 70:816–823

Hall AE, Hoffman GJ (1976) Leaf conductance response to humidity and water transport in plants. Agron J 68:876–881

Hall AE, Schulze E-D (1980a) Stomatal responses to environment and a possible interrelation between stomatal effects on transpiration and CO_2 assimilation. Plant Cell Environ 3:467–474

Hall AE, Schulze E-D (1980b) Drought effects on transpiration and leaf water status of cowpea in controlled environments. Aust J Plant Physiol 7:141–147

Hall AE, Schulze E-D, Lange OL (1976) Current perspectives of steadystate stomatal responses to environment. In: Lange OL, Kappen L, Schulze E-D (eds) Water and plant life. Ecol Stud Vol 19. Springer, Berlin Heidelberg New York, pp 169–188

Hall AE, Foster KW, Waines JG (1979) Crop adaptation to semi-arid environments. In: Hall AE, Cannell GH, Lawton HW (eds) Agriculture in semi-arid environments. Ecol Stud Vol 34. Springer, Berlin Heidelberg New York, pp 148–179

Hanks RJ, Allen LH, Gardner H (1971) Advection and evapotranspiration of wide-row sorghum in the Central Great Plains. Agron J 62:520–527

Herkelrath WN (1975) Water uptake by plant roots. Ph D Thesis, Univ Wisconsin, Madison

Hinckley TM, Schroeder MO, Roberts JE, Bruckerhoff DN (1975) Effects of several environmental variables and xylem pressure potential on leaf surface resistance in white oak. For Sci 22:201–211

Hsiao TC, Allaway WG (1973) Action spectra for guard cell Rb$^+$ uptake and stomatal opening in *Vicia faba*. Plant Physiol 51:82–88

Jarman PD (1974) The diffusion of carbon dioxide and water vapor through stomata. J Exp Bot 25:927–936

Jarvis PG (1971) The estimation of resistances to carbon dioxide transfer. In: Sestak Z, Catsky J, Jarvis PG (eds) Plant photosynthetic production manual of methods. Junk, The Hague, pp 566–631

Jarvis PG (1975) Water in plants. In: Vries de DA, Afgan NH (eds) Heat and mass transfer in the biosphere I. Transfer processes in the plant environment. Halsted, Washington, pp 369–394

Jarvis PG (1976) The interpretation of the variations in leaf water potential and stomatal conductance found in canopies in the field. Philos Trans R Soc London Ser B 273:593–610

Jarvis PG (1980) Stomatal response to water stress in conifers. In: Turner NC, Kramer PJ (eds) Adaptation of plants to water and high temperature stress. Wiley-Interscience, New York, pp 105–122

Jarvis PG, Slatyer RO (1970) The role of the mesophyll cell wall in leaf transpiration. Planta 90:303–322

Jeffree CE, Johnson RPC, Jarvis PG (1971) Epicuticular wax in the stomatal antechamber of Sitka spruce and its effects on the diffusion of water vapor and carbon dioxide. Planta 98:1–10

Johnsson M, Issaias S, Brogardh T, Johnsson A (1976) Rapid blue-light-induced transpiration response restricted to plants with grass-like stomata. Physiol Plant 36:229–232

Jones HG (1980) Interaction and integration of adaptive responses to water stress: the implications of an unpredictable environment. In: Turner NC, Kramer PJ (eds) Adaptation of plants to water and high temperature stress. Wiley-Interscience, New York, pp 353–365

Jones MM, Rawson HM (1979) Influence of rate of development of leaf water deficits upon photosynthesis, leaf conductance, water use efficiency, and osmotic potential in sorghum. Physiol Plant 45:103–111

Jury WA (1979) Water transport through soil, plant, and atmosphere. In: Hall AE, Cannell GH, Lawton HW (eds) Agriculture in semi-arid environments. Ecol Stud Vol 34. Springer, Berlin Heidelberg New York, pp 180–199

Kappen L, Oertli JJ, Lange OL, Schulze E-D, Evenari M, Buschbom U (1975) Seasonal and diurnal courses of water relations of the aridoactive plant *Hammada scoparia* in the Negev desert. Oecologia 21:175–192

Kaufmann MR (1976) Water transport through plants: current perspectives. In: Wardlaw IF, Passioura JB (eds) Transport and transfer processes in plants. Academic Press, London New York, pp 313–327

Landsberg JJ, Butler DR (1980) Stomatal responses to humidity: implications for transpiration. Plant Cell Environ 3:29–33

Lange OL, Lösch R, Schulze E-D, Kappen L (1971) Responses of stomata to changes in humidity. Planta 100:76–86

Lange OL, Schulze E-D, Evenari M, Kappen L, Buschbom U (1978) The temperature-related photosynthetic capacity of plants under desert conditions. III. Ecological significance of the seasonal changes of the photosynthetic response to temperature. Oecologia 34:89–100

Lemon ER, Stewart DW, Shawcroft RW, Jensen SE (1973) Experiments in predicting evapotranspiration by simulation with a soil-plant-atmosphere model (SPAM). In: Bruce RR et al. (eds) Field soil water regime. Soil Sci Soc, Am, Inc SSSA Spec Publ No 5, Madison, pp 57–76

Lösch R (1977) Responses of stomata to environmental factors-experiments with isolated epidermal strips of *Polypodium vulgare* 1. Temperature and humidity. Oecologia 29:85–97

Lösch R (1979) Stomatal responses to changes in air humidity. In: Sen DN, Chawan DD, Bansal RP (eds) Structure, function and ecology of stomata. Dehra Dun, pp 189–216

Loomis RS, Rabbinge R, Ng E (1979) Explanatory models in crop physiology. Annu Rev Plant Physiol 30:339–367

Louwerse W, Zweerder WVD (1977) Photosynthesis, transpiration and leaf morphology of *Phaseolus vulgaris* and *Zea mays* grown at different irradiances in artificial and sunlight. Photosynthetica 11:11–21

Meyer WS, Ritchie JT (1980) Resistance to water flow in the sorghum plant. Plant Physiol 65:33–39

Monteith JL (1965) Evaporation and environment. In State and movement of water in living organisms. Soc Exp Biol Symp XIX, Univ Press, Cambridge, pp 205–234

Mooney HA, Ehleringer JR (1978) The carbon gain benefits of solar tracking in a desert annual. Plant Cell Environ 1:307–311

Mooney HA, Gulmon SL, Rundel PW, Ehleringer J (1980) Further observations on the water relations of *Prosopis tamarugo* of the northern Atacama desert. Oecologia 44:177–180

Neilson RE, Jarvis PG (1975) Photosynthesis in sitka spruce (*Picea sitchensis* (Bong.) Carr.) VI. Response of stomata to temperature. J Appl Ecol 12:879–891

Nobel PS (1978) Microhabitat, water relations, and photosynthesis of a desert fern *Notholaena parryi*. Oecologia 31:293–309

Osonubi O, Davies WJ (1980a) The influence of plant water stress on stomatal control of gas exchange at different levels of atmospheric humidity. Oecologia 46:1–6

Osonubi O, Davies WJ (1980b) The influence of water stress on the photosynthetic performance and stomatal behaviour of tree seedlings subjected to variation in temperature and irradiance. Oecologia 45:3–10

O'Toole JC, Cruz RT (1980) Response of leaf water potential, stomatal resistance, and leaf rolling to water stress. Plant Physiol 65:428–432

Pallardy SG, Kozlowski TT (1979) Relationship of leaf diffusion resistance of *Populus* clones to leaf water potential and environment. Oecologia 40:371–380

Passioura JB (1973) Sense and nonsense in crop simulation. J Aust Inst Agric Sci 39:181–183

Passioura JB (1980) The meaning of matric potential. J Exp Bot 31:1161–1169

Penning de Vries FWT (1972) A model for simulating transpiration of leaves with special attention to stomatal functioning. J Appl Ecol 9:57–77

Ramos C (1981) Relationship between leaf conductance, CO_2 partial pressure and CO_2 uptake rate in leaves, and a test of a portable instrument for its measurement in the field. Ph D Thesis, Univ California, Riverside

Raschke K (1976) How stomata resolve the dilemma of opposing priorities. Philos Trans R Soc London Ser B 273:551–560

Raschke K (1979) Movements of stomata. In: Haupt W, Feinleib ME (eds) Physiology of movements. Encyclopedia of plant physiology new series Vol VII. Springer, Berlin Heidelberg New York, pp 383–441

Raschke K, Hanebuth WF, Farquhar GD (1978) Relationship between stomatal conductance and light intensity in leaves of *Zea mays* L., derived from experiments using the mesophyll as shade. Planta 139:73–78

Richter H (1973) Frictional potential losses and total water potential in plants: a reevaluation. J Exp Bot 24:983–994

Ritchie JT (1972) Model for predicting evaporation from a row crop with incomplete cover. Water Resour Res 8:1204–1213

Ritchie JT (1973) Influence of soil water status and meteorological conditions on evaporation from a corn canopy. Agron J 65:893–897

Rose CW, Byrne GF, Hansen GK (1976) Water transport from soil through plant to atmosphere: a lumped parameter model. Agric Meteorol 16:171–184

Rosenthal WD, Kanemasu E, Raney RJ, Stone LR (1977) Evaluation of an evapotranspiration model for corn. Agron J 69:461–464

Running SW (1976) Environmental control of leaf water conductance in conifers. Can J For Res 6:104–112

Running SW (1980a) Environmental and physiological control of water flux through *Pinus contorta*. Can J For Res 10:82–91

Running SW (1980b) Relating plant capacitance to the water relations of *Pinus contorta*. For Ecol Manage 2:237–252

Running SW, Waring RH, Rydell RA (1975) Physiological control of water flux in conifers. Oecologia 18:1–16

Schulze E-D, Küppers M (1979) Short-term effects of plant water deficits on stomatal response to humidity in *Corylus avellana* L. Planta 146:319–326

Schulze E-D, Lange OL, Kappen L, Buschbom U, Evenari M (1973) Stomatal responses to changes in temperature at increasing water stress. Planta 110:29–42

Schulze E-D, Lange OL, Evenari M, Kappen L, Buschbom U (1974) The role of air humidity and leaf temperature in controlling stomatal resistance of *Prunus armeniaca* L. under desert conditions. I. A simulation of the daily course of stomatal resistance. Oecologia 17:159–170

Schulze E-D, Hall AE, Lange OL, Evenari M, Kappen L, Buschbom U (1980) Long-term effects of drought on wild and cultivated plants in the Negev Desert. Oecologia 45:11–18

Shackel KA, Hall AE (1979) Reversible leaflet movements in relation to drought adaptation of cowpeas. *Vigna unguiculata* (L.) Walp. Aust J Plant Physiol 6:265–276

Sharp RE, Davies WJ (1979) Solute regulation and growth by roots and shoots of water-stressed maize plants. Planta 147:43–49

Sharpe PJH, De Michelle DW (1977) Reaction kinetics of poikilotherm development. J Theor Biol 64:649–670

Sharpe PJH, Wu H (1978) Stomatal mechanics: volume changes during opening. Plant Cell Environ 1:259–268

Sheriff DW (1979) Stomatal aperture and the sensing of the environment by guard cells. Plant Cell Environ 2:15–22

Shoemaker EM, Srivastava LM (1973) The mechanics of stomatal opening in corn (*Zea mays* L.) leaves. J Theor Biol 42:219–225

Slabbers PJ (1980) Practical prediction of actual evapotranspiration. Irrig Sci 1:185–196

Slatyer RO (1967) Plant-water relationships. Academic Press, London New York

Smith WK, Geller GN (1979) Plant transpiration at high elevations: theory, field measurements and comparisons with desert plants. Oecologia 41:109–122

Spanner DC (1973) The components of the water potential in plants and soils. J Exp Bot 24:816–819

Syvertsen JP, Cunningham GL, Feather TV (1975) Anomalous diurnal patterns of stem xylem water potentials in *Larrea tridentata*. Ecology 56:1423–1428

Tanner CB, Jury WA (1976) Estimating evaporation and transpiration from a row crop during incomplete cover. Agron J 68:239–243

Thorpe MR, Warrit B, Landsberg JJ (1980) Responses of apple leaf stomata: a model for single leaves and a whole tree. Plant Cell Environ 3:23–27

Turk KJ, Hall AE (1980a) Drought adaptation of cowpea. II. Influence of drought on plant water status and relations with seed yield. Agron J 72:421–427

Turk KJ, Hall AE (1980b) Drought adaptation of cowpea. III. Influence of drought on plant growth and relations with seed yield. Agron J 72:428–433

Turk KJ, Hall AE (1980c) Drought adaptation of cowpea. IV. Influence of drought on water use, and relations with growth and seed yield. Agron J 72:434–439

Turner NC (1974) Stomatal response to light and water under field conditions. In: Bieleski RL, Ferguson AR, Cresswell MM (eds) Mechanisms of regulation of plant growth. Roy Soc NZ Bull 12:423–432

Turner NC, Begg JE (1978) Responses of pasture plants to water deficits. In: Wilson JR (ed) Plant relations in pastures. CSIRO, Melbourne, pp 50–60

Waggoner PE (1969) Predicting the effect upon net photosynthesis of changes in leaf metabolism and physics. Crop Sci 9:315–321

Waring RH, Running SW (1978) Sapwood water storage: its contribution to transpiration and effect upon water conductance through the stems of old-growth Douglas fir. Plant Cell Environ 1:131–140

Weatherley PE (1970) Some aspects of water relations. Adv Bot Res 3:171–206

Wong SC (1979) Stomatal behavior in relation to photosynthesis. PhD, Thesis, Aust Natl Univ

Wong SC, Cowan IR, Farquhar GD (1978) Leaf conductance in relation to assimilation in *Eucalyptus pauciflora* Sieb. ex Spreng. Influence of irradiance and partial pressure of carbon dioxide. Plant Physiol 62:670–674

Wong SC, Cowan IR, Farquhar GD (1979) Stomatal conductance correlates with photosynthetic capacity. Nature (London) 282:424–426

9 Physiological Responses to Moderate Water Stress

K.J. Bradford and T.C. Hsiao

CONTENTS

9.1 Introduction

On a global basis, water is a paramount factor in determining the distribution
of species, and the responses and adaptations of a species to water stress are
critical for its success in any environmental niche. Numerous studies have reported a myriad of changes elicited by water stress. The changes observed
are dependent on the species under study and on the severity, duration, and
time course of the stress. Before reviewing the changes in detail, we will first
present an overview of stress and responses using the stress–strain concept
of physics. Next, we will discuss specific water-related parameters for quantifying
plant water status and briefly consider how changes in the parameters may
affect plant functions. This is followed by the main body which first reviews
and analyzes selected responses to water stress and then examines the integrated
adaptive behavior of whole plants.

   The intent of this chapter is to discuss selected topics from the personal
viewpoint of the authors. For more comprehensive coverage, other recent reviews
should be consulted (Paleg and Aspinall 1981; Turner and Kramer 1980).

9.2 Stress and Responses: an Overview

The numerous physiological responses of plants to water deficits generally vary
with the severity as well as the duration of the stress. Only the most sensitive
processes are altered by a very mild stress. As the stress increases, these changes
intensify, and additional processes become affected in accordance to their relative
sensitivities to the stress. If the stress is prolonged, there is more time for
the initial effects to lead to secondary and tertiary responses. These changes
with time, taken as a whole, often represent modulation of the system to meet
the demand of the altered environment. An example is leaf senescence during
drought, discussed in Section 9.8.3. Very few responses to water stress represent
true lesions, especially when the stress is not extremely severe. One exception
is the cavitation of water in the xylem under high tension (Milburn 1979;
see Chap. 5, this Vol.), which constitutes outright damage to the water transport
system. In many other cases, the changes effected by water stress which appear
to be damaging, probably represent operation of control mechanisms to adjust
the performance of the organism in accordance with the environmental constraint. Selected examples of this behavior are discussed in the following sections.

   A general conceptual framework of stress physiology may help to formalize
some of the aforementioned points and aid in the detailed examinations of
plant responses to water stress to follow. The framework is the physical model
of stress–strain relationships (Fig. 9.1). It should be pointed out at the onset,
however, that this simple analogy is useful only to a point. The term "stress"
is in common use in the physiological literature but its meaning has been
controversial at times (Kramer 1980; Levitt 1980). In physics and mechanics,
stress refers to the force applied to a body and strain is used to describe

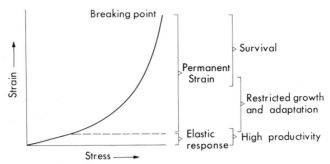

Fig. 9.1. Generalized stress–strain diagram of physical material, as a model for plant responses to water stress. Overall plant responses in terms of growth and productivity, corresponding to the regions of physical strain, are given on the *right margin* of the diagram

the deformation of the body resulting from the stress. In accordance with that usage, plant water deficiency would be the stress, and responses to the deficiency, the strain. In physics, stress and strain are usually introduced first under the topic of elasticity. In engineering, they are treated in depth under the topic of strength of materials. The names of these topics suggest strength and ability to resist on the one hand, and yielding and resilience on the other, behavior characteristics very pertinent to consideration of plant responses and adaptation to stresses.

The analogy can be extended to include magnitudes of stress and strain. Strain increases with each increment of stress, as seen in stress–strain diagrams (Fig. 9.1). A small amount of stress, when applied to a body, causes limited and reversible deformation. The original form is fully recovered when the stress is removed. As shown in the figure, this perfectly elastic response to stress holds only within the elastic limit. When deformation or strain is pushed above this limit by additional stress, the body is permanently deformed more and more as stress continues to rise. The final point on the diagram is reached when the body can strain no further and breaks under yet another increment of stress. In terms of environmental stresses and plant responses, the region of elastic strain represents stress levels which have little or no enduring effect on plant performance and productivity. An example could be the mild water stress encountered daily at midday by plants growing on well-watered soil in sunny weather. Diminution of the stress in the late afternoon and recovery overnight may be such that the daily overall growth is not inhibited. As stress becomes more than just very mild, however, the effects on plants are at least partly permanent. This is represented by the region of permanent strain above the elastic limit.

In the lower portion of the permanent strain region, growth and productivity are somewhat restricted, and adaptive responses and adjustment to the stress set in. In the upper portion of the permanent strain region, growth is virtually stopped, extensive damage due to the stress is obvious, and the plant is struggling to survive. The breaking point of strain is reached when stress is sufficiently severe to kill the plant. In our view, the interval of elastic strain on the ordinate

diagram (see Chap. 2, this Vol.). Ψ is dependent on water content because both of its key components, Ψ_π and Ψ_p, are theoretically functions of water volume in the protoplasm. Water content can be related conceptually to plant responses to water stress. For example, sufficient reduction in water content causes herbaceous plants to lose their normal shape and form, the maintenance of which is dependent on cell inflation by water. With sufficient reduction in cellular water volume, metabolites become significantly more concentrated and spatial relationships among organelles and membranes are substantially altered.

Turgor pressure is another parameter closely tied to tissue water status, but only in the water status region above the zero turgor point (Chap. 2, this Vol.). When nearly saturated tissue (RWC approaches 1.0) loses small amounts of water, Ψ_p drops steeply, as is the case for Ψ. Turgor pressure is extremely difficult to measure directly. The common procedure of estimating Ψ_p by $\Psi - \Psi_\pi$ is not without pitfalls, especially where Ψ and Ψ_π are measured on separate subsamples and using different techniques, each with its own inherent errors. Turgor pressure is known to be critical for expansive growth (see below). Although by definition Ψ_p is a unique function of the pressure in the water with atmospheric pressure as datum, from the viewpoint of physiological functions the key is not the absolute pressure Ψ_p, but the pressure differential ($\Delta\Psi_p$) across the plasmalemma-cell wall boundary. This point was made clear earlier in a detailed analysis (HSIAO 1973a). Consideration of Ψ_p instead of $\Delta\Psi_p$ is adequate in most natural situations, however, because the pressure outside the cell wall and in the intercellular air space is usually atmospheric.

Osmotic potential (Ψ_π) is yet another possible indicator of water stress. Its relationship to water volume is described by Morse's equation, making it a rather insensitive indicator because changes in water volume having functional significance are usually only a small fraction of the total. More importantly, Ψ_π obviously is also a function of the amount of solutes present. The latter quantity can be markedly affected by osmotic adjustment to water stress or salinity, or by variations in other environmental parameters such as light (ACEVEDO et al. 1979).

The foregoing discussion makes it clear that no single parameter is totally sufficient as the indicator of water stress, except for the most restricted situations. In the vast majority of the cases, a combination of Ψ and RWC or Ψ and Ψ_p provides much more insight than the use of any one of the three parameters. A major part of the current literature, however, still reports only Ψ.

Regardless of the indicator, it is helpful to identify a general reference point of water stress. The most frequently mentioned reference point is the level of water stress that just induces obvious wilting in leaves low in sclerenchyma tissue, such as those of annual crops. This level also corresponds approximately to the point of nearly zero turgor in cells (TURNER 1974) and the point when stomata close pronouncedly in response to the water stress in the bulk leaf tissue. Needless to say, CO_2 assimilation is also substantially restricted at that point. For many field-grown herbaceous crop species without a significant history of water stress, the wilting point falls in a Ψ range of -13 to -16 bar. When subjected to the preconditioning effect of water stress, however, herba-

ceous crop species capable of osmotic adjustment would show wilting only at substantially lower Ψ values, in some cases perhaps as low as -28 to -30 bar. In many tree and wild species, wilting as a visual symptom of water stress may not be observed due to the mechanical strength of the leaves. The Ψ value representing the point of near-zero turgor and threshold for stomatal closure may also be much lower than -16 bar, reflecting more solutes in the tissue (FERERES et al. 1978). When RWC is used as an indicator, however, there appears to be more unity among species and in the same species with varying growth history — the near-zero turgor point for the vast majority of leaves appears to be in the RWC range of 0.75 to 0.85.

As will be amplified below, many physiological processes are altered by water stress levels milder than those causing wilting and stomatal closure. The level of water stress that triggers perturbation in plant functions depends on the processes in question, as well as on the duration of the stress and preconditioning. In many cases, the thresholds correspond to high values of Ψ and remarkably small reductions in tissue water status may cause distinct deficiency responses. Indeed, for some processes such as expansive growth the threshold may not exist.

9.4 Effects of Stress on Growth and Underlying Metabolism

The ultimate goal of plant ecophysiology is to understand how environment and physiological processes interact to determine the growth and reproduction of plants. Just as the availability of water is a dominant factor of the physical environment, expansive growth (irreversible cell enlargement) is an overriding physiological event. On the short term, cellular expansion and utilization of substrates are intimately linked through feedback channels to all aspects of metabolism. On the long term, the expansion of leaves determines the active photosynthetic surface area and sets limits on the future growth potential of the plant. Thus, expansive growth can be viewed as an integrator of the environmental and metabolic events which influence overall plant productivity. For this reason, the various short-term physiological responses to water stress will be considered within the context of expansive growth. This will involve an outline of the physics of growth, followed by current ideas on the metabolic mechanisms underlying cellular expansion.

9.4.1 A Physical View of Expansive Growth

Expansive growth has long been known to be highly sensitive to variations in Ψ (see HSIAO 1973a). Various lines of evidence suggest that the initial effect of reduced Ψ on expansion is physical and is mediated by changes in Ψ_p. The best of such evidence is that obtained with giant internodal cells of *Nitella* whose Ψ_p could be monitored directly (GREEN 1968; GREEN et al. 1971). Sudden

and BOYER 1978; SILK and WAGNER 1980). The major uncertainty in these estimates is the magnitude of C, which may change during growth. For auxin-induced growth of soybean hypocotyls, BOYER and WU (1978) calculated that increases in E_g and C contributed about equally to the stimulation of growth rate. The change in C presumably resulted from an increase in membrane permeability to water, which is known to be sensitive to a variety of chemical and environmental stimuli (KUIPER 1972; LEE-STADELMANN and STADELMANN 1976).

The importance of C in regulating growth rates during water stress is a complex question (see Chap. 2, this Vol.). The magnitude of C determines the Ψ gradient within the tissue for a given rate of water flow, or growth. The importance of the auxin-induced increase in C may be to offset the larger $\Delta\Psi$ that would be required to sustain a higher flow rate. A similar increase in C during water stress would allow maintenance of the growth rate with a smaller $\Delta\Psi$ between the xylem and the expanding cells. Alternatively, if prolonged water deficit limits growth through effects on $\Psi_{p,th}$ or E_g, the magnitude of C will be less important as flow rates will be slow and $\Delta\Psi$ will be small. Much more experimental information is required before we can realistically evaluate the importance of C in determining the overall growth rate during water stress.

9.4.2.4 Cell Wall Synthesis

In addition to the factors discussed above, synthesis of new cell wall material is an essential component of steady-state growth. There is generally a close parallel between the incorporation of glucose into cell wall material and the rate of elongation (BAKER and RAY 1965; RAY 1962). In certain cases, however, wall synthesis can be divorced from its usual relation to growth. For example, elongation can occur in excised tissues without corresponding wall synthesis if additional substrates are not supplied. This is accompanied by an apparent thinning of the cell walls (RAY 1962). Certain inhibitors of elongation, such as 20 mM Ca^{2+}, do not prevent wall synthesis, leading to an increase in wall material and presumably thicker walls (BAKER and RAY 1965). It is possible that when elongation is prevented by water stress, wall synthesis might continue, producing small cells with thicker walls, as was reported for water-stressed cotton leaves (CUTLER et al. 1977). However, experiments using osmotic stress to reduce Ψ have found that wall synthesis is inhibited in parallel with growth, and wall thickness remains constant (BAYLEY and SETTERFIELD 1957; BAKER and RAY 1965), suggesting the existence of tight feedback links between wall expansion and wall synthesis.

9.4.2.5 Protein Synthesis

As with cell wall synthesis, protein synthesis is an obvious requirement for sustained cell enlargement. The myriad of functions of proteins in cellular

physiology as enzymes, structural and membrane components, etc., makes it unlikely that expansive growth could continue for very long without simultaneous protein synthesis. The rapidity with which inhibitors of protein synthesis will arrest growth has led to the concept of growth-limiting proteins (CLELAND 1971; PENNY 1971). These are postulated to be rapidly turned over so that when new synthesis is blocked, these essential proteins become depleted and growth ceases. More recent results have tended to confirm this hypothesis (BATES and CLELAND 1979; LADO et al. 1977).

On the other hand, mild water stress is known to inhibit protein synthesis as well as growth (reviewed by HSIAO 1973a). In rapidly expanding *Zea mays* leaves, a brief desiccation treatment that reduced Ψ only 2 or 3 bar caused a dramatic shift of polyribosomes to monoribosomes, which was interpreted to reflect a decrease in overall protein synthesis (HSIAO 1970). Similar results have been reported for several other species (MORILLA et al. 1973; BARLOW et al. 1977). DHINDSA and CLELAND (1975b) found that the application of pressure to osmotically stressed *Avena* coleoptiles did not reverse the inhibitory effect on protein synthesis, indicating that the response was not due to a reduction in tissue Ψ.

HSIAO (1970) originally suggested, on the basis of the sensitivity of growth and polyribosome changes to reductions in Ψ, that inhibition of protein synthesis may represent a feedback effect of slowed growth rates. Recently, SCOTT and coworkers (1979) compared polyribosome levels of mature and elongating wheat leaves as Ψ varied from -8 to -30 bar. Water stress caused a decline in the polyribosome percentage in the elongating leaves but had no significant effect in mature leaves. In the young tissue, the shift from polyribosomes to monoribosomes occurred concomitantly with the cessation of elongation. These data, confirmed by unpublished work of HSIAO on maize, indicate that there is a close relationship between expansion and protein synthesis in growing cells. These regulatory links must be very tight, as the reciprocal effects of water stress on growth and protein synthesis, and of protein synthesis inhibitors on growth, can both be expressed within a matter of minutes. How slowed growth rates affect the activity of ribosomes remains an intriguing question.

The inhibition of protein synthesis during water stress is not indiscriminate. Synthesis of some proteins is promoted by water stress while that of others is reduced (DHINDSA and CLELAND 1975a). BRADY and coworkers (1974) were able to show by a dual-labeling technique that water stress (91% RWC for 2 h) reduced the rate of synthesis of Fraction I protein in young wheat leaves. This included effects on both subunits of ribulose bisphosphate carboxylase, and there was a preferential loss of chloroplast polyribosomes. Interestingly, a similar decrease in the synthesis of Fraction I protein relative to other soluble proteins was induced by ABA (10^{-6} M). In contrast, DHINDSA and CLELAND (1975b) reported that ABA indiscriminately inhibited protein synthesis in *Avena* coleoptiles, which presumably synthesize very little RuBPCase. These provocative results have yet to be followed up in detail using modern molecular biology techniques.

As would be expected from the effects of water stress on protein synthesis, the activities of a large number of enzymes have been found to vary in response

to stress (see Todd 1972; Hsiao 1973a). These are too numerous to catalog here, but in general, enzyme activities are lowered by water stress except those involved in hydrolysis or catabolism, which often increase. Two well-studied enzymes exhibiting this pattern are nitrate reductase (NR) and ribonuclease (RNase), the former decreasing rapidly during water stress, the latter increasing in activity. These enzymes will be used as examples to illustrate the control mechanisms operating to regulate enzyme levels during water stress.

Slight reductions in water content (Huffaker et al. 1970) or Ψ (Morilla et al. 1973) resulted in a rapid decline in NR activity in barley and maize seedlings. Morilla and coworkers (1973) concluded that inhibition of enzyme synthesis, coupled with rapid turnover of the enzyme, was responsible for the loss of activity. Correlations between polyribosome levels and NR activity during stress and recovery, the prevention of restoration of NR activity by cyclohexi-mide after rewatering, as well as the insensitivity of the rate of decline in NR to water stress, support this hypothesis. Others (Plaut 1974; Heuer et al. 1979) have suggested that at least part of the inhibition of NR activity by water stress results from inactivation of existing enzyme, but more specific information on the rates of turnover is needed to establish this point.

Since NR is inducible by nitrate (Hewitt 1975), it is possible that water stress effects are an indirect result of reduced nitrate uptake. Shaner and Boyer (1976) showed that the level of NR in the tissue was related to the flux of nitrate from the roots, rather than to the tissue nitrate content or to Ψ. Reduced nitrate uptake by stressed roots in conjunction with stomatal closure and lessened transpiration resulted in a severe restriction of nitrate flux to the shoot. Appar-ently, nitrate in the leaf is compartmentalized so that only that in the transport path is effective in inducing NR. This example illustrates the integrative nature of plant response to water stress, with root ion uptake, stomatal control of transpiration, and leaf protein synthesis interacting to alter the activity of a key assimilative enzyme.

In contrast to NR, RNase activity increases as a result of water stress, but only when stress is quite severe (Maranville and Paulsen 1972). In isolated tobacco protoplasts, synthesis of the enzyme is induced by increases in the osmotic strength of the medium (Premecz et al. 1977), indicating that changes in protoplast volume or concentration of internal solutes is the triggering mecha-nism. RNase is also sensitive to modification by plant growth regulators, with ABA increasing and kinetin decreasing the activity in turgid plants (Arad et al. 1973; Sodek and Wright 1969). During water stress, however, these hormonal relationships can be reversed due to contrasting effects on leaf water balance. When barley leaves were pretreated with either ABA or kinetin and then stressed by desiccation or salinity, RNase activity was determined by the water status, rather than the hormonal treatment (Arad et al. 1973; Arad and Richmond 1976). ABA pretreatment tended to reduce the severity of the fall in Ψ, and also resulted in lowered RNase activity. Kinetin, on the other hand, enhanced the loss of tissue water and stimulated RNase activity. The hormonal effects were therefore reversed from those found in the absence of water stress. It appears that the specific hormonal controls operating in turgid tissue can be overridden when water deficit becomes excessive.

9.5 Synthesis and Transport of Growth Regulators in Response to Stress

As virtually all aspects of plant growth and development are influenced by both water stress and growth regulators, it is not surprising that the major plant hormones have been investigated with respect to water stress. The literature is too voluminous to be covered comprehensively here. Emphasis will be placed on the changes in endogenous levels of growth regulators in response to water stress and the possible consequences of these changes with respect to plant water balance, growth, and development. Other viewpoints can be found in previous reviews (ASPINALL 1980; DAVIES et al. 1980; ITAI and BENZIONI 1976; MANSFIELD et al. 1978; VAADIA 1976; WALTON 1980; WRIGHT 1978).

9.5.1 Indoleacetic Acid

Information on the effect of water stress on endogenous indoleacetic acid (IAA) levels is scarce and often conflicting. Diffusable auxin content of both *Helianthus annuus* and *Anastatica hierochuntica* decreased with decreasing soil water content (HARTUNG and WITT 1968). IAA in *Vicia faba* leaves, on the other hand, increased considerably during a drying cycle, but the response was relatively slow compared to the changes in ethylene and ABA levels (HALL et al. 1977). These studies suffer from poor characterization of Ψ and its components, and the degree and duration of stress varied widely. DARBYSHIRE (1971) measured a linear increase in IAA oxidase activity with decreasing Ψ between -2 and -15 bar in tomato, and suggested that leaf IAA content would be reduced as a result. This expectation was not supported in work with a wilty mutant of tomato, *flacca,* which contains higher than normal amounts of IAA-like activity, apparently due to a stimulation of IAA synthesis rather than to reduced degradation (TAL et al. 1979). However, it is not clear in this mutant which effects are caused by water stress and which result from altered hormonal relationships, particularly with respect to ABA. At present, no conclusions can be drawn concerning a specific relationship between Ψ and endogenous IAA levels.

There is evidence that basipetal auxin transport is inhibited by water stress ($\Psi < -10$ bar) (KALDEWEY et al. 1974; DAVENPORT et al. 1977, 1980). Ethylene synthesis may be involved here, as the gas is known to reduce auxin transport (BEYER and MORGAN 1971). The combination of ethylene production and reduced auxin transport is thought to be involved in the promotion of leaf abscission by water stress (see Sect. 9.8.2).

9.5.2 Gibberellins

Little is known of the effect of water stress on metabolism of gibberellins (GA). Endogenous GA activity declined rapidly in stressed lettuce leaves, and rose again during a subsequent recovery period (AHARONI et al. 1977). The

fall in GA activity preceded the rise in ABA content of the same tissue. These results are complicated by the use of detached leaves, which are simultaneously senescencing. Nonetheless, water stress (10% reduction in RWC) accelerated the rate of decline in GA (AHARONI and RICHMOND 1978). Gibberellins are known to be synthesized in roots as well as leaves (TORREY 1976), but effects of water stress on the sites of synthesis and transport of GA have not been studied. The paucity of information on endogenous GA during water stress prevents speculation as to their importance in physiological responses.

9.5.3 Ethylene

Increased ethylene production is a general response of plant tissues to environmental stresses, including water stress (YANG and PRATT 1978). Since ethylene is a gas, it has been suggested that stomatal closure during water stress might limit diffusion from the plant, leading to increased internal concentrations (EL-BELTAGY and HALL 1974). Further work has shown, however, that ethylene readily diffuses from leaves and stems, and that similar results are obtained whether ethylene emanation or internal accumulation are measured (WRIGHT 1980; ZERONI et al. 1977). This implies that water stress increases the rate of ethylene synthesis. The biosynthetic pathway of ethylene has recently been deduced, including the identification of a new intermediate, aminocyclopropanecarboxylate (ACC) (ADAMS and YANG 1979; LÜRSSEN et al. 1979). ACC is derived from S-adenosylmethionine (SAM), and is in turn converted into ethylene. The rate-limiting step in the sequence is the production of ACC, and most factors which accelerate ethylene synthesis act to stimulate the conversion of SAM to ACC (see YANG 1980 for review). As expected, when wheat leaves were allowed to lose 10% fresh weight, synthesis of both ACC and ethylene increased markedly (APELBAUM and YANG 1981). The mechanism by which water stress stimulates the activity of the ACC-forming enzyme remains unknown.

Ethylene has generally been considered to act near its site of synthesis, since long-distance transport of the gas is unlikely. In response to waterlogging or root anaerobiosis, however, ACC synthesis in the roots of tomato plants is accelerated, but conversion of ACC to ethylene is blocked (BRADFORD and YANG 1980, 1981). ACC accumulates in the roots and is transported in the xylem to the shoot, where in the presence of oxygen it is rapidly converted to ethylene. Thus, "ethylene" may be mobile in the plant in the form of its precursor, ACC. Waterlogging and water deficit are quite different stresses (BRADFORD and YANG 1981), and it is not known whether ACC transport is involved in the stimulation of ethylene production by reduced Ψ. It should, however, be considered as a possible mechanism for hormonal communication of stress responses within the plant.

9.5.4 Cytokinins

Information on how endogenous cytokinins (CK) are affected by water stress is quite limited, despite considerable speculation as to their role in plant re-

sponses to drought (ITAI and BENZIONI 1976; VAADIA 1976). Cytokinins are thought to be synthesized primarily in the roots, although they can be metabolized throughout the plant (VAN STADEN and DAVEY 1979). Xylem sap from droughted (ITAI and VAADIA 1965) or osmotically stressed (ITAI et al. 1968) roots contained considerably less CK activity per unit volume than that from control roots. When the stress consisted of an enhanced evaporative demand which caused only transient wilting of the leaves, CK in both root exudate and leaf extracts were reduced by 50% (ITAI and VAADIA 1971). ITAI et al. (1968) proposed that a reduction in CK export from the roots could be responsible for leaf senescence and protein synthesis inhibition in water-stressed plants. Unfortunately, subsequent work in this area has been virtually nil. Key data needed to establish the validity of the hypothesis, such as characterization of the degree and duration of stress required, the kinetics of CK transport during stress, the levels of CK in the leaf, and the specific CK involved, are not available.

The notion that a drop in CK export from the roots acts as a "signal" to the shoot of root distress remains provocative. ASPINALL (1980) has noted that "such a 'signal' would seem to be redundant during water stress, since shoot water potential falls more rapidly than root potential during stress". This depends to a certain degree, however, on how stomata act to regulate leaf Ψ during soil water depletion (BATES and HALL 1981). Stomata can also respond to other root stresses while leaf Ψ remains unaffected (BRADFORD and YANG 1981; SOJKA and STOLZY 1980). Whether CK are involved in these stomatal responses is unknown, but the concept of root-to-shoot communication of root status is still useful (JONES 1980). The physiology of CK in water-stressed plants deserves further experimental consideration.

9.5.5 Abscisic Acid

In mesophytic plants, the endogenous levels of abscisic acid (ABA) rise markedly in response to moderate water stress, apparently due to de novo synthesis (MILBORROW 1974; WALTON 1980). The increase is most dramatic in the leaves, but has also been observed in roots, stems, and xylem and phloem sap (HOAD 1975, 1978; WALTON et al. 1976; ZEEVAART 1977). Following the discovery that stomatal closure can be induced by ABA, considerable effort has been directed toward elucidating the relationship between the increase in ABA levels and stomatal behavior during water stress, as will be discussed below (Sect. 9.6.1). The present section emphasizes the regulation of ABA levels in the plant and possible nonstomatal effects of ABA.

In some cases, as when leaves are sampled at various times in a drying cycle, ABA content changes little until a "threshold" Ψ is reached, then it accumulates rapidly with a further fall in Ψ (ZABADAL 1974). If Ψ of detached leaves is reduced to various levels and then held constant to allow time for ABA accumulation, a more gradual rise in ABA content may be observed (WRIGHT 1977). At least part of the reason for the apparent threshold Ψ for ABA synthesis may be due to increasing stress duration at the same time that

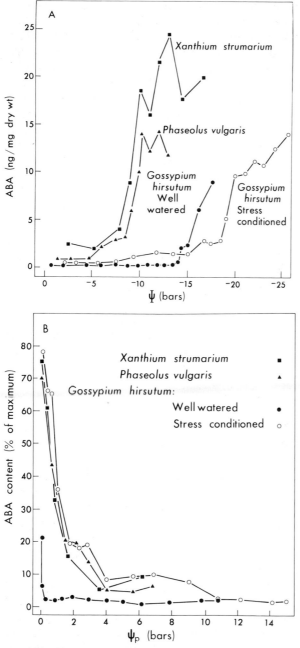

Fig. 9.2 A, B. Relationship of ABA accumulation to Ψ and Ψ_p. **A** Ψ of an excised leaf was determined as it dried with a pressure bomb and samples were taken for ABA determination. All samples were extracted at the same time, so that stress duration was identical. "Stress-conditioned" *G. hirsutum* plants had previously experienced eight cycles of wilting and recovery prior to measurement, and Ψ_π was 5.6 bar lower than in the well-watered plants. **B** Data of **A** plotted as a function of Ψ_p, which was determined from the pressure-volume curves obtained during the drying period. It is apparent that, despite the large variations in ABA response to Ψ, all the curves show a sharp increase in ABA accumulation as Ψ_p approaches zero. (Redrawn from Pierce and Raschke 1980)

Ψ is falling in rapid desiccation experiments. However, even when precautions are taken to exclude this complication, a plot of ABA content versus leaf Ψ still shows a marked change in slope as Ψ_p approaches zero (Fig. 9.2). If the Ψ corresponding to zero turgor is lowered by osmotic adjustment, the point of rapid ABA accumulation is also shifted (Fig. 9.2 A). It is likely, therefore, that the very large (up to 40-fold) increases in ABA content during water stress are triggered by the loss of leaf turgor.

The gradual rise in ABA content when turgor is low but above zero (Fig. 9.2 B) may be due to heterogeneity in Ψ_π or volumetric elastic modulus among leaf cells, broadening the range of Ψ over which individual cells would reach zero turgor, or to inherent differences in the turgor sensitivity of different cells. It is these smaller changes in ABA content which can occur before Ψ_p reaches zero which should perhaps attract our attention, as the combination of osmotic adjustment and stomatal closure often prevents the complete loss of turgor in field-grown plants (TURNER and JONES 1980). DAVIES and LAKSO (1978) found that the ABA content of apple leaves increased linearly with a decline in Ψ_p during a slowly developing water stress, even though Ψ_p did not fall below 5 bar. ACKERSON (1980) reported that repeated stress and recovery cycles resulted in an increase in the ABA content of turgid leaves, but had little effect on the amount of ABA accumulated upon wilting. It is interesting in this regard that well-watered cotton plants showed virtually no increase in ABA until Ψ_p was less than 1 bar, while plants which had experienced several stress cycles began to accumulate ABA when Ψ_p was still at least 9 bar (Fig. 9.2 B). Consequently, modification of the turgor sensitivity of ABA synthesis (or degradation) may be more closely related to adaptation to water stress than is the rate of ABA production or degree of accumulation when Ψ_p reaches zero.

The notion that small changes in endogenous ABA concentration might be physiologically significant has been invoked to explain kinetic discrepancies between increases in leaf ABA content and stomatal closure (see Sect. 9.6.1). These hypotheses suggest that the initial response to water deficit may be release of ABA from a "bound" or "compartmentalized" form as an initial response to stress, followed by stimulation of synthesis as a subsequent event (RASCHKE 1975). It is unlikely that free ABA is released by hydrolysis of ABA conjugates (probably ABA-glucosyl ester), as the conjugated forms represent only a small fraction of the total ABA, and they increase rather than decrease during wilting (MILBORROW 1978; ZEEVAART 1980).

Compartmentation remains a distinct possibility, both among cell types and within a given cell, and there is evidence that ABA is not uniformly distributed within cells. It has been thought that this might result from ABA synthesis occurring primarily in the chloroplasts (LOVEYS 1977; MILBORROW 1974), but this is now controversial (HARTUNG et al. 1981; WALTON 1980). Regardless of the site(s) of synthesis, the distribution of ABA among the cellular compartments seems to be determined primarily by pH gradients. HEILMANN and co-workers (1980) found that up to 80% of the total ABA content of illuminated spinach leaves can be contained in the chloroplasts, which they explained on the basis of the equilibration of a weak acid (pK$_a$ of ABA=4.8) between two

compartments of differing pH, assuming that the chloroplast membrane is permeable only to the undissociated species. Further results indicate that this assumption is probably valid, both for the chloroplast envelope and the plasma membrane, and that the transport of ABA does not seem to be carrier mediated (Gimmler et al. 1981; Kaiser and Hartung 1981). A difference in uptake of ABA into chloroplasts in light or darkness could be accounted for by the pH gradient which exists across the outer membrane under the two conditions (Heilmann et al. 1980). The hypothesis also predicts that ABA concentration will be very low in the vacuole, since it is slightly acidic, and Milborrow (1979) found that the "vacuolar" sap of citrus fruit vesicles did contain considerably less ABA than the remaining "cytoplasmic" fraction. Intracellular ABA concentration should therefore be greatest in the chloroplasts, intermediate in the cytoplasm, and least in the vacuole, the differences being accentuated in the light (Cowan et al. 1982).

If water stress causes ABA redistribution, then it should affect either the pH gradients or the membrane permeability to anionic ABA. Hartung and coworkers (1981) reported that osmotic stress caused release of ABA from isolated chloroplasts, which they attributed to a decrease in stromal pH due to water stress. In intact cells, however, decreases in Ψ largely affect Ψ_p, not cell volume or Ψ_π. It remains to be shown that changes in hydrostatic pressure will alter chloroplast pH or ABA compartmentation. Others have proposed that the initial effect of water stress is to increase the permeability of chloroplast membranes to ABA (Mansfield et al. 1978; Milborrow 1979). In light of the pH-dependent distribution model, this would require an increase in permeability to anionic ABA, as the membrane is already highly permeable to the protonated species. Such measurements have not been made on chloroplasts obtained from water-stressed plants. While there is now a testable hypothesis for the intracellular distribution of ABA, we still do not know how a fall in Ψ_p acts to alter ABA compartmentation or synthesis.

ABA is metabolized to phaseic acid (PA), dihydrophaseic acid (DPA), and ABA-glucosyl conjugates (see Walton 1980, for review). The ABA concentration in the leaf therefore reflects the relative rates of ABA synthesis and metabolism. Harrison and Walton (1975) concluded that both synthesis and metabolism were accelerated during water deficit, leading to a new, higher steady-state level of ABA in bean leaves. Zeevaart (1980) also found that metabolites continued to accumulate even when ABA levels remained constant in stressed *Xanthium* leaves. When the stress was relieved, ABA levels fell after a 1-h lag, and the PA accumulation rate increased. The rate of ABA catabolism increases when even slight turgor is restored following stress (Pierce and Raschke 1981). The synthesis and degradation of ABA seem to be finely balanced around the point of zero turgor to regulate the cellular ABA content.

The high level of ABA present in water-stressed leaves raises the question of whether transport to other parts of the plant occurs. Zeevaart (1977) presented evidence for the export of ABA and its metabolites in phloem exudate from stressed *Ricinus* leaves. Tracer studies in turgid plants also support the notion that ABA is mobile in the phloem (Bellandi and Dörffling 1974). Very high concentrations of ABA (up to 0.1 mM) were reported in phloem

sap exuding from cut pods of water stressed *Lupinus albus* (HOAD 1978). Steam girdling of petioles prevented export of ^{14}C-ABA applied to the leaves (HARTUNG 1976) and led to an increase in endogenous ABA levels (SETTER et al. 1980). In addition to compartmentation and rates of synthesis and degradation, translocation must also be considered as a mechanism for internal regulation of ABA levels.

Although HOAD (1975) concluded that ABA appearing in the xylem sap of stressed sunflower plants had originated in the leaves, roots of several species have been shown to synthesize ABA following water loss or osmotic stress (BARR 1973; MILBORROW and ROBINSON 1973; WALTON et al. 1976). Thus, it is likely that ABA levels increase in roots during water stress, but perhaps less markedly than in leaves. A major resistance to water transport in the plant occurs in the roots. Various authors have reported that treatment with ABA increases the hydraulic conductance (C) of the root system (GLINKA 1980; TAL and IMBER 1971), which would reduce the Ψ gradient required for water transport and maintain a higher leaf Ψ. Others, however, found either no effect (CRAM and PITMAN 1972) or a decrease (MARKHART et al. 1979) in C following ABA application. Even in cases where hydrostatic pressure (MARKHART et al. 1979) or suction (GLINKA 1977) were used to minimize the contribution of ion transport to the estimation of C, contrasting effects were observed. As the results of such experiments have been shown to be highly dependent upon growth conditions, methods of measurement, duration of treatment, species, and other factors (PITMAN et al. 1974a), such differences are perhaps not surprising.

A major source of variation, however, may reside in the widely differing concentrations of ABA employed. For example, KARMOKER and VAN STEVENINCK (1978) found maximum stimulation of volume flow through bean root systems at 0.5 µM ABA, with decreasing effects as the ABA concentration was increased to 10 µM. PITMAN and WELLFARE (1978) reported an initial stimulation of volume flow in barley roots followed by inhibition, but the ABA concentration used was 50 µM, which is at least 100-fold greater than the reported maximum ABA content of roots even following an episode of water stress (WALTON et al. 1976). Although the data for endogenous ABA levels in roots are limited, it would seem that studies with applied ABA should be restricted to concentrations in the range of 1 µM or less if the results are to have physiological significance. There is a clear need for more information on the endogenous ABA levels (and compartmentation?) in roots and how these change in response to water stress.

Estimations of C involve measurements of ion uptake and transport to the xylem, and these processes are also sensitive to ABA and water stress. Both water stress (from 98% to 88% RWC) and ABA (1 µM) had little effect on ion uptake into barley roots, but transport from roots to shoots was reduced, resulting in an accumulation of ions in the root (PITMAN et al. 1974b). But again, there are conflicting reports of stimulation of ion uptake and transport by ABA (COLLINS and KERRIGAN 1974; GLINKA 1980). Regardless of the fine details, all reports agree that ABA can markedly influence the ionic relations of roots. ABA could therefore play a role in the accumulation of solutes which

with the consequent reduction in transpiration as well as assimilation. The threshold behavior is most common in herbaceous crop species (Beadle et al. 1973; Davies et al. 1981; Turner 1974; Hsiao 1973a; Ludlow 1980), but is also often observed in woody species (Jarvis 1980). It is consistent with the concept of stomata serving as an overriding protective mechanism against excessive tissue water loss. Midday stomatal closure in many crops in the field when soil water depletes sufficiently is an example of such a response. For many herbs growing in the field under high irradiance and favorable environment, the threshold for stomatal closure in recently matured leaves in light lies in the range of -12 to -16 bar, provided that the plants have had no recent history of substantial water stress. With a history of stress and osmotic adjustment, the threshold can be much lower (Begg and Turner 1976; Ludlow 1980). The threshold may also differ for leaves of different ages and prior exposure to radiation (Jordan et al. 1975).

Stomata also close partially in many cases when air humidity is low and the evaporative demand is high, although the water status of the bulk leaf tissue is above the closure threshold. This response has been covered in detail in Chapter 7 this Volume. Since this behavior results in the immediate reduction in CO_2 assimilation and the conservation of water in spite of the absence of tissue water stress, it may be advantageous only in locations where the rainfall probability diminishes as the season progresses and competing species which may use up the water conserved in the soil are absent. Behavior of this kind may be called "pessimistic" (Jones 1980; Y. Vaadia personal communication), as it appears to anticipate the worst water supply situation in the future. Not surprisingly then, the literature leaves the impression that crop species selected for high productivity tend to show minimal or no stomatal response to humidity while trees and wild herbs often have marked responses. The interplay between stomatal responses to bulk leaf water status and to humidity have been analyzed by Ludlow (1980).

Stomatal closure due either to low leaf water status or high evaporative demand is based on changes in turgor balance between guard cells and surrounding epidermal cells. Because the mechanism is turgor-mediated, the notion is still held by some that excessive loss of leaf water, or differential loss of water between guard cells and their surroundings, can lead directly to changes in turgor balance and stomatal closure. Actually, the mechanism is much more complex, and is, in the words of Stålfelt, not just "hydropassive" but "hydroactive". The former term refers to stomatal movements arising as the result of the gain or loss of only water by cells, whereas the latter refers to stomatal movements resulting from gain or loss of solutes by cells followed by changes in water volumes. Many years ago, Stålfelt (1955) had repeatedly observed that as water stress developed in leaves, solute loss from guard cells, reduction in guard cell volume, and stomatal closure occurred simultaneously. The necessity of solute gain and loss from guard cells for more than just transient stomatal movement is demonstrated in the elegant analysis by Raschke (1979) of the mechanics of stomata. Here we will use a simpler approach similar to that of Boyer (1976) to make the same point. For stomata to open substantially, turgor in guard cells (Ψ_p^{gc}) must be much higher than turgor in subsidiary

cells (Ψ_p^{sc}) (MEIDNER and EDWARDS 1975; RASCHKE 1979). On the other hand, because of their adjacent positions and the lack of an impervious barrier to water transport, Ψ in guard cells and subsidiary cells must be in near equilibrium, in the absence of sudden stepwise changes in water status. Since $\Psi = \Psi_p + \Psi_\pi$,

$$\Psi_p^{gc} + \Psi_\pi^{gc} = \Psi_p^{sc} + \Psi_\pi^{sc}.$$

It follows that for $\Psi_p^{gc} \gg \Psi_p^{sc}$, $\Psi_\pi^{gc} \ll \Psi_\pi^{sc}$. That is, for stomata to open substantially, osmotic potential must be much more negative and solutes much more concentrated in guard cells than in subsidiary cells. Conversely, for stomata to close as a consequence of water stress or high humidity gradient, the turgor difference and hence solute difference between guard cells and subsidiary cells must be markedly reduced. Merely a redistribution of water between guard cells and their neighbors without an underlying movement of solutes would be insufficient to cause the changes in turgor needed to effect closure. Generally, the changes in Ψ_π and hence Ψ_p in guard cells associated with full opening and closing are in the range of 10 to 40 bar (HSIAO 1976; RASCHKE 1979).

STÅLFELT's early work did not identify the solute species involved in the hydroactive closing of stomata under water stress. Since K^+ and associated anions account for virtually all of the solutes being transported in and out of guard cells in stomatal movements elicited by changes in CO_2 concentration and light (reviewed by HSIAO 1976), it is no surprise that K^+ was also found to be the cationic solute underlying stomatal movement in response to changes in bulk leaf water status (HSIAO 1973b; EHRET and BOYER 1979). As the leaf undergoes water stress, stomata close concurrently with losses in stainable K^+ from guard cells. Changes in stomatal aperture and guard cell K^+ are well correlated, either as stomata close during water stress or as they reopen when stress is released (HSIAO 1973b). When water status of the leaf is either raised or lowered rapidly, stomatal movement lags behind the change in tissue water content but appears to be synchronous with variations in stainable K^+ in guard cells, as shown in Fig. 9.3. As the leaf tissue rapidly lost water during a 10-min drying period, stomatal aperture and stainable K^+ in guard cells declined only slightly. Subsequent to the drying, the tissue was kept in an air stream of 100% relative humidity for 30 min. During that time there was no further drying and the tissue maintained its water content, although stomata continued to close in parallel with K^+ loss from the guard cells. In fact, most of the decline in K^+ and aperture took place during the period when there was no further drop in tissue water content. These data suggest that the hydropassive component is insignificant in stomatal movement induced by variations in leaf water status. Stress apparently triggers the efflux of K^+ and anions from guard cells with the consequent diminution of turgor differences between guard cells and their neighbors, leading to stomatal closure.

Having verified the hydroactive nature of the stomatal closing elicited by water stress and demonstrated the key role for K^+, there remains still the question of how a reduction in leaf water status leads to K^+ efflux. A popular hypothesis, that water stress causes abscisic acid (ABA) accumulation which in turn leads to the efflux of K^+ from guard cells, was recently reviewed by

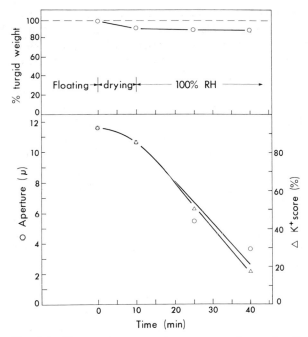

Fig. 9.3. Changes in stomatal aperture and guard cell K^+ in leaf discs of *Vicia faba* in response to water stress. *Above* Fresh weight of leaf discs as percent of turgid weight when floating on water, after drying in moving air, and while being kept in saturated moving air. *Below* Stomatal aperture and stainable K^+ score in guard cells of the leaf discs. Replicates of discs were taken from recently mature leaves and floated on water under moving air of controlled humidity and temperature. At time zero, the discs were removed from water and allowed to dry in the same moving air for the indicated duration, then transferred to moving saturated air to prevent further desiccation. Discs were removed at various times, two epidermal strips were taken from each disc, and the apertures in one strip under oil were measured microscopically. The other strip was stained for K^+ with cobaltinitrite, darkened by sulfide, and scored microscopically as percent of guard cell area occupied by the stain. Fischer (1971) has shown a linear relationship between K^+ content and percent of guard cell area stained. Data are means of 4 discs, with 20 stomata measured for aperture and 4 microscope fields scored for K^+ per disc. (Unpublished data of T.C. Hsiao)

Raschke (1979). While most of the evidence indeed indicates a mediating role for ABA in stomatal behavior in general and under conditions of gradually intensifying water stress in particular, some data are inconsistent with the hypothesis. These inconsistencies were pointed out in an earlier review (Hsiao 1973a) and are basically discrepancies between the time course of variations in ABA levels and stomatal behavior. When suddenly stressed, the accumulation of ABA in leaves can lag behind stomatal closure (Beardsell and Cohen 1975; Henson 1981; Walton et al. 1977). Generally ABA buildup in leaves becomes measurable only after 20 min to 1 h of stress (e.g., Wright 1969; Pierce and Raschke 1980a) but stomatal closure begins sooner (e.g., Fig. 9.3), often within 5 min from the start of the reduction in tissue water status (Graz-

IANI and LIVNE 1971; HENSON 1981; HSIAO unpublished). Upon rewatering of stressed plants, leaf ABA declines ahead of recovery in stomatal opening (BEARDSELL and COHEN 1975; LOVEYS and KRIEDEMANN 1973; LUDLOW et al. 1980). These discrepancies commonly are attributed to preferential localization of ABA in or near guard cells. Since guard cells constitute only about 1% of leaf volume (RASCHKE 1979), ABA content of bulk leaf tissue is a poor indicator of its concentration at the stomatal site. Recent results with a highly sensitive radioimmunoassay for ABA indicate that guard cell protoplasts are capable of synthesizing ABA in response to an osmotic stress (WEILER et al. 1982). On the other hand, there is some indication that ABA elicited by water stress is produced largely in the mesophyll and may be transported from there to the guard cells (LOVEYS 1977). Changes in pH within the mesophyll cells due to stress could result in an increase in ABA in the apoplast (COWAN et al. 1982), but experimental data on whether this occurs in vivo are lacking. Also, gaps exist as to how ABA acts to change the rate and direction of ion transport between guard cells and their neighbors. Further discussion of these points is found elsewhere (DAVIES et al. 1981; HSIAO 1976; RASCHKE 1979; WALTON et al. 1977).

Even less is known about the mechanism underlying stomatal response to humidity at relatively high leaf water status. LÖSCH and SCHENK (1978) found some correlation between stomatal aperture of, and stainable K^+ in, guard cells of *Valerianella locusta* as air humidity was varied. Upon a reduction or elevation in humidity, aperture decreased or increased respectively, but always ahead of decreases or increases in guard cell K^+. This is in contrast to the close correlation found between aperture and K^+ in the same plant when illumination was varied. The authors were unable to conclude whether the initial aperture change was hydropassive followed by stabilization and adjustment via K^+ transport, or whether the initial response was underlaid by changes in solutes other than K^+. It is not known if ABA plays a role in the humidity response.

9.6.2 Nonstomatal Effects of Water Stress on Photosynthesis

In the resistance network analysis of CO_2 assimilation, the intracellular resistance (r_i) represents all the "resistances" encountered by CO_2 in moving from the intercellular air spaces to the carboxylation sites in the chloroplasts. Since this includes dissolution of CO_2 in the cell wall water, movement across the wall, the membranes, and the cytoplasm to the sites of the carboxylase, as well as the biochemical reaction of carboxylation, r_i should be clearly distinguished from the epidermal resistance discussed above which involves only gaseous diffusion. Examination of r_i should provide a gross view of water stress effects on the photosynthetic processes downstream from stomata. It is unquestionable that under very severe stress, when tissue RWC is only a fraction of that under well-watered conditions, the photosynthetic apparatus will be damaged and the processes other than gaseous CO_2 transport inhibited. Therefore, the important question is not whether r_i can be increased by stress, but rather what stress severity will cause r_i to rise, what mechanisms underlie changes

in r_i, and what the importance of these changes is to plant adaptation to water stress conditions.

Early work indicated that the response of r_i to water stress can be quite variable, sometimes increasing at about the same water status as the threshold for stomatal closure, and other times remaining unchanged until very severe stress had developed (reviewed by HSIAO 1973a). More recent studies, while using improved gas exchange techniques and broadening the range of species tested, have still not uncovered the causes for the different behaviors of r_i under water stress (PEARCY 1982). In addition to possible inherent differences among species, certainly part of the variability must lie in the rates and degrees of stress development. Studies demonstrating little or no effect of stress on r_i down to the range of 60%–70% RWC often involved rapid imposition of stress, in a matter of less than one hour to a few hours (MEDERSKI et al. 1975; SLATYER 1973; TROUGHTON and SLATYER 1969). On the other hand, stress usually developed over a period of several days to weeks in studies showing marked effects on r_i (JONES 1973b; COLLATZ 1977; COLLATZ et al. 1976). There are contrasting data, however, particularly when osmotic adjustment is involved. For example, r_i of the perennial desert shrub *Larrea divaricata* increased about proportionally with the increase in stomatal resistance as stress developed rapidly in potted plants (MOONEY et al. 1977). In the natural environment, however, r_i stayed nearly constant down to a leaf Ψ of -49 bar and was relatively independent of stomatal behavior. JONES and RAWSON (1979) found a similar effect of the rate of stress development on r_i of *Sorghum*. In both cases, osmotic adjustment occurred during the slowly developing stress to maintain some turgor and presumably prevent alteration of the photosynthetic machinery. But even osmotic adjustment does not always insure an unaltered r_i. Cotton which had osmotically adjusted to drought assimilated at higher rates at low leaf Ψ, but at lower rates at high leaf Ψ, compared to unadjusted plants (ACKERSON and HEBERT 1981; OLIVEIRA and HSIAO 1980). Since stomatal conductance was higher in the adjusted plants than in the controls at any given leaf Ψ (ACKERSON and HEBERT 1981), r_i must have increased in the adjusted leaves in spite of the better maintenance of leaf turgor.

This latter example illustrates a conceptual problem which may underlie much of the controversy over water stress effects on r_i. If r_i is taken to represent all factors influencing the rate of assimilation of CO_2 from the intercellular spaces, then the conclusion that r_i increased in the stressed leaves is justified. However, for the resistance analog model to be valid, the photosynthetic rate must be proportional to the intercellular CO_2 concentration (c_i), which generally means making measurements at CO_2 levels well below ambient (JONES 1973a). Intercellular resistance is then estimated from the inverse of the assimilation versus c_i curve. At ambient CO_2 concentrations, other factors, such as electron transport rate or ability to regenerate RuP_2, may co-limit the assimilation rate, which will no longer be a linear function of c_i (Chap. 16, this Vol.). Thus, photosynthesis can be limited by nonstomatal factors even though the calculated r_i (determined at low c_i) remains unchanged.

If, in the example cited, water stress affected primarily the CO_2-saturated rate of photosynthesis, then the measured r_i (at low CO_2) could have remained

unaltered although the apparent r_i (at ambient CO_2) had increased. Assumption of the linear model for r_i leads to the conclusion that most of the reduction in photosynthesis due to water stress results from stomatal closure (SLATYER 1973). However, there are data suggesting that the degree to which stomata limit photosynthesis remains constant or even decreases during water stress due to associated alterations in the photosynthetic machinery (FARQUHAR and SHARKEY 1982; JONES 1973b; VON CAEMMERER 1981). This may even result in an increase in c_i in stressed plants, which has been reported to be the case for cotton (RADIN and ACKERSON 1981). The relative importance of stomatal versus nonstomatal limitations to photosynthesis may depend upon the rate of imposition, degree, and duration of water deficit. Systematic comparisons of the responses of stomata and r_i of selected species at various rates of stress development, and at both low and high c_i, should clear up much of the present confusion.

The biochemistry of photosynthesis is often divided into the light reactions and the dark reactions. Studies of the effects of water stress on the dark reactions have focused on RuP_2 carboxylase/oxygenase. The activity of this enzyme extracted from several C_3 crop species was found to decrease as stress developed over a period of several days or longer (JONES 1973b; JOHNSON et al. 1974; O'TOOLE et al. 1976). Although CO_2 assimilation followed the same general trend, r_i was only loosely related to RuP_2 carboxylase activity (JONES 1973b; O'TOOLE et al. 1976). With Sitka spruce (*Picea sitchensis*), the assayed activity of the enzyme remained about constant while r_i increased during the drying cycle, down to a needle Ψ of -30 bar (BEADLE and JARVIS 1977). The other enzymes reduced by slowly developing stress are carbonic anhydrase in cotton (JONES 1973b), and ribulose-5-phosphate kinase and PEP carboxylase in barley (HUFFAKER et al. 1970). Other photosynthetic enzymes are yet to be examined.

Water stress readily inhibits light-induced chlorophyll formation in etiolated leaves but has little or no effect on chlorophyll contents in green leaves of crop species (BOYER 1976; JONES 1973a; reviewed by HSIAO 1973a). Chlorophyll in Sitka spruce did not change significantly until needle Ψ reached -21 bar after slow drying (BEADLE and JARVIS 1977).

Early studies, conducted mostly in the 1960's on crop species, indicated that reactions in the chloroplasts, especially the light reactions, were inhibited by very severe stress (e.g., $<50\%$ RWC) but probably little affected by mild to moderate stress (reviewed by HSIAO 1973a). BOYER and BOWEN (1970), however, reported convincing data indicating that even moderate stress on sunflower leaves inhibited the activity of Photosystem II in chloroplast fragments isolated from these leaves. More severe stress, on the other hand, was necessary to affect chloroplast fragments from pea leaves. The inhibition of Photosystem II in sunflower was well correlated with the inhibition of CO_2 assimilation by intact leaves for the range of leaf Ψ from the beginning of to complete stomatal closure. FRY (1970) first reported an inhibition of electron transport, measured as Hill activity, for cotton chloroplast fragments isolated from severely stressed leaves. Later, FRY (1972) demonstrated that the inhibition was also present in the Ψ range expected for the stomatal threshold for cotton. BEADLE and JARVIS (1977) found, however, that electron transport in fragmented chloro-

plasts, measured as uncoupled Photosystems I and II activities, remained about constant as Sitka spruce underwent slow stress from a needle Ψ of -7 bar to about -28 bar, when assimilation became nil and the needles neared the point of shedding due to desiccation. Unfortunately, the data were quite variable from date to date and hence would not have shown gentle trends or small changes. Mohanty and Boyer (1976) found that the quantum yields of photosynthesis in intact leaves as well as of Photosystem II activity in isolated chloroplast fragments were reduced by stressing the plant. Quantum yield of leaf photosynthesis was also observed to be reduced in stressed *Larrea* by Mooney et al. (1977), but the reduction appeared to have accounted for only a part of the measured increase in r_i. These data indicate that basic aspects of light-harvesting and energy conversion were altered by stress. Interestingly, quantum yield of *Larrea* adapted to the Death Valley environment was not affected by stress down to leaf Ψ of -49 bar (Mooney et al. 1977).

Most exciting are the recent results of Govindjee et al. (1981) on chlorophyll *a* fluorescence transients, showing reduced ratio of maximum to minimum fluorescence (P/O) in intact leaves of *Nerium oleander, Atriplex triangularis,* and *Tolmiea menziesii* under water stress. They interpreted the data to be indicative of a blockage of electron flow on the water side of Photosystem II since Q, the electron acceptor of Photosystem II, must remain in a largely oxidized state for chlorophyll *a* fluorescence to be low under excitation. The sensitivity of the response was such that the authors actually proposed the use of the P/O ratio as an indicator of leaf Ψ, at least in the range of -9 to -40 bar. The changes were evident whether the stress developed in 1 h or over a period of days and were readily reversible upon rewatering. Unfortunately, no accompanying data on assimilation or other aspects of photosynthesis were presented.

In sunflowers, various features of electron transport and cyclic and noncyclic phosphorylation of isolated chloroplasts were shown to be inhibited by rapid stress in the range affecting stomata and CO_2 assimilation (Keck and Boyer 1974). Both phosphorylation systems were reduced to zero at -16 to -18 bar of leaf Ψ, about 5 bar below the zero turgor point and a stress level which still permitted some net photosynthesis in those leaves (Boyer 1976). Inhibition of Photosystems I and II activities was also only partial at these stress levels, indicating an uncoupling of phosphorylation from electron flow (Keck and Boyer 1974). In a later study conducted by Boyer and associates (Younis et al. 1979) on spinach, however, photophosphorylation by chloroplasts was reduced only somewhat at -15 bar and was still about 40% of the control rate at -25 bar. At -25 bar, the spinach leaves contained only about one third of the water compared to the control (Younis et al. 1979), and probably would have lost viability if kept at that water content for a number of hours.

By varying the water content of isolated chloroplasts drastically, Santarius and Ernst (1967) concluded that marked dehydration leads to reversible uncoupling of photophosphorylation from electron transport. Younis et al. (1979) succeeded in isolating coupling factor CF_1 from chloroplasts of rapidly stressed and control spinach leaves. CF_1 from stressed leaves exhibited less ATPase activity and much less tendency to bind the fluorescent analogs of ADP and ATP than CF_1 from control leaves. Circular dichroism spectra indicated that stress altered the conformation of CF_1 protein, probably in the random coil

region. Results with reconstitution experiments suggested that both CF_1 and the chloroplast membrane were altered by stress. The effects of stress were obvious at leaf Ψ of -16 to -18 bar, more so at still lower Ψ values, and were reversible in vivo but not in vitro. To date, these findings represent the only definitive evidence of a macromolecular structural alteration of functional significance induced by stress.

Reversibility represents a puzzling aspect of stress effects on chloroplast functions. Isolation and assay of chloroplast activities were usually carried out in identical media of relatively high Ψ whether the chloroplasts originated from stressed or control leaves. Thus, the effects of stress are residual and cannot be reversed in vitro, yet rewatering of the stressed plant effected quick recovery (BOYER 1976; YOUNIS et al. 1979). When chloroplasts from well-watered plants were stressed in osmotic solutions, similar effects on electron transport and photophosphorylation were observed but at reductions of chloroplastic volume much larger than those required if stressed in vivo (BOYER 1976; HSIAO 1973a; SANTARIUS and ERNST 1967). Further, the effects were reversed completely when the chloroplasts were placed back in the standard assay medium. In the case of the coupling factor, the CF_1 protein studied by YOUNIS et al. (1979) was stored in 2 M $(NH_4)_2SO_4$, Ψ of which should be less than -100 bar. Yet, CF_1 from the control leaves remained highly active, in contrast to the low activity of CF_1 from the stressed. All these observations point to some unique feature of the cytoplasmic environment playing a key role in mediating the effects of stress and of rewatering. What is more, the mediating role appeared to be all-encompassing, perhaps impinging upon the whole complement of light reactions.

A discussion of causal mechanisms of water stress effects on photosynthesis would not be complete without mentioning the recent proposals of OSMOND et al. (1980). As these authors note, environmental conditions conducive to water stress are virtually always associated with high light intensity. If leaves are exposed to very low CO_2 levels in the light, "photoinhibition" may occur due to damage to the photosynthetic apparatus. It is possible that when stomata close due to rapid water stress in the light, the reduction in c_i, coupled perhaps with some unknown mechanism induced by water stress, brings about photoinhibition, acounting for the reduction in quantum yield and increase in r_i. When stress develops gradually, plants may adjust both stomatal and nonstomatal components of photosynthesis in a coordinated manner, in accordance with the hypothesis of COWAN and FARQUHAR (see Chaps. 7 and 17, this Vol.). Some of the biochemical aspects of photoinhibition have been discussed recently by LORIMER and ANDREWS (1980) in a lucid review, along with alternative points of view. Experimental data are as yet too sparse for a proper evaluation of the importance of photoinhibition during water stress, but it remains a provocative possibility. The notion of coordinated adjustments under slow stress is well worth considering. Some early data already hinted at a concerted response of several components of the CO_2-assimilation complex (HSIAO 1973a, p. 531). It is likely that slow stress results in modified leaves, clearly distinct from control leaves in their photosynthetic characteristics, but with their functional units still tightly integrated. Further discussion of coordinated modulation of plant responses under stress is found in Section 9.8.

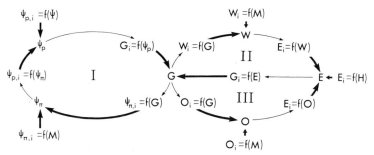

Fig. 9.4. Interdependence of expansive growth and underlying parameters. *G* expansive growth; *M* general metabolism (substrates, energy); *E* gross extensibility; *W* cell wall synthesis and metabolism; *O* synthesis of macromolecules other than cell wall; *H* hormonal effects. Each parameter is taken as a function of a number of other parameters. For example, $E = f(W, O, H)$. The component functions $E_i = f(W)$, $E_i = f(O)$, and $E_i = f(H)$ together determine the total E. *Heavy arrows* ($\rightarrow$) indicate the "summing" of the components or partials to make the whole. *Light arrows* ($\rightarrow$) indicate that the whole parameter in turn serves as the variable on which the partial of another function depends. Completion of loops is indicative of the interlocking nature of the various processes. Loops are labeled *I, II,* and *III* for easy reference. See text for further explanations

how it may be futile to attempt to find a "limiting" step once changes set in and are propagated with time. Some speculations and simplifying assumptions are necessary in constructing this chart, but the overview should be reasonably valid and certainly illustrates the integrated nature of the system.

In the chart (Fig. 9.4), the starting point, as before, is that the instantaneous growth rate (G) is a function of turgor pressure and gross extensibility of the wall (E). Following the mathematical concept of total derivative being the sum of the partials, we diagramatically show that G results from or is a sum of its partials or components (G_i, where $i = 1, 2$), one being the rate as a function of Ψ_p, and another, the rate as a function of E. Implicit in the equations for components [e.g., $G_i = f(\Psi_p)$] is the fact that all variables other than those explicitly shown are held constant. The figure shows that the independent variable Ψ_p in the equation for G_i, in turn, is dependent on tissue Ψ_π and Ψ. Further on, Ψ_π is in turn dependent on metabolism (M) and on G, thus completing a loop involving G, Ψ_p, and Ψ_π. The dependence of Ψ_π on metabolism is obvious, either for solutes generated internally or for those transported into the growing tissue. The dependence of Ψ_π on G is due to dilution by growth-associated increase in volume, as discussed earlier.

The other two loops in Figure 9.4 involve cell building blocks: cell wall and other macromolecules. In Section 9.4, it was pointed out that E is a function of hormonal activity (H) and cell wall synthesis and metabolism (W). W, in turn, is dependent on G, as well as on general metabolism (M). This completes loop II in the diagram. The third loop, connecting G, E, and synthesis of macromolecules other than cell wall (O), involves the most uncertainty. The most serious is that it is not known whether synthesis and metabolism of proteins and lipids directly affect extensibility of cells or indirectly influence it by affecting W. The loop is drawn arbitrarily through G, O, and E; it could well be through

G, O, W, and E. The evidence suggesting that protein synthesis (a part of O) under water stress is partly a function of G has been discussed (Sect. 9.4.2.4).

In Fig. 9.4, Loop I shows that a decrease in leaf Ψ can lead to reduction in Ψ_p and then in G. The reduction in G, in turn, leads to less volume dilution and hence a partial reestablishment of Ψ_p, thus allowing for resumption of growth, as observed with *Nitella* (GREEN 1968). Loop II shows that simultaneously with the adjustments in Loop I arising out of the initial reduction in Ψ, changes in wall metabolism and hence extensibility may take place. The reduced G may make the wall more extensible, as is found with *Nitella,* coleoptile systems (Sect. 9.4.2.1), and maize leaves (ACEVEDO et al. 1971) in cases of very short stress intervals. On the other hand, longer stress may lead to the opposite effect of apparent reduction in E (MEYER and BOYER 1972; MICHELENA and BOYER 1980; SHARP et al. 1979; HSIAO unpublished), giving rise to the phenomena of slower growth in spite of higher Ψ_p. Thus, with prolonged stress, the function $W_i(G)$ or $E_i(W)$ has apparently undergone a sign change. It is also conceivable that the apparent reduction in E may have arisen from modification of nonwall components in Loop III. There is virtually no information bearing on these points. The significance of "wall stiffening" with longer stress durations in adaptation is also not clear. We may speculate that once stress sets in and persists, it would be important for the plant to restrict expansive growth of leaves while it undergoes osmotic adjustment to maintain turgor for other purposes. Continued fast leaf growth would lead to the undesirable result of a larger surface for transpiration and greater water expenditure. One test of this hypothesis would be to compare effects of stress on extensibility of leaves with that of roots, as the argument of restricting expansion as an adaptive advantage would not hold for roots.

The above discussion, though considering only a small segment (expansive growth) of the whole, makes it clear that once stress persists beyond the initial period of minutes or a few hours, the apparent tight coordination among the various processes in the plant makes questions on cause–effect relations moot for many functions operating near a state of dynamic equilibrium. Only when the various control loops have just been perturbed by a nearly stepwise change in one of the parameters is the causal question pertinent.

9.8.2 Hormonal Interactions in Developmental Responses to Water Stress

The preceding discussion is particularly pertinent to hormonal interactions during water stress. Contrasting and counteracting effects of different growth regulators on a given developmental process are certainly the rule rather than the exception. The analysis or application of a single growth regulator often yields results which can only be interpreted in the light of possible alterations in synthesis or activity of other hormones. In addition, environmental stress can alter these functional relationships and their developmental consequences. This makes generalization difficult, particularly since regulatory mechanisms vary widely among species. Our approach here will be to describe some cases which have been examined in detail as examples of the types of interactions that

as the deeper layers (Hsiao and Acevedo 1974; Klepper et al. 1973; Ellis et al. 1977). Thus, the beneficial effect on water supply is more than just proportional to the change in the total root system.

There is uncertainty regarding the stress level necessary to cause the shift in root–shoot balance. In a short-term pot study of maize, Sharp and Davies (1975) found the change in root–shoot ratio to start in the same two-day period as when root and leaf Ψ began to decline and leaf elongation became notably suppressed by water stress. It is possible that root growth is favored over shoot growth mostly by stress levels not completely inhibitory to photosynthesis. Such stresses, by restricting leaf expansion, may leave more assimilates available for root growth. When stress is severe enough to suppress photosynthesis substantially, root growth would also be reduced.

The mechanism accounting for the favored root growth under water stress is not known. The situation is made complex by the fact that the mechanical strength of most soils increases dramatically as the soil dries, offering greater and greater impedance to root elongation. To overcome this impedance as well as the lower water potential, the roots osmotically adjust to continue growth in the drying soil (Greacen and Oh 1972). The adjustment is more pronounced in the growing region of the root tip than in the mature basal region of the root (Sharp and Davies 1979). This parallels the ability of the elongating regions of leaves to osmotically adjust more effectively than the mature leaves (Barlow et al. 1980; Michelena and Boyer 1980), but why root growth continues while leaf growth is inhibited remains puzzling. The hypothesized role of ABA in modifying root–shoot balance under water stress has been discussed in Section 9.5.5. As was pointed out, some data are inconsistent with the hypothesis and more studies are needed.

Osmotic adjustment throughout the plant in response to water stress constitutes another adaptive strategy to enhance available water in many soils. By building up osmotica in the cells, turgor and physiological functions can be maintained at low tissue Ψ. The ability to withstand low tissue Ψ permits the establishment of sufficient Ψ gradient within the plant to continue water absorption from soils of low Ψ values. How much additional water can be extracted from the soil is dependent on the degree of osmotic adjustment as well as on the moisture release characteristics of the soil. If the soil is coarse-textured and releases little water in the Ψ range between the Ψ values of the unadjusted and osmotically adjusted roots, then little additional water can be gained by the plant through the adjustment. If the soil is fine-textured and releases significant amounts of water in that Ψ range, the plant would increase its water supply considerably by osmotic adjustment. The extent of osmotic adjustment is highly variable among species, and is also affected by the speed of development of water stress (see Chap. 2, Vol. 12 C).

If the saving in water achieved by restricting canopy development and the maintenance or even enhancement of water supply through root development and osmotic adjustment are insufficient to prevent leaf Ψ from dropping substantially with time, sooner or later leaf Ψ will reach the threshold for stomatal closure. Initially, stomatal closure will be confined to the midday periods of peak irradiance and evaporative demand. As stress becomes more severe, howev-

er, stomata may open only briefly in the morning and close for much of the remaining part of the day (MacDowall 1963; Saugier 1976). In as much as they close and open in a matter of minutes, stomata constitute a dynamic means of controlling water loss and CO_2 assimilation. The direct response of stomata to humidity and postulated optimization of carbon assimilation and water use are discussed in Chapters 7, 17, and 18 of this Volume.

Loss of turgor and wilting often coincide with the point when leaf Ψ reaches the threshold value for stomatal closure. Wilting reflects the loss of mechanical strength of the tissue. When wilted, the lamina of many dicots droops and its petiole bends downward, resulting in a smaller projected area on the horizontal plane for the leaf (Turner 1974). If the leaf area index (LAI) is not very high, a droopy canopy would intercept less radiation than a turgid one when the sun is overhead, leading to a smaller radiation energy load and less evaporative demand on the crop at midday (Luxmoore et al. 1971; Rawson 1979). Thus, transpiration is reduced beyond that achieved solely by stomatal closure (Rawson 1979).

Stress-induced changes in leaf shape may involve specialized anatomical features. Leaf rolling in some grass species under water stress is thought to be due to volume changes in the bulliform or motor cells distributed longitudinally in rows along the adaxial side of the leaf. When severely stressed, the leaves can be tightly rolled into a needle shape and held nearly vertical. Rolling appears to start at about the same leaf Ψ as stomatal closure (Begg 1980; Jordan 1981; O'Toole and Cruz 1980) and contributes to reducing transpiration independently of stomatal closure (O'Toole et al. 1979). Radiation load on the crop decreases due to the more erect leaves and smaller light interception surface (Jordan 1982), and the transpiring surface area is reduced due to the overlapping lamina in the leaf cylinder.

If stress sufficiently severe to cause wilting and stomatal closure persists or intensifies, senescence of older leaves usually becomes evident in a matter of days (Boyer and McPherson 1975; Fischer 1973). Senescence generally starts with the oldest and the most shaded leaves and advances sequentially to the youngest as stress progresses. In most dicots, senescence culminates in abscission of the leaf. Shedding of leaves is well known as a means of adaptation to drought in native communities (Kozlowski 1976). Nutrients such as nitrogen, phosphorus, and potassium in the senescing leaves are mobilized for use in the remaining parts of the plant (Thomas and Stoddart 1980). Senescing leaves have lower stomatal conductance (Friedrich and Huffaker 1980; Wittenbach et al. 1980) and their stomata are more sensitive to water stress (Jordan et al. 1975). The more important effect in the long run, however, is that the green leaf area is reduced, accounting for much of the diminution in transpiration (Fischer and Kohn 1966).

The stress level which triggers leaf senescence is probably dependent on nitrogen nutrition and the stage of development, though definitive data are lacking. It is well known that nitrogen deficiency alone induces early senescence of older leaves, and water stress appeared to accelerate that further in one field study (Bataglia 1980). Senescence may also be more readily triggered if water stress occurs in the late stage of plant development, when the demands

sure, have received general recognition in the physiological literature only in the last few years (e.g., Begg 1980; Turner 1979), although some authors have called attention to them much earlier (e.g., Fischer and Hagan 1965; Hsiao and Acevedo 1974; Hsiao et al. 1976b). A more balanced approach in water stress physiology in the years to come should lead to a better understanding of the system as a whole.

Acknowledgments. The authors express their appreciation for the assistance of Ms. Wendy Hall and Ms. Val Rawlings in preparing the manuscript. Partial funding was provided by National Science Foundation Grant No. PCM 78-2371 to Wendy K. Silk and T.C. Hsiao.

References

Acevedo E, Hsiao TC, Henderson DW (1971) Immediate and subsequent growth responses of maize leaves to changes in water status. Plant Physiol 48:631–636

Acevedo E, Fereres E, Hsiao TC, Henderson DW (1979) Diurnal growth trends, water potential, and osmotic adjustment of maize and sorghum leaves in the field. Plant Physiol 64:476–480

Ackerson RC (1980) Stomatal response of cotton to water stress and abscisic acid as affected by water stress history. Plant Physiol 65:455–459

Ackerson RC, Hebert RR (1981) Osmoregulation in cotton in response to water stress. I. Alterations in photosynthesis, leaf conductance, translocation, and ultrastructure. Plant Physiol 67:484–488

Adams DO, Yang SF (1979) Ethylene biosynthesis: Identification of l-aminocyclopropane-l-carboxylic acid as an intermediate in the conversion of methionine to ethylene. Proc Natl Acad Sci USA 76:170–174

Adams PA, Montague MJ, Tepfer M, Rayle DL, Kuma HI, Kaufman PB (1975) Effect of gibberellic acid on the plasticity and elasticity of *Avena* stem segments. Plant Physiol 56:757–760

Aharoni N (1978) Relationship between leaf water status and endogenous ethylene in detached leaves. Plant Physiol 61:658 662

Aharoni N, Richmond AE (1978) Endogenous gibberellin and abscisic acid content as related to senescence of detached lettuce leaves. Plant Physiol 62:224–228

Aharoni N, Blumenfeld A, Richmond AE (1977) Hormonal activity in detached lettuce leaves as affected by leaf water content. Plant Physiol 59:1169–1173

Apelbaum A, Yang SF (1981) Biosynthesis of stress ethylene induced by water deficit. Plant Physiol 68:594–596

Arad S, Richmond AE (1976) Leaf cell water and enzyme activity. Plant Physiol 57:656–658

Arad S, Mizrahi, Richmond AE (1973) Leaf water content and hormone effects on ribonuclease activity. Plant Physiol 52:510–512

Aspinall D (1980) Role of abscisic acid and other hormones in adaptation to water stress. In: Turner NC, Kramer PJ (eds) Adaptation of plants to water and high temperature stress. Wiley and Sons, New York, pp 155–172

Baker DB, Ray PM (1965) Relation between effects of auxin on cell wall synthesis and cell elongation. Plant Physiol 40:360–368

Barlow EWR, Munns R, Scott NS, Reisner AH (1977) Water potential, growth and polyribosome content of the stressed wheat apex. J Exp Bot 28:909–916

Barlow EWR, Munns RE, Brady CJ (1980) Drought responses of apical meristems. In: Turner NC, Kramer PJ (eds) Adaptation of plants to water and high temperature stress. Wiley and Sons, New York, pp 191–205

Barnett NM, Naylor AW (1966) Amino acid and protein metabolism in Bermuda grass during water stress. Plant Physiol 41:1222–1230

Barr ML (1973) Biosynthesis of abscisic acid: Incorporation of radioactivity from ^{14}C mevalonic acid by intact roots. Plant Physiol Suppl 51:47

Bates GW, Cleland RE (1979) Protein synthesis and auxin-induced growth: Inhibitor studies. Planta 145:437–442

Bates LM, Hall AE (1981) Stomatal closure with soil water depletion not associated with changes in bulk leaf water status. Oecologia 50:62–65

Bayley ST, Setterfield G (1957) The influence of mannitol and auxin on growth of cell walls in *Avena* coleoptiles. Ann Bot 21:633–641

Bataglia OC (1980) Effects of nitrogen-water-relations on maize productivity. Ph D Dissertation, Univ California, Davis

Beadle CL, Jarvis PG (1977) Effects of shoot water status on some photosynthetic partial processes in Sitka spruce. Physiol Plant 41:7–13

Beadle CL, Stevenson KR, Neumann HH, Thurtell GW, King KM (1973) Diffusive resistance, transpiration, and photosynthesis in single leaves of corn and sorghum in relation to leaf water potential. Can J Plant Sci 53:537–544

Beardsell MF, Cohen D (1975) Relationships between leaf water status, abscisic acid levels, and stomatal resistance in maize and sorghum. Plant Physiol 56:207–212

Begg JE (1980) Morphological adaptations of leaves to water stress. In: Turner NC, Kramer PJ (eds) Adaptation of plants to water and high temperature stress. Wiley and Sons, New York, pp 33–42

Begg JE, Turner NC (1976) Crop water deficits. Adv Agron 28:161–217

Bell DT, Koeppe DE, Miller RJ (1971) The effects of drought stress on respiration of isolated corn mitochondria. Plant Physiol 48:413–415

Bellandi PM, Dörffling K (1974) Transport of abscisic acid-2-^{14}C in intact pea seedlings. Physiol Plant 32:365–368

Bengston C, Falk SD, Larsson S (1979) Effects of kinetin on transpiration rate and abscisic acid content of water stressed young wheat plants. Physiol Plant 45:183–188

Beyer EM, Morgan PW (1971) Abscission: The role of ethylene modification of auxin transport. Plant Physiol 48:208–212

Bisson MA, Gutknecht J (1980) Osmotic regulation in algae. In: Spanswick RM, Lucas WJ, Dainty J (eds) Plant membrane transport: Current conceptual issues. Elsevier/North Holland, Amsterdam, pp 131–146

Blackman VH (1919) The compound interest law and plant growth. Ann Bot 33:353–360

Boggess SF, Stewart CR, Aspinall D, Paleg LG (1976) Effect of water stress on proline synthesis from radioactive precursors. Plant Physiol 58:398–401

Boussiba S, Richmond AE (1976) Abscisic acid and the aftereffect of stress in tobacco plants. Planta 129:217–219

Boussiba S, Rikin A, Richmond AE (1975) The role of abscisic acid in cross-adaptation of tobacco plants. Plant Physiol 56:337–339

Boyer JS (1968) Relationship of water potential to growth of leaves. Plant Physiol 43:1056–1062

Boyer JS (1971) Nonstomatal inhibition of photosynthesis in sunflower at low leaf water potentials and high light intensities. Plant Physiol 48:532–536

Boyer JS (1976) Water deficits and photosynthesis. In: Kozlowski TT (ed) Water deficits and plant growth Vol IV. Soil water measurement, plant responses, and breeding for drought resistance. Academic Press, London New York, pp 153–190

Boyer JS, Bowen BL (1970) Inhibition of oxygen evolution in chloroplasts isolated from leaves with low water potentials. Plant Physiol 45:612–615

Boyer JS, McPherson HG (1975) Physiology of water deficits in cereal crops. Adv Agron 27:1–23

Boyer JS, Wu G (1978) Auxin increases the hydraulic conductivity of auxin-sensitive hypocotyl tissue. Planta 139:227–237

Bradford KJ, Yang SF (1980) Xylem transport of l-aminocyclopropane-l-carboxylic acid, an ethylene precursor, in waterlogged tomato plants. Plant Physiol 65:322–326

Bradford KJ, Yang SF (1981) Physiological responses of plants to waterlogging. Hort Science 16:25–30

Brady CJ, Scott NS, Munns R (1974) The interaction of water stress with the senescence

Fry KE (1972) Inhibition of ferricyanide reduction in chloroplasts prepared from water-stressed cotton leaves. Crop Sci 12:698–701

Gimmler H, Heilmann B, Demmig B, Hartung W (1981) The permeability of the plasma-lemma and the chloroplast envelope of spinach mesophyll cells for phytohormones. Z Naturforsch 36C:672–678

Glinka Z (1977) Effects of abscisic acid and of hydrostatic pressure gradient on water movement through excised sunflower roots. Plant Physiol 59:933–935

Glinka Z (1980) Abscisic acid promotes both volume flow and ion release to the xylem in sunflower roots. Plant Physiol 65:537–540

Goldbach H, Goldbach E (1975) Abscisic acid translocation and influence of water stress on grain abscisic acid content. J Exp Bot 28:1342–1350

Göring H, Bleiss W, Kretschmer H (1978) Stimulated elongation growth of coleoptile segments as a consequence of activated H^+ secretion after temporary turgor reduction. Biochem Physiol Pflanz 173:373–376

Govindjee, Downton WJS, Fork DC, Armond PA (1981) Chlorophyll *a* fluorescence transient as an indicator of water potential of leaves. Plant Sci Lett 20:191–194

Graziani Y, Livne A (1971) Dehydration, water fluxes, and permeability of tobacco leaf tissue. Plant Physiol 48:575–579

Greacen EL, Oh JS (1972) Physics of root growth. Nature (London) New Biol 235:24–25

Green PB (1968) Growth physics in *Nitella*: a method for continuous in vivo analysis of extensibility based on a micro-manometer technique for turgor pressure. Plant Physiol 43:1169–1184

Green PB, Erickson RO, Buggy J (1971) Metabolic and physical control of cell elongation rate – in vivo studies in *Nitella*. Plant Physiol 47:423–430

Green PB, Bauer K, Cummins WR (1977) Biophysical model for plant cell growth: auxin effects. In: Jungreis AM, Hodges TK, Kleinzeller A, Schultz SG (eds) Water relations in membrane transport in plants and animals. Academic Press, London New York, pp 30–45

Greenway H, Klepper B (1968) Phosphorus transport to the xylem and its regulation by water flow. Planta 83:119–136

Greenway H, Leahy M (1970) Effects of rapidly and slowly permeating osmotica on metabolism. Plant Physiol 46:259–262

Grenetz PS, List A JR (1973) A model for predicting growth response of plants to changes in external water potential: *Zea mays* primary root. J Theor Biol 39:29–45

Hall MA, Kapuya JA, Sivakumaran S, John A (1977) The role of ethylene in the response of plants to stress. Pestic Sci 8:217 223

Hanson AD, Hitz WD (1982) Water deficit and the nitrogen economy. In: Taylor H, Jordan W, Sinclair T (eds) Efficient water use in crop production. Am Soc Agron, Madison, Wisconsin, in press

Hanson AD, Nelsen CE (1978) Betaine accumulation and [^{14}C] formate metabolism in water-stressed barley leaves. Plant Physiol 62:305–312

Hanson AD, Nelsen CE, Everson EH (1977) Evaluation of free proline accumulation as an index of drought resistance using two contrasting barley cultivars. Crop Sci 17:720–726

Hanson AD, Nelsen CE, Pedersen AR, Everson EH (1979) Capacity for proline accumulation during water stress in barley and its implications for breeding for drought resistance. Crop Sci 19:489–493

Harrison MA, Walton DC (1975) Abscisic acid metabolism in water stressed bean leaves. Plant Physiol 56:250–256

Hartung W (1976) Effect of water stress on transport of [2-^{14}C] abscisic acid in intact plants of *Phaseolus coccineus* L. Oecologia 26:177–183

Hartung W, Witt J (1968) Über den Einfluß der Bodenfeuchtigkeit auf den Wuchsstoffgehalt von *Anastatica hierochuntica* und *Helianthus annuus*. Flora (Jena) Abt B 157:603–614

Hartung W, Heilmann B, Gimmler H (1981) Do chloroplasts play a role in abscisic acid synthesis? Plant Sci Lett 22:235–242

Haschke H-P, Lüttge U (1975a) Interaction between IAA, potassium and malate accumulation, and growth in *Avena* coleoptile segments. Z Pflanzenphysiol 76:450–455

Haschke H-P, Lüttge U (1975b) Stoichiometric correlation of malate accumulation with auxin-dependent K^+-H^+ exchange and growth in *Avena* coleoptile segments. Plant Physiol 56:696–698

Haschke H-P, Lüttge U (1977) Action of auxin on CO_2 dark fixation in *Avena* coleoptile segments as related to elongation growth. Plant Sci Lett 8:53–58

Heilmann B, Hartung W, Gimmler H (1980) The distribution of abscisic acid between chloroplasts and cytoplasm of leaf cells and the permeability of the chloroplast envelope for abscisic acid. Z Pflanzenphysiol 97:67–78

Henson IE (1981) Changes in abscisic acid content during stomatal closure in pearl millet (*Pennisetum americanum* (L.) Leeke). Plant Sci Lett 21:121–127

Heuer B, Plaut Z, Federman E (1979) Nitrate and nitrite reduction in wheat leaves as affected by different types of water stress. Physiol Plant 46:318–323

Hewitt EB (1975) Assimilatory nitrate – nitrite reduction. Annu Rev Plant Physiol 26:73–100

Hiron RW, Wright STC (1973) The role of endogenous abscisic acid in the response of plants to stress. J Exp Bot 24:769–781

Hoad GV (1973) Effect of moisture stress on abscisic acid levels in *Ricinus communis* L. with particular reference to phloem exudate. Planta 113:367–372

Hoad GV (1975) Effect of osmotic stress on abscisic acid levels in xylem sap of sunflower. Planta 124:25–29

Hoad GV (1978) Effect of water stress on abscisic acid levels in white lupin (*Lupinus albus* L.) fruit, leaves and phloem exudate. Planta 142:287–290

Hsiao TC (1970) Rapid changes in levels of polyribosomes in *Zea mays* in response to water stress. Plant Physiol 46:281–285

Hsiao TC (1973a) Plant responses to water stress. Annu Rev Plant Physiol 24:519–570

Hsiao TC (1973b) Effects of water deficit on guard cell potassium and stomatal movement. Plant Physiol Suppl 51:9

Hsiao TC (1976) Stomatal ion transport. In: Lüttge U, Pitman MG (eds) Encyclopedia of plant physiology new ser vol II. Transport in plants II, Part B, tissues and organs. Springer, Berlin Heidelberg New York, pp 193–221

Hsiao TC, Acevedo E (1974) Plant responses to water deficits, water use efficiency and drought resistance. Agric Meteorol 14:59–84

Hsiao TC, Acevedo E, Fereres E, Henderson DW (1976a) Stress metabolism: water stress, growth, and osmotic adjustment. Philos Trans R Soc London Ser B 273:479–500

Hsiao TC, Fereres E, Acevedo E, Henderson DW (1976b) Water stress and dynamics of growth and yield of crop plants. In: Lange, OL, Kappen L, Schulze E-D (eds) Water and plant life: problems and modern approaches. Ecol Stud Vol 19. Springer, Berlin Heidelberg New York, pp 281–305

Hsiao TC, Bradford KJ (1982) Physiological consequences of cellular water deficits. In: Taylor HM, Jordan WR, Sinclair TR (eds) Efficient water use in crop production. Am Soc Agron, Madison, Wisconsin, in press

Huang C-Y, Boyer JS, Vanderhoef LN (1975) Limitation of acetylene reduction (nitrogen fixation) by photosynthesis in soybean having low water potentials. Plant Physiol 56:228–232

Hüsken D, Steudle E, Zimmermann U (1978) Pressure probe technique for measuring water relations of cells in higher plants. Plant Physiol 61:158–163

Huffaker RC, Radin T, Kleinkopf GE, Cox EL (1970) Effects of mild water stress on enzymes of nitrate assimilation and of the carboxylative phase of photosynthesis in barley. Crop Sci 10:471–474

Itai C, Benzioni A (1976) Water stress and hormonal response. In: Lange OL, Kappen L, Schulze E-D (eds) Water and plant life: problems and modern approaches. Ecol Stud Vol 19. Springer, Berlin Heidelberg New York, pp 176–188

Itai C, Vaadia Y (1965) Kinetin-like activity in root exudate of water-stressed sunflower plants. Physiol Plant 18:941–944

Itai C, Vaadia Y (1971) Cytokinin activity in water-stressed shoots. Plant Physiol 47:87–90

Itai C, Richmond A, Vaadia Y (1968) The role of root cytokinins during water and salinity stress. Isr J Bot 17:187–195

Jackson MB, Hartley CB, Osborne DJ (1973) Timing abscission in *Phaseolus vulgaris*

L. by controlling ethylene production and sensitivity to ethylene. New Phytol 72:1251–1260

Jarvis PG (1980) Stomatal response to water stress in conifers. In: Turner NC, Kramer PJ (eds) Adaptation of plants to water and high temperature stress. Wiley and Sons, New York, pp 105–122

Jewer PC, Incoll LD (1980) Promotion of stomatal opening in the grass *Anthephora pubescens* Nees by a range of natural and synthetic cytokinins. Planta 150:218–221

Johnson KD, Rayle DL (1976) Enhancement of CO_2 uptake in *Avena* coleoptiles by fusicoccin. Plant Physiol 57:806–811

Johnson RR, Frey NM, Moss DN (1974) Effect of water stress on photosynthesis and transpiration of flag leaves and spikes of barley and wheat. Crop Sci 14:728–731

Jones HG (1973a) Limiting factors in photosynthesis. New Phytol 72:1089–1094

Jones HG (1973b) Moderate-term water stresses and associated changes in some photosynthetic parameters in cotton. New Phytol 72:1095–1105

Jones HG (1980) Interaction and integration of adaptive responses to water stress: The implications of an unpredictable environment. In: Turner NC, Kramer PJ (eds) Adaptation of plants to water and high temperature stress. Wiley and Sons, New York, pp 353–365

Jones MM, Rawson HM (1979) Influence of rate of development of leaf water deficits upon photosynthesis, leaf conductance, water use efficiency, and osmotic potential in sorghum. Physiol Plant 45:103–111

Jordan WR (1982) Whole plant response to water deficits: An overview. In: Taylor H, Jordan W, Sinclair T (eds) Limitations to efficient water use in crop production. Am Soc Agron, Madison, Wisconsin, in press

Jordan WR, Miller FR (1980) Genetic variability in sorghum root systems: implications for drought tolerance. In: Turner NC, Kramer PJ (eds) Adaptation of plants to water and high temperature stress. Wiley and Sons, New York, pp 383–400

Jordan WR, Morgan PW, Davenport TL (1972) Water stress enhances ethylene-mediated leaf abscission in cotton. Plant Physiol 50:756–758

Jordan WR, Brown KW, Thomas JC (1975) Leaf age as a determinant in stomatal control of water loss from cotton during water stress. Plant Physiol 56:595–599

Kaiser WM, Hartung W (1981) Uptake and release of abscisic acid by isolated photoautotrophic mesophyll cells, depending on pH gradients. Plant Physiol 68:202–206

Kaldewey H, Ginkel U, Wawczyniak G (1974) Auxin transport and water stress in pea (*Pisum sativum* L.). Ber Dtsch Bot Ges 87:563–576

Karmoker JL, Steveninck van RFM (1978) Stimulation of volume flow and ion flux by abscisic acid in excised root systems of *Phaseolus vulgaris* cv. Redland Pioneer. Planta 141:37–43

Katsumi M, Kazama H (1978) Gibberellin control of cell elongation in cucumber hypocotyl sections. Bot Mag Tokyo Spec Issue 1:141–158

Kauss H (1977) Biochemistry of osmotic regulation. In: Northcote DH (ed) Int Rev Biochem, Plant Biochem II, vol XIII. Univ Park Press, Baltimore, pp 119–140

Keck RW, Boyer JS (1974) Chloroplast response to low leaf water potentials. III. Differing inhibition of electron transport and photophosphorylation. Plant Physiol 53:474–479

King RW (1976) Abscisic acid in developing wheat grains and its relationship to grain growth and maturation. Planta 132:43–51

King RW, Evans LT (1977) Inhibition of flowering in *Lolium temulentum* L. by water stress: a role for abscisic acid. Aust J Plant Physiol 4:225–233

Klepper B, Taylor HM, Huck MG, Fiscus EL (1973) Water relations and growth of cotton in drying soil. Agron J 65:307–310

Koeppe DE, Miller RJ, Bell DT (1973) Drought-affected mitochondrial processes as related to tissue and whole plant response. Agron J 65:566–569

Kozlowski TT (1976) Water supply and leaf shedding. In: Kozlowski TT (ed) Water deficits and plant growth, vol IV. Academic Press, London New York, pp 191–231

Kramer PJ (1980) Drought, stress, and the origin of adaptations. In: Turner NC, Kramer PJ (eds) Adaptation of plants to water and high temperature stress. Wiley and Sons, New York, pp 7–20

Kuiper PJC (1972) Water transport across membranes. Annu Rev Plant Physiol 23:157–172

Labavitch JM (1981) Cell wall turnover in plant development. Annu Rev Plant Physiol 32:385–406

Labavitch JM, Ray PM (1974) Relationship between promotion of xyloglucan metabolism and induction of elongation by indoleacetic acid. Plant Physiol 54:499–502

Lado P, Rasi-Caldogno F, Colombo R (1977) Effect of cycloheximide on IAA- or FC-induced cell enlargement in pea internode segments. Plant Sci Lett 9:93–101

Ladyman JAR, Hitz WD, Hanson AD (1980) Translocation and metabolism of glycine betaine by barley plants in relation to water stress. Planta 150:191–196

Lahiri AN (1980) Interaction of water stress and mineral nutrition on growth and yield. In: Turner NC, Kramer PJ (eds) Adaptation of plants to water and high temperature stress. Wiley and Sons, New York, pp 341–352

Lee-Stadelmann OY, Stadelmann EJ (1976) Cell permeability and water stress. In: Lange OL, Kappen L, Schulze E-D (eds) Water and plant life: Problems and modern approaches. Ecol Stud Vol 19. Springer, Berlin Heidelberg New York, pp 268–280

Levitt J (1980) Stress and strain terminology. In: Levitt J (ed) Responses of plants to environmental stresses, Vol I, 2nd edn. Academic Press, London New York, pp 3–19

Lockhart JA (1965) An analysis of irreversible plant cell elongation. J Theor Biol 8:264–276

Loescher WA, Nevins DJ (1973) Turgor-dependent changes in *Avena* coleoptile cell wall composition. Plant Physiol 52:248–251

Lorimer GH, Andrews TJ (1980) The C_2 photo- and chemorespiratory carbon oxidation cycle. In: Hatch MD, Boardman NK (eds) The biochemistry of plants, vol VIII. Academic Press, London New York, pp 329–374

Lösch R, Schenk B (1978) Humidity responses of stomata and the potassium content of guard cells. J Exp Bot 29:781–787

Loveys BR (1977) The intracellular location of abscisic acid in stressed and non-stressed leaf tissue. Physiol Plant 40:6–10

Loveys BR, Kriedemann PE (1973) Rapid changes in abscisic acid-like inhibitors following alterations in vine leaf water potential. Physiol Plant 28:476–479

Ludlow MM (1980) Adaptive significance of stomatal responses to water stress. In: Turner NC, Kramer PJ (eds) Adaptation of plants to water and high temperature stress. Wiley and Sons, New York, pp 123–138

Ludlow MM, Ng TT, Ford CW (1980) Recovery after water stress of leaf gas exchange in *Panicum maximum* var. *trichoglume*. Aust J Plant Physiol 7:299–313

Lürssen K, Naumann K, Schröder R (1979) 1-Aminocyclopropane-1-carboxylic acid – a new intermediate of ethylene biosynthesis. Naturwissenschaften 66:264–265

Luxmoore RJ, Millington RJ, Marcellos H (1971) Soybean canopy structure and some radiant energy relations. Agron J 63:111–114

MacDowall FDH (1963) Midday closure of stomata in aging tobacco leaves. Can J Bot 41:1289–1300

Mansfield TA, Wellburn AR, Moreira TJS (1978) The role of abscisic acid and farnesol in the alleviation of water stress. Philos Trans R Soc London Ser B 284:471–482

Maranville JW, Paulsen GM (1972) Alteration of protein composition of corn (*Zea mays* L.) seedlings during moisture stress. Crop Sci 12:660–663

Markhart AH III, Fiscus EL, Naylor AW, Kramer PJ (1979) Effect of abscisic acid on root hydraulic conductivity. Plant Physiol 64:611–614

Marré E, Lado P, Rasi Caldogno F, Colombo R (1973) Correlation between cell enlargement in pea internode segments and decrease in the pH of the medium of incubation. I. Effects of fusicoccin, natural and synthetic auxins and mannitol. Plant Sci Lett 1:179–184

Masuda Y (1978) Auxin-induced cell wall loosening. Bot Mag Tokyo Spec Issue 1:103–123

Masuda Y, Sakurai N, Tazawa M, Shimmen T (1978) Effects of osmotic shock on auxin-induced cell extension, cell wall changes and acidification in *Avena* coleoptile segments. Plant Cell Physiol 19:857–867

McMichael BL, Elmore CD (1977) Proline accumulation in water-stressed cotton leaves. Crop Sci 17:905–908

McMichael BL, Jordan WR, Powell RD (1972) An effect of water stress on ethylene production by intact cotton petioles. Plant Physiol 49:658–660

McMichael BL, Jordan WR, Powell RD (1973) Abscission processes in cotton: induction by plant water deficit. Agron J 65:202–204

McNeil DL (1976) The basis of osmotic pressure maintenance during expansion growth in *Helianthus annuus* hypocotyls. Aust J Plant Physiol 3:311–324

Mederski HJ, Chen LH, Curry RB (1975) Effect of leaf water deficit on stomatal and nonstomatal regulation of net carbon dioxide assimilation. Plant Physiol 55:589–593

Meidner H, Edwards M (1975) Direct measurement of turgor pressure potentials of guard cells. J Exp Bot 26:319–320

Meyer RF, Boyer JS (1972) Sensitivity of cell division and cell elongation to low water potentials in soybean hypocotyls. Planta 108:77–87

Michelena VA, Boyer JS (1980) Growth and osmotic adjustment in maize leaves having low water potentials. Plant Physiol Suppl 65:8

Milborrow BV (1974) The chemistry and physiology of abscisic acid. Annu Rev Plant Physiol 25:259–307

Milborrow BV (1978) The stability of conjugated abscisic acid during wilting. J Exp Bot 29:1059–1066

Milborrow BV (1979) Antitranspirants and the regulation of abscisic acid content. Aust J Plant Physiol 6:249–254

Milborrow BV, Robinson DR (1973) Factors affecting the biosynthesis of abscisic acid. J Exp Bot 24:537–548

Milburn JA (1979) Water flow in plants. Longman, London New York

Mizrahi Y, Richmond AE (1972) Hormonal modification of plant response to water stress. Aust J Biol Sci 25:437–442

Mizrahi Y, Blumenfeld A, Richmond AE (1972) The role of abscisic acid and salination in the adaptive response of plants to reduced root aeration. Plant Cell Physiol 13:15–21

Mohanty P, Boyer JS (1976) Chloroplast response to low leaf water potentials. IV. Quantum yield is reduced. Plant Physiol 57:704–709

Molz FJ, Boyer JS (1978) Growth-induced water potentials in plant cells and tissues. Plant Physiol 62:423–429

Mooney HA, Björkman O, Collatz GJ (1977) Photosynthetic acclimation to temperature and water stress in the desert shrub *Larrea divaricata*. Carnegie Inst Yearb 76:328–335

Morgan JM (1980) Possible role of abscisic acid in reducing seed set in water-stressed wheat plants. Nature (London) 285:655–657

Morilla CA, Boyer JS, Hageman RH (1973) Nitrate reductase activity and polyribosomal content of corn (*Zea mays* L.) having low leaf water potentials. Plant Physiol 51:817–824

Munns R, Brady CJ, Barlow EWR (1979) Solute accumulation in the apex and leaves of wheat during water stress. Aust J Plant Physiol 6:379–389

Mussell H, Staples RC (1979) Stress physiology in crop plants. Wiley-Interscience, New York, 510 p

Nulsen RA, Turtell GW, Stevenson FR (1975) Response of leaf water potential to pressure changes at the root surface of corn plants. Agron J 69:951–954

Nye PH, Tinker PB (1977) Solute movement in the soil-root system. Stud Ecol, vol IV Univ California Press, Berkeley, 342 p

Oliveira EC, Hsiao TC (1980) Osmotic adjustment of cotton to water stress: time course and associated changes in growth and assimilation. Plant Physiol Suppl 65:6

Osmond CB (1976) Ion absorption and carbon metabolism in cells of higher plants. In: Lüttge U, Pitman MG (eds) Transport in plants II. Encyclopedia of plant physiology new ser vol II, part A, Springer, Berlin Heidelberg New York, pp 347–372

Osmond CB, Winter K, Powles SB (1980) Adaptive significance of carbon dioxide cycling during photosynthesis in water-stressed plants. In: Turner NC, Kramer PJ (eds) Adaptation of plants to water and high temperature stress. Wiley and Sons, New York, pp 139–154

O'Toole JC, Cruz RT (1980) Response of leaf water potential, stomatal resistance and leaf rolling to water stress. Plant Physiol 31:44–53

O'Toole JC, Crookston RK, Treharne KJ, Ozbun JL (1976) Mesophyll resistance and carboxylase activity. A comparison under water stress conditions. Plant Physiol 57:465–468

O'Toole JC, Cruz RT, Singh TN (1979) Leaf rolling and transpiration. Plant Sci Lett 16:111–114

Paleg LG, Aspinall D (eds) (1981) Physiology and biochemistry of drought resistance in plants. Academic Press, Sydney, 492 p

Pallaghy CK, Raschke K (1972) No stomatal response to ethylene. Plant Physiol 49:275–276

Parrondo RT, Smith RC, Lazurick K (1975) Rubidium absorption by corn root tissue after a brief period of water stress and during recovery. Physiol Plant 35:34–38

Pate JS (1980) Transport and partitioning of nitrogenous solutes. Annu Rev Plant Physiol 31:313–340

Pearcy RW (1982) Non-stomatal inhibition of photosynthesis by water stress. In: Taylor HM, Jordan WR, Sinclair TR (eds) Efficient water use in crop production. Am Soc Agron, Madison, Wisconsin, in press

Pearson RW (1966) Soil environment and root development. In: Pierre WH, Kirkham D, Pesek J, Shaw R (eds) Plant environment and efficient water use. Am Soc Agron, Soil Sci Soc Am, Madison, Wisconsin, pp 95–126

Penny P (1971) Growth-limiting proteins in relation to auxin-induced cell elongation in lupin hypocotyls. Plant Physiol 48:720–723

Penny P, Penny D (1978) Rapid responses to phytohormones In: Letham DS, Goodwin PB, Higgins TJV (eds) Phytohormones and related compounds – a comprehensive treatise, vol II. Elsevier, Amsterdam, pp 537–597

Petrie AHK, Wood JG (1938) Studies on the nitrogen metabolism of plants. I. The relation between the content of proteins, amino acids, and water in the leaves. Ann Bot 2:33–60

Pheloung P, Barlow EWR (1981) Respiration and carbohydrate accumulation in the water-stressed wheat apex. J Exp Bot 32:921–931

Pierce M, Raschke K (1980) Correlation between loss of turgor and accumulation of abscisic acid in detached leaves. Planta 148:174–182

Pierce M, Raschke K (1981) Synthesis and metabolism of abscisic acid in detached leaves of *Phaseolus vulgaris* L. after loss and recovery of turgor. Planta 153:156–165

Pitman MG, Wellfare O (1978) Inhibition of ion transport in excised barley roots by abscisic acid; relation to water permeability of the roots. J Exp Bot 29:1125–1138

Pitman MG, Lüttge U, Läuchli A, Ball E (1974a) Action of abscisic acid on ion transport as affected by root temperature and nutrient status. J Exp Bot 25:147–155

Pitman MG, Lüttge U, Läuchli A, Ball E (1974b) Effect of previous water stress on ion uptake and transport in barley seedlings. Aust J Plant Physiol 1:377–385

Plaut Z (1974) Nitrate reductase activity of wheat seedlings during exposure to and recovery from water stress and salinity. Physiol Plant 30:212–217

Premecz G, Olah T, Gulyas A, Nyitrai A, Palfi G, Farkas GL (1977) Is the increase in ribonuclease level in isolated tobacco protoplasts due to osmotic stress? Plant Sci Lett 9:195–200

Quarrie SA, Jones HG (1977) Effects of abscisic acid and water stress on development and morphology of wheat. J Exp Bot 28:192–203

Quebedeaux B, Sweetser PB, Rowell JC (1976) Abscisic acid levels in soybean reproductive structures during development. Plant Physiol 58:363–366

Radin JW, Ackerson RC (1981) Water relations of cotton plants under nitrogen deficiency III. Stomatal conductance, photosynthesis, and abscisic acid accumulation during drought. Plant Physiol 67:115–119

Raschke K (1975) Stomatal action. Annu Rev Plant Physiol 26:309–340

Raschke K (1979) Movements of stomata. In: Haupt W, Feinleib ME (eds) Physiology of movements. Encyclopedia of plant physiology new ser vol VII. Springer, Berlin Heidelberg New York, pp 383–441

Raschke K, Zeevaart JAD (1976) Abscisic acid content, transpiration, and stomatal conductance as related to leaf age in plants of *Xanthium strumarium* L. Plant Physiol 58:169–174

Rawson HM (1979) Vertical wilting and photosynthesis, transpiration, and water use efficiency of sunflower leaves. Aust J Plant Physiol 6:109–120

Ray PM (1962) Cell wall synthesis and cell elongation in oat coleoptile tissue. Am J Bot 49:928–939

Ray PM, Green PB, Cleland R (1972) Role of turgor in plant cell growth. Nature (London) 239:163–164

Rayle DL (1973) Auxin-induced hydrogen ion secretion in *Avena* coleoptiles and its implication. Planta 114:63–73

Reed NR, Bonner BA (1974) The effect of abscisic acid on the uptake of potassium and chloride into *Avena* coleoptile sections. Planta 116:173–185

Rehm MM, Cline MG (1973) Inhibition of low pH-induced elongation in *Avena* coleoptiles by abscisic acid. Plant Physiol 51:946–948

Rikin A, Richmond AE (1976) Amelioration of chilling injuries in cucumber seedlings by abscisic acid. Physiol Plant 38:95–97

Rikin A, Blumenfeld A, Richmond AE (1976) Chilling resistance as affected by stressing environment and ABA. Bot Gaz 137:307–312

Rubinstein B (1977) Osmotic shock inhibits auxin-stimulated acidification and growth. Plant Physiol 59:369–371

Sakurai W, Masuda Y (1977) Effect of indole-3-acetic acid on cell wall loosening: changes in mechanical properties and noncellulosic glucose content of *Avena* coleoptile cell wall. Plant Cell Physiol 18:587–594

Santarius KA, Ernst R (1967) Hill reaction and photophosphorylation of isolated chloroplasts in relation to water content. I. Removal of water by means of concentrated solutions. Planta 73:91–108

Saugier B (1976) Sunflower. In: Monteith JL (ed) Vegetation and the atmosphere, vol II. Case studies. Academic Press, London New York, pp 87–119

Scott NS, Munns R, Barlow EWR (1979) Polyribosome content in young and aged wheat leaves subjected to drought. J Exp Bot 30:905–911

Setter TL, Brun WA, Brenner ML (1980) Effect of obstructed translocation on leaf abscisic acid, and associated stomatal closure and photosynthesis decline. Plant Physiol 65:1111–1115

Shaner DL, Boyer JS (1976) Nitrate reductase activity in maize (*Zea mays* L.) leaves. II. Regulation by nitrate flux at low leaf water potential. Plant Physiol 58:505–509

Sharp RE, Davies WJ (1975) Solute regulation and growth by roots and shoots of water-stressed maize plants. Planta 147:43–49

Sharp RE, Osonubi O, Wood WA, Davies WJ (1979) A simple instrument for measuring leaf extension in grasses, and its application in the study of the effects of water stress on maize and sorghum. Ann Bot 44:35–45

Silk WK, Wagner KK (1980) Growth-sustaining water potential distributions in the primary corn root: A noncompartmental continuum model. Plant Physiol 66:859–863

Sinclair TR, Wit de CT (1975) Photosynthate and nitrogen requirements for seed production by various crops. Science 189:565–567

Singh TN, Paleg LG, Aspinall D (1973) Stress metabolism. III. Variations in response to water deficit in the barley plant. Aust J Biol Sci 26:65–76

Slatyer RO (1973) Effects of short periods of water stress on leaf photosynthesis. In: Slatyer RO (ed) Plant response to climatic factors. Proc Uppsala Symp 1970. UNESCO, Paris, pp 271–276

Smith FA, Raven JA (1979) Intracellular pH and its regulation. Annu Rev Plant Physiol 30:289–311

Sodek L, Wright STC (1969) The effect of kinetin on ribonuclease, acid phosphatase, lipase and esterase levels in detached wheat leaves. Phytochemistry 8:1629–1640

Sprent JI (1981) Nitrogen fixation. In: Paleg LG, Aspinall D (eds) Physiology and biochemistry of drought resistance in plants. Academic Press, Sydney, pp 131–143

Sojka RE, Stolzy LH (1980) Soil-oxygen effects on stomatal response. Soil Sci 130:350–358

Stålfelt MG (1955) The stomata as a hydrophotic regulator of the water deficit of the plant. Physiol Plant 8:572–593

Staden van J, Davey JE (1979) The synthesis, transport and metabolism of endogenous cytokinins. Plant Cell Environ 2:93–106

Steudle E, Cosgrove D (1981) Water relations of growing pea epicotyl. Abstr XIII Int Bot Congr, Sydney, August 21–28, p 247

Stevenson TT, Cleland RE (1981) Osmoregulation in the *Avena* coleoptile in relation to auxin and growth. Plant Physiol 67:749–753

Stewart CR, Hanson AD (1980) Proline accumulation as a metabolic response to water stress. In: Turner NC, Kramer PJ (eds) Adaptation of plants to water and high temperature stress. Wiley and Sons, New York, pp 173–189

Stewart CR, Boggess SF, Aspinall D, Paleg LG (1977) Inhibition of proline oxidation by water stress. Plant Physiol 59:930–932

Storey R, Ahmad N, Wyn Jones RG (1977) Taxonomic and ecological aspects of the distribution of glycine betaine and related compounds in plants. Oecologia 27:319–332

Stout RG, Johnson KD, Rayle DC (1978) Rapid auxin and fusicoccin-enhanced Rb^+ uptake and malate synthesis in *Avena* coleoptile sections. Planta 139:35–41

Stuart DA, Jones RL (1978a) Role of cation and anion uptake in salt-stimulated elongation of lettuce hypocotyl sections. Plant Physiol 61:180–183

Stuart DA, Jones RL (1978b) The role of acidification in gibberellic acid- and fusicoccin-induced elongation growth of lettuce hypocotyl sections. Planta 142:135–145

Tal M, Imber D (1971) Abnormal stomatal behavior and hormonal imbalance in *flacca*, a wilty mutant of tomato III. Hormonal effects on the water status in the plant. Plant Physiol 47:849–850

Tal M, Imber D, Erez A, Epstein E (1979) Abnormal stomatal behavior and hormonal imbalance in *flacca*, a wilty mutant of tomato. V. Effect of abscisic acid on indoleacetic acid metabolism and ethylene evolution. Plant Physiol 63:1044–1048

Thomas H, Stoddart JL (1980) Leaf senescence. Annu Rev Plant Physiol 31:83–111

Todd GW (1972) Water deficits and enzymatic activity. In: Kozlowski TT (ed) Water deficits and plant growth. Vol III. Academic Press, London New York, pp 177–216

Torrey JA (1976) Root hormones and plant growth. Annu Rev Plant Physiol 27:435–484

Troughton JH, Slatyer RO (1969) Plant water status, leaf temperature, and the calculated mesophyll resistance to carbon dioxide of cotton leaves. Aust J Biol Sci 22:815–827

Tully RE, Hanson AD, Nelsen CE (1979) Proline accumulation in water-stressed barley leaves in relation to translocation and the nitrogen budget. Plant Physiol 63:518–523

Turner NC (1974) Stomatal behavior and water status of maize, sorghum and tobacco under field conditions. Plant Physiol 53:360–365

Turner NC (1979) Drought resistance and adaptation to water deficits in crop plants. In: Mussel H, Staples RC (eds) Stress physiology in crop plants. Wiley-Interscience, New York, pp 343–372

Turner NC, Jones MM (1980) Turgor maintenance by osmotic adjustment: A review and evaluation. In: Turner NC, Kramer PJ (eds) Adaptation of plants to water and high temperature stress. Wiley and Sons, New York, pp 87–103

Turner NC, Kramer PJ (eds) (1980) Adaptation of plants to water and high temperature stress. Wiley and Sons, New York, 382 p

Vaadia Y (1976) Plant hormones and water stress. Philos Trans R Soc London Ser B 273:513–522

Verasan V, Phillips RE (1978) Effects of soil water stress on growth and nutrient accumulation in corn. Agron J 70:613–618

Volkenburgh van E, Cleland RE (1980) Proton excretion and cell expansion in bean leaves. Planta 148:273–278

Walton DC (1980) Biochemistry and physiology of abscisic acid. Annu Rev Plant Physiol 31:453–489

Walton DC, Harrison MA, Cote P (1976) The effects of water stress on abscisic acid levels and metabolism in roots of *Phaseolus vulgaris* L. and other plants. Planta 131:141–144

Walton DC, Galson E, Harrison MA (1977) The relationship between stomatal resistance and abscisic acid levels in leaves of water-stressed bean plants. Planta 133:145–148

Weiler EW, Schnabl H, Hornberg C (1982) Stress-related levels of abscisic acid in guard cell protoplasts of *Vicia fabe* L. Planta 154:24–28

Williams RF (1975) The shoot apex and leaf growth. Univ Press, Cambridge, 256 p

Wittenbach VA, Ackerson RC, Giaquinta RT, Hebert RR (1980) Changes in photosynthesis, ribulose bisphosphate carboxylase, proteolytic activity and ultrastructure of soybean leaves during senescence. Crop Sci 20:225–231

Wright STC (1969) An increase in the "inhibitor-β" content of detached wheat leaves following a period of wilting. Planta 86:10–20

Wright STC (1977) The relationship between leaf water potential (Ψ leaf) and the levels of abscisic acid and ethylene in excised wheat leaves. Planta 134:183–189

Wright STC (1978) Phytohormones and stress phenomena. In: Letham DS, Goodwin PB, Higgins TJV (eds) Phytohormones and related compounds: A comprehensive treatise, vol II. Phytohormones and the development of higher plants. Elsevier, Amsterdam, pp 497–536

Wright STC (1979) The effect of 6-benzyladenine and leaf ageing treatment on the levels of stress-induced ethylene emanating from wilted wheat leaves. Planta 144:179–188

Wright STC (1980) The effect of plant growth regulator treatments on the levels of ethylene emanating from excised turgid and wilted wheat leaves. Planta 148:381–388

Yang SF (1980) Regulation of ethylene biosynthesis. HortScience 15:238–243

Yang SF, Pratt HK (1978) The physiology of ethylene in wounded plant tissues. In: Kahl G (ed) Biochemistry of wounded plant tissues. De Gruyter, Berlin, pp 595–622

Younis HM, Boyer JS, Govindjee (1979) Conformation and activity of chloroplast coupling factor exposed to low chemical potential of water in cells. Biochim Biophys Acta 548:328–340

Zabadal TJ (1974) A water potential threshold for the increase of abscisic acid in leaves. Plant Physiol 53:125–127

Zeevaart JAD (1977) Sites of abscisic acid synthesis and metabolism in *Ricinus communis* L. Plant Physiol 59:788–791

Zeevaart JAD (1980) Changes in levels of abscisic acid and its metabolites in excised leaf blades of *Xanthium strumarium* during and after water stress. Plant Physiol 66:672–678

Zeroni M, Jerie PH, Hall MA (1977) Studies on the movement and distribution of ethylene in *Vicia faba* L. Planta 134:119–125

Zimmermann U (1978) Physics of turgor and osmoregulation. Annu Rev Plant Physiol 29:121–148

10 Desiccation-Tolerance

J.D. BEWLEY and J.E. KROCHKO

CONTENTS

10.1 Introduction

Productivity and geographical distribution of plant species are limited as much, if not more, by water stress than by any other environmental factor. Fully one-third of the exposed land mass is classified as arid or semi-arid while the remainder is subjected to seasonal or local variations in water supply. It is hardly surprising that a strong evolutionary impetus toward improved drought-resistance has resulted in a considerable array of adaptations at all levels of organization (ecological, morphological, physiological, and biochemical). Within this variety three basic strategies are recognizable: drought-evasion, drought-avoidance, and drought-tolerance (CLOUDSLEY-THOMPSON and CHADWICK 1964). Drought evasion (or escape) is seen most easily in the ephemeral annuals. Due to an abbreviated life-cycle these plants complete their vegetative growth and reproductive cycle during periods of moisture availability, surviving the intervening dry periods as desiccation-tolerant seeds. Drought-avoidance

is achieved primarily through adaptations that retard water loss and/or increase water absorption. Plants in which these features are well-developed effectively forestall internal water deficits when exogenous supplies are scarce. Drought-tolerance is a feature of plants capable of experiencing protoplasmic dehydration without permanent injury. Except for the seed stage, this latter mechanism is poorly developed in the majority of higher plants. Losses greater than 40%–90% of normal water content (LEVITT 1972), or equilibration with relative humidities of 91% to 98% (LEVITT et al. 1960) are lethal for most. By contrast, many lower plants (and some angiosperms) are remarkable in the ability of their vegetative tissues to withstand extreme drought, i.e., desiccation. Known also as poikilohydrous plants (WALTER 1955), poikiloxerophytes (HENCKEL and PRONINA 1968), or resurrection plants, these desiccation-tolerant plants are loosely defined by their unique ability to revive from an air-dry condition (the air being of low relative humidity). Plants that succumb to desiccation are called desiccation-sensitive, desiccation-intolerant or homoiohydrous (WALTER 1955) plants. Plants that can survive water deficits only by avoiding or resisting desiccation are desiccation-resistant plants, and these fall into the desiccation-intolerant category.

By far the majority of research on water stress in plants has involved desiccation-intolerant species. This is quite understandable, considering that poikilohydrous plants comprise a very limited proportion of native vegetation (even in the regions where they are found) and that they make an imperceptible contribution to agriculture. Generally, desiccation-tolerant plants have sacrificed productivity for survival in the regions to which they are adapted.

Much information is now available regarding the physiological and biochemical changes occurring in desiccation-intolerant species of plants during and after exposure to sub-lethal levels of water stress. Yet very little is understood of the factors responsible for a plant's susceptibility to severe water deficits, or of those that confer greater tolerance. Equally little is known about the basis for desiccation-tolerance per se. Nevertheless, some interesting information on the metabolism of desiccation-tolerant plants under stress has been gained over the past few years, which has necessitated a re-evaluation of established concepts of desiccation-tolerance and the proposal of new ones. These will be elaborated upon in subsequent sections. Some comparisons are made with desiccation-intolerant plants throughout this chapter. However, the reader should refer to others in this volume for a more detailed discussion of the effects of drought on homoiohydrous species.

Desiccation-tolerance in plants has been reviewed elsewhere recently (BEWLEY 1979; GAFF 1980), and the reader is directed to these publications for aspects not covered here.

10.2 Taxonomic Origins of Desiccation-Tolerance in Higher Plants

In addition to numerous examples of fungi, algae (DAVIS 1972), bryophytes and lichens the list of known desiccation-tolerant plants now includes approxi-

mately 60–70 species of ferns and fern-allies, and at least 60 species of angiosperms (Table 10.1). GAFF (1980), citing unpublished data, reported that 83 species of tolerant seed plants have been identified (see also Chaps. 2 and 4, this Vol.).

During the evolution of higher plants, the differentiation of vascular tissue and concomitant increases in plant size and complexity have led to the development of predominantly drought-avoidance mechanisms in species adapted to xeric regions. These kinds of adaptation have the advantage of enabling plants to continue growing during times of restricted water supply. As is now obvious, higher plants have not been restricted to this course despite the intricacies of their structure and physiology. Most are genetically capable of producing desiccation-tolerant reproductive propagules (seeds). The absence of gymnosperms from the survey (Table 10.1) (VIEWEG and ZIEGLER 1969; GAFF 1972) suggests that limitations on size for the successful re-establishment of water continuity in the xylem after drying may be important. The angiosperm examples are all herbs or small shrubs, rarely exceeding 1 m in height. The tallest reported are specimens of *Xerophyta eglandulosa* at 1.7 m (GAFF 1977). Drought-tolerance limits determined in the laboratory reveal that, as a group, the reviviscent angiosperms are more hardy than the ferns, although somewhat less so than either lichens or bryophytes (GAFF 1971, 1977). The disorganization of subcellular constituents that occurs in desiccation-tolerant seed plants during drying frequently is more severe than that observed in rehydrated mosses and ferns, or homoiohydrous plants subjected to sub-lethal levels of water stress (FELLOWS and BOYER 1978; GAFF and HALLAM 1974; GAFF et al. 1976; TUCKER et al. 1975). At least one-third of the desiccation-tolerant monocot species are poikilochlorophyllous (Table 10.1); they suffer the loss of the majority of their chlorophyll while retaining viability during drying.

Examples of desiccation-tolerant pteridophytes comprise greater than 0.65% of the recognized species in this taxon, and are found in a high proportion of families [10 out of 15 — after WILLIS (1973)]. Their distribution is pancontinental (Table 10.1). At present, desiccation-tolerance has been described for approximately 0.1% of monocot species and 0.01% of dicots, but it is very probable that more cases will be documented. Most of the desiccation-tolerant angiosperms are native to southern Africa (39 of the species included in Table 10.1), with fewer from other regions, and none from North America. The most drought-tolerant seed plant from North America is probably the desert shrub, *Larrea divaricata*. Its buds and immature leaves (but not mature leaves) survive considerable dehydration (RUNYON 1934) although the tolerance limitations of these organs have not been fully established. GAFF and LATZ (1978) have suggested that the relative abundance of tolerant species from southern Africa possibly reflects a longer duration of continuous aridity there; according to KOCH (1964) the Namib desert (which is drier than any area in Australia) has existed since the Cretaceous period.

Examples of desiccation-tolerant angiosperms are found in eight families belonging to five orders in this classification (after CRONQUIST, in RADFORD et al. 1974) (Table 10.1). The lack of close relationships among many of these suggests that the ability to withstand air-drying has evolved independently on

Table 10.1. Desiccation-tolerant vascular plants

		Family	Genus[c]	Location[d]	References
Pteridophyta[a]					
Lycopsida	Selaginellales	Selaginellaceae	Selaginella (10)	N. Am., S. Am., Afr.	1, 2, 3, 6, 8, 12, 20, 24, 28
Filicopsida	Pteridales	Sinopteridaceae	Cheilanthes (21)	N. Am., Afr., Aust.	3, 7, 8, 13, 20, 28
			Notholaena (6)	N. Am., S. Afr.	17, 19, 20, 26, 28
			Pellaea (7)	N. Am., S. Afr., Aust.	3, 6, 7, 8, 28
		Actiniopteridaceae	Doryopteris (2)	S. Afr., Aust.	2, 3, 7
		Hemionitidaceae	Actiniopteris (2)	S. Afr.	3
			Gymnopteris	N. Am.	28
			Paraceterach	Aust.	7
		Adiantaceae	Adiantum	S. Afr.	3
	Aspidiales	Aspleniaceae	Asplenium (4)	Afr.	3, 20
			Ceterach (2)	Eur., Med., S. Afr.	3, 20
			Pleurosorus	Aust.	7
	Schizaeales	Schizaeaceae	Mohria	S. Afr.	2, 3
	Davalliales	Oleandraceae	Arthropteris	S. Afr.	3
	Polypodiales	Grammitidaceae	Ctenopteris	Aust.	7
		Polypodiaceae	Polypodium (2)	N. Am., S. Afr.	3, 8, 23, 26
			Platycerium	W. Afr.	12, 13
Spermatophyta					
Angiospermae[b]					
Dicotyledonae	Hamamelidales	Myrothamnaceae	Myrothamnus (2)	S. Afr.	2, 6, 8, 14, 16, 24, 25, 26, 28, 29
	Scrophulariales	Scrophulariaceae	Craterostigma (4)	S. Afr.	2, 3, 6, 8, 24
			Chamaegigas[e]	S. Afr.	2, 6
			Illysanthes (2)	S. Afr.	3, 6
		Gesneriaceae	Boea	Aust.	6, 7, 8
			Haberlea[f]	Med.	6, 27
			Ramonda[f] (3)	Eur., Med.	6, 8, 20, 24, 27
	Lamiales	Labiatae	Satureja	S. Am.	30
Monocotyledonae	Cyperales	Cyperaceae	*Coleochloa (2)	S. Afr.	2, 3, 5, 6, 8, 24
			*Afrotrilepis	W. Afr.	6, 12, 13, 22
			*Carex[g]	C. Asia	6, 12

Order	Family	Genus	Distribution	References
	Gramineae	*Fimbristylis[h]	Aust.	6, 7
		*Cyperus[h]	S. Afr.	3, 5, 6
		*Mariscus[h]	S. Afr.	5, 6
		*Kyllinga[b]	S. Afr.	3, 5, 6
		Oropetium	S. Afr.	2, 5, 6, 8
		Microchloa (2)	S. Afr.	2, 5, 6
		*Eragrostis[h] (3)	S. Afr.	5, 6, 24
		*Sporobolus[h] (4)	Aust., S. Afr.	2, 5, 6, 7, 8, 24
		Brachyachne	S. Afr.	5, 6
		Micraira (6)	Aust.	6, 7
		Tripogon (2)	S. Afr., Aust.	5, 6, 7, 8
		*Eragrostiella	Aust.	7
		Poa	Aust., Med.	6, 7, 27
Liliales	Liliaceae	*Borya (3)	Aust.	4, 6, 7, 8, 9, 24
		Talbotia	S. Afr.	6, 8, 11, 24
	Velloziaceae	*Xerophyta (13)	Afr., S. Am.	2, 3, 6, 8, 10, 18, 21, 24

[a] Classification according to WILLIS (1973)

[b] Orders and Families according to CRONQUIST (in RADFORD et al. 1974)

[c] For genera containing more than one desiccation-tolerant species, the number is indicated in brackets. Genera denoted by an asterisk (*) contain at least one poikilochlorophyllous example

[d] Geographical distribution or collection site of desiccation-tolerant species: N. Am. (North America), S. Am. (South America), Aust. (Australia, New Zealand), C. Asia (central Asia), Eur. (Europe), Med. (southern Europe and/or Mediterranean), Afr. (Africa) or more specifically S. Afr. (southern Africa) and W. Afr. (West Africa)

[e] Only submerged leaves and immature floating leaves are desiccation-tolerant

[f] Desiccation-tolerance disputed by HENCKEL and PRONINA (1973)

[g] Desiccation-tolerance considered ambiguous by WALTER and STADELMANN (1968)

[h] Includes species in which desiccation-tolerance is confined to basal portion of leaf [and also bulbils (Poa bulbosa) or immature leaves (Sporobolus lampranthus)]

References: 1. EICKMEIER (1979); 2. GAFF (1971); 3. GAFF (1977); 4. GAFF and CHURCHILL (1976); 5. GAFF and ELLIS (1974); 6. GAFF and HALLAM (1974); 7. GAFF and LATZ (1978); 8. GAFF and McGREGOR (1979); 9. GAFF et al. (1976); 10. HALLAM and GAFF (1978a); 11. HALLAM and GAFF (1978b); 12. HAMBLER (1961); 13. HAMBLER (1964); 14. HENCKEL and PRONINA (1969); 15. HENCKEL and PRONINA (1973); 16. HOFFMANN (1968); 17. ILJIN (1957); 18. MEGURO et al. (1977); 19. NOBEL (1978); 20. OPPENHEIMER and HALEVY (1962); 21. OWOSEYE and SANFORD (1972); 22. RICHARDS (1957); 23. STUART (1968); 24. TYMMS and GAFF (1979); 25. VIEWEG and ZIEGLER (1969); 26. WALTER (1955); 27. WALTER and STADELMANN (1968); 28. WALTER and STADELMANN (1974); 29. ZIEGLER AND VIEWEG (1970); 30. MONTENEGRO et al. (1979)

desiccation through the ability of the tissue to avoid damage during drying and rehydration. There are, however, a substantial number of examples in the literature of poikilohydrous plants that do not conform metabolically or structurally as predicted by these theories; their responses to droughting are often very similar to those of homoiohydrous plants subjected to water deficits (although the level of stress required to elicit these changes may differ). While the ability to avoid excessive damage might be important in some desiccation-tolerant plants, it is evident that others do not undergo severe water deficits without exhibiting cellular changes, some of which might be regarded as quite extensive and involve perturbations of organelle structure (Sect. 10.5.3). According to BEWLEY (1979), what may be the critical features of desiccation-tolerance are the abilities (1) to limit damage during desiccation to a reparable level; (2) to maintain physiological integrity in the dry state so that metabolism can be reactivated quickly upon rehydration; and (3) to put a repair mechanism into effect upon rehydration, in particular to retain or regain integrity of membranes and membrane-bound organelles. These features will be examined in the following section.

10.5 Cellular Responses of Tolerant and Intolerant Plants to Desiccation and Rehydration

10.5.1 Plant Water Status

A meaningful assessment of the metabolism of plants of varying sensitivity to drought demands attention to the levels of water loss sustained. Accordingly, the designations defined by HSIAO (1973) will be used for clarification whenever possible. These are (1) mild stress: reduction in Ψ (water potential) by several bar or of RWC by 8–10%, (2) moderate stress: decrease in Ψ by less than 12–15 bar, or lowering of RWC by between 10–20%, and (3) severe stress: Ψ lowered more than 15 bar or RWC more than 20% (see Chap. 9, this Vol.).

Water deficits can affect cellular processes in one or more of the following ways: (1) through a decrease in turgor pressure; (2) by a reduction of the chemical potential or activity of water in cells; (3) by changes in spatial relations in membranes and organelles resulting from a decrease in volume of the protoplasm; (4) by effects of increases in solute concentrations caused by losses of water; (5) by alteration of structure of macromolecules resulting from dehydration (HSIAO 1973). It is considered that (1) [but not (2)] may influence plant metabolism at mild and moderate levels of stress, whereas (3) and (4) would have a greater influence at severe water deficits than at moderate stress levels, and (5) would be important at desiccating water contents. These generalities do not exclude the possibility that there may be cellular reactions or structures particularly sensitive (or resistant) to change via these mechanisms at suboptimal water contents (for detailed discussion of water status in tissues and cells see Chap. 2, this Vol.).

10.5.2 Osmotic Effects

Drought-resistant plants frequently are reported to have lower osmotic potentials than less hardy plants (HOSOKAWA and KUBOTA 1957; ILJIN 1957; LEVITT 1956; PARKER 1968; PATTERSON 1946). The relevance of this correlation to drought-tolerance mechanisms is ambiguous at best; it may simply reflect lowered tissue water content due to restricted water supply. Alternatively, reduced solute potentials may represent a drought-avoidance adaptation for increasing the water-retention capabilities of cells relative to their external environment (KLUGE 1976; LEVITT 1956; OPPENHEIMER 1960). Some plants are capable of actively increasing their stores of solute in response to water deficits (osmoregulation) (HSIAO et al. 1976; JONES and TURNER 1978; KLUGE 1976; MORGAN 1977). In these, avoidance adaptations are also involved if these changes effectively delay the loss of turgor (or restore turgor) to lower water contents than would have occurred otherwise (cf. HSIAO and ACEVEDO 1974).

Increases in free sugars and loss of starch commonly occur in plants [including a poikilohydrous angiosperm, *Xerophyta schnitzleinia* (OWOSEYE and SANFORD 1972)] during water stress (BASKIN and BASKIN 1974; KLUGE 1976; LEVITT 1972), although desiccation and rehydration of the poikilohydrous moss *Tortula ruralis* does not result in any substantial changes in starch or free sugar (sucrose) levels (BEWLEY and THORPE 1974; BEWLEY et al. 1978). Free proline accumulation also occurs in drought-stressed plants (e.g., BARNETT and NAYLOR 1966; BASKIN and BASKIN 1974; PÁLFI et al. 1973; SINGH et al. 1972; STEWART 1972), commencing at moderate to severe levels of water stress. The amounts of this amino acid accumulated have been positively correlated with drought-resistance in varieties and species of desiccation-intolerant plants (SINGH et al. 1972; WALDREN and TEARE 1974), but the validity of such correlations has been questioned (HANSON et al. 1977). Proline levels have been found to increase to different extents in a number of desiccation-tolerant higher plants (POURRAT and HUBAC 1974; TYMMS and GAFF 1979). But no correlations can be drawn between the extreme desiccation-tolerance of resurrection plants and their accumulated proline levels. Moreover, improved survival of desiccation cannot be invoked by exogenous application of proline (TYMMS and GAFF 1979). In the highly tolerant moss, *Tortula ruralis,* proline levels remain very low and unchanged during desiccation and rehydration (BEWLEY unpublished data).

When enzymes, structural proteins, nucleic acids, macromolecular complexes, etc. are desiccated in their native state the integrity of the molecules can be retained if some water remains associated with them to prevent the formation of unfavorable conformations (see reviews by HSIAO 1973; LEVITT 1972; PARKER 1972; TODD 1972), or fragmentation (DARBYSHIRE and STEER 1973). Hence the production or availability of substances (e.g., sugar, polyols, anions, amino acids – including proline) to maintain bound water content could be important features of desiccation-tolerance. Little work has been done to support or reject the possibility. Increased production of polyols by lichens (FARRAR and SMITH 1976) might have some importance in this respect, although some desiccation-tolerant plants (e.g., *T. ruralis*) do not appear to exhibit changes in the pool sizes of low molecular weight compounds such as sugars and amino acids

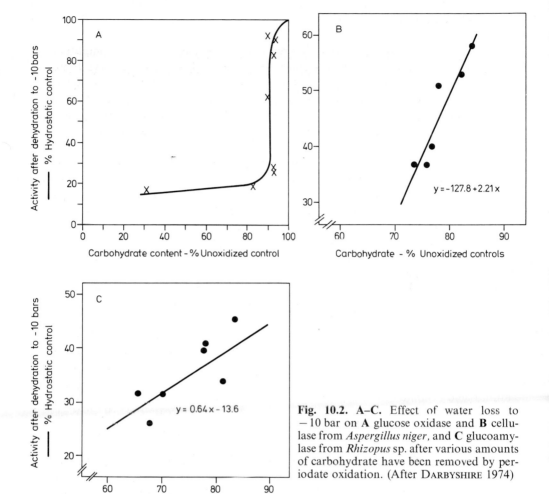

Fig. 10.2. A–C. Effect of water loss to −10 bar on **A** glucose oxidase and **B** cellulase from *Aspergillus niger,* and **C** glucoamylase from *Rhizopus* sp. after various amounts of carbohydrate have been removed by periodate oxidation. (After Darbyshire 1974)

(Bewley et al. 1978, Bewley unpublished data). Protection of some fungal enzymes against water stress may depend upon their conjugation with carbohydrate as glycosylated proteins (Darbyshire 1974). Removal of 10% or more of the carbohydrate associated with commercially available glucose oxidase, cellulase, and glucoamylase leads to a marked reduction in enzyme activity (Fig. 10.2). The universality of this feature in vivo and in desiccation-tolerant plants remains to be established. Protection against desiccation of chloroplast membrane structures by sugars has been proposed, their purported action being to stabilize proteins (Santarius 1969, 1973). Desiccation leads to the concentration of ions within cells, and the possibility that this results in some damage cannot be ignored. Tolerant plants must be able to neutralize these potentially damaging ion effects, or else accommodate and limit them.

10.5.3 Ultrastructural Changes

There appear to be few remarkable differences in the ultrastructural changes caused by air-drying in desiccation-tolerant plants and the changes observed in desiccation-intolerant plants following treatments at sublethal water deficits. However, there is a complicating factor in the interpretation of many of these studies. When water-stressed or desiccated plant tissues are prepared for microscopic examination, the fixation and embedding procedures frequently result in a partial rehydration of the material. Consequently, even though the water deficit present in the tissue at the time of fixation is known, the published results may represent the condition of cellular structures following the imbibition of additional water. Such an occurrence does not necessarily invalidate the observations, but it is probable that in some cases they represent dehydration–rehydration phenomena.

In desiccation-tolerant mosses after air-drying and a short period of rehydration the chloroplasts are swollen, with distended outer membranes, and the thylakoids are dilated (BEWLEY and PACEY 1978; NOAILLES 1974, 1977, 1978; TUCKER et al. 1975). The pattern of response to desiccation in poikilohydrous angiosperms exhibits one striking variation. Whereas tolerant dicots retain chlorophyll throughout a desiccation/rehydration cycle, in many of the tolerant monocots chlorophyll is degraded during drying. In viable air-dry samples of these "poikilochlorophyllous" plants the thylakoids are indistinct or reduced in number and the grana also are fewer or absent (ZIEGLER and VIEWEG 1970; GAFF and HALLAM 1974; GAFF et al. 1976). In some chlorophyll-retaining species (e.g., *Pellaea calomelanos* and *Talbotia elegans*) chloroplast integrity is maintained during desiccation and remoistening, while in other species (e.g., *Xerophyta villosa*) there is some loss of grana and thylakoids (GAFF and HALLAM 1974; HALLAM and GAFF 1978a, b). Vesicularization within the internal membranes of chloroplasts is common among desiccation-tolerant angiosperms (GAFF and HALLAM 1974; GAFF et al. 1976). However, some of the extreme disruptions observed in micrographs of *B. nitida* are probably artifacts of inadequate fixation (GAFF 1980).

Characteristically mitochondria become swollen and the cristae are indistinct in desiccation-tolerant plants after air-drying and rehydration and in desiccation-intolerant plants exposed to injurious levels of water stress (BEWLEY and PACEY 1978; FREEMAN and DUYSEN 1975; GAFF and HALLAM 1974; GAFF et al. 1976; HALLAM and GAFF 1978a, b; MARINOS and FIFE 1972; NIR et al. 1969; NOAILLES 1974, 1977, 1978; TUCKER et al. 1975; VIEIRA DA SILVA et al. 1974). Also numerous lipid droplets are observed in cells of both groups of plants after these stress treatments (BEWLEY and PACEY 1978; GAFF et al. 1976; NIR et al. 1969; NOAILLES 1977; SWANSON et al. 1976). Chromatin condensation may occur (MARINOS and FIFE 1972; NIR et al. 1969), although the nucleolus and nuclear membrane remain well defined in cells capable of recovery (GAFF et al. 1976; MARINOS and FIFE 1972; NIR et al. 1969; NOAILLES 1977; TUCKER et al. 1975).

The response of the intolerant semi-aquatic moss *Cratoneuron filicinum* to desiccation varies with the speed at which it loses water (BEWLEY and PACEY 1978; KROCHKO et al. 1978). Within the first hour of rehydration of this moss

after rapid desiccation the cytoplasm of all cells of the leaves (phyllidia) is disorganized, mitochondria are swollen and have an ill-defined internal structure, the outer chloroplast membrane is lost, and lamellae are dispersed. At the same time of rehydration after very slow desiccation only about 20% of the cells are similarly disrupted – the rest are fairly normal in appearance. After 24 h rehydration all cells of the rapidly desiccated moss are extensively disrupted, but about 50% of the cells of the very slowly dried moss retain their integrity.

The advantages of slow drying in nature have been alluded to in Section 10.3. Perhaps gradual water loss allows for controlled changes in the configuration of macromolecules which favor their stability or which facilitate limited (bio)chemical reactions and hence increases resistance to disruption by dehydration. Presumably even in very slowly dried *C. filicinum* some cells dry out more slowly than others, and these are the ones that survive. As will be evident in succeeding sections, rapid desiccation of *T. ruralis* causes considerably more metabolic disruption than slow desiccation, even though there is complete recovery after both speeds of desiccation. Leaves of many of the higher resurrection plants do not display the extraordinary desiccation-tolerance when detached (which allows them to dry quickly) that they do when dried (more slowly) on intact plants (Gaff 1980). Detached leaves of *Borya nitida* survive 0% relative humidity better if they are initially in the range of ~ -27 to -150 bar for 2 days as they dry.

10.5.4 Leakage and Membrane Integrity, and the "Repair" Concept

Little is known about the changes which the plasmalemma and tonoplast undergo during desiccation and rehydration, although leakage studies indicate that some changes do occur. Many of these studies have been reviewed by Simon (1974, 1978), who summarizes the evidence that dry viable seeds, lichens, yeasts, pollen, fungi, and their spores all leak solutes when placed in liquid medium. Leaked substances include amino acids, mono-, di- and tri-saccharides, sugar alcohols, organic acids, hormones, phenolics, phosphates, and various fluorescent materials and electrolytes. A common feature is that the major leakage of solutes is a transient phenomenon, often lasting only minutes after the addition of water. Prolonged loss of solutes is characteristic of irreversibly damaged tissues.

Desiccation-tolerant and -intolerant bryophytes exhibit leakage of electrolytes upon rehydration following desiccation (e.g., Gupta 1976, 1977c, 1979). An index of desiccation-tolerance for bryophytes has been devised based upon potassium retention within cells after storage at high and low relative humidities (Brown and Buck 1979). There is a good relationship between this index, tolerance of the plants to stress, and the availability of water in each bryophyte's habitat. An index of recovery has been devised also, which is a useful indication of a bryophyte's ability to survive brief and substantial desiccation stress, but it is less well-correlated to habitat water availability. Desiccation-tolerance and recovery indices have been proposed for lichens also (Buck and Brown 1979).

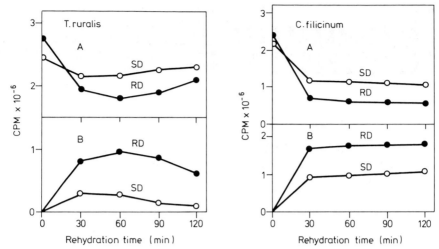

Fig. 10.3 A, B. Leakage of ^{3}H-leucine from the mosses *Tortula ruralis* and *Cratoneuron filicinum* on recovery from rapid desiccation (*RD*) and slow desiccation (*SD*). Changes in total radioactivity in the moss (**A**) and in radioactivity leaked into the bathing solution (**B**) during rehydration are shown. (After DHINDSA and BEWLEY 1977)

The extent of leakage from the one cell-thick phyllidia of the desiccation-tolerant moss *Tortula ruralis* on rehydration is determined by its prior speed of desiccation (Fig. 10.3). After slow drying, leakage is less than half that from rapidly desiccated moss and is similar to that from undried controls. After 1 h the leaked material in the medium is taken up by the moss again. Loss of material from both slowly and rapidly desiccated intolerant *Cratoneuron filicinum* is more extensive than from *T. ruralis* and is not reversed with time. Even so, it is less after slow than after rapid desiccation. The implication from these studies is that membranes of *T. ruralis* undergo certain reversible conformational changes during desiccation to retain their integrity. During slow desiccation these can be accomplished fully, but after rapid desiccation some repair mechanism must be put into effect quickly on rehydration. On the other hand, damage to *C. filicinum* membranes during desiccation and rehydration is apparently too extensive for repair, or the repair mechanisms themselves are damaged, or both.

Leakage from tissues has been explained in terms of changes which take place in the structure of membranes during water loss (SIMON 1974, 1978). Membranes are composed principally of proteins and phospholipids arranged in a fluid bilayer. Individual phospholipid molecules are lined up side-by-side with their polar groups facing the aqueous phase on either side of the membrane and with their hydrocarbon chains forming the hydrophobic central region (Fig. 10.4 A). This molecular organization is stabilized by the relationship between membrane components and water. Low angle X-ray diffraction patterns of isolated membranes have shown that 20%–30% hydration (above fully dried weight) is essential for maintenance of the lipoprotein association in membranes (FINEAN 1969; LUZZATI and HUSSON 1962). At lower water contents the mem-

Table 10.4. The relative amounts of the fatty acids in a phospholipid fraction of *Tortula ruralis* upon rehydration after fast and slow drying. (R.R.C. Stewart and Bewley unpublished data)

	Palmitic	Palmitoleic	Oleic	Linoleic	Linolenic	Eicosatrienoic	Eicosatetraenoic
	16:0	16:1	18:1	18:2	18:3	20:3	20:4
H	100	T	37	35	112	39	27
RD	100	T	38	36	115	36	26
R 15	100	T	36	37	98	29	19
R 45	100	T	31	35	99	27	18
R 75	100	T	34	37	114	39	26
R 105	100	T	37	36	113	34	23
SD	100	T	34	38	118	38	22
S 15	100	T	33	37	99	29	20
S 45	100	T	24	24	71	25	14
S 75	100	T	36	32	84	24	14
S 105	100	T	38	37	116	39	24

H: undesiccated moss; RD: rapidly dried moss within 1 h over silica gel; R 15–105: rapidly dried moss rehydrated from 15–105 min; SD: slowly dried moss over 3 h in an atmosphere of 65% R.H.; S 15–105: slowly dried moss rehydrated from 15–105 min. T: trace amounts

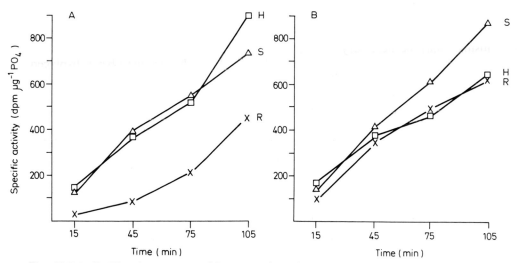

Fig. 10.5 A, B. The time course of incorporation of **A** acetate and **B** glycerol into fatty acids of the phospholipid fraction of *Tortula ruralis* in *H* control, undesiccated moss, *R* moss rehydrated after rapid desiccation and *S* moss rehydrated after slow desiccation. (By R.R.C. Stewart and Bewley unpublished data)

of membrane leakage. Rapidly desiccated moss leaks more upon rehydration (Fig. 10.3), but slowly desiccated moss undergoes the greater phospholipid changes (Table 10.4). Probably, then, the phospholipid component of the membrane plays an insignificant role in the control of leakage, and once again

we must invoke a role for the unstudied component — the protein. In desiccation-sensitive *C. filicinum* the proportions of $18:3$, $20:3$, and $20:4$ fatty acids in the phospholipid fractions are considerably less than in *T. ruralis*. As in *T. ruralis*, however, there are no changes in fatty acid composition during either rapid or slow desiccation. Upon subsequent rehydration of rapidly dried moss the levels of the above three unsaturated fatty acids decline over the last 2 h, but there are no changes after slow drying (STEWART and BEWLEY, unpublished data). But following both speeds of desiccation there is considerable leakage upon rehydration (Fig. 10.3) — again suggesting a lack of correlation between the status of phospholipids and the extent of leakage upon rehydration.

Alterations to membrane properties by lipid peroxidation could account for some of the observed cellular changes associated with desiccation and rehydration (SIMON 1974). A number of biological oxidations, both enzymatic and spontaneous, generate the free superoxide radical ($O_2^{\cdot-}$) which is cytotoxic, and in turn can react with H_2O_2 to produce singlet oxygen and the hydroxyl radical ($OH\cdot$) — highly potent oxidants (FRIDOVICH 1976). These can induce considerable destruction, particularly to large polymers like nucleic acids, protein and polysaccharides, and to membrane lipids (MEAD 1976). In hydrated tissues free radical production is normally controlled by free radical absorbents or scavenging reactions. One such scavenger is the enzyme superoxide dismutase (SOD) (FRIDOVICH 1975, 1976) which converts $O_2^{\cdot-}$ to H_2O_2, and this in turn can be removed by catalase. It is possible that water loss from cells of desiccation-intolerant plants can upset the balance between free radical producing and scavenging reactions in favor of the former, whereas in desiccation-tolerant plants the balance is maintained.

In desiccation-tolerant *T. ruralis* SOD and catalase activities increase during slow desiccation and lipid peroxidation (as shown by the production of malondialdehyde (MDA), a breakdown product of tri-unsaturated fatty acids with double bonds three carbons apart, e.g., $18:3$, $20:3$) decreases (Fig. 10.6 A–C). On rehydration lipid peroxidation rises again, but only to control levels, and enzyme levels decline. During rapid desiccation there are no changes, but on rehydration there is a sharp rise in lipid peroxidation, but SOD and catalase levels rise also, sufficiently, presumably, to limit peroxidation damage. Unfortunately, however, it is difficult to draw correlations between peroxidation damage (and the system for scavenging free radicals) and the status of fatty acids within the phospholipid fraction. It is surprising that the levels of MDA rise so quickly and to such an extent upon rehydration of rapidly desiccated moss (Fig. 10.6 C) when the changes in fatty acids (particularly $18:3$ and $20:3$) are small (Table 10.4). Also, there is little comparison between the small changes in peroxidation products on rehydration after slow desiccation, and the more substantial changes in phospholipid fatty acids. Perhaps, then, the substrates for peroxidation damage and for free radical damage are not to be found within the phospholipid (membrane) fraction, but in some other lipid fraction within the cell. As suggested earlier (Sect. 10.5.3), there is an accumulation of lipid droplets within the cells of some mosses during desiccation (including *T. ruralis*: BEWLEY and PACEY 1978) and it is these which might be the target for peroxidation reactions and protection. On theoretical grounds, the importance of SOD in limiting

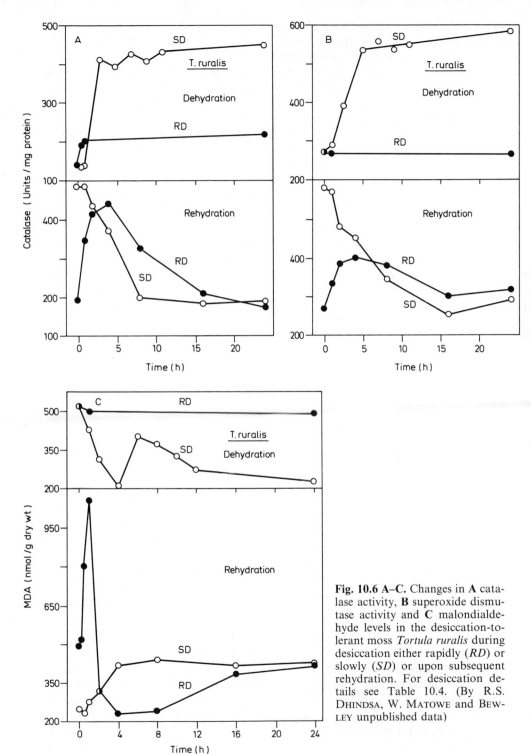

Fig. 10.6 A–C. Changes in **A** catalase activity, **B** superoxide dismutase activity and **C** malondialdehyde levels in the desiccation-tolerant moss *Tortula ruralis* during desiccation either rapidly (*RD*) or slowly (*SD*) or upon subsequent rehydration. For desiccation details see Table 10.4. (By R.S. Dhindsa, W. Matowe and Bewley unpublished data)

membrane peroxidation damage is debatable anyway. SOD is a soluble enzyme (FRIDOVICH 1975) and it may be unable to exert much influence over events taking place in the hydrophobic core of the lipid bilayer.

In desiccation-intolerant *C. filicinum* catalase and SOD decline during drying at either speed, and their activities decline precipitously on rehydration (DHINDSA, MATOWE and BEWLEY unpublished data). Lipid peroxidation, as shown by malondialdehyde production, is greatest on rehydration after slow desiccation, and is 2.5 times greater after 2 h than at the start of rehydration. Also it is 2 times greater than in rehydrated rapidly desiccated moss over the same time period. Yet, the decline in phospholipid fatty acids is considerably greater after rapid than after slow desiccation.

It is evident that desiccation causes perturbations to membranes of both tolerant and intolerant plants, resulting in leakage upon subsequent rehydration. The extent of these perturbations is affected by the speed at which water is lost — rapid desiccation being more deleterious than slow desiccation. Restitution of the membranes occurs upon rehydration of desiccation-tolerant plants, even though there is temporary leakage of low molecular weight solutes until this occurs. This restitution may involve de novo synthesis of membrane components involving the so-called "repair" mechanisms. Limited evidence to date suggests that changes to the phospholipid component due to desiccation and rehydration cannot easily be correlated with the increased leakiness of membranes.

10.5.5 RNA and Protein Synthesis

Very mild to moderate water stress reduces the level of protein synthesis in drought-sensitive vegetative tissues and protein synthesis does not recover in cells subjected to severe water loss (see references in HSIAO 1973; BEWLEY 1981; BEWLEY and LARSEN 1980).

Our understanding of the effects of desiccation on protein and associated RNA synthesis in desiccation-tolerant plants has come largely from studies on the gametophyte of the moss *Tortula ruralis*. There is a recent report that protein synthesis recovers in *Xerophyta villosa* and *Myrothamnus flabellifolia* after extended periods of hydration (GAFF and McGREGOR 1979 and cited in GAFF 1980), but little work has been done on the higher resurrection plants.

The effects of desiccation of *T. ruralis* on polysomes varies with the speed at which water loss takes place (GWÓŹDŹ et al. 1974). Rapidly desiccated moss contains about half the polysomes of the undesiccated control, but following slow desiccation polysomes are absent (Fig. 10.7). These losses of polysomes could be due to: (1) stress-induced production or activation of ribonucleases which degrade polysomes or, (2) ribosome run-off from mRNA, coupled with failure to reform an initiation complex under stress conditions. That ribosomes simply become detached from mRNA during water loss is an untenable alternative because in rapidly desiccated moss some polysomes are retained (Fig. 10.7).

Ribonuclease activity increases during both rapid and slow desiccation (Fig. 10.7), but it does so only after polysome levels have declined to their

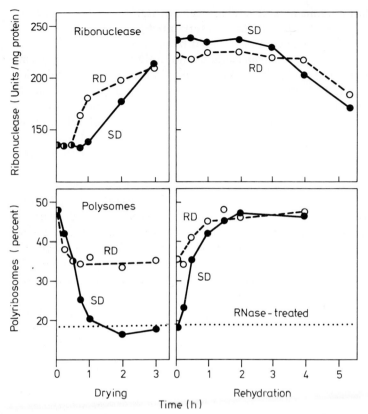

Fig. 10.7. Changes in ribonuclease (*top*) and polyribosomes (*bottom*) during rapid desiccation (*RD*) and slow desiccation (*SD*) of *Tortula ruralis,* and upon subsequent rehydration. For desiccation details see Table 10.4. (After DHINDSA and BEWLEY 1976a)

minimum (which suggests that the enzyme does not arise by de novo synthesis). Moreover, while the final ribonuclease level is the same for mosses dried at both speeds, the final polysome level is much higher after rapid desiccation. Thus the lack of temporal coincidence and quantitative correlation between the increase in enzyme activity and the polysome decrease suggests that ribonuclease is not the causative agent. Polysomes return to control levels within 2 h of rehydration after both speeds of desiccation, and yet ribonuclease levels do not decline until considerably later (Fig. 10.7). This, again, is indicative that ribonuclease is not involved in the regulation of polysome activity. Others (BLEKHMAN 1979) strongly invoke a role for ribonuclease in restricting protein synthesis during water loss from tolerant and intolerant plants, but no temporal correlations between polysome loss and enzyme levels have been made. An increase in ribonuclease as a result of water loss is clearly inadequate evidence for its participation in the cessation of protein synthesis.

   During desiccation at both speeds the ribosomal pellet (containing both polysomes and single ribosomes) decreases in its capacity to effect the formation

Table 10.5. Translation in vitro of poly(A)-containing messenger RNA from undesiccated and dry gametophytes of *Tortula ruralis*. (Based on DHINDSA and BEWLEY 1978)

RNA source	^{14}C-Leucine incorporation (cpm)
Fresh moss	9,175
Rapidly desiccated	7,976
Slowly desiccated	7,185
Deletions:	
No mRNA	693
No S-23	85

of peptide bonds, as shown by its increasing inability to utilize puromycin to form peptidyl-puromycin in an in vitro assay system (DHINDSA and BEWLEY 1976a). This is evidence that as polysomes decline the released ribosomes are not complexed with fragments of messenger RNA, whereas they would be if polysomes were degraded by ribonuclease. Similar results were obtained using moss maintained under steady-state water stress conditions (-10 to -60 bar) by polyethylene glycol (DHINDSA and BEWLEY 1976b). Hence ribosome run-off from messenger RNA, coupled with failure to reform an initiation complex, appears to be the primary cause of polysome loss during water loss. Presumably during desiccation at a rapid rate critical water loss occurs before run-off can be completed.

Since loss of polysomes during desiccation of *T. ruralis* is not due to their degradation by ribonuclease it is reasonable to expect that ribosomes exist in slowly desiccated moss, separated from messenger RNA. This is indeed the case (GWÓŹDŹ and BEWLEY 1975). Moreover, cytoplasmic ribosomal RNA (24 S and 17 S) and low molecular weight RNA (4–5 S) are not degraded during desiccation or on subsequent rehydration (TUCKER and BEWLEY 1976).

That messenger RNA also is conserved in the dry moss and is utilized on subsequent rehydration is inferred from the observation that protein synthesis can resume on rehydration of slowly desiccated moss even when most RNA synthesis is inhibited by cordycepin and actinomycin D (DHINDSA and BEWLEY 1978). Other studies on the qualitative aspects of protein synthesis have shown that similar proteins are synthesized before and after desiccation (either rapid or slow) even when RNA synthesis is inhibited on rehydration. This, again, argues for messenger RNA conservation during desiccation (DHINDSA and BEWLEY 1978). Direct and unequivocal evidence for the conservation of messenger RNA in dry *Tortula ruralis* has come from studies in which poly(A)-containing RNA has been extracted from rapidly and slowly desiccated moss, and then made to catalyze the synthesis of polypeptides in vitro (Table 10.5). Extractable poly(A)-messenger RNA activity in slowly desiccated moss is about 80% of that of fully hydrated controls: rapidly desiccated moss contains some 90% messenger RNA activity, although some presumably is conserved on polysomes. Poly(A)-containing RNA also has been extracted from the hydrated and dry gametophyte of *Polytrichum commune* (SEIBERT et al. 1976). Air-drying (claimed

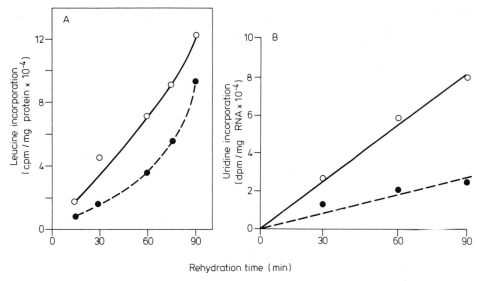

Fig. 10.8 A, B. Protein **A** and RNA **B** synthesis by *Tortula ruralis* on rehydration following rapid (— ● —) and slow (– ○ –) desiccation. For desiccation details see Table 10.4. (**A** after Gwóźdź et al. 1974, **B** by MJ Oliver and Bewley unpublished data)

to be slow drying) of *P. commune* does not result in any degradation of total extractable RNA, but whether or not polysomes are present in the dry moss is not indicated. Hence it is not known if the poly(A)-containing RNA is conserved in the free state, or if it is associated with ribosomes in polysomes. Nor, yet, is it known whether it has messenger RNA-like properties in vitro.

Following desiccation, *T. ruralis* (Bewley 1973a; Gwóźdź et al. 1974), *P. commune* (Seibert et al. 1976) and *Neckera crispa* (Henckel et al. 1977) recommence protein synthesis within a few minutes. In *T. ruralis* polysomes are restored to control levels within 2 h (Fig. 10.7), even after the moss has been stored in the dry state for 10 months (Bewley 1973b). Protein synthesis resumes at a faster rate after slow desiccation than after rapid desiccation (Fig. 10.8 A). The reason for this is not readily apparent, though, because polysomes are present already in rapidly desiccated moss, and resume activity on rehydration (Bewley 1973a), whereas for slowly desiccated moss to restart protein synthesis the recombination of separated messenger RNA and ribosomes must occur.

RNA synthesis in *T. ruralis* also recommences rapidly on rehydration after both speeds of desiccation (Gwóźdź et al. 1974; Dhindsa and Bewley 1978), and more quickly after slow desiccation than after rapid desiccation (Fig. 10.8 B). But the synthesis of neither messenger RNA nor ribosomal RNA appears to be essential for the re-establishment of protein synthesis (Tucker and Bewley 1976; Dhindsa and Bewley 1978). It is claimed that on rehydration of *P. commune* RNA synthesis is delayed by some 30–60 min (Seibert et al. 1976), although insensitivity of the experimental technique used could contribute to this apparent delay.

For comparative purposes, similar studies have been carried out using mosses which are not normally subjected to desiccation in their usual aquatic or semi-aquatic habitat. After rapid desiccation *Bryum pseudotriquetrum* does not retain any polysomes, and not only does it not reform any on rehydration but within 24 h even its ribosomes are degraded (BEWLEY et al. 1974). Subsequent studies on *Cratoneuron filicinum* (mis-identified in some publications as *Hygrohypnum luridum*) have shown that this moss retains a reduced number of polysomes in the dry state after rapid desiccation, compared to undesiccated controls (GWÓŹDŹ and BEWLEY 1975), and none following slow desiccation (MALEK and BEWLEY unpublished). Ribosomes increase as polysomes decline in the dried moss, and they retain their activity in vitro. On rehydration, however, activity of both polysomes and ribosomes decreases precipitously (GWÓŹDŹ and BEWLEY 1975), suggesting that it is rehydration, rather than desiccation, which is lethal. Predictably, after both slow and rapid desiccation protein synthesis fails to resume (KROCHKO et al. 1978). Even *C. filicinum,* however, is capable of losing a considerable amount of water before its capacity to resume protein synthesis is impaired. Loss of water to about 45% of original fresh weight is possible without a significant deleterious effect on protein synthesis on rehydration. Moreover protein synthesis can occur at -40 bar and can resume following a 6-h treatment with -60 bar of water potential imposed by polyethylene glycol (DHINDSA and BEWLEY 1977). Although this moss is intolerant of desiccation, and grows almost entirely immersed in water, it has a tolerance of water-stress which is greater than that of many terrestrial higher plants.

What is evident from the studies on *T. ruralis,* a desiccation-tolerant terrestrial moss, is that protein synthesis ceases as water is lost, and resumes again rapidly on rehydration. Protein synthesis itself is quite sensitive to drought stress, being reduced by about 50% at -20 bar water potential although a low amount occurs even at -60 bar (DHINDSA and BEWLEY 1977). Hence protein synthesis may not have a high resistance to drought stress (i.e., it may not continue under severe stress conditions) but it is tolerant of drought, in that the process can resume even after desiccation. Rapid resumption may be aided by the conservation of the components of the protein synthesizing complex in the dry state. This may be particularly important to those plants receiving only temporary hydration (e.g., by morning dew) and which have but a few hours to continue metabolism before becoming desiccated again. The effects of desiccation stress on the protein-synthesizing complex are unknown, although failure of re-initiation under stress is probably an important factor in the cessation of its activity. It may be that the components of the synthetic complex itself have an inherent tolerance of desiccation, for even extracted polysomes can be revived from the air-dry state (GWÓŹDŹ and BEWLEY 1975). It appears, however, that polysomes and ribosomes from desiccation-intolerant *C. filicinum* also retain their activity in the dry moss, as shown by in vitro assay, although they lose activity rapidly on rehydration. Hence it is likely that the possession of a stable protein-synthesizing complex which can withstand severe drought conditions is an important feature of desiccation-tolerant plants, but that other factors are more important in determining the absolute level of tolerance of the cells themselves.

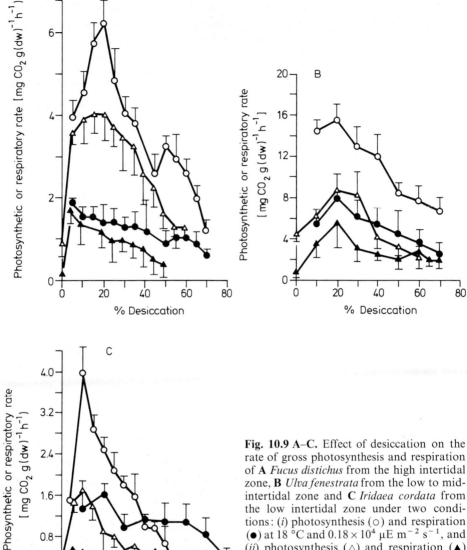

Fig. 10.9 A–C. Effect of desiccation on the rate of gross photosynthesis and respiration of **A** *Fucus distichus* from the high intertidal zone, **B** *Ulva fenestrata* from the low to mid-intertidal zone and **C** *Iridaea cordata* from the low intertidal zone under two conditions: (*i*) photosynthesis (○) and respiration (●) at 18 °C and 0.18×10^4 µE m^{-2} s^{-1}, and (*ii*) photosynthesis (△) and respiration (▲) at 10 °C and 0.15×10^4 µE m^{-2} s^{-1}. (After Quadir et al. 1979)

10.5.6 Photosynthesis and Respiration

These are by far the most-studied metabolic processes in desiccation-tolerant plants so, for convenience, our discussion is divided into sub-sections, each one dealing with a particular group of plants.

Table 10.6. The survival, photosynthesis (rate of evolution of oxygen in $\mu mol\ O_2 \cdot g$ wet wt^{-1} h^{-1}), and growth (mean $\pm$ S.E.) of three species of fucoid algae after drying for 5 h at 26 °C and 48%–52% R.H. (Based on SCHONBECK and NORTON 1978)

Position in eulittoral zone	Species	Rate of O$_2$ evolution			Growth	
		Before drying	After 5 h drying and 18 h recovery in sea water	% Original rate	% Gain in wt after 10 days in culture	Condition of thalli after 10 days in culture
Upper fringe	Pelvetia canaliculata	23 ± 1	21 ± 1	90	32	Healthy
Upper middle	Fucus spiralis	29 ± 3	13 ± 2	45[a]	3	Damaged near tips
Lower	Fucus serratus	25 ± 1	0	0	0	Dead

[a] This species will recover fully after longer periods of hydration

10.5.6.1 Algae

Several studies have shown that during drying of eulittoral algae photosynthetic capacity is gradually reduced, although most work has been done with nontolerant species which do not recover after severe water stress (CHAPMAN 1966). Photosynthesis in a variety of seaweeds in the middle and upper zones is maximal after some water loss (Fig. 10.9) [and about 25% loss from *Fucus vesiculosus* and *Ascophyllum nodosum* (BRINKHUIS et al. 1976; JOHNSON et al. 1974)], but then declines with declining fresh weight (Fig. 10.9). It is evident from Fig. 10.9 that the lower zone alga is considerably more sensitive to desiccation than those from the higher zones. Initially water loss from the surface of the fronds may enhance the uptake of CO_2, and hence an increase in photosynthesis, but as water loss progresses the photosynthetic mechanism is presumably disturbed. The kinetics of recovery of carbon fixation after drying of desiccation-tolerant marine algae do not appear to have been studied. Nevertheless, it is evident that the ability to tolerate desiccation and to resume photosynthesis and growth when resubmerged is greatest in species found highest on the shore, and is progressively less in species inhabiting successively lower levels (Table 10.6).

In the red alga *Porphyra* the primary photochemical mechanism of photosynthesis is stable in the dry state and on rehydration is reactivated instantaneously (FORK and HIYAMA 1973). During extensive water loss from desiccation-tolerant marine algae there is complete inactivation of photosynthetic partial processes, the first site that is sensitive to desiccation being the electron transport between photosystems II and I (WILTENS et al. 1978). In contrast, desiccation-intolerant algae do not recover following even limited water loss, suggesting irreversible chloroplast damage.

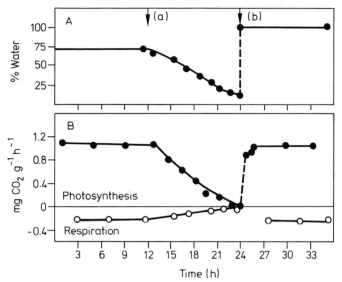

Fig. 10.10. A Water content and **B** carbon dioxide exchange during wetting and drying of the lichen *Ramalina maciformis*. *Arrow (a)* indicates the start of exposure to dry air and *arrow (b)* the time of rewetting by means of spraying. (After Lange 1969a)

Respiration in *A. nodosum, Chondrus crispus, Ulva lactuca, F. vesiculosus* and *Gigartina stellata* declines during drying (following a brief rise after some water loss in the last two species (Brinkhuis et al. 1976; Kanwisher 1957; Mathieson and Burns 1971) — see also Fig. 10.9 — and recovery on rehydration can occur after at least 80% water loss (Kanwisher 1957) (with the exception of *A. nodosum*). Similar observations have been made on other marine and freshwater species (Ogata 1968). Predictably, desiccation-tolerant terrestrial algae lose their capacity to respire and photosynthesize during drying, and recover these faculties on subsequent rehydration (Bertsch 1966; Brock 1975a; Fray-mouth 1928).

10.5.6.2 Lichens

The responses to drying of the whole lichen thallus are a combination of those of the algal (phycobiont) and of the fungal (mycobiont) component. Desiccation-induced changes in photosynthesis, for example, reflect the metabolic state of the algal component which, although it is only 3%–10% of the thallus by weight, is the fixer of carbon, subsequently transported as carbohydrate to the more massive fungal component. This latter is the major site of respiration. Several reviews have been written on the effects of environmental stresses on lichen survival and carbon assimilation (Farrar 1973, 1976; Harris 1976; Kappen 1973; Lange et al. 1975; Smith 1975) and the reader should consult these for details that are not presented here (see also Chap. 10, Vol. 12 C).

Little is known about the metabolic changes that lichens undergo during desiccation, although Lange (1969a) has demonstrated that water loss from

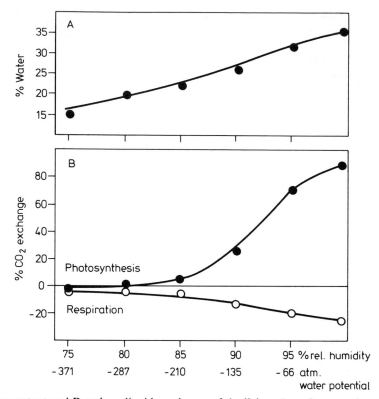

Fig. 10.11. A Water content and **B** carbon dioxide exchange of the lichen *Ramalina maciformis* in equilibrium with the water vapor pressure of air having different relative humidities and water potentials. CO_2 exchange at 10,000 lux is expressed as the percentage of that following spraying with water. (After LANGE 1969a)

Ramalina maciformis is paralleled by a continuous decline in CO_2 assimilation and dark respiration (Fig. 10.10). Recovery from desiccation has been studied under both field and laboratory conditions. In their natural habitat some desert lichens are rarely rewetted by rainfall, but rather resume their metabolism in atmospheres of high relative humidity and during early morning dew formation. Dry *Evernia* and *Ramalina* species can absorb sufficient water from moist air to resume CO_2 exchange; in fact, at relative humidities above 80% respiration and photosynthesis increase nonlinearly with increasing moisture content of the ambient air (BERTSCH 1966; LANGE 1969a). These lichens can achieve at least 90% of their maximum activities in water-saturated air, and yet under these conditions (where care is taken to prevent water condensing into droplets) the water content of *R. maciformis,* for example, reaches only 35% (Fig. 10.11). The compensation point of this species is reached at 80% relative humidity (10,000 lux, 10 °C), corresponding to a water content of about 20%, and a water potential close to −300 bar. Fixation of radioactive CO_2 by photosynthesis in *Lepraria membranaceae* has been observed at water potentials as extreme as −450 bar (BROCK 1975b).

When *R. maciformis* is allowed to absorb water from moist air (to a water content of 37%), on subsequent wetting of the thallus with liquid water (to 60% water content) there is an increase in CO_2 assimilation by only 20%. On the other hand, dark respiration more than doubles (LANGE 1969a). The reasons for this are not known, but these observations are of relevance to the environmental conditions to which this lichen is subjected in its natural habitat — the central Negev desert. Here the intervals between winter rainfalls can exceed 12 months, but this and other lichens are often moistened at night by humid air and by early morning dew. Before dawn the water content of the *R. maciformis* thallus may reach 31%, but the night temperatures are too low to allow for much respiration. As dawn breaks and the light intensity increases net assimilation of CO_2 occurs, but photosynthesis then declines within 2–3 h as the thallus loses water to the now drier, and warmer, air. Respiration also resumes, although less rapidly, but by the time optimal temperature conditions are reached the thallus has dried out again (LANGE et al. 1970). It has been calculated that, on a 24 h basis, the mg CO_2 yield of dry weight^{-1} by assimilation is 1.32 and loss by respiration is 0.78, to give a net yield of 0.54 mg g dry weight^{-1}, or an equivalent of 146 µg of organic carbon fixed (summarized by KAPPEN et al. 1975; LANGE et al. 1975). Further calculations, based on the fact that *R. maciformis* will be subjected normally to 198 dew events per annum in the central Negev, suggest a yearly increment of thallus growth of 8.4%. Not all desert-inhabiting lichens resume photosynthesis in response to increasing air humidities (GANNUTZ 1969): *Chondropsis semiviridis,* a native of Australian deserts, probably requires liquid water (dew or rain) (ROGERS 1971).

Most information on the metabolic responses of lichens to rehydration following desiccation has come from laboratory studies in which dried thalli have been rewetted with, and maintained on (or in) liquid water — conditions that might not be always ideal. Immediately on introduction to water there is an intense, but brief (1–2 min) nonmetabolic release of previously adsorbed gases (FARRAR and SMITH 1976; SMITH and MOLESWORTH 1973). This "wetting burst" is a purely physical process also exhibited by nonliving tissues and inert substances, and is of no significance to desiccation-tolerance. It is followed by a period of increased oxygen consumption and CO_2 output over and above basal levels of the undesiccated thallus, and this is known as "resaturation respiration", a phenomenon which may last for from one to many hours, or even days (FARRAR and SMITH 1976; RIED 1953, 1960; SMITH and MOLESWORTH 1973). Even when lichens are not fully dried they exhibit resaturation respiration on rehydration, e.g., *Peltigera polydactyla* after drying to only 40% of full saturation (SMITH and MOLESWORTH 1973). The length and magnitude of this resaturation respiration varies with species, and probably also with conditions of drying and period of desiccation. *C. semiviridis* dried in atmospheres of high relative humidity (hence probably slowly dried) showed very little resaturation respiration on rehydration, basal respiration rates being achieved within an hour (ROGERS 1971). Lichens hydrated by absorbing moisture from the air before being saturated with liquid water, show no resaturation respiration either (BERTSCH 1966; LANGE 1969a). The nature of the resaturation respiration is unknown, but it is claimed that in *Hypogymnia physodes* and *P. polydactyla,*

unlike basal respiration, it is cyanide-sensitive (FARRAR and SMITH 1976; SMITH and MOLESWORTH 1973). Whether this implicates mitochondria as the site of resaturation respiration has not been resolved. Resaturation respiration is also azide-sensitive in *P. polydactyla* and DNP-sensitive in *H. physodes*. But these inhibitors have different effects upon metabolism at different concentrations, and so it is unfortunate that the effect of only one concentration was reported. Information on the relationship between oxygen consumption, ATP production and ATP requirements of rehydrated thalli is not available.

The major substrates for respiration (including resaturation respiration) are polyols (e.g., mannitol and arabitol in the fungus, and ribitol in the alga), plus the nonpolyol sucrose (FARRAR and SMITH 1976; SMITH and MOLESWORTH 1973). The highest concentration of polyols is in the fungus, they having been modified from carbon skeletons provided by photosynthetic activity of the alga (SMITH 1975). The net loss of polyols from the thallus of *H. physodes* on rehydration exceeds that which can be accounted for by resaturation respiration alone. The balance is lost due to extensive leakage from alga and fungus into the surrounding medium during the first few minutes of rehydration (FARRAR and SMITH 1976).

Many mesic and xeric lichens cannot survive in a continuously wet habitat, and thrive only under conditions of alternating wet and dry periods. When lichens are rewetted by water vapor there is no leakage of polyols nor any resaturation respiration, and hence (although it has not been established) no depletion of the pools of respirable substrate. But in lichens from temperate climates, where wetting by rain is a common occurrence, there is a potential for depletion of respirable substrates. FARRAR (1976) has hypothesized that the establishment of a sizeable and readily accessible pool of respirable substrate is an important "physiological buffer", so that in times of metabolic stress imposed by alternate wetting and drying cycles substrate may be drawn from the pool, and hence degradation of insoluble cell components (e.g., carbohydrate and protein polymers) does not occur. In time, the pool is replenished by photosynthesis when favorable conditions prevail. If the polyol pool is depleted below a critical level then recovery from desiccation is not possible. Although this concept of physiological buffering is an interesting one, its application to lichens in their natural habitat needs to be established.

Very few studies have been conducted on the metabolism of plants at very low water contents. Using lichens placed in an atmosphere of tritiated water (THO) vapor, COWAN et al. (1979) have shown that different metabolic systems operate at different degrees of desiccation. These are summarized in Fig. 10.12 A and B for *Ramalina celastri* and *Peltigera polydactyla*. It is apparent that events associated with the tricarboxylic acid cycle (b) and related transaminations (a), and with sugar alcohol metabolism (f) operate to produce metabolites at lower water contents than do events associated with carbon fixation, i.e., sugar production (c) and sugar phosphate production (d), and with lipid synthesis (e). Macromolecule synthesis (g) proceeds only at high water contents. The α-oxo acids of the tricarboxylic acid cycle are unstable during desiccation, and it is suggested (COWAN et al. 1979) that amino acid synthesis at very low water contents results in the accumulation of an available store of stable intermediates

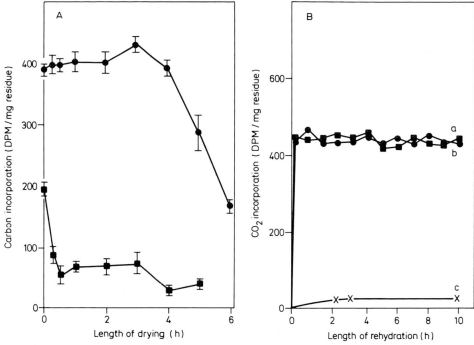

Fig. 10.17. A The effect of slow desiccation on nonautotrophic dark CO_2-fixation in *Tortula ruralis* (●) and *Cratoneuron filicinum* (■). **B** The recovery of dark fixation in *a* slow-dried and **b** fast-dried *T. ruralis* upon rehydration, and *c* in slow-dried *C. filicinum* upon rehydration. (Based on Sen Gupta 1977)

poorly after slower speeds of desiccation (Fig. 10.17). In vitro activities of PEP carboxylase, GOT and MDH do not decline during drying and subsequent rehydration of either *T. ruralis* or *C. filicinum* and so loss of dark-fixation ability is not the result of enzyme destruction within the latter. An alternate, but entirely speculative, possibility is that increasing water deficits cause a decline in acceptor molecules (e.g., PEP) or cofactors.

Dark CO_2 fixation has also recently been reported in the hydrated thalli of two lichen species at rates between 10% and 25% of photosynthesis (Kershaw et al. 1979). Dark fixation is depressed at low thallus water contents, in a similar manner to net photosynthesis.

10.5.6.4 Vegetative Tissues of Vascular Plants

The effects of mild to moderate water stress on CO_2 exchange by desiccation-intolerant higher plants has received considerable attention and there are several extensive reviews (in particular on the effects of drought on photosynthesis) (e.g., Boyer 1976; Cooper 1975; Hsiao 1973; see Chap. 9, this Vol.). Desiccation of intolerant species results in irreversible disruption of cellular organization and metabolism, although some photosynthetic reactions can occur at severe water deficits (Santarius 1967). In the desiccation-tolerant fern *Polypodium*

polypodioides both respiration and photosynthesis are reduced as water content declines, and below 35%–40% water content they cease (STUART 1968). Whether reduced photosynthesis due to water loss is mediated through effects on stomata or by changes in the chloroplasts, or both, has not been investigated, although the photosynthetic pigment content of *P. polypodioides* leaves is unaffected by desiccation. On rehydration of this fern, and of *Ceterach officinarum* (OPPEN-HEIMER and HALEVY 1962) respiration resumes at a higher level than in undesiccated controls. In *C. officinarum* it takes several days for respiration to return to control levels: data are not available for *P. polypodioides*. Photosynthesis resumes soon after rehydration in this latter species (STUART 1968). Desiccation of the poikilohydrous spikemoss *Selaginella lepidophylla* results in a decline in RuBP carboxylase activity by about 40%, but recovery of activity occurs within the first 24 h of rehydration – possibly by de novo synthesis of the enzyme (EICKMEIER 1979). Thus recovery of photosynthesis in this plant after desiccation may be facilitated by the high level of conserved RuBP carboxylase and its ability to quickly restore enzyme levels to normal.

Myrothamnus flabellifolia is a desiccation-tolerant angiosperm which can resume photosynthesis and respiration after long periods in the dry state (HENCKEL and PRONINA 1969; HOFFMANN 1968; VIEWEG and ZIEGLER 1969; ZIEGLER and VIEWEG 1970). A number of important soluble enzymes involved in these processes remain potentially active in the desiccated tissue (GÜNDEL, quoted by KLUGE 1976), and the chlorophyll and carotenoid content of the plant is unchanged during desiccation and rehydration (HOFFMANN 1968). It has been implied (KLUGE 1976) that desiccation-induced changes in membrane components of mitochondria and chloroplasts are responsible for the decline in gaseous exchange, and that their reconstitution on rehydration is essential for resumption of photosynthesis and respiration. Some suggestive evidence has been provided in electron microscope studies (HOFFMANN 1968; ZIEGLER and VIEWEG 1970; WELLBURN and WELLBURN 1976), but more extensive studies are required.

Not all desiccation-tolerant plants retain their photosynthetic pigments within intact chloroplasts during desiccation. The poikilochlorophyllous angiosperms lose both, and reconstitute or resynthesize them on rehydration (GAFF and HALLAM 1974; GAFF et al. 1976; MEGURO et al. 1977). Changes in gaseous exchange during drying and rehydration unfortunately have not been followed in these plants, although electron microscopy studies on organelle integrity have been carried out (see earlier). It is interesting to note that *Borya nitida* only survives desiccation if it is dried slowly, during which chlorophyll is lost, so that the dried plant is yellow. Rapid drying, which does not allow for destruction of chlorophyll, is fatal (GAFF and CHURCHILL 1976).

In concluding this section, it is apparent that in many desiccation-tolerant plants there is a considerable degree of conservation of the components of the respiratory and photosynthetic mechanisms. Perturbations may occur to the structure and contents of both mitochondria and chloroplasts early upon rehydration, but events are soon put in motion to reverse or repair these perturbations. Elucidation of the nature of these repair mechanisms is a fertile field for research.

10.6 Conclusions

While desiccation-tolerance is relatively prevalent in lower plants, this characteristic has been reacquired by a number of higher, vascular plants in unrelated
orders and families. Some poikilohydrous plants are able to survive in exposed,
uncompromising habitats, that less tolerant plants cannot survive, but others
are to be found only in areas where they are protected from the harshest
elements of their environment (particularly direct sunlight). Such protection
may allow plants to retain water longer, and hence increase their productivity,
or to lose water more slowly and thus make the appropriate cytoplasmic adjustments that will allow them to tolerate severe water loss.

There do not appear to be any common morphological features that distinguish poikilohydrous plants from intolerant species — tolerance of desiccation
can be attributed largely to properties of the protoplasm. Tolerant plants do
not undergo severe water deficits without perturbations to their metabolic and
cellular integrity, but critical features of desiccation-tolerance may be the abilities
to limit damage due to desiccation to a reparable level and to repair damage
quickly upon subsequent rehydration. The integrity of the majority of metabolic
systems (or at least of their components) is probably retained in the dry state,
and these systems are quickly reactivated upon rehydration. This is probably
also an important feature, for hydration of many poikilohydrous plants is a
transient phenomenon. Obviously, any plant in any environment can only survive
if it is able to achieve a net gain in its carbon status, and the adaptations
of poikilohydry can be viewed in relation to this fact (Eickmeier 1979). Poikilohydric plants can occupy habitats that are unavailable to intolerant plants because they can benefit, relative to potential carbon gain from (1) extreme desiccation (and sometimes temperature) tolerance, (2) utilization of dew or water
vapor for hydration (some species only), (3) rapid emergence from the quiescent
state and metabolic, including photosynthetic, recovery with the availability
of water. On the other hand, these benefits must be considered against the
potential carbon costs associated with (1) stored energy and/or time costs for
physiological reactivation upon rehydration, (2) physiological deterioration with
increasing time in the dry state, (3) low photosynthetic rates, and (4) decline
in membrane integrity permitting carbohydrate and nutrient losses during rehydration with liquid water. Different species have developed different ecological,
morphological, and (presumably) physiological adaptations to accomplish, ultimately, a net gain in their photosynthetic productivity.

References

Alpert P (1979) Desiccation of desert mosses following a summer rainstorm. Bryologist
    82:65–71
Barnett NM, Naylor AW (1966) Amino acid and protein metabolism in Bermudagrass
    during water stress. Plant Physiol 41:1222–1230
Baskin CC, Baskin JM (1974) Responses of *Astragalus tennesseensis* to drought. Changes
    in free amino acids and amides during water stress and possible ecological significance.
    Oecologia 17:11–16

Bérard-Therriault L, Cardinal A (1973) Importance de certains facteurs ecologiques sur la resistance a la desiccation des Fucales (Phaeophyceae). Phycologia 12:41–52

Bertsch A (1966) CO_2-Gaswechsel und Wasserhaushalt der aerophilen Grünalge *Apatococcus lobatus*. Planta 70:46–72

Bewley JD (1973a) Polyribosomes conserved during desiccation of the moss *Tortula ruralis* are active. Plant Physiol 51:285–288

Bewley JD (1973b) Desiccation and protein synthesis in the moss *Tortula ruralis*. Can J Bot 51:203–206

Bewley JD (1973c) The effects of liquid nitrogen temperatures in protein and RNA synthesis in the moss *Tortula ruralis*. Plant Sci Lett 1:303–308

Bewley JD (1979) Physiological aspects of desiccation tolerance. Annu Rev Plant Physiol 30:195–238

Bewley JD (1981) Protein synthesis. In: Paleg LG, Aspinall D (eds) Physiology and biochemistry of drought resistance in plants. Academic Press, London New York, pp 261–282

Bewley JD, Gwóźdź EA (1975) Plant desiccation and protein synthesis. II. On the relationship between endogenous ATP levels and protein synthesizing capacity. Plant Physiol 55:1110–1114

Bewley JD, Larsen KM (1980) Protein synthesis ceases in water-stressed pea roots and maize mesocotyls without loss of polyribosomes. Effects of lethal and non-lethal water stress. J Exp Bot 31:1245–1256

Bewley JD, Pacey J (1978) Desiccation-induced ultrastructural changes in drought-sensitive and drought-tolerant plants. In: Crowe JH, Clegg JS (eds) Dry biological systems. Academic Press, London New York, pp 53–73

Bewley JD, Thorpe TA (1974) On the metabolism of *Tortula ruralis* following desiccation and freezing: Respiration and carbohydrate oxidation. Physiol Plant 32:147–153

Bewley JD, Tucker EB, Gwóźdź EA (1974) The effects of stress on the metabolism of *Tortula ruralis*. In: Bieleski RL, Ferguson AR, Cresswell MM (eds) Mechanisms of regulation of plant growth. Roy Soc NZ Bull 12:395–402

Bewley JD, Halmer P, Krochko J, Winner WE (1978) Metabolism of a drought-tolerant and a drought-sensitive moss. Respiration, ATP synthesis and carbohydrate status. In: Crowe JH, Clegg JS (eds) Dried biological systems. Academic Press, London New York, pp 185–203

Biebl R (1962) Seaweeds. In: Lewin RA (ed) Physiology and biochemistry of algae. Academic Press, London New York, pp 799–815

Blekhman GI (1979) Factors behind changes of ribonuclease activity and characteristics of manifestations of this activity during dehydration of plants. Sov Plant Physiol 26:754–762

Boyer JS (1976) Water deficits and photosynthesis. In: Kozlowski TT (ed) Water deficits and plant growth vol IV. Academic Press, London New York, pp 153–190

Brinkhuis BH, Tempel NR, Jones RF (1976) Photosynthesis and respiration of exposed salt-marsh fucoids. Mar Biol 34:349–360

Brock TD (1975a) Effect of water potential on a *Microcoleus* (Cyanophyceae) from a desert crust. J Phycol 11:316–320

Brock TD (1975b) The effect of water potential on photosynthesis in whole lichens and in their liberated algal components. Planta 124:13–23

Brown DH, Buck GW (1979) Desiccation effects and cation distribution in bryophytes. New Phytol 82:115–125

Buck GW, Brown DH (1979) The effect of desiccation on cation location in lichens. Ann Bot (London) 44:265–277

Busby JR, Whitfield DWA (1978) Water potential, water content, and net assimilation of some boreal forest mosses. Can J Bot 56:1551–1558

Chapman ARO (1973) A critique of prevailing attitudes towards the control of seaweed zonation on the sea shore. Bot Mar 16:80–82

Chapman VJ (1966) The physiological ecology of some New Zealand seaweeds. In: Young EG, McLachlan JL (eds) Proc 5th Int Seaweed Symp Pergamon, Oxford, pp 29–54

Clausen E (1952) Hepatics and humidity, a study on the occurrence of hepatics in a

Hambler DJ (1964) The vegetation of granite outcrops in Western Nigeria. J Ecol 52:573–594

Hanson AD, Nelsen CE, Everson EH (1977) Evaluation of free proline accumulation as an index of drought resistance using two contrasting barley cultivars. Crop Sci 17:720–726

Harris GB (1976) Water content and productivity of lichens. In: Lange OL, Kappen L, Schulze E-D (eds) Water and plant life. Problems and modern approaches. Ecol Stud vol 19. Springer, Berlin Heidelberg New York, pp 452–468

Henckel PA, Pronina ND (1968) Factors underlying dehydration resistance in poikiloxerophytes. Sov Plant Physiol 15:68–74

Henckel PA, Pronina ND (1969) Anabiosis with desiccation of the poikiloxerophytic flowering plant *Myrothamnus flabellifolia*. Sov Plant Physiol 16:745–749

Henckel PA, Pronina ND (1973) The euxerophytic affiliation of *Haberlea rhodopensis* (Family Gesneriaceae). Sov Plant Physiol 20:690–692

Henckel PA, Kurkova EB, Pronina ND (1970) Effect of dehydration on the course of photosynthesis in homeohydrous and poikilohydrous plants. Sov Plant Physiol 17:952–957

Henckel PA, Satarova NA, Shaposhnikova SV (1977) Protein synthesis in poikiloxerophytes and wheat embryos during the initial period of swelling. Sov Plant Physiol 24:737–741

Hinshiri HM, Proctor MCF (1971) The effect of desiccation on subsequent assimilation and respiration of the bryophytes *Anomodon viticulosus* and *Porella platyphylla*. New Phytol 70:527–538

Hoffmann P (1968) Pigmentgehalt und Gaswechsel von *Myrothamnus*-Blättern nach Austrocknung und Wiederaufsättigung. Photosynthetica 2:245–252

Hosokawa T, Kubota H (1957) On the osmotic pressure and resistance to desiccation of epiphytic mosses from a beech forest, southwest Japan. J Ecol 45:579–591

Hsiao TC (1973) Plant responses to water stress. Annu Rev Plant Physiol 24:519–570

Hsiao TC, Acevedo E (1974) Plant responses to water deficits, water-use efficiency, and drought resistance. Agric Meterol 14:59–84

Hsiao TC, Acevedo E, Fereres E, Henderson DW (1976) Stress metabolism. Water stress, growth, and osmotic adjustment. Philos Trans R Soc London Ser B 273:479–500

Hutchinson J (1973) The families of flowering plants, 3rd edn. Oxford Univ Press, Oxon

Iljin WS (1953) Causes of death of plants as a consequence of loss of water: conservation of life in desiccated tissues. Bull Torrey Bot Club 80:166–177

Iljin WS (1957) Drought resistance in plants and physiological processes. Annu Rev Plant Physiol 8:257–274

Johnson WS, Gigon A, Gulmon SL, Mooney HA (1974) Comparative photosynthetic capacities of intertidal algae under exposed and submerged conditions. Ecology 55:450–453

Jones MM, Turner HC (1978) Osmotic adjustment in leaves of *Sorghum* in response to water deficits. Plant Physiol 61:122–126

Kanwisher J (1957) Freezing and drying in intertidal algae. Biol Bull 113:275–285

Kappen L (1973) Response to extreme environments. In: Ahmadjian V, Hale ME (eds) The lichens. Academic Press, London New York, pp 311–380

Kappen L, Lange OL, Schulze E-D, Evenari M, Buschbom U (1975) Primary production of lower plants (lichens) in the desert and its physiological basis. In: Cooper JP (ed) Photosynthesis and productivity in different environments. Univ Press, Cambridge, pp 133–143

Kershaw KA (1972) The relationship between moisture content and net assimilation rate of lichen thalli and its ecological significance. Can J Bot 50:543–555

Kershaw KA, Morris T, Tysiaczny MJ, MacFarlane JD (1979) Physiological-environmental interactions in lichens. VIII. The environmental control of dark CO_2 fixation in *Parmelia caperata* (L.) Ach and *Peltigera canina* var. *praetextata* Hue. New Phytol 83:433–444

Kluge M (1976) Carbon and nitrogen metabolism under water stress. In: Lange OL, Kappen L, Schulze E-D (eds) Water and plant life: problems and modern approaches. Ecol Stud vol 19. Springer Berlin Heidelberg New York, pp 243–252

Koch C (1962) The tenebrionidae of southern Africa. XXXI. Comprehensive notes on the tenebrionid fauna of the Namib desert. Ann Transvaal Mus 24:1–98

Krochko JE (1979) Metabolism of a desiccation-tolerant and desiccation-sensitive moss during drying and after rehydration: Respiration, photosynthesis, ATP levels and protein synthesis. MSc Thesis, Univ Calgary

Krochko JE, Bewley JD, Pacey J (1978) The effects of rapid and very slow speeds of drying on the ultrastructure and metabolism of the desiccation-sensitive moss *Cratoneuron filicinum*. J Exp Bot 29:905–917

Krochko JE, Winner WE, Bewley JD (1979) Respiration in relation to adenosine triphosphate content during desiccation and rehydration of a desiccation-tolerant and a desiccation-intolerant moss. Plant Physiol 64:13–17

Lange OL (1953) Hitze- und Trockenresistenz der Flechten in Beziehung zu ihrer Verbreitung. Flora 140:39–97

Lange OL (1969a) Ecophysiological investigations in lichens of the Negev desert. I. CO_2 gas exchange of *Ramalina maciformis* (Del.) Bory under controlled conditions in the laboratory. Flora 158:324–359

Lange OL (1969b) CO_2-gas exchange of mosses following water vapour uptake. Planta 89:90–94

Lange OL, Schulze E-D, Koch W (1970) Experimentell-ökologische Untersuchungen an Flechten der Negev-Wüste. II. CO_2-Gaswechsel und Wasserhaushalt von *Ramalina maciformis* (Del.) Bory am natürlichen Standort während der sommerlichen Trockenperiode. Flora 159:38–62

Lange OL, Schulze E-D, Kappen L, Buschbom U, Evenari M (1975) Adaptations of desert lichens to drought and extrme temperatures. In: Hadley NF (ed) Environmental physiology of desert organisms. Dowden, Hutchinson and Ross, Stroudsburg, pp 20–37

Larson DW (1979) Lichen water relations under drying conditions. New Phytol 82:713–731

Larson DW, Kershaw KA (1976) Studies on lichen-dominated systems. XVIII. Morphological control of evaporation in lichens. Can J Bot 54:2061–2073

Lechowicz MJ, Adams MS (1974) Ecology of *Cladonia* lichens. II. Comparative physiological ecology of *C. mitis, C. rangiferina* and *C. uncialis*. Can J Bot 52:411–422

Lee JA, Stewart GR (1971) Desiccation injury in mosses. I. Intra-specific difference in the effect of moisture stress on photosynthesis. New Phytol 70:1061–1068

Levitt J (1956) The hardiness of plants. Academic Press, London New York

Levitt J (1972) Responses of plants to environmental stresses. Academic Press, London New York

Levitt J, Sullivan CY, Krull E (1960) Some problems in drought resistance. Bull Res Counc Isr Sect D:8 173–179

Luzzati V, Husson F (1962) The structure of the liquid-crystalline phases of lipid-water systems. J Cell Biol 12:207–219

MacFarlane JD, Kershaw KA (1978) Thermal sensitivity in lichens. Science 201:739–741

MacFarlane JD, Kershaw KA (1980) Physiological-environmental interactions in lichens. IX. Thermal stress and lichen ecology. New Phytol 84:669–685

Mahmoud MI (1965) Protoplasmics and drought resistance in mosses. PhD Thesis, Univ California, Davis

Malek L, Bewley JD (1978a) Effects of various rates of freezing on the metabolism of a drought-tolerant plant, the moss *Tortula ruralis*. Plant Physiol 61:334–338

Malek L, Bewley JD (1978b) Protein synthesis related to cold temperatures in the desiccation-tolerant moss *Tortula ruralis*. Physiol Plant 43:313–319

Marinos NG, Fife DN (1972) Ultrastructural changes in wheat embryos during a "presowing drought hardening" treatment. Protoplasma 74:381–396

Mathieson AE, Burns RL (1971) Ecological studies on economic red algae. I. Photosynthesis and respiration of *Chondrus crispus* Stackhouse and *Gigartina stellata* (Stackhouse) Batters. J Exp Mar Biol 7:197–206

McKay E (1935) Photosynthesis in *Grimmia montana*. Plant Physiol 10:803–809

McKersie BD, Stinson RH (1980) Effect of dehydration on leakage and membrane structure in *Lotus corniculatus* L. seeds. Plant Physiol 66:316–320

winters. Low temperatures or ice crystal formation in the soil or conducting vessels limit or completely interrupt water transport. Within the temperate zone, this phenomenon occurs increasingly with proximity to the poles and also becomes more pronounced with increasing altitude in mountain areas. The amount of desiccation which trees, shrubs, and other perennial plants experience within their natural distribution areas, however, does not usually tax or exceed the reserve of water which can be lost without incurring injury. Only when plants are cultivated outside of their natural distribution area, or when they occur on the edge of their natural range (e.g., boreal and alpine forest limit) is it likely that the upper limit of their tolerance will be reached, or actually exceeded, with the result that winter desiccation injury occurs.

EBERMAYER (1873, 1901) was the first to attribute extensive winter damage in young pine plantations, which led to a massive shedding of brown needles, to winter desiccation, thereby establishing the frost desiccation theory. This was later challenged by NEGER (1915), NEGER and FUCHS (1915) and MÜNCH (1928a, b, 1933). They maintained that injuries which appeared in forest trees in low-lying areas following a harsh winter were purely freezing injuries. The rapid advance of experimental ecology from about 1920 on made it possible to investigate such phenomena more exactly. As a result, WALTER (1929a, b) and THREN (1934) found large decreases in the osmotic potential of several different plants during the winter in the vicinity of Heidelberg. This indicated that many plants suffer a considerable water deficiency if winters are severe, and that the previously described injuries were due to desiccation. MICHAEL (1963, 1966, 1967a, b) in Germany and SAKAI (1968, 1970) in Japan, very thoroughly tested the validity of the frost desiccation theory by studying trees in low-lying areas. Nevertheless, in more recent, predominantly forestry-oriented literature, injuries are frequently designated as frost desiccation injuries or attributed to the direct influence of frost without experimental verification. Thus, the controversial question first raised around the turn of the century, "frozen or desiccated", is still an important issue today.

At the alpine limit of tree and shrub growth the situation is clearer. Since the work of GOLDSMITH and SMITH (1926), numerous further investigations have shown that the plants for the most part dry out in the winter and that the severe damage seen along the upper limit of existence is due to winter desiccation injury (WARDLE 1971; LARCHER 1977; TRANQUILLINI 1979). Similar conditions are found at the boreal forest limit (HOLTMEIER 1974).

With respect to frost desiccation and its importance for plant distribution, only a few comprehensive descriptions exist (WALTER 1951, 1968; WALTER and KREEB 1970; LARCHER 1957, 1963, 1972; PARKER 1969; TRANQUILLINI 1963, 1976, 1979, 1980; HOLTMEIER 1974; PEARS 1977). Accordingly, this paper will attempt to describe the more recent experimental work on winter desiccation, and to identify those trends which are of particular relevance in clarifying the ecological significance of frost desiccation.

11.2 Water Uptake and Water Conductance

11.2.1 Soil Frost

The soil water easily available to plants, soil pore diameter 0.2–8 µm, freezes, according to LARCHER (1957) and SAKAI (1968), between 0° and −1 °C. At still lower temperatures plant uptake of soil water becomes negligible. LEIK-

OLA and PAAVILAINEN (1972) reported that an upward movement of water took place in tree trunks on warm days in late winter, even though the ground was still frozen. However, this could be explained as resulting from an internal vertical displacement of water following thawing of the conducting tissue (cf. SWANSON 1967).

How long plants remain cut off from the soil water supply depends on the length of time and the depth to which the soil freezes. This in turn depends on the prevailing air temperatures of the habitat, which can be very different from year to year, and on the soil properties, as well as on the depth of the snow cover and the length of time it remains, since this effectively isolates the soil from the influence of the air.

During severe winters in Tharandt, GDR (330 m), the ground froze to a depth of 1 m in areas devoid of snow. It remained frozen to a depth of 30 cm, a depth to which the roots of younger trees penetrate, for 3 months (December to March) (Fig. 11.1). If one considers only the $-1\,°C$ isotherm in Fig. 11.1, then the length of time during which plant water uptake could not have occurred is somewhat more than 2 months. Under natural snow conditions during a severe winter, the ground froze to a depth of only about 60 cm, but it likewise remained frozen to a depth of 30 cm for 3 months, and temperatures continued to fall periodically below $-1\,°C$. In other years the soil either did not freeze at all or else froze only for short periods of time (MICHAEL 1967a).

A comparable situation exists along the alpine forest limit where the depth to which the ground freezes depends decidedly on the depth of the snow cover. The latter can be extremely varied within a particular area due to local differences in wind and radiation. In a climatically normal year, the frost penetrated to a depth of only 20 cm in a heavily snow-covered location along the forest limit at Obergurgl (Tyrol) at an altitude of 2,000 m. In no instance did the temperature drop to $-1\,°C$ at this depth. At 30 cm depth the temperature remained constantly above $0\,°C$ (Fig. 11.1). In contrast, at a nearby, only lightly snow-covered location, the frost reached a depth of 1 m and remained to a depth of 30 cm from December through April, or 5 months. For 4 months the soil temperature actually remained below $-1\,°C$ (AULITZKY 1961). The roots of trees within the forest transition zone penetrate to this depth (cf. WARDLE 1968).

TURNER et al. (1975) and PLATTER (1976) also found conditions which fell within this range of extremes at altitudes of about 2,000 m. They reported that in habitats having little snow cover or in years of low snowfall the soil freezes to a depth of 30 cm, and they estimated that water uptake remains interrupted for a period of several months continuing into April. Interruption of water uptake in any case is always more prolonged at this than at lower altitudes (Fig. 11.1).

Within the boreal spruce forest zone of the Alaskan interior, soil temperature is extremely dependent on both the type of soil and on the vegetation cover. Under a stand of *Picea glauca* the soil temperature at a depth of 30 cm remained below $0\,°C$ for 4 months, in one year from December to the end of March, and in the following year from January until the end of April (VIERECK 1970). Thus conditions here resemble those found along the alpine forest limit (Fig. 11.1).

Table 11.1. Transpiration rate at 0.5 °C soil temperature in percent of the transpiration rate at 25 °C (KRAMER 1942)

Pinus taeda	13.7 ⎱	Southern distribution
Pinus caribaea	13.9 ⎰	
Pinus strobus	37.7 ⎱	Northern distribution
Pinus resinosa	25.0 ⎰	

0 °C than at 20 °C, due to increase in root cell resistance to water transport. This leads to a reduction in stomatal pore size and likewise a decrease in transpiration rate. According to KRAMER (1942), the rate of transpiration in different pine species already decreases when soil temperature drops below 25 °C. At temperatures under 15 °C, species having a more southerly distribution area show a greater decrease in the rate of transpiration than do species having a more northerly range of distribution (Table 11.1). KOZLOWSKI (1943) also found that at a soil temperature of 1 °C, the amount of transpiration in *Pinus taeda* and *Pinus strobus* was only 20%–30% of that occurring at 30 °C. According to HAVRANEK (1972), stomatal closure begins at a soil temperature of 5 °C in *Larix decidua* and *Picea abies* and, at 2 °C, transpiration has been reduced by about 50%, compared with the rate at 15 °C. In *Pinus radiata* seedlings, transpiration also decreases as soil temperature drops, due to a reduction in water uptake. The latter occurs in response to a lowering of root membrane permeability which begins just under 15 °C, the temperature at which these membranes are maximally permeable (BABALOLA et al. 1968). According to AN-DERSON and McNAUGHTON (1973) the water content of herbaceous plants from different altitudes was significantly lower at a soil temperature of 3 °C than at 20 °C. For plants from increasingly higher altitudes this difference became decreasingly significant. Thus, mountain plant species appear to be adapted to absorbing water at lower temperatures. This is also supported by the investigations of KAUFMANN (1975, 1977) which indicated that root resistance to water uptake increases with decreasing temperature, due to the greater viscosity of the water, and, at the same time, to changes in root membrane permeability. The latter begin to have a rapid effect under 14 °C in *Pinus radiata,* whereas in tree species of colder regions, such as *Picea engelmannii,* they are first effective under 7 °C.

Root conductivity is not only influenced directly by soil temperature, but also decreases as a result of the hardening processes which take place during the transition to winter dormancy. This transition is initiated by decreasing temperatures and daylength (PARSONS 1978).

11.3 Water Loss

During the frost period in which water transport is diminished or fully interrupted, plants must guard against excessive water loss in order to avoid a rapid increase in water deficit. In evergreen plants this is effected through

stomatal closure, whereby water loss occurs only via cuticular transpiration. In deciduous species winter water loss is restricted to transpiring stem axes. With progressive desiccation of plant organs, cuticular and peridermal transpiration can be further reduced through a dehydration of the cutinized layers at the surface which results in an increased diffusion resistance (PISEK and BERGER 1938; see also Chap. 6, this Vol.).

The effect of water loss on the winter water balance of plants, then, will depend on whether or not the stomata are closed in winter, and on the magnitude of cuticular transpiration resistance, and thus ultimately, on the amount of unavoidable water loss occurring under natural conditions, despite these resistances.

11.3.1 Stomatal Movements

One of the causes of stomatal closure in evergreen leaves at the beginning of winter is a rapid increase in the water saturation deficit which occurs when the ground frost penetrates to the root horizon and water ceases to be available (TRANQUILLINI 1957). As shown in Fig. 11.1, this usually occurs in December, at low as well as at high altitudes. The stomata of some plants, however, may already begin to narrow and close during the transition to winter dormancy (LARCHER 1972). According to PARSONS (1978), the stomata of *Cornus stolonifera* close, in the process of frost hardening, when freezing tolerance reaches $-12°$ to $-14 °C$. This could be brought about through an increase in the concentration of abscisic acid leading to stomatal closure (LITTLE and EIDT 1968; MITTEL-HEUSER and VAN STEVENINCK 1969). Moreover, in winter the crypts of sunken stomata become sealed with wax, whereby the effectiveness of stomatal closure is increased (JEFFREE et al. 1971; FAHEY 1979).

In the height of winter, during a lasting frost, stomata as a rule remain closed. This is true of plants in lower areas as well as of trees and dwarf shrubs of the subalpine zone (MICHAELIS 1934b; CARTELLIERI 1935; SCHMIDT 1936; TRANQUILLINI 1957; MICHAEL 1967a; TRANQUILLINI and MACHL-EBNER 1971; KÖRNER 1976; LARCHER 1977).

An important question is, when in the spring will an increase in water loss occur due to the reopening of stomata. According to TRANQUILLINI and MACHL-EBNER (1971) stomata of *Pinus cembra* needles open already in winter if the temperature remains at $10 °C$ for 24 h. Only in February and March will they remain closed under these conditions. In all months, however, a slight stomatal opening will occur if $20 °C$ temperatures continue for more than 24 h. *Rhododendron* leaves react considerably more rapidly to warm temperatures. CHRISTERSSON (1972) reported that after 4 days at $20 °C$, the behavior of *Picea abies* and *Pinus sylvestris* approximated that of nonhardened plants. That is, an increase in transpiration and a normal stomatal reaction to light and dark occurred.

Clearly, in the winter, periods with high temperatures do not last this long. Thus, KÖRNER (1976) found that under actual habitat conditions, the stomata of *Loiseleuria procumbens* and *Calluna vulgaris* at 2,170 m remain continuously

closed until the end of March, although on sunny days the leaves are warmed above 20 °C for short periods. In the Rocky Mountains of Wyoming, at 2,900 m, the stomata of *Pinus contorta* first open at the end of April, after 3 warm days and no night frost, if melt water has penetrated into the soil (Fahey 1979). At this time of the year night frost still induced renewed stomatal closure. *Picea abies* along the forest limit at the northern border of the Alps in Allgäu (FRG) first open their stomata in late winter, if the temperature rises above 8 °C. *Pinus mugo* reacts still more slowly; *Rhododendron,* on the other hand, considerably more rapidly (Michaelis 1934b).

11.3.2 Cuticular and Peridermal Transpiration Resistance

Depending on species, the rate of cuticular transpiration occurring under controlled conditions is very different. Rates range relatively from 1 (coarse-needled evergreen conifers) to 80 (thin-leaved herbaceous shade plants) (Pisek and Berger 1938). The transpiration rate is more important, in terms of surviving frost conditions, than either differences in water reserves or desiccation resistance (Pisek 1956). How effectively many plants can cut back on water loss by curbing stomatal transpiration is shown through comparisons of summer and winter transpiration: the winter water loss of North American conifers is only 1/50 to 1/250 of that occurring in autumn (Weaver and Mogenson 1919). In the vicinity of Leningrad (USSR), the winter transpiration of *Pinus sylvestris* was 300 to 400 times less than summer transpiration (Iwanoff 1924). The summer transpiration rate of *Picea abies* and *Pseudotsuga menziesii* located in Tharandt was 65 times the average occurring in the winter when the soil was frozen (Michael 1967a). According to Larcher (1977) the water use of *Loiseleuria procumbens* at the forest limit in Tyrol was 4.6 g dm^{-2} d^{-1} on good weather days in the summer and, with closed stomata in the winter only 0.05 g, or about 1/100 of the summer rate. The leaf diffusion resistance increased from 3.1 s cm^{-1}, with stomata open, to greater than 100 s cm^{-1} after stomatal closure in winter. The cuticular transpiration resistance in *Picea abies* reached enormously high values after longer periods of desiccation. In isolated annual shoots (water content 120% dry wt.), this resistance increased from around 100 s cm^{-1}, after 4 h of desiccation, to 3,600 s cm^{-1} after 124 h (water content 90% dry wt.) (Platter 1976). The leaf conductance (cuticular conductance) of some Alaskan conifers, following stomatal closure in the winter, amounted to 0.013–0.088 cm s^{-1} (*Picea glauca*), <0.001–0.033 (*Pinus contorta*) and <0.001–0.074 (*Pinus banksiana*) (Cowling and Kedrowski 1980).

The leafless shoots of deciduous plants also lose water in the winter (Kozlowski 1943). On a surface area basis, these shoots actually transpire considerably more than do shoots with needles. Water reserves are thus more quickly depleted, especially if the leaf excision scars have not yet completely healed, as a consequence of unfavorable climatic conditions in late fall (Gordiagin 1930). According to Platter (1976), under the same outside conditions, peridermal transpiration from *Larix decidua* axes is approximately equal to that of

Table 11.2. Average cuticular transpiration rate of detached 1-year-old shoots after several days of desiccation at 15 °C, 40% R.H., 10 klx and 3.5 m s^{-1} wind velocity in mg H$_2$O (g dry wt h)$^{-1}$ (PLATTER 1976)

		October	December
Picea abies	Valley floor	2.30	2.24
	Forest limit	2.56	3.12
	Tree limit	5.90	6.40
Pinus cembra	Forest limit	1.54	1.28
	Tree limit	2.71	3.66
Larix decidua	Valley floor	2.88	2.10
	Forest limit	4.88	2.71
	Tree limit	5.40	4.87

Picea abies shoots with needles, calculated on a dry weight basis. In *Pinus cembra* considerably less transpiration occurs (Table 11.2).

The cuticular transpiration resistance also depends, however, on the outside conditions under which the leaves and shoots developed. In order for complete development of the surface tissues of newly formed shoots to occur, a certain input of warmth and thus a certain amount of time is required. LANGE and SCHULZE (1966) established that, at low altitudes, cutinized layers of *Picea abies* needles require three months from the time of shoot elongation to reach their final thickness. At the forest limit *Picea abies* trees resume growth about 2 months later than in the valley (TRANQUILLINI et al. 1980). If, moreover, the summer is cool so that developmental processes proceed more slowly (HOLZER et al. 1979), then needles and shoots may not be able to mature fully before the onset of winter. BAIG and TRANQUILLINI (1976) as well as PLATTER (1976) were able to demonstrate that a progressive decrease in the thickness of the cuticular layers of all woody species occurs between the valley floor and the "krummholz" limit. Accompanying the reduction in the thickness of the cuticular layers, which may also involve compositional changes, is an exponentially increasing water permeability (cf. ROSSA and LARSEN 1980). The cuticular transpiration rate thus increases with altitude (Table 11.2). After 24 h in an environmental chamber, excised *Picea abies* shoots exhibited only cuticular transpiration. Their water loss was greater, the higher the altitude from which they originated. On the average, water loss in branches from the tree limit (2,100 m) was 2.26 times greater, and in those from the forest limit (1,900 m) 1.70 times greater than that of branches from the valley floor (1,000 m) (Fig. 11.2). That the degree of cuticular maturity decisively affects the magnitude of cuticular transpiration is also shown by the high cuticular transpiration values which are obtained following cool summers and following experimental shortening of the vegetation period (BAIG et al. 1974; TRANQUILLINI 1974; PLATTER 1976).

The cuticular transpiration resistance also varies depending on the origin of the plants. Seedlings of *Pseudotsuga menziesii,* grown from seeds of different altitudinal origin under the same conditions, became desiccated more slowly

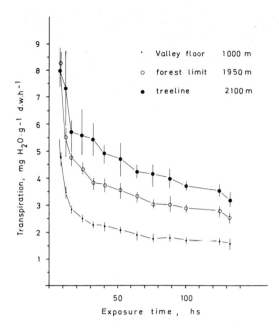

Fig. 11.2. Transpiration in detached 1-year-old shoots of *Picea abies* collected in March from the valley floor (1,000 m), the forest limit (1,950 m) and the tree limit (2,100 m) at Patscherkofel above Innsbruck, in the course of desiccation in a climate-controlled wind tunnel at 10 klx, 15 °C, 40% R.H. and 3.5 m s^{-1} wind velocity. The *steep drop of the curves* at the beginning of the experiment is due to hydroactive stomatal closure. The *smoother portion of the curves* from 20 to 30 h corresponds to the cuticular water loss after stomatal closure. The *vertical lines* indicate the range of variation of the individual measurements (Platter 1976)

Chart legend:
· Valley floor   1000 m
o forest limit   1950 m
• treeline   2100 m

Y-axis: Transpiration, mg H$_2$O·g^{-1} d.w.h^{-1}

X-axis: Exposure time, hs

in an environmental chamber if they came from populations growing at higher altitudes (Larsen 1978). Trees of higher altitudes are thus better adapted to withstanding desiccation stress than trees of lower altitudes. This adaptation counteracts to some extent the increased cuticular transpiration which is found in high mountain habitats as a result of an incomplete development of the cuticular layers. (For detailed discussion of cuticular resistances see Chap. 6, this Vol.).

11.3.3 Winter Transpiration in Natural Habitats

The amount of cuticular water loss occurring in a particular habitat will depend on the water vapor pressure gradient between the leaf surface and the ambient air (Gäumann and Jaag 1936; Slatyer and Bierhuizen 1964). This will become steeper when the wind decreases the boundary layer resistance and when the plant organs are heated above air temperature by the sun. In order to evaluate the effects of these two factors on the cuticular transpiration of conifers, the cuticular transpiration rate of *Picea abies* and *Pinus cembra* was measured at different wind velocities and air temperatures during a desiccation experiment. When wind velocity was increased from 4 to 10 m s^{-1}, the water loss in *Picea abies* increased at most only 10%, and in *Pinus cembra* around 21%. With a further increase in wind strength (15 m s^{-1}) the water loss did not increase significantly. If, on the other hand, with a constant dew point of 3 °C, air temperature was increased from 15 °C [9.5 mb vapor pressure deficit (v.p.d.)] to 20° or 25 °C, the transpiration rate at 20 °C (15.8 mb v.p.d.) increased by 30% (*Picea abies*) or almost 60% (*Pinus cembra*). The greatest increase occurred

Table 11.3. The influence of wind and temperature on the cuticular transpiration rate of 1-year-old and 2-year-old branches from *Picea abies* and *Pinus cembra* trees. Change in transpiration rate, in percent, with reference values obtained at 4 m s^{-1} and 15 °C air temperature. The average from trees of different altitudes (BAIG and TRANQUILLINI 1980)

	Picea abies		*Pinus cembra*	
	1-year-old	2-year-old	1-year-old	2-year-old
10 m s^{-1}	2.0	9.7	10.9	21.4
15 m s^{-1}	−1.0	6.6	23.2	25.5
20 °C	25.4	29.8	58.7	52.9
25 °C	129.4	117.1	182.5	173.4

at 25 °C (24.1 mb v.p.d.): 130% (*Picea abies*), 180% (*Pinus cembra*) (Table 11.3). Calculations of the cuticular transpiration resistance indicate that the increase which occurs at higher temperatures results essentially from an increase in the water vapor pressure gradient, and is not the result of stomatal opening.

From this one can see that a strong absorption of radiant energy leading to a heating of plant organs beyond air temperature will have a much greater impact on the rate of cuticular transpiration than will strong wind (BAIG and TRANQUILLINI 1980). However, it is primarily the wind factor which leads to an increase in winter transpiration in regions where strong, dry winds blow throughout the winter, as for example, in the Scottish Highlands (PEARS 1977). This will likewise be the case in the far north where radiation is very weak during the winter. In the subalpine zone, on the other hand, it is the radiative warming of plants that is decisive, above all in late winter. A great deal of impressive evidence demonstrating the occurrence of such radiative warming is available to us (MICHAELIS 1934a; PISEK and SCHIESSL 1946; TRANQUILLINI and TURNER 1961; SAKAI 1966, 1970; PLATTER 1976; LARCHER 1977). According to TRANQUILLINI and TURNER (1961), in April needles of *Pinus cembra* near the surface of the snow may reach a temperature maximum of almost 30 °C. In the extreme case, this is about 21.5 °C higher than the air temperature measured at the same time in a nearby Stevenson screen at 2 m height. Based on the air temperature in the direct vicinity of the branches, sun-exposed needles in the absence of wind had a temperature above air temperature of 17 °C.

Following determination of the rate of winter transpiration at the habitat site, an estimate can be made of the length of time until water reserves are depleted and injury may occur, if no water uptake is possible. In detached annual shoots of *Picea abies* in Tharandt, this time varied, depending on month, between 69 and 21 days (1-year-old shoots) or 47 and 21 days (2-year-old shoots). Water reserves were depleted more rapidly in *Pseudotsuga menziesii* branches, and likewise in branches of *Buxus sempervirens* (Table 11.4).

If one compares these time lengths with the time period during which the soil is continually frozen (Fig. 11.1) in a severe winter (78 days), it is readily apparent that these branches in intact plants must draw upon the water reserves of the adjoining branches and main stem or trunk, if they are to avoid a

11.5 Winter Injuries

11.5.1 Evidence of the Causes: Desiccation or Freezing Injuries

Climate-induced injuries are found to occur during the winter in different plants in different habitats, sometimes with varying frequency. Ever since EBERMAYER attributed such winter injury in young *Pinus sylvestris* to desiccation, and NEGER and MÜNCH argued in favor of the freezing hypothesis, this controversial question has remained unresolved. Experimental evidence which would substantiate the correctness of one view or the other is difficult to obtain, since low water contents measured at the first appearance of visible damage could have arisen secondarily as a result of injury. Thus, MICHAEL (1966) found that frost-killed branches became desiccated more quickly than living branches, under the same conditions (cf. ZEIDLER 1964). On the other hand, the presence of high water contents at the first appearance of injury does not rule out the possibility that the plants may have been desiccated at an earlier point in time and that the dead organs then became resaturated through a passive movement of water.

For this reason, it has been necessary to rely on indirect evidence as well, in interpreting the causes of winter injury. In many cases a striking parallelism exists between the amount of winter transpiration and the extent of injury. This has been shown to be true for different aged needles in different years, for plants in different habitats, and for different plant species (BAIG et al. 1974). For example, in a study of different conifer species in Hamburg, MEYER (1965) found a close relationship between the degree of winter injury after a cold winter, and the rate of cuticular transpiration determined through laboratory desiccation experiments with isolated needles and shoots. An increasingly greater release of water from these needles and shoots paralleled an increasingly greater severity of injury suffered during the winter by the corresponding plants in the field. According to IWANOFF (1924), winter transpiration is closely correlated with species distribution. Northern species transpire at lower rates than southern species. The high rate of winter transpiration in the latter is thus a primary factor determining the northern limit of their distribution.

Lending further support to the frost desiccation theory is the experimental work from HAVIS (1965). He reported that when the soil is artificially heated to prevent the formation of soil frost, either winter injuries do not occur, or else they are less strongly manifested.

It has been repeatedly claimed, after comparing minimum habitat temperatures with laboratory-determined frost resistances, that in certain habitats the observed winter injury could only have resulted from desiccation stress because habitat temperatures were not low enough for frost injury to occur. This conclusion is also contestable since frost resistance is usually determined on the basis of standardized cooling and thawing velocities which can, under certain conditions, be greatly exceeded in the habitat (TRANQUILLINI and HOLZER 1958). Injuries may then be evoked by only slightly freezing temperatures (WHITE and WEISER 1964; WENTZEL 1965; CHRISTERSSON and SANDSTEDT 1978). Repeated freezing and thawing can also lead to an intensification of injuries (VENN 1979).

Moreover, frost injuries can also arise in late winter–early spring when plant organs become rapidly de-hardened and highly susceptible to freezing damage in a subsequent cold period.

11.5.2 Conclusions: Implications for the Distribution of Plants

At low altitudes all perennial plants within their natural distribution areas are adapted to winter conditions. Some of course require snow protection or else suffer the loss of their semi-evergreen leaves (WALTER 1929a; THREN 1934; ROUSCHAL 1939; HAVIS 1965; HAVAS 1971).

Winter desiccation injuries may occur in forest plantations following severe winters. Young plants are especially endangered, and the question of provenance plays an important role as well, above all in introduced species such as *Pseudotsuga menziesii* in Europe (EBERMAYER 1901; MÜNCH 1928b; KOZLOWSKI 1958; OHNESORGE 1963; ZEIDLER 1964; SCHÖNHAR 1965; WENTZEL 1965; SAKAI 1968; OESCHGER 1973; LARSEN 1978; VENN 1979). That frequent and severe injuries or death occur in cultivations of exotic species following severe winters is understandable, and in many cases results from too little frost resistance (JAHNEL and WATZLAWIK 1956/57).

Various plant species growing near the limits of their natural distribution areas are likewise apt to suffer lethal disturbances in their winter water economies. This is the case for species with an atlantic distribution along their eastern border (WALTER 1929a, b), and for *Quercus robur* along its continental eastern border (GORDIAGIN 1930), as well as for many southern species along their northern border as a result of overly high transpiration rates, e.g., *Salix alba, Ulmus campestris, Tilia platyphyllos, Carpinus betulus* and *Evonymus europaea* (IWANOFF 1924; WALTER 1951).

Winter desiccation is also the primary cause of injury along the boreal forest limit, mainly because new shoots are unable to reach full maturity under the prevailing climatic conditions, and therefore transpire too strongly during the winter (HOLTMEIER 1971, 1974). This applies above all to afforestations composed of species of southern origin, and to the naturally occurring young plants.

Especially distinct, however, are winter desiccation injuries which occur at the upper limits of distribution of trees and dwarf shrubs in all mountains outside of the tropics, but especially in mountains of continental regions. Here the classic frost desiccation conditions prevail – long lasting soil freezing and intense radiative warming of plants. Up to the forest limit and into the lower portion of the dwarf shrub belt, frost desiccation injuries are rare. However, a sudden and dramatic increase occurs in the timberline ecotone and in the upper part of the dwarf shrub belt due, on the one hand, to more extreme climatic conditions, and on the other hand to the shorter time available for development of sufficient protection against cuticular evaporation. Species which require a lower input of warmth to complete this development and which can better restrict their transpiration, are thus in a position to spread to still higher

Studies with a number of species (HYDE et al. 1959; BAIN and MERCER 1966; MATTHEWS 1973; BEDFORD and MATTHEWS 1976; ROGERSON and MATTHEWS 1977; VAN ONCKELEN et al. 1980; BARLOW et al. 1980) show that after anthesis seed moisture content changes in three distinct phases. Initiation of each phase appears to be associated with some fundamental change(s) in the seed.

The first phase is initiated by onset of mitosis in the mature ovule, usually following fertilization. Dry matter accumulates at a constant rate, mostly as soluble sugar. Increase in moisture content is rapid, predominantly by osmotic uptake into vacuoles. This maintains a steep $\Delta\Psi$ between the developing seed, which has a low apparent turgor potential, and the rest of the plant (BARLOW et al. 1980). In most seeds the unicellular zygote completes its growth and development into the multi-cellular, fully differentiated embryo during this phase. Despite this intense mitotic and metabolic activity, the seed is incapable of germinating.

Onset of the second phase is characterized by an abrupt and sharp decline in the rate at which the seed accumulates water. This is not caused by inactivation of the conducting system, since dry matter continues to accumulate at the same rate, but by elimination of the $\Delta\Psi$ between the seed (wheat grain) and the rest of the plant (BARLOW et al. 1980). It appears that this phase is initiated when plastids become active sinks for sugars, which they polymerize into osmotically inactive starch. Osmotically active sugars move out of the vacuoles, which thereupon lose water. A sharp decline in respiratory activity takes place. This could be reversed (in peas) by supplying sugars, but not by maintaining high seed moisture content, and is therefore apparently a direct result of the fall in availability of reducing sugars and not at all related to the decrease in moisture content (ROGERSON and MATTHEWS 1977). Concurrently with these changes, the seeds become progressively more germinable, as well as more tolerant of desiccation. Both phenomena have been ascribed to the concurrent increase in integrity of the cell membranes, which is expressed by reduction in leakiness to electrolytes. In beans, the amount of ABA per seed (as well as per unit fresh weight) increases sharply during this phase (VAN ONCKELEN et al. 1980). This may be a response to the progressive desiccation on the one hand, and on the other it may be the cause of the progressive decline, and eventual cessation of growth. Full seedling vigor is reached only toward the end of this phase. In the developing wheat grain Ψ is remarkably unaffected by drastic changes in Ψ^{plant} throughout these two phases. This has been ascribed to high resistance in the water transport pathway into the grain (BARLOW et al. 1980).

The third phase is characterized by onset of a rapid fall in moisture content, which coincides with abrupt cessation in dry matter accumulation. These simultaneous changes indicate that this stage is initiated when the conducting system to the seed is no longer functional. In *Pennisetum americanum* translocation of assimilates into the grain (and consequently also accumulation of dry matter) stops when growth of the embryo into the basal endosperm crushes the transfer cells at the chalazal pad (FUSSELL and DWARTE 1980). In other cases the conducting system may become nonfunctional as a result of the change in the balance of growth regulators in the seed, related to its diminishing growth activity.

Does desiccation have a role in seed development, other than as an aid to dispersal? In developing barley grains germinability increased more rapidly when desiccation was accelerated, by dry weather, or by early harvest, and this has been ascribed to increase in conductance to water by the coats (WELLINGTON and DURHAM 1961; WELLINGTON 1964). An additional, or alternative mechanism is suggested by the finding that exogenous GA fails to induce hydrolytic activity in aleurone of developing grains, unless they were first desiccated, which also made them germinable (EVANS et al. 1975; NICHOLLS 1979). Gibberellin is present in the developing grain and this response to desiccation therefore plays a role in allowing the storage of food during development, preventing its utilization until dispersal. There are indications that desiccation acts in this way by inducing catabolism of ABA (VAN ONCKELEN et al. 1980).

Vital physiological processes take place in the dry seed and their rate depends, among other things, on its equilibrium moisture content. This affects the rate of metabolic processes involved in loss of primary dormancy, as well as the rate at which the coats become modified during after-ripening. Similarly, the rates at which vigor of dry seeds is reduced and their viability is lost as they age in storage are correlated with their moisture content (reviewed by MAGUIRE 1977). Phototransformation of the inactive (red-absorbing) form of phytochrome, P_r, to the active (far-red-absorbing) form, P_{fr}, and vice versa, can take place in dry seeds, but the former requires a higher moisture content. Thus, seed ripening in sunlight would tend to have a low P_{fr}/P_r ratio and require light for germination (MCARTHUR 1978).

12.3 Seed Water Relations During Germination

The kinetics of water uptake by the seed integrate the uptake by its individual parts. The different organs of the embryo, as well as the different tissues of the seed differ in chemical composition, physical organization, physiological activities, and water-retention characteristics (STILES 1948). They may therefore differ in swelling capacity, as well as in the direction of anisotropic swelling. Some of these differences play a role in water uptake and germination.

Uptake of water by the dry seed is characterized by an initial phase of rapid uptake with saturation kinetics, followed by a transition phase with very gradual to negligible uptake, and this is in turn followed by a third phase of rapid and exponentially increasing uptake.

12.3.1 Initial Phase

The kinetics of uptake during this phase are qualitatively the same in live and killed seeds. It has therefore been assumed that this is nonbiological adsorption and capillary uptake. However, this uptake becomes progressively temperature-dependent during the course of this phase (ALLERUP 1958) and this could not be accounted for by effects of temperature on the energy status of water,

or on its viscosity. Studies with embryos of Lima bean (WOODSTOCK and POL-
LOCK 1965; POLLOCK and TOOLE 1966; KLEIN and POLLOCK 1968) and soybean
(WEBSTER and LEOPOLD 1977; BRAMLAGE et al. 1978) showed that proliferation
and reorganization of the membrane system (plasmalemma, ER, mitochondria)
starts as early as 20 min after onset of rehydration. Chilling injury results from
brief exposures to low (5 °C) temperature during this early part of imbibition,
apparently by interfering with membrane reorganization. The rate of this process
is probably very temperature-dependent, even in chilling-insensitive seeds, such
as *Amaranthus retroflexus* (TAYLORSON and HENDRICKS 1972). As the membrane
system reorganizes, the relative contribution of osmosis to the overall uptake
of water also increases. This enhances the effects of temperature on the later
stages of uptake in this phase. Respiratory rate and oxidative phosphorylation
also increase rapidly early in the initial phase (PRADET et al. 1968), and this
can be ascribed to the early reorganization of the inner mitochondrial membrane
system (WEBSTER and LEOPOLD 1977).

Responsiveness of light-sensitive seeds to promotive irradiation increases
during the course of incubation. In lettuce, responsiveness increased progressively with initial hydration (BERRIE et al. 1974), and in *Chenopodium album* rate
of increase in responsiveness correlated well with rate of this rehydration (KARS-
SEN 1970). These authors have therefore attributed the increase in responsiveness
to the progressive hydration of phytochrome. However, in embryos of *Pinus
palustris,* spectrophotometrically detectable levels of phytochrome increased
markedly within minutes of contact with water, but physiological changes associated with the phytochrome system did not become evident until several hours
later (TOBIN and BRIGGS 1969). Furthermore, in lettuce, phytochrome becomes
fully hydrated at a considerably lower water content than that required for
full activity of its hypothetical reactant (HSIAO and VIDAVER 1971; LOERCHER
1974; DUKE 1978). Results with *Artemisia monosperma* (KOLLER et al. 1964),
Portulaca oleracea and *Rumex crispus* (DUKE et al. 1977) indicated that increase
in responsiveness could not be attributed to increase in level of phytochrome,
or its hydration, but to increase in availability of its hypothetical reactant.
In *Artemisia* and *Portulaca* responsiveness continued to increase long after the
seeds had become fully imbibed.

12.3.2 Transition Phase

Moisture content, respiratory rate, and morphology of the seed remain virtually
unchanged throughout this phase, but a variety of metabolic events have been
reported to occur, such as changes in levels, or activities of organelles (for
instance, polysomes). Stability of respiratory rate during this time indicates
that energy is primarily supplied for maintenance. The rate is sufficiently low
as not to deplete stored food. This is of obvious advantage, since it is commonplace for seeds to imbibe under conditions that are unfavorable for their germination.

The processes that take place during the transition phase may differ in
their operational levels of hydration (SPYROPOULOS and LAMBIRIS 1980). Such

differential requirements for hydration are probably the basis for the technique of "priming" seeds of economically important species for more rapid, or uniform germination, by allowing them to equilibrate with and stay for specific periods and at specific temperatures at controlled water potentials, usually by employing solutions of innocuous, high molecular weight polymers such as polyethylene glycol (HEGARTY 1978; KHAN et al. 1980/81). Priming apparently occurs in nature as well, for instance in some succulent halophytes whose seeds can withstand prolonged immersion in highly saline water and germinate fully upon transfer to pure water (UNGAR 1962; BOORMAN 1968). Priming by different means also occurs in nature. Seeds of many species remain in the transition phase until released by a specific environmental stimulus that either eliminates or inactivates an inhibitory factor, or causes the synthesis or activation of an essential factor. The significance of such responses is discussed in Section 12.1.2. In many cases the seeds can be dried after exposure to the promotive stimulus, yet retain its effects until they are rehydrated. In general, once responsiveness of the seeds to the promotive stimulus is achieved, the seeds remain in the transition phase, "poised" for immediate response (for instance, light-sensitive weed seeds in cultivated soil). In some species, exposure of the seeds to one or more cycles of alternate hydration and dehydration accelerates, or otherwise improves subsequent germination (reviewed by KOLLER 1955). In wheat (HANSON 1973), such treatment was particularly effective for germination under water-stress, or at sub-optimal temperature. Effectiveness depended on duration and temperature of the hydration phase, on conditions of dehydration and on the number of cycles. Treated grains exhibited accelerated activation of α-amylase and higher rates of respiration and of protein synthesis in the aleurone, but not in the embryo.

Among the variety of metabolic and structural changes that take place during the transition phase there may be some that tend to inactivate germination. Physical properties of the coats may become unfavorably modified (NEGBI et al. 1966), essential reactants may become depleted (DUKE et al. 1977), or inhibitory products may accumulate. Under any set of conditions germination would depend on the relative rates of the promotive and inhibitory processes (NEGBI et al. 1966). This may be one cause for the "secondary" dormancy which seeds of certain species enter under conditions that prolong their transition phase (KARSSEN 1980/81). Some of these inhibitory processes appear to require high levels of hydration and are blocked when the transition phase takes place under water stress (NEGBI et al. 1966; KOLLER 1970) and may be reversed by drying (VINCENT and CAVERS 1978). This is probably the underlying mechanism for the promotive effects and after-effects of exposure to water stress in seeds of *Taraxacum kok-saghyz* (LEVITT and HAMM 1943), to high levels of salinity in seeds of certain halophytes, such as *Suaeda depressa* (UNGAR 1962), *Plantago maritima* (BINET 1964) and *Limonium* spp. (BOORMAN 1968).

12.3.3 Growth Phase

The third phase of water uptake occurs only in viable, nondormant seed. Its onset coincides approximately with radicle protrusion and is therefore associated

with establishment of cellular extension growth. This accounts for the marked increase in respiratory activity and in oxygen requirements. Growth is initiated prior to radicle protrusion. In the wheat grain the embryo starts to grow during the transition phase. This involves metabolic and energy-requiring processes, but does not depend on supplies from the endosperm, as it takes place equally in excised embryos (on water) and (in intact grains) is not accompanied by increase in embryo dry weight. The increase in embryo fresh weight has been ascribed to water uptake by vacuolation in existing cells, starting with the coleorhiza and epiblast. In certain varieties this growth generates sufficient thrust to overcome the mechanical resistance of the coats. In others, germination is delayed because additional thrust must be generated by mobilizing stored food and this takes place after the scutellum had been rehydrated (WELLINGTON and DURHAM 1961) and had presumably released gibberellin.

12.3.4 Water as a Driving Force

It therefore appears that the growth phase is associated with a fundamental change in the mechanisms controlling seed water relations. Initiation of this phase appears to be the process that is most sensitive to water stress. A lower Ψ_o is required to suppress radicle elongation after germination than to suppress germination itself (HEGARTY and ROSS 1980/81). This difference may be ascribed to the mechanical resistance of the coats prior to radicle protrusion, which counteracts the thrust generated by the radicle. However, the fact that Ψ of seedlings becomes progressively lower (McDONOUGH 1975) suggests that this process may indeed have started before radicle protrusion. This mobilization of water provides the driving force for early growth of the embryo, by means of which it overcomes the mechanical resistance of the coats. Several studies, in which the thrust generated by the embryo was compared to the mechanical resistance of the coats, indicate that dormancy may act by blocking the osmotic mobilization of water. In *Juglans* the imbibed embryo achieves the capacity to generate sufficient pressure to fracture the endocarp only during cold treatment (CROCKER et al. 1946). In *Xanthium* the imbibed embryo of the upper (dormant) seed is incapable of generating sufficient thrust to exceed the resistance of its own coat, while that of the lower (nondormant) seed is (ESASHI and LEOPOLD 1968). In light-sensitive lettuce seed, osmotic inhibition of germination could be overcome by promotive irradiation with red light (KAHN 1960). Lower Ψ_o was required to produce the same inhibition in light than in darkness (REYNOLDS 1975). This could be explained on the basis of results by SCHEIBE and LANG (1965), who showed that the promotive action of light was expressed by increasing the growth capacity of the embryo itself. Furthermore, the P_{fr}-induced increase in the growth rate of the radicle by red light was limited to the initial stages of its growth. The subsequent growth rate was independent of the state of phytochrome (SCHEIBE and LANG 1967). Treatment of the lettuce embryo with red light caused a reduction in its water potential (NABORS and LANG 1971). In subsequent studies, CARPITA et al. (1979a, b) showed that Ψ

in axes of red-irradiated "seeds" was lower by 0.34 MPa than in far-red-treated "seeds" and this difference remained constant during subsequent growth. However, the initial difference in Ψ_s (0.1–0.2 MPa) became progressively less as Ψ_s increased in red-irradiated "seeds", indicating a decrease in Ψ_p. They suggest that the P_{fr}-mediated increase in the driving force for growth of the embryonic axis is an integrated function of cell-wall loosening and increase in osmotic constituents, as a result of activation of a proton pump.

12.4 Statics and Dynamics of Seed-Water Relations

Water uptake by seeds from its surrounding medium (e.g. soil) is controlled by the water energy status within and transportability of water between the various components of the seed-soil system (e.g. seed storage materials, embryonic tissues and coat, soil-seed interface zone and the soil bulk around or in contact with the seed). Initially, water potential in air-dried seeds is extremely low: -50 MPa to -100 MPa (BLACK 1968; HEGARTY 1978). When brought in contact with a moist environment, such as moist soil, humid air, or free water, the seed starts to take up water and the potential of the water in its tissues increases. The relationship between the seed water potential, Ψ^{seed}, and its water content yield characteristic sorption isotherms for different seed species, that depend on the seeds storage materials, as well as on the ambient temperature and solutes in the surrounding medium (MAYER and POLJAKOFF-MAYBER 1975). Similar relations between soil water content and water potential of the soil solution, Ψ^{soil}, depends on texture and structure of the soil and on solute species and concentrations in the soil solution (CHILDS 1969; HILLEL 1971; BAVER et al. 1972). Soil texture and structure govern the matric water potential component, Ψ_m, and the solute content and concentrations determine the osmotic water potential component, Ψ_s. Unless the soil is air-dry, water potentials in the soil are generally higher than in the dry seed. Water will therefore move along the potential gradient from the soil to the seed. However, water potential considerations alone can neither explain nor describe the kinetic aspects of water uptake during seed germination (KOLLER 1972). The kinetic aspects involve the rate of water movement, or water flux along the soil bulk-seed pathway. The water flux toward the seed depends on the water transmission properties of the soil bulk and at the seed-soil contact zone, e.g., soil water diffusivity, or soil capillary conductivity, and seed-soil contact impedance to water flow (COLLIS-GEORGE and HECTOR 1966; PHILLIPS 1968; HADAS 1969, 1970; SHAYKEWICH and WILLIAMS 1971; WILLIAMS and SHAYKEWICH 1971; HADAS 1974; HADAS and RUSSO 1974a, b; HADAS and STIBBE 1973).

These parameters of water potential and water transmission may change with time and soil water content, either by direct relation (e.g., seed metabolism, seed swelling, and seed-water contact) or independently of the process of water uptake (e.g., soil water content, potential and conductance). Effects of these various parameters on water uptake by the seed are discussed in detail below.

12.4.1 Soil Water Potential

It has long been established that the rate and final level of germination decrease with decreasing Ψ^{soil} (DONEEN and MCGILLIVRAY 1943; HUNTER and ERICKSON 1952; COLLIS GEORGE and SANDS 1959). Seeds that exhibit water sensitivity are exceptions to this.

Critical Ψ^{seed}. The ability to germinate and the rate of germination under low Ψ^{soil} depend on the seed species. A seed must absorb a minimal amount of water in order to germinate. This "critical hydration level" is species-specific and corresponds to the "critical Ψ^{seed}", below which germination cannot take place (HUNTER and ERICKSON 1952; MCGINNIES 1960; KAUFMANN 1969; HADAS and STIBBE 1973). HADAS and STIBBE (1973) have suggested that for each seed different critical hydration levels, or critical Ψ^{seed}, exist for various activities or growth processes. Different critical hydration levels probably control cell swelling, imbibition, cell expansion, and cell division (DASBERG 1971; HEGARTY 1978). Attainment of the "critical Ψ^{seed}" depends on the external Ψ^{soil} and seed soil contact. Therefore, it is important to study its dependence on the various soil water potential components contributing to the Ψ^{soil}.

Differential Effects of Ψ_S *and* Ψ_m. The total Ψ^{soil} is considered to consist of the sum of several components, as follows: gravitational potential, Ψ_g, which depends on the vertical position of the considered point in reference to a given datum; osmotic potential, Ψ_S, derived from the composition and concentrations of the dissolved solute species at the considered point in reference to pure water; pressure potential, Ψ_p, in water-saturated soil, or matric potential, Ψ_m, in unsaturated soil, derived from adsorptive and interfacial (capillary) attraction between soil water and soil matrix and dependent upon soil moisture content.

The two components directly involved in water transport to germinating seeds are Ψ_m and Ψ_S. Thus changes in soil water content and solute composition affect seed germination through changes in both these components of soil water potential. AYERS (1952) and RICHARDS and WADLEIGH (1952) have stated that seeds respond equally to equal changes of Ψ_m and Ψ_S. However, this statement holds as long as the seed coats are selectively permeable to solutes in the osmotic solutions and the seed has perfect contact with the surrounding medium (HADAS and RUSSO 1974a; MANOHAR and HEYDECKER 1974).

HEGARTY (1978) has stated that seeds immersed in water may lose various species of solute to the external solution due to leaky membranes during the imbibition. COLLIS-GEORGE and SANDS (1962) have concluded, from germination behavior, that although Ψ_m and Ψ_S may be of equal nominal free energy value, they do not have the same biological consequences. Their results support the possibility that solutes or ions of inorganic electrolytes move from the osmotic solution into the seed cells. Both reports indicate leaky or selectively permeable membranes in imbibing seeds. Osmotic solutions made of high molecular weight polyelectrolytes, as used by KAUFMANN (1969) and HADAS and RUSSO (1974a, b), show only similarity of equal consequences to germination

by both components, namely Ψ_S and Ψ_m. These facts suggest that the contribution of salts commonly found in the soil solution to the total Ψ^{soil} is small or ineffective as long as the seed coat or embryonic cell membranes are leaky or selectively permeable. It is probable that most salt effects on germination are related to ion toxicity. Biological systems differ in their tissue permeabilities to salts and in their susceptibility to stimulatory or toxic effects by different salts and ions found in osmotic solutions or in the soil. Sodium chloride (NaCl) and gypsum ($CaSO_4$) were reported to have toxic effects (UHVITS 1946; COLLIS-GEORGE and SANDS 1959; WIGGANS and GARDNER 1962), while nitrate salts have stimulatory effects on germination (Sect. 12.1.1).

A slight decrease in soil water matric potential, Ψ_m, has a greater effect on water uptake and germination retardation than a corresponding or greater decrease in the soil water osmotic potential, Ψ_S (UHVITS 1946; AYERS and HAYWARD 1948; WIGGANS and GARDNER 1959; COLLIS-GEORGE and SANDS 1959, 1962; McGINNIES 1960; COLLIS-GEORGE and HECTOR 1966; WILLIAMS and SHAYKEWICH 1971; HADAS and STIBBE 1973; HADAS and RUSSO 1974a, b). A change of 0.01 MPa in Ψ_m was found to cause the same consequences as a 1.0 MPa change in Ψ_S (COLLIS-GEORGE and SANDS 1962). The differences in effectiveness of these soil water potential components are due to the fact that slight changes in the matric water potential involve the recession of water from larger soil pores to smaller ones and are thus accompanied by simultaneous changes in the soil water conductivity and the seed-soil water contact area (SEDGLEY 1963; COLLIS-GEORGE and HECTOR 1966; HADAS 1970; HADAS and RUSSO 1974a, b). Consequently, the "critical Ψ^{seed}" cannot be directly related to the sum of the matric and osmotic components of Ψ^{soil}. The dependence of germination on Ψ^{soil} must be studied separately with respect to changes in the matric component and using high molecular weight substances for the osmotic component. HUNTER and ERICKSON (1952) determined the "critical Ψ_m values" of -1.25, -0.79, -0.66 and -0.35 MPa for seeds of corn, rice, soybeans and sugar beets, respectively. Values of -1.52 to -2.0 MPa, -0.7, -1.2, -0.6, and -0.35 MPa, were reported for sorghum, cotton, chickpea, pea, and clover seeds, respectively, by HADAS (1970), HADAS and STIBBE (1973), and HADAS and RUSSO (1974a, b). Ψ^{soil} values are of the soil bulk under static equilibrium conditions. However, the real values are even lower and should be calculated for the soil-seed interface by using dynamic water flow models (HADAS 1970; HADAS and STIBBE 1973; HADAS and RUSSO 1974b). Such computations yield, for a case of perfect seed soil-water contact, critical Ψ_m values of -1.4, -2.0, -0.45, -1.10, and -1.5 MPa for corn, sorghum, clover, cotton, and chickpea seeds.

Under natural conditions, changes in soil water contents due to precipitation, drainage, evaporation, and uptake by seeds are simultaneously accompanied by changes in Ψ^{soil}. During precipitation, the soil is wetted and its water potential increases, imposing no problems for water uptake by seeds. However, as the soil dries out during imbibition its water potential decreases and this may affect seed germination. Changes in Ψ^{seed}, as inferred from the change with time in water uptake rates by the seeds, were observed by HADAS (1976). Furthermore, germination rate and final level of germination decreased with a continu-

ous decrease in the Ψ_s of osmotic solutions during imbibition (HADAS 1977a, b). A greater total drop, or a greater rate of drop in Ψ_o caused larger decreases in germination rates and in final germination. These effects, which were observed for seeds in perfect contact with the osmotic solution, i.e., without limiting water conductivity, should be even more pronounced for similar changes in total Ψ^{soil}, where conductivity at the seed-soil interface changes with moisture content. HADAS (1977b) found good agreement between projected estimates of seed germination in osmotic solutions in the laboratory and final germination determined under field conditions.

Mechanical Effective Stress. Recently, COLLIS-GEORGE and HECTOR (1966), COLLIS-GEORGE and WILLIAMS (1968) and HADAS (1970, 1977a) examined the possibility that soil Ψ_m affects seed germination by its direct contribution to the mechanical effective stress within the soil matrix, which may physically inhibit the seed from swelling, thus reducing its capacity for imbibition, or for its embryo growth. However, data of HADAS (1970, 1977a) and SHAYKEWICH (1973) have shown that under natural conditions the range of normal stresses of mechanical nature found in the soil cannot impair seed germination.

12.4.2 Water Conductivity and Diffusivity of Soils and Seeds

Water uptake by seeds is a dynamic process and cannot be described, or its limiting factors defined, by an energetical approach alone, but rather by studying the kinetic aspects of the water transport process of the system, namely, the conductance to water across the bulk soil-seed interface and within the seed itself. Obviously, for a given water potential gradient a greater water flux will be attained at a higher soil water conductivity. Reviews by HADAS and RUSSO (1974a, b) show that in most of the reported experimental data relating germination to water uptake rates, the experimental procedures precluded differentiation between the specific effect of changes in Ψ_m, water conductivity, and/or in seed-soil contact area.

Water Conductivities in Soil-Seed System. Water movement in biological systems, across membranes, is best described by diffusion equations, rather than by equations of mass flow systems (PHILLIPS 1968; HADAS 1970; HADAS and RUSSO 1974a, b; see Chap. 17, Vol. 12A). Published values of apparent water conductivity of seeds are lower than those found in moist and wet soils (SHAYKEWICH and WILLIAMS 1971; WILLIAMS and SHAYKEWICH 1971; WARD and SHAYKEWICH 1972). The range of water conductivities of the soils reported was 1.3×10^{-1} m day^{-1} at matric potentials of -0.06 MPa to 3.2×10^{-7} m day^{-1} at -1.50 MPa, whereas the water conductivity of rape and wheat seeds was around 1.1×10^{-7} and 3.2×10^{-7} m day^{-1}, respectively. These values suggest that the soil and the seed conductivities to water are nearly equal only at very low water potentials, indicating that the water conductivity in the bulk soil cannot limit germination. The same conclusion is reached by comparing values of diffusivity to water for seeds and soils.

Diffusivity to Water in Soil-Seed System. Values of soil water diffusivities range from 5×10^7 to $4-5 \times 10^4$ m^2 day^{-1} for saturated soils to air-dried soils respectively (BRUCE and KLUTE 1956; RIJTEMA 1959; KUNZE and KIRKHAM 1962; DOERING 1965 — for sieved soils, and AMEMIYA 1965; HADAS 1974 — for aggregate soils). Values of water diffusivities for various seeds range from 1.7×10^2 to 1.5×10^{-6} m^2 day^{-1} for rape seeds (SHAYKEWICH and WILLIAMS 1971), 4.2×10^2 to 3×10^{-6} m^2 day^{-1} for wheat (WARD and SHAYKEWICH 1972), 8.9×10^0 to 5.9×10^1 and 2.0×10^1 to 8.4×10^2 m^2 day^{-1} for clover and chickpea seeds (HADAS 1970), 2.6×10^1 to 2.5×10^2 and 1.9×10^1 to 1.6×10^2 m^2 day^{-1} for soybean and corn seeds respectively (PHILLIPS 1968). The average seed water diffusivity increases with both the mean seed water content and soil water content and the range is largest in pure water (PHILLIPS 1968; HADAS 1970; SHAYKEWICH and WILLIAMS 1971; WARD and SHAYKEWICH 1972). Moreover, diffusivities to water of seeds immersed in osmotic solutions of different Ψ_S increase as the Ψ_S increases (HADAS and RUSSO 1974b; HADAS 1976). The data suggest that water distribution within the imbibing seed, as manifested by its relatively low average diffusivity to water, may be a limiting factor controlling imbibition, its rate, and consequently germination.

Soil-Seed Interface. Another rate-limiting process is water flow into the seed across the seed coat-soil interface and through the seed. This deduction is inferred from changes in the average water diffusivities of seeds immersed in osmotic solutions, moist soils and soil aggregates (HADAS 1970, 1976, 1977a).

Seed coat permeability to water is discussed in Sections 12.5.2 and 12.5.3. MORRIS et al. (1968) reported values of seed coat permeability to water for 11 varieties of snap beans. HADAS (1976) has reported that water diffusivity for seed coats of chickpea, pea, and vetch seed ranged from 3×10^0 to 3×10^2, 2.5×10^{-1} to 6×10^0 and 9×10^{-2} to 1.5×10^0 m^2 day^{-1} respectively. These values increased with increasing Ψ_S of the solutions.

Even though reported values of seed coat diffusivity to water are lower than those reported for whole seeds, their influence on water uptake by the seeds was hardly significant (HADAS 1976), but less permeable seed coats may severely impair water uptake. However, as pointed out, the fact that diffusivity to water of the seed coat is lower than that of the soil cannot explain the dependence of the imbibition rate on soil water conductivity, at least for chickpea, pea, and vetch, as reported by HADAS and RUSSO (1974a). In view of their data, as well as of those of others (WILLIAMS and SHAYKEWICH 1971; WARD and SHAYKEWICH 1972), this dependence is caused by change of hydraulic properties at the seed-soil water contact interface. Changes in water flow properties of the contact zone are a consequence of diminishing soil water content at the seed surface and in the soil adjacent to it (HADAS 1970; DASBERG and MENDEL 1971). These effects are more pronounced in a coarse-textured soil such as sand, or in coarsely structured soil (e.g., with large aggregates) in which the changes in the unsaturated soil water conductivity to water are greatest for a small change in the soil water content (AMEMIYA 1965; HADAS 1968).

12.4.3 Impedance to Water Flow at the Seed-Soil Interface

Under natural conditions rate of water uptake by imbibing seeds depends on changes in soil water content and soil hydraulic properties adjacent to the seed surface in contact with the soil particles and soil water (HADAS 1970; HADAS and RUSSO 1974b). These changes and the nonuniformity in water flow at the seed-soil contact interface can be lumped together into a flow parameter which is an index of resistance to water flow to the seed imposed by the seed-soil interface conditions (HADAS 1974, 1976). In most reports of the effects that Ψ^{soil} or hydraulic conductivity have on seed germination, measurements were carried out by using soil plugs, sintered glass, or other porous substrates. Water flow to the seeds was either restricted to a small portion of the seed surface or opposed by pressure of the densely packed material around the seed (COLLIS-GEORGE and SANDS 1959, 1962; COLLIS-GEORGE and HECTOR 1966; DASBERG 1971; SHAYKEWICH and WILLIAMS 1971; WILLIAMS and SHAYKEWICH 1971).

For these reasons the interpretation of the data was criticized by SEDGLEY (1963), HADAS (1970), HADAS and RUSSO (1974a), because the experimental procedures combined the effects of the seed-soil contact impedance to flow with the effects of soil water stress and conductance and normal mechanical stresses on germination. SEDGLEY (1963) has shown that improvement of seed-water contact increased imbibition and hastened germination. COLLIS-GEORGE and HECTOR (1966) calculated the seed coat area in contact with the wet soil and correlated it to the germination rate. They concluded that effects of Ψ_m per se are more important than the indirect control it exerts over the wetted seed-coat area, except at very high matric water potentials. Their analysis was incomplete since in both cases the dynamic aspects of water flow characterization, as given by the hydraulic conductivity of the contact zone, were not included (HADAS 1970; HADAS and RUSSO 1974b).

Contact Impedance. Since the hydraulic conductivity of the seed-soil interface cannot be determined, a procedure has been developed and tested (HADAS and RUSSO 1974a, b) that makes it possible to analyze separately the unique effects that the matric and osmotic components of water potential in the soil bulk, water conductivity, and the seed soil water contact impedance to water flow have on seed imbibition and germination. Their analysis for fully buried, or covered seeds combines the effects that the geometrical configuration, the hydraulic conductivity and Ψ_m at the interface have on water flow to the seed. The impedance factor found shows a good correlation with the wetted area of the seed and the soil conductivity to water. The analyses by HADAS and RUSSO (1974b), and HADAS (1974, 1976) furthermore show that for a given Ψ^{soil} and assuming a perfect seed-soil contact, an increase in the impedance to flow causes a smaller decrease than anticipated in the soil Ψ_m at the seed surface. The contact impedance increases as the seed wetted area, or the soil water conductivity, or both, decrease. Contact impedance for a given Ψ_m increases as the coarseness of the soil texture or structure increase. Thus, for a given seed size and soil Ψ_m the wetted seed coat area will decrease and

its contact impedance to flow will increase as the particle coarseness of their immediate surrounding increase. As a consequence, the water uptake rate, as well as the rate and final percentage of germination, will diminish as the proportion of large-sized soil crumbs increases (CURRIE 1973; HADAS 1974, 1977a).

These phenomena may become aggravated for seeds that are partially buried, or lying on the soil surface, since only a small part of the seed coat is in direct contact with the water films.

Contact impedances to water flow at the seed-soil interface of pea and chickpea were neither significantly high to delay water uptake or germination, nor did they increase further during the progress of imbibition (HADAS 1977a). Since these and many other seeds swell during imbibition, the increased volume of the seed compacts the soil adjacent to it and increases the total area in contact with it (HADAS 1970, 1977a). At the same time decrease in water content and diminishing pore sizes at the compacted soil-seed interface cause a marked decrease in water film contact points and hence in water conductivity at the interface. HADAS (1977a) has suggested that the reduction in film contact points and in conductance to water at the seed-soil interface overrides the increase in the total contact area. Swelling seeds on top of a moist soil cannot compact the soil, and thus one may expect a more pronounced increase in the contact impedance, lower rate of water uptake, and delayed germination.

12.5 Pathways for Entry of Water into the Seed

The exterior of the seed (dispersal unit) is never uniform, but exhibits an intricate surface sculpture, as well as specialized regions, such as hilum, micropyle, and chalaza (strophiole in the Leguminosae). The architecture and structure of the seed (dispersal unit) and water-repellant properties of its coats may have a profound influence on the geometry of the pathway for movement of water from the soil into the seed. Using artificial "soil" surfaces, HARPER and BENTON (1966) showed that germination of mucilaginous seeds was least sensitive to Ψ_m, while spiny and reticulate seeds were particularly sensitive. Sensitivity of smooth-coated seeds increased with their size. Dependence of germination on Ψ_m was greatly reduced when evaporative losses were cut. Germination at constant Ψ_m was affected by soil moisture content. However, MOTT (1974) found that features that improve soil-seed contact failed to improve germination on the soil surface. McWILLIAM and PHILLIPS (1971) have shown that whereas Ψ_s and Ψ_m have equivalent effects on germination of *Lolium perenne* and dehulled *Phalaris tuberosa*, the equivalence no longer holds in nondehulled *Phalaris* because the air gap between the hulls and the pericarp remains vapor-filled at low Ψ_m and causes an increase in resistance to absorption of soil water.

Anatomical studies indicate a structural complexity of the tissues, as well as a specialization of the cell walls from which these coats are made up. Internal to the seed coat are additional envelopes, such as the perisperm and endosperm, with their own physical and chemical peculiarities. Many of these features play

a role in the biological functions of the seed, namely in its dispersal and germination. Some of them play a role in water uptake (a) by acting as selectively permeable barriers, and/or (b) by restricting the entry of water through the coats (Christiansen and Moore 1959; Manohar and Heydecker 1964). Discussion of the anatomical and structural features of the seed coat is outside the scope of the present chapter.

12.5.1 Myxospermy

In species of Plantaginaceae, Linaceae, Brassicaceae, Euphorbiaceae, Onagraceae, Acanthaceae etc., the seed coats become mucilaginous when wet. The mucilage is rapidly formed by uptake of a relatively large volume of water that is then held in readily available form (high Ψ) in the immediate vicinity of the seed. Also, the contact area between the seed and soil water is greatly increased. These features may be of advantage in improving water uptake by the seed, for instance in coarse-textured soils (Dexter and Miyamoto 1959; Young and Evans 1973), but are of no advantage in the severe water relations at the soil surface (Mott 1974). On the other hand, myxospermy aggravates oxygen supply. In *Spinacia oleracea* (Cavazza 1953) and in *Hirschfeldia incana* (Negbi et al. 1966) this creates a positive response to reduced Ψ_m, while in *Blepharis persica* germination on the soil surface is inhibited by surface water and promoted by divalent ions, such as Ca^{2+} (Witztum et al. 1969). The ecological role of myxospermy is still problematic (Grubert 1974).

12.5.2 Selective Permeability

In seeds that exhibit selective permeability, water uptake is controlled by the osmotic, as well as by the matric components of the external water potential (Manohar and Heydecker 1964), and by the reflection coefficients for the molecular species of the solutes. These considerations must be kept in mind in studies involving osmotic control of seed water relations (Nabors and Lang 1971). Interpretation is complicated by the fact that osmotically active compartments, with different permeability properties, may exist within the seed. Simon (1974) and Simon and Wiebe (1975) have shown that selective permeability due to biological membranes might be influenced by environmental factors, either directly, for instance by effects of temperature on fluidity of the lipid phase (see also Labouriau 1978), or indirectly, for instance by effects of aeration on availability of energy by oxidative phosphorylation. Selective permeability changes during the course of rehydration, as membrane integrity improves. Selectively permeable coats control leakage of enzymes (Duke and Kakefuda 1981), metabolites, and growth regulators from rehydrating seeds before membrane integrity is established in the embryo and endosperm. Such leakage may not only deplete seed reserves, but also enhance microbial activity in the vicinity of the seed (Pollock and Toole 1966).

12.5.3 Impermeability to Water

In some seeds the coats are entirely impermeable to water, and only become permeable under the influence of specific environmental complexes. Some of these complexes are clearly related to the ecological niches that the species occupy. This is, for instance, the case with species such as *Rhus ovata* that occupy frequently burnt sites, whose impermeable inner seed coat cracks open above the micropyle and becomes permeable after brief exposures to temperatures that occur at the soil surface during brush fires (STONE and JUHREN 1951). In other cases, the environmental complexes that cause loss of impermeability regulate seed germination in ways that contribute to the successful survival and establishment of the seedlings (KOLLER 1972).

In other seeds, coat impermeability is discontinuous, thus restricting the entry of water to specific pathways, which are either few in number and localized, or more numerous and scattered more uniformly over the seed coat. These features must be taken into account in studies of the effect of the contact area on water uptake by the seed from the soil.

12.5.4 Identification of Pathways

Specific sites for entry of water through otherwise impermeable, or selectively permeable seed coats have been identified by blocking specific regions with water-impermeable material prior to soaking. Other techniques have employed water-soluble stains for imbibition. Sectioning the seeds at intervals during imbibition allows the progress of the wetting front in the seed to be followed. BERGGREN (1963), using such techniques, concluded that the pathway is related to the type of ovule from which the seed had developed: the hilum in seeds from campylotropous ovules, the chalaza — from anatropous, and the micropyle in those from orthotropous ovules. SPURNY (1973) has employed a cinematographic analysis to identify the pathway for entry and to follow the time-course of rehydration of individual regions of the seed coat and organs of the embryo during initial swelling and subsequent germination of pea seeds. Volatile stains (iodine) have been used to identify pathways through which water may enter only in vapor form (HYDE 1954). Seeds with less localized pathways for water entry do not lend themselves to similar procedures for identification of the pathways. Their existence can only be inferred indirectly by the fact that they can open and close, and that when open, the seed can take up water equally well when different regions of its coat are blocked artificially.

12.5.5 Hard-Seededness

Phenomenology. The most extreme, and therefore the most evident manifestation of seed coat impermeability to water is found in "hard" seeds, which take up water very slowly, or not at all when soaked. Such seeds are prevalent in the Papilionaceae, Mimosaceae, Caesalpiniaceae, Malvaceae and Convolvula-

ceae and exhibit extreme longevity in artificial storage, as well as in nature. Hard-seededness is therefore a major contribution to long-term availability of viable seeds in the soil, and thus to persistence of the species. Characteristically, when such seeds are soaked in water, individual seeds may imbibe and swell more or less abruptly and sporadically over long periods. The time-course of these events ("rate of imbibition") is temperature-dependent (FAYEMI 1957). Water apparently enters the seed very gradually. As the colloidal contents of the seed (up to and including inner layers of the coat) become rehydrated they change their spatial organization. This opens up new pathways for water entry into the seed and/or enlarges existing ones, thus changing a trickle into a flood. This explains the abrupt swelling after long delays.

Softening. Hard seeds can be artificially "softened" by a variety of means that attack the integrity of the coats, without damaging the interior, such as "scarification" by mechanical abrasion, or acid corrosion (PORTER 1949; KOLLER and COHEN 1959), "percussion" (="impaction") treatments (HAMLY 1932; HAGON and BALLARD 1970), or brief immersion in hot (80 °C) water (CHRISTIANSEN and MOORE 1959). Such treatments may attack the coat indiscriminately, but specific regions of the coat may be more susceptible. In nature, permeability is achieved by opening up specific pathways through the otherwise impermeable coats (see Sect. 12.6.4).

Establishment of Seed Coat Impermeability. Seed coat impermeability has been mostly studied in the Papilionaceae (QUINLIVAN 1971), because of their economic importance, but the findings can probably be extended to other families. According to BALLARD (1973) and WERKER et al. (1979), the impermeable layer is that of the palisade (or Malpighian) cells, which contain quinones and have external caps that are very hard, pectinaceous, and embedded in a suberin matrix.

HYDE et al. (1959) have shown that impermeability is absent during early seed development and increases rapidly soon after the rapid phase of moisture uptake by the seed comes to an end. In a more definitive study HYDE (1954) showed that as the seed ripens it loses most of its water rapidly by evaporation over its entire surface. When its water content had fallen (from 150%–200%) to 25%, the coats start to become impermeable. However, water loss continues, although at a much slower rate, by diffusion through the hilum, which has cracked open along the median groove by the tensions created in the drying and shrinking counter-palisade layer. This gradual water loss continues until an equilibrium is reached between Ψ inside the seed and in the surrounding atmosphere. As seed moisture content falls (to 14%) the palisade cells shrink laterally and the coats become impermeable. Thus, as the seeds became dehydrated during ripening their capacity to take up liquid water was equally high as long as their moisture content did not fall below 20% and then decreased markedly and exponentially as moisture content continued to fall to 14%. When ripening took place in atmospheres of controlled humidity the duration of impermeability was negatively correlated with this relative humidity. Thus, when the hilar fissure opens, it allows outward diffusion of water vapor, but

prevents entry of liquid water. It was further found that in dry air the hilar fissure opened rapidly and allowed loss of water vapor, while in wet air it closed rapidly and prevented the sorption of water vapor, thus acting as a one-way valve. As a result, seeds exposed to a fluctuating atmospheric humidity could only become progressively more dehydrated, equilibrating with the lowest humidity in the sequence.

Prematuration Conditioning. Germination responses may be quantitatively affected by the parental environment during seed ontogeny, as well as by the position of the seed in the fruit, or inflorescence (review by KOLLER 1972). These effects are also expressed in seed water relations.

   Exposure of barley plants to a short heat stress 3 weeks after awn emergence resulted in grains with a thinner coat, that took up water and germinated more readily (KHAN and LAUDE 1969). In hard-seeded Papilionaceae, seed coat impermeability, as well as its susceptibility to summer conditions, differs according to the position of the seed in the pod (KOLLER 1969; HALLORAN and COLLINS 1974). The photoperiodic environment at a late stage in pod development (GUT-TERMANN and EVENARI 1972) and length of the growing season of the parent plant apparently affect the ripening process of the seed coat and thus determine the degree of hard-seededness (QUINLIVAN 1965; EVENARI et al. 1966).

12.6 Optimization of Water Supply by Regulation of Germination

The general aspects of germination-regulating mechanisms as strategies for survival are discussed in Section 12.1.2. Water is one of the basic requirements for and plays a central role in the germination process. A considerably larger and more sustained supply of water is required for subsequent growth and survival of the seedling. Yet seeds are small and are therefore able to sample the availability of water only within a small volume of the surrounding soil. Clearly, such a small and localized sampling cannot provide a reliable indication as to whether or not the store of locally available soil moisture is sufficiently large. It thus appears that the probability of survival is actually enhanced by controlling the tendency of quiescent tissue to initiate growth upon rehydration. In this section we shall examine several strategies where the mechanism that regulates germination can be visualized as contributing to ensure the subsequent availability of soil moisture. We shall deal also with mechanisms that regulate the dispersal of the seeds (or more generally, the dispersal unit) in a way that also contributes to ensure the availability of soil moisture.

12.6.1 Optimal Soil Depth for Germination and Emergence

Seeds of most plants land on the soil surface after dissemination. This is where the radiant energy, convection, turbulent transfer, and gravitational flow com-

bine to create rapidly increasing moisture stress, telescoping to a minimum the period during which precipitated water remains available (McWILLIAM and DOWLING 1970). This is a precarious environment in which to germinate, yet germination in the more hospitable environment of deeper soil encounters difficulties in emergence resulting from the limitations of stored food and from the mechanical impedance by the drying surface layers of the soil (ARNDT 1965a, b). The relative effect of these two conflicting constraints will depend on soil physical conditions and moisture regime on the one hand, and on the nature of the particular seed on the other.

12.6.2 Physiological Depth-Gages

In most natural habitats the soil is undisturbed and its surface is compact. Consequently, the majority of the seed population inhabits a shallow layer at the surface, except where cracks develop. Germination that is triggered, accelerated, and synchronized by environmental conditions which are typical to the soil surface, such as light and/or extreme diurnal temperature fluctuations will help to maximize the utilization of the ephemeral supply of soil moisture at the surface. The energy and daily duration of light (KOLLER et al. 1964; WOOLEY and STOLLER 1978), as well as the amplitude of the diurnal temperature fluctuation, become strongly attenuated with soil depth. These regulatory mechanisms may therefore limit the depth from which the seedlings would have to emerge and the mechanical impedance that they would have to overcome.

A different situation exists in coarse-grained desert soils, where the balance between moisture relations and mechanical impedance at the surface makes the deeper soil layers more hospitable for germination. Inhibition by prolonged irradiation would act to restrict germination to a minimal soil depth in such habitats. This is the case with *Citrullus colocynthis* (KOLLER et al. 1963), whose large seeds are rich in food reserves and whose seedlings exhibit a high growth rate.

12.6.3 Regulation of Depth

In cultivated soil, the optimal depth of planting represents the compromise between the improving water relations and the deteriorating conditions for emergence with depth. The same strategy occurs naturally, unaided by man.

Geocarpy. Some species exhibit geocarpy and actively bury their seeds at a predetermined depth in the soil in the vicinity of the parent plant, while they are still developing. This is achieved in *Faktorovskya aschersoniana* (ZOHARY 1937) and in *Arachis hypogaea* by intercalary growth and positive geotropism of the basal part of the fertilized ovary — the gynophore (SMITH 1956); in *Trifolium subterraneum* by elongation and positive geotropism of the peduncle, followed by burrowing action of successive whorls of sterile calyces (KATZNELSON and MORLEY 1965); in the amphicarpic *Gymnarrhena micrantha* by contraction

of the main root prior to transformation of the retracting shoot apex to the reproductive state (KOLLER and ROTH 1964; UKO, unpublished). In addition, geocarpy may provide the rather general advantage of germinating where the parent had successfully completed its own life cycle. Seed burial may also be advantageous by providing some protection against predation.

Hygroscopic Mechanisms. Other species equip their dispersal units with means by which they bury themselves in the soil after dissemination. In *Erodium* spp., the mericarps come equipped with a long, hygroscopic style whose proximal part coils into a tight helix when dry and uncoils when wet (YOUNG et al. 1975). In *Avena sterilis* the same responses occur in the two awns of the dispersal unit (which consists of two fertile florets). In both species the base of the dispersal unit tapers to a sharp tip that carries barbs facing the rear. Diurnal fluctuations in atmospheric humidity result in cycles of coiling and uncoiling that screw the harpoon-like tip of the dispersal unit into the soil. The seed comes to rest at a depth determined on the one hand by the increasing attenuation of the humidity fluctuations and by the increasing mechanical resistance of the soil on the other. In all cases, the rather precise depth at which the seeds come to rest is evidently nonlimiting for emergence.

12.6.4 Seasonal Forecasting

Widespread regions of the earth are characterized by an alternation between a "wet" and a "dry" season, that differ in the abundance, predictability, and pattern of rainfall. With relatively few exceptions (e.g., "summer annuals" that occur where the dry season coincides with summer), the probability for survival and establishment is higher in the wet season, provided over-abundant germination does not increase competition. It is therefore of obvious value for plants to avoid germination in the unreliable soil moisture provided in the dry season and delay it till the onset of the wet season, when supply of moisture is more reliable. Most plants produce their seeds toward the end of the wet season. A requirement for "after-ripening" in such seeds may suffice to reduce the probability of precocious germination, but under field conditions this requirement is usually satisfied fairly early in the dry season. A widespread strategy for further delaying germination until the onset of the following wet season is exhibited by hard-seeded legumes, in which the hilar fissure acts as a one-way valve that under diurnal fluctuations in atmospheric humidity allows only the outward diffusion of water vapor from the seed (Sect. 12.5.5). However, when the atmospheric humidity rises very gradually, the seed becomes progressively rehydrated. Presumably, under such conditions the two superimposed layers that operate the hilar valve have time to become equally hydrated and expand simultaneously, leaving the fissure open (HYDE 1954). Alternatively, colloids inside the seed become hydrated and swell, stretching the coat, and prevent the valve from closing. In the natural environment, seed impermeability is thus progressively lost as the general level of atmospheric humidity gradually rises, with the approach of the wet season.

Quinlivan BJ (1965) The influence of the growing season and the following dry season on the hard seededness of subterranean clover in different environments. Aust J Agric Res 16:277–291

Quinlivan BJ (1966) The relation between temperature fluctuations and the softening of hard seeds of some legume species. Aust J Agric Res 17:625–631

Quinlivan BJ (1968) The softening of hard seeds of sand plain lupin (*Lupinus varius* L). Aust J Agric Res 19:507–515

Quinlivan BJ (1971) Seed coat impermeability in legumes. J Aust Inst Agric Sci 37:283–295

Reynolds T (1975) Characterization of osmotic restraints on lettuce fruit germination. Ann Bot (London) 39:791–796

Richards LA, Wadleigh CH (1952) Soil water and plant growth. In: Shaw BT (ed) Soil physical conditions and plant growth. Academic Press, London New York, pp 74–253

Rijtema PE (1959) Calculation of capillary conductivity from pressure plate outflow data with a non-negligible membrane impedance. Neth J Agric Sci 7:209–215

Roberts EH (1972) Dormancy: a factor affecting seed survival in the soil. In: Roberts EH (ed) Viability of seeds. Chapman and Hall, London, pp 321–359

Roberts EH, Smith RD (1977) Dormancy and the pentose phosphate pathway. In: Khan AA (ed) The physiology and biochemistry of seed dormancy and germination. Elsevier, Amsterdam, pp 385–411

Rogerson NE, Matthews S (1977) Respiratory and carbohydrate changes in developing pea (*Pisum sativum* L) seeds in relation to their ability to withstand desiccation. J Exp Bot 28:304–313

Scheibe J, Lang A (1965) Lettuce seed germination: evidence for a reversible light-induced increase in growth potential and for phytochrome mediation of the low temperature effect. Plant Physiol 40:485–492

Scheibe J, Lang A (1967) Lettuce seed germination: a phytochrome-mediated increase in the growth rate of lettuce seed radicles. Planta 72:348–354

Sedgeley RH (1963) The importance of liquid seed contact during the germination of *Medicago tribuloides*. Aust J Agric Res 14:646–654

Shaykewich CF (1973) Proposed method for measuring swelling pressure of seeds prior to germination. J Exp Bot 24:1056–1061

Shaykewich CF, Williams J (1971) Resistance to water absorption in germinating rape seed (*Brassica napus* L). J Exp Bot 22:19–24

Simon EW (1974) Phospholipids and plant membrane permeability. New Phytol 73:377–420

Simon EW, Wiebe HH (1975) Leakage during imbibition, resistance to damage at low temperature and the water content of peas. New Phytol 74:407–411

Smith BW (1956) *Arachis hypogaea*. Embryology and the effect of pod elongation upon embryo and endosperm growth. Am J Bot 43:233–240

Smith H (1973) Light quality and germination: ecological implications. In: Heydecker W (ed) Seed ecology. Butterworth, London, pp 219–231

Soriano A (1953) Estudios sobre germinacion. I. Rev Invest Agric 7:315–340

Spurny M (1973) The imbibition process. In: Heydecker W (ed) Seed ecology. Butterworth, London, pp 367–389

Spyropoulos CG, Lambiris MP (1980) Effect of water stress on germination and reserve carbohydrate metabolism in germinating seeds of *Ceratonia siliqua* L. J Exp Bot 31:851–857

Stiles IE (1948) Relation of water to the germination of corn and cotton seeds. Plant Physiol 23:201–222

Stone EC, Juhren G (1951) The effect of fire on the germination of the seed of *Rhus ovata* Wats. Am J Bot 38:368–372

Taylorson RB, Hendricks SB (1972) Rehydration of phytochrome in imbibing seeds of *Amaranthus retroflexus*. Plant Physiol 49:663–665

Taylorson RB, Hendricks SB (1977) Dormancy in seeds. Annu Rev Plant Physiol 28:331–354

Thomas H (1972) Control mechanisms in the resting seed. In: Roberts EH (ed) Viability of seeds. Chapman and Hall, London, pp 360–396

Tobin EM, Briggs WR (1969) Phytochrome in embryos of *Pinus palustris*. Plant Physiol 44:148–150

Uhvits R (1946) Effect of osmotic pressure on water absorption and germination of alfalfa seeds. Am J Bot 33:278–285

Ungar IA (1962) Influence of salinity on seed germination in succulent halophytes. Ecology 43:763–764

Vincent EM, Cavers PB (1978) The effects of wetting and drying on the subsequent germination of *Rumex crispus*. Can J Bot 56:2207–2217

Ward J, Shaykewich CF (1972) Water absorption by wheat seeds as influenced by hydraulic properties of the soil. Can J Soil Sci 52:99–105

Webster BD, Leopold AC (1977) The ultrastructure of dry and imbibed cotyledons of soybean. Am J Bot 64:1268–1293

Wellington PS (1964) Studies on the germination of cereals. 5. The dormancy of barley grains during ripening. Ann Bot (London) 28:113–126

Wellington PS, Durham VM (1961) Studies on the germination of cereals. 3. The effect of the covering layers on the uptake of water by the embryo of the wheat grains. Ann Bot (London) 25:185–196

Werker E, Marbach I, Mayer AM (1979) Relation between the anatomy of the testa, water permeability and the presence of phenolics in the genus *Pisum*. Ann Bot (London) 43:765–771

Wesson G, Wareing PF (1969) The role of light in the germination of naturally occurring populations of buried weed seeds. J Exp Bot 20:402–413

Wiggans SC, Gardner EB (1959) Effectiveness of various solutions for simulating drought conditions as measured by germination and seedling growth. Agron J 51:315–318

Williams AW, Elliott JR (1960) Ecological significance of seed coat impermeability to moisture in crimson, subterranean and rose clovers in a Mediterranean type climate. Ecology 41:785–790

Williams J, Shaykewich CF (1971) Influence of soil matric potential and hydraulic conductivity on the germination of rape seed (*Brassica napus* L.). J Exp Bot 22:586–597

Witztum A, Gutterman Y, Evenari M (1969) Integumentary mucilage as an oxygen barrier during germination of *Blepharis persica* (Burm) Kuntze. Bot Gaz 130:238–241

Woodstock LW, Pollock BM (1965) Physiological predetermination: imbibition, respiration and growth in Lima bean seeds. Science 150:1031–1032

Wooley JT, Stoller EW (1978) Light penetration and light-induced seed germination in soil. Plant Physiol 61:597–600

Young JA, Evans RA (1973) Mucilaginous seed coats. Weed Sci 21:52–54

Young JA, Evans RA, Kay BL (1975) Dispersal and germination dynamics of Broadleaf Filaree, *Erodium botrys* (Cav) Bertol. Agron J 67:54–57

Zohary M (1937) Die verbreitungsökologischen Verhältnisse der Pflanzen Palästinas. I. Die antitelechorischen Erscheinungen. Beih Bot Zbl 56:1–155

gules, bacteria and yeasts have not evolved such mechanisms (INGOLD 1965; GREGORY 1966). But even this generalization may have to be qualified since the finding by LaCHANCE et al. (1976) that strains of *Metschnikowia australis,* pathogens of brine shrimp, forcibly expel their needle-shaped spores from asci. Apparently, the propulsive force originates from a mucilage which, upon swelling, exerts the requisite force.

However, discharge adaptations may be difficult to evaluate because of their complexity. For example, SUSSMAN (1968) discusses the case of *Sphaerobolus stellatus,* which appears to discharge spores only during daylight hours under some circumstances, but will do so in the dark under others. Moreover, a discharge rhythm with a period of 10–12 days can override the other discharge mechanisms when the organism is kept under constant light and temperature, so this rhythm's effect upon spore release in nature must be evaluated in addition to the other factors.

Of the media for dissemination, air probably has been studied most intensively. According to the calculation of SUSSMAN and HALVORSON (1966), the theoretical terminal velocity of bacterial spores (0.00037 cm per second) probably is small enough to ensure that settling is more difficult than it is for larger spores, such as those of fungi, and for pollen (GREGORY 1961). In any case, given the presence of vegetative bacterial cells in the atmosphere along with spores, what seems to be unique about the latter is their survivability, not the fact that they can be dispersed in air. Nevertheless, viable cells of non-spore-formers as well as spore-forming bacteria are spread widely in the air and have been found in Antarctica, high elevations in temperate zones and over the Atlantic. Although spore-formers predominate in some of these habitats, vegetative cells also survive. Certain technical difficulties make the data less reliable than would be desired, such as the difficulty of distinguishing between colonies that arise from spores and vegetative cells, clumping of cells and the use of selective media.

Many data attest to the wide distribution of fungi through the air because of the intense study of plant pathogens over many years. A case in point is *Puccinia chondrilla,* the uredospores of which germinate at temperatures from 0° to 36 °C. This organism occurs as a pathogen in the cold continental climates of southern Siberia to the hot, mediterranean ones of Portugal and North Africa (HASAN and WAPSHERE 1973). That many other factors influence distribution in any medium may be seen in the data of SIMPSON et al. (1973) who have found that the spore's response to moisture is the determinant of geographical distribution of the parasites of cotton with which they worked.

Light is another factor that strongly affects the distribution of microorganisms in air. Thus, DOWDING (1969) and others have observed that nonpigmented conidia separated from one another lose viability rapidly when exposed to sunlight. In fact, the frequency of occurrence of viable spores in the air (ALI et al. 1976) over desert areas or in desert soils (NICOT 1960; RANZONI 1968) can be correlated with the resistance to insolation imparted by melanized walls, although resistance to desiccation must also play a part in survival in such regions. That resistance to ozone, an attribute aiding survival in the atmosphere, also is correlated with pigmentation of spores, has been shown by HIBBEN

and STOTZKY (1969). Moreover, the spores of the fungi that populate the surface of leaves, and those that are carried by birds, are black and appear to be adapted to withstand insolation as well (PUGH 1971, 1972). Organisms in similar environments, such as epiphytic parasites, very often produce mycelium, spores, and other structures that are melanized, whereas endophytic parasites form similar pigments only in structures that are produced outside the host (PARBERY and EMMETT 1977).

Dispersal by animals has been studied but much remains to be learned in this important field. For example, MASER et al. (1978) have pointed out that the role of small mammals as primary vectors in the dissemination of hypogeous mycorrhizal fungi makes the poisoning of forest rodents in timber management risky if healthy coniferous forests are to be maintained. Coprophilous ascomycetes, among other fungi, sometimes are dependent upon passage through the gut of mammals for the activation of their spores, as well as for food after germination. This is true as well for *Phytophthora megasperma;* the germination of its spores is increased from 5% to 93% after ingestion by the land snail, *Helix aspersa* (SALVATORE et al. 1973). Similar results were obtained by using enzymes of the animal. Birds are a means of transport (PUGH 1972) and are vectors of diseases as well (HUBALEK and RUSH-MUNRO 1973).

As for soil as a habitat in which spores appear to play a role, dry ones show a predominance of spore-formers and actinomycetes and, in turn, probably give rise to much of the dust from which airborne bacteria arise (DOETSCH and COOK 1973). According to MISHUSTIN (1956), the type of soil determines the proportion of spores and spore-formers found in this habitat. It would be interesting to know the distribution of spores and spore-formers in the different zones of soil, including the rhizosphere, etc., but the experiments are difficult because they require observation at the microscopic level so that spores can be distinguished from vegetative stages.

In the sea, about 80% of the bacteria are gram-negative, implying that only a minority can be spore-formers, although the details remain to be studied. Adaptation to the marine environment has taken place in some fungi which can sporulate and germinate in seawater (GARETH JONES et al. 1971; BYRNE and GARETH JONES 1975), although terrestrial fungi are less tolerant of this environment. The spores of a number of fungi have evolved the "tetraradiate" habit, which appears to be useful in anchoring these organisms under the turbulent conditions of streams (INGOLD 1975; WEBSTER et al. 1978).

13.4 Responsiveness

Microorganisms living in environments in which moisture, food, temperature, light, and other factors fluctuate gain selective advantage from mechanisms that ensure development when conditions are most favorable. Dormant spores and other propagules may serve this function by sensing the environment and germinating under appropriate conditions. Among microorganisms, such timing

all the types of soils used by Rosenzweig and Stotzky (1979) and conidia are more sensitive than hyphae in this instance. In controlled environments, *Bacillus cereus* prevents the germination of uredospores of *Puccinia allii* and the development of the rust disease of leek (Doherty and Preece 1978).

Some fungal spores form toxins that inhibit higher plants, as in the case of *Helminthosporium maydis* on maize leaves (Comstock and Martinson 1975), germinating uredospores of *Phakospora anachyrhizi* on soybean pods (Deverall et al. 1977) and *Alternaria kikuchiana* on pear leaves (Otani et al. 1975). The latter authors speculate that the reason that spores of *Penicillium citrinum* cannot penetrate pear leaves is that citrinin, a toxin exhibiting similar effects to those of *A. kikuchiana,* is produced only by the hyphae of the former fungus.

While bacteria frequently have been shown to have deleterious effects upon fungal spores, the reverse has been reported much less often.

Inhibitors from Higher Organisms

Most of the data available relate to higher plants although some evidence exists for animals as well. The literature on this subject is large and has been reviewed before so we shall discuss this field only briefly.

Volatile inhibitors from swelling seeds of a number of cultivated plants, including peas, beans, wheat, maize, and others severely inhibit the germination of spores of *Botrytis cinerea, Mucor racemosus* and *Trichoderma viride* (Catska et al. 1975). Experiments with these and other fungi suggest that the effectiveness of the toxins is dependent mainly upon the species of fungi tested, rather than upon the source of the toxin. Clonal and seasonal variation in substances inhibitory to spores of *Hypoxylon mammatum* were found in assays of the bark and wood of the quaking aspen (French and Mannion 1976). Spores of *Arthroderma curreri* are inhibited or killed by feather fats from certain birds, so its distribution is influenced by this means (Pugh and Evans 1970).

Phytoalexins, those substances arising in response to infection, often act to suppress spore germination as in the case of methyl-3,4-dimethoxycinnamate, which is produced by *Phaseolus vulgaris* and is inhibitory to uredospores of *Uromyces phaseoli* (Elnaghy and Heitefuss 1976). An interesting aspect of this interaction is that this phytoalexin also has been identified as the self-inhibitor of the germination of these spores.

The relationship between pathogenicity and sensitivity of spores to phytoalexins is an obvious ecological derivative of these data. Additionally, Afifi (1978) suggests that the effect of root exudates and volatile substances released from leaves upon fungal spores may influence the colonization of the rhizosphere and phyllosphere, respectively, especially in certain plant associations.

Self-Inhibitors of Germination

In contrast to the inhibitors discussed above which, when their effects are reversible, may impose a form of exogenous dormancy in spores, self-inhibitors are a means of inducing "constitutive" dormancy (Sussman and Halvorson 1966). These substances have been reviewed by the latter authors and by Sussman and Douthit (1973) and this review will be cursory.

Although many propagules can germinate even within sporocarps, such as the ascospores of the genus *Tympanis,* which form mycelium within asci (Ouel-

LETTE and PIROZYNSKI 1974), others are restrained from developing by the presence of self-inhibitors. Evidence that self-inhibitors are present includes the reduced capacity of spores to germinate in high concentrations, as in the case of the spores of *Smittium culisetae* (EL-BUNI and LICHTWARDT 1976). Other evidence is the increase in germination upon leaching or washing, as reported for oospores of *Albugo candida* by VERMA and PETRIE (1975). Nevertheless, the precautions discussed by SUSSMAN and DOUTHIT (1973) must be considered before conclusions are drawn on such evidence alone; once again, competition for food is an alternative that must be tested.

The self-inhibitor has been identified and in some cases its mode of action is known. The self-inhibitor in spores of *Agaricus bisporus* has been identified as carbon dioxide, according to RAST and her coworkers (GREUTER and RAST 1975; RAST and HOLLENSTEIN 1977), who have done detailed studies that suggest its locus of action to be succinic dehydrogenase, after the formation of oxaloacetate by carbon dioxide fixation (RAST et al. 1979). Other cases in which self-inhibitors have been identified include the rusts which, according to the work of MACKO and coworkers, produce a family of cinnamic acid inhibitors. Thus, the self-inhibitors from wheat stem rust, bean rust and stripe rust have been identified (MACKO et al. 1970), along with those of the snapdragon and sunflower rusts (MACKO et al. 1972), and that for the peanut rust (FOUDIN and MACKO 1974).

A controversy has developed over the identification of the self-inhibitor of spores of *Dictyostelium discoideum*, which has been identified as N^2-dimethylguanosine (2-dimethylamino-6-oxypurineriboside) by BACON et al. (1973). However, the toxicity of this compound to these spores has been challenged (TANAKA et al. 1974) and chromatography of an authentic sample and a crude spore extract showed clear differences between the two substances. Therefore, it is likely that N^2-dimethylguanosine is not the self-inhibitor from this organism. Recently, UCHIYAMA and ABE (1977) have accomplished the synthesis of the self-inhibitor, called discadenine, worked on by Tanaka and coworkers, establishing its structure to be 3-(3-amino-3-carboxypropyl)-6-(3-methyl-2-butenyl-amino) purine. An interesting attribute of this substance, in addition to its strong inhibitory effect on spores of *D. discoideum,* is activity on higher plants resembling that of cytokinin (NOMURA et al. 1977).

Prevention of the germination of spores in the immediate vicinity of their site of formation may help to ensure their dissemination. In other cases, germination may be suppressed until food becomes available, as seems to happen with spores of *Fusarium oxysporum,* the effect of the self-inhibitor of which is reversed by ethanol, a metabolite of glucose (OKAZAKI 1976).

13.4.2.2 Chemical Stimulators

Stimulators Produced by Other Organisms
It has been observed that the percentage germination of some spores is considerably greater in natural situations than in synthetic media, as in the case of basidiospores of the mycorrhizal fungus, *Rhizopogon luteolus,* which is part

of the rhizosphere (Theodorov and Bowen 1973). Such observations are widespread and a number of factors that stimulate spore germination have been described that originate from a broad range of organisms. For the most part, these substances have not been identified, nor is their mechanism of action known, except in a few cases. Bacteria produce substances that activate spores of *Dictyostelium discoideum* (Hashimoto et al. 1976; Dahlberg and Cotter 1978). A difference in the results of these two sets of workers lies in the lack of effect of *Escherichia coli* in the former case, which may be explained by differences in the strains of slime mold used.

Spores of *Bacillus subtilis* fail to germinate in acid forest soils unless fungal growth occurs nearby (Siala and Gray 1974). Volatile substances from *Ceratocystis fagacearum* stimulate the germination of spores of *Lactarius* spp. (Oort 1974), as do substances produced by the yeast *Rhodotorula glutinus* (Fries 1977), so even unrelated organisms can act identically upon the same spore, as in the case of the bacteria that affect *D. discoideum*. Animals also may activate spores during their passage through the gut of insect larvae (Lim 1977) and of rabbits (Harper and Webster 1964).

By far the largest number of stimulatory substances has been reported from higher plants: exudates and volatiles from seeds, roots and leaves, guttation drops, and extracts of pollen yield substances that stimulate spore germination. That these effects may have important consequences in nature is shown by the large increase in the infection of maize by *Fusarium graminearum*, the germination of the macroconidia of which is stimulated by pollen from the same plant (Naik and Busch 1978).

The chemical nature of germination stimulators is known in some cases and has been reviewed for fungal spores (Sussman 1965; Sussman and Halvorson 1966; Sussman 1976) and bacterial spores (Keynan and Evenchik 1969).

Morphogenic effects upon fungal spores also are induced by substances from higher plants. An important example of such effects is the formation of infection structures by some plant pathogens, a subject reviewed recently by Staples and Macko (1980). Substances that induce such effects include acrolein, which induces differentiation of infection structures in the wheat stem rust fungus (Macko et al. 1978). Factors of this kind may be part of the environment of stomata through which the germinating spore gains access to its host, according to Grambow and Riedel (1977) and others. Another effect on the differentiation of germinating spores is the induction of indirect germination, as in the case of sporangia of *Phytophthora infestans*, in response to factors in potato tubers (Walmsley-Woodward et al. 1975). Inducers of sporulation also occur that are produced by higher plants, but these will not be covered in this review.

The same organism can produce stimulators and inhibitors of spore germination. Volatiles from the leaves of *Ocimum basilicum* inhibit the germination of spores of several fungi, whereas the germination of spores of *Alternaria tenuis* and *Penicillium chermesinum* is enhanced (Afifi 1975a). Even within a single habitat, the rhizosphere, it has been shown that 11 species of bacteria antagonize the growth of the butt-rot fungus, *Fomitopsis annosa*, while 10 others are stimulatory (Orekhov 1974).

In an environment like soil, in which the available nutrient supply usually is low, there would be selective advantage for spores that germinate in response to chemical stimulators. For example, chemicals released by host plant roots in the rhizosphere appear to induce the development of pathogens, perhaps at times of the year when metabolic activity is high and environmental conditions favorable.

On the other hand, premature commitment to germinate, or a response induced by nonspecific signals from "decoy plants", may be deleterious. BLACK and DIX (1976) have shown that ferulic acid can stimulate the germination of several fungi even though they may not be able to utilize this substance as a substrate. In fact, the survival of sclerotia of *Sclerotium rolfsii* in soil is reduced when they are stimulated to germinate by volatile substances released by alfalfa hay (LINDERMAN and GILBERT 1969). Also, while cowpea exudates induce the germination of several species of *Fusarium,* the germ tubes and some conidia are lysed by the extracts within 48 h (ODUNFA 1978). A similar effect may help explain the difference in response of cultivars of pea to pathogenic fusaria (WHALLEY and TAYLOR 1976).

Self-Stimulators of Germination

When large inocula support germination better than small, the presence of self-stimulators is suggested, as with the spores of *Aspergillus* spp. studied by TOTH (1973) and those of *Ustilago cynodontis* studied by SHARMA and AGRAWAL (1978). An extreme instance of this kind is that of the arthrospores of *Geotrichum candidum,* the germination of which is stimulated when two or more spores are in contact with one another (ROBINSON 1973). A similar conclusion is suggested by the decrease in germination caused by washing spores of *Botrytis cinerea, Cephalosporium coccorum, Fusarium solani, Mucor racemosus, Trichoderma viride,* and *Verticillium dahliae* (AFIFI 1975b). The latter situation probably illustrates Lockwood's thesis that leaching of nutrients can inhibit germination of many spores (see Sect. 13.4.2.1.1). Reciprocally, the provision of the substance(s) washed away can stimulate the germination of spores previously deprived of nutrients.

Several reports exist of the enhancement of pathogenesis through the use of increased spore density, as in the case of chlamydospores of *Phytophthora palmivora* infecting papaya (RAMIREZ and MITCHELL 1975) and basidiospores of *Cronartium ribicola* infecting pine needles (HANSEN and PATTON 1977). However, it is not known whether this effect is due to self-stimulators of germination or to other phases in the process of infection.

A special case of self-stimulation involves the interaction of two different stages of an organism, such as the increased germination of spores of *Paxillus involutus* and *Leccinum scabrum* caused by factors from their respective mycelia (FRIES 1978). Spores of *Agaricus bisporus* represent a classic case of this kind and iso-valeric and iso-amyl alcohols may be the activators involved (LOSEL 1964). However, it remains to be established whether the parent mycelium is the sole producer of the activating substance or whether, as in the case of *Agaricus bisporus,* other microorganisms can produce the active factor as well.

A germination stimulator produced by spores themselves has been identified as pelargonaldehyde, which activates spores of the wheat stem rust (FRENCH and WEINTRAUB 1958).

References

Afifi AF (1975a) Effect of volatile substances from species of Labiatae on rhizospheric and phyllospheric fungi of *Phaseolus vulgaris*. Phytopathol Z 83:296–302

Afifi AF (1975b) Effect of colchicine on ribose and galactose absorption in relation to spore germination of some fungi. Indian Phytopathol 28:476–478

Afifi AF (1978) Effect of volatile substances released from *Origanum majorana* and *Ocimum basilicum* on the rhizosphere and phyllosphere fungi of *Phaseolus vulgaris*. Folia Microbiol 23:399–405

Ali MI, Salama AM, Tahani MA (1976) possible role of solar function on the viability of some air fungi in Egypt. Zentralbl Bakteriol Parasitenkd Infektionskr Hyg Abt 2 131:529–534

Arthur JC (1929) The plant rusts. Wiley and Sons, New York

Bacon CW, Sussman AS, Paul AG (1973) Identification of a self-inhibitor from spores of *Dictyostelium discoideum*. J Bacteriol 113:1061–1063

Black RLB, Dix NJ (1976) Utilization of ferulic acid by microfungi from litter and soil. Trans Br Mycol Soc 66:313–317

Borut ST (1960) An ecological and physiological study of soil fungi of the northern Negev (Israel). Bull Res Counc Isr Sect D8:65–80

Brian A, Dickinson CH, Goodfellow M (1977) Antagonistic interactions of phylloplane bacteria with *Drechslera dictyoides* (Drechsler) Shoemaker. Can J Microbiol 23:710–715

Byrne P, Gareth Jones EB (1975) Effect of salinity on spore germination of terrestrial and marine fungi. Trans Br Mycol Soc 64:497–504

Cardoso EJBN, Schmitthenner AF (1975) Influence of light on the germination of *Phytophthora cactorum* oospores. Summa Phytopathol 1:23–30

Catska V, Affifi AF, Vancura V (1975) The effect of volatile and gaseous metabolites of swelling seeds on germination of fungal spores. Folia Microbiol 20:152–156

Cole ALJ (1976) Fungal spore germination inhibitors from wheat leaves. Mauri Ora 4:3–7

Comstock JC, Martinson CA (1975) Involvement of *Helminthosporium maydis* race t toxin during colonization of maize leaves. Phytopathology 65:616–61

Cotter DA (1977) The effects of osmotic pressure changes on the germination of *Dictyostelium discoideum* spores. Can J Microbiol 23:1170–1177

Dahlberg KR, Cotter DA (1978) Activators of *Dictyostelium discoideum* spore germination released by bacteria. Microbios Lett 9:139–146

Denyer WBG (1960) Cultural studies of *Flammula alnicola* (Fr.) and *Flammula conissans* (Fr.) Gillet. Can J Bot 38:909–920

Desser H, Broda E (1965) Radiochemical determination of the endogenous and exogenous respiration of bacterial spores. Nature (London) 206:1270–1271

Deverall BJ, Keogh RC, McCleod S (1977) Responses of soybean to infection by, and to germination fluids from, urediniospores of *Phakospora pachyrhizi*. Trans Br Mycol Soc 69:410–416

Doetsch RN, Cook TM (1973) Introduction to bacteria and their ecology. Univ Park Press, Baltimore

Doherty MA, Preece TF (1978) *B. cereus* prevents germination of uredospores of *Puccinia allii* and development of rust disease of leek *Allium porrum* in controlled environments. Physiol Plant Pathol 12:123

Dowding P (1969) The dispersal and survival of spores of fungi causing bluestain in pine. Trans Br Mycol Soc 52:125–137

El-Buni AM, Lichtwardt RW (1976) Spore germination in axenic cultures of *Smittium* spp. (Trichomycetes). Mycologia 68:573–582

Elnaghy MA, Heitefuss R (1976) Permeability changes and production of antifungal compounds in *Phaseolus vulgaris* infected with *Uromyces phaseoli*. I. Role of the spore germination inhibitor. Physiol Plant Pathol 8:253–267

Foudin AS, Macko V (1974) Identification of the self-inhibitor and some germination characteristics of peanut rust uredospores. Phytopathology 64:990–993

French JR, Mannion PD (1976) *Hypoxylon mammatum* ascospore germination and mycelial growth on bark and wood media from young branches of trembling aspen. Can J Bot 54:1438–1442

French RC, Weintraub RL (1958) Pelargonaldehyde as an endogenous germination stimulator of wheat stem rust spores. Arch Biochem Biophys 72:235–237

Fries N (1977) Germination of *Laccaria laccata* spores in vitro. Mycologia 69:848–850

Fries N (1978) Basidiospore germination in some mycorrhiza forming hymenomycetes. Trans Br Mycol Soc 70:319–324

Gareth-Jones EB, Byrne P, Alderman DJ (1971) The response of fungi to salinity. In: Vie et milieu. 3rd Eur Symp Mar Biol Suppl 22:265–280

Garrett SD (1956) Biology of root-infecting fungi. Cambridge Univ Press, London New York

Gassner G, Niemann E (1954) Untersuchungen über die Temperatur- und Lichtabhängigkeit der Sporenkeimung verschiedener *Tilletia*-Arten. Phytopathol Z 21:367–394

Gerhardt P, Murrell WG (1978) Basis and mechanism of spore resistance: a brief preview. In: Chambliss G, Vary JC (eds) Spores Vol VII. Am Soc Microbiol Press, Washington, pp 18–20

Gold RE, Littlefield LJ (1979) Light and scanning electron microscopy of the telial, pycnial and aecial stages of *Melampsora lini*. Can J Bot 57:629–638

Grambow HJ, Riedel S (1977) The effect of morphogenically active factors from host and nonhost plants on the in vitro differentiation of infection structures of *Puccinia graminis* f. sp. *tritici*. Physiol Plant Pathol. 11:213–224

Gregory PH (1961) The microbiology of the atmosphere. Wiley-Interscience, New York

Gregory PH (1966) Dispersal. In: Ainsworth GC, Sussman AS (eds) The fungi Vol II. Academic Press, London New York, pp 709–732

Greuter B, Rast D (1975) Ultrastructure of the dormant *Agaricus bisporus* spore. Can J Bot 53:2096–2101

Gupta SK, Banerjee AB, Achari B (1976) Isolation of ethyl p-methoxycinnamate, the major antifungal principle of *Curcuma zedoaria*. Lloydia 39:218–222

Hansen EM (1976) Twenty-year survival of *Phellinus* (*Poria*) *weirii* in Douglas-fir stumps. Can J For Res 6:123–128

Hansen EM, Patton RF (1977) Factors important in artificial inoculation of *Pinus strobus* with *Cronartium ribicola*. Phytopathology 67:1108–1112

Harper JE, Webster J (1964) An experimental analysis of the coprophilous fungus succession. Trans Br Mycol Soc 47:511–530

Hasan S, Wapshere AJ (1973) The biology of *Puccinia chondrillina,* a potential biological control agent of skeleton weed. Ann Appl Biol 74:325–332

Hashimoto T, Blumenthal HJ (1978) Survival and resistance of *Trichophyton mentagrophytes* arthrospores. Appl Environ Microbiol 35:274–277

Hashimoto Y, Tanaka Y, Yamada T (1976) Spore germination promoter of *Dictyostelium discoideum* excreted by *Aerobacter aerogenes*. J Cell Sci 21:261–271

Hibben CR, Stotzky G (1969) Effects of ozone on the germination of fungus spores. Can J Microbiol 15:1187–1196

Hora FK, Baker R (1974) Abiotic generation of a volatile fungistatic factor in soil by liming. Phytopathology 74:624–629

Hsu SC, Lockwood JL (1969) Mechanisms of inhibition of fungi in agar by Streptomycetes. J Gen Microbiol 57:149–158

Hubalek Z, Rush-Munro FM (1973) A dermatophyte from birds, *Microsporum ripariae* sp. nov. Sabouraudia 11:287–292

Ingold CT (1965) Spore liberation. Oxford Univ Press, London, New York

Ingold CT (1975) Hooker lecture: convergent evolution in aquatic fungi: the tetraradiate spore. Biol J Linn Soc 7:1–25

Kato H, Yamaguchi T, Nishihara N (1977) Seed transmission, pathogenicity and control of ragi blast fungus and susceptibility of ragi to *Pyricularia* spp. from grasses, cereals and mioga. Ann Phytopathol Soc Jpn 43:392–401

Kenneth R, Muttath TI, Gerson U (1979) *Hirsutella thompsonii,* a fungal pathogen of mites. I. Biology of the fungus in vitro. Appl Biol 91:21–28

Keynan A, Evenchik Z (1969) Activation. In: Gould GW, Hurst A (eds) The bacterial spore. Academic Press, London New York, pp 359–396

Kirillova IP, Agre NS, Kalakutskii LV (1975) Temperature regimes of the formation and germination of *Thermoactinomyces vulgaris* endospores. Jzv Acad Nauk SSSR Ser Biol 6:910–913

Knaysi G (1948) The endospore of Bacteria. Bacteriol Rev 12:19–77

Kollmorgen JF, Jones LC (1975) The effects of soil-borne micro-organisms on the germination of chlamydospores of *Tilletia caries* and *T. foetida.* Soil Biol Biochem 7:407–410

LaChance MA, Miranda M, Miller MW, Phaff HJ (1976) Dehiscence and active spore release in pathogenic strains of the yeast *Metschnikowia bicuspidata* var. *australis:* possible predatory implications. Can J Microbiol 22:1756–1761

Lamanna C (1952) Biological role of spores. In: Symposium on the biology of bacterial spores. Bacteriol Rev 16:90–93

Lim TM (1977) Production, germination and dispersal of basidiospores of *Ganoderma pseudoferreum* on *Hevea.* J Rubber Res Inst Malays 25:93–100

Linderman RG, Gilbert RG (1969) Stimulation of *Sclerotium rolfsii* in soil by volatile components of alfalfa hay. Phytopathology 59:1366–1372

Lockwood JL (1977) Fungistasis in soils. Biol Rev Cambridge Philos Soc 52:1–43

Losel DM (1964) Stimulation of spore germination in organisms by living mycelium. Ann Bot (London) 28:541–554

Lucas CE (1947) The ecological effects of external metabolites. Biol Rev Cambridge Philos Soc 22:270–295

Lucas JA, Kendrick RE, Givan C (1975) Photocontrol of fungal spore germination. Plant Physiol 56:847–849

Macko V, Staples RC, Gershon H, Renwick JAA (1970) Self-inhibitor of bean rust uredospores: methyl 3,4-dimethoxycinnamate. Science 170:539–540

Macko V, Staples RC, Allen PJ, Renwick JAA (1971) Identification of the germination self-inhibitor from wheat stem rust uredospores. Science 173:835–836

Macko V, Staples RC, Renwick JAA, Pirone J (1972) Germination self-inhibitors of rust uredospores. Physiol Plant Pathol 2:347–355

Macko V, Staples RC, Yaniv Z, Granados RR (1976) Self inhibitors of fungal spore germination. In: Weber DJ, Hess WM (eds) The fungal spore: form and function. Wiley-Interscience, New York, pp 73–98

Macko V, Trione EJ, Young SA (1977) Identification of the germination self-inhibitor from uredospores of *Puccinia striiformis.* Phytopathology 67:1473–1474

Macko V, Renwick JAA, Rissler JF (1978) Acrolein induces differentiation of infection structures in the wheat stem rust fungus. Science 199:442–443

Maheshwari R, Sussman AS (1970) The nature of cold-induced dormancy in uredospores of *Puccinia graminis tritici.* Plant Physiol 47:289–295

Marx DH (1976) Synthesis of ectomycorrhizae on loblolly pine seedlings with basidiospores of *Pisolithus tinctorius.* For Sci 22:13–20

Maser C, Trappe JM, Nussbaum RA (1978) Fungal-small mammal interrelationships with emphasis on Oregon coniferous forests. Ecology 59:799–809

Mineo K, Uritani I (1976) Possible involvement of furanoterpenoid phytoalexins in establishing host-parasite specificity between sweet potato and various strains of *Ceratocystis fimbriata.* Physiol Plant Pathol 8:97–111

Mineo K, Uritani I (1978) Isolation and characterization of factors in sweet potato root which agglutinate germinated spores of *Ceratocystis fimbriata,* black rot fungus. Plant Physiol 62:751–753

Mishra RR, Pandey KK (1978) Studies on soil fungistasis: effect of certain physical and biological factors. Plant Soil 49:355–366

Mishustin EN (1956) The law of zonality and the study of microbial associations of the soil. Soils Fert 19:385–390

Mitchell DJ (1975) Density of *Pythium myriotylum* oospores in soil in relation to infection of rye. Phytopathology 65:570–575

Murrell WG (1967) Biochemistry of the bacterial endospore. In: Rose AH, Wilkinson JF (eds) Advances in microbial physiology Vol I. Academic Press, London New York, pp 133–251

Naik DM, Busch LV (1978) Stimulation of *Fusarium graminearum* by maize pollen. Can J Bot 56:1113–1117

Nickerson KW, Freer SN, van Etten JL (1981) *Rhizopus stolonifer* sporangiospores: a wet-harvested spore is not a native spore (unpublished)

Nicot J (1960) Some characteristics of the microflora of desert sands. In: Parkinson D, Waid JS (eds) The ecology of soil fungi. Univ Press, Liverpool, pp 94–99

Niel van CB (1975) Natural selection in the microbial world. The second Marjory Stephenson memorial lecture. J Gen Microbiol 13:201–217

Nomura T, Tanaka Y, Abe H, Uchiyama M (1977) Cytokinin activity of discadenine: a spore germination inhibitor of *Dictyostelium discoideum*. Phytochemistry 16:1819–1820

Odunfa VSA (1978) Root exudation in cowpea and sorghum and the effect on spore germination and growth of some soil fusaria. New Phytol 80:607–612

Okazaki H (1976) Stimulation of chlamydospore germination of *Fusarium oxysporum* f. sp. Raphani by volatile metabolites produced by mycelium. Ann Phytopathol Soc Jpn 42:442–449

Oort AJP (1974) Activation of spore germination in *Lactarius* species by volatile compounds of *Ceratocystis fagacearum*. Proc K Ned Akad Wet Ser C 77:301–307

Orekhov DA (1974) Interrelation between butt-rot fungus *Fomitopsis annosa* (Fr.) Karst and bacteria of the rhizosphere of trees. Mikol Fitopatol 8:245–249

Otani H, Nishimura S, Kohmoto K, Yano K, Seno T (1975) Nature of specific susceptibility to *Alternaria kikuchiana* in Nijisseiki cultivar among Japanese pears: V. Ann Phytopathol Soc Jpn 4:467–476

Ouellette GB, Pirozynski KA (1974) Reassessment of *Tympanis* based on types of ascospore germination within asci. Can J Bot 52:1889–1912

Parbery DG, Emmett RW (1977) Hypotheses regarding appressoria, spores, survival and phylogeny in parasitic fungi. Rev Mycol 41:429–448

Plotnikova Yu M, Andreev LN, Serez GV, Zaitseva LG (1977) Conditions of the formation of infectious structures of *Puccinia graminis tritici* in vitro. Izv Akad Nauk SSSR Ser Biol 1:90–94 (in Russian)

Pugh GJF (1971) Factors which influence the early colonization of organic matter by fungi. In: Organismes du sol et production primaire. IVth Int Colloq Soil Zool Paris, pp 319–327

Pugh GJF (1972) The contamination of bird's feathers by fungi. Ibis 114:172–177

Pugh GJF, Evans MD (1970) Keratinophilic fungi associated with birds. II Physiological studies. Trans Br Mycol Soc 54:241–250

Ramirez BN, Mitchell DJ (1975) Relationship of density of chlamydospores and zoospores of *Phytophthora palmivora* in soil to infection of papaya. Phytopathology 65:780–785

Ranzoni FV (1968) Fungi isolated in culture from soils of the Sonoran desert. Mycologia 60:356–371

Rast D, Hollenstein GO (1977) Architecture of the *Agaricus bisporus* spore wall. Can J Bot 55:2251–1162

Rast D, Stussi H, Zobrist P (1979) Self-inhibition of the *Agaricus bisporus* spore by CO_2 and/or γ-glutaminyl-4-hydroxybenzene and γ-glutaminyl-3,4-benzoquinone: a biochemical analysis. Physiol Plant 46:227–234

Robinson PM (1973) Chemotropism in fungi. Trans Br Mycol Soc 61:303–313

Rodrigues CJ Jr, Meideiros EF, Lewis BG (1975) Relationship between a phytoalexin-like response in coffee leaves (*Coffea arabica*) and compatibility with *Hemileia vastatrix*. Berk et Br Physiol Plant Pathol 6:35–42

Romine M, Baker R (1973) Soil fungistasis: evidence for an inhibitory factor. Phytopathology 63:756–759

Rosenzweig WD, Stotzky G (1979) Influence of environmental factors on antagonism of fungi by bacteria in soil: clay minerals and pH. Appl Environ Microbiol 38:1120–1126

Salvatore MA, Gray FA, Hine RB (1973) Enzymatically induced germination of oospores of *Phytophthora megasperma*. Phytopathology 63:1083–1084

Schauz K (1977) The role of light quantity and quality in spore germination and spordial production of the dwarf bunt of wheat, *Tilletia controversa* Kuehn. Phytopathol Z 89:134–145 (in German)

Schneider HA (1967) Ecological ectocrines in experimental epidemiology. Science 158:597–603

Sharma KD, Agrawal DK (1978) Cultural studies on *Ustilago cynodontis* (Pers) P. Henn. Indian J Microbiol 18:66

Shirata A (1978) Production of phytoalexin in cortex tissue of mulberry shoot. Ann Phytopathol Soc Jpn 44:485–492

Shirata A, Takahashi K, Takasugi M, Nagao S, Masamune R (1978) Antifungal and antibacterial activities of phytoalexins, moracin A and B, isolated from mulberry. Bull Seric Exp Stn (Tokyo) 27:647–660

Siala A, Gray TRG (1974) Growth of *Bacillus subtilis* and spore germination in soil observed by a fluorescent antibody technique. J Gen Microbiol 81:191–198

Simpson ME, Marsh PB, Filsinger EC (1973) Geographical localization of infections of cotton bolls with *Colletotrichum gossypii*. Plant Dis Rep 57:828–832

Smith Shirley N (1977) Comparison of germination of pathogenic *Fusarium oxysporum* chlamydospores in host rhizosphere soils conducive and suppressive to wilts. Phytopathology 67:502–510

Soper CJ, Whistler JM, Davies DJG (1976) The response of bacterial spores to vacuum treatments: II. Germination and viability studies. Cryobiology 13:71–79

Staples RC, Macko V (1980) Formation of infection structures as a recognition response in fungi. Exp Mycol 4:2–16

Sussman AS (1965) Physiology of dormancy and germination in the propagules of cryptogamic plants. In: Ruhland W (ed) Encyclopedia of plant physiology Vol XV/2, Springer, Berlin Göttingen Heidelberg, pp 933–1025

Sussman AS (1968) Longevity and survivability of fungi In: Ainsworth GC, Sussman AS (eds) The fungi Vol III. Academic Press, London New York, pp 447–486

Sussman AS (1976) Activators of fungal spore germination. In: Weber DJ, Hess WM (eds) The fungal spore: form and function. Wiley-Interscience New York, pp 101–137

Sussman AS, Douthit HA (1973) Dormancy in microbial spores Annu Rev Plant Physiol 24:311–352

Sussman AS, Halvorson HO (1966) Spores: their dormancy and germination. Harper and Row, New York

Sussman AS, Lowry RJ, Tyrrell E (1959) Activation of *Neurospora* ascospores by organic solvents and furans. Mycologia 51:237–247

Tanaka Y, Yanagisawa K, Hashimoto Y, Yamaguchi M (1974) True spore germination inhibitor of a cellular slime mold *Dictyostelium discoideum*. Agric Biol Chem 38:689–690

Theodorov C, Bowen GD (1973) Inoculation of seeds and soil with basidiospores of mycorrhizal fungi. Soil Biol Biochem 5:765–771

Toth JA (1973) The influence of spore number per surface unit on the course of germination in some *Aspergillus* species on solid medium. Acta Bot Acad Sci Hung 18:385–389

Uchiyama M, Abe H (1977) A synthesis of ($\pm$)-discadenine. Agric Biol Chem 41:1549–1552

Vary JC (1979) Bacterial spore germination. Spore Newsl 6:191

Verma PR, Petrie GA (1975) Germination of oospores of *Albugo candida*. Can J Bot 53:836–842

Walmsley-Woodward D, Lewis BG, Akerman AM (1975) Behaviour of *Phytophthora infestans* (Mont.) de Bary on potato tubers in relation to lenticel resistance. Physiol Plant Pathol 7:293–302

Warcup JH (1957) Chemical and biological aspects of soil sterilization. Soils Fert 20:1–5

Wearing AH, Burgess LW (1977) Distribution of *Fusarium roseum* "Graminearum" group 1, and its mode of survival in eastern Australian wheat belt soils. Trans Br Mycol Soc 69(3):429–442

Webster J, Sanders PF, Descals E (1978) Tetraradiate aquatic propagules in two species
    of *Entomophthora*. Trans Br Mycol Soc 70:472–479
Whalley WM, Taylor GS (1976) Germination of chlamydospores of physiologic races
    of *Fusarium oxysporum* f. sp. *Pisi* in soil adjacent to susceptible and resistant pea
    cultivars.Trans Br Mycol Soc 66:7–13
Wicklow DT, Zak JC (1979) Ascospore germination of carbonicolous ascomycetes in fungi-
    static soils: an ecological interpretation. Mycologia 71:238–242
Wood FA, French DW (1965) Microorganisms associated with *Hypoxylon pruinatum*. Myco-
    logia 57:766–775
Zemlyanukhin AA, Chebotarev LN (1973) Effect of visible light on the germination of
    mold spores. Biol Nauki 16:57–60 (in Russian)

14 Physiological Responses to Flooding

R.M.M. CRAWFORD

CONTENTS

14.1 Introduction

Flooding denotes an environmental transformation which is of limited but uncertain duration. Plants that are absent from flood-prone sites will include species that are directly injured by inundation of their roots, as well as species which remain physiologically viable but become inefficient competitors under these conditions. On the other hand, plants that inhabit flood-prone sites will include species that can grow actively in flooded soils, as well as other species that survive flooding in a quiescent or dormant condition. The adverse effects of flooding on unadapted species will therefore be discussed separately from the various reactions of flood-tolerant plants, as tolerance and intolerance of flooding does not necessarily depend on positive and negative aspects of the same phenomenon.

Despite the extensive research that has been carried out on flooding injury on agricultural crops (SCOTT RUSSELL 1977; CANNELL 1977), it is still difficult to make any generalizations on the initial causes of flooding damage to un-

adapted plants. In flood-tolerant species a certain degree of rationalization is possible (Hook and Crawford 1978), provided the type of flooding is defined. Whether or not the flood-water is moving, stationary, nutrient-rich, nutrient-poor of short or long duration has important implications for the survival strategy of the adapted plants.

The adaptations found in flood-tolerant plants do not include those of the truly aquatic species. Aquatic species do not suffer the stress of a sudden removal of oxygen from the soil atmosphere. In aquatic plants the greater part of the plant is in contact with a large body of free water and the problems of oxygen deficiency and toxin accumulation are largely avoided. By contrast, in the terrestrial plant adapted to withstand flooding, the amphibious nature of its existence creates problems both for the supply of oxygen and the removal of toxins produced either internally in the plant or externally due to the reducing conditions in the soil.

14.2 Flooding Injury

14.2.1 Symptoms

When examining the symptoms of flooding damage to plants it is often difficult to distinguish between the immediate and original causes of injury. Paradoxically, the commonest sign of the roots having an excess of water is the development of a water deficit in the leaves (Kramer 1951; Kramer and Jackson 1954). The wilting and defoliation that is found on flooding can be traced to an increased resistance to water flux in the roots (Mees and Weatherley 1957). Roots of intact tobacco plants that were sealed in a chamber where they received their nutrients in a spray began to reduce their water uptake within 6 min of starting to flush the root chamber with nitrogen (Willey 1970). The reduction in leaf water potential on flooding is not confined to flood-intolerant plants. Flooding of *Alnus glutinosa* also reduces leaf water potential, which is not lessened by the possession of adventitious roots (Gill 1975). Reduction in root aeration can reduce or cause imbalance in ion absorption (Lee 1977). Symptoms of mineral deficiency, in particular nitrogen, are a common symptom of flooding injury (Kramer 1969; Lee 1978). In barley nitrate level in the shoot is reduced to one third of that in the controls within 48 h of flooding. The shoot, however, still continues to grow and chlorosis rapidly develops in the lower leaves as nitrogen is translocated to the growing regions (Drew and Sisworo 1979). Other symptoms of flooding damage include epinasty (Jackson 1955) and alterations in tropic responses irrespective of whether or not the plants are injured by flooding (Kordan 1975; Bendixen and Peterson 1962).

In flood-sensitive species, root and shoot growth are usually rapidly reduced on flooding (Jackson 1979) and in particular the root tip may be damaged so that when aeration is restored, growth can be renewed only from the regions proximal to the stem (Morisset 1978). However, growth alone is not a reliable

indicator of the ability of a plant to survive flooding. Many well-adapted species reduce their growth when flooded and resume normal growth rates only when the water table has subsided below the main rooting zone (CRAWFORD 1972). Some wetland species even show improved growth when the water table is lowered. The growth of *Narthecium ossifragum* is increased when the drainage is improved (MILES 1976), as is also that of *Empetrum nigrum* (BELL and TALLIS 1974). In the swamp trees *Taxodium distichum* and *Nyssa sylvatica* growth is better in saturated soils that dry out between successive waterings (DICKSON and BROYER 1972).

14.2.2 Survival Time

No higher plant can endure prolonged anoxia. Even rice is unable to extend more than the coleoptile and the first seminal roots in the absence of oxygen (VARTAPETIAN et al. 1978). Much of the observed variation that is found in the relative endurance of higher plants to flooding can be accounted for in the varying time that it takes to kill different species by flooding. Sudden death due to flooding is normally observed only in species of well-drained habitats where inundation is a rare event, e.g., *Centaurium erythrea, Geranium molle* and *Luzula campestris* (CRAWFORD 1966). The most intolerant of all plants to flooding are those that contain cyanogenic glycosides. The stem and root bark of apricot, plum and peach trees is rich in cyanogenic glycosides and these species can be killed by as little as 24 h flooding due to anaerobic hydrolysis yielding free hydrogen cyanide (ROWE and BEARDSELL 1973). In warm greenhouse conditions reduction in yield in peas and tomatoes of up to 43% and 50% respectively can be caused by as little as 24 h flooding (ERICKSON and van DOREN 1960).

The most reliable data for the length of time that plants can survive flooding is found with trees. When water reservoirs have been completed without the trees being felled it is possible to collect accurate data on their growth and survival (GILL 1970). Table 14.1 lists the flooding survival time for a number of flood-tolerant trees. For most species the length of the flooding period is only critical if it occurs during the growing season. The tulip tree (*Liriodendron tulipifera*) can withstand prolonged flooding in the dormant season but will die after 4 days flooding in June (McALPINE 1961). This seasonal aspect of flooding tolerance has been documented for over 2,000 years. CATO (234–149 B.C.) in his work *De Re Rustica* stressed the need to avoid spring and autumn flooding of winter cereal crops.

If the water table is lowered for short periods, the length of time in which flooding can be endured is much lengthened. All-year-round flooding can be tolerated by some trees provided it happens only in isolated years (GILL 1970). In general even the most flood-tolerant of trees need to be unflooded for at least 55%–60% of the growing season. Once a habitat is flooded for more than 40% of the growing season it cannot be colonized by woody species although established trees may survive for a whole season. The upper limit of flooding tolerance in woody species appears to be related to the need to

Table 14.5. Percent air space in roots of various wet-land species of higher plants determined by weighing intact and disintegrated roots in pycnometer bottles. (Unpublished data of Crawford and Smirnoff). Mean values based on observations on whole root system unless otherwise stated

Species	Percentage air space $\pm$ S.E.
Nardus stricta (primary root)	45 ± 1.2
Eriophorum angustifolium	42 ± 1.9
Glyceria maxima (primary root)	35 ± 0.3
Eriophorum vaginatum	31 ± 1.8
Trichophorum caespitosum	26 ± 3.1
Juncus effusus	25 ± 3.5
Spartina townsendii	22 ± 1.4
Narthecium ossifragum (primary root)	19 ± 1.5
Deschampsia caespitosa	19 ± 2.7
Ranunculus lingua (primary root)	19 ± 0.4
Ranunculus lingua (lateral root)	12 ± 1.7
Lythrum salicaria	12 ± 1.8
Glyceria maxima (lateral root)	11 ± 0.8
Potentilla palustris	10
Nardus stricta	8 ± 2.0
Mentha aquatica	7 ± 0.6
Phalaris arundinacea	6 ± 0.6
Myosotis scorpioides	4.9 ± 0.7
Narthecium ossifragum (lateral root)	3.3 ± 1.4
Filipendula ulmaria	2.0 ± 0.5

tion (Table 14.5). Table 14.6 records the root porosity of a number of species from wet-land plants together with the oxygen reservoir capacity of the root air space. Two facts emerge. The first is that the oxygen reservoir capacity of root air spaces is extremely low. The high figure for *Eriophorum angustifolium* agrees with the findings of Armstrong (1975) in that the internal oxygen content will not support aerobic respiration for more than 2 h unless renewed. The second fact is that wet-land species differ greatly in the air space content of their roots. In *Filipendula ulmaria* the root air space is only 2%. There would appear, therefore, to be two classes of roots in wet-land species;

1. those which possess a degree of ventilation which allows oxygen to diffuse a certain distance below the water table; and

2. those roots where there is no evidence of any specialized ventilation system.

In the first group, the plants with specialized ventilation mechanisms, the monocots are predominant. The possession of an adventitious root system also aids ventilation. Furthermore, as adventitious roots are renewed annually it is not necessary for them to survive the prolonged period of anaerobiosis that inevitably arises during winter when the shoots die down and the water table rises. Adventitious root systems are also found in trees tolerant of flooding such as willow, where lenticel development is also well marked in the lower

Table 14.6. The capacity of root air space to serve as an oxygen reservoir calculated on the length of time that the air volume of the root could maintain full activity of aerobic dark respiration at 18 °C without replenishment (CRAWFORD and SMIRNOFF unpublished data) assuming that the oxygen content of the root atmosphere is 20%

Species	Oxygen reservoir capacity (min)	Oxygen consumption $\mu l O_2$ mg^{-1} dry wt. h^{-1}	Air space in ml g^{-1} dry wt.
Eriophorum vaginatum	126	0.362	3.81
Eriophorum angustifolium	102	0.781	6.62
Trichophorum caespitosum	67	0.168	0.94
Glyceria maxima	37	0.520	1.61
Ranunculus lingua	32	0.670	1.76
Juncus effusus	34	0.645	1.84
Carex curta	22	0.633	1.15
Lythrum salicaria	22	0.515	0.94
Narthecium ossifragum	14	0.388	0.46
Mentha aquatica	13	0.650	0.71
Lycopus europaeus	12	0.755	0.76
Potentilla palustris	9	0.520	0.39
Filipendula ulmaria	2	0.375	0.07

regions of the trunk and assists both the downward diffusion of oxygen and the upward movement of toxic substances such as ethanol and acetaldehyde (CHIRKOVA and GUTMAN 1972).

Apart from the cases where anatomical modifications assist root ventilation there are many cases where no such provision is found and the plant tissues are able to survive prolonged periods in an anaerobic environment. It would appear that here metabolic adaptation rather than ventilation is necessary for survival. The deeper anchoring roots of trees as well as the roots and perennating organs of most helophytes have frequently to endure hypoxia in winter and early spring, although the hazards of anaerobiosis will be reduced during dormant periods. In addition, there are striking examples from the flood-plain forests of the tropics where roots are able to endure prolonged periods of flooding and where there is no evidence of root ventilation. The flood-plain forest of the upper Amazon has to endure flooding to a depth of 8–10 m for periods that can be as long as 6 months (GESSNER 1968), and there is no evidence that in the still waters of the lagoons (Igapo) away from river currents there is any ventilation of the tree roots.

14.3.2 Adaptive Metabolic Responses to Anoxia

14.3.2.1 Aerobic Metabolic Rate

The demands on the root ventilation system can be reduced by lowering the metabolic rate after the roots have been flooded. When the roots of *Senecio aquaticus* are grown in a solution of low oxygen tension their anaerobic respiration rate is reduced by over 50% (LAMBERS et al. 1978). It must be noted,

Table 14.7. Substances reported to accumulate under anaerobic conditions in higher plants and animals. (References are intended only as a source of further information and do not indicate priority of discovery or complete range of occurrence)

Substance	Animal occurrence	Plant occurrence
Lactic acid	Vertebrate skeletal muscle[1]	Germinating seeds[2], tubers[3]
Pyruvic acid	Vertebrate skeletal muscle[1]	Willow roots[4]
Formic acid	Parasitic helminths[5]	–
Acetic acid	Bivalve molluscs, cestodes[6]	–
Acetoin	Nematodes[5]	–
Propionic acid	Molluscs, cestodes[5]	–
Butyric acid	Parasitic protozoa[5]	–
Succinic acid	Bivalve molluscs[6]	Seeds[2]
Malic acid	–	Roots of marsh plants[8, 9]
Shikimic acid	–	Iris and water lily roots[10]
Glycolic acid	–	Willow roots[4]
Ethanol	Parasitic protozoa[5], helminths[5]	Flood-intolerant roots and seeds[10]
Sorbitol	Insects[16]	–
Glycerol	Insects[16]	Alder roots[10]
Alanine	Sea turtles[7], molluscs[19]	Flood-tolerant roots[4]
Aspartic acid	Marine annelids[11]	Flood-tolerant roots[4]
Glutamic acid	Marine annelids[11]	Flood-tolerant roots[4]
Serine	–	Flood-tolerant roots[4]
Proline	–	Flood-tolerant roots[4]
Octopine	Cephalopods[12]	Crown-gall tissues[13]
γ-amino butyric acid	–	Tomato roots[14] and radish leaves[17]
Methyl butyrate	Parasitic nematodes[15]	–
Methyl valerate	Parasitic nematodes[15]	–
Glycerophosphate	Insects[16]	–
Hydrogen	Parasitic protozoa[5]	–
Ethylene	–	Roots and fruits[18]

References: 1 Hochachka and Storey 1975; 2 Wager 1961; 3 Davies et al. 1974; 4 Dubinina 1961; 5 von Brand 1966; 6 Gäde et al. 1975; 7 Hochachka et al. 1975; 8 Crawford and Tyler 1969; 9 Linhart and Baker 1973; 10 Crawford 1972; 11 Zebe 1975; 12 Hochachka et al. 1977; 13 Menage and Morel 1964; 14 Fulton et al. 1964; 15 Bryant 1971; 16 Gilmour 1965; 17 Streeter and Thompson 1972; 18 Pratt and Goeschl 1969; 19 de Zwaan and Wijsman 1976

the studies on ethanol accumulation (see Sect. 14.3.2.2) quantification of the importance of these substances is lacking in many of these studies due to the problems of movement up or out of the hypoxic root. One of the best-studied end-products of glycolysis is lactate, which serves to accumulate the oxygen debt in potato tubers and *Equisetum* rhizomes (James 1953), as well as for a brief period during the germination of seeds (Sherwin and Simon 1969). The extent to which pyruvate is able to serve as a proton acceptor during anaerobiosis (forming lactate) appears to be strictly limited. Davies (1973) has suggested that there is a switch to ethanol production from lactate as the pH of the cytoplasm drops. This is questioned by Smith and ap Rees (1979b) who found that lactate production ceased very quickly under total anoxia before any pH change was likely to have taken place.

MAZELIS and VENNESLAND (1957) suggested, on grounds of enzymatic equilibria that malic acid should serve as an end-product of glycolysis in plants. Under totally anoxic conditions and following the path of C^{14} from radioactive sucrose (U^{14}) SMITH and AP REES (1979b) were unable to detect any production of malate by the excised root apices of a number of flood-tolerant species. The only evidence that malic acid may play a role comes from an examination of the pool-size of this metabolite in the roots of plants that have been grown under flooded and unflooded conditions for periods varying from a few days to 1 month. In a study of a number of herbaceous species it was found that malate increased in concentration in the flood-tolerant species and fell in the intolerant (CRAWFORD and TYLER 1969). This interspecific difference was also shown to operate at a provenance level in a study of 20 populations of *Veronica peregrina*. Populations that came from a pond centre where they grew under flooded conditions increased their malic acid content when flooded. No regularity of behaviour could be found in plants taken from sites only a short distance away in the drier ground at the edge of the pond (LINHART and BAKER 1973). These studies, however, give no quantitative evidence as to how much of the presumed oxygen debt is accumulated by malic acid. KEELEY (1978) in a critical examination of the respective roles of ethanol and malate in accumulating a possible oxygen debt in the submerged roots of the swamp tupelo tree (*Nyssa sylvatica* var. *biflora*) showed that in the first month of flooding ethanol fermentation rates accelerate rapidly then fall to a low level after a year of inundation. Malic acid, on the other hand, reaches a peak later than ethanol and remains at this level to the end of the year's flooding observations. It is, therefore, suggested that as malic acid has a different time course in its accumulation, it does not serve as an alternative to ethanol in servicing the oxygen debt. It must be noted, however, that after 1 month's flooding, both ethanol and malate were higher than at the beginning of the experiment. As malic acid is a strong acid (stronger than lactic) its continued production requires a certain degree of translocation as well as electrical balancing with cation uptake and that it only accumulates when the degree of hypoxia is lessened by anatomical modification of the root.

In chick pea seeds (*Cicer arietinum*) malic and lactic acid and ethanol all increase during the typical period of hypoxia that occurs in the early stages of germination (ALDASORO and NICOLAS 1980). The maximum concentrations were reached for all three metabolites simultaneously 24 h after the beginning of the germination period. The concentration of malic acid increased one half as much that of ethanol. The peak in malic acid accumulation was matched by maximal activities for dark fixation of carbon dioxide and PEP carboxylase.

Thus in investigations in which intact plants are used, as when whole root systems still attached to the shoot are flooded, or in the course of germination of seeds, there are cases where malic acid accumulates and appears to match the role of ethanol in representing the anaerobic oxygen debt. It must be noted that malic acid accumulation under anoxia has not been observed in detached roots (SMITH and AP REES 1979b) and some doubt therefore remains in assessing its role in anaerobiosis.

the effects of waterlogging, nitrogen deficiency and root excision. New Phytol 82:315–329

Dubinina IM (1961) Metabolism of roots under various levels of aeration. Fiziol Rast 8:395–406

El-Beltagy AS, Hall MA (1974) Effect of water stress upon endogenous ethylene levels in *Vicia faba*. New Phytol 73:47–60

Erickson AE, Doren van DM (1960) The relation between plant growth and yield to oxygen availability. Proc 7th Int Congr Wis IV 54:429–434

Fewson CA, Nicholas DJD (1961) Utilization of nitrate by microorganisms. Nature (London) 190:2–7

Francis CM, Devitt AC, Steele P (1974) Influence of flooding on the alcohol dehydrogenase activity of roots of *Trifolium subterraneum* L. Aust J Plant Physiol 1:9–13

Fulton JM, Erickson AE, Tolbert NE (1964) Distribution of C^{14} among metabolites of flooded aerobically grown tomato plants. Agron J 56:527–529

Gäde G, Wilps H, Kluytmans JH, Zwaan DE A (1975) Glycogen degradation and end products of anaerobic metabolism in the fresh water bivalve *Anodonta cygnea*. J Comp Physiol 104:79–85

Garcia Nova F, Crawford RMM (1973) Soil aeration, nitrate reduction and flooding tolerance in higher plants. New Phytol 72:1031–1039

Gembrell RP, Patrick Jr WH (1978) Chemical and microbiological properties of anaerobic soils and sediments. In: Hook DD, Crawford RMM (eds) Plant life in anaerobic environments. Ann Arbor, Michigan, pp 375–423

Gessner F (1968) Zur ökologischen Problematik der Überschwemmungswälder des Amazonas. Int Rev Gesamten Hydrobiol 53:525–547

Gill CJ (1970) The flooding tolerance of woody species – a review. For Abstr 31:671–688

Gill CJ (1975) The ecological significance of adventitious rooting as a response to flooding in woody species with special reference to *Alnus glutinosa* (L.) Gaertn. Flora 164:85–97

Gilmour D (1965) The metabolism of insects. Oliver and Boyd, Edinburgh

Girton RE (1979) Effects of oxygen concentration on the respiration of excised root tip segments of maize and rice and of germinating grains of rice and buckwheat. Physiol Plant 46:58–62

Green MS, Etherington JR (1977) Oxidation of ferrous iron by rice (*Oryza sativa* L.) roots: a mechanism for waterlogging tolerance. J Exp Bot 28:678–690

Greenwood DJ (1968) Effect of oxygen distribution in the soil on plant growth. Proc 15th Easter Sch Agric Sci Univ Nottingham, pp 202–221

Hall TF, Penfound WT, Hess AD (1946) Water level relationships of plants in the Tennessee valley with particular reference to malaria control. J Tenn Acad Sci 21:18–59

Hayaishi O (1962) Biological oxidations. Annu Rev Biochem 31:25–46

Healy MT, Armstrong W (1972) The effectiveness of internal oxygen transport in a mesophyte (*Pisum sativum* L.). Planta 103:302–309

Hochachka PW, Storey KB (1975) Metabolic consequence of diving in animals and man. Science 613–621

Hochachka PW, Owen TG, Allen JF, Whittow GG (1975) Multiple end-products of anaerobic metabolism in diving vertebrates. Comp Biochem Physiol 50B:17

Hochachka PW, Hartline PH, Fields HHA (1977) Octopine as an end-product in the chambered Nautilus. Science 195:72–74

Hook DD, Crawford RMM (eds) (1978) Plant life in anaerobic environments. Ann Arbor, Michigan

Hook DD, Scholtens JR (1978) Adaptation and flood tolerance in trees. In: Hook DD, Crawford RMM (eds) Plant life in anaerobic environments. Ann Arbor, Michigan, pp 299–331

Horvarth RS (1974) Evolution of anaerobic energy-yielding pathways of the procaryote. J Theor Biol 47:361–371

Howeler RH (1973) Iron induced oranging disease of rice in relation to physicochemical changes in a flooded oxisol. Soil Sci Soc Am Proc 37:898–903

Int Rice Inst Annu Rep (1973) Los Banos, Laguna, Philippines, pp 100–104

Itai C, Vaadia Y (1965) Kinetin-like activity in root exudates of water-stressed sunflower plants. Physiol Plant 18:941–944

Jackson MB (1979) Rapid injury to peas by soil waterlogging. J Sci Food Agric 30:143–152

Jackson MB, Campbell DJ (1975a) Movement of ethylene from roots to shoots, a factor in the reponses of tomato plants to waterlogged soil conditions. New Phytol 74:397–406

Jackson MB, Campbell DJ (1975b) Ethylene and waterlogging effects in tomato. Ann Appl Biol 81:102–105

Jackson MB, Campbell DJ (1975c) Hormones and the responses of plants to waterlogged soil. Rep Agric Res Counc Letcombe Lab 1974:45–48

Jackson MB, Campbell DJ (1979) Effects of benzyladenine and gibberellic acid on the responses of tomato plants to anaerobic root environments and to ethylene. New Phytol 82:331–340

Jackson MB, Gales K, Campbell JD (1978) Effects of waterlogged soil conditions on the production of ethylene and on water relationships in tomato plants. J Exp Bot 29:183–193

Jackson WT (1955) The role of adventitious roots in recovery of shoots following flooding of the original root system. Am J Bot 42:816–819

Jaffre T, Heim R (1977) Accumulation du manganese par des éspèces associées aux terrain ultrabasiques de Nouvelle Caledonie. CR Acad Sci 284:1573–1575

James WO (1973) Plant respiration. Clarendon Press, Oxford

John CD, Greenway H (1976) Alcoholic fermentation and activity of some enzymes in rice roots under anaerobiosis. Aust J Plant Physiol 3:167–178

John CD, Limpinuntana V, Greenway H (1974) Adaptation of rice to anaerobiosis. Aust J Plant Physiol 1:513–520

Jones RL, Phillips IDJ (1966) Organs of gibberellin synthesis in light grown sunflower plants. Plant Physiol 41:1381–1386

Kandler O (1950) Untersuchungen über den Zusammenhang zwischen Atmungsstoffwechsel und Wachstumsvorgängen bei in vitro kultivierten Maiswurzeln. Z Naturforsch 5:203–211

Kawase M (1974) The role of ethylene in induction of flooding damage in sunflower. Physiol Plant 31:29–38

Keeley JE (1978) Malic acid accumulation in roots in response to flooding: evidence contrary to its role as an alternative to ethanol. J Exp Bot 29:1345–1349

Keeley JE (1979) Population differentiation along a flood frequency gradient: physiological adaptation to flooding in Nyssa sylvatica. Ecol Monogr 49:89–108

Kordan HA (1975) Oxygen and the establishment of normal shoot geotropism in germinating rice seedlings. Phytomorphology 25:201–205

Kramer PJ (1951) Causes of injury to plants from flooding of the soil. Plant Physiol 26:722–736

Kramer PJ (1969) Plant and soil water relationships. McGraw-Hill, New York

Kramer PJ, Jackson WT (1954) Causes of injury to flooded tobacco plants. Plant Physiol 29:241–245

Lambers H (1976) Respiration and NADH oxidation of the roots of flood-tolerant and flood-intolerant Senecio species as affected by anaerobiosis. Physiol Plant 37:117–122

Lambers H, Smakman G (1978) Respiration of the roots of flood-tolerant and flood-intolerant Senecio species: affinity for oxygen and resistance to cyanide. Physiol Plant 42:163–166

Lambers H, Steingrover E, Smakman G (1978) The significance of oxygen transport and of metabolic adaptation in flood-tolerance of Senecio species. Physiol Plant 43:277–281

Lee RB (1977) Effect of organic acids in the loss of ions from barley roots. J Exp Bot 28:578–587

Lee RB (1978) Inorganic nitrogen metabolism in barley roots under poorly aerated conditions. J Exp Bot 29:693–708

Linhart YB, Baker G (1973) Intra-population differentiation of physiological responses to flooding in a population of Veronica peregrina L. Nature (London) 242:275

Longmuir IR (1954) Respiration of bacteria as a function of oxygen concentration. Biochem J 57:81–87

15 Functional Significance of Different Pathways of CO_2 Fixation in Photosynthesis

C.B. Osmond, K. Winter, and H. Ziegler

CONTENTS

15.1 Introduction

The functional significance of different photosynthetic CO_2 fixation pathways is a question which can be answered in many ways, each being appropriate to certain scales of enquiry. In physiological ecology our purpose should be to integrate these different scales of enquiry as comprehensively as possible, and to show how photosynthesis contributes, directly or indirectly, to performance and survival of plants in diverse habitats. Studies of photosynthetic CO_2 fixation were afflicted with a post-Calvin cycle chauvinism in the 1950's, which may have been responsible for the slow and tentative revelation of the C_4 pathway of photosynthetic carbon assimilation in the USA and USSR (Burr et al. 1957; Karpilov 1960; Kortschak et al. 1965). Elucidation of this pathway undoubtedly stimulated new interest in the carbon metabolism of photosynthesis in the next decade (Hatch and Slack 1966, 1970; CC Black 1973) and led to an upsurge in comparative studies of higher plant photosynthesis (Black 1971; Björkman 1973). Largely as a result of this stimulus, the peculiar dark CO_2 fixation processes of succulent plants, known as crassulacean acid metabolism (CAM), were also recognized as a distinctive photosynthetic process (Kluge and Ting 1978; Osmond 1978). It also led to the present revival of interest in the photosynthesis of aquatic plants.

Discussions of the functional significance of different photosynthetic CO_2 fixation pathways usually emphasize plant productivity. In the physiological context, superior productivity may be evidence for superior adaptation, suggesting that component physiological systems are better fitted together, giving optimum performance in a particular habitat. Many ecological studies are based on records of plant occurrence (survival) in different habitats and it is not easy to anticipate the "manifold consequences in ecological relationships which may arise from two- to threefold differences in primary productivity" (Black 1971).

Because the biochemical processes relevant to this chapter have been reviewed at length by Trebst and Avron (1978) and Gibbs and Latzko (1979), and because many of the physiological processes are reviewed in companion chapters, our treatment of them is about inversely proportional to the publications available. In spite of the stimulus to ecophysiological studies of photosynthetic process in the last decades, relatively few experiments have given satisfying insights into the functional significance of different photosynthetic pathways in an ecological context. The techniques of reciprocal transplant and competition experiments, which might uncover evidence in support of many speculations, appear to hold little fascination for modern physiologists or ecologists. Few such experiments are available for review in this chapter, and we therefore hope to place the question of the functional significance of different pathways of CO_2 fixation into more appropriate contexts which might cause such experiments to become more commonplace in the future. Our main purpose is to attempt a critical evaluation of the large-scale experiments of nature, presented to us as complex patterns of photosynthetic response to seasonal and geographic climates, and displayed as patterns of distribution of plants with different photosynthetic pathways.

15.2 The Biochemical Context: Comparative Biochemistry of Photosynthetic CO_2 Fixation Pathways

In the whole of evolution the enzymic chemistry of photosynthetic CO_2 assimilation, "the lone reaction that counterbalances the vast expenditures of respiration, that reverses decomposition and death" (UPDIKE 1968), appears to have been successfully resolved in only one way. All three photosynthetic CO_2 fixation pathways ultimately depend on the photosynthetic carbon reduction cycle (PCRC) for net CO_2 fixation. The PCRC is a unique association of ribulose bisphosphate (RuP_2) carboxylase-oxygenase, a reduction step, and the enzymes of the reductive pentose-phosphate pathway which catalyze the fixation and reduction of CO_2 and permit the simultaneous regeneration of the carboxylation substrate. Although there are differences in the primary and secondary structure of RuP_2 carboxylase-oxygenase from different autotrophic organisms (AKAZAWA 1979), and some differences in kinetic properties of the enzyme (BADGER 1980; HOCH HIN et al. 1980, 1981), the chemistry of this "lone reaction" is essentially similar in all plants so far examined, with the possible exception of some bacteria (QUANDT et al. 1977). The reaction mechanism, as far as it is understood (LORIMER and ANDREWS 1973, 1981), also predisposes the carboxylase to also react as an oxygenase (Fig. 15.1), allowing O_2 and CO_2 to react with RuP_2 at the same active site on the enzyme, and thus to behave as competitive inhibitors. The products of oxygenation of RuP_2 are then consumed in reactions of the photorespiratory carbon oxidation pathway (PCOP) which is integrated with the PCRC (Fig. 15.1).

15.2.1 Biochemistry of a Compromise: the Integration of Reduction and Oxidation Pathways in C_3 Photosynthesis

The functional significance of the oxygenase activity of the fundamental carboxylase in photoautotrophic organisms is obscure. The reaction itself is inevitable when the carboxylase functions in photosynthetic systems which are in equilibrium with the present atmosphere of 210 mbar O_2 and 330 μbar CO_2. Presumably the oxygenase activity is a phylogenetic relic of the evolution of autotrophic CO_2 fixation in photosynthetic organisms which derived energy from processes other than the photolysis of water and which existed in a primitive reducing atmosphere rich in CO_2 (LORIMER and ANDREWS 1981). In the present atmosphere RuP_2 carboxylase in leaves of C_3 plants functions at something less than its K_m (CO_2) and in the vicinity of the $K_i(O_2)$ (see Chap. 16, this Vol.). If the PCRC in chloroplasts of C_3 plants was to function in isolation, a large part of the assimilated carbon would be excreted as P-glycolate. When isolated intact chloroplasts of C_3 plants are provided with limiting $^{14}CO_2$ in the presence of 210 mbar O_2, most of the ^{14}C is converted to glycolic acid and excreted to the suspending medium. Ultimately, the chloroplast is depleted of PCRC metabolites (KIRK and HEBER 1976).

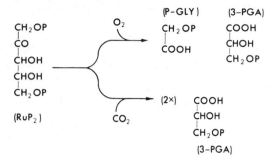

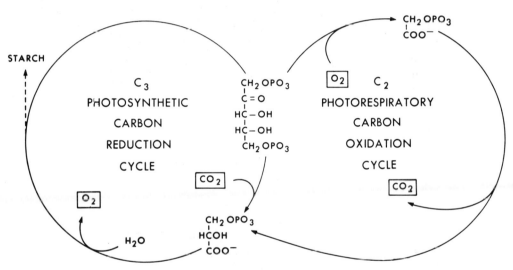

Fig. 15.1. Linkage of the photosynthetic carbon reduction cycle and the photorespiratory carbon oxidation cycle by RuP_2 carboxylase-oxygenase and its reaction products

The reactions of the PCOP in peroxisomes and mitochondria in cells of C_3 plants, reviewed by SCHNARRENBERGER and FOCK (1976), BERRY et al. (1978), LORIMER et al. (1978) and shown schematically in Fig. 15.2, conserve carbon which is lost from the chloroplast as a result of oxygenation. The integration of PCRC and PCOP, unlike RuP_2 oxygenase itself, can be viewed as functionally significant in several ways.

1. Integration of the reactions of the PCOP with those of the PCRC in C_3 photosynthesis permits the recovery of 75% of the carbon excreted from the PCRC as P-glycolate. Figure 15.2 shows that for each 2 mol of P-glycolate (C_2) formed as an inevitable consequence of oxygenation, 1 mol of 3-PGA (C_3) is returned to the chloroplast. The remaining 25% is released as the CO_2 of photorespiration and it is this CO_2 production which results in the relatively high CO_2 compensation point in leaves of C_3 plants. The flow of carbon through

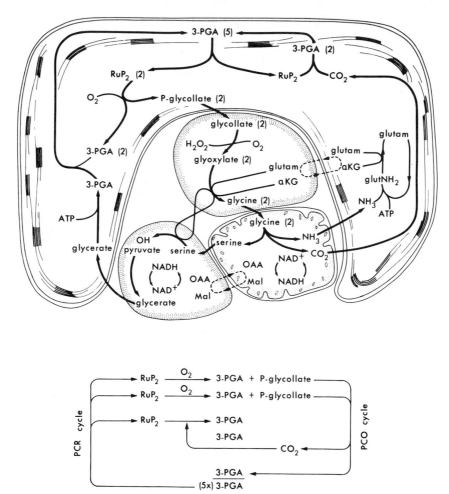

Fig. 15.2. Schematic outline showing the integration of the reduction and oxidation cycles at the CO$_2$ compensation point in leaves of C$_3$ plants, and the location of steps of the oxidation cycle in leaf chloroplasts, peroxisomes, and mitochondria

the PCOP following the oxygenation of RuP$_2$ also consumes ATP and reducing potential, and accounts for depression of the quantum yield in C$_3$ plants by O$_2$ (EHLERINGER and BJÖRKMAN 1977). The stoichiometry of carbon and energy metabolism in these integrated cycles is detailed in Chapter 16, this Volume.

2. Although only 75% of the carbon diverted from the PCRC as P-glycolate is recovered in the PCOP, it seems likely that all of the NH$_3$, released stoichiometrically with CO$_2$, must be recovered by the integrated PCRC and PCOP (LEA and MIFFLIN 1979; FARQUHAR et al. 1980). The fluxes of N through reactions of the PCOP are an order of magnitude greater than the capacity of leaves to assimilate NO$_3^-$, so the conservation of N in these reactions is essential.

3. Recent experiments suggest that by providing an internal source of CO$_2$, photorespiration and integration of PCRC and PCOP may have another impor-

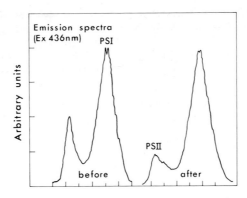

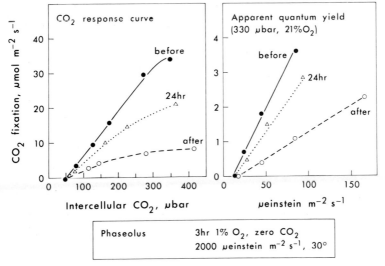

Fig. 15.3. Photoinhibition in leaves of *Phaseolus vulgaris* (C_3) after 3-h illumination in the absence of CO_2 and at low O_2 (no photorespiration), as shown by reduction in the capacity (CO_2 response curve), and efficiency (quantum yield) of photosynthesis. The fluorescence emission spectra indicate photosystem II has been selectively damaged. Partial recovery from photoinhibition is observed after 24 h in normal atmosphere. No photoinhibition is observed if leaves are kept at the CO_2 compensation point in 21% O_2. (After Osmond et al. 1980a)

tant function in terrestrial plants. If leaves of C_3 plants are exposed to normal light intensities in the absence of CO_2 and at low O_2 concentrations which prevent photorespiration, the orderly dissipation of photochemical energy does not take place. Under these conditions the excess excitation energy causes the destruction of photochemical reaction centers and photoinhibition results (Cornic 1976; Powles and Osmond 1978). Photoinhibition reduces both the capacity and efficiency of photosynthesis (Fig. 15.3), with substantial damage to photosystem II reactions in chloroplast thylakoids (Osmond et al. 1980a).

Conquest of land by higher plants presumably depended upon the evolution of stomatal mechanisms to control water loss in the water-limited habitat, and indeed stomata are found in the shoot of the first land plant, the leafless *Rhynia*. However, if stomata close tightly in the light and deprive the leaf of access to external CO_2, the limited capacity to use the products of photosynthetic light reactions may lead to photoinhibition. Internal sources of CO_2, such as photorespiratory CO_2 production in the PCOP might mitigate photoinhibition. In some species the production of large amounts of highly reduced secondary plant substances (terpenes etc.) under stress conditions might also serve as a sink for photochemical energy under conditions of limiting CO_2. However, proof of the significance of these hypotheses depends on the demonstration that, in arid habitats, stomata close sufficiently tightly in the light to allow the internal leaf atmosphere to decline to the CO_2 compensation point (see Chap. 7, this Vol.). Of course, the presence of 210 mbar O_2 in the present atmosphere ensures that C_3 plants are unlikely to suffer photoinhibition, even if stomata close completely. However, these speculations imply that it may be undesirable to attempt to eliminate photorespiration in land plants.

Not surprisingly, with the emphasis on photosynthetic rate as the determinant of plant productivity (BLACK 1971), substantial programs have been directed to the control of photorespiration. The wisdom of these is questionable because, as will be evident later, photosynthetic rate itself can rarely be shown to limit plant productivity. Indeed, there is good evidence that increased harvestable yield of C_3 crops such as wheat has been achieved by selecting varieties which have lower rates of photosynthesis per unit leaf area, but improved display of photosynthetic tissues (DUNSTONE et al. 1973). Moreover it seems improbable that the complex biochemistry of the PCOP would have evolved under natural selection if it was totally without function. In broad terms, photorespiration and the integrated PCRC and PCOP represent an adaptive compromise which compensates, at some cost, for imperfectations of the carboxylation mechanisms of plants in the terrestrial environment.

15.2.2 CO_2-Concentrating Mechanisms in Photosynthesis

The high affinity of RuP_2 carboxylase for CO_2 [$K_m(CO_2) \approx 20\ \mu M$] compared to the affinity for O_2 as an inhibitor [$K_i(O_2) \approx 300\ mM$] means that the oxygenation of RuP_2 can be largely prevented by a two-to threefold increase in CO_2 concentration. It is not surprising that, rather than devise a new chemistry of carboxylation, natural selection has favored plants which have evolved different mechanisms for effecting an increase in CO_2 concentration in the vicinity of RuP_2 carboxylase-oxygenase. The different photosynthetic pathways effectively serve this function and in each of these the diversion of carbon from the PCRC to the PCOP as a result of oxygenation during CO_2 fixation is largely prevented.

Three main types of CO_2-concentrating mechanism are known and these are based on the following physiological processes:

1. Intercellular transport of C_4 dicarboxylic acids in the symplast of adjacent cells in C_4 plants (Björkman 1971; Hatch and Osmond 1976).

2. Intracellular transport of malic acid across the tonoplast, into and out of the vacuole, in CAM plants (Kluge and Ting 1978; Osmond 1978; Lüttge and Ball 1979).

3. HCO_3^- transport systems in the plasma membrane of aquatic organisms (Badger et al. 1978; Raven 1981).

15.2.2.1 C_4 Photosynthesis

On the basis of anatomical observations, Volkens (1887), Haberlandt (1884) and Rhoades and Corvalho (1944) speculated on the possibility of a "division of labor" during photosynthesis in plants which displayed the Kranz arrangement of photosynthetic tissues. The C_4 pathway of photosynthesis is always associated with Kranz anatomy in the leaves in one or more of its complex forms (Carolin et al. 1975; Hattersley et al. 1977) and Karpilov (1960) proposed the term "cooperative photosynthesis" which aptly describes the coordinated functioning of component reactions in adjacent cells. During C_4 photosynthesis CO_2 is first assimilated into C_4 carboxylic acids in outer mesophyll cells and these acids are transported through the symplast to bundle-sheath cells. Here the acids are decarboxylated by one of three different pathways (Hatch and Osmond 1976; Edwards and Huber 1981), to yield CO_2 and a C_3 compound which is returned in the symplast to mesophyll cells where it serves again as substrate for the primary carboxylation reaction (Fig. 15.4). The CO_2 thus released is refixed by reactions of the PCRC in bundle-sheath chloroplasts. The concentration gradients of C_4 acids and the activity of the decarboxylase enzymes are such that CO_2 concentration in the bundle-sheath cells is about ten times greater than that in the atmosphere (Hatch 1971). The CO_2 concentrating mechanism is based on a spatial separation of carboxylation and decarboxylation events.

Under these conditions, O_2 inhibition of the carboxylase is largely overcome (Björkman 1971), oxygenation activity is inhibited by CO_2, and proportionally less carbon flows through the PCOP (Osmond and Björkman 1972; Schnarrenberger and Fock 1976). Because PEP-carboxylase is not sensitive to O_2, and as a result of the CO_2 concentrating mechanism, C_4 photosynthesis does not respond to O_2 partial pressure between 10 and 210 mbar. In this sense, C_4 photosynthesis is an elaborate accessory to the conventional C_3 pathway which is functionally significant in that it overcomes the inhibitory effects of 210 mbar O_2 on net CO_2 fixation in the present atmosphere. As noted by Black (1971) C_4 plants are thus potentially capable of substantially higher rates of CO_2 fixation. We shall later examine circumstances in which this potential may be realized.

Because the activity of PEP-carboxylase in mesophyll cells is so high, practically all CO_2 leaking from the PCRC in the bundle sheath can be refixed and returned as C_4 acids in the symplast. Thus C_4 plants display a CO_2 compensation point near to zero. In CO_2-free air Berry and Farquhar (1978) believe the CO_2 concentration in the bundle sheath cells is similar to that in C_3 meso-

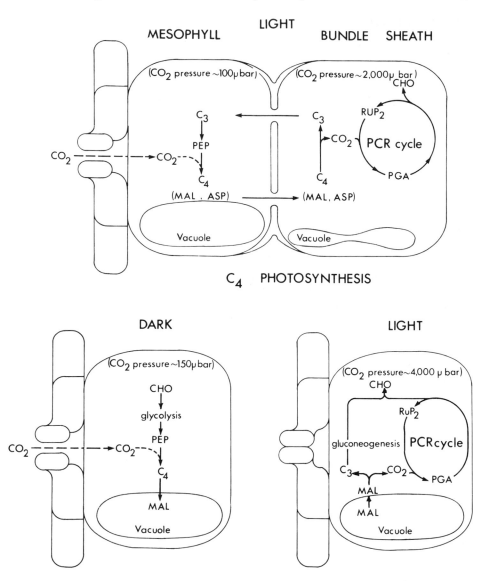

Fig. 15.4. Schematic outline of C_4 photosynthesis and CAM showing the biochemical analogies between the two pathways, as well as the differences in spatial (C_4) and temporal (CAM) organization of the component processes. (After BJÖRKMAN 1973)

phyll cells, but no methods have yet been devised to verify these assumptions. It is known that many C_4 plants have only low activities of PCOP enzymes in the bundle-sheath cells (HATCH and OSMOND 1976) and their capacity for photorespiration is not easily assessed (MOROT-GAUDRY et al. 1980). What is clear is that by concentrating CO_2 in the bundle-sheath cells, O_2 inhibition

C_4 plants on this account. It is naive, however, to interpret the functional significance of these pathways in such simple terms. There are "manifold consequences" of these biochemical processes which give rise to very different physiological responses to light, temperature, and water. These physiological parameters may be more important in determining plant responses to the rapidly increasing high CO_2 atmosphere, which will also almost certainly result in a hotter and more arid environment.

15.3 The Physiological Context: Comparative Responses of Plants with Different Photosynthetic Pathways to Environmental Factors

If our interpretation of the functional significance of the C_4 pathway in the biochemical context is correct, namely that it is a mechanism to overcome the deficiencies of RuP_2 carboxylase in the present atmosphere, then, as BJÖRK-MAN (1975, 1976) has pointed out, we can expect that the C_4 pathway might confer an advantage in terms of photosynthetic production under any conditions which tend to deplete intercellular CO_2 partial pressure in leaves. Other things being equal, we have no reason to suppose that possession of C_4 photosynthesis should be a liability in conditions in which CO_2 partial pressure was not limiting. By the same reasoning, if internal CO_2 generation in the light in photorespiration and CAM are important in protection against photoinhibition, we would expect these processes to confer an advantage in terms of stability of the photosynthetic apparatus under conditions which lead to CO_2 deprivation (OSMOND et al. 1980a). Investigations of a wide range of physiological responses of photosynthesis under laboratory and field conditions tend to confirm these hypotheses.

15.3.1 Comparative Water Economy of Different Photosynthetic Pathways

Since water vapor shares the same stomatal diffusion pathway as CO_2, water is inevitably lost when stomata open and CO_2 is absorbed. As discussed in Chapter 7, this Volume, stomatal conductance appears to adjust in response to the assimilatory capacity of the mesophyll tissue. That is, other things being equal, stomata open to the extent required to provide CO_2 at rates sufficient to meet the CO_2 fixation requirements of the metabolic pathway (WONG SC et al. 1979).

The CO_2-concentrating function of C_4 photosynthesis leads to steady-state CO_2 concentrations of about 100 μbar in mesophyll cells (Fig. 15.8) and about 2,000–3,000 μbar in bundle-sheath cells (HATCH and OSMOND 1976; WONG SC et al. 1979). As a consequence, CO_2 fixation in C_4 plants is practically CO_2-saturated in the normal atmosphere. On the other hand, C_3 plants in the normal atmosphere function with intercellular CO_2 concentrations in the vicinity of 220 μbar (WONG SC et al. 1979) and under these conditions CO_2 fixation rate is somewhat short of saturation with respect to CO_2, especially in high-N plants

Fig. 15.8. Photosynthetic CO$_2$ response curves of a C$_3$ plant (*Gossypium*) and a C$_4$ plant (*Zea*) grown at low and high levels of nitrogen nutrition. (Unpublished data, courtesy of S.C. WONG)

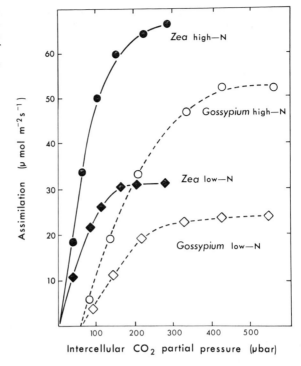

(Fig. 15.8). These marked differences in the operational intercellular CO$_2$ concentrations in C$_3$ and C$_4$ plants are achieved by maintenance of somewhat lower stomatal conductance in C$_4$ plants. Under exactly similar conditions of leaf temperature and leaf-air vapor pressure difference, the lower stomatal conductance of C$_4$ plants is responsible for substantially lower transpiration (E) from leaves of C$_4$ plants than from leaves of C$_3$ plants. Because the CO$_2$-concentrating mechanism of C$_4$ plants overcomes both O$_2$ inhibition of carboxylase and depresses oxygenase, assimilation (A) of C$_4$ plants in air is often greater than in C$_3$ plants. Consequently the transpiration ratio E/A is greater in C$_3$ plants than in C$_4$ plants: C$_4$ plants have a high water use efficiency (see Chaps. 7 and 17, this Vol.).

When C$_3$ and C$_4$ plants are compared under exactly similar conditions this distinction between the water economy is maintained at different levels of organization (LUDLOW and WILSON 1972), and it also persists over long growth periods (Table 15.4). However, these observations should not be taken to imply that the lower transpiration ratios of C$_4$ photosynthesis necessarily result in more water-efficient carbon acquisition under natural conditions. The ratio E/A is markedly dependent on the water vapor difference and hence leaf and air temperature during growth period. A C$_3$ plant growing in the cooler part of the year (a warm desert annual for example) could have a lower transpiration ratio than a C$_4$ plant which grows in the hot season.

The importance of taking seasonal activity patterns into account in comparative studies of the water economy of C$_3$ and C$_4$ plants is well illustrated in

at this low temperature, the C_4 plant had a higher light-saturated rate of photosynthesis (reviewed in OSMOND et al. 1980 b). However, the measured growth and calculated total carbon gain of the two species was about the same, because the greater quantum yield of *A. glabriuscula* compensated for its lower rate of CO_2 fixation at light saturation. A similar comparison was made between *Tidestromia oblongifolia* (C_4) and *Larrea divaricata* (C_3), two heat-tolerant species from desert habitats, when grown at 40 °C. The light response curves at this temperature showed that the C_3 species was inferior to the C_4 species both in terms of lower quantum yield and lower light saturated CO_2 fixation rate. Both the superior light-saturated CO_2 fixation rate and quantum yield in the C_4 plant at high temperature can be ascribed to the CO_2 concentrating function of the biochemical reactions.

15.3.3 Comparative Temperature Responses of Different Photosynthetic Pathways

The thermal stability of the photosynthetic apparatus, both at high and low temperatures, is determined by a variety of properties, none of which is unique to C_3, C_4, or CAM pathways of photosynthetic CO_2 fixation. These properties have been discussed in detail by BERRY and BJÖRKMAN (1980) and in Chaps. 10, 12, and 14, Volume 12 A, and for our purposes it is sufficient to note that they are primarily concerned with temperature responses of the photochemical reactions of photosynthesis, which in turn control the supply of energy to, and the activation of, different steps in the carbon assimilation pathways. In high light environments CO_2 fixation by C_4 pathway plants at higher temperatures is superior to that of C_3 plants, because the C_4 plants operate near to CO_2 saturation. In C_3 plants, oxygenase activity increases relative to carboxylase at high temperatures and photorespiration is greater. If the species being compared have similar intrinsic thermal stabilities, then this difference in response of C_3 and C_4 plants at high temperatures can be largely abolished by increasing the CO_2 partial pressure to levels which are saturating for the C_3 plant, or by reducing O_2 concentration. At lower temperatures the differences between C_3 and C_4 plants in rates of CO_2 fixation largely disappear. In cold, low-light environments the lower quantum requirement of C_3 plants may sometimes allow the daily carbon gain to exceed that of C_4 plants. Under such conditions the higher energy costs of C_4 photosynthesis may become a liability (OSMOND et al. 1980 b).

Although a large number of C_4 plants, particularly those of the NADP malic enzyme type, are unable to function effectively at low temperatures, CO_2 fixation in many other C_4 plants is not impaired by low temperature (BJÖRKMAN et al. 1976; LONG et al. 1975). CALDWELL et al. (1977a) showed that low growth temperature had little effect on the pulse-chase kinetics of $^{14}CO_2$ fixation in cool and warm desert C_4 *Atriplex* spp. Substantial changes in leaf morphology were noted in plants grown at low temperature, and substantial deposits of starch accumulated in both mesophyll and bundle-sheath cells, but by all criteria the carbon assimilation pathway was unaltered.

Impaired photosynthesis in C_4 plants which are sensitive to low temperature, such as the tropical grasses, is manifest in chlorosis, abnormal chloroplast structure, impaired photochemistry and subsequent severe disruption of the CO_2 fixation pathway (LUDLOW and WILSON 1971; TAYLOR and ROWLEY 1971; SLACK et al. 1974). It is conceivable that some of these changes are light-dependent following the chilling injury and the consequences of photoinhibition which follows whenever the capacity of illuminated chloroplasts to dispose of photochemical energy in an orderly fashion is impaired (OSMOND et al. 1980a; POWLES and CRITCHLEY 1980). Chilling injury impairs the capacity of chloroplasts to generate ATP and $NADPH_2$ and the excess excitation energy absorbed by the choroplasts may be dissipated in destructive oxidative processes, analogous to those responsible for photoinhibition following illumination of leaves in CO_2 free air under conditions which prevent photorespiration. Interestingly, when leaves of freezing-tolerant evergreens are exposed to high light intensity at low temperature, they too suffer impairment of photochemical reactions (MARTIN et al. 1978; ÖQUIST et al. 1978), presumably because at low temperature, slow carbon turnover limits the orderly dissipation of photochemical products (OSMOND 1981).

The temperature responses of CO_2 fixation in CAM plants have been widely discussed, but in most studies stomatal regulation of CO_2 supply has not been taken into account. Stomata of CAM plants are responsive to vapor pressure difference (OSMOND et al. 1979b; LANGE and MEDINA 1979) and this changes rapidly with leaf and air temperature. NOBEL (1976, 1977) and NOBEL and HARTSOCK (1978) showed the declining dark CO_2 fixation at high temperature was accompanied by stomatal closure in three hot desert CAM plants. In *Opuntia inermis* night temperature between 7° and 27 °C had little effect on malic acid synthesis, or on rate of CO_2 fixation in short-term measurements, until stomata began to close at higher temperature (OSMOND et al. 1979a, b). When leaf-air water vapor pressure difference was kept constant at 15° and 25 °C, stomata of *Kalanchoe pinnata* were slightly more open at 25 °C, but net carbon gain during the night was reduced by only 20% (K. WINTER unpublished). Furthermore, in many studies the capacity for CO_2 assimilation at high night temperature may be under-estimated by the inclusion of nonphotosynthetic, respiring tissues in the gas exchange curvette. It is not clear whether stomatal closure contributed to the sharp optimum (10 °C) for malic acid synthesis in *Echeveria columbiana* (MEDINA and DELGADO 1976). MEDINA and OSMOND (1981) established that the 15 °C optimum for dark CO_2 fixation in *K. daigremontiana* is not due to stomatal control of CO_2 uptake. Moreover, they showed that the reduction in dark CO_2 uptake at high temperatures was relatively lower in plants grown at high night temperatures and proposed that these temperature responses may be mediated by effects on transport of malate to and from the vacuole.

Comprehensive analyses of the effects of day and night temperature on the gas exchange patterns of CAM plants have been published by NEALES (1973a, b) and by LANGE and ZUBER (1980). The latter authors confirmed the observations of WAGNER and LARCHER (1981) who showed that *Sempervivum montanum* does not deacidify at low temperatures in the light and has instead

a net CO_2 exchange pattern similar to that of non-CAM plants. At higher temperatures some species such as *Caralluma negevensis* show substantial loss of CO_2 in the light (LANGE et al. 1979). There are several ways in which the temperature in the light period influences net CO_2 fixation of CAM plants. High temperature, at high light intensity, accelerates the rate of deacidification and may therefore increase the possibility of additional CO_2 fixation in the light. In some experiments, higher day temperatures increase the capacity for subsequent dark CO_2 fixation (GERWICK and WILLIAMS 1978; cf. NOBEL and HARTSOCK 1978).

15.3.4 Nutrition and Salinity in Relation to Different Photosynthetic Pathways

A wide range of photosynthetic responses to nutrition has been recorded but few of these have been investigated in such a way that the functionally significant relationships can be discerned. Some, such as the early stages of K^+ deficiency in maize (PEASLEE and MOSS 1968) can be attributed almost entirely to declining stomatal conductance, which is not surprising in view of the importance of K^+ fluxes in stomatal opening in many species (cf. RASCHKE 1975). TERRY (1979) reported that limiting Fe^{2+} supply controls the number of photosynthetic units per unit leaf area, and hence photosynthetic capacity.

The best-documented responses by far are those to nitrogen nutrition, in which declining photosynthesis in response to declining nitrogen is closely associated with the level of the major leaf protein, RuP_2 carboxylase-oxygenase (RYLE and HESKETH 1969; MEDINA 1970, 1971; NEVINS and LOOMIS 1970). As pointed out by BJÖRKMAN et al. (1976) and BROWN (1978), C_4 plants are likely to be very much more efficient in the use of nitrogen than C_3 plants. Because the CO_2 concentrating mechanism allows RuP_2 carboxylase in bundle-sheath cells of C_4 plants to function near CO_2 saturation, higher rates of photosynthesis can be sustained by lower concentrations of this enzyme in C_4 plants. In C_3 *Atriplex* spp. grown with adequate nutrition this enzyme comprises $41\%-56\%$ of soluble leaf protein whereas in a C_4 *Atriplex* spp. grown under the same conditions it comprises only 19%–21%. In *Tidestromia,* a C_4 plant which grows rapidly at 45 °C, this enzyme comprises only 4%–8% of soluble leaf protein. The high nitrogen use efficiency of C_4 plants may be of particular significance in hot arid regions with soils of low N status.

Similar arguments have been advanced by K. WINTER and S.C. WONG (unpublished) for CAM plants which may also occupy low nitrogen arid habitats or ephiphytic habitats in rainforests. Dark CO_2 fixation via PEP carboxylase, followed by the reassimilation of CO_2 at high internal concentrations, should require lower investment in RuP_2 carboxylase than conventional C_3 photosynthesis. *Kalanchoë pinnata* was grown at three levels of nitrogen nutrition in the expectation that low nitrogen plants might engage in a greater proportion of total CO_2 fixation in the dark than high N plants. Although this expectation was realized in gas exchange studies and practically no net CO_2 fixation in the late light period was observed in low-N plants, δ^{13} values, which should

be an integrated measure of the total carbon acquisition in light and dark, did not confirm this trend during long-term growth.

Photosynthetic responses to salinity have not been extensively studied. It was recognized that some halophytes show a requirement for Na^+ as a micronutrient ion (BROWNELL and WOOD 1957) and later it was shown that the requirement for this micronutrient appears to be restricted to C_4 plants (BROWNELL and CROSSLAND 1972). HUBER and SANKHLA (1976) reviewed many studies which have claimed to show that the level of NaCl supply may modify the pathway of photosynthetic CO_2 assimilation. Although salinity may often influence labeling patterns during photosynthetic assimilation of $^{14}CO_2$ in C_3 or C_4 plants, or cause shifts in the $\delta^{13}C$ value of C_3 halophytes (GUY et al. 1980), there is no evidence that the carbon assimilation pathway is essentially changed. Sodium-deficient C_4 plants remain functional C_4 plants in all respects (BOAG and BROWNELL 1979). The concept of balance between C_3 and C_4 pathways of carbon assimilation is itself probably erroneous. Even in so-called intermediate C_3/C_4 plants there is no convincing evidence, from $\delta^{13}C$ value for example, that a significant proportion of total carbon is assimilated by C_4 photosynthesis. RATHNAM and CHOLLET (1980) conclude that limited C_4 pathway activity in some so-called intermediate C_3/C_4 plants may effect some increase in CO_2 concentration in bundle-sheath cells and thereby account for the different O_2 sensitivity of CO_2 fixation, and of CO_2 compensation point, in these plants.

By and large, successful halophytes are those which are able to control NaCl accumulation to the shoot, use it for osmotic adjustment in the cell vacuole and prevent the interference of electrolytes in the normal functioning of leaf cells (OSMOND et al. 1980b). Salt-sensitive plants are by and large unable to achieve one or all of these functions. There is no reason to suspect that C_3, C_4, or CAM pathways of photosynthetic CO_2 fixation should facilitate the functionally important relationships. It could be argued that if NaCl transport to the shoot is largely dependent on transpiration, then shoots of C_4 plants with lower transpiration ratios may be better able to retain shoot salt load within manageable levels. However, to our knowledge there have been no comprehensive comparative analyses of the salt, water, and carbon economies of halophytes which bear on this speculation. Certainly the studies of WILLIAMS (reviewed in OSMOND et al. 1980b) show that salinity and low water potential in arid zone soils had similar effects on transpiration, growth, and transpiration ratios in C_3 and C_4 halophytes.

In most respects the effects of salinity on photosynthesis are mediated via water relations of the leaves and closely associated processes. It is not therefore surprising that the induction to CAM in succulent annuals such as *Mesembryanthemum crystallinum* in response to NaCl can also be brought about by any treatment which reduces water uptake, such as growth in nutrient solutions at low temperature or low O_2 partial pressure (WINTER 1979b). Although these plants are most commonly found in arid saline habitats which are seasonally arid, the change in CO_2 fixation pathway is a response to water stress, not to salinity per se. This change to CAM is functionally significant in that it allows net carbon gain and normal reproductive development to continue.

Some CAM plants show Na^+ deficiency symptoms when grown under conditions which maximize their dependence on dark CO_2 fixation (Brownell and Crossland 1974). *Bryophyllum tubiflorum* grown without Na^+ may suffer strongly reduced growth, but still exhibits all features of CAM and thus the implication that Na^+ is a "prerequisite for the onset of CAM" (Bloom 1979a) is misleading. It has also been suggested (Laetsch 1974) that salinity-induced CAM is analogous to malate synthesis as a balance of cation surplus (Osmond 1976). It has been further proposed that, in *M. crystallinum,* inorganic cations move between epidermis and mesophyll to balance the changing level of malate in the mesophyll during the day/night cycle (Bloom 1979b). These analogies seem to be irrelevant, because dark CO_2 fixation leads to the accumulation of equivalent amounts of malate anions and protons (hydrogen malate = malic acid) in mesophyll cells of *M. crystallinum,* as it does in all other CAM plants. There are no suitable analogies for the bidirectional fluxes of hydrogen malate in CAM (Lüttge and Ball 1979); the process is evidently unique.

15.3.5 Summary

In the physiological context the different pathways of photosynthetic CO_2 fixation can be viewed as the foundation of diverse responses of C_3, C_4, and CAM plants to environment. The biochemical properties of the pathways are such that, in leaves of C_3 plants in the present atmosphere, photosynthesis proceeds at an intercellular CO_2 partial pressure of about 200 μbar. In C_4 plants the biochemical properties permit the same or higher rates of photosynthesis with an intercellular CO_2 partial pressure of about 100 μbar so that, at given leaf temperature and water vapor pressure difference between leaf and air, C_4 plants can fix CO_2 at much lower water cost than C_3 plants because they can function with lower stomatal conductance.

If adequate water is available for transpiration, and the thermal stability of the photosynthetic apparatus is suited to high temperature, then this potential advantage of C_4 photosynthesis is likely to be better expressed at high temperature. The biochemical properties of CAM plants, which permit C_4-like CO_2 fixation in the dark by PEP carboxylase, enable carbon assimilation to proceed at very low water cost, at very low stomatal conductance. However, the physiological constraints arising from the storage of malic acid in the vacuole limit the capacity for nocturnal carbon assimilation in these plants. Additional carbon assimilation in the light by CAM plants is closely controlled by plant water relations. The relative contributions of CO_2 fixation in the dark and the light are discussed in the next section. Some CAM plants display a distinct temperature optimum for nocturnal CO_2 fixation; others do not. The physiological bases for these responses are not clear.

The biochemical processes of C_4 and CAM plants have higher intrinsic energy costs and hence lower quantum yields than C_3 plants. However, because these processes allow C_4 plants to function near saturating intercellular CO_2 partial pressure, leaves of these plants tend to display nonsaturating light response curves for photosynthesis. The dependence of CAM on light intensity

is a complex function of component processes separated in time, and the overall efficiency of light energy conversion is markedly dependent on stomatal responses to internal and external factors.

The functional relationship between nutrition and photosynthetic CO_2 fixation pathways is not yet well understood. Because the biochemical processes of C_4 and CAM pathways permit RuP_2 carboxylase to function at elevated intercellular CO_2 partial pressures, lower concentrations of this enzyme are needed to sustain high photosynthetic rates. Because this enzyme comprises the major leaf protein, both pathways may be considered to be nitrogen-efficient. In both C_4 and CAM pathways sodium has a specific but as yet undefined role.

15.4 The Ecological Context: Productivity and Survival in Different Habitats

The functional significance of different CO_2 fixation pathways in the ecological context will be displayed by natural selection to the extent that photosynthetic properties contribute to performance and survival of the whole plant in different habitats. The translation of carbon-assimilating processes into productivity of the whole plant is primarily determined by carbon allocation processes which are poorly understood. In the same environment, greater CO_2 assimilation rate on a leaf area basis of a C_4 plant may result in growth rates lower than those of a C_3 plant, if a greater proportion of the assimilated carbon is allocated to nonphotosynthetic structures in the C_4 plant. SLATYER (1970) showed that the initially higher net assimilation rate in C_4 *Atriplex spongiosa* declined to less than that of the C_3 *Atriplex hastata* after 3 weeks growth because the C_3 plant developed greater leaf area. On the other hand, survival of the organism may be determined by the allocation of assimilate between photosynthetic and reproductive structures, rather than on vegetative production.

Carbon allocation patterns are reflected in plant life forms, as discussed in Chapter 18, this Volume. With the exception of tree form *Euphorbia* spp. of Hawaii (PEARCY and TROUGHTON 1975), as well as Chenopodiaceae and Polygonaceae of Middle Asia (WINTER 1981), C_4 plants are shrubs and grasses. In some cool desert species, such as *Atriplex confertifolia,* root/shoot ratios of seven have been measured (CALDWELL and CAMP 1974). Most CAM plants are shrub-like with little biomass invested in roots and nonphotosynthetic tissues. Although some Cactaceae and Euphorbiaceae develop tree form, the stems and branches remain photosynthetic. In most Didiereaceae small succulent leaves capable of CAM are borne on woody stems with only a thin chloroplast containing cortex (WINTER 1979a), and in some species, leaves with normal C_3 photosynthesis are borne on green stems which carry out CAM (*Frerea indica,* Asclepiadaceae: LANGE and ZUBER 1977; *Euphorbia trigona,* Euphorbiaceae: EDER et al. 1981). These C_3 leaves are dropped in response to water stress.

Although allocation pattern is unlikely to be related to rates of translocation, it is important to note that C_4 grasses generally have translocation rates about twice those of C_3 grasses, and translocation in C_4 plants is two to three times

faster on a phloem area basis (LUSH and EVANS 1974). Moreover, C_4 plants generally translocate a greater proportion of recent photosynthate from leaves than do C_3 plants (HOFSTRA and NELSON 1969; LUSH and EVANS 1974; GALLAHER et al. 1975). Photosynthate which is not exported in the light is stored as starch and mobilized in the dark. In the C_4 plants *Paspalum dilatatum* and *Panicum maximum*, but not in C_3 *Lolium temulentum*, the mobilization of stored starch is abruptly slowed by night temperatures below 10 °C (LUSH and EVANS 1974) and this may be responsible for the accumulation of starch in leaves of many C_4 plants grown at low temperatures (HILLIARD and WEST 1970; CALDWELL et al. 1977a).

15.4.1 Environmental Effects on Allocation of Assimilates

There have been few comparative studies of the effects of environmental factors on assimilate partitioning in plants differing in photosynthetic CO_2 fixation pathway. However, interactions in other experiments serve to emphasize the importance of assimilate partitioning in modulating carbon-assimilating capacity in terms of productivity and survival.

It is commonly observed that decreasing light intensity causes an increase in the proportion of assimilate retained for leaf growth. The extent to which this increase in photosynthetic surface compensates for the reduction in photosynthetic capacity at lower light intensities varies between species. In sun plants such as *Amaranthus spinosus* (C_4) and *Datura stramonium* (C_3) there was no compensation at all, and relative growth rate declined more than proportionally with light intensity (SINGH and GOPAL 1973). In shade plants, the compensation is more effective, so that maximum relative growth rate is achieved at a fraction of full sunlight. It is quite impossible to generalize these relationships with respect to photosynthetic pathway, and indeed SINGH and GOPAL describe both "sun" and "shade" response types in two varieties of *Portulaca oleracea* (C_4) which grow intermixed in open habitats. The broad leaf variety maintained higher dry weight and seed production at decreasing light intensity, whereas the narrow leaf variety declined in dry weight and showed a more than proportional decline in seed production over the same range.

When *Avena sativa* (C_3) and *Amaranthus edulis* (C_4), or when *Panicum maximum* (C_4) and *Atriplex hortensis* (C_3) were grown alone or in mixed cultures, root weight of all species increased with decreased water supply (Fig. 15.12). However, in the C_4 plants the ratio root/shoot decreased, whereas in the C_3 plants this ratio increased. When the same experiments were run under shade and full sunlight, growth of the C_4 plants was stimulated by high light and low water supply, whereas growth of C_3 plants was inhibited (Fig. 15.13). The increased growth of C_4 plants was associated with a decrease in the shoot/root ratio. Evidently the higher water use efficiency of C_4 plants enables them to maintain higher leaf area under drier conditions and hence to attain higher rates of photosynthesis per plant and higher growth. Further experiments with C_3 and C_4 plants of different life forms are needed to determine whether, in competitive situations, water spared by C_4 plants is expended by C_3 plants.

Fig. 15.12. Dry weight of the aboveground and belowground parts of 12-week-old *Avena sativa* (C$_3$) and *Panicum miliaceum* (C$_4$) plants cultivated in pure culture or under competitive conditions on garden soil with different levels of ground water. *Avena*, pure culture ●---●, mixed culture with *Panicum* ○---○; *Panicum*, pure culture ●————●, mixed culture with *Avena* ○————○. Aboveground parts reach the highest value under competitive conditions on the driest soil in the C$_4$ plant, *Panicum*, under competitive conditions on the wettest soil in the C$_3$ plant *Avena*. The yield of *Panicum* is generally higher in mixed culture with *Avena*. The yield of *Avena* on the other hand is higher in pure culture. There is a tendency for higher dry weight in the belowground parts in the driest soil. (After ÖZTÜRK et al. 1981)

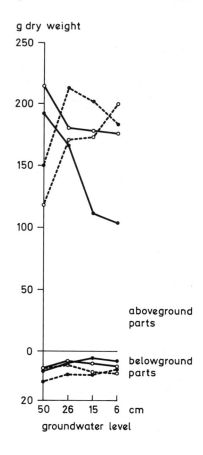

PEARCY et al. (1981) found limitation of water supply did not influence competitive interactions between C$_4$ *Amaranthus* and C$_3$ *Chenopodium*.

The effects of temperature on assimilate partitioning are likely to be very complex because leaf temperature is an important determinant of transpiration and hence of water acquisition by the root system. The vast difference between the root/shoot ratio of warm desert *Atriplex* spp. (C$_4$) in south eastern Australia (0.3) and of cool desert *A. confertifolia* (C$_4$) in Utah (7.0) may be related to the utilization of unpredictable superficial rainfall in Australia, and to the predictable winter recharge of the whole soil profile in Utah. In experiments with warm desert *Atriplex* spp. (C$_4$) in which only the air temperature was controlled, higher temperatures resulted in reduced allocation of carbon to root (NICHOLLS 1972) and increased total growth. In similar experiments with cool coastal *Atriplex* spp. (C$_3$) the same response was observed up to moderate temperatures, but at higher temperatures reduced growth was accompanied by an increase in the proportion of assimilates allocated to roots (Fig. 15.14). OSMOND et al. (1980b) suggested that these responses to temperature may be generalized. The response of cool coastal *A. hortensis* (C$_3$) matches that of C$_3$ winter annuals studied by DAVIDSON (1969a) and that of warm desert *A. argentea* (C$_4$) matches Davidson's observations with subtropical C$_4$ grasses.

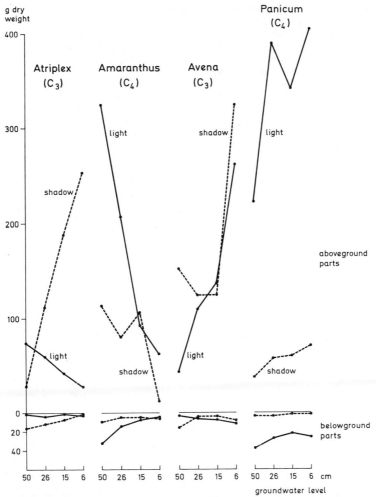

Fig. 15.13. Dry weight of the aboveground and belowground parts of 12-week-old plants of the grasses *Avena sativa* (C₃) and *Panicum miliaceum* (C₄) and of the herbaceous plants *Atriplex hortensis* (C₃) and *Amaranthus retroflexus* (C₄), cultivated in mixed culture of all four species on garden soil with different levels of ground water. One plot was grown in full light (——) and the other was shadowed to about 50% of the light intensity by a screen (---). The dry weight of the aboveground parts of C₄ plants was strongly promoted under full light conditions and — at least relatively to the C₃ plants — under dry soil conditions. The absolute dry weight of the belowground parts generally increases with decreasing soil moisture, while the shoot/root ratio shows variable values. (After Öztürk et al. 1981)

Clearly, these responses in well-irrigated plants indicate that assimilate partitioning in plants which are capable of CO₂ fixation at high temperatures is such as to reinforce their photosynthetic potential by maintaining the minimal allocation of photosynthate to roots commensurate with the water requirements of

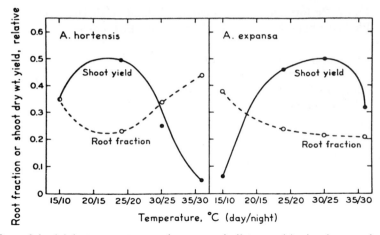

Fig. 15.14. The effect of day/night temperature regime on assimilate partitioning in a cool temperate C$_3$ plant (*Atriplex hortensis*) and a warm desert C$_4$ plant (*Atriplex expansa*) (reproduced from Osmond et al. 1980 b)

the plant. Even if adequate leaf water relations and CO$_2$ fixation capacity are maintained, the allocation of assimilate to roots rather than shoots will decrease productivity and growth. Whether the higher water use efficiency of C$_4$ plants enables them to maintain lower root/shoot ratios and hence higher productivity in water-limited environments remains to be determined.

DAVIDSON (1969b) developed a similar hypothesis with respect to the effects of nutrients on assimilate partitioning. He observed that the growth of shoots decreased, relative to the growth of roots during nutrient deficiency, and proposed that photosynthate was partitioned to roots in increase proportion to their functional activity, whether it be the absorption of water or nutrients. Because C$_4$ plants can achieve high rates of CO$_2$ fixation at lower leaf nitrogen concentrations, we might speculate that they would show differences in assimilate partitioning with respect to nutrient supply. To our knowledge no comparisons between C$_3$ and C$_4$ plants have been made.

The partitioning of assimilates between roots and shoots also changes in response to salinity, and the response is similar to the response to water stress. HOFFMAN et al. (1971) noted that depressed growth of cotton in response to salinity or water deficit was associated with an increase in the root/shoot ratio. In comparisons of halophytic C$_3$ and C$_4$ *Atriplex* spp. stimulation of growth in response to low levels of salinity was associated with a decrease in the root/shoot ratio as photosynthate was used to develop further photosynthetic tissue. At higher levels of salinity growth was depressed and the root/shoot ratio increased (OSMOND et al. 1980b). Salinity had little effect on the rate of CO$_2$ fixation of these halophytes over the range of salt concentrations tested, so that the growth response was controlled principally by the allocation of assimilates.

15.4.2 Performance (Productivity) of Plants with Different Photosynthetic Pathways in Relation to Environment

The range of maximum rates of net CO_2 fixation in air by C_3 and C_4 plants overlaps because plants differ, among other things, in the temperature optimum for photosynthesis. Table 15.5 shows that some C_3 plants adapted to high temperatures are capable of CO_2 fixation at rates comparable with those of high temperature-adapted C_4 plants. Some C_4 plants, which are adapted to low temperatures, show maximum CO_2 fixation rates comparable with other low temperature adapted C_3 plants. Clearly most of the C_4 plants listed in Table 15.5 are adapted to higher temperatures than the C_3 plants. However, GIFFORD (1974) pointed out that although at the highest natural light intensities a crop of *Zea* (C_4) at 29 °C showed 1.5 times higher CO_2 fixation than *Triticum* (C_3) at 14°–17 °C (equal leaf area indices), this advantage disappeared below about 60% full sunlight. Attenuation of the higher potential productivity shown by individual leaves of C_4 plants at high light intensity arises because in dense stands light levels are usually well below the noon maximum for most of the day. Moreover, night time respiratory losses of carbon are likely to be greater in high temperature habitats occupied by C_4 plants.

There is abundant evidence that differences in photosynthetic CO_2 fixation as a function of temperature in individual leaves are translated into differences in growth of individual plants irrespective of whether they are C_3 or C_4 plants. The dry matter yields of *Atriplex* spp. from cool coastal and warm interior habitats were compared when plants were grown under full sunlight, with adequate water at 15 °C day/10 °C night and 36 °C day/31 °C night. All the plants of cool coastal origin, whether C_3 or C_4, grew only half to one third as rapidly at 36°/31 °C compared to 15 °/10 °C (OSMOND et al. 1980b). All the C_4 plants of warm interior habitats grew three to five times more rapidly at 36°/31 °C compared to 15°/10 °C (OSMOND et al. 1980b).

GIFFORD (1974) compared maximum crop growth rates of C_3 and C_4 plants and concluded that "there is no apparent difference between the best examples of the two groups when grown in their own preferred environments". However, reappraisal of these and other data sets led other authors (LOOMIS and GERAKIS 1975; MONTEITH 1978) to conclude that C_4 crop plants do indeed have higher maximum short-term crop growth rates ($51–54$ g m^{-2} day^{-1}) than C_3 crop plants ($27–39$ g m^{-2} day^{-1}). The higher crop growth rates which have been reported for some C_3 plants, which were responsible for indistinct separation of C_3 and C_4 groups in Gifford's data, seem to have been obtained from small plots in which substantial lateral interception of light evidently permitted higher growth rates. This is, of course, an academic distinction, which is relevant to the efficiency of crop production and of little concern in natural communities where lateral interception of light is likely to be significant, but in which other factors such as water and nutrition are likely to be limiting. More extensive analyses of productivity in different ecosystems are given in Volume 12 D of this series.

The higher vegetative productivity (dry matter production) of C_4 plants relative to C_3 plants is sometimes a product of a longer growing season. Esti-

Table 15.5. Maximum values of net CO_2 fixation in C_3 and C_4 plants. (Data from GIFFORD 1974; BJÖRKMAN et al. 1975, and MOONEY et al. 1976)

Pathway and species	Leaf temp. (°C)	Net CO_2 fixation (nmol cm^{-2} s^{-1})
C_3 plants		
Camissonia claviformis	30	5.9
Typha latifolia	25	4.3
Triticum boeoticum	21	4.5
Medicago sativa	–	5.4
Glycine max	29	2.7
Helianthus annuus	–	2.8
C_4 plants		
Tidestromia oblongifolia	40	5.0
Saccharum hybrid	25	6.4
Pennisetum typhoides	35	6.4
Zea mays	32	5.5
Sorghum sudanense	28	5.7
Atriplex sabulosa	16	2.8

mates of long-term productivity of C_3 and C_4 plants are summarized in Tables 15.6, 15.7. Although the range of values for annual productivity overlaps between the two groups, full-year tropical C_4 plants, such as *Pennisetum* and *Saccharum*, are more productive than full-year tropical C_3 plants such as *Manihot*. The average growth rate over the whole season is only about 40% of the maximum crop growth rates disputed above, but these longer-term studies tend to confirm that the higher productivity of C_4 plants is based on higher growth rates. The maintained superior productivity of vegetative C_4 crop plants at low latitudes (*Saccharum, Pennisetum*) is about twice that of *Zea* (Fig. 15.15), presumably because selection for seed production has been at the cost of vegetative production. In fact, the productivity of C_3 root crops such as *Manihot* and *Beta* is comparable with that of C_4 plants such as *Zea* and *Cynodon* over a wide range of latitudes in which these plants are grown.

CAM plants are not noted for their high productivity because CO_2 fixation in the dark is limited by availability of substrate carbon and the capacity to store malic acid. However, in some communities CAM plants can attain relatively high biomass, nearly all of which is photosynthetically active surface. Estimates of maximum biomass of 100–300 t ha^{-1} for *Opuntia* in parts of eastern Australia (DODD 1940) indicate the potential productivity of this persistent organism. OSMOND et al. (1979a) estimate that at this biomass, which corresponds to a leaf area index of about 12–15, productivity of 30–40 g m^{-2} day^{-1} could be attained. The pineapple (*Ananas sativus*) is frequently cultivated at leaf area indices of 10–12 and sustains crop growth rates of 20 g m^{-2} day^{-1} and a productivity over two years of 34 t ha^{-1} yr^{-1} (BARTHOLOMEW and KADZIMIN 1975). Cultivated *Opuntia* spp. have yielded approximately 40 t ha^{-1} yr^{-1} over 2 years and harvests of 15–30 t ha^{-1} yr^{-1} of nopales have been recorded

pan evaporation and dryness ratio. They concluded that "there appear to exist adaptive properties of these families, in addition to the type of photosynthetic pathway, which favor their presence in arid regions". These observations thus suggest that the efficiency of water use during CO_2 fixation may be of less significance to survival in arid habitats than other properties shared by C_3 and C_4 plants in the Chenopodiaceae, Amaranthaceae, and Euphorbiaceae.

Tiezen et al. (1979) confirmed suggestions by Brown (1977) that those C_4 grasses occupying the most arid regions and growing during the hot dry season belong to the NAD-malic enzyme subtype of C_4 photosynthesis. They showed, for instance, that members of the Eragrostoideae and Aristideae occupied environments with the lowest available soil moisture, whereas members of the Paniceae and Andropogoneae (all C_4) were common to more mesic sites. This trend was also recognized by Vogel et al. (1978) who reported that 81% of the grasses in the Southern Kalahari were "aspartate formers" which presumably belong in this same biochemical sub-group of C_4 plants. It is difficult to imagine any biochemical or physiological basis for this correlation and presumably factors other than C_4 pathway sub-group are responsible for this distribution.

Statistical analysis of the distribution of members of the succulent families Cactaceae and Crassulaceae in North America (Teeri et al. 1978) showed that in both families distribution is highly correlated with climatic indices of dry habitats. However, the authors noted that Cactaceae were best correlated with habitats characterized by high evaporation, whereas Crassulaceae were best correlated with low precipitation regions. Unlike C_3 and C_4 pathways of CO_2 fixation, which can be assigned with some certainly on the basis of leaf anatomy, the presence of CAM and its contribution to total CO_2 fixation is not easily ascribed on the basis of morphological features such as succulence. There are succulent plants without CAM and CAM plants which are not succulent. However, succulents with CAM provide the most direct and readily evaluated evidence for the functional significance of different photosynthetic CO_2 fixation pathways.

15.4.4 The Compromise Between Productivity and Survival in CAM Plants

Ideally, to test the ecological significance of different photosynthetic pathways one should have access to the same or closely related genotypes which differ in that property alone. For this reason the few comparisons that have been made with C_3 and C_4 species of *Atriplex* have been especially valuable, and for this reason the prospect of functionally intermediate hybrids was particularly exciting (Osmond et al. 1980b). However, as far as is known there are no wild plants, or artificial hybrids which are functionally intermediate and which have been the subject of ecophysiological evaluation. Comparisons of the so-called intermediate C_3/C_4 species of *Panicum* would be rewarding (Brown and Brown 1975; Ku and Edwards 1978; Rathnam and Chollet 1980). There is no single genotype in which the potential advantages of a C_3 property can be evaluated against a C_4 property in response to the selective pressures of the environment. Yet in constitutive CAM plants (Osmond 1975) we may sepa-

rately evaluate the response and functional significance of CO$_2$ fixation in the dark (C$_4$-like) and the light (C$_3$-like) in relation to performance and survival in different habitats. Moreover, in inducible CAM plants, such as *M. crystallinum*, we are able to evaluate the induction of nocturnal CO$_2$ fixation and the decline in conventional C$_3$ photosynthesis in response to environmental factors.

These engaging possibilities have yet to attract much experimental proof. Because the $\delta^{13}C$ value in leaf succulents is a useful integrator of the contributions of CO$_2$ fixation in the dark and light, it has been used in pilot laboratory studies (OSMOND et al. 1976) and widely applied to infer patterns of carbon assimilation among succulent plants in the field. By and large, our enthusiasm in application of this technique in the field has exceeded our understanding of the processes involved. One notable example of this lapse concerns the contribution of CO$_2$ fixation in the light to total carbon gain in *Opuntia* under mesic conditions. More negative $\delta^{13}C$ values for specimens collected in more mesic sites (OSMOND 1975) suggested a substantial amount of net CO$_2$ fixation in the light in this stem succulent. Although this response in the patterns of CO$_2$ fixation was later confirmed in field experiments, it was found that nocturnal CO$_2$ fixation also increased markedly with improved plant water status, and this obscured any significant trend in the $\delta^{13}C$ value (OSMOND et al. 1979a). Other studies with stem succulents, under natural conditions and under experimental irrigation, confirm that although net CO$_2$ fixation in the light may sometimes be observed, it evidently contributes little to overall carbon gain (SUTTON et al. 1976; EICKMEIER and BENDER 1976; HANSCOMB and TING 1978; RUNDEL et al. 1979). Surveys of the $\delta^{13}C$ value of stem succulents in southern Africa, California, and Chile (MOONEY et al. 1974, 1977), confirm that most lie between $-10^0/_{00}$ and $-17^0/_{00}$ (Fig. 15.20), suggesting that most carbon is acquired by dark CO$_2$ fixation. Similar results were obtained with the endemic stem succulents of Madagascar (WINTER 1979a).

In contrast to the stem succulents, leaf succulents of the Crassulaceae known to be capable of CAM display much more variable $\delta^{13}C$ values which, in laboratory studies, are readily correlated with the proportions of CO$_2$ fixation in the light and dark (OSMOND 1975, 1978). Studies of samples from the field indicate three categories of CAM in leaf succulents:

1. Exclusive dark CO$_2$ fixation in species from very dry habitats, such as the Crassulaceae from Mexico (RUNDEL et al. 1979).
2. Sensitive responses to water stress with an increase in dependence on dark CO$_2$ fixation.
3. No dark CO$_2$ fixation in some succulents from natural habitats, but CAM can be induced under extreme conditions as was found in Central-European *Sedum* spp. (OSMOND et al. 1975; KLUGE 1977).

Sempervivum species from the driest habitats in the European Alps showed slightly less negative $\delta^{13}C$ values than those from moist habitats (OSMOND et al. 1975). Similar variations were found in *Dudleya* spp. from different habitats in the Santa Monica Mountains (TROUGHTON et al. 1977). More convincing evidence for this response along an aridity gradient was found in *Welwitschia mirabilis* by SCHULZE et al. (1976). In the most arid lichen desert regions of the Namib the $\delta^{13}C$ value averaged $-19.6\% \pm 1.0^0/_{00}$, whereas in the more

Kirk M, Heber U (1976) Rates of synthesis and source of glycolate in intact chloroplasts. Planta 132:131–141

Kluge M (1977) Is *Sedum acre* a CAM-plant? Oecologia 29:77–83

Kluge M, Ting IP (1978) Crassulacean acid metabolism: analysis of an ecological adaptation. Ecol Stud Vol 30. Springer, Berlin Heidelberg New York

Kortschak HP, Hartt CE, Burr GO (1965) Carbon dioxide fixation in sugar cane leaves. Plant Physiol 40:209–213

Kremer BP, Küppers U (1977) Carboxylating enzymes and pathway of photosynthetic carbon assimilation in different marine algae – evidence for the C_4-pathway? Planta 133:191–196

Kremer BP, Markham JW (1979) Carbon assimilation by different developmental stages of *Laminaria saccharina*. Planta 144:497–501

Kremer BP, Willenbrink J (1972) CO_2-Fixierung und Stofftransport in benthischen marinen Algen. I. Zur Kinetik der $^{14}CO_2$-Assimilation bei *Laminaria saccharina*. Planta 103:55–64

Kroh GC, Stephenson SN (1980) Effect of diversity and pattern on relative yields of four Michigan first year fallow field plant species. Oecologia 45:366–371

Ku SB, Edwards GE (1978) Photosynthetic efficiency of *Panicum hians* and *Panicum milioides* in relation to C_3 and C_4 plants. Plant Cell Physiol 19:665–675

Küppers U, Kremer BP (1978) Longitudinal profiles of CO_2 fixation capacities in marine macroalgae. Plant Physiol 62:49–53

Laetsch WM (1974) The C_4 syndrome: a structural analysis. Annu Rev Plant Physiol 25:27–52

Lange OL, Medina E (1979) Stomata of the CAM plant *Tillandsia recurvata* respond directly to humidity. Oecologia 40:357–363

Lange OL, Zuber M (1977) *Frerea indica*, a stem succulent CAM plant with deciduous C_3 leaves. Oecologia 31:67–72

Lange OL, Zuber M (1980) Temperaturabhängigkeit des CO_2-Gaswechsels stammsukkulenter Asclepiadaceen mit Säurestoffwechsel. Flora 170:529–553

Lange OL, Schulze E-D, Kappen L., Evenari M, Buschbom U (1975) CO_2 exchange pattern under natural conditions of *Caralluma negevensis*, a CAM plant of the Negev desert. Photosynthetica 9:318–326

Lea PJ, Mifflin J (1979) Photosynthetic ammonia assimilation. In: Gibbs M, Latzko E (eds) Photosynthesis II: Photosynthetic carbon metabolism and related processes. Encyclopedia of plant physiology new ser. Vol VI. Springer, Berlin Heidelberg New York, pp 445–456

Lerman JC (1975) How to interpret variations in the carbon isotope ratio of plants: biologic and environmental effects. In: Marcelle R (ed) Environmental and biological control of photosynthesis. Junk, The Hague, pp 323–335

Lerman JC, Deleens E, Nato A, Moyse A (974) Variation in the carbon isotope composition of a plant with Crassulacean acid metabolism. Plant Physiol 53:581–584

Lloyd NDH, Canvin DT, Bristow JM (1977) Photosynthesis and photorespiration in submerged aquatic vascular plants. Can J Bot 55:3001–3005

Long SP, Incoll LD, Woolhouse HW (1975) C_4 photosynthesis in plants from cool temperate regions with particular reference to *Spartina townsendii*. Nature (London) 257:622–624

Loomis RS, Gerakis PA (1975) Productivity of agricultural ecosystems. In: Cooper JD (ed) Photosynthesis and productivity in different environments. IBP Vol III. Univ Press, Cambridge, pp 145–172

Lorimer GH, Andrews TJ (1973) Plant photorespiration – an inevitable consequence of the existence of atmospheric oxygen. Nature (London) 243:359

Lorimer GH, Andrews TJ (1981) The C_2 photo- and chemorespiratory carbon oxidation cycle. In: Hatch MD, Boardman NK (eds) The biochemistry of plants: a comprehensive treatise Vol VIII. Academic Press, London New York, pp 329–374

Lorimer GH, Woo KC, Berry JA, Osmond CB (1978) The C_2 photorespiratory carbon oxidation cycle in leaves of higher plants: pathway and consequences. In: Hall DO, Coombs J, Goodwin TW (eds) Photosynthesis 77. Biochem Soc, London, pp 311–322

Lucas WJ (1975) Photosynthetic fixation of 14 carbon by internodal cells of *Chara corallina*. J Exp Bot 26:331–346

Lucas WJ (1976) The influence of Ca^{2+} and K^+ on $H^{14}CO_3^-$ influx in internodal cells of *Chara corallina*. J Exp Bot 27:32–42

Lucas WJ (1979) Alkaline band formation in *Chara corallina*. Plant Physiol 63:248–254

Lucas WJ (1980) Control and synchronization of HCO_3^- and OH^- transport during photosynthetic assimilation of exogenous HCO_3^-. In: Spanswick RM, Lucas WJ, Dainty J (eds) Plant membrane transport: current conceptual issues. Elsevier/North-Holland, Biomedica Press, Amsterdam New York, pp 317–327

Lucas WJ, Tyree MT, Petrov A (1978) Characterization of photosynthetic [14]carbon assimilation by *Potamogeton lucens* L. J Exp Bot 29:1409–1421

Ludlow MM (1976) Ecophysiology of C_4 grasses. In: Lange OL, Kappen L, Schulze E-D (eds) Water and plant life: problems and modern approaches. Ecol Stud Vol 19. Springer, Berlin Heidelberg New York, pp 364–386

Ludlow MM, Wilson GL (1971) Photosynthesis of tropical pasture plants. I. Illuminance, carbon dioxide concentration, leaf temperature and leaf-air vapour pressure difference. Aust J Biol Sci 24:449–470

Ludlow MM, Wilson GL (1972) Photosynthesis of tropical pasture plants. IV. Basis and consequences of differences between grasses and legumes. Aust J Biol Sci 25:1133–1145

Lüttge U, Ball E (1979) Electrochemical investigation of active malic acid transport at the tonoplast into the vacuoles of the CAM plant *Kalanchoe daigremontiana*. J Membr Biol 47:401–422

Lush WM, Evans LT (1974) Translocation of photosynthetic assimilate from grass leaves, as influenced by environment and species. Aust J Plant Physiol 1:417–431

Martin B, Martensson O, Öquist G (1978) Effects of frost hardening and dehardening on photosynthetic electron transport and fluorescence properties in isolated chloroplasts of *Pinus silvestris*. Physiol Plant 43:297–305

Medina E (1970) Relationships between nitrogen level, photosynthetic capacity and carboxy-dismutase activity in *Atriplex patula* leaves. Carnegie Inst Washington Yearb 69:655–662

Medina E (1971) Effect of nitrogen supply and light intensity during growth on the photosynthetic capacity and carboxydismutase activity of leaves of *Atriplex patula* ssp. *hastata*. Carnegie Inst Washington Yearb 70:551–559

Medina E, Delgado M (1976) Photosynthesis and night CO_2 fixation in *Echeveria columbiana* v. Poellr. Photosynthetica 10:155–163

Medina E, Minchin P (1980) Stratification of $\delta^{13}C$ values of leaves in Amazonian rain forests. Oecologia 45:377–378

Medina E, Osmond CB (1981) Temperature dependence of dark CO_2 fixation and acid accumulation in *Kalanchoe daigremontiana*. Aust J Plant Physiol 8:641–649

Medina E, Delgado M, Troughton JH, Medina JD (1977) Physiological ecology of CO_2 fixation in Bromeliaceae. Flora 166:137–152

Meinzer FC, Rundel PW (1973) Crassulacean acid metabolism and water use efficiency in *Echeveria pumila*. Photosynthetica 7:358–364

Miller AG, Coleman B (1980) Evidence for HCO_3^- transport by the blue-green alga (Cyanobacterium) *Coccochloris peniocystis*. Plant Physiol 65:397–402

Monteith LJ (1978) Reassessment of maximum growth rates for C_3 and C_4 crops. Exp Agric 14:1–5

Mooney HA, Troughton JH, Berry JA (1974) Arid climates and photosynthetic systems. Carnegie Inst Washington Yearb 73:793–805

Mooney HA, Björkman O, Ehleringer J, Berry JA (1976) Photosynthetic capacity of in situ Death Valley plants. Carnegie Inst Washington Yearb 75:410–413

Mooney HA, Throughton JH, Berry JA (1977) Carbon isotope measurements of succulent plants in southern Africa. Oecologia 30:295–306

Morot-Gaudry JF, Farineau JP, Huer JC (1980) Oxygen effect on photosynthetic and glycolate pathways in young maize leaves. Plant Physiol. 66:1079–1084

Morris I, Farrell K (1971) Photosynthetic rates, gross patterns of carbon dioxide fixation and activities of ribulose diphosphate carboxylase in marine algae grown at different temperatures. Physiol Plant 25:372–377

Mulroy TW, Rundel PW (1977) Annual plants; adaptations to desert environments. Bioscience 27:109–114

Neales TF (1973a) The effect of night temperature on CO_2 assimilation, transpiration and water use efficiency in *Agave americana* L. Aust J Biol Sci 26:705–714

Neales TF (1973b) Effect of night temperature on the assimilation of carbon dioxide by mature pineapple plants *Ananas comosus* (L.) Merr. Aust J Biol Sci 26:539–546

Nevins DJ, Loomis RS (1970) Nitrogen nutrition and photosynthesis in sugar beet. Crop Sci 10:21–25

Nicholls AO (1972) An analysis of the growth of seedlings of four *Atriplex* L. species in controlled environments. Ph D Thesis, Univ Melbourne

Nobel PS (1976) Water relations and photosynthesis of a desert CAM plant, *Agave deserti*. Plant Physiol 58:576–582

Nobel PS (1977) Water relations and photosynthesis of a barrel cactus, *Ferocactus acanthodes*, in the Colorado desert. Oecologia 27:117–133

Nobel PS (1980) Interception of photosynthetically active radiation by cacti of different morphology. Oecologia 45:160–166

Nobel PS, Hartsock TL (1978) Resistance analysis of nocturnal carbon dioxide uptake by a Crassulacean acid metabolism succulent, *Agave deserti*. Plant Physiol 61:510–514

Nobs MA, Pearcy RW, Berry JA, Nicholson F (1972) Reciprocal transplant responses of C_3 and C_4 Atriplexes. Carnegie Inst Washington Yearb 71:164–169

Öquist G, Martensson O, Martin B, Malmberg G (1978) Seasonal effects on chlorophyll-protein complexes isolated from *Pinus silvestris*. Physiol Plant 44:187–192

Österlind S (1951) Inorganic carbon sources of green algae. III. Measurements of photosynthesis in *Scenedesmus quadricauda* and *Chlorella pyrenoidosa*. Physiol Plant 4: 242–254

Österlind S (1952) Inorganic carbon sources of green algae. IV. Further experiments concerning photoactivation of bicarbonate assimilation. Physiol Plant 5:403–408

Öztürk M, Rehder H, Ziegler H (1981) Biomass production of C_3- and C_4-plant species in pure and mixed culture with different water supply. Oecologia 50:73–81

O'Leary MH (1981) Carbon isotope fractionation in plants. Phytochemistry 20:553–567

O'Leary MH, Osmond CB (1980) Diffusional contribution to carbon isotope fractionation during dark CO_2 fixation in CAM plants. Plant Physiol 66:931–934

Osmond CB (1975) Environmental control of photosynthetic options in Crassulacean plants. In: Marcelle R (ed) Environmental and biological control of photosynthesis. Junk, The Hague, pp 311–321

Osmond CB (1976) Ion absorption and carbon metabolism in cells of higher plants. In: Lüttge U, Pitman MG (eds) Transport in plants II. Encyclopedia of plant physiology, new ser Vol IIA. Springer, Berlin Heidelberg New York, pp 347–372

Osmond CB (1978) Crassulacean acid metabolism: a curiosity in context. Annu Rev Plant Physiol 29:379–414

Osmond CB (1981) Photorespiration and photoinhibition: some implications for the energetics of photosynthesis. Biochim Biophys Acta 639:77–98

Osmond CB, Björkman O (1972) Simultaneous measurements of oxygen effects on net photosynthesis and glycolate metabolism in C_3 and C_4 species of *Atriplex*. Carnegie Inst Washington Yearb 71:141–148

Osmond CB, Holtum JAM (1981) Crassulacean acid metabolism. In: Hatch MD, Boardman NK (eds) The biochemistry of plants: a comprehensive treatise Vol VIII. Academic Press, London New York, pp 283–328

Osmond CB, Ziegler H (1975) Schwere und leichte Pflanzen: Stabile Isotope im Photosynthesestoffwechsel und in der biochemischen Ökologie. Naturwiss Rundsch 28:323–328

Osmond CB, Allaway WG, Sutton BG, Troughton JH, Queiroz O, Lüttge U, Winter K (1973) Carbon isotope discrimination in photosynthesis of CAM plants. Nature (London) 246:41–42

Osmond CB, Ziegler H, Stichler W, Trimborn P (1975) Carbon isotope discrimination in alpine succulent plants supposed to be capable of Crassulacean acid metabolism (CAM). Oecologia 18:209–217

Osmond CB, Bender MM, Burris RH (1976) Pathways of CO_2 fixation in the CAM plant *Kalanchoe daigremontiana* III. Correlation with $\delta^{13}C$ value during growth and water stress. Aust J Plant Physiol 3:787–799

Osmond CB, Nott DL, Firth PM (1979a) Carbon assimilation patterns and growth of the introduced CAM plant *Opuntia inermis* in Eastern Australia. Oecologia 40:331–350

Osmond CB, Ludlow MM, Davis R, Cowan IR, Powles SB, Winter K (1979b) Stomatal responses to humidity in *Opuntia inermis* in relation to control of CO_2 and H_2O exchange patterns. Oecologia 41:65–76

Osmond CB, Winter K, Powles SB (1980a) Adaptive significance of carbon dioxide recycling during photosynthesis in water stressed plants. In: Turner NC, Kramer PJ (eds) Plant responses to water and high temperature stress. Wiley-Interscience, New York, pp 139–154

Osmond CB, Björkman O, Anderson DJ (1980b) Physiological processes in plant ecology: toward a synthesis with *Atriplex*. Ecol Stud Vol 36. Springer, Berlin Heidelberg New York

Osmond CB, Valaane N, Haslam SM, Uotila P, Roksandic Z (1981) Comparisons of $\delta^{13}C$ values in leaves of aquatic macrophytes from different habitats in Britain and Finland: some implications for photosynthetic processes in aquatic plants. Oecologia 50:117–124.

Park RB, Epstein S (1960) Carbon isotope fractionation during photosynthesis. Plant Physiol 36:133–138

Patten DT, Dinger BE (1969) Carbon dioxide exchange patterns of cacti from different environments. Ecology 50:686–688

Pearcy RW, Troughton JH (1975) C_4 photosynthesis in tree form *Euphorbia* species from Hawaiian rainforest sites. Plant Physiol 55:1054–1056

Pearcy RW, Tumosa N, Williams K (1981) Relationships between growth, photosynthesis and competitive interactions for a C_3 and C_4 plant. Oecologia 48:371–376

Peaslee DE, Moss DN (1968) Stomatal conductivities in K-deficient leaves of maize (*Zea mays* L.) Crop Sci 8:427–430

Philpott J, Troughton JH (1974) Photosynthetic mechanisms and leaf anatomy of hot desert plants. Carnegie Inst Washington Yearb 73:790–793

Picket-Heaps JD (1975) Green algae: structure, reproduction and evolution in selected genera. Sinauer Sunderland

Powles SB, Critchley C (1980) Effect of light intensity during growth on photoinhibition of intact attached bean leaflets. Plant Physiol 65:1181–1187

Powles SB, Osmond CB (1978) Inhibition of the capacity and efficiency of photosynthesis in bean leaflets illuminated in a CO_2-free atmosphere at low oxygen: a possible role for photorespiration. Austr J Plant Physiol 5:619–629

Powles SB, Chapman KSR, Osmond CB (1980) Photoinhibition in intact attached leaves of C_4 plants: dependence on CO_2 and O_2 partial pressures. Aust J Plant Physiol 7:737–747

Prins HBA, Wolff RW (1974) Photorespiration in leaves of *Vallisneria spiralis*: the effect of oxygen on the carbon dioxide compensation point. Proc Kon Ned Akad Wet Ser C 77:239–245

Quandt T, Gottschalk G, Ziegler H, Stichler W (1977) Isotope discrimination by photosynthetic bacteria. FEMS Microbiol Lett 1:125–128

Radmer RJ, Kok B (1976) Photoreduction of O_2 primes and replaces CO_2 assimilation. Plant Physiol 39:336–340

Raschke K (1975) Stomatal action. Annu Rev Plant Physiol 26:309–340

Rathnam CKM, Chollet R (1980) Photosynthetic carbon metabolism in C_4 plants and C_3-C_4 intermediate species. Prog Phytochem 6:1–48

Rau G (1978) Carbon-13 depletion in a subalpine lake: carbon flow implications. Science 201:901–902

Raven JA (1970) Exogenous inorganic carbon sources in plant photosynthesis. Biol Rev 45:167–221

Raven JA (1981) Nutritional strategies of submerged benthic plants: the acquisition of C, N, and P by rhizophytes and halophytes. New Phytol 88:1–30

Raven JA, Glidewell SM (1978) C_4 characteristics of photosynthesis in the C_3 alga *Hydrodic-tyon africanum*. Plant Cell Environ 1:185–197

Reed ML, Graham D (1977) Carbon dioxide and the regulation of photosynthesis: activities of photosynthetic enzymes and carbonate dehydratase (carbonic anhydrase) in *Chlorella* after growth or adaptation to different carbon dioxide concentrations. Aust J Plant Physiol 4:87–98

Rhoades MM, Carvalho A (1944) The function and structure of the parenchyma sheath plastids of the maize leaf. Bull Torrey Bot Club 71:335–346

Rundel PW (1980) The ecological distribution of C_4 and C_3 grasses in the Hawaiian Islands. Oecologia 45:354–359

Rundel PW, Rundel JA, Ziegler H, Stichler W (1979) Carbon isotope ratios of central Mexican Crassulaceae in natural and greenhouse environments. Oecologia 38:45–50

Ruttner F (1960) Von Kohlendioxyd und Kohlensäure im Süßwasser. In: Ruhland W (ed) Handbuch der Pflanzenphysiologie Vol I. Springer, Berlin Göttingen Heidelberg, pp 62–69

Ryle GJA, Hesketh JD (1969) Carbon dioxide uptake in nitrogen deficient plants. Crop Sci 9:451–454

Schantz HL, Piemeisel LN (1927) The water requirement of plants at Akron, Colorado. J Agr Res (Washington DC) 34:1093–1189

Schiegl WE (1970) Natural deuterium in biogenic materials. Influence of environment and geophysical applications. Ph D Thesis, Univ South Africa, Pretoria

Schiegl WE, Vogel JC (1970) Deuterium content of organic matter. Earth Planet Sci Lett 7:307–313

Schmidt H-L, Winkler FJ (1979) Einige Ursachen der Variationsbreite von $\delta^{13}C$-Werten bei C_3- und C_4-Pflanzen. Ber Dtsch Bot Ges 92:185–191

Schnarrenberger C, Fock H (1976) Interactions among organelles involved in photorespiration. In: Heber U, Stocking CR (eds) Transport in plants III. Encyclopedia of plant physiology new ser Vol III. Springer, Berlin Heidelberg New York, pp 185–234

Schulze E-D, Ziegler H, Stichler W (1976) Environmental control of Crassulacean acid metabolism in *Welwitschia mirabilis* Hook. fil. in its natural range of distribution in the Namib desert. Oecologia 24:323–334

Schulze E-D, Hall AE, Lange OL, Evenari M, Kappen L, Buschbom U (1980a) Long-term effects of drought on wild and cultivated plants in the Negev Desert. I. Maximal rates of net photosynthesis. Oecologia 45:11–18

Schulze E-D, Lange OL, Evenari M, Kappen L, Buschbom U (1980b) Long-term effects of drought on wild and cultivated plants in the Negev Desert II. Diurnal patterns of net photosynthesis and daily carbon gain. Oecologia 45:19–25

Simon H (1982) Tracer-Methoden in der Biologie. In: Hoppe W, Lohmann W, Markl H, Ziegler H (eds) Biophysik, 2nd ed. Springer, Berlin Heidelberg New York

Simon H, Palm D (1966) Isotope effects in organic chemistry and biochemistry. Angew Chem 5:920–933

Sims PL, Singh JS (1978a) The structure and function of ten Western North American grasslands. II. Intraseasonal dynamics in primary producer compartments. J Ecol 66:547–572

Sims PL, Singh GH (1978b) The structure and function of ten Western North American grasslands. III. Net primary production, turnover and efficiencies of energy capture and water use. J Ecol 66:573–579

Sims PL, Singh JS, Lauenroth WK (1978) The structure and function of ten Western North American grasslands. I. Abiotic and vegetational characteristics. J Ecol 66:251–285

Singh KD, Gopal B (1973) The effects of photoperiod and light intensity on the growth of some weeds of crop fields. In: Slatyer RO (ed) Plant response to climatic factors. UNESCO, Paris, pp 73–75

Slack CR, Roughan RG, Bassett HCM (1974) Selective inhibition of mesophyll chloroplast development in some C_4 pathway species by low night temperature. Planta 118:67–73

Slatyer RO (1970) Comparative photosynthesis, growth and transpiration of two species of *Atriplex*. Planta 93:175–189

Smith BN, Epstein S (1971) Two categories of $^{13}C/^{12}C$ ratios for higher plants. Plant Physiol 47:380–384

Smith FA, Walker NA (1980) Photosynthesis by aquatic plants: effects of unstirred layers in relation to assimilation of CO_2 and HCO_3^- and to carbon isotopic discrimination. New Phytol: 86:245–259

Søndergaard M (1979) Light and dark respiration and the effect of the lacunal system on refixation of CO_2 in submerged aquatic plants. Aquat Bot 6:269–283

Spalding MH, Stumpf DK, Ku MSB, Burris RH, Edwards GE (1979) Crassulacean acid metabolism and diurnal variations of internal CO_2 and O_2 concentrations in *Sedum praealtum* D.C. Aust J Plant Physiol 6:557–567

Spalding MH, Edwards GE, Ku MSB (1980) Quantum requirement for photosynthesis in *Sedum praealtum* during two phases of Crassulacean acid metabolism. Plant Physiol 66:463–465

Spence DHN (1976) Light and plant response in fresh water. In: Evans GC, Bainbridge R, Rackham O (eds) Light as an ecological factor Vol II. 16th Symp Br Ecol Soc. Blackwell, Oxford, pp 93–133

Spence DHN (1981) Zonation of plants in freshwater lakes. Adv Ecol Res

Steemann Nielsen E (1960) Uptake of carbon dioxide by the plant. In: Ruhland W (ed) Handbuch der Pflanzenphysiologie. Vol I. Springer, Berlin Göttingen Heidelberg, pp 70–84

Stewart KD, Mattox KR (1975) Comparative cytology, evolution and classification of the green algae with some consideration of the origin of other organisms with chlorophylls a and b. Bot Rev 41:104–135

Stowe LG, Teeri JA (1978) The geographic distribution of C_4 species of the dicotyledonae in relation to climate. Am Nat 112:609–623

Stumm W, Morgan JJ (1970) Aquatic chemistry. Wiley-Interscience, New York

Sutton BG, Ting IP, Troughton JH (1976) Seasonal effects on carbon isotope composition of cactus in a desert environment. Nature (London) 261:42–43

Szarek SR, Ting IP (1977) The occurrence of Crassulacean acid metabolism among plants. Photosynthetica 11:330–342

Szarek SR, Johnson HB, Ting IP (1973) Drought adaptation in *Opuntia basilaris*. Significance of recycling carbon through Crassulacean acid metabolism. Plant Physiol 52:539–541

Talling JF (1976) The depletion of carbon dioxide from lake water by phytoplankton. J Ecol 64:79–121

Taylor AO, Rowley JA (1971) Plants under climatic stress. I. Low temperature, high light effects on photosynthesis. Plant Physiol 47:713–718

Teeri JA, Stowe LG (1976) Climatic patterns and the distribution of C_4 grasses in North America. Oecologia 23:1–12

Teeri JA, Stowe LG, Murawski DA (1978) The climatology of two succulent plant families, Cactaceae and Crassulaceae. Can J Bot 56:1750–1758

Terry N (1979) The use of mineral nutrient stress in the study of limiting factors in photosynthesis. In: Marcelle R, Clijsters H, Pucke M van (eds) Photosynthesis and plant development. Junk, The Hague, pp 151–160

Thomas EA, Tregunna EB (1968) Bicarbonate ion assimilation in photosynthesis by *Sargassum muticum*. Can J Bot 46:411–415

Tieszen LL, Senyimba MM, Imbamba SK, Troughton JH (1979) The distribution of C_3 and C_4 grasses and carbon isotope discrimination along an altitudinal and moisture gradient in Kenya. Oecologia 37:337–350

Trebst A, Avron M (1978) (eds) Photosynthesis. I. Photosynthetic electron transport and photophosphorylation. Encyclopedia of plant physiology new ser Vol V. Springer, Berlin Heidelberg New York

Troughton JH (1979) $\delta^{13}C$ as an indicator of carboxylation reactions. In: Gibbs M, Latzko E (eds) Photosynthesis II. Encyclopedia of plant physiology new ser Vol 6. Springer, Berlin Heidelberg New York, pp 140–147

Troughton JH, Mooney HA, Berry JA, Verity D (1977) Variable carbon isotope ratios of *Dudleya* species growing in natural habitats. Oecologia 30:307–312

Updike J (1968) Couples. Fawcett, Greenwich

Van TK, Haller WT, Bowes G (1976) Comparison of the photosynthetic characteristics of three submerged aquatic plants. Plant Physiol 58:761–768

Vogel JC (1980) Fractionation of the carbon isotopes during photosynthesis. Springer, Berlin Heidelberg New York

Vogel JC, Fuls A, Ellis RP (1978) The geographical distribution of Kranz grasses in South Africa. S Afr J Sci 74:209–215

Volkens G (1887) Die Flora der ägyptisch-arabischen Wüste. Sitzungsber Preuss Acad Wiss Berl Phys Math Kl

Wagner J, Larcher W (1981) Dependence of CO_2 gas exchange and acid metabolism of the alpine CAM plant *Sempervivum montanum* on temperature and light. Oecologia 50:88–93

Weber JN, Woodhead P (1970) Carbon and oxygen isotope fractionation in the skeletal carbonate of reef building corals. Chem Geol 6:93–123

Weidner M, Küppers U (1973) Phosphoenolpyruvat-Carboxykinase und Ribulose-1,5-Diphosphat-Carboxylase von *Laminaria hyperborea* (Gunn.) Fosl: Das Verteilungsmuster der Enzymaktivitäten im Thallus. Planta 114:365–372

Westlake DF (1967) Some effects of low velocity currents on the metabolism of aquatic macrophytes. J Exp Bot 18:187–205

Willenbrink J, Rangoni-Kübbeler M, Tersky B (1975) Frond development and CO_2 fixation in *Laminaria hyperborea*. Planta 125:161–170

Williams GJ III (1974) Photosynthetic adaptation to temperature in C_3 and C_4 grasses. A possible ecological role in the short-grass prairie. Plant Physiol 54:709–711

Willis JC (1973) A dictionary of the flowering plants and ferns, 8th edn. Univ Press, Cambridge

Winter K (1978) Short-term fixation of 14-Carbon by the submerged aquatic angiosperm *Potamogeton pectinatus*. J Exp Bot 29:1169–1172

Winter K (1979a) $\delta^{13}C$ values of some succulent plants from Madagascar. Oecologia 40:104–112

Winter K (1979b) Photosynthetic and water relationships of higher plants in saline environments. In: Jefferies RL, Davy AJ (eds) Ecological processes in coastal environments. Blackwell, Oxford, pp 297–320

Winter K (1980) Carbon dioxide and water vapor exchange in the Crassulacean acid metabolism plant *Kalanchoe pinnata* during a prolonged light period. Plant Physiol 66:917–921

Winter K (1981) C_4 plants of high biomass in arid regions of Asia – occurrence of C_4 photosynthesis in Chenopodiaceae and Polygonaceae from the Middle East and USSR. Oecologia 48:100–106

Winter K, Lüttge U (1976) Balance between C_3 and CAM pathway of photosynthesis. In: Lange OL, Kappen L, Schulze E-D (eds) Water and plant life: problems and modern approaches. Ecol Stud Vol 19. Springer, Berlin Heidelberg New York, pp 323–334

Winter K, Troughton JH (1978) Photosynthetic pathways in plants of coastal and inland habitats of Israel and the Sinai. Flora 167:1–34

Winter K, Willert von DJ (1972) NaCl-induzierter CAM bei *Mesembryanthemum crystallinum*. Z Pflanzenphysiol 67:166–170

Winter K, Kramer D, Throughton JH, Card KA, Fischer K (1977) C_4 pathway of photosynthesis in a member of the Polygonaceae: *Calligonum persicum* (Boiss. & Buhse) Boiss. Z Pflanzenphysiol 81:341–346

Winter K, Lüttge U, Winter E, Troughton JH (1978) Seasonal shift from C_3 photosynthesis to Crassulacean acid metabolism in *Mesembryanthemum crystallinum* growing in its natural environment. Oecologia 34:225–237

Wong SC, Cowan IR, Farquhar GD (1979) Stomatal conductance correlates with photosynthetic capacity. Nature (London) 282:424–426

Wong WW, Benedict CR, Kohel RJ (1979) Enzymic fractionation of the stable carbon isotopes of carbon dioxide by ribulose-1,5-bisphosphate carboxylase. Plant Physiol 63:852–856

Yamaguchi T, Ikawa T, Nisizawa K (1969) Pathway of mannitol formation during photosynthesis in brown algae. Plant Cell Physiol 10:425–440

Ziegler H (1979) Diskriminierung von Kohlenstoff- und Wasserstoffisotopen: Zusammenhänge mit dem Photosynthesemechanismus und den Standortbedingungen. Ber Dtsch Bot Ges 92:169–184

Ziegler H, Osmond CB, Stichler W, Trimborn P (1976) Hydrogen isotope discrimination in higher plants: correlation with photosynthetic pathway and environment. Planta 128:85–92

Ziegler H, Batanouny KH, Sankhla N, Vyas OP, Stichler W (1981) The photosynthetic pathway types of some desert plants from India, Saudi Arabia, Egypt and Iraq. Oecologia 48:93–99

16 Modelling of Photosynthetic Response to Environmental Conditions

G.D. FARQUHAR and S. VON CAEMMERER

CONTENTS

16.1 Introduction

Photosynthesis is the incorporation of carbon, nitrogen, sulphur and other substances into plant tissue using light energy from the sun. Most of this energy is used for the reduction of carbon dioxide and, consequently, there is a large body of biochemical and biophysical information about photosynthetic carbon assimilation. In an ecophysiological context, we believe that most of today's biochemical knowledge can be summarized in a few simple equations. These equations represent the rate of ribulose bisphosphate (RuP₂)-saturated carboxylation, the ratio of photorespiration to carboxylation, and the rates of electron transport/photophosphorylation and of "dark" respiration in the light. There are many other processes that could potentially limit CO_2 assimilation, but probably do so rarely in practice. Fundamentally this may be due to the expense, in terms of invested nitrogen, of the carboxylase and of thylakoid functioning. To reach our final simple equations we must first discuss the biochemical and biophysical structures — as they are understood at present — that finally reduce the vast number of potentially rate-limiting processes to the four or five listed above. A diagrammatic representation of these processes is given in Fig. 16.1.

We then discuss integrated functioning in individual leaves of C_3 species, and later briefly discuss canopy photosynthesis. Models of C_4 photosynthesis are less well developed than those of C_3 photosynthesis; we discuss how they may be extended. (For description of these pathways of photosynthesis see also Chap. 15, this Vol.)

Models of leaf photosynthesis have been reviewed by Thornley (1976), Jassby and Platt (1976), and Tenhunen et al. (1980a). In this article we emphasize recent progress made in mechanistic models, but recognize the validity of other types (see Chap. 8, this Vol.) and give brief references to successful empirical models. Stomatal and boundary layer conductances affect the intercellular partial pressure of CO_2, C, and the leaf temperature, T. We examine responses of the rate of assimilation to C and T but do not consider submodels

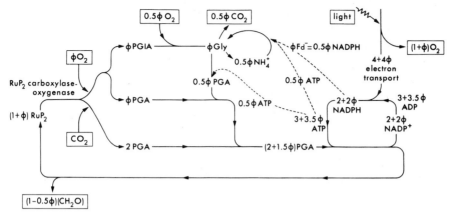

Fig. 16.1. Simplified photosynthetic carbon reduction (PCR) and photorespiratory carbon oxidation (PCO) cycles, with the cycle for regeneration of NADPH and ATP linked to light-driven electron transport. For each carboxylation, ϕ oxygenations occur. *Gly* glycine; *Fd⁻* reduced ferredoxin (assumed equivalent to $^1/_2$ NADPH); *PGA* 3-phosphoglycerate; *PGlA* phosphoglycolate. At the compensation point $\phi = 2$

of the response of stomatal conductance to environmental perturbations. These are dealt with in Chapter 8, this Volume (see also Chaps. 7 and 17, this Vol.).

16.2 Stromal and Extrachloroplastic Reactions

16.2.1 Kinetics of Ribulose Bisphosphate Carboxylase-Oxygenase

16.2.1.1 RuP₂ Saturated Rates

The currently accepted equation to describe the rate, V_c, of carboxylation of ribulose bisphosphate (RuP₂), in the presence of competitive inhibition by oxygen, and of saturating concentrations of RuP₂ is

$$V_c = W_c = \frac{V_{c\,max} C}{C + K_c(1 + O/K_o)}. \tag{16.1}$$

We denote RuP₂ carboxylase rates in general as V_c, and RuP₂ saturated rates as W_c. $V_{c\,max}$ is the maximum velocity, C and O are partial pressures of CO_2 and O_2, $p(CO_2)$ and $p(O_2)$ respectively, in equilibrium with their dissolved concentrations in the chloroplast stroma, K_c is the Michaelis-Menten constant for CO_2, and K_o is the Michaelis-Menten constant for O_2. This equation is used in the models of LAING et al. (1974), KU and EDWARDS (1977b), TENHUNEN et al. (1977), BERRY and FARQUHAR (1978), FARQUHAR et al. (1980), COOKE and RAND (1980), BAUWE et al. (1980) and RAVEN and GLIDEWELL (1981). Earlier attempts to include competitive inhibition by oxygen in models of leaf photosyn-

grated PCR and PCO cycles is, from Eq. (16.26)

$$\text{rate of whole chain electron transport} = 4\,V_c + 4\,V_o = (4 + 4\,\phi)\,V_c$$
$$= (4 + 8\,\Gamma_*/C)\,V_c. \qquad (16.35)$$

The enzyme which catalyzes the production of NADPH is $NADP^+$-ferredoxin reductase, which occurs after (reducing side of) PS I in the electron transport chain (ARNON 1977). There are approximately 500 chlorophyll (Chl) molecules per PS I in leaves (MELIS and BROWN 1980) and since 1 mol Chl is associated with 25 l stroma (HELDT and SAUER 1971), there are $1/(500 \times 25)$ mol of PS I sites per l stroma, i.e., the effective concentration of sites is approximately 80 μM (2 mmol/mol Chl). SHIN and OSHINO (1978) have purified the equivalent of 10.6 mg purified reductase from 2 kg fresh weight of spinach. A comparison of its diaphorase activity with that of the original crude homogenate suggests that 2 kg contains 424 mg reductase. Since the molecular weight of the dimer is 80,000 (SHIN et al. 1981) and assuming a chlorophyll content of 1 mmol/kg fr. wt. (VON CAEMMERER unpublished), this corresponds to one mol reductase per 204 mol Chl, or approximately 196 μM (4.9 mmol/mol Chl). The K_m for $NADP^+$ is only about 8 μM (SHIN 1971). Thus we have a situation analogous to the high concentration of RuP_2 carboxylase-oxygenase relative to the K_m for RuP_2. The rate of $NADP^+$ reduction should have a non-rectangular hyperbolic dependence on $[NADP^+]$, similar to that in Eq. (16.11) and (16.12). By analogy with Eq. (16.13) we can approximate the situation by

$$\text{rate} = 0.5\,J \cdot \min\{1, [NADP^+]/F\}, \qquad (16.36)$$

where again min $\{\ \}$ means "minimum of", and F is the concentration of $NADP^+$-ferredoxin reductase sites. Thus for maximum rates of electron transport, $[NADP^+]$ should be slightly greater than F. NADPH will be required in the stroma, and so the total pool $N_t (= [NADP^+] + [NADPH]$, should also be greater than F, which we estimated above as 5 mmol/mol Chl. LENDZIAN and BASSHAM (1976) report a value for N_t of 36 mmol/mol Chl.

The above considerations help to explain the discrepancy (LILLEY and WALKER 1979) between the in vivo concentration of ferredoxin (19–38 mmol/mol Chl or ~ 1 mM in the stroma) and that required in in vitro studies ($\sim 10\,\mu$M). To the extent that ferredoxin is soluble, it will need to be at a concentration in excess of the sum of PS I and reductase sites, for maximum rates of electron transport. Measurements are needed of the levels of pyridine nucleotides, ferredoxin, and reductase sites in the same chloroplasts.

16.3.4 ATP Production

16.3.4.1 Introduction

A situation analogous to the high concentration of reductase sites may exist for photophosphorylation, the conversion of ADP to ATP on the thylakoid

membranes. STROTMANN et al. (1973) have measured 0.42 g of coupling factor
(CF_1) per g Chl. CF_1 is the ATP synthetase without hydrophobic subunits
which anchor in the membrane. YOUNIS et al. (1977) found 0.4 to 0.5 g CF_1/
g Chl. Assuming CF_1 has a molecular weight of 325,000 (FARRON 1970), this
corresponds to 1.2 mmol/mol Chl, giving an effective concentration of 46 µM.
BERZBORN et al. (1981) have measured 1.5 mmol/mol Chl, or 62 µM. BERZ-
BORN and MÜLLER (1977) showed that the ratio depends on the irradiance
during growth. There are multiple binding sites for ADP, although usually
only two show tight binding, giving half-maximal binding at about 2 µM [ADP]
(McCARTY 1979). The concentration of tight binding sites, approximately
0.1 mM, is again much larger than the appropriate half-saturation concentration.
There is evidence that these tight binding sites are not necessarily the sites
of catalysis and various models of ATP synthesis have been suggested (McCARTY
1979). Some schemes and experiments (e.g., HOCHMAN and CARMELI 1981) still
favour two sites of phosphorylation, with as yet unknown affinities for ADP.
In our opinion, when structural and substrate forms of bound ADP are taken
into account, the dependence of the rate of photophosphorylation on the total
(bound and free) ADP concentration will probably be approximated by analogy
with Eq. (16.36) as

$$\text{rate} = \text{maximum rate} \cdot \min\{1, [\text{ADP}]/\mathscr{A}\}, \tag{16.37}$$

where $\mathscr{A}$ is the concentration of sites of ADP phosphorylation. Accurate measurements of $\mathscr{A}$ are needed.

At first sight it would appear from Eq. (16.37) that A_t ($=[\text{ADP}]+[\text{ATP}]$)
would only need to be slightly in excess of $\mathscr{A}$ (≈ 2 mmol/mol Chl). However,
this is not the case. A_t has variously been estimated as 70–100 (HEBER and
SANTARIUS 1970), 9.2 (LILLEY et al. 1977), 27 (WIRTZ et al. 1980) and 44 mmol/
mol Chl (GIERSCH et al. 1980a). This may be because a large concentration
of ATP is required to keep the reversible reaction between Ru5P and RuP_2
favouring production of the latter. Expressed differently, it is known that ribu-
lose-5-P kinase requires a large energy charge to support RuP_2 regeneration
(PREISS and KOSUGE 1976).

16.3.4.2 Non-Cyclic Photophosphorylation via Whole-Chain
Electron Transport

It is now widely accepted that three protons move across the thylakoid into
the stroma every time an ATP molecule is produced (SHAVIT 1980). From
Eq. (16.27) we see that in the steady state, the required

$$\begin{aligned}
\text{rate of proton production} \quad &= 9\ V_e + 10.5\ V_o = (9 + 10.5\ \phi)\ V_e \\
&= (9 + 21\ \Gamma_*/C)\ V_e. \tag{16.38}
\end{aligned}$$

The movement of one electron through the whole electron transport chain
results in the accumulation of two protons in the thylakoid spaces, one from
the splitting of water in PS II and one from the shuttle of reduced plastoquinone

across the membrane (Junge 1977). Thus if the proton production is by whole-chain electron transport alone, the required

$$\text{rate of whole chain electron transport} = 4.5\, V_c + 5.25\, V_o$$
$$= (4.5 + 5.25\, \phi)\, V_c = (4.5 + 10.5\, \Gamma_*/C)\, V_c. \quad (16.39)$$

16.3.4.3 Pseudo-Cyclic Electron Transport (Mehler Reaction)

Comparing Eq. (16.39) with Eq. (16.35) we see that there is a disparity of $(0.5 + 1.25\, \phi)\, V_c$. For this reason Farquhar and von Caemmerer (1981) developed equations to model the situation where the extra whole-chain electron transport was to an acceptor other than $NADP^+$, such as O_2, as occurs in the Mehler reaction (Mehler 1951). This reaction was reported to be half saturated at a $p(O_2)$ of 80 mbar (8%) (Radmer et al. 1978). An increased requirement for O_2 at high rates of electron transport may explain the observation by Viil et al. (1977) that at high $p(CO_2)$, photosynthetic rate is lowered when $p(O_2)$ is lowered from 210 to 5 mbar.

The required

$$\text{rate of electron transport to } O_2 = (0.5 + 2.5\, \Gamma_*/C)\, V_c, \quad (16.40)$$

which, with $\Gamma_* = 31$ and $C = 230$ µbar, respectively, is about 16% of the rate given by Eq. (16.35). This is comparable with the measured capacities of the Mehler reaction in higher plants (Heber et al. 1978; Marsho et al. 1979). Nevertheless, there are other mechanisms by which chloroplasts may meet the conflicting requirements for ATP and NADPH. The incorporation of nitrate into amino acids reduces the disparity. Other mechanisms are discussed in the following two subsections.

16.3.4.4 Cyclic Photophosphorylation

Whole-chain electron transport to $NADP^+$ alone leaves a deficiency in proton production of $(1 + 5\, \Gamma_*/C)\, V_c$. This could be met by a portion of the electron transport being cyclical around PS I. Since this cycle will probably only contribute one proton per electron involved, the required

$$\text{cyclic-electron transport} = (1 + 5\, \Gamma_*/C)\, V_c. \quad (16.41)$$

Farquhar and von Caemmerer (1981) considered this possibility and wrote an expression for whole-chain electron transport

$$J = \frac{J_{max}\, I}{I + K_I}, \quad (16.42)$$

where

$$K_I = \frac{9.4 + 10.9\phi}{4 + 4\phi} J_{max} \simeq 2.4 J_{max}. \quad (16.43)$$

In this case, J_{max} is the maximum rate of whole chain transport, while cyclic flow is occurring simultaneously. If the limitations to electron transport, other than irradiance, are common to both cyclic and non-cyclic flow, then J_{max} is $(4.5+5.25\ \phi)/(5+6.5\ \phi)$ times the rate which would occur in the absence of cyclic flow (FARQUHAR and VON CAEMMERER 1981).

16.3.4.5 DHAP/PGA Shuttle

A third mechanism which may contribute to the balancing of conflicting requirements is the DHAP/PGA shuttle. In this shuttle (WALKER 1976), which does not actually involve the thylakoid, DHAP is exported from the chloroplasts, and oxidized in the cytoplasm to yield ATP, NADH and 3-PGA, the latter returning to the stroma together with a proton. If we consider that x mol PGA return in this manner per mol of carboxylations, Eqs. (16.26) and (16.27) are replaced by

$$\text{rate of NADPH consumption} = (2+2\ \phi+x)\ V_c \tag{16.44}$$

$$\text{rate of ATP consumption} \quad = (3+3.5\ \phi+x)\ V_c \tag{16.45}$$

and the required rates of whole-chain electron transport become, respectively,

$$\text{rate} = (4+4\ \phi+2x)\ V_c \tag{16.46}$$

and

$$\text{rate} = (4.5+5.25\ \phi+1.5x)\ V_c. \tag{16.47}$$

If this were the *sole* mechanism for balancing requirements then (16.46) and (16.47) would have to be equated, yielding

$$x = 1+2.5\ \phi. \tag{16.48}$$

This, as we see later, would be energetically expensive for the chloroplast.

16.3.4.6 Photosynthetic Control of Whole-Chain Electron Transport

It is known that electron transport is reduced when a proton motive force (p.m.f.) occurs across the thylakoid membrane. This has been called photosynthetic control (WEST and WISKICH 1968). Thus each time a mole of ATP is produced on the stromal side, and 3 mol of protons move across the membrane, reducing the p.m.f., 1.5 mol of electrons (1.5 equivalents) should be able to move along the whole chain, or 3 mol cyclically around PS I, perhaps by removing limitations on the diffusion of reduced PQ (SIGGEL 1976). Thus

$$\text{rate of ATP production} = \tfrac{2}{3} \cdot \text{rate of whole chain electron transport}$$
$$+ \tfrac{1}{3} \cdot \text{rate of cyclic electron transport.} \tag{16.49}$$

and PCO cycles for limiting NADPH and ATP. Farquhar et al. (1980) derived an equation similar to (16.63 c) and numerical solutions of this equation were graphed by Berry and Farquhar (1978). All of these models are able, with differing degrees of precision, to match the CO_2, O_2 and temperature dependencies observed by Ehleringer and Björkman (1977). (It is interesting to note here that Ku and Edwards (1978) found that the quantum yield (mol CO_2 fixed per mol quanta absorbed) of wheat leaves was independent of temperature when the solubility ratio of O_2/CO_2 was kept constant. They recognized that this may, in part, be fortuitous.)

All of the published models cited above, while successful in predicting effects of environmental changes, were empirical in the sense that parameters were chosen in order to make the quantum yield close to observed values at high $[CO_2]$ or low $[O_2]$ (i.e., $C \gg \Gamma_*$). Hall (1979) chose a value for a fundamental parameter he called the "photochemical efficiency" and Farquhar et al. (1980) chose a value for the "fraction of light not effectively absorbed by chloroplasts". Eq. (16.63) suffer less from this deficiency. Under conditions where $C \gg \Gamma_*$, the quantum requirements (mol quanta absorbed per mol CO_2 fixed) become (a) 8.4, (b) 9.4, (c) 9.5, and (d) 12.6. Using white light, Ehleringer and Björkman (1977) observed requirements of 12.3 in one set of experiments and 13.7 in another, while Ku and Edwards (1978) found requirements of 12.0. Terry (1980), using red light, found values ranging between 8 and 11, but averaging 10.

Eq. (16.63) have other deficiencies. Firstly, there are chloroplastic requirements for ATP and NADPH outside the PCR and PCO cycles (Raven 1972) including additional amino acid biosynthesis, lipid metabolism and, in some cases, nitrate reduction. These will raise the apparent quantum requirement. Secondly, the quantum yields are measured at finite irradiances, often between 50 and 150 $\mu E\ m^{-2}\ s^{-1}$, where J may not necessarily increase linearly with I. From Eq. (16.32)

$$\frac{dJ}{dI} = \frac{2.1 J_{max}^2}{(I + 2.1 J_{max})^2} \tag{16.64}$$

and for case (b) (cyclic), from Eq. (16.43)

$$\frac{dJ}{dI} = \frac{K_1 J_{max}}{(I + K_1)^2}. \tag{16.65}$$

For $J_{max} = 200\ \mu Eq\ m^{-2}\ s^{-1}$, at $I = 100\ \mu E\ m^{-2}\ s^{-1}$, dA/dI becomes, for $C \gg \Gamma_*$, (a) 0.078, (b) 0.072, (c) 0.069, (d) 0.052, giving apparent quantum requirements of (a) 12.9, (b) 13.8, (c) 14.6, (d) 19.2. We see that case (d) would be energetically expensive. Inclusion of (b) in a strict comparison with the others may be misleading since with the same electron transport capacity J_{max} should be smaller in this case (cf. Sect. 16.3.4.4) giving a greater quantum requirement than 13.8. As was mentioned before, Eq. (16.32) may lead to an underestimate of dJ/dI.

In 21% oxygen, at normal CO_2 concentrations, and 25 °C, the apparent quantum requirements are increased, theoretically and in practice (Ehleringer

and BJÖRKMAN 1977) by about 40%; i.e., quantum yield is inhibited by about 30%.

16.5.3 Carboxylation Efficiency

16.5.3.1 Introduction

FARQUHAR et al. (1980) differentiated Eq. (16.61) to obtain

$$\frac{dA}{dC} = V_{c\,max} \cdot \frac{\Gamma_* + K_c(1+O/K_o)}{[C + K_c(1+O/K_o)]^2},\tag{16.66}$$

i.e., the slope, sometimes called the "mesophyll conductance" and, more appropriately, the "carboxylation efficiency" (KU and EDWARDS 1977b), should have a slight dependence only on CO_2 concentration because K_c is relatively large. Inclusion of activation effects [Eq. (16.14)] may lead to an even more linear response above the compensation point. At $C = \Gamma_*$

$$\frac{dA}{dC} = \frac{V_{c\,max}}{\Gamma_* + K_c(1+O/K_o)}.\tag{16.67}$$

VON CAEMMERER and FARQUHAR (1981) have measured dA/dC using gas exchange techniques and $V_{c\,max}$ using biochemical techniques and found good agreement between these results and Eq. (16.67). Leaves of *Phaseolus vulgaris* were used and the sources of variation were age, nitrogen nutrition, iron nutrition, previous irradiance, and CO_2 concentration during growth and defoliation.

16.5.3.2 Oxygen Dependence of Carboxylation Resistance

The inverse of dA/dC, the "carboxylation resistance", is

$$\frac{1}{dA/dC} = \frac{\Gamma_* + K_c(1+O/K_o)}{V_{c\,max}}\tag{16.68}$$

$$= \frac{K_c + (\gamma_* + K_c/K_o)\,O}{V_{c\,max}}\tag{16.69}$$

which is linearly dependent on oxygen concentration, as observed by KU and EDWARDS (1977b), with a slope of $(\gamma_* + K_c/K_o)/V_{c\,max}$.

Anomalous results have been reported by PEISKER and APEL (1971), who observed that the oxygen dependence of carboxylation resistance increased with oxygen concentration. PEISKER et al. (1979) also reported anomalous changes in carboxylation resistance at high temperatures and high O_2 concentrations. However, KU and EDWARDS (1977b) found no such anomalies.

16.5.3.3 Temperature Dependence of dA/dC

The temperature dependence of dA/dC is determined by the kinetic constants of RuP_2 carboxylase-oxygenase and their respective temperature dependencies.

FARQUHAR et al. (1980) used the temperature dependencies of K_c, K_o, $V_{c \, max}$ and $V_{o \, max}$, determined by BADGER and COLLATZ (1977). This model predicts that dA/dC should increase slowly with temperature (2% per degree at 25 °C) at normal $p(O_2)$, but be independent of temperature at zero $p(O_2)$. HALL (1979) used the same activation energies for K_c and K_o, but assumed an in vivo temperature optimum for $V_{c \, max}$ and $V_{o \, max}$ of about 30 °C. Recent data of WEIS (1981) appear to support this assumption. There is, as yet, no in vitro biochemical support. KU and EDWARDS (1977b) observed increasing "carboxylation efficiency" with increasing temperature, when expressed in terms of concentration in solution. When expressed in terms of partial pressures of CO_2, the increase was almost zero. PEISKER et al. (1979) observed that at normal $p(O_2)$, dA/dC were similar at 23 °C and 33 °C in wheat.

16.5.4 Transition from Limitation Due to RuP$_2$ Carboxylation Capacity to One Due to RuP$_2$ Regeneration Capacity

The above equations [(16.66)–(16.69)] apply only when RuP$_2$ is saturating. FARQUHAR et al. (1980) suggested that this would be so at low CO_2 concentrations, but that at higher $p(CO_2)$ a point is reached where RuP$_2$ regeneration is limiting, and the dependence on CO_2 changes in nature. Their prediction of a change in the response of A to C has been confirmed by VON CAEMMERER and FARQUHAR (1981) (see Fig. 16.5). To the extent that RuP$_2$ regeneration is limited by photophosphorylation, the dependence on C is given by Eq. (16.62c). Note that A continues to increase with C in this region as limiting ATP is diverted from the PCO cycle to the PCR cycle. Analyses of CO_2 exchange under high CO_2 concentration which ignore the RuP$_2$ limitation (SINCLAIR and RAND 1979) are unreasonable.

From Eq. (16.59) and (16.60c), we can predict that the transition from RuP$_2$ carboxylation limitation to RuP$_2$ regeneration limitation occurs at

$$C = \frac{K_c(1 + O/K_o) \, J/(4.5 V_{c \, max}) - 7/3 \Gamma_*}{1 - J/(4.5 V_{c \, max})}. \tag{16.70}$$

Note that the transition depends on the ratio $J/V_{c \, max}$ and since this ratio is somewhat conservative at the growth irradiance (VON CAEMMERER and FARQUHAR 1981), the transition C also tends to be conservative.

The change in CO_2 dependence moving from RuP$_2$ carboxylation limitation to RuP$_2$ regeneration limitation causes faster saturation than would occur due to the kinetics of RuP$_2$ carboxylase-oxygenase alone. Failure to recognize this has led TENHUNEN et al. (1977) to fit sunflower data at 25 °C with the physiologically unreasonable values of 0.45 μbar and 1 mbar for K_c and K_o respectively, and wheat data at 25 °C (TENHUNEN et al. 1980a) with $K_c = 12$ μbar and $K_o = 82$ mbar. TENHUNEN et al. (1980a) emphasized the linear relationship between A and C as indicating support for mesophyll resistance to diffusion. However, all that is needed for such a response is to use biochemically reasonable values for the kinetic constants. FARQUHAR et al. (1980) used 460 μbar and 210 mbar,

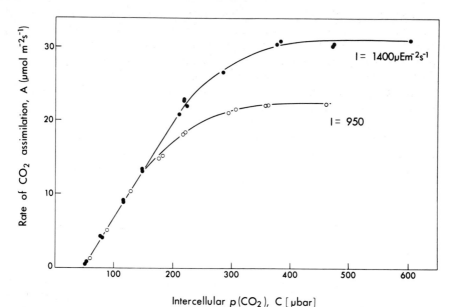

Fig. 16.5. Rate of CO_2 assimilation A, vs. intercellular partial pressure of CO_2, C, in *Phaseolus vulgaris* at an irradiance, I, of $1,400\ \mu E\ m^{-2}\ s^{-1}$ (●), and $950\ \mu E\ m^{-2}\ s^{-1}$ (○) at 28°C (after VON CAEMMERER and FARQUHAR 1981)

for K_c and K_o at 25 °C. There is still some uncertainty about exact values which, although reasonably consistent among higher C_3 land plants, may show a twofold variation (YEOH et al. 1981). All measurements indicate values much higher than those used by TENHUNEN.

At low CO_2 concentrations the response of A to C is not linear, as demonstrated by MEIDNER (1970). It is possible that this curvature may be due to carboxylase-oxygenase inactivation [cf. Eq. (16.14)].

16.5.5 Temperature Optimum

The dependence on temperature of the CO_2 assimilation rate, A, depends on that of its subprocesses, but the analysis is nevertheless complex (see also Chap. 10, Vol. 12 A). At normal $p(CO_2)$ and $p(O_2)$ the RuP_2 saturated rate, given by Eq. (16.61), increases with temperature. This dependence is greater at high $p(CO_2)$. At sufficiently high temperatures there is a decline due to increased day respiration, R_d. The latter effect is more pronounced at low $p(CO_2)$ since R_d then has a greater fractional impact on A. The temperature dependence of the RuP_2-limited rate, given by Eq. (16.62c) is affected more by that of J_{max}, and the optimum is closer to that of J_{max}, which occurs at lower temperatures. We show in Fig. 16.6 that by increasing the ratio $J_{max}/V_{c\ max}$, which tends to release the RuP_2 limitation, an increase in the temperature optimum is obtained.

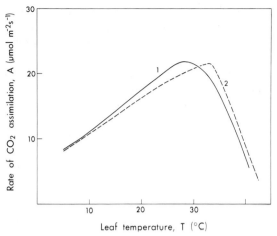

Fig. 16.6. Modelled rate of CO_2 assimilation, A, vs. leaf temperature, T, for two ratios of $J_{max}/V_{c\ max}$:

$$1 \quad \frac{J_{max}}{V_{c\ max}} = \frac{190\ \mu Eq\ m^{-2}\ s^{-1}}{115\ \mu mol\ m^{-2}\ s^{-1}} = 1.65, \qquad 2 \quad \frac{J_{max}}{V_{c\ max}} = \frac{210\ \mu Eq\ m^{-2}\ s^{-1}}{98\ \mu mol\ m^{-2}\ s^{-1}} = 2.14.$$

The irradiance is $2,000\ \mu E\ m^{-2}\ s^{-1}$, intercellular $p(CO_2)$ is 230 μbar

Increasing $p(CO_2)$ from a low level causes an increase in the optimum temperature, as does increasing the irradiance from a low level. Both also cause the temperature response to become sharper, as discussed by HALL (1979). All these phenomena are observed in practice (ENOCH and SACKS 1978; BERRY and BJÖRKMAN 1980). Decreasing the $p(O_2)$ from an initially high value causes a similar response as observed by JOLLIFFE and TREGUNNA (1968).

16.5.6 Resistance of the Intercellular Spaces

YOCUM and LOMMEN (1975) estimated the drop in the concentration of CO_2 at cells some distance from the substomatal cavities. They used equations developed to describe a system where enzymes are uniformly distributed in a diffusing medium without carriers for facilitated transport. They regarded the distributed cells as being analogous to the distributed enzymes, and estimated that the CO_2 concentration at the farthest distance from the substomatal cavities was 0.91 of that in the cavities, C_o. However, their dimensionless Michaelis-Menten constant, K_m/C_o, was probably too low by at least an order of magnitude, as they chose a value for K_m of only 25 μbar. The latter value was determined, presumably, using the erroneous method of assessing K_m from A vs C response curves, without considering electron transport and photophosphorylation limitations. If a more reasonable estimate of $K_m[=K_c(1+0/K_o)]$ is used in their equations, with the parameters they determined for an ivy leaf, the estimated drawdown in CO_2 concentration in remote regions of the intercellular spaces is negligible.

RAND (1977) estimated the maximum drawdown to be 50% of the substomatal concentration. His sink strengths were unreasonable and he subsequently (RAND 1978) revised this estimate to 2%–14%. The substomatal concentration is typically 220 μl 1^{-1} in C_3 species (WONG et al. 1979). COOKE and RAND (1980) estimated the intercellular air space (ias) resistance to be typically 0.25 m^2 s mol^{-1} for CO_2. PARKHURST (1977) has derived a three-dimensional model for CO_2 uptake in which he estimated an ias resistance of 6.3 m^2 s mol^{-1}. The reasons for the disparity are not obvious to us.

We now give independent estimates. The maximum drawdown, at cells most remote from the stomata, in a hypostomatous leaf assimilating uniformly throughout its volume is approximately $A_1 r_i/2$, where A_1 (μmol m^{-2} s^{-1}) is the flux of CO_2 into the lower surface, and r_i is the resistance to diffusion of CO_2 across the whole leaf through the intercellular spaces. In an amphistomatous leaf the maximum drawdown $\simeq \dfrac{A_1 A_2}{A_1+A_2} \cdot \dfrac{r_i}{2}$, where A_2 is the CO_2 flux into the upper surface. FARQUHAR and RASCHKE (1978) measured the resistance to the diffusion of helium across leaves of cotton and *Xanthium strumarium*. After allowing for stomatal and boundary layer resistances on each side of the leaf, and for the ratio of the diffusivities of CO_2 and helium in air, the total intercellular resistances were approximately 8 and 3.2 m^2 s mol^{-1} for cotton and *X. strumarium,* respectively. With $A_1=A_2=10$, and $A_1=8$, $A_2=5$, respectively, the maximum drawdowns are then 20 and 5 μl 1^{-1}. The average drawdowns in the leaves are approximately half these values.

At a whole leaf level these predictions for average drawdown may be mimicked by resistances to the diffusion of CO_2 in the intercellular air spaces of 0.5 and 0.2 m^2 s mol^{-1}, respectively, in agreement with the estimates of COOKE and RAND (1980). These resistances are relatively unimportant, but may underestimate the effects of close packing in, for example, sclerophyllous leaves.

16.5.7 Liquid-Phase Resistance

YOCUM and LOMMEN (1975) pointed out that most of the liquid diffusion path is within the chloroplasts themselves. They used the equations relevant to distributed sinks with Michaelis-Menten kinetics to examine CO_2 diffusion across a chloroplast. They estimated that the CO_2 concentration at the surface away from the wall would be 0.5 of that nearest it if the diffusing species were CO_2 alone. Unfortunately the K_m chosen for CO_2 was only 25 μbar and with a more appropriate value the drawdown is again very small. YOCUM and LOMMEN (1975) estimated that carbonic anhydrase activity would reduce the depletion to almost zero.

SINCLAIR et al. (1977) have developed equations to describe the net characteristics associated with both diffusion through cytoplasm and kinetics of RuP_2 carboxylase-oxygenase. When geometric characteristics of C_3 plants are used, certain simplifications are possible, but the equations still *appear* to depend on geometry. In fact the resulting equations may be further reduced to a description based on the amount of carboxylase per unit area of leaf, with no depen-

dence on liquid-phase resistance, or on cell geometry. Cooke and Rand (1980) treated the results of Sinclair et al. (1977) as an expression of "liquid-phase resistance", but the terminology in this case is inappropriate.

Hall (1971) estimated that the liquid-phase resistance contributed an effective resistance, in terms of gaseous diffusion of only $0.4 \, m^2 \, s \, mol^{-1}$. With a net assimilation rate of $20 \, \mu mol \, m^{-2} \, s^{-1}$, the depletion in partial pressure would then be only $8 \, \mu bar$. Considering carbonic anhydrase activity and the aqueous and lipid portions of the pathway, Raven and Glidewell (1981) estimated the liquid-phase resistance as 25 to $38 \, m^2 \, s \, mol^{-1}$ on a cell area basis. Nobel et al. (1975) observed a correlation between mesophyll cell surface area per unit leaf area and assimilation rate, irradiance during growth being the independent variable. In *Plectranthus parviflora* when the surface area ratio was 50, the assimilation rate was $7.3 \, \mu mol \, m^{-2} \, s^{-1}$. On this basis the above estimate of liquid-phase resistance would correspond to a depletion of 3.6 to $5.5 \, \mu bar$. However, ratios are often smaller, and assimilation rates are often higher in other species (Raven and Glidewell 1981), and if these changes do occur simultaneously the drawdown could be greater. Longstreth and Nobel (1980) found that with varying nutrition, cotton gave varying rates, but that the area ratio remained relatively constant (≈ 25). At the highest assimilation rate, $30 \, \mu mol \, m^{-2} \, s^{-1}$, Raven and Glidewell's estimate of liquid-phase resistance would correspond to a drawdown of 30 to $45 \, \mu bar$.

Farquhar et al. (1980) and Björkman (1981) have pointed out that an increase in mesophyll cell area is usually associated with increases in photosynthetic enzymes and electron carriers, which are the prime cause of increased assimilation rates. An excess of photosynthetic machinery per cell will cause inefficiency (Raven and Glidewell 1981), but there is little evidence that this problem occurs. A reduced ratio of surface areas, because it is generally accompanied by decreased photosynthetic capacity, does not necessarily cause a significant CO_2 drawdown.

16.5.8 On the Appropriate Measure of CO_2 Concentration

Summarizing the previous two sections, it appears that, unless there is bicarbonate pumping in cells, as occurs in some algae (Badger et al. 1980) and submerged macrophytes (see Chap. 15, this Vol.), the CO_2 concentration, C, at the sites of carboxylation is usually only marginally less than in the substomatal cavities. Farquhar et al. (1982) came to the same conclusion from considerations of observed carbon isotope fractionations. Controversy exists whether the most appropriate measure of C is the molar concentration in solution (Ku and Edwards 1977a, b, 1978) or the equilibrium partial pressure (Badger and Collatz 1977). The question will be resolved when it is known whether or not the CO_2 in solution is in equilibrium with that bound to the carboxylase sites. Ku and Edwards (1977a, b) have shown that much of the temperature dependence of various processes is reduced when the solubilities of CO_2 and O_2 are taken into account. However, it is unlikely that the kinetic constants are completely independent of temperature. If the molar concentration is the appro-

priate measure, the temperature dependence of the kinetic constants can still be treated in terms of partial pressures by absorbing the temperature dependence of solubility (HALL 1979).

16.6 Long-Term Effects of Environment on Leaf Photosynthesis

Photosynthetic CO_2-assimilation by leaves is affected by plant nutrition, light and temperature regimes, leaf age and other physiological factors. If analytical, mechanistic models are to be used to estimate the influence of individual components on the integrated performance, an understanding of which parameters may change and which are invariant under environmental changes is important. As discussed previously, there is evidence that the ratio $V_{o\,max}/V_{c\,max}$ is constant among species and under different growth conditions. Similarly the Michaelis-Menten constants for the RuP_2 carboxylase-oxygenase, K_c and K_o, are not affected by different growth conditions such as high temperature (BERRY and BJÖRKMAN 1980) and high $[CO_2]$ (YEOH et al. 1981). However, the amounts of carboxylase and of electron transport components may vary greatly. This has been shown by several authors. For example, BJÖRKMAN et al. (1972) and POWLES and CRITCHLEY (1980) found that RuP_2 carboxylase activity, $V_{c\,max}$, and maximum electron transport rate, J_{max}, were higher, on a leaf area basis,

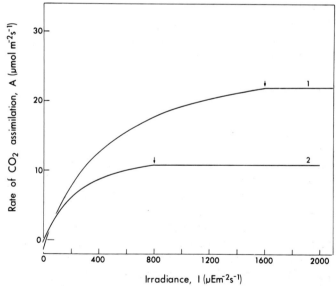

Fig. 16.7. Modelled rate of CO_2 assimilation, A, vs. irradiance, I: I represents high light grown plant with $V_{c\,max}=115\ \mu mol\ m^{-2}\ s^{-1}$ and $J_{max}=210\ \mu Eq\ m^{-2}\ s^{-1}$; 2 represents low light grown plant with $V_{c\,max}=57\ \mu mol\ m^{-2}\ s^{-1}$ and $J_{max}=105\ \mu Eq\ m^{-2}\ s^{-1}$. Values of J_{max} and $V_{c\,max}$ chosen are typical of those determined experimentally by the authors. Rates of day respiration have been scaled accordingly. *Arrows* indicate transition from RuP_2 regeneration limitation to RuP_2 carboxylation limitation

in plants grown at high light than in plants grown at low light (see Chap. 3, Vol. 12 A). The modelled effects are shown in Fig. 16.7. Plants grown at differing levels of nitrogen nutrition also have differing values of $V_{c\,max}$ and J_{max} (Medina 1969; von Caemmerer and Farquhar 1981). The decrease in CO_2-assimilation rate observed during leaf ageing is associated with a decline in $V_{c\,max}$ and J_{max}. Similarly the increase in CO_2-assimilation rate after defoliation of other leaves (Wareing et al. 1968) has been correlated with an increase in $V_{c\,max}$. Wong (1979) has shown that the lowered assimilation rate at normal $p(CO_2)$ of cotton plants grown at enhanced $p(CO_2)$, is associated with a lowered carboxylase activity.

Temperature adaptations may also to some extent be explained by changes in the amount and ratio of J_{max} and $V_{c\,max}$. Berry and Björkman (1980) reported that high temperature grown plants have less carboxylase than low temperature grown plants. This will cause an increase in the temperature optimum of CO_2-assimilation rate as discussed earlier. The temperature optimum of electron-transport rate itself did not change significantly in the example cited, although there was greater thermal stability at temperatures greater than the optimum.

Thus it appears that many longer-term environmental effects may be modelled by suitable changes in two key parameters, $V_{c\,max}$ and J_{max}.

16.7 C₄-Photosynthesis

The mathematical modelling of CO_2 assimilation by C_4-species is in its infancy. Nevertheless, many of the gas exchange characteristics observed with intact leaves have been predicted using models based on the known biochemical and anatomical characteristics. Peisker (1978a) and Berry and Farquhar (1978) predicted the low compensation point, insensitive to $p(O_2)$. Berry and Farquhar predicted the insensitivity of quantum yield to $p(CO_2)$, $p(O_2)$ and temperature, and the lack of O_2 effects on assimilation rate. They predicted that photorespiration should nevertheless continue at a low rate in the bundle-sheath cells, as observed in several studies and most recently by Morot-Gaudry et al. (1980). They also predicted the greater nitrogen use efficiency of C_4 plants, especially at higher temperatures.

Factors needing consideration in future models are the mechanism of action of phosphoenol pyruvate (PEP) carboxylase, the malate and aspartate inhibitions of PEP carboxylation, the feedback inhibition by free CO_2 of C_4 acid decarboxylation (Rathnam and Chollet 1980), and the higher K_c for RuP_2 carboxylase in C_4 species (Yeoh et al. 1981).

16.8 Canopy Photosynthesis

Photosynthesis of canopies of C_3-species has been the subject of a great deal of experimentation and modelling (Hesketh 1980; see also Chaps. 4–10, Vol.

12D). It is useful to examine how the equations for leaf photosynthesis may be utilized in this context.

Earlier we suggested that for an individual leaf the rate of assimilation should be given by

$$A = (1 - \Gamma_*/C) \cdot \min\{W_c, J'\} - R_d. \tag{16.71}$$

Since W_c and J' are usually correlated (VON CAEMMERER and FARQUHAR 1981) and since irradiance is often limiting in the canopy, we can expect that to a good approximation $W_c \leq J'$ for most leaves. Substituting for J' using Eq. (16.60c) we obtain the RuP_2 limited rate of assimilation for a single leaf (16.62c) and using Eq. (16.32) this yields

$$A = \frac{J_{max} I}{I + 2.1 J_{max}} \cdot \frac{C - \Gamma_*}{4.5 C + 10.5 \Gamma_*} - R_d. \tag{16.72}$$

The problem of predicting canopy photosynthesis, the rate of assimilation per unit ground surface, reduces to that of determining how J_{max}, R_d, I, T and C vary through the canopy, and integrating appropriately. It is possible that treatments could be developed which exploit the correlation that can occur between J_{max} and growth irradiance to predict how J_{max} is reduced lower in the canopy. Further, R_d may be correlated with A (ANGUS and WILSON 1976). Intercellular $p(CO_2)$ depends on stomatal conductance, but at a particular temperature is often insensitive to I (GOUDRIAAN and VAN LAAR 1978; WONG et al. 1979), except at low irradiances where contributions to photosynthesis are, in any case, minimal. The main problem, therefore, relates to the penetration, propagation and absorption of radiation (DE WIT 1965), which in turn depends on canopy structure (MONSI et al. 1973).

Regardless of the details of light absorption in the canopy, the irradiance dependence of canopy photosynthetic rate (per unit ground area) will be similar to that given by Eq. (16.72), but with J_{max} much greater than that for a single leaf, and with R_d summed over the whole canopy. This result may be seen in the classical papers of BOYSEN JENSEN (1932, 1949).

16.9 Empirical Models

At present, even in the models of short-term responses discussed earlier, the dependence of J_{max} on temperature is fairly empirical. So too are the effects of water stress and salinity. Models concerned with time scales in which $V_{c\ max}$, J_{max} and R_d change are also, of necessity, empirical at present. Models which successfully deal with these longer times include that of LANGE et al. (1977), in which the productivity of lichens is predicted. Even over the short-time scales discussed earlier, some authors have found it easier to make statistical analyses of gas exchange characteristics such as the response of A to appropriately spaced changes in C, T and I than to assume a particular underlying

biochemical structure (Enoch and Sacks 1978). Nevertheless it is probably easier for most ecophysiologists interested in C_3-photosynthesis to assume a structure such as the one described earlier, measure CO_2-assimilation rate under certain conditions, and fit values to $V_{c\ max}$, and to R_d and J_{max} and their temperature dependencies, using techniques similar to those described by Hall (1979). Hopefully further research and modelling of the mechanistic kind will continue to decrease the areas where empiricism is still required.

References

Angus JF, Wilson JH (1976) Photosynthesis of barley and wheat leaves in relation to canopy models. Photosynthetica 10:367–377

Armond PA, Schreiber U, Björkmann O (1978) Photosynthetic acclimation to temperature in the desert shrub, *Larrea divaricata*. II. Light harvesting efficiency and electron transport. Plant Physiol 61:411–415

Arnon DI (1977) Photosynthesis 1950–75: Changing concepts and perspectives. In: Trebst A, Avron M (eds) Photosynthesis I. Photosynthetic electron transport and photophosphorylation. Encyclopedia of plant physiology New Ser Vol V. Springer, Berlin Heidelberg New York, pp 7–56

Azcon-Bieto J, Farquhar GD, Caballero A (1981) Effects of temperature, oxygen concentration, leaf age and seasonal variations on the CO_2 compensation point of *Lolium perenne* L: Comparison with a mathematical model including non photorespiratory CO_2 production in the light. Planta 152:497–504

Badger MR, Andrews TJ (1974) Effects of CO_2, O_2 and temperature on a higg-affinity form of ribulose diphosphate carboxylase-oxygenase from spinach. Biochem Biophys Res Commun 60:204–210

Badger MR, Collatz GJ (1977) Studies on the kinetic mechanism of ribulose-1,5-bisphosphate carboxylase and oxygenase reactions, with particular reference to the effect of temperature on kinetic parameters. Carnegie Inst Washington Yearb 76:355–361

Badger MR, Kaplan A, Berry JA (1980) Internal inorganic carbon pool of *Chlamydomonas reinhardtii*. Evidence for a carbon dioxide-concentrating mechanism. Plant Physiol 66:407–413

Bassham JA (1979) The reductive pentose phosphate cycle. In: Gibbs M, Latzko E (eds) Photosynthesis II. Photosynthetic carbon metabolism and related processes. Encyclopedia of plant physiology New Ser Vol VI. Springer Berlin Heidelberg New York, pp 9–30

Bauwe H, Apel P, Peisker M (1980) Ribulose 1,5-bisphosphate carboxylase/oxygenase and CO_2 exchange characteristics in C_3 and C_3–C_4 intermediate species checking mathematical models of carbon metabolism. Photosynthetica 14:550–556

Berry JA, Björkman O (1980) Photosynthetic response and adaptation to temperature in higher plants. Annu Rev Plant Physiol 31:491–543

Berry JA, Farquhar GD (1978) The CO_2 concentrating function of C_4 photosynthesis. A biochemical model. In: Hall D, Coombs J, Goodwin T (eds) Proc 4th Int Congr Photosynthes. Biochem Soc London, pp 119–131

Berzborn RJ, Müller D (1977) Correlation of grana in chloroplasts with the variability in the size of 'photophosphorylation unit'. In: Coombs J (ed) Read Abstr, pp 30–31

Berzborn RJ, Müller D, Roos P, Andersson B (1981) Significance of different quantitative determinations of photosynthetic ATP-synthase CF_1 for heterogeneous CF_1 distribution and grana formation. In: Akoyunoglou G (ed) Proc Fifth Int Congr Photosynthesis Vol. III. Balaban Philadelphia, pp 107–120

Björkman O (1981) Ecological adaptation of the photosynthetic apparatus. In: Akoyunoglou G (ed) Proc Fifth Int Congr Photosynthesis Vol. VI. Balaban Philadelphia, pp 191–202

Björkman O, Badger MR, Armond PA (1980) Response and adaptation of photosynthesis to high temperatures. In: Turner NC, Kramer PJ (eds) Adaptation of plants to water and high temperature stress. Wiley and Sons, New York, pp 233–249

Björkman O, Boardman NK, Anderson JM, Thorne SW, Goodchild DJ, Pyliotis NA (1972) Effect of light intensity during growth of *Atriplex patula* on the capacity of photosynthetic reactions, chloroplast components and structure. Carnegie Inst Washington Yearb 71:115–135

Boysen Jensen P (1932) Die Stoffproduktion der Pflanzen. Fischer, Jena 108 pp

Boysen Jensen P (1949) The production of matter in agricultural plants and its limitation. Biol Med 21:1–28

Caemmerer von S, Farquhar GD (1981) Some relationships between the biochemistry of photosynthesis and the gas exchange of leaves. Planta 153:376–387

Čatský J, Tichá I (1979) CO_2 compensation concentration in bean leaves: Effect of photon flux density and leaf age. Biol Plant 21:361–364

Charles-Edwards DA (1978) Leaf carbon dioxide compensation points at high light flux densities. Ann Bot (London) 42:733–739

Chartier P, Prioul JL (1976) The effects of irradiance, carbon dioxide and oxygen on the net photosynthetic rate of the leaf: A mechanistic model. Photosynthetica 10:20–24

Collatz GJ (1978) The interaction between photosynthesis and ribulose-P_2 concentration – effects of light, CO_2 and O_2. Carnegie Inst Washington Yearb 77:248–251

Cooke JR, Rand RH (1980) Diffusion resistance models. In: Hesketh JD, Jones JW (eds) Predicting photosynthesis for ecosystem models Vol I. CRC Press, Boca Raton, pp 93–122

Cramer WA, Whitmarsh J, Widger W (1981) On the properties and function of cytochromes b-559 and f in chloroplast electron transport. In: Akoyunoglou G (ed) Proc Fifth Int Congr Photosynthesis Vol. II. Balaban Philadelphia, pp 509–522

Ehleringer J, Björkman O (1977) Quantum yields for CO_2 uptake in C_3 and C_4 plants. Dependence on temperature, CO_2 and O_2 concentrations. Plant Physiol 59:86–90

Enoch HZ, Sacks JM (1978) An empirical model of CO_2 exchange of a C_3 plant in relation to light, CO_2 concentration and temperature. Photosynthetica 12:150–157

Farquhar GD (1979) Models describing the kinetics of ribulose bisphosphate carboxylase-oxygenase. Arch Biochem Biophys 193:456–468

Farquhar GD, Caemmerer von S (1981) Electron transport limitations on the CO_2 assimilation rate of leaves: a model and some observations in *Phaseolus vulgaris* L. In: Akoyunoglou G (ed) Proc Fifth Int Congr Photosynthesis Vol. IV. Balaban Philadelphia, pp 163–175

Farquhar GD, Raschke K (1978) On the resistance to transpiration of the sites of evaporation within the leaf. Plant Physiol 61:1000–1005

Farquhar GD, Caemmerer von S, Berry JA (1980) A biochemical model of photosynthetic CO_2 assimilation in leaves of C_3 species. Planta 149:78–90

Farquhar GD, O'Leary MH, Berry JA (1982) On the relationship between carbon isotope discrimination and the intercellular carbon dioxide concentration in leaves. Aust J Plant Physiol 9:121–137

Farron F (1970) Isolation and properties of a chloroplast coupling factor and heat-activated adenosine triphosphatase. Biochemistry 9:3823–3828

Giersch Ch, Heber U, Kobayashi Y, Inoue Y, Shibata K, Heldt HW (1980a) Energy charge, photophosphorylation potential and proton motive force in chloroplasts. Biochim Biophys Acta 590:59–73

Giersch Ch, Heber U, Krause GH (1980b) ATP transfer from chloroplasts to the cytosol of leaf cells during photosynthesis and its effect on leaf metabolism. In: Spanswick RM, Lucas WJ, Dainty J (eds) Plant membrane transport: current conceptual issues. Elsevier/North-Holland Biomedical Press, Amsterdam New York, pp 65–79

Goudriaan J, Laar van HH (1978) Relations between leaf resistance CO_2-concentration and CO_2-assimilation in maize, bean, lalang grass and sunflower. Photosynthetica 12:241–249

Graham D, Chapman EA (1979) Interactions between photosynthesis and respiration in higher plants. In: Gibbs M, Latzko E (eds) Photosynthesis II: Photosynthetic carbon metabolism and related processes. Encyclopedia of plant physiology New Ser Vol VI. Springer, Berlin Heidelberg New York, pp 150–162

of water available to a plant. Therefore the period, T, during which the theory, as it has so far been developed, may apply must certainly be short in terms of relative changes in the amount of water in the soil explored by the roots of the plant.

17.2.2 The Transpiration Function

The movement of water vapour and CO_2 across the epidermis and boundary layer of a leaf may be expressed as

$$E = g \frac{e_i - e_a}{1 - \bar{e}/P} \tag{17.6}$$

$$A = 0.63 \, g \cdot (p_a - p_i) - \frac{\bar{p}}{P} E \tag{17.7}$$

where g is the conductance to vapour transfer, e_i and p_i are partial pressures of water vapour and CO_2 in the leaf internal air space, e_a and p_a are partial pressures of water vapour and CO_2 in the ambient atmosphere, $\bar{e} = (e_a + e_i)/2$, $\bar{p} = (p_a + p_i)/2$, P is atmospheric pressure, and the coefficient 0.63 is the ratio of the diffusion coefficients of CO_2 and water vapour in air. No allowance is made here for the fact that the ratio of the transfer coefficients for CO_2 and water vapour in the boundary layer is somewhat greater than 0.63 (see COWAN 1972), because the influence of the boundary layer on g is often relatively small compared with that of the stomata and in any event cannot be measured with great accuracy. Nor is cuticular transfer of water vapour considered (if it is appreciable, it may be approximately taken into account by replacing g in Eq. (17.6) by $g + g_c$, where g_c is cuticular conductance). Allowance is made in Eq. (17.6) for the influence of net mass transfer on vapour diffusion, and in Eq. (17.7) for the influence of vapour diffusion on CO_2 diffusion (see JARMAN 1974; VON CAEMMERER and FARQUHAR 1981). The second effect can reduce the effective transfer coefficient for CO_2 by as much as 20% in hot dry conditions, but has generally been neglected in treatments of gas exchange in leaves, including that of COWAN and FARQUHAR (1977).

Eqs. (17.6) and (17.7) do not by themselves define the interrelationship between E and A, because the partial pressures e_i and p_i are partly dependent on the fluxes. It may be assumed that the leaf internal air space is saturated with water vapour (see Chap. 1, Vol. 12 A). Therefore

$$e_i = e'(T_l) \tag{17.8}$$

where $e'(T_l)$ is saturation vapour pressure at leaf temperature T_l. From a consideration of the energy balance of a leaf, it may be shown (PEISKER 1977) that, to a very good approximation,

$$T_l = T_a + \frac{\Phi_0 - LE}{C_p g_b + 8\sigma T_a^3} \tag{17.9}$$

in which T_a is ambient air temperature, ϕ_o is the flux of solar and terrestrial radiation absorbed per unit area of leaf minus the flux of radiation that would be emitted per unit area of leaf if leaf temperature were the same as air temperature, L is the latent heat of vaporisation of water (44 kJ mol^{-1}), C_p is the molar heat capacity of air ($\approx 29.2 \text{ J mol}^{-1} \text{ K}^{-1}$), g_b is the conductance of the leaf boundary layer to transfer of sensible heat, and σ is the Stefan-Boltzmann constant ($5.9 \times 10^{-8} \text{ W m}^{-2} \text{ K}^{-4}$).

The final (and far more complicated) process to be considered is that of net carbon fixation in leaf mesophyll tissue. In the short term, the variables which primarily determine the net rate of fixation in a given leaf are internal partial pressure of CO_2, temperature, and irradiance. Thus

$$A = A(p_i, T_l, I). \tag{17.10}$$

Attempts to relate empirical measurements of net CO_2 fixation in leaves with the biochemistry of photosynthesis and respiration are progressively more successful, and have yielded models which go a long way towards defining the function above in terms of a small number of measurable metabolic parameters (see Chap. 16, this Vol.). However it is not yet clear whether rate of fixation is also affected in the short term by previous accumulation of photosynthate in the leaf, or by changes in leaf water potential as affected by rate of transpiration (see Chaps. 7 and 8, this Vol.). If it should prove necessary to extend the function to allow for such affects, it will greatly complicate the application of the optimization hypothesis.

The foregoing equations together constitute a relationship between rate of transpiration and rate of carbon assimilation, for the other variables that are in part dependent on the physiological functioning of a leaf, g, e_i, p_i, and T_l may in principle be eliminated. Of the remaining variables e_a, p_a and T_a are by definition independent of leaf function. Provided the optical properties and orientation of the leaf are not under physiological control (at least during the time-span considered) then variations in ϕ_o, I, and g_b stem entirely from variations in the radiation and wind environments. Variation in all of these environmental factors, and differences from leaf to leaf in the parameters of internal carbon metabolism may notionally be subsumed in the general spatial and temporal variables s and t, as in Eq. (17.1).

In practice the relationship between E and A must be found numerically, unless drastic simplifications to the system of equations are made (see COWAN 1977). The method is first to use Eqs. (17.6), (17.8) and (17.9) to determine E and T_l for various assumed magnitudes of g. Equation (17.7) and the model underlying Eq. (17.10) are then employed to find the corresponding magnitudes of A. Providing the differences in g are sufficiently small, the slope $\partial E / \partial A$ may be approximated as the ratio of finite differences.

17.2.3 Illustration

The surface in Fig. 17.2 depicts the transpiration function for a single leaf, $E(A, t)$, during the course of a day. It is a hypothetical example, being derived

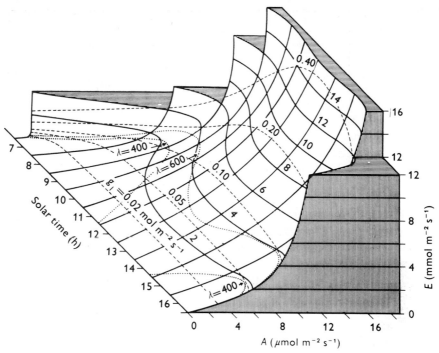

Fig. 17.2. A transpiration function for a single leaf during the course of a day. The *dotted lines* are optimal relationships between rate of transpiration, E, and rate of assimilation, A, corresponding to two constant magnitudes, $\lambda = 400$ and $\lambda = 600$, of $\partial F/\partial A$. The *broken lines* represent constant magnitudes of leaf conductance to vapour transfer, g_l

for a horizontal exposed leaf having assumed characteristics of C_3 photosynthetic carbon fixation and subject to an assumed diurnal variation in environment typical of a hot, dry, clear day in an arid sub-tropical environment (for details, see COWAN and FARQUHAR 1977). The diurnal behaviour of a leaf is represented by a particular trajectory on such a surface. The broken trajectories correspond to constant magnitudes of leaf conductance to gas exchange, g_l (the component of conductance g relating to the leaf epidermis, as distinct from that relating to the leaf boundary layer); the contours correspond to constant rates of transpiration. The dotted trajectories traverse the surface in such a way that the slope, $\partial E/\partial A$ is constant. As the surface is curved in the sence $\partial^2 E/\partial A^2 > 0$, they are optimal trajectories, two of an infinite number of optimal trajectories each one of which corresponds to a particular optimal variation in stomatal aperture and a particular magnitude of λ. Figure 17.3 shows a number of trajectories, represented as temporal variations in E and A. When λ is large, that is to say unit marginal cost is large, the optimal variations in gas exchange do not deviate greatly from those which would occur if leaf conductance were constant. With decreasing λ, the deviations become relatively greater. Gas exchange is increasingly confined to those periods, early in the morning and late in the afternoon, when irradiance and temperature are appropriate for rapid photosyn-

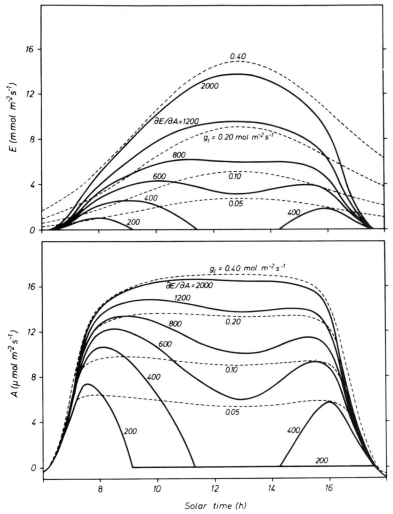

Fig. 17.3. Optimal time courses of rate of assimilation, A, and rate of transpiration, E, for various magnitudes of λ (*solid lines*). Also shown are A and E for various magnitudes of leaf conductance, g_l

thesis but, because the ambient vapour pressure deficit is relatively small, potential rate of transpiration is relatively small. COWAN and FARQUHAR (1977) pointed out that curves of the type shown in Fig. 17.3 resemble observations of gas exchange in plants out of doors, particularly those of LANGE et al. (1975) with wild plants in the Negev desert at various times of the year. However, the shapes of optimal variations in rate of transpiration and rate of assimilation depend not only on the magnitude of an undetermined parameter, λ, but also on characteristics of the physical environment, and of leaf orientation and exposure which are inevitably somewhat disturbed when leaves are placed in a gas exchange cuvette, and on characteristics of leaf internal metabolism which

are exceedingly difficult to determine. For these reasons it will be very difficult to test the optimality hypothesis with plants in their natural condition.

17.2.4 The Evidence

If diurnal variation in natural physical environment were regular and predictable, then optimization would require only that there be an appropriate circadian rhythm in stomatal aperture. But variation in environment is, in part, stochastic, and therefore optimization would require that the plant respond appropriately to stochastic changes. This is the justification for examining the variance of $\partial E/\partial A$ during a sequence of single-factor step changes in humidity, irradiance or temperature of the kind imposed in laboratory experiments. Of course one does not know what peculiarities of preconditioning may take place in glasshouse or growth cabinet. Only one experiment (FIELD et al. 1981) to determine degree of optimization has been conducted with a plant growing in the field, *Lepechinia calycina*. The results of that experiment, and also of laboratory experiments with *Nicotiana glauca* and *Corylus avellana* (FARQUHAR et al. 1980a), *Vigna unguiculata* (HALL and SCHULZE 1980), and *Pseudotsuga menziesii* (MEINZER 1982), demonstrate conservation in $\partial E/\partial A$. In all four investigations, changes in ambient humidity were imposed. HALL and SCHULZE changed temperature also; some of their results are illustrated in Fig. 17.4. No specific examination of $\partial E/\partial A$ with varying irradiance has yet been made.

Despite the paucity of quantitative information pertaining to $\partial E/\partial A$, there is strong circumstantial evidence that the optimization theory provides at least a first approximation to the truth. It relates to the qualitative characteristics of stomatal responses. Discussions of stomatal mechanisms in relation to optimization of gas exchange are to be found in COWAN (1977) and COWAN and FARQUHAR (1977) and will not be elaborated here, except in two respects. It was pointed out that optimization in some circumstances demands that stomata should respond directly to changes in external environmental conditions which influence rate of transpiration and rate of assimilation; that is to say, they should be capable of controlling gas exchange by a process of feed-forward, for only then is it possible for actual rate of transpiration to decrease when environmental changes tend to enhance rate of transpiration, or for intercellular partial pressure of CO_2 to increase when environmental changes tend to enhance rate of assimilation. That stomata are directly sensitive to difference in the partial pressure of water vapour across the epidermis had already been established (LANGE et al. 1971; SCHULZE et al. 1972; HALL et al. 1976). It has now been shown that stomatal movements due to changes in irradiance are predominantly of the feedforward kind (WONG et al. 1978) and that intercellular partial pressure sometimes increases with irradiance (SHARKEY and RASCHKE 1981; VON CAEMMERER unpublished). In short, the nature of the stomatal responses to the predominant environmental determinants of E and A is of the kind required to bring about optimization. Consider now spatial, rather than temporal, optimization, associated with differences in metabolic characteristics amongst leaves. There is much evidence, summarized by WONG et al. (1979)

Fig. 17.4. Components of $\partial E/\partial A =$ $(\partial E/\partial g)/(\partial A/\partial g)$ as functions of difference in leaf internal vapour pressure and external vapour pressure in *Vigna unguiculata*. Leaf temperatures: (●) 26 °C, (○) 30 °C, (▲) 34 °C. (Redrawn from HALL and SCHULZE 1980)

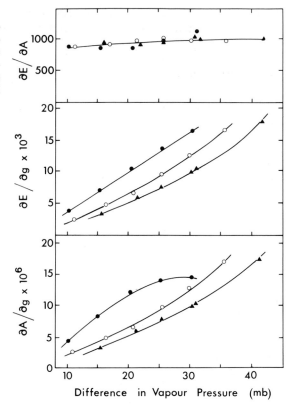

and in Chapter 7, this Volume, and recently confirmed by VON CAEMMERER (1981) that stomatal conductance is positively correlated with leaf mesophyll capacity for photosynthetic carbon fixation, whether differences in the latter are due to differences in age, in exposure to light, or in nutritional status. Assuming this correlation persists amongst the different leaves within one plant, it is clearly a phenomenon conforming qualitatively with the requirements of optimization.

Perhaps it is not too extravagant to summarize the argument in this way. Suppose that the hypothesis had been proposed, and its implications worked out, without knowing much of the responses of stomata; knowing only that the apertures of stomata may change in response to a variety of external physical, and internal physiological stimuli. Then, when it had been discovered that stomata indeed generally open in the light (to some extent, even in plants which are short of water), close in the dark (even in well-watered plants), close with increase in vapour pressure deficit (even to the extent that rate of water loss may be less than that at a lower deficit), and tend to be opened or closed as the intrinsic capacity of the leaf to fix carbon is large or small, the theory would surely have been thought a great success. That it has been developed with hindsight does not detract from its value in summarizing so much of what plants do in one neat relationship, $\partial E/\partial A = \lambda$. Doubtless the

behaviour is not in exact quantitative accord with the relationship, but certainly it tends to reduce water loss in relation to carbon gain. It presumably has been adapted towards doing so. F. Darwin (1898) put the matter thus: "When we remember the innumerable adaptations which serve to economise water, it is inconceivable that the closure of the stomata should not cooperate. Those who deny that the stomata close adaptively as a precaution against too great evaporation must assume, I imagine, that the closure on withering is a chance outcome or bye-product of the machine. They cannot deny, however, that this closure does effect an economy, and this makes it even more difficult to understand their position."

17.2.5 Some Problems

Whatever the worth of the empirical evidence that plants tend to optimize gas exchange, the theory is of limited conceptual value if it is without a plausible explanation as to why plants are so adapted. An explanation will have to contend with several problems. Firstly, the economy in water use that may be achieved appears generally to be small. Figure 17.5 shows results of some computations of daytime averages of rate of assimilation and rate of transpiration. They relate to three different radiation regimes, associated with three differing leaf orientations. The climatic circumstances, similar to those assumed in constructing Fig. 17.2, are shown in Fig. 17.6; they are chosen as typical of a hot, clear, dry day in an arid sub-tropical region. The characteristics

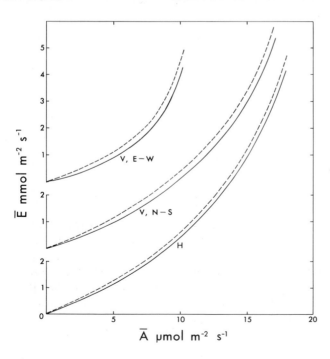

Fig. 17.5. Relationships between average daily rates of transpiration, $\bar{E}$, and assimilation, $\bar{A}$, in leaves of differing orientations: H horizontal; V vertical and E-W east-west; V vertical and N-S North-South. The *full curve* in each case is the optimal relationship, each *point* corresponding to a particular constant magnitude of λ. Each point on the *broken curve* corresponds to a constant magnitude of leaf conductance

Fig. 17.6. Climatic variables used in the computations shown in Fig. 17.5. T_a, e_a, u, g_b, I, and ϕ_o are respectively ambient air temperature, ambient vapour pressure, windspeed, boundary layer conductance, irradiance, and net radiation

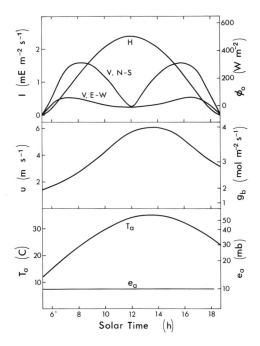

of leaf carbon metabolism are represented by the model of FARQUHAR et al. (1980b, see also Chap. 16, this Vol.). The lower of each pair of curves is the relationship between $\bar{E}$ and $\bar{A}$ that obtains if gas exchange is regulated optimally; the upper curve is that which obtains if stomatal conductance is constant. It is worth mentioning that much greater differences are found between the optimal and "constant-conductance" relationships when calculations are made for higher temperatures than those in Fig. 17.6. Nevertheless, if the theory is to have general validity, it must relate to conditions which occur frequently in the natural plant habitat.

A second problem that must be addressed relates to competition. Whatever the economy in water use that may potentially be achieved by optimization, and whatever the value of that economy to a plant growing in isolation, what can be the advantage of economy in a plant if the water conserved is available for use by competitors?

As suggested in Chapter 1, this Volume, competition might demand that λ is very large, and this leads one to the central question that cannot be answered by studying short-term regulation only: what is the optimal magnitude of λ? If optimization is in some way to be related to fitness, then the roles of carbon fixation and water use must be considered over periods which are at least long enough to encompass significant relative plant growth and development. How, on such a time scale, does the function of short-term reversible regulatory mechanisms relate to longer-term irreversible adjustments, associated for example with partitioning of carbon to leaves and roots?

These various problems will be touched on in the remainder of this chapter.

that the plant will not, in fact, die (the growth rate of plants that will die before reaching maturity is of no interest). Relative growth rate is proportional to rate of assimilation per unit area of foliage, other things, such as carbon partitioning for leaf growth, being equal. Therefore the problem is solved by finding the condition that the probable average rate of assimilation in a surviving plant is maximum. Let the probability of a plant surviving a period T, where T is long compared with t_1, be $\exp(-MT)$. The probability of the last rain-free interval within this period being between t and $t+dt$ is, from Eq. (17.11), $(1/\tau)\exp(-t/\tau)\,dt$. Only if $t<t_1$ will the plant have survived. As the probability of the plant having survived the sum, $T-t$, of all the previous intervals is $\exp[-M(T-t)]$ it follows that

$$\exp(-MT)=\int_0^{t_1}\frac{1}{\tau}\exp(-t/\tau)\cdot\exp[-M(T-t)]\,dt$$

leading to the equation

$$M\tau=\exp\left[\frac{-t_1}{\tau}(1-M\tau)\right] \tag{17.13}$$

This has two real roots: M is to be taken as the root $\neq 1/\tau$. Let the probable average rate of assimilation in a surviving plant be $\hat{A}$. Then $\hat{A}$ must satisfy the integral equation

$$\hat{A}T\exp(-MT)=\int_0^{t_1}\left[\int_0^t\overline{A}(t')\,dt'+\hat{A}\cdot(T-t)\right]\cdot\frac{1}{\tau}\exp(-t/\tau)\cdot\exp[-M\cdot(T-t)]\,dt$$

from which it may be shown that

$$\hat{A}=\frac{1}{\tau(1-Mt_1)}\int_0^{t_1}\overline{A}(t)\cdot[(M\tau)^{t/t_1}-M\tau]\,dt \tag{17.14}$$

Eqs. (17.13) and (17.14) were first derived, as particular results of a more general analysis, by Dr. H.N. Comins, to whom I am greatly indebted. The presupposition made here, that probable relative mortality, M, and probable average rate of assimilation remain constant with time, requires comment. It is valid of the period T is independent of any particular rainfall event. But it is not strictly valid, for example, if the beginning of the period is chosen to coincide with a rainfall (as it would implicitly tend to be if taken at the time of seed germination). In that instance, mortality would be zero during the first t_1 days of the period. However, the analysis by Dr. Comins shows, *inter alia*, that, for all the numerical examples presented in this chapter $(t_1/\tau>2)$, the probable relative mortality, and the probable average rate of assimilation, within the following t_1 days would differ from the asymptotic estimates provided by Eqs. (17.13) and (17.14) by no more than a few percent. The convergence is greater the greater the magnitude of t_1/τ.

The next step is to find the condition that the integral in Eq. (17.14) is an extremum. As $\overline{A}$ is uniquely related to $\overline{E}$, and $E = q\phi - F(\phi)$ from Eq. (17.12), the integrand has the form $Q = Q(t, \phi, \dot{\phi})$. Therefore the Euler equation is

$$\frac{d}{dt}\left(\frac{\partial Q}{\partial \dot{\phi}}\right) - \frac{\partial Q}{\partial \phi} = 0$$

or

$$\frac{d}{dt}\left\{\frac{q}{\lambda}\left[(M\tau)^{t/t_1} - M\tau\right]\right\} + \frac{1}{\lambda}\frac{dF}{d\phi}\left[(M\tau)^{t/t_1} - M\tau\right] = 0$$

with $\lambda = \partial\overline{E}/\partial\overline{A}$ as before. Integration yields

$$\lambda = \lambda_0 \frac{(M\tau)^{t/t_1} - M\tau}{1 - M\tau} \exp\left(\frac{1}{q}\int_0^t \frac{dF}{d\phi} dt'\right) \tag{17.15}$$

where $\lambda_0 = \lambda$ at $t = t_0$. The magnitude of λ_0 is not arbitrary. It must be chosen so $\phi = 1$ at $t = t_1$.

Equation (17.15) determines the time course of $\overline{E}$ and $\overline{A}$ following rain. As it determines the time course of $\overline{E}$ and $\overline{A}$ it also determines the probable average growth rate of plants which survive, $\hat{A}$, as defined by Eq. (17.14), and the corresponding probable average rate of water use, $\hat{E}$, which is defined by an equation analogous to (17.14).

17.3.3 Interpretation

If rainfall occurred at regular intervals, and the soil water available to a plant was not subject to depletion by physical processes or the action of competing plants, then plants would tend to assimilate and transpire water at constant rates from day to day so that the available water was almost, but never quite, exhausted at the end of each rain-free period. The total water loss corresponding to a given total of carbon uptake is a minimum when the rates of loss and uptake are constant, provided the sense of the curvature of the $\overline{E} = \overline{E}(\overline{A})$ relationship is that shown in Fig. 17.6 (a fact first pointed out by COWAN and TROUGHTON 1972).

Opposed to the influence of curvature in the $\overline{E} = \overline{E}(\overline{A})$ relation are influences associated with randomness in the occurrence of rainfall and depletion of the available soil water by other processes. A plant should fix carbon and use water rapidly immediately after rain, partly because a second fall of rain may occur shortly, and partly because the rate at which some of the other competing processes extract soil water is dependent on soil water content, and is greatest when the content of water is greatest. The rates should then decline with time because the risks of further water use increase; the reserve of available water is diminished, while the expectation of replenishment by rain is not increased. Of course, there is no risk unless competing processes continue to remove water as soil water content approaches the critical level. In fact there is always

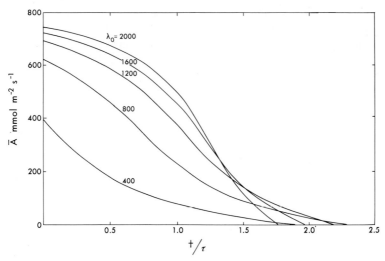

Fig. 17.8. Optimal variations of mean daily rate of assimilation, $\overline{A}$, with time, t, following rain. τ is the average interval between rainfalls. λ_o is the magnitude of $\partial\overline{E}/\partial\overline{A}$ at $t=0$

some loss of water from soils even when they have become too dry to support higher plant life.

All of these considerations are incorporated in Eq. (17.15). The equation shows how λ decreases with time; to put it graphically, how the plant slides down the curve in Fig. 17.7. The rate of descent depends on the statistics of rainfall as represented by the terms involving τ. It also depends on the way in which the processes which compete for soil water vary with soil water content. The term $dF/d\phi$ will invariably be negative; if $|dF/d\phi|$ is large — that is to say, F is very much diminished with decrease in water content — then λ will decline rapidly. But it may also be shown that λ_o is increased. Thus the plant uses the available water early in order that it should not be lost.

Some illustrations are shown in Figs. 17.8, 17.9 and 17.10. It has been assumed that $q/\tau = 500$ mol m^{-2} day^{-1}, and $F=100$ mol m^{-2} day^{-1} (a case with F varying with water content is discussed later). Thus a constant rate of transpiration $E=400$ mol m^{-2} day^{-1} would lead to the exhaustion of available water within the average period, τ, between successive periods of rain. If the plant did not transpire at all, the available water would be lost in a period five times as long.

Figure 17.8 shows the decline of $\overline{A}$ with time for various magnitudes of λ_o. Three points need to be emphasized. The graph does not imply that $\overline{A}$ runs the full time course shown after each fall of rain; the length of time actually run varies stochastically in accordance with the function P(t). Secondly, the times at which $\overline{A}$ becomes zero are not the critical times, t_1, corresponding to $\phi=1$. Optimization requires that gas exchange cease before the available water is exhausted. Whether or not a plant, having reached this stage, will die depends on whether the next rain occurs before the processes contributing

Fig. 17.9. Probable average assimilation rate (*right ordinate*) of surviving plants, Â, and the relative critical time t_1 (*left ordinate*), as functions of λ_o, the magnitude of $\partial\bar{E}/\partial\bar{A}$ immediately following rain. τ is the average interval between rainfalls

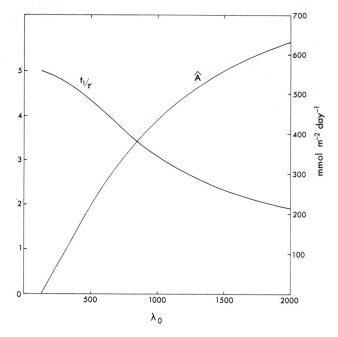

to F remove the remaining available water. Thirdly, the critical times are different for the different time courses in Fig. 17.8.

The significance of the parameter distinguishing the different curves in Fig. 17.8 becomes clear in Fig. 17.9, which shows the average probable assimilation rate Â, computed from Eq. (17.13), and the critical time relative to the average period between falls of rain, t_1/τ, as functions of λ_o. When λ_o is small, Â is small. However t_1 is large, implying that plants operating in this way are relatively unlikely to die from drought. When λ_o is large, Â is large and t_1 is small. Plants operating in this way grow rapidly but are relatively likely to die from drought.

In the next section the quantities Â and t_1 will be translated in terms of growth and mortality. But this may be an appropriate juncture at which to address the inevitable question: what physiological mechanism might be associated with optimization of this kind? A possible answer is made obvious by plotting the optimal daily rate of evaporation, Ê, against the deficit of soil water, ϕ, as in Fig. 17.10. The decline in rate of evaporation is, of course, associated with a decline in leaf conductance; and increase in soil water deficit would lead to a decrease in the potential of water not only in the soil, but in the plant itself. We may suppose that the actual responses of stomata to changes in plant internal water relations have become adapted towards optimization of the kind described. These responses, it is becoming clear, are associated with a complex hormonal regulation system (see Chap. 9, this Vol.). They are feedback responses, as distinct from the feedforward responses required to optimize stomatal behaviour in relation to variation in the environment of the foliage.

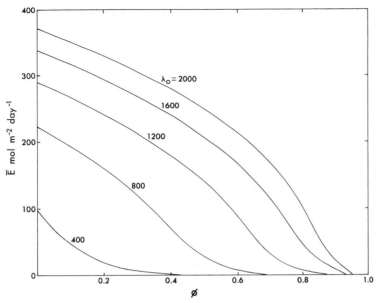

Fig. 17.10. Optimal variations of mean daily rate of transpiration, $\bar{E}$, with soil water deficit, ϕ

17.3.4 Growth and Mortality

An equation for plant relative growth rate that is in common use may be expressed in the form

$$G = \left(\frac{1}{W}\frac{dW}{dt}\right) = \alpha\left[\frac{S}{W}\hat{A} - \beta\right] \tag{17.16}$$

where W is the amount of carbon in the plant in moles, S is leaf area, $\hat{A}$ is the rate of assimilation in moles per unit area, α is the "growth efficiency" and β is the proportion of the plant carbon lost in unit time in association with "maintenance respiration". Typical magnitudes of α and β are 0.75 and 0.015 day^{-1} (HESKETH et al. 1980; HUNT and LOOMIS 1979).

The curves in Fig. 17.11 correspond to those in Fig. 17.9. The probable average relative growth rate of a surviving plant, G, has been calculated from Eq. (17.16) with S/W being taken as 0.1 m^2 mol^{-1}. The probable relative mortality, M, derives from Eq. (17.13) with τ being taken as 10 days. It is seen that M is an accelerating function, and G is a decelerating function, of λ_o. We may take G as a rough indication of the reproductive capacity of an individual mature plant, but the significance of the relation between G and M in terms of population dynamics depends on many factors that are beyond the compass of this article. Nevertheless, in certain circumstances the quantity G-M is related to the relative increase in a plant population. It is seen that it has a maximum. That it happens to fall within the range of λ_o considered is, of course, a result

Fig. 17.11. Probable average relative growth rate of surviving plants, G, and probable average mortality, M, as functions of λ_o, the magnitude of $\partial \overline{E}/\partial \overline{A}$ immediately following rain

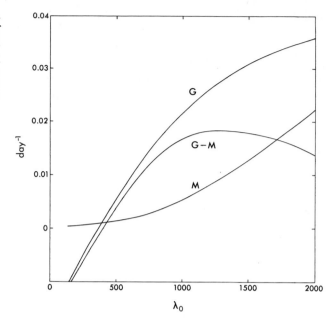

Fig. 17.12. Probable average mortality, M, as a function of probable average relative growth rate, G. The *full curve* is the optimal relationship; the *broken curve* represents long term regulation, with an absence of short-term regulation (i.e. constant leaf conductance during each day). The *dotted curve* represents the result of maintaining constant conductance at all times

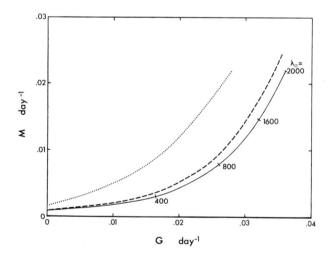

of the particular numbers that have been used as a basis for computation, but, insofar as water resources are of major importance in limiting the performance of terrestrial plants, it seems likely that the relationship between growth, as it affects soil and plant hydrology, and mortality, as it is affected by soil and plant hydrology, should exhibit an optimum within the domain of real physiological and environmental conditions. But rather than attempting to discuss its location, it is perhaps better simply to graph M as a function of G, as in Fig. 17.12, and remark, as of the first figure in this article, that if the

abscissa is a measure of benefit and the ordinate of cost, then the curve is one of increasing costs.

Two other curves are shown in Fig. 17.12. One is the relationship between G and M corresponding to a constant rate of assimilation, $\bar{A}$, and transpiration, $\bar{E}$. Plainly the decrease in mortality for a given growth rate (or the increase in growth rate for a given mortality) associated with optimal variation as compared with no variation is very large indeed. The other relationship is based on the assumption that $\bar{E}$ and $\bar{A}$ are constant within each day (see Fig. 17.7), but are varied optimally from day to day. The cost of such an imperfection in short-term regulation is appreciable when expressed in terms of M.

17.3.5 Competition

It is unrealistic to assume that the independent loss of water F is constant with time, as has been done in the previous numerical examples. The physical processes of evaporation and drainage in the soil will surely decrease as soil water content decreases. It has been noted that if F decreases with ϕ, then λ and therefore $\bar{E}$ and $\bar{A}$ must be initially larger and then decrease more rapidly with time. But what happens when the loss of water F is partially due to the uptake by the root systems of competing plants leads to more subtle considerations.

Let us compare two populations of plants, identical in all respects except that in one the root systems do not overlap, and in the other each plant shares its water resources with n others (n need not be integral, as the root systems may only partially overlap). Then, if we adapt Eq. (17.12) to describe the overlapping case we must replace q by $(n+1)q$ and F by $n\bar{E}+(n+1)F$. Clearly the net result is that the equation remains unchanged. As Eq. (17.14) is also unaffected, the optimal solution is still described by Eq. (17.15). This might be expected, because there is nothing to be gained or lost on the average by individual plants in having overlapping root systems (provided we neglect the diversion of photosynthate involved in creating more extensive, but no more productive root systems).

However, another argument leads to a very different result. If we make the same replacements to q and F, but now directly in Eq. (17.15), then

$$\lambda = \lambda_0 \frac{(M\tau)^{t/t_1} - M\tau}{1 - M\tau} \exp\left[\frac{1}{q}\int_0^t \frac{dF}{d\phi}dt'\right] \cdot \exp\left[\frac{n}{(n+1)q}\int_0^t \frac{d\bar{E}}{d\phi}dt'\right] \tag{17.17}$$

This equation represents an optimisation that cannot be bettered by any *individual* plant as a result of its choosing a slightly different behaviour. It is akin to an "evolutionary stable strategy" (see Maynard-Smith and Price 1973). It is different from the strategy represented by Eq. (17.15). That is the strategy which is optimal for a community of plants as an entity. When it was assumed that depletion of available water was in part due to the activity of competing plants *before* evaluating the optimal strategy, it was implicitly assumed, also, that the characteristics of an advantageous mutation would automatically and

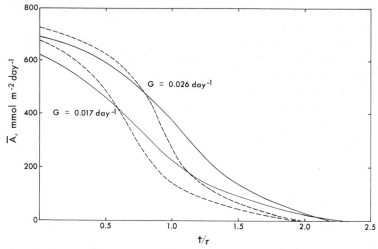

Fig. 17.13. Optimal variations, without competition (–) and with competition (---), in the mean daily rates of assimilation, $\bar{A}$, corresponding to two magnitudes of the probable average growth rate, G

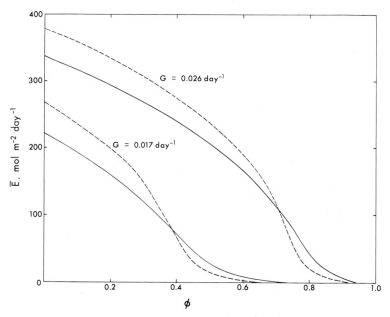

Fig. 17.14. Optimal variations of mean daily rates of transpiration, $\bar{E}$, with soil water deficit, ϕ, corresponding to the variations in Fig. 17.13

immediately be transferred to all members of the plant community. By so doing competition in any real sense of the word was excluded. Figure 17.13 shows two optimal time courses of $\bar{A}$ extracted from Fig. 17.7 ($\lambda_o = 1,200$ and 800). The probable growth rates, G, are 0.026 and 0.017 day^{-1}. The broken

curves are also optimal time courses, yielding the same two probable growth rates, but computed using Eq. (17.17) with $n = 1$. The difference in the shapes of the curves is clear and needs no comment. What is not obvious is that the competitive plants use more water in achieving the same probable growth rate. As a result, their mortality, M, is increased by about 3%. The variations in daily rate of transpiration with soil water deficit are shown in Fig. 17.14.

17.4 Discussion and Conclusions

It is a gross simplification to assume that the only reversible effect of water depletion on plant functioning is stomatal closure, and that all irreversible effects are concentrated in a single catastrophe at a particular, critical soil water deficit. Nevertheless, the separation of the reversible and irreversible does provide an insight to certain aspects of the regulation of gas exchange in plants. Because of the unpredictability of rainfall, there is an adaptive advantage in conserving water by closure of stomata, quite apart from any immediate influence of water "stress" on plant metabolism. The conservation is not, of course, conservation in an absolute sense. It is conservation with respect to carbon fixation. That is why it has been possible to identify it with reduction in the probability of death due to drought corresponding to any particular probable rate of growth. Other things being equal, we may associate probable rate of growth with probable rate of reproduction. Therefore the variables G and M come close to defining the Malthusian fitness of a species, insofar as water deficiency may be the dominant limitation on fitness. However, there is no reason to suppose that the hypothesis of optimization is relevant only with plants in habitats that are generally arid. Severe droughts occur in mesic regions also. Even were they to do so at intervals much longer, on the average, than the life span of any individual plant, it is possible that they exert a considerable selection pressure for optimal regulation of water use. Nor are the principles of optimization changed when competition is taken into account. It might, perhaps, have been supposed that individual plants would waste water in a community in which there is strong competition for water. The truth is that they do tend to take up and lose water more rapidly when it is available, but do not neglect to fix as much carbon as possible in relation to the water used. As the theory of evolutionary stable strategies indicates, there is a sense in which the community as a whole is wasteful, but it is one which has no relevance to the individual.

None of these general conclusions is likely to be altered if we allow that plant carbon metabolism is affected by the state of plant water. Optimization would still require that $\partial E/\partial A$ be maintained nearly constant in the short term, and that E and A should decline with increase in soil water deficit. Of course, the determination of $\partial E/\partial A$ would be greatly complicated if it were necessary to take into account the influence of short-term changes in plant water relations due to changes in rate of transpiration, Eq. (17.10) being replaced by $A = A\ (p_i,$

T_1, I, E). And it would no longer be possible to describe the decline in $\bar{A}$ and $\bar{E}$ in terms of decrease in the parameter λ, as in Eq. (17.15), if the relationship between $\bar{E}$ and $\bar{A}$ were to change with increase in soil water deficit. Indeed it may be shown that $\partial\bar{E}/\partial\bar{A}$ would increase if the intrinsic decline in photosynthetic metabolism with increase in ϕ were sufficiently large, as was in fact observed by FARQUHAR et al. (1980a).

To introduce an empirical description of the direct effects of diminishing water supply on plant metabolism into the mathematical treatment of the implications of the optimization would tend to confound an important question: to what extent may the effects themselves be also a manifestation of optimization? If conductance and rates of gas exchange should decline with increase of soil water deficit as a precautionary measure, so to speak, it follows that other physiological disturbances might be explicable as economic consequences of this. A particularly dramatic example is that of leaf abscission. Leaves become inefficient when conductance becomes small, because they continue to lose some water through the cuticle without taking up much CO_2 through the stomata. This topic could have been treated by including cuticular transpiration in E, the transpiration function then making a positive intercept with the E-axis (see JONES 1980. Parenthetically JONES correctly pointed out that there is then a region, corresponding to small conductances, in which $\partial^2 E/\partial A^2 < 0$. Optimization demands that the plant avoid operating in such a region. For an account of other circumstances in which $\partial^2 E/\partial A^2 < 0$ and their implications see COWAN and FARQUHAR 1977). Cuticular transpiration has not been treated in this way here, because it is not under stomatal control. However it may be controlled in another, rather drastic way. If the risk of further water loss exceeds the potential worth of the established capacity for carbon fixation, then the leaf should be excised. The circumstances in which the risk exceeds the potential worth depends on the magnitude of $\partial G/\partial M$ at which the plant operates. In other words, the excision strategy should be tuned in a way which relates to the stomatal optimization of conductance, as indeed should all other strategies relating to the compromise between carbon gain and water loss. An example of this principle, relating to short-term regulation, is given by COWAN (1978). In those plants that make rapid adjustments of leaf angle in a way depending both on atmospheric environment and plant internal water relations, optimization suggests that $\partial E/\partial A = \lambda$ shuld be the same whether conductance or angle is taken as the physiological parameter linking E and A. Likewise long-term changes in leaf angle (or reflectance, or size) should be related to $\partial G/\partial M$.

It will have been noticed that no explicit allowance for the role of growth per se in optimization has been made. If the area of foliage increases at the same relative rate as the available water capacity of the extending root zone, then the parameter q remains constant. If the roots are extending into soil in which the water is no more and no less subject to depletion by competing processes than is that in the established root zone, then the function $F(\phi)$ is also invariant with time. Then the mathematics remains unchanged. In point of fact, however, it seems probable that increase in q, or decrease in $F(\phi)$, or both, do take place with seedling development. SILCOCK (1977) found that seedlings in semi-arid Queensland, Australia were most likely to die in the

first 14 days after emergence. After 30 days deaths were relatively few (11%–17%) of the original population, and after 60 days the average relative mortality was only 3% per week. Changes in root:shoot ratio also seem to take place in response to decrease in the availability of water. However, the adaptive advantage, if one exists, of investing a greater proportion of photosynthate in water-gathering organs as distinct from photosynthesizing organs is not clear. As leaf conductance and rates of gas exchange decline, there would seem to be a diminishing need for water-gathering tissue. Perhaps the need for a disproportionately increasing root system stems from a decrease in the efficiency of roots in taking up water rather than an increased need for water (see Chaps. 1 and 3, this Vol.). For an elementary treatment of the relationship between optimization theory and carbon partitioning to roots and leaves see COWAN (1978).

The principle of optimization that has been expounded in this chapter is simply one of balancing risk of water use against benefit of carbon fixation in a changing environment. It has been illustrated with respect to diurnal variation in leaf microenvironment, and variation in soil water supply on a time scale characterized by the average interval between falls of rain. It presumably has relevance also to plant functioning on time scales appropriate to the life histories of plants, and to seasonal variations in environment. A premonition of its development in this wider context is provided in the next chapter of this volume.

References

Caemmerer von S (1981) On the relationship between chloroplast biochemistry and gas exchange of leaves. PhD Thesis, Aust Natl Univ, Canberra

Caemmerer von S, Farquhar GD (1981) Some relationships between the biochemistry of photosynthesis and the gas exchange of leaves. Planta 153:376–387

Courant R, Hilbert D (1953) Methods of mathematical physics Vol I. Wiley-Interscience, New York

Cowan IR (1972) Mass and heat transfer in laminar boundary layers with particular reference to assimilation and transpiration in leaves. Agric Meteorol 10:311–319

Cowan IR (1977) Stomatal behaviour and environment. Adv Bot Res 4:117–228

Cowan IR (1978) Water use in higher plants. In: McIntyre AK (ed) Water, planets, plants and people. Aust Acad Sci, Canberra, pp 71–107

Cowan IR (1981) Coping with water stress. In: Pate JS, McComb AS (eds) The biology of Australian plants. Univ West Australia Press, Nedlands, pp 1–32

Cowan IR, Farquhar GD (1977) Stomatal function in relation to leaf metabolism and environment. In: Jennings DH (ed) Integration of activity in the higher plant. Univ Press, Cambridge, pp 471–505

Cowan IR, Troughton JH (1972) The relative role of stomata in transpiration and assimilation. Planta 106:185–189

Darwin F (1898) Observations on stomata. Philos Trans R Soc London Ser B 190:531–621

Farquhar GD, Schulze E-D, Küppers M (1980a) Responses to humidity by stomata of *Nicotiana glauca* L. and *Corylus avellana* L. are consistent with the optimisation of carbon dioxide uptake with respect to water loss. Aust J Plant Physiol 7:315–327

Farquhar GD, Caemmerer von S, Berry JA (1980b) A biochemical model of photosynthetic CO_2 fixation in leaves of C_3 species. Planta 149:78–90

Field C, Berry JA, Mooney HA (1982) A portable system for measuring carbon dioxide and water vapour exchange of leaves. Plant Cell Environ 5:179

Hall AE, Björkman O (1975) Model of leaf photosynthesis and respiration. In: Gates DM, Schmerl RB (eds) Perspectives of biophysical ecology. Ecol Stud 12. Springer, Berlin Heidelberg New York, pp 187–202

Hall AE, Schulze E-D (1980) Stomatal response to environment and a possible interrelation between stomatal effects on transpiration and CO_2 assimilation. Plant Cell Environ 3:467–474

Hall AE, Schulze E-D, Lange OL (1976) Current perspectives of steady state stomatal responses to environment. In: Lange OL, Kappen L, Schulze E-D (eds) Water and plant life, problems and modern approaches. Ecol Stud 19. Springer, Berlin Heidelberg New York, pp 169–188

Hesketh JD, Alberte RS, Jones JW (1980) Predicting dark respiration in the soil-plant system. In: Hesketh JD, Jones JW (eds) Predicting photosynthesis for ecosystem models, vol I. CRC Press, Boca Raton, pp 69–84

Hunt WF, Loomis RS (1979) Respiration modelling and hypothesis testing with a dynamic model of sugar beet growth. Ann Bot 44:5–17

Jarman PD (1974) The diffusion of carbon dioxide and water vapour through stomata. J Exp Bot 25:927–936

Jones HG (1976) Crop characteristics and the ratio between assimilation and transpiration. J Appl Ecol 13:605–622

Jones HG (1980) Interaction and integration of adaptive responses to water stress: the implications of an unpredictable environment. In: Turner NC, Kramer PJ (eds) Adaption of plants to water and high temperature stress. Wiley-Interscience, New York, pp 353–365

Lange OL, Lösch R, Schulze E-D, Kappen L (1971) Responses of stomata to changes in humidity. Planta 100:76–86

Lange OL, Schulze E-D, Kappen L, Buschbom U, Evenari M (1975) Photosynthesis of desert plants as affected by internal and external factors. In: Gates DM, Schmerl RB (eds) Perspectives of biophysical ecology. Ecol Stud 12. Springer, Berlin Heidelberg New York, pp 121–143

Maynard-Smith J, Price GR (1973) The logic of animal conflicts. Nature (London) 246:15–18

Meinzer (1982) The effect of vapour pressure on stomatal control of gas exchange in Douglas fir – Pseudotsuga menziesii. Oecologia (in press)

Peisker M (1977) Transpiration and CO_2 uptake at varying stomatal aperture. In: Unger K (ed) Biophysikalische Analyse pflanzlicher Systeme. Fischer, Jena, pp 151–153

Schulze E-D, Lange OL, Buschbom U, Kappen L, Evenari M (1972) Stomatal responses to change in humidity in plants growing in the desert. Planta 108:259–270

Sharkey TD, Raschke K (1981) Separation and measurement of direct and indirect effects of light on stomata. Plant Physiol 68:33–40

Silcock RG (1977) A study of the fate of seedlings growing on sandy red earths in the Charleville district, Queensland. Aust J Bot 25:337–346

Wong SC, Cowan IR, Farquhar GD (1978) Leaf conductance in relation to assimilation in Eucalyptus pauciflora Sieb. ex Spreng. Plant Physiol 62:670–674

Wong SC, Cowan IR, Farquhar GD (1979) Stomatal conductance correlates with photosynthetic capacity. Nature (London) 282:424–426

18 Plant Life Forms and Their Carbon, Water and Nutrient Relations

E.-D. Schulze

CONTENTS

on the environment (e.g., *Oryza sativa, Sorghum vulgare*). Annuals occur in almost all climatic regions of the world (WALTER 1968, 1973) and are found in most open habitat communities as early successional species following disturbance. In animal ecology the equivalent "strategy" is performed by fugitive species which are specialized to survival in unpredictable habitats (r-strategy: STEARNS 1976; GRIME 1979). Annual plants are most successful in semi-arid and arid regions, where they may predominate over other plant forms following rainfall, even though during dry periods perennial woody plants appear to be the dominant plant form. However, because the whole life cycle must be completed in a single growing season, annuals are not very effective in arctic and alpine environments. In these vegetation zones they contribute <1% of the general flora (BILLINGS and MOONEY 1968). Although endemism and subspecies are common in annuals, some have a wide range of distribution, and one of the few cosmopolitan representatives is *Poa annua*.

18.2.3.2 Carbon Allocation and Ecological Features of Perennial Herbaceous Plants

Perennial herbaceous plants are similar to annuals in that they maintain living non-photosynthesizing parts. The significant difference between annual and perennial plants (herbaceous and woody) occurs with respect to dry matter production in successive years. Annuals rely solely on successive generations of new individuals for the continuation of dry matter production, whereas in perennials production is directed to the prolonged survival of the plant individual. (In animal ecology referred to as k-strategy: STEARNS 1976). In a seasonally cold or dry environment, for example, perennials accumulate and store carbohydrates or lipids to ensure survival and growth of the same individual in successive years. The stored reserves of buds or rhizomes enable the perennial plants to start growth more quickly at the onset of the growing season. Seed production may be delayed in a given growing season. Although the storage of reserves is discussed as being of ecological significance for survival of the individual in seasonal climates, it is important to realize that humid tropical environments are also dominated by perennial plants.

   During occupation of bare land in the process of succession, a population of perennials cannot increase its dry matter as rapidly as annuals because of differences in carbon allocation after germination and because of the differences in seed yield following the initial years of colonization. But after several years and with the accumulation of reserves and deeper-established root systems, perennials are more successful in interspecific competition mainly through competition for light. Also production of seeds may then be quite high. As a result, the perennial plant community usually succeeds the annual pioneers. Yet since the critical leaf area index is constant in a closed plant community (see Sect. 18.2.4) for a given radiation climate and plant species, an upper limit to the increase in size of the individual exists. This may be a significant distinction between perennial herbaceous and woody species. If the living non-photosynthetic but supporting portion of the plant increases, the maintenance respiration also increases. Accordingly, for a given partitioning ratio [Eqs. (18.3)

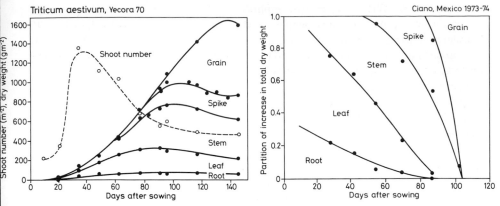

Fig. 18.3. A Distribution of total dry weight (including roots) and life shoot number during development in a crop of the dwarf spring wheat variety Yecora 70 grown under conditions of optimal agronomy. (After FISCHER 1975.) **B** Approximate distribution of various organs of a wheat plant during increase in total dry weight at different times in the life of the canopy shown in Fig. 18.7A. The figure does not consider transfer of dry matter from one organ to another after temporary storage in the former. Transfer from the stem, which decreases in dry weight, to grain, thereby augmenting its increase in dry weight, is quite important from day 110 onwards

are allocated for the formation of roots and leaves. Stem formation reaches its maximum just before anthesis. At that time the flow of carbohydrates is partitioned such that the assimilates of the flag leaf primarily serve the formation of the seed head, whereas the lower leaves mainly supply stem and root with assimilates for anabolic and catabolic processes. At the time of flower formation root growth slows down and leaf growth declines rapidly. At the end of the life cycle only seeds show a net increase in weight. The same principles as shown in Fig. 18.3 may apply for most annual species, although some may mobilize stored carbohydrates for seed formation (*Sorghum*, aubergines: DONALD and HAMBLIN 1976; CLAUSSEN and LENZ 1979) or redistribute carbon flow at stress (maize: JURGENS et al. 1978).

The following paragraphs discuss those growth characteristics of annuals which appear to be of greatest significance for their existence in natural environments.

18.3.1.1 The Phenological Control of Growth in Annuals

The phenological control of germination, growth, flowering and fruiting is probably quite similar in different plant life forms, but since completing the life cycle in one season is crucial for the reproductive success of annuals, some of the implications of this are discussed.

The environmental factors which control phenological development are different in plants, depending on their origin. Many tropical species are day-neutral and in these growth processes may be triggered by temperature, water status or other factors, whereas non-tropical plants are generally strongly dependent

---

plant in which carbohydrates were distributed with the ratio of 0 growth of new leaves and non-photosynthetic tissues respectively, at a rate of CO_2 assimilation and respiration. Neglecting competition for tween leaves it is predicted that within 3 years this plant would be larger than the opposite case with a ratio of 0.3/0.7 for leaf and non-thetic biomass growth. As an example of this principle, MONSI and (1970) mentioned the growth and competition of lianas and rainfo Lianas allocate relatively more carbohydrates into leaf area develope do trees, but use the latter as support in order to expose their leav daylight above the canopy. Through this "light parasitism" the lia covers the host plant and eventually even causes its destruction. The d of an increase in the allocation of carbohydrates for leaf growth, namel ing the photosynthetic area as well as decreasing the new growth of r tissues, explains the frequent observation of a close correlation betwe rates and leaf area. Even within the same genus, EL-SHARKAWY et showed three-fold differences in net photosynthesis of 24 *Gossypiu* but dry matter accumulation was associated with the rate of leaf area ment and not with photosynthesis.

Theoretically, therefore, in order to obtain maximal growth, it ma effective to maximize the portion of photosynthates allocated to l leaves. This has, in fact, been done in wheat cultivars. EVANS and 1 (1970) have compared wheat from all stages of its evolution as a c found that photosynthetic rate per unit flag leaf area has fallen b 3 in highly productive modern cultivars compared with the diploid *boeoticum*, but flag leaf area and duration has increased considerably grain size. However, there is an upper limit to which leaf area can be since there is an increased self-shading effect at high leaf density due to amounts of supporting tissues and leaves. Figure 18.2A shows th rates are dependent on leaf area index, LAI (integral of projected per unit ground area), but as leaf area increases the growth rate maximum value. Thereafter, it may decline. The existence of an LAI for herbaceous plants was debated by McCREE and TROUGHTO At the turning point of the slope (critical LAI: BROUGHAM 1958) a in LAI and its associated CO_2 uptake will not counterbalance the of CO_2 uptake in the existing leaf area because of self-shading. The c might still continue to gain in biomass, but at a lower rate.

If all leaves were horizontal and opaque and were arranged to soil surface completely, then a LAI of 1 would be sufficient to u incident photosynthetically active radiation. Communities of *Petasite* which have a LAI of about 2 are so efficient in shading the un that they even build a stage of subclimax during succession. In n communities LAI ranges between 3 and 19 (Table 18.3), and may in conifers (WARING et al. 1978: LAI of 53 taking total needle su not projected leaf area as a basis). Plant growth and life form stron optimum LAI through leaf angle and clustering and vertical distri leaves. For example, leaf disposition in kale tends to be horizontal sugar beet has more erect foliage. At increasing LAI, fewer leaves

---

and (18.4)] the net production of the individual becomes smaller with increasing plant size. Eventually, one expects that a limit is reached where the primary production will be zero for a given leaf biomass and the plant individual will be maintained by respiration but no further growth will occur. Perennial herbaceous plants differ from woody species with respect to respiratory carbon loss in the non-photosynthetic plant portion. In herbaceous species, this remains to a large degree alive. Additionally herbaceous perennial plants lack secondary growth.

Perennial herbaceous plants may complete their life cycle after 2 years (biennials) while others require many years (perennials sensu strictu). They may flower but once, like all biennials or like *Agave deserti*, which directs all of its stored carbon into seed production at the end of a 10–30-year lifetime. Others flower repeatedly upon reaching maturity or under extreme conditions, perennial herbaceous plants may reproduce only vegetatively. Unfavourable dry or cold seasons may be endured in an evergreen state (many temperate zone grasses in winter) or as dormant buds (arid and temperate zone grasses at drought), rhizomes or bulbs. It is clear that within the category of perennial herbaceous plants a large variety of structural types occur (SCHMITHÜSEN 1968). Herbaceous perennials are most successful in environments where cold temperatures, shade, seasonal drought, wetness or mechanical disturbance create extreme but stable conditions. They lose efficiency when the probability of rainfall is low or the rainy season is of short duration, in which case annuals are more successful.

Perennial herbaceous plants occur further north than all other vascular plants (*Saxifraga oppositifolia*: 83°39′ northern latitude: HOLMEN 1957) and occupy the cold deserts (*Puccinellia* sp.: BILLINGS and MOONEY 1968). They are the only vascular plants on the Antarctic continent (*Deschampsia antarctica*, WALTER 1968). *Stellaria decumbens* reaches the highest altitude known for higher plants (6,136 m, Himalaya, SWAN 1967), and *Allocasia macrorpa* shows the lowest known light saturation at 80 µmol photons $m^{-2} s^{-1}$ on the forest floor in a subtropical rain forest (BJÖRKMAN et al. 1972). Herbaceous perennials are predominant in vegetation types which cover about a fourth of the earth's land surface, namely the subtropical grasslands and the temperate and boreal steppes. Together with scattered trees they are dominant constituents of the subtropical savannah. Herbaceous perennials also dominate in regions of natural forest vegetation, as long as regular disturbance by grazing or mowing excludes competition from woody species. Within temperate and tropical forest regions perennial herbaceous plants contribute major portions of the forest floor vegetation.

18.2.3.3 Carbon Allocation and Ecological Features of Woody Plants

Woody plants are characterized by secondary growth and by the continuous conversion of structural tissue into non-living and therefore non-respiring biomass. This dry matter remains an integral part of the individual, essential to its functioning. It is part of the conducting system, it allows physical support of the large body of biomass, and it may also act as a storage reservoir (e.g.,

for water, nutrients or carbohydrates). The process of wood fo
improves the carbon balance with respect to respiratory CO_2 l
with herbaceous plants on a relative scale. Trees and shru
a prolonged life cycle. The germination and seedling stage
over an entire growing season and is followed by a saplin
last for several years. Flowering and fruiting is further redu
to perennial herbaceous species. Many trees reach maturity
decades (*Picea excelsa* stands 60–70 years) and may even t
only periodically (every 3–8 years). In contrast, there are also
produce abundant fruit (*Malus, Salix, Pinus*), but only after ye

However, in addition to other physiological and hydrc
on growth, there is also a limitation to growth in woody plan
when the respiratory rates of the living portion of the stem
the rate of carbon supply of the foliage. As with herbace
point an increase in non-photosynthetic biomass is possible o
drate is allocated into growth of new foliage. This leads to
leaf biomass and therefore to further deterioration of the ca
situation can be observed in seedling establishment on for
the oldest living tree, *Pinus aristata*, which is more than 4,0
age is reached partially because of the low rate of wood
semi-arid alpine environment of California, but also because c
of the supporting stem and root which probably acts to r
between photosynthesizing and non-photosynthesizing li
MARCHE 1969). Trees and shrubs differ mainly with respect
which are primarily determined by differences in branchir
the extent of apical dominance.

Trees and shrubs are generally long-lived, with maximum
about a hundred years (most northern temperate forest tr
1,000 years. The age of a single *Larrea tridentata* indivic
to be more than 11,000 years (VASEK 1980). Because of t
dimensions, trees outcompete all other plant forms in a lo
provided environmental conditions allow establishment. The
vulnerable stage in the life cycle of a woody species becar
with other plant life forms. Many temperate-zone tree spe
effectively in the shade of the parent tree where other plant spe
(e.g., *Fagus*). This may be in contrast to tropical environmer
have a greater chance of survival at larger distances from
because of highly specialized seed-predators (e.g., Bruchid:
explained tree species diversity in tropical rainforest enviror
of this mechanism.

18.2.4 Leaf Area Index and Light Interception

For plant growth the carbon-partitioning between leaf ar
growth of non-photosynthesizing tissues becomes increasing
age of the individual. MONSI (1968) made a growth estimate

---

structural costs for protection against adverse climatic conditions (e.g., heat, cold or desiccation) and predation (ZWÖLFER 1978), which in turn, will favour an evergreen leaf biomass.

Low nutrient uptake reduces the amount of nutrients available for incorporation into new living biomass. In particular a shortage of phosphorus and nitrogen severely affects the photosynthetic capacity (see Chap. 7, this Vol.). In this case photosynthetic production will be reduced. In addition it is expected that the partitioning of carbohydrates will favour construction of a larger root biomass for nutrient uptake. Again, the functioning of the plant at low carbon input and high carbon costs for nutrient-uptake are expected to be achieved by the maintenance of leaf biomass (see Sect. 18.3.2.2).

Plant water stress is associated with an imbalance of water uptake and water loss. SCHULZE et al. (1980) showed that long-term water stress reduced the photosynthetic capacity of several contrasting species. This, in principle, should lead to perennial leaf forms if a recovery after stress is possible, an evolutionary trend followed by numerous desert xerophytes. But in contrast to carbohydrates and nutrients, in terms of water the conditions are more complicated, since the storage capacity of water is generally very low in relation to the turnover rates. Significant storage capacity is found only in special cases e.g., large trees (HINCKLEY et al. 1978), succulents, or bottle trees (WALTER 1973). Therefore the probability and seasonality of water availability strongly governs the success of deciduous or evergreen plant forms (see Sect. 18.3.3.3).

AXELROD (1966) suggested that the present geographical distribution patterns of evergreen and deciduous plant forms in the northern and southern hemisphere have evolved since the Cretaceous period, mainly in response to habitat conditions. But the competitive balance which may exist between plant forms of a specific habitat in the northern or southern hemisphere may be seriously disturbed by the introduction of an exotic species. For example, alpine and arid tree lines in the southern hemisphere, e.g., in New Zealand, can be changed dramatically following the introduction of northern hemisphere species such as *Pinus radiata* and *Pinus contorta*. Therefore the success of a certain plant life form in a specific habitat is always related to the ability of the neighbour species of the community which is strongly influenced by geological history.

18.3 The Influence of the Environment on the Growth Characteristics of Specific Plant Life Forms

In the following an attempt is made to describe those relations between structural forms, growth and environment which may be most significant for the main groups of plant life forms.

18.3.1 The Influence of Environmental Conditions on the Growth Characteristics of Annuals

The development of wheat is shown in Fig. 18.3 as an example of growth in annual plants (FISCHER 1975). In the early growth stages all photosynthates

---

on photoperiod. With respect to annuals of seasonally dry and cold environments, the phenological control generally operates so that the life cycle is largely completed during a period of favourable growth conditions. Certainly, exceptions are found in nature, e.g., summer annuals in deserts may germinate after the first winter rains, but complete the main part of their life cycle, including flower and fruit formation, under extreme conditions of summer drought (*Salsola inermis*, EVENARI et al. 1971).

The control of germination is the first and major step of phenological control of annuals (see Chap. 11, this Vol.).

After germination the steps of development are triggered by various environmental factors depending on the day-neutrality (of the species. Photoperiodic control of development explains hastened development after germination at the end of the wet season, in many non-tropical annuals, since calendar date rather than germination is a better predictor of the termination of the wet season (FISCHER and TURNER 1978). In *Anagallis arvensis* 24 days were required for floral initiation at an 11 h photoperiod, but only 9 days were necessary at a 15 h photoperiod (SINGH and GOPAL 1973). This pattern may be altered by water stress. Sudden or severe stress has been shown to delay floral initiation in annuals. More commonly, however, floral initiation was found to be stress-insensitive and flowering generally hastened slightly (TURNER and BEGG 1977). This may be different in principle in perennial herbaceous plants, where stress prolongs rather than hastens development, e.g., *Daucus carota* (DALE 1974). Temperature (heat sums) seems to be the principle environmental trigger for phenological development in many day-neutral species (HALL et al. 1979).

18.3.1.2 Seed Production

Seed production is the main event in the life cycle of an annual, and annuals maximize the commitment of growth to seed production (HARPER and OGDEN; see also Chap. 16, Vol. 12 C). Table 18.2 shows that seed production in wild annual species is comparable to that of cultivated crops, and the yield of wheat without fertilizer may be less than that of *Thlaspi arvense* (BEST and McINTYRE 1975). Crop plants and wild annuals may allocate an average of 30%, in many cases even more than 50% of their above ground dry matter product (defined as harvest index: HI) to seed formation which is more than in a perennial plant community. DONALD and HAMBLIN (1976) provide a comprehensive review of harvest indices of cereals and their dependence on environmental factors. DE RIDDER et al. (1981) gave a complete review comparing wild and cultivated species.

The grain yield of annual cereals is affected by all environmental factors acting on floral initiation and on photosynthesis during grain filling. Therefore, seed yield is determined by a subtle balance of factors determining seed number and seed size (FISCHER and TURNER 1978). It is necessary to distinguish between determinate and indeterminate annuals. Many annuals including several grain crops from the temperate or cold arid region are determinate, i.e., flowering respresents an abrupt and irreversible end to further vegetative growth. In this

Table 18.2. Harvest indices (yield per aboveground biomass %) for some wild and cultivated species (HARPER and OGDEN 1970; DONALD and HAMBLIN 1976; DE RIDDER et al. 1981)

Helianthus annuus	14–40	*Trigonella arabica*	42
Carthamus tinctorius	16–25	*Zea mays*	38–49
Senecio vulgaris	25–27	*Oryza* var.	39–56
Chrysanthemum segetum	26–27	*Triticum* tall var.	25–36
Calendula officinalis	27	*Triticum* short var.	38–41
Matricaria matricarioides	35		

case environmental conditions during particular growth periods such as temperature during floral initiation, or drought during anthesis can irreversibly affect yield. In contrast, many species evolved from the semi-arid subtropical and tropical environments are indeterminate (*Arachis, Vigna*). In these species drought stress may prevent flowering and vegetative growth, but both may be resumed if favourable conditions return. Indeterminate species retain the capacity for high seed yield even after a period of severe stress (TURK and HALL 1980). In contrast, with certain indeterminate crops (tomato, cotton) factors stimulating vegetative growth (e.g., N-fertilization, irrigation) will negatively affect yield above a certain optimum (DONALD and HAMBLIN 1976).

The source/sink relationships of assimilate partitioning in annuals are certainly more complicated and still unclear (e.g., FARRAR 1980). It was suggested that the demand for assimilates determines the photosynthetic rate (KING et al. 1967), although this is still controversial and can be reproduced with pruned plants only. Ear photosynthesis may contribute 13% to grain filling and awns may increase that proportion to 34% (EVANS et al. 1972). Although the effect of awns is still under discussion, they appear to be advantageous with late drought (HALL et al. 1979). That additional factors besides source and sink determine yield is shown by the observation that insect attack may increase plant yield in some species because of early removal of apical dominance (HARRIS 1974).

Water stress severely affects seed yield in annuals not only under natural conditions but also in crops (HSIAO et al. 1976). In this respect it must be considered that the major portion of arable land for annual crops occurs in semi-arid environments. In the annual weed *Senecio vulgaris* the relative change in carbohydrate allocation during water stress (Fig. 18.4; HARPER and OGDEN 1970) indicated that total dry matter production under the high stress treatment was strongly suppressed (only 2% of the well-watered treatment) and dry matter was allocated mainly into the root leaving little or no surplus for seed formation. Similar responses are found in perennial species (HEIM et al. 1979; EVENARI et al. 1977). A close relationship was found between relative dry matter production or yield and water use (DE WIT 1958), which seems to be related not to leaf water potential but to the cumulative water stress experienced (TURK and HALL 1980). Despite the changes in absolute growth and yield numbers with stress, it is remarkable that annuals have the ability to maintain their HI for a considerable range of water stress provided stress develops early or is mild and evenly distributed over the life cycle (DAY et al. 1978).

and roots may be shed continually (tropical environments) or seasonally (temperate and arid environments) without the death of the individual. Under seasonally arid or cold conditions dieback of the aboveground parts may leave only a dormant main bud and very few living roots containing reserves for new growth (e.g., *Stipagrostis obtusa*). Therefore the annual gain in living biomass of the individual may be very low although the seasonal primary production may be quite high. A typical example of this response type is found for the energy flow through grassland ecosystems (SIMS and SINGH 1978). Despite the great amount of total energy being captured, the seasonal energy balance shows only a minute increase of the perennially persisting energy of the system. From the numerous interactions, the following paragraphs discuss those which appear to be most significant for the success of perennial herbaceous plants in relation to other plant forms.

18.3.2.1 Growth Initiation and Carbon Allocation

It is obvious that perennial herbaceous plants have a major advantage over annuals due to the fact that the life cycles need not be completed in a single season. Furthermore, vegetative growth and photosynthesis may start from stored reserves at a time before annuals can germinate and can continue after annuals are occupied with seed production. Under identical environmental conditions, this leads to a higher total net primary production in perennial pasture grasses than in annual crops (DE WIT 1968). Because of the limited time for vegetative growth in annuals, some have evolved mechanisms to prolong the growing season. Winter annuals, such as winter wheat, achieve higher yields than spring wheat by having a greater interval between seedling establishment and flowering (DONALD 1963). The special feature of biennials in terms of dry matter production was emphasized in this context by WALTER (1973).

Perennial herbaceous plants have special adaptations for initiating rapid growth from buds and stored carbohydrates, especially in extreme environments such as arctic alpine areas (BILLINGS 1974). A large number of arctic alpine plants in the northern and southern hemisphere have shoot and flower buds, which are initiated 1 year, in some Greenland species even 2 years (SØRENSEN 1941), before flowering. Shoot elongation and flowering may then occur very quickly after snow melt (WIELGOLASKI and KÄRENLAMPI 1975). The reproductive period may also be extended by postponing fruit development. In *Braya* (= *Sisymbrium*) *humilis,* the fruiting inflorescence regularly overwinters and completes development during the following summer (BILLINGS and MOONEY 1968).

In perennial herbaceous species a relatively large proportion of carbohydrates is translocated to the belowground system (MARSHALL and SAGAR 1968 and others). Only a relatively small portion is used as reserves, but a large portion serves for growth of the underground root or rhizome system. There are very few studies on the root turnover rate of herbaceous and graminoid species. CHRISTIE (1978) found a root turnover rate of 1.1–2.9 g day^{-1} m^{-2}, which suggests that roots of an Australian *Astrebla* grassland may live on the average 2–3 years.

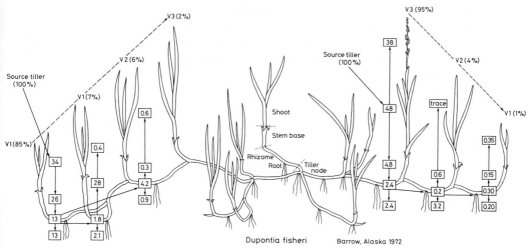

Fig. 18.5. Distribution of ^{14}C radioactivity in tiller compartments of single plants as influenced by tiller age. Values are percentage of the total radioactivity recorded from the tiller. *V1* is a tiller with excerpted leaves in its first season of shoot production; *V2* is a tiller in its second year of aboveground growth; *V3* and *V4* are tillers in their third and fourth year of growth aboveground. Flowering normally takes place in (*V3*) or (*V4*). The *dotted line* represents the total translocation per tiller. *Squares* and *arrows* represent translocation into the different organs. (After ALLESSIO and TIESZEN 1978)

In *Dupontia fisheri* (Fig. 18.5) only about $^1/_3$ of all newly photosynthesized carbohydrates remained in the leaf for expansion whereas $^2/_3$ were translocated from the leaf; 13% of the total carbon gain was allocated to the rhizome for vegetative spreading of the clone, but export to new tillers of the rhizome declined as soon as these newly grown parts were sustained by their own photosynthesis. Thereafter a young tiller might translocate 15% of its carbohydrate gain to older sprouts. There it is used mainly in the rhizome formation of 2-year-old sprouts or may be added to the reserves of neighbouring 1-year-old sprouts. In contrast, only 1% of the photosynthates were allocated from old tillers to young organs. After 3 years, sufficient carbohydrates were accumulated to support flowering. At that stage carbohydrates were redistributed. Only about 5% of the photosynthates were allocated to the rhizome and root and a large proportion was used for flower formation.

The pattern of carbon translocation is similar in many grasses, even those in habitats more favourable to growth, e.g., *Agrostis tenuis* and *Festuca pratensis* (HARRIS et al. 1979) and *Phleum pratense* (WILLIAMS 1964). However, generalizations are not possible in the case of dicotyledonous herbs since most work has been conducted with graminoid species. Under conditions of stress the carbon allocation pattern changes immediately. In *Medicago sativa* defoliation resulted in a rapid translocation of carbohydrates from the root to the new leaves and stems and a partial defoliation of *Lolium perenne* delayed the normal age-related decline of photosynthetic rates in the remaining main shoots (GIFFORD and MARSHALL 1973). The assimilate partitioning also changes under

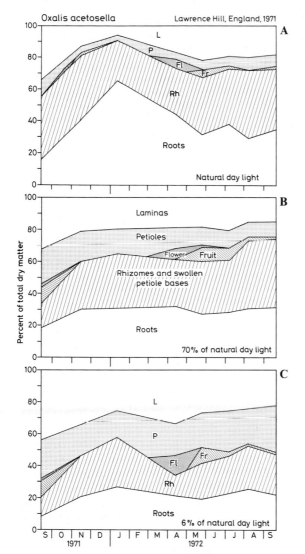

Fig. 18.6. A–C Dry matter allocation to different organs of *Oxalis acetosella* grown from cuttings under three light regimes of natural light; **A** 70%; **B** 27%; **C** 6% of natural midday light. (After Packham and Willis 1977)

natural conditions of low carbon fixation, e.g., shade. In this case plants export a greater portion of their assimilates to growing leaves as shown in Fig. 18.6 for *Oxalis acetosella* (Packham and Willis 1977). Thus, the root/shoot ratio, which is high for alpine and arctic plants, becomes very low in shaded habitats. Shade leaves are also broader and thinner than sun leaves (Eagles 1973). A carbon allocation pattern similar to that of *Oxalis acetosella* is found in shade grown *Lolium temulentum,* but this may change to favour of translocation to roots following 2–3 days of exposure to high light intensity (Ryle and Powell 1975).

The adaptations to shade and the competition between sun- and shade-tolerant plants may be more complicated than is obvious from growth analysis,

since unrelated factors may be of significance. For example, *Cirsium palustre,* a shade-avoiding species, and *Geum urbanum,* a species avoiding exposed conditions, show similar growth under conditions of shade in the vegetative phase. However, only *Geum* continued to grow until fruit ripening. *Cirsium* developed a high leaf area in the shade but the stems were too weak to support themselves and collapsed, thus flowering was not achieved (PONS 1977). This shows that special environmental conditions may initiate a growth form which causes physical self-damage to an extent that the species is not reproductive in that habitat.

18.3.2.2 The Storage of Reserves

In a seasonal climate the storage of reserves, such as carbohydrates and lipids, is fundamental to the extension of the life cycle and initiation of growth in the following season as soon as conditions are favourable. Storage seems to be a principle ecological feature of herbaceous perennials and a basis for their success in arid and cold climates.

The development of bulbs and rhizomes as storage organs has been most commonly viewed as an adaptation to cold and dry seasons. Geophytes are typical elements of the mediterranean and the steppe vegetation. Despite this it should be noticed that many herbaceous plants of the humid tropics also develop rhizomes and in many cases are even planted as crops (e.g. *Allocasia, Zingiber*). One may say that although rhizomes and bulbs occur in both humid tropical and seasonal climates, as far as we know, they appear to have ecological significance only in the latter.

The seasonal change in the carbohydrate and lipid reserves reflects the growing activity of the plant (e.g., BILLINGS and MOONEY 1968). In *Polygonum bistortoides* carbohydrates were stored in large amounts in roots and rhizomes at the end of the growing season (Fig. 18.7 A). But with breaking of dormancy in the following summer 50% of the rhizome reserves were used in a 1-week period of early and rapid shoot growth (MOONEY and BILLINGS 1965). Figure 18.7 B shows that in *Primula glutinosa* the energy content of the whole plant drops significantly during the time of spring growth, indicating that photosynthesis does not balance growth and maintenance respiration.

FONDA and BLISS (1966) found in alpine regions that carbohydrate reserves may ensure growth even during adverse climatic periods within the growing season. There appears to be a tendency for carbohydrate contents to decrease with increasing altitude (MOONEY and BILLINGS 1965), although in some species (*Chinochloa rigida* and *C. macra*) the reserves in the root increased with altitude when growth was significantly retarded (PAYTON and BRASCH 1978). In alpine habitats, whenever plants are covered with snow during the summer period, carbohydrate reserves decrease and may not be restored during that season (BILLINGS and MOONEY 1968).

Although quite a large amount of information is available on the growth of herbaceous plants in alpine and arctic habitats, very little knowledge is available on carbohydrate storage in plants of arid regions.

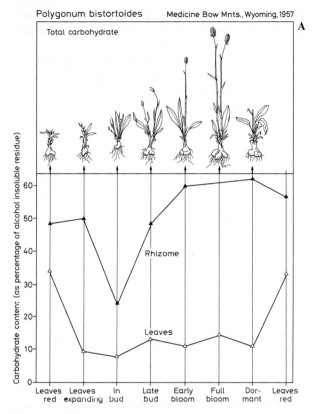

Fig. 18.7. A Annual growth and carbohydrate cycle of *Polygonum bistortoides*. (After Mooney 1963; Mooney and Billings 1965.) **B** Annual cycle of the energy content and of the carbohydrate reserves for *Primula glutinosa* and lipid reserves for *Saxifraga bryoides* (*black* high content; *hatched area* low content; *dotted area* traces; *white area* no content). (After Moser et al. 1977)

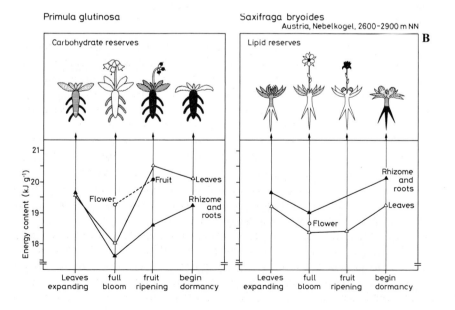

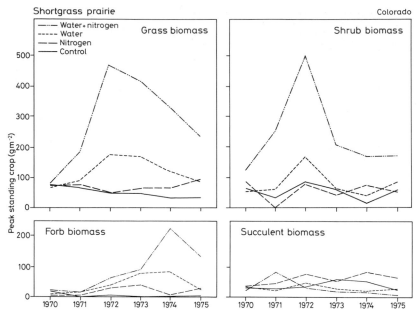

Fig. 18.8. Response of a grassland ecosystem to natural water stress, nitrogen fertilization (0.015 kg N m^{-2} in the first year and 0.005 kg N m^{-2} in subsequent years), and irrigation plus nitrogen fertilization (sprinkler irrigation to maintain soil matric potential between 0 and 0.8 bar at 10 cm soil depth plus 0.005 kg N m^{-2}). Average soil water content was 14% for the control and about 20% for the watered treatment. The *curves* show the peak standing crop of each year. (After DODD and LAUENROTH 1979)

18.3.2.3 Competition Between Graminoids and Dicotyledonous Herbaceous Species

The complex competitive interactions between graminoid and dicotyledonous herbaceous perennials have been investigated mainly in agricultural systems (DONALD 1963). Light penetration is one important factor in competition (see Sect. 18.2.4). Grasses tend to have erect leaves in the upper layers of the herbaceous vegetation, which allow sufficient light to penetrate to the horizontal lower leaves and to dicotyledonous herbaceous species at ground level.

Graminoid species have a basal meristem and a dense system of adventitious roots and seem more successful in extracting nutrients or water from the soil than other herbaceous plants. Dicotyledonous herbs may invade larger soil volumes but are not as efficient at obtaining water and nutrients for growth from a small soil volume or horizon. Under arid conditions (Fig. 18.8) the peak standing crop of grasses increased about six-fold in 2 years when the plants were fertilized and irrigated, but irrigation alone results in only a two-fold increase and fertilization without irrigation had no effect. The biomass of the half-shrub *Artemisia frigida* increased also, whereas succulents showed no response. The peak standing crop of forbs increased only after 3 to 4 years of water and fertilizer treatment. Similar findings were obtained in wet and

boggy habitats (Summers 1968) and under alpine conditions (Wielgolaski et al. 1975). The conclusion of Van Keulen (1975) that productivity of deserts is limited mainly by the supply of nitrogen is not correct in view of the above-mentioned grassland experiment.

Agriculturally, equilibrium in a man-made community of grasses and legumes can be maintained by withholding nitrogen and thus retarding grass growth as soon as it begins to dominate by shading the legume which grows close to the ground. In contrast grass growth is activated as soon as the nitrogen release from the legume nodules permits. A competitive equilibrium can be achieved in temperate *Lolium/Trifolium* pastures (Harris 1974; Brougham 1958) or in subtropical *Panicum/Macroptilium* pastures (Ross et al. 1972).

The strong response of the graminoid species in Fig. 18.8 was accompanied by a ten-fold increase in root biomass (Detling 1979). The ability of grasses to rapidly initiate root growth from the adventitious root system may be one reason for the success of this plant form under arid conditions, since moisture always accelerates microorganism activity and thereby increases nitrogen availability. Grasses respond readily after fire for similar reasons (Payton and Brasch 1978). Bare soil of burned areas may become dryer than unburned controls to such a degree that growth is retarded earlier in a dry season (Redmann 1978). Thus, in areas subject to burning, only those species which are activated most quickly, namely the grasses, eventually succeed. Additionally, grasses, e.g., *Agrostis tenuis,* appear to be more effective in uptake of phosphorous than forbs, e.g., *Trifolium repens,* and this difference increased in favour of *Agrostis tenuis* during water stress (Jackman and Mouat 1972). It remains unclear whether it is the availability of nutrients or the decline in uptake metabolism of the plant which first ceases with water stress. If grass growth in an arid environment is selectively harvested by grazing, a succession occurs leading not to forbs but to woody plants. The available water may at first be used by both, but woody species eventually suppress the other herbaceous plant forms through defense mechanisms against grazing and competition for light (Walter 1973).

18.3.3 The Influence of Environmental Conditions on Growth Characteristics of Woody Shrubs and Bushes

It was pointed out in Section 18.2.3.3 that woody species are characterized by a larger potential growth of permanent functional biomass, whereas herbaceous plants generally may increase their plant volume each season but die back to relatively small, perennial storage organs. In woody plants the biomass of stems and roots therefore increases continually over time, although there is a superimposed seasonal variation in biomass because of shedding of plant parts. Although the secondary growth of wood is the major distinction between herbaceous and woody plant life forms, it appears justified with respect to the competitive importance of height growth to distinguish between shrubs or bushes, which have prostrate growth or little apical dominance, and trees, with a dominating vertical growth.

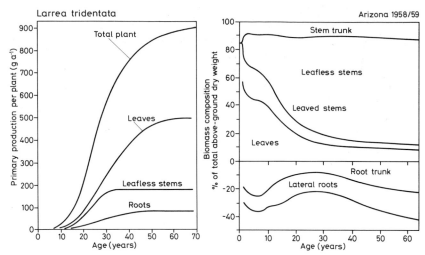

Fig. 18.9. Annual primary production of different organs and estimated relative composition of the shoot and root of *Larrea tridentata* of different ages. (After CHEW and CHEW 1965)

Carbon partitioning of shrubs is exemplarily shown in Fig. 18.9 for *Larrea tridentata*. It is quite obvious that the relative proportion of leaves decreases continually although annual leaf production increased. Partitioning of assimilates does not change significantly beyond age 30. With increasing age the carbon balance is more likely to become disturbed in unfavourable years. Growth patterns similar to those shown for *Larrea* are also found in temperate and arctic zone shrubs and bushes e.g., *Calluna vulgaris* (CHAPMAN and WEBB 1978). In many arctic and alpine shrubs, however, this ratio remains favourable by production of adventitious roots from a prostrate stem which acts comparably to a rhizome in herbaceous plants (e.g., *Salix arctica:* TIESZEN 1978).

The maintenance of a positive annual carbon balance in a large plant body over many years seems to be a functional problem which requires special adaptations in woody plants. Therefore, following the general discussion of Section 18.2.5 the consequences of the evergreen and deciduous habit in shrubs and bushes will be treated in the following paragraphs.

18.3.3.1 Evergreen and Deciduous Growth as Related to the Carbon Balance

Foliage longevity is significant for the survival in shaded habitats. Through a reduced leaf turnover at a comparable rate of total plant assimilation, a greater proportion for maintenance respiration and growth is achieved on a long-term basis. In fact low light intensity of shady habitats generally causes prolonged longevity of foliage in different plant forms. Leaf longevity increased in herbaceous *Oxalis acetosella* in shady habitats (PACKHAM and WILLIS 1977); the palm *Livistonia subglobosa* maintained leaves about 3 years in full daylight, but 12 years in the forest understory (MONSI 1960); 85-year-old spruce (*Picea*

abies) had 12-year-old needles on similar age twigs only in the shade and not in the sun crown (SCHULZE et al. 1977a).

Low temperatures and a short vegetation period reduce the carbon input of plants especially in arctic/alpine environments (MOSER 1973). However, with respect to the evergreen or deciduous habit, general conclusions are not obvious. Both life forms occur in the arctic and alpine region. The carbon balance of plants is the result of a number of processes which favour either deciduous or evergreen plant life forms. A decrease in the length of the growing season would promote evergreen structures rather than deciduous leaves. The young leaves of deciduous species are in danger of suffering severe damage by late frost if bud break is early. Evergreen species avoid this critical period in the early season, since bud break is generally later in evergreen than in deciduous species. Therefore, evergreens are able to start CO_2 assimilation earlier in the season than deciduous species. But the length of the growing season is only one of several factors which determine the plant carbon balance. The rate of CO_2 assimilation was found to be three times higher in arctic deciduous *Betula nana* and *Salix arctica* than in evergreen *Ledum palustre* (JOHNSON and TIESZEN 1976). One may consider that the lower photosynthetic capacity of the evergreen leaf in comparison to the deciduous one is the structural cost of being cold- or drought-tolerant. The annual carbon gain per unit dry weight was higher in the deciduous *Rubus chamaemorus* and *Betula nana* than in the evergreen *Andromeda polifolia* and *Empetrum hermaphroditum* species (JOHANSSON and LINDER 1975). However, annual carbon investment into new foliage was found to be as much as three to four times higher in the deciduous than in the evergreen types. But damage by ice or wind and frost drought may cause the evergreen carbon balance to deteriorate. In summary JOHNSON and TIESZEN (1976) come to the conclusion that net carbon gain over the total life span of a leaf may be quite similar for deciduous and evergreen tundra species even though photosynthetic capacity and growth pattern may differ markedly.

Cushion plants are a special plant form typical of arctic and alpine environments. These are plant tufts of woody or herbaceous species which build a dense, cushion-like cover close to the ground. Because of a high boundary layer resistance, the microclimatic conditions within the cushion of *Loiseleuria procumbens* may exhibit a temperature increase of up to 15 °C above ambient (Fig. 18.10) which may even be close to the upper limit of heat tolerance in an alpine environment (LARCHER 1977). Since humidity is generally above 80% at reduced wind within the cushion, water stress was not found even with low humidities in the external air (KÖRNER and DE MORAES 1979). GRABHERR and CERNUSCA (1977) concluded that conditions within the cushion were more favourable than those outside during 83% of the 140 days of the growing season for this plant, and that this period was 49 days longer within the cushion than in an open shrub. Probably the carbon balance within the cushion is additionally improved by CO_2 supply from soil respiration, although this has not been investigated. Despite these favourable aspects of "cushion"-stature, photosynthesis of leaves in the lower strata of the cushion will be very negatively affected by self-shading from the upper strata.

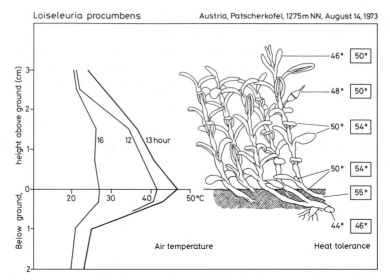

Fig. 18.10. Vertical temperature profiles in a cushion of *Loiseleuria procumbens* at 12 h, 13 h and 16 h of a clear summer day. Highest temperatures were 47.5° C at the soil surface, air temperature was 19.4° C at 10 cm above canopy and 16.6° C at 2 m above canopy. The heat tolerance is characterized by that temperature which was endured with 50% damage during cultivation following $^1/_2$ h treatment at that temperature. *Single numbers* indicate the actual heat tolerance at the time of climate measurements. *Numbers in squares* indicate the "potential" heat tolerance after a period of hardening. (After LARCHER 1977)

18.3.3.2 Evergreen and Deciduous Growth as Related to the Nutrient Balance: Xeromorphy and Sclerophylly

SCHIMPER (1898) recognized that xeromorphous plants occur on bogs with ample moisture supply. He interpreted this as "physiological drought" due to inhibition of water uptake by lack of oxygen. Since then it has been demonstrated that these plants may not be suffering water stress (SMALL 1972a), and that nutrient deficiencies, especially N, P and trace minerals (Cu) are responsible for the structural changes in the plant which are generally referred to as xeromorphic features (refer to the excellent review by SMALL 1973). These features include reduced stature, reduction of internode length, perenniality, and leaf modifications such as small size, small cells, thick cuticle and others (SHIELDS 1950). A sub-set of xeromorphic features is included in the term "sclerophylly", which refers to the "hardness" of leaves due to cutinization, sclerification, silicification and dehydration.

Sclerophylly appears to be associated with a relative decrease in protein rather than with an increase in fibre content per unit dry matter (Fig. 18.11). Additionally there is a correlation between protein and P content in sclerophyllous leaves (LOVELESS 1961). Plants growing in nutrient-deficient environments utilize their available nutrients very efficiently although high transpiration can help nutrient uptake. Bog species reabsorb significantly more N from their foliage preceding leaf-fall than non-bog species (SMALL 1972b). The potential

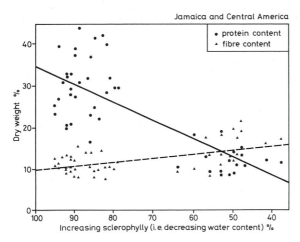

Fig. 18.11. Relative dry weight of protein content (*triangles*) and relative dry weight of fibre content (*circles*) as related to decreasing water content as measure of increasing sclerophylly of 19 evergreen Jamaican bushland species and 31 mesomorphic Central American species. (After LOVELESS 1961)

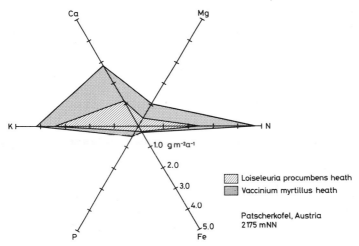

Fig. 18.12. Annual mineral uptake of a *Loiseleuria* heath and a *Vaccinium* heath. (After LARCHER 1977)

photosynthesis which a species could achieve during the time a unit nitrogen remained in the plant before being lost through leaf fall was found to be 235% higher for evergreen bog species than for bog deciduous species and even 275% higher than in non-bog deciduous species. One would therefore expect evergreen forms to be more widely distributed under nutrient-deficient conditions (i.e., humid tropical environments). The evergreen alpine *Loiseleuria procumbens* occupies habitats where leaves can incorporate only half as much N and P as the deciduous *Vaccinium myrtillus* incorporates in its habitat (Fig. 18.12).

It is not clear why, under conditions of limited nutrient supply, plants do not invest all extra carbon into a more extensive root system but produce leaves which require a great amount of structural carbohydrates. Apparently

a limit is reached, at which the investment of additional roots together with their requirement for proteins exceeds the gain of additional nutrient uptake (e.g., in lateritic soils). In this case protection against environmental extremes and predation with secondary plant compounds (MORROW and MOONEY 1974) would appear to be more "productive" than increased rooting in terms of carbon return and nutrient conservation. However, this interpretation should be tested with additional experimental evidence. Hypothetically it may be considered that in nutrient-deficient environments carbon is produced in excess, since any further growth would require additional nutrients, and excess carbohydrates are deposited in cell walls or cutin and waxes, which do not require nutrients, leading to sclerophylly. Therefore both leaf longevity and sclerophylly appear to be adaptive mechanisms under nutrient-deficient conditions.

18.3.3.3 Evergreen and Deciduous Growth as Related to the Water Balance

Under arid conditions the evergreen habit is not necessarily more indicative of a limitation in water supply than the deciduous form (Sect. 18.2.5). It was even found that the deciduous form is more adapted to extremes of aridity than the evergreen form in mediterranean climates (MOONEY und DUNN 1970), in the Californian coastal sage vegetation (POOLE and MILLER 1975), and in the Sonoran (SZAREK and WOODHOUSE 1977) and Saharan desert (STOCKER 1971). The evergreen microphyllous tree *Olneya tesota* maintained a favourable water balance and a low rate of photosynthesis year-round. In contrast, in the deciduous *Ambrosia deltoidea* plant water potentials decreased from -10 bar at high rates of photosynthesis to almost -100 bar in the drought deciduous stage (Fig. 18.13). In the case of the evergreen life form, stress due to high evaporative demand in the atmosphere is avoided. They have a deep-reaching root system and are restricted to special habitats where at least some groundwater is available. In contrast drought deciduous plants have a shallow root system and water stress in both soil and atmosphere is tolerated albeit in a defoliated state. Thus they are able to inhabit very dry habitats of irregular or discontinuous water availability.

Under arid conditions evergreen and deciduous life forms are the extremes in a large variety of intermediate cases. One interesting form is the seasonal leaf dimorphism described for several Irano-Turanian and Saharan species (EVENARI et al. 1971). *Poterium spinosum,* an eastern mediterranean shrub, develops three sets of leaves as drought proceeds, each distinctly different. The ecological significance of this phenomenon is not clear, although it was proposed as a water-saving mechanism (ZOHARY 1961). Conservation of water could also be achieved through deciduousness, and the investment of carbohydrates into construction of new sclerophyllous summer leaves has not been shown to contribute with significance to the carbon balances of the plant in leaf dimorphous *Zygophyllum dumosum* and *Artemisia herba-alba* (SCHULZE et al. 1980). One is tempted to view seasonal dimorphism as a form of retarded growth occurring under stress and, perhaps, with unsufficient nutrient supply. SCHÄFER (1973) showed that the activity of microorganisms in a mediterranean climate is high only during winter (when moist) and that they remain in a dormant state

The energy balance of a stand of winter deciduous *Fagus silvatica* shows strong seasonal variation (Fig. 18.14 A). About 40% of incoming radiation reaches the forest floor before and only 8.6% after spring leaf growth. This seasonal change in radiation climate does not exist in coniferous forests where permanently only 1.6% to 7.2% of incoming radiation reaches the ground (Mitscherlich et al. 1965). The supply of photosynthetically active light directly affects herbaceous plants. In deciduous forests, therefore, the life cycle of many species on the forest floor is restricted to the time before tree leaf growth in spring (Goryshina 1969). These species do not survive in the permanent shade of afforested conifers. The temperature climate affects herbaceous ground vegetation indirectly. If a comparison is made with the altitudinal adiabatic temperature decrease, the effect of an evergreen canopy on a warm summer day is comparable to a 1000-m altitudinal variation (Mitscherlich and Künstle 1970). The temperature effect is reversed in the deciduous forest in spring. Very high temperatures occur within the litter when temperatures are close to freezing in the open field. The high temperatures rapidly activate geophytes. The temperature climate also very likely affects soil microorganisms. The acidification of the soil in coniferous stands is related to the C/N ratio of the litter, but this effect may be enhanced by the micrometeorological differences in soil temperature.

Very few comparative studies of the water budgets of evergreen and deciduous forests have been reported and even then important information is lacking due to measurement and theoretical problems. In the temperate zone all studies report that on the average, total annual interception (evaporation of water from wet leaves) was 15%–20% higher for conifers than for broad-leaved trees (Benecke 1976; Mitscherlich et al. 1966), (Fig. 18.14 B). Loss of intercepted water from *Pseudotsuga* may even reach 36%–66% of gross rainfall (Fritschen et al. 1977). The variability arises from the fact that interception depends strongly on the frequency and average duration of canopy wetness. The result is that the water budget and the water gain for groundwater may be 20% higher in broad leaved forests than in coniferous stands (Stanhill 1970). It may be concluded that a coniferous evergreen forest in Middle Europe is not only cooler and continually darker but also drier than a deciduous one.

The implications of evergreen and deciduous leaves for the carbon balance of trees are similar to those of shrubs (Sect. 18.3.3.1). Evergreen conifers have lower maximal rates of photosynthesis (4–6 mg CO_2 g^{-1} h^{-1}) than broad-leaved deciduous trees (10–14 mg CO_2 g^{-1} h^{-1}). In contrast, conifers have a higher wood production (0.8–1.6 kg m^{-2} a^{-1}) than broad-leaved trees (0.6–0.9 kg m^{-2} a^{-1}) (Bonnemann and Röhrig 1972). Deciduous leaves of *Fagus silvatica* and *Betula verrucosa* have a higher photosynthetic gain per dry weight and year than conifers (Fig. 18.15). The low photosynthetic capacity of the coniferous needle is not counterbalanced sufficiently by a prolonged growing season, since a short photoperiod, low light and low temperatures restrict photosynthetic activity in autumn and spring in the European climate. Conditions are different in summer-dry and winter-mild climates, e.g., the Pacific Northwest of North America.

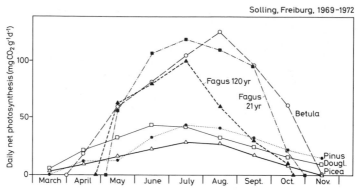

Fig. 18.15. Seasonal change of daily net photosynthesis for winter deciduous *Fagus silvatica* and *Betula verrucosa* and evergreen *Pinus silvestris*, *Pseudotsuga douglasii* and *Picea abies*. (After SCHULZE 1970; SCHULZE et al. 1977a; KÜNSTLE and MITSCHERLICH 1977)

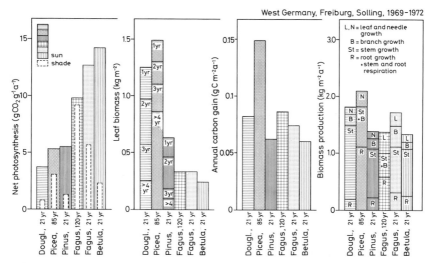

Fig. 18.16. Annual gain of net photosynthesis per gram leaf dry weight, leaf biomass of the canopy per m² stand, annual carbon gain of the stand and annual stand biomass production of evergreen *Pseudotsuga douglasii*, *Picea abies*, *Pinus silvestris* and winter deciduous *Fagus silvatica* and *Betula verrucosa*. (After SCHULZE 1970; SCHULZE et al. 1977a; KÜNSTLE and MITSCHERLICH 1977)

The differences in growth between the deciduous and evergreen form are a consequence of leaf longevity. The annual growth of new foliage is less in conifers than in deciduous trees (Fig. 18.16) but total leaf biomass is higher, because needles are maintained for up to 12 years in *Picea excelsa* (SCHULZE et al. 1977b). Therefore, despite a lower carbon gain per unit leaf weight, but because of a higher accumulation of total leaf biomass the annual carbon gain is greater for conifers than for deciduous trees. The significance of the old foliage for growth in conifers is shown in defoliation experiments. Removal of 1- to 2-year-old needles caused a 51% decrease in growth of *Pinus radiata*

(Rook and Whyte 1976). Needle retention time increases in *Pinus* with elevation and aridity and reaches a maximum of 45 years in *Pinus longaeva* (Evers and Schmid 1981).

The implications of these findings appear to be significant for the understanding of successional stages and geographical distributions of tree forms. Broadleaved trees grow more rapidly than evergreens during the sapling stage, as is known from successional *Populus, Betula,* and *Alnus,* because evergreen forms have to accumulate leaf biomass over many years before maximal productivity is achieved. With decreasing length of the growing season the annual costs of construction of deciduous leaves increase relative to the total carbon gain. Hence, evergreen trees are more efficient in the boreal climate and deciduous trees occur only on very nutritious soils at their northern and eastern border (Klötzli 1976) or after disturbance (e.g., along water ways). However, evergreen trees are replaced by deciduous bushes, e.g., *Salix* and *Betula* in the transitional regions between the boreal forests and tundras. One may hypothesize that the metabolic costs of maintenance increase during dark periods lasting several months and also that the risk of snow and ice damage or eating away of the perennial needles becomes greater for the evergreen tree in the subarctic environment. Therefore, deciduous species are again more competitive in the tundra region, particularly as shrubs with a lower level of respiratory costs. However, the interaction of deciduous *Betula tortuosa* and the evergreen *Pinus* and *Picea* in the oceanic arctic region is certainly not sufficiently understood (see Walter 1973). Also in the continental boreal and alpine climates which are characterized by extremely low winter temperatures but a distinct and warm summer evergreen and deciduous strategies are again both successful (*Larix decidua, L. sibirica, Pinus cembra*).

18.3.4.2 The Alpine Tree Line

At high altitude the alpine tree line represents the most abrupt change in plant dominance on a large geographical scale. It is a zone where the extension of forests is terminated by natural climatic barriers and competition. The major climatic constraints at high altitude are the decreasing length of the vegetation period, which is accompanied by decreasing temperatures and evaporative demand, but increasing radiation, wind and snow cover. The ecology of the alpine tree lines is discussed in Chapter 11, this Volume. Figure 18.17 gives a schematic presentation of the main functional processes.

At low temperatures the photosystem apparently becomes more susceptible to photoinhibition by high light (Van Hasselt and Strickwerd 1976). This effect, together with chlorophyll destruction due to increasing UV light causes a decrease in the rate of net photosynthesis at higher elevation (Caldwell 1979). The annual primary production is also reduced due to the decreased length of the growing season. The main effect of the reduced carbon gain and the decreasing time of vegetative growth is the incomplete development of protective tissues in the evergreen needles. The effects of this become obvious mainly in late winter when low soil and air temperatures restrict water uptake and water transport. At high radiation needle temperature may rise above freez-

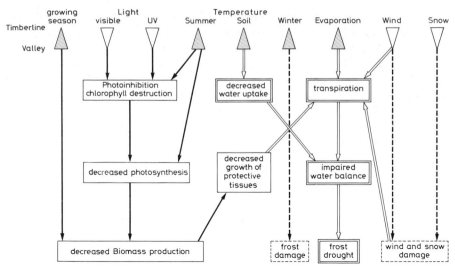

Fig. 18.17. Schematic presentation of environmental factors, which decrease in absolute value on a gradient from the valley to the timberline (*hatched triangles*) and which increase in absolute value (*open triangles*), influencing and restricting plant functions related to carbon relations (*solid arrows*) and to water relations (*open arrows*) and physical damage (*broken line*). The interaction of these factors and functions constrains tree growth at the alpine timberline

ing and despite closed stomata, the needle will lose water by cuticular transpiration. The result is a decrease of water content below a critical value resulting in "frost drought". Low temperatures are not decisive for the survival of conifers in alpine habitats. Frost tolerance is adequate for the minimum habitat temperatures (PISEK et al. 1967; see also Chap. 13, Vol. 12A) and is determined by photoperiod and hardening (SCHWARZ 1970). Wind may act as an additional factor by reducing boundary layer resistance although this effect is negligible when stomata are closed; see also Chap. 15, Vol. 12A. However, wind may cause physical damage to the xylem of the stem and of the needles, which again would enhance frost drought (MARCHANT and CHABOT 1978). It may very well be that the needle is partially separated from the stem by wind and that water stress develops in this half-damaged needle.

The environmental conditions are different for shrubs and needles which are buried beneath snow and which are thus protected against climatic extremes, but which may suffer from drought and frost as soon as they are exposed e.g., by wind (LARCHER 1963). Because of this and because of the decreasing density of the forest canopy and the concomitant increase in light in the understory, low shrubs and herbs are increasingly successful as ground vegetation within the upper alpine forest region. This competitive interaction of trees and other plant life forms is very pronounced at the tree line of *Eucalyptus pauciflora*, the sole tree line species on mainland Australia. It has been found to survive up to several hundred meters above timberline when transplanted into cleared

plots (SLATYER personal communication). Seedling establishment does not occur in undisturbed shrub- and grass-dominated alpine vegetation.

In the New Zealand alpine region northern hemisphere conifers grow successfully up to 300 m higher in altitude than the native *Nothofagus*. Seedlings of *Nothofagus* are rather photo-sensitive and re-establishment occurs only under the protection of the crown of adult trees. The result is a very distinct and closed alpine forest line. This is in contrast to the sun-tolerant pine seedlings of the northern hemisphere which may re-establish independent of the main stand. Although the discrepancy between the tree- and forest line in Europe has been repeatedly attributed to the influence of man (ELLENBERG 1978), *Pinus aristata* shows a similar pattern of crippled growth forms and a separation of forest- and tree line in Nevada in areas where human disturbance is absent. It is alternatively suggested that whether or not the tree line and forest line coincide may strongly depend on the species and on the competitive situation during the stage of seedling establishment.

18.3.4.3 The Arid Tree Line

The ecological significance of the tree trunk is generally discussed in terms of light competition with other plant forms. Trees are also effective carbohydrate (GÄUMANN 1935) or nutrient (BURROWS 1976) storage bodies, although this may not be so different in principle from shrubs or herbaceous plants. However, trees are the only morphological types of plant life form other than highly specialized succulents, which can store considerable amounts of water and use this store during the course of a day. This does not only apply to specialized forms such as bottle trees (*Adansonia digitata, Brachychiton australe*) but also to temperate zone forest trees (HINCKLEY et al. 1978). Even in the humid climate of Scotland *Pinus silvestris* relies significantly on water stored in the sapwood over short periods (WARING et al. 1979).

Despite this storage capacity, tree growth is retarded with decreasing precipitation. WARING et al. (1978) found a decreasing leaf area with increasing drought. Additionally, a redistribution of carbohydrates favouring root growth occurs. A root/leaf dry weight ratio of 7.8 was found in the trees and shrubs of a tree savannah (LAMOTTE 1975). This increased to 9.4 and 11.4 with increasing drought in a shrub savannah and in an open savannah respectively.

The significance of drought for tree existence becomes obvious along an environmental gradient of a desert dry valley. The height of *Acacia constricta* (Fig. 18.18) decreased linearly with soil drought experience ($\Psi_{soil \times week}$). At 400 "bar weeks" tree height was almost the same as for the desert shrub *Larrea tridentata*. At this point there was no competitive advantage of the tree structure. Both trees and shrubs exhibit further reductions in height as water stress increases and eventually reach the same height as the low half-shrub *Krameria glandulosa* (BALDING and CUNNINGHAM 1974).

WALTER (1973) has schematically described the competitive strategies of trees and grasses under semi-arid conditions. Trees and bushes have a large and deep root system whereas grasses are characterized by a dense adventitious root system in the upper horizon. With high rainfall sufficient water reaches

Fig. 18.18. Plant height of a tree (*dots: Acacia constricta*), a shrub (*triangles: Larrea tridentata*) and a half-shrub (*circles: Krameria glandulosa*) in a desert valley as related to cumulative soil water potential. (After BALDING and CUNNINGHAM 1974)

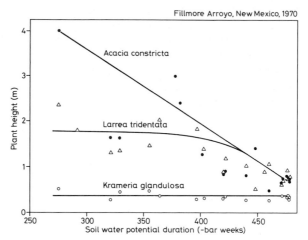

the low soil horizon to be used by trees, which grow rapidly and suppress grasses through competition for light. Australian *Acacia aneura* even exhibits a special growth form of erect branches which allow rain to be captured in a funnel fashion and channelled along the stem into the lower soil profile towards the roots. Furthermore the shading of the evergreen tree crown reduces soil evaporation close to the tree (SLATYER 1961; PRESSLAND 1976). With lower rainfall and retarded tree growth, the competitive advantage of trees in respect to light gathering decreases. At this stage grasses gain in dominance since they are more efficient at water uptake in the upper soil layers. Indirect evidence for these relationships can be seen in the dominance of trees and shrubs in stony habitats where grasses are unable to develop their dense root system. In contrast, sandy soils are grass-dominated as well as clay soils where water does not penetrate deeply.

On a phytogeographic scale the evergreen and deciduous tree habit is distributed in arid regions such that either one or the other form dominates vegetation. In the North Sahara the evergreen tree habit is dominant. The reverse holds for the South Sahara where deciduous *Acacia* ssp. are by far more common. STOCKER (1976) suggested that evergreen trees are adapted to the combination of cold winter and summer drought in the North Sahara, similarly to mediterranean shrubs, but that deciduous trees are favoured in the Sahel where summer rains occur, but where the mild winter is characterized by extreme and prolonged drought. In contrast, the arid regions of Australia are dominated by evergreen *Eucalyptus* and *Acacia*. WALTER (1968) pointed out a principle difference between the Australian and African semi-arid environments. Africa has a strict dry season of several months, whereas Australia has very irregular but recurring rainfalls throughout the year, although marked dry seasons do occur in North and Southwest Australia. Under conditions of uncertain but repeated rainfall evergreen sclerophyllous species appear to be more successful than deciduous trees, since the latter may have to replace foliage several times per year. Additionally, phytogeographical observations confirm that, similarly to shrubs, the ever-

green structure in trees is better adapted to atmospheric drought, whereas the deciduous tree is more adapted to soil aridity.

18.4 The Effect of Plant Life Form on Biomass, Productivity and Water Use Efficiency in Different Vegetation Zones

The latitudinal zones of the earth's vegetation are dominated by different plant life forms (e.g., Troll 1956; Walter 1973, 1968). Tree vegetations generally occupy habitats of higher rainfall, with the exception of arctic and alpine climates, whereas shrubs and grasses generally succeed at the drier end of the scale. High rainfall may partially compensate for a long dry period. This section will investigate the extent to which plant form determines the accumulated biomass, primary production and water use efficiency of different vegetation types. Although numerous biomass studies have been conducted, it is very difficult to find data with complete and sufficient information for such a comparison (Table 18.3; see also Chaps. 4–9, Vol. 12D).

Certainly tree vegetation has the highest total biomass (Fig. 18.19), but when a comparison is made between different forest types it is remarkable that conifers of the temperate and boreal zone may reach and even exceed the total biomass of temperate and tropical broad-leafed forests. Despite the large variability in the primary production of forest stands, which is related to differences in temperature and drought between the various study sites, it can be seen that a 10- to 40-fold difference between species in A_{max} at the leaf level (Sect. 18.2.1) is reduced to only a factor of 2 to 4 at the primary production level. For forest vegetations this variation becomes even smaller if the differences in annual growing season are considered. Coniferous forests have the highest monthly primary production of all forest types. The large potential advantage of the deciduous tree at the leaf level is attenuated and even reversed at the stand level when compared with the coniferous tree (see Sects. 18.3.4.1 and 18.2.4).

In natural vegetation primary production of tropical and temperate grasslands may reach the same order of magnitude as forest vegetations, but a large variation within the data mainly due to drought is apparent. Extremely high biomass production was reported by Walter (1981) for Siberian river flood plain vegetation of tall herbaceous plants. Leaf area index and leaf biomass are quite similar in grasslands and broad-leaved forests. As discussed in Section 18.2.4 it is the supply of radiant energy which eventually limits productivity in the temperate and tropical region independent of plant life form. Biomass and P_N decrease in the arctic and arid environment, but in these regions where vegetation types are not "light-limited", the diversity of plant life form increases (Whittaker and Niering 1975).

The similarity of P_N per month of growing season (Fig. 18.19) implies that the water use efficiency (WUE) corrected for differences in evaporative demand may be rather similar in various vegetation types as long as water is available. It may be quite different if water availability is diminished, but usually then

Vegetation	Maximum biomass kg m⁻²	Leaf biomass kg m⁻²	Primary production kg m⁻² a⁻¹	Leaf area index m² m⁻²	Max. height m	Rainfall mm	Growing season months	References
Tropical rainforest	41–65	1–3.5	6–17					LIETH 1975; RODIN et al. 1975
Manaus, Amazone	47.3	0.90	1.8	5.2	38	2000	12	KLINGE 1976a, b, JORDAN and UHL 1978
Thailand	41	0.76	2.7	6.7	56	1867	12	KIRA 1978
S. Thailand[a]	36.5	0.84	2.9	12.3[b]	36	2696	12	OGAWA et al. 1965a, b; KIRA et al. 1967[b]
Peninsular Malaysia	(34.6)	0.78	2.7	6.9	58	2054	12	KIRA 1978
Tropical seasonal forest	42		1.6–2.5	6–10				LIETH 1975
S.W. Cambodia	38.2	0.73	–	7.4	44	3700	9	HOZUMI et al. 1969a, b, c
Côte d'Ivoire	29.1	0.25	1.3	3.2	50	2000	10	MÜLLER and NIELSEN 1965
C. Thailand, dry evergreen forest	18.6[b]	0.71	1.8	8.6	23	1290	9	OGINO et al. 1967
C. Thailand, dry Dipterocarpus forest	9.0[b]	0.18	0.7	0.82	16	1290	9	OGINO et al. 1967
Evergreen temperate forest broadleaved								
Evergreen oak (Castanopsis/ Cyclobalanopsis)	46.7	0.67	1.8	6.7	24	2680	10	KIRA et al. 1978
Distylium racemosum[a]	(32.1)	1.14[b]	2.1	8.8[b]	25	5700	11	KIRUMA 1960
Cinnamomum camphora	(21.5)	0.47	(1.36)	4.9	17	2300	7	SATOO 1968
Castanopsis cuspidata	9.4	0.84	2.3	8.9	8	1800	11	TADAKI 1968
Evergreen temperate forest coniferous								
Tsuga sieboldii	73.2	1.02	0.9	7.4	27	2800	9	ANDO et al. 1977
Abies firma	64.7	1.78	1.1	9.2	31	2800	9	ANDO et al. 1977
Pinus radiata	31.6	1.0	2.5	7.5	31	1500	12	ROOK and BENECKE, personal communication
Summer deciduous forest broadleaved	18–58		0.4–2.5	3–12				LIETH 1975; DUVIGNEAUD et al. 1971, WHITTAKER 1975
Smoky Mts cove forest	(58.5)	0.60	(1.3)	6.2	34	700	–	WHITTAKER 1975
Fagus crenata	36.9	0.41	1.1	6.8	22	2500	6	OGINO et al. 1976
Fagus crenata	(36.4)	0.38	1.2	7.9	29	–	6	MARUYAMA 1977
Fagus silvatica	30.4	0.37	1.1	6.0	26	1065	5	ELLENBERG 1978
Querceto-Coryletum	31.6	0.35	1.5	5.7	24	800[a]	5	DUVIGNEAUD et al. 1971

Table 18.3 (continued)

Vegetation	Maximum biomass kg m^{-2}	Leaf biomass kg m^{-2}	Primary production kg m^{-2} a^{-1}	Leaf area index m^2 m^{-2}	Max. height m	Rain-fall mm	Growing season months	References
Querceto-Crataegetum	18.6	0.31	1.2	4.4	20	800[a]	5	DUVIGNEAUD et al. 1971
Querceto-Betuletum	20.4	0.33	1.3	4.8	21	800[a]	5	DUVIGNEAUD et al. 1971
Betula maslimowitziana	(11.7)	0.22	(0.6)	4.1	20	1200	5	SATOO 1974a
Populus tremuloides	(20)	0.50	(1.2)	7.4	18	800	—	WHITTAKER and NIERING 1975
Populus davidiana	(11.5)	0.22	(0.9)	2.4	20	1200	5	SATOO 1956
Summer deciduous forest coniferous								
Larix leptolepis	(16.4)	0.36	(1.26)	4.2	19	1800	5	SATOO 1970a b
Metasequoia glyptostroboides	(8.9)	0.43	(1.62)	8.5	17	1800	7	SATOO 1974b
Boreal forest	20–92		0.2–1.5	7.19				LIETH 1975; WHITTAKER and NIERING 1975
Pseudotsuga menziesii	150	1.5–2.0	1.2	15.0	80	2400	5	WARING and FRANKLIN 1979
Pseudotsuga menziesii	(92)	2.5	(1.34)	19.0	45	800	—	WHITTAKER and NIERING 1975
Abies veitchii	(31.1)	1.88	(1.3)	10.6	20	2000	7	TADAKI et al. 1970
Abies lasiocarpa	(42)	1.60	(1.0)	14.0	35	800	—	WHITTAKER and NIERING 1975
Abies concolor	(32)	1.70	(1.3)	18.0	40	800	—	WHITTAKER and NIERING 1975
Pinus ponderosa	(30)	0.68	(0.7)	7.0	25	800	—	WHITTAKER and NIERING 1975
Thujopsis dolabrata	(16)	4.4	(1.92)	17.9	9	2300	6	SATOO 1974c
Picea abies	17	0.21	0.67	4	15	400	6	GORTINSKY 1975
Mediterranean and semi-arid scrub	26		0.25–1.5	4–12				LIETH 1975
Eucalyptus socialis, E. dumosa	6.7	0.24	(0.24)	0.67	7	407	4–6	BURROWS 1976
Acacia aneura, (100yrs)								
Eucalyptus populnea (55yrs)	7.0	0.70	(0.33)	1.96	10	467	2–3	BURROWS 1976
Eucalyptus ssp. (Malle) (13yrs)	3.9	0.30	(0.54)	0.85	3.3	407	4–6	BURROWS 1976
Calif. evergreen comm.	(2.8)	0.53	(0.67)	2.6	3–4	410	6–7	MILLER et al. 1977; MILLER and POOLE 1979; POOLE and MILLER 1978
Chile evergreen comm.	(1.2)	0.34	(0.25)	2.0	3–4	440	6–7	
Tropical grassland	<5		0.02–3.4	1–7				
Eragrostis, India	4.45	2.73[a]	4.55[b]	8.5[a]	2.00	1134	9–10	SINGH and JOSHI 1979

Senna, India	1.29	0.43	0.83	3.4	0.90	1257	9–10	Singh and Joshi 1979
Dichanthium, India	1.25	0.52	0.98	6.7	0.90	1030	9–10	Singh and Joshi 1979
Cenchrus, Australia	0.55	0.15	0.34	1.6[a]	0.40	650	3	Christie 1978
Thyridolepis, Australia	0.23	0.12	0.20	1.3[a]	0.40	660	3	Christie 1978
Temperate Grassland	<3		0.02–1.3	5–16				Lieth 1975
Phalaris arundinacea meadow CSSR	3.05	1.39	2.15	4.2	1.0	520	6–7	Rychnovská 1979
Festuca sulcata meadow, CSSR	2.51	0.96	1.09	1.3	0.5	520	6–7	Rychnovská 1979
Alopecurus pratensis meadow, CSSR	2.23	1.01	1.48	3.9	0.8	520	6–7	Rychnovská 1979
Mixed prairie, Hays, Cottonw., Dickinson, Matador	2.68	0.11	0.89	0.57[a]	–	425	6–7[c]	Sims and Coupland 1979
Shortgrass prairie, Pentax, Pawnee, USA	1.83	0.07	0.81	0.37[a]	–	422	7[c]	Sims and Coupland 1979; Brown 1974
Desert Grassland Jornada, USA	0.34	0.05	0.22	0.26[a]	–	228	10[c]	Sims and Coupland 1979
Bouteloua/Fouqueria	0.26	0.15	0.28	3.2	0.5/3	400	8[c]	Whittaker and Niering 1975
Desert	0.1–4		0.01–0.25	<1				Lieth 1975
Artemisia terrae-albae	4.29	0.14	0.76	–	0.7	120	6	Rodin 1979
Atriplex confertifolia	2.47	0.1	0.12	0.92	0.5	244	4–5	Caldwell et al. 1977
Ceratoides lanata	2.18	0.07	0.08	0.96	0.3	244	4–5	Caldwell et al. 1977
Haloxylon persicum	0.89	0.05	0.10	–	5	170–110	7	Rodin 1979
Larrea divaricata	0.43	0.04	0.14	0.93	1.5	300	8[c]	Whittaker and Niering 1975;
Haloxylon ammadendron	6.35	0.3	1.6	–	7	114	7	Rodin 1976
Tundra	0.1–3		0.1–0.4	0.5–1.3				Lieth 1975
Subarctic tundra	1.1–5.8	–	0.1	0.1–0.6		–	–	Wielgolaski 1975
Arctic tundra	0.6–1	–	0.1–0.5	0.6–3.3		–	–	Wielgolaski 1975
Alpine *Loiseleuria procumbens* heath	3.78	0.35	(0.29)	2.6	0.03	950	4–5	Schmidt 1977
Alpine *Vaccinium* heath	3.60	0.54	(0.49)	5.3	0.15	950	4–5	Schmidt 1977

() Above ground. [a] Estimate uncertain. [b] Probably overestimated. [c] Thermal potential growing season.
Personal communication with: T. Kira, T. Satoo, J.S. Singh, P.C. Miller, M.M. Caldwell, B. Burrows, E.K. Christie, M.J. Trlica, F.E. Wielgolaski, R.H. Whittaker, H. Klinge, E. Medina, U. Benecke, D. Rook, P.L. Sims, H.A.I. Madgwick.

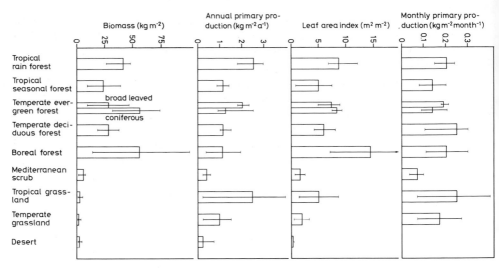

Fig. 18.19. Biomass, annual primary production, leaf area index and monthly primary production during the growing season of different vegetation formations according to Table 18.3. *Columns* averages; *line* range of conditions given in Table 18.3

growth is also retarded (Fischer and Turner 1978). De Wit (1958) proposed that plant growth (P_N) is directly related to the ratio of the cumulative transpiration ($\sum E$) divided by the daily free evaporation ($\sum E_0$):

$$P_N = n \frac{\sum E}{\sum E_0}. \tag{18.9}$$

The data of De Wit (1958) show that the "n" value varied between 10 and 14 g dry weight m^{-2} day^{-1} for many C_3 species at different locations in the Great Plains. It was 21–23 g dry weight m^{-2} day^{-1} for C_4 crops.

According to De Wit (1958) the linear relationship between total dry matter production and transpirational water use, which was observed repeatedly, is due to the differences in evaporative demand. Fischer and Turner (1978) showed that, despite a large variation in WUE, the product of $WUE \cdot E_0$ is rather constant in field experiments with C_3 plants, including desert shrubs. The C_4 species *Zea mays* had a higher "n" value. Fischer and Turner (1978) maintain that although intensive consideration has been given to the many possible ways in which WUE may be affected by genotype and environment, the variation in WUE can be attributed largely to two factors, namely the evaporative demand in the atmosphere and the primary carboxylation enzyme in photosynthesis. These results imply that plants maximize WUE to such an extent that P_N is not very different between plant life forms in dry regions, provided allowance is made for differences in E_0 or that plants have not evolved means to control WUE at the canopy level. Apparently, there is a discrepancy between results based on a determination of WUE from total dry matter production and canopy transpiration and the results on T/P ratios at the leaf level

which is not only determined by the vapour pressure deficit but also by stomatal response. Under natural conditions stomata are generally closed to such a degree that the plant assimilates CO_2 at the leaf level at less than 80% of its maximal rate (SCHULZE et al. 1980; LANGE et al. 1974). Therefore, although $WUE \cdot E_0$ may be constant for C_3 or for C_4 plants, it is not clear to what extent this WUE is also under stomatal control. Since $\sum E_0$ is related to the vapour pressure deficit of the air, the expression $\sum E / \sum E_0$ represents an expression of an average conductance of the canopy, $\bar{g}$. Furthermore, since P_N is related to the average CO_2 assimilation of the canopy, $\bar{A}$, one may rewrite Equ. 18.9 into $\bar{A}/\bar{g} =$ constant. Since the intercellular CO_2 concentration of the mesophyll is generally being expressed as "$c_i = c_a - A/g$" one could interpret the "n" factor of DE WIT to represent an average depletion of CO_2 in the mesophyll, which is different for C_3 and C_4 plants.

For ecological understanding of the primary production as related to the total water budget of the vegetation, interceptive water loss must be included in the consideration. WEBB et al. (1978) showed that P_N of semi-arid vegetation types was linearly related to average evapotranspiration (i.e., transpiration plus interception plus soil evaporation) above a minimum amount of water which may represent soil evaporation in open vegetation. However, this relation does not exist for forest systems, which were not water stressed mainly because of interceptive water loss. (For detailed discussions of productivity of different ecosystems see Vol. 12 D).

18.5 Conclusions

It is appropriate to enquire, first, what plant life forms do; second, how they do it. Only then is enough understanding present for the third question, if it may be asked at all, namely, "why they do it". Phytogeographical observations of the earth's vegetation have led to the first question and very practical systems for plant life form description were developed in order to classify and to compare the vegetation zones of the earth. The second problem, of how plant life forms operate, has been the subject of many decades of ecophysiological, physiological and biochemical work. It is obvious that we are presently able to understand some single plant processes even at the molecular basis. However, the integration of this knowledge into whole plant processes is still very limited. Therefore, it might not be appropriate at all to enquire into the third question, "why they do it", at this stage.

The present chapter has tried at its beginning to make assumptions about the "strategies" by which different plant life forms may operate. Strategy is used in the sense of animal ecology (ZWÖLFER 1978; STEARNS 1976) as an adaptive response which has been selected under ecological pressures. It is proposed that the performance of a specific plant life form in its natural habitat might be "measured" by the marginal returns of carbon relations, which means the extra carbon return per unit carbon, water or nutrient investment in an

organ. It is hypothesized that the composition of plant life forms in the vegetation of the earth is governed by these rules. The way, in which plants could regulate carbon returns at limited carbon, water, or nutrient supply is seen in the regulation of carbon allocation into photosynthetic and non-photosynthetic biomass and in the regulation of leaf longevity.

A hypothesis as to "why plant life forms do it", is presently mathematically and experimentally not developed. There are almost no experimental studies known which investigate the immediate change of carbon returns due to a perturbation in the water and nutrient relations, but numerous descriptions of performance under certain conditions have been made. Therefore, extrapolations are not possible. In spite of this the implications of the foregoing assumptions were explored in terms of competitive features in different life forms and the result of this was compared with the behaviour and success of certain plant life forms in their natural vegetation. It appears that it is not the unfavourable season that determines the success of a specific plant life form, as was suggested by RAUNKIAER (1904), but the carbon relations during the favourable season. The environmental constraints during the growing season determine the plant life form of those species which can persist in a vegetation and compete with others. All species appear to have a large degree of adaptability to the climatic conditions of their habitat at the CO_2 assimilation level. Therefore, the adaptations to different environments occur with carbon allocation, which determines the structural forms of annuals, herbaceous perennials and of deciduous and evergreen woody shrubs and trees. These categories allow a functional insight into the phytogeographical composition of different vegetation types, although it is quite clear that the present study has taken only the simplest cases into account for each group; the phytogeographical diversity of species remains unexplained. The major reason for this is the complete lack of experimental evidence. The comparative study of plant life forms has been strongly neglected and we are still at the level of asking "what plant life forms do". Only for annual species we may be at a stage, mainly for crop species, to know, "how they do it". But solving this question, though it is essential for understanding the mechanisms of succession in natural communities, remains an important goal for further research. The ecological significance, which results from various growth strategies at the carbon allocation level, may be obvious whenever more is known about the functional bases of "success" and "fitness" and their role in community stability and organization.

Acknowledgement. This work was supported by the "Sonderforschungsbereich 137" of the Deutsche Forschungsgemeinschaft and by a grant from the Research School of Biological Sciences which enabled me to use the unique library facilities of the Australian National University. Some of the ideas expressed in this chapter developed during many discussions and in cooperation with Prof. Dr. I.R. COWAN, Prof. O.L. LANGE, Prof. Dr. A.E. HALL and Dr. G.D. FARQUHAR. I am grateful for this fruitful partnership. I thank Prof. E. BECK, Dr. U. BENECKE, Dr. R.A. FISCHER, Dr. H.G. JONES, and Prof. H. ZWÖLFER for reviewing the manuscript. Numerous personal communications were necessary for the compilation of Table 18.3 and I wish to thank these authors. Main appreciation, however, is given to Mrs. M. BALL and Mrs. L. TENHUNEN, who went to great pains to correct my English.

References

Allessio ML, Tieszen LL (1978) Translocation and allocation of ^{14}C-photoassimilate by *Dupontia fisheri*. In: Tieszen LL (ed) Vegetation and production ecology of an Alaskan arctic tundra. Ecol Stud Vol 29. Springer, Berlin Heidelberg New York, pp 393–413

Ando T, Chiba K, Nishimura T, Tanimoto T (1977) Temperate fir and hemlock forests in Shikoku. In: Shidei T, Kira T (eds) Primary productivity of Japanese forests. JIBP Synthesis Vol 16. Univ Press, Tokyo, pp 213–245

Axelrod DI (1966) Origin of deciduous and evergreen habits in temperate forests. Evolution 20:1–15

Balding FR, Cunningham GL (1974) The influence of soil water potential on the perennial vegetation of a desert arroyo. Southwest Nat 19:241–248

Benecke P (1976) Soil water relations and water exchange of forest ecosystems. In: Lange OL, Kappen L, Schulze E-D (eds) Water and plant life. Ecol Stud Vol. 19 Springer, Berlin Heidelberg New York, pp 101–132

Best KF, Macintyre GI (1975) The biology of Canadian weeds. 9. *Thlaspi arvense* L. Can J Plant Sci 55:279–292

Billings WD (1974) Adaptations and origins of alpine plants. Arct Alp Res 6:129–142

Billings WD, Mooney HA (1968) The ecology of arctic and alpine plants. Biol Rev 43:481–529

Björkman O, Ludlow MM, Morrow PA (1972) Photosynthetic performance of two rainforest species in their native habitat and analysis of their gas exchange. Carnegie Inst Yearb 72:94–102

Bonnemann A, Röhrig E (1972) Baumartenwahl, Bestandesgründung und Bestandespflege. Waldbau auf ökologischer Grundlage, Vol 2. Parey, Hamburg, Berlin

Bornkamm R (1970) Über den Einfluß der Konkurrenz auf die Substanzproduktion und den N-Gehalt der Wettbewerbspartner. Flora 159:84–104

Boysen-Jensen P (1932) Die Stoffproduktion der Pflanzen. Fischer, Jena

Brougham RW (1958) Interception of light by the foliage of pure and mixed stands of pasture plants. Aust J Agric Res 9:39–52

Brouwer R (1963) Some aspects of the equilibrium between overground and underground plant parts. Jaarb Inst Biol Scheikd Onderzoek (IBS) pp 31–39

Brown LF (1974) Photosynthesis of two important grasses of the shortgrass prairie as affected by several ecological variables. PhD Thesis, Colo State Univ, Fort Collins

Brown LF, Trlica MJ (1977) Interacting effects of soil water, temperature and irradiance on CO_2 exchange rates of two dominant grasses of the shortgrass prairie. J Appl Ecol 14:197–204

Burrows WH (1976) Aspects of nutrient cycling in semi-arid Mallee and Mulga communities. PhD Thesis, Aust Natl Univ, Canberra

Caldwell MM (1979) Plant life and ultraviolet radiation: some perspective in the history of the earth's climate. Biol Sci 29:520–525

Caldwell MM, White RS, Moore RT, Camp LM (1977) Carbon balance, productivity, and water use of cold-winter desert shrub communities dominated by C_3 and C_4 species. Oecologia 29:275–300

Candolle De AP (1818) Regni vegetabilis systema naturale Vol I. Treuttel et Würtz, Paris

Chapman SB, Webb NR (1978) The productivity of a *Calluna* heathland in Southern England. In: Heal OW, Perkins DF (eds) Production ecology of British moors and montane grasslands. Ecol Stud Vol 27. Springer, Berlin Heidelberg New York, pp 247–269

Chew RM, Chew AE (1965) The primary productivity of a desert-shrub (*Larrea tridentata*) community. Ecol Monogr 35:355–375

Christie EK (1978) Ecosystem processes in semi-arid grasslands. I. Primary production and water use of two communities possessing different photosynthetic pathways. Aust J Agric Res 29:773–787

Claussen W, Lenz F (1979) Die Bedeutung des Assimilatstaus in den Blättern für die Regulierung der Nettophotosyntheserate bei Auberginen (*Solanum melongena* L). Angew Bot 53:41–52

Clements FE (1920) Plant indicators. The relation of plant communities to process and practice. Carnegie Inst Washington Publ 290

Dale HM (1974) The biology of Canadian weeds. 5. *Daucus carota*. Can J Plant Sci 54:673–685

Day W, Legg BJ, French BK, Johnston AE, Lawlor DW, Jeffers WDeC (1978) A drought experiment using mobile shelters: The effect of drought on barley yield, water use and nutrient uptake. Agric Sci 91:599–623

Detling JK (1979) Processes controlling blue grama production on the short grass prairie. In: French NR (ed) Perspectives in grassland ecology, Ecol Stud Vol 32. Springer, Berlin Heidelberg New York, pp 25–42

DeWit CT (1978) Simulation of assimilation, respiration and transpiration of crops. Simulation Monographs. PUDOC, Wageningen

Dodd JL, Lauenroth WK (1979) Analysis of the response of a grassland ecosystem to stress. In: French NR (ed) Perspectives in grassland ecology. Ecol Stud Vol 32. Springer, Berlin Heidelberg New York, pp 43–58

Doanald CM (1963) Competition among crop and pasture plants. Adv Agron 15:1–118

Donald CM, Hamblin J (1976) The biological yield and harvest index of cereals as agronomic and plant breeding criteria. Adv Agron 28:361–405

Drude O (1887) Die systematische und geographische Anordnung der Phanerogamen. In: Schenk A (ed) Handbuch der Botanik Vol III/2. Trewendt, Breslau, pp 175–496

Drude O (1928) Pflanzengeographische Ökologie. In: Abderhalden's Handbuch der biologischen Arbeitsmethoden, Abt XI. Urban and Schwarzenberg, Berlin Wien, pp 1–56

Duvigneaud P, Kestemont P, Ambroes P (1971) Primary productivity of the temperate deciduous forests of Western Europe. In: Duvigneaud P (ed) Productivity of forest ecosystems. UNESCO, Paris, pp 259–270

Eagles CF (1973) Effect of light intensity on growth of natural populations of *Dactylis glomerata* L. Ann Bot (London) 37:253–262

Ellenberg H (1978) Vegetation Mitteleuropas mit den Alpen in ökologischer Sicht, 2nd edn. Ulmer, Stuttgart

El-Sharkawy M, Hesketh J, Muramoto H (1968) Leaf photosynthetic rates and other growth characteristics among 26 species of Gossypium. Crop Sci 8:670–674

Evans LT, Dunstone RJ (1970) Some physiological aspects of evolution in wheat. Aust J Biol Sci 23:725–738

Evans LT, Bingham J, Jackson P, Sutherland J (1972) Effects of awns and drought on the supply of photosynthate and its distribution within wheat ears. Ann Appl Biol 70:67–76

Evenari M, Shanan L, Tadmor N (1971) The Negev. The challenge of a desert. Harvard Univ Press, Cambridge, Mass

Evenari M, Lange OL, Schulze E-D, Kappen L, Buschbom U (1977) Net photosynthesis, dry matter production, and phenological development of apricot trees (*Prunus armeniaca* L.) cultivated in the Negev Highlands (Israel). Flora 166:383–414

Ewers FW, Schmid R (1981) Longevity of needle fascicles of *Pinus longaeva* (Bristlecone Pine) and other North American pines. Oecologia 51:107–115

Farrar JF (1980) Allocation of carbon to growth, storage and respiration in the vegetative barley plant. Plant Cell Environ 3:97–106

Fekete G, Szujkó-Lacza J (1971) A survey of the plant life-form systems and the respective research approaches. III. Raunkiaer's life-form concept. The application of life-forms in the characterization of phytoclimate and vegetation analysis. Ann Hist Nat Mus Nat Hung Botanica 63:37–50

Fischer RA (1975) Future role of physiology in wheat breeding. In: Johnson VA (ed) Proc 2nd international winter wheat congress. Univ Neb Misc Publ 32:178–196

Fischer RA, Maurer R (1978) Drought resistance in spring wheat cultivars. I. Grain yield responses. Aust J Agric Res 29:897–912

Fischer RA, Turner NC (1978) Plant productivity in the arid and semiarid zones. Ann Rev Plant Physiol 29:277–317

Fonda RW, Bliss LC (1966) Annual carbohydrate cycle of alpine plants on Mt Washington, New Hampshire. Bull Torrey Bot Club 93:268–277

Fritschen LJ, Hsia J, Doraiswamy P (1977) Evapotranspiration of a douglas fir determined with a weighing lysimeter. Water Resour Res 13:145–148

Gäumann E (1935) Der Stoffhaushalt der Buche im Laufe eines Jahres. Ber Schweiz Bot Ges 44:157–334

Gifford RM, Marshall C (1973) Photosynthesis and assimilate distribution in *Lolium multiflorum* Lam. following differential tiller defoliation. Aust J Biol Sci 16:517–526

Gloser J (1977) Photosynthesis and respiration of some alluvial meadow grasses: responses to soil water stress, diurnal and seasonal courses. Acta Sci Nat Acad Sci Bohemoslovacae Brno NS 11:1–36

Good R (1974) The geography of the flowering plants. 4th edn. Longman, London New York

Gortinsky GB (1975) Productivity of forests of the European part of the USSR. In: Resources of the biosphere (Synthesis of the Soviet studies for the International Biological Programme) Vol I. Leningrad, NAUKA, pp 34–42

Goryshina TK (1969) Prevernal photosynthesis in the leaves of nemoral herbaceous plants after overwintering. Bot J Acad Nauka CCCP 54:919–923

Grabherr G, Cernusca A (1977) Influence of radiation, wind, and temperature on the CO_2 gas exchange of the alpine dwarf shrub community *Leuseleurietum cetrariosum*. Photosynthetica 11:22–28

Grime JP (1979) Plant strategies and vegetation processes. Wiley and Sons, New York

Grisebach A (1872) Die Vegetation der Erde nach ihrer klimatischen Anordnung. Ein Abriß der vergleichenden Geographie der Pflanzen. Engelmann, Leipzig

Hall AE, Schulze E-D (1980) Stomatal response to environment and a possible interrelation between stomatal effects on transpiration and CO_2 assimilation. Plant Cell Environ 3:467–474

Hall AE, Foster KW, Waines JG (1979) Crop adaptation to semi-arid environments. In: Hall AE, Cannell GH, Lawton HW (eds) Agriculture in semi-arid environments, Ecol Stud Vol 34. Springer, Berlin Heidelberg New York, pp 148–179

Harper JL, Ogden J (1970) The reproductive strategy of higher plants. I. The concept of strategy with special reference to *Senecio vulgaris* L. J Ecol 58:681–698

Harris P (1974) A possible explanation of plant yield increases following insect damage. Agroecosystems 1:219–225

Harris W (1974) Competition among pasture plants. V. Effects of frequency and height of cutting on competition between *Agrostis tenuis* and *Trifolium repens*. NZ J Agric Res 17:251–256

Harris W, Pandey KK, Gray YS, Conchman PK (1979) Observations on the spread of perennial ryegrass by stolons in a lawn. NZ J Agric Res 22:61–68

Hasselt Van PR, Strickwerd JT (1976) Pigment degradation in discs of the thermophilic *Cucumis sativus* as affected by light, temperature, sugar application and inhibitors. Physiol Plant 37:253–257

Heim G, Landsberg JJ, Watson RL, Brian P (1979) Eco-physiology of apple trees: Dry matter production and partitioning by young golden delicious trees in France and England. J Appl Ecol 16:179–194

Hellmuth EO (1968) Eco-physiological studies on plants in arid and semi-arid regions in Western Australia. I. Autecology of *Rhagodia baccata* (Labill.) Moq. J Ecol 56:319–344

Hinckley TM, Lassoie JP, Running SW (1978) Temporal and spacial variations in the water status of forest trees. For Sci Monogr 20:1–72

Hodgkinson KC, Johnson PS, Norton BE (1978) Influence of summer rainfall on root and shoot growth of a cold-winter desert shrub *Atriplex confertifolia*. Oecologia 34:353–362

Holmen K (1957) The vascular plants of Peary Land, North Greenland. Medd Groenl 124:1–149

Hozumi K, Yoda K, Kokawa S, Kira T (1969a) Production ecology of tropical rain forests in southwestern Cambodia. I. Plant biomass. Ibid 6:1–51

Hozumi K, Yoda K, Kira T (1969b) Ibid. II. Photosynthetic production in an evergreen seasonal forest. Ibid 6:57–81

Hozumi K, Yoda K, Kira T (1969c) Production ecology of tropical rain forests in southwe-
stern Cambodia. II. Photosynthetic production in an evergreen seasonal forest. In:
Kira T, Iwata K (eds) Nature and life in Southeast Asia Vol 6. Jpn Soc Promotion
Sci, Tokyo, pp 57–81
Hsiao TC, Ferreres E, Acevedo E, Henderson DW (1976) Water stress and dynamics
of growth and yield of crop plants. In: Lange OL, Kappen L, Schulze E-D (eds)
Water and plant life. Ecol Stud Vol 19. Springer, Berlin Heidelberg New York, pp 281–
306
Huffaker CB (1959) Biological control of weeds with insects. Ann Rev Entomol 4:251–276
Humboldt von A (1806) Ideen zu einer Physiognomik der Gewächse. Cotta, Tübingen
Jackman RH, Mouat MCH (1972) Competition between grass and clover for phosphate.
II. Effect of root activity, efficiency of response to phosphate, and soil moisture. NZ
J Agric Res 15:667–675
Janzen DH (1971) Seed predation by animals. Annu Rev Ecol Syst 2:465–492
Johansson LG, Linder S (1975) The seasonal pattern of photosynthesis of some vascular
plants on a subarctic mire. In: Wielgolaski FE (ed) Fennoscandian tundra ecosystems.
I. Plants and microorganisms. Ecol Stud Vol 16. Springer, Berlin Heidelberg New York,
pp 194–200
Johnson DA, Tieszen LL (1976) Above ground biomass allocation, leaf growth, and photo-
synthesis patterns in tundra plant forms in arctic Alaska. Oecologia 24:159–173
Jordan CF, Uhl C (1978) Biomass of a "terra firme" forest of the Amazon basin. Oecol
Plant 13:287–400
Jurgens SK, Johnson RR, Boyer JS (1978) Dry matter production and translocation in
maize subjected to drought during grain fill. Agron J 70:678–682
Keulen Van H (1975) Simulation of water use and herbage growth in arid regions. PUDOC
Wageningen
Kiese O (1971) The measurement of climatic elements which determine production in
various plant stands. In: Ellenberg H (ed) Integrated experimental ecology. Ecol Stud
Vol 2. Springer, Berlin Heidelberg New York, pp 132–142
King RW, Wardlaw IF, Evans LT (1967) Effect of assimilate utilization on photosynthetic
rate in wheat. Planta 77:261–276
Kira T (1978) Community architecture and organic matter dynamics in tropical lowland
rain forests of southeast Asia with special reference to Pasoh Forest, West Malaysia.
In: Tomlinson PB, Zimmermann MH (eds) Tropical trees as living systems. Cambridge
Univ Press, London, pp 561–590
Kira T, Ogawa H, Yoda K, Ogimo K (1967a) Comparative ecological studies on three
main types of forest vegetation in Thailand. IV. Dry matter production, with special
reference to the Khao Chong rain forest. In: Kira T, Iwata K (eds) Nature and life
in Southeast Asia Vol 6. Jpn Soc Promotion Sci, Tokyo, pp 149–174
Kira T, Ogawa H, Yoda K, Ogino K (1967b) Ibid. IV. Dry matter production, with
special reference to the Khao Chong rain forest. Nature Life SE Asia (Kyoto) 5:149–174
Kira T, Ono Y, Hosokawa T (1978) Biological production in a warm-temperate evergreen
oak forest of Japan. JIBP Synthesis Vol 18. Univ Press, Tokyo
Kiruma M (1960) Primary production of the warm-temperate laurel forest in the southern
part of Osumi Peninsula, Kyushu, Japan. Misc Rep Res Inst Natl Recour (Tokyo)
52/53:36–47
Klinge H (1976a) Root mass estimation in lowland tropical rain forests of central Amazonia,
Brazil. III. Nutrients in fine roots from giant humus podsols. Trop Ecol 16:28–38
Klinge H (1976b) Bilanzierung von Hauptnährstoffen im Ökosystem tropischen Regenwalds
(Manaus) – Vorläufige Daten. Biogeographica 7:59–77
Klötzli F (1976) Grenzen von Laubwäldern in Europa. Ber Dtsch Bot Ges 89:371–380
Körner CH, Moraes De JAPV (1979) Water potential and diffusion resistance in alpine
cushion plants on clear summerdays. Oecol Plant 14:109–120
Körner CH, Scheel JA, Bauer H (1979) Maximum leaf diffusive conductance in vascular
plants. Photosynthetica 13:45–82
Künstle E, Mitscherlich G (1977) Photosynthese, Transpiration und Atmung in einem
Mischbestand im Schwarzwald. IV. Bilanz. All Forst Jagdztg 148:227–238

Laing DR, Fischer RA (1977) Adaptation of semi-dwarf wheat cultivars to rainfed conditions. Euphytica 26:129–139

LaMarche VC (1969) Environment in relation to age of Bristlecone Pine. Ecology 50:53–59

Lamotte M (1975) The structure and function of a tropical savannah ecosystem. In: Golley EB, Medina E (eds) Tropical ecological systems. Ecol Stud Vol 11, Springer, Berlin Heidelberg New York, pp 179–222

Lange OL, Schulze E-D, Evenari M, Kappen L, Buschbom U (1974) The temperature related photosynthetic capacity of plants under desert conditions. I. Seasonal changes of the photosynthetic response to temperature. Oecologia 17:97–110

Larcher W (1963) Zur spätwinterlichen Erschwerung der Wasserbilanz von Holzpflanzen an der Waldgrenze. Ber Naturwiss Med Ver Innsbruck 53:125–137

Larcher W (1976) Ökologie der Pflanzen. UTB 232, 2nd edn. Ulmer, Stuttgart

Larcher W (1977) Ergebnisse des IBP-Projektes „Zwergstrauchheide Patscherkofel" Sitzungsber Oesterr Akad Wiss Math Naturwiss Kl Abt I 186:301–371

Lieth H (1975) Primary production of the major vegetation units of the world. In: Lieth H, Whittaker RH (eds) Primary productivity of the biosphere. Ecol Stud Vol 14. Springer, Berlin Heidelberg New York, pp 203–215

Loomis RS, Gerakis PA (1975) Productivity of agricultural ecosystems. In: Cooper JP (ed) Photosynthesis and productivity in different environments. Univ Press, Cambridge IBP 3:145–172

Loveless AR (1961) A nutritional interpretation of sclerophylly based on differences in the chemical composition of sclerophyllous and mesophytic leaves, Ann Bot (London) 25:168–184

Marchant PJ, Chabot BF (1978) Winter water relations of tree-line plant species on Mt Washington, New Hampshire. Arct Alp Res 10:105–116

Marshall C, Sagar GR (1968) The interdependence of tillers in Lolium multiflorum Lam – a quantitative assessment. J Exp Bot 19:785–794

Maruyama K (1977) Beech forests in the Naeba Mountains. Part I. Comparison of forest structure, biomass and net productivity between the upper and lower parts of beech forest zone. In: Shidei T, Kira T (eds) Primary productivity of Japanese forests. JIBP Synthesis Vol 16. Univ Press, Tokyo, pp 186–201

McCown B (1978) The interaction of organic nutrients, soil nitrogen, and soil temperature and plant growth and survival in the arctic environment. In: Tieszen LL (ed) Vegetation and production ecology of an Alaskan arctic tundra. Ecol Stud Vol 29. Springer, Berlin Heidelberg New York, pp 435–456

McCree KJ, Troughton JH (1966) Non-existence of an optimum leaf area index for the production rate of white clover grown under constant conditions. Plant Physiol 41:1615–1622

Meusel H (1978) Wuchsform und ökogeographisches Verhalten von Bupleurum spinosum Gouan im Vergleich mit einigen nahe verwandten Arten. Bot Jahrb Syst 99:222–248

Miller PC, Bradbury DE, Hajek E, La Marche V, Thrower NJ (1977) Past and present environment. In: Mooney HA (ed) Convergent evolution in Chile and California. Mediterranean climate ecosystems, US/IBP Synthesis 5. Dowden, Hutchinson and Ross, Stroudsburg, pp 27–72

Miller PC, Poole DK (1979) Patterns of water use by shrubs in Southern California. For Sci 25:84–98

Mitscherlich G, Künstle E (1970) Untersuchungen über die Bodentemperatur in einigen Nadel- und Laubholzbeständen in der Nähe von Freiburg/Br. Allg Forst Jagdztg 141:129–133

Mitscherlich G, Moll W, Künstle E, Maurer P (1965) Ertragskundlich-ökologische Untersuchungen im Rein- und Mischbestand. II. Wind, Globalstrahlung und Bestandeshelligkeit. Allg Forst Jagdztg 136:149–257

Mitscherlich G, Moll W, Künstle E, Maurer P (1966) Ertragskundlich-ökologische Untersuchungen im Rein- und Mischbestand. IV. Niederschlag, Stammablauf und Bodenfeuchtigkeit. Allg Forst Jagdztg 137:1–12

Monsi M (1960) Dry-matter reproduction in plants. I. Schemata of dry-matter reproduction. Bot Mag 73:81–90

Monsi M (1968) Mathematical models of plant communities. In: Eckardt FE (ed) Functioning of terrestrial ecosystems at the primary production level. UNESCO, Paris, pp 131–149

Monsi M, Murata Y (1970) Development of photosynthetic systems as influenced by distribution of matter. In: Prediction and measurement of photosynthetic productivity. PUDOC, Wageningen, pp 115–130

Mooney HA (1963) Physiological ecology of coastal, subalpine and alpine populations of *Polygonum bistortoides*. Ecology 44:813–816

Mooney HA, Billings WD (1965) Effects of altitude on carbohydrate content of mountain plants. Ecology 46:750–751

Mooney HA, Dunn EL (1970) Photosynthetic systems of mediterranean climate shrubs and trees of California and Chile. Am Nat 104:447–453

Mooney HA, Ehleringer JR (1978) The carbon gain benefits of solar tracking in a desert annual. Plant Cell Environ 1:307–312

Mooney HA, Ehleringer JR, Berry JA (1976) High photosynthetic capacity of a winter annual in Death Valley. Science 194:322–324

Mooney HA, Ferrar PJ, Slatyer RO (1978) Photosynthetic capacity and carbon allocation patterns in diverse growth forms of *Eucalyptus*. Oecologia 36:103–111

Morilla CA, Boyer JS, Hageman RH (1973) Nitrate reductase activity and polyribosomal content of corn (*Zea mays* L.) having low leaf water potentials. Plant Physiol 51:817–824

Morrow PA, Mooney HA (1974) Drought adaptations in two Californian evergreen sclerophylls. Oecologia 15:205–222

Moser W (1973) Licht, Temperatur und Photosynthese an der Station „Hoher Nebelkogel" (3184 m). In: Ellenberg H (ed) Ökosystemforschung. Springer, Berlin Heidelberg New York, pp 203–223

Moser W, Brzoska W, Zachhuber K, Larcher W (1977) Ergebnisse des IBP-Projektes „Hoher Nebelkogel 3184m". Sitzungsber Oesterr Akad Wiss Math Naturwiss Kl Abt I 186:387–419

Müller D, Nielsen J (1965) Production brute, pertes par respiration et production nette dans la forêt ombrophile tropicale. Forstl Forsoegsvaes Dan 29:69 160

Nicholson JE (1973) Growth stress differences in Eucalypts. For Sci 19:169–174

Ogawa H, Yoda K, Kira T, Ogino K, Shidei T, Ratanawongse D, Apasutaya C (1965a) Comparative ecological studies on three main types of forest vegetation in Thailand. I. Structure and floristic composition, Nature Life SE Asia (Kyoto) 4:13–48

Ogawa H, Yoda K, Ogino K, Kira T (1965b) Ibid. II. Plant biomass. Ibid 4:49–80

Ogino K (1977) A beech forest at Ashiu – biomass, its increment and net production. In: Shidei T, Kira T (eds) Primary productivity of Japanese forests. JIBP Synthesis, Vol 16. Univ Press, Tokyo, pp 172–186

Ogino K, Ratanawongse D, Tsutsumi T, Shidei T (1967) The primary production of tropical forest in Thailand. SE Asian Stud (Kyoto) 5:121–154

Orshan G (1973) Morphological and physiological plasticity in relation to drought. In: McKell CM, Blaisdell JP, Goodin JR (eds) Wildland shrubs – their biology and utilization, USDA forest service. Gen Tech Rep INT-1:245–259

Packham JR, Willis AJ (1977) The effects of shading on *Oxalis acetosella*. J Ecol 65:619–642

Payton IJ, Brasch DJ (1978) Growth and nonstructural carbohydrate reserves in *Chinochloa rigida* and *C. macra*, and their short-term response to fire. NZ J Bot 16:435–460

Penning de Vries FW (1975) Use of assimilates in higher plants. In: Cooper JP (ed) Photosynthesis and productivity in different environments. IBP 3. Cambridge London New York Melbourne, pp 459–480

Pisek A, Larcher W, Unterholzner R (1967) Kardinale Temperaturbereiche der Photosynthese und Grenztemperaturen des Lebens der Blätter verschiedener Spermatophyten. I. Temperaturminimum der Nettoassimilation, Gefrier- und Frostschadensbereiche der Blätter. Flora (Jena) Abt B 157:239–264

Pons TL (1977) An ecophysiological study in the field layer of ash coppice. III. Influence of diminishing light intensity during growth on *Geum urbanum* and *Cirsium palustre*. Acta Bot Neerl 26:251–263

Poole DK, Miller PC (1975) Water relations of selected species of chaparral and coastal sage communities. Ecology 56:1118–1128

Poole DK, Miller PC (1978) Water related characteristics of some evergreen sclerophyll shrubs in central Chile. Oecol Plant 13:289–299

Pressland AJ (1976) Soil moisture redistribution as affected by throughfall and stemflow in an arid zone shrub community. Aust J Bot 24:641–649

Raunkiaer C (1904) Biological types with reference to the adaptation of plants to survive the unfavourable season. In: Egerton FN (ed) History of ecology, life forms of plants and statistical plant geography. Arno Press, New York, Reprint 1977

Redmann RE (1978) Plant and soil water potentials following fire in a northern mixed grassland. J Range Manage 3:443–445

Richards PW (1952) The tropical rainforest. An ecological study. Univ Press, Cambridge

Ridder De N, Seligman NG, Keulen Van H (1981) Analysis of environmental and species effects on the magnitude of biomass investment in the reproductive effort of annual pasture plants. Oecologia (in press)

Rietz Du GE (1931) Life-forms of terrestrial flowering plants. Acta Phytogeogr Suec 3:1–95

Rodin LE (1976) Primary productivity of desert communities in North Africa and Asia. Probl Desert Dev 3–4:55–65 Ashkhabad

Rodin LE (1979) Productivity of desert communities in central Asia. In: Perry RA, Goodall DW (eds) Arid-land ecosystems: structure, functioning and management Vol I. Univ Press, Cambridge, pp 273–298

Rodin LE, Bazilivich NJ, Rozov HN (1975) Productivity of the world's main ecosystems. In: Reichle DE, Franklin JF, Goodall DW (eds) Productivity of world ecosystems. Natl Acad Sci, Washington, pp 13–26

Rook DA, Whyte AGD (1976) Partial defoliation and growth of 5-year-old *Radiata* pine. NZ J For Sci 6:40–56

Ross PJ, Henzell EF, Ross DR (1972) Effects of nitrogen and light in grass-legume pastures – a systems analysis approach. J Appl Ecol 9:535–556

Rychnovská M (1978) Energy flow and relevant processes in a meadow ecosystem. In: Sen DN (ed) Environmental physiology and ecology of plants. Bishen Singh Mahendra Pal Singh, Dehra Dun, pp 315–322

Rychnovská M (1979) Ecosystem synthesis of meadows. Energy flow. In: Coupland RT (ed) Grassland ecosystems of the world: analysis of grasslands and their uses. IBP 18. Univ Press, Cambridge, pp 165–169

Ryle GJA, Powell CE (1975) Defoliation and regrowth in the graminaceous plant: The role of current assimilate. Ann Bot (London) 39:297–310

Saeki T (1960) Interrelationship between leaf amount, light distrubition and total photosynthesis in a plant community. Bot Mag 73:55–63

Satoo T (1956) Materials for the study of growth in stands. III. Amount of leaves and production of wood in an aspen (*Populus davidiana*) second growth in Hokkaido. Bull Tokyo Univ For 51:33–51

Satoo T (1968) Materials for the studies of growth in stands. 7. Primary production and distribution of produced dry matter in a plantation of *Cinnamomum camphora*. Bull Tokyo Univ For 64:241–275

Satoo T (1970a) Primary production in a plantation of Japanese larch, *Larix leptolepis*: A summarized report of JPTE-66 KOIWAI. J Jpn For Soc 52:154–158

Satoo T (1970b) A synthesis of studies by the harvest method: Primary production relations in the temperate deciduous forests of Japan. In: Reichle DE (ed) Analysis of temperate forest ecosystems. Ecol Stud Vol I. Springer, Berlin Heidelberg New York, pp 55–72

Satoo T (1974a) Primary production relations in a natural forest of *Betula maximowicziana* in Hokkaido: materials for the studies of growth in forest stands. 1. Bull Tokyo Univ For 66:109–117

Satoo T (1974b) Primary production relations of a young stand of *Metasequoia glyptostroboides* planted in Tokyo: materials for the studies of growth in forest stands. 13. Bull Tokyo Univ For 66:153–164

Satoo T (1974c) Primary production relations in plantations of *Thujopsis dolabrata* in the Noto Peninsula: materials for the studies of growth in forest stands. 12. Bull Tokyo Univ For 66:139–151

Schäfer R (1973) Microbial activity under seasonal conditions of drought in mediterranean climates. In: DiCastri F, Mooney HA (eds) Mediterranean type ecosystems. Ecol Stud Vol 7. Springer, Berlin Heidelberg New York, pp 191–198

Schimper AFW (1898) Pflanzen-Geographie auf physiologischer Grundlage. Fischer, Jena

Schmidt L (1977) Phytomassevorrat und Nettoprimärproduktivität alpiner Zwergstrauchbestände. Oecol Plant 12:195–213

Schmithüsen J (1968) Allgemeine Vegetationsgeographie, 3rd edn. De Gruyter, Berlin

Schulze E-D (1970) Der CO_2-Gaswechsel der Buche (*Fagus silvatica* L.) in Abhängigkeit von den Klimafaktoren im Freiland. Flora 159:177–232

Schulze E-D, Fuchs MI, Fuchs M (1977a) Spacial distribution of photosynthetic capacity and performance in a montane spruce forest of Northern Germany. I. Biomass distribution and daily CO_2 uptake in different crown layers. Oecologia 29:43–61

Schulze E-D, Fuchs M, Fuchs MI (1977b) Spacial distribution of photosynthetic capacity and performance in a mountain spruce forest of Northern Germany. III. The significance of the evergreen habit. Oecologia 30:239–248

Schulze E-D, Hall AE, Lange OL, Evenari M, Kappen L, Buschbom U (1980) Long-term effects of drought on wild and cultivated plants in the Negev Desert. I. Maximal rates of net photosynthesis. Oecologia 45:11–18

Schwarz W (1970) Der Einfluß der Photoperiode auf das Austreiben, die Frosthärte und die Hitzeresistenz von Zirbe und Alpenrose. Flora 159:258–285

Shackel KA, Hall AE (1979) Reversible leaflet movements in relation to drought adaptation of cowpeas, *Vigna unguiculata* (L.) Walp. Aust J Plant Physiol 6:265–276

Shields LM (1950) Leaf xeromorphy as related to physiological and structural influences. Bot Rev 16:299–447

Sims PL, Coupland RT (1979) Producers. In: Coupland RT (ed) Grassland ecosystems of the world: analysis of grasslands and their uses. IBP 18. Univ Press, Cambridge, pp 49–72

Sims PL, Singh JS (1978) The structure and function of ten western North American grasslands. IV. Compartmental transfers and energy flow within the ecosystem. J Ecol 466:983–1010

Singh JS, Joshi MC (1979) Primary production. In: Coupland RT (ed) Grassland ecosystems of the world: analysis of grasslands and their use. IBP 18. Univ Press, Cambridge, pp 187–217

Singh KP, Gopal B (1973) The effects of photoperiod and light intensity on the growth of some weeds of crop fields. In: Slatyer RO (ed) Plant responses to climatic factors. Ecology and conservation 5. UNESCO, Paris, pp 77–85

Singh JS, Yadava PS (1974) Seasonal variation in composition, plant biomass and net primary productivity of a tropical grassland at Kwukshetra, India. Ecol Monogr 44:351–375

Slatyer RO (1961) Internal water balance of *Acacia aneura* F. Muell. in relation to environmental conditions. UNESCO Arid Zone Res 16:137–146

Small E (1972a) Water relations of plants in raised *Sphagnum* peat bogs. Ecology 53:726–728

Small E (1972b) Photosynthetic rates in relation to nitrogen recycling as an adaptation to nutrient deficiency in peat bog plants. Can J Bot 50:2227–2233

Small E (1973) Xeromorphy in plants as a possible basis for migration betweeen arid and nutritionally deficient environments. Bot Not 126:534–539

Smith EM, Hadley EB (1974) Photosynthetic and respiratory acclimation to temperature in *Ledum groenlandicum* populations. Arct Alp Res 6:13–27

Sørensen T (1941) Temperature relations and phenology of the northeast Greenland flowering plants. Medd Groenl 125:1–305

Stanhill G (1970) The water flux in temperate forests: Precipitation and evapotranspiration. In: Reichle DE (ed) Analysis of temperate forest ecosystems. Ecol Stud Vol I. Springer, Berlin Heidelberg New York, pp 247–256

Stearns SC (1976) Life-history tactics: A review of the ideas. Q Rev Biol 51:3–47
Stocker O (1971) Der Wasser- und Photosynthesehaushalt von Wüstenpflanzen der mauretanischen Sahara. II. Wechselgrüne, Rutenzweige und stammsukkulente Bäume. Flora 160:1–43
Stocker O (1976) The water-photosynthesis syndrome and the geographical plant distribution in the Saharan desert. In: Lange OL, Kappen L, Schulze E-D (eds) Water and plant life. Ecol Stud, Vol 19. Springer, Berlin Heidelberg New York, pp 506–522
Summers CF (1968) Production in montane dwarf shrub communities. In: Heal OW, Perkins DF (eds) Production ecology of British moors and montane grasslands. Ecol Stud Vol 27. Springer, Berlin Heidelberg New York, pp 263–276
Swan LW (1967) Alpine and aeolian regions of the world. In: Wright HE Jr, Osborn WH (eds) Arctic and alpine environments. Indiana Univ Press, Blommington, pp 29–54
Szarek SR, Woodhouse RM (1977) Ecophysiological studies of Sonoran Desert plants. II. Seasonal photosynthesis patterns and primary production of *Ambrosia deltoidea* and *Olneya tesota*. Oecologia 28:365–375
Szujkó-Lacza J, Fekete G (1969) A survey of the plant-form systems and the respective research approaches I. Ann Hist Nat Mus Natl Hung 62:129–139
Tadaki Y (1968) Studies on the production structure of forest (XIV). The third report on the primary production of a young stand of *Castanopsis cuspidata*. J Jpn For Soc 50:60–65
Tadaki Y, Hatiya K, Tochiaki K, Muyauchi H, Matsuda U (1970) Studies on the production structure of forest (XVI). Primary productivity of *Abies veitchii* forests in the subalpine zone of Mt Fuji. Bull Gov For Exp Stn 229:1–22
Tieszen LL (1978) Vegetation and production ecology of an Alaskan arctic tundra. Ecol Stud Vol 29. Springer, Berlin Heidelberg New York
Troll C (1956) Das Wasser als pflanzengeographischer Faktor. In: Ruhland W (ed) Handbuch der Pflanzenphysiol Vol 3, pp 750–786
Turk KJ, Hall AE (1980) Drought adaptations of cowpeas. II. Influence of soil water deficits and evaporative demand on plant water status and relation with seed yield. Agron J (in press)
Turner NC, Begg JE (1977) Response of pasture plants to water deficits. In: Wilson JR (ed) Plant relations in pastures. CSIRO, Melbourne, pp 50–66
Turner NC, Jones MM (1980) Turgor maintenance by osmotic adjustment: A review and evaluation. In: Turner NC, Kramer PJ (eds) Adaptation of plants to water and high temperature stress. Wiley-Interscience, New York London, pp 87–104
Vasek FC (1980) Creosote bush: long-lived clones in the Mojave desert. Am J Bot 67:246–255
Walter H (1968) Die Vegetation der Erde. II. Die gemäßigten und arktischen Zonen. Fischer, Stuttgart
Walter H (1973) Die Vegetation der Erde. I. Tropische und subtropische Zonen, 3rd edn. Fischer, Jena Stuttgart
Walter H (1979) Vegetation und Klimazonen, 4th edn. UTB 14. Ulmer, Stuttgart
Walter H (1981) Über Höchstwerte der Produktion von natürlichen Pflanzenbeständen in NO Asien. Vegetatio 44:37–41
Waring RH, Franklin JF (1979) Evergreen coniferous forests of the Pacific Northwest. Science 204:1380–1386
Waring RH, Emmingham WH, Gholz HL, Grier CC (1978) Variation in maximum leaf area of coniferous forests in Oregon and its ecological significance. For Sci 24:131–140
Waring RH, Whitehead D, Jarvis PG (1979) The contribution of stored water to transpiration in Scots Pine. Plant Cell Environ 2:309–318
Warming E (1884) Über perenne Gewächse. Bot Centralbl 18:184–188
Warming E (1895) Plantesamfund. Grundtrack af den økologiske plantegeografi. PG Philipsen, Kjøbenhavn
Warming E (1909) Ecology of plants. An introduction to the study of plant communities. Clarendon, Oxford
Warming E (1923) Økologiens Grundformer. Udkast til en systematisk ordning Rackke IV, 2 København. K Vidensk Selsk Skr Naturvidensk Math Afd 8

Watanabe I (1976) Transformation factor from CO_2 net assimilation to dry matter in crop plants. Jpn Agric Res Q 10:114–118

Watson DJ (1958) The dependence of net assimilation rate on leaf area index. Ann Bot NS 22:27–54

Webb W, Szarek S, Lauenroth W, Kinerson R, Smith M (1978) Primary productivity and water use in native forest, grassland, and desert ecosystems. Ecology 59:1239–1247

Whittaker RH (1973) Handbook of vegetation science. Ordination and classification of communities. Vol V. Junk, The Hague

Whittaker RH (1975) Communities and ecosystems, 2nd edn. MacMillan, New York

Whittaker RH, Niering WA (1975) Vegetation of the Santa Catalina Mountains, Arizona. V. Biomass, production, and diversity along the elevation gradient. Ecology 56:771–790

Wielgolaski FE (1975) Primary production of tundra. In Cooper JP (ed) Photosynthesis and productivity in different environments. IBP 3. Univ Press, Cambridge, pp 75–106

Wielgolaski FE, Kärenlampi L (1975) Plant phenology of Fennoscandian tundra areas. In: Wielgolaski FE (ed) Fennoscandian tundra ecosystems. I. Plants and microorganisms. Ecol Stud Vol. 16. Springer, Berlin Heidelberg New York, 94–102

Wielgolaski FE, Kjelvik S, Kallio P (1975) Mineral content of tundra and forest tundra plants in Fennoscandia. In: Wielgolaski FE (ed) Fennoscandian tundra ecosystems. I. Plant and microorganisms. Ecol Stud Vol 16. Springer, Berlin Heidelberg New York, pp 316–332

Williams RD (1964) Assimilation and translocation in perennial grasses. Ann Bot NS 28:419–425

Wit CT De (1958) Transpiration and crop yields. Versl Landbouwkd 2 onderz Agr Res Rep 64. 6. PUDOC, Wageningen

Wit CT De (1968) Plant production. Misc Pap Landbouwhogesch Wageningen 3:25–50

Zohary M (1961) On the hydro-ecological relations of the Near Eastern desert vegetation. In: Plant water relationships in arid and semi-arid conditions. UNESCO Arid Zone Res 16:199–212

Zwölfer H (1978) Mechanismen und Ergebnisse der Co-Evolution von phytophagen und entomophagen Insekten und höheren Pflanzen. Sonderbd Naturwiss Ver Hamburg 2:7–50

Zwölfer H (1980) Distelblütenköpfe als ökologische Kleinsysteme: Konkurrenz und Koexistenz in Phytophagenkomplexen. Mitt Dtsch Entoml Ges 2:21–37

Author Index

Page numbers in *italics* refer to the references

Taxonomic Index

Page numbers in **bold face** refer to tables or figures

Subject Index

Page numbers in **bold face** refer to tables or figures

Encyclopedia of Plant Physiology

New Series · Editors: A. Pirson,
M. H. Zimmermann

Physiological Plant Ecology

Editors of Volume 12A–D: O. L. Lange,
P. S. Nobel, C. B. Osmond, H. Ziegler

Volume 12 A:

Physiological Plant Ecology I

Responses to the Physical Environment

1981. 109 figures. XV, 625 pages
ISBN 3-540-10763-0

Contents:

G. S. Campbell: Fundamentals of Radiation and
Temperature Relations. – *K. J. McCree:* Photosyn-
thetically Active Radiation. – *O. Björkman:*
Responses of Different Quantum Flux Densities. –
D. C. Morgan, H. Smith: Non-Photosynthetic
Responses to Light Quality. – *F. B. Salisbury:*
Responses to Photoperiod. – *M. M. Caldwell:* Plant
Response to Solar Ultraviolet Radiation. –
S. Ischikawa: Responses to Ionizing Radiation. –
W. N. Wheeler, M. Neushul: The Aquatic Environ-
ment. – *S. W. Jeffrey:* Responses to Light in Aquatic
Plants. – *J. A. Berry, J. K. Raison:* Functional
Responses of Macrophytes to Temperature. –
M. Aragno: Responses of Microorganisms to Tem-
perature. – *P. L. Steponkus:* Responses to Extreme
Temperatures. Cellular and Sub-Cellular Bases. –
W. Larcher, H. Bauer: Ecological Significance of
Resistance to Low Temperature. – *L. Kappen:*
Ecological Significance of Resistance to High Tem-
perature. – *P. S. Nobel:* Wind as an Ecological
Factor. – *P. W. Rundel:* Fire as an Ecological
Factor. – *P. Benecke, R. R. van der Ploeg:* The Soil
Environment . –
Author Index. – Taxonomic Index. – Subject Index.

Springer-Verlag
Berlin
Heidelberg
NewYork

In preparation

Volume 12 C:

Responses to the Chemical and Biological Environment

ISBN 3-540-10907-2

Contents:
The Ionic Environment and Plant Ionic Relations. –
Osmoregulation. – Halotolerant Eukaryotes. –
Halotolerant Prokaryotes. – Physiology and Eco-
logy of Nitrogen Nutrition. – Influence of
Limestone, Silicates and Soil pH on Plants. –
Toxicity and Tolerance in the Responses of Plants
to Metals. – Ecophysiology of N_2-fixing Systems.
– Ecophysiology of Mycorrhizal Symbioses. – Eco-
physiology of Lichen Symbioses. – Interactions
between Plants and Animals in Marine Systems. –
Ecophysiology of Carnivorous Plants. – Host-
Parasite Interactions in Higher Plants. – Virus-
Ecology – 'Struggle' of the Genes. – Ecophysiology of Zoophilic Pollination. – Physiological Eco-
logy of Fruits and Their Seeds. – Physiological and
Ecological Implications of Herbivory. – Interactions
between Plants.

Volume 12 D:

Ecosystem Processes: Mineral Cycling, Productivity and Man's Influence

ISBN 3-540-10908-0
In preparation

Contents:
Nutrient Allocation in Plant Communities:
Mineral Cycling in Terrestrial Ecosystems. –
Nutrient Cycling in Freshwater Ecosystems. –
Nutrient Cycling in Marine Ecosystems. –
Modelling of Growth and Production. – Produc-
tivity of Agricultural Systems. – Productivity of
Grassland and Tundra. – Productivity of Desert
and Mediterranean Climate Plants. – Productivity
of Temperate Deciduous and Evergreen Forests. –
Productivity of Tropical Forest and Tropical Wood-
land. – Phytoplankton Productivity in Aquatic
Ecosystems. – Effects of Biocides and Artificially
Introduced Growth Regulators: Physiological
Basis. – Effects of Biocides and Artificially Intro-
duced Growth Regulators: Ecological Implica-
tions. – Eutrophication Processes and Pollution of
Fresh Water Ecosystems Including Waste Heat. –
Ecophysiological Effects of Atmospheric Pollu-
tants. – Ecophysiological Effects of Changing
Atmospheric CO_2 Concentration. – Man's
Influence on Ecosystem Structure, Operation,
and Ecophysiological Processes.

Part D: Physiological Plant Ecology IV
Ecosystem Processes: Mineral Cycling, Productivity and Man's Influence

Contents Part A, C and D

Contents Part B

C.B. Osmond
Department of Environmental Biology
Research School of Biological
Sciences
Australian National University
Box 475, Canberra City 2601/
Australia

J.B. Passioura
CSIRO Division of Plant Industry
P.O. Box 1600
Canberra City, A.C.T. 2601/Australia

P.W. Rundel
Department of Ecology and
Evolutionary Biology
University of California
Irvine, California 92717/USA

J. Schönherr
Institut für Botanik und Mikrobiologie
der Technischen Universität München
Arcisstraße 21
D-8000 München 2/FRG

E.-D. Schulze
Lehrstuhl Pflanzenökologie
der Universität Bayreuth
Universitätsstraße 30
D-8580 Bayreuth/FRG

A.S. Sussman
Horace H. Rackham School of Graduate
Studies and Division of Biology
University of Michigan
Ann Arbor, Michigan 48109/USA

W. Tranquillini
Forstliche Bundesversuchsanstalt
Außenstelle für subalpine Waldforschung
Rennweg 1
A-6020 Innsbruck/Austria

M.T. Tyree
Department of Botany
University of Toronto
Toronto M5S 1A1/Canada

P.E. Weatherley
Department of Botany
University of Aberdeen
St. Machar Drive
Aberdeen AB9 2UD/United Kingdom

K. Winter
Lehrstuhl für Botanik II
der Universität Würzburg
Mittlerer Dallenbergweg 64
D-8700 Würzburg/FRG

H. Ziegler
Institut für Botanik und Mikrobiologie
der Technischen Universität München
Arcisstraße 21
D-8000 München 2/FRG

M.H. Zimmermann
Harvard University
Harvard Forest
Petersham, MA 01366/USA

List of Contributors

J.D. BEWLEY
Department of Biology
University of Calgary
Calgary, Alberta T2N 1N4/Canada

K.J. BRADFORD
Department of Vegetable Crops
University of California
Davis, California 95616/USA

S. VON CAEMMERER
Department of Environmental Biology
Research School of Biological
Sciences
Australian National University
Box 475, Canberra City A.C.T. 2601/
Australia
Present address:
Plant Biology Laboratory
Carnegie Institution of Washington
290 Panama Street
Stanford, California 94305/USA

I.R. COWAN
Department of Environmental Biology
Research School of Biological
Sciences
Australian National University
Box 475, Canberra City A.C.T. 2601/
Australia

R.M.M. CRAWFORD
Department of Botany
The University
St. Andrews
Fife KY16 9AL/United Kingdom

H.A. DOUTHIT, Jr.
Division of Biology
University of Michigan
Ann Arbor, Michigan 48109/USA

G.D. FARQUHAR
Department of Environmental Biology
Research School of Biological
Sciences
Australian National University
Box 475, Canberra City A.C.T. 2601/
Australia

A. HADAS
Institute of Soils and Water
Agricultural Research Organization
Volcani Center
P.O. Box 6
Bet Dagan 50250/Israel

A.E. HALL
Department of Botany and Plant
Sciences
University of California
Riverside, California 92521/USA

T.C. HSIAO
Department of Land, Air and Water
Resources
University of California
Davis, California 95616/USA

P.G. JARVIS
Department of Forestry and
Natural Resources
University of Edinburgh
King's Buildings
Edinburgh EH9 3JU/United Kingdom

D. KOLLER
The Hebrew University of Jerusalem
Department of Agricultural Botany
Rehovot/Israel

J. KROCHKO
Department of Biology
University of Calgary
Calgary, Alta T2N 1N4/Canada

J.A. MILBURN
Department of Botany
University of New England
Armidale, N.S.W. 2351/Australia

Professor Dr. O.L. LANGE
Lehrstuhl für Botanik II der Universität Würzburg
Mittlerer Dallenbergweg 64, 8700 Würzburg/FRG

Professor P.S. NOBEL
Department of Biology
Division of Environmental Biology
of the Laboratory of Biomedical and Environmental Sciences
University of California
Los Angeles, California 90024/USA

Professor C.B. OSMOND
Department of Environmental Biology
Research School of Biological Sciences
Australian National University
Box 475, Canberra City 2601/Australia

Professor Dr. H. ZIEGLER
Institut für Botanik und Mikrobiologie
der Technischen Universität München
Arcisstraße 21, 8000 München 2/FRG

ISBN 3-540-10906-4 Springer-Verlag Berlin Heidelberg New York
ISBN 0-387-10906-4 Springer-Verlag New York Heidelberg Berlin

Library of Congress Cataloging in Publication Data. Main entry under title: Physiological plant ecology II. (Encyclopedia of plant physiology; new ser., v. 12 B) Bibliography: p. Includes index. 1. Plant-water relationships. 2. Plants, Effect of carbon dioxide on. 3. Plants–Assimilation. 4. Botany–Ecology. I. Lange, O.L. (Otto Ludwig) II. Title: Carbon assimilation. III. Series. QK711.2.E5 new ser., vol. 12 B 581.1s 82-10342 [QK870] [581.1].

Typesetting, printing and bookbinding: Universitätsdruckerei H. Stürtz AG, Würzburg.
2131/3130-543210

Physiological Plant Ecology II

Water Relations and Carbon Assimilation

Edited by

O.L. Lange P.S. Nobel C.B. Osmond H. Ziegler

Contributors

J.D. Bewley K.J. Bradford S. von Caemmerer I.R. Cowan
R.M.M. Crawford H.A. Douthit Jr. G.D. Farquhar A. Hadas
A.E. Hall T.C. Hsiao P.G. Jarvis D. Koller J. Krochko
J.A. Milburn C.B. Osmond J.B. Passioura P.W. Rundel
J. Schönherr E.-D. Schulze A.S. Sussman W. Tranquillini
M.T. Tyree P.E. Weatherley K. Winter H. Ziegler
M.H. Zimmermann

With 153 Figures

Springer-Verlag Berlin Heidelberg New York 1982

Encyclopedia of
Plant Physiology

New Series   Volume 12 B

Editors

A. Pirson, Göttingen
M. H. Zimmermann, Harvard

EXPLORATION
CONSERVATION
PRESERVATION

A Geographic Perspective
on Natural Resource Use

THIRD EDITION

PREFACE

Natural resource conservation has been an important college-level course for several decades, and many good texts have been written on the subject. Moreover, in the nearly 30 years since the first Earth Day, students' interest in environmental issues has remained high. The textbooks most often used since the early 1970s have reflected the ideals of the recent environmental movement, with its concern for natural environmental processes, pollution control, the population explosion, and depletion of mineral and other resources.

The environmental movement of the 1960s and 1970s was one of idealism. Throughout the 1970s and 1980s those ideals became incorporated into many aspects of government policy, business practice, and the everyday concerns of the general population. Since the late 1980s, we have seen both a renewal of environmental concerns with a global focus and a maturation of our understanding of the interdependence of economic processes and environmental protection. Today natural resource issues have great emotional and political significance, and form one of the most central elements of our economic and social lives. As we near the next century we are obliged to examine the diverse facets of these issues.

In this book, we integrate physical, economic, social, and political considerations into our examination of the major natural resource issues facing the world today. We take the view that none of these four factors alone determines the suitability of a resource for any particular use at any time. Rather, a dynamic interplay between these factors causes continuing changes in methods and rates of resource exploitation. The title *Exploitation, Conservation, Preservation* includes three value-laden and politically charged words that have been at the heart of the natural resources debate over the last century. The subtitle, *A Geographic Perspective on Natural Resource Use*, reflects the traditional use of geography, which integrates studies of physical and human phenomena to understand human use of the earth.

Although the authors share this approach to the subject, we have contrasting scientific and philosophical views. With the exception of the epilogue we have avoided, as much as possible, taking any one point of view. Instead, we have attempted in most cases to include a wide range of opinions and interpretations of natural resource issues, in the hope that this will provide both a balanced review and a basis for discussion. At the same time, no commentary on natural resources can be free of political content, and we recognize that this book must inevitably be influenced by its authors' personal views. We hope that students reading this book will learn to recognize and understand the political content of our discussions as well as others' presentations and arguments on these issues.

In this edition we have made use of several global environmental databases that are now available. These are invaluable instructional tools that have the potential to transform a course in environmental conservation from one that helps students to understand the issues to one in which they learn how to analyze and quantitatively evaluate the significance of resource patterns and trends. We have used a small fraction of these data to illustrate some of the more important topics covered in this text, but we encourage students and instructors using the book to exploit these data more fully, and especially to be aware of changing conditions over time. Fortunately, the Internet and those who have made their data available on it have made this much easier than it was just a few years ago.

In this regard, we are establishing a new web-based resource for users of this book. It will consist of updates on important topics (equivalent to new or updated issue boxes) and links to other web sites with useful data related to this text. The URL for this is **www.wiley.com/college/cutter**

Those familiar with the previous editions will recognize many changes, most significantly the consolidation of agriculture and rangeland into a single chapter on food, consolidation of the water quantity and quality chapters, and an entirely new chapter on sustainability. These changes were made primarily to highlight the interconnectedness of these resource issues. As before, a glossary has been included for students' use.

In producing the third edition we have benefited not only from those who worked on previous editions, but also from several people who contributed specifically to this one. In particular, we would like to thank Jerry Mitchell, Rick Collins, Tracy Fehl, and Bill Lace at South Carolina, and Andrea Kuyper and Mark Petrie at Miami who helped with bibliographic and statistical research. Many reviewers offered useful critiques including Kirstin Dow (University of South Carolina), Leslie Duram (Southern Illinois University), Tom Orton (Concordia Lutheran University, Austin), John Hayes (Salem State College), Melissa Savage (UCLA), Roger Balm (Rutgers University), Neil Salisbury (University of Oklahoma), Paul Knuth (Edinboro University of Pennsylvania), Chris Steele (State University of New York, Binghamton), Clarence Head (University of Central Florida), Marvin Baker (University of Oklahoma), Solomon Isiorho (Indiana Purdue University), Norman Stewart (University of Wisconsin) and Marshall Parks (Indiana State University).

We would like to acknowledge the Wiley staff: Nanette Kauffman and Barbara Bredenko, our Acquisitions Editors; Catherine Beckham, Marketing Manager; Sandra Russell, Production Editor; Dawn Stanley, Designer; Kim Khatchatourian, Photo Editor and Edward Starr, Illustration Editor.

We also thank our families: Langdon, Nathaniel, Megan, Debra, Sarah, Levi, Peg, and Oliver who continue to be understanding of the time pressures we face. The authors accept all responsibility for any errors, and we share credit with everyone who helped us for any praise this book may receive.

Susan L. Cutter
William H. Renwick

CONTENTS

PHOTO CREDIT LIST

Chapter 1
Figure 1-2: ©Steve Morgan/FSP/Gamma Liaison. Figure 1-4: ©Grant Heilman/Grant Heilman Photography.

Chapter 2
Figure 2-3: ©Jonathon Nourok/Tony Stone Images/ New York, Inc. Figure 2-4: ©Jacques Jangoux/Photo Researchers.

Chapter 3
Figure 3-1: /Index Stock. Figure 3-2: ©W.A. Raymond/ Corbis-Bettmann. Figure 3-3: ©Tim Barnwell/Stock Boston/ PNI. Figure 3-4: Courtesy U. S. Department of the Interior, Bureau of Reclamation, B. D. Glaha. Figure 3-5: /Tribune Media Services.

Chapter 4
Figure 4-3: ©Nicholas Parfitt/Tony Stone Images/ New York, Inc. Figure 4-4: Leland J. Prater/Courtesy U.S. Forest Service. Figure 4-10: Courtesy NOAA/National Weather Service. Figure 4-13: ©Betty Press/Woodfin Camp & Associates/ PNI.

Chapter 5
Figure 5-4: Courtesy United Nations. Figure 5-7: ©Craig Sillitoe/Black Star. Figure 5-12: J. Isaac/Courtesy United Nations.

Chapter 6
Figure 6-10a: ©Grant Heilman/Grant Heilman Photography. Figure 6-10b: Erwin Cole/Courtesy USDA. Figure 6-11: ©Joe Munroe/Photo Researchers. Figure 6-12: Doug Wilson/Courtesy USDA. Figure 6-13: ©Grant Heilman/Grant Heilman Photography. Figure 6-14: ©Billy E. Barnes/Tony Stone Images/ New York, Inc. Figure 6-15: John McConnell/Courtesy of USDA. Figure 6-17a: E. W. Cole/Courtesy Soil Conservation Service. Figure 6-17b: Courtesy USDA. Figure 6-17c: Tim McCabe/Courtesy USDA. Figure 6-17d: Gene Alexander/Courtesy Soil Conservation Service.

Chapter 7
Figure 7-3: Courtesy USDA/Forest Service. Figure 7-4: A. S. Sudhakaran/Courtesy United Nations.

Chapter 8
Figure 8-3: ©James H. Carmichael/The Image Bank. Figure 8-4: ©Novosti/Gamma Liaison. Figure 8-7: ©Edward R. Degginger/Bruce Coleman, Inc./ PNI. Figure 8-9: Courtesy Tennessee Valley Authority.

Chapter 9
Figure 9-8: ©Sygma. Figure 9-9: ©Dennis Capolango/ Black Star.

Chapter 10
Figure 10-5: Department of Water Resource. Figure 10-11: ©Kirk Condyles/Impact Visuals. Figure 10-12: ©Grant Heilman/Grant Heilman Photography. Figure 10-13: ©Daniel S. Brody/Stock Boston.

Chapter 11
Figure 11-1: ©Anthony Suau/Gamma Liaison. Figure 11-4: ©Joel W. Rogers/Earth Images. Figure 11-8: ©Grant Heilman/Grant Heilman Photography. Figure 11-11: ©Gabe Palacio/Aurora/ PNI.

Chapter 12
Figure 12-4: ©Sigrid Estrada/Gamma Liaison. Figure 12-5: Schmidt-Thomsen/ Landesdenkmalamt Westfalen-Lippe Munster, Germany.

Chapter 13
Figure 13-6: Don Green/Courtesy Kennecott Copper Corporation. Figure 13-7: W. I. Hutchinson/Courtesy U.S. Forest Service. Figure 13-8: ©Paul Souders/Gamma Liaison. Figure 13-10: Courtesy Reynolds Aluminum Recycling Company.

Chapter 14
Figure 14-6: ©Grant Heilman/Grant Heilman Photography. Figure 14-8: Courtesy U. S. Nuclear Regulatory Commission. Figure 14-11: Courtesy State of New Mexico Department of Energy, Minerals and Natural Resources Department. Figure 14-12: Courtesy Pacific Gas & Electric Company.

Chapter 15
Figure 15-4: ©Index Stock.

CHAPTER 1

NATURAL RESOURCES: THOUGHTS, WORDS, AND DEEDS

WHAT IS A NATURAL RESOURCE?

Have you ever wondered what went into the manufacture of the pencil you are now using? A seed germinated and consumed soil nutrients, sprouted and was warmed by the sun, breathed the air, was watered by the rain, and grew into a beautiful straight tree. The tree was cut down. Perhaps it rode a river's current, was stacked in a lumberyard, and was sawn into small pieces. This wood was transported to a factory, where it was dried, polished, cut, drilled, inserted with graphite (which is made from coal), and painted. Then consider how the pencil made its way to you. It has been packaged attractively with appealing letters painted down its side, shipped via truck, and stored in a warehouse. Your pencil's active life will not end with you, for it may be used by other hands and minds if you lose or discard it.

Where are the natural resources in that description? *Resources* are things that have utility. *Natural resources* are resources that are derived from the Earth and biosphere or atmosphere and that exist independently of human activity. The seed, tree, soil, air, water, sun, and river are all natural resources. They are out there, regardless of whether or not human beings choose to use them. They are the *"neutral stuff"* that makes up the world, but they become resources when we find utility in them (Hunker 1964).

Now, consider the role of human effort in the creation, sale, and use of that pencil. First, in addition to natural resources, nonnatural resources are needed, such as saws, labor, and the intelli-gence to create the pencil. But what motivates people to select and use some portions of the neutral stuff so that they become resources while other things are neglected? It is here that we are able to isolate the subject matter of this book: the interactions between human beings and the environment or the neutral stuff. When geographers focus on natural resources, we are asking: What portions of the Earth's whole have people found of value? Why? How do these values arise? How do conflicts arise, and how are they resolved? Neutral stuff may exist outside of our use, but it becomes resources only within the context of politics, culture, and economics. Let us begin, then, to try to understand how and why resources emerge, are used, and fought over.

Resource Cognition and Value

A resource does not exist without someone to use it. Resources are by their very nature human-centered. To complicate the picture, different groups of people value resources differently. Let's look at the role of environmental cognition in the emergence of resource use.

Environmental cognition is the mental process of making sense out of the environment that surrounds us. To cognize, or think, about the environment leads to the formation of images and attitudes about the environment and its parts. Because we constantly think and react to the environment, our cognition of it is constantly changing on some level. Nonetheless, certain elements of environmental cognition will remain stable throughout our lives. Many factors influence our cognition of resources and thus how they will be used. These factors can be grouped into five broad categories: (1) cultural background; (2) view of nature; (3) social conditions; (4) scarcity; and (5) technological and economic factors (see Fig. 1.1).

With regard to the first category, there are many different cultures in the world, and each has a different system of values. What has value and meaning in one culture may be regarded as a nuisance in another. More to the point, the value and meaning assigned in one culture may be the complete opposite of the meaning and value of that resource in a different culture. Whaling provides a classic example. Native Americans, especially the Inuit, historically used whales as a source of food and the whale's fat as fuel. Later, the Inuit used whale bones in their arts and crafts, a usage that continues to the present. Today, most Americans appreciate the majesty and beauty of these marine mammals and value them, not as a consumable resource (food and fuel), but as an aesthetic one. Whale watching in California and New England draws thousands of people to view these migratory mammals in their natural habitat. Harvesting whales for food produces high seas protests

against commercial whaling vessels, actions that garner world headlines and public sympathy (Fig. 1.2).

The mesquite, a deep-rooted drylands shrub, is another example of cultural differences. Ranchers in West Texas feel the need to fight the thirsty mesquite because they perceive that it dictates what will flourish and what will wither and die in the semiarid environment. Range grasses are shallow rooted and do not compete well with mesquite, which thus deprives range animals of a source of food. As one popular magazine reported, "the rancher enjoys with his mesquite the same relationship that Wile E. Coyote maintains with the Roadrunner in the children's cartoon; the rancher will try anything short of nuclear weapons to conquer mesquite" (*Time*, March 1, 1982). Yet, not too long ago, the Indians of the American Southwest lived quite harmoniously with the now pesky mesquite. The mesquite was used for fuel and shade, while the bush's annual crop of highly nutritious beans was a staple resource. Even diapers were fashioned from the bark. Today mesquite is popular as a fuel for gourmet barbecues.

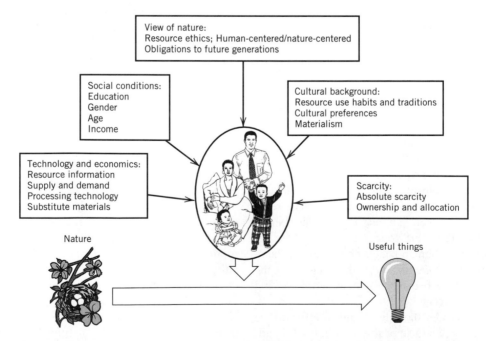

Figure 1.1 Factors involved in resource-use cognition include cultural evaluation, view of nature, social change, economic and technological factors, and resource scarcity.

Figure 1.2 Society's view of nature. Nature can be viewed as a commodity or as a scenic wonder in need of preservation. These Greenpeace activists believe that killing whales is immoral, and use dramatic actions such as this to call attention to their beliefs. In Norway, whales have been eaten for years and many regard this as morally no different from eating any other animal.

A society's view of itself relative to its natural environment is a second indicator of how it will ultimately use natural resources. On an idealized spectrum, different worldviews range from human domination and control of nature (technocentrism) to living in harmony with it (ecocentrism) (Pepper 1996). Of course, there is variation within any one group; not all members will agree on their view of nature. These underlying philosophical ideas form the basis for many of the modern environmental movements (Chapter 3).

Social conditions the third category, influences the value and use of resources. The composition of societies is constantly changing. People grow older, richer, and poorer, and the cultural makeup of societies changes. All of these factors, particularly ethnicity, gender, education, and income, influence how societies cognize and use resources. For example, higher-income households in the United States use more energy than do lower-income households. In colonial New England, lobsters were fed to indentured servants as a cheap food resource. It was not until the late nineteenth century and the influx of southern European immigrants, who regarded the lobster highly, that it became a valuable culinary delicacy.

Cognition of future resources is colored by historical and current use; cognitions also change over time. As a result, planning for future uses of natural resources must take account of these changes. Economists, politicians, and industrialists find it difficult to make accurate forecasts of future resource uses. We may overlook today a resource that will become invaluable in 20 years. Specifically, the solid waste we produce and discard today may be a source of raw materials in the future, and we may see mining reclamation projects in old landfills.

The fourth factor influencing natural resource cognition and use is resource scarcity. As a natural resource becomes scarce or is cognized as becoming scarce, its value may increase. This scarcity may be of two different types. *Absolute scarcity* occurs when the supplies of that resource are insufficient to meet present and future demand. The exhaustibility of all supplies and known reserves of some resources is possible, if improbable. The dwindling supply of certain land resources such as wilderness could conceivably lead to an absolute scarcity. *Relative scarcity* occurs when there are imbalances in the distribution of a resource rather than the insufficiency of the total supply. This imbalance can be either short or long term. Climatic fluctuations resulting in floods, droughts, or frost routinely cause relative shortages of fresh produce. Open space was not considered a resource until it became relatively scarce in urban areas. Then it became something to be valued, protected, and incorporated into urban redevelopment plans. Relative scarcity also results when one group is able to control the ownership or distribution of resources at the expense of another group. In the energy crises of the early and mid-1970s, Americans were told by both environmental and industry experts that the supply of oil and gas was dwindling—and that it would be impossible to meet future demand because of the absolute scarcity of the resource. Yet, in the 1990s, we see lower prices and a more than adequate supply, suggesting that relative scarcity was in fact the cause of the energy crisis.

Finally, the fifth set of factors that influence resource cognition and use are technological and economic, both of which are basic to understanding the role of scarcity. Technological factors relate to our knowledge and skills in exploiting resources. Groundwater is not a resource until it is made available by drilling a well and installing pumps or other means to bring it to the surface. Desert lands have little agricultural value unless we possess the technical capability to collect and distribute irrigation water, at which time they may become very valuable. Deuterium in the oceans is not at present a resource, except for its use in weapons. However, if we learn how to control the fusion reaction for energy production in the future, it may become a resource.

Economic factors combine technology and cognition, as reflected in our pricing system. That is, the value or price of a good is determined by its physical characteristics as well as our ability and desire to exploit those characteristics. In a capitalist economy, a commodity will not be exploited unless it can be done at a profit. Therefore, as prices change, things become (or cease to be) resources. A deposit of iron ore in a remote location may be too expensive to exploit today, but if prices rise substantially it may become profitable to exploit and sell that ore; at that time it becomes a resource.

Rarely is the status of a resource determined by technological, cognitive, or economic factors alone; usually it is a combination of all three. The nuclear power industry is a good example. The development of fission reactors and related technology was necessary for uranium to become a valuable energy resource. But rapid expansion of nuclear-generating capacity depends on this energy source being economically competitive with other sources, such as coal and oil. Coal has become costly to use, in part because of concerns about the negative environmental effects of global warming, air pollution, and mining. These concerns helped make nuclear power competitive. But the belief that nuclear power is unsafe necessitated modifications in plants that drove up the cost of nuclear power to the point where it is no longer economically attractive. In addition, many people, citing environmental and health fears, reject nuclear energy at any price. The interplay of these forces will continue to affect the choice of nuclear power relative to other energy sources for some time.

Kinds of Resources

There are various ways to classify resources. We can ask how renewable they are and who benefits from them. *Perpetual resources* (Fig. 1.3) are resources that will always exist in relatively constant supply regardless of how or whether we exploit them. Solar energy is a good example of a perpetual resource; it will continue to arrive at the Earth at a reasonably constant rate for the foreseeable future. In the past, the atmosphere and precipitation were regarded as perpetual resources. Recently, however, their quality and the absolute supply of rainfall in some locations have been questioned.

Resources that can be depleted in the short run but that replace themselves in the long run are called *renewable* or *flow resources*. Forests, most groundwater, and fisheries are good examples. Although they can be depleted by harvesting in excess of the replacement rate, if given sufficient time and the right conditions, natural processes will replace them. The key to maintaining the availability of renewable resources is keeping our rate of use at or below the rate of natural replacement.

Nonrenewable or *stock resources* exist in finite supply and are not being generated at a significant rate in comparison to our use of them. Once they are used up that is the end of them. Most geologic resources, such as fossil fuels and mineral ores, are of this type, as is wilderness.

Finally, *potential resources* are not resources at present, but may become resources in the future depending on cognitive, technological, and economic developments. Their potential depends in part on decisions made about them today. Should we make decisions that eliminate them from consideration (such as allowing a plant or animal species to become extinct), then there is no chance of our discovering a resource value in them. Some contemporary examples of potential resources that have recently come into use are

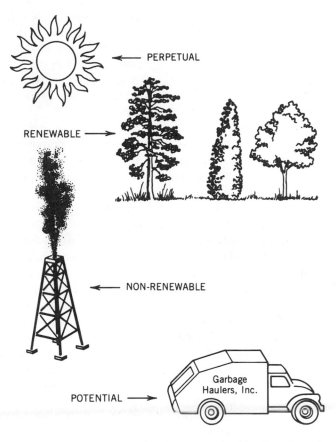

Figure 1.3 The four traditional resource classifications. In reality, a resource can shift from one category to another.

solid waste as an alternative fuel or material source and wastewater that might be treated and used in irrigation or other purposes.

Limits to Resource Classification

Although these definitions are relatively clear, to a large extent the status of any resource as perpetual, renewable, or nonrenewable depends on the time scale in which we view it and on how we manage the resource. Even though rainfall on the global level is reasonably constant from year to year, in many areas the quality of that water has been changed by industrial and auto emissions that produce acid rain. On a longer time scale, there is evidence that we may be causing global climatic changes, resulting in increases or decreases in rainfall at the regional level, if not worldwide. Soil, generally regarded as a renewable resource, will recover some degree of its natural fertility if left fallow for a few years. But if accelerated erosion removes a substantial por-

tion of the soil profile, the ability of that soil to support plants that restore nutrients and organic matter may be impaired. It may be centuries before the soil is again productive. That time period is probably too long to consider the soil renewable in human terms.

Similarly, groundwater is generally considered a renewable resource, but in many areas, particularly desert areas where it is so important, the natural rate of recharge is very low, and in some cases there is presently little or no recharge. In these cases the groundwater is effectively a stock resource; once it is used it is lost forever. For these reasons, the traditional definitions of resources tell us little about the true nature of particular resources. In fact, they may be harmful, leading us to think that a renewable resource *will* always be available regardless of how we exploit it. These classifications illustrate, however, that not all resources are equal to the demands put on them. They also indicate the importance of examining the detailed characteristics of resources and their ability to meet our needs under varying conditions.

CONSERVING RESOURCES: WHAT DOES IT MEAN?

Like Mom and apple pie, few politicians would ever admit to being opposed to the conservation of natural resources, but just as certainly people disagree on what conservation means. Some believe that it means limited or no use of certain resources. A person with this point of view might maintain that no air pollution is acceptable and that wilderness cannot be wilderness if there are any people in it. Others feel that conservation means efficient use. They argue that a resource should be used to produce the greatest possible human good. Resources are beneficial but only if they are used; disuse is seen as waste. Some of the history of the development of these two viewpoints in the United States is discussed in Chapter 3.

The disagreement, however, is even more complex than this. There are many definitions of "efficient," because few agree on what is truly beneficial. Is profit the highest benefit? Or is spiritual renewal the best use? If a beautiful valley is filled with four houses to the acre, each resident has a home and a quarter acre of land. Is this a more efficient and beneficial use than making the valley into a park, so that many more can enjoy it, albeit less often?

In addition, how much time should be considered for use of a resource? Should its beneficial use be spread over many years, in small amounts? Or should we gain all the benefits we can now and use other resources in the future? Do future generations have the same rights to a present resource as do people currently living, even though we can't tell whether they will actually want to use it? In some cases these questions can be answered in rational terms, but often they are philosophical or political in nature and may be considered in the context of *environmental ethics*.

Another central question relating to environmental ethics is whether nonhuman entities have rights, independent of those assigned by humans, and if so what those rights are. For ex-

ample, many people believe that animals have a right to exist and that to deliberately kill them for any reason is immoral. Some may attach similar rights to plants. Or one might feel that it is acceptable to kill animals for human necessity, such as for food, but not for sport or convenience.

Some people may extend rights to nonliving entities, such as mountains or rivers. For example, some Native American groups believe that to plow the ground is to cut into the flesh of the Earth, while others would regard mining on a sacred mountain as an offense to the spirits of that mountain (Nash 1989; Stone 1993).

The dominant view in the United States today, at least as it is manifested in current resource-use practices, is quite different from all the foregoing. This view focuses on human needs and assigns rights only to humans. It considers plants, animals, and the nonliving parts of Earth to have value only to the extent assigned by humans. A bald eagle, for example, has value as our national symbol, and we prohibit killing it for that reason. Old Faithful geyser is unique and well known, and we would not tolerate turning the site into a parking lot. But we do not attach special values to "ordinary" natural things.

Environmental Ethics: Some Examples

Clearly, a wide range of views of nature and natural resources within human society have arisen. We have no intention of evaluating these different views or of making judgments about them— that is for the individual alone. As a society, we attempt to arrive at consensual value statements, usually through political processes, and our social expressions of values change through time.

As examples of the diversity of ethical views of natural resources that exist today, and the implications of these views for natural resource policy, we can consider two different positions: a nature-centered view and a human-centered view. These two positions represent a strong contrast, but they are not necessarily extremes. Neither could be considered a majority view in the world today, but each includes elements that many people would agree with, at least to a limited extent. We present these two views solely as illustrations of the diversity of opinions that are brought to bear on the subject of this book.

A Nature-Centered View of Natural Resource Management   Consider the following statements:

1. Nature, including individual organisms, species, and ecosystems, has inherent value. Humans exist as one species among many, and like any species, we have the right to use nature to the extent necessary to maintain our existence. But because humans have intelligence and power that is much greater than that of any other species, we have a special obligation to use that intelligence and power wisely, and not damage other organisms or their habitats unnecessarily.
2. Nature is the basis of the resource base we enjoy. While many materials we use are synthesized from inanimate substances, our most important resources —food, water, and oxygen—are produced by biogeochemical processes in nature. The function of these processes must therefore be allowed to continue unmodified by humans.
3. In addition to an obligation to nature itself, we have an obligation to future generations of humans to leave them with an environment that is at least as healthy, productive, and diverse as the one we have inherited. We must not make any assumptions about the desires, needs, or technological abilities of future generations that would limit their opportunity to lead satisfying and fruitful lives.
4. Humans are using resources at rates never before experienced on Earth, and these rates will probably double in the next 50 years. Human participation in Earth's biogeochemical cycles is globally significant and locally dominant. Most natural resource systems are fundamentally altered, and many are severely stressed. Growth in population and resource use over the next few decades will increase the degree to which natural resource systems are altered, and many resource systems will be stressed beyond the limits of utility.

These four statements sound reasonable enough and are not likely to offend many people. If we accept them as good environmental values, what resource management policies do they require? Clearly, they demand that we minimize our modifications of natural systems. Actions such as deforestation, soil erosion, pollution, or emissions that lead to global warming cause either permanent or long-term alteration of the environment, probably resulting in species extinctions or at the very least substantial alterations of natural systems.

These statements demand that our resource-use activities be completely sustainable, in the sense that everything we use from nature must be recycled and replaced at rates equal to our use. If we harvest the trees in a forest, we must allow them to regenerate, and we must do so in ways that do not prevent species that depend on mature forests from occupying them. If we use the soil to grow crops, we must do so in ways that do not deplete soil fertility. We should not use nonrenewable resources such as fossil fuels, for to do so deprives future generations of their use. We might mine metal ores, provided that we make it possible to supply future needs of those metals through the recycling of already-mined materials.

We cannot depend on future generations to have better technology than we have, for to do so would limit future opportunities. If we create radioactive wastes, we must dispose of them in ways that will protect future generations from harm indefinitely, without requiring others to manage those wastes. Human-induced climate change is an especially severe violation of these values, for it will likely have many far-reaching impacts on future natural resource availability. We must therefore cease all emissions of gases that we believe will lead to climatic change.

A Human-Centered View of Natural Resource Management   What happens if we take another ethical position, one that is more human-centered? How does this position influence resource-use practices? Consider these statements:

1. Our primary concern should be to improve the quality of life for all humans. Quality of life includes both material goods such as food, shelter, consumer goods, and good health, and intangibles such as education, security, and aesthetic values including beauty in human and natural creations.
2. Human culture is so diverse that the value of these intangibles cannot possibly be fixed, but rather varies from individual to individual, from time to time, and from one geographic location to another. Material goods, on the other hand, are universally important, and their value is measured in monetary terms with relative ease.
3. Throughout history, the single most important determinant of the material quality of life has been the ability of human societies to create goods from the natural resources that surround them. This ability is more dependent on human factors such as technology and wealth than on the inherent qualities of natural resources. For example, if we

were in need of containers for cooking food, iron ore would be worthless without the knowledge of how to convert it to metal pans. With sufficient knowledge, however, we can make suitable cooking containers from a vast range of natural resources—not only other metals but also ceramics and many other materials.

4. Disparities in quality of life between rich and poor are large, and a significant portion of Earth's human population has a quality of life that most people regard as unacceptably low. For the poorer portion of Earth's population, economic development would have a much greater impact on quality of life than improvement in environmental quality.

This second group of statements, like the first one, contains few things that could be disputed. But you can probably see that they will lead us in a very different direction for resource use than those suggested by the first group.

Most significantly, by making quality of life for humans our primary concern we immediately relegate the needs of other species and the habitats they occupy to a secondary role. This does not mean that we are driven to destroy other species; rather, in weighing a decision on how to manage a given environment, we need only concern ourselves with the value of that species to us and not with its inherent value.

For example, consider the tall-grass prairie ecosystem that once occupied the eastern Great Plains of the United States. Today this ecosystem is virtually nonexistent, except for a few remnant patches and some places where we are attempting to restore what we think this ecosystem originally consisted of. We don't know how many species were lost through the destruction of this ecosystem, let alone what they were. In its place, however, we have farms that produce enormous amounts of food—the wheat, corn, and soybeans from which we make bread and which we feed to livestock to produce meat. These lands produce ample good-quality food for hundreds of millions of people. Which use of the land brings the greatest improvement in the quality of life? Tall-grass prairie or amber waves of grain?

What about the future? Should we be concerned about preserving specific environments or resources for future generations? While we should be concerned about the future, we cannot possibly anticipate society's needs and abilities more than a few generations in the future. If we look back to the 1890's, the internal combustion engine had only just been developed, use of electricity was in its infancy, and airplanes were still just dreams. Who could possibly have anticipated that plastics would replace steel in automobiles, that plywood and particle board could replace sawn lumber, or that telecommunications could replace physical transport of some commodities? Technological and social change would make resources that are insignificant today vital and today's precious commodities worthless, and these changes can happen very quickly. It would be foolishly arrogant of us to think that we can make decisions about resource needs 100 years in the future.

Finally, we would be irresponsible to pass up the opportunity to significantly improve the quality of life for humans alive today, just to preserve a resource that might or might not be useful in the future. In the poorer countries of the world, millions of people (especially children) die each year from conditions like diarrhea caused by untreated drinking water, or respiratory ailments caused by indoor air pollution from wood-fired cookers and similar sources (Cutter 1995). This suffering could be relieved through the provision of safe drinking water supplies, sewage treatment plants, or electricity to power cooking stoves. If curtailing use of fossil fuels cost money that could otherwise be used to install water treatment systems, would it be right to do so just to keep the planet from being a few degrees warmer 100 years from now? If a large dam could be built that would generate hydroelectricity, would it be right to not build that dam for the sake of preserving habitats and species that would be replaced by the reservoir?

What Values Do You Bring to the Natural Resources Debate? The values that we adopt individually or as a society are central to our decisions about resource management. As suggested by the title, this book will present many viewpoints regarding resource use along a spectrum from those who advocate full use (or exploitation) to those who would conserve (or balance efficient use with protection) to those who would preserve (or remove from use those resources in need of full protection). *Exploitation* is the complete or maximum use of a resource for individual profit or societal gain. *Conservation* is the wise utilization of a resource so that use is tempered by protection to enhance the resource's continued availability. *Preservation* is the nonuse of a resource by which it is fully protected and left unimpaired for future generations.

As we proceed through the book, we will examine a broad range of resource issues, each of which has many facets and many possible outcomes. You will find that in evaluating these issues you will need to know how you feel about such questions as the inherent value of nature or the extent of our obligations to future generations. Take some time to think about these questions as you go! For examples of others' ideas, see articles by Hardin (1974), Plant (1989), Tobias (1988), Warren (1990), Weiss (1990), and White (1967).

Nature, Economics, and The Politics of Natural Resource Use

We believe that a combination of natural, economic, and political factors determines resource use. This means that the study of natural resources must be interdisciplinary and integrative. Integrative approaches must also rely on increasingly specialized work on particular aspects of resource problems, and so we must be able to think in both specific and inclusive ways (Clawson 1986). Most modern views of natural resources use systems thinking to achieve this integration, and that approach will be used here. To illustrate this view, consider the availability of a basic mineral commodity, such as a metal ore (Fig. 1.4). What determines how much of the mineral we will use?

Ores exist in rocks in a wide range of conditions and with a wide range of qualities. Thus, some deposits might be mined relatively cheaply, whereas others are costly to mine. There are also deposits that are as yet undiscovered but that might be found if one made a careful effort to do so (which is more likely if substantial profits are to be gained from mining the ore).

From the standpoint of a consumer of a mineral, availability depends on whether someone is able and willing to sell at a price the consumer is willing to pay. Willingness to sell usually depends on ability to do so profitably, which de-

Figure 1.4 Ore mine. The mining of iron ore in northern Minnesota provided the backbone of the regional economy for over a century.

pends on a combination of the costs of mining and processing and the market price. Economic factors affecting both costs of mining and consumer willingness to pay include general levels of wealth and economic activity and many more specific aspects of a national or world economy. Social goals and policies also come into play in that they affect both consumer preferences and environmental policies relating to mining activities, for example.

Figure 1.5 is a simplified representation of how all these factors interact in determining how much of a mineral is used. Clearly, being able to consider economics, geology, environmental regulation, marketing, and technology simultaneously has advantages. We also must rely on specialists who can analyze the details of individual components of that system. This book will examine both integrative and specific problems.

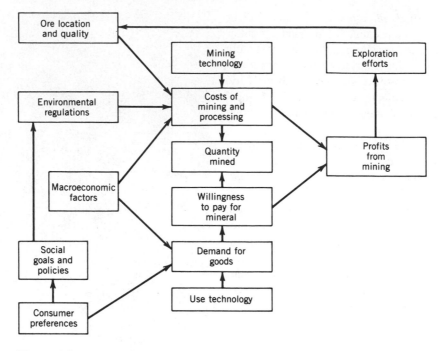

Figure 1.5 A schematic representation of the interaction between natural, economic, and political factors in determining mineral availability and use. Quantity mined is most immediately determined by mining costs and market price, but these are in turn affected by a wide range of economic, technological, and social factors.

THE SYSTEMS APPROACH

In the fourth century B.C., Aristotle stated that the whole is greater than the sum of its parts. This view, more fully developed over the centuries, argues that we should understand the entire world by examining all of it at once rather than looking at each of its constituent parts and then adding them up. During the twentieth century, this holistic view has gained acceptance in many fields of study. It was formalized in the scientific community in the 1950s under the heading of *general systems theory* (von Bertalanffy 1950).

Systems thinking is a way of viewing the world. The focus is on the comprehensive treatment of a whole by a simultaneous treatment of all parts. A systems approach not only examines the parts individually, but also looks at how they interact both with each other and as part of the entire system. Geographers use the systems approach to make sense of both natural and human

systems and to better understand why the two interact as they do.

As we saw with the example of the pencil, natural resource use involves elements of both human and physical systems. Examples of natural systems are forest ecosystems, the hydrologic cycle, and atmospheric circulation. Human systems include technological, economic, and social systems. Figure 1.5 is a highly simplified illustration of these systems as they apply to mineral resources. The complexity and interrelatedness of human and natural systems make the systems approach particularly important. Natural resources cannot be viewed simply as parts of the physical environment or as commodities that are bought and sold. Instead, they must be considered in the context of the many natural and human factors that affect them, and with concern for the potentially far-reaching impacts of changes in resource use.

The need for an integrated systems approach to natural resource use was made abundantly clear in the late 1980s when it appeared that the "spaceship Earth" was rapidly deteriorating. Droughts plagued the northern Plains states, raw sewage and medical waste fouled the nation's beaches, the depletion of the ozone layer became fact, not conjecture, and unprecedented tropical deforestation continued. Dire predictions of ecological collapse and environmental degradation echoed throughout the world. Environmental disasters so dominated the news that in their annual Woman or Man of the Year Issue, *Time* magazine selected the "Endangered Earth as Planet of the Year" for 1988.

As we progress into the next century, environmental concerns will influence every aspect of our lives both here and abroad (Issue 1.1). The halcyon days of rapid exploitation are over and are being replaced by more conservation-oriented strategies that emphasize sustainable development, less resource use, and more awareness of the longer term consequences of resource use (Fig. 1.6). Understanding the complexities of these human and physical systems and their interaction is essential as we fulfill our stewardship of the planet. You can make a difference, and we hope that this book will help you realize that.

GENERAL OUTLINE OF THE BOOK

In this book, the analysis of natural resources and management policies has both physical and human foci. We stress the interrelations among the physical attributes of resources, their role in economic systems, and the political and social factors that govern decision making about their use. We take the view that, even though resources can be classified as perpetual, renewable, nonrenewable, or potential at any given time, they are dynamic and subject to modification or redefinition. Human activity has as much effect on the nature of resources as do natural processes.

Part I focuses on the basic human and natural components of resource use. Chapter 2 provides an overview of the economics of natural resource use, including pricing systems, demand elasticities, externalities, and the relationship between economic growth and resource use. In Chapter 3 the decision-making processes governing resource use and the historical origins of current conservation philosophies in the United States are discussed. Chapter 4 provides a review of the ecological bases of natural resources. Chapter 5 examines the human population system.

Part II deals with specific resource issues. These issues include agriculture and food production (Chapter 6), forests (Chapter 7), biodiversity and habitat (Chapter 8), marine resources (Chapter 9), water resources (Chapter 10), urban air pollution (Chapter 11), regional and global air issues (Chapter 12), minerals (Chapter 13), energy resources (Chapter 14),

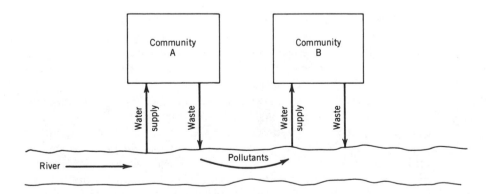

Figure 1.6 The external effects of one system on another. Communities A and B rely on the river as a source of drinking water and a receptacle for their waste. Unfortunately, Community B, because of its downstream location, must use the water after it has been polluted by Community A's waste.

ISSUE 1.1: European Integration and the Environment: EEA and EIONET

Europe has undergone rapid changes during the 1990s, and this situation can be expected to continue into the next century. It has become more prosperous than at any other time since before World War I, and its economy is more fully integrated today than it has ever been. Economic integration and prosperity are in large part attributable to the establishment of the European Economic Community, or European Union as it is known today.

The EU began in the 1950s as an economic association, with the aim of improving the standard of living in member states through elimination of internal trade barriers, while economically linking nations so as to reduce the likelihood of war. Since then, it has grown and become a political as well as an economic association. As economic cooperation has expanded it has been necessary and desirable for the member nations to act in concert on other matters such as social and environmental policy. For example, social policy is often carried out through taxation and subsidies: taxing alcoholic beverages and tobacco or subsidizing rail systems. Social policies are thus linked to economic policies.

With the ratification of the Maastricht Treaty (1992), 15 countries became member states of the European Union (Austria, Belgium, Denmark, Finland, France, Germany, Greece, Ireland, Italy, Luxembourg, Netherlands, Portugal, Spain, Sweden, and the United Kingdom). The EU is working toward a goal of an internal market with no barriers to the movement of goods, labor, or capital. This means the complete removal of any import restrictions, taxes, or regulations that could interfere with business across the international boundaries of the member nations. Many of the less contentious steps that must be taken, for example, elimination of import tariffs and standardization of product safety requirements and similar specifications, have already been achieved. More difficult matters, such as the complete elimination of barriers to international movements of labor, still remain. It is possible that a completely integrated and barrier-free internal market may not be achieved immediately, but most of the important barriers are likely to be significantly lowered, if not removed alto-

gether. A unified currency (the EURO), for example, has already been established.

In 1990 the EU established the European Environment Agency (EEA) whose purpose is to provide the EU with objective and comparable information for environmental protection, to inform the public about the state of the environment, and to provide the necessary technical and scientific support to achieve those goals. The 15 member states of the European Union together with Iceland, Liechtenstein, and Norway, are the current members of the EEA. One of the agency's first goals was to establish the European Environment Information and Observation Network (EIONET).

The primary function of the EEA is to monitor and assess the quality of the environment, pressures on it, and areas of environmental sensitivity. The EEA acts as a centralized clearinghouse for aggregated environmental data from all member states. As such, they are especially interested in transboundary and global implications of environmental quality including the socioeconomic dimensions. Current priority areas include air quality/atmospheric emissions; water quality; status of soil and flora/fauna; land use and natural resources; waste management; noise emissions; hazardous substances; and coastal protection. The EIONET is the monitoring network for the EEA and consists of national monitoring centers from each of the member states. Thus, all data collection and management is the primary function of EIONET.

But the environmental movement in Europe today is subject to a wide range of pressures. Many nations with diverse cultural and political systems are involved. The desire to improve living standards and stimulate trade provides the stimulus for economic cooperation, but because environmental and economic policies are closely intertwined, any improvement in economic conditions cannot be achieved without environmental improvement. It is too soon to evaluate the effectiveness of the European equivalent to our Environmental Protection Agency, but it is clearly a step in the right direction for building a cooperative and comprehensive environmental policy within the European Union (European Environment Agency 1996).

and, lastly, a chapter on the transition to global sustainability (Chapter 15). We conclude with an epilogue that provides our own personal views of the future.

REFERENCES AND ADDITIONAL READING

Clawson, M. 1986. Integrative concepts in natural resource development and policy. In R.W. Kates and I. Burton, eds. *Geography, Resources, and Environment*, Vol. II, pp. 69–82. Chicago: University of Chicago Press.

Cutter, S. L., 1995. The forgotten casualties: women, children, and environmental change. *Global Environmental Change: Human and Policy Dimensions* 5(3): 181–194.

Easterbrook, G. 1995. *A Moment on the Earth.* New York: Viking.

Ehrlich, P. and A. Ehrlich, 1991. *Healing the Planet.* Reading, MA: Addison-Wesley.

Engel, J. R. and J. G. Engel, eds. *Ethics of Environment and Development.* London: Bellhaven Press.

European Environment Agency, 1996. European Environment Agency: Putting Information to Work. ON-LINE: http://www.eea.dk/

Gore, A. 1989. An ecological Krystallnacht. Listen. *New York Times*, March 19, p. E27.

_____. 1992. *Earth in the Balance: Ecology and the Human Spirit.* Boston: Houghton Mifflin.

Hardin, G. 1974. Living on a lifeboat. *Bioscience* 24:10.

_____. 1985. *Filters Against Folly.* New York: Basic Books.

Hunker, H. L., ed. 1964. *Erich W. Zimmermann's Introduction to World Resources.* New York: Harper & Row.

Kates, R. W. and I. Burton, eds. 1986. *Geography, Resources, and Environment*, Vols. I and II. Chicago: University of Chicago Press.

Kaufman, W. 1994. *No Turning Back: Dismantling the Fantasies of Environmental Thinking.* New York: Basic Books.

Kiss, A. and D. Shelton. 1993. *Manual of European Environmental Law.* Cambridge, UK: Grotius Publications.

McKibben, B. 1989. *The End of Nature.* New York: Random House.

Nash, R. A. 1989. *The Rights of Nature: A History of Environmental Ethics.* Madison: University of Wisconsin Press.

Ophuls, W. and A. S. Boyan, Jr. 1992. *Ecology and the Politics of Scarcity Revisited.* New York: W. H. Freeman.

O'Riordan, T. 1986. Coping with environmental hazards. In R.W. Kates and I. Burton, eds. *Geography, Resources, and Environment.* Vol. II, pp. 272–309. Chicago: University of Chicago Press.

Pepper, D. 1996. *Modern Environmentalism.* New York: Routledge.

Plant, J. ed. 1989. *Healing the Wounds: The Promise of Ecofeminism.* Philadelphia: New Society Press.

Smil, V. 1987. *Energy, Food Environment.* Oxford: Clarendon Press.

Southwick, C. H. ed. 1985. *Global Ecology.* Sunderland, MA: Sinauer Associates.

Stone, C. D. 1993. *The Gnat Is Older Than Man: Global Environment and Human Agenda.* Princeton: Princeton University Press.

Tobias, M. ed. 1985. *Deep Ecology.* San Diego: Avant Books.

von Bertalanffy, L. 1950. An outline of general systems theory. *Brit J. Philos. Sci.* 1(2): 134–165.

Warren, K. 1990. The power and promise of ecological feminism. *Environmental Ethics* 12: 125–147.

Weiss, E. B. 1990. Our rights and obligations to future generations for the environment. *Am. J. Int. Law* 84: 198–207.

Welch, S. and R. Miewald, eds. 1983. *Scarce Natural Resources: The Challenge to Public Policy-making.* Beverly Hills, CA: Sage Publications.

White, G. F. 1969. *Strategies of American Water Management.* Ann Arbor: University of Michigan Press.

White, Lynn, 1967. The historical roots of our ecological crisis. *Science* 155:1203–1207.

For more information, consult our web page at ***http://www.wiley.com/college/cutter***

STUDY QUESTIONS

1. Pick an object you are familiar with—an item of clothing, a desk, whatever. List the natural resources that were probably used to make it. Which ones were renewable and which were nonrenewable? What portion of the value (retail price) of the object represents the cost of the raw natural resources, and what portion is attributable to human labor?

2. Do you eat meat? Do you wear leather? Define the extent to which you feel responsible for the welfare of the animals you use and those you don't

(pets, for example). What are the moral bases of your decisions in this regard? In a few sentences, can you define the limits of your personal obligations to other species?

3. Examine the contents of your garbage container at home. Make a brief list of the major categories of materials present. For each of these, write down a potential use and what you think would have to change in your society in order for this potential resource to become useful and economically valuable (instead of having negative value as waste).

CHAPTER 2

ECONOMICS OF NATURAL RESOURCES

INTRODUCTION

Decisions on the exploitation, conservation, and preservation of natural resources are always made within the context of a particular culture, with its own economic system. This can be a centrally planned socialist economy or, at the other extreme, an unregulated capitalist system based exclusively on the pressures of the marketplace. Most countries today have economies somewhere in between these two. No matter what the political or social system, a mechanism must exist for the exchange of goods and services. In most societies, this mechanism is price—the value society places on an item.

The price of a good or service is usually represented by its monetary equivalent. In some cases, however, a good or service can have less tangible value. For example, although many in the United States consider clean water and free-flowing streams valuable, it is difficult to place a monetary value on such a resource. Today, resource economists have begun to view natural resources differently from other commodities and suggest ways in which economies can include an accounting of the degradation or conservation of natural resources. In the past, a clean and healthy environment was seen by industry and development as "too expensive" in the face of economic reality.

Economists have been debating the nature of economic systems and the relationship between economic growth and environmental quality for decades. The neoclassical view of economics as open systems unrestrained by environmental limits (either natural resources or residuals disposal) is seriously being questioned. In the 1960s, a lone voice in the economic wilderness dubbed this neoclassical view "cowboy economics." Boulding (1966) advocated replacing cowboy economics with by a more sensible perspective in which economic systems are closed systems, with economic processes constrained by negative feedback effects. According to this "spaceship Earth" view of economic systems, every effort must be made to recycle materials, reduce wastes, conserve exhaustible energy resources and seek more "limitless" energy sources such as solar. Kneese et al. (1971) refined this perspective in their *materials balance* principle. This approach suggests that wastes are pervasive in the economic system and thus require a production system in which inputs and outputs (wastes or pollution) are balanced. The primary contribution of the materials balance approach was the recognition of the need for residuals management. Further refinements were made calling for steady-state economic systems (Daly 1996) in which the objective is to establish the lowest rate of throughput of energy and matter, not to maximize the output of goods and services. Finally, the entropy concept (a measure of disorder in a system) was used to explain how economies will decline as predicted by the second law of thermodynamics. Georgescu-Roegen (1976) proposed a bioeconomic program based on the flow of solar energy and the minimal depletion of terrestrial matter (resources). Most environmental economists now favor a *steady-state* or *sustainable* view of economic systems.

William D. Ruckelshaus, first administrator of the U.S. Environmental Protection Agency (EPA), calls for the development of a "sustainability consciousness"—toward a way of living that does not destroy the environment but keeps it healthy for future use. Ruckelshaus (1989) states that such a consciousness requires the following beliefs:

- The human species is part of nature. Its existence depends on its ability to draw sustenance from a finite natural world; its continuance depends on its ability to abstain from destroying the natural systems that regenerate this world.
- Economic activity must account for the environmental costs of production.
- The maintenance of a livable global environment depends on the sustainable development of the entire human family.

This chapter provides a look at the evolution of thought on the dilemma of economics and environment, as they have moved from being natural enemies to being natural allies. Specifically, we examine the role of economics in natural resource management. Three questions provide the focus for our discussion.

1. What are the economic characteristics of natural resources? Natural resources are commodities regulated in part by supply, demand, and price, but several unique characteristics of natural resources alter the economic use we make of them.
2. How do we place a value on a natural resource? To operate within an economic system, a value or price of a resource must be determined. Yet, many values of a resource may not be reflected in price. Deciding on the value of a resource is the key to understanding how economic pressures influence both the use and management of a resource.
3. How do economic forces influence the management of a resource? Short-term pricing mechanisms might dictate the use and management of a resource quite differently than pricing systems based on long-term social needs.

Economics and the Use of Resources

Characteristics of Natural Resources

Natural resources are the basic building blocks in the production system; they are raw materials. Because little of their value is derived from human inputs such as labor, they generally have a lower value per unit than other commodities. The value of a standing forest, for example, is rarely more than the cost of owning the land for a period of time, and usually it is much less. When the trees are cut they are somewhat more valuable, but milling and drying add much more value. By the time the wood is made into a house or a piece of furniture, the price of the standing tree accounts for a very small portion of the value of the finished product; most of the value was added after the tree was grown. In a few cases natural resources have a high value "in the ground," but in these instances it is the consumer that drives the price up, if demand is greater than the amount of the resource available.

A second important characteristic of natural resources is that over short periods of time supply is relatively inelastic. Most natural resources require substantial capital investment and planning to bring them into production. For example, suppose the demand for a particular metal increases significantly. To a certain extent, existing mines can step up activity by hiring more miners and buying more equipment. But a large increase in production will probably require that new mines be opened. This may require geologic exploration, but even if the deposits are known and owned by mining companies, they must still build roads and other facilities to allow extraction, sink the initial mine shafts, and build housing for labor, before extraction can actually begin. All of these activities take time, generally years, and so in the short run the supply cannot keep up with increased demand. This means that the supply cannot be stretched quickly: supply is inelastic.

The inelastic nature of many resources can encourage wide fluctuations in price. For example, the prices of most mineral commodities are notoriously volatile. Part of this volatility is inherent in the production and supply system of the resources themselves, and part of it is in the psychology of the market. During the energy crisis of the early 1970s, when imports from the Middle East were dramatically reduced, the price of gasoline at the pump more than doubled in a matter of months. In the years since then, gas prices have become very sensitive to real and apparent shortages in the supply. In 1989, for example, when the *Exxon Valdez* spilled its oil cargo along the Alaska shoreline, the price at the pump rose overnight in both the United States and Great Britain, even though the spill was irrelevant to the supply of gasoline. Simultaneously, the intangible value of pristine coastline and healthy wildlife rose incalculably across the nation within a period of days (Fig. 2.1). "Price gouging" was an issue again in 1990, when gas prices soared following Iraq's invasion of Kuwait.

Coffee prices are another example. Good market prices for coffee (one of Colombia's primary export commodities) kept that country's external debt significantly lower than that of its other Latin American neighbors during the mid-1980s debt crisis in the region. Increased production globally led to falling prices for coffee starting in 1987. In the early 1990s coffee prices rose sharply upon news of a bad harvest in Brazil. Each of these price fluctuations has worldwide repercussions for farmers, consumers, and the processors and handlers between.

Small changes in demand as well as supply can cause a dramatic rise or fall in price, yet there is little that the producers can do in the short run to assure a steady, long-term trend. To illustrate, bitter cold snaps occasionally hit the eastern United States. Consumer demand for fuel oil and propane supplies reduces existing supplies to low levels. Almost overnight, prices for fuel oil and propane may skyrocket to double and triple what they were earlier in the month. When warmer weather returns, consumer demand slackens, and home heating fuel prices once again fall.

Whenever possible, a relatively high degree of substitutability among raw materials is desirable. Not only can one metal be substituted for another in, say, an automobile, but recently plastics, fiberglass, carbon fibers, and other synthetic materials have begun to replace metals for many purposes. Beet sugar can substitute for cane sugar; coal can substitute for natural gas. Although this substitutability contributes to stability for the makers of finished products, it often leads to considerable volatility in natural resources markets. The endless pattern of boom and bust cycles in one-employer mining towns is one of the sadder human consequences of this volatility.

For some natural resources, particularly minerals, supply is theoretically infinite, assuming we are able to pay a high enough price. Most metals exist in the earth's crust in much greater total quantities than we have need for; the prob-

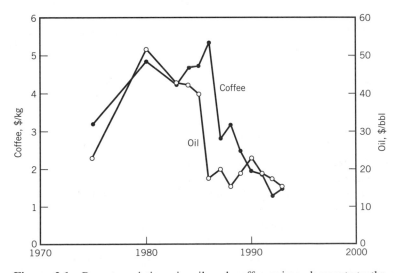

Figure 2.1 Recent variations in oil and coffee prices demonstrate the volatility of natural resource commodity markets. The similarity in the patterns is coincidental. *Source:* World Resources Institute, 1996.

lem is that in only a limited number of locations are they found in high enough concentrations or close enough to the surface to allow them to be extracted at a profit. But as long as we are willing to pay a little more to obtain them, then we can dig a little deeper, or refine less concentrated ores, and still obtain the desired commodity. At some point, we will find that it is cheaper to recycle used metals than to mine new ores, and it is then that we will be able to supply much of our new requirements by recycling. When we also consider the substitutability of most substances, it seems unlikely that we will encounter a situation in which we run out of raw materials. On the other hand, the theoretical supply of energy may or may not be infinite, depending on what technologies are available to us, and activities such as mining and recycling may well be limited by shortages of energy.

Pricing Systems

Natural resources are commodities, and we value them for their ability to provide the basic needs of life: food, clothing, shelter, and happiness. As commodities, they are exchanged among individuals, groups, and nations using some sort of pricing system as a medium of exchange. This pricing system can have a major impact on how resources are used. Resource price is dictated both by a society's determination of resource value (discussed in the next section) and by the economic system in use.

Economic Systems

Although there are three major types of economic systems in the world—commercial, centrally planned, and subsistence—only commercial and centrally planned economies produce a surplus of goods. In a commercial economy, prices are set by the producers who sell goods and services. Producers are characterized by a profit motivation and pressure to produce at low cost. This motivation usually leads to specialization, thus allowing more efficient production. A producer will try to do one thing well instead of many things in a mediocre way: there is greater profit in using this approach. Profit and efficiency are balanced by market forces, where supply and demand govern the price and quantity of goods exchanged. In other words, a producer can be efficient and offer a high-quality product, but once he or she enters the world market, certain economic forces are at work that are beyond the control of the individual company, and dreamed-of profits are not guaranteed. In a commercial economy, the use and allocation of natural resources are governed by many forces, especially market competition and profit maximization. Producers respond to these forces to protect their own best interests. Examples of commercial economies include the United States and Canada, European and most Latin American countries, India, Japan, and South Africa.

In a centrally planned economic system, the government controls the resources. Producers market goods and services to the central government, which in turn controls the supply and price according to its own objectives. These objectives can range from monetary gain to social and economic equality, goals that are not normally found in a commercial economy. China and Cuba are examples of centrally planned economies. However, the failure of socialist governments in eastern Europe and the former Soviet Union to consider environmental values in their planning, and the difficulty of recognizing amenity values in a materialist society, have contributed to the severe environmental problems evident there.

Regardless of the type of economic system in place, a price is set on a resource, thus permitting exchange and use by society. Several different approaches can be used to determine price. For example, Marxists follow the *labor theory* of value, which states that the price of a good is determined by the amount of labor required to produce it. An alternative approach is the *consumer theory* of value, which says that value is determined by how much a consumer is willing to pay. Still another view is the *cost theory*, which says that in a competitive system different producers will compete by reducing prices until they equal the cost of production. Finally, the *production theory* emphasizes the inputs of some critical commodity, for example, energy. That is, the value of goods is a function of the energy required to produce them, and thus they are priced accordingly. Although each of these theories addresses at least one aspect of the value of resources, in the final analysis it is the interaction of supply and demand that determines both the price of a good and the quantity sold at that price.

Supply and Demand

In a market economy, supply and demand are the primary factors determining price. The relations among supply, demand, and price tell us the amount of a good demanded by consumers and the amount the producers are willing to supply, depending on price. As price increases, the amount consumers are willing to buy decreases. Conversely, as price increases, the amount that producers are willing to sell increases. The intersection of these two functions determines the equilibrium price and quantity sold (Fig. 2.2). If there is a change in conditions, say, increasing scarcity of a commodity, then it will cost producers more to supply that commodity and they will either require a higher price to produce the same amount or they will supply less at the same price. In either case, the supply function shifts up and to the left, with the result that price increases and quantity sold decreases. Similarly, a change in the value consumers place on a commodity will change the demand function, with appropriate changes in price and quantity sold. This process assumes perfect competition, which exists only when no individual consumer or producer can exert influence on the market, and when all producers and consumers have full information and access to the market. Obviously, perfect competition does not exist in the real world, so these assumptions are violated in many cases.

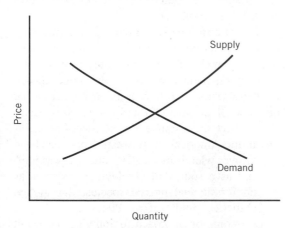

Figure 2.2 Classic supply, demand, and price relationships. As supply decreases and demand increases, prices also increase. Conversely, as supplies increase and demand decreases, prices also fall.

Market Imperfections

Unfair competition causes price to be determined by factors other than supply and demand, and this situation results in an imperfect market. A *monopoly* exists when a single buyer or seller dominates the market. Monopolistic or *oligopolistic competition* describes what happens when a few buyers or sellers either follow a price leader in fixing the price of a commodity or engage in discriminatory practices to set prices so as to maximize their own profits. Their purpose is to restrain competition by keeping prices artificially high.

There are many resource oligopolies in the world today, and these are normally referred to as cartels. A *cartel* is a consortium of commercial enterprises that work together to limit competition. These cartels can either be similar industries (such as refineries) or resource-rich exporting countries. In the latter case, these countries band together for economic advantage to fix the world prices of their commodity. The Organization of Petroleum Exporting Countries (OPEC) is a good example of a cartel. OPEC consists of 12 member nations: Algeria, Gabon, Indonesia, Iran, Iraq, Kuwait, Libya, Nigeria, Qatar, Saudi Arabia, United Arab Emirates, and Venezuela. OPEC nations supply around 40 percent of the world's supply of crude oil (World Resources Institute 1996). Other examples of cartels include those controlling copper and bauxite.

Finally, trade agreements and trade barriers can create unfair competition, leading to competitive advantages for some nations. The tensions between free trade and protective regulation are most pronounced in the environmental arena. Protectionist producers want to restrict the importation of goods that can outcompete them in the marketplace because of cheaper labor costs or materials. Tariffs (which by definition distinguish between domestic and imported goods) increase the price of imports, often resulting in limiting the market through the use of quotas on the amount of goods allowed into the country. On the other hand, the trade community is worried about the use of trade barriers as a form of "eco-protectionism" used to restrict sales of goods produced in environmentally harmful ways in the exporting nation (Vogel 1995). The disparity in national environmental regulations is a continuing source of strain in the international trade community. However, trading alliances and economic integration such as those in the European Union and in North America are helping to improve the domestic environmental policies of less green trading partners.

DETERMINING RESOURCE VALUE: QUANTIFYING THE INTANGIBLES

Not all resources have a value that can be quantified and expressed in monetary terms. Clean air is one example; an unobstructed view of the landscape is another. Yet these resources are increasingly part of the picture in determining the use we make of our Earth. As mentioned in the chapter introduction, only in the past few years have economists begun to look for ways that the environment and the marketplace can work together instead of being pitted against each other. Let us look at the historical development of the marketing of the environment.

The most widely used techniques to determine the value of intangibles such as clean air and scenic views have been cost-effectiveness analysis and benefit-cost analysis. *Cost-effectiveness analysis* simply involves summing all the costs and monetary returns involved in a single plan to determine the expected return on investment. *Benefit-cost analysis*, on the other hand, compares all the costs and benefits of several different plans. It requires an understanding of the social context—the alternative values placed on a resource by different sectors of the society—within which the balancing of costs and benefits is made.

Cost-effectiveness analysis helps the decision maker determine the least costly and most efficient strategy for carrying out a project or exploiting a resource once the decision has been made to proceed. Benefit-cost analysis is a tool for helping society make choices on the allocation of resources, whereas cost-effectiveness analysis aids the individual firm or agency in implementing that decision. Benefit-cost analysis evaluates alternative uses of a resource within a particular social context, and it usually seeks to find the alternative that has the greatest ratio of total benefits to total costs.

Benefit-Cost Analysis

Because benefit-cost analysis has been the building block of both environmental protection and exploitation, we will examine it in greater detail. When a shopper goes to the supermarket, he or she is constantly making choices of what and how much to buy. How long will that small jar of peanut butter last? Is it worth it to me to buy a larger jar at a lower unit price? Do I really need steak or should I settle for hamburger? Economic theory tells us that making such decisions usually involves thinking about the costs and benefits of each item and purchasing those items whose benefits appear to outweigh costs. Intangibles enter the picture even here, however, if the consumer considers the health aspects of cholesterol, fiber, and fats when choosing foods.

The balancing process observed in the supermarket can also be found in natural resource economics. Decisions on whether or not to build a dam, invest in new timberland, or clean up a polluted river usually involve some sort of benefit-cost analysis. This analysis can range from the elaborate accounting used to justify large government water projects to simple judgments made by individual farmers, foresters, or fisherfolk. In either case, a value is placed on expected costs and benefits, and the two values are then compared within a particular time frame. Some sort of price must be placed on all the factors in the resource decision: the price of the resource in question and the price of improvements or costs of damages to resources and society expected to result from a project.

Benefit-cost analysis involves a number of factors, including price, interest rate, and time. Since the analysis frequently must take into account nonmonetary variables, the value chosen for these factors can have a major impact on the outcome of the analysis and the resulting decision on how the resource is to be used. For example, in the American Northwest, debate has been raging over what is of greater value: trees as lumber and as a source of employment or trees as habitat for an endangered species, the spotted owl (Mitchell 1990; Yaffee 1994).

One common approach to applying the result of a benefit-cost analysis is to determine the ratio by separately summing the costs and benefits over time, then dividing benefits by costs. A benefit cost (B:C) ratio greater than 1 indicates that benefits are greater than costs and the project should go forward. A B:C ratio can be very misleading when the analysis includes potential environmental impacts. Any project will presumably have some environmental impacts, regardless of benefits or costs. These impacts should be applied to either the calculation of costs (by addition) or the calculation of benefits (by subtraction) and must be used consistently. Another problem is that the present value of future costs or benefits depends on the interest or discount rate used in the calculations (Turner et al. 1993). Small changes in interest rates can result in very large differences in project costs. Despite these problems, B:C ratios are frequently used to evaluate or justify public works projects.

Frequently, the organization conducting a benefit-cost analysis has a vested interest in some particular outcome, leading to a bias in estimates of resource values that favor that outcome. This is especially true for estimates of amenity resources such as recreation or a scenic view. When several different pricing methods are available for incommensurable resources, it is tempting to choose the pricing method that gives the desired result—either high or low depending on the wishes of the person doing the analysis. As a result, benefit-cost analyses are frequently biased and must be used with caution.

Quantifying Value

When faced with a decision about whether or not to permit lumbering in a National Forest, a resource manager seeks various types of information to include in an analysis of benefits and costs. Some of this information, like the value of standing timber, the cost of replanting trees after harvest, or the increased water yield as a result of cutting the forest, can be expressed in monetary terms. Other information is more speculative, such as the value of wildlife habitat lost and the resulting decline in the number of hunters and fisherfolk. These so-called incommensurables and intangibles can frustrate benefit-cost analysis, forcing the decision maker to create an artificial or *shadow price* for that resource.

Incommensurables are effects (both benefits and costs) that cannot readily be translated into a monetary value or price. *Intangibles* are incom-

mensurables that cannot be measured at all—they are truly outside the analysis. The trick in benefit-cost analysis is to separate the incommensurable effects from the intangible effects (see Issue 2.1). Although it is impossible to assign a value to intangibles, we can place a value or shadow price on incommensurables. In any assessment of the benefits and costs of resource exploitation, it is necessary to define the limitations of such methods in order to quantify these incommensurable effects.

Economists employ a broad range of techniques to establish the shadow price of incommensurable resources. Three of the most commonly used techniques are discussed here.

Willingness to pay is a method in which potential users of a resource are asked how much they are willing to pay for access to the resource. Conversely, one could ask how much society would have to pay the individual not to use the resource (avoidance costs). An example would be a survey of beach users to determine how much they are willing to pay to use the beach or how much they would have to be paid not to go to the beach. The value of the latter could be used to estimate the value of recreation losses caused by an oil spill on the beach (Fig. 2.3). The former could be used to justify importing beach sand to keep an eroding beach the way it is. One specific method for measuring willingness to pay is the *contingent valuation method (CVM)*. This method employs a questionnaire to ask users (and often nonusers as a comparative group) a series of questions on how much they would pay for that new park or how much they would be willing to pay to preserve their view of the coastline. Such a questionnaire often contains a number of possible scenarios such as the following CVM study of the Monongahela River (Desvouges et al. 1987):

Scenario 1: Keep the current river quality (suitable for boating only) and don't allow further decay.
Scenario 2: Improve the water quality from the current levels (boating) to where fishing could take place.
Scenario 3: Improve the water quality even more to make it swimmable.

Respondents in this study were asked how much they were willing to pay for each. The dollar value was then averaged across groups (users/nonusers)

ISSUE 2.1: What Is the Value of a Human Life?

Estimating the value of services provided to humans by an ecosystem (see Issue 2.2), in the form of materials produced, pollutants absorbed, or amenities provided, is a complex accounting task that involves a very large number of price estimates and assumptions but relatively few fundamental moral questions. The value of a human life, on the other hand, can only be measured in moral terms. We could never put a dollar figure on it. Or can we? Should we?

Like it or not, there may be good reasons to calculate the value of a human life. One reason is that our governments take actions to protect human life, through laws and regulations requiring seat belts in automobiles, controlling air pollution, maintaining safe drinking water, and the like. These measures cost money, and although one might think that any cost is justified when a human life is at stake, this is not necessarily true. The costs of life-saving measures are borne ultimately by consumers. These consumers' disposable income is reduced as a result.

It is a well-known fact that wealthy people tend to live longer than poor people. This is because the less money we have, the less likely we are to visit a doctor for a regular checkup, buy fresh vegetables instead of canned, take nutritional supplements, or perhaps move from a polluted area to a cleaner one. If a certain amount of money is taken out of the economy to pay for safety, then some people may suffer poorer health as a result because their income will have been reduced to pay for that safety. Inexpensive ways of saving lives (seat belts, for example) are cost-effective, but expensive ones may not be. One estimate is that a loss of $10 million from the U.S. economy results in one added death due to people's reduced in-

come. If this is true, we should not spend more than $10 million for safety per life saved—to do so would cost more lives than are saved (Passell 1995). In other words, we have just estimated the value of human life in the United States at about $10 million.

In the United States and other wealthy countries, most people have access to good food and health care, and the added cost of safety can be borne relatively easily without endangering health. Safety measures costing millions of dollars per life saved can be justified. In poor countries, however, many people suffer because they lack access to food and health care. In India, for example, average per capita income is around $300. A person earning this amount per year may not be able to afford clean drinking water and has a significant risk of sickness and death resulting from contaminated water. Providing such a person with enough money to buy clean drinking water or to buy clean fuel to boil water could easily save a life. In these situations, spending for safety is much harder to justify; even a small loss of income could significantly increase the risk of death. In a poor country, it takes only a small amount of added income to save a life. In a rich country, saving lives costs much more. Put another way, the value of a life in a rich country is greater than one in a poor country.

Does this valuation of life sound a little scary or at least morally questionable? Of course it does. But consider this: In the United States, insurance companies and courts routinely place monetary values on human life. Suppose a plane crashes and the airline is found to be at fault. The survivors of passengers killed in the crash can sue the airline for compensation for the loss of

to produce a demand curve for water quality. Users were consistently higher in their willingness to pay in all three scenarios than nonusers ($45.30 for users and $14.20 for nonusers for Scenario 1 and $20.20 for users and $8.50 for nonusers for Scenario 3). Interestingly, the nonusers' willingness to pay is greater than zero, suggesting that the

river has a public value at its current quality level. In other words, respondents did not want to see further deterioration in water quality and were willing to pay a considerable amount to achieve that goal.

A second technique is determining *proxy value* or the value of similar resources elsewhere. This

their loved ones. If the person killed was, say, a 32-year-old brain surgeon with an annual income of $300,000 expecting to work to age 65, then the income lost to her family over the next 33 years is $10 million. If the person killed was a 75-year-old pensioner then there is no lost income. In fact, the death releases money that would have been used to sustain the pensioner. The court would likely award much more compensation to the survivors of the surgeon than to those of the pensioner. We thus estimate the value of a life in terms of the income he or she would earn. And, simply put, wealthy people's lives are worth more than those of poor people.

Individuals also place monetary values on their own lives on a routine basis, though usually not consciously. For example, suppose you are shopping for a new car. The model you want to buy is equipped with standard brakes, but an optional automatic braking system could be purchased for $500. Suppose that over the five-year period during which you expect to own the vehicle the chance of you or one of your passengers dying in a crash is 1 in 1000 and that the automatic brakes would reduce that to 1 in 2000. Is the braking system worth the price to you? In the five-year period, your $500 investment would save 1/2000 of a life, giving a cost of $1 million per life saved. If you decide that the automatic braking system is too expensive, then you are implying that the value of your own and your passengers' lives is less than $1 million each. If, on the other hand, you decide that the braking system is worth the investment, then you are valuing a life at more than $1 million. This neglects other benefits you receive from the system, such as nonfatal crashes avoided and the peace of mind

resulting from the added safety. Note that a rich person would be more likely to buy the braking system than a poor one. Once again rich people's lives are valued more highly than those of the poor.

In an era of global trade and manufacturing, with industrial activities and the pollution they create being shifted from wealthy countries to poor ones, these questions of the value of human life can take an interesting twist. Suppose an industrial activity generates pollution that may shorten the lives of people living near the industry. Suppose that industry also generates income for those people. If this industry were located in a wealthy country, the people would be unlikely to tolerate a significant amount of life-threatening pollution. But in a poor country, the added income from the industry might improve their lives to an extent that they would be better off with the pollution than without it. The number of lives saved by people being able to afford clean drinking water might be more than the number of lives lost to lung disease caused by the pollution.

If this is true, then would it be a good thing to move dirty or dangerous industries from rich countries to poor ones? Most people would respond emphatically, no. To do so is morally repugnant. We should find ways to increase the income of developing countries without also increasing pollution levels. We should never trade pollution for money, let alone trade one life for another. But the question does make us think a little bit about tradeoffs between environment and economic development. Perhaps it might lead one to think twice about condemning environmental degradation in poor countries, when that degradation is directly connected to economic development.

technique estimates the value of a day's hunting, for example, by summarizing the hunter's investment in supplies, time, and travel and dividing this figure by the number of days of hunting. This is an estimate of the value that would have resulted if the project or exploitation did not occur in the first place. Another example is the decline

in commercial fish harvest due to the destruction of their habitat by an oil spill.

The third technique is called *replacement cost*. This is simply the cost of replacing the resource that is being used, such as substitution of clean sand for polluted sand on a beach fouled by an offshore oil spill. Often there is no market for

Figure 2.3 Oil spills are an obvious and expensive form of pollution. We value coastal resources highly, and demand cleanups after spills like this one at Huntington Beach, California. Usually when oil is spilled there is an easily identifiable party responsible, and the cost of the clean up can be borne directly by those causing the pollution.

the replacement of extramarket goods, for the resources are not substitutable.

The accuracy varies when using these and other methods of estimating the shadow prices of resources. It is important to recognize the limitations of such techniques as well as their ability to provide the necessary data for a benefit-cost analysis. They are useful in placing a comparable value (price) on those resources that normally do not have one, but only within the limitations we have discussed.

MANAGEMENT AND ALLOCATION OF RESOURCES

Economic forces shape the price and utility of a resource (Fig. 2.4). For example, oil shale in western Colorado and Wyoming was valuable enough to extract and process when the world's oil price was high, but when that price dropped, oil shale became too expensive as a source of oil. Economic forces also affect who gets to use a resource and how it is managed. When the North American deserts were seen as valueless a century ago, they became a place of exile for Native

Americans who were displaced from more valuable lands elsewhere. Recently, however, rich mineral deposits have been found on many of these "valueless" tribal lands. In some cases, tribal corporations and private industry have agreed on mutually beneficial business deals. Overall, the influence of economics on management decisions can best be classified into three categories. These are ownership of the resource, social costs, and the economics of the individual company or firm.

Ownership

Many natural resources are held in communal rather than private ownership. This is true both for resources that are government owned, such as National Forests and offshore mineral rights, and for resources for which no formal ownership is designated, such as air or the water in the oceans. Although these resources are commonly owned, that is, owned by everyone, they are exploited by private individuals and corporations for their own profit. This discrepancy between ownership and management responsibility causes problems. These types of resources are called *common property resources* because they are owned by

Figure 2.4   This rainforest in Brazil is being cleared because its value to the owner is greater as pasture then as forest. It is being burned rather than harvested for wood because the cost of cutting, transportation and marketing are greater than the market value of the wood that would be produced.

everyone, even though they may only be used by a few who have the technical and economic means to do so.

This conflict was described by Garrett Hardin (1968) in his classic article entitled "The Tragedy of the Commons." Hardin argued that commonly owned resources are nearly always overexploited. The reason why is that while the costs of exploitation are shared among all the owners of the resource, the benefits accrue to the individual, and so it is always in the individual's interest to increase exploitation, even to the point of overexploiting the resource. Hardin concludes that there must be some institutional arrangement that prohibits overuse and encourages conservation.

For example, if a group of people all dump sewage into the same body of water, they all suffer, but for any one person to not dump sewage would be foolish from a purely economic standpoint. This person would still suffer everyone else's sewage and would not reap the full benefit of his or her reduction in pollution. As a consequence, some governing body may step in, and through that body all agree to regulate their exploitation of the resource for mutual benefit.

In some cases this is relatively easy, and in others it is not. When large corporations are both exploiters and employers and thus politically powerful, or when enforcement of restrictions is difficult, then overuse and degradation of commonly held resources can result. For example, throughout the 1980s the United States avoided taking serious action to control emissions that contributed to acid rain, out of concern for the burdens these emission controls would place on steel mills and power plants that were basic components of the United States' midwestern economy. Only after intense pressure from both environmentalists and Canada, which received much of the acid rain caused by U.S. emissions, was significant action finally taken. The responsibility for management of these common property resources is a major issue in air, water, and ocean resources as we will see in later chapters.

In the last few years, a new approach to the commons problem has emerged: How can government make it profitable to the individual to protect the commons? We can call this approach "the opportunity of the commons," in which government creates economic incentives that promise increased profits to a company that decreases its pollution output.

How might this work? In the case of acid rain, Stavins (1989) reports on a plan that would give pollution credits to companies that contribute to solving the acid rain problem. If a company lowered its emissions below the level required by law, it could make deals with the difference—to delay compliance with another regulation or to sell accumulated pollution-compliance points to a company that remains in violation of the law. This would earn a profit for the first company and a delay for the second. Pollution credits could thus be bought and sold among companies to allow the marketplace to decide the cheapest way to reduce smokestack emissions. But why restrict this plan to companies? Why shouldn't environmentalists be allowed to buy pollution rights (or credits) from publicly owned utilities and then retire the facility? In 1989 the going rate for the right to discharge a ton of sulfer dioxide per year in this case was between $1000 and $2000 per ton (Hershey 1989). By 1993 sulfur dioxide pollution credits were selling between $250 and $400 per ton (Dao 1993), making them much more accessible to environmentalists. Each year a significant amount of pollution credits is purchased by environmental organizations, preventing some pollutants from being emitted.

But can we trust the bottom line, a purely market-oriented approach to environmental protection? Even advocates for this approach warn that the market is limited as a tool for protection: while companies wheel and deal for points and profits, pollutants are still produced, and the commons continues to absorb them. Government remains a necessary tool to force industry to internalize the cost of pollution, but this command and control approach is becoming increasingly ineffective. Government has its own problems to address, for government-owned enterprises such as the Tennessee Valley Authority and nuclear weapons facilities have been among the nation's most notorious and prolonged polluters and have voiced opposition to increased pollution abatement measures. How can industry be required to produce fewer pollutants? Let's look at economic concepts that, if made into law, would encourage industry to create fewer pollutants.

Social Costs

In commercial economies, both the producer and consumer bear the costs of production. These production systems are termed efficient if they maximize output (finished goods or services) per unit cost of production. Economists today recognize that not all production systems are truly efficient. Certain spillover effects from the production system may enter the environment and affect consumers disproportionately. These spillover effects are called *externalities* because they are commodities that change hands outside the marketplace, without a price being agreed upon by the principals. Environmental externalities are the unwanted byproducts of modern industrial processes and usually consist of pollutants such as heat, toxic chemicals, or sediment. These pollutants or *residuals*, as they are sometimes called, are normally discharged into one of the many common property resources—air, water, and public land—and this is where conflict arises.

The problem with externalities is that they have clear environmental and social impacts. A private or government-operated producer wants to minimize costs and maximize profits, which ultimately forces the local community in which the factory or plant is located to absorb the externality. In most cases, the conflict is between a private company and a community, as the following example shows. Chemsweet Inc. is located upstream from Farmer Green. Chemsweet routinely discharges chemicals into the stream that Green uses to irrigate her crops. Eventually, the crop is damaged as a result of the contaminated water. Any costs that are attributed to these spillover effects or residuals are called external costs. Chemsweet Inc. does not incur any cost for polluting the stream, yet costs are imposed on neighbors like Farmer Green. Not only does Farmer Green bear the costs of a reduced harvest (and less profit), but she must also pay for a new source of water or lose her crop entirely. The transfer of pollution from Chemsweet to Farmer Green took place outside the market system, and thus the costs incurred by Farmer Green are not reflected in the price of the manufactured good that Chemsweet Inc. produces.

Social costs are those costs to society that not only involve externalities but also include the cost of producing the good in the first place. In most cases, natural resource use does not fully embrace this in the pricing structure, and we are thus left with the problem of managing and coping with these externalities or residuals.

Residuals management is a major part of natural resource economics. Several techniques have been developed for understanding and managing residuals, and these usually involve economic or pricing mechanisms or government intervention in the form of pollution regulations. Residuals management is the term used to describe the first technique.

Residuals management (or materials/energy balance as it is also known) is a process used to describe and quantify the inputs and outputs of a production system including the residuals. The economic model that first described this process was developed by Kneese, Ayers, and d'Arge (1971). Residuals management advocates a steady-state production system in which inputs and outputs are balanced. The residuals, or waste products, are either fed back into the production system (recycled) or released into the environment. Specific techniques have been developed to manage residuals. A *residuals tax* or effluent charge was first proposed by Kneese and Bower (1971) as a method of controlling residuals. This can also be called the *polluter pays principle*. Producers of goods would pay for the residuals they discharge, with taxes levied against firms in relation to how much pollution they release to the environment. A residuals tax would force the polluter to bear the true social costs of production and contamination of common property resources by internalizing the externalities. It would encourage the polluter to reduce the quantity of residuals, for the tax would be in direct proportion to the amount discharged. This fee would then be used either to clean up the environment or to compensate those consumers adversely affected by the pollution. In the early 1990s, a number of "green taxes" or more specifically "carbon taxes" were proposed to reduce greenhouse gas emissions, but most of these failed for lack of popular support.

Another technique of residuals management is the *throughput tax*, or disposal charge. Producers of goods would be charged a materials fee that would reflect the social costs of disposal of the residuals. This tax would be passed on to the consumer in the form of increased prices for the commodity. Although a throughput tax might provide an incentive to recycle and make products last longer, many of the disposal charges currently used, such as deposits on beverage containers, are discriminatory against consumers. These types of taxes influence the price of a commodity beyond the simple demand and supply accounting (Issue 2.2).

Economics of the Individual Firm

Microeconomics refers to the economics of the firm or individual company. In a commercial system, most resource exploitation is undertaken by the firm rather than by society as a whole, and so it is worthwhile to examine some microeconomic activities that affect natural resource decisions.

One problem affecting many resources is a tendency for firms to maximize the rate at which resources are used instead of spreading that use out over a long period of time. The reason for this practice is fairly simple. Firms earn profits by investing money (capital) in the physical plant needed for production (land, machinery, etc.) and in other production inputs (energy and labor) in order to produce an output that can be sold for more money than was invested. The producer's costs in producing a given output can be divided into two categories, fixed costs and variable costs. *Fixed costs* are bills that must be paid regardless of how much of a product is made in a given time. Fixed costs are primarily the costs of owning the means of production (the physical plant). If the money needed to set up a plant was borrowed, then the interest expenses on that loan are fixed costs. *Variable costs* consist of labor, energy, transportation, and similar inputs in the production process itself, and these vary according to the rate of production. Variable costs are a relatively constant fraction of the selling price of the goods produced, although some levels of output are more efficient than others.

Let us assume that a given investment is required to open up a particular mine. Afterward, variable costs vary in direct proportion to the rate of extraction of minerals. The faster the minerals are extracted, the greater the profit will be, for the fixed costs need be borne for a shorter period of time. In practice, variable costs per unit output are low at high rates of production because of economies of scale. However, variable costs may increase at very high rates of production because of the need for greater capital and labor inputs to maintain high rates of production. The optimal

ISSUE 2.2: The Value of Nature

In the present era of neoliberal free-market economics, policymakers argue that solutions to environmental problems must be based on the market, a system of trading goods and services at prices that reflect society's valuation of them. This requires establishing prices for environmental goods and services such as biomass production and pollution dispersal that are currently traded but not in the marketplace. This is easier in some cases than in others. For relatively small areas and limited resources, it can be done fairly easily. But for large areas comprising a wide range of interdependent resources, the task is much more difficult, and the results are much less reliable.

In recent years, several attempts have been made to place price tags on the natural resources of large areas, including countries and even the entire planet. Because such estimates are necessarily crude, it is difficult to use the results to make decisions on specific resource exchanges as in a market. Rather, they are intended mostly as wakeup calls, showing the importance of natural resources' contributions to the wealth and prosperity of nations. And as natural resource accounting methods improve in the future, the potential for making real market-based decisions increases.

Natural resource valuations (like any financial balance sheet) take two fundamental forms: stocks (assets and debts) and flows (income and expenditures). Accountings of stocks, the total wealth of an individual, company, or country at any given time, are useful in determining the market price of an object if it is to be sold. This is not very meaningful in the case of, say, a country, unless the accounting is done repeatedly on a regular basis using consistent methods. For example, should the total wealth of a nation decline from one period to the next, then the resources or savings are being drawn down; the resource base is being mined, and future generations will have less to work with. Alternatively, accountings of flows show how much of a country's income comes from various sources, such as manufacturing, mining, and agriculture. When the productivity of natural systems is valued in this way, we can estimate the importance of natural processes in supplying humankind with our daily needs relative to our own labor. Recently, accountings of both types have been attempted.

An accounting of the wealth of nations must recognize that such wealth takes many forms, and to a certain extent one form may be substituted for another. For example, meat can be obtained by relying almost entirely on natural resources, by raising cattle on natural grasslands. Meat can also be produced by feeding them grain such as corn, using some natural resources but supplementing them with tractors, chemicals, and the farmer's skills. Or we can just use money to buy meat from someone else.

The World Bank calculated the wealth of nations by summing produced wealth (factories, goods, money), human and social capital (educated, healthy people capable of creating wealth through their labor), and natural capital (land, soil, water, forests, etc.). Calculations of natural resource value involved applying a particular value per hectare to each type of land, multiplying by the number of hectares of that land, and adding in wealth in the form of geologic resources such as oil or minerals. Not surprisingly, countries like Japan

rate of production is, of course, determined by a combination of fixed and variable costs. Fixed costs always make the optimal rate of output higher. As interest rates go up, the need to recover the initial investment in a short time period increases, hence the need to increase rates of production.

As a result of these pressures, demands are made on the firm to maximize the rate of production, regardless of whether it is good conservation policy in the long run. This generalization strictly applies only to a single facility, such as a single mine or a single forest unit. A large corporation owning many mines will vary its total output not by varying output at every mine simultaneously but by closing or opening mines. That is how it keeps its fixed costs as low as possible. But in most cases the extracting firm will

and Germany have a large portion of their wealth in the form of human capital, while Russia and Canada have large amounts of natural capital. The total wealth of the world was estimated at $86,000 per person, comprised of 20 percent natural resources, 16 percent produced wealth, and 64 percent human capital. These measures allow us to evaluate the depletion of natural capital as an oil field is exploited, for example, in comparison to the increase in ability to generate wealth that may be represented by investing of oil revenues in industry or education (World Bank 1995).

Evaluating the amount of income produced by nature each year, as opposed to the amount of stored wealth, follows a similar approach: estimating the per-hectare amount of income generated from a particular ecosystem and multiplying by the total area of that ecosystem on earth's surface. In one recent study, 17 different kinds of services were evaluated, including such functions as gas and climate regulation, provision and regulation of water flows, soil formation, nutrient cycling, waste treatment, pollination, food production and recreation (Costanza et al. 1997). For each of 16 biomes, estimates of the value of services provided were collected. Most of these estimates were based on contingent valuation—asking how much society would be willing to pay for a given amount of soil formation, for example, if we were able to increase such a process. The total value of these services per year was estimated at about $33 trillion, or a little less than double the gross world product of $18 trillion. Ecosystem services are not counted as part of gross product calculations, which only measure goods and services produced by humans. Of the

$33 trillion figure, the service with the largest value is soil formation, estimated at $17.1 trillion per year; recreation comes second at $3.0 trillion, and nutrient cycling is third at $2.2 trillion. Among biomes, coastal systems produce the most income—$12.6 trillion per year, followed by the open ocean ($8.4 trillion) and wetlands ($4.9 trillion) (Costanza et al. 1997).

Both the World Bank and Costanza studies are very rough approximations, and many uncertainties surrounded the actual values they estimated. But if we make the assumption that the two studies are in the right neighborhood, then some conclusions are possible. First, both studies make it clear that natural resources are very important to our well-being. Second, most of our stock of wealth is in human rather than natural form, whereas most of our income is derived from natural rather than human processes. In other words, nature produces a large amount of income from a relatively small amount of capital, while people store much more capital but produce a more modest amount of income from it. Perhaps the most critical issue, however, may not be measuring the value of nature. We all recognize, for example, that the biological productivity of the world's oceans is of enormous value or that air pollution increases costs for health care. The key question is how to get these costs internalized in our markets, so that our resource use recognizes these costs and damage to resources is minimized. The more we understand about the enormous value of the natural contributions to our well-being, the more likely we will be to incorporate these values in our day-to-day management of resources.

be pressured to maximize the rate of extraction to recover fixed costs, often at the expense of the environment.

Another important aspect of the firm relative to natural resources is the degree of liquidity of its assets, or how easily the firm can sell out if it needs to. Remember that the goal of any company is to turn a monetary investment into monetary return, and production of a particular commodity is

simply a means to that end. An oil company consists of a group of people who have particular expertise in finding, extracting, and selling oil, and who also own the equipment needed to do those things. If that oil company has an opportunity to invest its capital in a housing development or a soft drink bottling plant and receive a greater return on investment than it would in drilling for oil, then it will do so. Only the existing investment in oil-related equipment and experience prevent an oil company from taking its money elsewhere if the financial opportunities are more attractive in some other business.

BUSINESS AND THE ENVIRONMENT: RECENT TRENDS

Diversification and Multinational Corporations

One significant business trend in the 1970s and 1980s was toward *diversification* of large corporations. Tobacco companies bought soap companies; oil companies bought electronics companies; and steel companies bought oil companies. Among other things, this diversification serves to protect large companies from unfavorable market conditions in particular sectors of the economy. It also serves to weaken a company's commitment to the long-term stability of a particular enterprise or resource.

For example, recent decades have witnessed a major increase in corporate ownership of farms. In the 1970s this increase was spurred by rapidly rising land prices that attracted speculative investments. In several areas of the United States, large diversified corporations have become major holders of agricultural land. If they carry on a policy of maximizing return on investment, then they may adopt farming practices that lead to excessive soil erosion. In this instance, as in many others, the best interests of business are not the best interests of society as a whole.

Historically, the large forest product (lumber and paper) companies have been an exception to this tendency of corporations to be interested only in short-term returns. Although many of the forest products companies are diversified, they also own large tracts of land that require decades to produce harvestable trees. This creates a tendency for these companies to maintain a long-term, environmentally healthy commitment to their land.

Another important trend of the last few decades has been the formation and growth of *multinational corporations* (MNCs). These are companies that operate in several countries or own or collaborate with companies in several countries. They have the ability to shift re-sources, production, and marketing activities from one country to another depending on where potential profits are greatest. They are generally large enough to have major control over markets in individual nations, if not at the world level. Their ability to move money and commodities internationally greatly limits the controls that individual governments have over them, and thus it is more difficult to force consideration of social costs in decision making.

The environmental record and corporate role of MNCs in environmental management is subject to intense debate. Some advocates feel that the MNCs are industry innovators and that with advanced technology and an enhanced environmental ethos they will make significant contributions to upgrade plants to meet environmental standards. The investment in pollution control (in the absence of strict environmental regulation) will ultimately be based on minimizing the present and future investment costs of MNCs while offsetting any potential political or social conflict, including adverse public opinion (Roysten 1985). Pollution prevention pays is not only the anthem of environmentalists, but also the rallying cry of 3M Corporation, which cleaned up its operations and saved money in the process.

Industry detractors believe that many MNCs deliberately seek pollution havens in developing countries in order to reduce their pollution control costs or their residuals costs. An example of this is multinational behavior and the disposal of hazardous wastes. In recent years, new controls have been established on the disposal of hazardous wastes in the United States and other wealthy nations. As a consequence of stricter regulations which increased the costs of hazardous waste disposal, industrialized countries looked for other disposal options, including the transboundary shipment of these hazardous wastes. Thus the U.S. EPA is required by law to fully inform waste recipients of what they are getting. However, government officials are often lax in providing host countries with the opportunity to turn down a waste shipment or to list the wastes that the country was about to receive. Poorer countries, for whom the fees paid by polluters are very tempting, are uniting to combat "toxic terrorism" (Deery Uva and Bloom 1989). The Basel Convention (1989) is a multilateral treaty adopted by 116 countries and the European Union in an effort to manage the hazardous waste trade. The majority of the provisions are designed to ensure that hazardous wastes are controlled in an environmentally sound manner that protects both the rights of exporting and importing countries. As a result of these efforts, waste minimization (the reduction of waste at its source) is now a major issue for industry. It is also helping to focus attention on conservation and recycling efforts at the individual firm level. A global pollution consciousness is in the making, with the understanding that a pollutant produced on one side of the globe can affect life on the other side.

Multinational corporations have also had the effect of greatly increasing the degree of worldwide economic integration. Markets for resources are controlled by world supply and demand rather than at the national level. A shortage of a commodity in one country causes increases in prices in other countries.

The Greening of Business

Cleaning up the environment is a profit-making enterprise. The environmental control industry (solid waste companies, consulting companies, hazardous treatment firms, and so on) generates over $100 billion a year in revenues, with many companies growing by 20 to 25 percent per year (Schiffres 1990). The companies that are involved in cleaning up environmental pollution (oil spills, hazardous waste, solid waste, medical waste, asbestos, and so on) constitute one of the fastest-growing industrial sectors of the economy and will surely be growth industries as long as reducing environmental pollution is a government priority. Manufacturers and distributors of environmentally safe consumer products have increased their sales and clout in the marketplace. Firms that specialize in environmental analysis and testing will also experience rapid growth during the decade.

Investor interest in environmental stocks is also growing as environmentally concerned citizens put their money where their mouths are. Just as socially responsive investing was important during the 1980s (no military weapons contracts or business in South Africa), environmentally responsive investing was also important during the 1990s. Several mutual funds specialize in environmental stocks. Consumers can even choose among a variety of different bank cards with the logo of their favorite environmental group emblazoned across their Visa or Master Charge card, with a small percentage of the proceeds donated to the group.

As a result of enhanced consumer and stockholder concern for the environment, stricter environmental regulations, and the increasing costs of waste disposal (especially hazardous wastes), individual firms are seeking new ways to internalize their pollution costs. Pollution prevention strategies are one such mechanism gaining in importance in the industrial sector. It is more efficient (economically) to prevent pollution in the first place than to clean it up after the fact. The EPA's pollution prevention program assists industry in devising such strategies that not only save money but clean up the environment as well.

Finally, business schools have also joined the environmental bandwagon. Environmental management courses are now being added to business curricula across the country at the behest of corporate sponsors who feel that students are totally ignorant about the business impact of environmental issues. Environmental issues can have far-reaching implications, ranging from capital expenditures to cash flow to redesign of manufacturing processes.

Deregulation

The 1980s and 1990s have seen the rise of neoliberalism, a view that favors greater reliance on the private sector and free trade to promote economic development. Neoliberalism was on the rise even in the 1970s, but it triumphed with the demise of socialism in Europe. One manifestation of this change has been the trend toward deregulation of business, both in capitalist and in centrally planned economies. Deregulation has had enormous impacts on every aspect of society. Although in the United States the term deregulation is often mentioned in the context of industries such as banking and telecommunications, natural resource use has also been dramatically changed. Let us consider some examples from the United States.

In the 1980s, early in the Reagan administration, the financial securities industry in the United

States was deregulated. Deregulation unleashed a wave of corporate takeovers in which asset-rich companies have been purchased and "restructured," usually involving the sale of valuable assets that generate relatively little income and concentration on the remaining profitable sectors of a business. This has increased pressure on natural resource companies to maximize short-term return on investments rather than managing for long-term income stability. For example, in 1985 the Pacific Lumber Company, holder of the largest remaining privately-owned old-growth forests in the United States and a company known for practicing sustainable forestry, was purchased by a "corporate raider" who went deeply into debt to buy the company and subsequently raised rates of harvesting in order to increase income and pay off the debt (see Issue 7.1).

In 1996 the Freedom to Farm Bill was passed in the United States, deregulating U.S. agriculture, which continued a trend begun in the 1980s. The bill eliminated linkages between government subsidies and some important farm management decisions, and increased the financial risk to farmers associated with variations in commodity prices. The full effects of this deregulation remain to be seen, but if deregulation continues, it may result in increased pressure for maximizing short-term yields at the expense of long-term soil conservation. It is also likely to accelerate the decline of the small family farm, whose demise for many years has been slowed by government subsidies (see Chapter 6).

In the late 1990s deregulation of the electric generation industry is under consideration. It will enable competition among different producers of electricity, instead of the regulated monopolies that have existed since the establishment of electric utilities. Deregulation is expected to open up opportunities for small generating companies to enter the business, possibly using unconventional technologies. It could therefore make it possible for photovoltaics, small-scale hydroelectric, or other renewable energy technologies to become commercially established.

As seen in these examples, deregulation may have positive or negative effects on resource conservation. In some cases, regulation has protected resources and encouraged conservation by allowing (or requiring) long-term goals and broader social needs to be considered by resource managers and users. In these cases, deregulation usually results in a focus on short-term monetary gains rather than on meeting the needs of a broader group of stakeholders. In other cases, where government regulation and subsidies have encouraged waste or discouraged innovation, deregulation opens up opportunites for much more efficient, and therefore conservation-oriented, resource management.

Conclusions

The business of natural resource use is no different from any other business. It is governed by the same need to turn investment into profit as quickly as possible, and it is subject to the same vagaries of economics caused by fluctuating interest rates, inflation, and the ups and downs of business cycles. Although we often blame our government, big corporations, foreign governments, or natural calamities for problems related to natural resource supply or prices, in almost all instances the real causes of the problem can be traced to economic constraints on the businesses involved and the simple desire of companies to make as much profit as possible. In centrally planned economies, economic development has always been favored over environmental protection. This has been made exceedingly clear in the past few years as eastern and central European countries have been found to have some of the worst air and water pollution in the world. Environmental degradation is extensive in many of these countries, and as a result of the pro-democracy movements, the rest of the world is slowly learning of the disastrous level of pollution. It is hoped that the greening of eastern and central Europe will continue.

Natural resources are of fundamental importance to us all, not least because many of them are commonly owned. Decisions involving natural resources are therefore likely to have external costs and social effects that businesses do not normally consider. Government intervention is necessary to modify the management process, so that intangible resources, long-term needs, and social costs can be managed along with the commodities that move through our economic system.

REFERENCES AND ADDITIONAL READING

Abramowitz, J. 1997. Valuing nature's services. In L.R. Brown, ed., *State of the World, 1997*. New York: W. W. Norton.

Boulding, K. E. 1966. The economics of the coming spaceship Earth. In H. Jarrett, ed., *Environmental Quality in a Growing Economy*. Baltimore, MD: Johns Hopkins University Press.

Costanza, R., R. d'Arge, R. de Groot, S. Farber, M. Grasso, B. Hannon, K. Limburg, S. Naeem, R. O'Neill, J. Paruelo, R. Raskin, P. Sutton, and M. van den Belt. 1997. The value of the world's ecosystem services and natural capital. *Nature* 387: 253–260.

Daly, H. E. 1973. *Towards a Steady State Economy*. San Francisco: W. H. Freeman.

_____ . 1996. *Beyond Growth: The Economics of Sustainable Development*. Boston: Beacon Press.

Dao, J. 1993. A new, unregulated market: selling the right to pollute. *New York Times*, February 6, pp. A1, A24.

Deery Uva, M., and J. Bloom. 1989. Exporting pollution: The international waste trade. *Environment* 31(5): 4–5, 43–44.

Desvouges, W. H., V. K. Smith, and A. Fisher. 1987. Option price estimates for water quality improvements: a contingent valuation study of the Monongahela River. *Journal of Environmental Economics and Management* 14: 248–267.

Feder, B.J. 1989. Group sets corporate code on environmental conduct. *New York Times*, September 8, p. D1.

Fowler, E. 1990. Careers: Environment courses in M.B.A. study. *New York Times*, March 13, p. D22.

Friends of the Earth. 1981. *Progress as if Survival Mattered*. San Francisco: Friends of the Earth.

Georgescu-Roegen, N. 1976. *Energy and Economic Myths*. New York: Pergamon Press.

Group of Seven. 1989. Paris communique by the Group of Seven. *New York Times*, July 17, p. A7.

Hardin, G. 1968. The tragedy of the commons. *Science* 162: 1243–1248.

_____ . 1972. *Exploring New Ethics for Survival: The Voyage of the Spaceship Beagle*. New York:Viking.

Hershey, R. D., Jr. 1989. New market is seen for "pollution rights." *New York Times*, June 14, p. D1.

Kneese, A. V., R. V. Ayres, and R. C. d'Arge. 1971. *Economics and the Environment: A Materials Balance Approach*. Baltimore, MD: Johns Hopkins University Press.

_____ . and B.T. Bower, eds. 1971. *Environmental Quality Analysis: Theory and Method in the Social Sciences*. Baltimore, MD: Johns Hopkins University Press.

Krutilla, J.V., and A. Fisher. 1975. *The Economics of Natural Environments*. Baltimore, MD: Resources for the Future/Johns Hopkins University Press.

Mackerron, C. B. 1989. Special report on cleaning up: Lucrative markets abound in environmental services. *Chem. Week*, October 11, pp. 21–26.

MacNeill, J. 1989. Strategies for sustainable economic development. *Sci. Amer.* 261(3): 154–165.

Markham, J. M. 1989. Paris group urges "decisive action" for environment. *New York Times*, July 17, p. A1.

Mitchell, J. G. 1990. War in the woods II: West Side story. *Audubon* 92(1) (January): 82–121.

O'Riordan, T. and R. K. Turner. 1983. *An Annotated Reader in Environmental Planning and Management*. Oxford: Pergamon Press.

Passell, P. 1992. Cheapest protection of nature may lie in taxes, not laws. *New York Times*. November 24, p. C1.

_____ . 1995. How much for a life? Try $3 million to $5 million. *The New York Times*, January 29, p. D3.

Rees, J. 1985. *Natural Resources: Allocation, Economics, and Policy*. London: Methuen.

Roysten, M. G. 1985. Local and multinational corporations: Reappraising environmental management. *Environment* 27(1): 12–20, 39–43.

Ruckelshaus, W. D. 1989. Toward a sustainable world. *Sci. Amer.* 261(3): 166–175.

Schiffres, M. 1990. A cleaner environment: Where to invest. *Changing Times* 44(2) (February): 33–39.

Stavins, R.N. 1989. Harnessing market forces to protect the environment. *Environment* 31(1): 5–7, 28–35.

_____ . and B.W. Whitehead. 1992. Dealing with pollution: market-based incentives for environmental protection. *Environment* 34 (7): 6–12.

Tolba, M. K., O. A. El-Kholy, E. El-Hinnawi, M.W. Holdgate, D. F. McMichael, and R. E. Munn. 1992. *The World Environment 1972–1992*. London: Chapman & Hall.

Turner, R. K., D. Pearce, and I. Bateman. 1993. *Environmental Economics: An Elementary Introduction*. Baltimore, MD: Johns Hopkins University Press.

Vogel, D. 1995. *Trading Up: Consumer and Environmental Regulation in a Global Economy*. Cambridge, MA: Harvard University Press.

World Bank. 1995. Monitoring Environmental Progress: A Report on Work in Progress—Washington: World Bank.

World Resources Institute. 1996. *World Resources 1996–97*. New York: Oxford University Press.

Yaffee, S. L. 1994. *The Wisdom of the Spotted Owl.* Washington, DC: Island Press.

For more information, consult our web page at *http://www.wiley.com/college/cutter*

STUDY QUESTIONS

1. When you buy a chicken at the grocery store, you pay a price that is divided (ultimately) among the grocery store, the chicken producer, the grain farmer, the transportation companies involved between these, and the many suppliers that provide each of these entities with materials they need in their businesses. At each of the steps along the way—grain farm, chicken farm, and grocery store—environmental externalities are generated. Make a list of the important environmental externalities generated from this process.

2. List the major environmental externalities associated with operating an automobile. Suggest three different ways these costs could be internalized.

3. Discuss why the externalities associated with operating automobiles are not likely to be eliminated in the United States any time soon.

4. Conduct a survey of your friends and classmates to determine how much they would be willing to pay to (1) preserve an acre of old-growth forest that would otherwise be harvested (a one-time investment); or (2) reduce sulfur emissions in the United States (or your country) by 50 percent (an annual fee). Multiply the result by the population of the country to estimate the value of these environmental improvements (assuming your friends and classmates are representative of the entire population).

5. Air pollution generated by a facility such as a coal-fired electric power plant constitutes an environmental externality that could be eliminated either by regulations (such as requiring the electric company to control its emissions under threat of a criminal penalty) or by a market-based system in which the costs of controlling emissions would be borne by those who benefit from generating it or those who would benefit from improved air quality. Discuss the advantages and disadvantages of each approach.

CHAPTER 3

ENVIRONMENTAL HISTORY, POLITICS, AND DECISION MAKING

INTRODUCTION

Government policy is a key determinant of how natural resources are exploited and conserved. In the United States, the policies that control natural resource use have been developed over three centuries by both governmental and private actions. Governmental policy is a product of the political process, constrained by history and precedent. The political process in turn is essentially one of confrontation and compromise among many different interests, both economic and ideological. International environmental policies are the outgrowth of cooperation between nations. Unfortunately, international policy often is difficult to produce because of wide disparities in legal, economic, and social systems, which exacerbate major differences between nations (Hempel 1996). Once these differences are ironed out, however, participation in an international treaty is only voluntary. Nations cannot be compelled to abide by treaties because of the concept of *national sovereignty* (Murphy 1994). In other words, a country has the right to look after its own interests first and foremost, and what happens within its territorial boundaries is that country's business. So, the enforcement of international treaties is even more doubtful because there are no international police, no international taxation mechanism to support enforcement, and you can't take a country to court without its permission. One last complicating issue for international environmental policy involves the transboundary nature of contaminants and the common property nature of many resources (Porter and Brown 1996).

This chapter examines the history of human impact on the environment worldwide, and the development of natural resource policy, with a particular focus on the United States. The policy process is described, along with the various ideological and economic interest groups that are the major forces behind environmental management practices at both the national and global levels.

NATURAL RESOURCE USE: A HISTORICAL PERSPECTIVE

Human history can be viewed as a process of increasing ability to manipulate and alter usable aspects of the physical environment. For example, in the early stages of human evolution, at least 2 million years ago, the natural environment was largely unaffected by humans. Small numbers of protohumans in their hunting bands, using simple technology (bone, stone, and wood tools and hunting pits), were generally capable of competing with animal species. Like animals, protohumans were also at the mercy of climate and topography and did not have the technological skills to master the earth's more difficult climates. Thus, they were best able to utilize the food and shelter resources of open and coastal lands, locations that were far more vulnerable to natural hazards such as floods than to any alteration by people.

The first human tool to have a major environmental impact was fire. Early humans used it to drive animals into traps; when agriculture was developed between 10,000 and 7000 B.C., fire was used to clear land for crops and to create grazing areas for livestock. Fire is the only example in which the capacity of modern technology to alter the environment is matched by that of the pretechnological humans. The deliberate use of fire introduced three types of environmental effects: (1) it was widespread, affecting a large area; (2) it was a repetitive process and could cover the same areas at frequent intervals; and (3) it was highly selective in its effects on animal and plant species, having a negative effect on some, while encouraging those with rapid powers of recovery or resistance to fire (Nicholson 1970). The environmental result was to improve the yield of certain species for human use and to modify the vegetation cover. These early effects were confined largely to tropical, subtropical, and temperate forests and grasslands, as well as some wetlands.

At least 10,000 years ago the human race had spread to all continents except Antarctica. With the shift from hunting and gathering to agriculture, human culture developed more sophisticated food production tools for planting, harvesting, and transporting. Also, in drier areas in the Middle East and later elsewhere, large-scale irrigation works were built. The sedentary life of the agriculturalist went hand in hand with the development of cities. These two developments, agriculture and urbanization, led for the first time to a substantial change in land use, from natural to human-made forms of productivity, in the form of fields, streets, homes, and irrigation ditches. The development of cities led to large-scale environmental disruption and change because of the concentration of large populations and the wide areas in which land was cultivated, grazed, cleared of trees, and subjected to erosion to support the urban population. In addition, through the domestication of plants and animals, people were able to direct the energy and nutrients of an ecosystem to produce more of certain foods than the environment would naturally. This in turn permitted the growth of human populations beyond the limits set by their pre-agricultural patterns. Thus, agriculture raised the *carrying capacity* of the earth to support human beings.

After about 1000 B.C., humans began to move freely around the world, and rulers began to dominate large regions from a distance. Settlements and their impacts were no longer necessarily small in scale or localized in effect. The era of European colonialism that began in the fifteenth century A.D. placed the environments and resources of far-distant lands under their control. These colonial powers were interested in removing and using resources, with little regard for environmental consequences either abroad or close to home. The advent of industrialization led to a global-scale use of fuel and mineral resources that altered or destroyed local and regional ecosystems, perhaps ultimately affecting global climate and other environmental patterns (Simmons 1989; Turner et al. 1990).

The last three millennia, and particularly the last 500 years, have seen a transformation in the kinds and scales of natural resource use in the world (Turner and Butzer 1992). Early societies depended primarily on locally available resources with relatively little trade, whereas now most of the goods we consume come from quite far away. Resource-use systems have become complex, with a wide variety of goods utilized in everyday life. This increasing complexity has isolated us somewhat from the basic raw materials provided by the environment and has made us more dependent on human systems of resource manipulation and distribution. There clearly are innumerable ways of making a living in the world today. No single commodity or geographic area is indispensable, and resource management has become a task of selecting which resource utilization techniques are most appropriate for our needs at any given time.

DEVELOPMENT OF NATURAL RESOURCE POLICY

Natural resource policies are established at a variety of levels—local, state, national, regional, and international. As you might expect, the decision making, mechanisms, and impacts of these policies vary not only between different states in the United States but also from country to country.

U.S. Environmental Policy

The history of natural resource policy in the United States from the seventeenth century to the present can be divided into different phases, but these do not have distinct beginning and ending dates and often overlap. The following is a summary of some of the major actions and events that form the basis of much of the United States' contemporary conservation philosophy and policy.

Phase 1: Exploitation and Expansion (1600–1870)   When the early European settlers arrived in North America, they found a vast continent with natural resources in apparently limitless supply, compared to the more urbanized and developed Europe. Their goal was to establish stable and profitable colonies. To accomplish this goal, the European landholders who controlled settlement promoted population growth and resource extraction to maximize their security and prosperity. The colonial economy was, by design, based on exporting raw materials to industrial Europe, with agriculture for domestic food production. The enormous land area of North America was the primary resource for this economic development, and exploitation of its natural resources was the means to the desired end.

The forests that covered most of the eastern third of the continent were seen partly as a resource and partly as a nuisance. Wood was needed for fuel and construction purposes, but the vast amount of forest compared to productive agricultural land meant that timber cutting was a low-value land use. The forests, then, were cleared as rapidly as possible to make room for agriculture. In addition, the prevailing aesthetic attitudes toward forests were different. Forests were seen as unproductive, undesirable, and dangerous, whereas agricultural land was productive, attractive, and secure (Fig. 3.1). Except in a very few cases, regulations limiting the clearing of forests were unknown, as was the notion of natural resource conservation. This exploitative attitude toward the land prevailed for about the first 250 years of European occupation of North America, until the middle or late 1800s (Cronon 1984). The growth of an industrial economy in the nineteenth century had little effect on this attitude, except perhaps to increase the demands of urban populations for food, timber, and, later, coal. Forests were first culled of the most valuable trees, and later the remaining timber was generally clear-cut and often burned. Agriculture in many areas was largely cash cropping of a very few crop types, and except for liming soils in some areas, little was done to maintain, let alone enhance, soil fertility. As a result, soil erosion was rapid, and de-

clines in fertility forced abandonment of land after only a few years, particularly in the southeastern United States (Dilsaver and Colten 1992).

As the nation expanded westward, political as well as economic goals required rapid settlement and development of the Great Plains. With each major territorial expansion from the Louisiana Purchase in 1803 to the Alaska Purchase in 1867 (the annexation of Texas excepted), the federal government acquired possession of vast acreages. In the early nineteenth century, much government land was sold to provide income to the fledgling republic as well as to promote settlement. Several laws were passed in the mid-1800s to promote settlement, largely by transferring government-owned lands to private ownership either for free or at a nominal cost. The most notable among these laws were the *Homestead Act* of 1862, the *Railroad Acts* of the 1850s and 1860s, the *Timber Culture Act* of 1873, and the *Mining Act* of 1872.

The Homestead Act and the Railroad Acts were specifically designed to encourage settlement, especially in the Great Plains. The Homestead Act gave any qualified settler 160 acres free of charge, and the Railroad Acts granted large

Figure 3.1 A mixed landscape of forest and farms has replaced the near-continuous forest that covered most of the eastern United States when Europeans began migrating here in the seventeenth century. Clearing the forests was viewed by individuals and their governments as an improvement of the resource base.

rights of way to the railroad companies to finance construction of transcontinental and other rail lines that would further accelerate settlement of the West. Most of the land granted to the railroads was sold to other private interests, but substantial acreages remain in railroad ownership today, particularly in California. The Timber Culture and Mining Acts granted free access to forests and minerals to anyone willing to exploit them. There were widespread abuses of these privileges, which resulted in land companies and speculators acquiring vast acreages at nominal expense. Although these laws were successful in stimulating settlement and economic development, in many cases they encouraged excessive exploitation by artificially depressing the price of resources. Environmental degradation usually followed, as with the forests of the upper Midwest (Michigan, Wisconsin, and Minnesota) in which much timber was lost to wasteful logging practices and fires, and soil was lost to accelerated erosion.

The primary themes of this era included resource exploitation for economic prosperity and land transfers from public to private ownership. In fact, this era is best characterized by the massive land transfers from federal to private ownership, be it the individual, developers, or selected industries such as the railroads.

Near the end of this phase, the practice of promoting exploitation of resources for economic growth was limited somewhat by the growth of the conservation movement. Exploitative policies continued into the twentieth century, however, with legislation such as the Reclamation Act of 1902, which provided for the development of water at public expense for crop irrigation in the arid West. Today, natural resource exploitation for economic prosperity is still the basis of government management of mineral resources such as coal and oil, as well as being an important consideration in other areas such as water and rangelands.

Phase 2: Early Warnings and a Conservation Ethic (1840–1910)   As the westward expansion continued, Americans escalated their efforts to exploit the environment for their own needs, and with improved technology, settlers had a much easier job of "taming the land." For example, the mechanization of farming enhanced the settlement of the Great Plains. McCormick's grain reaper allowed the timely harvest of wheat. Steel plows developed by John Deere helped to break up the prairie soil for cultivation (Fig. 3.2). The cotton gin provided a mechanical means to sort lint from the cotton, and barbed wire allowed farmers and ranchers to demarcate property. As a result of many of these mechanical inventions, wildlife populations were particularly hard hit as they were either displaced from their ecosystem, outcompeted by the domesticated animals (cows and sheep), or succumbed to harsh winters and the rifle.

During the time when settlement was rapidly advancing westward with the government's stimulation and encouragement, a few individuals

Figure 3.2   An early tractor plowing prairie soil for wheat production in Oregon about 1890. The development of equipment such as this encouraged specialization in agriculture and strengthened links between agricultural and industrial sections of the economy.

were suggesting that the exploitation of resources was too rapid and too destructive. In general, these persons were intellectuals and academics who did not enjoy popular audiences for their criticisms; thus, the effects of their writings were limited at the time. Eventually, however, their warnings were heard by decision makers in government, and this led to a new concern for conserving and preserving resources.

Among the early American writers advocating wilderness preservation were Ralph Waldo Emerson and Henry David Thoreau, who argued on philosophical grounds in the 1840s and 1850s against continued destruction of natural areas by logging and similar activities. George Perkins Marsh's *Man and Nature, or Physical Geography as Modified by Human Action*, published in 1864, was perhaps more influential in the conservation versus exploitation debate. Marsh was both a public servant and a scientist, which led him to advocate government action to protect natural resources. Although a native of Vermont, Marsh traveled widely in the Mediterranean lands, areas long damaged by overgrazing. He saw a parallel between the Mediterranean situation and the damage done by sheep grazing in the Green Mountains in his home state. In *Man and Nature*, Marsh argued that humans should attempt to live in harmony rather than in competition with nature (Fig. 3.3). More important, Marsh argued that natural resources were far from inexhaustible. This book was widely read and had considerable influence on Carl Schurz,

who later became Secretary of the Interior under President Rutherford Hayes in 1877.

Phase 2 included a series of developments in the late nineteenth century, when many of the basic doctrines of the government's natural resource conservation policy were established. The primary tenet was that land resources should be managed for long-term rather than short-term benefits to the general population. This phase, dominated by concern for forest resources and to a lesser extent wilderness preservation, began in the 1860s and was marked by the first significant government action aimed at restricting exploitation of natural resources. One important governmental action was the formation, in 1862, of the Department of Agriculture's Land Grant College System, which was designed to help improve the management and productivity of agriculture and forestry through improved education. The establishment of the Cooperative Extension Service by the Smith-Lever Act of 1914 also helped to improve conservation education by linking the local farmer to agricultural experts in the state universities.

By the late nineteenth century, the forests of much of the eastern United States were either entirely cut over or were rapidly disappearing. Thus, it is not surprising that the forest resource was the first focus of the emerging conservation efforts in the 1870s. Carl Schurz launched an attack on corrupt and wasteful practices in timber harvesting on federal lands and brought the severity of the problem to the public eye. In 1872

Figure 3.3 Formal gardens. Formal gardens like those in Manteo, North Carolina, show our love for nature's forms but, more important, our domination over it.

the Adirondack Forest Reserve Act halted the sale of state forest lands, an action that eventually led to the creation of the Adirondack Forest Preserve (now Adirondack State Park). The most significant development during this period was the passage, in 1891, of a rider on a public lands bill that gave the President the authority to set aside forested lands by proclamation, thus reserving them from timber cutting. President Benjamin Harrison quickly began withdrawing land from timber cutting, and in 1897 additional reservations by President Grover Cleveland brought the total forest reserves to about 40 million acres (16 million ha). The federal government thus had established what would later become the National Forest System, but at the time it had no real management policy for these lands. In 1898 Gifford Pinchot was appointed as the first Chief Forester. Pinchot was trained as a forester in Europe, where the field was well established. He brought with him knowledge of the scientific basis for land management, in particular the notion of *sustained yield* forestry. The principle of sustained yield management of renewable resources has since been firmly incorporated into all aspects of official federal policy, although there is some debate as to whether the principle is truly followed in practice.

In 1901 Theodore Roosevelt became president, and his administration represented the culmination of this phase of America's natural resource history. Roosevelt was an adventurer and an outdoorsman, and thus had a personal appreciation for the values of undeveloped land, particularly the still untouched wilderness areas of the western United States. Pinchot was one of his key advisers, and with the forester's advice, Roosevelt added large acreages to the nation's forest reserves. In 1905 the United States Forest Service was established with Gifford Pinchot as its first chief, and "forest reserves" became National Forests. By the end of Roosevelt's administration, these reserves totaled 172 million acres (70 million ha). Later, large acreages were added to the National Forests in the eastern United States after the passage of the Weeks Act in 1911, which provided for federal acquisition of tax-delinquent cutover lands.

Theodore Roosevelt was also instrumental in expanding what would later become the National Park System. Yellowstone was reserved as a National Park in 1872, and several other parks were created during this period. Roosevelt protected the Grand Canyon from development by invoking the Antiquities Act. Passed in 1906, this act was intended primarily to allow the President to preserve national historic sites such as buildings and battlefields. Roosevelt, however, used it to create the Grand Canyon National Monument, which later became a National Park. Some 90 years later, in 1996, Bill Clinton used this same act to preserve thousands of acres of wilderness in Utah. Finally, near the end of his presidency, Roosevelt sponsored the first White House Conference on Conservation, further bringing the issue to public attention and concern.

Another important figure during this period was John Muir, who founded the Sierra Club in 1892. Muir was a strong preservationist and wilderness advocate, whose primary area of interest was the Sierra Nevada Range of California. The Yosemite region was one of his favorite spots, and he led the battle to protect the area from damage by sheep grazing by establishing what would later become Yosemite National Park.

One of the most significant battles of Muir's life was fought over the preservation of Hetch-Hetchy Valley. This valley is adjacent to Yosemite Valley and was very similar in scenic beauty. Hetch-Hetchy was, however, a convenient source of water for the growing city of San Francisco and an excellent dam site. Muir fought hard to prevent the damming of the Tuolumne River but eventually lost in a battle with a former ally in the conservation movement, Gifford Pinchot. Although Pinchot was a conservationist, he believed in conservation as a means of maintaining the productive capacity of natural resources. To prevent development was contrary to the notion that resources could be used for the general benefit of the population, and Pinchot opposed Muir in the debate over Hetch-Hetchy. In the end, the development interests prevailed, and today the valley is a reservoir providing water and electricity to the cities of northern California. Almost a century later, there is occasional talk of draining Hetch-Hetchy and restoring the valley to its original state.

The Hetch-Hetchy controversy made clear the distinction between conservationists, who encourage careful husbanding of resources yet do not condemn their use, and preservationists, who would stop all use or development on the basis that some areas and resources are too valuable to be used. This second phase ushered in major achievements in resource conservation and saw the establishment of the principles of both sustained yield management and preservation of outstanding natural features for future generations. This period also witnessed the emergence of two of the major ideological camps, the preservationists and the conservationists, which still dominate debates over natural resources today.

Phase 3: Conservation for Economic Recovery (1930–1940)

The Great Depression of 1929– 1941 and Franklin Roosevelt's New Deal of the 1930s had more impact on all aspects of modern domestic policy than events in any other period in American history, and natural resource use was no exception. The Depression provided the impetus for massive programs aimed at relief, recovery, and prevention of similar problems in the future. Most of the major programs of this period were primarily economic rather than conservation-oriented in emphasis. The Civilian Conservation Corps, for example, did not represent a major new policy but rather was a make-work program that put many of the unemployed to work on conservation projects, principally planting trees and maintaining or constructing park facilities. In contrast, two major agencies established by the New Deal, the Tennessee Valley Authority (TVA) and the Soil Conservation Service (SCS), were aimed at correcting problems that, if not major contributors to the Depression, were very much worsened by it.

The Appalachian region of the Southeast had long been economically depressed and was among the areas hardest hit by the Depression. The forests were largely cut over, farms were not competitive with those in the Midwest, soil erosion and flooding were particularly severe, and no significant industrial employment was available. The TVA was the first major effort to address this wide range of problems in an integrated regional resource management and economic development program. The major elements of the program were the construction of dams for hydroelectric power generation and flood control, with the power generated being used to support new industries, particularly fertilizer and later munitions production. Forests were replanted to control erosion, and many smaller erosion control measures were instituted, in part to protect the newly created reservoirs from sedimentation. Today the TVA is mostly an electric power-generating authority, but it has an important legacy in natural resources. It represents the recognition that good natural resource management and economic vitality are interdependent, and that to ensure long-term economic stability both must be undertaken together.

In addition to dam construction in the Tennessee Valley, many large dams were completed in the arid western states, including the Hoover Dam on the Colorado River (Fig. 3.4) and several dams in the Columbia River basin. These were seen as important government investments in agriculture and electric power generation, which would help revitalize agriculture and provide new sources of energy for industry.

The agricultural expansion in the Midwest and Great Plains during the late nineteenth and early twentieth centuries took advantage of the naturally fertile soils of that region, and farming was successful without significant inputs of fertilizers or other means to maintain soil fertility. Severe soil erosion was widespread, but it took the economic collapse of the 1930s and the ensuing dust bowl conditions in portions of the Midwest and Great Plains to focus attention on the problem. Several dry years on land that was marginal for farming, combined with economic hardship brought on by low farm prices, led to severe wind erosion in Oklahoma, Colorado, and nearby areas, forcing thousands off the land (Worster 1979).

The Soil Erosion Service, created in 1933, was established in response to these problems. Hugh Hammond Bennett became the first director of the newly renamed Soil Conservation Service (now known as the Natural Resources Conservation Service) in 1935. He led an extensive research effort to determine the causes of soil erosion and the means to prevent it. This resulted in the development and implementation of many important soil conservation techniques, which yielded dramatic reductions in soil erosion in much of the nation. The Agricultural Adjustment Administration, forerunner to the Agricultural Stabilization and Conservation Service (now known as the Farm Service Agency) was established to provide payments to farmers who reduced crop acreage. This not only reduced farm surpluses, but also helped support prices and reduced the rate of soil erosion.

Figure 3.4 Hoover Dam. This 1938 Bureau of Reclamation photo shows the multipurpose dam that spans the Colorado River at the Nevada–Arizona border. Hoover Dam and its reservoir, Lake Mead, provide flood protection, water storage, hydroelectric power, and recreation. These benefits typify the goals of the governmental public works projects during the 1930s and 1940s.

Some of the subsidy programs established in the New Deal continued through the 1990s, but are being phased out (see Issue 6.3).

Another significant piece of legislation of this period was the *Taylor Grazing Act* of 1934, which established a system of fees for grazing on federal lands, with limitations on the numbers of animals that could be grazed. This law was a partial response to the widespread accelerated erosion caused by overgrazing. The act also closed most of the public lands to homesteading, effectively ending the large-scale transfer of public lands to private ownership that had begun in 1862. Today, these public lands are administered by the Bureau of Land Management. The Natural Resources Planning Board was another milestone of resource management in the FDR years and was a major step toward establishing long-term comprehensive natural resources planning.

In summary, the FDR years saw important advances in federal resource management and conservation activities. Most of the new programs were conceived as a result of the Depression and were designed to alleviate the problems of the time as well as prevent future mismanagement of resources. The need for careful management of renewable resources, particularly soil and water, was recognized, and the close relation between economic and resource problems became clear.

Phase 4: The Environmental Movement (1962–1976) The years 1940 to 1960 witnessed few new developments in conservation policy. The 1940s were dominated by war, and the economic recovery and ensuing prosperity of the 1950s diverted attention from natural resources issues. There was, however, considerable progress in soil, water, and forest conservation, expanding on the achievements made under FDR. The major federal actions of this period were largely in the area of recreational activities, with the expansion of the National Parks and similar recreational areas in response to increased use by the American public.

By the 1960s, attention became focused on the quality of life available to Americans, and natural resources became more broadly defined. Two significant books published in 1962 and 1963 called attention to this expanded view of natural resources and signaled the beginning of a new era in which environmental pollution was recognized as a major threat to natural resources and the quality of life.

One of these books was *The Quiet Crisis* (1963), by Stewart Udall, Secretary of the Interior under President John F. Kennedy. In this work Udall presented much of the history of natural resource use in the United States, particularly focusing on the destruction of natural environments and wildlife. He called for renewed attention to the human effects on the environment, echoing many of the sentiments of G. P. Marsh 100 years earlier. The other book was Rachel Carson's *Silent Spring* (1962), which described the effects of pesticides on the ecosystem and predicted drastic environmental consequences of continued pollution.

Throughout the 1960s, a popular movement for pollution control grew, led largely by scientists, such as Barry Commoner and Paul Ehrlich, student activists, and a few government officials such as Stewart Udall. Many influential authors argued that the environment was severely damaged already and that urgent action was needed to restore its health and prevent further damage to both natural and managed ecosystems. A major focus of the movement was the disparity between a limited resource base on "spaceship earth" and a rapidly growing world population that already faced severe shortages of food and raw materials. A long list of laws was passed in the late 1960s and early 1970s aimed at reducing pollution, preserving wilderness and endangered species, and promoting ecological considerations in resource development. Some of the more important of these were the Wilderness Act of 1964, the Clean Air Act of 1963 and its amendments of 1970 and 1977, the Federal Water Pollution Control Act of 1964 and its amendments of 1972, the Coastal Zone Management Act of 1972, the Endangered Species Act of 1973, and the National Environmental Policy Act of 1970 (NEPA). The laws relating to specific resource problems such as air and water pollution have been the most important in terms of improving environmental quality, and they are discussed in more detail later in this and other chapters.

The National Environmental Policy Act (NEPA) represents the first comprehensive statement of United States environmental policy and is illustrative of the character of this phase of American natural resources history. Section 101 of NEPA contains a statement of the federal government's environmental responsibilities. These are to:

1. fulfill the responsibilities of each generation as trustee of the environment for succeeding generations;
2. assure for all Americans safe, healthful, productive, and aesthetically and culturally pleasing surroundings;
3. attain the widest range of beneficial uses of the environment without degradation, risk to health or safety, or other undesirable and unintended consequences;
4. preserve important historic, cultural, and natural aspects of our national heritage, and maintain, wherever possible, an environment which supports diversity and variety of individual choice;
5. achieve a balance between population and resource use which will permit high standards of living and a wide sharing of life's amenities; and
6. enhance the quality of renewable resources and approach the maximum attainable recycling of depletable resources. (CEQ 1980: 426–427).

These are lofty goals, but they reflect the idealism of the time as well as the far-reaching concerns of the environmental movement. They emphasize quality of life, preservation, or maintenance rather than exploitation, and the concern with a limited and finite resource base supporting a rapidly growing population. NEPA also established the requirement for environmental impact statements in order to ensure compliance with its policies.

Phase 5: Pragmatism and Risk Reduction (1976–1988) By the late 1970s a complex set of laws, regulations, and procedures was in place, along with a bureaucracy to administer them. The mass of environmental legislation generated in the preceding decade was being translated into everyday action, and the energy crises of the mid-1970s re-emphasized the need for resource conservation. Substantial improvements in environmental quality were being made, particularly in the areas of air and water pollution. With an upsurge of public concern about the effects of pollution and toxic chemicals on health, the Toxic Substances Control Act and the Resource Conservation and Recovery Act were signed into law in 1975 and 1976, respectively. The Comprehensive Environmental Response, Compensation, and Liability Act (Superfund) was signed into law in 1980, whose purpose was to reduce the toxicity, mobility, and volume of hazardous wastes and to clean up existing hazardous waste sites. The Superfund Amendments and Reauthorization Act (SARA), passed in 1986, further clarified the goals of the Superfund program to enhance the long-term prevention of health effects through waste reduction and better treatment and incineration of wastes. Land disposal of hazardous wastes was not considered a viable policy option. Risk reduction as environmental policy placed the Environmental

Protection Agency in the leading role. However, scientific uncertainty regarding the nature of toxic risk, coupled with the scale and complexity of abandoned waste sites and over 5000 known toxic chemicals, resulted in very little cleanup and standard setting during this phase. Inadequate funding for enforcement and cleanup, compounded by a lack of agency and governmental priorities, exacerbated the situation.

At the same time, public debate shifted away from the rather abstract issues of ecological stability and environmental quality toward economic problems. With a downturn in the national and world economy, some began to see the costs of improving environmental quality as contributing to economic problems and others saw environmental initiatives as simply too expensive for the benefits derived. When President Reagan took office in 1980, he rode a tide of political conservatism that turned away from the idealism of the 1960s and focused more on stimulating economic development. Public lands policy shifted from federal management and conservation to state or private control of resources and exploitation to improve supplies of raw materials, especially energy. Federally owned coal, which had not been sold during earlier administrations because of an oversupply of minable coal, was once again made available to the industry. In its rush to divest the federal government of its holdings, the Interior Department sold coal leasing rights in many areas at below market value. Pollution abatement efforts by the federal government were reduced in favor of state and local control over these policies. Attention was also turned toward reducing the costs of pollution control to industry. Clearly, resource conservation had entered a new phase that considered the economic aspects of resource decisions along with the ecological goals established in the 1960s and 1970s.

Phase 6: The New Environmental Consciousness: Global and Local Responsibility (1988–)

During the late 1980s, a new awareness of global environmental issues re-emerged. The spaceship earth philosophy, which had been popular 20 years earlier, fell out of favor in the intervening years as predicted catastrophes (widespread famines, climate change, and species extinctions) failed to materialize, and environmentalists who voiced these fears were regarded as alarmist or, worse, catastrophists! (Gore 1992; McKibben 1989). But a number of dramatic events in the mid-1980s, including the nuclear accident at Chernobyl and the "discovery" of the Antarctic ozone "hole," made people aware of the global scale of environmental problems. They were no longer problems of the smelly smokestack in town, but a real source of threat to the planet. Environmental protection was fast becoming an international concern, one requiring cooperation between developed and developing nations. A key event in this phase was the UN Conference on Environment and Development, discussed later in this chapter.

International Policy

At the international level, the evolution of environmental policy took a different path (Kamieniecki 1993). Prior to World War II, a few international environmental agreements existed, as did a number of international institutions. Most of the early agreements concerned migratory birds and marine life (fur seals, whales). Institution building during this time included the well-known World Meteorological Organization founded in 1873 (to coordinate weather observations) and the International Council of Scientific Unions in 1919 (to coordinate international science).

The UN System, 1944–1972

International environmental policy and institutions got their real start with the founding of the United Nations in 1945. As this international organization evolved, more specialized programs and subagencies were founded. The International Union for the Conservation of Nature and Natural Resources (IUCN) (1948) included both nation-state and nongovernmental members. Others operated under the auspices of the United Nations including the International Maritime Organization and the World Health Organization (WHO).

Also established during this period were two important financial institutions—the International Monetary Fund and the World Bank. The World Bank's mission is to provide financial assistance to developing countries in order to help improve economic conditions. Initially, the World Bank was the leading financier of many of the economic development projects that accelerated environmental decline in the developing world such as large dams. Since 1985, the World Bank has funded environmental restoration projects to minimize resource degradation and pollution of habitats. Finally, the Food and Agriculture Organization (FAO) was established in 1945 to improve nutrition and the standard of living among the world's rural residents. Some of the more important global institutions are listed in Table 3.1.

While this period reflected substantial growth of the United Nations' infrastructure, it also ushered in the era of environmental diplomacy and the negotiation of environmental treaties (Susskind 1994). The enhanced protection of whales was one of the first big success stories for international environmental policy. The 1946 International Convention for the Regulation of Whaling established the International Whaling Commission to preserve and manage these marine mammals, which is still in effect today (see Chapter 9). Similarly, the conservation of transboundary resources and the global commons were of utmost concern and were reflected in a number of important treaties on plant protection (1951), preventing oil pollution of the seas (1954), fishing resources (1958), and pristine Antarctica (1959, 1964). The most significant treaty during this time, however, was the 1963 Nuclear Test Ban treaty, which prohibited the testing of nuclear weapons in the air, under water, or in outer space (CIESIN 1997; Tolba et al. 1972).

The 1972 Stockholm Conference   Most of the United Nations' work is done through conferences and the meetings that prepare for them. This is a slow deliberative process that allows all member nations to participate in the drafting of the policy (Table 3.2). Once the treaties are drafted, they are presented to member states for signature and ratification.

One such conference that many people point to as the turning point in the international environmental arena was the 1972 UN Conference on the Human Environment held in Stockholm. This conference produced divergent opinions among member nations. The industrialized world was concerned about pollution from increasing industrial activity and the need to preserve natural resources, while the developing nations argued that poverty and the inefficiency of resource use

Table 3.1   Global Institutions with Environmental Interests

Institution	Date Established	Mandate
Food and Agriculture Organization (FAO)	1945	Raise nutritional levels and standards of living, improve food production, better conditions of rural populations
General Agreement on Tariffs and Trade (GATT)	1946	Expand international trade and remove trade/tariff barriers
International Atomic Energy Agency (IAEA)	1957	Monitor nuclear programs for peaceful uses
International Maritime Organization (IMO)	1958	Responsible for sea safety, international shipping, and protection of the marine environment from shipping
UN Educational, Scientific, and Cultural Organization (UNESCO)	1945	Promote peace and security through education, science, and culture
World Health Organization (WHO)	1948	Improve the health of the world's population
UN Children's Fund (UNICEF)	1946	Provide assistance for children's health and welfare services
UN Development Program (UNDP)	1966	Assist developing countries in social and economic development programs
UN Environment Program (UNEP)	1972	Coordinate and stimulate environmental action, monitor global environmental trends

Source: Tolba et al. 1992.

caused by underdevelopment were the primary issues. Despite the often rancorous debate, the Stockholm conference was a defining moment for international environmental policy. It led to the establishment of the UN Environment Programme (UNEP), which collects and disseminates environmental data. UNEP now plays a leading role in developing and implementing international environmental policy.

In 1987 the UN World Commission on Environment and Development published its influential report: *Our Common Future* (WCED 1987) linking resource degradation to unsustainable development practices. Ushering in a new emphasis on sustainability, the Bruntland report (named for the Norwegian Prime Minister Gro Harlem Brundtland who chaired the Commission) fostered a new recognition among the world's countries on the interconnectedness of human development, resource decline, and pollution.

Marking the twentieth anniversary of its Stockholm Conference on the Human Environment (1972), the United Nations held its Earth Summit in Rio de Janeiro in June 1992. The UN Conference on Environment and Development (UNCED) was designed to forge a new path in international cooperation on environmental protection and sustainability. The United States sent a large contingent led by the newly elected Vice President, Al Gore. New agreements were signed at the Earth Summit (climate change and biodiversity). In addition, a new intergovernmental infrastructure was created to monitor progress on Agenda 21, the series of goals and principles adopted at the conference (Haas et al. 1992; Jordan 1994; Parson et al. 1992) (Issue 3.1). These achievements indicate a new and perhaps unprecedented period of international cooperation to facilitate the sustainable use of the earth's natural resources. It remains to be seen how long this new awareness will last or how important it will be in changing policies and behavior. It is clear, however, that unprecedented popular support has developed for the establishment of an international agency to solve environmental problems (Dunlap et al. 1992). In many nations,

Table 3.2   Selected Major International Treaties/Conventions

Date	Place	Treaty
1959	Washington, DC	Antarctic Treaty and Convention
1963	Moscow	Nuclear Test Ban Treaty
1971	Ramsar	Convention on Wetlands of International Importance
1972	London	Ocean Dumping Convention
1972	London	Biological Weapons Convention
1973	Washington, DC	Convention on International Trade in Endangered Species (CITES)
1978	London	Protocol on the Prevention of Pollution from Ships (MARPOL)
1979	Bonn	Convention on Conservation of Migratory Species of Wild Animals
1982	Montego Bay	Convention on the Law of the Sea (UNCLOS)
1985	Vienna	Vienna Convention for the Protection of the Ozone Layer
1987	Montreal	Montreal Protocols on Substances That Deplete the Ozone Layer
1989	Basel	Basel Convention on the Control of Transboundary Movements of Hazardous Wastes and Their Disposal
1992	Rio de Janeiro	Framework Convention on Climate Change (FCCC)
1992	Rio de Janeiro	Convention on Biological Diversity
1997	Kyoto	Kyoto Protocol to the Framework Convention on Climate Change

residents are keenly aware of the linkage between environmental problems and their own health and welfare.

The years following Rio were a mix of successes and failures (Flavin 1997). While the link between environment and development has been recognized, the goal of an environmentally sustainable global economy has not been achieved. Carbon emissions are climbing, biodiversity is declining, world population is increasing, and millions more people are living in poverty. Despite this pessimism, grass-roots activism has increased through which people are implementing practical plans for solving local environmental problems. This "grass-roots" spirit throughout

the world is giving new meaning to the old slogan, "Think globally, act locally."

CURRENT NATURAL RESOURCE POLICY

The history of policy development for natural resource use reviewed in the previous section shows that at one time or another government decision making motivated many important goals, many of which are embodied in present policy. These goals can be grouped into four general categories: to promote economic development; to conserve resources for the future; to

ISSUE 3.1:   IN FAIRNESS TO ALL: AGENDA 21 AND ENVIRONMENTAL EQUITY

One of the greatest obstacles in international environmental diplomacy is the sharp divide between industrialized and developing nations. This North/South conflict, as many call it, has led to many divisions among nations often causing them to fall along the lines of haves and have nots. As part of the Earth Summit, an attempt was made to reduce these sharp economic divisions among nations. Through the application of equity, the Earth Summit tried to convince nations of the need for sustainability—not just in the developing world but among the most industrialized nations as well.

Agenda 21 provides the blueprint for achieving sustainability. But it is much more than that. It also provides a framework for implementing a code of conduct or fairness among nations as they strive to meet the ambitious goals of the Earth Summit.

Equity has many forms. For example, *social equity* refers to the differences in social, economic, and political forces in the consumption of resources and the ability to degrade environments. The transboundary shipment of hazardous wastes from industrialized countries in Europe to poorer nations in Africa is one example of social inequity; closer to home, dumping your garbage in another poor community is another example. *Generational equity* is perhaps the most important form of *environmental equity*. Generational equity embodies the concept of fairness to future generations. By

this we mean that our generation has a responsibility to our children to leave the environment in the same or better condition than what was left to us. This type of generational stewardship is most often seen in the preservation of wild areas (Biosphere Reserves, National Parks) and more recently in biodiversity treaties. The last form of equity is *procedural*, which applies to the ways in which laws and treaties are applied in a fair way.

Agenda 21 has 27 specific principles, and close to half of these directly address some form of equity. For example, Principle 3 states the right of all people to development to meet the environmental needs of present and future generations (generational equity). Principle 22 recognizes the rights of indigenous people and communities, while Principle 20 encourages the full participation of women in environmental management in development (social equity). Finally, Principle 11 proposes that environmental standards reflect the context within which they apply (procedural) and argues that universal codes might affect some nations more than others.

It remains to be seen whether these equity goals will be achieved, for it will require not only a rethinking of international relations but a potential redistribution of wealth as well. In other words, Earth's resources must be shared for the benefit of all, not just for a select few (United Nations 1992).

protect public health; and to preserve important natural features.

Clearly, the most frequent motivation for government actions with respect to natural resources has been to promote economic development. This began with the land divestitures of the eighteenth and nineteenth centuries and continues today in the management of our national forests, offshore oil resources, rivers, and grazing land. The construction of major dams and reservoirs on rivers for hydroelectric power generation, irrigation, or flood control addresses this goal. Economic development was the motivation when the United States increased mineral lease sales in the 1980s, with development rights being sold at below-market value to stimulate production. It is also the primary justification for one of the basic tenets of public land management policy in the United States, that of multiple use. The concept of multiple use was incorporated into the U.S. Multiple Use and Sustained Yield Act of 1960 and was restated in NEPA, but it originated much earlier.

In encouraging economic development, the companion to the multiple use concept is the idea of *sustained yield*, which aids in achieving the second goal, to conserve resources for future generations. This is the fundamental principle of renewable resource management established by Pinchot in forest management, but it applies equally to the mission of the U.S. Natural Resources Conservation Service and indeed to every agency that manages natural resources. More recently, sustainability has been the approach used to reconcile economic development goals within environmental limits (Chapter 15).

The third goal, to promote public health, is the basis for most pollution control legislation. Many of the early American laws regulating potential health hazards in the environment were enacted at the state level, and major federal actions in this area did not appear until the late nineteenth and early twentieth centuries. Today most of the water and air quality standards established by governments are based on health criteria and risk assessments. At the international level, environmental health is a key objective of the World Health Organization. Treaties limiting emissions of ozone-destroying chemicals are motivated primarily by health concerns.

The fourth major goal of natural resource policy is to preserve significant natural features that

are valuable for aesthetic or scientific reasons, if not for economic ones. This is the aim of the extensive legislation enacted regarding wilderness preservation and protection of endangered species, and it is the principal mission of the National Park Service and the United Nations' Biosphere Reserves (Chapter 8). This goal also forms the basis of some water-quality criteria, and it is considered one of the uses of public lands incorporated in multiple use planning.

Many natural resource policies combine these different goals. A U.S. example is water pollution control, which not only protects the public health but also provides recreational, aesthetic, and economic benefits to fisheries. All the agencies involved in resource management address these multiple goals in devising management strategies, and this combination of purposes also plays an important role in creating political coalitions to enact new laws. Together they form the basis for resource management decisions.

After decades of polarization and politicization, environmental issues now have broad political support in the United States and most other industrial nations (Paarlberg 1996). Conservation and environmental issues became part of the national and international agenda in such diverse areas as national security, international trade, and population policies. International concerns over acid rain, global warming, and tropical deforestation, to name but a few, fueled the international debate on how to best manage these resources. Domestic concerns such as clean air and toxic emissions still provide a focus for American Earth Day observances (April 22), a gentle reminder not of how far we've progressed, but of how much farther we need to go to protect the environment (Fig. 3.5).

HOW DECISIONS ARE MADE

Resource Decision Making in the United States

Several different groups are involved in any decision over the use of natural resources: resource managers, social agents, and interest groups. Membership in these groups is not constant, for any individual may shift from one role to another as the decision-making process unfolds (Fig. 3.6).

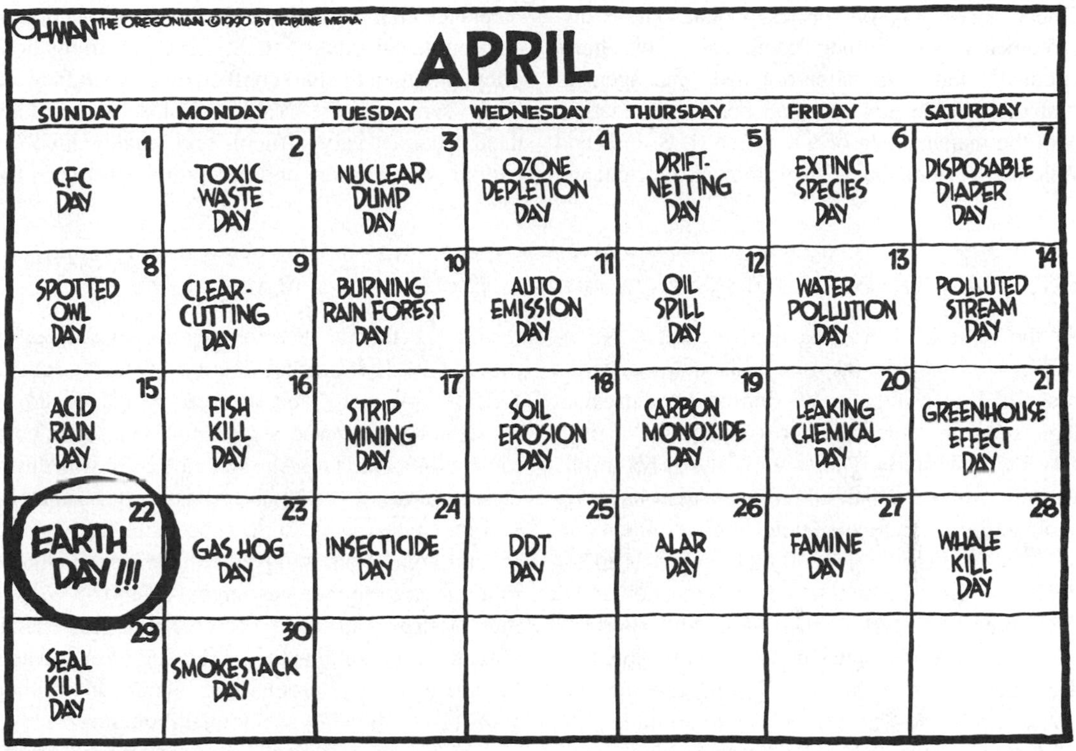

OLIMAN THE OREGONIAN ©1990 BY TRIBUNE MEDIA

APRIL

SUNDAY	MONDAY	TUESDAY	WEDNESDAY	THURSDAY	FRIDAY	SATURDAY
1 CFC DAY	**2** TOXIC WASTE DAY	**3** NUCLEAR DUMP DAY	**4** OZONE DEPLETION DAY	**5** DRIFT-NETTING DAY	**6** EXTINCT SPECIES DAY	**7** DISPOSABLE DIAPER DAY
8 SPOTTED OWL DAY	**9** CLEAR-CUTTING DAY	**10** BURNING RAIN FOREST DAY	**11** AUTO EMISSION DAY	**12** OIL SPILL DAY	**13** WATER POLLUTION DAY	**14** POLLUTED STREAM DAY
15 ACID RAIN DAY	**16** FISH KILL DAY	**17** STRIP MINING DAY	**18** SOIL EROSION DAY	**19** CARBON MONOXIDE DAY	**20** LEAKING CHEMICAL DAY	**21** GREENHOUSE EFFECT DAY
22 EARTH DAY!!!	**23** GAS HOG DAY	**24** INSECTICIDE DAY	**25** DDT DAY	**26** ALAR DAY	**27** FAMINE DAY	**28** WHALE KILL DAY
29 SEAL KILL DAY	**30** SMOKESTACK DAY					

Figure 3.5 Celebrating Earth Day. Despite three decades of environmental concern and activism, we still have a long way to go.

A resource manager is the individual or agency that is in immediate contact with the resource and has a direct stake in how that resource is used or misused. Examples of resource managers include an individual farmer concerned with soil erosion, a forest ranger charged with managing a particular national forest, or the Secretary of the Interior, who manages the resources under his or her jurisdiction—parks, public lands, and so on.

Resource managers are subject to outside influences or social agents also called stakeholders. These range from the forest rangers' superiors in the Department of Agriculture to the United States President, who oversees the Secretary of the Interior. These social agents provide technical expertise and direction to the individual managers in the field. The goals, objectives, and responsibilities of the social agents are broader than those of the resource manager. Social agents are thus influenced by interest groups who have a stake in how a resource is eventually used. Special interests range from timber companies seeking access to a national forest to supermarket chains buying farm produce to environmental groups seeking to preserve a piece of nature.

Conflicts between participants inevitably lead to disagreement over management policies. One example is whether to manage forests for water yield,

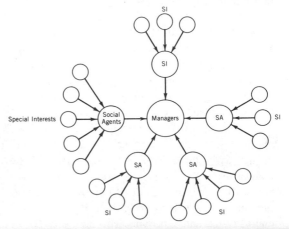

Figure 3.6 Participants in the resource-use decision-making process. Individuals may shift roles, depending on the resource issue under consideration.

timber harvesting, or species habitat. These disagreements are further complicated by goal-oriented and mitigation-oriented management strategies. Some governmental bodies are charged with the management of a resource (U.S. Fish and Wildlife Service), that is, they are goal-directed; and others are charged with regulation and protection of environmental quality (U.S. EPA), or mitigation-oriented. Often the two conflict, even when they are in the same agency. (Table 3.3) Decision making then becomes very difficult and usually involves conflict, cooperation, and compromise between the

---

ISSUE 3.2: THE POLITICS OF U.S. ENVIRONMENTAL LEGISLATION: THE ALASKA LANDS BILL

At the national level, the fundamental decision-making process is the congressional legislative process. Laws are initially drafted by individual legislators or, more commonly, groups of legislators and their staffs. They are discussed before the various congressional committees that have responsibility for particular areas of government policy. These committees modify the proposals and, if approved, forward them to the full Senate or House of Representatives for amendment and approval. When, usually after much debate and revision, they are passed by both houses of Congress, they are forwarded to the President for signing into law. At each stage of the process, resource managers, social agents, and interest groups make their positions known, and their opinions may be either incorporated or ignored in the proposed legislation. Each law is unique, and each is subjected to different forces depending on the course the process takes from initial proposal to final enactment. An example of the politics of environmental legislation is the Alaska National Interest Lands Conservation Act (ANILCA) passed in 1980. This act, better known as the Alaska Lands Bill, is a good example because the battles over it were particularly intense and involved many different actors. Few environmental laws in recent decades have been as controversial as this one.

Alaska has an area of about 375 million acres (152 million ha), and virtually all of this land was federally owned when Alaska became a state in 1959. The terms of the Statehood Act, however, required that 104 million acres (42 million ha) eventually be turned over to the state. In 1971 the Alaska Native Claims Act was passed, which paved the way for construction of the Alaska pipeline by providing a settlement of the land claims of the native peoples. This act called for 44 million acres (18 million ha) to be turned over to the natives. But before these lands could be transferred, the federal government had to decide, by the end of 1978, which lands it would retain in federal ownership, and of these which would be preserved as wilderness and which would be open to development. The Alaska lands issue was thus a classic battle of preservation versus development, and the stakes were high: spectacular and unique natural areas containing potentially very valuable mineral and timber resources. The battle took much longer than was expected, and to prevent development of some areas while Congress debated, President Carter proclaimed about 44 million acres (18 million ha) as national monuments.

The House of Representatives was the first to take up the Alaska lands issue, in 1977. Morris Udall, a leading environmentalist in Congress, introduced a bill that would place nearly 170 million acres (69 million ha) in the "four systems": the national parks, wildlife refuges, forests, and wild and scenic rivers. In contrast, a proposal introduced by Alaska Representative Don Young would place only 25 million acres (10 million ha) in the four systems and another 57 million acres (23 million ha) in a joint state-federal management area to be managed for multiple uses. The battle lines were drawn, and the special interests went to work. One of the most effective of these was the Alaska Coalition, a group of conservation organizations that banded together to press for a preservation-oriented bill. On the other side were the state of Alaska, which wanted as much development potential as possible, and industry groups such as the American Mining Congress and the Western Oil and Gas Association. In the numerous negotiations the various proposals were modified, and eventually they were narrowed to two: the Udall bill and another that would have preserved much less land. Public sentiment for preservation was mobilized by the Alaska Coalition, which produced and distributed literature

resource manager, social agents, and interest groups. In addition, conflicting environmental ideologies complicate the matter further (Pepper 1996).

Ultimately, federal decisions are made by Congress and then implemented by the appropriate agency such as the Environmental Protection Agency or the Department of the Interior (Issue 3.2). Passing an environmental bill in Congress is fraught with partisanship and compromise, and often the finished bill (which is based on the compromise between the House and Senate versions) is not as strict as environmentalists would like.

and films depicting the spectacular wilderness. In the end, this sentiment was very important, and the Udall bill passed by a wide margin.

Once the House had passed its bill, the Senate began deliberations on its own versions of the bill. In general the Senate was less conservation-minded than the House, although there was a powerful group of senators who supported a bill very similar to the House-passed bill. But the bill that finally emerged from committee in the Senate was rather different, including substantial reductions in areas designated as wilderness and more access for development in other areas. This was far from acceptable to the two Alaskan Senators, Ted Stevens and Mike Gravel, who vowed to filibuster to prevent passage of a bill that would not meet the desires of the state. The debate became heated, and at one point the Senate went into closed session after a shouting match between Stevens and Colorado Senator Gary Hart. Eventually, Stevens and Gravel's attempts at a filibuster failed as the Senate voted to cut off debate. The Senate version finally passed and placed 104 million acres (42 million ha) in the four systems, substantially less than the 127 million acres (51 million ha) in the House bill. Wilderness designation was made for 67 million acres (27 million ha) in the House bill, but only 57 million acres (23 million ha) in the Senate version, and mineral exploration was permitted in some wildlife refuges.

After the Senate passed its bill, the House again took up the issue under threats of a filibuster if it failed to agree to the Senate version. Finally, it did accept the Senate version of the bill, and in late 1980 the bill was signed by President Carter. It was most certainly a compromise but not an entirely happy one. Morris Udall said that he got most of what he wanted, but that some provisions were still unacceptable to him which he hoped would be modified in the next Congress. Alaska Representative Don Young was pleased that the bill did permit more mineral exploration than the original House bill, but he, too, said he wanted to change things in the next Congress to permit even more exploration and development.

Throughout the debate on the Alaska Lands Bill, the changing strengths and fortunes of the actors could be seen. Conservationists were buoyed by support from the Carter administration, particularly Interior Secretary Cecil Andrus. In the midst of the debate, the Alaska legislature was repealing income taxes and rebating millions of dollars to its citizens as a result of accumulating oil revenues, actions that earned no extra sympathy for their demands for resource development. Carter and most environmental groups hailed the bill as the Carter adminstration's most significant environmental achievement. Mike Gravel was defeated in a primary election during the height of the debate, and one of the major issues was his inability to force the Senate to recognize Alaska's interests. At the same time, industry won some crucial battles, and most of the valuable mineral and timber resources are now open to development.

The congressional process is one of compromise, and the most effective means for compromise is to make sure everyone gets something they want. Each actor and each interest group is given at least token recognition of its interests in an attempt to gain support for the final outcome. The particular characteristics of that outcome—which interests get more of what they want and which get less—is dependent on the strengths of their various power bases. In the case of the Alaska Lands Bill, the environmentalists had much more popular support than their opponents, and the result was a bill that is generally regarded as a significant achievement for conservation.

International Environmental Decision Making

As mentioned previously, environmental decisions at the international level are conducted through conferences and conventions. However, some regional organizations also have environmental policy interests; often these organizations also serve as economic or strategic alliances such as the European Union (EU) and the Organization of American States (OAS). The most successful of these regional environmental efforts has been the United Nations' Regional Seas Program. Member nations that border many of these important seas, such as the Caribbean or Mediterranean, participate in multinational treaties designed to protect the sea from the overexploitation of its biotic resources and to reduce land-based pollution originating from the bordering nations. Relatively few conflicts arise inasmuch as every regional nation has a vested interest in protecting this shared common property resource. In many instances, regional alliances are more effective than global treaties in curtailing transboundary pollutants and the degradation of common property resources.

THE DECISION-MAKING PROCESS

The legislative process and diplomacy are not the only ways environmental law is made. For example, over 50 U.S. federal entities are involved in natural resources policy and decision making (Table 3.3). Many times overlapping jurisdictions, different goals, and antagonistic staffs result in interagency squabbling over the management of specific resources. There are also intra-agency conflicts between temporary political appointees who head the agencies and their professional civil servant staffs. How these agencies go about making decisions and implementing policy is crucial to our understanding of natural resources management, especially in the United States.

Nongovernmental organizations (NGOs) are not-for-profit entities that operate at national and international levels. Increasingly, NGOs are becoming a considerable force in environmental decision making. In the environmental area, their primary purpose is to improve the human condition and manage resources in a sustainable

Table 3.3   Federal Agencies with Major Responsibility for Environmental Policy or Management

Department of the Interior	Department of Defense
National Park Service	Army Corps of Engineers
Bureau of Land Management	Departments of Army, Navy, and Air Force
Fish and Wildlife Service	Department of Transportation
Biological Survey	Department of Labor
Geological Survey	Occupational Safety and Health Administration
Minerals Management Service	Department of Health and Human Services
Bureau of Reclamation	Food and Drug Administration
Surface Mining Reclamation and Enforcement	Environmental Protection Agency
Department of Agriculture	Executive Office of the President
Forest Service	Council on Environmental Quality
Natural Resources Conservation Service	Federal Emergency Management Agency
Farm Service Agency	Other Independent Agencies
Department of Commerce	Tennessee Valley Authority
National Oceanographic and Atmospheric Administration	Bonneville Power Commission
United States Coast Guard	Water Resources Council
Department of Energy	National Science Foundation/National Research Council/National Academy of Science
Federal Energy Regulatory Commission	Nuclear Regulatory Commission
National Center for Appropriate Technology	Great Lakes Basin Commission
Nuclear Waste Policy Act Project Office	

way. They apply pressure to government to act responsibly. In this way, they act like both special interests and social agents. Most NGOs were started in the 1980s, but a few were operating much earlier. Examples of NGOs include the Worldwide Fund for Nature, Catholic Relief Services, Rainforest Action Network, Greenpeace, and the Sierra Club.

Organizations

There are few differences between how organizations make decisions and how you do. Their decisions differ from yours only in scale and complexity. As we saw in the previous chapter, private industry makes decisions based on the "bottom line." Governmental and other public organizations are less motivated by profit margins. Instead, their decisions are usually made in response to human needs and require government efforts for implementation. Government agencies are influenced by the opinions of others, such as lobby groups or political action committees. In addition, these decisions can be influenced by the motivations and political philosophy that underlie the decision makers' choices. Finally, decisions will often be avoided because they are painful in terms of conflict between the governmental entity and the other groups or individuals. This results in nondecision, which in fact becomes a form of decision making. Non-decision making is more pervasive in the United States than most people realize (O'Riordan 1981).

In theory, responsible, objective decisions are possible, but in practice many factors bias both decision makers and their conclusions, resulting in less than perfect decisions. One of these factors is the constraint imposed by organizational tradition—we have always done things this way, and there is a tradition to maintain. Moreover, there are constraints imposed by bureaucratic procedures, such as the endless arguments between regional and home offices or between divisions of the same organization. Conflicts between regional offices of the EPA and Washington headquarters are well known. Some constraints on decisions also are imposed by the demands of the executive role. A decision maker may feel that she cannot show friendliness to subordinates, for it might be construed as a sign of weakness and would hamper negotiations with a lobbyist or other interest groups.

Perhaps one of the most important constraints is the lack of objective standards for assessing alternative outcomes, which can force the decision maker to be sympathetic to social and political pressures and special interests. Decision makers often rely on stereotypes, such as believing that the information of uneducated people is always unreliable, resulting in biased decisions. Bias can be introduced by an individual decision maker's cognition of his or her role and intuitive assessment of the likelihood of the success or failure of the chosen course of action. And, of course, decisions are often made with insufficient or imperfect information, particularly in the case of environmental contaminants.

Strategies

Given that we live in an imperfect world with many complexities, it is surprising that we have been able to make sound environmental decisions at all. Decision making in natural resources management is divided into three general categories: satisficing, incrementalism, and stress management. *Satisficing* is the consideration of two policy alternatives at a time, which are examined sequentially and compared to one another. The best choice is then selected from these two. The goal of the satisficing approach is to look for the course of action or alternative that is just good enough and meets a minimal set of requirements. This type of approach is cost-effective because the full range of alternatives is not researched, which would be too costly in time and money, thus, the collective resources of the decision maker or agency are used more efficiently. A negative aspect of this strategy is the limited range of alternatives from which to select the best choice. Satisficing is an appealing approach to managers because it is simple, and it is used in many other areas besides resource-use decision making.

Incrementalism is used when the problem or resource issue is not clearly defined or when there are conflicting goals, values, or objectives. Incremental decisions are made by "muddling through" as they come across an administrator's desk. Administrators may not know what is wanted, but they do know what should be avoided. As a result, incrementalism is not used to set broad policy guidelines as is the satisficing strategy, but rather to alleviate the shortcomings in the present policy in its day-to-day administration. This approach is regularly used to cope with the bureaucratic politics that often result in com-

Table 3.4   Selected Public Interest and Environmental Groups

Advocacy	Litigation
Clean Water Action Project	Environmental Defense Fund
Common Cause	Natural Resources Defense Council
Cousteau Society	The Public Citizen
Defenders of Wildlife	Public Interest Research Group
Ducks Unlimited	
Earth First!	Research/Education
Earth Island Institute	Center for Marine Conservation
Environmental Action Foundation	Center for Science in the Public Interest
Friends of the Earth	Center for the Study of Responsive Law
Fund for Animals	Center for Research on Endangered Plastic Pink Flamingos
Fund for Renewable Energy and the Environment	Citizen's Clearinghouse of Hazardous Waste
Greenpeace	Conservation Foundation
Izaak Walton League	Environmental Law Institute
League of Conservation Voters	Institute for Local Self Reliance
National Audubon Society	Population Reference Bureau
National Wildlife Federation	Resources for the Future
The Nature Conservancy	World Resources Institute
Physicians for Social Responsibility	WorldWatch
Planned Parenthood	
Rainforest Action Network	Industry
Sierra Club	American Petroleum Institute
Trout Unlimited	American Water Well Association
Union of Concerned Scientists	Atomic Industrial Forum
The Wilderness Society	Chemical Manufacturers Association
World Wildlife Fund	Edison Electric Institute
Zero Population Growth	Keep America Beautiful
	National Solid Waste Management Association

promising and shifting coalitions. Incrementally made decisions are often disjointed and seemingly contradictory, and reflect minute changes in policy.

The third strategy, *crisis management*, is the approach most commonly used in government today. Crisis management is the response to an issue once it becomes a critical problem. It begins with a seat-of-the-pants planning effort to come to grips with the looming impact of the problem, and policy is then determined on a piecemeal basis to deal with the immediate problem at hand. There may be little consideration of long-term effects in the rush to get something done quickly. For example, when it was realized that certain industries contributed to local air pollution, regulations were put into effect in the 1970s that required higher smokestacks so that the pollutants would not afflict nearby communities. In the long run, this decision led to larger negative impact, as these airborne pollutants contributed to the acid rain problem leading to major deforestation and water pollution problems hundreds of miles from the smokestacks. Thus, with crisis management choices, there is no time for a discussion of larger policy questions. All decisions must be made immediately and implemented as quickly as possible, with very little time to discuss all the alternatives or the implications of new rules and regulations. Unfortunately, many of our environmental regulatory agencies routinely operate in this fashion.

You might think that the cumulative effect of all these imperfections in the decision-making process would prevent good decisions from ever being made. Some might agree. In fact, however, with most decisions of this nature there is a wide range of opinion on how problems should be approached, and in most cases only a portion of the population could be completely satisfied with the result. That is, of course, the nature of the political process. But the important thing to recognize is that the push and pull of politics goes on at many levels of decision making—not just at election time. The administrator and enforcer are just as susceptible to the forces that sway decisions as is the legislator.

The Role of Public Interest

The public interest can be defined in many ways because there are many different "publics." At the international level, for example, who constitutes "the public" and what is the public interest? At the national level, perhaps these are easier questions to address, largely because of our penchant for opinion polls.

There are many types of public interest groups, each with a particular cause and management style. Some groups are conservative and work with lobbyists. Other groups are more radical and often take their message to the forest, oceans, or streets, wherever they can command media attention. Table 3.4 lists some of the different types of public interest environmental groups that are active today. This is not an exhaustive list but is provided simply to illustrate the diversity and abundance of different "public interests." It is important to understand that environmental groups make decisions just like any other organization and are subject to the same pressures and stresses. Just because it is the Sierra Club or the Natural Resources Defense Council does not mean that their decisions are perfect and unbiased. They operate just like any other organization or governmental agency.

Public opinion regarding environmental issues has always been strong, yet this support has not been translated into electoral power. In the last decade, in particular, the public has endorsed stronger environmental laws even if improved environmental quality means higher prices and costs (Dunlap 1987, Dunlap and Mertig 1992). Recent polls confirm the notion that public support for environmental protection remains high not only in the United States but in other countries as well (Dunlap et al. 1993).

Despite this overwhelming support, environmental issues still do not decide national elections. At the national level, this concern is often tapped by environmental activist groups that are able to mobilize public support and increase their membership and ultimate lobbying positions. During the early Reagan years, membership in many environmental organizations rose markedly, largely in response to Reagan's anti-environmental policies (Gottlieb 1994). The environment remained a hot political topic in the 1990s with the elections of President Clinton and Vice President Gore (a strong environmentalist). Even Congress was supportive until the environmental backlash of 1994. The attempt to reduce environmental regulations as part of Newt Gingrich's Contract with America was severely denounced by the American people who have maintained their pro-environment stance. As a result, the Republican Congress backed off and "rediscovered" environmental issues by the end of that congressional session. From the mid-1990s onward, however, environmental problems took a back seat to more pressing national problems such as the economy, health care, and crime (Kaufman 1994).

THE "NEW" ENVIRONMENTAL POLITICS

Two additional factors currently influence environmental decision making: the increased role of private industry as an environmental innovator; and the shift from top-down policies to more localized innovations.

In many countries, especially the United States, private businesses are the major environmental policy innovators. Take, for example, the ISO 14000 program that is a standardized compliance auditing system. ISO 14000 sets up a standardized reporting system so that companies can see whether their customers or vendors comply with a given country's environmental laws. ISO 14000 also sets up periodic third-party audits of vendors to monitor such compliance. For example, Levi Strauss, the blue jean manufacturer, buys denim from a variety of vendors, some in the United States, others in Singapore, Taiwan, and so forth. If one of these vendors is contaminating the environment in its stone washing (bleaching) process, for example, Levi Strauss (the parent organization), not the local vendor, is sued. In an effort to control product and environmental liability, then, many private industries have agreed to ISO 14000. While motivated by reducing their own liability, the private sector has actually helped local manufacturers comply with local environmental regulations, or else the big companies will simply take their business elsewhere. Obviously, this provides a strong incentive to follow the letter of the environmental law be it here in the United States or abroad.

The second factor is a shift from the top-down legislative approach in which Congress passes national laws and states adhere to them to a more bottom-up one in which individual states set policy that are ultimately nationalized. Compromise politics is especially important when governmental power is divided between two political parties. Nonetheless, one of the most significant legacies of the Reagan administration was to shift environmental responsibility from the federal government to state and local governments. The result was a fundamental transformation in how laws are made in the United States. Beset by inactivity at the national level, state legislators devised their own laws to tackle pollution issues within their state but not exclusive to them. For example, in 1987 legislators in Sacramento, California, insisted that refiners change the mix of ingredients in gasoline to inhibit evaporation since these vapor fumes were a major source of hydrocarbons in Southern California. New York, New Jersey, and the six states in New England followed suit a year later. By 1989 the EPA announced a major national program for controlling evaporation of unburned fuel. California is clearly the policy innovator for clean air legislation, for it has the worst air quality in the nation and hence the greatest need to clean it up. Another innovative state is New Jersey, which experienced the garbage crisis before anyone else. In response to the mounds of solid waste generated daily by its residents, the state developed a comprehensive recycling master plan that mandates the recycling of 25 percent of the municipal solid waste stream. This program has become a model for the rest of the nation.

Why are these interstate problems being solved at the state rather than the national level?

Some point to the fact that many states have such severe pollution problems (e.g., Los Angeles smog) that they cannot wait for Washington to act. As a consequence, if California acts and doesn't fall flat on its face, other states may adopt California's programs. In addition, aggressive national lobbyists don't often frequent state houses, which means that the likelihood of passing a controversial piece of legislation (meaning one that industry does not favor) is greater at the state than the national level. Finally, some argue that state legislators are more in tune with political change and thus more responsive to local environmental concerns. This immediately translates voter support for environmental concerns into political action. The trend at the national level is less clear.

As we have tried to convey in this chapter, natural resource policy is determined by choices and compromise. There is no right or wrong policy, nor is there a good or bad one. To render these subjective evaluations depends on your own perspective and role in the decision-making process.

References and Additional Reading

Carson, R. L. 1962. *The Silent Spring*. Boston: Houghton Mifflin.

Commoner, B. 1966. *Science and Survival*. New York: Viking Press.

Consortium on International Earth Science Information Network (CIESIN). 1997. Web page for their international treaties (ENTRI): http://www.ciesin.org/entri

Council on Environmental Quality (CEQ). 1980. *Environmental Quality: The Eleventh Annual Report*. Washington, DC: U.S. Government Printing Office.

_____ . 1986. *Environmental Quality: The Seventeenth Annual Report*. Washington, DC: U.S. Government Printing Office.

Cronon, W. 1984. *Changes in the Land: Indians, Colonists and the Ecology of New England*. New York: Hill & Wang.

Dilsaver, L. M., and C. E. Colten, eds. 1992. *The American Environment*. Lanham, MD: Rowman & Littlefield.

Dunlap, R. 1987. Polls, pollution, and politics revisited: Public opinion on the environment in the Reagan era. *Environment* 29(6): 6–11, 32–37.

_____ . 1992. Trends in public opinion toward environmental issues: 1965–1990. In R. E. Dunlap and A. G.

Mertig, eds. 1992. *American Environmentalism: The U.S. Environmental Movement 1970–1990.* New York: Taylor & Francis, pp. 89–116.

_____ , G. H. Gallup, Jr., and A. M. Gallup, 1992. Of global concern: Results of the health of the planet survey. *Environment* 35 (9): 6–15, 33–39.

Easterbrook, G. 1995. *A Moment on the Earth: The Coming Age of Environmental Optimism.* New York: Viking Press.

Flavin, C. 1997. The legacy of Rio. In L. R. Brown et al., eds., *State of the World 1987.* Washington, DC: Worldwatch Institute, pp. 3–22..

Gore, A. 1992. *Earth in the Balance: Ecology and the Human Spirit.* Boston: Houghton Mifflin.

Gotlieb, R. 1994. *Forcing the Spring.* Washington, DC: Island Press.

Haas, P. M., M. A. Levy, and E. A. Parson. 1992. How should we judge UNCED's success? *Environment* 34 (8): 6–11, 26–33.

Hardin, G. 1985. *Filters Against Folly.* New York: Penguin Books.

Hempel, L. C. 1996. *Environmental Governance: The Global Challenge.* Washington, DC: Island Press.

Huth, H. 1957. *Nature and the American: Three Centuries of Changing Attitudes.* Berkeley: University of California Press.

Jordan, A. 1994. Paying the incremental costs of global environmental protection: The evolving role of GEF. *Environment* 36 (6): 12–20, 31–36.

Kamieniecki, S., ed. 1993. *Environmental Politics in the International Arena: Movements, Parties, Organizations, and Policy.* Albany, NY: SUNY Press.

Kaufman, W. 1994. *No Turning Back: Dismantling the Fantasies of Environmental Thinking.* New York: Basic Books.

Lainre, R. D., and T. A. Barron. 1988. The environmental agenda for the next administration. *Environment* 30(4): 16–20, 28–29.

Leopold, A. 1949. *A Sand County Almanac and Sketches Here and There.* New York: Oxford University Press.

McKibben, B. 1989. *The End of Nature.* New York: Random House.

Marsh, G. P. 1864. *Man and Nature, or Physical Geography as Modified by Human Action.* New York: Scribner.

Murphy, Al. 1994. International law and the sovereign state: Challenges to the status quo. In G. J. Demko and W. B. Wood, eds., *Reordering the World: Geopolitical Perspectives on the 21st Century.* Boulder, CO.: Westview Press, pp. 209–224.

Nash, R. 1982. *Wilderness and the American Mind,* rev. ed. New Haven: Yale University Press.

Nicholson, M. 1970. *The Environmental Revolution: A Guide for the New Masters of the World.* New York: McGraw-Hill.

O'Riordan, T. 1981. *Environmentalism.* London: Pion.

_____ , and R. K. Turner. 1983. *An Annotated Reader in Environmental Planning and Management.* Oxford: Pergamon Press.

Paarlberg, R. L. 1996. A domestic dispute: Clinton, Congress, and international environmental policy. *Environment* 38 (8): 16–20, 28–33.

Parson, E. A., P. M. Haas, and M. A. Levy. 1992. A summary of the major documents signed at the Earth Summit and Global Forum. *Environment* 34 (8): 12–15, 34–36.

Pepper, D. 1996. *Modern Environmentalism.* New York: Routledge.

Porter, G., and J. W. Brown. 1996. *Global Environmental Politics, 2nd ed.* Boulder, CO: Westview Press.

Simmons, I. G. 1989. *Changing the Face of the Earth: Culture, Environment, and History.* Oxford: Basil Blackwell.

Susskind, L. E. 1994. *Environmental Diplomacy: Negotiating More Effective Global Agreements.* New York: Oxford University Press.

Swem, T., and R. Cahn. 1983. The politics of parks in Alaska. *Ambio* 12: 14–19.

Tolba, M. K. et al. 1992. *The World Environment 1972–1992.* New York: Chapman & Hall.

Turner, B. L., and K. W. Butzer. 1992. The Columbian encounter and land use change. *Environment* 34 (8): 16–20, 37–44.

_____ , W. C. Clark, R. W. Kates, J. F. Richards, J. T. Matthews, and W. B. Myers, eds. 1990. *The Earth as Transformed by Human Action.* Cambridge: Cambridge University Press.

Udall, S. 1963. *The Quiet Crisis.* New York: Holt, Rinehart.

United Nations. 1992. *Agenda 21: Programme of Action for Sustainable Development.* New York: United Nations.

Vale, T. R., ed. 1986. *Progress Against Growth: Daniel B. Luten on the American Landscape.* New York: Guilford Press.

Wood, W. B., G. J. Demko, and P. Motson. 1989. Ecopolitics in the global greenhouse. *Environment* 31(7): 12–17, 32–34.

World Commission on Environment and Development (WCED). 1987. *Our Common Future.* Oxford: Oxford University Press.

Worster, D. E. 1979. *Dust Bowl: The Southern Plains in the 1930s.* Oxford: Oxford University Press.

_____ , 1993. *The Wealth of Nature: Environmental History and the Ecological Imagination.* New York: Oxford University Press.

For more information consult our web page at *http://www.wiley.com/college/cutter*

STUDY QUESTIONS

1. The phrase "Think globally, act locally" has taken on new meaning in the past decade. What kinds of actions can you take in your local area that might ultimately lead to some reduction in global consumption or pollution?

2. What are the major differences between international environmental policies and those developed for individual countries?

3. How have the following laws/treaties/conventions shaped natural resource policies over the last two decades?
   (a) NEPA
   (b) Homestead Act
   (c) Nuclear Test Ban Treaty
   (d) Stockholm Conference
   (e) Superfund

4. Go and visit your local city or town government meeting when officials are holding discussions on an environmental issue. How do they make decisions? How does it compare to what goes on nationally? How is their decision-making process different from yours?

5. Who are the important stakeholders in your area who influence environmental policy? In what ways is this influence manifested?

CHAPTER 4

ECOLOGIC PERSPECTIVES ON NATURAL RESOURCES

Natural resources, by definition, are produced by natural processes. Some resources such as metal ores or fossil fuels were produced by processes operating millions of years ago and in human time scales are essentially fixed. But most of the natural resources that we depend on today are continually being produced and replenished. Resource use that is truly sustainable in the long run must be based on these renewable resources. An ecological perspective on natural resources focuses on the role of natural processes in sustaining human activity rather than on human controlled processes.

An ecological view of resource management is also a nature-centered view. As discussed in Chapter 1, this view holds that:

- Nature has inherent value.
- Natural processes provide us with many, if not all, of the resources on which we depend.
- We have an obligation to future generations of humans to leave them with an environment that is at least as healthy, productive, and diverse as the one we have inherited.

If natural processes are the basis of resource use, and if we are to preserve the integrity of these processes to achieve sustainability, then we must learn to use resources in such a way that the basic structure of natural systems remains unaltered. This requires considerable knowledge of these natural systems. Although some may argue that we can never adequately understand nature in all its complexity, we can benefit from a careful description and analysis of nature.

This chapter introduces the basic concepts for an ecological perspective on natural resources, which derives from the scientific study of natural processes operating on Earth's surface. We will first summarize the physical environments that exist on the planet, their extent, and our use of them. We will then describe a few of the processes that function in these environments to create and maintain the resources we use. Finally, we will examine some of the ecological consequences of the enormous burden humans are placing on Earth's natural resource systems.

EARTH'S RESOURCE ENVIRONMENTS

The heart of the study of *ecology* is the interrelationship between animals and plants and the living and nonliving components and processes that make up their environment. This is why the study of ecological systems is so basic to the conservation of natural resources. Without an understanding of how natural systems work, we cannot begin to conserve, manage, and protect them.

An *ecosystem* is a system in which matter and energy are exchanged among organisms and with the larger environment. The ecosystem receives inputs of energy and material, which are stored, utilized, or flow through the ecosystem and leave as outputs. Interaction between the physical environment of the Los Angeles basin and the human patterns imposed on it produces a complex picture of inputs and outputs (Fig. 4.1). In this urban ecosystem, inputs include raw materials and

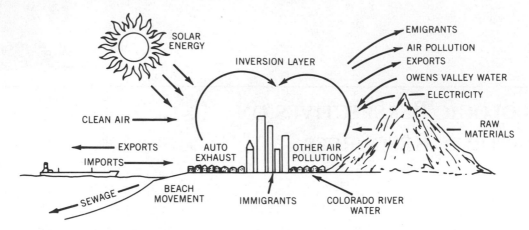

Figure 4.1 An urban ecosystem. This simplified and idealized model of the Los Angeles urban ecosystem shows some of the physical, social, and economic inputs and outputs.

other imports, migration of new residents, relatively clean Pacific air, water supplies, and electric power. Within greater Los Angeles, products are created for export, such as air pollution, and emigrants move on in search of other opportunities. This diagram is a simplification and presents only a few of the major elements that make up the input-output model of an urban ecosystem.

An ecosystem can encompass a large or small geographic area and usually consists of several organisms whose needs and requirements are complementary, so that the available resources are used in a stable and nondepleting fashion. It can be difficult to define the precise boundaries of an ecosystem, for organisms are often participants in more than one. *Ecotones* or transitional zones are the more flexible alternative to outlining a sharp boundary. Within a single ecosystem, researchers tend to separate the plants and animals into *communities*, which consist of groups of interacting local populations. Finally, the ecologist can examine the individual organism's function in this larger system.

Although much of the research on ecosystems has focused on small scales such as individual communities or relatively homogeneous ecological regions, there is growing recognition that the entire Earth may be viewed as a single environmental system. Events occurring in one area may have such far-reaching impacts as to be essentially global in nature. For example, deforestation in the Amazon basin and other tropical areas is a significant contributor to the worldwide increase in atmospheric carbon dioxide content, which could lead to global climatic changes. Fluctuations in ocean circulation in the eastern Pacific were recognized as a factor in the decline of the Peruvian anchovy fishery in the 1960s, but now we also recognize that these events play a major role in weather patterns throughout the Earth. The explosion at the nuclear reactor at Chernobyl in the Soviet Union in 1986 spewed a plume of radioactive pollutants that spread across most of Europe and was detected at monitoring stations around the world.

The integrated nature of the world environmental system is the basis of the *Gaia hypothesis*, a controversial but stimulating view of the Earth (Lovelock 1979). The Gaia hypothesis suggests that the Earth functions as a unified, self-regulating ecological system that has internal feedback mechanisms not unlike those of a single organism. For example, changes in carbon dioxide content may cause changes in rates of plant photosynthesis, which in turn will remove carbon dioxide from the atmosphere.

Bioregions

One way to look at the world's land resources is in terms of their general ecological characteristics. A region's resources and environmental capabilities are closely tied to the basic characteristics of its ecosystems, which are themselves related to the prevailing geologic, topographic, soil, and climatic environment. Ecological regions, or *biore-gions*, can serve as a valuable framework for environmental management decisions—a framework that is based primarily on natural resources rather than their use by humans, although human factors can be combined with natural ones in classifying resource areas. The explanation for delimiting bioregions is that they form a rational basis for resource assessment and management decisions. Such regions have a certain amount of internal homogeneity, and presumably similar policies should be applied within them, whereas different ecological areas may demand different policies. Unfortunately, political boundaries usually have little correspondence to natural ones, and it is often more expedient to base resource management strategies on the political map than on the ecological map. But at somewhat smaller scales, within nations or cooperating groups of nations, bioregions offer considerable potential for guiding the management process.

Ecosystems are also useful to the researcher because they are large enough to be a reasonably representative slice of the environment, yet not so large as to be unmanageable. Ecosystems are themselves ultimately part of larger systems. At the broadest level is the *biosphere*, the worldwide envelope of organic and inorganic substances within which all life functions. Envision the millions of tiny and large ecosystems that make up the biosphere, and try to comprehend the awesome complexity of the interactions and "meshing of gears" that have developed over billions of years so that this global system can function smoothly.

The concept of *biome* helps us make sense of the patterns of interaction between plants, animals, and the physical environment. A biome is a major ecological unit within which plant and animal communities are broadly similar, both in their general characteristics and in their relations to each other and to the physical environment. Because biomes are defined on the basis of organism-environment interactions, it is within each of the world's major biomes that the researcher can make sense of individual ecosystems.

Figure 4.2 is a map of the major world biomes. Looking first at the equator, we see that the equatorial or tropical rainforest is an exuberant response to a rainfall schedule that is year-round and frequent, with little variation in day length or seasonal change. The resulting vegetation cover is a complex array of broad-leaved evergreens, trees that constantly shed some leaves but are never bare. A larger diversity of species is found in the rainforest than anywhere else. For example, an acre of forest in the northeastern United States might sustain five to ten tree species, whereas an acre of tropical rainforest might yield several times that many. In addition, tropical species are often unique to only a very small area of rainforest, unlike their northern counterparts, which are found over a very wide geographic area. Tropical rainforests straddle the equator, with the largest areas found in the Amazon basin (Brazil), in Indonesia and the Southeast Asian peninsula, and in Africa's Congo basin.

South and north from the equator we find a seasonally drier climate and a correspondingly less heavily vegetated biome called *savanna*, which occurs near latitude 25 degrees north and south, notably in Africa, South America, and Southeast Asia. Most savanna is located in the tropical wet and dry climate zone and is characterized by heavy summer rainfall and an almost completely dry winter season. The characteristic vegetation varies from open woodland with grass cover to open grassland with scattered deciduous trees (Fig. 4.3). Researchers generally agree that much of Africa's savanna is derived not from natural processes but from the human use of fire. If this is true, savanna is perhaps the oldest of human-shaped landscapes.

The dry climates that produce the desert biome are found in two locations worldwide: in the subtropical latitudes as the result of high-pressure zones and in the midlatitudes in continental interiors far from ocean moisture. Deserts vary from the cartoon image of bare rock and blowing sand dunes where no rainfall is recorded year after year to areas with shrubs and 100 to 300 mm of rain a year. *Potential evapotranspiration*, or the amount of water that would be evaporated or transpired if it were available, is much higher, leading to a water deficit. Desert vegetation consists of plants with special structural adaptations that enable them to store moisture, to retain it under waxy leaves, and to search for it via long root systems. These species complete their brief life cycles during the short rainy season.

The subtropical deserts are the largest on Earth and include the Sahara Desert, which stretches across Africa eastward to join the Arabian, Iranian, Afghani, and Pakistani deserts. Other sub-

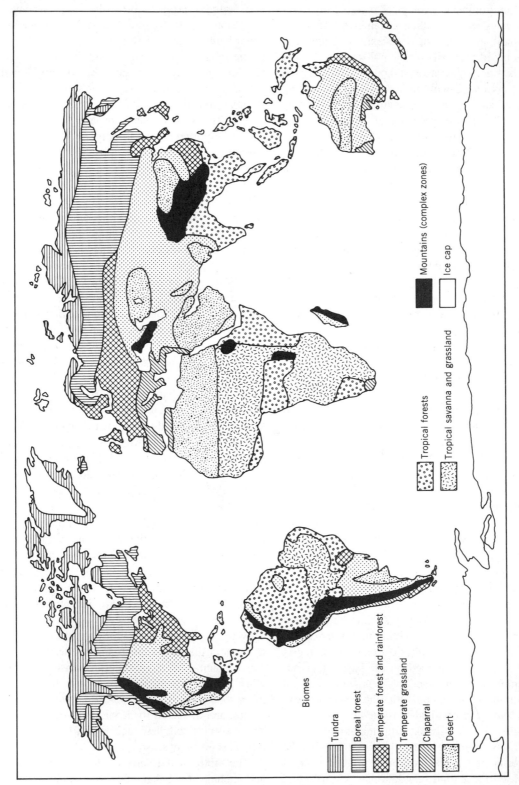

Figure 4.2 The world's major biomes. The broad geographical distribution illustrates the diversity of ecosystems found throughout the world.

Biomes

Tundra
Boreal forest
Temperate forest and rainforest
Temperate grassland
Chaparral
Desert

Mountains (complex zones)
Ice cap
Tropical forests
Tropical savanna and grassland

Figure 4.3 Tropical savanna in the Serengeti Plains of Tanzania. This landscape has been influenced by humans for many thousands of years, but today human exploitation is being limited so that the remaining wild animal populations can be preserved.

tropical deserts are found in the southwestern United States, northern Mexico, Australia, Chile, Peru, and southern Africa. Continental deserts are found in the interiors of Northern Hemisphere continents: between the Caspian and Aral seas in the former Soviet Union, the Gobi Desert in Mongolia, and between the Rocky Mountains and the Sierra-Cascade Ranges in the United States.

The Mediterranean biome is named after the region that stretches around the Mediterranean Sea, characterized by a cool, moist winter and a hot, dry summer. Typical vegetation consists of a thorny, glossy, and sometimes impenetrable mass of fire-prone species called *chaparral*. Mediterranean climate and chaparral are found in other coastal locations between 30 and 45 degrees latitude north and south of the equator, including coastal Southern California, Chile, South America, and parts of southern Australia.

The midlatitude *grasslands* are found at 30 degrees north and south latitude in semiarid interior areas. With not quite enough moisture to support trees and shrubs, these fire-prone grasslands once stretched from Texas to Alberta and Saskatchewan in North America, before being put to the plow in the nineteenth and twentieth centuries. Ecologists sometimes half-jokingly refer to the ecosystem that replaced the grass-

lands in the central United States as the corn–hog biome. The grasslands of South America in Argentina and Uruguay also have been converted to agricultural development. The grassland steppes of Asia extend from the Ukraine east as far as Manchuria in China.

The vast midlatitude or *temperate forests* (Fig. 4.4) once stretched from 30 to 50 degrees north and south latitude across the eastern United States, much of northwestern Europe, eastern China, Japan, and small areas of South America, Australia, and New Zealand. With the colonization and population growth of the last several centuries, much of this deciduous (in the United States) and mixed deciduous/evergreen (in Europe) woodland cover has been removed. The characteristic climate of this region is cold winters and warm summers, with average annual precipitation generally equal to or greater than potential evapotranspiration.

The *boreal*, or northern coniferous forest, biome is located between 50 and 60 degrees north latitude (there being no significant land mass at this latitude south of the equator). In contrast to the diversity of the tropical rainforest, the number of species in this biome is extremely limited. These woodlands stretch in a belt across Alaska, Canada, and as far south as the northern portions

Figure 4.4 A stand of old-growth broadleaf deciduous forest in the Nicolet National Forest of Wisconsin. Much of this biome, especially in North America and Europe, has been either replaced by agriculture or significantly altered by harvesting in the last few hundred years. Old-growth stands like the one in this photo are rare.

of Michigan, New York, and New England in North America. In Europe this belt continues across Scandinavia and Russia. The vegetation cover is dominated by fir, spruce, pine, and larch, which have thick needles and bark to withstand the cold. In the far north, trees only one meter high may be one hundred or more years old.

At this tree line boundary the *tundra* biome begins, generally poleward of 60 degrees north and south latitude. The average temperature of the growing season does not exceed 50 degrees for more than a few weeks, which prohibits tree growth. Much of this area is underlain by permafrost, or permanently frozen ground. With low precipitation, the tundra is often called a frozen desert; in its brief thaw, like the warm deserts, a low and colorful mat of shrubs, mosses, lichens and grasses temporarily springs up. The tundra region contains substantial storages of carbon, which may be released if climate warms substantially.

The preceding descriptions present a highly simplified picture of a complex patterning of biomes. There are numerous exceptions to the commonly occurring biomes, caused by microclimate, soil variability, and human impact. The main point to note is that vegetation and climate have interacted over millions of years, resulting in adaptive vegetation patterns. We should remember that substantial portions of these biomes have been altered by the work of humanity, and that is the cause of much discussion and dissent among those who would conserve and those who would develop and alter the landscape.

Human Use of the Land

The land area of the world (excluding Antarctica) totals about 13 billion hectares (Fig. 4.5). The best data on world land use are provided by the Food and Agriculture Organization (FAO) of the United Nations. The FAO classifies land as *arable* (land that is capable of producing crops through cultivated agriculture), permanent pasture (land that is suitable and available for grazing animals, regardless of the dominant vegetation type), forest and woodland, and other (including parks, urban areas, roads, deserts, and other nonagricultural areas). Based on this classification, about 11 percent of the world's land is used for arable agriculture and another 26 percent for permanent pasture. Thirty-two percent of the world is in forest and woodland, while 31 percent is in other uses. The continents vary considerably in the proportions of land in these uses. For example, Oceania, Africa, and South America are only about 6 percent arable whereas Asia and North/Central America have between 13 and 16 percent arable land (World Resources Institute 1996). Europe's arable land increased from 5 to 26 percent between 1990 and 1994, not because of agricultural land conversion, but because of the reclassification of Russia. This statistical artifact (see Issue 4.1) is complicating our understanding of longer term trends at the continental scale.

The portion of land in each of these uses is changing (Table 4.1). During the last decade, minor but significant increases took place in the amount of arable land: an increase of about 1.3 percent worldwide. The largest increases were in Africa, South America, Asia, and Oceania. The increases in arable land were caused by expansion of cultivation into areas that were previously forested to meet the food demands of a rising population (see Chapter 6). In the wealthier parts

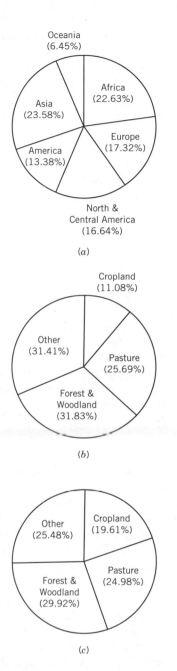

Oceania
(6.45%)

Asia
(23.58%)

Africa
(22.63%)

Europe
(17.32%)

America
(13.38%)

North &
Central America
(16.64%)

(a)

Cropland
(11.08%)

Other
(31.41%)

Pasture
(25.69%)

Forest &
Woodland
(31.83%)

(b)

Other
(25.48%)

Cropland
(19.61%)

Pasture
(24.98%)

Forest &
Woodland
(29.92%)

(c)

Figure 4.5 World land area and land use, excluding Antarctica. (*a*) Land areas of the continents. (*b*) Use of the world's land area. (*c*) Use of land in the United States. *Source:* World Resources Institute 1996.

of the world (North America and Europe), the amount of arable land decreased. In much of the world, especially Africa, South America, and Asia, forest cover has been declining while permanent pasture has been increasing. This is a re-

sult of forests being cleared for grazing or arable agriculture. Estimates of the total amount of change vary, but generally forest cover decreased about 1 to 4 percent during the 1980s. The fact that woodlands are being cleared to make way for cultivation indicates that agriculture is being forced onto poorer and poorer land, with concomitant increases in problems of erosion, unfavorable moisture conditions, poor fertility, and so on. The amount of land in "other" uses changed little overall, but locally significant changes occurred as a result of urban development, land degradation, and the establishment of large areas for parks and wildlife reserves.

The total land area of the United States is 957 million hectares. This consists of about 20 percent cropland, 25 percent pasture and range, 30 percent forest, and 25 percent other. This land-use pattern has undergone many changes since the Europeans arrived in North America. Obviously, little cropland existed prior to European settlement, and there was substantially more forest. Most of the forest clearance took place during the eighteenth and nineteenth centuries, and forest area reached a minimum in the late 1800s or early 1900s—earlier along the eastern seaboard and later in the central and western states. As settlement and agriculture spread westward from the early 1600s to the 1920s, forestlands in the east were cleared and tall-grass prairie was plowed under. Land that wasn't cleared for farming or pasture was cleared for other purposes, usually to provide fuel and building materials. But as the productivity of agriculture grew in the nineteenth century, eastern lands less suitable for farming were abandoned and gradually reverted to woodland, so that much of the eastern United States today is reforested. But the tall-grass prairie of the eastern plains and most of the forest of the central states have been replaced by farms; thus, what was once oak forest or grassland is now fields of corn, soybeans, and wheat.

In addition to this dramatic land-use change, there have been equally drastic changes covering smaller areas such as natural preserves, cities, and other developed areas. Urban lands now occupy about 6 percent of the country, and transportation uses occupy another one percent. Reservoirs also have taken substantial areas. The amount of land in urban uses continues to increase at about 1.3 percent per year (CEQ 1994).

Rural areas are also being committed to new uses, most importantly as parks and wildlife areas. National Parks occupy over 3 percent of the land area of the United States, and national wildlife refuges and designated wilderness areas each cover an additional 8 percent of the nation's land (CEQ 1994).

About a third of the land in the United States is publicly owned. In areas of the eastern United States that were territories in the original British colonies, the British government granted land to various companies and private individuals or the states granted land as payment for military ser-vice. Almost all the land in the east has been in private hands since the late eighteenth century. But most of the land west of the Mississippi River (excluding Texas) was acquired by the U.S. government by treaty or purchase. Through homesteading, grants to railroads, and other means, most of the more productive land came under private ownership, mostly in the second half of the nineteenth century. But semiarid and arid areas and high mountain areas that were not desirable for agriculture remained unclaimed into the early twentieth century. Many of the moun-tainous areas were reserved as National Forests,

---

ISSUE 4.1: WHAT HAPPENS WHEN THE GEOGRAPHY CHANGES?

The rise of democratic republics in the aftermath of the fall of the communist empire has pro-foundly altered world affairs. The Soviet Union no longer exists; in its place we have 15 independent countries. Czechoslovakia is now Slovakia and the Czech Republic. When the United Nations was formed in 1945, there were 51 members states; in 1989 there were 157; and today there are 182.

What do these geopolitical changes have to do with conservation of natural resources? The sim-ple answer is everything! Most of the compara-tive statistics on population, economics, and the environment are reported by individual country. In 1989 the total land area of the Soviet Union was 2190 hectares. Because the Soviet Union no longer existed as a separate political entity in 1990, the statistics on land area were divided among its successor states, of which Russia is the largest (1699 hectares). Although the total amount of land hasn't changed at all, the way we politically carve it up and report data on it has.

This change in how we report statistical data also affects continental comparisons. Both the United Nations and the World Resources Institute report individual country and continental aver-ages. The Soviet Union spanned two continents, so which continent gets allocated what land? In the statistical reports, Russia, Belarus, Estonia, Latvia, Lithuania, Moldova, and the Ukraine are categorized as being in Europe, whereas Armenia, Azerbaijan, Georgia, Kazakhstan, Kyrgyz Repub-lic, Tajikistan, Turkmenistan, and Uzbekistan are listed as being in Asia.

One of our biggest headaches in this regard in-volves comparing countries or continents over some period of time. For example, if we try to ex-amine changes in arable land from 1980 to 1995 (see Table 4.1), the task becomes very difficult. In order to compare the 1995 and 1980 data, we must sum all the individual country-level data and gen-eralize to the old geography. If we parcel out the 1980 data to individual countries, the original data may not be available. While we may already be convinced that geography matters in natural re-sources and environmental issues, perhaps now we can really appreciate just how important it really is.

In addition to the impacts of these geographic changes on statistical trends, the economic collapse of the Soviet Union and eastern Europe had far-reaching consequences for the world resource trends. For example, the steady increase of total world carbon dioxide emissions was halted in 1989, and total emissions remained relatively steady be-tween 1989 and 1994. Emissions were increasing in most of the world, but the dramatic drop in coal combustion that took place in Russia and eastern Europe was enough that in some years world totals actually declined. Similarly, a dramatic decrease in grain production in the former Soviet Union in the early 1990s was enough to significantly reduce world grain supplies. We will discuss these trends in more detail in later chapters of this book.

Table 4.1 World Land Use, 1970–1994 (in millions of hectares)

	Africa	North & Central America	South America	Asia	Europe	Oceania	USSR	Total
Land area 1994	2963	2137	1753	3085	2260	849	0	13048
(% of world)	23	16	13	24	17	7	0	100
Land area 1990	2964	2137	1753	2678	473	849	2190	13044
(% of world)	23	16	13	21	4	7	0	100
Arable land 1994	190	274	115	520	316	52	0	1467
(% of region)	6	13	7	17	14	6	0	11
Arable land 1990	187	273	111	472	139	53	229	1463
(% of region)	6	13	6	18	29	6	10	11
Arable land 1985	180	274	105	461	140	52	232	1445
(% of region)	6	13	6	17	30	6	11	11
Arable land 1980	175	274	101	456	141	49	232	1427
(% of region)	6	13	6	17	30	6	11	11
Arable land 1970	165	269	82	448	146	46	233	1389
(% of region)	6	13	5	17	31	5	11	11
Permanent pasture 1994	884	366	495	1047	179	429	0	3399
(% of region)	30	17	28	34	8	50	0	26
Permanent pasture 1990	901	364	494	798	82	430	327	3397
(% of region)	30	17	28	30	17	51	15	26
Permanent pasture 1985	890	364	484	741	84	440	326	3331
(% of region)	30	17	28	28	18	52	15	26
Permanent pasture 1980	894	358	475	694	86	453	322	3283
(% of region)	30	17	27	26	18	53	15	25
Permanent pasture 1970	893	357	451	650	89	453	315	3208
(% of region)	30	17	26	24	19	53	14	25
Forest/woodland 1994	713	824	932	557	947	200	0	4172
(% of region)	24	39	53	18	42	24	0	32
Forest/woodland 1990	717	824	945	532	158	201	942	4319
(%ofregion)	24	39	54	20	33	24	43	33
Forest/woodland 1985	715	800	931	538	156	201	929	4269
(% of region)	24	37	53	20	33	24	42	33
Forest/woodland 1980	727	807	927	552	155	201	929	4298
(% of region)	25	38	53	21	33	24	42	33
Forest/woodland 1970	732	831	925	580	150	201	913	4333
(% of region)	25	39	53	22	32	24	42	33
Other land 1994	1177	673	212	962	818	161	0	4003
(% of region)	40	32	12	31	36	19	0	31
Other land 1990	1158	676	203	876	94	165	692	3864
(% of region)	39	32	12	33	20	19	32	30
Other land 1985	1177	699	233	939	92	156	704	3999
(% of region)	40	33	13	35	19	18	32	31
Other land 1980	1167	699	249	976	90	146	708	4036
(% of region)	39	33	14	36	19	17	32	31
Other land 1970	1173	680	294	1000	88	149	729	4113
(% of region)	40	32	17	37	19	18	33	32

Source: Food and Agricultural Organization, 1996.

and so most federally owned land consists of these arid and mountainous areas in the western United States. Almost 30 percent of U.S. land is in federal ownership, another 10 percent is state owned or owned by Native Americans, and the remaining 60 percent is in private hands (U.S. Bureau of the Census 1997).

Land-use decisions are probably the most important single issue in environmental management, for land use essentially defines what kinds of resources we exploit and the extent of environmental impact associated with our activities. If a parcel of land is used for agriculture, then not only does this contribute to our total food production but it also means that runoff from that land will contain certain byproducts of agriculture (sediment, nutrients, and pesticides) in nonpoint water pollution. The use of a land parcel for one purpose has implications for other parcels: urban growth may mean a demand for recreational lands nearby or the need for watershed protection in other areas to supply a growing population with drinking water.

In most of the world, land-use decisions are made through some process of balancing competing interests. In market economies, allocation of land among various uses is generally determined by the relative income that can be generated at any given time. Agricultural land near cities is sold for urban development because those uses generate greater profits for the landowner than agriculture. Similarly, farmers shift land among crops, pasture, and other uses depending on production costs and the return on investment for various commodities.

Governments play a role in this process. Public interests are served by the allocation of land to transportation, parks, water resources, defense, and similar common needs. In most countries, patterns as well as types of land uses are regulated. In the United States this regulation is accomplished by zoning laws, usually at the local level, which are generally designed to separate incompatible uses, such as industry and residences. Land-use regulations also help ensure adequate open space, such as through the designation of greenbelt areas around cities, and for environmental protection as in restrictions on development in wetland areas and prohibition of waste disposal on floodplains.

As populations grow and land becomes more scarce, competition for land resources and the intensity of debates over land-use decisions inevitably increase. Many examples of such problems exist, ranging from the restriction of oil exploration or timber harvesting from wildlife refuges to local debates over where to locate a sewage treatment plant.

ENERGY TRANSFERS AND MATERIAL FLOWS

Energy in ecosystems (and human systems) is ultimately derived from the sun. This energy passes through a series of storages via many paths, before finally being returned to space as radiant energy. Two fundamental laws govern all energy transfers: the first and second laws of thermodynamics.

The *first law of thermodynamics* is the *law of conservation of energy*, but it also governs conversion of matter into energy. It simply states that in any energy transfer, the total amount of energy is unchanged; energy is neither created nor destroyed. Another way of saying this is, "You can't get more out than you put in." The second law is called the *law of entropy*, and it is a little less obvious than the first. It states that any time energy is converted from one form to another, the conversion is inefficient. Energy is always converted to a less concentrated form or dissipated as heat. Another way of saying this is, "Not only is it impossible to get more out than you put in, but you can't even break even." Entropy is a measure of the degree of organization present. Greater entropy means greater disorganization or randomness. The following two examples may help to illustrate these concepts.

The first example is the conversion of solar energy to food energy by *photosynthesis*, producing all the food needed to feed humans and other organisms. A leaf on a plant is exposed to sunlight, and this stimulates a chemical reaction in which carbon dioxide and water are converted to carbohydrates, with oxygen given off as a byproduct. In the process, however, the leaf must be heated, causing a loss of energy by radiation or convection from the leaf surface. In addition, water must be moved through the leaf stem to deliver nutrients to the leaf and is also evaporated by the leaf as a cooling mechanism. This water loss involves a conversion of water from liquid to vapor form, which requires energy. Finally, plants must also respire. Respiration is a process in which food energy is converted to heat energy, which is then dissipated. When all these things are considered together in an energy budget for a single plant or for an entire plant community, only a very small fraction of the incoming solar energy is converted to food energy or biomass, generally about 1 percent or less. The rest of the energy is reflected, reradiated, or used in the conversion of liquid water to water vapor.

A coal-fired electric-generating plant provides a second example. Coal is formed by the chemical modification of formerly living matter, mostly plants. The energy released was first stored by plant photosynthesis at some time in the geologic past. When the coal is burned, some heat is lost in the smokestack, but most of the heat is used to convert water to steam. The steam then drives turbines, which drive generators, which in turn produce electricity. The steam is cooled in the process but not enough to condense it, although it must be returned to the boiler as water. To do this it must be cooled, usually by dissipating the heat in the nearest river or other body of water. Heat is also produced by the generator and by friction in moving parts, and this must be dissipated as well. In the end, only about 35 percent of all the heat stored in the coal is finally converted to electric energy. The rest is dissipated as heat, either in the stack gases or in the steam condensing system. This dissipation of energy is an example of entropy.

Just as energy flows through an ecosystem in a cyclic manner, so do materials necessary for life—carbon, oxygen, nitrogen, potassium, water, and many others. The paths these substances take in the environment are called *biogeochemical cycles*. Some biogeochemical cycles are dominated by large storages in the atmosphere; the nitrogen cycle is a good example of this type. Others are dominated by terrestrial storages, usually in rocks and sediment. The phosphorus, potassium, sulfur, and calcium cycles are examples of this latter type. Although the cycles differ because of the different chemical and biological processes regulating them, the patterns are generally similar.

These environmental cycles are of enormous importance in regulating natural processes and strongly affect the viability of natural resources. They provide the major means by which resources are renewed following harvesting. For example, when a forest is logged, the environmental system of the forest is drastically altered. Removal of trees causes a reduction in evapotranspiration, with a corresponding increase in water moving both through and over the soil. This increased water movement, together with the decay of plant matter left behind (stumps and smaller branches and leaves), contributes to a greatly increased removal of nutrients from the area, both dissolved and as part of soil particles. Were it not for weathering, nitrogen fixation, and other additions of nutrients over time to replace these losses, the soil would be less able to support the regrowth of the forest for future harvest. Similarly, grazing, cultivation, and water resource development depend on replacement of substances by these natural cycles. In addition, the timing of these cycles may place significant constraints on human use in the same way that finite, or stock, resources impose constraints. Clearly, "renewable" resources also have an element of finiteness.

The operation of biogeochemical cycles also has implications for activities that disturb some portion of the cycle, by either removing or introducing substances. The use of nitrogen fertilizers in agriculture causes a substantial increase in the inorganic nitrogen content of the soil. This increase benefits crop plants, but it also leads to greater leaching of nitrogen by water and hence greater nitrogen concentrations in rivers and lakes draining agricultural areas. This added nitrogen causes serious pollution problems in some areas, for it not only modifies aquatic ecosystems to trigger algal blooms but it also poses a danger to humans if it is consumed in drinking water. By modifying the nitrogen inputs to the soil, we also change conditions farther downstream, often with undesirable consequences. The total amount of biologically available nitrogen introduced into the environment is enormous, exceeding total natural fixation of nitrogen (Vitousek 1994). A second example relates to the use of pesticides in the environment. An insecticide may be intended to act on only one small component of an ecosystem—the population of some particular insect species—

but the food chain can carry both food and un-wanted substances to other organisms, with un-foreseen and damaging effects (Issue 4.2).

Thus, biogeochemical cycles serve as conduits for energy and matter from one part of the environ-ment to another. They also cause the effects of human activities to extend beyond the immediate area of impact. For these reasons, we have become increasingly aware of the interrelatedness of natural resources, particularly renewable resources, and of the need to understand these phenomena com-pletely in order to manage these resources properly. Next we will discuss four of the important biogeo-chemical cycles: the nitrogen, phosphorus, carbon, and hydrologic cycles.

Carbon Cycle

One of the most important biogeochemical cycles is the carbon cycle (Fig. 4.6), which utilizes large storages in the atmosphere, in living organisms, and in rocks. Carbon dioxide in the atmosphere enters plant leaves and through photosynthesis is incorporated in living matter to form a basic part of starches, sugars, and other foods. As it passes through the food chain, carbon dioxide is returned to the atmosphere by respiration of consumers and decomposers. But significant amounts of organic matter accumulate in soils, marshes, and lake bot-toms, and this organic matter is largely carbon. Some of it may be oxidized from time to time, but most is semipermanently stored in sediment. In

---

ISSUE 4.2: *SILENT SPRING* VERSUS *OUR STOLEN FUTURE*

When *Silent Spring* was first published more than 30 years ago, it warned of the dangers of syn-thetic pesticide usage, especially DDT. In this book, first serialized in *The New Yorker* maga-zine, Rachel Carson eloquently explained how these persistent chemicals damaged the environ-ment and how they were accumulated in species, including humans. Both industry and government criticized and tried to discredit the book by at-tacking its author, claiming she was not a scien-tist, but just an extremely emotional woman (Hynes 1989). Despite her master's degree in marine biology from Johns Hopkins University, Carson was not taken seriously until the Presi-dent's Science Advisory Committee produced its own report a year later confirming her findings. *Silent Spring* has sold millions of copies world-wide and laid the foundation for governmental action in protecting the environment. It is truly a classic in the environmental field.

Our Stolen Future picks up where Rachel Car-son left off. Written by two scientists and an en-vironmental journalist (Theo Colburn, Dianne Dumanoski, and John Peterson Myers), the 1996 book chronicles the effect of synthetic chemicals on reproductive systems. Providing evidence from laboratory experiments, wildlife studies, and human epidemiological data, the book illus-trates the role of these hormone-disrupting chem-icals and how they are affecting the reproductive and growth-regulating systems of many species. Worldwide human male sperm counts have dropped by nearly 50 percent in the last decade, and nearly one-quarter of American couples have infertility problems. Frogs are disappearing in the upper Midwest, and defective sexual organs have been found among alligators in Florida. These problems are not specific to the United States but have been found in other industrialized countries as well.

In response to public concern about these re-productive toxins or endocrine disrupters as they are more formally known, the Environmental Protection Agency (EPA) established a large re-search initiative to establish the linkage between these synthetic substances and reproductive health. Unfortunately, we still don't quite know which specific chemicals pose the greatest risks to endocrine functions. Nor do we know how widespread they might be in the environment. However, as a precautionary measure, both the Food Quality Protection Act and the Safe Drink-ing Water Act passed in 1996 mandate that the EPA begin screening and testing for endocrine disrupters by 1999. While it's too soon to judge whether our future has indeed been stolen, it's not too late to ask that environmental toxic re-leases be reduced for the benefit of all species.

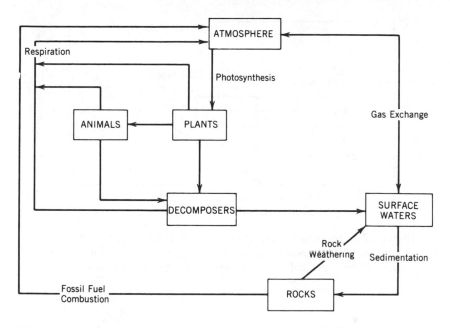

Figure 4.6   The carbon cycle. Carbon is stored in the form of carbon dioxide in the atmosphere, in plants, and in the decayed remains of organic organisms found in rocks and oceans. Fossil fuel combustion has altered the normal carbon cycle by removing carbon from terrestrial storage, burning it, and returning it to the atmosphere faster than it can be placed into storage.

addition, large amounts of carbon exist in the oceans, both in living organisms and as dissolved carbon dioxide. Carbon is continually deposited on the ocean floor in sediment, which over time becomes sedimentary rocks. Limestone, which is primarily calcium carbonate ($CaCO_3$), is formed in this way, as are fossil fuels. Carbon in rocks reenters the atmosphere through combustion of fossil fuels. In the last few hundred years, humans have removed and burned much more carbon from terrestrial storages of coal, oil, and natural gas than has been returned in that time, and the atmospheric concentration of carbon dioxide has increased accordingly (see Chapter 12). In addition, clearing of forests and depletion of soil organic matter by poor land management practices have reduced these storages of carbon and contributed to the increase of atmospheric carbon dioxide. Regrowth of forests, on the other hand, removes carbon from the atmosphere.

Nitrogen and Phosphorus

Nitrogen comprises about 80 percent of the Earth's atmosphere, and most of the Earth's nitrogen is in the atmosphere at any given time

(Fig. 4.7). Nitrogen is also an essential nutrient and a fundamental component of many proteins. Nitrogen cannot be directly used by most organisms in its gaseous form, and for it to be available to living matter it must be fixed or incorporated in chemical substances such as ammonia, nitrates, or organic compounds that plants are able to use. Some nitrogen is added directly to the soil as impurities in rainfall, but the much more important mechanism is the action of nitrogen-fixing bacteria, some of which live in association with plant roots. These bacteria are able to extract nitrogen directly from the air. Some plants, such as legumes, have symbiotic or mutually beneficial relationships with particular nitrogen-fixing bacteria, but many other plants also accommodate nitrogen-fixing bacteria, and some nitrogen fixers are not dependent on the environment of plant roots at all. Once nitrogen is incorporated into organic matter, it follows much the same route as energy in the food chain, passing from producer to consumer and ultimately to decomposer. Decomposers return nitrogen to the soil in mineral forms such as

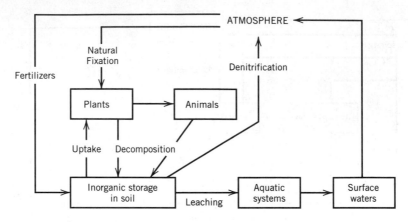

Figure 4.7 The nitrogen cycle. The atmosphere provides the primary storage of nitrogen, which is unusable by plants in its gaseous state and must first be converted by nitrogen-fixing bacteria before it can be used by plants.

ammonia that are again available to plants. In addition, nitrifying bacteria convert nitrogen from ammonia to nitrates and eventually to the gaseous forms N_2O, NO, and N_2, which are returned to the atmosphere. Finally, some nitrogen is leached from the soil or incorporated in runoff and makes its way into groundwater, rivers, lakes, and the sea, from which it can be returned to the atmosphere.

The phosphorus cycle (Fig. 4.8) is a good example of a biogeochemical cycle that is dominated by terrestrial rather than atmospheric storage. Phosphorus, an essential nutrient, is found primarily in rocks and enters the soil by the weathering of those rocks. But many rocks contain little phosphorus, and areas underlain by nonphosphate rocks must derive their phosphorus from trace amounts contained in rainfall. Once in the soil, phosphorus travels through the food chain, ultimately being returned to the soil by decomposers. Considerable amounts of phosphorus are leached or eroded from the soil, however, and this phosphorus eventually accumulates in the sea, where it is concentrated in the bones of fish. As the fish die and their bodies decay, phosphorus is deposited on the ocean floor and eventually is incorporated in sedimentary rocks. Fish-eating birds excrete large amounts of phosphorus, and their dung, or guano, which accumulates on rocks or offshore islands where seabirds roost, is an important source of phosphate fertilizer. Fish bones from processing plants are also used as fer-

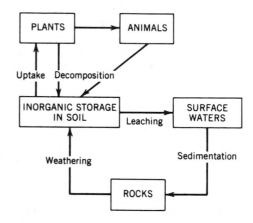

Figure 4.8 The phosphorus cycle. Phosphorus naturally enters the environment through the weathering of rocks. Human uses of phosphorus include phosphate fertilizers and detergents.

tilizer in some parts of the world. In the United States, most of our phosphate fertilizer is derived from the mining of phosphate-rich rocks.

Hydrologic Cycle

Another example of an important environmental cycle is the hydrologic cycle (Fig. 4.9), which is not a biogeochemical cycle in the same way as the others just discussed but is more of a regulator of flows of nutrients and energy. The hydrologic cycle is the set of pathways that water takes as it passes from atmosphere to Earth and back (Fig.

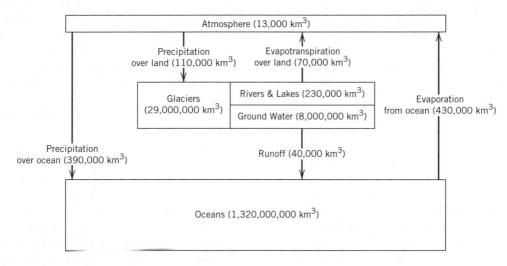

Figure 4.9 The hydrologic cycle. Water flows in the environment play a major role in regulating material and energy cycles.

4.10). It is regulated primarily by climate, but the terrestrial components of the cycle—rivers, lakes, soil, and groundwater—are also regulated by the characteristics of surficial materials and by topography. Analysis of water budgets, which quantify various components of the hydrologic cycle, is essential for water management.

Beginning with the atmosphere, water is delivered to the Earth's surface by precipitation. Rain strikes the leaves of plants, and some remains there and is evaporated, but most reaches the soil surface. Once on the soil, the water may either evaporate, soak into the soil, or run off. Several factors determine how much water soaks in and how much runs off, but the primary controls are the rate at which rain fails, or precipitation intensity, and the ability of the soil to soak up water, or its *infiltration capacity*. These fac-

Figure 4.10 Precipitation. Moisture held in storage in the atmosphere precipitates out as rain, illustrated by this thunderstorm. The water is used by plants, runs off into surface waters, or percolates through the soil for storage as groundwater.

tors are of critical importance in controlling soil erosion, and they will be discussed later in that context. Water that runs off the soil surface or through the regolith enters stream channels and becomes surface water. Through gravity, surface waters flow to the ocean via rivers, lakes, swamps, and so on. Depending on climatic factors such as atmospheric humidity and temperature, varying amounts of surface water are lost by evaporation. Water is temporarily stored in the soil, where it becomes available to plants. As they use water, it is returned to the atmosphere by evapotranspiration from their leaves. Water that is not used by plants percolates into the ground, where it eventually reaches a level below which the pores in the rocks are saturated, known as the *water table*. Water in this saturated zone is called *groundwater* and flows by gravity, and over long periods of time it may return to the surface in valleys and become surface water. The rate of flow of groundwater is considerably less than that for surface water, and depending on subsurface characteristics, very large amounts of water may be stored there. Groundwater flow is primarily responsible for maintaining river flow during dry periods between rains. Eventually, most water is returned to the atmosphere, either by evapotranspiration by plants or by evaporation from surface waters, particularly the oceans. Some water may be stored for such long periods of time, such as in groundwater, ice caps, and isolated deep water bodies. Water in such long-term storage is removed, for all practical purposes, from the cycle.

Food Chains

Ecosystems consist of all the living organisms in a defined geographic area, together with all the physical entities (soil, water, dead organic matter, and so on) with which they interact. As such they are exceedingly complex, and the energy and material transfers within them are difficult to quantify. Several important studies of energy transfers within ecosystems have been done, however, and from these some generalizations are possible. As one type of organism in an ecosystem consumes another, a pattern of energy flow through the ecosystem is set up, called a *food chain* (Fig. 4.11). Some food chains are simple—for example, when a plant is consumed by a rabbit, which is consumed by a fox. Such a

simple chain is usually part of a more complex food web in which several animals and plants may be dependent on one another. Many organisms eat more than one kind of food and may in turn themselves be appealing to several other species.

Energy is transferred from one trophic level to another within the chain or web. Terrestrial green plants are producers, as they convert solar energy to food energy at the first trophic level. Consumers can in turn be classified as primary consumers, which feed on producers at the second trophic level, secondary consumers, which feed on primary consumers at the third trophic level, and so forth. In addition there are decomposers, which feed on dead organic matter and return nutrients to the soil or water where they become available to producers. There may be fourth- or fifth-level consumers, but rarely do we find more than five in an ecosystem, for the energy produced at the first level has been mostly consumed at intermediate levels. Human beings are able to take advantage of the food energy at different levels because we can consume energy in the form of both plants and animals. There is some debate over whether or not we are wasteful of the world's food energy because our diets are high in animal products. It is generally more efficient in terms of energy production and consumption to obtain our food directly at the first trophic level.

Figure 4.11 illustrates a relatively simple food chain. Notice that at each step in the system, energy is either stored as biomass (the living and dead organic matter in an ecosystem) or used in respiration. Most of the energy consumed at any given level is used in organism metabolism, with only a small percentage being stored, as biomass, and available for the next higher level to consume.

Carrying Capacity

No matter how complex or simple the ecosystem, its component organisms are always working to reproduce themselves and to find adequate food. Obviously, the number of organisms cannot exceed the amount of food available to them for very long, or the stability of the ecosystem will be threatened. For an ecosystem to sustain itself, population size and food supply must be balanced over the long run, although there can be short-term fluctuations. As a result, we find an intricate relationship between the size of populations of the dif-

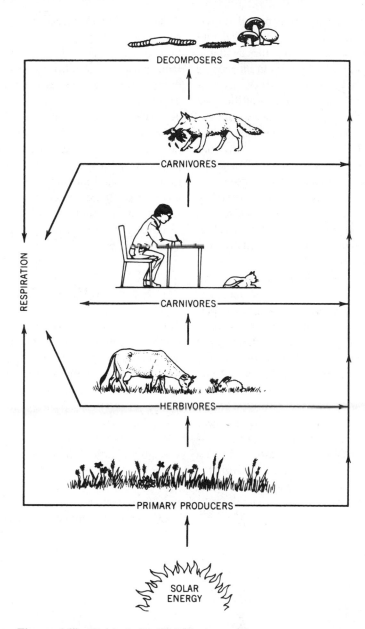

Figure 4.11   Food chain. Herbivores, or primary consumers, eat producers and are then consumed by carnivores. Sometimes a food chain can support additional trophic levels of consumers, before decomposers take their turn.

ferent species in an ecosystem and their competitive or complementary food needs relative to other populations in that ecosystem. These relationships can change over time, as the ecosystem's population dynamics shift in response to internal and external changes. *Carrying capacity* is the number of individuals of a given species that can be sustained

by an ecosystem over a long period of time without environmental degradation.

With ample food, living space, good health, and no predators, a species population could grow at its *biotic potential*. This is the maximum rate of population growth resulting if all females breed as often as possible, with all individuals surviving past their reproductive period. Obviously, a species breeding at an exponential rate of increase would soon outstrip the available food supply for it and other species in its ecosystem. Just as obviously, various types of environmental resistance, such as exhaustion of the food supply, adverse weather, and disease, would ensure keeping the population at a level far below its biotic potential. In systems terms, environmental resistance is a good example of negative feedback. For example, as a population grows, its food consumption in-creases and food becomes more difficult to find. As food becomes scarce, competition for food intensifies and survival of organisms to reproductive age is less likely, and thus population growth is reduced.

Although these inhibitions on population growth prevent exponential rates of increase, there are several fairly predictable growth patterns for populations within ecosystems (Fig. 4.12). An S-shaped growth curve describes a population with only a small difference between the rates of growth (birth and immigration) and decline, as a result of disease, predation, uncertain food supply, and other forms of resistance. Over time, however, the population may increase more rapidly as long as there is enough food and other necessities. Eventually, the resources that a population demands may exceed those available for its use, and environmental resistances such as disease and malnutrition will put a damper on the rate of increase.

The near-level portion of the S-shaped curve suggests a zero growth rate in which births plus immigrations equal deaths plus emigrations. In fact, this is an equilibrium situation in which biotic potential equals environmental resistance. The carrying capacity for this species in this ecosystem has been reached, which is the maximum number of organisms of one species that can be supported in the given environmental setting. Extinction of a species can occur when a population fluctuates dramatically, dropping so low that the species cannot reproduce quickly enough to remain in competition with others for available resources. These factors provide the biological basis for renewal resources management.

The Scope of Human Impact

Scientists have been aware of the human impact on the environment for a century or more (Marsh 1864). Agriculture and urbanization have generated the most dramatic transformations of the natural landscape (Goudie and Viles 1997; Turner et al. 1990). While often regionally specific, the global patterns of agriculture and urban changes have irrevocably altered natural ecosystems in all parts of the world.

In the 1960s, spurred by books such as *Silent Spring* (Carson 1962), environmental scientists became more interested in local and regional impacts, such as pollutants in a river or acid deposi-

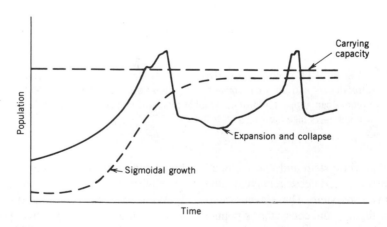

Figure 4.12 Population patterns in ecosystems. Populations can stabilize below carrying capacity. If the carrying capacity is exceeded, however, populations collapse and dieback can occur.

tion in a lake. This research demonstrated that many systems were indeed profoundly altered by such pollutants. In the 1970s, more extensive global-scale data collection networks began to be assembled, so that by the 1980s sufficient data had been amassed to allow rough estimates of human impacts at the global scale, especially in the area of climate change and its impacts. Finally, in the 1990s, Colburn et al. (1996) alerted the public to the dangers of toxic substances in the environment and their links to reproductive problems in species, including humans. This section examines some of the results of the recent research on pollution impacts, focusing on toxic substances. Other forms of water and air pollution are discussed in Chapters 10, 11, and 12.

The Extent of Environmental Pollution

One of the most significant human impacts on the environment in recent decades has been the creation and release of a wide variety of chemical substances into the environment, some of which have significant adverse effects on natural organisms or on humans. Ecological processes are very important in the study of toxic substances, both because ecosystems are affected by toxic substances and because ecological processes, like the biogeochemical cycles discussed earlier, are important in distributing toxic substances through the environment. Problems associated with toxic substances are discussed throughout this book in relation to various resource issues. The following sections provide an introduction to some of the general problems and characteristics of toxic substances.

Toxic Substances   Divergent definitions of toxic substances are used in different circumstances; here we will consider a toxic substance to be any substance in the environment that is harmful to humans, plants, or animals at very low concentrations. In practice, most of the toxic substances we examine are hazardous to humans and other animals, and by low concentrations we usually mean parts per million or less. Thousands of toxic substances are of environmental concern, and lists of known toxic substances change frequently as new information on toxicity or environmental concentrations becomes available. Toxic substances are derived from a multitude of human and natural sources and move along many different environmental pathways. In the follow-

ing sections, we provide a glimpse of the diversity of toxic substances and their sources.

Manufacturing activities are an important source of toxic substances in the environment, and in the United States polluters are required to report toxic substance releases through a system known as the Toxic Release Inventory (TRI). The total reported releases and transfers of toxic substances amounted to about 5.45 billion pounds (2.47 billion kg) in 1994, or an average of about 2.3 pounds per acre of land (2.58 kg/hectare) per year. Obviously, not all releases are ultimately deposited on land, and this average is not particularly meaningful for any one place, but it gives an indication of the magnitude of the situation. The majority of TRI releases (69%) are actually discharged into the air, with another 15 percent injected underground or released onto the land (13%) (U.S. EPA 1996). Table 4.2 lists the top 12 chemicals released in the greatest quantities. While most of the dirty dozen are released into the air, 72 percent of the phosphoric acid and 92 percent of the zinc compound releases are onto land, and 66 percent of the hydrochloric acid and 84 percent of the ammonia nitrate releases are injected underground.

Many toxic substances are released to the environment deliberately and for beneficial purposes. Pesticides are an obvious example. In 1995 over 1.2 billion pounds (545 million kg) of pesticides were produced in the United States, and most of

Table 4.2 Quantities of Specific Chemical Releases Reported Under the Toxic Release Inventory, 1994

Chemical	Total Releases (lb)
Methanol	255,767,000
Hydrochloric acid	214,952,000
Ammonia	205,801,000
Toluene	168,959,000
Xylene (mixed isomers)	108,936,000
Carbone disulfide	83,385,000
Zinc compounds	81,765,000
Methyl ethyl ketone	79,361,000
Phosphoric acid	78,766,000
Dichloromethane	63,775,000
Ammonium nitrate (solution)	60,546,000
Chlorine	60,432,000

Source: U.S. Environmental Protection Agency, 1996.

these were released into the environment in applications ranging from large-scale agricultural uses to individual use of insect repellents. Another example is the use of tributyl tin as an anti-fouling agent in marine paints.

Lead is an important toxic substance that has received much attention in recent years. It is toxic to humans and has been used as an additive in motor fuels for decades. In the early 1970s increasing concern over air pollution led to the requirement that cars be equipped with catalytic converters to reduce hydrocarbon emissions. Lead in fuel damages these converters, and so lead-free gasoline was introduced, with the added benefit of reduced lead emissions. Today all gasoline sold in the United States is lead-free, and cars with or without catalytic converters are using lead-free gasoline. As a result, lead concentrations in the air and water decreased markedly in the 1980s (see Chapter 11).

Many toxins have natural origins besides their human-caused presence in the environment. For example, most toxic metals are present in rocks and soils and are naturally released to water and biota through rock weathering and water flow in soils. Many plants produce toxic organic chemicals, some of which are released directly by plants and others which are produced by processes of biochemical decay.

Under most circumstances, these natural sources of toxic substances do not present major problems, either because the concentrations involved are low or because ecosystems are adapted to them. However, in some circumstances human activities aggravate, or are aggravated by, these natural sources. One example occurs when toxic substances have both human and natural sources. Metals are a good example. Several metals are natural constituents of water but usually in relatively low concentrations. In some cases, however, human sources of these metals may cause the total concentrations to rise to toxic levels, creating or increasing hazards to humans and other organisms. Another possibility is that toxins are present in relatively harmless forms naturally, but human actions release these toxins to the environment. An example would be acid precipitation, which may result in a decrease in soil pH and thus cause metals that were in insoluble forms to be released and taken up by plants or enter surface water. Natural substances may also combine with pollutants of human origin to produce new toxic

substance problems. For example, a group of substances called trihalomethanes is produced in drinking water from the combination of natural organic substances (such as the products of plant decay in streams) and chlorine added to water to reduce bacterial concentrations.

The fact that some toxic substances have both natural and human origins makes management and control efforts particularly difficult. It may be possible to control some human sources but not all, and sometimes we eliminate human sources and still find the pollutant present because of natural sources. If a pollutant is found in the environment, it is often difficult to determine how much of it is natural and how much is human in origin. These uncertainties are often used to political advantage by those attempting to point a finger at polluting industries, for example, or by those trying to avoid pollution control efforts.

Once pollutants are introduced into the environment, they migrate within it and their concentrations change as a result. The processes of pollutant movement in the environment are critical in understanding and evaluating their impacts on resources. In the following sections, we will examine three different mechanisms by which the concentrations of pollutants change through time: pollutant decay, bioconcentration, and physical transport from one place to another.

Pollutant Decay Some pollutants decay gradually in the environment and become less toxic over time. This is true for compounds such as pesticides but not for elements such as metals. Biochemical decay may be accomplished in organisms that ingest pollutants, or it may take place as a result of exposure to water, sunlight, and other substances in the environment. Some pollutants are very stable in the environment, and it is this stability that may cause them to become a problem. Persistent pesticides, so named because they are relatively stable in the environment, are an example. Many compounds of carbon, hydrogen, and chlorine (chlorinated hydrocarbons) are resistant to decay. Persistent pesticides such as DDT and chlordane are examples of chlorinated hydrocarbons that have been restricted from use in the United States because of their danger to organisms and the environment.

Other pollutants decay quite rapidly, and their concentrations decrease through time. Most of the pesticides in use today do decay in the environment and so have relatively short-term impacts. As a rule, this decay is advantageous, although it sometimes requires that pesticides be applied in higher concentrations to overcome the effects of rapid decay.

Bioaccumulation and Biomagnification

Some pollutants are selectively accumulated by organisms that consume or are exposed to them in the environment, and in many cases this is an important mechanism of toxicity. This is called *bioaccumulation* and is particularly important for metals and some organic compounds. Plants and animals absorb pollutants through their food, through skin contact, or through the air. If the pollutant has a tendency to bind with other substances in the organism, then it may accumulate over time. Usually, the pollutant will accumulate in a particular part of the organism; for example, iodine tends to accumulate in the thyroid gland. As this accumulation continues, the concentration of the pollutant in an individual organism rises, sometimes to toxic levels.

Biomagnification is a process whereby the concentration of a substance in animal tissues is increased step by step through a food chain. As a rule of thumb, it takes about 10 kg of food to make 1 kg of tissue in the consumer. If a substance has a tendency to be retained in animal tissues rather than metabolized or excreted, then its concentration in those tissues could be increased by as much as 10 times for every step in the food chain. When a food chain has many steps, the ultimate concentration in the top predator may be quite high.

Many of the persistent pesticides accumulate in fatty tissues of animals and tend to be concentrated in the food chain. Although concentrations in most waterways now generally range from not detectable to parts per billion, fish and bird tissues frequently contain DDT and other pesticides at the parts per million level. Average concentrations of DDT and its metabolites in human tissues in the United States were about 8 ppm in 1970, 5 ppm in 1976, and less than 1 ppm in 1990 (CEQ 1994). Other hazardous substances that have become bioconcentrated include polychlorinated biphenyls (PCBs) and strontium-90, which tends to concentrate in bone tissues. Persistent pesticides are generally found in higher concentrations in aquatic sediment than in the water, and they will be found in animal and human tissues for a long time.

Pollutant Transport

Because toxic substances are dangerous at relatively low concentrations, transfers of small amounts from one place to another may be of significance. Many processes are involved, including transport in surface and groundwater, in air, dust, and sediment, and through organisms. Often a pollutant deposited in one medium turns up in another. For example, organic compounds in wastes disposed of in a landfill may enter groundwater, flow into surface water, be taken up by fish, and be passed through the food chain. Or soil in a mine tailings pile containing high concentrations of metals may be eroded by wind and transported considerable distances before being deposited.

Management problems become more complex as a result of the low concentrations that must be examined and the mobility of toxic substances from one medium to another. Not the least of these problems is the expense of sampling and analyzing environmental materials for concentrations of a wide range of substances at the parts per million (ppm) or parts per billion (ppb) level. Laboratory analyses for some substances cost in excess of $1000 each, in addition to sampling costs. But more troublesome is the development of regulatory mechanisms that deal with several different media simultaneously. For example, a substance may be relatively benign when found in soil but be very hazardous in water. Regulations governing disposal of wastes on land must include some means to evaluate the likelihood that pollutants will enter water and the concentrations in which they may occur. Such regulations become extremely complex and are both difficult and costly to enforce.

Uncertainty in Toxic Substances Management

Managing toxic substance pollution presents many problems, but perhaps the most difficult one is that decisions must be made with less than adequate information. In the first place, a great number of substances (at least several hundred) may be toxic to humans or other organisms. For many of these we have little information on the exact concentrations at which toxicity occurs and even less information on their concentrations in the environment. Assessment of the risk to humans associated with exposure to a substance becomes one of extrapolation from very limited information, and the conclusions we draw are necessarily shaky (Cutter 1993; National Research Council 1994, 1996). On the one hand, we seek to eliminate any chance of adverse health impacts associated with a pollutant. However, we cannot do so with any certainty unless we reduce exposures to very low levels, often at very high (and weakly justified) costs.

Careful and painstaking research by ecologists provides a strong argument for thoughtful management of resources. Ecosystems are so complex that one can never assume that an action will only affect the immediate location. The vast body of ecological research that has accumulated in the last few decades has shown that the interconnectedness of ecosystems almost always leads to more far-reaching and often unexpected effects. Without a recognition of this fact, disruption in natural systems is likely to occur and lead to further disruption of connected systems or possibly to a domino effect in which distantly related systems and organisms may suffer.

We must always remember that the ecological viewpoint is open to political uses, as are all scientific approaches. Ecosystems are both real and abstract (Kormondy 1969). It is the abstract idea of interrelatedness that can be used by individuals or organizations eager to protect some special interest from change or development. They may argue that because everything is interrelated, then if a certain stream is dammed, this act will eventually lead to the collapse of civilization or life on Earth. Ecology as a serious field of study makes no such sweeping guarantees or generalities. In the context of resource management, it needs to be used in a sober and factually based manner.

Human Impact on Biogeochemical Cycles

One of the startling conclusions of global-scale studies of biogeochemical cycles is that human impact is sufficiently large that it is easily recognizable at the global scale. Even though 71 percent of the Earth's surface is water, and human population is heavily concentrated in a small portion of the land area of the planet, the quantities of basic substances—carbon, nitrogen, water, and so on—processed by humans is a significant part of the global total. This is especially obvious in the case of the carbon cycle described earlier but is no less significant for other biogeochemical cycles. Here we describe two examples in more detail: the hydrologic cycle and the food chain.

Hydrologic Cycle   Less than 3 percent of the world's water is fresh, but most of this is found in glaciers. The fresh water that is accessible to humans is found in lakes, rivers, and the soil. This amounts to a total of perhaps 200,000 km^3. Groundwater is more plentiful, perhaps as much as 8 million km^3, but this is a storage that cannot be depleted indefinitely and is only replaced by surplus surface water. Surplus surface water is derived from net precipitation: the difference between precipitation and evapotranspiration. Worldwide, this net precipitation on land areas totals about 40,000 km^3. This is the renewable supply of water that is available for river flow and for replacing depleted soil and groundwater.

Humans withdraw water from lakes, rivers, and wells and use it for irrigation, industrial and commercial purposes, consumption by humans and domestic animals, and other purposes (Fig. 4.13). The total amount of water withdrawn from the hydrologic cycle worldwide is a little over 3000 km^3, or about 8 percent of the total. Of the water that is withdrawn, some is evaporated in the atmosphere, especially from irrigated lands. The remainder is returned to rivers and lakes after use, usually with waste products added. The total withdrawals for agricultural uses are estimated to be about 2880 km^3 per year, with 65 percent of this or 1870 km^3 evapotranspired to the atmosphere by irrigated crops, and another 415 km^3 evaporated from other uses, mostly reservoirs in arid and semiarid areas (Postel et al. 1996). Thus, the average runoff from the continents to the oceans is decreased by human activities by 6 percent or 2285 km^3. Most of this depletion occurs in the drier parts of the populated world, such as Asia and western North America, and in these regions the net depletion of runoff is much higher—virtually 100 percent for some basins.

The Food Chain   Photosynthesis by green plants is the basic process that creates food for virtually all living organisms. *Net primary production* (NPP) is the net amount of biomass created by the plants in an ecosystem, after respiration by those plants is deducted. The

Figure 4.13   Irrigation of crops, as is being carried out by these women in Gambia, uses most of the water withdrawn for human use worldwide.

world's biomes differ greatly in the amount of NPP that occurs in them. Wetlands and tropical rainforests are the most productive environments, sometimes producing 2000 to 4000 grams of biomass (dry weight) per square meter of area per year. At the other end of the spectrum are deserts and polar regions where NPP is only a few grams or tens of grams per square meter per year. The total amount of NPP that occurs in the world includes all the food that is available to support life—human and otherwise. This is estimated to be about 220 petagrams (1 Pg = 10^{18}g) per year (Vitousek et al. 1986).

How much of this primary production is consumed by humans? Vitousek et al. (1986) estimated that humans consume about 0.8 Pg from cultivated land directly, but an additional 6.4 Pg are consumed by domestic animals, harvested as wood from forests, or caught in the world's fisheries, for a total of 7.2 Pg or 3.2 percent of total global NPP consumed or used directly by humans and their domestic animals. They extended their calculations to include that portion of NPP that is either controlled by humans or lost due to poor land management. Productivity controlled by humans would include the waste portions of

crop plants or trees burned in shifting cultivation. Poor land management includes the decreased productivity of farmlands due to soil erosion and declining soil fertility. When these additional portions of global NPP are included, Vitousek and others estimate that humans directly consume, control, or waste about 39 percent of terrestrial NPP and about 25 percent of global NPP.

The global-scale estimates described in the preceding paragraphs are very rough, but they provide an indication of the magnitude of the human impact on Earth's biological processes. What they show is that human participation in biogeochemical cycling, whether the hydrologic cycle, the food chain, the carbon cycle, or other cycles, accounts for a significant portion of the total amounts of materials processed. We can no longer consider humans to be just one of many species on the planet, consuming a portion of its output but otherwise not altering it. We are not merely nibbling at the edge of the natural world. We are major, if not dominant, processors of material, intentionally controlling or inadvertently altering many ecological systems. And at the local scale, in those environments most intensely used by humans, we have profoundly altered natural processes to the extent that entire biomes have been destroyed and replaced by new, human-made and human-controlled systems.

ECOLOGICAL CONCEPTS IN RESOURCE MANAGEMENT

If humans are now the dominant players in the world's ecological systems, then we need to act accordingly. Whether we are concerned for the health and longevity of all species or just our own, we need to manage the Earth in ways that will maintain its ability to support life. In this section, we will describe four principles of environmental management that derive from an ecological view of natural resources.

Any Given Environment Has Finite Carrying Capacity

Earlier in this chapter, we discussed the concept of carrying capacity. This concept was originally developed for application to natural and human-managed systems, in which we might want to know how many organisms could be supported in a given area. The concept can be extended to human use of a given system as a way to suggest the extent to which we can use that system without damaging it. For example, we might calculate how much sewage a river can absorb, breaking it down and removing the waste products, without significantly degrading water quality. In this case, "significantly" might be defined in terms of maintaining sufficient dissolved oxygen to support a diverse aquatic community.

The problem with applying the carrying capacity concept to human use of the Earth arises when we ask how many humans can be supported by a given resource base. To do this we must make assumptions about what level of resource consumption constitutes an adequate level of human support and what level of environmental degradation is acceptable. For rabbits or elephants, we usually define support as meaning a level of food supply and habitat that will allow the population to reproduce itself, without worrying too much about whether the animals are hungry or well-fed, uncomfortable or happy. But with humans we recognize that reproduction alone doesn't necessarily mean an acceptable quality of life. If people are poor and die young because of inadequate

food supply, then we might argue that the carrying capacity of a system has been exceeded even though the population can still reproduce itself.

Nonetheless, the idea of a finite carrying capacity for any given system is useful, provided we can agree on a definition of acceptable environmental quality and quality of human life. If, for example, we can agree that a forest must be maintained with a sufficient number of large trees to support those species that depend on mature forests for their survival, then we can agree on what level of harvest would be sustainable in that system. Questions such as these are at the core of the debate over maintaining habitat for biodiversity preservation (see Chapter 8).

Be Aware of Limiting Factors

One of the most important principles relating populations to ecosystem characteristics is the *principle of limiting factors*. Usually, many factors (nutrients, physical site characteristics, etc.) are necessary for an organism to exist, and the availability of these factors varies from site to site, with some factors plentiful while others are rare. An organism requires different environmental conditions in varying degrees or in different amounts, and there is no reason to assume that every condition is avaiable in exactly the amount required. Small changes in limiting factors may have profound effects; similar changes in non-limiting factors may have little or no effect.

Plant nutrients provide a simple example. A particular plant may require sunlight, water, a stable substrate, and a variety of nutrients from the soil. These nutrients may include nitrogen, phosphorus, potassium, magnesium, copper, zinc, and many other elements. They may all be available in plentiful supply except one, say, phosphorus. The plant's rate of growth will be restricted by the lack of phosphorus, even though there is more than enough of the other nutrients. In this situation, nitrogen fertilizer applied to the soil will do nothing to help the plant, but phosphorus fertilizer will be very effective. Phosphorus is thus said to be the limiting factor in this case.

Nutrients are not the only factor that can be limiting. Sunlight, carbon dioxide, frost, or any other environmental characteristic that an organism requires may be limiting. If substances are present in excessive quantities that may poison an organism, they can also be considered limiting.

Predators are often limiting factors for animal populations. It is usually difficult to determine just what factor or factors are limiting in any given situation, but clearly this information is essential to predicting the effects of environmental changes on ecosystem development and illustrates the critical importance of sound environmental knowledge for informed resource management.

Minimize Disruption by Mimicking Nature

A third principle of ecological management of natural resources is that human resource systems should mimic nature whenever possible. This principle follows from the study of ecosystems and from the experience of unanticipated consequences of human modifications to ecosystems. Although the scientific study of ecosystems has advanced tremendously in recent years, we are still far from being able to accurately predict ecosystem states and processes. This is due to the enormous complexity of food webs and interactions between individuals, species, and communities.

The study of ecosystems has shown that these natural systems and the organisms they include have developed over millions of years of evolution and adaptation. Each and every species in a community has adapted characteristics that allow it to exist in a specialized niche. Species interact with other species in a community, sometimes competitively, sometimes symbiotically, but always in ways that continue the exchange of energy and matter within the system and perpetuate its existence.

Experiences in recent decades have shown that attempts to control nature have more often than not ended in problems larger than those we hoped to solve. Control of predators results in a mushrooming of prey populations. Control of agricultural pests using insecticides results in the development of strains resistant to pesticides. In the face of this unpredictability and recurring management failures, many ecologists conclude that we are not likely to be able to control natural systems with any reliability, and we are better off to let these systems manage themselves to the extent possible.

One way to promote the systems' self-management is to use management strategies that exploit natural processes by mimicking them, working with nature rather than against it. For example, the history of agricultural pest control is one of many failures and only modest successes. The largest problems are those associated with human health effects, estimated to include 20,000 deaths per year worldwide; in the United States alone about 67,000 people are poisoned annually due to pesticides (Pimentel et al. 1992). Additional problems include damage to nontarget organisms, development of pesticide resistance, crop product losses, and water pollution.

Although these problems are balanced against the benefits of pesticide use, many argue that unintended negative effects can be reduced by adopting an alternative strategy called *integrated pest management* (IPM). This approach utilizes more intensive management, combining use of crop rotations and crop combinations that reduce pest infestations, biological control methods such as introduction of pest predators, and limited use of pesticides. The IPM approach recognizes that some pest losses are inevitable, but if the natural pest-resisting capabilities of an agricultural ecosystem are exploited, much less chemical pesticide need be used, minimizing the unintended negative impacts of pest control.

Close the Loops

Biogeochemical cycles are, ultimately, closed loops at the global scale. Carbon that is taken up in photosynthesis passes through the food chain, is released to the atmosphere, and is taken up in photosynthesis again. Nitrogen in the atmosphere is fixed in the soil, taken up in plants, converted to nitrate when plants decay, leached by soil water and transported to a river, converted to a gas through denitrification, and released to the atmosphere.

The gross imbalances in biogeochemical cycles that are resulting in a steady increase in atmospheric CO_2 concentrations, or that are causing typical nitrogen concentrations in human-impacted rivers to be 100 times their natural levels, are a result of human-caused transfers of materials. Many of these transfers go just one way. Carbon is taken out of the Earth in the form of fossil fuels but is not put back again. Atmospheric nitrogen is converted to fertilizer and pumped into the soil, but our crops do not remove all of this nitrogen from the soil and much is left to contribute to water pollution.

If, every time we moved a quantity of matter from one place to another or changed it from one form to another, we made sure that an equivalent quantity were transferred in the other direction, then these problems would be alleviated. Carbon would not accumulate in the atmosphere, water would not be polluted, and resource use would be indefinitely renewable.

Of course, this is impossible in many cases. Fossil fuels cannot be replaced; to do so would require energy, which would defeat the purpose of using them. In fact, the second law of thermodynamics means that we would use more energy putting the fuels back in the ground than we could get out! But failure to close the loop means that we are creating an imbalance in Earth's biogeochemical cycles, which ultimately will damage other parts of the environment. The only solution, then, is to limit our use of resources to those that can be replaced, recycled, or reused. In the case of energy, this means abandoning the use of fossil fuels and relying only on the various forms of solar energy. In the case of nitrogen fertilizers, it means limiting our use to just the amount that can be taken up by the crops we plant and harvest, so that no excess remains to pollute water.

CONCLUSION

It will never be possible to manage all resources according to such strict ecological principles, and probably we wouldn't want to do so. But an ecological viewpoint on natural resources holds that environmental problems derive from violating these principles, and to the extent that we are able to change how we use resources and return to production and consumption practices that are more like the natural processes that existed before humans occupied the Earth, the more likely we are to protect the environment and resources for future generations.

REFERENCES AND ADDITIONAL READING

Asner, G. P., T. R. Seastedt, and A. R. Townsend. 1997. The decoupling of terrestrial carbon and nitrogen cycles. *BioScience* 47: 226–234.

Carson, Rachel. 1962. *Silent Spring*. Boston: Houghton Mifflin.

Colburn, T., D. Dumanoski, and J. P. Myers. 1996. *Our Stolen Future*. New York: Dutton.

Council on Environmental Quality (CEQ). 1994. *Environmental Quality, 24th Annual Report*. Washington, DC: U.S. Government Printing Office.

Cushman, J. H. 1995. Freshwater mussels facing mass extinction. *New York Times*, October 3, 1995, p. B5.

Cutter, S. L. 1993. *Living with Risk*. London: Edward Arnold.

Detwyler, T. R., and M. G. Marcus, eds. 1962. *Urbanization and Environment*. Belmont, CA: Duxbury Press.

DeYoung, R., and S. Kaplan. 1988. On averting the tragedy of the commons. *Environmental Management* 12: 273–283.

Food and Agriculture Organization, 1996. FAOSTAT, http://apps.fao.org/

Goudie, A., and H. Viles. 1997. *The Earth Transformed*. New York: Blackwell.

Houghton, R. A. 1994. The worldwide extent of land-use change. *BioScience* 44: 305–329.

Hynes, H. 1989. *The Recurring Silent Spring*. New York: Pergamon.

Kirchner, J. W. 1989. The Gaia hypothesis: Can it be tested? *Rev. Geophy.* 27(2): 223–235.

Kormondy, E. J. 1969. *Concepts of Ecology*. Englewood Cliffs, NJ: Prentice-Hall.

Lovelock, J. E. 1979. *Gaia, a New Look at Life on Earth*. Oxford: Oxford University Press.

Marsh, G. P. 1864. *Man and Nature, or Physical Geography as Modified by Human Action*. New York: Scribner.

Myers, N., ed. 1989. *The Gaia Atlas of Planet Management*. London: Pan Books.

National Research Council. 1994. *Science and Judgment in Risk Assessment*. Washington, DC: National Academy Press.

_____. 1996. *Understanding Risk: Informing Decisions in a Democratic Society*. Washington, DC: National Academy Press.

Pimentel, D., et al. 1991. Environmental and economic effects of reducing pesticide use. *BioScience* 41: 402–409.

_____. 1992. Environmental and economic costs of pesticide use. *BioScience* 42: 750–760.

Postel, S. L., G. C. Daily, and P. R. Ehrlich. 1996. Human appropriation of renewable fresh water. *Science* 271: 785–788.

Robertson, G. P. 1986: Nitrogen: regional contributions to the global cycle. *Environment* 28(10): 16–20, 29.

Simmons, I. G. 1981 *Ecology of Natural Resources*, 2nd ed. Philadelphia: W. B. Saunders.

Turner, B. L., W. C. Clark, R. W. Kates, J. F. Richards, J. T. Matthews, and W. B. Meyer, eds.

1990. *The Earth as Transformed by Human Action.* Cambridge: Cambridge University Press.

U.S. Bureau of the Census. 1997. *Statistical Abstract of the U.S.* Washington, DC: U.S. Government Printing Office.

U.S. Environmental Protection Agency. 1996. *TRI Public Data Release Report.* Washington, DC: Office of Prevention, Pesticides, and Toxic Substances, U.S. EPA.

Vitousek, P., et al. 1986. Human appropriation of the products of photosynthesis. *BioScience* 36: 368–373.

Vitousek, P. M. 1994. Beyond global warming: ecology and global change. *Ecology* 75: 1861–1876

World Resources Institute. 1996. *World Resources 1990–97.* New York: Oxford University Press.

For more information, consult our web page at *http://www.wiley.com/college/cutter*

Study Questions

1. Using your local community as an example, list some of the adverse effects of biogeochemical cycle disruptions. Are these disruptions produced locally (e.g., activities that are going on in your community), transferred from someone else's activities either upwind or upriver, or resulting from larger-scale global phenomena? Why is it important to consider the likely source of the disruption?

2. Keep a diary of the chemical products you use in any given day such as shampoos, laundry detergent, dish soap, and deodorant. Examine each for chemicals used. How many of these products contain synthetic substances? Can you think of non-synthetic substitutes that might accomplish the same thing? (*Hint:* vinegar, baking soda, lemon juice, and baby powder) How many alternatives did you discover?

3. How does geographic scale help us understand the differences between communities, ecotones, and ecosystems?

4. Why is the concept of bioregions useful in environmental management? What are some of the major characteristics of the world's major biomes?

5. Given the current trends in land-use changes shown in Table 4.1, what might these land uses look like in the year 2010? in the year 2030?

CHAPTER 5

THE HUMAN POPULATION

The world's population is increasing rapidly. In 1985 global population was estimated at 4.84 billion, and by 1997 it had reached 5.85 billion. In 1997 one-fifth of this total, or 1.22 billion, lived in China, the world's most populous country, with another 967 million living in India. The United States had 269 million people (Population Reference Bureau 1997).

As the world's population increases, so does its use of resources. Environmentalists and population theorists such as Paul Ehrlich and Lester Brown and economists such as H. E. Daly and N. Georgescu-Roegen continue to warn of increased population pressures on natural resource consumption. People must be fed, housed, and clothed, and the more people there are, the more food resources, housing materials, and fibers must be produced. Other theorists, such as economist Julian Simon and writer Ben Wattenberg, are confident that population growth does not mean a drop in the standard of living.

The population problem, or crisis to some, is not a recent phenomenon. In 1798, the British economist *Thomas Malthus* foresaw some of the world's current population problems. Malthus wrote that populations increase in size geometrically; that is, they double in size in a fixed time period. Geometric growth is shown by the upward-trending curve in Figure 5.1. Malthus also wrote that food supplies increase arithmetically; that is, they increase by addition of a fixed amount in a given time period. Arithmetic growth is shown as a straight line in Figure 5.1. Eventually, he said, population growth would outstrip the food resources (assuming, of course, no new resources were developed) with catastrophic consequences—mass starvation,

poverty, and economic and social collapse. The history of population growth and food production since Malthus' time has been very different from what Malthus predicted. Population has indeed grown rapidly, but food production has grown even faster. The crisis he predicted has not materialized.

Debates continue today over the relationship between population growth and resource scarcity. *Neo-Malthusians* take the same perspective as Malthus, yet they argue for strong birth control measures to postpone or delay population growth to a level below the limit of resource availability. Advocacy of birth control to stabilize population growth, instead of expecting nature to do the job through famine and war, differentiates neo-Malthusianism from the original Malthusians.

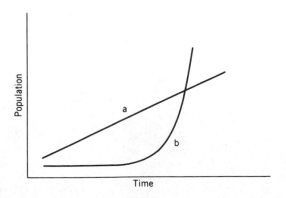

Figure 5.1 Arithmetic versus geometric growth. Arithmetic growth (*a*) follows a straight line, increasing by the same number each year. Geometric growth (*b*) follows a curve, increasing by the same percent each year.

A nineteenth-century critic of Malthus, Karl Marx, stressed that there was no single theory of population growth and resource use. Increased population growth did not by itself, as Malthus suggested, result in excessive resource use and a lowered standard of living. Marx believed that poverty was caused by the economic system, which exploited labor for the benefit of the elite. The cause of poverty was economic, he stated, not solely an increase in numbers of people.

In the twentieth century, Esther Boserup (1965, 1981) and Julian Simon (1981, 1986) have suggested that population growth may be beneficial in providing a stimulus for improving the human condition. They suggest that population growth intensifies land use, resulting in increased agricultural production. The end result is that all individuals benefit from the increased production and thus achieve a higher standard of living. They suggest that Malthus incorrectly assumed that increased population led to increased poverty, starvation, and war.

Today some population experts anticipate some form of population catastrophe in the near future. Others, however, are confident that human needs can be met no matter how large the world's population becomes. The following historical perspective and some of today's population numbers may help you decide where you stand on this issue.

A BRIEF HISTORY OF POPULATION GROWTH

Although we cannot accurately measure the world's human population in the distant past, demographers and archaeologists, among others, have developed low to high ranges for population size and growth over thousands of years. These estimates change, of course, with the unearthing of new evidence such as ancient communities, new dating methods, and new theories. The world's human population at the end of the most recent ice age, about 10,000 years ago, was somewhere between 2 and 10 million people. It had taken perhaps 1 to 2 million years for the population to grow to this size. When we consider that population has burgeoned to 5.8 billion in the past 10,000 years—and most of that in the last 300 years—it is clear that extraordinary changes have taken place in all aspects of human life in order to adjust to this astonishing growth.

From 8000 B.C. to A.D. 1 the population doubled almost six times, to between 200 and 400 million (Fig. 5.2). The doubling time was more

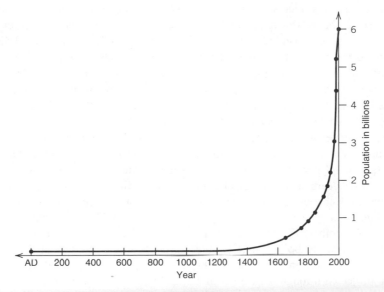

Figure 5.2 World population growth. World population growth was slow and steady until about 1700 to 1750. Since then, the world's population has expanded rapidly.

than 1000 years. One should realize that this growth was not steady and smooth. A close look would reveal sudden rises and drops owing to the vagaries of famine, war, and disease over small and large regions. The tendency, however, was toward growth. Between A.D. 1 and 1750, growth continued at about the same rate, ultimately reaching 750 million by 1750. Though scholars differ, the technological developments of agriculture and irrigation no doubt had much to do with this population increase. After 1750 the world's population began its modern climb, starting in Europe. It took only 150 years, from 1750 to 1900, for the world's population to double from 750 million to 1.5 billion. The population doubled once again between 1900 and 1965, a two-fold increase in 65 years, and will nearly double between 1965 and 2000.

Where was the growth, and where is the growth likely to occur in the future? After 1750, Europe's population mushroomed, and the resulting crowding and poor conditions had a great impact on the settlement of the Americas, Australia, and New Zealand and on European imperialism worldwide. Europe needed raw materials to support its astonishing human and economic growth, and those resources were available in Africa, Asia, the Americas, and the Indian subcontinent. During the twentieth century, the benefits of the Scientific Revolution that led to Europe's boom—the germ theory of disease, ideas about cleanliness, vaccinations, agricultural improvements—were introduced to the rest of the world, and population growth shifted to Europe's former colonies.

Doubling time is the number of years it takes a population to double in size assuming a constant rate of natural increase. The lower the number of years to double in size, the faster the growth rate. In the mid-1960s when the world's population was growing at 2.0 percent per year, the doubling time of world population was about 35 years. By 1997, with a growth rate of 1.4 percent per year, it had increased to about 47 years. This change in doubling time shows the weakness of the assumption of a constant rate of increase. For example, in 2044, a date 47 years from 1997, the world's population will almost certainly be less than double the 1997 level. If population growth trends existing in 1997 are projected through the twenty-first century, the world's population would reach 9 billion by 2050 and 10 billion by the year 2100. At the national and regional level, great differences in growth rates exist (Table 5.1). Some countries, notably in Africa and southwest Asia, have growth rates well over 3 percent per year, with doubling times under 25 years. Other areas, particularly Europe, have virtually zero population growth.

World population growth has slowed significantly since the late 1960s, and in the early 1990s the growth rate slowed even more, surprising many demographers. Fertility rates are dropping rapidly in much of the world, and estimates of future population have been revised downward repeatedly. There are now clear signs that the period of rapid population growth centered on the 20th century is coming to an end. Present growth rates cannot be extrapolated very far into the future, however. Many factors, such as war, disease, social pressure, government programs, immigration and emigration, may affect the doubling time on a year-to-year basis as population projections illustrate. Since we don't have crystal balls to peer into the future, these population forecasts are often more art than science.

BASIC DEMOGRAPHICS

Many factors have contributed to this dramatic increase in world population. One is the development of a broader worldwide food base because of increased trade; another is humanity's eventual development (after a two-century-long period of fluctuation) of a rise in overall disease resistance, which was also a result of increased trade and travel. It has been suggested as well that population began to rise in the wake of better medical technology and theory, leading to a drop in infant and child mortality rates and an increased life span for large segments of the world's population. Let us discuss the possibilities and implications of present and future growth rates.

We will examine two dimensions of the world population picture. The first includes the rate and causes of population growth and is called *population dynamics*. The second is the location of growth, that is, its spatial distribution around the world. Both are essential to our understanding of current and future population trends. In examining population dynamics, the first question is: How and why do populations grow? Two factors are

Table 5.1   Demographic Characteristics of Selected Countries, 1995

Country	Population (1000s)	Growth Rate (%/year)	Crude Birth Rate (births/1000 population)	Crude Death Rate (deaths/100 population)	Total Fertility Rate
World	5,846,871	1.4	23	9	2.9
Argentina	35,798	1.3	20	8	2.7
Australia	18,439	1.0	14	7	1.8
Bangladesh	125,340	1.8	30	11	3.4
Brazil	167,661	1.3	21	8	2.4
Canada	30,337	1.1	12	7	1.7
China	1,226,275	0.9	16	7	1.8
Colombia	37,852	1.9	25	6	2.9
Congo (Kinshasha)	47,590	2.8	47	15	6.6
Cuba	10,999	0.4	13	7	1.5
Egypt	64,824	1.9	28	9	3.5
Ethiopia	57,099	2.3	45	21	6.9
France	58,609	0.4	12	9	1.7
Germany	82,072	0.0	9	11	1.2
Guatemala	11,686	2.7	36	7	4.9
India	966,783	1.7	26	9	3.3
Indonesia	209,774	1.5	23	8	2.7
Iran	67,540	2.1	33	6	4.5
Italy	56,831	− 0.1	9	10	1.2
Japan	125,689	0.2	10	8	1.4
Mexico	96,807	1.8	26	5	3.0
Myanmar	46,525	1.7	29	13	3.8
Nigeria	107,286	3.0	43	13	6.2
Pakistan	132,185	2.2	35	11	5.1
Peru	25,595	2.0	27	6	3.4
Philippines	76,104	2.1	29	7	3.6
Poland	38,615	0.0	10	10	1.4
Romania	22,463	− 0.3	10	12	1.2
Russia	147,306	− .03	10	15	1.4
South Africa	42,209	1.5	27	12	3.2
South Korea	45,949	1.0	16	6	1.8
Spain	39,108	0.1	9	10	1.2
Tanzania	29,899	2.6	41	17	5.6
Thailand	59,451	1.0	17	7	1.9
Turkey	63,528	1.6	22	5	2.5
Ukraine	50,448	− 0.6	10	16	1.4
United Kingdom	57,592	0.2	12	11	1.6
United States	267,955	0.9	15	9	2.1
Vietnam	75,124	1.5	22	7	2.6
Yemen	15,857	3.3	43	11	7.2

Source: U.S. Bureau of the Census, 1997.

important in understanding global population growth: rates of natural growth/decline and the age structure of a population. A third factor, immigration/emigration, is an important consideration at the national or regional level but does not influence global trends.

Birth, Death, and Fertility

Natural growth (sometimes called natural increase or decrease) is a simple measure of population growth that examines the differences between births (fertility) and deaths (mortality) in a given group. *Birth* and *death rates* are normally expressed as rate of occurrence per 1000 people. For example, if 3000 babies were born in a population of 150,000, then the birth rate would be 20 per 1000. *Natural increase* is the difference between birth and death rates and is expressed as a percentage figure. About 4 million people were born in the United States in 1997 and about 2.4 million died, causing a net natural increase of 1.6 million. Net legal immigration added a further 4.5 to 5 million (about 80% of them undocumented) to the U.S. population during this time.

Annual growth rates must be considered in combination with the actual population figure. A low annual growth rate of a small population is significantly different from a comparable annual figure for a much larger population. India and Myanmar, for example, had similar annual growth rates of 1.7 percent in 1997. India, with a base population of 968 million, increased by 16 million annually. Myanmar, on the other hand, with a population base of 46.5 million, added only 790,000 to its population that year.

One of the most important factors in population growth today is the birth rate. The more babies are born, the more a population grows. Birth rates in the world today are typically between about 10 and 50 per 1000 population. Birth rates are controlled mostly by the *fertility rate*, a measure of the average number of children a woman has in her reproductive years (ages 15 to 49). Birth rates are also affected by the age structure of a population. If there is a large number of young women in a population, the birth rate will be higher, while in an older population birth rates are lower because more women are beyond child-bearing years.

On a global scale, the total fertility rate was 2.9 in 1997. The rate is significantly higher in the less industrialized nations (3.4) than in the more industrialized nations (1.6). There are also some very distinct regional differences. For example, Africa had a total fertility rate of 5.1 versus 2.8 in Asia and 1.4 in Europe.

Death rates are more closely related to the age structure of a population than are birth rates. Countries with older populations have higher death rates than those with younger populations. Death rates are also affected by factors such as nutrition and the availability of health care, and so high death rates also occur in very poor countries, even though their populations may be relatively young. Death rates in the world tend to be between about 5 and 20 per thousand, much lower than typical birth rates. This difference between birth rates and death rates results in population growth.

Recent trends in world population growth rates and average fertility rates are shown in Figure 5.3. The global population growth rate was relatively low in 1950, because death rates in poorer countries were still high. But improved medicine and hygiene caused significant reductions in mortality, and population rose rapidly. Average fertility rates at this time were about 5. Between 1957 and 1962, population growth plummeted as a result of famine in China brought on by crop failures during the Great Leap Forward. This was the government's attempt to dramatically increase food production by planting even where conditions were not favorable. Population growth rebounded quickly, however, and remained over 2 percent per year through the rest of the 1960s. Significant declines in fertility began in the early 1970s. By 1980 the average world fertility rate was below 4, and in 1997 it dropped to 2.9. This decline in fertility directly affected birth rates and thus population growth. In Japan and some European countries fertility has dropped well below replacement level, and if it remains low populations may decline. This is problematic in countries like Japan which do not have high rates of immigration (Issue 5.1).

One of the most important reasons for a decline in the rate of natural growth in the United States has been a steady decline in the number of children born per family. In 1990, for example, the total fertility rate among American women was 2.1. This means that, on the average, every American woman has two live births during her lifetime. The total fertility rate in the United States has steadily declined since the 1950s (Table 5.2), al-

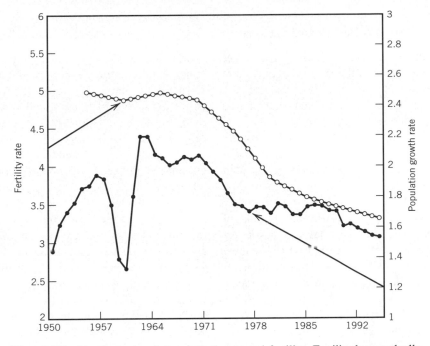

Figure 5.3 Trends in population growth rate and fertility. Fertility has gradually declined since the mid-1960s, and the population growth rate has followed a similar course. The dramatic dip in the world's population growth rate is a result of a dramatic increase in mortality and a decrease in fertility that occurred during the Great Leap Forward in China. *Source:* World Resources Institute, 1996.

though from 1985 until 1995, a small increase is apparent, as the "baby boom" generation nears the end of their reproductive years.

For decades, debate has persisted on the question of whether or not high-growth nations should work to decrease their fertility rates. As an example, the People's Republic of China (now with a total fertility rate of 1.8) instituted a one-child limit for all families (Fig. 5.4) during the 1970s. Although the policies varied from province to province, in some areas the birth of a second child resulted in the loss of state medical and school aid, ostracism, and official criticism. A third pregnancy brought strong pressure from the community for an abortion (Greenhalgh and Bongaarts 1987).

Accustomed to large families and desirous of having boys, many Chinese found it very difficult to live with this policy. Reports of female infanticide, though true, remain very controversial, because those who favor population control do not like to admit to such abuses, which often provide ammunition to those who would abolish all limits to growth. In recent years, Chinese policies have eased somewhat as urban-rural and ethnic differences have begun to play a role in family planning.

For the past 25 years India has struggled to reduce birth rates by providing various economic and social incentives, as well as involuntary measures. Its most recent census revealed, however, that growth rates did not decline significantly between 1970 and 1990. In some countries, fertility has declined primarily as a result of government-sponsored family planning programs. Not all of these programs have been successful, and many countries have exhibited continued high fertility rates.

Zero population growth (ZPG) is a term indicating the number of births that will simply replace a population, without further growth. It takes a total fertility rate of about 2.1 in developed nations or 2.7 in developing nations to maintain a population at a constant size, assuming a stable age structure and no net migration. The difference is explained by higher mortality rates in the developing nations, which require a higher birth rate to offset losses. A total fertility

ISSUE 5.1: JAPAN'S DECLINING POPULATION

Japan is a densely populated nation: it averages 332 people per square kilometer, as compared to 105 in France and 28 in the United States. But population growth is not a problem in Japan; in fact, the opposite is a greater concern. The total fertility rate in Japan is just 1.5, well below replacement level. If the population starts to decline, real estate begins to lose value, the labor supply shrinks, and the economy contracts. And that state of affairs has some leaders worried.

Japan's situation is very similar to that of many other advanced industrial and postindustrial societies. In fact, in the early 1990s there were 26 countries with fertility rates below 1.75, 23 of them in Europe. The other 3 were Japan, Singapore, and South Korea—the 3 wealthiest countries in Asia outside the Middle East (World Resources Institute 1996).

The main reasons for low fertility rates in Japan, as in most of the other countries with similar rates, are familiar and most of them related to wealth. Wealth is associated with a number of factors that all lead women to choose to have fewer children. Foremost among these are employment opportunities, which usually conflict with child-rearing. Education is important, because it increases employment opportunities; social conditions that open the same doors to women as to men are also important. The fact that women are working outside of the home does not mean that they can't have children, but it usually indicates that they prefer to have fewer children. It isn't easy raising two kids and working full time, but raising five or six kids and working full time is nearly impossible. Education and employment opportunities also lead to a reduced rate of teen pregnancy: Japan's teen pregnancy rate is among the lowest in the world (UNICEF 1996). The age at marriage is also a factor: women who marry at an older age tend to have fewer children than those who marry young.

In the last half of the twentieth century, Japan has seen a steady decline in fertility rates, mirroring its economic growth. Demographic changes for this period are illustrated in the graphs on the next page, including the trend of total fertility and the population pyramid. Immediately following World War II, Japan, like the United States and many other countries, experienced a baby boom. Total fertility rates in the early 1950s were well above 2, families of 3 and 4 children were common, and the population grew at nearly 1.5 percent per year. The babies born in this period were in their mid-40s in 1997, and they form the broadest portion of the population pyramid. But the total fertility rate declined steadily after the baby boom, and the lack of people in their mid-30s in 1997 is clear in the narrowing of the pyramid at that level. The overall growth rate of population fell to 0.9 percent annually in the early 1960s.

Then in the early 1970s the fertility rate increased again. This appears because the total fertility rate is calculated from the number of births divided by the number of women of childbearing age: 15–49. But most babies are born to mothers in their 20s and relatively few are born to women in their late 30s and 40s. In the early 1970s in Japan, there was a disproportionately large number of women in their 20s because of the baby boom two decades earlier. This caused a temporary increase in the total fertility rate. The fertility of the large population of baby-boom women contributed to a surge in the overall growth rate of population, reaching rates similar to those during the postwar baby boom.

Adjusting for the number of women in each age cohort, we can see that fertility has steadily declined, reaching 1.5 in the mid-1990s. The overall population growth rate reached 0.3 percent per year in 1995 and is still declining. The population pyramid shows the result of declining fertility: in 1995, the number of people aged 0–5 was only 56 percent of the number of people aged 45–49. Thus, if fertility continues at this low rate and if no net immigration takes place, the population will begin to decline, and rapidly. The population decrease will be especially dramatic in 2020–2040, when the baby boomers will die. If fertility rates continued at around 1.5, then the population could fall to just 55 million in the year 2100, as compared to its present level of 125 million (Kristof 1996).

In a world of rapidly growing populations, why should a population decline in some areas

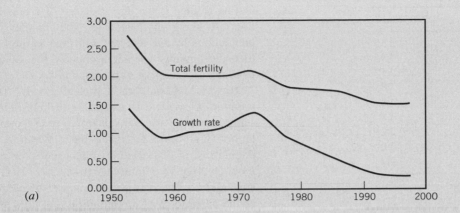

(a)

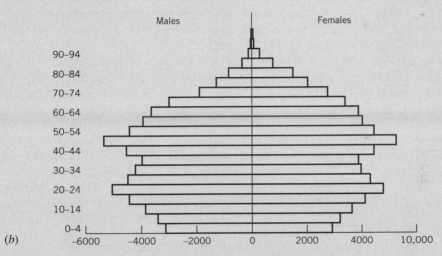

(b)

Demographic trends in Japan. Fertility and growth rates have declined since 1953 (*a*) resulting in a declining population (*b*). Data in the population pyramid are for 1995. *Sources:* World Resources Institute, 1996; United Nations, 1994.

be a problem? If people could move easily from one country to another, and from one society to another, then it wouldn't be a problem. But such migrations generate problems, usually in the receiving country. Some of these problems are a result of differences in education and job skills: if immigrants come from poor countries, they are less likely to possess the skills needed to contribute to the economy of a wealthy nation to which they would migrate. But other problems are rooted in racism and ethnocentrism and lead to tensions between cultures. Examples are everywhere: Koreans in Japan, Turks in Germany, Algerians in France, Latinos in the United States. If these problems could be solved, then rich countries with stable populations could absorb some of the excess population from other parts of the world. Unless fertility rates start to increase in countries like Japan, increasing the number of immigrants these countries admit will be the only way to avert economic decline.

Table 5.2 U.S. Fertility
Rates, 1950–1995

Year	Rate
1950	3.3
1960	3.4
1970	2.5
1975	1.8
1980	1.8
1985	1.8
1990	2.1
1993	2.0
1995	2.1

Source: U.S. Census Bureau, 1996.

rate of less than 2.1 would eventually lead to population decline, assuming no net immigration. To achieve ZPG globally, a total fertility rate of about 2.5 is needed, but a much lower rate (below *replacement levels*) would be needed in some regions to stabilize population. Even if a ZPG fertility rate were reached, which is highly unlikely in this century, the population would continue to expand simply because of the age structure of the world population. In other words, a disproportionate number of young people have yet to reach their child-bearing years.

Age Structure

The second factor that contributes to overall population change is the age structure of a population. A short discussion of the profiles of populations by age and sex will give us the key to understanding whether a country has an expanding, declining, or stable population.

How is a population's profile drawn? The *population pyramid* is a visually striking representation of the age and sex structure of a population (Fig. 5.5). To make up a pyramid, a population is classified in age groups or *cohorts* by five-year intervals (0–4, 5–9, 10–14, etc.) and by sex. The actual number of people or the percentage of a population that falls into each of these age categories is then graphed. The percentage of males in specific age groups is shown on the left and the percentage of females on the right. The general shape of the pyramid indicates the relative growth of the population.

For example, a rapidly expanding population such as the Congo's (Fig. 5.5*a*) has a very broad base because a large percentage of the population is less than 14 years of age; that is, many children are being born to each mother. The average fertility rate of Congolese women is 6.7, and the birth rate is 47.5 per 1000 population. Many of

Figure 5.4 One-child family policy in China. The Chinese government has encouraged late marriage and has imposed economic penalties on families with more than one child. This has resulted in a significant lowering of the country's fertility rate. The wall poster in Chengdu, Sichuan Province, praises the merits of one-child families.

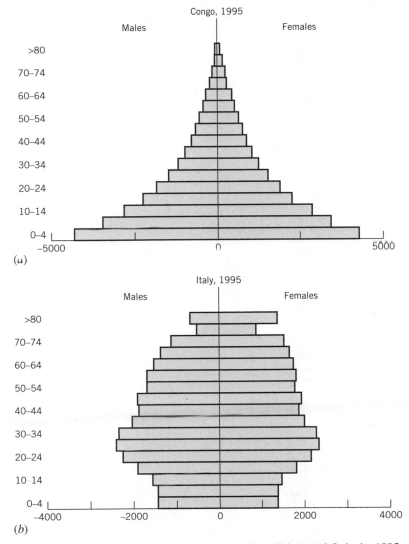

Figure 5.5 Population pyramids for Congo (then Zaire) and Italy in 1995. Congo's population pyramid is broad at the base indicating that it is young and growing rapidly. Italy's pyramid has near-vertical sides, indicating that the number of children is about the same as the number of middle-aged people, and the population is not growing. *Source:* United Nations, 1994.

the developing nations have population pyramids of this shape. One hundred years ago, the U.S. population had a similar shape, as did the countries of Europe.

Stable or declining populations such as those of Italy (Fig. 5.5b) have population pyramids with narrower bases. As the population ages, the actual number or percentage in each cohort declines due to mortality. Italy's fertility rate is 1.5—below replacement level—causing the pyramid to be narrow at the base. The low birth rate of 10.1 is attributable to both low fertility

and a relatively small proportion of women in child-bearing years.

The effect of changing fertility on changing age structures is evident in data from Brazil (Fig. 5.6). In 1960 Brazil had high fertility rates characteristic of developing countries at that time and a similarly broad-based population pyramid. But during the 1970s and 1980s both fertility and birth rates declined rapidly (see Issue 5.2), and by 1995 a distinct narrowing of the pyramid's base was evident. The pyramid for 2030, as projected by the United Nations, shows continued

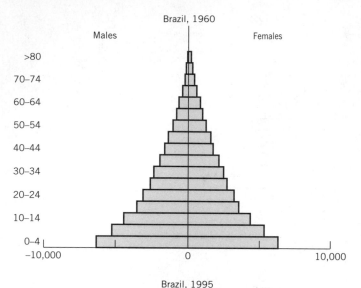

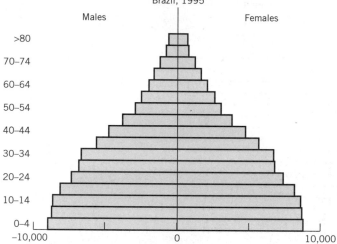

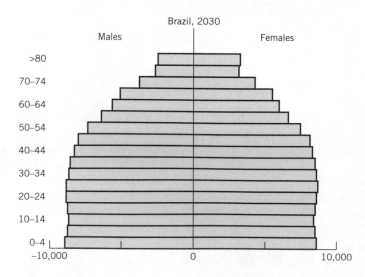

Figure 5.6 Population pyramids for Brazil: 1960, 1995, 2030. Initially characterized by high birth rates in 1960, Brazil's population growth in 1995 reflected a more stable population. Projected growth also indicates a stable population. *Source:* United Nations, 1994.

ISSUE 5.2: BRAZIL'S FERTILITY RATE DROPS NEARLY 50 PERCENT: WHY?

An unanticipated development has occurred in Brazil. Since 1970, the fertility rate in this huge South American country has declined by more than one-half—from 5.75 children per woman to about 2.4 in 1996 (Population Reference Bureau 1997).

While other countries have experienced rapid, precipitous drops in fertility, these examples either took place in the developed world or are the result of strong government policies, such as China's stringent one-child policy and government-led programs in Colombia and Mexico. Conspicuous policy failures also have occurred, such as in India, where all the family planning campaigning in the world cannot seem to make a dent in the birth rate. To make Brazil's situation all the more puzzling, its present population of 160 million is overwhelmingly Roman Catholic, a religion that dis- courages birth control, and Brazil's government has no government birth control policy.

This fertility drop has several known causes. The first is the government's withdrawal from the fertility issue. In the 1960s, Brazil's military government encouraged big families, and both government and church were hostile to family planning. What has changed is that both authorities are now silent on the subject and allow couples to decide for themselves. Universal access to contraception has also helped. In the 1960s, only 5 percent of fertile married women used contraceptives; today that figure is 66 percent. In a Roman Catholic country, it is not surprising that abortions are illegal; nor is it surprising that so many are carried out. Nevertheless, 3 million illegal abortions take place annually in Brazil.

The improved status of women has also contributed to Brazil's fertility decline. There is close to an 85 percent literacy rate among Brazil's women, a rate that is comparable to that of most developed nations. Education has increased the range of choices among Brazilian women. For example, the two most popular forms of birth control are the pill and female sterilization, which require Brazil's women to take an active role in determining their own fertility. Birth control pills can be purchased without a prescription, and the largely irreversible tube–tying choice has been made by 27 percent of married Brazilian women (the U.S. level is 17 percent). Only 0.8 percent of Brazil's married men have opted for sterilization.

Brazil's constitution mandates a four-month maternity leave. This law, passed in 1988, was intended to encourage women both to work and to have babies: however, in actuality women workers find they are penalized for remaining fertile. Many employers now demand sterility certificates as a precondition for hiring or conduct regular urine pregnancy tests of their female workers. This punitive response certainly suppresses childbearing among Brazil's working women.

Economic changes within the family and Brazilian society are also important. In the classic tradition of the demographic transition, family size declines as real income rises; this was the experience in Europe and North America. In Brazil, however, real income has declined in a stagnant 1980s economy, but the poor maintain that they cannot afford more children, even though many babies die before their first birthdays, victims of unsanitary conditions and malnourishment. Finally, and perhaps most importantly, the role of television has been extremely influential. Researchers maintain that in the absence of real prosperity, Brazilians are absorbing the values of the good life by watching television—an image of urban life that does not always reflect reality.

In order for fertility levels to drop, proponents of the demographic transition state that a population must become urban and industrialized and experience a rise in quality of life. In addition to educational advancements, television (in particular the hugely successful evening soap operas) emphasizes that sexuality and procreation can be separated, that large families are poor and miserable, and that small families are affluent. In the absence of real prosperity, Brazil's population—especially its women—has made the move to low birth rates on the basis of expectations alone.

low fertility—a pyramid that is approaching the near-vertical pattern characteristic of stable populations. This is just a projection, and we really don't know exactly what Brazilian fertility rates will be in the next few decades. But we do know how many young girls are alive today, and this number, when multiplied by the fertility rate for each cohort, helps us predict the total number of children who will be born to those women as they enter child-bearing years.

The three pyramids in Figure 5.6 provide an excellent illustration of how the total population grows as a consequence of a period of high birth rates but increasing longevity of the population resulting from improved nutrition and medical care. With high death rates and low life expectancy a pyramid shaped like Brazil's in 1960 could represent a stable population (although by this time Brazil's population was already growing rapidly). The lower death rates and greater longevity typical of wealthier nations today means that the pyramid of a stable population is shaped more like Brazil's in 2030.

The United States has seen significant variations in fertility in the last few decades. Right after World War II and into the 1960s, the U.S. fertility rate was at a modern-day high, as explained earlier. These baby boomers have not been reproducing at the high rate of their parents, and even with their huge numbers, the number of people under age 14 has decreased since 1970. As the baby boom cohort ages, so does the overall age of the U.S. population. The median age in 1970 was 28, in 1980 it was 30, and by 1995 it was 34 and it is expected to reach 36 by the end of the century. Declining birth rates and the general aging of the *baby-boom* cohort of the 1950s, coupled with a long life expectancy, account for this trend.

Migration

Migration, which includes immigration and emigration, is the movement of individuals from one location to another. It has no influence on global population projections, but it does have a significant impact at national, regional, and local population levels. Migration flows are caused by lack of economic opportunities, group conflicts between and within nations, and environmental disruption. These flows can be permanent or temporary.

The populations of many countries are affected by migration. In the short run, refugees may flee or be forced from their homes during war or famine and migrate to nearby nations, with the intention of returning home when conditions improve (Fig. 5.7). Often such short-term migration becomes permanent. In the long run, regions of high population growth or poor economic conditions tend to be areas of net emigration, while those with strong economies

Figure 5.7 Rwandan refugees in a camp in Tanzania, following the civil war in 1994. Most of them were eventually repatriated.

and a need for labor tend to be regions of net immigration.

In the world today, Europe and North America have substantial net immigration. Early migration to North America was of two basic types. Free immigrants came in search of a better life, and forced immigrants, or slaves, helped make life easier for others. By the late nineteenth century, mass migration greatly increased the flow as entire ethnic or regional groups decided collectively to move to the United States and Canada, largely in search of better economic opportunities, as conditions became too crowded in "the old country."

Since World War II, the international migration flow has to a large extent been reversed, with the largest percentage of migrants moving from less industrialized nations to European and North American urban areas. The principal destinations of transnational migrants from 1950 onward have been the United States, Canada, Australia, and New Zealand, with large numbers moving to Europe and Great Britain as well. All of these countries currently have low birth rates, and the native population is stabilizing or shrinking. These new immigrants account for much of the increase in population in these countries. This trend has been accelerated by war and genocide, for example, the expansion of the Vietnamese population in the United States since the end of the Vietnam War or the increase in the Congo of refugees from Rwanda.

As a result of increasing numbers of migrants to the industrialized world, some countries have devised restrictive policies for immigration, maintaining that the immigrants are stealing wages from native-born citizens. Of course there is usually a large component of fear and dislike—racism—among natives regarding these new residents. Though often disliked, the peoples of the Middle East, Asia, and Africa are allowed to enter industrialized nations on a temporary basis to work the jobs that declining populations cannot or will not fill. In Europe these temporary residents are called *guest workers*. Fears of an unending flood of illegal immigrants from Mexico into the United States is a perennial source of controversy in the United States.

This situation is only a symptom of a larger problem, that is, population pressure and perceived lack of opportunity in many less industrialized nations. People are both pulled off the land into the cities by the attractive opportunities available there and pushed off the land because economic opportunities in rural areas are limited. A move to the regional or capital city brings little satisfaction because these areas are overcrowded and cannot provide basic services (sanitation, electricity, and housing) for the new immigrants.

This situation will continue as long as rural populations in poorer countries perceive that economic opportunity remains greater elsewhere. When the population boom hit Europe in the eighteenth century, the overcrowded countries had empty lands for the population to spread into; where the land was not empty, as with the native populations of the Americas, the Europeans simply conquered by force. Today the peoples of Asia and Africa have no empty lands to spread into. The situation is somewhat better in Central and South America, although even there the industrialized, environmentally sensitive countries have chastised the governments for their environmentally destructive methods of settlement. Many peasants still remain landless, thus increasing the likelihood of poor stewardship of the land.

Trends in Population Growth

When we examine current rates of population change due to natural increase and migration, we see significant population growth at rates that, if continued, will cause dramatic changes in all aspects of life in just a few decades. But how are rates of population growth changing? Can present rates be extrapolated into the future? The answer is yes and no. Significant changes in population growth are occurring, and these cannot be predicted beyond a few decades. On the other hand, we know some important parts of the population puzzle, especially the numbers and ages of people alive today, and so we can predict the near future with relative certainty.

The demographic transition is a widely used generalization of past population change that can be used to illustrate these processes (Fig. 5.8). It is a pattern generalized from the history of population in Europe in the last two centuries. Prior to the Industrial Revolution with its attendant social changes and medical advances, most human populations had both high fertility rates and high mortality rates together with relatively stable populations. In recent centuries in the industrialized nations, mortality rates began to decline as a

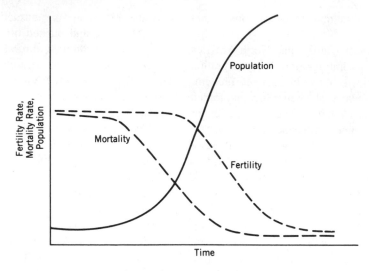

Figure 5.8 The demographic transition. Preindustrial populations have generally had high birth rates and death rates. When death rates fall before birth rates, population rises rapidly.

result of increased standards of living and medical care. This decline preceded the decline in fertility. The result was a period of time in which birth rates were substantially greater than mortality rates, and population increased accordingly.

This period of increase was characterized by a particularly broad-based population pyramid. It was also during this era, the eighteenth and nineteenth centuries, that the large populations of Europe found an outlet by settling in North America, Australia, and other frontier areas. Later, social changes brought about in part by the Industrial Revolution led to a decline in fertility in the industrialized nations, so that the base of the population pyramids narrowed and populations stabilized. Thus, Europe and the Americas have passed through their own period of intense population growth.

In the mid-twentieth century, much of the developing world is experiencing a similar demographic transition, though much more rapidly than occurred in Europe. Death rates declined dramatically in midcentury, and the decline in birth rates followed a few decades later. The various positions of countries in the demographic transition can be seen in Figure 5.9, which shows birth rates and death rates for the countries listed in Table 5.1. Countries like Ethiopia and Nigeria are in the middle of the transition.

They have high birth rates because both have high fertility rates and relatively young populations. At the same time, they still have high death rates because of poor nutrition and health. Countries like Indonesia, Brazil, and Mexico are further along in the transition. They have much lower fertility rates than Ethiopia or Nigeria, and so their birth rates are lower. Economic conditions in these countries are also somewhat better, and this in combination with very young populations means that death rates are very low. Finally, countries such as France and Russia have very low birth rates, as a result of low fertility and older populations. But an older population also means higher death rates, as can be seen in the graph.

Although it appears that the period of great difference between birth and death rates (and hence rapid population growth) in developing nations will be relatively brief, the base population was large to begin with and the growth rate was also large. To this we add the confounding problem that we do not have available continents with relatively low populations of easily subdued people to serve as outlets for excess population, as the Americas were available to Europeans a century or two ago. Thus population pressures in Africa and Asia will be particularly significant for the next few decades.

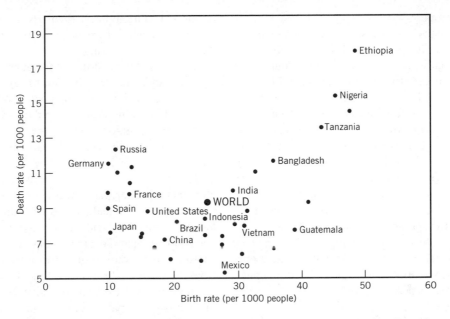

Figure 5.9   Birth rates and death rates for the countries listed in Table 5.1. Countries early in the demographic transition plot on the upper right. Countries in mid-transition show low death rates and declining birth rates, and plot in the lower center of the graph. As population growth slows and the population ages, death rates rise; countries in this phase of the transition plot at the left-hand side of the graph. *Source:* World Resources Institute, 1996.

THE DISTRIBUTION OF POPULATION AND POPULATION GROWTH

The world's population is far from evenly distributed. It is concentrated in five major regions of the world: east Asia (especially China and Japan), southeast Asia (Indonesia, Vietnam, Myanmar), south Asia (India, Pakistan, Bangladesh), Europe (European Union, Russia), and eastern North America (United States, Canada). Sixty percent of the world's population lives in Asia (Fig. 5.10); China and India together account for about 38 percent of the world's population.

Rich and Poor Regions

Currently, the most rapid population growth is taking place in the less industrialized countries. Based on the medium variant of recent UN projections, population worldwide will rise to 8.67 billion by 2035, an increase of 2.96 billion. This growth is overwhelmingly concentrated in the less industrialized nations. Only about 70 million of the 2.96 billion increase in world population expected between 1995 and 2030 will take place

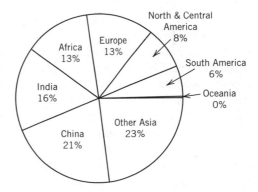

Figure 5.10   World population distribution. Most of the world's population is concentrated in Asia, with the remaining population more evenly distributed among the continents except Oceania, which is the least populated. *Source:* World Resources Institute, 1996.

in the more industrialized countries; the other 2890 million, nearly 98 percent of the projected growth, will occur in the less industrialized countries (United Nations, 1994). Between 1970 and 1990, fertility declined significantly in all parts of the world, but in the industrialized nations this decline brought fertility levels to below replacement in many countries. The demographic momentum of the post–World War II baby boom caused continued population growth, but by the turn of the century this momentum will be expended, and little further population growth is expected. In the less industrialized nations, however, population will continue to grow, both because of high fertility (though lower than past levels) and relatively young populations. Thus, while less industrialized countries in 1995 represented about 80 percent of the world's population, in 2030 this portion will be about 86 percent. Europe and Africa in 1995 had similar populations, each representing about 13 percent of the world. In 2030 Europe will represent only 9 percent, while Africa's share of world population will be 18 percent.

Increasing Urbanization

Much of the world's population growth since the 1960s has occurred in urban places in both the industrialized and less industrialized nations (Fig. 5.11), and this trend is expected to continue. Movement away from rural areas, where in most cases the population was largely food self-sufficient, has complicated the population pressures in the less industrialized nations. It certainly has intensified the pressures on usable resources, including space, water, and food, and it taxes national abilities to promote social and economic welfare. This trend toward increasing urbanization is a major problem facing the less industrialized nations in the future. At the present time about half of the world's people live in urban areas. About 90 percent of the world's population increase between 1995 and 2025 is expected to take place in urban areas.

POPULATION CONTROL STRATEGIES

Since the 1960s, when the population problem was recognized internationally, various programs have been instituted to control population, primarily through controlling fertility. Some of these programs have been quite coercive, such as forced sterilization or tax penalties for large families. Others have focused on increasing opportunities for women through education and economic development. Some strategies have concentrated on individual behavior, particularly use of contraceptives, whereas others have taken a broader social view, emphasizing economic factors. We now know that many different factors affect fertility rates, and it is often difficult to say which are the most effective in reducing population growth.

Family planning programs in the United States were first institutionalized in the form of birth control clinics in the 1920s. The first birth control clinics were established in New York City by Margaret Sanger, a leader in the women's rights movement. Sanger was concerned with the suffering of women who had too many children, spaced too close together, with no options for fertility control other than illegal abortions. The first birth control clinics were designed to liberate women from the traditional roles of wife and breeder and to allow women to exercise active control over the number and spacing of the births of their children. These early clinics met with strong resistance, in much the same way that the equal rights movement would meet resistance over half a century later. For a time in the United States, diaphragms were illegal and had to be smuggled in from Europe by birth control advocates.

The link between a woman's role in her society and her desire to increase or decrease the size of her family is a strong one, however. An understanding of women's roles in society is a prerequisite for any successful family planning effort.

Socioeconomic Conditions and Fertility

In those nations where standards of living and increased literacy have helped to improve women's status, fertility has declined (see Issue 5.2). Several specific factors have influenced the decline in fertility, including increased educational levels of women, increased female employment outside the home, and marriage at a later age. All of these changes create conditions that motivate women to limit the size of their families. In much of the world social conditions that affect fertility, such as women's employment outside the home, are changing as people move to cities and industrial employment expands. This may be one of the factors contributing to the decline in fertility.

Increased educational levels have opened opportunities other than motherhood to many

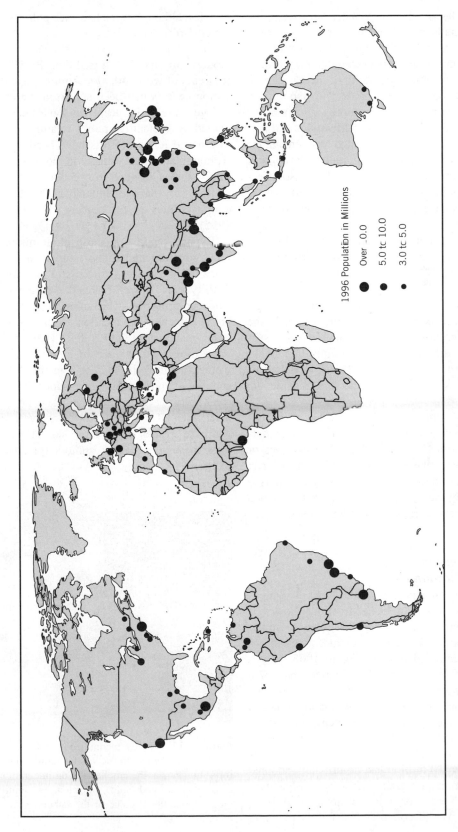

Figure 5.11 Major metropolitan areas of the world, 1996. In the early 1990s, the total urban population of the world surpassed the number living in rural areas.

1996 Population in Millions

Over 10.0

5.0 to 10.0

3.0 to 5.0

women. The acquisition of more knowledge not only has made these women more aware of family planning and contraceptive information but has also increased their knowledge of the need for family planning. In addition, increased education influences one's goals and aspirations, and as a woman receives more education she may seek new alternatives or life-styles and perhaps a career. Lastly, educated women realize the value of education and want to have their own children educated as well. To do so effectively and in some cases economically, these women feel the need to limit the size of their families.

Increased female employment outside the home is another factor that has contributed to declining fertility rates. The need for two income earners in North American households is a response to increasing economic pressures. With a large percentage of women now in the labor force, large families are not as easily sustained as when women were mainly homemakers. According to the U.S. Census, over half of the nation's married women work outside the home.

Delaying the age of marriage has also contributed to declining fertility. If a woman is marrying later in her life, in her late twenties or early thirties, the number of children she can bear will be smaller. This practice has been used for years in the People's Republic of China as a family planning method and has shown mixed results.

Contraception and Family Planning

Family planning programs are generally voluntary. In the less industrialized nations, however, many countries have found it necessary to implement compulsory programs or incentives to encourage family planning. Prior to 1965, only a handful of less industrialized nations had officially supported family planning programs. The international spread of family planning began after 1965 and quickly gained momentum in the next ten years (Fig. 5.12). By 1975, only 3 of the 38 less industrialized nations with populations greater than 10 million had no officially adopted family planning programs. These were Myanmar, Peru, and North Korea. Five years later, all but a few Third World countries had family planning

policies, although some had such policies only on paper (Brown et al. 1989).

Indonesia's example illustrates the use of modernism mixed with tradition. By 1980, after ten years of work, 40,000 information and distribution centers had been set up in the country's villages. Free contraceptives have been accompanied by a relentless public relations campaign. These and related efforts have been successful. Although abortion is illegal in Indonesia, the fertility rate has dropped from 5.6 to 2.7 today. The number of married Indonesian women using contraceptives is 50 percent (United Nations 1995).

Experts report that those programs receiving good governmental support and economic assistance will be the most successful in reducing the fertility rate. A well-planned program must include not only the distribution of contraceptives but also increased education about their use. The bitter reaction to India's IUD (intrauterine device) program is a case in point. Many Indian women adopted the IUD as a method of contraception. Family planning personnel would visit rural villages and, after medical examinations, insert the IUDs. The doctors, however, failed to warn the women of potential side effects. When these became apparent, rumors spread and the

Figure 5.12 Family planning in Jendouba, Tunisia. Education is the key to success for family planning efforts. In Tunisia, the emphasis is on integrating health care (maternal and child), nutrition, and family planning. Notice the absence of the fathers in this family planning class.

program virtually collapsed overnight. Similar reactions to the IUD have followed in the United States, with class action suits on one particular type, the Dalkon shield.

In the United States, fertility rates have risen slightly since the mid-1980s, from 1.8 to 2.1 in 1997. The number of abortions has been fairly steady since the mid 1980s, although the rate per 1000 women has declined. Women are seeking more educational opportunities and postponing marriage to a later age. They also have more choices on when and if to start a family, choices that were not as socially acceptable two decades ago.

SUMMARY

The rate of population growth worldwide is clearly dropping. The reasons vary from one culture to another, and in many cases the causes for declining fertility are not clear. It is impossible to say whether population control programs, industrialization and employment opportunities for women, access to birth control, or other factors are most responsible for the change. One thing is certain, however, fertility rates can and do change very rapidly. At the moment they are declining in most of the world, and most demographers expect this trend to continue.

If current trends persist for the next few decades, we can expect world population to grow at a much slower rate than it did in the 1960s and 1970s. The next doubling of population will probably take much longer than is implied by the current doubling time of a little over 50 years. In fact, many predict that world population will stabilize at the level of 10 to 11 billion, in which case it would never double its current size. Demographic data often hold surprises, however, and such predictions must be read with caution.

Even though population growth is slowing, it is still a major factor in the world resource picture. A 50 percent increase in world population in the next three to four decades is a near certainty, and if new people consume resources at rates similar to the present ones, the environmental consequences will be dramatic. We will turn our attention to these consequences in the remainder of this book.

REFERENCES AND ADDITIONAL READING

Boserup, E. 1965. *The Conditions of Agricultural Growth: The Economics of Agrarian Change under Population Pressure.* London: Allen & Unwin.

_____. 1981. *Population and Technological Change.* Chicago: University of Chicago Press.

Brooke, J. 1989. Decline in births in Brazil lessens population fears. *New York Times,* August 8, p. A1.

Brown, L. R., and H. Kane. 1994. *Full House: Reassessing the Earth's Population Carrying Capacity.* New York: W. W. Norton

_____. et al. 1989. *State of the World, 1989.* Washington, DC: Worldwatch Institute.

Chen, L. C., W. Fitzgerald, and L. Bates. 1995. Women, politics, and global management. *Environment* 37 (1): 4–9, 31–33.

Daly, H. E. 1977. *Steady–State Economics.* San Francisco: W. H. Freeman.

Durning, A. B. 1989. *Poverty and the Environment: Reversing the Downward Spiral.* Worldwatch Paper no. 92. Washington, DC: Worldwatch Institute.

Ehrlich, P. R., and A. H. Ehrlich. 1990. *The Population Explosion.* New York: Simon & Schuster.

Erlich, P. 1968. *The Population Bomb.* New York: Ballantine Books.

Georgesu–Roegen, N. 1979. Comments on papers by Daly and Stiglitz. In V. K. Smith, ed., *Scarcity and Growth Reconsidered.* Baltimore, MD: Johns Hopkins University Press.

Greenhalgh, S., and J. Bongaarts. 1987. Fertility policy in China: Future options. *Science* 235: 1167–1172.

Hardin, G. 1993. *Living Within Limits: Ecology, Economics, and Population Taboos.* New York: Oxford University Press.

Harkavy, O. 1995. *Curbing Population Growth: An Insider's Perspective on the Population Movement.* New York: Plenum Press.

Harvey, D. 1974. Population, resources, and the ideology of science. *Economic Geography* 50: 256–277.

Hohm, C. F., and Lori Justin Jones. 1995. *Population: Opposing Viewpoints.* San Diego, CA: Greenhaven Press.

Jacobson, J. L. 1988. *Environmental Refugees: A Yardstick of Habitability.* Worldwatch Paper no. 86. Washington, DC: Worldwatch Institute.

Kristof, N. D. 1996. Baby may make 3, but in Japan that's not enough. *New York Times,* October 6, 1996, p. A3.

Lutz, W. 1994. *The Future Population of the World: What Can We Assume Today?* London: Earthscan Pub.

Malthus, T. R. 1976. An essay on the principle of population. In P. Appleman, ed. *An Essay on the Principles of Population: Text, Sources and Background, Criticism.* New York: W. W. Norton.

Mazur, L. A. 1994. *Beyond the Numbers: A Reader on Population, Consumption, and the Environment.* Washington, DC: Island Press.

Mink, S. D. 1993. *Poverty, Population, and the Environment.* Washington, DC: World Bank.

Moffett, G. D. 1994. *Global Population Growth: 21st Century Challenges.* Ithaca, NY: Foreign Policy Association.

Newland, K. 1977. *Women and Population Growth: Choice Beyond Childbearing.* Worldwatch Paper no. 16. Washington, DC: Worldwatch Institute.

_____ . 1980. *City Limits: Emerging Constraints on Urban Growth.* Worldwatch Paper no. 38. Washington, DC: Worldwatch Institute.

Population Reference Bureau. 1995. *1995 World Population Data Sheet.* Washington, DC: Population Reference Bureau.

_____ . 1997. *World Population and the Environment.* Washington DC: Population Reference Bureau.

Preston, S. H. 1986. Population growth and economic development. *Environment* 28(2): 6–9, 32–33.

Sen. G. 1995. The World programme of action: A new paradigm for population policy. *Envirnoment* 37 (1): 10–15, 34–37.

Simon, J. 1981. *The Ultimate Resource.* Princeton, NJ: Princeton University Press.

_____ . 1986. *Theory of Population and Economic Growth.* Oxford/New York: Basil Blackwell.

_____ . 1990. *Population Matters: People, Resources, Environment, and Immigration.* New Brunswick, N.J.: Transaction Publishers.

Stein, D. 1995. *People Who Count: Population and Politics, Women and Children.* London: Earthscan.

Stokes, B. 1980. *Men and Family Planning.* Worldwatch Paper no. 41. Washington, DC: Worldwatch Institute.

United Nations. 1994. *The Sex and Age Distribution of the World Populations: The 1994 Revision.* New York: United Nations.

_____ . 1995. *The World's Women 1995: Trends and Statistics.* New York: United Nations.

U.S. Bureau of the Census. 1996. *Statistical Abstract of the U.S.* Washington, DC: U.S. Government Printing Office.

UNICEF. 1996. Japan has lowest teen birth rate. ONLINE: United Nations Children's Emergency Fund. http://www.unicef.org/pon96/inbirth.htm.

Urban Institute. 1989. *U.S. Immigration Reform and Control Act and Undocumented Immigration to the United States. In Cooperation with the Rand Program for Research and Immigration Policy.* Washington, DC. Urban Institute.

Wattenberg, B., and K. Zinsmeister, eds. 1985. *Are World Population Trends a Problem?* Washington, DC: American Enterprise Institute for Public Policy Research.

World Resources Institute. 1996. *World Resources 1996–97.* New York: Oxford University Press.

For more information, consult our web page at ***http://www.wiley.com/college/cutter***

Study Questions

1. What is the significance of geometric versus arithmetic growth?
2. Why is the spatial distribution of population growth so important? Which nations or regions are growing most rapidly? Why? Which regions are not increasing in population?
3. Why do some people resist birth control measures? What incentives do some nations provide to use them?
4. What are the current major migration patterns? How do you explain these large-scale movements of people?
5. If you gaze into your crystal ball, what will the world population patterns be like in 2010? in 2025?

CHAPTER 6

AGRICULTURE AND FOOD PRODUCTION

Several resource issues are of particular importance in predicting and planning for future world supplies of food. These issues include the variability of rainfall patterns in lands already marginal for agriculture, overgrazing, competing land uses, ancient cultural traditions, and the efficiency of using meat for food. In this chapter we will look at the quantity and quality of agricultural resources and food production globally and within the United States.

Although food production is a global issue, local conditions vary tremendously around the world. Some regions chronically underproduce and either face widespread malnutrition or must import a large portion of their food needs. Others, like the United States, have ample productive capacity and only limited ability to sell surpluses overseas, so that much land is idle and the industry as a whole continues to shrink relative to the rest of the national economy.

International trade in agricultural commodities will become more significant in the coming decades. Trade and specialization have transformed agriculture in most of the world, and this trend will continue. In the United States, this means the continued decline of the traditional small family farm, and a shift toward large farms run as businesses, increasingly owned by corporations. American farmers today serve markets around the world, and production is thus affected by world market and trade factors. Although American agriculture is immensely productive and the United States is a major food exporter, it has yet to make a significant contribution to alleviating food shortages in the developing world.

Food production is probably the most important natural resource issue facing the world today. Population growth, though slower than in the 1960s, is still more rapid than at any other time prior to the twentieth century. This growth necessitates a continuing expansion of agricultural output. The expansion must take place in the context of severe constraints on the availability of agricultural land and on the ability of natural biogeochemical cycling processes to supply agricultural inputs (such as water) and absorb waste products (such as nitrogen). Thus, we must achieve a near doubling of agricultural output over the next half-century or so through more intensive use of existing lands while minimizing the environmental impacts of that intensification.

Plants that are now our major crops have been carefully bred for generations just like our major food animals. For optimal production, herders and ranchers need to provide high-quality food for livestock and ensure that grazing land is not overused. Most of the world's grazing lands are in semiarid climates, for in these low-rainfall areas the land generally cannot support arable agriculture without irrigation. Palatable grasses and low shrubs, however, are available to livestock. Animals are grazed on other lands too, usually mountainous areas and forests, both of which are unsuited for agriculture. In the United States, cattle grazing was the early backbone of the western states' economy, and in fact it contributes to much of the region's folklore. Today raising and selling cattle is part of the nation's agribusiness industry. Often, conflicting demands are made on the land available for grazing, and a debate ebbs and flows over the comparative value of meat versus grain production for national and global food supplies.

FOOD PRODUCTION RESOURCES

The world's food supply is based on about 30 major crops. The top 7 (wheat, rice, maize, potatoes, barley, sweet potatoes, and cassava) have annual harvests of 100 million metric tons or more, and these 7 account for more than half the harvest of the top 30 crops. In terms of global meat supply, 7 species provide more than 95 percent of all meat production. Cattle, poultry and pigs supply most of our meat, followed by much smaller contributions from lamb, goat, buffalo, and horse. Total world production of poultry has been growing rapidly and recently surpassed global pork production.

Great disparities exist in the amounts and kinds of food consumed in rich and poor nations, with rich nations eating not only more but better (Fig. 6.1). In the wealthy countries of North America and Europe, the average consumption of food (as measured by the amount that reaches the consumer—not all of this is necessarily eaten) is typically 120 to 140 percent of the needed caloric intake. In most of the poorer areas of the world, average food consumption is closer to 100 percent of need. And of course this is the average—some people in a society consume above average, and so others are inevitably underfed. The following paragraphs describe these patterns in greater detail.

Crops
The total land area of the world is about 32 billion acres (11 billion ha). Of this total, only about 13 percent is presently *arable*, or suitable for cultivated agriculture. Figure 6.2 is a map showing the distribution of arable land in the world. Arable land is not uniformly distributed in relation to population. Asia has the most arable land, but it also has an immense population to feed. On the other hand, North America only has 12 percent arable land and a relatively small population (see Table 4.1 in Ch. 4). When we consider that American agriculture generally produces higher yields per acre than systems where fertilizers and pesticides are less avail-

able, these disparities from one area to another are even greater.

Agricultural production has been increasing steadily since the 1960s. Between 1960 and 1990 world food production doubled and per capita production increased about 15 percent (Fig. 6.3). The rate of increase in both total and per capita production was largest in Europe and Asia, where increases in production dramatically outpaced population growth (Table 6.1). Food production also grew faster than population in South America. In Africa production increases have not kept pace with population growth, and as a result per capita food production there declined about 10 percent between 1960 and 1990. In North America production generally increased, although there were wide variations in output from year to year.

Much of the increase in food production since 1960 is attributable to the *Green Revolution*. The Green Revolution is a name applied to a series of agricultural innovations developed between 1945 and 1965 for the purpose of increasing food production in poor countries. These innovations included the development of new varieties of wheat and rice that were capable of much higher yields than traditional varieties, especially when fertilizer is applied (Easterbrook 1997). The Green Revolution is largely responsible for preventing widespread famines that were predicted in the 1960s.

Since 1990 global trends have changed, largely as a result of the collapse of the former Soviet Union. Food production in the former Soviet Union dropped nearly 40 percent between 1990 and 1994, and world grain inventories were substantially reduced. Thus while food production has continued to increase in most parts of the world, events in the former Soviet Union have caused world averages to be fairly constant in the 1990s.

Food security means that all people have both physical and economic access to the basic food they need to function normally (World Resources Institute 1996). Many nations in the world are now faced with a food security crisis that will only accelerate in the future. Food security is affected by scarcities (see Chapter 2) and by physical and economic access. Physical access includes poor distribution networks, lack of storage facilities, or civil strife. Economic access includes a country's ability to pay for food imports or the individual household's capability to generate enough income to pay for food. Even if

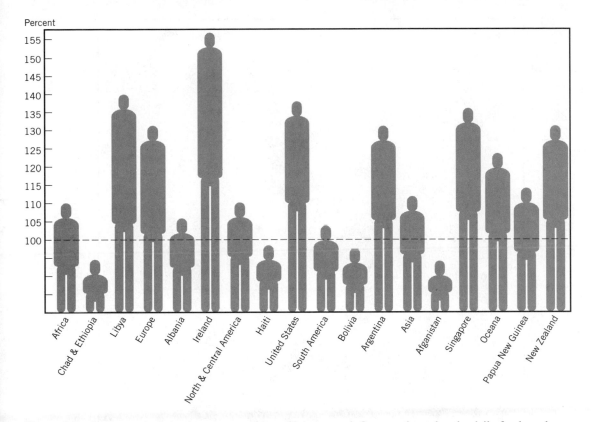

Figure 6.1 Average caloric intake as a percentage of human need. On a continental scale, daily food needs appear to be met, but notice the great disparity between the high and low values for individual countries on each continent. *Source:* World Resources Institute, 1996.

these factors were alleviated, there are still longer term consequences of chronic undernutrition that affect the physical and mental well-being of many of the world's people (Hildyard and Sexton 1996).

A recent FAO study found that 27 nations had food security problems, 7 of which were deemed critical in 1990–1992. The majority of these countries are located in Africa (Fig. 6.4). Faced with rising costs of fuel oil, conversion to cash crops for sale or export, rising populations, warfare, and uncertain weather, these and other countries are waging a continuing struggle to attain food self-sufficiency. For example, the civil war in Rwanda produced hundreds of thousands of refugees, necessitating humanitarian food aid. In 1993–1994, global food aid rose to 4.5 million metric tons (World Resources Institute 1996), almost a fourfold increase since 1980!

Livestock

About 12 percent of the world's population are dependent on livestock production for both food and income. Patterns of life dependent on livestock developed thousands of years ago in Asia and Africa and are still important in many world regions. Most of the world's *pastoralists* are located in Africa (55%), Asia (29%), and parts of Central and South America (15%). The traditional *pastoral nomad* is not oriented toward the production of large quantities of meat and dairy products for market. Instead, products of the sheep and goat herds of Asia and the cattle herds of Africa are used locally or traded on a small scale. The past 100 years have seen a decline in the number of these pastoral nomads as a result of settlement in permanent locations. The process of *sedentarization* has been enforced by governments that encourage herding

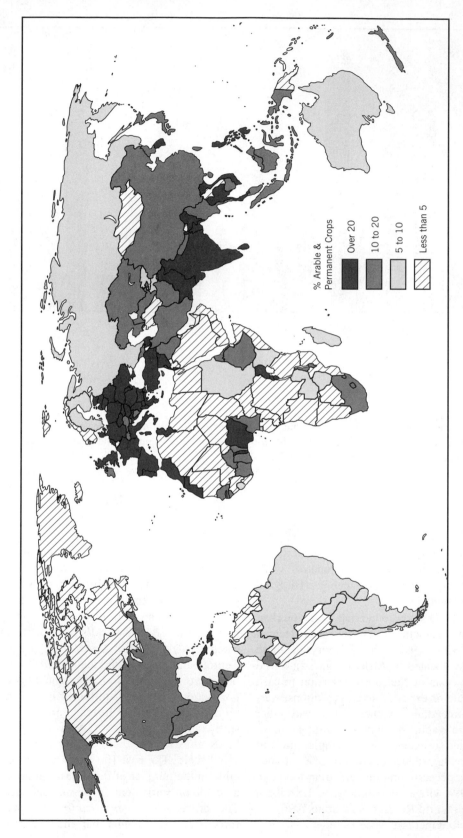

Figure 6.2 World agricultural land. Percent arable land and land in permanent crops, 1991–93. *Source:* World Resources Institute, 1996.

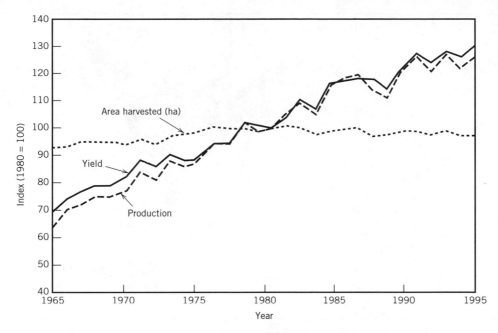

Figure 6.3   Trends in food production, 1965-1995. World cereal production. Production has increased steadily since the 1960s. Area harvested has remained relatively steady so that the increase in production is primarily a function of yield.

Table 6.1   Per Capita Food Production Indices 1965–1995

Region	1965	1975	1985	1995	% change 1985–1995
Africa	109.8	109.1	97.3	95.2	- 2.2
Asia	72.8	78.7	92.9	112.6	+21.2
Europe	74.6	87.3	99.7	92.1	- 7.6
North/Central America	91.2	99.6	107.2	101.7	- 5.1
Oceania	98.3	103.5	105.1	108.6	+ 3.3
South America	82.4	88.0	99.5	105.8	+ 6.3
World	86.4	92.2	99.3	100.4	+ 1.1

Source: FAOSTAT, 1996.

groups to settle in villages and that control the crossing of national borders. In addition, many nomads have left their herds and families for work in urban areas.

In other agricultural systems, livestock are of varying importance. For example, in the wet rice cultivation regions that provide food for the populations of the Far East, there is little room on cultivated acreage for growing animal feed. Thus, meat and dairy products play only a small

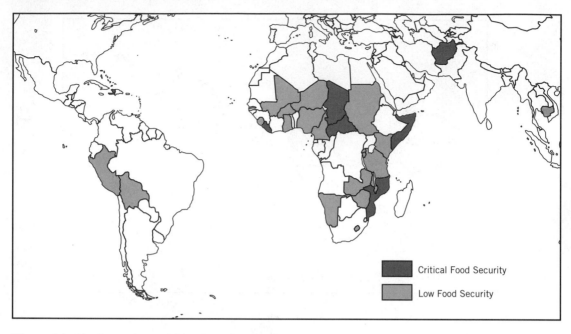

Figure 6.4   Food security problems in the early 1990s. Those countries experiencing critical food security issues include Afghanistan, Central African Republic, Chad, Haiti, Liberia, Mozambique, and Somalia. Low food security dominates portions of sub-Sahelian Africa as well as Bolivia and Peru. *Source:* World Resources Institute, 1996.

role in the diet of southern and eastern Asia. This situation is changing, however, as rising incomes stimulate more meat consumption, and American-style fast-food chains and the high-status appeal of beef make inroads into the traditional eating habits of the region.

With the nineteenth-century settlement of drier areas in the Americas and Australia, it became environmentally and financially feasible to raise and transport large numbers of livestock for transport to distant markets. The vast open stretches of shrub and grassland were well-suited for grazing, for there was not enough rainfall for any other agricultural system except for risky *dry farming* (farming in semiarid areas without irrigation). Important differences exist between the traditional Asian and African pastoralism and cattle raising in the more recently settled drylands. One is that livestock raising in the Americas and Australia is oriented toward meat instead of milk consumption. The newer system is also more highly dependent on a technologically complex

set of elements, including truck transport, antibiotics, and other food supplements.

Another element of these newer livestock raising patterns is the grazing land itself, which can be brought more fully under the control of human managers than was technologically possible for Old World nomads. The main tool available to the nomad for range improvement or alteration was fire. The American farmer can alter vast stretches of land with defoliants, irrigation systems, and newly introduced seeds and can use helicopters, trucks, and bulldozers as tools. Even with these new developments, however, the problems of overuse, degradation, and erosion loom as large in these modern systems as they have for millennia in the drylands of Asia and Africa.

The sharp rise in population in these areas has led to an ever-increasing demand for food. In addition, improvements in the overall standard of living and increased use of animal protein in fulfilling dietary needs have resulted in a subsequent increase in *ruminant* resources (cattle, sheep, and goats). While cattle, sheep and goat populations increased after the 1950s, the rate of growth slowed during the 1990s, which showed a slight decline in ruminants between 1990 and 1995 (Fig. 6.5). World cattle populations increased by only 2 percent, while goats increased by 11 percent. Sheep populations declined by 10 percent during this period. However, other livestock populations have dramatically increased, such as pigs (12%) and chickens (48%). The equine, buffalo, and camel populations have increased since the early 1980s. Regionally, substantial increases in livestock resources occurred in Asia (chickens, pigs, sheep, and goats), Latin America (cattle, buffalo, and chickens), and Africa (cattle, buffalo, chickens, sheep, and goats). Decreases in ruminant populations were found in North America, Oceania (sheep and goats), and western Europe (cattle, sheep).

This increase in animal populations means a rise in the use of grazing lands and is thus a major cause of land degradation in places like Africa. However, about three-fourths of the world's ruminants are no longer totally raised on range resources as countries increasingly move toward intensive livestock production. Farming and the use of forage crops such as alfalfa now contribute to the animals' feed. This is the pattern in the developed world but even more so in the developing

countries (Fig. 6.6). For example, in China, 23 percent of livestock feed is derived from grains, compared to 68 percent in the United States (World Resources Institute 1996). What this means is that most of the grains consumed in the United States are by livestock, not people.

The U.S. Agricultural Resource Land Base

About 70 percent of U.S. land is classified as agricultural land. "Agricultural land" is a broad term, however, and includes cropland, rangeland, forestland, and pastureland. Cropland, or land on which crops are presently grown, comprises only about 25 percent of agricultural land. The cropland area of the United States amounts to about 1.5 acres (0.6 ha) per person, as compared with the global average of 0.8 acre (0.32 ha) per person.

America has always been a land of agricultural abundance, with a large area of arable land and a relatively small population. Through the first two centuries of European settlement in North America, agriculture was based largely on a fertile soil resource, supplemented in some sectors by cheap slave and indentured labor. In the mid-nineteenth century, the opening of the Great Plains was facilitated in part by the development of the steel plow, one of many major innovations contributing to the growth of U.S. agricultural production.

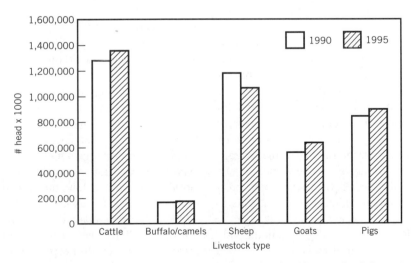

Figure 6.5 World livestock resources. The number of ruminant animals has remained constant during the 1990s with slight increases in cattle, goat, and pig populations. *Source:* World Resources Institute, 1996.

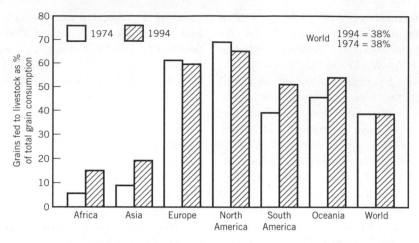

Figure 6.6 Grain consumption by livestock. The worldwide percentage of grain fed to livestock has remained unchanged since 1974, although there are significant regional variations. *Source:* World Resources Institute, 1996.

Today the U.S. agricultural system is among the most technologically advanced in the world.

American agriculture is based on high and continual inputs of capital and replacement of animal power and human labor by machines, which has resulted in drastic reductions in the number of farms and farm workers. This has culminated in an agricultural system that, unlike those in traditional societies, is operated as a complex of small and large businesses whose primary goal is earning money rather than producing food for subsistence. This system has come to be known as *agribusiness*.

U.S. agriculture dominates food exports in the world economy, with American grain exports accounting for over half of the world total. American agriculture feeds many more people than live in the United States, and there is potential for even greater food exports. In addition, the average American consumer pays a much smaller portion of disposable income for food than the average consumer in most of the rest of the world.

Farming in the United States has been profitable at times and unprofitable at others, as is illustrated by recent trends in area harvested, yields, and total production of corn (Fig. 6.7). In the early 1970s, increasing world demand for grain and government policies favoring exports stimulated farmers to increase production. Area planted expanded, and with relatively favorable weather, yields and total production rose substantially. This

period was also one of considerable investment in agricultural land and machinery. But bumper harvests in the late 1970s kept prices down, while inflation continued to force costs and interest rates up. In the mid-1980s, a decline in profitability, coupled with government policies aimed at reducing production, led to a substantial decline in area harvested, with associated production declines. In the late 1980s, the situation improved as a result of a combination of lower interest rates, lower acreages planted, and stable prices for inputs such as fuel and chemicals. In the 1990s, farming was again becoming profitable.

Because the United States exports so much food, American agricultural prosperity is closely linked to world agricultural markets. These markets exert an important influence on agriculture in both the rich and the poor nations. In recent decades, the general pattern has been one of government policies that encourage production by keeping domestic prices high and that encourage exports by subsidizing such sales. This keeps world market prices low, thus making it difficult for poorer nations to export agricultural products. At the same time, many developing nations have followed policies that also keep their domestic prices low in order to keep food within reach of their poorer citizens. Low domestic prices discourage production, and most developing nations lack the foreign currency needed to import enough food to meet their needs. The situation is

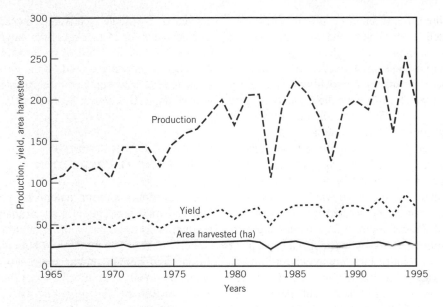

Figure 6.7 U.S. corn production, 1965–1995. Area harvested (in millions of hectares) has remained relatively steady, while yields (expressed as kilograms per hectare) have increased slightly. Year-to-year variations in production (in millions of metric tonnes) are mostly caused by yield variations, although some fluctuations (such as the dip in area harvested in 1993) are attributable to government policies. *Source:* FAOSTAT 1997.

therefore one of considerable imbalance: the United States and other wealthy nations overproduce and the developing nations underproduce in a world market that makes it increasingly difficult for rich nations to sell to poor ones.

Modern American Agricultural Systems

American agriculture today includes both mixed and monocultural cropping systems. *Mixed cropping* systems are agricultural systems that combine several different crops in a single farm unit. They usually include crops for both human consumption and fodder (animal feed). Mixed cropping is used in areas where several different crops can be grown with roughly the same profit per acre and in dairy farming areas. A typical dairy farm in the northeastern United States might include corn and alfalfa grown for fodder for dairy cattle, with milk marketed for cash income. By producing several different animal and vegetable products simultaneously, mixed farming systems make efficient use of the land resource while minimizing susceptibility to unfavorable weather or market conditions for any

one commodity. Mixed systems benefit from crop rotation, in which the crops grown on a given parcel of land are changed from year to year or season to season, thus reducing depletion of particular nutrients. These farmers also may make greater use of plants by feeding otherwise unused parts of plants to animals and by returning some organic matter to the fields in the form of manure.

Monoculture is an agricultural system in which just one crop is cultivated repeatedly over a large area. Other, much more distinctive characteristics of modern monocultural systems include a reliance on technology (in the form of machines), specialized plant varieties, fertilizers, and pesticides. This technological agriculture is most fully developed in the United States but is found in most of the wealthy nations of the world as well. Monoculture is necessary to take advantage of the labor-saving benefits of machines. Additional benefits include economies of scale and more efficient marketing. The plant varieties bred not only produce high yields but also have a large degree of uniformity in plant dimensions and ripening time. If an entire 160-acre field is to be harvested at one time by machines that harvest eight rows at a pass, then clearly all the plants must mature at the same time. A food production system that is primarily monocultural is a highly specialized one. It must have the capacity to store produce over long time periods and transport it efficiently from one area to another.

One consequence of the uniformity of plants in monocultural systems is their susceptibility to disease and pest infestation. If an insect that can successfully attack a particular variety takes hold, large fields can be devastated quickly. For this reason, substantial inputs of pesticides are normally required. Many of these specialized plant varieties also require large inputs of fertilizer or irrigation water to realize maximum yields. In addition, the machines, fertilizers, and chemicals require large amounts of energy, in the form of fossil fuels and electricity, to operate or produce.

Monoculture under these conditions produces very high yields of uniformly high quality. As a result, the value of crops on a per acre basis is very high. But to achieve this high-value harvest, much capital is needed to purchase the inputs of production—land, machines, seed, fertilizer, and so on. It is a capital- and energy-intensive system rather than a labor-intensive one. In recent years, capital has become an increasingly costly input for American farmers, and at the same time there is growing concern about the negative aspects of agricultural chemicals. There are indications that American agriculture may be turning away from intensive use of chemicals, although it is not clear whether other factors of production (such as labor) would be substituted or yields per acre would be allowed to decline. These trends will be discussed in more detail later in this chapter.

U.S. Rangeland Resources

There are about 240 million hectares of rangeland in the United States. In addition, about 130 million hectares of woodland can be grazed. Most U.S. rangeland is found in the 17 western states. Only 1 percent is in the 31 eastern states, mostly in the South. Any potential for increased grazing in the East depends on more intensive grazing of forests or the removal of forest cover.

More than half of the rangelands in the United States are on private lands, mostly east of the Rocky Mountains. In the six Great Plains states, 98 percent of the range is privately owned, and this area accounts for 25 percent of the range grazed in the lower 48 states. West of the Rockies much of the range is federally owned; in the Pacific Northwest, federal land supplies more than half of the grazed range (U.S. Forest Service 1981).

NATURAL RESOURCES FOR AGRICULTURAL PRODUCTION

The connection between natural resource condition and food production is an intimate one, but production is not dependent on natural resources alone. Rather, it is a function of both natural conditions and human management. For example, plants obviously require soil, water, and sunlight to grow. But the soil must also be managed in ways that promote plant growth; seeds that will produce the food we need must be planted at the right time and tended as they grow. Crops must be harvested, processed, stored, and distributed to consumers. All of these things are essential to the food production system. In examining the geographical variations in food production today, as well as the possibilities for increasing that production in the future, we need to consider the role each of these factors plays in food production. In this section, we will consider soil, water, fertilizers and pesticides, seed, labor and machines, animals, and distribution infrastructure.

Soil

Soil is the uppermost part of the Earth's surface, which has been modified by physical, chemical, and biological processes over time. It is the essential medium for plant growth, and it is a complex and dynamic mixture of solid and dissolved mineral matter, living and dead organic matter, water, and air. Soil is formed over long periods of time, usually thousands of years.

Many factors affect soil formation, including climate, parent material, topography, erosion, and biological activity. Climate affects soil by determining the amount of water that may enter the soil from rainfall and the amount that can be drawn from the surface by evaporation. Climate also determines soil temperatures, which are important in regulating chemical reactions in the soil as well as influencing plant growth. *Parent material* is the mineral matter on which soil is formed.

It affects the soil by supplying the mineral matter that forms the bulk of the soil. Parent material has a fundamental influence on *soil texture*, which is the mix of different sizes of particles, and on the chemical characteristics of the soil.

Topography influences soil primarily by regulating water movement within and over the soil. On slopes, water moves down and laterally through the soil, providing drainage. In low-lying areas water accumulates, and soils may become waterlogged. Along stream courses sediment may accumulate, producing fertile alluvial soils. Topography also affects the rate of erosion. *Erosion* is the removal of soil by running water or wind. It is a natural process that can be greatly accelerated by human influences such as vegetation removal. The rate of erosion relative to the rate of new soil formation is an important determinant of soil characteristics.

Finally, biological activity makes soil the distinctive, living, dynamic substance it is, rather than just an accumulation of sterile rock particles. Biological activity includes the growth and decay of plants and animals in and above the soil. It contributes organic matter to the soil, which constitutes the basic storage of nutrients for most ecosystems. Biological activity also aids in the physical modification of the mineral soil by contributing organic acids that break down rocks, by exerting physical forces that fracture rocks, and by stirring and aerating the soil so that water and air may penetrate below the surface. Vegetation cover regulates water losses by evapotranspiration and protects the soil from excessive erosion. The type of vegetation is also important in determining soil characteristics. For example, the thick grass cover of a prairie leads to the development of an organic-rich and uncompacted topsoil that is not usually found in forest soils. In short, biological activity plays a fundamental role in soil formation and helps maintain the ability of soils to support life.

The way in which individual soil particles group together in aggregates is called *soil structure*. Soil structure is important in determining the water-holding capacity of soil and the speed with which water soaks into and through the soil. Plowing, compaction, oxidation of organic matter, extraction of nutrients by plants, or desiccation can sometimes destroy soil structure to the detriment of its water-holding properties.

Soils develop slowly from unweathered bedrock to a complete soil profile. The rate of new soil formation varies from place to place, but as a rule it is very slow in human terms, requiring hundreds to tens of thousands of years. Erosion is part of the natural soil system, and soil eroded from the surface must be replaced by formation of new soil from parent material. If the soil erosion rate is high, then the soil may not develop as thickly or as completely as in areas of low erosion rates.

Soils vary greatly in their ability to support agricultural production, depending on their fertility, water-holding characteristics, temperature, and other factors. *Soil fertility* is defined as the ability of a soil to supply essential nutrients to plants, which is dependent on both the chemical and textural properties of the soil. Generally, soils that have a high proportion of clay and organic matter also have high fertility, for these substances have the ability to store and release nutrients. Sandy soils, on the other hand, generally have lower amounts of nutrients available to plants, although as little as 10 to 15 percent fine particles may be sufficient to supply the needed nutrients. The abundance of various elements in the soil, such as phosphorus and calcium, is also important. This is often controlled by the chemical composition of the bedrock and the degree of leaching of these nutrients by water percolating through the soil.

The *water-holding capacity* of a soil is determined primarily by its texture. As a rule, coarse-textured soils have low capacities to store water, whereas clayey soils can hold large volumes of water in the upper parts of the profile. At the same time, however, clay soils may be poorly drained, with the tendency to become waterlogged, which prevents air from reaching plant roots. Waterlogging is particularly common in humid areas, on floodplains, or on other flat land. In addition, irrigated areas often experience waterlogging if irrigation causes a rise in the local groundwater table.

The productive capabilities of soils are thus of fundamental importance in determining what plants can be grown, what particular management techniques should be used, and what typical yields will be. The U.S. Natural Resource Conservation Service has developed a system, called the *Land Capability Classification System*, for assessing and classifying this productive capacity (Table 6.2). There are eight major capability classes, designated I through VIII, with classes I through IV indicating arable land and classes V through VIII indicating land useful for grazing or forestry. For both agriculture and other uses, the first category includes land that is nearly ideal for production, with little or no limitations of fertility, drainage, and so on. The next two classes include land with increasing degrees of limitations, including such problems as poor drainage, excessive erosion hazard, poor water-holding capacity, and the like. The fourth class is land that is generally not usable. Note that the land in the United States is about equally divided between suitability for agriculture and suitability for forestry or grazing, and that in each of these groups about 80 percent of the land has some limitations for use. This further indicates the great importance of proper land management techniques that are adapted to the inherent capabilities and limitations of each land unit.

Such capability classifications are just part of the work of the U.S. Department of Agriculture's Natural Resource Conservation Service (NRCS), which includes nationwide mapping of soil types, their physical characteristics, and their productive capabilities. These maps are of great use to farmers and land-use planners in their attempts to make the best possible use of the soil resource (Fig. 6.8).

Water

Water is essential to plant growth and is supplied to crops naturally by rainfall and artificially by irrigation. Rainfall farming is entirely dependent on the weather to provide a sufficient, but not excessive, supply of moisture to plants. With not enough moisture, plants wither and die; with too much, the soil cannot be worked, crops rot in the field, or roots suffocate from lack of air. The amount and timing of rainfall are major determinants of what can be grown, where, and when. In areas without irrigation, rainfall variability is a major cause of year-to-year variations in yields. Droughts, early rains, and late rains take their tolls in crop failures or low yields in many regions of the world each year. Some climatologists feel that in the future climates will change or become more variable; if this is the case, yield fluctuations will become an even greater problem than they are today (Issue 6.1).

In those parts of the world where rainfall is sufficient and reasonably dependable, crops can be

Table 6.2   Land Capability in the United States

Capability Class		% US Nonfederal Land
Suitability for arable agriculture		
I	Few limitations on use	3
II	Moderate limitations for agricultural uses	20
III	Severe limitations that reduce the choice of plants or require special conservation practices	20
IV	Very severe limitations for cropping	13
Suitability for grazing or forestry		
V	Few limitations for pasture or woodland uses	2
VI	Moderate limitations for pasture or woodland uses	19
VII	Very severe limitations for pasture or woodland uses	20
VIII	Generally suitable only for wildlife, recreation, or aesthetic purposes	3

Source: Soil Conservation Services, 1980.

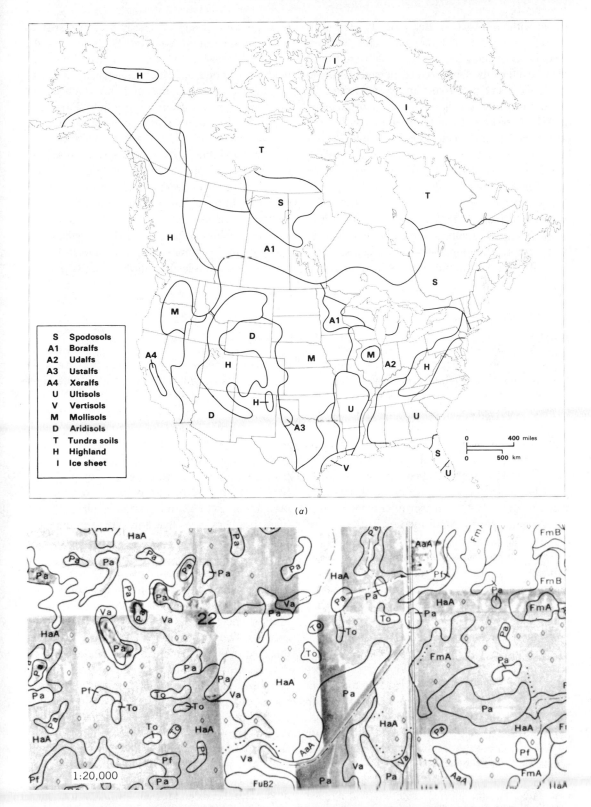

Figure 6.8 Soil maps. (*a*) Generalized map of soils of North America. (*b*) Detail of a U.S. Soil Conservation Service soil map of an area in southern Minnesota, illustrating local variability in soil types.

grown without irrigation. But about 17 percent of the world's arable lands are productive because water has artificially been made available to plants. Also, much of the land deemed potentially arable will become so only through irrigation. Most of the world's irrigated land is in seasonally dry regions of Asia. China and India together contain 40 percent of the world's irrigated land; the United States has about 8 percent of all irrigated land in the world. The distribution of irrigated lands in the United States is illustrated in Figure 6.9.

Four major types of *irrigation* are used in the world today: flood, furrow, sprinkler, and drip. *Flood irrigation* involves inundating entire fields with water or allowing water to flow across entire fields. The most widespread use of flood irrigation

is in growing paddy or sawah rice, primarily in southern and eastern Asia. Rice fields are quite flat and bounded by dikes. During the wet season the fields are flooded, and rice seedlings are planted in standing water. Later the fields are drained, and the rice ripens in a relatively dry field. Flood irrigation is also used to irrigate pastures in some areas. *Furrow irrigation* (Fig. 6.10a) also requires very flat land, but in this case the water flows between rows of plants, which are grown on low ridges. Water is delivered to the furrows by small ditches or in pipes and applied as needed throughout the growing season.

Sprinkler irrigation (Fig. 6.10b) requires substantially more equipment than flood or furrow irrigation. In sprinkler irrigation, water is pumped

ISSUE 6.1:   AGRICULTURE, CO_2, AND CLIMATE: THE ONLY CERTAINTY IS CHANGE

When extreme weather occurs, one of the most obvious and immediate effects is on agriculture. Farming is vulnerable to a wide variety of bad weather: cool spring weather delays growth, wet spring weather delays planting, autumn rains prevent harvesting, and drought and early frost damage crops. All of these take their toll on crop yields. At the same time, there can be especially good weather: summer rain, dry weather to help crop ripening, and warm spring weather sometimes contribute to bumper crops in the United States. Weather variability has obvious impacts on agricultural production, and although the American consumer rarely notices these effects directly in other parts of the world, these variations mean, literally, feast or famine. In countries vulnerable to food shortages, a drop in production has an immediate impact on diet and health.

Climatologists are predicting changes in global weather, largely as a result of increasing atmospheric CO_2 concentrations. What does this mean for agriculture? Will the changes be good or bad? Will higher atmospheric CO_2 levels mean more plant growth? The effects of CO_2-induced climatic change on agriculture are difficult to predict, but it seems likely that they will be significant.

It is generally recognized that global warming associated with the greenhouse effect will include a wide variety of climatic shifts and not simply a

rise in temperature. The temperature rise will be significant but perhaps not the most important aspect of climate change. There may be shifts in storm tracks and in the prevailing wind and pressure patterns. In some locations this may mean warmer or wetter weather, and in other places cooler or drier weather. Many forecasters anticipate hot and dry conditions in the central United States, which would probably be damaging to corn production. But a warming trend would also make many northern areas that now have summers that are too short and cool for crops more favorable for agriculture.

Although climatologists working with global climate models may make predictions of how the climate in a given place may change, a great degree of uncertainty surrounds such specific predictions. Only recently has a consensus emerged that average temperature worldwide will increase, and as yet there is little agreement on conditions in specific agricultural areas. It is reasonable to assume, however, that within the next decade or two we will have a clearer idea of how regional-scale climatic patterns will change (or are changing right now). When this knowledge is available, we will be in a better position to analyze likely shifts in growing regions for various crops. But these changes will probably take place over decades, and our past experience of world

under pressure to nozzles and sprayed over the land. Nozzles may be fixed or moved across a field manually or automatically. Sprinkler irrigation usually results in much higher evaporative losses than other methods, but in areas of very permeable soils seepage losses are important, so that sprinklers are preferred to furrow irrigation. *Drip irrigation* is a relatively recent development and is used primarily in orchards and vineyards. Each plant has a small pipe that delivers water at a controlled rate directly to the base of the plant. The water drips out very slowly so that little is lost to evaporation or to seepage. Although it is an expensive system to install, it is cost effective in areas where water is scarce.

Irrigated agriculture generally produces high yields as long as water is available. This is because the other environmental characteristics of dry lands, plentiful sunshine, and warm temperatures are conducive to crop growth. This high productivity is not without its costs, however, and in many areas of the world waterlogging, salt accumulation, groundwater depletion, and disease are serious side effects of irrigation. In some areas, salinization is severe enough that it is forcing abandonment of formerly productive land. In parts of the arid western United States, much of the environmental damage associated with irrigation can be attributed to government policies that provided water at artificially low prices. These subsidies encourage inefficient use of water, such as for production of hay. This excessive use has

agricultural patterns makes it clear that climate is only one of several factors affecting agricultural production. Unforeseen changes in other factors, such as mechanization, development of new crop varieties, or economic factors, may contribute at least equally with climate in determining the future geography of crop production. In addition, the complex biochemical interactions between increased atmospheric CO_2 and plant growth adds another layer of unpredictability.

Carbon dioxide not only plays a central role in the earth's atmospheric circulation but is also an essential input to photosynthesis. The concentration of carbon dioxide in the atmosphere affects the rate at which plants remove that gas from the air and store it as biomass: the more CO_2 in the air, the faster plants photosynthesize. If plants grow faster, then crop yields may also increase.

To understand the importance of this effect, we must recognize that different plants use different biochemical processes in photosynthesis. Two of these are the C_3 and C_4 processes. C_3 plants, including wheat, barley, rice, and potatoes, respond well to increases in atmospheric CO_2, whereas C_4 plants such as corn, sorghum, and sugarcane do not (Parry 1990). Increases in CO_2 concentration also affect the efficiency of water use by plants: the more CO_2 present, the less water is used per unit of plant growth. This means that in areas of water shortage, higher CO_2 concentrations are likely to have beneficial effects on production. In addition, when plants grow in a CO_2-enriched atmosphere, their stomata are open less, causing them to lose less water to evaporation. This increases the efficiency of plant water use, and in dry areas this could mean that less water is needed for irrigation.

Predicting the effects of these changes on world agricultural production is clearly impossible at this time. The effects at any given place depend on what varieties of crops are grown, whether water availability is an important limiting factor, and how other factors of production (fertilizer, seed, energy, machinery, and so on) change—too many unknowns even for the most careful analyses. But we can make three simple generalizations. First, farmers need to be prepared for change. They should avoid growing crops that are easily damaged by unusual weather and should concentrate on varieties that are relatively robust. Second, we should expect the geography of crop production to change: areas that are important for one crop today may be growing something different in the future, areas that have no crops today may become productive, and currently viable regions may cease to produce. And third, agricultural research needs to be directed toward developing new crops and adapting old ones to a wide array of possible future climatic conditions.

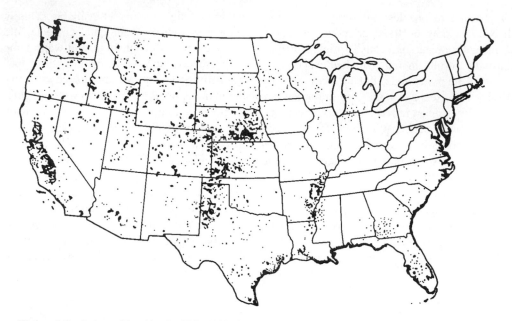

Figure 6.9 Irrigated land in the U.S. 1987. *Source:* Bajwa et al., 1987.

contributed greatly to the salinity problems in the lower Colorado River.

Although in most of the world's farming regions water already is being used intensively, significant opportunities exist to increase irrigation. One older estimate suggests a potential for irrigating an additional 248 million acres (100 million ha) between 1988 and 2000, accounting for about two-thirds of the projected increase in arable land in that time period (Alexandratos 1988). Water resources are already stressed in much of the world, however, especially in semiarid areas. Increases in irrigated land will therefore be limited. Greater opportunities lie in increasing the efficiency of irrigation, not expanding its current use.

Fertilizers and Pesticides

Average yields of grains worldwide more than doubled between 1960 and 1990, owing mostly to increases in the use of *fertilizers*. Fertilizer use increased over four times in that same 30-year period. While fertilizer is already being used at high rates in the U.S. and Europe, significant production increases from expanded fertilizer use are still possible in poorer countries. One of the main reasons for this prominence is the development of high-yielding plant varieties that require

large inputs of fertilizer to realize their potential. In addition, fertilizers may make production possible on otherwise marginal land.

The three most important nutrients required by plants are nitrogen, phosphorus, and potassium. Nitrogen is ultimately derived from the atmosphere, but it is made available to plants by nitrogen-fixing bacteria. It is the nutrient that is most often deficient and that is most widely applied to crops. Additions in amounts of 45 to 90 pounds/acre (50 to 100 kg/ha) may increase yields from 1.5 to 3 times, depending on plant variety and inherent soil fertility. Natural gas is an important raw material in the manufacture of most nitrogen fertilizers. The most commonly used forms are ammonia (NH_4) and urea ($CO[NH_2]_2$). Phosphorus is usually present in small quantities in soils, but it is often found in relatively unusable forms. It is usually applied as superphosphate or as phosphoric acid, which are manufactured from phosphate rock or from guano (bird dung) deposits found in some coastal areas. In soils, potassium generally is found in larger quantities than phosphorus because it is a more abundant constituent of most rocks. Plants also demand it in large quantities, and in many areas potassium fertilization is important. In some areas, local soil conditions or

Figure 6.10   Irrigation methods. (a) Furrow irrigation in Texas, (b) Center pivot sprinkler irrigation in Nebraska.

the particular needs of plants require that other fertilizers be added, with lime (a source of calcium and magnesium as well as a regulator of soil pH) being the most common.

Organic fertilizers (primarily manure) have historically been the most important source of nutrients, especially nitrogen. Organic fertilizers also help maintain good soil structure and water-holding capacity by keeping soil organic matter content high. In the wealthy nations, inorganic fertilizers are now more important, but in the developing nations manure is still a common fertilizer. In most areas, manure supplies are quite limited, and manure is more difficult to apply than other forms of fertilizer. Manure is low in nutrient content relative to synthetic fertilizer and is not capable of providing the large inputs of nutrients demanded by high-yielding crop varieties. Increasingly, therefore, inorganic sources of nutrients have been replacing organic sources, and this trend can be expected to continue.

Pesticide is a general term referring to any of a number of chemical agents used to control organisms harmful to plants, including insects, fungi, and some types of worms. Pesticides include insecticides, rodenticides, fungicides, and others. Herbicides are used to control weeds. The use of pesticides and herbicides has accounted for a large part of recent increases in crop yields, particularly in the wealthier nations. Thousands of different kinds of pesticides and herbicides are in use, and the vast majority are complex organic compounds manufactured using petroleum as an important raw material. Among insecticides, organochlorines, organophosphates, and carbamates are important types.

The large-scale use of pesticides in agriculture began in the 1950s. Among the first widely used insecticides were organochlorines such as DDT, aldrin, dieldrin, and chlordane. In the 1960s and 1970s, these were largely replaced by organophosphates for most uses, in part because insects began to develop resistance to the effects of organochlorines and in part because organophosphates break down more rapidly and therefore are less likely to accumulate in the environment. Today many different types of chemicals and application methods are used (Fig. 6.11). Among the small-grain crops, pesticides and herbicides are used most intensively on corn, soybeans, and sorghum. Most fruits and vegetables are susceptible to damage by insects, fungi, and other pests, and various pesticides are used depending on specific circumstances.

The dangers of pesticides have been discussed since the early 1960s, and as a result, their application has been regulated in many ways. But in general their use has increased continuously since their introduction. As will be discussed in a later section, there are now signs that this trend may be reversed.

Seed

Ever since the development of agriculture, farmers have practiced crop improvement through seed selection. Observant of the variations in a single crop, farmers saved seed from those plants that possessed the characteristics they preferred and planted them the following year. Over a period of thousands of years, this process led to the development of the world's major modern crops. One of the most spectacular examples of this long-term process is maize, or corn. Since 6000 B.C., corn has been altered from a small grain head to its present size and productivity. The success of hybrid corn varieties was a major factor contributing to a large increase in acreages of corn planted in the United States over the past few decades.

Since the early twentieth century, the application of Mendel's laws of genetics accelerated the process of selection. Following the successes of hybrid corn, new varieties of wheat and rice were developed as part of the Green Revolution. Many of these new varieties were bred to produce high yields when adequately fertilized. They were bred to be shorter in stature so that plants would not collapse under the weight of heavier grains they supported. More recently, advances in bioengineering are making it possible to manipulate the genetic material directly, so that alterations can be made in a single generation of a plant species. Not only does this allow the creation of

Figure 6.11 Aerial application of insecticide to lettuce field in California.

new plant varieties, but also hybrid seeds tend to produce more vigorous plants than nonhybrid varieties, and thus substantial increases in yield have been achieved. Those farmers who can afford to pay for these sophisticated seeds can choose among a wide array of disease, insect, and drought resistance, and for specific fruit or grain size, flavor, ripening time, packing and processing qualities, and so on.

There is some evidence that, at least in the United States and other countries with technologically advanced agriculture, the "miracle seed" productivity is leveling off. This change is in large part due to diminishing returns from the addition of more fertilizer and the continuing use of high-yielding varieties. Experts argue, however, that there is still room for greatly increased productivity in the developing world, where the use of chemical fertilizers and improved seed varieties is increasing. Others are more pessimistic about genetically-engineered crops (Steinbrecher 1996).

In recent years, controversy in the seed development industry has focused on the granting of seed patents to large agribusiness concerns. Such patents allow seed developers to collect royalties for use of seeds and thus provide a greater economic incentive for research and development into new crop varieties. But some see this development as yet another cost for farmers and consumers and another potential barrier to increasing production. In addition, the abandonment of older low-yielding varieties is threatening some of these varieties with extinction, though efforts are being made to preserve seeds in gene banks (see Chapter 8).

Labor and Machines

To grow crops, soil must be tilled, weeds removed, and plants harvested. Until the nineteenth century in North America, most of this work was done by human and animal labor, using simple tools such as plows and hoes. In much of the developing world, the work is still done by human and animal power. But increasingly, machinery driven by fossil fuels predominates (Fig. 6.12). In the nonindustrialized countries, an impetus toward mechanization was introduced as part of the Green Revolution "package."

In the United States, Canada, and other countries dependent on mechanized production, the percentage of the labor force employed as farmers has dropped steadily. In 1850, 64 percent of the U.S. labor force was made up of farmers; this figure had dropped to 2.5 percent by the mid 1990s. In the early days of mechanization, these millions of workers were absorbed by the availability of industrial jobs in cities. However, during the last three decades, the demand for underskilled labor in industry also dropped, aggravating problems of unemployment. In addition, much of the remaining nonmechanized farm work is performed by seasonal and permanent legal and illegal immigrants to the United States.

The technological developments in agriculture involving farm machinery have had their greatest effects in the industrialized, wealthier nations. For example, grain production was revolutionized through a series of inventions. The plow evolved from a wooden horse- or ox-drawn implement to today's gang plow with up to 16 blades capable of plowing 10 acres (4 ha) per hour. The reaping and threshing of grain were once done with sickles, scythes, and human muscle power. Today the diesel-powered combine both harvests and threshes grain at a rate of up to 12 acres (5 ha) an hour. These machines need a single human operator who rides in an air-conditioned cab (Issue 6.2).

The amount of petroleum products required to fuel this mechanical transformation is enormous. In comparing total energy inputs with total energy outputs per hectare of land, the energy efficiency of modern, machine-powered, and chemical-intensive agriculture is substantially lower than that of traditional animal-powered methods (Swaminathan and Sinha 1986), but yields per acre are higher under energy-intensive techniques. The largest uses in mechanized agriculture are fuels for tillage, planting, harvesting, transport, and water pumping for irrigation. In addition, heat and light are needed for livestock and poultry production, crop drying, and frost protection. Energy is also utilized in the form of agricultural chemicals, and this amounts to more than a third of the total energy used in U.S. agriculture. The dependency of U.S. agriculture on fossil fuels leads farm interests to resist energy-conservation measures or carbon emission controls that would involve increases in fuel prices.

Animals in the Food Production System

Meat production plays an important role in many agricultural systems. One important function of meat is to provide a source of concentrated pro-

Figure 6.12   Combine harvesting of wheat in Washington.

tein in the diet. While adequate protein can be obtained from purely vegetable diets, the availability of animal protein adds some flexibility in meeting human nutritional requirements. A second important function of meat production is to take advantage of biomass that is not digestible by humans. Grass and shrubs, for example, are not acceptable food for humans, but cattle, sheep, and goats have the ability to digest these plants and convert them to meat and dairy products that humans can use. Other animals, especially pigs and chickens, are able to consume human food wastes and convert them into usable food.

In many ways, then, meat production complements arable agriculture, thus increasing the total amount of food we can harvest from a given amount of land. At the same time, in many animal production systems domestic animals compete with humans for food. This is particularly the case in North America and Europe, where most meat is produced not by feeding grass and other inedible materials to animals but by feeding them the same grains that we could eat, grown on land that could produce grain for direct human consumption. The efficiency of converting vegetable food energy to animal food energy in the United States is about 5 percent; that is, 20 calories of food energy as feed (range grasses and grains in the feedlot) are needed to produce one calorie of food energy as meat on the table.

If the food used to produce meat is grown on land that could be used to grow grain for human consumption, then we are in effect substituting a substantial amount of vegetable food for a small amount of meat, which would seem to be unwise in a world short of food. About two-thirds of the grain grown in the United States is fed to livestock; the proportion is similar in Europe. On the other hand, meat produced by grazing animals on land that is not otherwise usable for food production represents an important increase in available food supplies. Thus, range animals can be a means of converting otherwise unusable vegetable matter to valuable food, even if the efficiency of conversion is relatively low (Fig. 6.13). It is when livestock are fed high-quality corn and other grains that questions of efficiency and equity arise.

Most of the world's prime grazing lands are natural grasslands found in semiarid and subhumid areas. The ability of grasses to grow rapidly when conditions are favorable, combined with the variability of precipitation in semiarid areas, leads to seasonal and annual variations in the amount of grass that grows in grassland areas. This means that the number of herbivores that can be supported by the land also varies. Under natural conditions, populations of these grazing animals such as rodents and deer are kept in check by competition for available food. But the population levels of domestic animals are controlled by humans, not by natural conditions. To maximize animal production in the short run, herders often exceed

ISSUE 6.2:   THE DIGITAL FARMER

Precision agriculture is carefully tailored soil and crop management that fits the different conditions found in each field. It allows the farmer to customize chemicals, fertilizers, and seeds to achieve the greatest output per acre while decreasing input costs. Improving the farmer's marginal return requires more precise data about crop yields and their variability within individual farm fields and ushered in a new "high-tech" approach to farming. Some people call it global positioning system (GPS) farming, and others simply refer to the new agriculturalists as digital farmers. For geographers, it's an exciting application of spatial knowledge and use of geographic information processing technology.

In many parts of the Midwest today, you can see GPS antennas on farm equipment and computers with GIS (Geographic Information Systems) packages in the air-conditioned cabs. Accuracies between one and two feet make it possible to develop field-specific inputs to maximize yields and minimize costs. Farm equipment has been fitted with a variety of sensors to monitor everything from rate of fertilizer application to amount of corn cut.

During spring planting, for example, data on crop inputs (fertilizers, pesticides, seeds) are recorded. The sensing devices attached to the planter or the fertilizer and pesticide applicators are electronically connected to GPS units that geocode the information for the real-time computer input maps. The specific longitude and latitude of the application are stored in the computer. At the end of the day, the farmer can download the data and produce an input map of his field. Throughout the season, the farmer can record additional fertilizer and pesticide applications, soil moisture, and so forth and again create maps of inputs for the season.

When harvesting begins, yield monitors (attached to the combine) transmit the data to disk but also display it on a computer screen in the cab. Data are received every 1 to 3 seconds so that the farmer can see (in real time) how much corn is being yielded. Later, these stored data can be used to make a digital map of yields at a 1- to 3-meter scale.

The most exciting development for the farmer is the yield map that illustrates the variability in yield in the fields. Low-yielding spots can be identified and inputs altered for the next crop or growing season. The ability to see the distribution of yield can result in significant savings in fertilizers, for example. Why add more fertilizers to an area that is already highly productive? In this way, the farmer can begin to think about the agronomic relationships that might produce such variability such as mistakes in fertilizer or pesticide applications, drift from a neighbor's pesticide application, diseases, or micro-zonations in soil fertility or nutrients.

Farming in the twenty-first century will require advanced degrees not only in agronomy but possibly geography. Hopefully, students with interests in agriculture can see how this spatial information helps in the management of our food resources. Perhaps others are wondering what geography can contribute to natural resources management. One answer is digital farming.

the carrying capacity of the land, which results in damage to the vegetation.

Grazing affects plants in several ways. Plants are reduced in size by grazing, which usually inhibits their ability to photosynthesize and grow. Animals damage plants by trampling, which is particularly detrimental to young plants. The reduction in plant cover caused by grazing leads to a deterioration in soil conditions that also inhibits plant growth. On the positive side, the seeds of some plant species are spread by grazing animals, either by being eaten and excreted or by being attached to fur. Other plant species may be inhibited from reproducing under grazing pressure, for example, if their seeds are digested. Finally, grazing may stimulate plant growth by reducing competition among plants for moisture or nutrients. Thus the plants may be able to replace some of the biomass taken by animals.

Range plant species vary in their ability to survive and reproduce under grazing pressure. Some species may be able to quickly regenerate

Figure 6.13 These cattle are converting grass into food on semiarid rangeland in Colorado that probably would not be agriculturally productive as cropland.

leaves lost to animals, whereas others cannot. Some are relatively unaffected by trampling, and for others trampling is fatal. Most importantly, some species are more palatable to grazing animals and thus are eaten first, and others are less palatable and are eaten only after the desirable forage is consumed. These differences in susceptibility of plants to grazing impact are the basis of the ecological changes that result from grazing (Fig. 6.14).

Range ecologists classify plant species in a particular area as decreasers, increasers, or invaders. *Decreasers* are plant species that are present in a plant community but decrease in importance (as measured by numbers of plants or percentage of ground covered) as a result of grazing. They are generally the most palatable plants, but they may also include species that are negatively affected by animals in other ways, such as by trampling. *Increasers* are species that were present prior to grazing which increase in importance as a result of grazing. They may be less palatable species, or they may increase simply because there is less competition from the decreasers for water or nutrients. *Invaders* are species that were not present prior to grazing but are able to colonize the area as a result of the change in conditions.

No species can be classified as decreaser, increaser, or invader without reference to a particu-

lar site. A species may be an increaser in one area and an invader in another, or it may be a decreaser in one area and an increaser in another. For example, big sagebrush (*Artemisia tridentata*) is present on much of the rangelands of the United States, and over most of this area it is an increaser (Fig. 6.15). Although it is high in nutrients, it is unpalatable to cattle and sheep except when other forage is unavailable. Big sagebrush is also unaffected by trampling. In some areas of the American West, it was insignificant or not present prior to the onset of grazing in the nineteenth century, but today it is a dominant species. In these areas it is an invader.

ENVIRONMENTAL IMPACTS OF FOOD PRODUCTION

Agricultural activities represent an enormous transformation of natural ecosystems occurring over very large portions of the Earth's surface. As such, they inevitably cause vast environmental impacts. Many of these impacts occur beyond the farm field, such as water pollution from agricultural runoff, air pollution from blowing dust, or dispersal of agricultural chemicals. Off-site impacts such as these are considered in Chapters 10 and 11 of this book. Here we consider those impacts that degrade the quality of agricultural resources for their primary function of producing food. We focus on two processes: soil erosion and rangeland degradation.

Soil Erosion

Soil erosion on agricultural lands takes place through three major processes: overland flow (or runoff), wind, and streambank erosion. Of these processes, overland flow erosion is the most visible and widespread, and in most agricultural areas it is quantitatively the most important. Wind erosion occurs on exposed soil if strong winds blow at times when the soil surface is relatively dry. Streambank erosion is limited to fields that border streams, and though locally significant it is not a major factor in soil erosion worldwide.

How Erosion Happens   Accelerated *overland flow* erosion is primarily the result of intense rainfall on bare ground. Raindrops striking a bare soil surface break up clumps of soil into

Figure 6.14 Much of the rangeland of the western United States has been degraded by a century of grazing. In many areas grass cover has been replaced with shrubland like this in Nevada.

Figure 6.15 Sagebrush rangelands in New Mexico.

individual particles. These are moved by the splash made on raindrop impact and compact the soil surface so that water is less able to soak in, thus reducing the *infiltration capacity*, or the maximum rate at which soil will absorb water. When the precipitation intensity exceeds infiltration capacity, water flows across the surface as overland flow rather than soaking in. When overland flow rates are particularly high, small stream channels called rills may be formed to carry the water away.

Soil erosion due to overland flow varies considerably from place to place. Some areas are extremely susceptible to erosion, whereas in other areas it is a minor problem. Some of the major factors influencing the severity of erosion are topographic factors such as slope steepness, the inherent susceptibility of the soil to erosion, the intensity and frequency of rainfall, and the cropping and management practices of the farmers.

Cropping and management practices are very significant to overland flow erosion. Cropping practices include what kinds of crops are grown and when they are planted. Row crops, such as corn and soybeans, tend to allow more erosion than do continuous cover crops such as wheat or hay. If the field is bare during part of the year, then that will be the time when there is the greatest susceptibility to erosion. As the plants grow and mature, they cover a greater amount of the ground and erosion susceptibility decreases. In most cases, the time of planting is dictated by plant characteristics and weather, but in some situations particular crops that provide greater cover at times of more erosive rainfall may be chosen. In addition, the decision of whether or when to plow stubble under has effects on erosion susceptibility. This is an example of a management practice. Others include the choice of various conservation techniques such as contour plowing, terracing, or minimum tillage, practices that are discussed in following sections.

Wind erosion occurs when there is a combination of high wind velocities and a soil surface that is easily eroded. High wind velocities are obviously dependent on weather conditions, and some areas are windier than others. Wind erosion is greater at times when the soil surface is dry, and for this reason wind erosion is generally a greater problem in arid than in humid regions. Vegetation cover is more important, for it controls wind speed at the soil surface. Plants are very effective in reducing surface wind velocities, and wind erosion is negligible under vegetation cover.

Extent of the Problem Accelerated soil erosion is found on virtually all cultivated lands, but the extent of the problem varies greatly from place to place (Pimentel, 1995; Crosson, 1995, 1997). The results of a U.S. Department of Agriculture survey of sheet and rill erosion on U.S. lands (U.S. Department of Agriculture 1989) are summarized in Figure 6.16a. The greatest rates of soil erosion are found in the Southeast and in the Corn Belt states, with average rates ranging from 4 to 6 tons per acre (8 to over 12 tons/ha) per year. Wind erosion is mapped in Figure 6.16b. It is most severe in the western Great Plains states, at rates similar to those of rill erosion in the East. The sum of wind and water erosion is mapped in Figure 6/16c. Rates of 4 to 6 tons/acre (8 to over 12 tonnes/ha) per year correspond to a loss of about 0.2 to 0.4

inch (0.5 to 1 cm) from the soil surface in 10 years. If we recognize that the top 4 to 12 inches (10 to 30 cm) of most soils hold the greatest proportion of the nutrients and organic matter, then these rates may lead to removal of much of this very fertile layer in just a few decades.

Soil Conservation Techniques Over the years, many techniques have been developed to control erosion while still allowing efficient agricultural production. Some of these techniques, such as crop rotation, have been known for centuries, whereas others have been developed fairly recently. Some of the important ones are discussed in this section.

Crop rotation is a farming method that is aimed primarily at maintaining soil fertility, but by so doing plant growth is enhanced and erosion reduced. Crop rotation simply means that over a period of several years the crops grown on a field will change in a systematic pattern. Some crops demand more of some nutrients than others, and by changing crops from year to year excessive depletion of nutrients can be prevented. Typical rotation patterns may include fallow periods or plantings of crops like alfalfa that restore some nutrients to the soil. Often such crops are plowed under rather than harvested; this technique is called green manuring. Crop rotation may also allow the ground to be covered a greater percentage of the time, thus reducing erosion. Some rotation patterns may repeat one or more crops, such as a rotation of corn, corn, oats, and hay. In the short run, this technique may require planting less profitable crops in some years, which may reduce the farmer's ability and willingness to use it.

Contour plowing, another important soil conservation method, involves plowing across a slope, or on the contour, rather than up and down a slope. Contour plowing reduces erosion by causing water to be trapped in the furrows where it can soak in, rather than running down the furrows and causing erosion. Thus, it is also a water conservation technique. On hilly land, contours are rarely straight, and so contour plowing requires plowing in curvy lines across a field. Similarly, field boundaries rarely follow the contours, and so this usually results in irregular-shaped patches and some unused land, making it more time-consuming and perhaps less profitable for

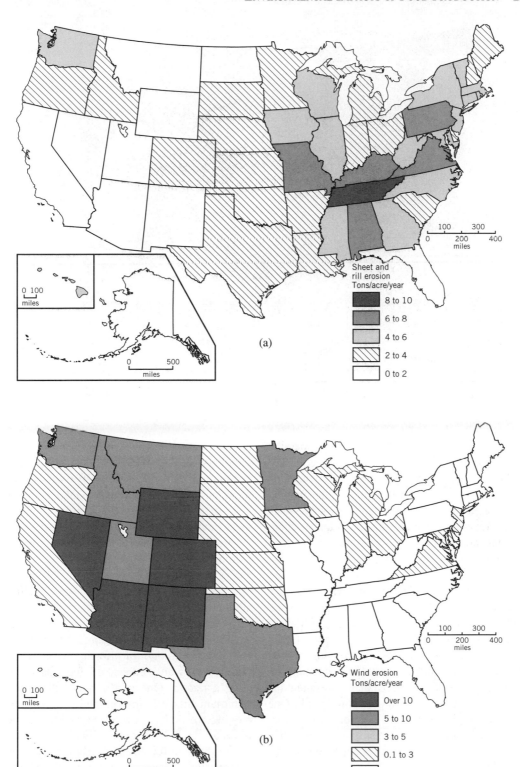

Figure 6.16   Soil erosion on U.S. cropland, 1992. Rates of sheet and rill erosion (*a*), wind erosion (*b*) combine to demonstrate the extent of total erosion (*c*) (page 132), geographically dominant in the western states.

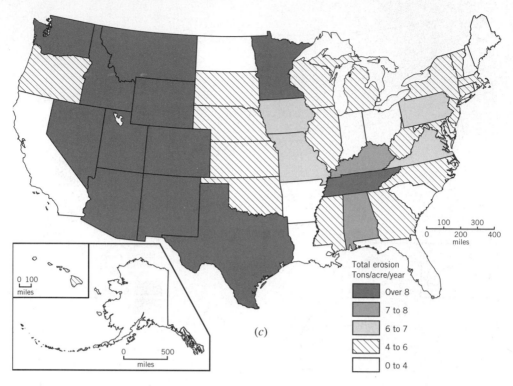

100   300
0   200   400
miles

0 100
miles

(c)

0   500
miles

Total erosion
Tons/acre/year

Over 8

7 to 8

6 to 7

4 to 6

0 to 4

Figure 6.16   (continued)

the farmer than plowing in straight rows parallel to the borders of a rectangular field.

Contour plowing is often used in conjunction with *terracing*. Terracing involves constructing ridges or ditches parallel to the contours, which trap overland flow and divert it into drainage channels, thus preventing it from continuing downslope and causing erosion. In some parts of the world, notably Southeast Asia, terraces are constructed with flat surfaces for ponding of water and rice production. In the United States most terraces are subtle ridges on sloping fields, and in many cases the farmer plows and plants on them as if they were not there. Contour plowing, terracing, or crop rotation may be combined with *strip cropping*, in which crops are planted in parallel strips along the contour or perpendicular to prevailing winds. One strip may be planted with a less protective crop or left fallow, while the adjacent strip has a protective cover. Soil eroded in one area is deposited nearby, and little of the soil is lost.

With regard to wind erosion, the most useful prevention methods are stubble mulching and windbreaks. Stubble mulching simply means leaving plant residue on the ground between growing seasons rather than plowing it under immediately after harvest. Windbreaks are lines of trees planted perpendicular to the most erosive winds. Both of these techniques act to reduce wind velocity at the soil surface and thus reduce erosion. Some of these methods are illustrated in Figure 6.17.

Another conservation technique that is rapidly gaining acceptance is *minimum tillage*, or *conservation tillage*. It includes a variety of techniques that seek to reduce erosion by maximizing the amount of crop residue that is left on the soil surface and by maintaining soil structure conducive to infiltration rather than runoff. Most do this by reducing the amount of plowing, which also conserves energy and reduces the fuel costs of operating a tractor. One of the major drawbacks of minimum tillage is that instead of physically removing weeds by plowing, herbicides are sometimes used to a greater extent, which increases the risk of the harmful side effects of these chemicals. Conservation tillage has been widely adopted in much of North America and is helping to reduce erosion without taking land out of production.

Decisions on how to manage agricultural land are made by individual farmers, who, like any individuals operating businesses in the short run, are concerned primarily with maximizing their incomes. Farmers are aware of the threat of erosion to the productivity of their lands (which in the long run destroys their capital base), and most feel that more should be done to prevent it. The problem is that their management decisions must consider the costs of inputs of seed, fertilizer, irrigation water, fuel, pesticides, and so on, relative to the value of the crops that will be produced. Inputs of fertilizers and pesticides will generally result in substantial increases in crop yields, and

so variations in these inputs are much more significant to short-term returns than long-term reductions in inherent soil fertility caused by erosion. Most farmers in the United States today, especially those with smaller operations, are struggling under enormous debts, and farm prices have not been high enough to pay off loans and provide a comfortable profit. This profit is necessary if farmers are to restrict planting, invest in erosion control structures, or otherwise constrain their activities.

Government officials concerned with soil conservation have recognized this problem and since

(a)

(b)

(c)

(d)

Figure 6.17   Soil conservation methods. (a) Windbreaks in Wisconsin. (b) Contour plowing and terraces in Iowa. (c) Contour strip cropping in Maryland. (d) Chiseling to till soil while leaving mulch on the surface in South Dakota.

the 1930s have implemented programs to ease the economic burden of soil conservation. One important method is payments to the farmer in exchange for planting soil-conserving cover crops such as alfalfa instead of more profitable, but non-protective, crops. Such payments can serve a second purpose, that of reducing farm production so as to increase prices. In addition to these payments, subsidies are made available from time to time to pay for capital improvements such as construction of terraces or gully control. Finally, Natural Resource Conservation Service extension agents provide technical assistance to farmers by making available information on different erosion control methods and ways to incorporate them into a profitable farm management plan.

In spite of these measures, the erosion problem persists. In the late 1970s and early 1980s, economic difficulties led farmers to plant on more and more land, rejecting cover crops in favor of more profitable row crops. In 1996, the U.S. government decided to phase out most crop subsidy programs by 2003, and with them incentives to reduce soil erosion will also be lost. The large machinery in use today is not well suited to terraced fields, and in many areas terraces have been destroyed. These trends have prompted new warnings on the severity of the erosion problem, but no new government programs have emerged to deal with it. Many experts feel that as long as new agricultural technologies can increase yields at the same time as erosion control reduces either yields or profits, few farmers will do much to control erosion. Although farmers might be willing to accept mandatory programs to control erosion, they would only be willing to do so if society as a whole, through the government, compensated them for reduced incomes.

Rangeland Degradation

Range, or grazing land, provides forage for limited numbers of domestic animals. *Overgrazing* occurs when the number of animals on these lands exceeds carrying capacities. Several areas of the world, notably the dry lands around the Mediterranean Sea, have been long overgrazed, with resulting problems of devegetation, erosion, and ultimately the threat of desertification. *Desertification* is land degradation in dryland regions resulting mainly from adverse human impact. It occurs in parts of all the major semi-arid regions of the world and affects some of these regions more than others.

The Global Perspective A number of factors contribute to the degradation of the world's rangelands. Overgrazing, the expansion of cultivation, the conversion of rangeland to cropland, and increased human population pressures are all taking their toll on rangeland conditions worldwide. There are four types of soil degradation: water erosion and wind erosion, which strip away nutrients from the soil and the soil itself, and physical and chemical processes, which reduce the productivity of the soil (Table 6.3).

One of the first baseline studies to estimate world land degradation patterns, the Global Assessment of Soil Degradation Desertification (GLASOD), found that 1.9 billion hectares (17% of all vegetated land) of land showed signs of human-induced degradation, 11% of it labeled as moderate, severe, or extreme (World Resources Institute 1993). Worldwide, about 35% of the human-induced soil degradation is caused by overgrazing, 30% by deforestation, 28% by agricultural activities, 7% by overexploitation for fuelwood use, and the remaining 1% by industrialization (World Resources Institute 1992). Regionally, these causes vary in their importance. In Africa, overgrazing is the leading cause of soil degradation (Dodd 1994), in North and Central America it's agricultural activities, and in Asia and South America, deforestation is the leading cause of land degradation. Figure 6.18 is a world map showing areas of moderate, severe, and extreme degradation. As you can see, those areas of serious concern are in Eurasia, the Middle East, China, and North and Central America. The areas of major concern include small areas with severe degradation or moderate degradation over larger areas.

Rangeland Degradation in the United States Rangeland decline is widespread in the United States, where serious problems of degradation exist on much of the nation's range, especially in the Southwest. It has been estimated that 37 percent of North America's arid lands are in a state of "severe" desertification. Within the United States, perhaps 225 million acres (91 million ha) (about 25% of the rangeland total) are in a state of "severe" or "very severe" desertification (Dregne 1997; Sheridan 1981a). In the early 1990s, the

Table 6.3   Types of Human-Induced Soil Degradation

Type	Definition	Processes Involved
Water erosion	Loss of topsoil through the action of water	Sheet or surface erosion Rill and Gully formation
Wind erosion	Decrease in vegetative cover, thus exposing topsoil to potential removal	Overgrazing, Agricultural practices Deforestation, Fuelwood removal
Chemical deterioration	Loss of soil nutrients	Salinization Acidification Pollution
Physical deterioration	Reduction in soil quality for agriculture	Compaction Waterlogging

NRCS began a program intended to reduce problems of rangeland degradation, and in 1997 39 percent of the U.S. rangeland no longer has serious resource problems, while 61 percent of rangeland and 46 percent of permanent pasture had serious ecological problems (Natural Resources Conservation Service 1997).

One case study helps illustrate the contribution of poverty, carelessness, and fluctuating climatic conditions on rangeland degradation. In the case of the Navajo Indians of Arizona and New Mexico, very severe degradation is caused by too many people, with few economic alternatives, being crowded onto too little land. During the past century, the Navajo population has multiplied by a factor of ten, while the land available has only tripled. From the late 1930s, when the U.S. government first tackled the overgrazing problem, the Navajo's sheep population grew from an estimated 1.3 million to 2.17 million in the early 1980s (Sheridan 1981b). When one considers that the U.S. government believes that the 15-million-acre (6-million-ha) Navajo reservation has a carrying capacity of 600,000 sheep, the problem of overgrazing becomes quite clear.

What are the environmental effects of this overgrazing, and why do the Navajo continue this practice? Most of the land surface of the reservation is badly eroded, and the plant cover the animals rely on for food is not being maintained. Until recently the Navajo have had few alternatives, and conflicts between traditional livelihood patterns and high unemployment rates (over 60%) forced the Navajo to continue their overgrazing practices. Since sheep and cattle herding remain the major source of income for many Navajo, they are naturally unwilling to reduce animal population levels to reach what they see as a U.S. government-generated ideal called carrying capacity that could threaten their own security.

AGRICULTURAL POLICY AND MANAGEMENT

Throughout the world, in capitalist and socialist economies alike, agriculture is considered to be of fundamental importance to national welfare—including social and cultural issues as well as economic prosperity and food supply. As a result, virtually every government in the world intervenes in the agricultural system in a variety of ways. These interventions take many forms, including production subsidies, price regulation, commodity management, research and education programs, and direct regulation of farm practices. Some programs have been more successful than others, but nearly everywhere such management has profound impacts on how food is produced and distributed.

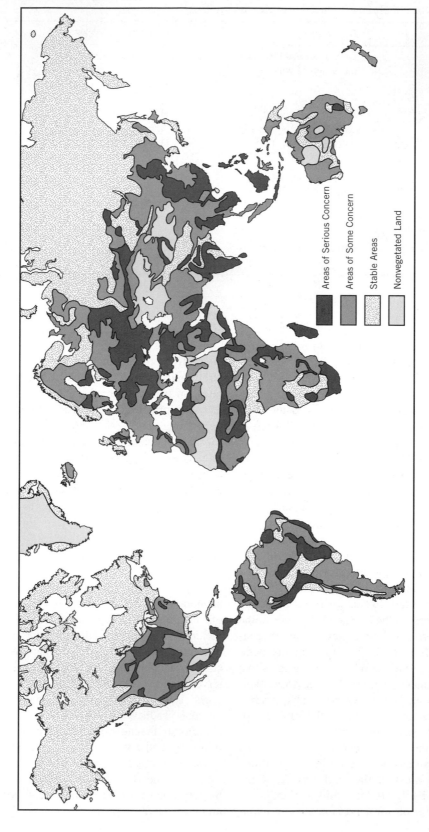

Figure 6.18 Soil degradation. Areas of serious concern for land degradation are located in the world's prime agricultural belts as well as highland areas. *Source:* World Resources Institute, 1992.

- Areas of Serious Concern
- Areas of Some Concern
- Stable Areas
- Nonvegetated Land

Subsidies

Some of the most successful policies in recent decades have been those that have stimulated production through providing financial subsidies to farmers. In the United States, for example, the thrust of most U.S. agricultural policies has been to subsidize agricultural income and maintain higher prices than would occur in a free market, while restraining production and pursuing conservation goals. Most of these policies were instituted in the 1930s as part of the New Deal programs and continued in place until the mid-1990s. The subsidies took many forms, including loans that are not repaid if a crop failed, direct payments in compensation for taking land out of production, and insurance against crop failure resulting from bad weather or disease, and targeted subsidies to help with conservation-related investments.

Subsidies are also responsible for the enormous increase in agricultural production that took place in Europe from the 1950s to the 1990s. The Common Agricultural Policy instituted there established uniform prices for all member nations in the European Union. Prices were set high enough so that the least efficient farmers (or those farming the poorest land) could still stay in production. At these high prices, the more efficient farmers operating on more fertile land could make substantial profits. They cultivated all the land they could, invested in new equipment, and prospered. These policies have generated more production than the market can absorb, and the government has accumulated surpluses of agricultural commodities. Some of these surpluses have been sold on the world market, usually at prices below domestic levels, while others have been given to famine relief and welfare programs. These policies also created new erosion problems where there were few before, for example, hilly land formerly in pasture was brought into grain production to take advantage of high grain prices.

In the mid-1980s these problems became more acute, and in the context of government budget-cutting and the trend toward reduced governmental intervention in markets, many of these subsidies are being reduced. In the United States, the most dramatic change took place with passage of the Food Security Act of 1996, also known as the Freedom to Farm Bill (Issue 6.3).

Sustainable Agriculture

In every agricultural region of the world, negative impacts of agriculture are being felt. The effects of soil degradation and agricultural pollution are more severe in some areas than in others, but there is universal recognition that while food production must increase to meet the needs of a growing population, the productive capacity of agricultural lands must be preserved and nurtured. Farm practices that seek to balance production and preservation are known as *sustainable agriculture.*

Although it is difficult to define precisely which farming techniques constitute sustainable agriculture, they generally involve intensive soil conservation measures and minimal use of pesticides and inorganic fertilizers. At the present time, the number of farmers using these methods is relatively small, mostly in specialized crops such as fruits and vegetables. But the number of farmers producing grain, meat, and dairy products using sustainable methods is increasing, and this trend is likely to continue as long as the costs of chemical inputs remain high and the need to maximize yield per acre is low.

One key feature of the drive toward sustainable agriculture is the reduced use of farm chemicals, especially pesticides. Pesticides have been a boon to modern technological agriculture, but they also have harmful side effects. The side effects of most concern are health hazards to agricultural workers using the pesticides, health effects on the general population through contamination of food, water, and air, and adverse ecological effects.

The most severe human health hazards of pesticides are those associated with the occupational exposure of farm workers handling the substances. Workers in the field at the time of application are exposed, as are those handling crops at harvest time. Accidental exposure is also a major concern. Although pesticides have been regulated to limit effects beyond the farm as well as on it, major problems remain. For example, the nonpersistent pesticides that are generally used today do not accumulate in high concentrations in the environment. However, they are highly toxic at the time they are applied, hence those in contact with pesticides at that time are most at risk.

The general population is also exposed to agricultural chemicals, primarily through con-

ISSUE 6.3:   Deregulating Agriculture in the United States

Since the New Deal era of the 1930s, the U.S. government has taken an active role in managing the nation's agricultural output. Its main goals were to reduce problems of overproduction and depressed crop prices; encourage soil conservation; and subsidize farm income. These goals were achieved through a variety of programs, but most guaranteed that farmers would receive at least a certain minimum price for their crop, regardless of market fluctuations or low yields. In return, farmers agreed to limit the amount of land that was planted and to farm in ways that would help conserve the soil.

Prior to the institution of these programs, farming was a much more risky business than it is today. In periods of low prices, farmers would plant more so as to increase their income and compensate for the low prices. This led to greater supplies of farm commodities, which drove down prices further to levels that were often below the costs of planting. The New Deal programs were intended to stabilize farm production and increase farm income, and they were reasonably effective.

One problem with the government programs was that they tended to create surpluses. The government would set a price for a commodity that was sometimes higher than the market price, and it would promise to buy the farmer's produce at that higher price, even if the market didn't demand it. The result was that the government accumulated large stocks of grain and other commodities, especially in the late 1970s. Some was distributed domestically and overseas in food aid programs, but storage and distribution costs were high. Another problem with the programs was the cost of the income subsidies. In 1993, income supports totaled over $13 billion, representing an 8 percent boost in farm income above that earned from sale of crops. But the criticism that eventually led to deregulation was an ideological one: that they represented government manipulation of the market, and in the 1990s the prevailing political sentiment was that businesses and the market should be left alone—deregulated.

Deregulation of the farm sector began in the Reagan administration in the 1980s, with gradual reductions in the level of subsidies. But the largest step toward deregulation came in 1996, with passage of the Freedom to Farm Bill, also known as the Federal Agriculture Improvement and Reform Act. The Freedom to Farm Bill sets U.S. farm policy through 2002. It eliminates acreage idling programs and allows farmers to plant any crop except fruits and vegetables on land receiving subsidies. In addition, it removes the link between income support payments and agricultural commodity prices, leaving farmers more exposed to the vagaries of the market. Farmers must still comply with conservation programs to receive subsidies. The subsidy levels fixed by the law vary from year to year, reaching a high of $5.8 billion in 1998 and declining to $4.0 billion in the last year of the program. In comparison, the average payments for 1987–1995 were $5.3 billion per year. Thus, early in the program the bill represents a substantial increase in average subsidy level, without the usual strings attached. In addition, expectations for the last few years of the 1990s were that world demand for grain would be relatively high because world grain inventories were low. Fixing payments at the average value from the early 1990s would thus represent a significant increase in subsidy over expected levels, making the increased risk to farmers politically more palatable, as well as financially attractive.

The impacts of this policy change remain to be seen. One likely result is that by increasing the degree to which farm income is determined by market prices, the economic advantages will go to the more efficient farmers (the ones able to earn the highest profits) while less efficient farmers will have a harder time staying in business. To the extent that large farms have economies of scale that make their operations more profitable, this contributes to the continuing decline of the family farm and its replacement by corporate-scale operations. A second result is that by making farmers more dependent on the market, and presumably on relatively short-term financial constraints, the bill may remove some of the incentive for farmers to conserve the soil. This will be particularly true if subsidy levels continue to decline after 2002, weakening the incentive to participate in conservation programs in order to qualify for subsidies.

sumption of foods containing these substances but also through transport of pollutants in water and air. Although these exposures are less acute than those faced by agricultural workers, the number of people affected is much greater.

The combined hazards of pesticide use are great, but so too are the benefits in terms of increased yields. Concern for the problems associated with massive pesticide use has prompted research on alternative methods of pest control, most importantly integrated pest management. This approach recognizes that several different means can be used to control pests, including pesticides, crop rotation and other habitat controls, biological controls such as predator introduction, and other techniques. No single technique is likely to be completely successful in any given place, but for each particular set of agricultural needs and pest problems it should be possible to use a mix of different control techniques tailored to the situation. This approach will require considerable research and development before it can be widely used, but it offers the greatest promise in solving pest problems without poisoning humans or the environment.

Many scientists and others concerned with the use of agricultural chemicals have long warned of dangers and advocated alternative approaches. But for the most part the governmental and university researchers and advisers who guide U.S. agricultural technology have maintained that productive agriculture depends on substantial chemical inputs.

There are recent indications of a major policy change in this area. In 1989, the National Academy of Sciences released a report describing a five-year study of practices and yields on farms that successfully use few or no chemical inputs (Schneider 1989). The study examined farms that have successfully eliminated or dramatically reduced use of chemical fertilizers and pesticides. The farms in the study were from a wide range of environments and produced crops such as corn, soybeans, wheat, and garden vegetables. Using innovative methods, they were able to produce these crops with yields per acre and profits that rivaled those of conventional farms. Most of the farms studied relied on intensive management, including techniques such as crop rotation, biological pest control, special cultivation techniques, and highly selective use of pesticides. The most intriguing aspect of the study is the reaction it received in Washington, DC: officials of

the U.S. Department of Agriculture, which is usually strongly supportive of conventional techniques, were pleased with the report and welcomed the recommended changes in agricultural practices.

This development came at a time of increasing evidence that farmers are working to reduce pesticide use. Examination of recent trends in pesticide use, for example, suggests that insecticide use is on the decline. Herbicides, which are used intensively in modern minimum-till and no-till methods, are still used intensively, but their use does not appear to be growing, even though more and more farmers are adopting reduced tillage techniques. Agriculture's reduced use of these chemicals is likely to improve many aspects of the food system, from the health of farm laborers to reduction of pesticide residues in processed foods, as well as reductions in groundwater pollution. The recent passage of the Food Quality Protection Act is one example. This act requires that pesticide tolerance settings reflect risk standards that are definable by modern scientific methods rather than absolutely zero risk. The bill also includes both dietary and nondietary (e.g., lawns) exposures and pays particular attention to certain high-risk groups such as children, infants, and farm workers—groups that might need extra precautions if they ingest too much of the pesticide.

Rangeland Management

The best way to manage rangelands is to maintain animal populations at or below carrying capacity. Carrying capacity varies from location to location and from year to year. Range ecologists have developed techniques for estimating carrying capacity based on vegetation type, average precipitation, soil characteristics, and other data. Because it remains difficult to predict rainfall months in advance, planning herd sizes to suit range conditions is sometimes a problem. Under ideal conditions we can determine fairly closely just how many animals should be allowed to occupy a given piece of land and under what conditions. The problem is that herders sometimes have limited flexibility when they have to decide about how many animals they can keep on a given piece of land, and there is usually an incentive to own more rather than fewer animals than the land can sustain. Overgrazing is the result.

Rangeland that is damaged by overgrazing is not lost forever; it will recover if grazing pressure is reduced or if rains improve plant growth. In contrast to this passive method, several active techniques can be used to improve range quality. These include mechanical, chemical, and biological control of undesirable plants, and burning, seeding, fertilization, and irrigation (Vallentine 1989). Mechanical brush control by plowing, bulldozing, or dragging heavy chains across the land is widely used to control sagebrush, mesquite, juniper, and other undesirable species. In some cases, the slash from such operations is burned, and in others it is left as an erosion control measure. In some areas, goats are used to control woody species, for they will strip plants of leaves and eat entire seedlings while cattle will not. Care must be taken that the goats do not overgraze the range, however, or desirable species will also be lost.

Most range management issues are complicated by the fact that populations are sparse and resources are often commonly owned. This is certainly the case in the United States, where much rangeland is under the control of the Bureau of Land Management.

The availability of free or low-cost forage on federally owned lands was essential to the profitability of the developing cattle industry. In addition to leasing the water and forage rights on government property, many ranchers obtained title to vast areas of federal land by evading the acreage limitations imposed by the 1862 Homestead Act (see Chapter 3). By the early twentieth century, the use of barbed wire had created boundaries to the great American pasture, and the days of open-range cattle and sheep drives wound down. These drives were replaced by truck and train transport to regional markets, notably Chicago, Minneapolis, Omaha, Dallas, and Denver.

The federal government has imposed several constraints on the traditional independence of the western rancher beginning with the founding of the National Forest System (1905), passage of the Taylor Grazing Act (1934), and the establishment of the *Bureau of Land Management (BLM)* in 1946. Initially, ranchers were not permitted to let animals graze in the National Forest reserves, but a nominal fee system later permitted the land to be opened for use. Battles have raged ever since over the government's right to control numbers of cattle and the seasonality of grazing. The Taylor Grazing Act organized federal lands

into a system of 144 grazing districts for joint management by the federal government and local stock raisers. Some cattlemen resisted this scheme and attempted to turn management of these lands over to the state governments. However, the effects of overgrazing were evident, and the Taylor Grazing Act's range rehabilitation plans received Congressional support. The act was passed, but it remained underfunded and subject to constant disagreement between federal and local interests (Stegner 1981a).

Today, 22,000 ranchers lease grazing rights from the BLM to graze 4 percent of the nation's beef cattle. A recent estimate suggests that ranchers lease lands at bargain prices. In 1982, for example, the BLM collected $20.9 million in grazing fees. The fair market value of these grazing rights indicates that $104 million should have been collected (Baker 1983). More recently, monthly grazing fees on public lands cost $1.40 per animal, whereas grazing on private land costs an estimated $8.85 per animal. The government subsidy ($7.45) provides a strong incentive for ranchers to graze on government lands regardless of the quality of the forage. By 1990, grazing fees had increased to $1.81 per animal unit, and in 1995, this was raised to $3.96 per animal unit month.

The BLM took over the administration of these and other public lands from the General Land Office and administered them in a similar manner until 1976. In that year Congress passed the *Federal Land Policy and Management Act (FLPMA)*, which brought together thousands of pieces of legislation related to public land management. It also increased the BLM's power to manage its 270 million acres (109 million ha) for the public good, with *multiple use* and *sustained yield* as guiding principles. Through the use of inventories, comprehensive plans, and public participation, the control of America's public lands began to slip away from the ranching, timber, and energy interests that had been influential at the state level (Nothdurft 1981; Stegner 1981b).

From their inception, the BLM and predecessor agencies have struggled to reduce overgrazing. Today's grazing allotments (number of animals permitted per acre) were established according to 1930s estimates of historical rangeland use. It has been suggested that the 1930s cattlemen provided the government with inflated figures of past cattle populations. Thus, in agreeing to reduce their allotments, many ranchers may in fact do very little.

Rangeland improvement measures are used on both private and public lands. The federal government, particularly the BLM, plays a major role in attempting to repair some of the damage done by overgrazing in the past. In 1979, BLM began a 20-year program to improve the rangeland it administers, including range improvement on 139 million acres (55 million ha) and erosion control on 148 million acres (60 million ha). The goal of the program is to double annual forage production on BLM lands from 5.6 million to 11.2 million tons (5.1 to 10.2 million tons) annually. However, these efforts were stymied by the lack of a national level assessment of rangeland health. Although federal agencies monitor range conditions and ecological status on nonfederal lands, there is no comparable program for federal lands. Instead, each federal agency must maintain its own inventory. As such, there is no comparable inventory of the status of rangelands for federally owned lands (National Research Council 1994).

CONCLUSION

Debate continues regarding the future of world agriculture. There are millions of hungry people in the world today, yet crop production increases are leveling off in the "breadbasket" nations of the world. Self-sufficiency in food production is far from a reality in many nations. Furthermore, cropland losses continue to decline globally as agricultural land gives way to expanding cities, or the land is degraded to such an extent that it loses its fertility.

Many food production experts in the wealthier nations encourage further transferral of mechanized agriculture to the less affluent, with the implication that the American system should be adopted worldwide. This would have to be accompanied by a massive industrialization program to employ the billions of farmers and families pushed off their land by mechanization. Such a transformation has immense social, environmental, and economic implications.

Many countries are attempting to stimulate a return to small-scale, subsistence-oriented farming for their rural residents but are fighting a massive flow of people to the cities. It is unlikely that these plans can be effective without a strong guarantee to farmers that they can turn a profit growing food for themselves and others. This is impossible under most present-day land-ownership and cash-crop-oriented systems.

In the United States, technological improvements will probably continue to produce increases in crop yields, and the country will continue to be a major food exporter. Concerns for the future of agricultural resource development revolve mainly around the problems of energy efficiency, pesticide use, and soil erosion. Energy prices are particularly important to farm income. Although energy prices fluctuate, it seems clear that in the long run they must increase. There is growing concern over the ecological and health effects of pesticide use, as pests become resistant to them and as farmers turn more to chemical than to mechanical means for controlling weeds. At the same time, there are indications that in the United States, at least, pesticide use may have peaked, and farmers may be embarking on a new technological revolution that will both reduce pollution and conserve soil. Nonetheless, soil erosion continues at unacceptable rates in many areas of the United States. Although it will probably not be an acute problem causing abandonment of land, it will be a chronic problem that will ultimately force farmers to increase inputs of fertilizer and possibly organic matter to replace lost nutrients and to improve deteriorating soil structure. All of these factors will further increase the cost of producing food and fiber. Thus, it seems that the United States will continue to be an important food provider but that food prices will probably have to rise substantially in the next few decades to allow this production to take place.

REFERENCES AND ADDITIONAL READING

Alexandratos, N. 1988. *Agriculture Toward 2000.* Rome: Food and Agriculture Organization.

Bajwa, R. S., W. M. Crosswhite, and J. E. Hostetler. 1987. *Agricultural Irrigation and Water Supply.* USDA Agricultural Information Bulletin 532. Washington, DC: U.S. Department of Agriculture.

Baker, J. 1983. The frustration of FLPMA. *Wilderness* 47(163) (Winter): 12–24.

Crosson, P. 1995. Soil erosion estimates and costs. *Science* 269:461–462.

_____. 1997. Will erosion threaten agricultural productivity? *Environment* 39(8): 4–9, 29–31.

Dale, E. E. 1930. *The Range Cattle Industry*. Norman: University of Oklahoma Press.

Dodd, J. L. 1994. Desertification and degradation in Sub-Saharan Africa. *BioScience* 44(1): 28–34.

Dregne, H. 1977. Desertification of the world's arid lands. *Economic Geography* 52: 332–46.

Easterbrook, G. 1997. Forgotten benefactor of humanity. *The Atlantic Monthly* 279(1): 74–82.

Food and Agriculture Organization, 1996. FAOSTAT, http://apps.fao.org/

Gardner, G. 1996. *Shrinking Fields: Cropland Loss in a World of Eight Billion*. Worldwatch Paper no. 131. Washington, DC: Worldwatch Institute.

Hilyard, N. and S. Sexton. 1996. Too many for what? The social generation of food "scarcity" and "over population." *The Ecologist* 26(6): 282–289.

National Academy of Sciences. 1972. *The Genetic Variability of Major Crops*. Washington, DC: National Academy of Sciences.

National Research Council. 1994. *Rangeland Health: New Methods to Classify, Inventory, and Monitor Rangelands*. Washington, DC: National Academy Press.

Nothdurft, W. E. 1981. The Lands Nobody Wanted. *Living Wilderness* 45(153): 18–21.

Parry, M. 1990. The potential impact on agriculture of the greenhouse effect. *Land Use Policy* 7 : 109–123.

Pimentel, D., *et al*. 1995. Environmental and economic costs of soil erosion and conservation benefits. *Science* 267: 1117–1123.

Schneider, K. 1989. Science Academy says chemicals do not necessarily increase crops. *New York Times*, September 8, p. A1.

Sheridan, D. 1981a. Can the public lands survive the pressures? *Living Wilderness* 45(153): 36–39.

_____. 1981b. Western rangelands: Overgrazed and undermanaged. *Environment* 23(4): 14–20, 37–39.

Soil Conservation Service, 1980. *America's Soil and Water: Condition and Trends*. Washington, DC: U.S. Government Printing Office.

_____. 1987. *Basic Statistics, 1982 National Resources Inventory*. Iowa State University, Statistical Laboratory, Statistical Bulletin 756. Ames: Iowa State University, Statistical Laboratory.

Stegner, W. 1981a. Land: America's history teacher. *Living Wilderness* 45(153): 5–7.

_____. 1981b. If the sagebrush rebels win, everybody loses. *Living Wilderness* 45(153): 30–35.

Steinbrecher, R. A. 1996. From Green Revolution to gene revolution: The environmental risks of genetically engineered crops. *The Ecologist* 26(6): 273–281

Swaminathan, M. S. and S. K. Sinha, eds, 1986, *Global Aspects of Food Production*, Oxford: Tycooly International.

Tolba, M. K., O. A. El-Kholy, E. El-Hinnawi, M. W. Holdgate, D. F. McMichael, and R. E. Munn. 1992. *The World Environment 1972–1992: Two Decades of Challenge*. London: Chapman & Hall.

United Nations Environment Programme. 1992. *World Atlas of Desertification*. London: Edward Arnold.

U.S. Department of Agriculture. 1981. *RCA Appraisal Parts I and II*. Washington, DC: U.S. Government Printing Office.

_____. 1989. *The Second RCA Appraisal, Soil, Water, and Related Resources on Nonfederal Land in the United States, An Analysis of Condition and Trends*. Washington, DC: U.S. Government Printing Office.

_____. 1996. *1995 Farm Bill: Guidance of the Administration*. Washington, DC: U.S. Government Printing Office.

U.S. Forest Service. 1981. *An Assessment of the Forest and Rangeland Situation in the United States*. Forest Research Report No. 22. Washington, DC: U.S. Government Printing Office.

U.S. Natural Resource Conservation Service. 1997. *A Geography of Hope*. Washington: U.S. Government Printing Office.

_____. 1997b. National Resource Inventory, http://www.nhq.nrcs.usda.gov/NRI/intro.html

Vallentine, J. F. 1989. *Range Development and Improvements*. 3rd ed. San Diego: Academic Press.

World Resources Institute, 1992. *World Resources 1992–93*. New York: Oxford University Press.

_____. 1996. *World Resources 1996–97*. New York: Oxford University Press.

For more information, consult our web page at ***http://www.wiley.com/college/cutter***

STUDY QUESTIONS

1. Americans pay much less for food (as a percentage of their income) than do most other people in the world. Is it a good thing that our food prices are low? Should we pay more so that farmers can

operate in ways that conserve resources more effectively?

2. Most of the world's food is produced in the same country in which it is consumed, although international trade in food is increasing. What are the impacts of increasing international food trade on food availability in poor countries? in rich countries?

3. Does the meat production system in the United States and other wealthy countries, in which meat is produced by feeding grain to animals, affect the availability of food in other parts of the world? If we ate less meat, would this make more food available?

4. How do you feel about pesticides used in the production of the food you eat? How much more would you be willing to pay for food produced without the use of pesticides?

5. Identify the major categories of environmental impacts of agriculture (both cropland and rangeland) where you live.

CHAPTER 7

FORESTS

Forests are the natural vegetation in biomes that have ample soil moisture and a sufficient growing season. They occupy areas of poor soil and steep slopes as well as high-quality lands. Because trees can survive on marginal lands, many forests remain intact even when there is great demand for agricultural land. Forests are found in virtually all humid and subhumid regions of the world, from the tropics to the margins of the tundra.

About 4.1 billion hectares, or about 32 percent of the Earth's land surface (excluding Antarctica) are covered with forest and woodland (World Resources Institute 1996) (Fig. 7.1). This portion has changed considerably over the centuries, generally decreasing as cultivated land has expanded. The original forest cover of the Earth may have approached 50 percent of land area (again, excluding Antarctica).

The remaining forests of the world are generally inhabited at much lower densities than farmland, but the lack of dense population does not mean a lack of economic importance. Forests supply a wide range of commodities for humans and other organisms, including fiber for fuel, lumber and paper, wildlife habitat for both hunting and biodiversity purposes, carbon uptake and storage, water purification and recycling, and recreation.

In addition, forests are under threat from many sources, and as a result Earth's forestland area is decreasing. Trees are being harvested for fiber, mostly for fuel. In many areas, forests are being cleared for other purposes, primarily agriculture (both crops and pasture). In industrial regions forests are being damaged by air pollution, especially acid deposition. Conse-

quently, forests are the subject of considerable competition and controversy worldwide. In this chapter we will explore some of the contrasting uses of forests and the ways these uses impinge on each other.

FORESTS AS MULTIPLE-USE RESOURCES

The fact that forests occupy lands that are not always suited to agriculture, grazing, or other uses does not mean that they are low-value lands. Rather, forests are among the most widespread, versatile, and easily exploited of the world's natural resources. They are used for fuel, construction materials, and paper. The water that is shed by forests in humid areas is usually clean and plentiful, inviting the construction of dams and other facilities to capture and use the water. Forests are the home to diverse wildlife, both plant and animal. Forests have long served as food sources for peoples who occupy the forests and farmlands near them, providing sustenance for birds, monkeys, deer, squirrel, and many other animals.

In the twentieth century, new uses of the forest have emerged with values sometimes even greater than fuel and fiber. These new uses focus on the qualities of the relatively undisturbed forest, especially its biodiversity. Trees are valued not just for the quality of the wood they contain, but for their roles in forest ecosystems and food chains. An old dead tree, once seen simply as lifeless wood better used for lumber, is now the home to a myriad of species that depend on such dead trees for their existence. Trees that were once only curiosities or

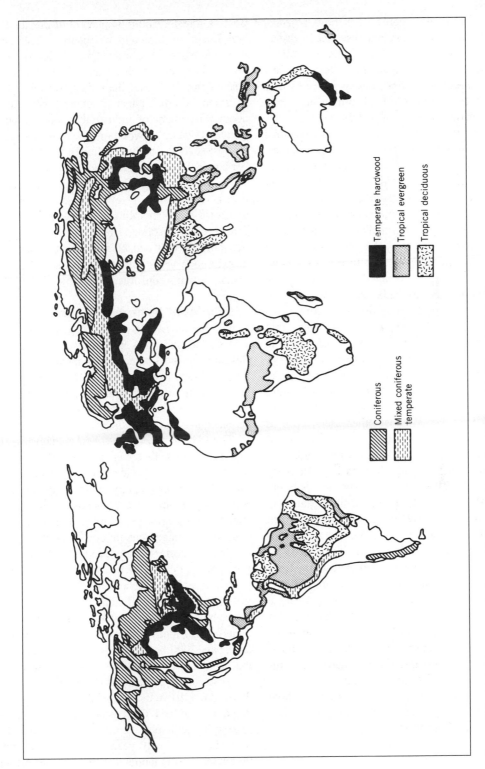

Figure 7.1 Major forest areas in the world. Forests occupy about 30 percent of the world's land areas.

Coniferous

Mixed coniferous temperate

Temperate hardwood

Tropical evergreen

Tropical deciduous

botanists' academic interests are now potential sources of medicines to fight diseases in distant cities. Users of the forest include the wealthy of those remote cities, who travel to the forest to view its diversity and uniqueness, to experience its solitude, or to respect its role in absorbing the excess carbon dioxide emitted by industrial society.

Forests thus present a paradox: it is a resource that is at once vastly abundant and yet scarce. Forests and their lands are used for an extraordinarily wide range of activities, and those who use and manage the forest resource disagree sharply over how much forest there is and how it should be used. For the decision maker in a paper products company, there may be more forest than could ever be needed, because forests are renewable when properly managed. In contrast, the wilderness preservationist believes that a second-growth forest is profoundly different from a forest that has never been cut and maintains that forested wildlands should be protected from the ax forever. Prospectors and miners, yet another interest group, do not care about the trees so much as what lies underneath them. All these groups have incompatible management and use goals for forestlands. Most other users, such as the wide array of people who visit forests for leisure activity, are not at such extreme odds.

The existence of multiple uses is particularly significant because most forests are publicly owned (Brooks 1993). In the United States 45 percent of forestland is publicly owned; in Canada 94 percent is public. The average for industrial countries is 56 percent. Ownership of forests in less industrialized countries in the tropics is less clear. Nominally, the vast forests of the Amazon, central Africa, and southeast Asia are mostly publicly owned, but public management and authority may be difficult to establish at the local level. In much of the world's forests, however, management decisions are made by government agencies that are subject to political pressure from various interests groups (Issue 7.1). Forest management is thus as much a political as a scientific process.

FORESTS AS FIBER RESOURCES

In the mid-1990s, an estimated 3.4 billion cubic meters of wood are harvested annually from the world's forests. About 54 percent of this total was consumed for fuel and charcoal; the remainder was processed into sawn lumber, plywood and other panel products, and paper. Sawn lumber represents more than half the industrial (nonfuel) use of wood, whereas paper production accounts for about 30 percent of industrial wood production. Total harvesting of wood has increased steadily in the last several decades, although the rate of timber harvesting appears to be leveling off.

In many parts of the world the total area of forest is declining. Nevertheless, the ultimate goal of the timber industry should be to harvest forests on a sustained-yield basis: to take only that amount that can be replaced by new forest growth each year. Unfortunately, actual practice doesn't always conform to this objective.

Principles of Sustainable Forestry

Forests are renewable resources. Trees can be harvested, and new trees will grow to replace them. Sustainable forest management means managing a forest in such a way that it will produce a given amount of timber each year indefinitely. If we harvest more than that amount, then we are exceeding the sustainable yield of the forest.

The key question for a forest manager is: How much timber can be cut each year without exceeding the sustainable yield? The answer depends on many factors, principally relating to how fast a forest can replace itself. These factors include tree species characteristics, climate, soil characteristics, and management practices. Growth rate is not only important to the productivity of a given forest but critical to the question of sustainability.

If a forest is to be managed sustainably, then trees must be given sufficient time to replace themselves before they are harvested. As an illustration, let us assume that we have a tract of original forestland, say, 2000 hectares. Moreover, let us assume that this forest takes 100 years to replace itself. Suppose we cut 20 hectares of land each year (Fig. 7.2a). After 10 years we have 200 hectares, or 10 percent of the land, that has been cut. If it begins to regrow immediately, then these 200 hectares have forest that is up to 10 years old, and the remaining 90 percent of the land still has mature forest more than 100 years old. After 20 years, if we cut at the same rate, we have 200 hectares that are 11 to 20 years old and 200 hectares that are less than 10 years old. If we continue to harvest at this rate for

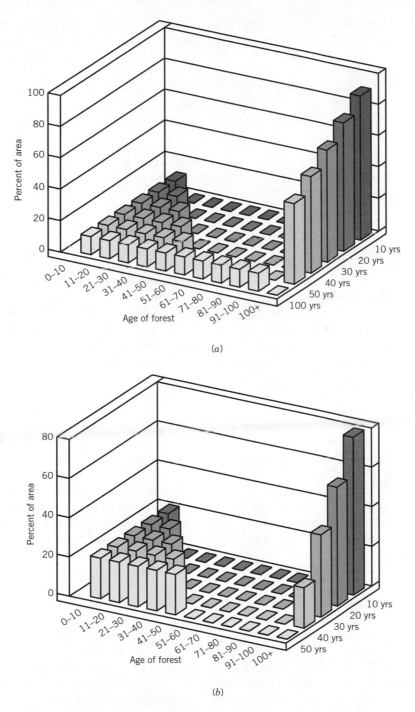

Figure 7.2   Effect of forest harvesting on the age distribution of forests. As forests are harvested, new trees may grow in their place. (*a*) If the rate of harvest in area per year is less than 1/n times the total forest acreage, where n is the number of years required for a forest to reach maturity, then the forest can be harvested at that rate indefinitely. (*b*) If forests are harvested at a high rate, then the area of harvestable forest declines and eventually is depleted, requiring an interval without harvesting before trees reach maturity and harvesting can begin again.

100 years, then eventually we have the same portion of land in each age class. Furthermore, every 10 years 200 hectares of forest reach maturity and are available for harvest.

Now consider the example in Figure 7.2*b*. In this case we cut 40 hectares of forest each year. After 10 years, we have 400 hectares of forest that is less than 10 years old and 1600 hectares of mature forest. If we continue to cut at this rate, after 50 years we have no more mature forest, with our oldest trees only 50 years old. If we are to wait until the trees are 100 years old to harvest them, we will have to wait another 50 years before we can harvest here again.

ISSUE 7.1: CHIPKO: GRASS-ROOTS ENVIRONMENTALISM, OR A STRUGGLE FOR ECONOMIC DEVELOPMENT?

Deforestation is a major issue on the southern flanks of the Himalayas. The region is an area of rapid population growth and large demands for wood (mostly for fuel but also for construction). It is also a region of rugged mountains, where slopes are steep and removal of the forest is contributing to greatly accelerated erosion, depleting soil fertility and causing problems of sediment accumulation and flood management downstream. One area where this deforestation is especially problematic is a region in the Indian state of Uttar Pradesh, known as the Garhwal Himalayas. There a political movement known as Chipko was at the forefront of a struggle over management of these forests. Chipko became an international symbol of grass-roots opposition to unsustainable commercial resource exploitation. But geographer Haripriya Rangan (1996) suggests another interpretation of the Chipko movement and provides some interesting insights into the linkages between environmentalism and other political movements.

The Garhwal Himalayas is a region of northern India, with rugged terrain and limited economic opportunities. It is marginal both within India and within the state of Uttar Pradesh, one of India's most populous states. As such, it is a region of relative poverty and limited political influence. When India won its independence from Britain in 1947, the people of the region supported themselves through subsistence agriculture, forestry, service of pilgrims' needs, and trade across the Himalayas. In the early 1960s, India fought a series of border wars with Pakistan and China, and the Garhwal gained strategic significance. Trade across the Himalayas was eliminated, and the Indian government took control of significant areas of forestlands for defense purposes, reducing the already limited economic opportunities. When Green Revolution agricultural technologies were adopted in the early 1970s, Garhwal was further marginalized. These technologies require significant capital investment for irrigation and purchase of chemicals. In the level land of the Indo-Gangetic Plain, the core of Uttar Pradesh, such investment was feasible. But in the hilly terrain of Garhwal it was more expensive, and capital was even more limited. As a result, cash cropping was less feasible, and subsistence farming remained dominant.

To obtain fuel and raw materials for crafts and to supplement their incomes through selling wood, the people of Garhwal harvested wood from the forests of the area. But these forest resources became more scarce, largely because of commercial harvesting on lands controlled by the state government of Uttar Pradesh. Much of this harvesting was carried out by contractors from outside Garhwal, employing migrant laborers who were also drawn from outside the region. Thus, this harvest did little to contribute to the local economy, and the Uttar Pradesh government was not sympathetic to requests that timber be made available to local harvesters. A protest movement grew, and from 1973 to 1975 villagers staged protests in which they went into the forests and clung to the trees, preventing them from being cut. A local forest contractor, Sunderlal Bahuguna, became a leader of the movement. Environmentalism was a potent force at that time, and Bahuguna cited the need to preserve forests for use by local harvesters against the forces of wanton exploitation in order to maintain ecological integrity for the benefit of all. Chipko means, literally, to stick to something or to hug it. The image of people hugging the trees

Thus, the area of forestland that can be harvested each year on a sustainable yield basis is:

$$\frac{\text{AREA OF FORESTLAND AVAILABLE}}{\text{NUMBER OF YEARS TO MATURITY}}$$

The numerator in this equation is obviously limited by the total amount of forestland in any given area, and in general this amount has been decreasing as land has been allocated to other uses such as agriculture, grazing, recreation, or habitat preservation. Increasing demand for forest products therefore requires that the denominator of the equation must be decreased to make more forestland available for harvesting. This has been

to prevent others from harvesting them became a powerful symbol for environmentalists.

At this time, the government of Indira Gandhi was embarking on a program of nationalizing important industries. The Chipko leaders, demanding greater local access to the forests, met little success in their negotiations with Uttar Pradesh officials. So when they appealed for help from the national government, it used the opportunity to take control of the forests and to institute strong controls on forest management. These controls included requiring consent from the national government prior to any large-scale harvests, prohibition on harvesting certain tree species, and a ban on harvesting above elevations of 1000 meters in the Himalayas.

One result of these measures was that both immediate economic opportunities and longer-term development projects in Garhwal were significantly curtailed. Declining administrative budgets in forestry agencies made it difficult for them to respond to local needs. Road construction, for example, cannot be carried out without a permit, and delays in issuing such permits slowed not only road construction but also irrigation development and electrification. Compounding the problem was the fact that while much of the impetus for forest protection came from the national government, the Garhwal forests were still administered by Uttar Pradesh. Despite the victory of the Chipko movement, the people of Garhwal still did not have either access to their forests or a significant political role in their management. The resulting tensions fueled new demands for the separation of Garhwal from Uttar Pradesh, creating a new state of Uttaranchal. Like Chipko, the central issues were economic: control over forest resources and infrastructure for economic development. Unlike Chipko, the movement for a state of Uttaranchal used the threat of violence to make its voice heard.

What was the Chipko movement? What did it mean? From the perspective of environmentalists, it was a heroic struggle of people whose livelihood was directly dependent on natural resources, and who sought to prevent excessive exploitation by outsiders simply interested in short-term economic gain. The people *hugged the trees*, clearly demonstrating their concern for nature and environmental preservation. Chipko is seen as similar to the Rubber Tappers movement in Brazil, a confrontation between those wishing to exploit the forest sustainably (without clearing the trees) and those who would exploit it through deforestation. The message is that local control of natural resources is a route to sustainability and that, left to themselves, people with a long tradition of local resource use will protect those resources.

On the other hand, the struggle in Garhwal can be seen as one for economic development. The Chipko movement emerged because the people of Garhwal were being denied access to a local resource, and instead outsiders were being allowed to exploit that resource without regard for the needs of local inhabitants. Hugging the trees was a means to prevent this exploitation and regain control of the forests for themselves. When the Chipko movement took the direction of increasing external control of the forest resource, it fell apart as a grass-roots movement, although it lived on as an international environmental legend. In its place we have a new movement, this time explicitly focused on local control. The message is that such control of natural resources is necessary for economic development to truly benefit local populations and that economic considerations, not environmental ones, are central (Rangan 1996).

achieved in two ways: by increasing growth rate through various forest management techniques and by decreasing the size of trees that we harvest. In the following paragraphs we will explore the variables in this equation in more detail.

Forest Management

Forests are managed in many different ways, in terms of both the kinds of uses occurring in them and the specific techniques employed in these uses. If we consider the use of forests as sources of fiber, the most obvious aspect of management is how, when, and at what rate timber is harvested. But the ways in which the forest is managed between harvests is equally important.

Harvest Techniques A variety of harvesting techniques are used in forestry management. Not all of them can be used interchangeably because each has specific goals and impacts. The three most important are *shelterwood cutting*, *selective cutting*, and *clear-cutting*. Another method for harvesting also discussed in this section is chipping or biomass harvesting, a technique generally used for less valuable wood on small lots.

Shelterwood cutting is a several-stage process requiring thinning and cutting. First, trees of poor quality are removed from both the forest floor and the stand itself. This opens up the forest floor to more light, enhancing seedling growth and reducing competition. The remaining trees provide some shelter for the seedlings. When the seedlings take root and become established, some of the remaining mature trees are harvested. Shelterwood cutting is an efficient technique in small plots with relatively homogeneous tree species. It is costly in terms of labor inputs in larger acreages and so is not widely practiced on large tracts of commercial forestlands.

Selective cutting is normally used only in forests of mixed age or in forests with trees of widely varying economic value. The mature trees of the most desirable species are harvested, while the others are left intact. In an oak–hickory forest, for example, the mature oaks might be selectively cut, leaving immature oaks, mature hickories, and other species standing. Selective cutting is used primarily in hardwood forests. When used in mixed-species forests, selective cutting leads to a loss of diversity, which can have negative impacts on wildlife and other sectors of the forest environ-ment. Selective cutting is costly and appropriate only when the value of the harvested trees is high relative to those left uncut.

Clear-cutting is the most widely used method of harvesting and also the most controversial. About two-thirds of U.S. timber production is harvested this way. The technique involves cutting all the trees regardless of size or species and is appropriate when the trees are relatively uniform in species and age or when it would provide the most desirable form of regeneration. Clear-cutting, however, does remove the entire forest canopy and may lead to soil erosion and wildlife habitat destruction. It also leaves a more scarred landscape than other harvest-ing techniques. Clear-cutting produces much more timber per unit of acre harvested than selective cut-ting or shelterwood cutting.

Loggers recently have developed a method for consuming whole trees of any size and shape, from any size tract. This biomass harvesting turns trees into wood chips that may then be used to make pulp or fuel wood-fired power plants. Chips are easier to handle in large quantities than logs and can be quickly loaded on trucks, railroad cars, or ships for transport to pulp mills or power plants. Loggers may cut selectively or consume all stand-ing timber, depending on the requirements of the job and stipulations of the landowner. This method has great economic appeal for harvesting the vast majority of U.S. forestlands—the small parcels in private hands. It is also being used in the developing world, where forests are being cut and exported to industrialized countries for processing into pulp and paper.

Silviculture Once a forest is harvested, the land is available for regeneration and growth of new trees. The period of regeneration and subse-quent growth is a time for management to maxi-mize growth rates and thus minimize the time needed to produce a harvestable stand of trees. In-tensive silviculture on productive lands—tree farming—can produce much larger yields of tim-ber than would occur in natural forests, just as cul-tivated crops produce much more food than could be collected from unmanaged ecosystems.

The incentive to establish intensive silviculture as a forest management strategy results from a shortage of timber available for harvest. In areas where timber resources are abundant, such as North America until the mid-twentieth century or the Amazon basin today, it may be cheaper simply to harvest the standing timber and move on to new land than to invest in regrowing timber for harvest decades in the future. But if the price of standing timber is high enough and if growth rates are strong enough that newly planted land can be harvested in the foreseeable future, then the investment in regeneration and management is justified. In some countries, governments require replanting, or invest in replanting themselves, so that timber will be available for future generations, even though such investments might not be justified by short-term returns.

One region where intense silviculture is practiced today is the southeastern United States, especially the Atlantic Coastal Plain. This is an area of warm temperatures, abundant rainfall, but relatively poor soils that support only limited agriculture. The soils are quite capable, however, of supporting pine plantations that grow very rapidly in the subtropical climate. The dominant tree species planted in this region is loblolly pine. Trees are planted almost immediately after harvest of the preceding crop. They are fertilized and treated with pesticides to limit insect damage. Stands may be thinned to encourage growth, and fire is used to reduce understory growth that would compete for moisture and nutrients. By using these techniques, harvestable stands of trees with diameters up to 30 cm (1 foot) are produced in as little 20 to 35 years. The expansion of timber production using these methods has been especially rapid in the twentieth century, encouraged by the development of plywood, fiberboard, and paper manufacture that can make use of small trees.

Forest Products Technology

Uses of Wood To better understand the changing supply and demand for timber and their relation to sustainable forestry, it is necessary to understand the uses to which wood is put. In most of the world, harvested wood is generally used for fuel. Wood supplies the domestic heating and cooking needs of half the world's population and is the dominant use of timber in most developing nations (Brooks 1993; United Nations 1992). In the industrialized world, wood is no longer a major fuel, and most wood is used for industrial purposes. In the United States, for example, fuel was the major use until the mid-nineteenth century, when it was surpassed by growth in lumber use. Gradually,

fuelwood was replaced by other energy sources, and this use plummeted after the 1930s (Clawson 1979). In the 1970s and 1980s, fuelwood use expanded greatly, and today it is again a major use of wood in the United States.

Beginning around 1900, wood began to be used to make plywood and pulp for paper, and these uses have increased steadily ever since. Demand for lumber also follows cycles in new housing construction. Today, for example, pulp production demands almost as much wood as lumber in the United States. In addition, wood chips and sawdust are now used to make boards rather than using whole pieces of wood. Production of these fiber-based structural panels continues to grow. Today about 35 percent of all wood harvested in the United States is used for sawn lumber, while about 25 percent is used to make pulp and paper products. About 10 percent of U.S. wood is used for plywood and similar products, while 30 percent is used for fuel (World Resources Institute 1996).

These varying uses require different kinds of wood. For example, just about any kind of wood can be burned, although hardwoods are better than softwoods for this purpose. Lumber, on the other hand, requires trees that are straight and as great in diameter as possible—in other words, old trees. Most lumbering requires softwoods, but specialized industries such as furniture construction use hardwoods. Plywood is made from large sheets of veneer only millimeters thick that are glued together. These sheets are not sawn from logs; they are peeled from a turning log with a large blade that can cut sheets that are hundreds of feet long. This means that plywood manufacture does not need logs of large diameter. Much younger trees can be used, provided they are softwoods, relatively straight, and free from knots. Similarly, pulp production is not dependent on any particular size of log, and the tree species is more important than age. Particle board and similar products are made using waste from other processes.

Impacts on Timber Requirements The transition from lumber as the main nonfuel use of wood to use of manufactured wood products such as plywood, particle board, and paper has profound impacts on the requirements of the timber industry. The most significant of these has been to decrease the need for large (and therefore old) trees and allow harvesting of small, young trees in their place. For example, in the 1800s most of the timber industry in northern Maine was focused on the white pine. This tree grew straight and tall in the old-growth forest and produced very high-quality lumber: long boards with straight grain and relatively few knots. Loggers operating in Maine at that time took the white pine first and left other species standing. Today, the forest products industry in Maine is dominated by paper production. Much smaller trees are used (mostly spruce), most of them being harvested from second-growth forests. A higher portion of the trees are used, because smaller logs can be made into pulp where they would not be useful for lumber. Clear-cutting is thus the preferred harvesting technique, as opposed to selective-cutting in the 1800s.

The ability to manufacture large pieces of wood such as plywood from small trees reduces the dependence of the lumber industry on old-growth forest and makes possible a shift toward using "fiber farms" rather than forests to supply our needs for building materials and paper. This shift is already taking place in the southeastern United States, where fast-growing pines are planted, intensively managed, and harvested in cycles as short as 20 to 25 years. The trees only grow to diameters of perhaps 30 cm in this time, but this is adequate for pulp, pulpwood, and particle board.

In the United States, lumber prices have been low enough that sawn boards remain the material of choice for most housing construction—the main use of such lumber. But if prices for lumber should rise significantly, we have the ability to replace it with other materials. Such changes are already taking place. A new home in the 1950s would likely have been built with plywood sheathing (the inner layer of the outside walls) and sawn wood siding. Today the sheathing on new homes is usually either a type of particle board called oriented strand board, made from small flakes of wood, or a foil/paper-covered plastic foam board, and siding is more likely to be vinyl than wood. If prices for the 2-by-4 and 2-by-6 boards that form most of the framing in new houses rise, they can be replaced with metal studs, like those already used in most commercial construction. And new plastic- and paper-based materials are also available to substitute for these boards if needed.

The significance of these changes is that should we decide that nontimber uses of forests, especially old-growth forests, are of great enough value, then the technology exists to replace this sawn lumber with other products relatively easily. It is just a matter of having the price of lumber rise sufficiently that substitute materials become more attractive. Manufactured wood products made from younger trees and nonwood substitutes, if cheaper than lumber, could meet our needs.

NONFIBER USES OF FOREST RESOURCES

Habitat

Trees are more long-lived than other plant types, and they take a long time to mature. Primarily because of their large size, trees contain large amounts of nutrients stored in living biomass. Forests are ecosystems in which most of the available nutrients accumulate in live trees over a long period of time. Relatively small amounts of nutrients are contained in herbs, shrubs, or the soil. In an experimental forest in New Hampshire, it was found that annual uptake rates of nutrients are a small fraction of the total amounts in storage. Restoration of ecosystem nutrients after forests are clear-cut may take several decades (Likens et al. 1978). For most tree species, the rate of growth (as measured by biomass) is relatively slow when the tree is young, primarily because it is small and does not have a large photosynthetic capacity. Growth rate increases as the tree gains a larger total leaf area and declines as it reaches maturity.

In many forests, the amount of stored biomass reaches a steady state in which old trees die and their nutrients are taken up by younger ones. For a large portion of the world's forests, cyclic disturbances kill all or nearly all the trees at the same time, releasing nutrients and beginning a new cycle of forest growth. These can include fire, disease or insect infestation, windstorms, or other disturbances.

The significance of old-growth forest habitat is at the center of debates over the impacts of timber harvesting. In many of the world's forest regions today, most forestland has already been harvested at least once and therefore contains young, second-growth timber. In these areas, relatively little land that has never been cut remains. This old-growth forest, undisturbed by humans for at least hundreds of years, contains species that are rare or nonexistent in second-growth forest. Each of these species is associated with a particular micro-habitat to which it is best suited. For example, some species nest in or feed in standing dead trees. As old trees decay, they become home to a myriad of insects and other invertebrates who live in and feed on the rotting wood. These in turn are food for birds, small mammals, and even foraging bears. Others, like the marbled murrelet and the spotted owl, two endangered bird species that inhabit the old-growth forest of the Pacific Northwest, nest only in very tall trees. Without these old tall trees, these and many other species are threatened with extinction (Maser 1994).

Water Resources

Forests are found in the more humid parts of the Earth's land surface, where mean annual rainfall exceeds evapotranspiration. The excess water becomes runoff that is available for human use. Forest vegetation has two contrasting impacts on that runoff. It protects the quality of the water but may decrease its quantity. In most cases, maintaining good water quality is a prime concern and so takes precedence.

Water quality is usually very good in forest areas because forest soils are very permeable. The continuous vegetation cover, high productivity, annual leaf fall, and large amount of standing biomass support a diverse community of organisms that live in the soil and maintain its ability to absorb water. Because most water arrives at streams by subsurface paths rather than running across the surface, natural soil erosion rates are low.

When a forest is harvested, the soil may be disturbed, increasing the amount of overland flow and erosion, with negative impacts on water quality. The extent of impact depends on the kind of disturbance and the terrain. If the forest is clear cut using heavy machines, with logs being dragged across the ground, the soil is often damaged. On the other hand, if the use of machines and dragging is minimized, the damage can be minor or insignificant. Steep slopes are much more susceptible to increased erosion caused by logging than are flat areas. Road-building is often one of the most damaging aspects of logging operations, especially in steep mountainous areas where road cuts and fills increase the likelihood of landsliding, which adds

much more soil and rock to streams. Landsliding has been especially severe in the Himalayas, the Andes, and the Pacific Northwest of North America. Accelerated erosion associated with deforestation is a major water-quality problem in the Pacific Northwest and has been one of the causes of the decline in salmon populations there.

In addition to regulating overland flow and erosion, forests play a critical role in evapotranspiration. Like all green plants, trees use water. When water is plentiful, they use about the same amount as any vegetation type would use, but when water is limited, as it is for at least part of the year in most climates, trees may use more water than grasses and other low vegetation. This is because trees typically have deeper and more extensive root systems, which allows them to use water stored in the soil below the reach of shallow-rooted plants. For this reason, in a dry season, trees may stay green when grasses turn brown.

If maximizing the amount of runoff is a goal of watershed managers, then this effect of trees may be undesirable. Accordingly, some area managers actually discourage the growth of trees, or replace trees with grasses, as a means of decreasing evapotranspiration and thus increasing runoff. Care must be taken in such operations to ensure that the conversion of vegetation does not degrade water quality.

When a large forest region is deforested, the decrease in evapotranspiration may actually reduce the amount of water vapor in the air and thus reduce precipitation. For decades trees have been planted in China in the belief that this practice will lead to an increase in precipitation, although there is little evidence to support this.

The interior of the Amazon basin ultimately receives its water vapor from evaporation in the Atlantic Ocean. But before Atlantic water can reach the interior it falls as precipitation and is evapotranspired back to the atmosphere. Most of the water vapor reaching the interior has been cycled through vegetation at least once on its way west across South America. Some climatologists have raised concerns that if large areas of the Amazon are deforested and evapotranspiration is reduced, the moisture supply to the western Amazon can be restricted, reducing rainfall there. As yet this argument is supported mostly by climate models, with little observational evidence of changing precipitation associated with deforestation.

Recreation

In many countries, especially wealthier ones, forests are important recreational resources. They are relatively undeveloped and thus have open space available for hiking, camping, and other outdoor activities. They are often in mountainous areas that offer other amenities such as skiing, climbing, and the cooler weather of high elevations. Because they serve as habitat for game animals, they can be preferred areas for hunting and fishing.

Recreational use of forests usually has relatively little impact on the forest and thus is compatible with most other uses. The one use with which recreation is incompatible is logging. During logging operations recreational use is not possible, and after logging the damage to the forest lingers for some years until significant regrowth has occurred. In many cases, recreation and logging can coexist in the same forest region. The maintenance of roads for logging is also advantageous in increasing access for vacationers. Lumber companies in such areas may leave buffer strips of forest along roads, rivers, and lakes to preserve the impression of forest for visitors. The greatest problem involving recreation and logging is that recreational users and the businesses that cater to them have formed a significant interest group that is usually opposed to logging. They thus increase the likelihood of political conflict over forest management issues.

In northern Maine, for example, much of the forest is owned by paper companies that actively manage the land for fiber production and harvesting. These companies also own many of the important access roads to the area and open them to the general public, greatly increasing recreational opportunities. One of the major recreational resources of the area is the Allagash Wilderness Waterway, a popular wilderness canoe route. The canoeists who travel this route do so out of a desire to see the undeveloped and unaltered landscape, and many of these canoeists also want to preserve that landscape. When controversies develop regarding the use of these lands (which is regulated by State and Federal law), these environmentalists are likely to be on the side of preservation rather than logging, creating some tension between paper companies and recreational users. In most cases, however, the mutual interests of both groups are recognized, and they can coexist in the same landscape.

Carbon Storage

Much of the concern about tropical deforestation has focused on its impacts on the global carbon cycle. This concern is well-founded, for the tropical forests play a dominant role in this important cycle. At the same time, we should not forget that fossil fuel combustion discharges vastly more carbon dioxide into the atmosphere than does deforestation. When we consider the role of forests in carbon cycling, we need to examine two dimensions of the problem: carbon processing and carbon storage. Both are important, but each is affected differently by forest management practices.

Although they occupy less than 40 percent of the world's land area, forests play a dominant role in biogeochemical cycling between the biosphere and the atmosphere. In the carbon cycle (see Chapter 4), carbon is removed from the atmosphere in photosynthesis, stored in living and dead biomass, and released through respiration. Forests occupy the well-watered parts of the planet and thus have high rates of primary productivity compared to arid and semiarid areas. As a result, forests are responsible for an estimated 70 percent of the total carbon exchange between the terrestrial biota and the atmosphere. Annually, the world's forests absorb and release about 4 gigatons of carbon through net photosynthesis and respiration (Waring and Schlesinger 1985). For comparison, total annual emissions of carbon from industrial sources is about 6 gigatons. Although the *gross* absorption of carbon by forests is significant, the *net* absorption is much smaller. In fact, for the world's forests as a whole, more carbon is lost by burning than is stored by net photosynthesis.

The total amount of carbon stored in the world's forests and woodlands contains about 765 gigatons of carbon—more than 100 times the annual amount emitted to the atmosphere by fossil fuel combustion. About 60 percent of the carbon stored in forests is in tropical forests (Waring and Schlesinger 1985). When forests are cleared and burned or allowed to decay, this carbon is released into the atmosphere. The total amount of carbon released from the biota each year is estimated at about 1 gigaton, most of which comes from tropical forests. When forests are cut and the wood is used for lumber or paper, the carbon contained in those products is not returned to the atmosphere. Instead, at least some of it is stored in the products from which the wood and paper are made. The amount of net storage depends on how the products are used and disposed of. Lumber in buildings and paper in landfills do not return to the atmosphere immediately but may do so over a long period of time.

If a forest is cleared and allowed to regrow, then carbon is taken out of the atmosphere through forest growth. During the early years of forest regrowth, the net storage of carbon is significant: perhaps as much as 1000 tons of carbon per square kilometer of forest per year in a rapidly growing tropical forest. In many parts of the world, particularly in previously cleared areas that are now regrowing such as eastern North America, forests are storing carbon.

Forests are therefore very significant to the world's carbon cycle in both the processing and storage of carbon. When forests are cleared and replaced with other land uses (such as pasture), there is a net loss of stored carbon and an increase in atmospheric CO_2. On the other hand, when forests are allowed to regrow and are managed for sustainable forestry, there is no net release of carbon to the atmosphere in the long run.

The Role of Fire

Trees are susceptible to fire. Annually, tens of thousands of forest fires burn millions of hectares of land in North America, Asia, and other forest regions. Many species have adapted to this situation by developing mechanisms for rapid regeneration after fire, including sprouting from the root crown and seeds that are released or germinate only after being heated. Other species have characteristics that protect against fire damage, such as low flammability or particularly thick bark.

In the past, fire was believed to be harmful to forests, but today forest fires are recognized as a natural and important part of most forest ecosystems (Mott 1989; Romme and Despain 1989). Fires cause major, if temporary, disruption of the forest ecosystem. They consume dead and living biomass and, if severe enough, kill most or all the trees. Water use and evapotranspiration are greatly decreased by the loss of live trees and shrubs, which results in increased runoff. This runoff causes accelerated erosion and large losses of nutrients from the forest soil. Downstream, the eroded soil and nutrients contribute to sediment and dissolved solid loads in streams, and may contribute to eutrophication in lakes.

Fires also have beneficial effects. They allow the release of nutrients stored in dead biomass, which stimulates growth after the fire. They also remove old stands of timber that are particularly susceptible to insect or disease infestation, thus inhibiting the spread of pests. Removing the forest canopy allows sunlight to reach ground level and promotes rapid growth of early successional species, thereby beginning the forest reestablishment process. Most importantly, however, frequent fires allow accumulated fuel to be burned off relatively harmlessly, preventing the severe fires that occur in areas of high-fuel buildup. In many commercial forests, such as the loblolly pine forests of the southeastern United States, ground fires are deliberately set from time to time to kill off plants that compete with the pines, so as to maintain an even-aged stand.

Forest ecosystems vary in their susceptibility to fire and thus in how frequently fires occur. *Fire frequency* is the average number of years between successive forest fires at a given site. Some forests, like the chaparral woodlands of Southern California, are particularly susceptible to fire and have natural fire frequencies of 20 to 60 years. The pine forests that grow on areas of very sandy soils along the east coast of the United States also experienced frequent fires under natural conditions. Most forests, such as those in the mountainous western United States and Canadian north, have natural fire frequencies of 100 to 400 years. Fire frequency depends on many factors, including the rate of fuel accumulation, fuel moisture levels, and ignition sources.

There are three basic kinds of forest fires. *Ground fires* are fires that burn within the organic matter and litter of the soil. They smolder slowly and have little effect on trees. *Surface fires* burn on the ground surface, consuming litter as well as the herbaceous and shrubby vegetation of the forest floor. They burn faster than ground fires and may clear all the low vegetation of the forest, but they have little effect on large trees. Finally, *crown fires* burn treetops as well as low vegetation, usually killing all or almost all above-ground vegetation. These fires are the most destructive to timber, wildlife, and the soil. Fires vary greatly in the temperatures that develop within the canopy and at ground level. Crown fires are much hotter than surface fires, but wind, fuel availability, and moisture levels are important influences on fire temperatures. Hotter fires are more destructive than cooler ones, particularly in that they consume greater amounts of organic matter. This results in greater post-fire erosion and nutrient losses and retards the process of forest regeneration.

Prior to 1972, the long-standing policy of the U.S. Forest Service, U.S. National Park Service, and other forest management agencies was to fight all naturally started fires. Paradoxically, this strategy exacerbated damage from fires. The easiest fires to extinguish are those that start during relatively wet or low-wind conditions. These low-temperature fires cause only minor damage to the forest, while performing the valuable function of consuming available fuel.

The fires that are hardest to put out are those that occur during particularly dry, windy conditions, or that burn in areas where lots of fuel is available. These fires tend to have relatively high temperatures and are more likely to be crown fires rather than surface or ground fires. By extinguishing the less harmful low-temperature fires, firefighters have permitted huge amounts of fuel to build up on the forest floor, which eventually will lead to the more severe crown fire. As a result, forest fires are less frequent in many areas today than they were prior to human interference. Natural fires occur in some ponderosa pine forests every one to two decades, and now fires may not recur on a given site for centuries. When a fire does strike after a century of fuel buildup, it is likely to be a very damaging one.

Many Americans have grown up with the image of Smokey the Bear in his ranger hat warning us to "extinguish all fires, crush your smokes," and so on. With Smokey around to convince us that all fires are bad, it has been very difficult to bring public and expert opinion around to the idea that several small fires are better than one big fire (Fig. 7.3).

Even without the public's general awareness, most U.S. agencies involved in forest management had adopted a "let-burn" policy by the middle of the 1970s. National Parks have been conducting scientific studies to understand the fire history of their particular regions, and many use deliberately set fires as a positive part of their management program (Romme and Despain 1989). The National Park Service and the Forest Service formulated a common set of guidelines on the use of fire: (1) the use of fire must be tai-

Figure 7.3   Smokey the Bear. A long-time symbol of the Forest Service's policy of fire suppresssion, he is also used in antilitter promotions (as pictured) and in several other Forest Service campaigns.

lored to the environmental specifications and history of each site; (2) naturally set fires are allowed to burn if the timing and location are right; (3) unplanned human-caused fires are to be put out; and (4) prescribed burns can be used only when conditions are right—cool and wet—so that the fire will not spread beyond the desired area.

DEFORESTATION AND REFORESTATION: THREE EXAMPLES

Forests are not inexhaustible and have been severely depleted in many areas of the world. In some cases, as in most of the wealthy nations, forests have recovered in recent decades and continue to be important renewable resources (Rice et al. 1997). But in many of the poorer countries, rapid population growth and rising fossil fuel prices have caused great increases in demand for wood, primarily for fuel. In these areas, wood is in critically short supply, and *deforestation* is causing accelerated erosion and soil degradation.

The world's forests have been dramatically altered by human activity, to the extent that the amount of forest today is only about two-thirds of the original forest prior to widespread human disturbance. This reduction of forest cover has occurred over several thousand years, especially in Europe and east Asia, but deforestation has accelerated along with population growth in the last 300 years, especially in the New World. The most important reason for forest clearance has been the creation of cropland; many of the world's 1.5 billion hectares of cropland were once forest. But forest has also been cleared for grazing, fuel, and lumber.

Much of the forestland that remains has also been altered by temporary clearance followed by regeneration. Large portions of the tropical forest region are subject to shifting cultivation, and forestlands that have been harvested have regenerated either partially or completely.

The Amazon Forest
More than 45 percent of the world's tropical rainforests have been cleared, and the rate continues at about 0.8 percent annually (World Resources Institute 1996). Ecologists are concerned about the long-term effects of this clearing on soil resources, species diversity, and global biogeochemical cycling as well as the social impacts on native human populations. Rising demand for fuel and building materials, as well as a desire to open new lands for farming, suggests that the worldwide forest resource is in dire jeopardy. Associated with the depletion of the rainforests is a concern that the byproducts of wood burning— for warmth, for cooking, for processing into other products, and for land clearance—may be contributing to global warming and loss of biodiversity.

In tropical areas, most notably the Amazon River basin in South America, deforestation is proceeding rapidly to make way for other land uses (Fig. 7.4). The Amazon rainforest covers about 7 million square kilometers, which is roughly equivalent to 90 percent of the area of the contiguous United States, and extends into nine countries. In Brazil alone, 4.9 million square

Figure 7.4   Clearing a tropical rainforest in the western Amazon, Brazil.

kilometers—the size of the United States west of the Mississippi River—is classified as Amazonian forest.

Until the 1960s, very little development of any kind took place in the Amazon, except for a few settlements along the major rivers. But development has expanded more or less continuously in the region in the post–World War II years as its resources were increasingly seen as providing the basis for both individual and national economic gain. Construction of the capital city, Brasilia, 1500 kilometers from the Atlantic coast, began in 1957, and a highway connecting it with Belém on the Amazon River was built in 1958. This and other roads opened up the region to development, primarily cattle ranching and small farming.

Deforestation proceeded rapidly. In the early 1970s, less than 1 percent of the Brazilian Amazon had been cleared; by 1989, more than 10 percent had been cleared (Moran 1993). The rate of clearance was especially great in the 1980s, reaching rates in excess of 20,000 square kilometers, or about 0.5 percent of the original forest area of the Brazilian Amazon, per year. Some estimates placed the rate of clearance at almost 1 percent per year. In the late 1980s and early 1990s, international concern about the Amazon reached a peak, and under pressure from environmental organizations the Brazilian government began to restrict forest clearance. The rate of forest loss declined somewhat in the early 1990s, although estimates of actual clearance vary widely.

Many environmentalists argue that Amazonian deforestation is a matter of grave concern and should be prevented if possible. The primary concerns expressed are as follows.

- **Loss of biodiversity** The tropical rainforests constitute only about 7 percent of the world's area, yet contain more than half the world's species (Wilson 1988). Areas as small as a few hectares may contain hundreds of tree species and many thousands of animal species. Key to the problem is the fact that most of these species are not even identified, let alone having understood life cycles. We don't know either the true extent of their range or the conditions that are necessary for their survival. Nonetheless, based on a few limited studies and many extrapolations, we believe that large numbers of species will become extinct as deforestation proceeds.

- **Emissions of carbon dioxide** Tropical forests are important to global carbon cycling for two reasons. First, they store large volumes of carbon in living biomass, and when this biomass is destroyed through clearance and burning the carbon is released into the atmosphere. It is estimated that perhaps 15 percent of the total global emissions of CO_2 are derived from land-use change, with deforestation the largest part of this figure. If forests are replaced with pasture or cropland and are not allowed to regrow, then this release of carbon is permanent. Second, the tropical forests have very high rates of productivity and so have an enormous capacity to absorb carbon from the atmosphere. Perhaps 20 percent of total global photosynthesis takes place in the tropical forests. Recent measurements suggest that gross uptake of carbon in the Amazon forests themselves is about 0.6 gigaton of carbon annually, or about 10 percent of total global emissions to the atmosphere (Keller et al. 1996). If these are replaced with less productive ecosystems, then removal of carbon from the atmosphere by photosynthesis will be reduced.

- **Disruption of the regional hydrologic cycle** The Amazon basin receives over 2 meters of rainfall annually. This water is derived from evaporation in the Atlantic Ocean to the east and is carried inland on the tropical easterly circulation. As water is carried westward, it falls from the atmosphere as precipitation and is returned through evapotranspiration. The interior western portions of the Amazon basin are 2000 to 3000 kilometers from the Atlantic and so derive a substantial amount of their moisture from water that was evapotranspired from forests to the east. On average about 30 percent of the rain that falls in the Amazon is derived from local evapotranspiration, but in the western portions of the basin the proportion is much higher. If forests were removed, the amount of evapotranspiration would decrease. This would increase the amount of runoff, perhaps causing more erosion, but more importantly it will decrease atmospheric humidity and thus precipitation in the interior. Hypothetically, a permanent decrease in the amount of rainfall could result.

- **Destruction of indigenous cultures** The Amazon is home to numerous groups of people who have lived with the forest as their home for millennia. These people have developed an intimate knowledge of the resources the forest has to offer, and they have learned to exploit these resources on a sustainable basis through a combination of hunting, gathering, and low-intensity shifting cultivation. Expansion of Western culture, agriculture, and industrialization not only removes the forest, which is their home, but also exposes these people to the ravages as well as the benefits of global trade. Some may find this a positive effect, while others view it negatively. In any case, it represents both a significant disruption of established life-styles and a potential loss of the cultural knowledge of indigenous peoples.

While these concerns are serious ones, proponents of logging and development in the Amazon can point to the fact that much of North America, including virtually all the deciduous forest of eastern Canada and the United States, was cleared between the seventeenth and nineteenth centuries. The extent and rate of deforestation in this case are similar to those in the Amazon. Much of what was cleared, especially in the eastern United States, has since regrown, but in the process of deforestation some species went extinct, soil was eroded, and indigenous cultures were destroyed. Some would argue that this damage should not be repeated; others would say that such a decision should be left to the Brazilians.

The Siberian Forest

The Siberian forest is vast, encompassing about 605 million hectares (Shvidenko and Nilsson 1994). This amounts to about 20 percent of the total forest area of the world and about 70 percent of the boreal or northern coniferous biome. It extends from the Ural Mountains in the west to the Pacific Ocean in the east, an expanse of about 8000 kilometers. The extent of forestlands within Siberia is equivalent to about two-thirds the total land area of the United States.

As discussed in Chapter 4, the boreal forest is characterized by relatively low species diversity. Most of the Siberian forest is coniferous forest (predominantly pine, cedar, spruce, larch, and fir), though portions are dominated by birch and aspen, particularly in the east. The climate of the area is one of extremes, and about 65 percent of the forest is underlain by permafrost (permanently frozen ground). Forest growth rates are relatively slow because of the cold climate and low amounts of solar radiation, but the cool climate also serves to reduce rates of organic matter decomposition. As a result, large amounts of carbon are stored in living and dead biomass. The total carbon stored in the Siberian forest has been estimated at 30 gigatons, or about six times the total amount of carbon emitted to the atmosphere by fossil fuel combustion worldwide. The forest acts as a net sink of carbon, absorbing about 0.4 gigaton annually (Shvidenko and Nilsson 1994).

Industrial-scale exploitation of the Siberian forest began after World War II, at a time when large amounts of timber were needed to reconstruct Eastern Europe and to support the rapidly expanding economy of the Soviet Union. During the 1980s, about 800,000 hectares were clear-cut annually—on the order of 0.1 percent of the total Siberian forest (Shvidenko and Nilsson 1994). This rate declined by about half between 1988 and 1993 as a result of the general economic decline in the Soviet Union/Russia during that period. Harvest fell to only one-third of the amount allowable under forest management practices in place at the time (Korovin 1995).

Throughout this period, forest harvest has been carried out primarily by clear-cutting, using heavy machinery and with minimal concern for protection of the soil, efficient collection of wood, or regeneration. Soil erosion problems have been widespread. Of particular concern is damage to permafrost, in places where it underlies the forest. Removal of trees results in a warming of the ground and melting water in the soil. This both encourages erosion and makes revegetation more difficult. Replanting of harvested areas has been almost nonexistent, with the forest left to regenerate naturally. Fires are also widespread, consuming about 1 to 1.5 million hectares annually.

Despite these problems, vast resources are available for use. In 1988, of approximately 544 million hectares classed as forest and managed by

government forest authorities, about 272 million hectares, or half, were classified as active commercial forests, 179 million hectares are available for harvest but are not being exploited because of their low value or high costs of extraction; and 94 million hectares are protected (Shvidenko and Nilsson 1994). The Siberian forest thus represents an enormous natural resource available for commercial exploitation, and a significant increase in harvest rates is possible. The recent history of the region and its place in the world may help encourage such an increase.

Three factors are at work. First, the transition to a market economy creates opportunities for entrepreneurs to invest in the forest products industry, establishing new businesses and markets. In some cases, the government agencies responsible for forest management have themselves encouraged exploitation as a means of securing their own funding. In other cases, large tracts of land have been leased to foreign forest products companies, which are beginning to harvest timber and export the logs. Second, Russia today has an enormous need for foreign exchange, and timber trade is an obvious potential export. It therefore has welcomed offers from Japanese, Korean, and European companies to develop timber resources. Most of these are joint ventures between Russian and foreign entities. Third, political instability and the increased autonomy of regional governments reduces the authority of central resource management agencies to control exploitation. Regional or local authorities are said to have sold timber that is officially protected by the national government. In some instances, there is no single central authority with clear responsibility for management decisions. In others, the same agency responsible for conservation is also the one that collects the income from timber exploitation (Acharya 1995; Korovin 1995).

The U.S. Forestland

The United States includes about 290 million hectares of forestland. Most of the U.S. forest resources are concentrated in the Pacific Northwest, Alaska, and the East and Southeast regions (Fig. 7.5).

At the time of the European settlement of North America, forests covered about two-thirds of the United States. This forest was both a resource and an obstacle to the early settlers. It provided fuel and building materials but at the same time stood in the way of land clearance for agriculture. Timber was plentiful in most areas in the seventeenth and eighteenth centuries, and no one had to go far for wood. By the mid-nineteenth century, however, population and economic growth began to exert a great demand for wood, and supplies were diminishing. Local or regional shortages developed in the northeastern United States as the focus of timber harvesting moved west to the Great Lakes states. Writer and explorer Henry David Thoreau traveling by canoe in the wilderness of central Maine found it notable to record the presence of towering white pines, as these were being harvested from remote areas even in the first half of the nineteenth century. Thoreau also complained of a chronic shortage of firewood in central Massachusetts.

Land area in forest cover continued to decline into the early twentieth century, largely due to clearing of land for agriculture. By 1920, however, forestland clearance had slowed. The increasingly productive agricultural lands of the Midwest had been competing with eastern agriculture for some time, and beginning in the nineteenth and continuing into the early twentieth century, farmland was rapidly being abandoned, primarily in areas within and east of the Appalachians. This farmland gradually reverted to forest, and as a result forest acreage in the lower 48 states has increased about 20 percent in the last 60 years.

The history of U.S. forest exploitation is one in which, region by region, forests have been rapidly exploited to the point of exhaustion, and then abandoned as new resources were opened up farther west. In many cases, the forest has regrown after abandonment, although the quality of second-growth forest seldom matches that which was destroyed in the first place. At the end of the twentieth century, we are cutting the last of the original old-growth, and the remaining forest is almost exclusively second-growth, and much of that is relatively young (see Issue 7.2).

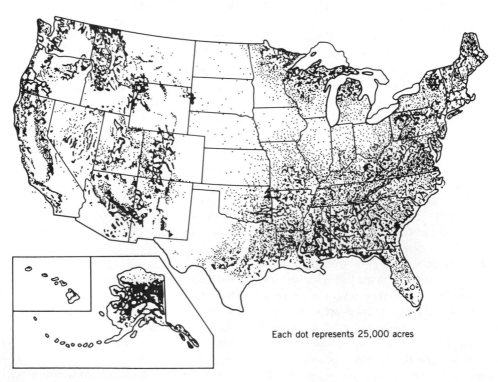

Each dot represents 25,000 acres

Figure 7.5 Forestlands in the United States. The nation's forests are concentrated in the East, Southeast, Pacific Northwest, and Alaska.

Despite this abuse, many of our forests are in good shape in comparison to those in many other nations (McKibben 1995). In fact, after 300 years of continual and often extravagant logging, the U.S. forest resource today is considered abundant and resilient, according to many measures. About two-thirds of the U.S. forestlands are rated as commercial forests. This means that the land is capable of growing at least 20 cubic feet of wood per acre (1.4 m³ of wood per hectare) in a fully stocked stand on an annual basis (U.S. Forest Service 1992). The timber produced is therefore commercially profitable. The remaining one-third of forestland is classified as noncommercial and is categorized as parks, wildlife habitat, recreation, and wilderness.

Commercial forestland in North America is differentiated by type of vegetation or tree species and is divided into hardwoods and softwoods. Hardwood forests generally consist of broadleaf and deciduous trees such as oak, maple, and hickory. In the United States, hardwood forests are located primarily in the northern and southern regions of the eastern half of the country (Fig. 7.6). Commercial hardwood stands are used largely for furniture making and flooring, although they are also important for heating. The total acreage of hardwood stands in North America is greater than that of softwoods, but the timber is commercially less valuable because of the greater difficulty in harvesting and lower demand.

Softwoods are conifers, usually evergreens. The primary North American species are spruce, pine, and cedar, whose wood is softer and grain is farther apart than in hardwoods. Softwoods are used primarily for paper products, lumber, and plywood. Softwood forests are located throughout North America but dominate in the Pacific Coast, Rocky Mountain, and Southern National Forest Service Regions. Softwoods supply about 80 percent of total lumber consumption in the United States.

Forest ownership is critical to forest management and timber supply (Table 7.1). The National Forests, administered by the U.S. Forest

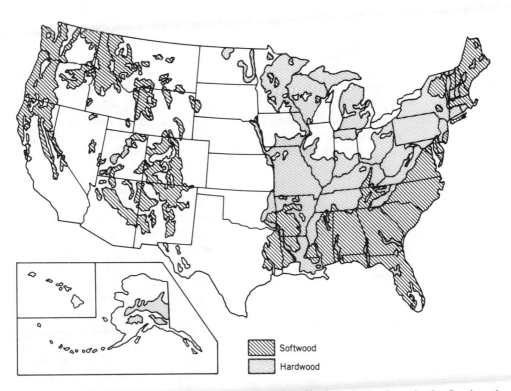

Figure 7.6 U.S. commercial forest by type and region. Hardwoods dominate in the South and East, and softwoods in the Southeast, Northeast, West, and Alaska. *Source:* Haden-Guest et al., 1956

Service, include about 17 percent of all commercial forestland. An additional 3 percent are administered by other federal agencies, notably the Bureau of Land Management. Eight percent are in state and county ownership, including state forestlands. The forest products industry owns about 14 percent of the commercial forest, mostly in the Southeast and with smaller holdings in northern New England and the Pacific Northwest. Finally, 57 percent of the commercial forestland in the United States is privately owned in small holdings and on farms. Thus, only a small portion of private, commercial forestland is owned by the forest industry itself. The federal government controls about one-fifth of commercial forestland. When we consider that most of the forests in "other private" ownership is in small holdings that are not easily accessible to the forest products industry, it becomes clear that less than half of the commercial forest is really available for harvest, and most of this is in government ownership.

When ownership patterns are examined on a regional basis, a number of interesting trends emerge (Fig. 7.7). Federal ownership dominates the western forests and is managed mostly by the Forest Service and the Bureau of Land Management. The timber industry dominates the ownership of forestland in Maine, South Carolina, and Florida. Private holdings by farmers and other individuals are the dominant type of ownership in the East. As a result of these patterns, public policies on forest issues also have a strong regional focus, with most of the controversy between government and the timber industry concentrated in the West.

Table 7.1 Ownership of forestlands in the United States

Ownership	Area (million hectares)	% of Commercial Forestland
U.S. Forest Service	34	17
Other federal	5	3
State and county	14	7
Forest industry	28	14
Other private	116	59
Total	198	100

Source: U.S. Forest Service 1992.

Because most of the forests in the United States are secondary forests (they have already been cut once and are regrowing), much of the timber is relatively young. Trees are fairly small and thus less valuable for lumber than the larger trees found in old-growth forests. At the same time, younger forests grow faster than old forests. Indeed, an old-growth forest doesn't grow at all—old trees die and decay at roughly the same rate that new trees are produced. Thus, in volume terms the U.S. forests are growing slightly more timber than is being cut, and the standing volume of timber is steadily increasing. But on an age basis, the amount of timber in mature forests with large trees is decreasing.

Similarly, at the aggregate level, we are presently harvesting below the long-term sustainable level. But aggregate statistics assume that all commercial forestland is available for harvest at some time or another, and this is not the case. Most of the commercial forest is in small private holdings. If a forest products company is to harvest this timber, it must make agreements with individual landowners, one at a time. Because not every landowner will want to sell timber at the same time, this means that if this timber is to be harvested, it must be taken from small, scattered parcels. This greatly increases management and transportation costs and makes harvesting such timber prohibitively expensive.

The forest products industry thus prefers to concentrate in a few regions of the country where sufficient forestlands exist to take advantage of economies of scale. In the United States, this is principally the Southeast, northern New England, and the Pacific Northwest, with smaller operations in the Rocky Mountains and the northern Great Lakes. In the Southeast and in Maine, the forest products industry controls most of the commercial forestland, and it manages this land intensively. Trees are replanted after harvest, and are cut on a relatively short cycle (as short as 20 to 30 years in the Southeast). These smaller trees are used mainly for plywood and paper manufacture. Sawn lumber operations are concentrated in the Pacific Northwest, where substantial areas of old-growth forest still exist. The old-growth forest there has been significantly re-

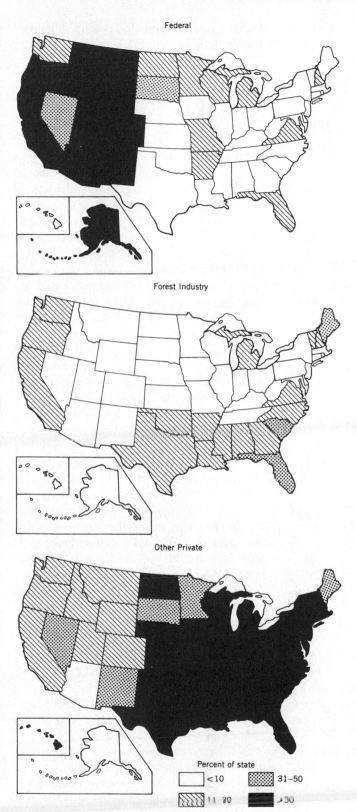

Figure 7.7 Ownership of commercial forestland. Federal ownership is dominant in the West and Alaska. Forest-industry ownership is most evident in the West, South, and Northeast. Other private holdings dominate in the East. "Percent of state" refers to the percentage of commercial forestland in each state by ownership category.

duced since the 1940s, however, and environmentalists want to stop logging of the old-growth and preserve what remains. In the short run, this will force curtailment of some logging operations and substitution of foreign (mostly Canadian) for domestically produced lumber. But in the long run the forest products industry will have to learn to rely more heavily on second-growth forests and the smaller trees they contain (Issue 7.2).

ISSUE 7.2: THE PACIFIC LUMBER SAGA

Probably the most intense environmental debate of the 1980s and early 1990s in the United States has been the controversy over management of the old-growth forests of the Pacific Northwest. These forests are the last fragment of old-growth that once covered much of the nation and that have been systematically cleared since the Europeans arrived four centuries ago. As loggers have headed westward across the country, they have harvested timber faster than it could regrow, knowing that more is always available a little further west. Now that harvest has reached the west coast, and with the end of the old-growth in sight, the battle to save what remains has intensified.

The battle between logging and forest preservation has been waged throughout the Pacific Northwest, but nowhere more intensely than around a 3000-acre tract known as the Headwaters Forest, owned by Pacific Lumber Company. This tract is both the focal point of a controversy and an excellent illustration of how a capitalist society makes choices about natural resource use.

The story begins in the early 1980s. Pacific Lumber (PL) was a small company whose stock was publicly traded, but it was run as a family operation. Its operations were based in Scotia, a company town on the northern California coast, about 200 miles north of San Francisco, where PL owned 189,000 acres of forestland, including several thousand acres of old-growth redwood. PL was a paternalistic company that took care of its employees, many of whom came from families that had worked for the company for generations. PL was the center of the community and accepted certain responsibilities associated with that role. It managed its forests on a sustained-yield basis so that the children and grandchildren of its employees would be able to live and work there, as had their parents and grandparents. Wages were good and work was steady, and the company intended to keep things that way.

But in the early 1980s a new phenomenon emerged on Wall Street, in which financiers sought out companies whose stock was undervalued; that is, they could be acquired for less than the market value of the companies' assets. An undervalued company was vulnerable to becoming the target of a hostile takeover, in which an offer is made to buy a controlling share of a company's stock, and if sufficient shares are accumulated, then the new owners take control of the company. Corporate raiders, as the purchasers were known, would buy a company, financing the deal with high-yielding "junk" bonds, sell the more liquid assets as quickly as possible to pay off the bonds, and be left with a smaller, yet still profitable, company. A wave of such hostile takeovers swept the nation's business community in the 1980s, facilitated in part by deregulation of the securities and banking industries. Pacific Lumber's vast holdings of forests and a significantly overfunded pension fund were attractive assets, while its stock price was relatively low because of the company's modest profits and stock dividends. It was ripe for the picking.

The raider was Maxxam Corporation, controlled by a Houston financier named Charles Hurwitz. With financing arranged by Michael Milken (who would later be convicted of several federal offenses related to his junk-bond operations), Hurwitz bought the company in 1985 for $840 million, perhaps half of its true value. The acquisition plan called for selling off some peripheral parts of the business, taking about $50 million from the pension fund, and dramatically increasing the rate of harvest to generate sufficient cash flow to pay off the expensive junk bonds quickly. This is exactly what happened, and by the late 1980s the company was running at maximum capacity, with most workers on mandatory 58-hour work weeks, harvesting timber as fast as possible.

The environmental community was outraged, particularly at the potential loss of old-growth forest. The old-growth of the Pacific Northwest is home to several endangered species that appear to be unable to survive in young second-growth. The

CONCLUSION

Forests are areas of low-population densities, primarily because they are found in areas that are not as suitable for farming as other areas. But this does not diminish their importance as resources. Increasing world population and resource use will inevitably increase pressures on the forest resource, and conflicts over its use will increase accordingly. Because a large part of the world's forestlands are

heart of PL's holding, a 3000-acre tract that came to be known as the Headwaters Forest, was the largest remaining piece of privately held old-growth. More than half of the remaining old-growth is preserved in state and National Parks. Even worse, the redwoods were being harvested at an accelerated rate to pay off junk bonds rather than to provide a livelihood to the people of Humboldt County. To the environmentalists, it was clearly a case of greed against good, of raping the forest to create short-term gains for the rich.

Leading the battle for the environmentalists, or at least at the forefront of it, was EarthFirst!, a loose-knit organization of radical environmentalists who believe in protecting the environment at nearly any cost. They use a variety of nonviolent tactics, including demonstrations, street theater, and obstruction, but occasionally they aggressively attacked the machinery of destruction, a tactic known as monkey-wrenching. Of all the forms of monkey-wrenching used in the Pacific Northwest, the most controversial is tree-spiking. This involves driving a long metal spike deep into a tree, where it isn't visible from the outside but where it will destroy the blade of a saw when the tree is cut or milled, often with great danger to the operator of the saw and others in the vicinity. Once a tree is spiked, it is valueless to a lumber company, and if a sawyer knows it is spiked then the tree won't be harvested. But if a spiked tree is cut, then serious injury or death can be the result. Needless to say, such tactics enraged both timber harvesters and moderate environmentalists, as a result of which EarthFirst! publicly renounced tree-spiking.

Through the late 1980s and climaxing in 1989, demonstrations and counter-demonstrations were held in the forest, at Pacific Lumber's mill in Scotia, and at Maxxam's corporate headquarters in Texas. Some of these demonstrations turned violent, and two of EarthFirst!'s leaders were injured when a pipe bomb exploded in their car. Countless lawsuits were filed to stop the takeover or the

logging, some continuing into the late 1990s. Eventually, the Federal government was drawn into the controversy, and a deal was negotiated whereby the Federal government would acquire the Headwaters Forest from Pacific Lumber. It appears, therefore, that this tract will be protected.

What are the lessons of the Pacific Lumber saga? There are many and they vary depending on your point of view. One view is that PL was mismanaged before the takeover, with the result that its shareholders were getting a poor return on their investment and the stock was undervalued. The takeover was simply a process whereby a more effective (i.e., more profitable) management strategy was introduced that significantly increased the income that could be generated from PL's lands, and the shareholders were rewarded with a significant increase in dividends and the value of their shares. With allowances for some potentially illegal aspects of the way the takeover occurred, this view is essentially correct.

But was PL really mismanaged? If we look beyond just the shareholders, and consider a broader community of interested parties, the *stakeholders*, perhaps PL was very well managed. The stakeholders in this case include those who benefit from the high quality of the ecosystems in the area—its high biodiversity and good water quality, for example. They also include future generations who might benefit from the forests, either through employment at PL and businesses that serve it and its employees, or through appreciation of the incommensurable values of the forest. In accelerating the rate of timber harvest, Hurwitz and the Maxxam shareholders took profits for themselves, at the expense of the wider community of stakeholders, whose interests were not recognized by the marketplace. Those stakeholders were forced to use other channels—demonstrations, lawsuits, and ultimately government investment through acquiring the forest in order to voice their interests in management of the resource (Harris 1996; Newton 1990).

either government-owned or subject to strong governmental controls on their use, the process of decision making regarding use of the forest will largely be a political one, as is clear in the examples of Amazonian, Siberian, and U.S. forests.

References and Additional Reading

Acharya, Anjali. 1995. Plundering the boreal forests. *Worldwatch* 8:(3): 20–29.

Brooks, David J. 1993. *U.S. Forests in a Global Context*. U.S. Forest Service, Rocky Mountain Forest & Range Experiment Station, General Technical Report RM-228.

Christensen, N. L., et al. 1989. Interpreting the Yellowstone fires of 1988. *Bioscience* 39: 678–685.

Clawson, M. 1979. Forests in the long sweep of U.S. history. *Science* 204: 1168–1174.

Council on Environmental Quality. 1981. *Environmental Trends*. Washington, DC: U.S. Government Printing Office.

Fearnside, P. M. 1990. The rate and extent of deforestation in Brazilian Amazonia. *Environmental Conservation* 17: 213–226.

Gusewelle, C. W. 1992. Siberia on the Brink. *American Forests* 98(5/6): 17–20.

Hapen-Guest, S., et al. 1956. *A World Geography of Forest Resources*. New York: Ronald Press.

Harris, David. 1996. *The Last Stand*. San Francisco: Sierra Club Books.

Keller, M., D. A. Clark, C. B. Clark, A. M. Weitz, and E. Veldkamp. 1996. If a tree falls in the forest . . . *Science* 273: 201.

Korovin, G. 1995. Problems of forest management in Russia. *Water, Air and Soil Pollution* 82: 13–23.

Likens, G. E., et al. 1978. Recovery of a deforested ecosystem. *Science* 199: 492–496.

Lugo, A. E. 1988. The future of the forest: ecosystem rehabilitation im the tropics. *Environment* 30(7): 16–20, 41–45.

Maser, Chris. 1994. *Sustainable Forestry: Philosophy, Science and Economics*. Delray Beach, Fl.: St. Lucie Press.

McKibben, B. 1995. An explosion of green. *The Atlantic Monthly*. (April): 61–83.

Moran, E. F. 1993. Deforestation and land use in the Brazilian Amazon. *Human Ecology* 21: 1–21.

Mott, W. P., Jr. 1989. Federal fire policy in national parks. *Renewable Resources Journal* 7: 5–7.

Newton, Lisa H. 1990. The chainsaws of greed: The case of Pacific lumber. In W. M. Hoffman, R. Frederick, and E. S. Perry, eds., *The Corporation, Ethics and the Environment*. New York: Quorum Books.

Rangan, Haripriya. 1996. From Chipko to Uttarancahal: Development, environment and social protest in the Garhwal Himalayas, India. In R. Peet and M. Watts, eds., *Liberation Ecologies: Environment, Development, Social Movements*. New York: Routledge.

Rice, R. E., R.E. Gullison, and J. W. Reid. 1997. Can sustainable management save tropical forests? *Scientific American*. 276(4): 44–49.

Romme, W. H., and D. G. Despain. 1989. The Yellowstone fires. *Scientific American*. 261(5): 37–46.

Shvidenko, A., and S. Nilsson. 1994. What do we know about the Siberian forests? *Ambio*. 23: 396–404.

Skole, D., and C. Tucker. 1993. Tropical deforestation and habitat fragmentation in the Amazon: Satellite data from 1978 to 1988. *Science* 260: 1905–1910.

United Nations. 1992. *Conservation and Development of Forests*. Rio de Janeiro, Brazil: UN Conference on Environment and Development.

U.S. Forest Service. 1992. *Forest Resources of the United States*. Washington, DC: U.S. Government Printing Office.

Waring, R. H., and W. H. Schlesinger. 1985. *Forest Ecosystems: Concepts and Management*. London: Academic Press.

Wilson, E. O., and F. M. Peters, eds. 1988. *Biodiversity*. Washington, DC: National Academy Press, pp. 3–20.

World Resources Institute. 1996. *World 1988 Resources 1996–97*. New York: Oxford University Press.

For more information, consult our web page at *http://www.wiley.com/college/cutter*

Study Questions

1. List the major timber and nontimber uses of forestland. For each use, identify the ways in which the use is compatible or incompatible, with other uses of the forest.

2. When the forests of the upper midwestern United States were cleared, the wealth that was generated (and some of the lumber) was used to build cities such as Chicago, which themselves contain the capital goods that their populations use today to generate wealth. To some extent, then, one form of capital (the forest) converted into another (the city). Was this a good thing?

3. List the uses of forest products that you encounter in a day. For each, identify a substitute material that

could be used instead of a tree. How would the environmental impacts of using the substitute be different from the impacts of using the tree?

4. How is an old-growth forest different from a second-growth forest? How much is lost (or gained) in the conversion?

5. Forestlands in the United States owned by the forest products industry generally yield more wood per acre than publicly owned commercial forests. This is because many of the privately owned forests are more intensively managed. Should privatization of forestlands be encouraged?

CHAPTER 8

BIODIVERSITY AND HABITAT

Biological diversity refers to both the genetic variability among individuals of a species and the abundance of individuals within a species. Wide variations in genetic traits increase the likelihood that at least some individuals of a given species will survive environmental change. The number of different species and the abundance of individuals in that species are also indicators of biological diversity in a particular ecosystem. The most ecologically diverse environments are the tropical forests, where there is a much greater abundance of plant and animal species than in any other single biome.

Species extinction is a fundamental threat to biological diversity. The death of an individual represents the loss of an organism capable of reproducing the same form as other individuals in the species. The death of individuals is a natural process. The death of an entire species is an irreversible process in which both the basic form and the reproductive potential are lost. The contribution of the species to the vitality of the planet is also lost. Species extinctions occur naturally, but humans have dramatically accelerated the pace and process in the last few centuries.

Human activities often result in the reduction of biological diversity through the destruction and simplification of natural habitats. Urban sprawl leads to an increase in the amount of asphalt and concrete at the expense of fields, forests, marshlands, and other valuable habitats. Modern farming and forest cultivation result in single-crop patterns over broad areas, maintained by chemicals that destroy unwanted species.

These practices endanger the genetic and ecological diversity of plant and animal communities.

Since the 1960s, the cry has been heard regarding the destruction and alteration of habitats and species. In 1962, Rachel Carson raised the concern in *Silent Spring* that pesticides would cause widespread extinctions (see Chapter 3). researchers and naturalists such as Eckholm (1978), Campbell (1980), and Ehrlich and Ehrlich (1970, 1981) argued that when forests are clear-cut, when meadows are paved, when rivers become sewers, we are destroying species with potential value—both economic and amenity value. These writers maintained that species and habitat destruction have reached epidemic proportions worldwide. By the late 1980s, concern over species destruction—and the implications for life on Earth—were no longer confined to gloom and doom debates on college campuses and in government offices. Newspapers, magazines, and the electronic media dramatically increased coverage of issues such as the destruction of the world's rainforests, the killing of rhinoceroses, and the plight of wolves (Allman 1988; Linden 1989).

In this chapter, we explore the problems of biodiversity and habitat conservation. We begin by examining why we are concerned with the destruction of a resource that has little obvious economic value, but that has become a prime focus of the environmental movement. We will then review the available information on the extent of species extinctions and the processes causing them. Finally, we will focus on efforts to reduce threats to biodiversity.

THE VALUE OF BIODIVERSITY

Loss of biodiversity has several consequences. Ecosystems are undermined when plant and animal species are destroyed or when they move into new areas. The possibility of using as yet untried species for food, fuel, fiber, or medicine disappears when they are eradicated. Human appreciation and understanding of nature are also diminished by species and habitat loss (Cairns 1995). Many people question the ethics of human beings to deny other species the right to exist (Chapter 1). Most profoundly, even from a completely selfish, homocentric point of view, it is feared that removal of even a few species from the web of life could cause a chain reaction, leading to widespread ecological disaster.

Ecological Interactions

The science of ecology has taught us that everything is connected to everything, and a change in one part of an ecosystem inevitably has implications elsewhere. At the level of individual links in a food web, when a plant species is eliminated, either locally or globally, the species that directly or indirectly rely on it, including insects, higher animals, and other plants, can be adversely affected.

The stability of ecosystems, in terms of their ability to maintain populations of organisms, is often enhanced by the diversity of organisms they contain. Not all ecosystems are made more stable by increased numbers of species, but in some, diversity helps contribute to stability by providing a supply of different species that are all capable of carrying on food processing. If one species declines in number as a result of some disturbance such as disease, then other species are available to occupy that niche. The metaphor of not putting all one's eggs in a single basket is an appropriate one.

For example, grasslands are subject to large environmental swings, particularly in available soil moisture. Indeed, grasses dominate midlatitude semiarid environments largely because they are able to lie dormant during dry spells but grow rapidly when moisture is available, as well as returning rapidly after fire. The original grasslands of North America contained a wide variety of grass and other herbaceous species. This diversity helped them withstand wide environmental swings because drought-tolerant species could take over in dry spells, or species resistant to a particular disease or insect could expand when other species were suffering. The North American grasslands of today are much less diverse than were the original ecosystems, and this loss of diversity is believed to have contributed to a loss of stability as well (Tilman 1996).

Diversity does not always lead to stability, however. For example, although the diversity of an ecosystem may contribute to its overall stability in terms of maintaining biomass and energy transfers, greater diversity may not make it easier for individual species to avoid local extinction. The complexity of food webs in diverse ecosystems may cause individual species to suffer wider population swings than would occur in a simpler system (Moffat 1992).

Potential Resources

In addition to maintaining the resource functions of ecosystems currently in use, nature contains many things that we might use at some time in the future. Food and medicine are the most often-cited potential uses of wild plants and animals, but many other uses are imaginable, including chemicals, fiber resources, and erosion control.

Of all naturally occurring species, plant and animal, it is estimated that humans have found uses for less than one-tenth of 1 percent of the total. The enormous majority are untested and unknown regarding their potential beneficial uses. It is known that at least 75,000 species of plants have edible parts, yet the world today relies almost entirely on about 30 plant species for its food supply, mostly wheat, rice, maize, millet, and rye. Given the stress on the world food production system that is expected as population grows in the coming decades, it seems a good idea to reexamine some of the 7000 plant species that humans have used for food during our occupancy of the earth and to conduct research on newly discovered plant species with promising value.

In recent years, researchers have looked at the possibility that previously unused or even despised plant species could be used for food, fiber, and medicine. For example, mesquite, a weedy nuisance on western cattle ranges, is now being promoted as a potential world food source. It produces abundant annual crops of a highly nutritious bean, once a staple for the region's Native Americans. Mesquite wood has become popular as a fuel in gourmet cooking, commanding a high price in some urban markets. Another recent discovery—recent to modern science, at least—is the buffalo gourd, used for at least 9000 years by the Native Americans. This widespread wild plant provides vegetable oil, protein, and starch of high quality and thrives on very little water (Kazarian 1981). Since humans depend on a narrow range of crop species for food, the discovery of new food resources is very important. The Central American amaranthus produces seeds that contain a high-quality protein that could be of use to protein-deficient human societies. Eelgrasses, grown in salt water, offer a potential substitute for grains in some heavily populated coastal areas.

The potential for significant environmental changes in the world caused by climate change or other factors may generate the need for new plant resources. For example, new crop varieties will have to be developed to take over from those currently in use if climate in important agricultural regions becomes unsuitable for varieties currently produced (Crosson and Rosenberg 1989; Wilson 1992). To that end, a 13-organization network of agricultural research establishments, the Consultative Group on International Agricultural Research (CGIAR), was formed to promote the development of new crops and agricultural techniques worldwide (Table 8.1).

Many of our most valuable medicines are derived from plants (Cox and Balick 1994). In the United States, for example, 25 percent of all prescription drugs involve active ingredients derived from plants. Sales of these totaled about $15.5 billion in 1990 (Reid 1995). Vincristine, discovered in the mid-1950s, is an alkaloid found in a Madagascar periwinkle. The chemical causes a decrease in white blood cell counts and has been used to fight cancer and cancerlike diseases. Quinine, an alkaloid in Cinchona bark, was used to treat malaria until synthetic quinine was developed in the 1930s. Digitalis, from foxglove, is widely used to treat chronic heart failure by stimulating the heart to pump more blood and use less energy. A number of well-known pain killers, including morphine and codeine, are derivatives of the opium poppy (Ehrlich and Ehrlich 1981).

Bee venom has been used to relieve arthritis, and the venom of the Malayan pit viper is used as an anticoagulant to prevent blood clots and to lessen the danger of heart attack (Ehrlich and Ehrlich 1981). Animals also provide important models for studying human diseases. The Mexican salamander, for example, is an endangered species that is being used in the study of injured heart muscles.

The medicinal use of plants and animals is a particularly compelling argument for conservation of not only ecosystems but also the indigenous cultures of people who occupy them. Indigenous peoples have intimate knowledge of the plants and animals of the regions they inhabit, and they use many of them for medicinal purposes. The people of the Amazon not only depend on the forest for their own medicines, but also have the knowledge that may help others use the forest beneficially.

In the southwestern United States and adjacent Mexico, native peoples are known to have made use of some 450 wild plants. Anthropologists contend that many of these desert-adapted species could be of value to modern society. Guayule is a shrub grown in northern Mexico and Texas. Before 1910 it supplied 10 percent of the world's rubber (Ehrlich and Ehrlich 1981); the latex in the guayule shrub is very similar to that in the rubber tree. Jojoba, a shrub related to boxwood, has seeds that contain a liquid wax. This wax, which makes up as much as 60 percent of the jojoba bean's weight, can be used for lubricating metal parts and other purposes once served by sperm whale oil, the use of which is now outlawed. Another seemingly unlikely possibility for development is the all-American goldenrod, whose leaves contain up to 12 percent natural rubber. It is easy to grow, can be mowed and baled, and resprouts without annual sowing. Euphorbia lathyrius, a desert shrub, might yield 10 to 20 barrels of crude oil per acre if cultivated (Johnson and Hinman 1980). These are just a few of the thousands of potentially useful plant species that make a strong economic argument for preserving not only rare but also abundant species.

The Inherent Value of Species

Perhaps the most compelling reason many people are deeply concerned about loss of biodiversity is unrelated to the material benefits of ecological stability, scientific and educational values, or po-

Table 8.1   The Centers and Purposes of the Consultative Group
on International Agricultural Research (CGIAR) System

Centro Internacional de Agricultura Tropical (1966), Calí, Colombia
Improve production of beans, cassava, rice, and beef in the tropics of the Western Hemisphere

Centro Internacional de la Papa (1971), Lima, Peru
Improve the potato in the Andes and develop new varieties for the lower tropics

Centro Internacional del Mejoramiento de Maiz y Trigo (1943), Mexico City, Mexico
Improve maize, wheat, barley, and triticale

International Board for Plant Genetic Resources (1974), Rome, Italy
Promote an international network of genetic resources (germ-plasm) centers

International Center for Agricultural Research in the Dry Areas (1977), Aleppo, Syria
Focus on rainfed agriculture in arid and semiarid regions in North Africa and West Asia

International Crops Research Institute for the Semi-Arid Tropics (1972), Andhra Pradesh, India
Improve the quantity and reliability of food production in the semiarid tropics

International Food Policy Research Institute (1974), Washington, D.C., U.S.A.
Address issues arising from governmental and international agency intervention in national, regional, and global food problems

International Institute of Tropical Agriculture (1967), Ibadan, Nigeria
Responsible for improvement of worldwide cowpea, yam, cocoyam, and sweet potato, and cassava, rice, maize, and beans, among others

International Laboratory for Research on Animal Disease (1974), Nairobi, Kenya
Help develop controls for trypanosomiasis (transmitted by the tsetse fly) and theileirosis (transmitted by ticks)

International Livestock Centre for Africa (1974), Addis Ababa, Ethiopia
Conduct research and development on improved livestock production and marketing systems, to train livestock specialists, and to gather documentation for livestock industry

International Rice Research Institute (1960), Los Banos, Philippines
Select and breed improved rice varieties and maintain a germ-plasm collection bank

International Service for National Agricultural Research (1980), The Hague, The Netherlands
Strengthen national agricultural research systems

West Africa Development Association (1971), Monrovia, Liberia
Promote self-sufficiency in rice in West Africa and improve varieties suitable for the area's agroclimate and socioeconomic conditions

---

ªYears in parentheses indicate year of establishment.
Source: Crosson and Rosenberg 1989, p. 134.

tential resources. Rather, it is the belief that we, as humans, have an obligation to respect the rights of other species to exist (see Chapter 1). While a belief in animal rights is fundamental to many of the world's cultures, it is not a significant part of the Christian tradition that dominates much of the Western world. But today many environmental-

ists believe in some fundamental rights for non-human species, and this is a motivating factor in their concern for loss of biodiversity. This ethical argument centers on the rights of nonhuman entities merely to exist, regardless of any usefulness to humans. Ehrenfeld (1981) argues that all living things have a right to coexist on the planet. Humans, possessing the power to destroy and alter plant and animal species, should exercise stewardship in preserving plant and animal species. This nonhomocentric view represents only one of the arguments for preserving biological diversity.

On the other hand, many would take a neo-Darwinian view of extinctions that would regard humans as just another species; in this perspective, the extinctions caused by humans are no different from mass extinctions of the past such as the disappearance of the dinosaurs. This view might maintain that species should be allowed to die because they have been unable to compete successfully with humans and other species. Furthermore, we should feel no guilt about species extinction because it is a natural process, and we should not have to keep rare species alive at great cost to human society.

The Pace and Processes of Extinction

The number of species on Earth is unknown, but some guesses can be made. At present, about 1.7 million species have been identified and described. We know that a much greater number have not been identified, but actual numbers of unidentified species can only be estimated by extrapolation. One example of such an estimate is based on studies of canopy beetles in tropical trees. One species of tropical tree was found to have 163 species of canopy beetles that only lived in that species of tree. If each of the about 50,000 tree species had 163 specific canopy beetles, then there would be 8 million species of canopy beetles on Earth. About 40 percent of known insects are beetles, so we can guess that there might be about 20 million species of insects on Earth. Obviously, this is only a guess, but it gives us an idea of the amount of diversity that may exist (Pimm et al. 1995).

Some types of organisms are better known than others. Vertebrates are fairly well known, for example. We have identified about 45,000 species of vertebrates, and it is estimated that the total number of species is 50,000 to 55,000. Insects, on the other hand, are less well known. About 950,000 have been described, and the estimates of the total number of insect species range from 2 million to 100 million! Most estimates of the total number of all species range between about 3 million and 100 million. A recent United Nations Environment Program report suggests a reasonable estimate of about 14 million (United Nations Environmental Program 1995; World Resources Institute 1996).

Because we are uncertain about the total number of species present on the planet, we are similarly uncertain about the number of these that have become extinct recently, or are threatened with extinction. One recent assessment suggests that about 12 percent of roughly 4300 mammal species and 10 percent of 9700 bird species are currently threatened. This is in addition to 58 mammals and 115 birds known to have become extinct in the past 400 years (World Conservation Monitoring Centre 1992). This same assessment estimates that 3 to 4 percent of fish and reptile species and only a fraction of a percent of insects are known to be threatened. Obviously, we know much more about some groups of organisms, such as mammals, than we do about others, such as insects.

Extinction is a natural process, and so data about numbers of species estimated to be threatened or to have gone extinct recently should be considered in relation to natural extinction rates. Again, much uncertainty exists, but most estimates suggest rates of perhaps one extinction per species per million years over geologic time. If we have 10 million species on the planet today, this would suggest an average of perhaps 10 extinctions per year. Over the past century, rates of extinction may have been 10 to 100 times higher than this estimated geologic rate (Pimm et al. 1995). Between 1600 and 1900, for example, the rate of species extinction was one species every four years, and this escalated to one species per year between 1900 and 1980. By 1993, the estimates for mammal and bird extinctions were one to three species per year (Council on Environmental Quality 1994). These extinction rates among better-known groups are sometimes used as indicators of overall extinction rates. It may be that the numbers of insect species known to be threatened are low simply because we have much less information about insects than we have about vertebrates.

In the United States, nearly one-quarter of all species are possibly extinct; almost half of these are freshwater mussels, amphibians, freshwater fish, and birds (Table 8.2). Regionally, the number of presumed or possibly extinct species is greatest in California and Alabama (Fig. 8.1). The lowest rates are in the upper Great Plains and Rocky Mountain states and Washington.

Table 8.2   Species at Risk in the United States

Group	Percent Vulnerable[a]	Percent Imperiled[b]	Percent Extinct or Possibly Extinct[c]
Amphibians	14.0	23.9	2.5
Birds	5.4	5.8	2.3
Butterflies/skippers	12.3	4.0	0.5
Crayfish	17.3	32.8	0.9
Conifers	12.2	14.0	0.0
Dragonflies/damselflies	10.4	7.6	0.4
Ferns	11.9	8.9	0.7
Flowering plants	16.6	15.8	0.9
Freshwater fish	14.1	22.0	2.6
Freshwater mussels	16.4	39.7	11.8
Mammals	9.1	7.28	0.2
Reptiles	11.9	6.1	2.9
Tiger beetles	13.6	6.3	0.0

[a]*Vulnerable populations are rare, typically 3000–10,000 individuals.*
[b]*Imperiled populations have fewer than 3000 individuals.*
[c]*Possibly extinct or presumed extinct had known historical occurrences but no current occurrences.*
Source: Stein and Flack, 1997.

In the United States, we make a distinction between *endangered species*, which are defined as those in danger of becoming extinct throughout all or a significant part of their natural ranges, and *threatened species*, which are those species likely to become endangered in the near future. As of 1997, the Fish and Wildlife Service listed a total of 858 species as endangered in the United States only, with an additional 521 so listed for foreign areas (Fig. 8.2). Another 222 species were listed as threatened in the United States only, and 39 for foreign areas (U.S. Bureau of the Census 1997). Freshwater invertebrates are among the most hard-hit groups.

Even though a species may not be extinct, zoologists worry about the consequences of inbreeding among the relatively few members of a small population. A small group of animals may not be enough for a breeding population. Within a few generations of inbreeding, negative recessive traits may become prevalent, and the species can die out, a victim of its own genetic weaknesses. For example, some of California's rare Tule elk have short lower jaws, which makes eating difficult. This may be the result of breeding within the small group of animals that biologists used to establish the herd. Today researchers advocate a more sophisticated use of genetics when attempting to reestablish species. For example, "embryo banks" preserve the frozen genes of some vanishing species. Another solution is to use more animals for the initial breeding population; however, there is just not enough room in wildlife refuges to maintain larger populations. Fewer than 5 percent of the world's preserves have the space for a genetically diverse breeding population of large wild mammals. It is probable that, in a crowded world, species survival will depend on human genetic technology.

Causes of Biodiversity Loss

Many different factors play a role in decreasing numbers of individuals and species, but nearly all of them are related to human impacts. Some

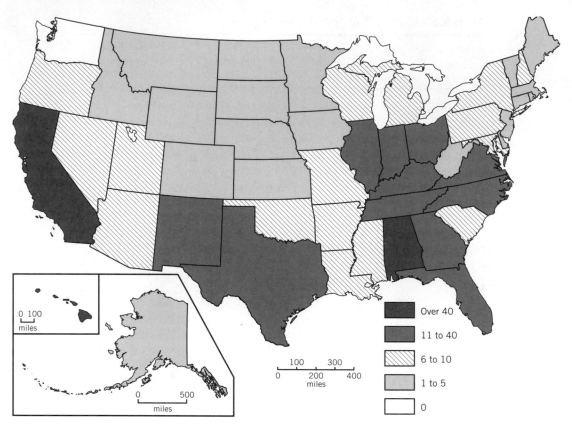

Figure 8.1 Number of presumed or possibly extinct species in the United States, 1997. The highest rates are found in the central states, portions of the Southeast, Texas, New Mexico, California, and Hawaii. *Source:* Stein and Flack, 1997.

of these impacts are direct, as through hunting, while others are indirect, caused by habitat modification or introduction of foreign species (Fig. 8.3). One study of the known causes of animal extinctions in the last 400 years found that 23 percent were caused by hunting, 36 percent by habitat destruction, and 39 percent by species introductions (World Conservation Monitoring Centre 1992). Although these figures are only rough estimates, they do indicate that each of these three processes is significant. In the following paragraphs we will examine them in more detail.

Habitat Modification For thousands of years, humans have been altering animal and plant species and the places they inhabit, or *habitats*, and life forms have been affected correspondingly. Concern about human impacts on the biosphere has been mounting in the Western

world since at least the nineteenth century. More recently, scientists have used the term *criticality* to characterize environmental zones where human activity has so severely degraded the natural environment that economic activity and human habitation are virtually impossible. Furthermore, the likelihood of environmental restoration of these regions to their former condition is almost hopeless (Kasperson et al. 1996). A good example of a critical environmental zone is the Aral Sea. Located in semiarid central Asia, the Aral Sea was the world's fifth largest freshwater lake (Fig. 8.4). Large-scale irrigation to produce cotton diverted the sea's main feeding streams. The Aral Sea has lost one-half of its surface and 70 percent of its volume since the 1950s. Fishing, once a thriving industry along the seashore, is no longer viable as salinization has killed most of the fish species. Evaporative salts blow into the agricultural areas, and pesticide and

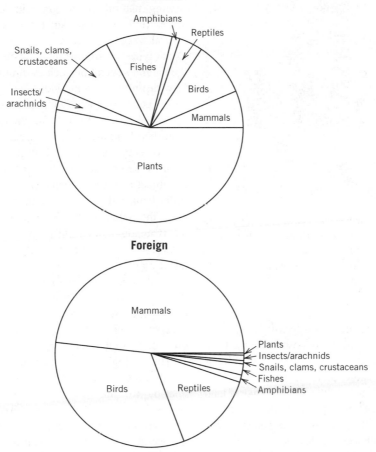

United States

Amphibians

Reptiles

Snails, clams,
crustaceans

Fishes

Insects/
arachnids

Birds

Mammals

Plants

Foreign

Mammals

Plants
Insects/arachnids
Snails, clams, crustaceans
Fishes
Amphibians

Birds   Reptiles

Figure 8.2   Threatened and endangered species, 1996.   Plants and mammals make up the largest percentages of threatened and endangered species. However, when comparing the United States to the rest of the world, mammals, birds, and reptiles are more at risk globally while fishes, crustaceans, insects, and plants are more vulnerable in the United States.   *Source*: U.S. Bureau of Census 1996, p. 240.

Figure 8.3   Harvesting old-growth timber, such as this in the Hoh forest of Washington, threatens species such as the spotted owl and the marbled murrelet. Intense controversy continues in both the United States and Canada over the ecological impacts of logging old-growth forests in the Pacific Northwest.

Figure 8.4 The Aral Sea, a vast inland water body that has shrunken because runoff has been diverted to irrigation use, is one of the more dramatic examples of human impacts on the hydrologic cycle.

completely transformed the landscape, such as replacing natural vegetation with crops or urban areas. Moderate disturbance means replacement of natural vegetation cover with secondary successional types, or significant and continuing stress to the natural vegetation such as through overgrazing. Low disturbance would indicate coverage with natural vegetation or a very low population density.

At the regional level, the greatest amounts of disturbed land are found in areas of high population density, especially Europe and Asia (Fig. 8.5). In Europe about two-thirds of the land area is subject to high disturbance. Extensive areas of little-disturbed land are found in Africa (principally the Sahara), Russia (Siberia), North America (Canada), and South America (the Amazon basin). Most of these relatively undisturbed habitats are areas of low biological activity either because they are deserts or very cold regions. The Amazon basin is a significant exception, being a large region with very high productivity and biodiversity. This helps explain why there is such great concern about deforestation there.

fertilizer use have reduced soil fertility to such an extent that even agriculture is now threatened.

While not formally designated as critical environmental zones, large parts of the world have been altered by human activity. For the world land areas as a whole, 24 percent is estimated to be subject to high levels of disturbance, 28 percent moderate levels, and 48 percent low levels of human disturbance (World Resources Institute 1994). In this classification, areas of high disturbance have

The biological consequences of past land-use changes are dramatic. The European lion was extinct by A.D. 80; wolves vanished along with Europe's forest cover. Similarly, wolves and bears were driven from the eastern United States in the eighteenth and nineteenth centuries by a combination of habitat loss and hunting. As the extent of forests grew in the past century, so too did the

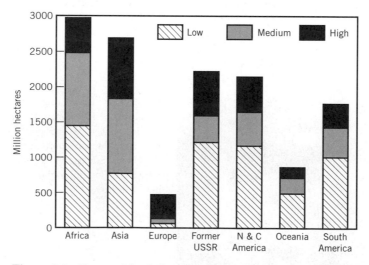

Figure 8.5 Extent of land disturbance in the world. *Source:* World Resources Institute, 1996.

range of the bear and the wolf. These species are growing in numbers today, sometimes generating new conflicts with humans.

The American bison or buffalo, whose vast herds impeded agricultural settlement and held up trains for hours, was almost wiped out in the second half of the nineteenth century, through a combination of hunting and habitat loss. Today, the American bison lives in protected refuge areas where populations are stable or growing. Often, the populations become so large that they spill over into private lands such as those surrounding Yellowstone National Park. The number of bison being herded commercially for meat production is also increasing, as ranchers in the northern Great Plains learn that the buffalo's natural adaptation to that environment means that they can be produced with lower costs than domestic cattle.

The greatest concern about habitat loss today is focused on the tropical forests. As discussed in the previous chapter, the world's rainforests are being cleared at a rate approaching 1 percent per year, and perhaps 55 percent of the total has already been cleared. Using conservative estimates of a total of 2 million species in the remaining forested areas, Wilson (1989) suggests that we are losing from 4000 to 6000 species a year to extinction in our tropical forests alone; this is 10,000 times the natural rate of extinction.

Species Introductions The human role is not always one of destruction; often we are responsible for the swift spread of species to new areas. It is estimated, for example, that one-eighth of California's plant species are exotic species—that is, imported from other places. The dominance of introduced species is particularly severe on islands, which typically have low natural species diversity because of their remoteness from other land. A recent study of Hawaii, for example, found a total of 21,368 species of organisms of all types present on the islands. Of these, about 41 percent are endemic to Hawaii. Twenty percent are known to have been introduced, and the remaining 49 percent are of unknown status (Mlot 1995). The total above excludes about 10,000 nonnative commercial species used in agriculture or as ornamental plants. If these were included, then a minimum of 45 percent of the islands' species would be nonnative.

Such a high density of foreign species can make it difficult for native species, which are not adapted to such competition, to withstand extinction. For example, many bird species are estimated to have gone extinct as a result of the introduction of rats on these islands by Europeans. Hawaii has lost at least 18 species of birds since European settlement (Pimm et al. 1995).

In addition to introducing species that were not present before, humans have created habitats that favor some species over others. The suburbs offer a very comfortable habitat for deer, coyote, squirrel, and raccoon. The white-tailed deer population in the United States had dropped to 500,000 in 1900; with control over hunting, their numbers have risen to at least 13 million, at least as many as when Europeans first arrived. Today many people regard them as a nuisance species, eating crops and suburban shrubbery, and creating a hazard on the roadways. Other introduced species that have transformed the landscape include kudzu (the South), eucalyptus trees (California), hydrilla (freshwater ecosystems), and zebra mussels (freshwater lakes) (Issue 8.1). These biological invaders are especially troublesome in Florida where the state spends nearly $25 million a year to combat exotic flora in order to protect agriculture and tourism (Burdick 1995).

Hunting Hunting is a third major cause of species extinctions. Many large mammals went extinct in North America at the end of the Pleistocene glaciations, including the wooly mammoth and the giant sloth. Some of these extinctions are believed to have been a result of excessive hunting. Settlement of Pacific islands by Polynesian peoples is estimated to have resulted in the extinction of over 2000 bird species, or about 15 percent of the world total, within the last few thousand years.

In spite of the fact that much of the Amazon's forest cover remains relatively undisturbed, many animal species are already significantly affected by humans. Hunting is the principal culprit, being carried out both by indigenous peoples and colonizers. Commercial exploitation of Amazon fauna has increased substantially since European occupation, and includes manatees, turtles, caiman, deer, peccary, otters, and various cats, primates, and birds. Several species have become locally extinct as a result (Redford 1992).

Another example is that of the black rhinoceros of Africa, whose population is dropping rapidly because of poaching—from 65,000 in

1970 to fewer than 4000 today. The animals are killed simply to obtain their horns, which are sold for thousands of dollars each and used as daggers and aphrodisiacs in Asia and the Middle East. In Namibia, wildlife authorities are actually dehorning the animals to save their lives. In Zimbabwe—poachers are shot and sometimes killed by wildlife authorities (Rees 1988). In these international examples, the situation is exacerbated by human population pressures on insufficient and marginal lands. When a family is pushed off their land to make way for a wildlife preserve, it is no wonder that they may be tempted to turn to poaching.

Sport hunting is also a problem in some areas, though less so now than in the past. The classic example in North America is the passenger pigeon. In 1810, the total passenger pigeon population was estimated at about 5 billion. During most of the nineteenth century, killing these birds for food or sport was easy, for they could be shot down in the hundreds by aiming into their roosting places at night or by firing at random as they flew overhead. The passenger pigeon was extinct in the wild by 1899, and the last one died in the Cincinnati, Ohio Zoo in 1914.

CONSERVATION OF BIODIVERSITY

What can be done to prevent this loss of biodiversity? Unfortunately, so much of the problem is caused by habitat loss and species introductions, our options are very limited. The main causes of habitat loss are the expansion of human settlement (especially agriculture) and deforestation. These processes cannot be reversed or significantly slowed in an era of rapidly expanding

---

ISSUE 8.1: THE MASS EXTINCTION OF FRESHWATER MUSSELS

Probably the most dramatic example of human-caused extinctions in North America is one that has been going on for decades, is well known to biologists and water-quality specialists, and yet receives very little public attention. It is occurring among freshwater mussels, a group of organisms that is particularly diverse in North America. Perhaps one of the reasons that the fate of mussels receives so little attention is that the problem is both widespread and long-standing. No critical environmental battles will be won or lost over mussels—their fate is already sealed by the land-use patterns that have become established in eastern North America in the last 300 years.

Freshwater mussels were once widespread in the rivers of eastern North America. They are filter feeders, drawing water through their bodies and filtering out fine particles of food—both dead organic matter such as leaves falling from streamside trees and living organisms such as microscopic plants and animals. Individual mussels may live several decades. They have developed a unique reproductive style, in which the larvae attach themselves to the gills or fins of fish and grow there for a few weeks before dropping to the stream bottom to grow and mature to adults. In the process, the mussels are spread up and downstream with the host fish. Many mussel species have become very specialized and require certain species of host fish for their reproduction.

North America has a wide variety of mussels. Roughly 300, or about one-third of all mussel species in the world, are native to North America. Most are found in the perennial streams and lakes of the eastern part of the continent, and half of them are in trouble. Of the 300 originally occurring here, about 20 are considered extinct and another 130 are either listed as threatened or proposed for listing (Cushman 1995). As a group, mussels are in worse shape than any other major type of animal.

Many factors have contributed to the decline of the mussels, all related to human activity and none easy to manage. When Europeans arrived in North America, they found many rivers teeming with mussels and quickly exploited the resource. Some were harvested for food, while others were collected for the shells. A major industry developed in the nineteenth century in the upper Mississippi and other areas using mussel shells to make buttons and other mother-of-pearl objects; today most buttons are made from plastic. Water quality is a

human population. Similarly, while some species introductions are intentional, many more are inadvertent consequences of human travel and trade, which also are not likely to be curtailed significantly in the near future. Several important initiatives have been undertaken, with both limited success and in some cases, much controversy.

It is difficult to estimate the biological, social, and economic impact of biodiversity loss. Because of this uncertainty, the wisest course is to apply the "precautionary principle." This simply means we need to err on the side of reversing the trends in species extinctions and biodiversity reduction. If we don't, then the species are gone forever.

Species Protection

One approach to biodiversity conservation is to protect threatened and endangered species at the species level (Table 8.3). This includes actions

such as prohibiting killing or trading in endangered species, efforts to preserve small amounts of habitat required to maintain a local population, and captive breeding programs.

The most significant program aimed at restricting hunting and trade in endangered species is the Convention on International Trade in Endangered Species of Wild Fauna and Flora (CITES). This international treaty regulates and controls commerce in endangered species and other species threatened by overharvest. The treaty negotiations began in 1973, with representatives from 80 countries. By 1996, it had been ratified by 128 countries, including the United States. CITES prohibits international trade in the most endangered species and their products and requires export licenses for some species and their products. Initially, only animal species were included, but beginning in 1992 commer-

much more pervasive problem. As filter feeders, mussels are exposed to large volumes of water and thus are very vulnerable to pollution. Both chemical pollutants and increased sediment caused by soil erosion have contributed to the mussel decline. Dams are another factor. They are barriers to migration of fish and mussels, fragmenting populations and limiting reproductive potential. If the host fish cannot pass a dam, then the portion of a river isolated by the dam can no longer receive introductions of mussels from beyond the dam. If a disturbance such as a flood or an episode of poor water quality should wipe out the species locally, then replenishment is not possible. Dams also create areas of slow-moving water and sediment deposition, which is detrimental to those species requiring gravel-bed streams and swift currents. Declines in certain host fish species may also contribute to the problem.

Finally, in recent decades the introduction of Zebra mussels has caused a new problem. Zebra mussels are a European freshwater species that were introduced to the Great Lakes in the 1970s and has since spread throughout the Great Lakes and the Mississippi and Ohio River systems. They are relatively small filter feeders that attach

themselves to hard substrate such as rocks, piers, boat bottoms, and other mussels. Zebra mussels grow and reproduce rapidly and cause a myriad of problems wherever they occur. In Lake Erie, Zebra mussels have eliminated 90 percent of the native mussels, and similar problems have been identified in the Ohio River system (Nature Conservancy 1997; Neves 1997).

Because many of the factors contributing to mussels' decline are pervasive and fundamental to the way we use resources today—agricultural runoff and dams in particular—they will probably continue to suffer. They are also not a particularly glamorous type of animal and so won't receive the attention that wolves, bears, or whales receive. Mussels have been called a "canary species." Like a canary in a mine, warning miners of bad air, they provide an early indicator of an unhealthy ecosystem. They are especially sensitive to a wide range of environmental impacts, and their high sensitivity is the reason they have been so hard-hit in recent decades. They are a sign of the widespread impact humans are having on the environment and, to some, a warning of future problems that should be avoided.

Table 8.3   Protecting Wildlife by Law

United States

- The Lacey Act, 1900
  Outlaws interstate trade of wildlife harvested or possessed against the laws of that state.

- Migratory Bird Treaty Act, 1918
  Prohibits hunting or injury to migratory wild birds moving between the United States, Mexico, and Great Britain (Canada).

- Migratory Bird Conservation Act, 1929
  Authorized purchase of new lands for waterfowl refuges.

- Migratory Bird Hunting Stamp Act, 1934
  Requires hunters (age 16 and over) to buy a federal waterfowl stamp prior to hunting migratory waterfowl.

- Pittman-Robertson Act, 1937
  Raises money for state wildlife conservation programs using excise taxes on rifles, shotguns, ammunition, and archery equipment.

- Marine Mammal Protection Act, 1972
  Bans the killing and importing of whales and most marine mammals; the moratorium can be waived for indigenous hunting and scientific takings if the current status of the species warrants it.

- Endangered Species Act, 1972
  Provides federal protection to species designated as threatened or endangered.

- Fisheries Conservation and Management Act, 1976
  Restricts foreign fishing in U.S. territorial waters; established regional fisheries managment councils to determine fisheries conservation and management policies.

Major Land-based International Treaties

- Convention on International Trade in Endangered Species of Wild Fauna and Flora (CITES)
  Regulates international trade and transit of certain animals, plants, their parts, and resulting products.

- Convention on Wetlands of International Importance Especially as Waterfowl Habitat, 1971 (Ramsar)
  Provides a framework for the conservation of wetlands and the designation of wetlands of international importance.

- Convention on the Conservation of Migratory Species of Wild Animals, 1979
  Protects migratory wild animal species.

- North American Waterfowl Management Plan, 1986
  Concluded cooperative agreement between the United States and Canada to restore sufficient wetland habitat to reestablish waterfowl populations to 1970 levels.

- Convention on Biological Diversity, 1993
  Provides framework for international cooperation in conserving biological diversity.

Source: World Resources Institute 1993, 1994.

cially important timber species were added to the list of banned species. Enforcement is left up to the individual treaty nations and varies according to national motivation, economics, and ability. As a result, international trade in endangered species has increased, despite the efforts of CITES.

Most of the traded species originate in developing countries and are imported to markets in developed nations. The illegal wildlife trade is often as lucrative as illegal drug trafficking but without the risks. Products made of ivory and rhino horn and furs from South American ocelots and jaguars and from North American lynxes, bobcats, otters, and wolves are all protected under CITES, but the trade continues. Collectors of rare birds and animals, such as the South American macaw or the Asian cockatoo, pay up to $8000 for one of these endangered species, thus providing a market for the illegal trade.

The most notorious example of poaching is the insatiable demand for elephant-tusk ivory and the impact this demand has had on the African elephant, *Loxodonta africana*. In 1979, there were 1.5 million of these majestic beasts; today that number stands at around 600,000. It is estimated that a hunter can kill 200 to 300 of these animals daily, although in 1989 the collapsing market for ivory reduced elephant poaching by nearly 80 percent in most of Africa (World Resources Institute 1993). All the countries that ratified the CITES treaty have agreed to a certain legal quota of elephant ivory; however, it is estimated that 80 percent or more of ivory harvesting and trade takes place illegally. Nearly a decade ago, the United States announced a total ban on the importation of any African ivory, even via indirect routes such as Hong Kong. A number of African countries have also called for a total ban on the international ivory trade; and in Kenya, the message was made clear in a dramatic pyre of fire that consumed tons of confiscated ivory (U.S. Fish and Wildlife Service 1989).

In addition to these efforts to protect species in the wild, about 200 species are being conserved in captivity (World Resource Institute 1994). Many of these have only a few dozens of individuals alive in the world. Some, like the California condor program, are attempting to reintroduce these species to the wild, with limited success (Pattee and Mesta 1995). Others are simply preserving the species in captivity with little hope of establishing a wild population in the near future. The bald eagle presents a different story. Habitat loss, hunting, and poisoning by pollutants (especially DDT) led to such a decline in the population that Congress passed protection plans in 1940 to save our national bird. Twenty years later, the number of these birds was still declining (with only 417 breeding pairs in the lower 48 states). By 1978, the bald eagle was officially listed as endangered. However, recovery was imminent, and by 1993 4000 nesting pairs were recorded (Council on Environmental Quality

1994). In 1994 its status was changed from endangered to threatened.

Such efforts can be extremely expensive. One extreme example is Florida's dusky sparrow. During the 1970s, the U.S. government spent over $2.5 million to buy 6.25 acres (2.5 ha) on Florida's east coast to create the St. John's River Refuge for the dusky sparrows. By 1981, there were five male sparrows living in a large cage (for their own safety), and a sixth male was believed to be alive in the wild. There were no known females in existence. How did this highly artificial situation develop?

The sparrows' original island habitat had been flooded to control mosquitoes around Cape Canaveral. Fires and drainage of marshes had further destroyed the birds' nesting and living area. Scientists proposed that the males be allowed to mate with a close relative, the Scott's seaside sparrow; after five generations, the offspring would be nearly full-blooded dusky sparrows. The suggestion was turned down in 1980, when the U.S. Fish and Wildlife Service decided that this hybrid sparrow would not meet the requirements of the Endangered Species Act. The agency instead gave a "pension" of $9200 per sparrow to care for them until their death.

The last surviving member, Orange Band, an aging male with gout, died in June of 1988 in luxurious captivity. Using new techniques, his keepers studied his genetic makeup and found that he and the other duskies were not really a separate subspecies after all—at the genetic level, they were identical to the common seaside sparrow that lives in abundance along the Atlantic. The scientists suggest that nineteenth-century taxonomic classifications should be updated with twenty-first-century biotechnology when species are being kept alive at great cost, to make absolutely sure that these organisms are definitely entitled to their own separate grouping. Before he died, Orange Band was the father of two near-pure "duskies," who were released into the wild to prosper with their genetically identical relatives along the beach (Wilford 1989).

In contrast to superficially insignificant species such as a sparrow, the need to conserve potential agricultural species is much clearer. Humans depend on only a few dozen plant species for food. A substantial loss of any one of these crops in a given year would almost certainly lead to widespread human starvation. How might such a loss occur? Modern agricultural technology has led to greater uniformity in the world's crops. The seed sown in a field is genetically uniform, minimizing irregularities in the mature crop and making the plants easy to harvest by machine. Unfortunately, a genetically uniform crop also means that the individual plants are all equally vulnerable to attack from pests and diseases. If such a crop is exclusively planted over a wide geographic area, the food supply of an entire region could be drastically reduced in a very short period of time. In Salina, Kansas, researchers at the Land Institute are working on these problems from a novel perspective. They see present-day agribusiness as disruptive to the soil and to water supply, and they argue that sustainable agriculture is possible by developing farm fields that imitate the native prairie. Working with native prairie species that today's farmers regard as weeds, these researchers hope to make the native perennials into major food crops that can be harvested year after year with little plowing and with no use of herbicides and pesticides. The resulting fields would be a complex mixture of several productive food crops that are difficult to harvest but that are environmentally and ecologically healthy (Luoma 1989).

Crop species are also endangered by a decrease in their genetic diversity and by the disappearance of wild relatives (Cohen et al. 1991). It is therefore necessary to maintain germ-plasm banks of the wild relatives of our principal crops. Agricultural experts can interbreed the positive characteristics of these plants, such as resistance to particular diseases, with the high productivity of the crop plants. In the event of an ecological disaster that eradicated the entire crop, we would have a well-preserved, genetically less vulnerable replacement to fall back on. The likelihood of such a large-scale disaster is exceedingly small, however, because experts have learned to provide seed with greater built-in diversity, following a near disastrous failure of the America corn crop in the early 1970s (National Academy of Sciences 1982). Modern crop plants are very sophisticated genetic packages.

Germ-plasm banks are also a refuge of last resort for threatened plant species. Even if the plant dies out, its genetic makeup is preserved in case

of a need to revive the species. Unfortunately, this is impossible for the great numbers of species eradicated by the clearing of tropical rainforests, which are not catalogued or noted by the scientific community, much less collected and preserved.

A clearinghouse for germ-plasm collection and research is the National Plant Germplasm System (NPGS), managed by the U.S. Department of Agriculture. It has over 400,000 accessions, and new ones are added at a rate of 7000 to 15,000 a year. The NPGS collects, preserves, evaluates, and distributes U.S. and international plant germ-plasm resources. In addition, 19 U.S. botanical gardens have formed a network called the Center for Plant Conservation. When a rare plant's habitat is destroyed, a number of the plants are moved to these protected gardens. A self-perpetuating 50-plant collection of each species is then grown in the belief that this number of plants will hold most of a species' possible genetic variations. In addition, seeds of each species are stored in freezers, and a few are thawed every five years and tested for continuing germination viability.

Habitat Conservation

Another method of protecting species is to protect their habitats, those areas best suited to species' needs. The amount of land under some form of protection from development has grown dramatically in recent years, and today accounts for about 6 percent of the world's land area (excluding Antarctica). A key part of this protection is the Biosphere Reserve Program of the United Nations Educational, Scientific, and Cultural Organization (UNESCO). The number of biosphere reserves worldwide has risen rapidly since the early 1970s, with the main objectives of conserving diverse and complete biotic communities, safeguarding genetic diversity for evolutionary and economic purposes, educating the public and training people in conservation, and providing areas for ecological and environmental research. In 1994, there were 327 biosphere reserves in 80 countries covering about 217 million hectares, less than 1 percent of the world's land area. Roughly two-thirds of these reserves are found in developing nations. To qualify as a biosphere reserve, an area must have outstanding, unusual, and complete ecosystems, with accompanying harmonious traditional human land uses. A reserve consists of a largely undisturbed core area surrounded by one or more buffer zones of human occupancy. Scientific research and training are carried on between the core and buffer zones, and local communities are encouraged to involve themselves in this approach to the preservation of older human and natural ecosystems (Fig. 8.6). At present, certain biomes such as mountains are well represented in the reserve system, whereas others, including tropical, subtropical, warm-arid, and intermediate areas, have very little protection (U.S. Man and the Biosphere Program 1997).

The United States has 47 officially designated Biosphere Reserves as of the mid 1990s. One biosphere reserve is the Pinelands National Reserve (PNR) of New Jersey, which was designated a U.S. National Reserve in 1978 and made part of the international network in 1983. The PNR is also part of the U.S. Experimental Ecological Reserve network. What makes the Pinelands so ecologically valuable?

Often known as the Pine Barrens, this distinctive area covers about 990,000 acres (400,000 ha) of sandy soils on the coast and inland in south-central New Jersey (Fig. 8.7). Threatened on all sides and from within by accelerated development, the Pine Barrens supports a wide variety of plant and animal life in upland, aquatic, and wetland environments, including 39 species of mammals, 59 species of reptiles and amphibians, 91 species of fish, 299 species of birds, and over 800 different kinds of vascular plants. Of the 580 native plant species, 71 are in jeopardy. Over a hundred of these are at the northern or southern limits of their geographic range, creating a unique and irreplaceable mix of species (Good and Good 1984). The area was long used by Native American tribes, but human population numbers remained low until recent decades. However, pressure has grown to develop the Pine Barrens for residential, retirement, recreational, military, and commercial purposes. The layers of national and international protection will do a lot to ensure the continued integrity of this largely intact natural area.

Habitat protection has a long history in the United States. Theodore Roosevelt was the first President to propose the establishment of na-

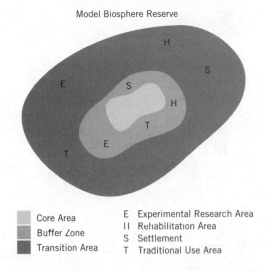

Model Biosphere Reserve

Core Area	E Experimental Research Area
Buffer Zone	II Rehabilitation Area
Transition Area	S Settlement
	T Traditional Use Area

Figure 8.6 Biosphere Reserve conceptual map. Biosphere Reserves typically consist of a core area with strict protection to achieve conservation objectives; a buffer zone where limited activities are permitted as long as they are compatible with conservation; and transitional areas where sustainable resource management practices are developed.

tional wildlife refuges. During his presidency, the first national wildlife refuge was established in 1903 at Pelican Island, Florida, for herons and egrets. This was the beginning of the National Wildlife Refuge System, which is currently managed by the Fish and Wildlife Service of the U.S. Department of the Interior. The system provides sanctuaries for endangered and threatened species of plants and animals (Fig. 8.8).

The National Wildlife Refuge (NWR) system currently has a total of 494 units covering 89.2 million acres. Unfortunately, many of these refuges are severely polluted, to the extent that birds nesting in them are producing deformed or stillborn offspring. The most notorious of these is the Kesterson NWR in California, which has become a collecting basin for the chemically laden runoff from surrounding farmlands. Other federal protection programs include the National Wilderness Preservation system (95.44 million acres) and the Wild and Scenic Rivers system (10,516 river miles). Estuarine research reserves contribute another 402,000 acres, and if we include our National Parks (80.3 million acres), then the

Figure 8.7 The Pinelands of New Jersey are an island of protected, relatively undeveloped land in the intensely urbanized eastern United States.

nation's total habitat conservation programs protect more than 265 million acres. As shown in Table 8.4, the expansion of habitat protection has increased significantly since 1960. The federal government is not the only agency in the United States involved in the protection of wildlife habitat. There are many wildlife refuges in the form of state game preserves, as well as many private and public interest organizations, such as the Nature Conservancy, the Trust for Public Lands, and the Izaak Walton League, that purchase critical habitat lands and preserve them from encroachment.

Despite the successes, degradation of species habitat sometimes continues inadvertently (Issue

Table 8.4 Habitat Protection in the United States, 1960–1995 (in million acres unless otherwise noted)

System	1960	1970	1980	1990	1995
National Parks	26.2	29.6	77.0	80.1	83.2
National Wildlife Refuges	17.3	29.2	69.9	89.1	92.3
National Wilderness Areas	a	10.4	79.7	95.0	103.7
National Wild and Scenic Rivers (miles)	b	868	5,662	9,318	10,734
National Estuarine Research Reserves	c	c	.22	.26	.4

a Did not exist until 1964.
b Did not exist until 1968.
c Did not exist until 1975.

Source: Council on Environmental Quality, 1994.

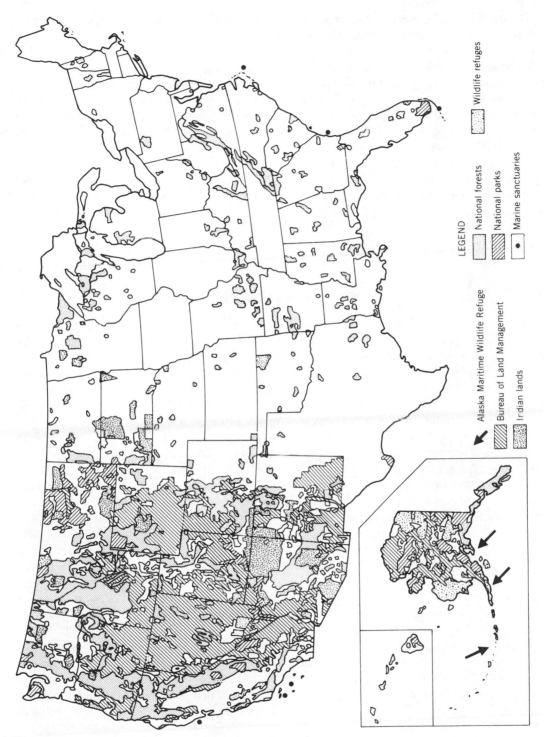

Figure 8.8 Public lands in the United States. Not all of these lands are completely protected from overexploitation. Some are managed for preservation goals, others for conservation goals. *Source:* Council on Environmental Quality, 1989.

LEGEND

National forests
National parks
Marine sanctuaries
Wildlife refuges

Alaska Maritime Wildlife Refuge
Bureau of Land Management
Indian lands

8.2). The maintenance of biological diversity requires an assessment of existing conditions and the monitoring of trends. One such program is the Gap Analysis Program (GAP) run by the National Biological Survey. Based on remote sensing and Geographic Information System (GIS) techniques, GAP analysis maps landcover, the distribution of wildlife, and landownership patterns to identify potential "gaps" in protection, hence the name. The GAP has been quite successful in identifying those areas most at risk using these geographical techniques and influencing land acquisition and conservation management programs at the local, state, and federal levels (LaRoe et al. 1995).

The Endangered Species Act

The United States has taken an active role in the protection of species. The most comprehensive piece of legislation regulating protection of all species of flora and fauna is the Endangered Species Act (ESA), passed in 1973. The ESA essentially bans acts such as hunting that directly affect threatened endangered species, and it also forbids government actions that would result in the loss of critical habitat for threatened or en-

---

ISSUE 8.2: ECOTOURISM: LOVING WILD PLACES TO DEATH

Many people are eager to experience nature first hand and often do so in their own backyards, public parks in their neighborhoods, or recreational areas in their communities. The more adventurous travel great distances to commune with nature, visiting remote and relatively unspoiled places in Central and South America or Africa. Some of the most popular destinations are the Galapagos National Park (Ecuador), Amboseli National Park (Kenya), Nepal, and Australia's Great Barrier Reef Marine Park.

Nature travel, or *ecotourism*, has become a big business with many countries depending on revenues as a source of foreign currency. In Kenya, for example, ecotourism generates more than 30 percent of its foreign currency—more than the exports of coffee or tea, its primary agricultural crops.

The demand for tourism has nearly doubled since the 1970s. Now, there are more than 450 million international tourist arrivals, many of these seeking ecotourist destinations. The irony is that once "discovered" as a tourist attraction, these environments become threatened by too many visitors. Kenya's Amboseli Park, for example, receives more than 200,000 visitors a year, many of them one-day excursions from Nairobi looking for the safari animals (elephant, lion, leopard, cape buffalo, and rhinoceros). In the United States' Yosemite Park, more than 3 million people visit annually, most of them concentrated in the Yosemite Valley. Traffic is so congested that the National Park Service restricts entrance to the Park during many summer weekends. In the mid 1990s, more than 267 million people visited our National Parks annually. The most popular were Great Smoky Mountain, Grand Canyon, Yosemite, Yellowstone, Olympic, and Rocky Mountain, all with more than 2.5 million visitors each.

What has all this attention wrought? Wildlife in many of these protected areas are now threatened. Cheetahs in Amboseli Park, for example, have changed their hunting patterns from dawn to dusk in order to avoid the tourists. Development pressures abound in these areas as entrepreneurs seek to provide tourist-related facilities such as lodging, food establishments, and the like. In foreign areas, many of the cultural resources of the areas are lost, and local people are either forced to relocate or adapt to the new development.

While the goals of ecotourism are laudable—to satisfy tourists while maintaining environmental protection and helping the local economy—it may be too much of a good thing. Although many tour operators and visitors are sensitive to environmental concerns, some are not. Despite the concern for environmentally responsible travel, perhaps the increasing numbers of visitors simply means we are just loving our National Parks to death! (Boo 1990; World Resources Institute 1993).

dangered species. The ESA is strong legislation that can significantly limit actions that might affect endangered species. Because of this strength, the law has been controversial ever since its passage.

The ESA requires that the Department of the Interior (in the case of nonmarine species) or the National Marine Fisheries Service (in the case of marine species) identify threatened or endangered species. It makes it illegal to capture, kill, sell, transport, buy, possess, import, or export any species on the endangered or threatened list. The act also requires the Departments of the Interior and Commerce to delineate the habitats of endangered and threatened species and to map these critical habitats, which are a prerequisite for species survival. It then forbids destruction of critical habitats as a result of dam-building, highway construction, housing developments, or other projects supported in whole or in part by federal monies. This final provision is the one that has generated the most controversy.

The controversy started immediately after passage of the act, when a small fish was identified that was believed to be threatened by completion of the Tellico Dam in Tennessee (Fig. 8.9). The Tellico Dam controversy ultimately resulted in amendments to the act in 1978, requiring closer consultation between government offices enforc-

ing the ESA and sponsors of capital improvement projects to avoid long and costly disputes over the fates of both the endangered species and the construction project. The amendments also allowed some exceptions to comprehensive species protection. Specifically, a major project can go ahead if it can be shown clearly that the benefits of the project outweigh and overshadow the species preservation issue. Exceptions to the ESA can be granted by six high-ranking (cabinet and subcabinet) officials and one representative of the state affected. Environmentalists have named this group the God Committee.

When it came into office in 1981, the Reagan administration was not kind to the endangered species legislation. The secretary of the Interior resisted the inclusion of new species on the endangered and threatened lists, even though the Fish and Wildlife Service had identified 2000 species that were eligible for listing. Amendments to the ESA in October 1982 stated that the Department of the Interior would consider only biological factors, not habitat destruction, in evaluating a species for listing. This resulted in a precipitous drop in the number of species considered for protection (Bean 1983). Nonetheless, in the summer of 1988 the U.S. Senate renewed the Endangered Species Act by the largest margin ever, largely because of a rising outcry of public

Figure 8.9   The Tellico Dam, Tennessee.

opinion against the environmental destruction encouraged by the Reagan administration (Pope 1988; U.S. Fish and Wildlife Service 1988).

Renewal of the act did not end the controversy, however. New debates arose, this time with terrestrial habitats as the focus. Old-growth forest was dwindling in the Pacific Northwest (see Chapter 7), and two endangered species of birds that depend on old-growth forest habitat were identified: the spotted owl and the marbled murrelet. Environmentalists made the case that continued logging of old-growth timber in the National Forests constituted a violation of the ESA, and the courts agreed, forcing a curtailment of logging activities. Elsewhere in the nation similar conflicts emerged over such issues as suburban development in the habitat of the California red-legged frog, logging old-growth timber in the Southwest, home of the Mexican spotted owl, expanding populations of wolves and grizzly bears in the northern Rockies, and preservation of habitat for the red-cockaded woodpecker in the Southeast. When the Republicans gained control of Congress in 1994, the ESA was targeted for substantial reform, particularly with the aim of restoring the rights of property owners to manage (develop, clear-cut) their land without government interference. In April 1995, Congress imposed a moratorium on new species listings while it debated reforms. The moratorium was finally lifted by a court order in May of 1996. The congressional session ended without action on the bill, but it is certain to remain a controversy with reform likely.

The Convention on Biological Diversity

The Convention on Biological Diversity is an international treaty aimed at promoting biodiversity conservation worldwide. It was developed in a series of negotiations leading up to the 1992 United Nations Conference on Environment and Development in Rio de Janeiro (see Chapter 3) and was signed by most of the nations of the world at that conference. The United States initially refused to sign the treaty, but after Clinton's election the United States signed. By 1997, 161 nations had ratified the treaty which went into effect in 1993. As of 1988, the United States had not ratified the treaty.

The Convention is more an agreement to work toward biodiversity conservation than it is a com-

mitment to binding action; nonetheless, it represents a major step forward in this area. It includes provisions obligating member nations to

- cooperate with other nations in conserving biodiversity
- develop plans and programs to conserve biodiversity
- establish systems of protected areas
- provide financial support for in-situ conservation
- include biodiversity conservation in national decision making
- establish programs for scientific and technical education and training for biodiversity conservation

One contentious issue surrounding the treaty was the question of how much money wealthy countries would provide for implementation of the treaty in poorer nations and how these funds would be controlled. But the issue that generated the most controversy concerned control of genetic resources and the profits to be earned from their use. The treaty establishes national sovereignty over genetic resources contained within a nation's borders, prohibiting collection and export of specimens without a government's permission. In addition to establishing this national ownership of genetic material, the treaty calls for unrestricted international transfer of technologies utilizing genetic resources. This would mean, for example, that if a company developed new seed varieties or medicines, these technologies should be made freely available worldwide rather than having the intellectual property rights surrounding the technology held by the developing country. The United States and other wealthy nations with companies involved in biotechnology are concerned about protecting intellectual property rights, and argue that genetic materials and the technologies that make use of them should be privately owned and distributed through market mechanisms. This would ensure that those developing these technologies would have the incentive to do so and would also provide for payment of royalties to the countries where genetic resources originate.

Another point of controversy surrounding the Biodiversity Convention is the mechanism for funding biodiversity conservation measures. The convention states clearly that the wealthy nations of the world should be responsible for the lion's share of the funding responsibility. Most wealthy nations have accepted this statement in principle, but debate continues over how much control the donor nations should have over how the money is spent, as opposed to the recipient countries responsible for evaluating biodiversity and developing and enforcing measures to conserve it (Raustiala and Victor 1996).

BIODIVERSITY: CRITICAL ISSUES FOR THE FUTURE

One question that frequently appears in the biodiversity debate is whether the central concern is preserving species or preserving habitat. The simple answer is to do both! With the exception of a few animals large and interesting enough to be preserved in zoos, most plant and animal species will not survive unless their native habitats are also preserved. If the entire land area of the world is converted to significantly altered ecosystems such as cities, farms, pastures, and plantation forests, many species will indeed become extinct. We cannot preserve species without also preserving habitat. What remains to be resolved, however, is just how much habitat will be preserved. Substantial areas were set aside during the past decade for biodiversity and habitat conservation, and additional areas came under management that would allow limited development but still preserve some habitat. But in much of the world, the United States included, pressures are mounting to limit the extent of such setaside land, and to allow continued or expanded development and resource extraction on the remaining wild lands. For the most part, this debate will take place at the national level, as it is in the United States through consideration of the Endangered Species Act.

A second key issue is the balance between the desire to maintain biodiversity and the need to maintain or improve standards of living, especially among the world's poor. Without question, biodiversity conservation is primarily a concern of the rich, who have the luxury of being able to worry about preserving species in which they have no material interests. In the United States and other wealthy nations, where public sentiment for biodiversity conservation is strong, mandating not only preservation of individual species but also the ecosystems that support them and other unknown species depends on the political will to legislate such protection. To be sure, such measures do have some economic disadvantages—loggers may become unemployed or landowners may be unable to reap all the potential value from their property. But these people usually have other opportunities. For example, in Washington and Oregon, where the ESA's impacts on the logging industry are of greatest concern, unemployment has generally been below the national average largely because of growth in the high-technology industries. But in Brazil, or Congo, or India, the preservation of remaining undisturbed or little-disturbed habitats has relatively little weight in comparison to meeting the basic needs of millions of people. Thus, when a large hydroelectric project or forest harvesting scheme is proposed for such areas, the environmental impacts are usually discussed at the international level, while in the areas directly affected the debates usually center around who will gain and who will lose economically or politically. The extreme contrasts in wealth between rich and poor nations will continue to make international cooperation on biodiversity difficult.

REFERENCES AND ADDITIONAL READING

Bean, M. J. 1983. Endangered species: The illusion of stewardship. *National Parks*, July/August, pp. 20–21.

Boo, E. 1990. *Ecotourism: The Potentials and Pitfalls.* New York: World Wildlife Fund.

Burdick, A. 1995. Attack of the aliens: Florida tangles with invasive species. *New York Times*, June 6, p. B8.

Cairns, J., Jr. 1995. Ecosocietal restoration: reestablishing humanity's relationship with natural systems. *Environment* 37(5): 4–9, 30–33.

Campbell, F. T. 1980. Conserving our wild plant heritage. *Environment* 22(9): 14–20.

Cohen, J. I., J. T. Williams, D. L. Plucknett, and H. Shands. 1991. Ex situ conservation of plant genetic resources: Global development and environmental concerns. *Science* 253: 866–872.

Council on Environmental Quality. 1989. *Environmental Trends.* Washington, DC: U.S. Government Printing Office.

_____. 1994. *Environmental Quality.* Twenty-Fourth Annual Report. Washington, DC: U.S. Government Printing Office.

Cox, P. A., and M. J. Balick. 1994. The ethnobotanical approach to drug discovery. *Scientific American* 270(6): 82–87.

Crosson, P. D., and N. J. Rosenberg. 1989. Strategies for agriculture. *Scientific American* 261(3): 128–135.

Culotta, Elizabeth. 1995. Bringing back the Everglades. *Science* 268: 1688–1690.

Cushman, J. H. 1995. Freshwater mussels facing mass extinction. *New York Times*, October 3, 1995, p. B5.

Daily, Gretchen C. 1995. Restoring value to the world's degraded lands. *Science* 269: 350–353.

Eckholm, E. 1978. *Disappearing Species: The Social Challenge*. Worldwatch Paper no. 22. Washington D.C.: Worldwatch Institute.

Ehrenfeld, D. W. 1981. *The Arrogance of Humanism*. Oxford: Oxford University Press.

Ehrlich, P., and A. Ehrlich. 1970. *Population, Resources, and Environment: Issues in Human Ecology*. San Francisco: W. H. Freeman.

_____ . 1981. *Extinction: The Causes and Consequences of the Disappearance of Species*. New York: Ballantine Books.

Good, R. E., and N. F. Good. 1984. The Pinelands National Reserve: An ecosystem approach to management. *Bioscience* 34: 169–173.

Johnson, J. D., and C. W. Hinman. 1980. Oils and rubber from arid land plants. *Science* 208: 460–464.

Kasperson, J. X., R. E. Kasperson, and B. L. Turner II. 1996. Regions at risk: Exploring environmental criticality. *Environment* 38(10): 4–15, 26–29.

Kazarian, R. 1981. Plant scientists get closer to developing buffalo gourd as a commercial food source. *Environmental Conservation* 8(1): 66.

LaRoe, E. T., G. S. Farris, C. E. Puckett, P. D. Doran, and M. J. Mac, eds. 1995. *Our Living Resources: A Report to the Nation on the Distribution, Abundance, and Health of U.S. Plants, Animals, and Ecosystems*. Washington, DC: U.S. Department of the Interior, National Biological Survey.

Lemonick, M. D. 1994. Winged victory. *Time*, July 11, p. 53.

Linden, E. 1989. Playing with fire. *Time*, September 18, pp. 76–85.

Luoma, J. R. 1989. Prophet of the prairie. *Audubon* 91(6): 54–60.

Mlot, Christine. 1995. In Hawaii, taking inventory of a biological hot spot. *Science* 269: 322–323.

Moffat, A. S. 1996. Biodiversity is a boon to ecosystems, not species. *Science* 271: 1497.

Myers, N. 1993. Tropical forest: The main deforestation fronts. *Environmental Conservation* 20: 9–16.

National Academy of Sciences. 1982. *Genetic Vulnerability of Major Crops*. Washington, DC: National Academy of Sciences.

Nature Conservancy. 1997. Vermont's freshwater mussels: Uniqueness and diversity, now under siege. ONLINE: The Nature Conservancy. http://www.tnc.org/infield/State/Vermont/science/mussels.htm.

Neves, R. 1997. Partnerships for Ohio River Mussels. ONLINE: U.S. Fisheries and Wildlife Service. http://www.fws.gov/~r3pao/eco_serv/endangrd/news/ohio_rvr.html.

Pattee, O. H., and R. Mesta. 1995. California condors. In LaRoe, E. T., G. S. Farris, C. E. Puckett, P. D. Doran, and M. J. Mac, eds. *Our Living Resources: A Report to the Nation on the Distribution, Abundance, and Health of U.S. Plants, Animals, and Ecosystems*. Washington, DC: U.S. Department of the Interior, National Biological Survey, pp. 80–81.

Pimm, S. L., G. J. Russell, J. L. Gittleman, and T. M. Brooks. 1995. The future of biodiversity. *Science* 269: 347–350.

Pope, C. 1988. The politics of plunder. *Sierra* 73(6), November/December: 49–55.

Raustiala, K., and D. G. Victor. 1996. Biodiversity since Rio: The future of the Convention on Biological Diversity. *Environment* 38(4): 16–20, 37–45.

Redford, K. H. 1992. The empty forest. *Bioscience* 42: 412–422.

Rees, M. D. 1988. Undercover investigation breaks rhino horn trafficking ring. *Endangered Species Technical Bulletin* 13(11–12): 6–7.

Reid, W. V. 1995. Biodiversity and health: prescription for progress. *Environment* 37(6): 12–15, 35–39.

Sale, K. 1985. *Dwellers in the Land, the Bioregional Vision*. San Francisco: Sierra Club Books.

Stein, B. A., and S. R. Flack. 1997. Conservation priorities: The state of U.S. plants and animals. *Environment* 39(4): 6–11, 34–39.

Tilman, D. 1996. Biodiversity: Population versus ecosystem stability. *Ecology* 77: 350–363.

Tolba, M. K., O. A. El-Kholy, E. El-Hinnawi, M. W. Holdgate, D. F. McMichael, and R. E. Munn. 1992. *The World Environment 1972–1992: Two Decades of Challenge*. New York: Chapman & Hall.

United Nations Environmental Program. 1995. *Global Biodiversity Assessment*. Cambridge University Press.

U.S. Bureau of the Census. 1997. *Statistical Abstract of the United States*. Washington, DC: U.S. Government Printing Office.

U.S. Fish and Wildlife Service. 1988. Congress reauthorizes and strengthens the Endangered Species Act. *Endangered Species Technical Bulletin* 13(11–12): 1, 11.

_____ . 1989. U.S. bans ivory imports. *Endangered Species Technical Bulletin* 14(6): 1, 6–8.

U.S. Man and the Biosphere Program. 1997. Web Page http://www.mabnetamericas.org/brprogram/

Vitousek, P. M., H. A. Mooney, J. Lubchenco, J. M. Melillo, 1997. Human domination of Earth's ecosystems. *Science* 277: 494–499.

Wedin, David A., and D. Tilman. 1996. Influence of nitrogen loading and species composition on the carbon balance of grasslands. *Science* 274: 1720–1723.

Wilford, J. N. 1989. Fallen breed of sparrows isn't so rare. *New York Times*, February 8, p. D25.

Wilson, E. O., ed. 1988. *Biodiversity*. Washington, DC: National Academy Press.

_____ . 1989. Threats to biodiversity. *Scientific American* 261(3): 108–117.

_____ . 1992. Biodiversity: Challenge, science, opportunity. *American Zoologist* 34: 5–11.

_____ . 1992. *The Diversity of Life*. Cambridge, MA: Bellknap Press of Harvard University Press.

World Conservation Monitoring Centre. 1992. *Global Diversity: Status of the Earth's Living Resources*. London: Chapman and Hall.

World Resources Institute. 1993. *The 1993 Information Please Environmental Almanac*. Boston: Houghton Mifflin.

_____ . 1994. *World Resources 1994–95*. New York: Oxford University Press.

_____ . 1996. *World Resources 1996–97*. New York: Oxford University Press.

For more information, consult our web page at *http://www.wiley.com/college/cutter*

STUDY QUESTIONS

1. Is a native species more important than a nonnative species? Why?

2. Find out what species are listed as threatened or endangered where you live. What kind of habitat do they need to survive? What areas of this habitat remain? What are the major threats to this habitat?

3. For each of the three main causes of extinction—habitat loss, hunting, and species invasions—identify a species in your area that has been affected by each.

4. The eastern United States was deforested between 1600 and 1900, with unknown loss of biodiversity. Does this history mean that we have no right to criticize other countries causing deforestation today? Why or why not?

5. Should it be illegal for a private property owner to alter habitat in such a way as to endanger a species? Should a property owner be compensated by the government for lost income caused by such a restriction?

CHAPTER 9

MARINE RESOURCES:
COMMON PROPERTY DILEMMAS

INTRODUCTION

No one nation owns the world's oceans or controls the resources found in them. The oceans, then, are a *common property resource*. Common property resources cannot be managed by a single individual, nation, or corporation because without some form of governmental or international regulation to allocate resources among users, individuals have little incentive to preserve or protect resources for future generations (Chapter 2). Historically, those nations that could exploit the world's marine resources, such as oil, fish, whales, and minerals, simply did so.

Although we usually think of the earth and its resources in terms of land area, about 71 percent of the earth's surface is covered by water, most of it in the oceans. Earth is a water planet. Virtually all living and nonliving resources are somehow influenced by the oceans.

The living and nonliving resources of the sea have slightly different characteristics than those found on land. First, they are often unseen and thus unmeasurable and uncountable. It is impossible, for example, for a fisheries biologist to know exactly how many fish there are in a given ocean area. It is also difficult to know the size of an oil field in deep water offshore, for exploration technology used on land will not work in the marine environment. Second, the oceans are the ultimate diffuser and therefore the ultimate pollution sink. Oceanic pollutants, for example, can travel immense distances, confounding attempts to identify and regulate the polluter.

Finally, despite a number of international treaties, the question of who owns the majority of the oceans and the resources found within them is still unanswered. On land, governments and individuals claim, occupy, and defend areas based on legally binding boundaries using easily recognized geographic features. Ownership of the oceans is less clear and depends on the current use of the ocean area or the political, technological, or military power of a country or private corporation. For example, U.S. companies seeking to mine deep ocean minerals cannot obtain commercial financing until legal ownership of sections of the deep ocean bottom is established either by international treaty or by unilateral action by the U.S. government. Such disputes are common, and resource managers frequently focus on who should have access to ocean resources rather than on how those resources should be allocated and used.

THE MARINE ENVIRONMENT

Physical Properties

The physical properties of seawater, the rotation of the earth, and the hydrologic cycle shape the distribution of marine resources and control the ocean's impact on terrestrial ecosystems. We will discuss three important properties of seawater—salinity, temperature, and dissolved oxygen. Salinity and temperature are especially important in determining the circulation of the oceans, while dissolved oxygen is necessary for animals to survive in the ocean.

Salinity Seawater is a solution of minerals and salts of nearly constant composition throughout the world. Sea salts, a product of billions of years of terrestrial erosion, contain at least traces of most elements found in the earth's crust. Six elements, however, comprise more than 98 percent of all sea salts (Table 9.1). On the average, a kilogram of seawater contains 35 grams of salt, or 35 parts per thousand (ppt) salt. These salts are dissolved in variable amounts of water, and slight differences in the *salinity* of seawater can influence the speed and direction of ocean currents and the vertical mixing of surface and bottom waters.

Salinity change may also have a major impact on the ocean's living resources. For example, it governs the spawning time of oysters and other shellfish on the east coast of the United States and the shrimp migrations in the Gulf of Mexico. Juvenile shrimp can tolerate the wide-ranging salinities (0–25 ppt) found in coastal areas; adult shrimp can only survive in ocean waters of 35 ppt salinity. Thus, the success of the shrimp fishing season is largely dictated by rainfall and freshwater river discharge, which dilute sea water and thus affect salinity.

As salinity changes, the density of seawater also changes. Fresh or low-salinity water will float on top of heavier, saltier water to create *stratified estuaries* in coastal areas and *haloclines* in the open ocean. Such stratification can complicate efforts to protect shellfish beds and to monitor pollutants, and can even threaten public drinking-water supplies. For example, at the mouths of rivers fresh water flows over denser sea water, and a wedge of salt water usually underlies freshwater at the surface. At the mouth of the Delaware River, near Philadelphia, the movement of the salt wedge is dictated by the volume of freshwater flow in the Delaware River. If river flow is low, salty ocean water creeps up Delaware Bay, threatening Philadelphia's drinking-water intake. Conversely, seasonal high flows of fresh water lower the salinity in the oyster beds downstream of Wilmington, Delaware, discouraging the spread of oyster parasites and predatory oyster drills. The size and movement of the salt wedge in this partially stratified estuary affects everything from commercial fishing to the drinking-water supplies for over 3 million people.

Temperature Water temperature and water temperature gradients (*thermoclines*) are other physical aspects of the ocean environment that influence the conservation and management of marine resources. The worldwide distribution of the ocean's surface-water temperature depends on the general supply of heat available from the sun. Surface temperature is highest at the equator and declines northward and southward, toward the poles. Total heat loss from the ocean waters (as opposed to the temperature of the water itself) also declines as one moves away from the equator, but not at the same rate. The difference between a surplus of heat at the equator and relatively little elsewhere results in the global heat-transfer mechanisms (air and water currents) that shape our weather. The oceans, then, can be viewed as a giant weather machine. The major ocean currents in the world are illustrated in Figure 9.1.

A change in ocean water temperatures can have a worldwide impact. A phenomenon called the Southern Oscillation describes the interannual fluctuation between warm *El Niño* conditions and cold *La Niña* ones. In the late fall of each year, a warm current, which local fishermen call El Niño, develops along the coasts of Ecuador and Peru. At irregular intervals, a much

Table 9.1 Composition of Dissolved Sea Salts in Seawater

Element	Percentage
Chlorine	55.0
Sulfur	7.7
Sodium	30.6
Magnesium	3.7
Potassium	0.7
Calcium	0.7
Minor elements (bromine, carbon, strontium)	1.6
Total	100.0

Source: Gross 1971, p. 57.

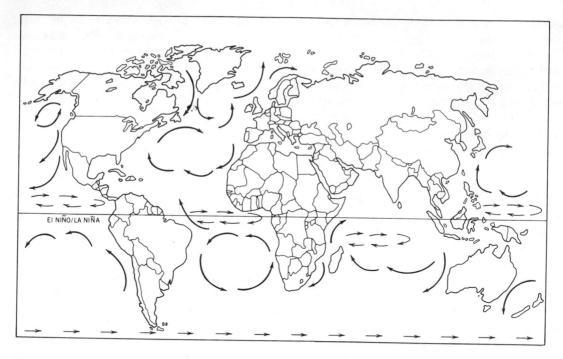

Figure 9.1 Major ocean currents of the world. The large ocean bodies have circular flow patterns, called *gyres*, which are clockwise in the Northern Hemisphere and counterclockwise in the Southern Hemisphere. Superimposed on this pattern are smaller currents, such as the equatorial countercurrents. Periodic disruptions of circulation, labeled El Niño/La Niña, occur in the eastern Pacific.

larger ocean warming occurs at the same time of year along the same coast but stretching westward along the equator, two-thirds of the way across the Pacific Ocean. This large-scale warming completely reverses the wind and current systems of the Pacific Ocean, influencing worldwide weather patterns and causing rare winter/spring hurricanes, floods, and droughts. La Niña has the opposite effect in that warm surface waters are driven westward, thus drawing cold water to the surface in the east.

Variations in temperature and salinity also drive global-scale ocean circulation patterns. For example in the North Atlantic, water cools and sinks, then flows southward, around Africa, across the Indian Ocean, and rises in the tropical western Pacific. This deep-water flow has a surface counterpart that returns water to the North Atlantic. Such flows are important in redistributing heat from one part of the planet to another. Changes in such currents over time are believed to play a role in climate variability.

Dissolved Oxygen The last important physical feature of the oceans that affects marine conservation and management is *dissolved oxygen*, the total amount of oxygen present within a body of liquid, in this case water. Dissolved oxygen is absolutely essential for aquatic life.

The distribution of dissolved oxygen is controlled by exchanges with the atmosphere, photosynthesis of phytoplankton, and respiration of oxygen-consuming biota. The solubility of a gas such as oxygen is a function of water temperature; the lower the temperature, the more dissolved oxygen. The vertical distribution of dissolved oxygen in the oceans is also a function of currents and of photosynthetic activity of phytoplankton in the *euphotic zone*. Dissolved oxygen levels generally decline with depth. The deep oceans, however, are rarely devoid of oxygen (or *anoxic*) because cold, deep water generally contains more oxygen than is consumed by the limited populations of animals in deep water. Dissolved oxygen is a key variable in determining the distribution of living resources in the sea and the sensitivity of the oceans to pollutants. For example, many of the fisheries die-offs in the ocean in recent years have been linked to a combination of factors, including weather, currents, and pollution. The pollution stimulates algal growth and creates conditions that are very similar to the *eutrophication* processes in shallow lakes. The results are localized anoxic conditions, resulting in massive fish and shellfish kills.

Habitat and Biological Productivity

Major Productive Regions   One of the keys to managing marine resources is determining where the resources are found and in what quantities. In terrestrial environments, you can see, count, and often map the precise location or habitat of a particular wildlife species or plant. In the ocean, you cannot. Measurement is always indirect, and you must rely on limited data and educated guesses.

Several key physical features tend to influence the distribution of resources, including topography, currents, upwelling areas, salinity gradients, water depth, thermoclines, and prevailing weather conditions. For living resources, mapping these physical features provides data for delineating key habitats of individual species. The fact that many living marine resources tend to be strongly influenced by one of these physical features is not coincidental.

The biological productivity of the oceans is highly variable and dictated by a combination of bottom topography, salinity, water temperature, sunlight, and currents. We can spatially delimit three major productive regions of the oceans—estuaries, near-shore and continental shelf waters, and the deep ocean. Each of these has a different level of importance to marine fisheries and food resources.

An *estuary* is an enclosed coastal water body that has a direct connection to the sea and a measurable dilution of seawater by fresh water from the land. Estuaries are transition zones where fresh and salt water mix in a shallow environment that is also strongly influenced by tidal currents. Estuaries can be classified as ecotones (see Chapter 4) or transitional areas between two distinct natural systems, terrestrial and marine. Ecotones generally have a greater diversity of species and higher biological productivity than the natural systems on either side. This "edge ef-

fect" is especially true in estuaries. The primary productivity of estuaries is 20 times as high as a typical forest (Odum 1971).

Since phytoplankton and other primary producers serve as the basis for most marine food chains, the majority of fish and shellfish caught for human consumption are dependent on estuaries during at least a portion of their life cycle. A few species are permanent estuarine residents, but the majority of fish species migrate between estuaries and near-shore and continental shelf waters to spawn or feed. Estuaries are also important nursery areas for immature fish and shellfish. Many fish move between marine and freshwater environments. *Anadromous* fish breed in freshwater and live their adult lives in the sea, whereas *catadromous* breed in the sea and live in rivers as adults. Estuaries play a key role in the migration of anadromous and catadromous fish such as Pacific salmon, the American eel, and the striped bass (see Issue 9.1). Fisheries biologists estimate that 75 to 90 percent of all fish and shellfish caught by commercial and recreational fishermen in the United States are in one way or another dependent on estuaries.

Near-shore and *continental shelf* waters are the second geographic division. They encompass a much larger portion of the world's total ocean area (7 to 8%) than estuaries (which occupy 2 to 3%), yet are less biologically productive. They slope from the shoreline out to a depth of approximately 656 ft (200 m) and are affected by geologically recent changes in sea level. The continental shelves are the submerged coastal plains that were above water as late as the last Ice Age, 15,000 years ago. Often low and marshy in prehistoric times, and subject to repeated burial and changes in pressure as sea level fluctuated, today the continental shelves are a major source of petroleum reserves.

The waters above the continental shelves are also the site of the majority of the world's fisheries. Close to highly productive estuaries, continental shelves are subject to wind-driven and tidal currents and are shallow enough to permit constant mixing of warm surface waters and cool, nutrient-rich bottom waters. The primary productivity of the shelves is approximately double that of the open ocean. One key feature of the continental shelf region is *upwelling*, in which wind-driven surface currents move away from the shoreline and deep, nutrient-rich water is drawn to the surface, creating exceptionally productive areas (Fig. 9.2).

Upwelling occurs on a large scale along the western edge of continents and, to a lesser extent, in specific portions of the shelf such as Georges Bank off the coast of Massachusetts. Nearly 99 percent of all fish production occurs in estuaries and continental shelves, and the majority of continental shelf fisheries are concentrated in upwelling regions.

Compared to the continental shelves, the *deep oceans* are a biological desert, even though they encompass 90 percent of the earth's ocean area. They are only half as productive as continental shelves, with most biological activity concentrated in the euphotic zone, where sunlight penetrates. At present, only a few important fisheries are found

---

ISSUE 9.1: SALMON IN THE PACIFIC NORTHWEST

The Pacific Northwest of North America is a region with a long history of reliance on natural resources, especially forests, fisheries, and hydroelectric power. These three resource bases are highly interdependent, with the forests as the keystone. Forests protect the soil from excessive erosion, helping to maintain high water quality. Hydroelectric power is dependent not only on ample supplies of water, but also on keeping reservoir sedimentation rates low. Salmon need clean water and unobstructed, free-flowing streams, and are suffering under the double threat of excessive sediment loads and impounded rivers. The natural resource base of the region is in trouble, and salmon are the most acute symptom of the problem.

Salmon are anadromous fish. They spend most of their adult lives in the open ocean—the North Pacific in this case—but they breed in fresh water. The salmon of the Pacific Northwest swim upstream in rivers draining to the Pacific, and they spawn in gravel-bed headwaters of streams draining the Rockies, Cascades, and coast ranges. Several species of salmon exist in the area, including chinook, chum, coho, pink, and sockeye; each of these species may be subdivided into relatively distinct populations. The salmon spawn in the same streams in which they were born and raised, making them particularly susceptible to local extinction.

In California, Idaho, Oregon, and Washington the problem is severe. Salmon are gone from about 40 percent of their historical breeding ranges, and the remaining populations levels are much reduced (CPMPNAS 1996). The total area in which they are threatened, endangered, or locally extinct is about two-thirds of their previous range in these states. Further north, in British Columbia and Alaska, salmon populations are in relatively good shape, although local problems exist. The worst problems are found in areas far inland, such as the headwaters of the Columbia River, where salmon would have to travel large distances through rivers that have been severely altered by human activity. Several factors are involved in the decline of salmon, including fishing, dams, freshwater habitat loss, hatcheries, and natural variations in ocean conditions.

Fishing, in both the ocean and rivers, is a factor in the decline of the salmon. The peculiar life cycle of the salmon makes fisheries management especially difficult. The ocean catch of salmon draws from populations that spawn in Alaska and Canada, as well as the Pacific Northwest. When a salmon is caught in the open ocean, the fisher has no way of knowing where that fish breeds. Similarly, the number of fish in a given region of open ocean may be high, even though those fish include individuals from an endangered population. Fishers from northern ports oppose restrictions on their catch because populations that breed in more northern streams are still plentiful.

The Pacific Northwest is a region of abundant water, and many dams are used for generating hydroelectricity and storing irrigation water. These include a few very large dams, such as the Grand Coulee, Hells Gate, and Dworshak dams in the Columbia River system, which are so large that they prevent all passage of fish upstream or downstream. Salmon are extinct from areas upstream of these dams. In addition, there are many smaller dams, some of which prevent salmon migration and some of which allow fish to pass. Fish

in the deep ocean, and the most valuable of these is tuna. As coastal nations have claimed the fishery resources of their continental shelves, deep ocean fisheries are becoming increasingly important to nations such as Japan and Russia, which have relatively little continental shelf area that is under their direct control.

FISHERIES

The importance of the ocean as a potential food resource is increasing. In the 1970s, about 9 percent of the protein consumed by the world's population came from marine fish and shellfish. In the 1990s, the figure was 16 percent and increas-

ladders are helpful but do not completely replace the natural channel that was obliterated by the dam. In most of the larger dams some mortality is associated with migration, so that the cumulative effect of a series of dams may be quite severe.

Water-quality and habitat degradation is another serious problem. Salmon require clear, cool, gravel-bed streams for spawning, while the young fish (smolts) require both clean water and a diverse habitat, with large organic debris (logs) and vegetation near the channel. Human activities, especially agriculture and forestry, have severely altered habitats in many salmon streams. Timber harvesting, for example, results in greatly accelerated erosion, especially in steep terrain. This adds sediment to the rivers, sometimes covering the stream bed with sand and silt instead of the gravel that salmon must have for spawning. Clearing vegetation along streambanks also contributes to the problem. Vegetation both shades the water, keeping it cool and oxygenated, and logs that fall in streams create habitat diversity which the smolts require, both for finding food and hiding from larger predators.

Hatcheries have been used for decades to increase the salmon population, but now it appears, ironically, that hatchery fish have had a negative impact on natural salmon populations. The introduction of large numbers of hatchery fish has reduced genetic diversity in natural populations, created competition with the natural population for food resources, and caused displacement of natural populations from spawning streams.

Finally, conditions in the open ocean determine the growth and survival rates of salmon and thus the number that return to spawn. These ocean conditions are not well understood, but it is known that they vary over time. It appears that the recent decline in salmon populations is at least partly caused by natural variations in the ocean environment. Thus, the population may recover partly, but it also may decline again in the future as those ocean conditions change again.

Several alternatives are available for protecting the salmon from further decline and potentially restoring populations, but nearly all involve constraints on other resource uses. Because dams are such an important contributor to the problem, significant changes in dam operations would be necessary to help solve it. Among the changes that have been proposed are structural modifications to the dams, drawing down reservoirs when the salmon are migrating seaward to speed water flow and thus shorten the smolts' journeys, diverting water around hydroelectric turbines, and even transporting smolts around dams in trucks or barges. All of these alternatives involve either very large costs, or significant losses in hydroelectric generation, or both. As regards land use, reduction of sediment and other pollutant inflows to streams would mean restrictions on agricultural activities, to conserve soil and reduce nutrients and chemicals in runoff. The salmon problem provides a powerful argument for significant restrictions on timber harvesting, potentially including prohibitions on clear-cutting in steeply sloping areas or the requirement of broad buffer strips along streams. In any case, it is clear that the natural resources of this region are closely interdependent, and effective management of the salmon problem will inevitably require consideration of a broad range of issues affecting many different environments, regions, and governments (CPMPNAS 1996).

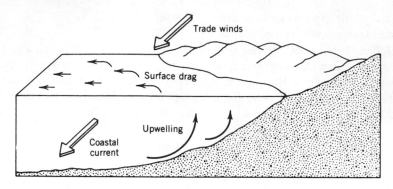

Figure 9.2 Upwelling. This natural event is caused by wind-driven currents that move away from a coastline. Nutrient-laden water is drawn upward to replace the water moved at the surface. Regions of upwelling are generally areas of very productive fisheries.

ing steadily (Tolba et al. 1992; World Resources Institute 1996). This rising demand for protein and the leveling off of agricultural production in many parts of the world resulted in a rapid climb in the world's catch of fish (Fig. 9.3) and a significant increase in aquaculture. In the early 1990s, for example, one quarter of all fish for food was produced by aquaculture.

Fisheries Production

Nearly 70 percent of all marine fish caught are eaten by people as fresh or frozen fish. The remaining 30 percent of the catch is reduced to fish meals, which are made into fertilizers, animal feed (primarily chicken feed), or oils that are used in paints and other industrial products.

Fishery resources are unevenly distributed

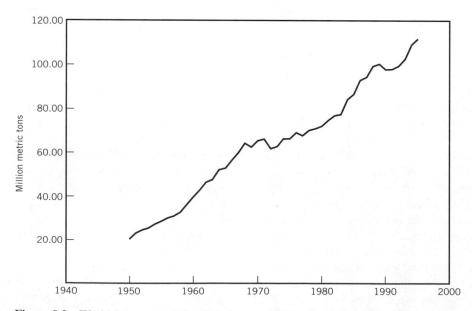

Figure 9.3 World fish catch, 1950–1995. *Source:* UN Food and Agriculture Organization, 1997.

around the globe in both fresh and salt water, and nearly 90 percent of the total fish catch is in marine waters (Food and Agriculture Organization 1997). The leading fishing nations in the world are China, Japan, Peru, Chile, Russia, and the United States. Ten nations account for nearly 70 percent of the world's total fish production (Table 9.2). Regionally, the northwestern Pacific Ocean is the primary fishing region, followed by the northeastern Atlantic Ocean and the southeastern Pacific Ocean. Many of the leading fishing nations, Japan and Russia in particular, do not fish solely in their own territorial waters. For example, Russia and Japan utilized all the world's marine fishing areas except the Arctic Ocean. Other major fishing countries tend to concentrate their fishing activities in regional waters, though not exclusively so. Chile does utilize the southern Atlantic Ocean off the coast of Antarctica, and China also uses the western Africa fishing region. Access to fish is therefore a key issue in ocean management, with countries such as the United States using fisheries as a "food weapon" when we disagree with the internal politics or political controversies in other nations. Disagreements over marine resources have even resulted in armed conflicts between nations, such as the 1970s Cod Wars between Iceland and Great Britain, and the continued disputes over territory such as Antarctica.

Table 9.2 Leading Marine Fishing Nations, 1995

	Metric Tons Caught
China	8,363,000
Peru	8,273,000
Chile	7,270,000
Japan	4,587,000
Russia	3,787,000
United States	3,580,000
Indonesia	2,422,000
Thailand	2,354,000
Norway	2,284,000
India	2,071,000

Source: Food and Agriculture Organization (FAOSTAT), 1997.

Commercial landings in the United States totaled 3.6 million metric tons in 1995 (U.S. Bureau of the Census 1997). The five major species in volume caught were Alaskan pollock, menhaden (the oil is used primarily in industry), salmon, crab, and flounder. In terms of dollar value, the most important species were crab, salmon, shrimp, pollock, and lobsters. In 1995, U.S. commercial landings were valued at $3.8 billion.

Fisheries in Distress

Worldwide, most of the important fisheries have either been severely depleted or are being heavily exploited. In the 1990s, the Canadian cod fishery closed, placing 40,000 people out of work. In addition, the groundfish (cod, haddock, and yellowtail flounder) fishery in Georges Bank, one of the United States' most productive fishing areas, collapsed because of overfishing. In the early part of the decade, the Food and Agriculture Organization (FAO) estimated that two-thirds of the marine fishing stocks were fished beyond their maximum productivity (World Resources Institute 1996). Overfishing and degradation of coastal ecosystems by pollutants were the primary causes of fisheries depletion. Although there was an increase in global fish catch after the 1980s, marine harvests declined from 77.7 percent of the global catch in 1993 to 75 percent in 1995. The global trends don't show this decrease because aquaculture was increasing at a faster rate. Regionally, the northern Atlantic fishing grounds have seen dramatic declines in cod catches since the mid 1980s. In the Northwest Pacific region, all fish stocks are exploited beyond sustainable levels. In response to fisheries depletion, the type of species caught has shifted from high-value fish such as cod and haddock to lower value fish such as sardines and anchovies. Unfortunately, these lower value species are not used for human consumption but are processed into fish oil and fish meal.

MINERALS FROM THE SEABED

Energy Resources

The United States and other nations are becoming increasingly dependent on the oceans for energy production. The share of traditional energy sources such as oil and gas from offshore areas is growing, and several nontraditional sources of energy from the oceans are under development (Chapter 14).

Approximately 30 percent of the earth's exploitable hydrocarbons are believed to exist beneath marine waters, with 90 percent of these unexplored. The majority of the explored oil and gas deposits are found on the continental shelf, near land-based oil and gas reserves. The U.S. outer continental shelf, for example, is roughly 1.8 million sq mi (4.7 million km^2) in size. This is comparable to the 1.7 million sq mi (4.4 million km^2) of geologically favorable land in the United States that currently supports most domestic oil and gas production. There is a good chance, then, that the offshore regions under U.S. control could produce at least as much oil and gas as is currently produced on land. A similar pattern can be found worldwide.

The contribution of offshore oil to total production has been growing steadily for many years. In 1992, world offshore oil production was 900 million metric tons, or about 20 percent of total production. The United Kingdom (utilizing North Sea reserves) is the leading offshore oil-producing nation, followed by the United States and Saudi Arabia. Global offshore natural gas production has also increased since 1980, reaching 358 billion m^3 in the early 1990s (World Resources Institute 1996). The United States (particularly the Gulf Coast) is the leading offshore natural gas producer, with about 29 percent of world total producion, followed by the United Kingdom and Norway. In 1995, for example, U.S. offshore wells produced $14 billion in sales of crude oil and natural gas (U.S. Bureau of the Census 1997).

The growth of offshore oil and gas production depends on the ability to drill for hydrocarbons in ever-deeper water. Early efforts at offshore drilling were simple extensions of land-based techniques in water less than 20 ft (6 m) deep. Advances in drilling technology, semi-submersible drilling-rig designs, offshore pipelines, and other equipment now permit construction of conventional drilling platforms in up to 1000 ft (305 m) of water (Fig. 9.4). In fact, the technology for drilling temporary exploratory wells has outstripped the technology for building permanent platforms needed to bring an area into regular production. Exploratory wells have been drilled in up to 5000 ft (1.5 km) of water, thus opening up large areas of the continental slope and even deep ocean areas to possible development.

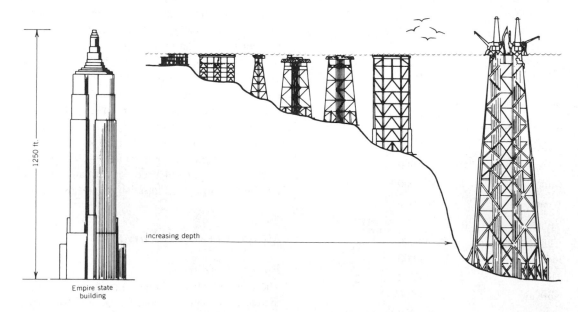

Figure 9.4   Changes in offshore oil drilling technology since 1940. Production oil drilling platforms were installed in 20 ft of water in the 1940s. By 1983, permanent platforms exceeded 1250 ft, approximately the height of the Empire State Building.

Deep-Seabed Minerals

For hundreds of years, sand, gravel, coal, tin, gold, and diamonds have been mined from the sediments beneath shallow-water areas around the world. By the early 1970s, mineral deposits found in the deep ocean became technically and economically exploitable. Many of these mineral deposits contain strategic minerals such as cobalt, which is currently imported by industrial nations, including the United States (see Chapter 13). Of particular interest to the developed nations are manganese nodules. These potato-sized lumps are common features of the seafloor in water from 2.5 to 3.5 mi (4 to 6 km) in depth. The nodules are composed of hydrated oxides of iron and manganese, which often form around a nucleus of shell, rock, or other material, just as the pearls that oysters create form around a grain of sand. Manganese nodules are found in all the world's oceans, although the grade (percentage of various metals) and coverage (weight and number per area) vary. The eastern Pacific Ocean several hundred miles south of Hawaii appears to feature exceptionally dense nodule deposits, containing minerals in sufficient quantity to permit commercial exploitation (Albarede and Goldstein 1992; Broad 1994; Knecht 1982) (Fig. 9.5).

Exploitation of seabed minerals requires an investment of many millions of dollars. For example, U.S., Japanese, and European mining companies are interested in gaining access to the billions of tons of deep-seabed minerals that are expected to become available as technology improves. But in order to protect their investment, these mining companies would demand guaranteed and probably exclusive access to this resource. The exploitable fields of seabed nodules, however, are in deep ocean waters, beyond any single nation's jurisdiction. Problems such as the lack of scientific knowledge, huge capital investments required for mining, and the vagaries of the minerals marketplace have all contributed to the lack of development of these seabed resources.

MANAGEMENT OF MARINE RESOURCES

The Problem of Ownership

As discussed earlier in this chapter, most of the world's oceans are a common property resource. Part of the ocean is globally common property, while some is nationally common property, although the boundaries between what is controlled internationally and nationally can be difficult to identify. The ownership problem may well be the largest single contributor to overexploitation of marine resources.

First, it is important to understand where control of marine resources by a single nation stops and where international control begins. Diplomats and international law experts make a distinction between control over ocean space and control over the use of ocean space. For example, international treaties recognize a 12-nautical-mile

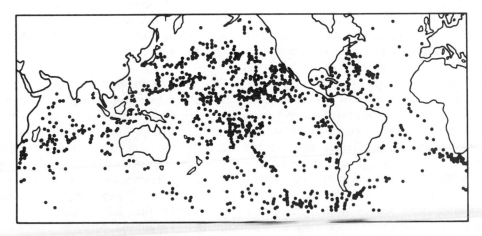

Figure 9.5 Manganese nodules in the oceans. Scientific research vessels have found accumulations of manganese nodules at these locations over the last 100 years. *Source:* Heath, 1982.

(22.2 km) territorial sea along a nation's coast-lines as the exclusive territory of that nation. Both ocean space (including bottom sediments) and the use of that space by fishing vessels, navy ships, mineral companies, or anyone else are controlled by the individual nation. Other types of jurisdiction or "ownership" are less clear. Many coastal nations claim control over all fishing resources within 200 nautical mi (370 km) of shore. Yet national control over other activities in this 200-mi area, such as the transit of military vessels of hostile nations, is not recognized by international law. In some cases, even particular types of fish, such as tuna, do not fall under the jurisdiction of individual coastal nations. In short, the definitions of jurisdiction and owner-ship of marine resources can vary with the distance from shore and the type of marine activity (Fig. 9.6).

Most of the world's nations accept four gen-eral types of jurisdiction over marine resources. *Internal waters* include bays, estuaries, and rivers and are under the exclusive control of the coastal nation. In the United States, jurisdiction over the resources found in these internal waters is shared between federal and state governments. Most states and some municipalities control fish-ing and shellfishing, while the states and the fed-eral government share jurisdiction over water pollution, dredging, and other activities.

The *territorial sea*, a band of open ocean adja-cent to the coast, is measured from a baseline on the shore out to a set distance. Most countries, in-cluding the United States, claim a 12-nautical-mile- (22.2-km) wide zone. A few nations, including Somalia, Peru, Ecuador, El Salvador, and Benin even claim a 200-nautical-mile- (370-km) wide territorial sea. A coastal nation controls all activities, such as fishing, within its territorial sea—except for the right of "innocent passage" by foreign vessels. A Japanese fishing boat can, for example, pass between the Aleutian Islands off Alaska, without permission from the state or federal government, but it cannot drop nets and proceed to fish. A foreign military vessel may also pass through territorial waters unhindered, as long as it remains outside the internal waters of the coastal nation. Curiously, the right of inno-cent passage through the territorial sea does not include aircraft. Foreign aircraft must seek per-mission to enter U.S. air space before moving

within 12 nautical miles (22.2 km) of shore. In the United States, the coastal states manage fish-eries and oil drilling in the territorial sea, while the federal government patrols and protects it.

The third type of jurisdiction is the 188-nauti-cal-mile (348 km) *exclusive economic zone* that was created by the *Law of the Sea Treaty* (UNC-LOS). For a discussion of *UNCLOS*, see the fol-lowing section. The exclusive economic zone (EEZ) is a special-use area where activities such as fishing and oil drilling are controlled by the coastal nation, while other activities are not. In 1946, the United States claimed exclusive juris-diction over its outer continental shelf, which ex-tends out to a depth of about 660 ft (200 m) of water, to control oil and gas development. In 1976, the United States created a 200-nautical-mile Fishery Conservation Zone, claiming con-trol over all fish and shellfish except the highly migratory tuna. Many other nations subsequently adopted this idea and made similar claims. The Law of the Sea Treaty creates a single EEZ that includes fishing and all forms of mineral extrac-tion, no matter what the water depth. Control over other activities in the EEZ is less clear. Some nations (including the United States) claim jurisdiction over ocean dumping and water pollu-tion, and others (excluding the United States) claim jurisdiction over the movements of vessels and oil spills in this zone. When taken together, the territorial sea plus the EEZ gives a nation control over 200 nautical miles of the oceans bor-dering them.

Finally, the *high seas* are those ocean areas that are beyond the jurisdiction of any individual na-tion. Traditionally, the limits to activities on the high seas are set by international treaties, such as the Law of the Sea.

The Law of the Sea Treaty

There is a long history of confusion over who owns or controls the oceans. Hundreds of con-flicting territorial claims have been made by coastal nations, many of which either clash with or ignore international treaties signed in 1958 on territorial seas and the outer continental shelf. There are over 90 independent nations in the world today that did not exist when the 1958 treaties were signed. Many of these nations are landlocked, underdeveloped, or both, and most are ex-colonies with boundaries and economies

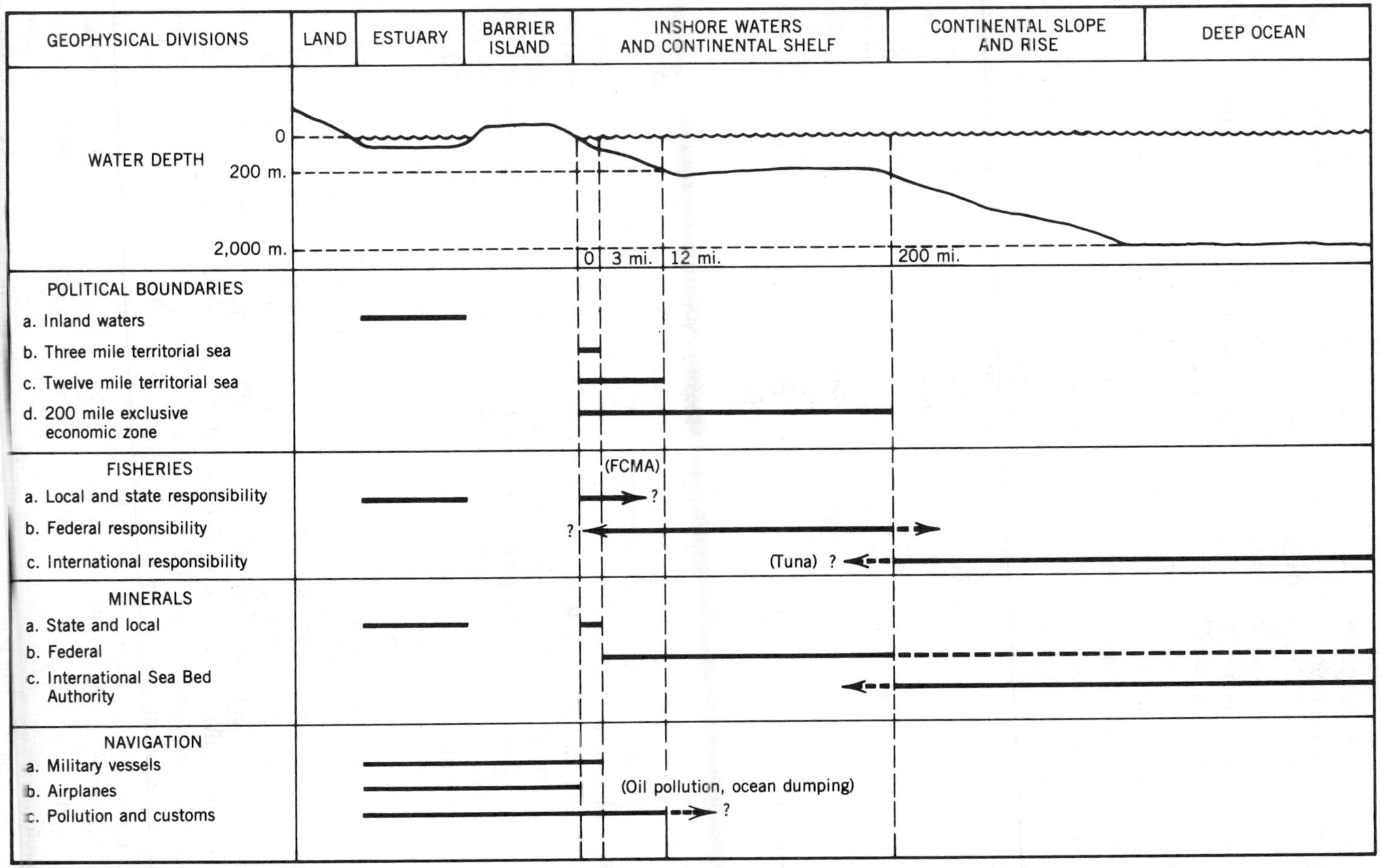

Figure 9.6 U.S. East Coast maritime boundaries. The United States claims jurisdiction over various portions of the sea for different purposes. Dashed lines indicate shared jurisdictions, question marks indicate disputed or ambiguous boundaries.

that were originally designed to benefit only the colonial power.

Maritime boundary problems coupled with the desire of many newly independent countries to allocate or reallocate marine resources led to negotiations over a new Law of the Sea Treaty. Negotiations started in 1974, with over 160 nations participating, and lasted until 1982, when a final version was approved. A total of 135 nations initially signed the treaty, and 148 have ratified it. The treaty did not take full effect until 1994 and is now in force for 115 nations. Many of the world's major fishing nations (including the U.S.) are not yet party to this treaty.

The Law of the Sea Treaty clarifies boundary claims by establishing internationally agreed-upon limits on the territorial sea, continental shelf, and exclusive economic zone. It establishes a universal 200-nautical-mile (370-km) economic zone, giving the coastal nation exclusive control over exploitable resources, such as fish, oil, and gas. It also preserves the right of free navigation through this zone by foreign ships, airplanes, and submarines.

Without right of innocent passage, a universal 12-nautical-mile (22.2-km) territorial sea would effectively close off 175 straits or narrow passages through which the majority of shipping travels. The most important of these are the straits of Gibraltar, Dover, Hormuz, and Malacca. The Strait of Gibraltar is 8 nautical miles (15 km) wide and is the major point of access to the Mediterranean Sea. The Dover Strait is the easternmost part of the English Channel and is 17.5 nautical miles (32 km) wide. Virtually all oil imported into northern Europe by ship passes through this narrow portion of the English Channel. The Strait of Hormuz, while only 20.7 nautical miles (38 km) wide, is perhaps the most important in the world. It is located between Iran and Oman in the Persian Gulf. All the oil transported by ship from the Middle East must pass through this vital and strategic strait. The Straits of Malacca (8.4 nautical miles or 16 km wide) lies between the Malay Peninsula and the island of Sumatra. Ship traffic between the Indian and Pacific oceans must use either this strait or others in Indonesian waters. All of Japan's imported oil from the Middle East traverses this strait.

The rights of neighboring nations to regulate traffic, including aircraft, through straits have never been clear. At the insistence of the United States and other nations, the Law of the Sea Treaty creates an internationally recognized "right-of-transit passage" through straits, permitting unimpeded access as long as ships and aircraft comply with minimal navigational rules. This right-of-transit passage is one of the most significant provisions of the treaty. The industrial nations with large navies insisted on this provision, at the expense of less developed countries, which border most of the straits in question.

The treaty also provides for the regulation of pollution and the conservation of living resources, including increased protection of marine mammals. Finally, the treaty allows for the exploitation of deep-seabed minerals but states that these resources constitute the common heritage of humankind. Although the developed nations possess the technology and knowledge of deep-seabed mining, the fruits of this expertise would have to be shared by all nations. In other words, those developed nations would not have exclusive right to the resources, even if they were the only ones with the technology and knowledge to get to them.

Marine Pollution Problems

The oceans are so large that we often think of them as a place where we can discard the unwanted byproducts of civilization. This attitude runs the gamut from passively allowing pollutants in streams and rivers to make their way to the ocean to actively and deliberately burying wastes in the ocean. There are three major sources of marine pollution: oil spills, hazardous materials spills, and ocean dumping.

Oil Spills Many major transportation accidents involving oil tankers have occurred (Fig. 9.7). The most famous of these include the wrecks of the *Torrey Canyon*, which spilled 700,000 barrels (95,200 tonnes) of oil off the southern coast of England in 1967; the *Amoco Cadiz*, losing 1,628,000 barrels (221,410 tonnes) off the French coast in the English Channel in 1978; and the wreck of the *Exxon Valdez* in 1989, spilling 260,000 barrels (35,374 tonnes) of oil into Prince William Sound in Alaska (Fig. 9.8). The resulting pollution of the ocean from these spills, including land-based effects, was quite extensive (Audubon 1989; Fairhall and Jordan 1980; Winslow 1978).

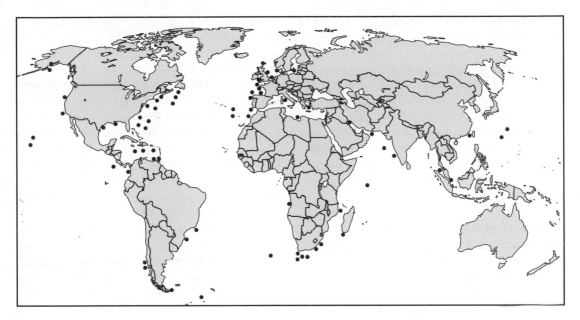

Figure 9.7   Major tanker oil spills, 1962–1996. Each dot represents a spill of over 5000 tons.

Tanker accidents are important pollution episodes, yet only 12 percent of the total world input of petroleum into the marine environment is a result of these accidents (Farrington 1985). Oil spills also occur in ports and harbors, from stationary offshore drilling platforms, and through runoff from land-based facilities (Freudenburg and Gramling 1994). In the United States alone, there were roughly 9400 reported accidents in 1993 in marine waters with 465,000 barrels (63,200 tonnes) of oil spilled (Council on Environmental Quality 1995). The majority of these were in inland waters, specifically river channels and ports and harbors. Offshore oil exploration and drilling accounts for less than 5 percent of the total world's oil pollution of the oceans, although at times the local impacts are quite severe. For example, in 1979–1980, over 2.7 million barrels of crude oil were spilled in the Gulf of Mexico as a result of the blowout of IXTOC-1, a Mexican-owned oil well in the Bay of Campeche. The drifting oil spill caused an international dispute when it washed ashore on beaches in Texas, destroying wildlife and habitat and severely affecting recreational and fishing industries in the region. During the 1991 Persian Gulf War, Iraq intentionally spilled 3 million barrels in the Gulf.

Figure 9.8   Oil spills. Oil spilling from the *Exxon Valdez* (at left); unspilled oil is being transferred to the ship (at right).

Hazardous Materials Spills Transportation of hazardous materials on the high seas is increasing as developed nations seek new disposal options for the byproducts of their industrialization. In the United States the number of reported hazardous materials spills in marine waters has been relatively constant, although the quantity spilled has been highly variable. The majority of these incidents (33%) occurred in river channels, but the amount spilled in the territorial sea is more significant. Most spills take place in coastal waters.

Ocean Dumping Ocean dumping, one of the major contributors to ocean pollution, includes the disposal of sewage sludge, industrial and solid waste, explosives, demolition debris, radioactive materials, and dredge spoils (Fig. 9.9).

Dredged material, by weight the most significant material currently being dumped in the oceans, accounts for over 90 percent of the waste disposed of in the marine environment. This material comes from the removal of bottom sediments from rivers, harbors, and intercoastal waterways to allow navigation in these water courses. Uncontaminated sediment (or spoil) poses little environmental risk. In the United States, dredged material was traditionally dumped in estuaries and on tidal wetlands. Concern over protecting these productive areas has led to a shift to near-shore and continental shelf dumping of dredged materials, although this varies by region.

Contaminated sediment that is loaded with toxic materials, such as cadmium, lead, copper, and polychlorinated biphenyls (PCBs), poses another problem. Bottom sediments in many ports and rivers contain high levels of toxic pollutants left over from decades of uncontrolled dumping and pollution. These sediments are usually immobile if undisturbed, but during dredging activities they become suspended in the water. The cost of disposing of such polluted sediments on land is significantly greater than ocean disposal, yet scientific evidence on the safety of various ocean disposal techniques is lacking.

In some parts of the world, sewage sludge and industrial wastes are a major source of contaminants in the marine environment. Although great efforts have been made to upgrade sewage treatment plants onshore to reduce water pollution, the result has been a higher volume of sewage sludge that needs disposal. In 1972, the U.S. Congress passed the Marine Protection, Research, and Sanctuaries Act, which, among other things, requires a permit for ocean dumping. In 1977, the act was amended to encourage land disposal of sewage sludge after 1981. Ocean disposal of sewage sludge therefore declined rapidly throughout the United States, with the exception of the New York Bight, the area of the Atlantic just off New York City because of a temporary exemption granted to them (Squires 1983; Swanson and Devine 1982). After years of wrangling, New York finally ended ocean dumping of its sludge in 1991.

Figure 9.9   A garbage barge in New York harbor, target of a Greenpeace protest.

Nonpoint pollution also contributes to marine pollution. In coastal areas, the problem results from septic tanks and combined sewer/stormwater systems. Although *nonpoint sources* (pollution that comes from diffuse sources such as atmospheric dustfall or moving ships) are difficult to measure, officials estimate that they are an even greater threat to the marine environment than are *point sources* (sources that are easily identified on a map, such as pipelines).

Finally, there is one other major contributor to the pollution of marine waters. The accumulation of nonbiodegradable plastics in the oceans has increased during the last two decades. Originating from land-based activities as well as trash thrown overboard from ships, plastics float on the ocean's surface for decades (Wilber 1987). The primary effect of plastic is on marine animals. It has been estimated that 100,000 marine mammals die each year either by ingesting the plastic or by becoming entangled in it (U.S. Congress 1987). Many more seabirds meet their fate in this way. The plastic pollution problem of the world's oceans has now become a global concern.

Protecting Marine Ecosystems
Control of Marine Pollution Because of their common property nature, international efforts to control pollution at sea are also important. The London Dumping Convention of 1972 is the primary international treaty on marine waste disposal and, more importantly, the only one to which the United States is signatory. The treaty prohibits the dumping of "blacklisted" substances (organohalogens, mercury, cadmium, plastics, oils, radioactive materials, and biological and chemical warfare agents) in waters seaward of the inner boundary of the territorial sea. The Oslo Convention of 1974 regulates the dumping and incineration of wastes by most European countries, and this treaty applies to Arctic, northern Atlantic, and North Sea waters. At-sea incineration is no longer practiced in the North Sea.

One of the most effective international treaties on marine pollution is the International Convention for the Prevention of Pollution from Ships 1973, 1978 (referred to as MARPOL 73/78). This treaty attempts to reduce pollution from ships, including oil, chemicals, and plastics. Also as a response to the *Exxon Valdez* spill in 1989, the International Convention on Oil Pollution Preparedness, Response, and Cooperation was signed. This treaty sets requirements for oil spill contingency plans and mechanisms for cooperation between transboundary spills. Finally, the United Nations Environment Program's (UNEP) Regional Seas program has been instrumental in developing regional action plans for marine pollution from ocean dumping, oil spills, and land-based sources (Table 9.3).

In U.S. territorial waters, four different federal laws govern pollution and wastes in the marine environment. The Clean Water Act (see Chapter 10) was instrumental in banning sludge dumping in the New York Bight. The act also provided construction grants for sewage treatment plants and combined sewer/stormwater overflow systems. In addition, the act provided funds for the development of management programs for nonpoint source pollution and the control of toxic pollutants. The 1990 amendments to the Coastal Zone Management Act also require local and state governments to implement controls for coastal pollution control, especially nonpoint sources. The Shore Protection Act of 1988 regulates the deposit of trash and medical debris in U.S. coastal waters.

The Marine Protection, Research, and Sanctuaries Act (MPRSA) was originally passed in 1972 and was designed to (1) regulate the disposal (dumping and pipeline discharge) of wastes into the marine environment and (2) control the level of pollution in these waters. Marine waters are defined as those waters seaward of the territorial sea (3 mi or 4.8 km). The act restricts the transportation and dumping of wastes in the open ocean and regulates the dumping and discharge of solid waste, sludge, industrial waste, dredged materials, radioactive waste, and biological and chemical warfare agents in marine waters. The act was amended and reauthorized in 1985 and became known as the Ocean Dumping Act.

Finally, the 1990 Oil Pollution Act provides coordinated federal assistance for oil spills in U.S. waters and was enacted shortly after the *Exxon Valdez* spill. The act has a number of major provisions, including the requirement for double hull tanker ships, and the development of oil spill emergency response plans by vessel and facility owners. The act also establishes liability for oil spills shared between shipowners, onshore facilities, deep-water port owners, and offshore facility owners. The most important provision, however, is the creation of the Oil Spill Liability

Table 9.3 Pollution Reduction Elements in Regional Seas Program

Regional Seas[a]	Emergency Response	Control Ocean Dumping	Control Land-based Pollution	Protected Areas
Antarctic	•			
North Sea	•			
Baltic Sea	•		•	•
Arctic/North Atlantic Nordic		•	•	
Mediterranean	•	•	•	•
Persian	•		•	
West Central Africa	•			
Southeast Pacific	•		•	•
Red Sea	•			
Wider Caribbean	•			•
East Africa	•			•
South Pacific	•	•		
East Asia				
South Asia				

[a]*Treaty not yet in force. Antarctic through Nordic Sea programs were in effect prior to the establishment of UNEP's Regional Seas program.*
Source: World Resources Institute, 1992, p. 183.

Trust Fund. This fund, based on a five cent per gallon tax on oil, is designed to pay damage claims to injured third parties.

Marine Sanctuaries The Marine Protection, Research, and Sanctuaries Act (1972) also had some preservation elements. It designated marine sanctuaries in the oceans and Great Lakes with the intent to preserve or restore these areas for their conservation, recreation, ecological, or aesthetic value. The National Marine Sanctuary Program (administered by the National Oceanic and Atmospheric Administration) was established to designate and manage nationally significant marine areas. Such areas would be classified based on specific criteria, including the representativeness of the marine ecosystems, research potential, recreational or aesthetic values, or uniqueness (historical, geological, ecological, or oceanographic). Sanctuaries range in size from less than 1 sq mi to over 5327 sq mi. Although they are managed under multiple-use guidelines, human use is balanced with the maintenance of the health and viability of the ecosystem. The first two sanctuaries included in the program in 1975 were the U.S.S. *Monitor* (off the coast of North Carolina) and Key Largo (off the Florida Keys). The act was amended in 1984, and by 1996, 14 units were included in the sanctuary program covering roughly 13,800 nautical miles.

Within the United States, there is also a National Estuarine Research Reserves program that is designed to protect and restore the ecosystem health of important estuaries (Council on Environmental Quality 1995). Municipal discharges, urban runoff, agricultural and industrial sources of pollution all contribute contaminant loads in estuaries affecting shellfish production but recreational value as well. The rate of decline in some of these most productive estuaries—Chesapeake Bay, Puget Sound, and the Mississippi Delta—is cause for concern.

At the international level, marine protection programs take many forms. There are about 1300 coastal and marine protected areas in over

87 countries (World Resources Institute 1996). The International Union for the Conservation of Nature (IUCN) drafted policy guidelines in 1988 for setting up marine protection programs. As is the case with many resources, protection is determined by the individual country. Some areas are protected in parklike settings where wildlife protection and tourism are stated management objectives, and other marine parks are more preserve-oriented with limited or restricted human use. Australia's Great Barrier Reef Marine Park is the best example of a protected marine resource. It was established in 1975, and the governing authority has the right to regulate and prohibit activities inside the park as well as those activities outside the park that may pollute or otherwise harm the reef ecosystem. The primary purpose of the park is to promote the human use of the park in a manner consistent with the preservation of the ecosystem.

Example: Exploitation and Protection of Marine Mammals

Exploitation of whales and other marine mammals has been taking place for thousands of years but became a problem when it reached industrial scales in the eighteenth and nineteenth centuries. Commercial whale-hunting brought several species to the brink of extinction, and in response international agreements have resulted in significant reduction, but not elimination, of whale harvesting. Whale conservation problems provide an excellent illustration of the scientific, social, and political dimensions of marine resource management.

Whale Populations   The exact population sizes of marine mammals occupying the world's oceans are unknown, although we do have estimates for specific species. Marine mammals include great whales, small whales, dolphins and porpoises, sirenians and otters, and seals and sea lions.

Many factors influence the number of marine mammals in any given region. Often, the best knowledge we have regarding their population is derived from historical data on whaling and harvesting and current information about their reproductive biology, natural mortality, and habitat. In the case of whales, defining habitat is problematic. For example, the distribution of the California gray whale is relatively easy to determine because their breeding areas are limited to several shallow lagoons on the west coast of Mexico and portions of their north-south migration routes follow the edge of the continental shelf along the western coast of North America. Both the lagoons and continental shelf are physical features that can be easily mapped. On the other hand, the distribution of other great whales such as the fin, right, and blue whales is greatly dependent on the concentration of food supplies such as krill and plankton. In turn, the distribution of krill and plankton is dependent on currents and weather conditions, thus making it highly variable. Therefore, the key feeding areas for these species could change from year to year.

Estimates of whale populations are extremely difficult to produce, although we can make some educated guesses based on historical and catch data. For example, Table 9.4 provides the best estimates of the virgin population of selected species before harvesting began, as well as current population estimates.

The international regulation of whaling is a classic example of the problems with managing a common property resource. The introduction of the harpoon gun and steam-powered whaling vessels in the late 1800s, coupled with the advent of the seagoing factory ship in the early twentieth century, revitalized the whaling industry of Moby Dick fame. This new technology permitted the exploitation of larger, faster species of whales, such as the blue whale, and the processing of oil, bone, and meat at sea. Several European nations developed fleets of small vessels, called whale catchers, centered around a large factory ship. These fleets caught several different species in both Arctic and Antarctic waters, raising concerns about overfishing as early as 1920. The first international whaling treaty, signed in 1931, proved ineffective. The International Whaling Commission (IWC) was therefore established in 1946, ostensibly to protect and ensure species survival. Currently, 39 countries are members of the IWC.

Regulation of Whaling   The wording of the preamble to the 1946 International Convention for the Regulation of Whaling, which created the IWC, is a good example of the difficulty associated with using a scientifically rational management approach on a common property resource such as whales. The treaty directs that the IWC safeguard for future generations the great natural

Table 9.4   Whale Abundance

Whale	*Virgin*[a]	*Current Population*
Blue	175,000–228,000	under 5000
Humpback	115,000	20,000
Bowhead	30,000–54,700	under 8500
Right	100,000–200,000	1000–4000
Fin	448,000–548,000	50,000
Sei	256,000	65,000
Sperm	2,400,000–2,700,000	N.A.[b]
Gray	15,000–20,000	21,000
Minke	140,000	904,270
Pilot	N.A.[b]	780,000

[a] *Estimates of population before harvesting began.*
[b] *N.A. = not available.*
Sources: Brownell, Ralls, and Perrin 1989; Council on Environmental Quality 1982; U.S. Department of Commerce 1985; World Resources Institute 1988, UNEP 1994; World Wildlife Fund 1997.

resources represented by the whale, while also increasing the size of whale stocks to bring the population to an "optimal level" to make possible the orderly development of the whaling industry. Is the objective of the IWC to protect whales, encourage industry development, or both? More than half a century's effort to manage whales by the IWC indicates that nations generally will seek to protect whales only when it is in their national interest to do so. The 1946 treaty creating the IWC permits member nations to object to and then legally ignore the quotas established by the Commission and its scientific committees. Thus, in 1986 when the IWC formally declared a complete moratorium on all commercial whaling at the urging of the United States and other non-whaling member nations, Japan and the Soviet Union formally objected and were initially allowed to set their own quotas. In 1987, Norway and the Soviet Union ceased commercial whaling, as did Japan in 1988. Under the IWC moratorium, however, countries can still obtain special permits to harvest whales for subsistence purposes for native populations (Inuit) and for scientific research.

International efforts to protect whales are complicated by the slow reproductive rates of these marine mammals. For example, one of the reasons cited in support of the international whaling conventions was the Pacific bowhead whale. The world catch for this species peaked in the mid-1800s, and the IWC's first act was to ban all further commercial harvest. However, right and bowhead whale populations have not recovered despite 40 years of complete protection. It appears that the slow reproductive rate of these species is responsible for the inability of the small, dispersed populations to grow rapidly.

Recent whaling follows a pattern of heavy exploitation of one species, leading to a dramatic population decline and a shift to another species. For example, 11,559 blue whales were caught in 1940, declining to less than 2000 in 1960 and 613 in 1965. The catch of the slightly smaller fin whale peaked at 32,185 in the mid-1950s and dropped to 5057 by 1970. The harvest of the still smaller sei whale was minimal until 1960, when it then rose and subsequently declined (Council on Environmental Quality 1981a). Similarly, the minke whale catch totaled about 60,000 during the early 1980s. The recovery of the minke whale population since the moratorium has been rapid. Current estimates place the population at around 900,000, a population large enough to support small-scale whaling, which was in fact recommended by the IWC's scientific committee, but not formally adopted by the entire IWC because of strong opposition by environmentalists. The trends in whale harvesting (Fig. 9.10) during the last decade illustrate the effectiveness of the IWC moratorium.

The failure of international efforts to regulate whales has caused an interesting reaction. In 1976, the United States adopted legislation linking the permitted harvest of fish within U.S. waters by foreign nations to their adherence to IWC quotas. Thus, when Japan refused to abide by the IWC's moratorium in 1983, the United States withheld 100,000 metric tons of Japan's 1984 allocation of fish to be caught off Alaska and threatened to limit fishing further if Japan's objections to the IWC were not withdrawn. Several other nations adopted a similar strategy.

In the United States, marine mammals are protected under the Marine Mammal Protection Act, which was passed in 1972. This legislation is similar to the Endangered Species Act (see Chapter 8)

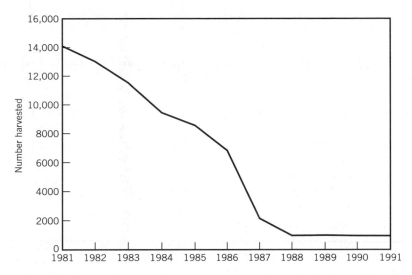

Figure 9.10   Whale catches 1980–1991. Since the 1980s whale catches have steadily declined and have remained flat as a consequence of the 1986 IWC moratorium on whaling. *Source:* United Nations Environment Program, 1993.

but applies only to marine species. The act places a moratorium on harvesting these animals in U.S. territorial waters and prohibits the import of animals or animal products except for public display or scientific purposes. Currently, 15 marine mammals are listed as endangered and 3 as threatened.

Multinational agreements on marine mammal protection are limited, however. Over 92 countries have some type of law regarding marine mammals, but only three (New Zealand, the United States, and the Republic of the Seychelles) have comprehensive protection of marine mammals. The Republic of the Seychelles has gone so far as to declare itself a marine mammal sanctuary and can impose a sentence of up to five years in prison on anyone who kills or harasses a marine mammal. Unfortunately, an agency such as the IWC has no real enforcement powers and must rely on economic sanctions and on the diplomacy of its member nations. Non-whaling nations such as the United States often cite the need to protect whales as an aesthetic resource. But this perception does not carry much weight in whaling nations, such as Japan, Norway, and Russia, where whales have economic value. Thus, international management of common property resources such as whales often de-

pends on resolving differences over the perceived value of the resource in question.

Conclusion

As a common property resource, the ocean is accessible to all nations. Responsibility for allocation and management of the ocean's vast resources is clouded by lack of certainty surrounding ownership of the resource. International efforts, such as the IWC and the Law of the Sea Treaty, are important steps in recognizing this dilemma and in appreciating the value and wisdom of conserving this resource.

One of the most critical issues facing our marine environment is coastal development, which destroys valuable wetlands and coral reefs. In addition, municipal sewage discharge and dredging sediments add to the destruction of estuarine environments, the most biologically productive of all. Oil and hazardous materials releases in coastal, territorial, and international waters continue to pose problems. Lastly, and perhaps most importantly, the overexploitation of marine fisheries is a major worry. Because of the over exploitation, many nations are turning to fish farming (or aquaculture) to meet the increasing food demand. Aquaculture normally takes place in near-shore estuarine environments, precisely those environments that are subject to intense land-based development and pollution.

Historically, the oceans were thought of in superlative terms, capable of providing food, transport, recreation, solitude, and dumping grounds in an apparently unlimited supply. As with other once-"infinite" natural resources, however, the oceans, like the air, are now an increasingly regulated part of the global village. Marine science research indicates that, like the atmosphere above, the oceans are integrative and interactive. Pollutants travel worldwide and the effects of overfishing are global as well. However, marine scientists are also quick to admit that we still have very little understanding of how the oceans operate and what their role is in climate change. Hence, there is a two-sided battle between, on the one hand, the conservation and political leaders of the world's wealthy nations, who call for research and ocean-use restrictions; and, on the other hand, the emerging countries of the world that are trying to stake a claim to their share of the last great common property resource.

REFERENCES AND ADDITIONAL READING

Albarede, F., and S. L. Goldstein, 1992. World map of Nd isotopes in sea-floor ferromanganese deposits. *Geology* 20: 761–763.

Audubon. 1989. Wreck of the *Exxon Valdez* (special issue). *Audubon* 91(5): 74–111.

Bohnsack, J. A. 1996. Marine reserves, zoning, and the future of fishery management. *Fisheries* 21(9): 14–16.

Broad, W. J. 1994. Plan to carve up ocean floor riches nears fruition. *New York Times*, March 29, 1994, p.C1.

Brownell, R. L., Jr., K. Ralls, and W. F. Perrin, 1995. Marine mammal biodiversity: Three diverse orders encompass 119 species. *Oceanus* 38(2): 30–33.

_____ . 1989. The plight of the "forgotten" whales. *Oceanus* 32(1): 5–12.

Clark, J. R. 1996. *Coastal Zone Management Handbook*. Boca Raton, FL: Lewis Publishers.

Committee on Protection and Management of Pacific Northwest Anadromous Salmonids (CPMPNAS). 1996. *Upstream: Salmon and Society in the Pacific*

Northwest. Washington, DC: National Academy Press.

Council on Environmental Quality. 1995. *25th Annual Report*. Washington, DC: U.S. Government Printing Office.

_____ . 1981a. *Environmental Trends*. Washington, DC: U.S. Government Printing Office.

_____ . 1982. *Environmental Quality 1982. 13th Annual Report*. Washington, DC: U.S. Government Printing Office.

CIESIN.
ONLINE: *http://sedac.ciesin.org/entri*

Fairhall, D., and P. Jordan. 1980. *The Wreck of the Amoco Cadiz*. New York: Stein & Day.

Farrington, J. W. 1985. Oil pollution: A decade of research and monitoring. *Oceanus* 28(3): 3–12.

Food and Agriculture Organization. 1987. *Yearbook of Fishery Statistics*. Vol. 52, *Catches and Landings*; Vol. 53, *Fishery Commodities*. Rome: United Nations, Food and Agriculture Organization.

Food and Agriculture Organization, Fisheries.
ONLINE: *http://www.fao.org/waicent/faoinfo/fishery/fishery.htm*

Foster, N. M., and J. H. Archer. 1988. The National Marine Sanctuary Program: Policy, education, and research. *Oceanus* 31(1): 5–17.

Freudenburg, W. R., and R. Gramling, 1994. *Oil in Troubled Waters*. Albany: SUNY Press.

Gross, M. G. 1971. *Oceanography*. 2nd ed. Columbus, Ohio: Merrill.

Heath, G. R. 1982. Manganese nodules: Unanswered questions. *Oceanus* 25(3): 37–41.

Knecht, R. W. 1982. Deep ocean mining. *Oceanus* 25(3): 3–11.

Odum, E. P. 1971. *Fundamentals of Ecology*. Philadelphia: W. B. Saunders.

Rasmusson, E. M., and J. M. Hall. 1983. El Niño: The great equatorial Pacific Ocean warming event of 1982–1983. *Weatherwise* (August): 166–175.

Russell, D. 1996. The world's fisheries: State of emergency; The crisis comes home. *E Magazine* (September/October): 38–41.

Sissenwine, M. P., and A. A. Rosenberg. 1993. U.S. fisheries. *Oceanus* (Summer): 48–55.

Squires, D. F. 1983. *The Ocean Dumping Quandary: Waste Disposal in the New York Bight*. Albany, NY: SUNY Press.

State of the Union Message, Ronald Reagan. 1980. *New York Times*, January 24,1980, p. A12.

Swanson, R. L., and M. Devine. 1982. Ocean dumping policy. *Environment* 24(5): 14–20.

_____ , and C. J. Sinderman. 1979. *Oxygen Depletion and Associated Benthic Mortalities in New York Bight*, 1976. NOAA Professional Paper 11. Washington, DC: U.S. Department of Commerce.

Tolba, M. K. et al., eds. 1992. *The World Environment 1972–1992*. London: Chapman & Hall.

United Nations Environmental Programme. 1993. *Environmental Data Report 1993–1994*. Cambridge, MA: Blackwell.

U.S. Bureau of the Census. 1997. *Statistical Abstract of the United States*. Washington, DC: U.S. Government Printing Office.

U.S. Coast Guard. 1984. *Polluting Incidents in and around U.S. Waters, 1983 and 1984*. Washington, DC: U.S. Government Printing Office.

U.S. Congress. Office of Technology Assessment. 1987. *Wastes in Marine Environments*. 0TA-0334. Washington, DC: U.S. Government Printing Office.

U.S. Department of Commerce, National Oceanic and Atmospheric Administration, National Marine Fisheries Service. 1985. *Annual Report 1984/85 Marine Mammal Protection Act of 1987*. Washington, DC: U.S. Government Printing Office.

Wilber, R. J. 1987. Plastic in the North Atlantic. *Oceanus* 30(3): 61–68.

Winslow, R. 1978. *Hard Aground. The Story of the Argo Merchant Oil Spill*. New York: W. W. Norton.

World Resources Institute. 1988. *World Resources 1988–89*. New York: Basic Books.

_____ . 1993. *The 1993 Information Please Environmental Almanac*. Boston: Houghton-Mifflin.

_____ . 1996. *World Resources 1996–97*. New York: Oxford University Press.

World Wildlife Fund. 1997. Whales in the wild. ON-LINE: *http://www.wwf.org/species/whales*

For more information, consult our web page at ***http://www.wiley.com/college/cutter***

STUDY QUESTIONS

1. What importance do estuaries and coastal areas have for marine fisheries?
2. What are the major factors contributing to the decline of marine fisheries?
3. Describe some of the major achievements and failures of the International Whaling Commission. What are the major factors that have contributed to these successes/failures?
4. What waste materials are commonly dumped in the oceans? Is this dumping any worse than land disposal of these wastes?
5. How effective is the protection provided, both internationally and in the United States, for marine mammals?

CHAPTER 10

WATER QUANTITY AND QUALITY

The necessity of water as a resource for all life, humans included, is obvious. All life forms require it to some degree, and they require water within certain ranges of quality. Water is essential to life in part because it is an excellent transporter of other substances. It is sometimes called the universal solvent in that a wide range of chemicals (though certainly not all chemicals) are readily dissolved in it. As a result, water serves to deliver nutrients to organisms, especially plants, as well as remove waste products. The movement of water between the atmosphere, the oceans, and the land is a fundamental part of earth's biogeochemical cycling systems. Water carries heat to the atmosphere when it evaporates from the ocean surface and condenses in the atmosphere to form precipitation. It also carries many other substances with it as it flows from the land to the sea or when it falls as precipitation.

As described in Chapter 4, humans have dramatically altered the hydrologic cycle, both locally and globally. These alterations come from our use of water for irrigation, our modification of the earth's vegetation cover, and our withdrawal of water from rivers, lakes, and subsurface aquifers for domestic and industrial use. The quantity of water we are withdrawing is enormous. In some regions, no more water is available for withdrawal and once-large reservoirs, both underground and on the surface, are significantly depleted. In other regions, what water is available is so polluted it is not usable.

As you can see, water-quality and water-quantity issues are closely linked. The more water we use, the more wastewater we generate. If water is withdrawn from a river for human use, then less water remains in the river for waste dilution, and stream quality suffers. Poor water quality limits the human use of water supplies, and demands for improved water quality are placing significant limits on expanding water use.

The combination of significant water-supply depletion and water-quality degradation means that water resources are increasingly stressed, especially in the more populated areas of the world. In the Middle East and south and central Asia, water-quality and -quantity problems are already acute, straining international relations. And in many wealthier countries, water-quantity and quality issues are major constraints on future resource development. In this chapter we will examine these problems by first reviewing issues associated with water quantity and quality and then discuss the interactions between the two.

WATER SUPPLY AND ITS VARIABILITY

Water storages on the land are of two basic types: surface water and groundwater. Both of these function as important storages in the hydrologic cycle. *Surface water* is liquid water and floating ice above the ground surface, in rivers, swamps, lakes, or ponds. It is derived from direct precipitation or from subsurface sources.

Groundwater is water below the ground surface, in a saturated zone below the *water table* (Fig. 10.1). The water table is simply the top of the saturated zone in which water fills pore spaces and cracks in rocks or sediments. Soil moisture above the water table is not considered part of groundwater. Groundwater is derived from downward percolation of rainfall through the soil and in some areas from seepage of surface water. In addition, many areas of the world have substantial "fossil" groundwater storages that are derived from past humid conditions and are not being significantly replenished today. A porous body of material containing groundwater is called an *aquifer*. If the water table is free to rise with additional water, the aquifer is said to be unconfined; if there is an impermeable layer overlying the aquifer, it is described as confined. Such impermeable layers are called *aquicludes*, and they are particularly important in segregating relatively clean groundwater from brackish or contaminated groundwater.

Surface water and groundwater flow from high to low elevations. Surface water flows according to the shape of the land, following channels to the sea. But groundwater flows according to the slope of the water table and the permeability of the materials through which it moves. *Permeability* refers to the speed with which water will flow through a porous medium such as rock or sediments. The steeper the slope of the water table, or the greater the permeability of the ground, the faster water will flow. Usually, the shape of the water table approximately parallels the shape of the land, so that groundwater flows

from upland areas toward lowlands, but this is not always the case. For example, variations in the permeability of subsurface materials may affect flow rates and directions, sometimes causing drainage divides for groundwater to be different from those for surface water. The locations of permeable and impermeable areas of rock or sediments not only affect groundwater flow patterns but also determine where water is stored and available.

Spatial Variation in Surface Supply

The renewable supply of fresh water is directly determined by precipitation and evapotranspiration rates (Chapter 4), with runoff being the difference between the two. The greatest water availability may not be in areas of high precipitation, if these areas also have high evapotranspiration. Figure 10.2 is a world map of renewable water supply. Rainfall in some areas, such as the Amazon basin, is so large that very high amounts of runoff occur despite high evapotranspiration rates. Tropical areas with seasonal precipitation patterns such as the monsoon areas of south Asia have high amounts of water available in the rainy season but limited water supply in the dry season. Relatively high amounts of runoff occur in humid portions of the midlatitudes where evapotranspiration rates are lower.

Unfortunately, the world's population is not evenly distributed with respect to water availabil-

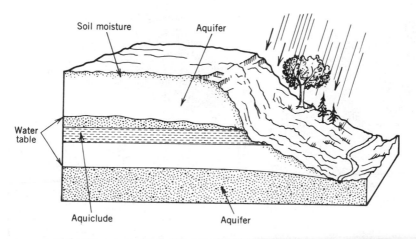

Figure 10.1 Groundwater and surface water. Water that is below the surface, filling spaces in rocks or sediments, is called groundwater. Surface water is water in lakes, streams, and reservoirs.

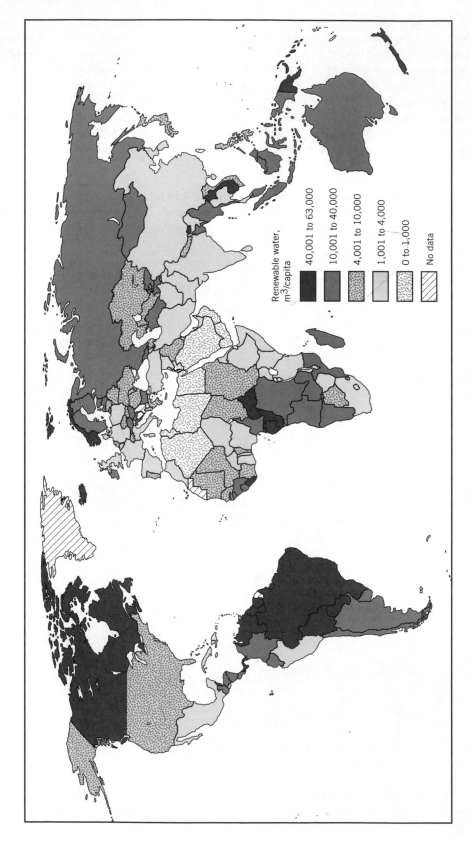

Figure 10.2 Renewable supply of water per capita, cubic meters per year, 1995. Data from World Resources Institute, 1996.

ity; thus, much of the world's water is not accessible to large population concentrations. About one-sixth of the world's renewable fresh water flows in the Amazon, a relatively unpopulated region. In contrast, India and China have about 40 percent of the world's population, yet their climates yield only about 12 percent of the world's fresh water. On a per capita basis, Asia is the driest continent, with an average of fewer than 4000 cubic meters per person per year (Table 10.1). In reality, most Asians have much less water available than this, because much of that continent's runoff is found in relatively unpopulated portions of Siberia. North and Central America have, on average, about four times as much water per person as Asia. But this average also is deceiving, for most of the runoff from North America is found in the northwestern and eastern parts of the continent, with relatively little in the southwestern United States and Mexico.

Temporal Variability

Runoff, the renewable supply of fresh water, is extremely variable in time, and usually the water is least available when it is most needed. Mean monthly discharges for rivers typically vary by one or even two orders of magnitude, depending on seasonal amounts of precipitation and evapotranspiration. This means that if the average flow in the driest month is 5 m^3/sec, the flow in the wettest month may be 50 or 500 m^3/sec. Flows are more variable in small rivers and less variable in large rivers. In the tropics, seasonal variations in river flow usually correspond to seasonal patterns of rainfall. In midlatitude climates, low-flow periods usually occur in the summer because

Table 10.1   Global Water Availability

Region/Country	Renewable Water Supply (km^3/year)	1995 Population (millions)	Renewable Water per Capita (m^3/year)
Africa	3996.0	728,074	5488
Kenya	30.2	28,261	1069
Zaire	1019.0	43,901	23,211
Asia	13,206.7	3,457,957	3819
China	2800.0	1,221,462	2292
Japan	547.0	125,095	4373
Europe	6234.6	726,999	8576
Italy	167.0	57,187	2920
Norway	392.0	4337	90,385
Oceania	1614.3	28,549	56,543
Australia	343.0	18,088	18,963
Papua New Guinea	801.0	4302	186,192
North/Central America	6443.7	419,260	15,369
Costa Rica	95.0	3035	27,745
United States	2478.0	263,250	9413
South America	9526.0	319,790	29,788
Brazil	6950.0	161,790	42,957
Chile	468.0	14,262	32,814
World	41,022.0	5,716,426	7176

Source: World Resources Institute, 1996.

plants are using more water at this time. Summer is also the time when demand for water is higher, because crops and lawns must be irrigated.

Because of this temporal variability, the amount of water we can count on withdrawing from a river is much less than the total amount that flows in it over the year. In addition, precipitation variations from one year to the next further reduce the amount of water we can depend on from rivers. An example of short- and medium-term variation in stream flow is shown in Figure 10.3. The drought years of the 1930s stand out. This period serves as the baseline record of low flow, because there has not been a prolonged period of drought since that time.

Water Supplies and Storage

As you have seen, the natural supply of water in the world is highly variable, with some countries (like Brazil) having very large renewable supplies of water per capita and others (like China) having to divide a modest amount of water among a large number of people. But natural supply alone does not ensure water availability. As Figure 10.4 shows, any water-supply system must have the following four components: collection system, storage facility, transportation system, and distribution system. Water-supply engineers design and construct water systems in

a variety of ways, and where possible incorporate natural features in one or more of these components. In virtually all cases, the collection system is natural: it is the *drainage basin* of a river or a groundwater aquifer, or some combination of the two. Rivers are particularly efficient concentrators of surface runoff. As a result, usually little is done to modify collection systems, although vegetation conversion to increase water yield or improve water quality has been used in some areas. Aquifers are much more dispersed conveyors of water. Water flows toward low points in the water table, and when a well is drilled to pump water out, the local water table is depressed. This causes water to flow toward the well, which is exactly what is desired. By drilling wells in particularly porous, permeable underground materials, we can tap into aquifers that have a ready supply of available water.

Storage is necessary to smooth out the natural variations in water availability and to save surplus water from high-rainfall seasons for dry seasons or periods of high demand. Under ideal conditions, a storage facility can allow average withdrawals to equal long-term average flow, and short-term withdrawals can far exceed average flows. In practice, however, average withdrawals are rarely this large. Storages cannot trap all the water during times of flood, and water must be

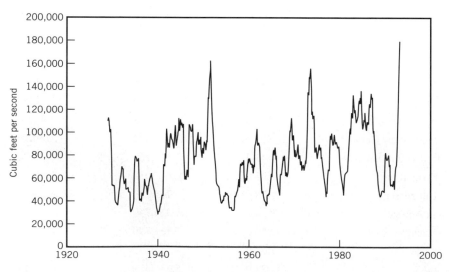

Figure 10.3 Average annual discharge of the Missouri River, 1928–1993. Seasonal variations in discharge have been smoothed out of the data. Flows in wet years are more than four times greater than those in dry years. *Source:* U.S. Geological Survey, 1998

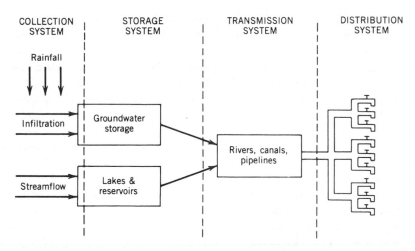

Figure 10.4   Components of a water-supply system. The component with the lowest capacity limits the capacity of the entire system.

left for in-stream uses. Nonetheless, short-term withdrawals—for periods of weeks or less—frequently can exceed average inflows in large reservoirs.

Surface-water storage is accomplished by constructing dams on rivers and impounding water in artificial lakes behind the dams. The amount of water that can be stored is a function of the shape of the valley and the height of the dam. The ideal dam site is a relatively narrow and deep valley (where the dam is built) with a broad and deep valley just upstream. In addition, the valley that is to be inundated should be underlain by impermeable rocks and be relatively unpopulated, and the land should have lower long-term value than the reservoir replacing it.

Transportation and distribution systems can be of many types, depending mostly on the distance between collection site and use area and the nature of the final use. In many cases, transportation distances are so short that the entire system is essentially just a distribution system. These facilities include canals, pipelines, and natural river channels, or any combination of these (Fig. 10.5). The choice of which type of conduit to use depends primarily on terrain, the volumes of water to be carried, the distances involved, and the need to protect against seepage or quality deterioration along the way.

It should be clear by now that, although water supply is constrained by natural factors, water de-

Figure 10.5   The California Aqueduct. This aqueduct carries water from the northern Sierra Nevada to agricultural lands in California's Central Valley.

velopment in the form of engineering works also affects water availability. The extent of water development can be evaluated only relative to what is naturally available, and that in turn is subject to debate because there are different definitions of what is "available water." One indication of the extent of water use can be gained by comparing withdrawals to natural runoff (Table 10.2).

Before proceeding, let us define a few terms that describe these aspects of water use. *Withdrawal* is the removal of water from a surface or groundwater source for a variety of purposes such as municipal, industrial, or irrigation use. *Consumptive* use is the use of that water in such a way that it is not returned to the stream or aquifer; instead, it is returned to the atmosphere by evapotranspiration. *In-stream* uses do not require removal of the water from a river or lake; these include navigation, wildlife habitat, waste disposal, and hydroelectric power generation.

Withdrawals can exceed stream flow because not all of the water withdrawn is consumed; some is returned to the stream. Nonetheless, these withdrawals place a heavy demand on water resources, particularly because they compete with in-stream uses. In the Colorado River basin, for example, a series of power plants at major dams generates about 4 percent of the nation's hydroelectric power, and plants in the Pacific Northwest (mostly in the Columbia River basin) generate almost 50 percent of U.S. hydroelectric power. If water is withdrawn and consumed rather than returned for this in-stream use, energy production will be drastically reduced.

In more densely populated areas of the country, the most important in-stream use is maintenance of water quality. Sufficient flow must be available to dilute and transport sewage effluents and other pollutants, as well as to provide habitat for aquatic life. The U.S. Fish and Wildlife Service estimates the flows necessary to support aquatic habitat and recreation. It has found these flows to be generally 80 to 90 percent of total stream flow in the eastern United States and 40 to 60 percent of total flow in most of the western states (Water Resources Council 1978). Navigation is another important in-stream use that competes with other in- and off-stream uses for the water in our rivers. Depletion of stream flows caused by consumptive off-stream use, particularly irrigation, is a major problem in semiarid and arid portions of the United States (Fig. 10.6).

One way to overcome this variability is to build reservoirs to store excess water from the high-flow season for use in the low-flow season. Around the world, over 36,000 large dams have been built for a variety of purposes, including hydroelectric power generation, flood control, and water storage for later withdrawal. About half of these dams are in China (Issue 14.1), and about 5500 are in the United States. The total storage capacity of the reservoirs they impound is over 5000 km^3, or 12 percent of the world's total annual runoff, and this is growing rapidly. In some regions, the amount stored in reservoirs is much greater than the annual flow; in the Colorado River basin, for example, reservoirs store about four years' average runoff.

In addition to these artificial storages, many natural lakes provide freshwater supplies. The Great Lakes of North America are the principal water supplies of Chicago, Cleveland, Toronto and other cities on their shores. Unlike reservoirs, however, these lakes cannot be easily drawn down to provide water during dry spells without severely affecting ecosystems and coastal communities. In practice, large lakes are available as major water supplies for irrigation or for urban populations only.

Groundwater is a more important storage of water for human use. The total volume of water stored in relatively accessible groundwater aquifers is estimated at about 9000 km^3, or roughly one-fourth of global annual runoff. Much more—perhaps as much as 4 million km^3—exists in deeper aquifers, though most of this amount is not economically accessible. Most small-scale and domestic water-supply systems use groundwater, whereas large industrial and commercial users depend mainly on surface water.

Typically, groundwater storages are replenished relatively slowly, taking years to centuries or more to replace the total volume of a given aquifer. As a result, it is possible to withdraw water much faster than it is replaced, a practice known as *groundwa-*

Table 10.2   U.S. Water Withdrawals by Basin

Basin	Percentage Available Water[a]
Mississippi	21
New England	6
Mid-Atlantic	20
Colorado	92
Great Basin	110

[a] *Withdrawal of surface water/natural runoff expressed as a percentage.*

Source: U.S. Geological Survey, 1998.

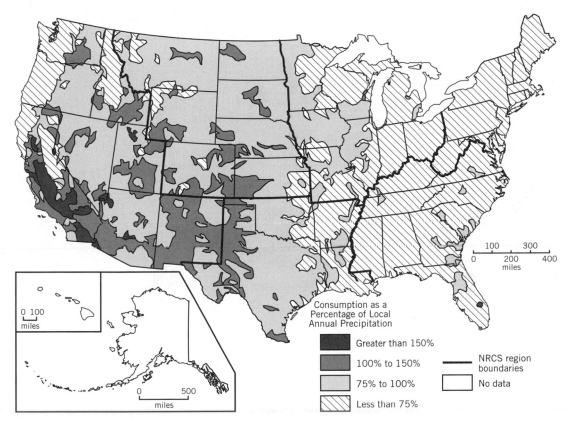

Figure 10.6   Water-depletion areas of the United States. The east generally has a surplus of water while the arid west is rapidly depleting its water supply. *Source:* U.S. Department of Agriculture 1989, p. 71.

ter mining. This practice is all too common, especially in the semi-arid and arid parts of the world. In a few countries in the Middle East, total withdrawals of water exceed the renewable supply, indicating significant *overdraft* of groundwater at the national level. In many other countries, including the United States, groundwater overdrafts are common at the local or regional level.

One impact of groundwater overdraft is declining well levels, often requiring that wells be deepened for withdrawals to continue. In coastal areas, usually a boundary exists between fresh water and salt water in the ground. Salt water is denser and so is found underneath the fresh water. A decline in the elevation of the freshwater table causes *saltwater intrusion*, an inland movement of the salt/fresh boundary, which contaminates wells and makes them unusable for drinking water. When this happens, generally the only recourse is to close the wells and find alternative sources of water, most often wells farther inland. This prob-

lem is particularly acute on the coastal plain of the eastern United States and in some areas of coastal California (Fig. 10.7). There are also examples of saltwater intrusion into inland aquifers in areas where saline groundwater underlies fresh water. In some areas, notably coastal Texas, southern Arizona, and central California, groundwater overdrafts are causing *subsidence*, or sinking of the land. In Texas, this is contributing to coastal flooding, particularly in suburban Houston, while in Arizona large fissures have opened in the ground.

In the western Great Plains, the most important overdraft problem is in the area underlain by the Ogallala aquifer. This aquifer is a thick, porous layer of sand and gravel that underlies an extensive area from Nebraska to Texas. It contains a large amount of water but has an extremely low recharge rate. Because most of this area is too dry for rainfall farming, groundwater-based irrigation has been rapidly expanding since the 1950s. The rate of withdrawal is enormous, exceeding the recharge

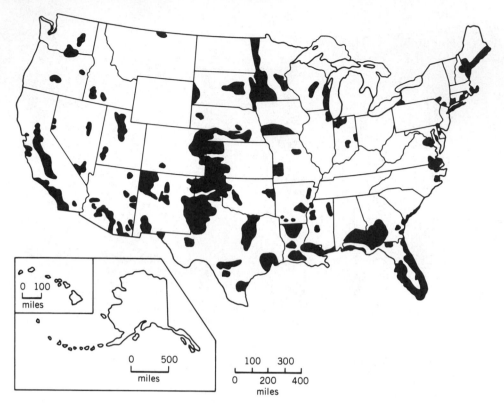

Figure 10.7 Areas of the United States where groundwater decline is of state or local concern. *Source:* U.S. Department of Agriculture 1989, p.71.

rate by 100 times in some areas. The Ogallala aquifer initially allowed the rapid development of irrigated agriculture in the High Plains, but its depletion will lead to an end of irrigated agriculture in the region and hasten the decline of economic growth. In the Arkansas-White-Red rivers region, which includes much of the Ogallala aquifer, groundwater overdrafts represent over 60 percent of all groundwater withdrawals. Another area of extreme overdraft is the Texas-Gulf region, where overdrafts account for 77 percent of all groundwater withdrawals. For the nation as a whole, about 37 percent of all groundwater withdrawals are overdrafts (U.S. Department of Agriculture 1989).

THE DEMAND FOR WATER

Water is used for a wide variety of purposes that have very different quantity, quality, and timing characteristics. The type of use can be evaluated by whether it takes place in the stream or elsewhere and by whether the water is returned to the stream after use.

Water demands fluctuate from year to year depending on weather patterns. In wet or cool years, demand is usually lower, whereas in dry years demand is greater. To evaluate long-term trends, it is useful to average these short-term fluctuations. For example, in the United States both water withdrawals and consumption have risen steadily since the 1960s (Fig. 10.8). Since 1980, freshwater withdrawals and consumption have declined somewhat. Surface water remains the primary source of water withdrawals (80%), a pattern evident from the 1950s. Groundwater withdrawals have increased since the 1950s.

Regional U.S. demand is greatest in the western states, especially Idaho, Montana, and Wyoming (Fig. 10.9). These states have the largest per capita withdrawals, with water used for irrigating sugar beets, potatoes, corn, and beans. The smallest per capita withdrawals are in New England, New Jersey, and Maryland; most of this water is used for industrial purposes and steam electrical generation. However, with the growth of metropolitan areas in the arid West,

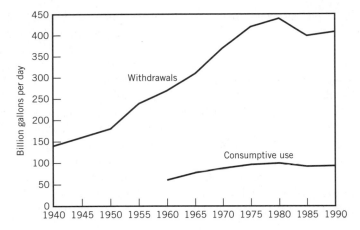

Figure 10.8   Trends in U.S. freshwater withdrawals and consumption, 1940–1990. *Source:* U.S. Bureau of the Census 1997, p. 233.

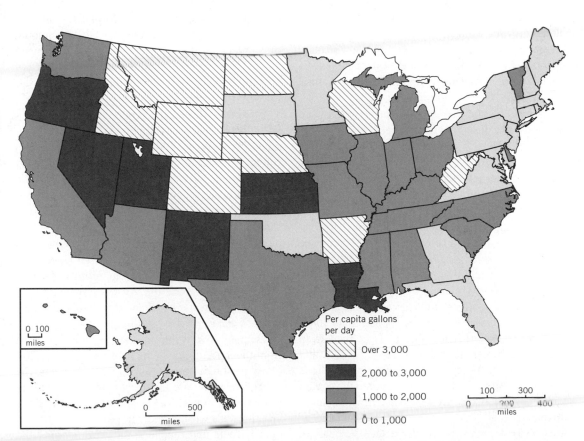

Figure 10.9   Water withdrawals by state, 1990. Per capita water withdrawals are highest in the upper Great Plains states, primarily due to irrigation. *Source:* U.S. Bureau of the Census, 1997, p. 232.

more demands will be placed on this scarce resource (Issue 10.1).

Off-Stream Uses

Withdrawal and consumptive uses of water are often defined by specific categories (or functions) of use. These include public supply, rural supply (domestic and livestock), industrial, irrigation, and hydroelectric power generation (an in-stream use).

Public and rural supplies include both domestic and commercial uses of water, including those familiar to us in our everyday lives at home or at work—washing, cooking, drinking, lawn water-ing, sanitation, and the like. Nearly 90 percent of the U.S. population is served by municipal water-supply systems; the remainder have individual domestic systems (usually wells).

Agricultural uses, principally irrigation, con-sume more fresh water than any other use. Worldwide, agriculture uses about 69 percent of total freshwater withdrawals (Table 10.3). This portion tends to be higher in developing than in industrialized countries, even those with rela-tively high amounts of rainfall. In addition to constituting the largest withdrawal of water, irri-gation is by far the most consumptive of all

---

ISSUE 10.1: WATER POLITICS IN THE WESTERN UNITED STATES

When questions on the availability and cost of water arise, elected officials in the Southwest often transform themselves into reptile-like crea-tures with the fangs of a rattlesnake and the changing colors of a chameleon. Water is per-haps the most parochial issue in Western politics and can force urbane, socially activist liberals to demand that government get off the backs of the people, while free market conservatives de-mand more government regulation over natural resources.

Access to and use of both surface water and groundwater has historically been governed by "use it or lose it" water rights laws in states like Arizona, California, Colorado, and Utah. On the basis of water rights granted to riparian property owners at the time of statehood or early land grants by state and federal governments, access to water supplies is generally governed by his-toric water uses. These water rights can be bought and sold independently of actual land-ownership. In addition, the water itself is a com-modity subject to sale.

Two basic systems of law govern the allocation of water. *Riparian doctrine* is applied to all states east of the 100th meridian and is derived from English common law. The water is owned and controlled by those who own the riparian land, which is defined as the land adjacent to the stream or upon which the stream flows. Riparian land-owners are allowed to use the water as long as their use does not substantially reduce the quantity or quality of water available to other riparian users. Furthermore, the rights cannot be lost be-cause of nonuse. In the West, a different system prevails. There water is allocated using a *prior ap-propriation system* based on a "use it or lose it" principle. Prior appropriation recognizes that the water is a finite resource and allocates the amount of available water to users on a predetermined basis. This protects agriculture and, with the heavy governmental subsidies up until the 1980s, has al-lowed water prices in the West to remain low.

Since the 1930s, the federal government has been the primary developer of new water sup-plies in the West. Federal agencies such as the Bureau of Reclamation and the Bureau of Land Management have had significant impact on the Western waterscape, ranging from major dam construction to more localized irrigation and canal systems. These large-scale water develop-ment projects helped populate the West and brought agriculture to the region. However, the days of large-scale, government-sponsored water projects are over, and the West is now entering a new phase in water conflicts: city dwellers versus farmers and ranchers.

Demand for water in the West has shifted from the agricultural to the urban sector. Because of a virtual halt in new federal water projects, the politics of water are heating up again and pitting farmers and ranchers against city dwellers. Since urbanites are willing and can pay more for water than farmers and ranchers, they are winning the

major uses. Typically 80 percent or more of irrigation water is used consumptively rather than being returned to surface water.

In the United States, about one-third of water withdrawals are for irrigation. To conserve more of the water, irrigation systems must become more efficient. Irrigation efficiency is defined as the volume of applied water in the root zone that is used by the crop. It is expressed as a percentage of the volume of water diverted from surface sources or pumped from groundwater supplies (U.S. Department of Agriculture 1989, p. 75). Drip irrigation is one of the most efficient application methods (90%), while flood, furrow, and sprinklers average between 60 and 80 percent efficiencies.

Industry takes the second-largest share of the world's water withdrawals, about 23 percent. The portion withdrawn for industry is highest in Europe, where it averages 55 percent. Industrial uses include a wide range of activities, including water used for washing products in the manufacturing process, removing waste materials, and cooling. The greatest withdrawals of water in the industrial sector are for cooling thermal electric power plants, typically in once-through cooling systems. Very little of this water is consumed, however.

battle over water at the moment. In Arizona, for example, urban water use exceeds natural runoff creating a deficiency. In 1980, the state forbade further groundwater over drafting in the Phoenix and Tucson regions. Urban development continued unabated, however, as the urban centers merely found other sources of drinking water for their residents. Phoenix, for example, bought 50,000 acres (20,235 ha) of farms (many in adjacent counties), including their water rights, and pumped the groundwater into the Central Arizona Project canals for use as municipal drinking water. Salt Lake City and St. George, Utah, have bought more than 100,000 acre-feet of water by purchasing shares of canal and ditch companies. To quench their thirst, metropolitan regions in the arid West look to more rural counties and purchase agricultural land to get the water. The water is now worth more than the land itself. A precedent for such water grabs was fictionalized in the movie *Chinatown*, which was based on a real event. Owens Valley, California, is located about 300 mi (483 km) northeast of Los Angeles. Between 1920 and 1950 the city of Los Angeles bought 75 percent of the valley's land and thus its water. The water was then sent by canal to Los Angeles. Some argue that this event helped shape the destiny of Los Angeles, making it one of the country's largest metropolitan regions.

What can be done about the thirsty West? Although some Westerners argue for halting development and sending the new immigrant easterners packing, this is unlikely. Alternative sources of water, conservation, or new strategies for water allocation must be developed to meet current and projected demands. Marketing water that has already been allocated is now viewed as a substitute for government-subsidized water projects. Water has long been traded among Western irrigation districts, but now urban centers are vying for some of the action. Speculators and private brokers are actively involved in water marketing. Western water rights are being purchased at increasing rates by investment firms (which anticipate that their initial investment can only increase in value over time). Oil companies that originally purchased the water rights for oil shale development during the 1970s soon realized the value of this water for urban uses, and private developers. Farmers were encouraged to sell water as a commodity, not just the rights to the water. In this way, water can be bought and sold like other natural resources such as grain or minerals. However, many states have reacted strongly. Texas, for example, completely outlaws interbasin transfers of water, and New Mexico and Wyoming prohibit out-of-state water transfers, largely to prevent thirsty Californians from taking their water. So while the metropolitan regions of the West increase in population and thirst, their search for water continues. Only time will tell how effective water marketing is in quenching the insatiable demand for water in the West (Steinhart 1990).

Table 10.3 Water Withdrawn for Various Purposes[a]

Region/Country	Per Capita Withdrawal (m³/year)	Domestic (%)	Industry (%)	Agriculture (%)
Africa	199	7	5	88
Kenya	87	20	4	76
Zaire	10	61	16	23
Asia	542	6	9	85
China	461	6	7	87
Japan	735	17	33	50
Europe	626	14	55	31
Italy	986	14	27	59
Norway	488	20	72	8
Oceania	586	64	2	34
Australia	933	65	2	33
Papua New Guinea	28	29	22	49
North/Central America	1451	9	42	49
Costa Rica	780	4	7	89
United States	1870	13	45	42
South America	332	18	23	59
Brazil	246	22	19	59
Chile	1626	6	5	89
World	645	8	23	69

[a]*The agricultural category includes plant irrigation and livestock; the industrial includes water for cooling thermoelectric plants; and the domestic includes residential and commercial users, as well as municipal providers.*

Source: World Resources Institute, 1996.

The manufacturing of paper and steel, the production of petroleum, coal, and chemicals, and food processing are also important industrial uses of water. Most of this water is used for cooling or washing purposes and thus is not heavily consumptive. Although industrial withdrawals are generally increasing, in some cases they are actually decreasing as water-quality controls force factories to remove wastes before discharging water and to release less. Industrial users are turning away from once-through systems toward water-recycling systems in which they use water over and over, reducing discharges of waste to the environment.

Domestic uses take the least water, generally less than 10 percent except in urbanized regions with relatively less industry and irrigation, such as South America and Oceania. Among the important domestic uses are cooking, laundry, bathing, toilet flushing, and, in North America, lawn irrigation. Total water use in public water systems in the United States averages about 750 liters (200 gallons) per person per day, including commercial uses such as restaurants and other service businesses. Domestic water use is not heavily consumptive—only about 20 percent in the United States, and much of this is in irrigating lawns.

Within the U.S., the states with the highest consumptive use are Arizona, Arkansas, Kansas, Nevada, New Mexico, and South Dakota (Table 10.4). More than half of the freshwater withdrawals in these states are for plant and animal agriculture. Kansas has the highest percentage consumptive use (72.5%), while New Jersey has the lowest (1.6%). It should be noted that the

Table 10.4 Water Source and Consumptive Use by State, 1990

State	Source		Consumptive
	% Surface	% Ground	Use (%)[a]
Alabama	95	5	5.6
Alaska	83	17	4.0
Arizona	58	42	66.2
Arkansas	40	60	52.8
California	68	32	44.7
Colorado	78	22	41.3
Connecticut	97	3	2.1
Delaware	94	6	4.3
Florida	74	26	17.5
Georgia	81	19	15.4
Hawaii	78	22	22.9
Idaho	61	39	30.9
Illinois	95	5	4.2
Indiana	93	7	4.8
Iowa	83	17	9.5
Kansas	28	72	72.5
Kentucky	94	6	7.2
Louisiana	86	14	17.0
Maine	93	7	4.5
Maryland	96	4	2.0
Massachusetts	94	6	3.5
Michigan	94	6	6.4
Minnesota	76	24	26.7
Mississippi	27	73	49.4
Missouri	89	11	7.6
Montana	98	2	22.4
Nebraska	46	54	47.3
Nevada	68	32	50.4
New Hampshire	95	5	2.0
New Jersey	95	5	1.6
New Mexico	49	51	59.2
New York	95	5	3.0
North Carolina	95	5	4.4
North Dakota	95	5	8.5
Ohio	92	8	7.7
Oklahoma	46	54	39.5
Oregon	91	9	37.5
Pennsylvania	90	10	5.9
Rhode Island	95	5	3.4
South Carolina	95	5	4.9
South Dakota	58	42	58.3
Tennessee	95	5	2.7
Texas	69	31	35.8
Utah	73	27	49.8
Vermont	93	7	4.6
Virginia	94	6	3.3
Washington	82	18	35.6
West Virginia	84	16	11.1
Wisconsin	90	10	7.1
Wyoming	95	5	35.9
Total	80	20	23.0

[a]The ratio of consumptive use as a percentage of total freshwater withdrawals.

Source: U.S. Bureau of the Census, 1990, p. 232.

high consumptive states derive a substantial portion of their freshwater supplies from groundwater sources.

In-Stream Uses

In addition to these off-stream uses, many important water uses take place in rivers or lakes, without withdrawing water from them. And while these uses do not result in any removal of water from the environment (except in the case of reservoir evaporation), they do require considerable amounts of water and they compete with off-stream uses. Within a river basin, water taken in one area may not be available in another. For example, if water is held in storage in a reservoir, then it is not part of downstream flow. If water must be released from a reservoir to generate hydroelectric power, then it cannot be held as storage for dry-season use.

Waste Dilution Probably the most important in-stream use of water is for waste dilution. Virtually all rivers in populated areas are used to remove wastes. The more water present and flowing in a river, the lower the concentration of pollutants will be, and thus the better water quality will be. So just removing water from a river reduces water quality, regardless of whether any pollutants are added in the process. This use will be discussed in more detail in the context of water quality.

Navigation The major rivers of the world, especially in industrialized countries, carry large amounts of freight. In the United States, for example, inland waterways carry about the same amount of freight (on a weight basis) as is delivered to or from ocean ports. Barge operations on rivers are constrained by river depth, for rivers are typically shallow and large barges may require 3 m or more of water depth to operate. Withdrawals of water from a river reduce depth and thus the usefulness of the river for navigation.

Hydroelectric Power Hydroelectric power is generated by storing water behind a dam and releasing it through turbines when electricity is needed. Hydroelectricity supplies about 9 percent of U.S. electric production, or 4 percent of total energy production. Because electricity cannot be stored in large quantities, timing of hydroelectric

power production is relatively inflexible. If the peak demand for electricity occurs at the same time as peak flow (as in the Colorado River basin, for example) all the better. But if peak demand occurs when flow is low, then water availability limits electric production. In addition, the large dams best suited to generating electricity inundate large areas and alter river habitats, causing additional economic and ecological dislocations.

Wildlife Habitat and Fisheries Although many rivers are severely degraded by pollution, these systems contain habitats necessary for the maintenance of important ecological communities and sport and commercial fisheries. These habitat values depend on maintaining good water quality, which in turn depends on water quantity. If the flow in a river is depleted to the point that additions of waste cause high pollutant concentrations, then habitat suffers. One common consequence is lowered dissolved oxygen levels and subsequently impoverished fish communities. In extreme circumstances fish kills occur, caused by low dissolved oxygen or by introduction of toxic substances.

Recreation In many rivers, recreational uses—mostly fishing and boating—are significant. These uses normally require high water quality for maintaining reasonably natural conditions and good fish habitat, safe swimming, and minimizing odors. They also require adequate flow, both for maintaining water quality and for floating boats. Recreational uses also make demands on streambank areas, in addition to the water in the channel.

Much competition prevails among in-stream and off-stream uses in the populated parts of the world. Water quality has degraded, and public concern about this degradation has risen to the point that further increases in pollutant concentrations are unacceptable. The combination of population growth and rising standards of living causes increased demand for off-stream uses of water as well as increased waste generation, yet rivers cannot absorb more waste. Nor can we afford to reduce rivers' waste-assimilating capacity by withdrawing more water. Finally, concern about the ecological impacts of large dams has made such projects increasingly controversial, if not impossible. The United States virtually ceased constructing large dams around 1980; such projects continue in developing countries but with much opposition from international environmental organizations. These factors together mean that further growth in water supplies will be very limited and that per capita water use must decrease significantly in the coming decades.

WATER QUALITY

Impurities in water come from many different sources, both natural and human, and it is often difficult to separate the two. When we speak of *pollution* or pollutants, we are usually referring to substantial human additions to a stream or lake's load of an impurity or impurities. A polluted stream must be defined relative to its condition unaffected by human activity rather than in absolute terms. Similarly, acceptability of given levels of contamination depends on what use we make of the water. For drinking water, absolute levels are important and standards for drinking water are established by governmental and other agencies.

Pollutants come from diverse human-made and natural sources. One way to classify pollutant discharges is by point versus nonpoint sources. A *point source* is a specific location such as a factory or municipal sewage outfall. A *nonpoint source* is a source that, as far as we know, originates from a large, poorly defined area. Runoff, subsurface flow, and atmospheric sources of water pollution are the primary nonpoint sources.

Major Water Pollutants
and Their Sources

Some pollutants, such as iron or suspended particulates, may have very large natural sources, so that human activities only marginally increase concentrations. Other pollutants, such as synthetic pesticides, are produced only by humans. Most common impurities, however, are contributed by both human and natural processes. Therefore, except in extreme cases, human pollution is difficult to define quantitatively. Furthermore, in a complex system such as a drainage basin, a given pollutant may have many different sources, including urban runoff, industrial effluents, municipal sewage, and even atmospheric precipitation. Once in a stream system, pollutants are removed by deposition or broken down or combined with other impurities to make new substances, or their concentrations are increased by chemical or biological processes. If a known quantity of a substance is put in a waterway, the amount that leaves may be greater or less, depending on the nature of the substances and the processes acting on it. Under these circumstances, it is virtually impossible to determine accurately the relative contributions of pollutant sources or to predict future contamination levels with confidence.

The list of substances that are of concern in water-quality assessments is getting longer every year. In part, this expansion is the result of advances in the analytic capabilities of laboratories and the increasing availability of water-quality data. But still there are so many substances that could be measured in a water sample, and the analyses are so complex and costly, that usually only a few major or index pollutants are determined. Most analyses summarize pollution levels with parameters such as *total dissolved solids (TDS)* or *biochemical oxygen demand (BOD)*. The following sections describe, in general terms, some major classes of pollutants, their sources, human health effects, and impacts on aquatic ecology. These categories are somewhat arbitrary and are intended to indicate the diversity of the pollutants found in our waters, rather than provide exhaustive coverage of them. The major pollutants, their sources, and environmental effects are shown in Table 10.5 and described in the following paragraphs.

Disease-Causing Organisms Of the many living things found in natural or polluted waters, only a small fraction can be regarded as important pollutants from a human standpoint. These are the bacteria, viruses, and parasites that cause disease in humans and livestock. The earliest awareness of water pollution as an important human problem came from the recognition that water, particularly drinking water, transmits many diseases. Among the infectious diseases communicated largely through drinking water are cholera, typhoid fever, hepatitis, and dysentery, but many other less known diseases are also transmitted in this manner. Most of these are transmitted through human or animal wastes; hence sewage pollution is their primary source. Many different organisms are potentially dangerous, and just one individual in a large amount of water may be sufficient to cause infections.

Table 10.5 Major Water Pollutants, Their Sources, and Environmental Effects

Pollutant Type	Major Sources	Indicator Measurements	Major Effects on Aquatic Life	Major Effects on Human Use
Disease-causing agents	Sewage releases; municipal discharges, urban and agricultural runoff, feedlots	Coliform bacteria	Few	Health hazard for human consumption and swimming, shellfish contamination
Oxygen-demanding wastes	Sewage; municipal discharges, industrial discharges	Biochemical oxygen demand (BOD), chemical oxygen demand (COD)	Oxygen depletion Loss of diversity, elimination of intolerant organisms, fish kills	Unpleasant odor if severe
Plant nutrients	Agricultural runoff, municipal and industrial discharges	Phosphorus, nitrogen, ammonia	Increased algal growth resulting in elevated turbidity, sedimentation of organic matter, oxygen depletion (eutrophication)	Ammonia toxicity in infants
Suspended particulates	Runoff and erosion, municipal and industrial discharges	Suspended solids, turbidity	Reduced light penetration and reduced photosynthesis, alteration of stream-and lake-bottom environment by sedimentation	Filtration required before consumption; damage to turbines and other machinery
Dissolved solids	Natural sources (rock weathering), municipal and industrial discharges, urban and agricultural runoff	Total dissolved solids, pH, alkalinity	Loss of diversity, elimination of intolerant organisms, fish kills due to altered pH or toxicity of effect unless concentrations are high	Health effects at elevated concentrations of some substances

Toxic substances	Pesticides, industrial activities, runoff from developed areas	Bioassays, analyses for specific chemicals	Bioaccumulation, toxicity for some organisms	Health hazards for consumption of water or organisms that concentrate toxins
Heat	Thermal electric power plants, industrial discharges, deforested stream banks	Temperature	Oxygen depletion causing loss of diversity, elimination of intolerant organisms, increase in warm-water species	None
Radioactivity	Natural sources, mining radioactive wastes	Radioactivity	None except in extreme situations	None except in extreme situations; fear of radiation may limit use

The presence of *coliform bacteria* is used as an indicator of the possibility of contamination by infectious organisms. Coliform bacteria live in great numbers in human and animal digestive systems. They are not dangerous in themselves, but their presence indicates the possibility that disease-causing organisms could also inhabit the water. Chlorination of public water supplies has eliminated these diseases from common occurrence in the developed nations, although disease outbreaks occasionally occur. In areas without such water treatment, as in most developing nations, water-borne diseases are a major problem. For example, it is estimated that billions of cases of diarrhea occur annually in Africa, Asia, and Latin America, resulting in perhaps 3 to 5 million deaths each year, mostly children (Meybeck et al. 1989; United Nations Environment Program 1997; World Resources Institute 1996). Many other diseases are transmitted via organisms such as snails or insects that live in water, schistosomiasis and malaria being well-known examples. However, infection results from insect bites, skin contact, and other means rather than ingestion; hence, these organisms are not usually considered components of water quality.

Plant Nutrients Although aquatic plants need many different substances for growth, algal growth requires just a few key substances, primarily nitrogen and phosphorus. Nitrogen is available to plants in the form of nitrate (NO_3), nitrite (NO_2), and ammonia (NH_4), while phosphorus is available mostly as phosphate (PO_3). In natural systems, nitrogen is derived primarily from the decay of plant matter. Phosphorus, on the other hand, is made available by the weathering of phosphorus-bearing rocks and enters streams either directly in groundwater or surface water or through decay of organic matter. Nitrogen and phosphorus are found in large quantities in sewage, and they enter waterways by the decay of organic particulates and by being dissolved in sewage treatment plant effluent. Runoff from urban and rural areas is also an important source. The close association between intensive agriculture and nitrogen in streams is clearly seen in Figure 10.10. Water in densely populated areas, such as the mid-Atlantic states, also has high nitrogen concentrations, which is derived from a combination of agricultural and urban sources.

When one or both of these nutrients are the factors limiting algal growth, their introduction stimulates rapid algal growth, also called blooms. The algae then die and decay, releasing still more nutrients and adding to BOD. In swift-flowing rivers, this extra BOD loading is a relatively minor problem, but in sluggish rivers and standing bodies of water serious problems can result. One effect of increased nutrients in surface water is *eutrophication*, which is the process whereby a water body ages over geologic time, with the water becoming progressively shallower and nutrient rich. In North America, eutrophic lakes typically support species such as carp and catfish, whereas geologically young *oligotrophic* lakes support pike, sturgeon, whitefish, and other species that require higher oxygen levels or cooler temperatures. In summer, lakes commonly develop a *stratification*, or layering, which prevents mixing of bottom and surface waters. If algal blooms occur, the algae settle to deeper waters, where decay depletes oxygen and deep-water fish suffocate. The absence of oxygen can also cause anaerobic decomposition of organic matter on the bottom, which produces unpleasant odors and may make water unsuitable for drinking or affect the aesthetic quality of a river or lake.

In drinking water, phosphorus is not a problem because it is an essential nutrient that humans require, and we generally ingest far more in food than in drinking water. Nitrate and nitrite, however, do present health hazards. When ingested in high concentrations, these lead to methemoglobinemia, in which the blood's ability to carry oxygen is impaired. In addition, ingestion of nitrate or nitrite may lead to the formation of compounds called nitrosamines, some of which have been found to cause cancer in animals, but the carcinogenic potential in humans is unknown.

In much of the central United States as well as parts of Canada and Europe, application of large amounts of nitrogen fertilizers to cropland has resulted in elevated nitrate concentrations in both surface and groundwater. This is particularly a problem for homes and communities that depend on this water for drinking. Surveys of rural residential wells in the central United States have revealed that in many areas 10 to 50 percent of wells have nitrate concentrations approaching the maximum allowable concentration of 10 ppm, and in some areas 20 percent or more have nitrates above

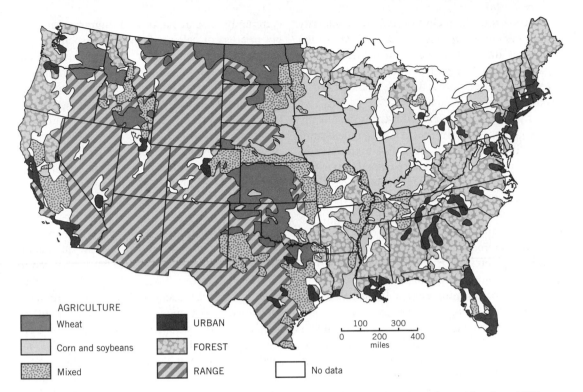

AGRICULTURE

◼ Wheat

▢ Corn and soybeans

▦ Mixed

◼ URBAN

▦ FOREST

▨ RANGE

▢ No data

100   300
0   200   400
miles

Figure 10.10 Nitrogen concentrations in U.S. streams. *Source:* From Smith, Alexander and Lanfear, 1993.

10 ppm. The problem is less severe in most developing countries because fertilizer application rates are lower, but nitrate levels are climbing worldwide as use of nitrogen fertilizer increases.

Oxygen-Demanding Wastes Organic matter is the pollutant that places the greatest burden on a stream or lake as a pollution assimilator. Particulate organics are small bits of living or dead and decaying plant and animal matter. They are broken down by bacteria in the water, which use dissolved oxygen in the process. The most widely used measure of oxygen-demanding wastes is biochemical oxygen demand (BOD). BOD indirectly measures the amount of dissolved oxygen that is required to decompose the organic matter. A stream with a high BOD loading will consequently have a low concentration of dissolved oxygen (DO). The depletion of oxygen and increased nutrient levels are primarily responsible for the ecological degradation of rivers and lakes.

Organic matter is derived from surface runoff, internal production by algae, agricultural wastes, various industries, especially food processing and paper pulp, and sewage. The relative contributions of these sources vary from one area to another, but historically large point sources have been responsible for the most severe cases of organic particulate pollution. These point sources include feedlots, pulp mills, sewage systems, and other major dischargers. In areas where treatment facilities have been installed and upgraded, such as most industrialized countries, these sources have been reduced in importance. In the United States, this most noticeable form of pollution has been significantly reduced since the 1950s. As a result, water quality has significantly improved in many streams both large and small, and fish populations have recovered dramatically.

Sediment By weight, sediment is the largest pollutant in our waters. It is measured along with organic particles as total suspended particulates in a water sample, and it consists of particles of soil and rock that are eroded from the land and from stream beds. Erosion is a natural process, and the movement of sediment through a river system helps to maintain the ecological integrity of that system. However, the accelerated erosion of agricultural lands and erosion associated with urban construction and similar activities have greatly increased the sediment loads of many streams.

For practical purposes, sediment is chemically inert and thus has little direct effect on the chemical quality of water. However, fine-textured sediment plays a role in the transport and deposition of trace substances in water. In this way, it can carry pesticides and nutrients from agricultural fields, as well as a wide range of harmful substances contained in urban runoff. Most sediment is easily filtered from water in drinking-water treatment plants, and thus health hazards associated with sediment pollution are minimal.

The major harmful effects of sediment are economic, including damage to turbines and pumps, and reduction in reservoir capacity as sediment is deposited in impoundments. In extreme cases, sediment also may reduce stream channel capacity and contribute to flooding. Excessive sediment loads also modify stream habitats and restrict fish reproduction. High sediment loads associated with logging activities have contributed to the decline of salmon populations in the Pacific Northwest of North America, for example (see Issue 9.1). Some fish are sensitive to chronic high suspended sediment loads, which clog gills, restrict vision, or otherwise interfere with normal activity. There are also a few examples, especially in the western United States, where reduction in sediment loads by reservoir construction has caused detrimental effects downstream, notably erosion in the Grand Canyon and on West Coast beaches.

Dissolved Solids Dissolved solids form a major part of the load of most rivers, and they include many different elements and compounds. Most of these are derived from rock weathering and soil leaching, and thus geographic variations in concentrations are often attributable to varying bedrock types. Hardness ($CaCO_3$ and related minerals) is a major indicator of dissolved minerals. Calcium carbonate is a good example of a substance derived from natural sources, primarily from marine sedimentary rocks. In areas of limestone bedrock, such as Florida and many areas of the central United States and Canada, hardness is

commonly several hundred milligrams per liter, but in areas of calcium-poor rocks, such as New England and the Canadian Shield, values of 5 to 25 mg/liter are typical. For most trace minerals, regional variations are attributable to natural factors, whereas local "hot spots" are almost always human-made. Many different inorganic minerals are found in water, and it is impossible to make generalizations about their effects on humans or the environment. Many minerals are essential nutrients in trace quantities, but virtually all have detrimental effects at higher concentrations.

Toxic Substances A wide variety of substances that are harmful at very low concentrations (parts per million or less) are introduced to surface and groundwater. Although many of these substances occur naturally, we are most concerned about those that are introduced by human activity. Among the most troublesome are organic chemicals. They include herbicides, insecticides, and a wide variety of industrial organic chemicals such as benzene, carbon tetrachloride, polychlorinated biphenyls (PCBs), chloroform, and vinyl chloride. In addition, oils and grease can be included in this category, although they are usually found at higher concentrations than the other compounds.

These toxic substances are a major concern because many of them are toxic, carcinogenic, or both. They can be dangerous if present in only parts per billion or parts per trillion, particularly if they are accumulated in tissues or biomagnified in the food chain. Adverse health effects may not be observed until many years after exposure; consequently, there is great uncertainty as to what substances are dangerous and at what levels of exposure. Many more years of intensive research are needed to understand the hazards associated with these substances.

In surface waters, toxic substances are usually diluted so that they are present only in very low concentrations, generally parts per trillion. They are found in higher concentrations in fine-grained sediments in many waterways, with runoff sources being particularly important. In groundwater, dilution is very slow and much higher concentrations have been found than in most surface waters.

Many metals are toxic to plants and animals at relatively low concentrations and so are a concern in surface water and groundwater. Some are also essential nutrients to certain organisms. Among the metals that are often identified as important toxic pollutants in water are arsenic, barium, cadmium, chromium, cobalt, copper, lead, manganese, mercury, nickel, silver, and zinc. The degree of health hazard associated with these metals depends on whether they are chemically or physically available to organisms. Most metals are relatively insoluble in water and tend to become associated with particulates. Metals bound to particulate matter are easily removed by filtration, and thus are less available to organisms than are dissolved forms. The solubility of most metals in water is affected by pH, with solubility increasing as pH decreases. Acid precipitation may therefore increase problems of metal pollution, as acidic water dissolves metals in soil and sediments and causes them to enter the food chain.

Heat Electric power generation, petroleum refining, and many other industrial processes depend on the production and dissipation of large amounts of thermal energy—heat. For example, typical efficiency levels in electric generation are 32 to 36 percent. This means that about a third of the energy produced at a power plant is converted to electricity, and the other two-thirds must be dissipated as heat, usually in condensing steam. Any industrial process that requires heating and cooling will produce waste heat, and water is the most effective means of dissipating that heat. Depending on the amount of heat discharged and the rate at which it is dispersed by receiving waters, the temperature increase of the water may be as much as 10° to 20°C, though usually it is less. Another cause of *thermal pollution* in streams is the removal of vegetation that shades the water. This is particularly severe when an area is deforested. Stream corridors, where shade trees are left along the streambanks, are effective in preventing this pollution.

Heat in water has little direct effect on humans; warm water may be less pleasant to drink, but it is no less safe. The primary detrimental effects of thermal pollution are to fish, because most fish have critical temperature ranges required for survival, and these ranges differ among species. Spawning and egg development in lake trout, walleye, and northern pike, for example, are inhibited at temperatures above 48°F (9°C). Smallmouth bass and perch will not grow at temperatures above about 84°F (29°C), whereas growth of catfish is possible at temperatures as high as 93°F (34°C). In some cases, thermal discharges have benefited commercial fisheries by making otherwise cool water suitable for species that require warmer temperatures, but generally the effects are negative. Equally important is the effect of temperature on dissolved oxygen concentrations. The amount of oxygen that can be dissolved in water decreases with increasing tem- perature; water at 92°F (33°C) holds only about half the oxygen that water at 32°F (0°C) will hold. At high temperatures, then, increased rates of bacterial activity put more demand on oxygen supplies just when saturation concentrations are low. Many fish kills are caused by a combination of high BOD and high temperatures, particularly in summer.

Radioactivity Radioactivity, or the emission of particles by decay of certain radioactive substances, is a subject of public concern today. Ionizing radiation, consisting primarily of alpha, beta, and gamma radiation, is derived from many natural and human-made sources. The sievert is a unit that describes all ionizing radiation in terms of the biological damage it causes. On the average, Americans receive a dosage of about 100 millisieverts (0.1 sievert) per year from natural sources and another 80 millisieverts from artificial sources, primarily diagnostic X rays. The radiation from natural sources comes mostly from cosmic radiation (the sun) and from terrestrial materials (rocks, bricks, and concrete). An average of about 15 to 20 millisieverts come from radioactive potassium-40 found in bone tissue.

Radioactive substances in water are derived primarily from rock weathering, particularly by groundwater. The greatest amount of radioactivity in water is from potassium-40, but this source is probably only about 1/100 of the amount derived from food sources. However, some substances tend to become concentrated in bone tissues, particularly strontium-90, radium-226, and radium-228. In certain areas, these isotopes occur in groundwater, and if the concentration is high, an increase in the risk of bone cancer is possible. In areas of mining or industrial operations that process rocks with high radionuclide content, local radioactive water pollution may occur. In general, however, surface waters dilute these substances to the extent that concentrations are lower than those found in natural groundwater.

Groundwater Pollution Problems

Groundwater pollution is a serious problem in industrialized countries, and stems from municipal and industrial sources as well as from agriculture. Groundwater represents a large storage of water that is replaced very slowly. Whereas typical flow velocities for rivers are measured in meters per second, groundwater is likely to flow at rates of meters per day to meters per year. In most cases, flow distances are quite large, and it takes decades to millennia to replace contaminated water in an underground reservoir, if it can be replaced at all. This has two important consequences. First, once an aquifer is contaminated, it is lost for an indefinite period of time, except for uses not affected by the contaminants. Second, the contamination being discovered in wells today may result from pollutant discharges that occurred years in the past, and chemicals dumped today may not show up in well water for years to come. Not only are flow rates low, but the purification processes that remove particulates and bacteria are not as effective against human-made chemicals such as chlorinated hydrocarbons. Such chemicals as seep into an aquifer are likely to remain there with little or no dilution or degradation.

Many different sources of groundwater contamination exist, including municipal and industrial landfills, industrial impoundments, household septic systems, and waste disposal wells (Fig. 10.11). Municipal and industrial landfills are used to dispose of nearly every kind of waste imaginable, most of it relatively harmless but some of it quite dangerous. Industrial landfills may receive much greater volumes of toxic materials, and most of the sites that pose the most immediate threat to human health are those in which industrial wastes have been discarded on the ground or in landfills. Municipal landfills, of which there are thousands in the United States, also receive hazardous wastes from household, commercial, and industrial sources, though generally in small quantities. In the past, landfills were often located on whatever land was available rather than in areas that were geologically suited for waste disposal. Until recently, little care has been taken to see that *leachate* (liquid seeping out of the base of a landfill) does not percolate down to an important aquifer.

Industrial impoundments such as storage lagoons and tailings ponds are another important cause of groundwater pollution. Lagoons may

Figure 10.11   A toxic waste lagoon near the Shenandoah River, Virginia. Sources of groundwater contamination include septic tanks, landfills, lagoons, and waste-disposal wells.

Figure 10.12   Waste-settling lagoon at a paper mill in Minnesota. Paper manufacturing is a major source of water pollutants.

be used to temporarily store liquid wastes prior to disposal, reprocessing, or other use (Fig. 10.12). If they are unlined, as most are, liquid wastes can percolate into groundwater. In still other cases, wastes may be intentionally pumped into the ground as a disposal method. In confined, unusable aquifers this can be a safe practice, but leakage may occur. Tailings ponds, or impoundments used to trap mining debris, sometimes cause severe contamination with acids or metals.

Household septic tanks with leach fields are used for sewage disposal in about one-quarter of all homes in the United States. Properly designed, constructed, and maintained septic systems are effective water purifiers, returning clean water to the ground and nutrients to the soil. They are generally used when population density is relatively low, such as in rural or low-density suburban areas.

WATER POLLUTION CONTROL

Because of the many different sources and kinds of water pollution, control is a complex and expensive problem. Wastewater discharged by point sources can be treated by a variety of methods, but nonpoint sources must be controlled through land management.

Wastewater Treatment

Sewage treatment methods include primary, secondary, and tertiary techniques. *Primary treatment* consists of removal of solids by sedimentation, flocculation, screening, and similar methods. Primary treatment may remove about 35 percent of BOD, 10 to 20 percent of plant nutrients, and none of the dissolved solids. *Secondary treatment* removes organic matter and nutrients by biological decomposition, using methods such as aeration, trickling filters, and activated sludge (Fig. 10.13). It became widely used

Figure 10.13 Activated sludge tanks at a sewage treatment plant in Wisconsin.

in the United States during the 1960s. This treatment Kremoves about 90 percent of BOD, 30 to 50 percent of nutrients, and perhaps 5 percent of dissolved solids. *Tertiary methods* have only come into widespread use in the last decade or so, and still only a small proportion of communities have tertiary treatment. There are many methods, and they vary considerably in their effectiveness, but generally they remove 50 to 90 percent of nutrients and dissolved solids. Treatment methods for industrial wastewater are usually specific to the type of wastes being considered. Many industries discharge into municipal sewage systems rather than treat wastes on site, although pretreatment is often required.

Prior to the early twentieth century, little was done to control water pollution in most of the world. The problem of contamination of water supplies by sewage was identified in Europe in the seventeenth century, but the solutions were to change drinking-water supplies rather than to try reducing pollution. Beginning around 1900 and growing rapidly by the 1940s, wastewater treatment was instituted in larger cities in the industrialized world. In the United States, a few states had water pollution control laws by the 1940s, and the 1948 Federal Water Pollution Control Act provided impetus for construction of treatment plants. By 1960, however, only about 36 percent of the population served by sewers had wastewater treatment, and this was almost exclusively primary treatment. The remaining 64 percent were served by sewer systems with no treatment at all.

Awareness of water pollution problems increased dramatically in the 1960s, especially in the industrialized world. In the United States, for example, new federal laws in 1961 and 1965 greatly increased nationwide efforts at pollution control, mostly by providing funds for construction of treatment plants. By 1970, over 85 million Americans were served by treatment plants, or 52 percent of those with sewer systems. The most ambitious and comprehensive law to date, the Federal Water Pollution Control Act of 1972 and its amendments of 1977, 1980, and 1987 now form the basis of our nationwide pollution control efforts. By the early 1990s, over 60 percent of the population was served with secondary sewage treatment plants, double the portion with such treatment in 1980 (Issue 10.2).

In the industrialized world, virtually all urban residents are served by sewage collection and treatment systems of some kind. In Japan, Canada, the United States, and western Europe, secondary treatment systems are most common. But in the developing world, urban sewage systems are not universal. In Latin America, about 80 percent of the urban population is served by sewage collection systems, in Asia about 60 percent have such service, and in Africa the figure is only 53 percent (World Resources Institute 1996). Sewage collection does not necessarily mean treatment—in poor countries the sewage is typically piped to rivers or the sea untreated. In these less industrialized regions of some countries, a large percentage of the population lives in rural areas, where sanitation systems are uncommon.

Nonpoint Pollution Control

Nonpoint sources are the most difficult to control. In rural areas, they consist primarily of suspended and dissolved solids, nutrients, and pesticides contained in runoff, either dissolved or in particulate form. In agricultural areas, control of overland flow can do much to limit these sources because soil eroded by water often contains harmful pollutants such as pesticides and nutrients. As you recall from Chapter 6, such management practices are often difficult to establish or enforce. In urban areas, runoff from streets, parking lots, and similar surfaces usually contains large amounts of suspended solids and BOD as well as many toxic substances. In cities with combined storm and sanitary sewers, runoff is routed through the treatment system, but during storms the treatment plant cannot handle the increased flow, so that sewage and runoff are discharged in an untreated form. Sewage discharge has generally been regarded as the more serious problem, and most cities have converted or are converting to separate sanitary and storm sewer systems. This eliminates the problem of untreated sewage discharges but does little to solve the problem of urban runoff pollution, as stormwater is discharged directly without treatment. In newly developing areas, storage basins can be incorporated into stormwater systems to retain runoff temporarily or permanently, and these may be useful in reducing runoff pollution. But in developed areas the control of urban runoff is usually prohibitively expensive.

Pollution Prevention

The cost of pollution control becomes a major problem as the amount of control increases. As a general rule, controlling the worst pollution is relatively cheap per unit of pollutants removed. But as pollution control requirements become more stringent, the costs of cleaner water increase. For example, consider the conventional technologies used in primary, secondary, and ter-

tiary treatment described earlier. Tertiary treatment using carbon-absorption filters is much more expensive than primary treatment using a settling tank. In the industrialized countries, by the late 1980s demands for pollution control remained strong, but costs were beginning to escalate. In the United States, for example, the goal of "fishable and swimmable" water by 1985 remained in place, but the costs of achieving that goal were so great that it ceased to be practical using conventional technologies.

As a result of this and other factors, a new approach known as *pollution prevention* emerged. This approach focuses on activities that reduce pollutants in the first place, rather than on removing them from wastewater before it is discharged to the environment. The idea of pollution prevention first caught on in industries which, faced with requirements that they comply with strict pollution standards, sought ways to minimize the cost of compliance. When engineers and plant managers started to look at alternative ways of dealing with these compliance problems, they found that modifying their practices so as to stop generating pollutants in many cases cost much less than removing pollutants from their effluents.

As the pollution prevention idea caught on, it came to be recognized as the best, and perhaps the only practical, means for achieving higher levels of water quality than could be reached with conventional approaches. Government regulatory agencies began to promote voluntary pollution prevention as an alternative to more stringent regulations, and corporations learned that other benefits were to be gained from voluntary actions to reduce pollution (see Chapter 15). The result has been a significant number of environmental success stories in areas such as paper, chemicals, and general manufacturing.

Much of the impetus for pollution prevention came from forces that only affected the business sector most strongly, such as consumer demand or government regulatory pressure. These forces are less significant for polluters in the government sector, and reduction of pollution from municipal sewage has been much less. Pollution prevention in municipal systems starts with the individual and thus has been limited to those individuals who have chosen to modify their practices on their own, regardless of what their neighbors do. Positive results have been much less visible.

ISSUE 10.2: Water Pollution Legislation in the United States

The Federal Water Pollution Control Act of 1972 (now called the *Clean Water Act*) established a federal goal of making all waters clean enough to fish and swim in by 1985. It contains provisions for establishing effluent standards for industries and municipal treatment plants, and for comprehensive local planning to reduce both point and nonpoint pollution. Municipal plants were required to achieve secondary treatment by 1977 and "best practicable" technology by 1983. Similarly, industries were required to use the best practicable technology by 1977 and the best available technology by 1983. All point discharges are required to obtain discharge permits under a National Pollutant Discharge Elimination System (NPDES), which was originally administered by the EPA, but today most states have taken over the permitting process. Permits allow discharges only within limits established by the permitting agency.

The actual conditions for issuance of permits are determined primarily by the permitting agency, and these conditions have changed with changing public opinion and availability of funds. During the 1970s, for example, the Environmental Protection Agency was relatively rigorous in enforcing compliance with effluent standards, although deadlines for compliance were frequently postponed. During the 1980s, however, standards in some areas were relaxed, because some argued that water quality was already good enough or that improved treatment would not result in significant improvement of water quality. One example of this administrative modification of the law came in 1982, when the EPA announced that it would no longer require secondary treatment for certain cities (including New York) discharging wastes into coastal waters.

The importance of nonpoint sources (particularly when major point sources are controlled) is recognized by the Clean Water Act, which requires the establishment of local or regional farming to reduce nonpoint pollution. Plans vary from one area to another depending on the nature of the sources and local needs. Most plans include provisions for runoff and sediment control at construction sites, as well as guidelines for nonpoint pollution control in new developments. In some urbanized areas, measures such as street sweeping were instituted. As with the measures for controlling point sources, local plans are subject to modification by the agencies concerned, depending on local needs and desires, because of the technical difficulty of controlling nonpoint pollution. As a result, actual implementation of the guidelines of the federal law is highly variable from place to place and time to time.

In 1977, the Clean Water Act Amendments were passed. One of the more important achievements of this law was to focus government regulatory efforts on toxic substances rather than on the more conventional pollutants such as BOD or nutrients. Under this law, EPA has established industry-specific effluent limits for many common toxic substances and has developed a system of monitoring certain index contaminants as a means to reduce monitoring costs.

During the 1980s, most of the efforts at water pollution control were led by the states, as the Reagan administration sought to reduce the federal role in this area. The administration of pollutant discharge permit programs was turned over to state regulatory agencies, which in many cases enforce regulations that are more stringent than federal criteria. Efforts at reducing point-source pollution from sewage continued, and many new

Quality, Quantity and the Water-Supply Problem

Relations Between Quality and Quantity

Although many significant improvements have been made in water quality in the last few decades, especially in wealthier countries, water quality remains a critical problem worldwide. In

wealthy countries, ecological impacts of water pollution are the focus of most public attention to water issues. Restoring degraded ecosystems, especially fisheries, and protecting endangered species are the topics in the headlines and on regulators' agendas. Drinking-water quality still serves to galvanize public opinion and draw attention to water pollution problems, however. In

treatment facilities were built. In 1987, the U.S. Congress overrode a Reagan veto of a bill continuing federal subsidy of these efforts and passed the Water Quality Act.

The Water Quality Act recognizes and reiterates the need for strong regulatory control of nonpoint sources of toxics and other pollutants. The act continues the effluent standards based on designated use through the NPDES permit process. The legislation also tightens the control on point-source polluters and provides additional money for control of nonpoint sources through state grants. The Water Quality Act also strengthens the protection of specialized environments like estuaries and wetlands. Finally, the Water Quality Act of 1987 instructs states to establish clean water strategies and assessments of nonpoint sources of pollution.

As a result of these and other legislative efforts, ter quality has improved in many areas. By 1978, virtually all sewer systems had treatment, with most of these having secondary treatment or better. Water-quality violation rates for some pollutants have declined markedly in major rivers. The Cuyahoga River, near Cleveland, Ohio, once notorious for catching fire repeatedly in the 1950s and 1960s, is no longer flammable. Lake Erie, pronounced dead by environmentalists in the 1960s, has shown some signs of improvement. But generally progress has not been as dramatic as had been hoped. The regulations were effective in reducing industrial discharges in many areas, and industries made substantial investments in pollution control equipment. Municipal pollution control efforts depended on both local revenues and federal assistance, and often a lack of funds or political disputes delayed treatment plant construction. For example, a 1980 estimate by the EPA indicated that 63 percent of the major municipal treatment facilities were not in compliance with the 1977 deadline for secondary treatment (Council on Environmental Quality 1980). Difficulties experienced by municipalities in meeting federal requirements have led to some relaxation of the regulations.

Under the 1977 Clean Water Act Amendments, states classified their streams according to the uses they should support, including fish propagation, fish maintenance, drinking, swimming, and boating. A 1994 survey of water quality indicated that in that year, of a total of over 615,800 stream miles assessed, 57 percent had water quality that fully supported the designated uses, 29 percent had quality that partially supported the designated uses, and the water quality in 14 percent of the miles provided no support of the designated uses (Council on Environmental Quality 1994). An earlier study also found that between 1972 and 1982, 84 percent of total assessed river miles had maintained existing quality, 13 percent had improved in quality, and quality was degraded in 3 percent (General Accounting Office 1986).

Throughout the 1980s, construction of improved treatment facilities continued, resulting in locally improved water-quality conditions. The total population served by secondary treatment or better is now 127 million, while fewer than 2 million people are still relying on direct discharges of untreated sewage into the nation's lakes and streams (U.S. Environmental Protection Agency 1988). Although on a per capita basis we are discharging less, the nation is still growing. Improvements in some areas are offset by degradation in less developed areas. In addition, the overwhelming importance of nonpoint sources and the difficulty in controlling them are a major barrier to further water-quality improvements.

1996 the U.S. Congress passed legislation (The Safe Drinking Water Act Amendments) that would require drinking-water purveyors to inform their customers, once each year, of the presence of regulated substances in their water even if concentrations were below levels considered hazardous. Such notices would stimulate more widespread public awareness of water-quality issues, and it is hoped that this awareness would lead to improvements in water quality.

Water-supply limitations in most wealthy countries are increasing. In the United States for example, population is increasing at about 1 percent per year, so that even if we did not increase individual water use our total withdrawals for domestic consumption would increase. More and more people are moving to the Sunbelt states which are often more arid environments, yet they still want their dishwashers and green grass lawns. As a consequence, per capita water use in public systems is increasing at about 0.7 percent per year (U.S. Bureau of the Census 1995). In Florida water demand has risen to the point that Tampa is considering building a desalinization plant to meet its drinking water needs.

How can we remove more water from rivers and thus reduce their capacity to dilute and remove wastes, while at the same time demanding lower pollutant concentrations? The answer, of course, is to reduce our output of pollution. But advanced sewage treatment is expensive, and publicly owned treatment works have been slow to respond to calls for reduced discharges. Instead, industrial and agricultural water users have been forced to reduce their use of water. In the case of U.S. industry, pressure to reduce water pollution under the 1972 Clean Water Act ultimately led to industries reducing withdrawals by replacing once-through systems with processes to clean and recycle water within the plant, or dispose of wastes in some other way such as through a municipal sewage treatment plant or conversion to solid form and disposal in a landfill. The decline in industrial use in the early 1980s was also partly caused by the slump in heavy industrial activity in that period. Agricultural uses also declined in the 1980s but for other reasons. Much water withdrawn for irrigation is taken from groundwater in arid and semiarid portions of the country. Groundwater overdrafts in these areas have significantly depleted supplies, and some areas have essentially run out of usable water. Increases in energy costs for pumping also reduced agricultural water use.

Water Quality in Developing Regions
Water-quality problems in most developing countries are a stark contrast to those in the wealthy world. While drinking water is a concern in wealthy countries, even the worst drinking-water problems there pale in comparison to those faced by the majority of residents in developing countries. In 1994, over 2.7 billion people, or nearly half of the world's population at that time, did not have access to sanitation services (Fig. 10.14). In less industrialized countries, only about one-third of the population has access to sanitation. New sewage systems are being built, but the number of

people served by these systems is growing slower than population, so that the number without access to sanitation services is increasing. The problem is especially acute in rural areas. Even where sewage is collected, most is discharged to surface waters untreated. Dissolved oxygen levels on average declined in low-income countries in the 1980s, reflecting an increase in sewage and industrial wastes discharged to rivers in that period. Fortunately, there has been steady improvement in making safe drinking water available in developing countries. In 1994 about 75 percent of people in less industrialized countries had access to safe drinking water, and that portion is increasing steadily (Fig. 10.15). Nonetheless, it is estimated

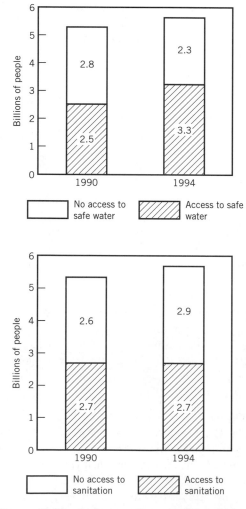

Figure 10.14 Access to safe water and sanitation in low-income countries. *Source:* World Bank, 1992, p. 46.

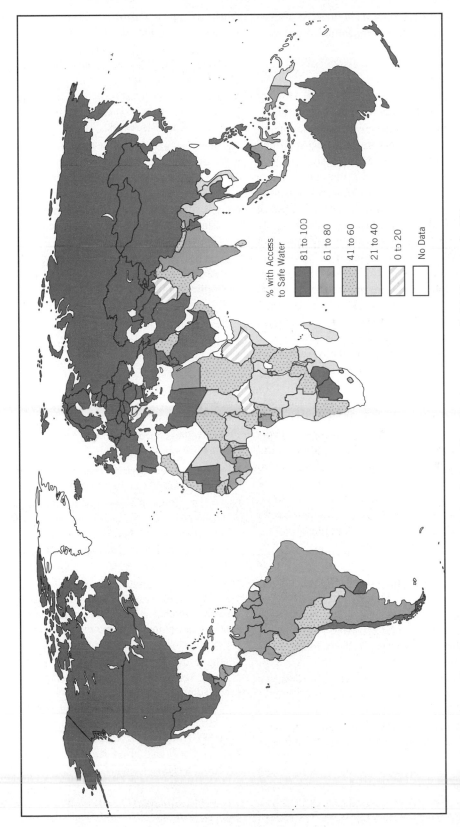

Figure 10.15 Spatial distribution of safe drinking water. Notice the large disparities in access to safe drinking water in Africa. *Source*: World Resources Institute, 1996.

that every year over 3 million children die of diarrhea caused by consuming contaminated water.

Conclusion

Clearly, the world's water problems are acute. Most of the world's available water supplies are already in use, and those that are not in use are found in places where population densities are very low. Water supplies in the world's megacities are a major source of concern. Poor sanitation resulting in waterborne diseases is still the leading cause of sickness and death worldwide. Water-supply scarcity and contamination are critically important in Africa, Asia, Latin America, and west Asia. Currently, about one-third of the world's population have moderate to severe problems with access to fresh water. It is estimated that in 2050, around 3 billion people will face severe water shortages (United Nations Environment Program 1997).

Opportunities for increasing the quantities of water available to people are few. The only means for making significant amounts of new water available on a renewable basis is construction of large dams to store runoff from wet seasons, making it available in dry seasons, but this option is limited by environmental, political, and financial constraints. As the world's population increases to nearly 10 billion in the next few decades, improving access to clean water can be achieved only through decreases in per capita consumption and increases in water reuse.

References and Additional Reading

Anon. 1993. Communicating water quality risk issues to the public. Stillwater, OK: Cooperative Extension Service, Division of Agriculture, Oklahoma State University, June 1993 (891), 7 p.

Council on Environmental Quality, 1980. *Environmental Quality, 1980*. Washington, DC: U.S. Government Printing Office.

_____. 1993. *Twenty-fourth Annual Report: Environmental Quality 24*. Washington, DC: U.S. Government Printing Office.

Crutchfield, S. R., L. Hansen, and M. Ribaudo. 1993. *Agricultural and Water Quality Conflicts: Economic Dimensions of the Problem*. Washington, DC: U.S. Department of Agriculture, Economic Research Service.

Gilpin, A. 1995. *Environmental Impact Assessment*. Hong Kong: Cambridge University.

Meade, R. H. 1995. *Contaminants in the Mississippi River, 1987–1992*. U.S. Geological Survey Circular 1133.

Meybeck, M., D. Chapman, and R. Helmer. 1989. *Global Freshwater Quality: A First Assessment*. Oxford: Basil Blackwell.

National Research Council. 1991. *Toward Sustainability: Soil and Water Research Priorities for Developing Countries*. Washington, DC: National Academy Press.

Opie, J. 1993. *Ogallala: Water for a Dry Land*. Our Sustainable Future series V.1. Lincoln: University of Nebraska Press.

Postel, S. 1989. *Water for Agriculture: Facing the Limits*. Worldwatch Paper no. 93. Washington, DC: Worldwatch Institute.

_____. 1992. *Last Oasis: Facing Water Scarcity*. New York: W. W. Norton.

Reisner, M. 1986. *Cadillac Desert: The American West and Its Disappearing Water*. New York: Viking Penguin.

Reuss, Martin, ed. 1993. *Water Resources Administration in the United States: Policy, Practice and Emerging Issues*. East Lansing: Michigan State University Press; Bethesda, MD: American Water Resources Association.

Rogers, P. 1993. *America's Water: Federal Roles and Responsibilities*. Cambridge, MA: MIT Press.

Sexton, R. 1990. *Perspectives on the Middle East Water Crisis: Analysing Water Scarcity Problems in Jordan and Israel*. London: Overseas Development Institute; Sri Lanka: International Irrigation Management Institute.

Shah, T. 1990. *Sustainable Development of Groundwater Resources: Lessons from Amrapur and Husseinabad Villages, India*. London, England: Overseas Development Institute; Colombo, Sri Lanka: International Irrigation Management Institute.

Smith, R. A., R. B. Alexander, and K. J. Lanfear. 1993. *Stream Water Quality in the Coterminous United States*—Status and Trends of Selected Indicators During the 1980's. National Water Summary 1990–91—Stream Water Quality, U.S. Geological Survey Water-Supply Paper 2400.

Steinhart, P. 1990. The water profiteers. *Audubon* 92(2): 38–51.

Stone, J. A., and D. E. Legg. 1992. Agriculture and the everglades. *Journal of Soil and Water Conservation* 47(3): 207–215.

United Nations Environment Program. 1997. *Global Environmental Outlook*. New York: Oxford University Press.

U.S. Bureau of the Census. 1997. *Statistical Abstract of the United States*. Washington, DC: U.S. Government Printing Office.

U.S. Department of Agriculture. 1989. *The Second RCA Appraisal: Soil, Water, and Related Resources on Nonfederal Land in the United States, Analysis of Condition and Trends*. Washington, DC: U.S. Government Printing Office.

U.S. Environmental Protection Agency. 1998. *Environmental Progress and Challenges: EPA's Update*. Washington, DC: U.S. Government Printing Office.

U.S. Geological Survey. 1998. ONLINE: *http://water.usgs.gov/*

U.S. General Accounting Office. 1986. *The Nation's Water: Key Unanswered Questions about the Quality of Rivers and Streams*. Washington, DC: U.S. Government Printing Office.

Valentine, J., and J. Carochi. 1993. Making a difference agencies can, will, do work together to solve nonpoint source pollution problems. *Journal of Soil and Water Conservation* 48: 401–406.

Water Resources Council. 1978. *The Nation's Water Resources, 1975–2000*. Washington, DC: U.S. Government Printing Office.

World Bank. 1992. *World Development Report, 1992: Development and the Environment*. New York: Oxford University Press.

World Resources Institute. 1996. *World Resources 1996–97*. New York: Oxford University Press.

For more information, consult our web page at *http://www.wiley.com/college/cutter*

STUDY QUESTIONS

1. What pollutants are most significant in agricultural areas? What pollutants are mostly derived from industrial sources? What pollutants are mostly derived from sewage?

2. Where does your drinking water come from? What are the most important sources, or potential sources, of pollution affecting that water? Where does your wastewater go? What pollutants are discharged as part of your wastewater? What are the likely effects of these pollutants on the receiving water body?

3. For a river near you, list all the significant uses of the waterway, including in-stream and off-stream uses. Which ones are most dependent on good water quality? Which ones are not affected by water quality?

4. Visit the home page of the U.S. Geological Survey (http://www.usgs.gov) and download information on streamflows for a stream near you. If possible, find a stream with at least a 30-year record. Make a graph of streamflow through time, and examine the fluctuations in water availability over time. How much is available in the driest year in the record, as compared to the average?

CHAPTER 11

THE AIR RESOURCE AND URBAN AIR QUALITY

INTRODUCTION

Although air quality may appear to be a recent issue to many people, some parts of the United States and Europe have been plagued with air pollution problems since the Industrial Revolution. *Pollution* is normally defined as a human-caused addition of impurities to the air. However, many of the same substances that humans release to the atmosphere, such as dust, also come from natural sources. While naturally-derived impurities are not really pollution, we must consider them as we attempt to manage environmental quality. Air pollution is a significant health hazard; acute episodes can cause death while lower, prolonged pollution levels also adversely affect health. Some of the more prolonged air pollution episodes can even be classified as disasters. For example, 20 people died in Donora, Pennsylvania, in 1948, and 4700 people lost their lives in London, England, in 1952 due to thick smog (Elsom 1987). In another example, nearly 6000 people were treated for "smog poisoning" in Tokyo during a 1970 oxidant and sulfate episode. All of these disasters were the result of a combination of meteorological conditions and excessive emissions of sulfur from coal burning. The situation today is not so dramatic, yet in some parts of the world we find that major pollution episodes require both industry and individuals to curtail their activities on a fairly regular basis.

On a global level, emissions of traditional air pollutants (sulfur dioxide and particulates) continue to rise, particularly in developing countries. Air pollution in many of the world's cities chronically plagues local residents from Auck-land to Zagreb. On the basis of one estimate, Shenyang and Xian, in the People's Republic of China, and Lahore, Pakistan, have the highest concentrations of sulfur dioxide and particulates, respectively, anywhere in the world (World Resources Institute 1996). Central Europe's air pollution is more dangerous and more widespread than in any other industrialized nation (Fig. 11.1). Bangkok exceeds the World Health Organization's health guidelines by a factor of ten! Mexico City, however, still retains its title as the world's worst air-polluted city. Excessive amounts of ozone, lead, and other contaminants spew forth daily from the city's 2.8 million vehicles and 36,000 factories, most of which have no pollution control equipment (Rohter 1989). In addition, emissions of carbon monoxide and other so-called greenhouse gases have far-reaching regional and global consequences, which will be discussed in Chapter 12.

AIR POLLUTION METEOROLOGY

Composition and Structure of the Atmosphere

The atmosphere is divided into several layers, based on temperature and gaseous content. The *homosphere*, or lower atmosphere, extends from sea level to an altitude of 50 mi (80 km) (Fig. 11.2). It is called the homosphere because the gases are highly diffused, so that they act as a single gas. These gases include nitrogen (78%), oxygen (21%), carbon dioxide (0.03%), and inert gases, such as argon, neon, helium, and krypton

Figure 11.1 Copsa Mica, Romania, a city where industrial air pollution contributes to an exceptionally high death rate.

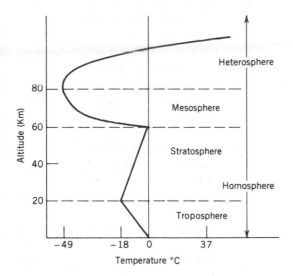

Figure 11.2 Temperature variation with altitude in the atmosphere. Most pollution is found in the troposphere, but some pollutants are carried to the stratosphere.

(less than 1%), and trace concentrations of several other substances.

The homosphere is further divided into the troposphere, stratosphere, and mesosphere. The *troposphere* is the layer in which humans live and extends from sea level to approximately 8–9 mi (13–14 km). In this layer, temperature steadily decreases with altitude, at an average rate of 3.5°F/1000 ft (6.4°C/km). This rate is called the *environmental lapse rate*.

The next layer is the *stratosphere*. Air temperatures gradually increase with altitude until they reach 32°F (0°C) at an altitude of about 30 mi (50 km). The protective ozone (O_3) layer is located in the stratosphere; this layer serves as a shield in protecting the earth's surface and the troposphere from harmful ultraviolet radiation.

The third layer of the homosphere is the *mesosphere*. Here, temperatures decrease with altitude, reaching a low of −120°F (−83°C) at approximately 50 mi (80 km) altitude.

Air pollutants are not confined to the lower parts of the troposphere. Certain concentrations of contaminants may have disastrous effects at higher altitudes by inducing global changes in climate. Similarly, ozone is considered a pollutant in the troposphere but becomes an essential gas necessary to protect human health in the stratosphere.

Role of Meteorology and Topography

Air pollution problems are the result of two factors: excessive emissions of pollutants and insufficient atmospheric dispersal. The first factor is the reason most cities have pollution problems and most rural areas do not. The second explains much of the variation in pollution problems from one city to another and why some very small cities have pollution problems as severe as those in major metropolitan regions.

Atmospheric dispersal of pollutants depends on air motion, both horizontal and vertical. Horizontal movements, or winds, carry pollutants away from cities. On windy days, the air in most cities is generally cleaner, and on calm days it is dirtier. Horizontal movements also contribute to vertical motions, which play a more direct role in air pollution. Despite the reputation that some cities have for being windy, average wind speeds do not vary much from place to place, and wind speed is not an important factor in explaining spatial variations in pollution.

Vertical movement in the atmosphere and low-pressure systems such as wave cyclones result from wind-generated turbulence and convection. Convection in turn is a result of differential heating of the lower layers of the atmosphere by sunlight, whereby the warmer layers become less dense and therefore rise, while cooler layers sink. Regional circulation patterns, characterized by areas of high and low pressure, can be seen as a larger-scale form of convection. The normal temperature pattern—cooler air at higher elevations—prevails when there is sufficient vertical mixing through the lower atmosphere. Sometimes, however, warmer air overlies cooler air, a condition called a *temperature inversion* (Fig. 11.3). An inversion keeps the atmosphere stable and thus inhibits vertical motions. Such inversions are the major meteorological factor in most air pollution problems.

Temperature inversions are caused by several different processes, including subsidence, radiation, and advection. A *subsidence inversion* develops when an air mass sinks slowly over a large area, as is common in a high-pressure cell. The atmosphere is compressed as the air mass sinks, and higher layers are warmed more than lower layers, resulting in an inversion. Subsidence inversions are formed over large areas (thousands of square kilometers), usually at relatively high altitudes, but can occur as low as 1000 m above the surface. The weather that produces them (slow-moving high-pressure cells) also produces sunny conditions and gentle winds, which contribute to photochemical smog formation and poor dispersal of pollutants. Subsidence inversions are responsible for most of the severe pollution episodes in large cities east of the Rocky Mountains and also contribute to problems in mountainous areas.

Radiation inversions also develop in clear, relatively calm weather, but, unlike subsidence inversions, they are a diurnal phenomenon. On clear nights, the ground radiates heat upward, and the absence of clouds allows this radiation to escape to the upper atmosphere and into space. The result is that the ground cools more than the atmosphere, thus cooling the air near the ground so that it becomes cooler than air higher up. Radiation inversions are fairly thin and usually temporary, but cold air drainage can cause them to thicken and thus slow their dispersal in the morning. In hilly or mountainous areas, the dense, cooler air near the ground flows downhill, accumulating in valleys and producing a large pool of cool air. In hilly areas, most cities are situated in the valley bottoms and thus the inversion traps the city's pollutants in the valleys. Valley walls prevent pollutants from dispersing horizontally, and the inversion keeps them from dispersing vertically. Valley inversions, often reinforced by subsidence inversions, are responsible for pollution problems in many cities in western North America, including Denver, Salt Lake City, Albuquerque, and Mexico City.

The third type of temperature inversion, the *advection inversion*, is a problem primarily on the West Coast of the United States, where local winds in the form of sea breezes blow off the Pacific Ocean. Before reaching land, air passes over the cold ocean current along the coast of California, and the lower layers of the air are cooled by contact with this water and thus become cooler than the air above. These inversions are usually of moderate thickness, from a few hundred to 1500 m or more. Los Angeles, San Diego, and, to a lesser extent, the San Francisco Bay area are bordered on the east by mountains that prevent pollutants from being dispersed inland. The particularly severe pollution problems of these cities are essentially the result of the presence of the mountains combined with very persistent advection inversions (Fig. 11.4).

In addition to dispersion, two other aspects of weather are important in understanding air pollution problems. These are sunlight and atmospheric humidity. Sunlight contributes to the formation of photochemical smog, and such smog is therefore

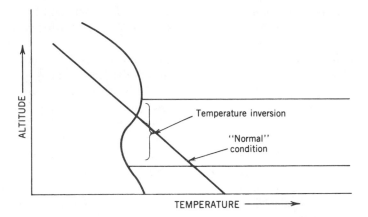

Figure 11.3 Temperature inversions. A temperature inversion consists of a layer in which temperature increases with altitude instead of decreasing. This temperature change prevents vertical circulation through the inverted layer.

Figure 11.4 Smog in Los Angeles, California. Per capita emissions in Los Angeles were low, but weather conditions limit dispersal of pollutants.

more severe on sunny days than on cloudy ones. Cities that have a lot of sunshine have more photochemical smog than do those in cloudy areas. High-altitude cities, such as Denver and most other cities in the Mountain West, have particularly intense sunlight because of the thinner atmosphere, and this is an important factor in their pollution problems. In areas of high sulfur oxide emissions, atmospheric humidity is more of a problem, because water and oxygen combine with sulfur oxides to form sulfates and sulfuric acid. In areas of high humidity, high sulfur emissions and foggy days can be more dangerous than dry days.

The various combinations of these factors make the problems of each metropolitan region different. Some cities suffer mostly from photochemical smog, whereas others have the greatest problems with particulates or carbon monoxide. Some cities have pollution episodes that last only a day or two, and others have much longer ones. In the Northeast United States, for example, pollution is usually the most severe in summer and fall, because that is when emissions are highest (high electrical demand and increased automobile usage) and subsidence inversions most frequent. In the Mountain West, winter is usually the time of the most persistent inversions, and thus pollution is worse. Local variations in wind direction or speed also contribute to variations in pollution. These regional and local differences in weather conditions are the major factor in explaining differences in pollution problems. They also influence the management of these pollution problems where local, regional, national, and sometimes international approaches to air pollution control are needed.

MAJOR POLLUTANTS

Air pollutants can come from both natural and nonnatural sources, with the latter being the most important in the United States. Some natural sources of pollutants include smoke from forest fires, hydrocarbons from coniferous trees and shrubs, dust from a variety of sources, volcanic eruptions, and pollen. Natural sources can be quantitatively significant, even dominant in some places. But in those areas with severe pollution—most urban areas—human-made (*anthropogenic*) sources are much more important, especially in the United States.

Anthropogenic sources of air pollutants are either stationary or mobile. *Stationary sources* are site specific and include stack emissions from refineries, smelters, electric power plants, and other manufacturing industries. *Mobile sources* are those that are not site specific. They include automobiles, motorcycles, buses, trucks, airplanes, trains, ships, boats, and off-highway vehicles.

Particulate Matter (PM)
Particulate matter includes any solid or liquid particles, such as soot, fly ash, dust, pollen, and various chemicals, and metals, such as arsenic, cadmium, and lead. Extremely small particles (less than 10 microns) are more likely to cause adverse health effects, such as respiratory distress and asthma. Other adverse health effects of particulates include the direct toxicity of some of the metals and chemicals and aggravation of cardiorespiratory diseases, such as bronchitis and asthma. Suspended particulates also have been linked to lung cancer. Aside from health, some of the negative effects involve the corrosion of metals and the soiling and discoloration of buildings and sculptures. More important, suspended particulates both scatter and absorb sunlight, thus reducing visibility. They also provide nuclei on which condensation can occur, which increases cloud formation.

Particulates are produced primarily by stationary sources, especially those industries that use coal as a fuel source, such as power plants, steel mills, and fertilizer plants. Construction activities, quarry operations, and solid waste disposal (burning) also contribute minor percentages of particulate emissions. Natural sources of suspended particulates are volcanic eruptions, forest fires, and wind erosion.

Sulfur Dioxide (SO_2)
Sulfur dioxide is a colorless gas with a strong odor. It is highly reactive in the presence of oxygen and moisture and forms sulfuric acid, a corrosive chemical. SO_2 stings the eyes and burns the throat. More important, SO_2 contributes to respiratory diseases, including bronchitis, emphysema, and asthma; chronic exposures can permanently impair lung functions. SO_2 also corrodes metals, discolors textiles, and speeds the deterioration of building material, especially stone and metals. Perhaps the most significant effect of SO_2 is its role in the formation of acid rain and the resulting damage and decrease in plant growth (see Chapter 12). SO_2 emissions are a direct result of burning sulfur-bearing fossil fuels and smelting sulfur-bearing metal ores. Certain industrial processes, notably petroleum refining, also contribute SO_2 to the atmosphere. The most significant natural source of SO_2 is volcanic eruptions.

Nitrogen Oxides (NO_x)
Nitrogen oxide emissions include nitrogen monoxide (NO) and nitrogen dioxide (NO_2). Nitrogen dioxide is a reddish-brown gas that aggravates respiratory diseases and increases susceptibility to pneumonia and lung cancer. NO_2 also causes paints and dyes to fade. There are, however, two effects of NO_x that cause it to be considered a major pollutant. The first is its crucial role as an ultraviolet light absorber in the formation of photochemical smog, or ground-level ozone. Second, and perhaps more important, NO_x is a factor in the formation of acid rain. Gaseous nitrogen is usually inert, but it combines with O_2 at high temperatures in internal combustion engines and furnaces to form NO_x. Thus, the primary sources of NO_x are power plants and motor vehicle exhaust.

Carbon Monoxide (CO)
Carbon monoxide (CO) is a tasteless, odorless, colorless gas. It combines with hemoglobin in the

blood, reducing its oxygen-carrying capacity and damaging some of the functions of the central nervous system. In small doses, CO impairs some mental functions as well, resulting in headaches and dizziness. In large doses, CO causes death.

Most CO pollution results from the incomplete combustion of carbon materials, including fossil fuels. There are some natural sources of CO, such as forest fires and decomposition of organic matter. Most of the anthropogenic CO emissions in urban areas are from transportation (mobile) sources, with an additional contribution from stationary sources, including industry and power plants.

Ozone (O_3) and Volatile Organic Compounds (VOCs)

Ozone is a photochemical *oxidant* that is the most important component of photochemical smog. In combination with volatile organic compounds (VOCs), NO_x, and sunlight, oxidants comprise the now famous Los Angeles-type smog. In simplified form, the process is as follows: sunlight causes NO_2 to break down into NO and monatomic oxygen (O). This O atom combines with O_2 to form O_3. In addition, VOCs, O_2, NO, and NO_2 interact to form both ozone and a class of compounds called peroxyacetyl nitrates (PAN), which, like ozone, are harmful photochemical oxidants.

Photochemical oxidants are eye and respiratory irritants, and prolonged exposures will aggravate cardiovascular and respiratory illnesses. Other effects include deterioration of rubber, textiles, and paints, and reduced visibility and vegetation growth. Leaves and fruit seem to be the most highly susceptible to oxidants, the effects of which result not only in injury but also in leaf drop and premature fruit. Since oxidants are produced in chemical reactions in the atmosphere, there is no direct source of emissions other than the sources for VOCs and NO_x.

Volatile organic compounds are released through the incomplete combustion of carbon-containing fuels and through the evaporation of fossil fuels from natural gas pipelines, gas tanks, and gas station pumps. Methane, propane, ethylene, and acetylene are some of the specific compounds generically called VOCs. Although many VOCs are suspected carcinogens, their most significant effect on air quality is their role in the formation of photochemical smog.

Most of the anthropogenic VOC emissions are from stationary industrial and fuel-combustion sources, with the remainder emitted by transportation. There are some natural sources of VOCs such as coniferous forests, but they are relatively insignificant in their contribution to urban pollution problems.

Lead (Pb)

Lead is a nonferrous, heavy metal that occurs naturally. In the atmosphere, lead occurs in the form of a vapor, dust, or aerosol. Lead acts as a cumulative poison in the human body, causing general weakness and impaired functioning of the central nervous system. High lead levels in children contribute to neurological damage and learning disabilities. Ingestion can lead to severe anemia and even death.

Lead is often added to high-octane gasoline to reduce engine knock. However, this practice was banned in the United States in the 1970s, so all gasoline is now unleaded. This is not true in other world regions. The primary sources of lead in the atmosphere are vehicle exhaust from lead additives in gasoline, lead mining and smelting, and manufacturing of lead products, such as batteries. Volcanic dust, the major natural source of lead, contributes less than 1 percent of total emissions. Another source of lead in the air is cigarette smoke.

URBAN AIR POLLUTION: THE GLOBAL CONTEXT

In evaluating pollution, we must distinguish between ambient concentrations (pollutants existing in the air) and emissions (pollutants discharged to the air). *Ambient data* measure the concentrations of pollution in the air that are recorded at specific monitoring locations. Using the appropriate health standards, ambient data indicate how close we are to achieving clean air. *Emissions data*, on the other hand, are actual estimates of the amount of pollutants released into the air from tailpipes or smokestacks. They illustrate how well the regulations on industrial and vehicular emissions are working. The distinction between ambient levels (the concentration of the pollutant in the air) and emissions levels (how much is coming out of tailpipe or smokestack) is an important one, especially when we consider air pollution control measures.

The World's Megacities

The world's population is now about 50 percent urban, and the proportion living in cities will continue to grow. Urbanization, though still greater in wealthy countries than in poor ones, is growing rapidly especially in the developing world. In 1995, there were 15 cities in the world with populations over 10 million; of these, 11 are in developing countries (World Resources Institute 1996). The megacities are places of significant, if not severe, air pollution, although such pollution problems also occur in hundreds, perhaps thousands, of smaller cities as well.

Monitoring Network In 1973, the World Health Organization (WHO) set up a global program to assist countries in monitoring air pollution. Shortly thereafter, the United Nations Environment Program (UNEP) set up its Global Environmental Monitoring System (GEMS), which now represents more than 175 sites in 75 cities in about 50 countries. More than one-third of the sites are in developing countries (Tolba et al. 1992). The six main pollutants of concern in urban areas are sulfur dioxide, nitrogen oxides, carbon monoxide, ozone, particulate matter, and lead. All of these are monitored by GEMS.

In many developing countries, however, indoor pollution is more of a health risk to millions of people who burn biomass fuels (wood, crop residues, dung) for stoves for cooking and heating. Women and children are most at risk from carbon monoxide and other contaminants (Cutter 1995). According to WHO, biomass burning is the major indoor air pollution problem in the world today.

Air-Quality Patterns Air pollution in urban areas is a local problem, although there are some transboundary considerations as we will see in the next chapter. This means that global estimates of total emissions by pollutant are difficult to quantify. However, we do know that industrialized countries accounted for 40 percent of the SO_2, 52 percent of the NO_x, 71 percent of CO, and 23 percent of PM emitted in 1991 (Tolba et al. 1992). Ambient levels are a little easier to quantify, and estimates suggest that nearly 900 million people living in urban areas, worldwide, are exposed to unhealthy levels of sulfur oxides, while more than a billion are exposed to particulate levels that are so high they are termed a health hazard.

In one of the first detailed assessments of air quality in urban areas, PM was found to be the most prevalent air pollutant in 17 of the 20 largest world cities (megacities) (UNEP/WHO 1992). Mexico City exceeds WHO concentrations for all pollutants by more than a factor of two for four of the six (ozone, SO_2, PM, and CO) (Table 11.1).

There is no systematic collection of information on the health risks and effects of air pollution in most of the megacities. Moreover, only 6 of the 20 have adequate assessment monitoring networks (United Nations Environment Program 1994). Suffice to say that as these cities increase in size, consume more energy, and use more automobiles, the level of air quality will deteriorate to dangerous levels unless air pollution control measures are implemented quickly.

Economic Development and Air Pollution

Despite the fact that the greatest quantities of pollutants are emitted by relatively wealthy countries, some of the worst air pollution problems are found in the developing world. For example, Mexico City has the worst air quality of any city in the world. Concentrations of suspended particulate matter in major Chinese cities are an order of magnitude higher than those in similar-sized cities in North America. Severe air pollution problems occur in Bangkok, Lahore, Delhi, Cairo, and many other smaller cities. Respiratory problems are a major cause of death in many cities in the developing world.

Why do many cities in developing countries have severe air pollution problems, even though per capita energy consumption levels are much lower? Several factors are important. First, cities are centers of industrial activity, and many cities in developing countries are experiencing rapid industrialization. In such countries, industrial development is often a higher priority than environmental protection, and so restrictions on industrial emissions are usually not as severe as in wealthy countries. In addition, the funds needed to install pollution control equipment are less readily available. Industrial emissions may therefore be substantial, even though the value of industrial output is usually not as great as in developed-world cities.

Table 11.1   Comparative Air Quality in the World's Megacities

City	SO_2	PM	Pb	CO	NO_x	O_3
Bangkok	L	S	M	L	L	L
Beijing	S	S	L	NA	L	M
Bombay	L	S	L	L	L	NA
Buenos Aires	NA	M	L	NA	NA	NA
Cairo	NA	S	S	M	NA	NA
Calcutta	L	S	L	NA	L	NA
Delhi	L	S	L	L	L	NA
Jakarta	L	S	M	M	L	M
Karachi	L	S	S	NA	NA	NA
London	L	L	L	M	L	L
Los Angeles	L	M	L	M	M	S
Manila	L	S	M	NA	NA	NA
Mexico City	S	S	M	S	M	S
Moscow	NA	M	L	M	M	NA
New York	L	L	L	M	L	M
Rio de Janeiro	M	M	L	L	NA	NA
São Paulo	L	M	L	M	M	S
Seoul	S	S	L	L	L	L
Shanghai	M	S	NA	NA	NA	NA
Tokyo	L	L	NA	L	L	S

S = *Serious problem, WHO guidelines exceeded by more than a factor of two.*
M = *Moderate to heavy pollution. WHO guidelines exceeded by up to a factor of two.*
L = *Low pollution. WHO guidelines normally met.*
NA = *No data available.*

Source: United Nations Environment Program/World Health Organization, 1992.

Second, even though cities in developing countries may have fewer automobiles per capita than the wealthy countries have, they still have quite a few. In most cases, this is a relatively recent phenomenon, and there has not been time or money to build urban highway networks like those in wealthier countries. As a result, traffic jams are nearly perpetual. Where it may take an hour or less to go 30 miles by auto in a U.S. city, much shorter journeys in developing-world cities often take two hours or more. In the process, cars are running continuously, emitting pollution in the stop-and-go traffic at much higher rates per mile than if they were moving faster. In addition, a higher proportion of vehicles are older, not equipped with the sophisticated pollution control devices required on cars in the United States, or not maintained as well.

URBAN AIR POLLUTION IN THE UNITED STATES

Air Pollution Monitoring in the United States

The U.S. government has identified several pollutants, called criteria pollutants, that are the focus of its air-quality management efforts. *Criteria pollutants* are those specific contaminants that adversely affect human health and welfare, for which the U.S. Environmental Protection Agency (EPA) has set *ambient air-quality* standards. *Primary standards* are designed to protect human health, and *secondary standards* are designed to protect human welfare (property and vegetation).

Legislative Mandates The original enabling legislation establishing air pollution control was the Clean Air Act, passed in 1963. Amendments to that legislation, the Air Quality Act of 1967 and the Clean Air Act Amendments of 1970, provided the framework for air resource decision making at both the regional and national level. The Clean Air Act Amendments of 1970 established standards for ambient air quality for the five major pollutants and provided timetables for achieving those standards.

The Clean Air Act Amendments of 1977 further refined the monitoring of air pollutants and clarified previous legislation. The 1963, 1967, 1970, and 1977 acts are collectively known as the *Clean Air Act.* The 1977 amendments required standard monitoring of the criteria pollutants and standardized reporting methods. Under this legislation, the EPA was to review the standards for criteria pollutants and establish deadlines for compliance with the standards. States were to meet the primary standards for SO_2, NO_x, and PM by 1981 and the primary standards for O_3 and CO by 1987.

The Clean Air Act expired in 1982. However, all the rules and regulations in effect at that time were still valid. In 1982, Congress passed a continuing resolution that provided appropriations and legal authority to the EPA to continue the air-quality program under the 1977 amendments. In essence, this placed the legislation on a hold status while it was debated in Congress. The Reagan administration wanted to relax standards as well as limit provisions for transboundary pollution problems, such as acid rain. In the fall of 1990, Congress finally passed a revision of the Clean Air Act (CAAA). The new law mandates a 50-percent reduction in sulfur dioxide emissions to help reduce acid rain. It also requires a phaseout of CFCs and other ozone-destroying chemicals in an effort to curtail stratospheric ozone depletion. To help alleviate urban air pollution problems, the new Clean Air Act requires lower vehicular emissions of nitrogen oxides (60% reduction) and hydrocarbons (40% reduction) and cleaner-burning gasoline, particularly in the country's smoggiest cities. The 1990 revisions call for a 90-percent reduction in the output of toxic emissions, particularly the 189 known toxic and cancer-causing chemicals. Provisions in the Clean Air Act on acid rain and other transboundary issues are discussed in the following chapter.

National Ambient Air-Quality Standards (NAAQS) Under the 1970 amendments, a national network of air-quality control regions (AQCRs) was established (Fig. 11.5). There are 247 AQCRs, with monitoring stations in 3000 counties in the United States (National Commission on Air Quality 1981). Data from each of these regions are stored in a national aerometric database, and monitoring is done on a county level. In 1979, problems with the frequency and accuracy of monitoring data led the EPA to standardize and regulate the monitoring network. State and local monitoring sites were thus incorporated into a national system, with consistent and uniform readings, including frequency, type of pollutant, and placement of monitoring stations (central city versus suburban location). Ambient air-quality data are submitted to the EPA's Aerometric Information Retrieval System (AIRS) where trends (10-year and 5-year) in air quality are monitored.

Primary and secondary standards were established under the Clean Air Act for criteria pollutants (Table 11.2). As stipulated by the 1977 amendments, these standards were subject to review and revision prior to the 1982 reauthorization. In July 1987, new standards were promulgated for particulate matter based on size. These smaller particles (designated PM_{10} and so on for sizes less than 10 microns in diameter) cause the most serious health threat since they become lodged in lung tissue and remain in the body for significant lengths of time. Currently there are debates on lowering the standard to PM_{05} (less than 5 microns).

The Nondegradation Issue Interesting quirks in the clean air legislation began to emerge in the mid-1970s, and these involved conflicts between economic development and air quality. The intent of the 1970 amendments was to keep clean air clean, while cleaning up dirty air. Primary standards for the criteria pollutants were to have been met by 1975. But there were no provisions or policies for those areas that were already clean in 1970. Industry noticed this and began to relocate into these relatively clean areas. The EPA did not take action on this issue, which became known as Prevention of Significant Deterioration (PSD), until the Sierra Club filed a legal suit over the Kaiparowitz energy facility in southern Utah.

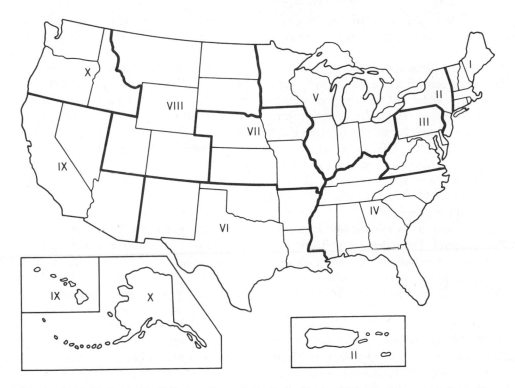

Figure 11.5 Federal Air Pollution Control Regions. *Source:* U.S. Environmental Protection Agency, 1980.

Table 11.2 National Ambient Air-Quality Standards (NAAQS), 1995

Pollutant	Averaging Time	Primary	Secondary
PM_{10}	Annual arithmetic mean	50 µg/m³	Same as primary
	24-hour	150 µg/m³	Same as primary
SO_2	Annual arithmetic mean	80 µg/m³ (0.03 ppm)	N.A.
	24-hour	365 µg/m³ (0.14 ppm)	N.A.
	3-hour	1300 µg/m³ (0.50 ppm)	N.A.
CO	8-hour	10 µg/m³ (9 ppm)	No secondary standard
	1-hour	40 µg/m³ (35 ppm)	No secondary standard
NO_2	Annual arithmetic mean	100 µg/m³ (0.053 ppm)	Same as primary
O_3	Maximum daily 1-hour average	235 µg/m³ (0.12 ppm)	Same as primary
Pb	Maximum quarterly average	1.5 µg/m3	Same as primary

Source: U.S. Environmental Protection Agency, 1995.

In response to a court order, the EPA established its PSD policy, which effectively limits the extent to which clean air can be degraded by managing economic growth in various regions (National Research Council 1981). The entire United States was divided into three classes. Class I areas could not have any increases in particulate (PM) or SO_2 levels. All National Parks and National Wilderness Areas were designated mandatory Class I areas, which limits industrial growth in the area. Most of the Class I areas are located in the western half of the country (Fig. 11.6).

Class II areas allow for moderate development and industrial growth. All areas of the country that were not mandatory Class I regions were assigned to this group. The states were then given the opportunity to change this designation to Class I or Class III. Class III areas permit significant industrial growth and residential development. Changes into Class III areas, however, require environmental impact statements, public hearings, and EPA approval.

There was and still is considerable debate over the PSD program. These debates are particularly acute in the western half of the country, where issues over energy development, industrialization, and pristine areas are hotly contested.

National Trends

The United States has had air pollution control measures for more than two decades, during which time noticeable improvements in air quality have been made. However, some parts of the country still exceed the primary health standards, posing serious risks to human health and the en-

vironment. In 1993, slightly more than 79 million people lived in areas that did not meet air-quality standards. By 1995, 127 million people were living in areas designated as nonattainment for one or more of the criteria pollutants. Overall, air quality in the United States has improved, but there are still some problem pollutants, most notably ozone. Advances in pollution control have been offset by more people creating increasing demand for heating/cooling, and driving more miles.

Emissions Significant decreases in emissions of criteria pollutants have been recorded since the Clean Air Act first was implemented. Nitrogen oxides, however, have shown an increase during the last two decades (Fig. 11.7, Table 11.3). Total suspended particulate emissions have declined by 77 percent since 1970 and by a little more than 4 percent since 1990. Fugitive dust from agricultural erosion, construction, and so forth increased in the first half of the decade, on the order of 1 percent per year. Although some improvement has been made in emissions from industrial sources due to the installation of control equipment, particulate emissions from

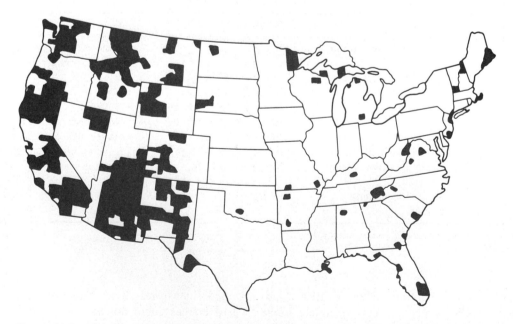

Figure 11.6 Class I counties. These counties have been designated as Class I areas because they have the best air quality. Therefore, new industrial growth in these areas is somewhat restricted *Source:* U.S. Environmental Protection Agency, 1980.

mobile sources remain problematic. Emissions standards for diesel automobiles and tailpipe standards for diesel trucks and buses took effect in 1988, helping to reduce particulate emissions from transportation sources. However, fugitive sources (Fig. 11.8), account for the overall increase in PM_{10} emissions.

The largest and most persistent source of SO_2 emissions is coal-burning electric power plants. Emissions have declined during the last decade, largely as a result of the switch from coal and high-sulfur oil to natural gas and low-sulfur oil. The recent trend shows an 18-percent decrease in SO_2 emissions from 1990 to 1995. In 1995, 18 million tons of SO_2 were emitted into the atmos-

phere. The increased use of emission control devices by industry (especially the chemical sector) and the recovery of sulfuric acid at smelters have contributed to the decline (Council on Environmental Quality 1995).

Emissions of nitrogen dioxide fluctuated during the last decade. While emissions were reduced from stationary sources (electrical utilities and industrial boilers), transportation sources have increased slightly despite advances in emissions control on highway vehicles. There are simply more people driving more miles. In 1995, 22 million tons of NO_2 were released.

Since oxidants are byproducts of chemical reactions, we have no direct emissions data for

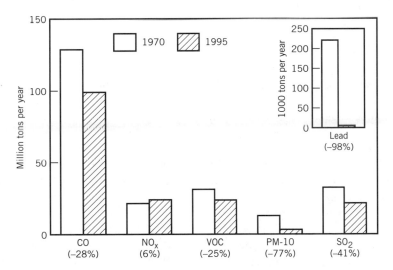

Figure 11.7   Change in U.S. emissions, 1970–1995. All criteria pollutants decreased in emissions with the exception of nitrogen oxides. *Source:* U.S. Bureau of Census, 1997.

Table 11.3   Percentage Change in U.S. Emissions of Selected Pollutants

Decade	PM_{10}	SO_2	NO_x	VOC	CO	Lead
1940-1950	+7.3	+12.1	+36.9	+22.0	+9.6	N.A.
1950-1960	-9.2	-0.6	+40.1	+16.8	+6.9	N.A.
1960-1970	-16.2	+40.2	+45.9	+25.3	+16.7	N.A.
1970-1980	-45.9	-16.9	+12.9	-15.5	-9.7	-65.8
1980-1990	-44.9	-13.4	-1.0	-8.9	-13.0	-92.4
1990-1995	-4.5	18.3	5.5	2.9	-0.5	-12.0
1970-1995	-76.6	-41.2	+5.6	-25.4	-28.1	-97.7

Source: U.S. Bureau of the Census, 1997.

Figure 11.8   Blowing dust from unvegetated areas such as this site in Nebraska contributes to particulate pollution problems.

them. However, we do have emissions data for both precursors: nitrogen oxides (already described) and volatile organic compounds. VOC emissions were down by only 3 percent during the period 1990–1995, but 23 million tons of VOCs were still emitted. The majority of VOC emissions continue to come from highway and off-highway vehicles (Fig. 11.9).

Two-thirds of the carbon monoxide emissions are from vehicles. Thus, emissions reductions in vehicles are offset by the increased number of vehicles and vehicle miles driven. However, between 1990 and 1995, there was a decrease in CO emissions. Pollution control and the retirement of older vehicles without catalytic converters have helped bring about the decline.

One of the greatest success stories in emissions reductions is lead, the use of which declined by 98 percent between 1970 and 1995. The phaseout of lead in motor fuels began in the early to mid 1970s and was virtually completed by the mid 1980s. As a result, ambient lead levels declined by over 75% during that 10-year period. Total emissions in 1995 were around 5000 tons, as compared to over 219,000 tons in 1970. Point sources now account for the major emissions, with metal processing representing about 40% of the total (U.S. Census Bureau 1997).

Ambient Concentrations   Overall ambient concentrations of the criteria pollutants have declined since 1985. PM_{10} ambient concentrations decreased by 15 percent between 1990 and 1995, for example. In 1985, 290 areas did not achieve air-quality standards for one or more of the criteria pollutants, and by 1990 this was reduced to 274 metropolitan areas exceeding air-quality standards. In 1996, the number of nonattainment areas dropped to 171 (U.S. Environmental Protection Agency 1995). Regionally, these nonattainment areas are concentrated in the Northeastern corridor between Washington, DC and Boston, and throughout California. Nearly one-third of the nonattainment areas have especially high particulate matter readings. This is the case in the arid West where wind-blown agricultural dust continues to degrade the air quality.

The construction of tall stacks by industry in the 1970s dispersed sulfur dioxide emissions far from the local source. The result was that ambient conditions at the local level improved even though emissions increased. The pollutants were simply transported farther downwind to more remote areas. There were 60 nonattainment areas for sulfur dioxide in 1985, and this figure dropped to 43 in 1995 (U.S. Environmental Protection Agency 1995). Despite the overall decline in sulfur dioxide ambient levels, the problem still

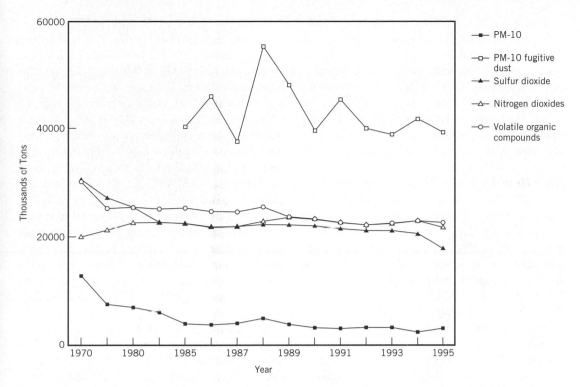

Figure 11.9 Emissions trends by source, 1970–1995. Note the differences in sources of pollutants. *Source:* U.S. Bureau of Census, 1997.

exists in those areas that burn high-sulfur coal to generate electricity, where nonferrous smelters operate, and where steel and chemical plants and pulp and paper mills predominate, such as in the intermontane West and the Great Lakes states.

Ambient concentrations of NO_x have also improved, except for a slight increase in 1984. Since then, however, ambient levels have remained relatively constant in the 1990s. Los Angeles-Long Beach, California, is the only area in the country that failed to meet the ambient air-quality standard for nitrogen oxides since 1990. There are currently no recorded violations of the annual average nitrogen dioxide standard anywhere in the country except for Los Angeles.

The trends in ozone concentrations tell a mixed story. For example, high levels were found in 1983 and 1988 and were attributed largely to meteorological conditions that favored the formation of ozone. The number of areas where the ozone standard was violated dropped from 368 in 1985 to 51 by 1990. In 1995, 43 metropolitan areas were in nonattainment. Again, California has the worst ambient ozone levels in the country. In the greater Los Angeles area, the standard was exceeded 67 days in 1995 (U.S. Bureau of the Census 1997). The San Joaquin Valley had 35 days exceeding the ozone standard, while the Riverside-San Bernardino area exceeded it 26 days. Nationally, 51 million people are exposed to unhealthy levels of ozone yearly (Council on Environmental Quality 1993). Although stationary sources do contribute to the problem, EPA control efforts focus on auto emissions by stressing motor vehicle inspections and maintenance. In addition, major life-style changes may be required to significantly reduce ozone levels in some of the nation's harder-hit sunshine states.

Ambient concentrations of CO have also declined, again because of emissions controls on automobiles. In 1996, EPA designated 31 areas as nonattainment for CO, with only one, Los Angeles, classified as serious. In 1995, for example, Los Angeles had 14 days when it failed to meet the CO standard, compared to the next highest city, Fairbanks, Alaska, which had 9 such days.

Finally, lead concentrations in urban areas (where most of the monitoring stations are located) show significant improvement. There has been a steady decline in ambient lead levels as well. Some areas, however, have still not met the ambient standard. These urban areas include St. Louis, Nashville, and their ambient levels are a function of their proximity to nonferrous smelters and other point sources of lead emissions.

How Healthy Is the Air You Breathe?

In an effort to standardize monitoring efforts nationwide, the EPA adopted a uniform air-quality index in 1978. This index, the *Pollution Standards Index*, or PSI, is a health-related comparative measure based on the short-term national ambient air-quality (NAAQS) primary standards for criteria pollutants. It is widely used to report daily air-quality readings to the public.

The PSI integrates concentrations of nitrogen dioxide, sulfur dioxide, carbon monoxide, ozone, and particulate matter (PM_{10}) for an entire monitoring network into a single value, which ranges from 0 to 500 (Table 11.4). When the levels for all five of these pollutants are below NAAQS primary standards, the air is called good or moderately polluted (PSI values 0–99). When ambient concentrations of any of the criteria pollutants exceed their primary standard, the PSI reading is in the 100–500 range depending on the concentration level. PSI values in the 100–200 range are labeled unhealthful; values from 200 to 300 are called very unhealthful; and values in excess of 300 are labeled hazardous.

Public warnings are issued when PSI values rise above the "good air" value of less than 100. An air-quality alert is called when PSI values range from 100 to 200; at this time, persons with heart or respiratory ailments should reduce physical exertion. An air pollution warning is given when the PSI ranges from 200 to 300. During a warning, elderly and other persons with heart and lung diseases should remain indoors. Industry is also asked to curtail emissions temporarily, until the warning is removed. An air pollution emergency is called when PSI readings exceed 300. Then the general population is advised to refrain from outdoor activities, and persons with heart and lung diseases are advised to remain indoors and minimize their physical activity. Industry and motorists are asked to curb emissions through lower production and less driving, respectively.

Overall air quality in metropolitan regions is improving. Selected metropolitan regions had an average number of 37 days of unhealthful air (above 100 on the PSI) in 1984, and this dropped to 12 days by 1993 and by 1995 it was down to 8 (Council on Environmental Quality 1993; U.S. Environmental Protection Agency 1995). Although the national trend exhibits signs of improvement, six metropolitan areas, (five in Southern California, and Houston, TX) had air-quality alerts (PSI>100) for the equivalent of a month or more.

Southern California still has the most troublesome air quality. In 1984, Los Angeles had 204 days with PSI levels greater than 100, but by

Table 11.4   Comparison of Pollution Standards Index (PSI) Values

PSI Value	PM[a]	SO₂[a]	CO[b]	O₃[c]	NO₂[c]	Descriptor
400 +	875 +	2000 +	46.0 +	1000 +	3000 +	Very hazardous
300–399	625–874	1600–1999	34.0–45.9	900–1099	2260–2999	Hazardous
200–299	375–624	800–1599	17.0–33.9	480–899	1130–2259	Very unhealthful
100–199	260–374	365–799	10.0–16.9	240–479	N.R.[e]	Unhealthful
50–99	75d–259	80[d]–364	5.0–9.9	120–239	N.R.	Moderate
0–49	0–74	0–79	0–4.9	0–119	N.R.	Good

[a] *24 hr, μg/m³.*
[b] *8-hr, μg/m³.*
[c] *1-hr, μg/m³.*
[d] *Annual primary NAAQS.*
[e] *N.R. = no index value reported at concentration levels below those specified by "alert level" criteria.*

Source: Council on Environmental Quality, 1980, pp. 156–157.

1995, it had decreased to a mere 106 days (or a little over three months). There are, however, year-to-year fluctuations that are often more reflective of local conditions than of any success in pollution abatement (Fig. 11.10). While Southern California has the distinction of the worst air pollution in the nation, it is also one of the most innovative regions for pollution reduction strategies (Issue 11.1).

Air-Quality Control and Planning

Economic Considerations In 1993, $109 billion was spent in the United States for pollution abatement and control (U.S. Bureau of the Census 1997). Nearly 29 percent of this amount, or $32 billion, was for air-quality control alone. Pollution abatement accounted for 94 percent of the expenditures. About $13 billion was spent on abatement for stationary sources of air pollution, while another $13 billion was spent on emissions reductions from cars and trucks. The government (federal, state, and local) spent $500 million (less than 2% of all air pollution abatement expenditures). Industry spent nearly $21 billion (67%) for air pollution abatement, and consumers spent another $8 billion (27%). Governmental regulation, monitoring, and research cost another $1.7 billion.

Clean air is a costly business and in an era of fiscal austerity, the return on investments in air pollution reduction must be demonstrated. EPA's Pollution Prevention Program (see Chapter 2) is one example of the need for the government to forge private partnerships and to make it cost-effective for industries to comply.

Another example is EPA's *bubble approach* to stationary source control. Instead of considering each smokestack as an emitter, which was the previous policy, the EPA now views the entire plant as a point source. Thus, it allows emissions from one smokestack to exceed standards as long as another stack at a different location in the same plant has compensating reductions. As long as the emissions from the entire plant do not exceed the standards, then the plant is not in violation of the Clean Air Act and thus not subject to criminal prosecution. This policy allows the plant to average emissions from all stacks, allowing internal decision making about what is most appropriate for the plant. Production levels and expenditures for control equipment are made by the plant management, as long as the total emissions are below federal limits.

Control Programs Until recently, it was thought that vehicle exhaust emissions offered the greatest potential for decreasing mobile source contributions to the nonattainment of NAAQS. However, the newest model cars already remove up to 95 percent of the emissions. Real improvements in vehicle emissions will come from a switch from gasoline as a fuel and from reductions in the number of vehicles and miles driven.

Vehicle exhaust emissions have been federally regulated since 1968 and have become increasingly strict (Table 11.5). The emissions standards apply only to the newer model year cars and trucks; older models have less stringent controls. Increased fuel efficiency is another way

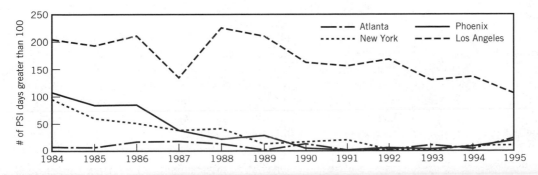

Figure 11.10 Air quality in selected metropolitan areas, 1984-1995. Overall air quality has improved in these cities, but Los Angeles still has the worst air quality of any major metropolitan area in the United States.

to reduce emissions. Smaller, more fuel-efficient cars produce less pollution. During the 1980s, fuel efficiency standards were rolled back to 26 mpg to ease pressures on U.S. auto makers. The result was that Americans began driving bigger and less fuel efficient cars, thereby producing more air pollution. In early 1989, the fuel efficiency standard was increased to 27.5 mpg as a result of increased pressure to reduce smog. Today, Americans are still driving bigger cars such as minivans and sport utility vehicles with lower fuel efficiencies.

One area specifically addressed by the 1990 CAA is the requirement for cleaner burning fuels. For example, in 1992 oxygenated fuel was introduced as a method for reducing CO emissions and improving total fuel combustion especially in colder areas. In 1993, limits on the sulfur content in diesel fuel came into effect. Also, regulations for cleaner, reformulated gasoline to reduce hydrocarbons and toxic emissions were put in place in the mid-1990s especially in non-attainment areas. Lastly, California has required that a certain number of cars sold in the state have zero emissions. This has prompted automobile companies to increase production of these vehicles (Issue 11.2).

State inspection and maintenance programs for vehicles in order to monitor emissions on a yearly basis are one method to control mobile sources. Unfortunately, there are no uniform requirements for such programs, and as a result there is great variation from state to state, with California's being the most stringent. Under the new CAA, enhanced vehicle inspection and maintenance, including stricter tailpipe and evap-

ISSUE 11.1: SMOG CITY, USA

"I love LA," echoes the refrain from a song about the city of angels. But how much longer will Los Angeles residents be feeling this way if they must begin to wear gas masks before venturing outside in the warm California sun? People in Los Angeles are becoming less enamored of their city as increased air pollution continues to choke not only their city but all of Southern California and as the costs of curbing it escalate.

Good air quality has been a persistent problem in Southern California since Juan Rodriguez Cabrillo first discovered the Bahia de los Fumos (Bay of Smokes) in 1542. By 1877, air pollution, in the form of dust from the streets, was so bad it prompted one citizen to remark: "It does not allow invalids with lung disease to remain here" (Weaver 1980, p. 197). By 1944, the term *smog* (smoke and *fog*) was coined to describe the brown haze that hung over the Los Angeles basin. With postwar urbanization and industrialization, the now famous Los Angeles smog worsened, and residents began to experience discomfort and adverse health effects. Smog alerts became commonplace, and, as early as the 1950s, people were advised to curtail their outdoor physical activities.

Four decades later, the smog problem remains. In March 1989, the South Coast Air Quality Management District (AQMD) finally decided to confront the Southern California icon, the single-passenger automobile. The AQMD developed a 20-year strategy for cleaning up the air by proposing and passing an innovative and far-reaching plan. The plan covers 13,350 sq mi (34,600 km^2) of Southern California and its 15 million inhabitants, as well as their 7 million cars and 2 million trucks and other vehicles.

The primary goal of the AQMD is to improve air quality by changing residents' everyday habits in the Los Angeles Basin. Restrictions have been placed on activities ranging from driving and parking to use of powered lawn-care tools and even backyard barbecues. Ultimately, this may change how cities are organized in the future.

The plan has 123 specific actions that involve not only residents but also industry. It placed a number of limits on sources of air emissions. Restrictions on car use included the elimination of free parking in some downtown locations and an increase in registration fees for motorists with more than one car. Emissions standards for diesel engines were tightened, and paints and solvents were reformulated to decrease emissions.

All over the city, businesses and industry began changing. The local dry cleaners had to in-

Table 11.5   Exhaust Emission Standards
for Automobiles

Model Year	Standard (g/m^3)		
	VOC	CO	NO_x
Pre–1968	8.2	90.0	3.4
1968–1971	4.1	34.0	N.A.[a]
1972–1974	3.0	28.0	3.1
1975–1976	1.5	15.0	3.1
1977–1979	1.5	15.0	2.0
1980	0.41	7.0	2.0
1981	0.41	3.4	1.0
1987	0.41	3.4	1.0
1991	.025	3.4	0.7
1996	.025	3.4	0.7

[a] N.A. = not available.

Source: National Commission on Air Quality, 1981; Renner, 1988; U.S. Environmental Protection Agency, 1997.

orative emissions control, are now under development. Electric-powered vehicles are another option, particularly for localized commuting, within metropolitan areas.

The most obvious way to reduce vehicle emissions is to force people to drive less. Admittedly, this is a rather impractical solution to the problem, given the increasing number of motor vehicles and trucks on the road. During the last decade, the number of cars and buses increased by 25 percent, while the number of trucks using diesel engines increased by 40 percent. The number of miles driven, however, doubled. So any improvement in emissions control was more than offset by the increase in vehicle miles driven. Under the new legislation, states are required to rethink their planning and transportation services provision so as to consider them within the con-

stall a combined wash/dry system to reduce VOC emissions when clothes are moved between machines. Some paint shops switched to water-based paints with fewer solvents. Body shops began to use a lower-pressure spray to reduce the amount of paint in the air.

At the same time, the AQMD established its RECLAIM pollution trading program. Originally covering 300 firms, RECLAIM allows companies to buy pollution credits on the "smog exchange." Using annual emissions for 1989 or 1990 (the company chooses) as a base, industries can either cut their own annual emissions or buy the unused portion of emissions (credits) from another firm. Because the base year of 1989 was quite high, emissions could actually increase. This is precisely what happened between 1993 and 1996.

In 1993, Southern California had its lowest emissions in more than a decade, owing largely to the recession in the region caused by the downsizing of the aerospace industry. As the economy picked up, so did emissions. From 1993 to 1996, emissions rose from their 1993 low values (remember the targets were set on 1989 emissions), so that the AQMD has now fallen 60 percent short of its emissions reduction goals. By 1997, the RECLAIM program was ex-

panded to more than 1000 industries in an effort to increase compliance. Emissions targets were set at 38 tons of VOCs daily compared to 31 tons in 1993. Under this new plan, the target emissions were slightly higher than those in the 1994 plan, but the rate of decline was faster since the timetable for emissions reductions was shortened from 2010 to 2005 in order to meet the federal ozone health standard.

As one might guess, the debate about the AQMD plan continues. Since Southern California already has the toughest air pollution legislation in the country, there was no alternative other than this complete overhaul. Legal challenges and business threats will no doubt fuel the fire over whether or not the costs exceed the benefits. The costs are astounding—around $1.7 billion annually (Cone 1997). Opponents claim that the benefits are not nearly that great, and proponents say it must be done to protect the health and welfare of residents. This far-reaching plan is the first of its kind in the nation and will surely serve as a model for other urban areas whose air pollution problems are worsening. A major change in life-style and the pattern of business is occurring in Southern California. Los Angeles has said yes to clean air, but at what cost? (Cone 1993; Reinhold 1989; Stevenson 1989; Weisman 1989.)

ISSUE 11.2: HOW CLEAN ARE ELECTRIC VEHICLES?

The United States Environmental Protection Agency, as well as several state and local governments, is pushing hard for an increase in the number of electric vehicles in use, and the automobile industry is responding in a major effort to develop the new cars. Major hurdles are yet to be overcome, including developing a battery storage system that provides adequate power without making the vehicle too heavy, and establishing the infrastructure that will allow vehicles to be recharged easily and quickly. Costs are another significant problem, although presumably these would be reduced by economies of scale once electric vehicles become commonplace.

The government is encouraging the use of electric vehicles primarily to reduce air pollution problems in urban areas. Electric vehicles are touted as zero-emission vehicles, but a more accurate phrasing is zero-tailpipe-emission vehicles. This is because generating the electricity to run these vehicles also produces emissions, but at an electric power plant rather than in the vehicle. So are we really reducing pollution, or are we just moving it from one place to another?

A typical electric vehicle is much more energy efficient than a gasoline-powered vehicle. This is because nearly all the energy consumed in the vehicle is used to move it down the road. In a conventional vehicle with an internal combustion engine, most of the energy produced by fuel combustion is lost as waste heat, dissipated via the engine's cooling system. Of course, the electricity used to power an electric vehicle may have been produced from combustion of fossil fuels—in the United States, about three-fourths of all electricity is produced this way. In a typical fossil-fueled power plant, only about one-third of the energy consumed is converted to electricity, and the rest is discharged into a waterway or the atmosphere as waste heat. But even accounting for this loss of energy in generating electricity,

text of meeting air-quality goals. In 1998, for example, 22 cities were required to have a new fleet of public transportation vehicles (taxis, buses) that met more stringent tailpipe emissions standards than automobiles.

Stationary-source control involves installing mechanical devices on smokestacks and switching from high-sulfur to low-sulfur fuels. Fitting gasoline pumps with pollution control equipment is another method currently in use to prevent hydrocarbons from escaping at the gas station (Fig. 11.11). There are over 27,000 major stationary sources of air pollution in this country alone. The EPA considers "major" any plant that produces more than 100 tons of pollutants per year. Stack scrubbers, precipitators, and filters are costly capital investments for industry, especially for facilities with old, outdated plants. For example, industry spent $4 billion on capital expenditures for air pollution abatement and another $6 billion in operating costs in 1994 alone (U.S. Bureau of the Census 1996). The chemical and petroleum industries had the largest air pollution control expenditures.

Compliance with federal standards is spotty. Unfortunately, no systematic assessment of compliance has been made at the national level since 1980. Reductions in enforcement actions as a result of cuts in the federal budget and decentralization of the federal role in air-quality control during the Reagan administration obviously have not improved air quality. Air pollution control is expensive and requires federal action and support from both industry and consumers.

Toxics in the Air

Over 70,000 synthetic chemicals are available in the world today. Although the effects of immediate (acute) exposures to human health and the environment may be known, scientific information on the effects of lower-level, longer-term exposures is often incomplete or missing. Disasters such as the 1984 release of methyl isocyanate in Bhopal, India, which killed more than 2000 people, do occur, though not frequently. Perhaps of greater concern are the daily emissions of airborne toxic substances that result in chronic exposures. Unfortunately, we have very little in-the energy efficiency of electric vehicles is much greater than that of conventional vehicles.

With regard to air pollution, electric vehicles are significantly cleaner than conventional vehicles. This is because of the increased energy efficiency of electric vehicles, since the combustion of fuels takes place in a power plant, where control of combustion temperatures, oxygen levels, and emissions is much easier than in an internal combustion engine. In terms of the pollutants of greatest concern in urban areas, electric vehicles would generate a very small fraction of the hydrocarbons and carbon monoxide produced by conventional autos, as well as a somewhat lower amount of particulates and NO_x. In addition, the pollution created in power plants supplying electric vehicles can be generated outside the city and discharged higher in the atmosphere, whereas that generated by cars today is released on city streets where large numbers of people breathe. Most United States electricity (55% or so) is generated using coal, and this coal produces large amounts of sulfur emissions. Fueled this way, electric vehicles produce more sulfur emissions than their conventional-powered counterparts.

In the long run, then, if we were to convert a substantial portion of our vehicle fleet from conventional fuels to electric power, we would see an overall decrease in air pollution in cities. If we generate that extra electricity from coal, then we may see an increase in sulfur emissions, but these could be partly controlled at the source through use of sulfur-reducing technologies such as fluidized bed combustion. The problem, as always, is one of cost. Are the environmental gains large enough to justify an enormous investment in converting to an electric vehicle fleet? In the short run many would say no. But in the long run, electric vehicles may be necessary if we want to preserve our access to personal transportation without further environmental degradation.

formation on the number of deaths attributed to longer term exposures to toxic chemicals in the air we breathe.

For years, the EPA has been grappling with the problem of air toxics that are emitted from a wide range of mobile and stationary sources, including incinerators, municipal waste sites, plastics and chemical manufacturing plants, and sewage treatment plants. The agency's first approach was to regulate the source emissions for a small number of toxic pollutants, even though hundreds of organic compounds, many with carcinogenic or mutagenic properties, are routinely emitted into the air. The National Emission Standards for Hazardous Air Pollutants (NESHAP), for example, monitors criteria pollutants and has set emissions standards for eight toxics: asbestos, beryllium, mercury, vinyl chloride, arsenic, radionuclides, benzene, and coke oven emissions. Under the 1990 CAA, emissions standards for 188 extremely hazardous substances are being phased in over the next decade. This should reduce "routine" toxic emissions into the air. Furthermore, the EPA has implemented toxic emissions reductions for the following industries—dry cleaners, coke ovens, industrial solvent users, and chromium electroplating factories—in an effort to reduce heavy metal and perchlorethylene emissions.

Underlying the current EPA policy was the assumption that emissions are directly related to ambient quality and thus human exposure. However, the air toxics problem is complex and requires an integrated approach in managing toxic substances and exposures from a variety of sources and media. As a result, the EPA is now using an exposure assessment methodology that measures all the exposures of toxics regardless of media (e.g., air, water, land). In this way, we can understand the total burden placed on the environment from toxic releases. The largest obstacle to widespread use of this method may be the myriad of environmental laws that restrict an agency's ability to undertake integrated studies of human exposures from different media as well as institutional inertia.

Under Title III of the Superfund Amendments and Reauthorization Act (1986), industry was re-

Figure 11.11 The rubber boot on this gasoline pump nozzle captures hydrocarbon-rich vapors that are expelled from a fuel tank as it is filled with gasoline, reducing the amount that are discharged to the atmosphere. Measures such as these have become increasingly important in capturing so-called fugitive emissions of hydrocarbons.

quired to report on the quantities of toxic emissions for about 320 chemicals. In the first survey, the EPA found that 2.7 billion pounds (1.2 million metric tons) of toxic chemicals were emitted into the air in 1987, significantly more than anyone thought (U.S. Environmental Protection Agency 1989b). Unfortunately, this is a conservative estimate, for it excludes those toxic emissions from autos, toxic waste dumps, and, most importantly, companies that produce less than 75,000 pounds (34.1 metric tons) of toxic materials. The chemical industry is the largest source of toxic emissions, with 308 million pounds released during 1994.

Indoor Air Pollution

Indoor air pollution has become a major health issue in the United States. As houses and buildings become more energy efficient, concentrations of pollutants build up because of lack of ventilation in both the winter and summer. Many people spend as much as 90 percent of their time indoors. The problems of indoor air pollution have received widespread attention during the last decade. Potential health effects range from short-term symptoms such as headaches, nausea, and throat irritations to longer-term health problems like lung disease and even cancer. There are a wide array of pollutants coming from a variety of sources like tobacco smoke, building materials, gas ranges, cleaning agents, and drinking water.

Home, Work, and School The most serious pollutant in the home is tobacco smoke (especially the benzene it contains), followed by radon and particulates from wood-burning stoves. Other sources of pollutants include some consumer products such as paint thinners and wood conditioners. Formaldehyde, which is often used in furniture, foam insulation, and some wood products, is a major source of volatile organic compounds; hence, the manufacturers recommend use of these products in "well-ventilated areas." Other sources of VOCs are carpets and carpet adhesives, latex paint, and products made from particleboard, such as bookcases.

We sometimes hear complaints about "sick buildings" that cause their inhabitants to complain about eye and throat irritations, drowsiness, headaches, and so on. The likely sources of many of these ills are elevated pollution levels within the buildings, often caused by the same agents that create elevated levels at home. Heating, ventilating, and air conditioning systems can bring biological contaminants indoors and circulate them throughout buildings, causing allergic reactions to pollen and fungi, as well as promoting more serious bacterial and viral infections. Asbestos, once used widely for insulation and fireproofing, is a known carcinogen. Some of the highest concentrations of asbestos have been found in the nation's schools. In 1986, Congress passed the Asbestos Hazard Emergency Response Act, which required all schools to inspect for asbestos-containing materials and to develop plans to remove them. The role of tobacco smoke in increasing benzene levels, together with the increased cancers that result from "passive smoking," has resulted in restrictions on smoking in most public and private buildings and on airplanes. The recent California law to ban smoking in bars and clubs is good example.

Radon Radon is a tasteless, colorless, odorless gas that is a natural byproduct of the decay of radium. Radium occurs naturally in many different types of soils and rocks, and radon enters buildings through cracks or openings in the foundations or basements. A study by the EPA suggests that radon may account for between 5000 and 20,000 lung cancer deaths each year (U.S. Environmental Protection Agency 1988a). The EPA estimates that up to 8 million homes nationwide may have radon levels exceeding 4 picocuries per liter, their indicator of high risk. The radon problem is found everywhere, and high-risk areas can be identified using geological maps to identify uranium-rich rocks. Elevated levels of radon were once thought to occur only in winter but are now found during summer months as buildings remain airtight to keep cool with air conditioning.

Despite the relatively high risk, radon can often be controlled at the individual homeowner level. Once a radon test is done, exposure can be lessened by sealing cracks in the basement, installing home ventilation systems, removing radium-tainted soil, and, if all else fails, relocation. Educational materials and testing kits are often available free of charge from individual state governments. The most comprehensive educational and testing programs are found in Florida, Maine, New Jersey, New York, and Pennsylvania (where the problem was first "discovered" in 1984). New Jersey has the most active educational and testing program, and Pennsylvania offers low-interest loans for home repairs to ameliorate radon exposure.

SUMMARY

As we have seen, the quality of our air resource has improved in some regions of the country but has worsened in others. Instead of cleaning up pollutants, we often exacerbate the problem by shifting from one pollutant source to another or simply transferring the problem to greater distances. Internationally, the problem of urban air pollution is increasing as many of the world's developing countries become more urbanized.

Cleaning up the air resource is costly and will entail cooperation between industry, government, and citizens. Unless we are willing to don gas masks every time we venture outside, it is essential that we reduce our reliance on the automobile and decrease fossil fuel use. Industry must also do its part by making fuels burn more efficiently and reducing the amount of toxins that are routinely emitted into the air we breathe. Unfortunately, reducing emissions entails substantial costs for both industrial polluters and consumers. While tangible emission reductions have been achieved, further reductions will require substantial capital investments or changes in the way we live. It remains to be seen whether we have the political will to force these improvements in air quality.

REFERENCES AND ADDITIONAL READING

Cone, Marla. 1997. Revised anti-smog plan is unveiled. *Los Angeles Times*, October 20, p. A3.

_____ . 1995. AQMD's smog plan for L.A. Basin Okd. *Los Angeles Times*, January 24, p. A3.

Conservation Foundation. 1982. *State of the Environment*. Washington, DC: Conservation Foundation.

_____ . 1987. *State of the Environment: A View Toward the Nineties*. Washington, DC: Conservation Foundation.

Council on Environmental Quality. 1980. *Environmental Quality, 1980. 11th Annual Report*. Washington, DC: U.S. Government Printing Office.

_____ . 1981. *Environmental Quality, 1981. 12th Annual Report*. Washington, DC: U.S. Government Printing Office.

_____ . 1982. *Environmental Quality, 1982. 13th Annual Report*. Washington, DC: U.S. Government Printing Office.

_____ . 1995. *Environmental Quality, 1993. 25th Anniversary Report*. Washington, DC: U.S. Government Printing Office.

Crawford, M. 1990. Scientists battle over Grand Canyon pollution. *Science* 247: 911–912.

Cutter, S. L. 1987. Airborne toxic releases: Are communities prepared? *Environment* 29(6): 12–17, 28–31.

_____ . 1995. The forgotten casualties: women, children, and environmental change. *Global Environmental Change* 5(3): 181-194.

_____ , and W. D. Solecki. 1989. The national pattern of airborne toxic releases. *Professional Geographer* 41(2): 149–161.

Dudek, D. J., and J. Palmisano. 1988. Emissions trading: Why is this thoroughbred hobbled? *Columbia Journal of Environmental Law* 13: 217–256.

Elsom, D. 1992. *Atmospheric Pollution: A Global Problem*. Cambridge, MA: Basil Blackwell.

Fleischaker, M. L. 1983. Converting the converters: Tampering with cars and the Clean Air Act. *Environment* 25(8): 33–37.

Goldsmith, J. R., and L. T. Friberg. 1977. Effects of air pollution on human health. In Arthur C. Stern, ed., *The Effects of Air Pollution*. 3rd ed. Chapter 7, pp. 457–610. New York: Academic Press.

Lave, L. B., and E. P. Seskin. 1977. *Air Pollution and Human Health*. Baltimore, MD: Johns Hopkins University Press for Resources for the Future.

_____ . 1989b. Automakers plea on pollution. *New York Times*, July 21, p. D1.

Liroff, R. A. 1986. *Reforming Air Pollution Regulation: The Toil and Trouble of EPA's Bubble*. Washington, DC: Resources for the Future.

Machado, S., and S. Ridley. 1988. *Eliminating Indoor Pollution*. Washington, DC: Renew America Project.

Miller, E. W., and R. Miller. 1989. *Environmental Hazards: Air Pollution*. Santa Barbara, CA: ABC-CLIO publishers.

National Commission on Air Quality. 1981. *To Breathe Clean Air*. Washington, DC: U.S. Government Printing Office.

National Research Council. 1979. *Airborne Particles*. Baltimore, MD: University Park Press.

_____ . 1981. *Prevention of Significant Deterioration of Air Quality*. Washington, DC: National Academy Press.

Reinhold, R. 1989. Southern California takes steps to curb its urban air pollution. *New York Times*, March 18, p. A1.

Renner, M. 1988. *Rethinking the Role of the Automobile*. Worldwatch Paper no. 84. Washington, DC: Worldwatch Institute.

Rohter, L. 1989. Mexico City's filthy air, world's worst, worsens. *New York Times*, April 12, p. A1.

Smith, K. R. 1988. Air pollution: Assessing total exposure in the United States. *Environment* 30(8): 10–15, 33–38.

Stavins, R. N. 1989. Harnessing market forces to protect the environment. *Environment* 312(1): 4–7, 28–35.

Tietenberg, T. 1985. *Emissions Trading: An Exercise in Reforming Pollution Policy*. Washington, DC: Resources for the Future.

Tolba, M. K. et al. 1992. *The World Environment 1972-1992*. London: Chapman & Hall.

United Nations Environment Program 1994. *Environmental Data Report 1993-94*. Cambridge, MA: Basil Blackwell.

United Nations Environment Program/World Health Organization. 1992. *Urban Air Pollution in Megacities of the World*. Cambridge, MA: Basil Blackwell.

U.S. Bureau of the Census. 1997. *Statistical Abstract of the United States, 1997.* Washington, DC: U.S. Government Printing Office.

U.S. Environmental Protection Agency. 1980. *Environmental Outlook.* EPA-600/8-80-003. Washington, DC: U.S. Government Printing Office.

_____ .1988a. *Environmental Progress and Challenges: EPA's Update.* EPA-230-07-88-033. Washington, DC: U.S. Government Printing Office.

_____ . 1988b. *Anthropogenic Emissions Data for the 1985 NAPAP Inventory.* EPA-600/7-88-022. Research Triangle Park, NC: U.S. Environmental Protection Agency.

_____ . 1995. *National Air Quality and Emissions Trends Report 1995.*
ONLINE *http://www.epa.gov/oar/aqtrnd95/tap.html*
_____ . 1997. *Motor Vehicles and the 1990 Clean Air Act.*
ONLINE http://www.epa.gov/docs/omswww/11-vehs.htm

Weaver, J. D. 1980. *Los Angeles: The Enormous Village 1781–1981.* Santa Barbara, CA: Capra Press.

Weisman, A. 1989. L.A. fights for breath. *New York Times* Magazine, July 30, pp. 14–17, 30–33, 48.

World Resources Institute. 1987. *World Resources 1987.* New York: Basic Books.

_____ . 1988. *World Resources 1988–89.* New York: Basic Books.

_____ . 1996. *World Resources 1996-97.* New York: Oxford University Press.

Zurer, P. S. 1988. Study traces most SO_2 emissions to burning of moderate-sulfur coal. *Chemical and Engineering News*, June 27, pp. 40–41.

For more information, consult our web page at *http://www.wiley.com/college/cutter*

STUDY QUESTIONS

1. What is an inversion, and how does it affect air pollution? How do sunlight and atmospheric humidity affect air pollution?
2. What are the criteria pollutants? For each one, what are the major emission sources? What emissions cause photochemical smog?
3. What has the government done to prevent air-quality deterioration in relatively clean areas? in nonattainment areas?
4. Does your city meet all federal air-quality guidelines? What pollutants are the greatest problems? What are the major sources of pollution in your city?
5. Summarize the trends in emissions and ambient concentrations for each major pollutant over the last several years. What is the difference among them?
6. How do cities in developing countries and those in wealthy countries differ in the kinds of pollution problems they face and in their potential solutions?
7. Economic development leads to increased industrial activity and fuel use, but it also makes possible investments to reduce air pollution. Overall, do you think economic development will improve air quality in developing world cities, or worsen it?
8. Why are toxic substances in the air of particular concern? Are toxics a more important problem than conventional pollution?

CHAPTER 12

REGIONAL AND GLOBAL ATMOSPHERIC CHANGE

Traditionally, air pollution has been a local concern, but recently it has taken on global significance in light of recent scientific evidence about climate change and the destruction of the protective stratospheric ozone layer by anthropogenic air pollutants. Although the pollutants may have a specific local or regional source, their effects are so widespread and there are so many sources that the emissions and their impacts often transcend national boundaries. This phenomenon is called *transboundary pollution*. In this chapter we discuss three major transboundary issues facing the planet today: acid deposition; stratospheric ozone depletion; and climate change.

ACID DEPOSITION

Acid deposition is a general term that refers to the deposition of acids and substances that contribute to soil acidification, carried by rainfall, snow, and dust particles falling from the atmosphere. Although normal rainfall is slightly acidic, air pollution, particularly emissions of sulfur and nitrogen oxides, have greatly increased the acidity of rainfall over wide areas in the last several decades. It is a regional rather than a local consequence of fossil fuel combustion, having been identified as a problem in the eastern United States, Canada, Europe, China, and southern Brazil (Fig. 12.1). Acid deposition has broad-ranging environmental effects, including damage to vegetation and structures and reduced surface-water quality. It will no doubt continue to be an important environmental issue in industrialized

and industrializing regions of the world in the years to come (Hedin and Likens 1996).

Formation and Extent

Acids are substances that give up a proton (hydrogen nucleus) in a chemical reaction. The acidity of solutions is measured on the pH scale, which gives the negative logarithm of the concentration of hydrogen nuclei in a solution. A pH of 7 is neutral, and numbers less than 7 are increasingly acidic. A pH greater than 7 indicates alkaline conditions. Rainwater is slightly acidic, even under natural conditions. Carbon dioxide dissolves in water to form carbonic acid, a weak acid of about pH 5.6. Other natural sources of acids exist in the atmosphere, including sulfur compounds emitted from volcanoes and nitric acids created by lightning passing through the atmosphere. The relative contributions of these other sources to the acidity of rainfall are not known, but the pH of natural rainfall is variable, slightly lower than 5.6, and perhaps as low as 5.0. Acid precipitation, on the other hand, has much lower pH values, commonly in the low 4's and sometimes in the low 3's, about the same as vinegar. A drop of one unit on the logarithmic pH scale represents a tenfold increase in acidity, so these are substantial differences.

Acid deposition is a significant and widespread problem in three regions of the world—eastern North America, central and northern Europe, China, and Japan—and is locally important in many others. These three major regions of acid deposition are all industrial areas with large amounts of coal use and major emissions of sul-

270

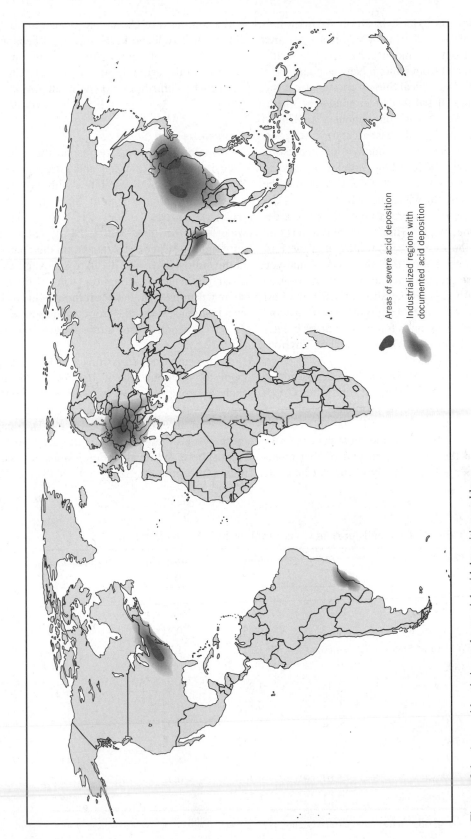

Figure 2.1 Areas with existing and potential acid deposition problems.

Areas of severe acid deposition

Industrialized regions with documented acid deposition

fur and nitrogen oxides. In North America precipitation pH is in the low 4's over a large area extending from the mid-Atlantic coast to southern Ontario and from Ohio to New England.

The U.S. Geological Survey coordinates a National Trends Network that monitors the chemistry of precipitation throughout the United States. In comparing the eastern and western portions of the country, a number of interesting trends appear (Table 12.1). Sulfates are two to three times more prevalent in the East than in the West. In addition, while the sulfate trend is declining in the East, there is no evidence of a decline in the West. Nitrate concentrations are greater in the East. We also know that the East has more precipitation than the West. When you consider the greater amount of "wet" deposition coupled with the concentration of acids, the East has a much more significant problem. Sulfate and nitrate wet deposition is four to five times greater in the East than in the West (Council on Environmental Quality 1995).

In Europe the most severe acid deposition is found in Germany, Poland, and the Czech Republic, but significant problems occur over much of Europe. Less data are available on acid deposition in China, but the most severe problems are in the southeastern part of that country. Coal is used intensively in the northeast as

in the southeast of China, but the acidity of precipitation is reduced in the northeast because of a higher input of neutralizing alkaline dust derived from the arid regions to the west. Chinese emissions contribute to acid deposition in Japan.

Emissions and Sources

Two major pollutants are responsible for acid deposition, sulfur dioxide and nitrogen oxides. Sulfur dioxide (SO_2) combines with oxygen and water in the atmosphere to form sulfuric acid (H_2SO_4). Nitrogen oxides (NO_x) combine with water to form nitric acid (HNO_3). These acids are found in water droplets and on dust particles in the atmosphere, and they are deposited on the ground either in precipitation or in dry dust. The chemical processes that form these acids are not instantaneous; they take from minutes to days to occur, depending on atmospheric conditions (Fig. 12.2).

Sulfur dioxide emissions derive primarily from the combustion of impure fossil fuels, such as coal and fuel oil. Globally, anthropogenic sources of sulfur account for 55 to 80 percent of all emissions (UNEP 1993). Most of these emissions originate in the Northern Hemisphere. While sulfur emissions are declining in the industrialized nations (Table 12.2)

Table 12.1 Trends in Acid Concentrations in U.S. Precipitation

Year	pH (units)	Sulfate (mg/l)	Nitrate (mg/l)	Precipitation (cm)
1985				
Eastern	4.42	2.04	1.25	107.1
Western	5.13	0.82	0.71	62.0
United States	4.56	1.63	1.07	91.9
1990				
Eastern	4.48	1.80	1.17	122.6
Western	5.21	0.80	0.87	66.2
United States	4.62	1.47	1.07	103.7
1994				
Eastern	4.48	1.71	1.24	111.9
Western	5.07	0.76	0.92	62.0
United States	4.61	1.38	1.13	94.5

Source: Council on Environmental Quality, 1995, p. 441.

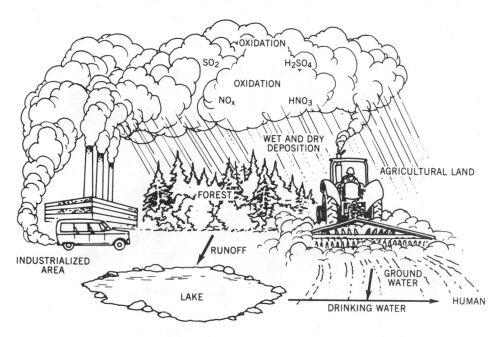

Figure 12.2   Formation and deposition of acid rain. Sulfur and nitrogen oxides emitted from industries, automobiles, and other sources are oxidized in the atmosphere to form nitric and sulfuric acids. These are deposited on the land, either in precipitation or in dry dustfall, and affect vegetation, soil, and water quality. *Source:* U.S. Environmental Protection Agency, 1980.

Table 12.2   Anthropogenic Emissions of Sulfur Dioxide and Nitrogen Oxides in Selected Countries

Region/ Country	Percent Change SO_2 1980–1990	Percent Change NO_x 1980–1990
North America		
Canada	-18	-1
United States	-10	-3
Asia		
China	+50	+50
India	+53	+53
Japan	-29	- 9
Korea	+23	+52
Pakistan	+92	+41
Europe		
Czechoslovakia	-17	- 7
France	-64	- 4
Germany	-16	- 5
Poland	-22	-15
United Kingdom	-23	+10
Former Soviet Union	-18	+23
Belarus	-24	+ 3
Russia	-16	+18
Turkmenistan	+115	+135
Ukraine	-28	- 9

Source: United Nations Environment Program, 1993, pp. 44–47.

they are noticeably increasing in rapidly developing countries such as China, Pakistan, and Turkmenistan. Nitrogen oxide emissions follow a similar pattern.

In the United States, the areas with the largest sulfur emissions are in the urban industrial areas of the Midwest, particularly the region extending from Illinois to Pennsylvania (Fig. 12.3*a*). Most of the sulfur emissions are from coal-fired power plants, which are heavily concentrated in the region and account for the majority of all sulfur dioxide emissions nationally. These electricity-producing plants burn coal that is higher in sulfur content than the coal burned in the West. It recently was estimated that moderate-sulfur coal (which accounts for 40% of the total coal burned) is a prime source of emissions, accounting for 49 percent of all sulfur dioxide emissions. In addition, older, smaller electrical utilities emit larger amounts of sulfur dioxide than newer facilities. In Canada, smelting is a major contributor of sulfur. A nickel smelter at Sudbury, Ontario, was, for years, one of the largest single point sources of sulfur dioxide in the world. In Europe, sulfur emissions are greatest in the heavily industrialized regions of central Europe.

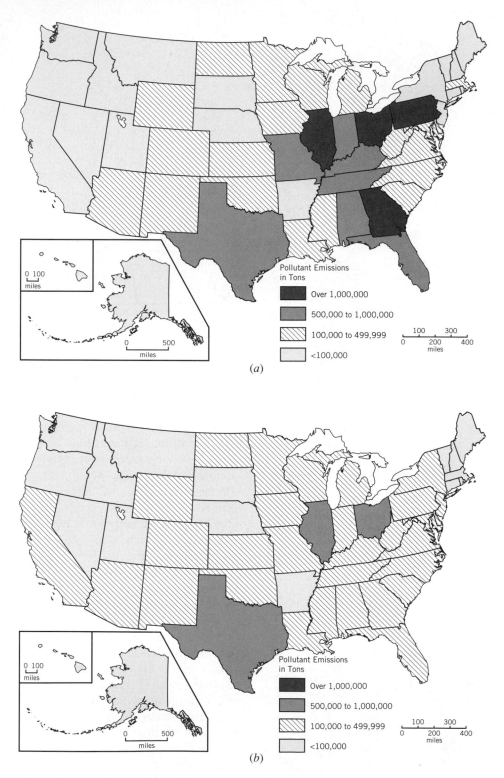

Figure 12.3 Sulfur dioxide and nitrogen oxide emissions, which contribute to the formation of acid precipitation. In 1997, sulfur dioxide emissions were greatest in the Ohio Valley states and Georgia (*a*), while nitrogen oxide emissions were more dispersed, with Texas, Illinois, and Ohio having the most (*b*). *Source:* U.S. Environmental Prrotection Agency, 1998.

The pattern for nitrogen oxide emissions is somewhat similar to that for sulfur dioxide (Fig. 12.3b) but the emissions are lower. Illinois, Texas and Ohio have the highest levels. There is a lower concentration of nitrogen oxide emissions in New England and the Pacific Northwest.

Effects on the Environment

Acid deposition has many effects on the environment, most of which are poorly understood at present. Among those recognized first were effects on lakes and aquatic life. Acid-neutralizing substances, such as calcium and magnesium compounds, are leached by water as it passes through the ground. In areas of calcium-rich rocks or soil, there are more than enough neutralizing substances to buffer most of the downstream effects of acid deposition. In areas of more acidic soils or in headwater areas where the water does not pass through much soil or rock before entering streams and lakes, the problem is more severe. In the Adirondacks of New York, for example, several high-altitude lakes have become so acidic that most fish cannot survive in the water. In some areas, lime has been added to lakes in an attempt to buffer the acids, but this has had limited success and is viewed as only a temporary solution to the problem (Patrick et al. 1981).

In addition to its effects on fish life, acid deposition contributes to slower growth and increased disease susceptibility in trees. Many mechanisms are involved, including mobilization of soluble metals in the soil, leaching of nutrients (especially calcium), and harm to soil biota that are vital to nutrient cycling. On Camels Hump Mountain in Vermont, spruce trees have been dying for several years. A drop in the pH tends to make minerals more soluble and thus increases their uptake by plants. Aluminum is of particular concern because of its toxic effects on plants. Analysis of cores from these trees suggests markedly increased accumulations of aluminum leached from the soil since 1950. Damage to spruce has also been documented in the Adirondacks. The main damage to red spruce, for example, is at 3000–4000 ft (914–1219 m) in the boreal zone of the Green Mountains (Vermont) and the Adirondacks (New York). In west Germany,

trees have died over 232 sq mi (60,000 ha), and another 14,672 sq mi (3.8 million ha) of forests are reported to be severely damaged (French 1990). In addition, about 35 percent of all European forests are now damaged as a result of acid deposition, approximately 1.9 million sq mi (49.6 million ha) (French 1990; Little, 1995) (Fig. 12.4).

Concerns have been voiced about acid rain and its effect on drinking water supplies and human health. Most metals are relatively insoluble in water at near-neutral pH, but as pH decreases, their solubility increases. Aluminum in soils, for example, may be leached out by acid rain and lead to an increase of aluminum concentrations in surface water. Lead, derived from both natural and human sources, is found in lake and stream sediments. As pH decreases, lead concentrations in water may increase. In addition, copper and other metals used in water-supply and distribution systems may be dissolved if the water becomes too acidic. Concern with these problems prompted officials in Massachusetts to add lime to Quabbin Reservoir, the major source of water for metropolitan Boston.

Finally, acid deposition contributes to the corrosion of building stone and exposed metal, including steel rails, unpainted metal surfaces on bridges and buildings, and so forth (Fig. 12.5). The economic costs of these effects are difficult to estimate, but they are believed to be substantial. The cost of pollution damage to European forests is estimated to be nearly $30 billion per year (World Resources Institute 1992). Damage estimates resulting from acid deposition are spotty, and their effect on crops, forests, human health, or buildings has not as yet been calculated.

Control and Management

Acid deposition can be controlled by the same methods used to control sulfur dioxide and nitrogen oxide concentrations in urban areas, including burning low-sulfur fuels, installing sulfur scrubbers, and reducing combustion temperatures. However, it is virtually impossible to link deposition in one area to emission sources in another because of the large number of sources broadly distributed over vast regions. In addition, NO_x, another component of acid rain, also derives from mobile sources (vehicles).

Figure 12.4   These trees in the Black Forest of southern Germany are dying because of the effects of air pollution, especially acid deposition. Documented damage to this famous forest helped galvanize public opinion, forcing action to reduce sulfur emissions in Germany.

Control of acid deposition is costly. Coal combustion is preferred in many areas because it is relatively cheap; switching to other fuels or to low-sulfur coal increases costs. Emission controls like scrubbers or advanced technologies such as fluidized bed combustion allow higher-sulfur coal to be burned, but these measures also bear high costs.

Because acid deposition affects large regions rather than just isolated areas, the solutions to the problem must also be regional, and this has been one of the primary barriers to reducing acid deposition. Failure to recognize the regional dimension to the problem delayed corrective actions. In the United States, for example, the 1970 Clean Air Act was aimed at urban air pollution problems, and its goal was to reduce pollutant concentrations in those areas. One of the techniques used was tall smokestacks, which dispersed the pollutants over a larger area in lower concentrations. This reduced local pollutant concentrations but also helped to spread sulfur and nitrogen oxides over larger areas by placing pollutants into stronger upper winds, thus adding to the acid deposition problem at remote locations.

The U.S. government was slow to act on the problem, but the 1990 Clean Air Amendments (CAA) set goals for emissions reductions. The CAA called for a 2 million ton reduction in nitrogen oxide emissions and a 10 million ton reduction for SO_2 by 2000. To achieve that goal, EPA's Acid Rain Program is using a variety of mechanisms to encourage energy efficiency and pollution prevention by industry and automobiles. To achieve SO_2 emissions reductions, EPA has set a national cap of 8.95 million tons of sulfur emissions annually by fossil fuel power plants. The EPA allocates emissions allowances, and it is up to each individual plant to decide how to meet them. The concept of trading allowances between different plants owned by the same utility, or trading allowances from one utility to another, is generally regarded as a success. In 1993, for example, 150,000 allowances were traded on the Chicago Board of Trade at prices of $122 to $450 per allowance.

Early in the program prices rose rapidly, but in the mid-1990s the market softened and prices fell significantly in 1996. Low prices for emission allowances mean that utilities can emit more

Figure 12.5 Destruction of sandstone sculpture caused by air pollution in Germany. The sculpture was installed in 1702; photo (at left) was taken in 1908; and photo (at right) was taken in 1969.

sulfur, and have less of an incentive to reduce pollution. In order for the price to rise either the government must issue fewer permits for sale, or environmental interests must be willing to purchase substantial numbers of permits and thus prevent sulfur from being emitted.

International agreements are needed to solve transnational pollution problems because some countries cause pollution and others suffer its effects. Persuading one country to pay for cleaning up the environment somewhere else may be difficult. During its tenure in the 1980s, the Reagan administration maintained that there was insufficient evidence of damage caused by acid deposition to warrant major reductions in sulfur and No_x emissions, but by 1991, agreement was reached with Canada to significantly reduce emissions on both sides of the border. By 1995, sulfate concentrations in rain were decreasing significantly, although concentrations of nitrates remained high.

The convention on Long-Range Transboundary Air Pollution (LRTAP) signed in 1979 by most European countries as well as the United States and Canada specifically addressed transboundary pollution issues. In 1987, a protocol to the 1979 convention, Reduction of Sulphur Emissions or Their Transboundary Fluxes by at Least 30 Percent (referred to as the 30 Percent Club), was ratified by 16 European countries and later joined by 5 others. The 30 Percent Club agreed to reduce sulfur dioxide emissions by at least 30 percent of 1980 levels in order to reduce transboundary pollution problems. Some of the largest sulfur dioxide emitters, notably the United States, the United Kingdom, and Poland, have not signed this protocol. Not all countries have achieved the promised reductions, but some have done better than a 30-percent reduction so that the average reductions for the 21 countries were 33 percent by 1990 (World Resources Instititute 1994). In addition to the sulfur protocol, a similar agreement was reached in Sofia, Bulgaria, in 1988 to limit nitrogen oxide emissions by freezing them at their 1987 levels. The Sofia protocol was signed by 24 nations, including the United States.

Stratospheric Ozone Depletion

Another global air pollution problem involves the accumulation of ozone-depleting chemicals (ODCs), such as chlorofluorocarbons (CFCs), which contribute to a loss of ozone in the stratosphere. Ozone intercepts ultraviolet radiation from the sun, and so one of the results of ODCs in the stratosphere is that more ultraviolet radiation reaches the earth's surface. This radiation is responsible for biological damage to plants and animals. Increased radiation may decrease photosynthesis, water use efficiency, leaf area, and ultimately crop yields by as much as 30 percent. Crops such as corn, soybeans, wheat, tomatoes, lettuce, and cotton seem to be the most affected in laboratory studies. Among non-agricultural environments, aquatic ecosystems may be most damaged, with estimates suggesting that a 25-percent reduction in ozone would result in a 35-percent reduction in the productivity of these ecosystems and their fish populations.

From a human standpoint, increased ultraviolet radiation would produce an increase in the number of skin cancers worldwide in the coming years. Every one percent decline in ozone is linked to a 4- to 6-percent increase in skin cancers. There could be 150 million new skin cancers resulting in 3 million deaths in the next 50 years in the United States alone. Some scientists also feel that ultraviolet radiation plays a role in depressing the human immune system, thus lowering the body's resistance to infections and disease.

Chlorofluorocarbons also play a role in the troposphere similar to that of carbon dioxide; they absorb longwave radiation and thus enhance the greenhouse effect. Although they are present in much lower concentrations, they are much more effective than carbon dioxide in raising atmospheric temperatures.

The worldwide response to the threat of ozone depletion represents a significant success story in international management of a commonly owned resource. The following sections describe the events contributing to that success, and some problems that remain to be solved.

Ozone-Depleting Chemicals

Chlorofluorocarbons (CFCs) are the most important ozone-depleting chemicals. CFCs are a class of synthetic substances that were originally developed for use in refrigeration. First discovered in 1930, these chemicals became widely used because they are neither toxic nor flammable. Marketed by E.I. du Pont de Nemours & Company under the trademark Freon (CFC-12), these chemicals have amazing versatility and hence many industrial applications. Over time, new chemical formulations were discovered and new applications were found for CFCs. CFC-113, for example, was one of the most widely-used members of the family. Its sole use is as a solvent, and it is used to clean everything from microchips in computers to dry-cleaned clothes.

CFCs were widely used in cooling and foam blowing. For example, before use was restricted by law in the United States, about a third of all CFCs were used as coolants for refrigeration and air conditioning, including the air conditioning in cars. Another third were used as blowing agents or synthetic rigid foams (insulation, styrofoam ice chests and cups, and fast-food containers) or flexible foams (furniture cushions and foam pillows). Other important uses included industrial solvents and aerosol propellants. The use of CFCs in aerosol sprays was discontinued in the U.S. in 1979.

Halons are a related family of compounds that contain bromine, a more potent destroyer of stratospheric ozone. It is speculated that per unit emitted halons cause 20 times the damage to the ozone layer as CFCs. Because of their superb fire-retardant properties, halons (Halon-1211, -1301, -2402) are used primarily in fire extinguishers. Finally, carbon tetrachloride (an intermediate product in the production of CFCs) and methyl chloroform also affect ozone. Carbon tetrachloride is used in chemical and pharmaceutical applications, but its impact on ozone depletion is minor when compared to that of the other ODCs. Methyl chloroform is used as an industrial degreasing agent and as a solvent in paints and adhesives.

Emissions of CFCs steadily increased over the years. In 1931, less than 220 million pounds (100 metric tons) were released; by 1976, worldwide CFC emissions peaked at 1.6 billion pounds (707,000 metric tons). A downturn in CFC emissions occurred between 1976 and 1983, but by 1986, CFC emissions were again quite high, averaging 1.5 billion pounds (671,600 metric tons) (World Resources Institute 1988). As discussed later in this chapter, emissions decreased dramatically in the 1990s, and it appears that stratospheric ozone concentrations will begin to recover early in the 2000s.

The Ozone Hole Is Discovered

One property of CFCs that makes them so useful is that they are chemically inert and therefore very stable. Unfortunately, this property also influences their adverse effect on the atmosphere as they remain intact, accumulating rather than breaking down and being removed. The atmospheric lifetime for CFCs, for example, ranges from 65 to 400 years (Table 12.3). This stability allows them to reach the stratosphere, where they are broken down by intense solar radiation, and their components enter into other chemical reactions. One of these reactions reduces the amount of ozone in the stratosphere. The process is quite simple, but a brief background on its scientific discovery is needed.

In 1985, a group of atmospheric scientists reported a 40-percent reduction in stratospheric ozone during the spring over Antarctica, where they were gathering data. Thus, the existence of the "Antarctic *ozone hole*" was established. During the sunless Antarctic winter (summer in the United States), the air mass is extremely cold, cold enough to freeze water vapor. Polar stratos-

pheric clouds are formed, and chemical reactions on the ice crystals convert chlorine from nonreactive forms to the more reactive hydrogen chloride and chlorine nitrate, which are sensitive to sunlight. As the Southern Hemisphere spring approaches, sunlight appears and releases the chlorine, which starts a chemical chain reaction that transforms ozone (O_3) into oxygen (O_2). The chlorine remains in the stratosphere to initiate many more chain reactions.

In one of the worst years (1987), 50 percent of the ozone over Antarctica was destroyed. Recent evidence indicates that CFC-derived chlorine is also destroying the ozone layer in the Arctic region as well, with 2 to 8 percent of the stratospheric ozone depleted (Fig. 12.6). With global air circulation patterns, the chlorine could easily be transported to midlatitudes, and this is what concerns scientists. In the late 1990s, springtime (October) averages of the ozone over Antarctica were 50 to 70 percent less than they were 30 years earlier. The ozone hole is expected to reach its greatest extent early in the next century, perhaps as soon as 2000 (Council on Environmental Quality 1993; Kerr 1996).

Reducing ODCs: The Montreal Protocol

In 1974, a group of U.S. scientists postulated that CFCs added chlorine to the stratosphere and through a series of complex chemical reactions reduced the amount of ozone. As a partial re-

Table 12.3   Ozone-Depleting Chemicals

Chemical	Atmospheric Lifetime (Years)	Contribution to Ozone Depletion (%)
CFC-11	65	26
CFC-12	130	45
CFC-13	400	
CFC-113	90	12
CFC-114	200	
CFC-115	400	
Carbon tetrachloride	50	8
Methyl chloroform	7	5
Halon-1301	110	4
Halon-1211	25	1

Source: Tolba et al., 1992

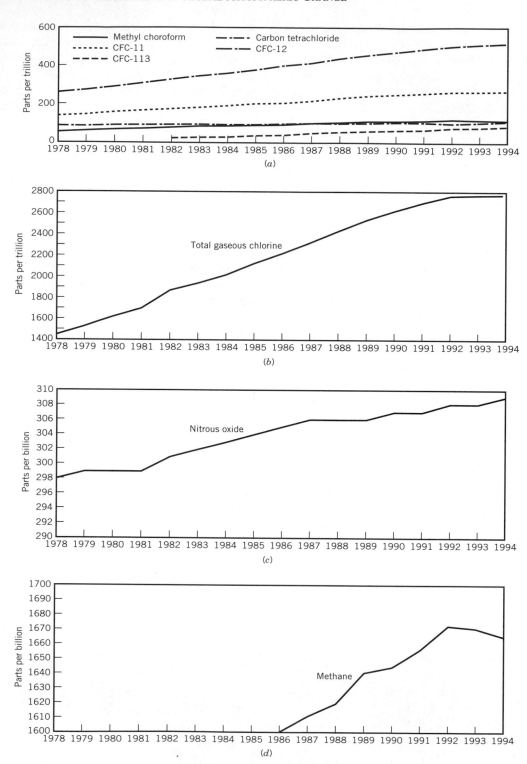

Figure 12.6 Atmospheric concentrations of ozone-depleting chemicals, 1978-1994. Concentrations generally rose rapidly in the 1980s, but the rate of increase declined significantly in the early 1990s. (*a*) Concentrations of methyl chloroform have declined since 1992. Chlorine (*b*) and nitrous oxides (*c*) show steady increases while methane (*d*) concentrations appear to have peaked. *Source:* World Resources Institute, 1996.

sponse to this concern over potential ozone depletion, the United States banned CFCs as aerosol propellants in all nonessential applications (ranging from hair sprays to deodorants to furniture polish). U.S. production of CFCs dropped by 95 percent. Considering that the United States and the European Community account for 84 percent of all CFC output, this was significant. Canada, Sweden, Norway, Denmark, and Finland also banned the use of CFCs as propellants in spray cans. The rest of the European Community (EC) was slower to respond and delayed action until 1980, when it cut aerosol use by 30 percent of 1976 levels (Conservation Foundation 1989). Because of CFCs' stability, the drop in production and use did not significantly alter the amount of CFCs in the atmosphere. With the discovery of the so-called *ozone*

hole in 1985 in Antarctica, the theoretical relationship between CFC use and ozone depletion became fact and widely accepted by scientists, policymakers, and the public. The time was ripe for international action (Table 12.4).

In 1985, 28 nations participated in the Vienna Convention on the Protection of the Ozone Layer. This meeting was designed as a legal instrument to protect the atmosphere as a resource by reducing the use of CFCs. The conferees were able to agree in principle to protect the atmosphere, but in practical terms they were unable to agree on CFC control. The United States, Canada, and Sweden, for example, wanted an immediate freeze on CFC production and a gradual phaseout of its use. European Community members wanted a freeze in production at existing levels. In early 1986, the Chemical Manufactur-

Table 12.4   Policy Milestones in Ozone-Depleting Substances

1978   UNEP Coordinating Committee for the Ozone Layer established
1985   Vienna Convention for the Protection of the Ozone Layer held
1987   Vienna Convention enters into force; 19 nations ratify
1987   Montreal Protocol on Substances That Deplete the Ozone Layer held
      Regulates consumption and production in the following manner:
        1. CFCs frozen at 1986 levels in 1990; 20% reduction in 1993; 50% reduction in 2000
        2. Halons frozen at 1986 levels by 2005
        3. Developing countries given 10-year exclusionary period
1989   Montreal Protocol enters into force; 23 nations ratify
1990   London Amendment to Montreal Protocol ratified
      Accelerates production and consumption phaseouts:
        1. CFCs reduced by 20% in 1993; 50% in 1995; 85% in 1997; phaseout in 2000
        2. Halons reduced by 50% by 1995; phaseout (except for essential uses) by 2000
        3. Carbon tetrachloride emissions reduced by 85% in 1997; phaseout in 2000
        4. Methyl chloroform emissions frozen in 1993; reduction by 30% in 1995; 70% in 2000; phaseout in 2005
        5. Other fully halogenated CFCs reduced by 20% in 1993; 85% in 1997; phaseout in 2000
1991   Interim Multilateral Fund established to provide financial assistance to developing countries to meet timetable for phaseout
1992   Vienna Convention now ratified by 82 nations
      Montreal Protocol now ratified by 76 nations
      London Amendment to the Montreal Protocol ratified by 19 nations
1992   London Amendment to the Montreal Protocol enters into force; 20 nations ratify
1994   Copenhagen Amendment to the Montreal Protocol ratified
      Accelerates complete phaseout of CFCs by January 1, 1996
1995   Nobel Prize in chemistry awarded to Paul Crutzen, F. Sherwood Rowland, and Mario Molina for discovery that trace amounts of gases can profoundly change the upper atmosphere.
      Copenhagen Amendment to the Montreal Protocol enters into force
1996   Production of CFCs in developed countries ceased

Source: Tolba et al., 1992, 37.

ers Association, an industry group, supported production limits. du Pont, the developer of Freon, vowed to find a substitute for CFCs within five years.

By 1987, significant international concern had been raised, resulting in the negotiation of the *Montreal Protocol* (officially known as the Montreal Protocol on Substances That Deplete the Ozone Layer). The treaty, which has since been ratified by over 125 countries, became effective January 1, 1989. It froze the production of CFCs by European Community members at mid-1989 levels and called for 50-percent reductions in emissions globally by 1999. The treaty permitted developing countries to increase CFC use for ten more years, while allowing the former USSR to continue production through 1990. Finally, the Montreal Protocol limits the use of halons as fire-suppressant chemicals.

In early 1989, the European Community countries went a step further and agreed to totally eliminate the use of CFCs by the end of the century. The United States supported this move, resulting in the total ban of CFC production by 65 percent of the world's producing countries. In 1990, an amendment to the Montreal Protocol called for the complete elimination of CFC use by 2000. Two years later, another amendment to the Montreal Protocol (the Copenhagen Amendment) accelerated the CFC phaseout to January 1, 1996. Finally, by January 1, 1996, all developed nations ceased their production of CFCs. As of 1996, 44 nations had ratified the Montreal Protocol, and 27 the London Amendments.

The result of these agreements has been dramatic. In the late 1980s, it was widely believed that the concentrations of ODCs in the stratosphere would increase well into the twenty first century. A decade later, in the late 1990s, concentrations of ODCs are declining and there is evidence that the ozone hole may have reached its worst level, and improvement is beginning. Projections indicate that ozone levels could recover to their 1979 levels by 2050, although continued release of halons from fire extinguishing systems may slow recovery (Kerr 1996). If these trends continue, significant international cooperation in managing a global common resource will have been achieved.

Problems remain however. In the mid-1990s production actually rose in China and other countries not required to eliminate CFC production, raising concerns that the global phaseout of CFCs might take a little longer than expected. Some of this increased production may have supplied a growing black market in CFCs smuggled into countries in which use has been curtailed (see Issue 12.1).

GLOBAL CLIMATE CHANGE

Climate is naturally variable, from year to year and over longer periods of time. While natural climate variations cause problems, we are normally content to live with them—we have no choice. Human-caused climate change is another matter, however. Concern about the climatic impacts of increasing carbon dioxide (CO_2) in the atmosphere began decades ago but has been especially vocal since the early 1970s. In the 1970s, considerable controversy arose over whether elevated CO_2 would cause warming, cooling, or neither. By the late 1990s, most scientists agreed that climatic warming would result from increased CO_2, in the atmosphere and many believed that the warming had already begun.

The Greenhouse Effect

The earth's atmosphere is a partially and differentially transparent medium with respect to energy and regulates flows of energy between space and the earth's surface. Since it is relatively transparent to the wavelengths of most solar radiation, sunlight passes through the atmosphere relatively unimpeded. The energy returned to space by the earth has longer wavelengths than that of sunlight. The atmosphere is only partly transparent to these wavelengths, and much of the outgoing radiation is temporarily trapped in the atmosphere, which keeps the atmosphere warmer than it would otherwise be. Several atmospheric components are responsible for this action, among them water vapor, methane, ozone, CFCs, nitrous oxides, trace gases, and carbon dioxide. These are collectively known as *greenhouse gases,* and they have natural as well as human sources. The ability of carbon dioxide to admit shortwave solar radiation but absorb outgoing longwave terrestrial radiation causes atmospheric warming, and has been called the *greenhouse effect.* In terms of its impact on atmospheric tem-

ISSUE 12.1:   BLACK MARKET FREON

Freon is the du Pont trade name for CFCs. Since January 1, 1996, CFCs, halons, carbon tetrachloride, and methyl chloroform (also called ozone-depleting substances) have been outlawed in the United States as part of the implementation of the Montreal Protocol. When the Montreal Protocol was ratified in 1987, it set a timetable for phasing out ozone-depleting chemicals by the year 2000 for the developed countries and the year 2010 for developing countries. However, in the early 1990s, developed nations agreed to a January 1, 1996, deadline.

CFCs were widely used coolants in refrigerators, freezers, room air conditioners, and car air conditioning units. With the ban, new coolants are now required for these consumer products. However, what do you do with the old appliances? More importantly, how do you get your older car serviced?

Recycled Freon is available from discarded freezers, refrigerators, and unit air conditioners. The government also stockpiled Freon (and other CFCs) in anticipation of potential shortages once the ban took effect. In 1989, for example, one pound of Freon cost around $1. Now with the recent governmental excise tax ($5.35 per pound), the average price has jumped from between $8 and $20 per pound.

Since 1991, all cars and trucks have been required to use a more environmentally friendly product. While older cars can be retrofitted to use the new refrigerants, most have not been converted despite the relatively low cost ($200–300).

This means that in 1996 there were about 140 million cars in the United States that still used Freon.

Unfortunately, the demand for Freon exceeded the legal supply. In addition, the legal supplies are costly: more than 20 times the price on the black market. A canister (30 pounds) costing $160 in Tijuana was worth $600 in Santa Ana less than 100 miles north. The result was a thriving black market in Freon. Some governmental officials estimated that nearly $200 million in tax revenues were lost due to illegal smuggling.

Smugglers mostly operate in India, Russia, and China where the CFCs are still legal. They ship the contraband through Canada or Mexico into the United States. In 1994, for example, customs officials seized 1.5 million pounds of Freon worth an estimated $18 million. In 1996, authorities figured that $500 million of Freon was smuggled into the United States, making it a bigger trade commodity than illegal guns. Obviously, much more is coming into the country undetected.

Consumers have no way of knowing the source of Freon when they have their car serviced. Often the mechanics might not know either. Black marketers will continue to supply the banned substance until such time as older car owners finally realize it is both economical and environmentally sound to spend the $200 to $300 needed to convert their cars than to continue to support the illegal smuggling operations. It just might be cheaper and more environmentally responsible to simply roll down your windows (Goldberg 1996; *San Diego Daily Transcript* 1996).

---

perature, water vapor is the most important greenhouse gas. The warming of the atmosphere as a result of human-caused increases in greenhouse gas concentrations is known as *global warming*.

Greenhouse Gases

The amount of heat stored in the atmosphere and its distribution within different layers and regions of the atmosphere play an important role in regulating atmospheric circulation and ultimately climate. The carbon dioxide content of the atmosphere (about 0.037% of the atmosphere in

1998) has changed considerably throughout the history of the earth. A billion or more years ago, it was probably much higher than today. During the Carboniferous Era, about 280 to 345 million years ago, much of the land surface of the globe was covered with vast swampy forests. The fossil fuels we burn today are derived from carbon taken from the atmosphere and stored in those forests and other ecosystems in the past.

Atmospheric carbon dioxide content also fluctuates on a seasonal basis. In the Northern Hemisphere, the concentration of carbon dioxide varies about 5 ppm within a given year. The maximum occurs in April; as plants photosynthesize and store carbon throughout the summer, the carbon dioxide content steadily decreases. It reaches a minimum in October and then climbs back up as more plant matter decays than grows. The annual cycle shows the close relation between carbon dioxide in the atmosphere and processes at the earth's surface. The global carbon cycle is the biogeochemical cycle that human activity has affected the most. This will result in significant climatic changes within the next several decades and may cause a profound impact on the global environment. The long-term effects of increased atmospheric CO_2 are highly uncertain, however, because we still have an inadequate understanding of atmospheric dynamics. For example, global warming could cause water vapor concentrations to rise and thus increase the greenhouse effect, but it could also create more cloud cover which might have the opposite effect.

Sources and Sinks   Greenhouse gases have a wide variety of sources and sinks, depending on biogeochemical cycling and human activities. Some of the major natural sources of greenhouse gases include decomposition in wetlands (methane) and microbial processes in soil and water (nitrous oxides). Anthropogenic sources include fossil fuel consumption and land-use change. The oceans, soil, and biomass are important sinks of CO_2.

Since the early nineteenth century, we have steadily increased our extraction and combustion of fossil fuels, returning stored carbon to the atmosphere as carbon dioxide. Not all the carbon dioxide emitted stays in the atmosphere; a substantial amount enters the oceans, and some is stored in living biomass. Not all fuels contribute the same amount of carbon dioxide when burned. Coal contains about 75 percent more carbon per unit of energy than natural gas, whereas oil contains about 44 percent more. Coal and oil combustion thus release more CO_2 to the atmosphere than natural gas.

Globally, more carbon is currently being released from the biota than is absorbed by it as a result of land-use activities. It is estimated that about 20 percent of carbon dioxide emissions come from deforestation and the loss of soil carbon due to soil degradation. Tropical deforesta-

tion is the largest source related to land-use change. In some parts of the world, forest growth is causing net removal of carbon from the atmosphere and storage in the biota.

Most atmospheric methane comes from natural processes, particularly anoxic decomposition of organic matter. Natural methane sources include decomposition in rice paddies and swamps, the action of anaerobic bacteria on plant material in the intestines of ruminants (cows, sheep, and camels) and wood digestion by termites. Anthropogenic sources contribute significantly less and include the combustion of fossil fuels (natural gas in particular) and biomass (clearing of forests), and landfills.

Nitrous oxide (N_2O) is another greenhouse gas that contributes to the greenhouse effect. In addition, nitrous oxide acts as a catalyst for stratospheric ozone removal. Nitrous oxide is derived primarily from anthropogenic sources, including the combustion of fossil fuels, the use of nitrogen-rich fertilizer, and deforestation.

Atmospheric Concentrations   Since the nineteenth century, the atmospheric content of carbon dioxide has been steadily increasing (Fig. 12.7). The rate of increase is itself escalating, a result of the growth in fossil fuel use worldwide. Prior to the Industrial Revolution it was about 280 ppm, and in 1980 it was 340 ppm. By 1990 the concentration was 354 ppm, and in 1994 it was 359 ppm (Table 12.5) (World Resources Institute 1996). Between 1970 and 1995, global concentrations of carbon dioxide rose by

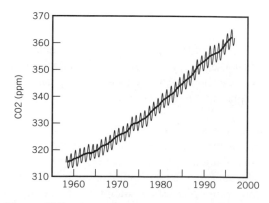

Figure 12.7   Atmospheric concentrations of carbon dioxide. *Source:* Keeling and Whorf, 1997.

Table 12.5   Trends in Ambient Levels of Key Greenhouse Gas Emissions

	CO_2 (ppm)	Methane (ppb)	NO_x (ppb)	CFC-11 (ppt)	CFC-12 (ppt)
Preindustrial	280	700	285	0	0
1990	354	1645	307	249	469
1994	359	1666	309	261	509
Current rate of change	0.5	0.5	0.2	5.0	5.0
Atmospheric lifetime	50-200	10	150	65	130

Source: Tolba et al., 1992; World Resources Institute, 1996.

10 percent or about 0.4 percent per year (World Resources Institute 1996). Nitrous oxides and methane concentrations also increased. Ambient concentrations of methane have more than doubled in the last 300 years, from 665 to around 1666, and are currently increasing at about 0.5 percent per year. The rate of increase of nitrous oxide is 0.2 percent per year.

Emission Trends   Carbon emissions from fossil fuel combustion were 6.25 billion metric tons (23 billion tons as carbon dioxide) in 1996. The overwhelming majority of these were from industrial activity. In fact, emissions from industrial activity have increased by 40 percent over the past 20 years. The vast majority of the CO_2 emissions are from the burning of fossil fuels (82%), especially petroleum and coal (Fig. 12.8a). The

United States is the largest source of CO_2 emissions, followed by China, Russia, and Japan (Table 12.6). Among the major global emitters, the United States still had the highest per capita rate (19.1 metric tons per person in 1994), more than four times the world average (5.3 metric tons per person in 1994). Globally, the United Arab Emirates has the highest per capita dioxide emissions (42 metric tons per person) as a consequence of petroleum production, including gas flaring, and a relatively small population (2.9 million). The regional variation in per capita emissions (Fig. 12.9) highlights the contributions of the industrialized nations.

Methane emissions averaged 270 million metric tons in 1992, the majority coming from industrial activity, followed by livestock (Fig. 12.8b). Regionally, China and India are the largest

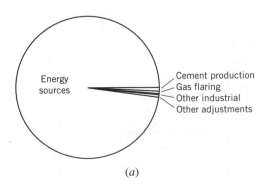

(a)

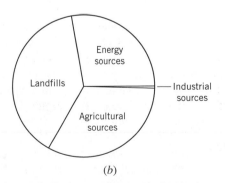

(b)

Figure 12.8   Emissions sources for CO_2 (a) and methane (b) for 1993. Carbon dioxide emissions come almost entirely from fossil fuel combustion. Cement production, gas flaring and other sources account for only 4 percent. Anthropogenic methane emissions come from landfills, energy sources such as unburned fossil fuels, and agricultural sources primarily wet-rice cultivation. *Source:* World Resources Institute, 1996.

Table 12.6 Regional Contributions to Greenhouse Gas Emissions (in million metric tons)

Continent	Industrial CO_2	Land Use CO_2	Anthropogenic Methane	Pct. World Total
Africa	715.8	730.0	21.0	5.7
Europe	6866.5	11.0	53.0	27.0
North/Central America	5715.5	190.0	35.0	23.1
South America	605.0	1800.0	21.0	9.4
Asia	7118.3	1300.0	140.0	33.3
Oceania	297.2	38.0	5.8	1.3

Source: World Resources Institute, 1996.

methane emitters, followed by the United States and Russia. In China, rice cultivation and coal mining produce more than 80 percent of the methane emissions. For India, it is a combination of livestock and wet rice cultivation. The methane emissions in the United States are more mixed, with solid waste dominating, followed by oil and gas production, coal mining, and livestock. A similer situation obtains for Russia, where oil and gas and livestock production dominate.

Impacts

Greenhouse gas emissions could cause a rise in global temperatures during the next century. Though seemingly small, this rise could have many significant impacts, including inundation of coastal areas caused by sea-level rise, increased variability in weather, and extreme weather events. Because of the climate's inherent variability it is difficult to tell whether observed climate change is natural or human in origin. We do know that global average temperature has risen about 1°C in the last century, and many believe that this is a result of increased CO_2 in the atmosphere.

A key question regarding the historic rise in temperature is as follows: Is the warming part of natural climatic variability, or is it a result of human activities? Those who argue that the warming may be natural note that the period from about 1500 to 1750 was distinctly cooler than the preceding centuries. This cool spell, known as the Little Ice Age, still may be coming to an end as a result of unknown natural processes, with temperatures returning to levels that existed several centuries ago. On the other hand, the recent warming coincides with the in-

crease in atmospheric CO_2 since the Industrial Revolution, and it is logical to see that correlation in cause-and-effect terms.

In the early 1990s, significant advances were made in climatic modeling that help to answer the question of causality. Modelers' analyses began to include changes in the atmospheric concentrations of sulfur oxides. These substances, emitted primarily through coal combustion, have a cooling effect on the atmosphere. When the effects of sulfur oxides are included, the models are able to produce both spatial and temporal patterns of change that are very similar to those observed in historical data. The similarities suggest a "fingerprint" of human impact, supporting the hypothesis that the observed warming is indeed a result of increased CO_2.

If the models are correct, then predicting future warming depends on predictions of future fossil fuel use. These are, of course, highly uncertain. In the 1960s and 1970s, fossil fuel use was rising rapidly, and projections indicated that the atmospheric concentration of CO_2 would double by sometime in the twenty-first century. But in the 1990s the rate of increase in atmospheric CO_2 slowed, largely as a result of the economic collapse in the former Soviet bloc. The 1995 report of the Intergovernmental Panel on Climatic Change makes projections based on a range of assumptions and suggests that earth's climate may warm by as little as 1°C and as much as 3.5°C by 2100 (Houghton et al. 1996).

What will be the impacts of such a climate change? The answer to that question is even more uncertain than the temperature change itself. Perhaps the most worrisome potential impact is related to people living in vulnerable areas such as

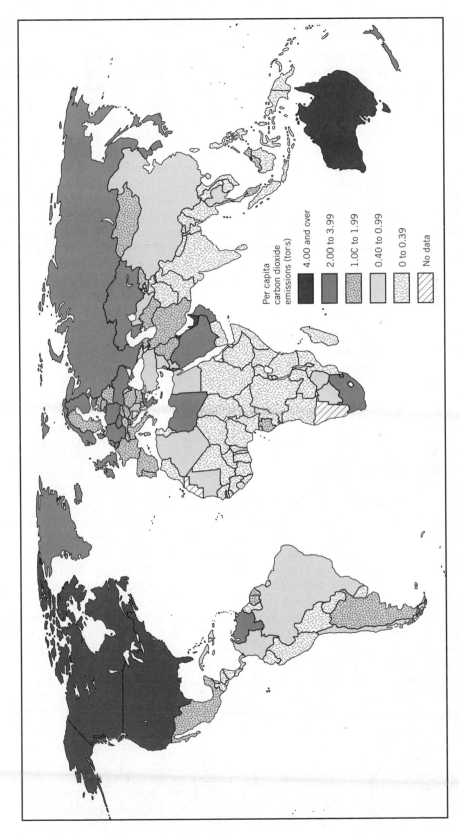

Figure 12.9 Per capita CO$_2$ emissions. With the exception of a few energy-producing states in the Middle East, the highest per capita emissions are in wealthy industrial countries. U.S. per capita emissions are about 5 times the world average and about 50 times those in sub-Saharan Africa.

Per capita
carbon dioxide
emissions (tons)

4.00 and over

2.00 to 3.99

1.00 to 1.99

0.40 to 0.99

0 to 0.39

No data

287

coasts and semiarid regions (Schneider 1997). A rise in sea level could displace millions of people from their current homes. The amount and rate of rise are highly uncertain but could be as much as 3 to 6 ft (1 to 2 m). The combined effects of these changes would inundate low-lying coastal areas, submerge coastal wetlands, increase coastal erosion, increase flood and storm damage from coastal storms, and increase the salinity of groundwater in low-lying areas, thus threatening drinking-water supplies. Bangladesh and Egypt are among the most vulnerable countries, where a 6-ft (2-m) rise in sea level would result in a 20-percent reduction in inhabitable land area in each country. China is also vulnerable, as are several small island nations such as the Maldives, Kirabati, and Tuvalu, which are threatened with

near-complete inundation. In the United States a similar rise would destroy 50 to 80 percent of our coastal wetlands and between 10 and 28 percent of the land area in Louisiana, Florida, Delaware, Washington, DC, Maryland, and New Jersey. Major changes in vegetation and land use would occur and have significant impacts on human society. If the predicted sea level changes are greater than 3 to 7 ft (1 to 2 m), then these effects will be even more pronounced and cover more of the world's low-lying areas (see Issue 12.2).

Another area of concern is the impact on agriculture. This impact will depend on both changes in temperature and precipitation, as well as the direct effects of CO_2 itself. Increases in atmospheric carbon dioxide cause more rapid plant growth, but some plants respond more dramati-

ISSUE 12.2: The Costs of Global Warming

In 1992, the countries of the world met in Rio de Janeiro and committed themselves to talking about doing something about CO_2 emissions. Again in 1995 and 1996 in Berlin, and in 1997 in Kyoto, the countries of the world again committed themselves to trying to reduce CO_2 emissions. But global CO_2 emissions continued their rise, which had been temporarily halted in the early 1990s by the economic collapse of eastern Europe. Despite the fact that the Intergovernmental Panel on Climate Change concluded in 1995 that there was strong evidence that human-induced global warming was occurring, and despite the fact that climate changes are probably the most profound and far-reaching impacts we have ever had on our environments, as of 1997 little of substance had been done to reduce CO_2 emissions. The reason for this lack of action is, of course, the enormous cost—perhaps as much as 4 percent of gross world product—involved in converting the world economy from one dependent on fossil fuels to one relying on less polluting sources of energy (Stevens 1995).

But what are the economic costs of not reducing CO_2 emissions? No one knows, and no one even has a very good guess, because no one knows exactly what climate changes will occur. Climate is made up of weather—storms and high pressure centers, clear skies and clouds, north winds and

southern breezes. These circulation patterns are, in turn, driven by the distribution of heat in the atmosphere. Common sense tells us that because CO_2 is affecting heat in the atmosphere, circulation, and hence weather, should change. But at the present time our knowledge of the atmosphere is still too crude to be able to predict what areas will actually get warmer or cooler, wetter or dryer. Thus, estimates of the impacts on agriculture, for example, are impossible. Some places that are on the dry margins of the arable earth may get wetter and so more productive, or they might get drier and become unusable for farming. We just don't know.

One industry that is widely expected to be hurt by global warming is the insurance industry, and many believe these costs are already appearing. In the early 1990s, several very expensive natural disasters occurred. The biggest of these in terms of monetary value was Hurricane Andrew, which struck southern Florida in 1992. Andrew's damages were estimated at $25 billion, of which $16 billion were covered by insurance. Had Andrew hit Miami directly instead of the southern margins of the city, the insured losses might have been as high as $50 to $60 billion. Other major storms in this period included floods in China in 1991 and 1994, in Italy in 1994, on the Mississippi River in 1993, and severe windstorms in northern Europe

cally than others. For example, soybeans respond much more than corn, and silver maple responds more than sycamore. These differences may lead to significant agricultural and ecological impacts. For example, some concern has been expressed about shifts in the range of forest species, increased forest fires, and the economic consequences of these factors on the forest industry. The impacts on agriculture also include shifts in the ranges of crops, increases in agricultural pests and livestock diseases, and shifts in the demands for irrigation.

Changes in regional climates resulting from warming are very hard to predict (Karl, Nicholls and Gregory 1997). Circulation changes might cause today's extreme weather to become the norm 50 years from now. Summers in the midcon-

tinental regions of North America, southern Europe, and Siberia, which are now some of the world's most productive agricultural regions, may become so dry that they will be unable to grow wheat. On the other hand, areas that are now marginal for agriculture may become more favorable. Droughts, floods, and similar problems could become commonplace rather than rare.

Greenhouse Politics and Emissions Stabilization

The United States is the leading source of carbon dioxide emissions, yet it was slow to acknowledge the importance of global warming and thus develop a comprehensive climate change strategy. It was also slow in joining the greenhouse politics parade.

in 1990. In just seven years, from 1990 to 1996, the insurance industry worldwide racked up losses from weather-related natural disasters totaling over $65 billion—over three times the total losses of the previous 30-year period (Worldwatch Institute 1997). Many insurance companies were put in serious financial trouble, and some were wiped out altogether.

We don't know whether these disasters are a result of global warming, or whether this is simply a string of bad luck. Some believe that an increase in atmospheric temperature causes an increase in the intensity of circulation and the severity of storms, but this is only a hypothesis. But whether or not they were caused by global warming, there are good reasons for the insurance industry, in particular, to be concerned. First, global warming is expected to cause a rise in sea level. If sea level rises only a few tenths of a meter, the damage caused by coastal storms can increase exponentially. A combination of increased storm frequency and slightly higher sea level is deadly. Second, insurance rates are based on past experience. The history of storms and the damages they cause give insurers an idea of how much they are likely to lose in a given year, and they charge rates that, over a period of time, will provide them with sufficient assets to cover those losses. But if cli-

mate is changing, then history is not a good predictor of the future, and that means that the insurance companies' rates may be too low. Finally, we might think that while some kinds of disasters could get more common, others might become less so. This is partly true, but insurance companies worry most about the big events that cause most of their losses. A few extra years without major disasters helps insurers a little, but a few extra years with major disasters can bankrupt a corporation. And because insurance companies are themselves major investors and also sell some of their contracts to other companies (called reinsurers), major disasters can send shock waves through financial businesses worldwide.

As a consequence of these disasters, the insurance industry has become a significant player in discussions on controlling CO_2 emissions. It lobbied intensively at the Berlin conferences, siding with a coalition known as the Alliance of Small Island States in proposing an international insurance pool that would help cover the costs of disasters related to climate change. Contributions to the fund would be based on GNP and CO_2 emissions. In this way, insurance companies would shed some of the risk of the disasters, with the costs at least partly borne by the countries responsible for rising CO_2 levels in the atmosphere.

In June 1988, a number of nations met in Toronto under the auspices of the United Nations to develop a far-reaching plan to protect the atmosphere. The Intergovernmental Panel on Climate Change (IPCC) recognizes that in order to merely stabilize carbon dioxide levels, a 50- to 80-percent reduction in carbon dioxide emissions is needed immediately. The panel's goal is to reduce carbon dioxide emissions by 20 percent by 2005, with an equitable distribution of reductions per country. This recommendation was obviously a compromise since many countries wanted an immediate freeze on emissions, whereas others oppose restrictions (the United States, Japan, and eastern and central European countries) because they are viewed as too costly.

The Framework Convention on Climate Change (FCCC) was adopted in May 1992 and signed by over 150 countries, who agreed to stabilize emissions of greenhouse gases. The treaty entered into force in March 1994. It calls for reducing emissions by the year 2000 to 1990 levels. The treaty also has other elements which promote our understanding of the emissions as well as actions we can take to reduce them. All countries must provide a periodic greenhouse gas inventory which takes into account the global warming potential of various gases and their production within that country. The Framework also called for countries to produce an action plan that outlines their proposals for reducing emissions by 1997.

In 1993, the United States adopted its Climate Change Action Plan. Among the actions planned are forest protection and industry/government partnerships for emissions reductions in electric utilities. Under the 1990 Clean Air Act, greenhouse gas emissions from transportation sources are also restricted. However, the U.S. plan relies heavily on voluntary measures, which may or may not work.

Work on a treaty to control carbon emissions continued between 1992 and 1997. Preliminary negotiations were carried out in a series of meetings held in Berlin in 1994 and 1995. In these sessions several positions became clear. The United States, a few other major emitters, and the oil-producing nations strongly opposed significant reductions in emissions. Most European nations favored significant reductions in emissions below 1990 levels. Such reductions were easier for the Europeans to achieve because a decline in coal use was already underway there. An alliance of small island nations concerned about rising sea level also favored significant reductions. Most of the poorer countries argued that the major emitters—especially the United States—bore responsibility for controlling carbon dioxide. These poorer countries were not willing to reduce emissions and potentially restrict their economic growth unless major reductions occurred in the United States and other rich countries first. Among these poorer countries is China, where emissions are growing rapidly. If current trends continue, China will become the world's largest emitter of CO_2 in the first decade of the twenty-first century (Drennen and Erickson 1998).

These negotiations culminated in Kyoto, Japan in December 1997 where an agreement known as the Kyoto Protocol was signed. The United States agreed to reduce emissions to 7 percent below 1990 levels by 2010, but only on the condition that credit for emissions reductions could be traded internationally, much as sulfur emissions permits are traded in the U.S. The Kyoto conference failed, however, to resolve the difficult issues of exactly how such trades would be carried out. The conferees set a deadline for late 1998 for agreement on this issue.

In addition, the Kyoto Protocol would have to be ratified by signatory nations before it became binding. Political resistance to the treaty in the Republican-controlled U.S. Senate is intense, and ratification of the treaty is highly unlikely in the near future unless significant modifications are made.

Reducing greenhouse emissions will require governmental intervention and personal responsibility. Stabilizing emissions will be costly and probably borne by most of the industrialized nations. However, they are not the only major emissions sources. Global reductions in greenhouse gas emissions require personal responsibility as well as equitable strategies that achieve the goals in the Framework without deleteriously affecting any one nation or population subgroup.

A WARMER FUTURE OR?

No one knows the geographic extent of the predicted climatic changes or the exact timing. Most scientists agree that some changes are likely, perhaps within the next several decades. These effects will be slow to come; to prevent them, we would have to act now or, better yet, have acted a few decades ago. For the present, the best that can be done is to become more aware of transboundary pollution problems and the difficulty they pose for environmental management.

Worldwide, both tropospheric and stratospheric pollution levels have worsened and will rise as developing countries become more urban and industrialized. The long-term consequences of altering the earth's atmospheric chemistry are already generating global concern. Tough economic and political action must be undertaken, and international cooperation is critical if we are to protect this common property resource for future generations.

Success in managing problems associated with international air pollution has so far been spotty. By 1997, the regional problem of acid deposition had been effectively addressed in Europe, but less so in the United States and work is just beginning in eastern Asia. Even in Europe, where the commitment to reduce emissions is strongest, acid deposition continues to be a severe problem. The international agreements to control ozone-depleting chemicals have been quite effective, to the point of reducing emissions and their damaging effects even faster than was envisioned in the 1980s. But negotiations to reduce carbon emissions produced only commitments to *attempt* reductions, which so far have had few meaningful results. The future of these international efforts remains cloudy.

REFERENCES AND ADDITIONAL READING

Abrahamson, D. E., ed. 1989. *The Challenge of Global Warming*. Covelo, CA: Island Press.

Anon. n.d. *Climate Action Report*. Submission of the United States of America Under the United Nations Framework Convention on Climate Change. Washington, DC: U.S. Government Printing Office.

Bolin, B., R., Doos, J. Jager, and R. A. Warrick, eds. 1986. *The Greenhouse Effect, Climatic Change and Ecosystems*. SCOPE 29. New York: John Wiley.

Conservation Foundation. 1989. The ozone protocol: A new global diplomacy. *Conservation Foundation Newsletter*, Vol. 4.

Consortium for International Earth Science Information Network (CIESIN). 1997. Environmental Treaties and Resource Indicators (ENTRI) ONLINE: *http://sedac.ciesin.org/entri/*

Council on Environmental Quality. 1993. *Environmental Quality. 24th Annual Report*. Washington, DC: U.S. Government Printing Office.

_____ . 1995. *25th Anniversary Report*. Washington, DC: U.S. Government Printing Office.

Dovland, H. 1987. Monitoring European transboundary air pollution. *Environment* 29(10): 10–20, 27–29.

Drennen, T. E., and J. D. Erickson. 1998. Who will fuel China? *Science* 279: 1483,

Flavin, C. 1989. *Slowing Global Warming: A Worldwide Strategy*. Worldwatch Paper no. 91. Washington, DC: Worldwatch Institute.

_____ . 1997. Climate change and storm damage: the insurance costs keep rising. *WorldWatch Magazine* 10:1: 10–11.

French, H. 1990. *Clearing the Air: A Global Agenda*. Worldwatch Paper no. 94 Washington, DC: Worldwatch Institute.

Goldberg, C. 1996. A chilling change in the contraband being seized at borders. *New York Times*, November 10, p. 34.

Hansen, J., et al. 1981. Climate impact of increasing atmospheric carbon dioxide. *Science* 213: 957–966.

Hedin, L. O. and G. E. Likens. 1996. Atmospheric dust and acid rain. *Scientific American*. 275 (6): 88–92.

Houghton, J. T., L. G. Meira Filho, B. A. Callendar, and N. Harris, eds. 1996. *Climate Change 1995: The Science of Climate Change*. Cambridge: Cambridge University Press.

Karl, T. R., N. Nicholls, and J. Gregory. 1997. The coming climate. *Scientific American*. 276 (5): 78–83.

Keeling, C. D., and T. P. Whorf. 1997. Atmospheric CO_2 concentrations—Mauna Loa Observatory, Hawaii, 1958–1996 (revised August 1997). ONLINE: *http://cdiac.esd.ornl.gov/ndp001.html*.

Kerr, R. A. 1995. It's official: first glimmer of greenhouse warming seen. *Science* 270: 1565–1567.

_____ . 1996. Ozone-destroying chlorine tops out. *Science* 271: 32.

Little, C. E., 1995. *The Dying of the Trees: The Pandemic in America's Forests*. New York: Viking/Penguin.

Luoma, J. 1988. The human cost of acid rain. *Audubon* 90(4): 16–29.

_____ . 1989. Crop study finds severe ozone damage. *New York Times*, February 2, p. C4.

National Research Council. 1983. *Acid Deposition: Atmospheric Processes in Eastern North America*. Washington, DC: National Academy Press.

Patrick, R., et al. 1981. Acid lakes from natural and anthropogenic causes. *Science* 211: 446–448.

San Diego Daily Transcript. 1996. Smugglers make hot case from air conditioner chemical. October 14. ONLINE: *http://sddt.com/files/li...0_14/DN96_10_14_cad.html*

Schneider, D. 1997. The rising seas. *Scientific American* 276 (3): 112–117.

Schneider, S. H. 1989a. The greenhouse effect: science and policy. *Science* 243: 771–782.

_____ . 1989b. *Global Warming: Are We Entering the Greenhouse Century?* San Francisco: Sierra Club Books.

Scholle, S. R. 1983. Acid deposition and the materials damage question. *Environment* 25(8): 25–32.

Stevens, W. K. 1995. Price of global warming? Debate weighs dollars and cents. *New York Times*, October 10, 1995, p. B6.

Stone, R. 1994. Most nations miss the mark on emission-control plans. *Science* 266: 1939.

Tolba, M. K., et al., eds. 1992. *The World Environment 1972–1992.* New York: Chapman & Hall.

United Nations Environment Programs. 1993. *Environmental Data Report 1993–94.* Cambridge, MA: Basil Blackwell.

U.S. Environmental Protection Agency. 1980. *Acid Rain.* EPA-600-79-036. Washington, DC: U.S. Government Printing Office.

_____ . 1988. ONLINE: *http://www.epa.gov:6703/air-wdcd/owa/afs.count*

World Resources Institute. 1987. *World Resources 1987.* New York: Basic Books.

_____ . 1988. *World Resources 1988–89.* New York: Basic Books.

_____ . 1992. *World Resources 1992–93.* New York: Oxford University Press.

_____ . 1994. *World Resources 1994–95.* New York: Oxford University Press.

_____ . 1996. *World Resources: A Guide to the Global Environment 1996–97.* New York: Oxford University Press.

Worldwatch Institute. 1997. Worldwatch database diskette. Washington, DC: Worldwatch Institute.

For more information, consult our web page at *http://www.wiley.com/college/cutter*

STUDY QUESTIONS

1. International negotiations to control emissions of ozone-depleting chemicals were quite successful, even leading to accleration of the timetable for control. In contrast, efforts to control CO_2 emissions have been an almost complete failure. What are the main reasons for the differences in these two outcomes?

2. Who will be the winners and who will be the losers if global climate changes significantly over the next 50 years?

3. Examine Chapters 6–10 in this book, and make a list of all the important resource issues that might be significantly affected by global warming.

4. What changes in energy policy would be necessary for a significant reduction in acid deposition in the eastern United States?

5. What changes in energy policy would be necessary for a significant reduction in CO_2 emissions in the United States?

6. What countries should be asked to make the greatest sacrifices to control global CO_2 emissions? Should all countries bear equal responsibility, or should responsibility be proportionate to emissions?

CHAPTER 13

NONFUEL MINERALS

INTRODUCTION

In Chapter 1 we stated that resources are defined by their use. They fluctuate in response to changing human evaluations of resources as commodities and our abilities to use them. This is particularly true for minerals. For most minerals there is nothing inherent in the substance that makes it valuable. The value of a mineral derives from its usefulness in a given situation, which is largely a function of technology and cost relative to other materials. Our use of minerals therefore changes frequently as technology and as economic and political conditions change. The physical characteristics of resources, including supply, may be relatively unimportant in determining use.

Minerals are defined differently in various contexts. For the purposes of this book, minerals are substances that come from the earth, either from solid rocks or from soils and other deposits. Minerals include fossil fuels, such as coal, oil, and natural gas, but these are discussed separately in Chapter 14. The nonfuel minerals include metal ores, phosphate rock, asbestos, salt, precious stones, clay, gravel, building stone, and similar materials. Minerals are valued for their physical properties, such as strength, malleability, corrosion resistance, electrical conductivity, and insulating or sealing capacity, and they are fundamental to any industrial system. Table 13.1 lists major minerals, some of their uses, and major world producers.

An important feature of mineral resources is that most are traded internationally. Usually, a relatively small number of countries dominate the production of a particular mineral, many countries are consumers, and a few are self-sufficient. A country may have substantial quantities of a mineral available, the capacity to extract it, and the need to use it, but this does not necessarily mean that it will produce the mineral domestically. If sufficient quantities are available on the world market at prices below domestic production costs, then the mineral will be imported. In, addition, socal or economic conditions in major producing or consuming nations can significantly affect world markets and have far-flung impacts on the status of mineral resources. We must therefore examine mineral resources on a global scale.

RESERVES AND RESOURCES

Reserves is an important term used to describe the availability of minerals to a production system. Reserves of a mineral are the supplies available for use at the present time. Their location and physical characteristics are known, and they can be extracted using present technology and under prevailing economic conditions. Reserves are a subset of resources, which also include deposits that are unavailable for use at present because of poor geologic knowledge or unfavorable economic or technological conditions, but which might become available in the future. *Unidentified resources* are those that have not yet been discovered, whereas *subeconomic resources* are those that may have been discovered but cannot be extracted at a profit at current prices.

The distinction between reserves and resources is illustrated in Figure 13.1. The hori-

Table 13.1 Major Mineral Uses and Producers

Mineral	Major Uses	Major Producing Nations
Antimony	Flame retardants, transportation, batteries	China, Russia, South Africa, Bolivia
Arsenic	Wood preservatives, glass manufacturing, agricultural chemicals	China, Chile, France
Asbestos	Roofing products, friction products, gaskets	Russia, Canada, Kazakhstan, China
Barite	Well drilling fluids, chemicals	China, U.S., India, Morocco
Bauxite	Packaging, building, transportation, electrical	Australia, Guinea, Jamaica, Brazil
Beryllium	Metal alloys in aerospace and electrical equipment, computers	U.S., China, Brazil, Russia
Bismuth	Pharmaceuticals, chemicals, machinery	Peru, Mexico, China
Boron	Glass, agriculture, fire retardants,	Turkey, U.S.
Bromine	Fire retardants, agriculture, petroleum additives	U.S., Israel, United Kingdom
Cadmium	Coating and plating, batteries, pigments	Japan, Canada, Belgium, U.S.
Cesium	Research and development, electronic and medical applications	Canada, Namibia, Zimbabwe
Chromium	Metallurgical and chemical industry, refractory industry	South Africa, Kazakhstan, India
Cobalt	Superalloys, catalysts, paint driers, magnetic alloys, cemented carbides	Canada, Zambia, Russia, Australia
Columbium	High-strength low-alloy steels, carbon steels, superalloys	Brazil, Canada
Copper	Building construction, electric and electronic products	Chile, U.S., Canada, Russia
Diamond	Machinery, mineral services, stone and ceramic products, abrasives	Australia, Russia
Diatomite	Filter aid, fillers	U.S., France, Former USSR
Feldspar	Glass, pottery	Italy, U.S., Thailand, South Korea
Fluorspar	Metal processing	China, Mexico, South Africa
Gallium	Optoelectronic devices, integrated circuits	Germany, Russia, Japan
Garnet	Petroleum industry, filters, transport	U.S., Australia, China, India
Germanium	Fiber-optics, infrared optics, detectors	U.S.
Gold	Jewelry manufacturing, electronics	South Africa, U.S., Australia
Graphite	Refractories, brake linings, packings	China, South Korea, India
Gypsum	Cement retarder, agricultural land plaster	U.S., China, Canada, Iran
Helium	Cryogenics, welding cover gas, pressurizing and purging, controlled atmospheres	U.S., Former USSR, Algeria
Ilmenite	Titanium pigments	Australia, South Africa, Canada
Indium	Coatings, solders and alloys, electrical components and semiconductors	Canada, Japan, France
Iodine	Animal feeds, catalysts, chemicals	Japan, Chile, U.S.

(continued on next page)

Table 13.1 Major Mineral Uses and Producers (continued)

Mineral	Major Uses	Major Producing Nations
Iron Ore	Steel	China, Brazil, Russia, Australia
Kyanite	Refractories	South Africa, France, India
Lead	Batteries, fuel additives	Australia, U.S., China, Peru
Lime	Steel furnaces, water treatment, construction	China, U.S.
Lithium	Ceramics, glass, aluminum, lubricants	Chile, Australia, Russia
Magnesium	Metal refractories, aerospace, auto components	U.S., Canada, Norway, Russia
Manganese	Construction, machinery, transportation	South Africa, China, Ukraine
Mercury	Chlorine and caustic soda, electronic and electrical applications, paints	Spain, China, Algeria
Molybdenum	Machinery, electrical, transportation	U.S., China, Chile, Canada
Nickel	Metal alloys, stainless steel	Russia, Canada, New Caledonia
Perlite	Building construction, filter aid, horticulture	U.S., Turkey, Greece
Phosphate Rock	Fertilizer	U.S., China, Morocco & Western Sahara
Platinum Group	Automotive, electronic, chemical	South Africa, Russia, Canada
Potash	Fertilizer	Canada, Germany, Belarus, Russia
Pumice	Building blocks	Italy, Turkey, Greece
Quartz Crystal	Electronics	U.S., Brazil
Rare Earths	Petroleum catalysts, metallurgical, ceramics	China, U.S., Former USSR
Rhenium	Petroleum catalysts, superalloys	U.S., Chile, Peru, Canada
Rutile	Titanium pigment, titanium metal, welding	Australia, South Africa, Sierra Leone
Scandium	Metallurgical research, halide lamps, lasers	China, Kazakhstan, Madagascar
Selenium	Electronics, glass, chemicals and pigments	Japan, U.S., Canada, Belgium
Silicon	Metal alloys	China, U.S., Russia, Ukraine
Silver	Photography, electronics	Mexico, Peru, U.S., Australia
Strontium	Color television picture tubes, magnets	Mexico, Turkey, China, Iran
Sulfur	Fertilizer, chemicals	U.S., Canada, China, Mexico
Talc	Ceramics, paint, paper, plastics	China, U.S., Japan
Tantalum	Electronics, machinery	Australia, Brazil, Canada
Tellurium	Iron and steel, catalysts and chemicals	Canada, Japan, Peru
Thallium	Electronics, pharmaceuticals, alloys	U.S., Canada
Thorium	Nuclear fuel, electrical	Australia, Brazil, Canada, India
Tin	Cans and containers, electrical, construction	China, Indonesia, Brazil, Bolivia
Titanium	Aerospace, chemical	Japan, Russia, Kazakhstan
Tungsten	Lamps, electrical, metalworking	China, Kazakhstan, Russia
Vanadium	Transportation, machinery and tools, building	South Africa, Russia, China
Yttrium	Television monitors, lasers, alloys, catalysts	China, Former USSR, Australia
Zinc	Metal plating, alloys	Canada, Australia, China
Zirconium	Foundry sands, refractories, ceramics	Australia, South Africa, Ukraine

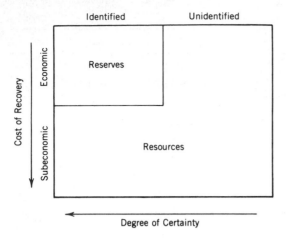

Figure 13.1 Reserves and resources. The boundary between reserves and resources is not fixed. It shifts with new discoveries, price changes, and other technological and socioeconomic factors. *Source*: Modified from Brobst and Pratt, 1973.

zontal axis of the diagram represents varying degrees of certainty about the existence or nature of deposits of a particular mineral. The vertical axis represents differing economic values of the deposits, that is, the varying economic profitability of extraction. All occurrences of a given mineral are contained symbolically within the boundaries of the diagram. For nonfuel minerals, this may include already-used and discarded resources, such as those in landfills. Use of nonfuel minerals does not destroy them but may convert them to a less usable form.

The boundaries between reserves and other resources in Figure 13.1 shift over time. Shifts in these boundaries result primarily from three factors: (1) economic conditions; (2) technology of extraction and use; and (3) geologic information. The economic profit ability of extraction varies considerably, depending primarily on the price of the commodity. As price goes up, more and more deposits, either of lower grade or costing more to extract, become profitable to mine. Similarly, if price falls, only high-quality or cheaply extracted deposits can be mined at a profit, and the quantity of reserves shrinks. Prices for minerals often fluctuate widely, as discussed in Chapter 2. Fluctuations in the level of production in the economy as a whole affect demand

and price for raw materials, and competition between substitutable materials can also cause price variations.

Technology is another factor that is of importance, mainly as it affects the costs of mineral extraction and processing. For example, during the nineteenth and early twentieth centuries, high-quality iron ore was shipped in essentially raw form from Lake Superior ports to steel mills on the lower Great Lakes. In time the high-grade ores were depleted, and transportation costs per unit of steel became prohibitive. The development of a means for concentrating a lower-grade ore, called taconite, into enriched pellets at the mining site reduced transportation costs and allowed renewed mining activities. This technological development made lower-grade ores economically extractable, which they had not been in the past. Technological and social changes can also cause increases in the costs of extraction. Recently, environmental regulations have required changes in mining techniques to minimize environmental disruption. These changes have increased the cost of extraction, thus tending to decrease reserves. Underground mining of coal is another example; stricter safety standards for miners have increased the costs of mining coal underground. In some cases, this has contributed to the shift from subsurface to surface mining of coal.

Geologic exploration does not directly affect the profitability of extracting minerals but instead brings new deposits to light. If these are extractable at current prices and with current technology, they become reserves. Changes in geologic information are generally more important in long-term trends in reserves rather than in the short term. For most minerals there are identified deposits that will last at least a few years, and price fluctuations cause much more variation in reserves than do increases in information. It takes time to acquire new geologic information. Easily located surficial deposits have mostly been identified, and new deposits must be found beneath the surface or in very remote areas. Geologic structures and rock types must be carefully mapped, possible mineral associations checked with geochemical surveys, gravity surveys conducted, and so forth. When a potential deposit is located, it is usually necessary to drill test boreholes and analyze many rock samples before there is any certainty of the nature and extent of a deposit. The sophisticated exploration techniques available today help us to see the subsurface in greater detail rather than significantly speeding the process of exploration.

AVAILABILITY OF MAJOR MINERALS

Geology of Mineral Deposits

There are so many different important minerals, and the geology of their deposits is so varied, that it is impossible to describe the specific conditions of all mineral occurrences. However, it is useful to discuss some general principles and examples of several major types of mineral deposits.

Minerals differ greatly in their crustal abundance, that is, in the percentage of the earth's crust that is composed of particular minerals. Iron, for example, makes up about 5 percent of the earth's crust and aluminum about 8 percent. Gold, on the other hand, is only about one-billionth of the earth's crust, and copper and zinc are each about one ten-thousandth. These fractions obviously affect the frequency with which we find usable deposits of these elements. Some minerals are valuable because of the particular chemical or molecular structure in which they are found, and the frequency of such occurrences may be high or low. Carbon is a relatively plentiful element, for example, but diamonds, a crystalline form of carbon, are quite rare.

Many minerals, especially metal ores, tend to be formed by similar geologic processes. For example, if rocks are heavily fractured by stresses in the earth's crust, at high temperatures, then *hydrothermal mineralization* can take place. In this process, various elements dissolved in subsurface water flow below the surface, within the crust. If the chemistry and temperature of the water change in certain ways, then certain minerals are deposited in surrounding rocks, creating concentrations of those minerals. Many valuable ores are created in this manner and tend to be found near each other in mineralized districts. Mountain building often includes hydrothermal activity, and as a result many of our important mineralized districts are in mountainous areas.

Shields are areas of very old igneous and metamorphic rocks that form the ancient cores of continents, and they are another geologic environment that has yielded large amounts of valuable minerals. In most of the world shields are buried under other rocks, but large-surface shield areas occur in Canada, Africa, Australia, and elsewhere. Because of their age, these areas contain different mineral assemblages than do most younger rocks, and many shield areas are very rich in metal ores. Important deposits of iron, nickel, copper, zinc, and other metals are found in the Canadian shield in Ontario and Quebec, for example.

Whereas concentrated metal ores are usually found in metamorphic rocks, many areas of sedimentary rocks yield important minerals. Lead, zinc, and uranium are sometimes found in commercially extractable quantities in sedimentary rocks. Some substances, most notably gold and diamonds, are found in *placer deposits*. These are deposits of sand or gravel in which denser particles have been concentrated by the action of running water. Mining them usually requires excavating large volumes of sediment to recover small quantities of minerals.

Another process that concentrates minerals at the earth's surface is *weathering*, or the gradual breakdown of rocks by mechanical and chemical processes. Weathering can selectively remove some elements while leaving others in the soil. Bauxite, the most important ore of aluminum, is formed in this way in humid tropical environments.

These few examples help to show the range of environments in which minerals are found. Some minerals show up in several different types of deposits, but many are located only in restricted geologic circumstances. Common minerals, such as iron, are found all over the globe, and the quality of those deposits varies greatly. As a rule, very high-grade deposits are relatively rare, but if industry is willing to accept slightly lower grade deposits, more is always available. This is certainly true for common elements such as iron and aluminum. The United States has little high-quality aluminum ore, and most of our best iron ore has been used. As a result, the United States imports most of its iron and aluminum ore from other countries. But should those foreign sources become too expensive, substantial domestic low-grade deposits are available. Rarer minerals, such as chromium, platinum, molybdenum, and vanadium, are found in commercial concentrations in fairly restricted locales. Only a few countries dominate world production and marketing for those minerals, and in some cases even low-grade domestic deposits are unavailable.

Variations in Reserves and Resources

Minerals can be regarded as stock or nonrenewable resources in that the amount available in rocks is finite. Thus it is possible to examine how much is in the ground relative to present and projected future demand. But this is not as easy as it might seem for the following reasons. First, the amounts of mineral resources in the ground are extremely large, and the real question is how large the reserves are relative to demand. The amount of a mineral reserve available, however, is heavily dependent on price. A doubling in price, for example, may produce a 10- or 100-fold increase in reserves. Price increases also stimulate exploration, which may further increase reserves through new discoveries. In this way, minerals act as flow resources rather than stock resources.

Second, an increasing number of minerals are recycled and thus, from the point of view of human production systems, are becoming renewable resources. Over 40 percent of U.S. iron and steel supplies are derived from recycled material, and about half the nation's lead consumption is met from recycled material. When the price of minerals rises, so does the economic attraction of recycling, and the contribution of recycled materials will undoubtedly increase in the future.

Third, there is a high degree of *substitutability* for most minerals. If we run short of steel, we can often use aluminum. If we run short of aluminum, we can use magnesium or synthetic materials. Substitution may not be possible for all uses of a material, but partial substitution usually alleviates supply problems and keeps the material available for necessary uses. This substitutability is one factor causing demand for minerals to be highly elastic, changing significantly with variations in price.

Taken together, these factors mean that future demands for minerals are difficult to predict and may be significantly affected by small changes in prices and technologies. In addition, a distinction must be made between short- and long-term availability. In the short term, perhaps over periods of less than 5 to 10 years, sharp fluctuations in mineral prices are common (Fig. 13.2). These fluctuations both reflect and cause variations in supply or demand, presenting very real problems when they occur (Fig. 13.3). We often misunderstand the nature of these crises, however. They are not the result of the world running out of a mineral; rather they are a consequence of the va-

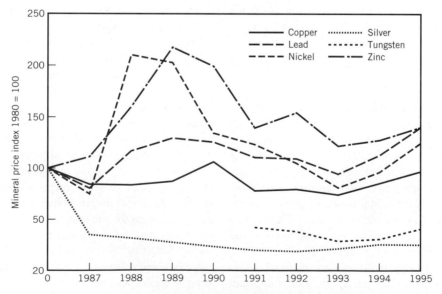

Figure 13.2 Indices of prices for selected minerals, 1980–1995 (1980 = 100). Mineral prices are highly variable; in general, prices for these minerals climbed in the 1980s, but fell dramatically in the 1990s. *Source*: U. S. Geological Survey, 1996.

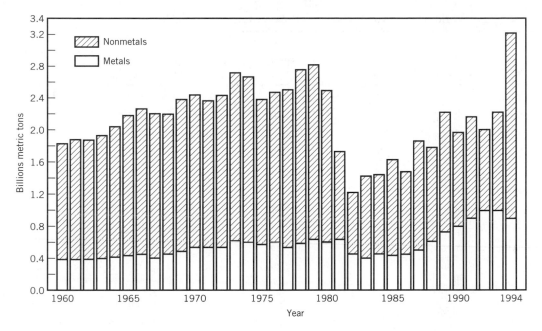

Figure 13.3 Trends in ore production at domestic mines 1960–1995. Metal production has remained relatively consistent during this period, whereas nonmetal production has varied considerably. *Source*: U.S. Geological Survey, 1996.

garies of the world economic and political system. In the long term, however, we will never "run out" of any minerals. We may find that a particular mineral has become too expensive to justify using it, and, in that sense, it may become unavailable. For groups of minerals, worldwide demand may cause a long-term trend of increasing prices, which would likely reduce demand for those minerals.

World Reserves and Resources

In the long run, mineral availability is determined by the level of economic activity, technological changes, and geologic considerations. Although these factors cannot be predicted with certainty, the current status of reserves relative to demand is indicative of future mineral availability and use. Table 13.2 is a listing of current world reserves of major minerals in relation to world consumption. Also included are some of the materials that could be substituted for the mineral in question for some of its major uses. The first column of numbers lists 1995 world production of various minerals. For some minerals the data are incomplete because data from some nations were unavailable or because proprietary data were withheld. In addition, actual consumption may differ from production for some minerals if invento-

ries were depleted or increased. Nonetheless, the figures are reasonably representative of current world conditions. The second column of numbers consists of ratios of 1995 world reserves to 1995 production, as reported by the U.S. Geological Survey (1996). These represent the number of years that current reserves would last at 1995 rates of production. The final column in the table lists some of the materials that could be substituted for several of the uses of the minerals if supplies were limited or prices climbed significantly. Substitution is usually possible only for some uses, whereas for other uses substitution is not currently feasible. In most cases the use of these substitute commodities would result in either increased costs or reduced quality of product, and in some cases new product development would be needed. After all, if these substitutes were suitable under present economic and technological conditions, they would already be in use.

Examination of current reserves indicates that for most minerals, currently identified deposits of economically recoverable materials are sufficient to meet world demand for several decades. If demand increases, as is likely for most minerals, the adequacy of current supplies will be somewhat less. On the other hand, changes in eco-

Table 13.2 World Reserves and Resources Relative to Demand for Minerals

Mineral	1995 Production (1000 metric tons unless otherwise noted)	Reserves (years)	Substitutes
Antimony	108	39	titanium, zinc, tin and several other metals
Arsenic	43	20	synthetic organic chemicals
Asbestos	2390	Large	cellulose fiber, glass fiber
Barite	4250	40	celestite, limenite, iron ore
Bauxite	109,000	211	clay
Beryllium	0.347	n/d	steel, titanium, graphite
Bismuth	3.2	34	several depending on product
Boron	3000	57	several depending on product
Bromine	430	n/a	chlorine, iodine, aniline
Cadmium	18.9	29	zinc
Cesium	n/a	n/a	rubidium
Chromium	10,600	349	none for ferrochromium
Cobalt	19.5	205	barium, nickel, manganese
Columbium	13.5 million kg	259	vanadium, molybdenum, tantalum
Copper	9800	32	aluminum, titanium, steel
Diamond	50 million carats	20	boron, corundum, silicon carbide
Diatomite	1500	533	many
Feldspar	6300	Significant	clays, talc, nepheline syenite
Fluorspar	4070	52	olivine, dolomitic limestone
Gallium	n/a	n/a	organic chemicals, indium phosphide
Garnet	110	Moderate	diamonds, quartz sand, cubic boron nitride
Germanium	45000 kg	n/a	silicon, gallium, zinc selenide
Gold	2.2	20	palladium, platinum, silver
Graphite	720	29	calcined petroleum coke
Gypsum	103,000	Large	lime, lumber, masonry, steel
Helium	114 million m^3	n/a	argon, hydrogen
Ilmenite	3310	82	rutile, synthetic rutile
Indium	15	17	gallium arsenide, silver, zinc oxide, hafnium
Iodine	15 million kg	n/a	bromine, chlorine, antibiotics
Iron ore	1,000,000	150	ferrous, scrap iron
Kyanite	280	Large	synthetic mullite, clays, bauxite
Lead	2800	24	plastics, aluminum, tin
Lime	120,000	Adequate	limestone, gypsum, cement
Lithium	6.3	349	several
Magnesium	311	Sufficient	aluminum, zinc, calcium carbide
Manganese	7300	93	none
Mercury	3.1	42	lithium, nickel-cadmium, indium
Molybdenum	118	47	chromium, vanadium, tungsten
Nickel	920	51	aluminum, plastics, titanium

(continued on next page)

Table 13.2 World Reserves and Resources Relative to Demand for Minerals (continued)

Mineral	1995 Production (1000 metric tons unless otherwise noted)	Reserves (years)	Substitutes
Perlite	1700	412	pumice, vermiculite, slag
Phosphate rock	137,000	80	none
Platinum group	130,000 kg	431	paladium
Potash	26,200	321	none
Pumice	11,700	n/a	shale, clay, diatomite
Quartz crystal	n/a	Large	synthetic quartz crystals
Rare earths	72	1389	many
Rhenium	29,200 kg	86	iridium, tin, gallium, indium
Rutile	360	83	ilmenite, titaniferous slag
Scandium	n/a	n/a	none in most applications
Selenium	1.89	37	silicon, cadmium, tellurium
Silicon	3200	Ample	various metals and alloys
Silver	14	20	aluminum, rhodium, tantalum
Strontium	190	36	barium
Sulfur	52,000	27	none in most applications
Talc	7900	Large	clay, calcium carbonate, kaolin
Tantalum	340,000 kg	65	columbium, aluminum, glass, tungsten
Tellurium	n/a	n/a	selenium, bismuth, germanium
Thallium	15,000 kg	25	several
Thorium	n/a	n/a	yttrium, magnesium alloy
Tin	180	39	aluminum, glass, paper, plastic
Titanium	35	4	zirconium, super alloy metals
Tungsten	20	105	ceramics
Vanadium	35	286	columbium, manganese, platinum
Yttrium	0.73	699	few for most applications
Zinc	7070	20	aluminum, plastics, magnesium
Zirconium	0.9	36	chromite, olivine dolomite, columbium

n/a—not available
n/d—not delineated
Source: U.S. Geological Survey, Office of Minerals Information, 1996.

nomic and technological conditions, in addition to geologic exploration, will almost certainly result in increases to reserves. Finally, should shortages of any of these minerals develop, higher prices will stimulate substitution of other substances or increased recycling, resulting in reduced demand. At the world level, then, it seems likely that most of these minerals will continue to be available for the foreseeable future.

This is not to say that localized, short-duration shortages will not take place. As discussed earlier, in many cases a few countries, or a few mines, may dominate world production. For example, 4 countries control about 70 percent of the world's bauxite production, 6 countries produce 90 percent of all manganese, and 65 percent of phosphate rock comes from 3 countries. Nearly 95 percent of the platinum group metals are produced by two countries—South Africa and Russia. Moreover, one firm, Norilsk Nickel in northern Siberia, produced 62 percent of the world's palladium, 27 percent of the world's nickel, and 22 percent of the world's platinum in 1994, enough to influence the world price of these commodities (Kotov and Nikitina 1996). Closure of a few mines or short-term restrictions in trade could easily result in market shortages and dramatic price changes.

One factor that sometimes leads to these short-term supply fluctuations is the *cartels* that artificially control supplies of minerals. The cartels that have been formed, notably those in tin, copper, and bauxite, have been unsuccessful in manipulating world markets (see the discussion of OPEC in Chapter 14). Their lack of success has been due to several factors. In some cases, important producers have refused to join because of political differences with other producers or lack of cooperation with other cartel members. In addition, many countries have large stockpiles of minerals that were accumulated for military uses in times of war that are now being used to manipulate supplies and prices. Most minerals are simply not in short enough supply nor critical enough to world economies to allow a group of producers to put significant pressure on consuming countries. The result has been a continuation of a relatively unregulated market at the global level. For those developing nations that are mineral-rich and derive substantial foreign exchange from mineral exports (Congo, Gabon, Zimbabwe, and Malaysia are examples), this situation has thwarted many plans to substantially increase national income through market manipulation of metals and minerals.

The diamond cartel provides a good example. One company, De Beers of South Africa, controls 80 percent of the world's rough diamond trade. Starting in 1990, diamonds from Angola and the former Soviet Union republics began flooding the market. The glut of illicit diamonds had two causes: illegal mining in the Lunda Norte province in Angola by garimpeiros, or prospectors, who flooded to the region in search of riches; and increased smuggling in Russia once its economic crisis worsened during the early 1990s after the breakup of the Soviet Union. This upsurge in supply forced De Beers to consider either reducing the price of their dia-

monds or buying the illicit diamonds themselves. De Beers spent nearly $200 million to purchase diamonds from Russia and Angola in order to maintain its control of the rough diamond market (MacLeod 1992).

U.S. Production and Consumption

Although most minerals are essentially global commodities, inasmuch as supply and demand are dominated by worldwide markets rather than national policies, it is useful to examine the domestic situation in the United States with respect to mineral supply and consumption. The United States is the largest single consumer of many materials, and conditions here are of considerable importance in the world market. Domestic conditions are sometimes the focus of policy debates relating to strategic material needs or environmental impacts of mining. Because non-fuel mineral production adds significant income to many states (Fig. 13.4), these policy debates often produce strong regional divisions.

Table 13.3 summarizes the U.S. mineral situation for selected minerals in 1995. The first column of numbers shows U.S. production; the second illustrates average apparent consumption in 1995 as a percentage of world production during the same year. The final column lists the U.S net import reliance, or the percentage of our consumption that was supplied by imports.

Several important generalizations can be made from these data. First, the United States consumes a substantial portion of world production of many minerals. Typically, the United States, with about 5 percent of the world's population, consumes between 10 and 30 percent of world production. This is roughly the same proportion as that of world energy production consumed by Americans and simply reflects the United States' large population, advanced level of industrialization, and high standard of living. Interestingly, many of the minerals for which our consumption is particularly high are associated with technologically advanced industries like aerospace and electronics. On the other hand, our consumption of iron ore and bauxite is at levels more appropriate to our population.

Second, U.S. domestic reserves of many minerals vary considerably, being virtually nonexistent for some minerals and very large for others. Important minerals for which our domestic reserves

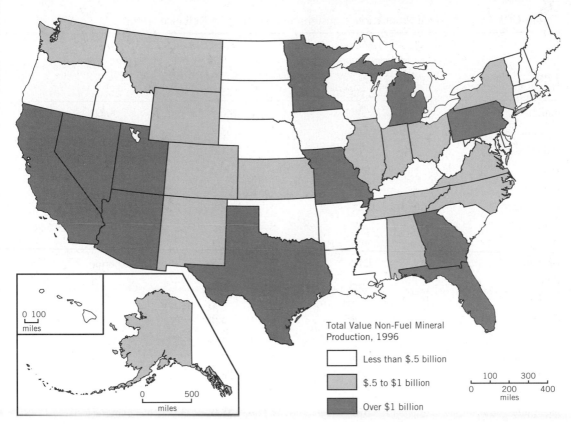

Figure 13.4   Total value of nonfuel mineral production, 1996. The mining states in the west produce high value minerals like gold and silver, in Minnesota and Michigan it is iron-ore, and in Florida phosphate. *Source*: U.S. Bureau of the Census, 1997.

are quite small include bauxite, chromium, cobalt, manganese, nickel, and the platinum group metals. The United States has abundant reserves of copper, iron ore, magnesium, molybdenum, rare earths, thorium, vanadium, and numerous other minerals.

Third, the United States is a major trader of minerals and is dependent on imports for such important commodities as bauxite, chromium, cobalt, graphite, iron ore, manganese, tin, tungsten, and zinc. The United States is a net exporter of boron, industrial diamonds, magnesium, phosphate rock, and others. Note that for some minerals there is essentially no domestic production, but our import reliance for these minerals is well below 100 percent. For example, we have no domestic chromium production, but we only imported 78 percent of our needs in 1995. The balance of our consumption was met with recy-

cled chromium. Recycling was also important for iron, aluminum, lead, copper, and tin.

STRATEGIC MINERALS AND STOCKPILING

Although effective mineral cartels or other political organizations have yet to significantly restrict supplies of minerals, the possibility of such restriction is of some concern to the United States government. This is particularly true in the case of minerals that are significant to military/industrial production and that are imported from nations with unstable or unfriendly governments.

This dependency issue has been recognized for many years. The U.S. government has therefore defined certain minerals to be of strategic or critical importance to the welfare of the country and has developed policies to prevent shortages.

Table 13.3 U.S. Mineral Production, Consumption, and Import Reliance, 1995

Mineral	Production (1,000 metric tons unless otherwise noted)	Consumption as % of world (includes U.S. production where available)	Import Reliance (%)
Antimony *	W	46.5	60
Arsenic	n/a	55.8	100
Asbestos *	9	1.0	46
Barite	600	40.2	65
Bauxite *	W	3.6	99
Beryllium *	0.225	57.6	Net exporter
Bismuth *	W	46.8	W
Boron	602	9.5	Net exporter
Bromine	211	46.5	Net exporter
Cadmium *	1.3	8.5	20
Cesium	n/a	n/a	n/a
Chromium *	n/a	5.0	78
Cobalt *	n/a	43.0	82
Columbium *	n/a	28.8	100
Copper *	1890	26.2	6
Diamond[1] *	115 million carats	n/a	Net exporter
Diatomite	670	35.0	Net exporter
Feldspar	770	12.0	Net exporter
Fluorspar *	48	14.8	92
Gallium	n/a	n/a	n/a
Garnet	53.3	40.8	Net exporter
Germanium	10,000kg	55.5	n/a
Gold	0.32	16.6	Net exporter
Graphite *	n/a	4.1	100
Gypsum	17,300	25.1	30
Helium	117 million m^3	68.8	Net exporter
Ilmenite	W	W	W
Indium	n/a	28.6	n/a
Iodine *	1.8 million kg	32.0	62
Iron Ore	62,000	7.5	18
Kyanite	W	W	W
Lead *	390	51.8	15
Lime	18,500	15.6	1
Lithium	W	W	Net exporter
Magnesium	140	53.7	Net exporter
Manganese *	n/a	9.7	100
Mercury *	W	W	W
Molybdenum *	59	24.6	Net exporter

(continued on next page)

Table 13.3   U.S. Mineral Production, Consumption, and Import Reliance, 1995 (continued)

Mineral	Production (1,000 metric tons unless otherwise noted)	Consumption as % of world (includes U.S. production where available)	Import Reliance (%)
Nickel *	1.65	17.3	61
Perlite	719	45.8	8
Phosphate Rock	45,500	31.8	Net exporter
Platinum Group*	2000 kg	n/a	n/a
Potash	1460	21.6	74
Pumice	544	6.5	29
Quartz Crystal *	0.5	n/a	n/a
Rare earths	28.7	40.8	2
Rhenium	18,000 kg	W	W
Rutile *	W	W	W
Scandium	W	W	n/a
Selenium	.36	28.6	33
Silicon	390	18.1	33
Silver *	1.5	n/a	n/a
Strontium	n/a	W	100
Sulfur	11,800	26.7	18
Talc *	1050	12.3	Net exporter
Tantalum *	n/a	138.23	80
Tellurium	W	n/a	n/a
Thallium	n/a	4.7	100
Thorium *	n/a	n/a	n/a
Tin*	Negligible	26.1	84
Titanium *	W	60.0	W
Tungsten *	W	79.5	87
Vanadium *	W	W	W
Yttrium	n/a	47.9	100
Zinc *	600	20.6	41
Zirconium	W	W	W

n/a—not available
W—Withheld to avoid disclosing company proprietary data
* —Strategic mineral
[1] U.S. production is for synthetic diamonds while world production is for mined diamonds.
Source: U.S. Geological Survey, 1996.

Strategic minerals are those essential for defense purposes for which the United States is totally dependent on foreign sources. Examples of strategic minerals are cobalt, chromium, manganese, and platinum. *Critical minerals* are also necessary for national defense, but the United States can meet some of its demand through domestic sources and supplies from friendly nations. Examples of critical minerals are copper, nickel, and vanadium. It is an interesting quirk of geography that much of the U.S. supply of strategic minerals comes from two nations;

South Africa and Russia. Over 30 minerals have been identified as having strategic or critical importance, and these minerals are indicated in Table 13.3 by asterisks. The following examples illustrate that importance.

Chromium is used to harden steel and make it resistant to corrosion. It is an essential component of stainless steel and is found in ball bearings, surgical equipment, mufflers, and tailpipes. It is used in the defense industry in armor plating and weapons and for many parts of piston and jet engines. The leading world producers of chromium are South Africa and Kazakhstan. The United States imports about 78 percent of its chromium, mainly from South Africa, Turkey, and Zimbabwe.

Cobalt is a metal used in the aerospace industry. It is a high-temperature alloy used in the manufacture of jet engines, cutting tools, magnets, and drill bits. It is also used in electronics equipment, especially in computers, television receivers, and transmitters. The primary producers of cobalt are Congo, Zambia, Canada, Norway, Finland, and Russia. The United States is heavily reliant on imported cobalt, mostly from Zambia, Norway, and Canada.

Other strategic minerals are those in the platinum group, which includes six different minerals with similar properties. These metals—platinum, iridium, palladium, oridium, rhodium, and ruthenium—are resistant to corrosion and are used to catalyze chemical reactions. Other applications include catalytic converters in automobiles, petroleum refining, electroplating, electronics, and fertilizer manufacture. The major world producers of platinum group metals are Russia, South Africa, Canada, and Japan. The United States imports about 90 percent of its platinum, primarily from South Africa, the United Kingdom, and Belgium.

Manganese is essential in steel manufacture and thus has many industrial and military applications. It is added to molten steel to remove oxygen and sulfur, thus hardening the steel. Ukraine, South Africa, China, and Australia are the world's major producers, providing about 62 percent of the world's manganese supply in 1995. The United States imports most of its manganese from South Africa, Gabon, France, and Brazil. The presence of large quantities of presently subeconomic manganese in deep-ocean beds was an important part of the United States' reluctance to sign the Law of the Sea Treaty, as we saw in Chapter 9.

Stockpiling, or maintaining large storages of commodities, is one method the United States has chosen to protect itself from restrictions in supplies of strategic minerals. The danger of minerals dependency has been recognized since the turn of the century, but actual stockpiling did not begin until shortly before World War II. In 1949, the U.S. Strategic Stockpile was created to avert shortages of minerals during wartime. The intent was to purchase and store materials in sufficient quantities to meet defense and national security needs for a three-year period, which is presumably long enough for alternative supplies to be developed in the event of a cutoff of supply from other nations. Ninety-three substances, not all of them minerals, were on the list. Congress did not appropriate funds for procurement, however, and the stockpile was well below the official goals for many years. Recently, procurement has increased, and the stockpile is at or over 100 percent for many materials, prompting the government to sell some of the material in the stockpile. For example, in 1995 the government sold excess minerals from the stockpile valued at $414 million. It has also occasionally used the stockpile to influence mineral prices through trading or threatening to trade in stockpiled commodities.

Stockpiling is an important policy because it protects a nation from the short-term interruptions of supply and rises in price to which minerals are susceptible. Stockpiling in the United States has historically implied preparedness for war. It is unlikely that limited regional wars would cut off supplies from all major mineral suppliers, and in the case of all-out world war it is improbable that the United States would exhaust the three-year supply of industrial minerals. Nonetheless, the strategic stockpiles are very good guarantees against short-term reductions in supplies caused by an industrial collapse or prohibition of trade in one or two countries. From the standpoint of national economic health, it makes sense to guard against such events.

In summary, the market for most minerals is a world market in which a relatively small number of suppliers sell to a large number of customers. In the long term, the availability of some minerals is essentially infinite, but for others there will be substantial increases in price, leading to conservation, recycling, development of substitute materials, and other means for reducing demand for expensive materials. In the short term, prices fluctuate widely, stimulating changes in sources and uses of minerals, and creating some economic distress in sensitive industries. Even though the production of many minerals is concentrated in a small number of countries, because those nations lack political agreement and depend on exports for foreign exchange, and because of the substitutability of materials, the formation of effective cartels is unlikely. The volatility of mineral prices makes stockpiling useful for insulating national production systems from catastrophic changes in the world market.

MINING IMPACTS AND POLICY

Environmental Considerations

Mineral extraction has significant environmental and social effects. Individual mines are often very large, as economies of scale are important in maintaining profitability. Few mineral ores are more than 30 percent pure, and some are less than 1 percent pure. Thus, large quantities of ore must be processed to obtain relatively small amounts of finished product (Fig. 13.5). If the mine is at the surface, such as the open-pit mine shown in Figure 13.6, the area disrupted can be quite large. In addition, it is often necessary to remove large amounts of undesired rock to get at an ore body, further increasing the area disturbed.

Unused rock and the waste from processing operations must be disposed of (Fig. 13.7). These materials, called *tailings*, often are processed using large amounts of water and are deposited in tailings ponds. Often these ponds are themselves quite large. The water pumped from mines after use in extraction or in ore processing is usually of low quality. In many cases it is highly acidic, and it is usually contaminated with the minerals being mined. The resultant pollution of receiving waters is often severe. The huge volume of ore-bearing rock to be processed requires that pro-

cessing take place near the mine; thus, many mine sites are also locations for smelting or other methods of purifying minerals. Most of these processes produce large emissions of air pollutants, particularly sulfur oxides and metals. These emissions may be of such quantity as to severely damage vegetation and soils in the surrounding area (Fig. 13.8). Sudbury and Wawa, Ontario, and Palmerton, Pennsylvania, are examples of areas where vegetation destruction is so severe that it is clearly visible on satellite photographs.

Mine sites are generally dictated by the presence of ore, not by the environmental suitability of the location for a large-scale industrial operation. Many of the mines in the Rockies and Sierra Nevada are in areas of considerable natural beauty, in or near important resort areas. In a region with extensive mining activities, the environmental consequences can be widespread (Issue 13.1). Although long-abandoned mines and ghost towns may be appealing to tourists, modern mines and associated support facilities generally are not.

Social Impacts

In addition to environmental effects, mining has many important social and economic effects in the areas where it occurs. Most mining towns are isolated, away from major urban centers, and frequently in mountains (Fig. 13.9). The populations of mining towns are almost entirely dependent on the mines for employment and income. When the mine is operating, they prosper, but when it is not operating, they become impoverished. Mine operations are governed by the prices of the materials mined, which, as we have shown, tend to fluctuate widely. When demand for a mineral drops, causing a reduction in price, production is usually reduced by closing whole mines rather than reducing production a little at all mines. This is because economies of scale are important in mining, and it is often more economical to close a mine entirely than to run it at a reduced level. Mining towns thus go through repeated boom-and-bust cycles, alternating between full employment and extreme unemployment (Issue 13.2). The toll this takes in the lives of the mine workers and other residents is understandably severe.

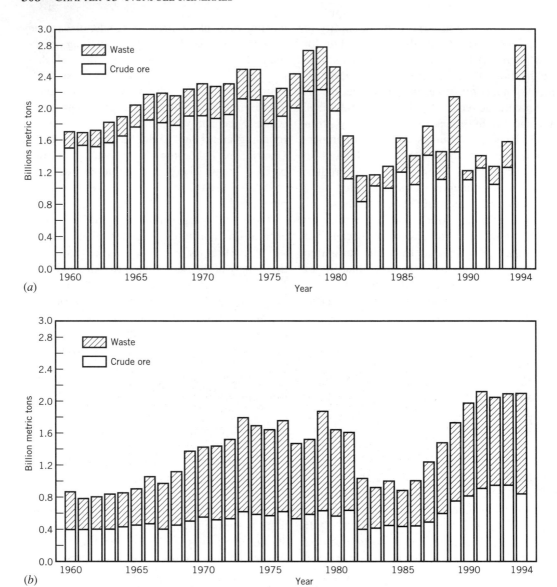

Figure 13.5 Metal ore and waste production at domestic mines, 1960–1995. Less waste (mine spoils) is produced by mining for nonmetals (*a*) such as phosphate, sand and gravel, and crushed stone, than for metal ores (*b*) like lead, copper, and iron ore. *Source*: U.S. Geological Survey, 1996.

Nonfuel Minerals Policy

Most of the minerals policy in the United States is still guided by the 1872 Mining Act which provided unlimited access to public lands for mineral exploration. Specifically, the Mining Law gives U.S. citizens and corporations the right to prospect for certain minerals on federal lands and allows them to file claims to mine and sell whatever minerals they find. The law does not provide for any payment to the federal government for minerals mined on federal lands. Despite repeated attempts to reform the 1872 Mining Law, most notably in 1997, the law still guides much of the United States' nonfuel minerals policy. Since the Mining Law was passed more than a century ago, the regulation of mining activities and environmental impacts is done on an ad hoc basis. Reforms are intended to

Figure 13.6 The Bingham Canyon copper mine in Utah—one of the world's largest open pit mines.

Figure 13.7 Spoil piles from hydraulic mining for gold in California.

Figure 13.8 Destruction of forests and associated wildlife is intense in the vicinity of Sudbury, Ontario, where acid emissions from nickel smelting have fallen on soils lacking adequate buffering capacity.

ISSUE 13.1: THE NEW GOLD RUSH: PROSPECTING IS POISON

Gold has a special allure to mining prospectors. For centuries, it has been associated with wealth and affluence. The Spanish conquest of the Americas was largely driven by the quest for gold. In the Andes, the Inca and Chibcha Indians were quite distinguished artisans in their use of the element. The Gold Museum, in Bogotá, Colombia, houses one of the most impressive collections of pre-Columbian gold artifacts in the world.

Gold rushes have come and gone, resulting in many boom-and-bust local economies and environmentally ravaged lands. The latest gold rush is in Venezuela. As an attempt to revitalize its mining sector, the Venezuelan government recently permitted gold mining in one of the country's most environmentally sensitive regions, Bolívar. The Caroní River runs through this region, supplying most of the drinking water for the state. The river feeds the Gurí Dam which produces more than 70 percent of the country's electricity. Canaima National Park is located in the southern section of Bolívar. More than 40 percent of the mining in Bolívar, according to government estimates, occurs in the Imataca Forest Reserve.

The mining process involves blasting the soil with powerful water jets (hydraulic mining). The sediments are carried into the tributaries and downstream. Increased sedimentation could threaten the power production potential of the Gurí Dam. In addition, the pools of water left behind become wonderful habitat for mosquitoes, many of whom are malaria carriers. To separate the gold from other minerals, mining companies often use cyanide, mercury, and other toxic substances. These substances are dumped into holding ponds (and seep into the ground) or are washed into the nearest stream. High levels of mercury have already been detected in the lower Caroní basin. Local people avoid the fish, which was once a staple in their diet. The incidence of Down's syndrome and the number of birth defects in Bolívar are among the highest in the entire country.

Venezuela's largest mine, Minerven, run by the state-owned mining company, operates no differently than dozens of smaller scale operations. All use hydraulic mining, and the larger facilities tend to use cyanide rather than mercury in the separation process. The relaxation of environmental laws to promote large-scale mining is an attempt by the government to promote sustainable development in southern Bolívar state (Schemo 1996).

Halfway around the world, the town of Bergama, Turkey, has been the site of confrontations for over 3000 years starting with the ancient Greeks and Romans and moving on to Alexander the Great and, much later, the Crusades. In 1989, gold was found. Eurogold, a French-based company backed by the Turkish government, wants to open the country's first modern gold mine. Currently under construction, the pit mine is just eight miles south of Bergama, a major tourist spot. About 300,000 people live in the area around the mine, which also happens to be located in a seismically active area. An earthquake could rupture the liner beneath the waste pool thereby releasing cyanide. In 1938, the region suffered a major earthquake in which many villages were totally destroyed.

The mine is being built according to the most modern of standards. There is a clay and polyethylene sealer beneath the waste pool. However, residents are fearful of the vast amounts of water (diverting it from agriculture) and the ever present cyanide. Nevertheless, the mine began operations in late 1997 (Kinzer 1997).

As gold prices fluctuate ($36 per ounce in 1970, $613 per ounce in 1980, $385 in 1990, $292 in 1998), prospecting will increase. Whether the return on the investment is achieved may be less important than the environmental disruption caused by the current mining practices. The get rich quick scheme to assist developing economies may in the end bring about their economic demise.

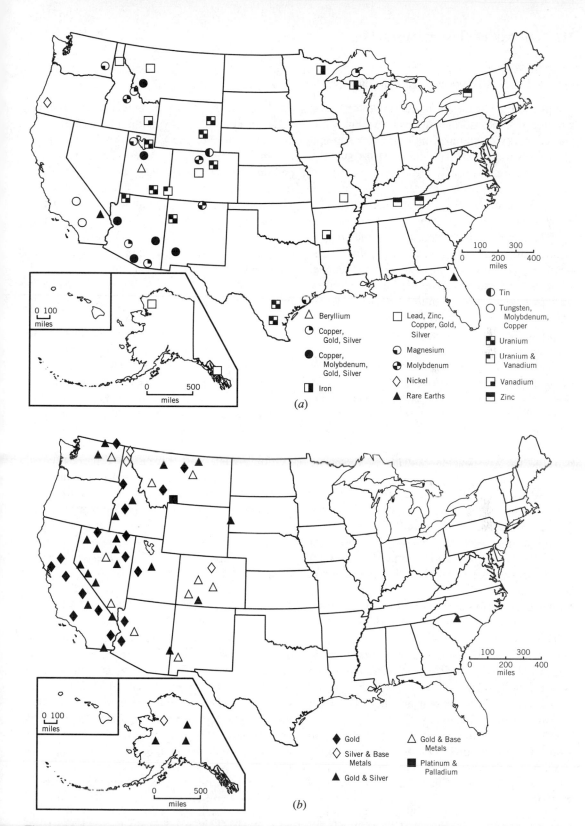

Figure 13.9 Major domestic metal (*a*) and precious metals (*b*) producing areas. Notice the concentration of mines in the west. In the east, most of the metal mining is for zinc and rare earths. South Carolina stands out as the only eastern state to mine gold and silver. *Source*: U.S. Geological Survey, 1997.

ISSUE 13.2: LIVING WITH BOOM AND BUST

Boom and bust, cycles of rapid growth and catastrophic decline, occur wherever mining dominates a local or regional economy. When national or world production of minerals drops slightly, mines that are marginally profitable close operation, while those with larger profit margins stay open. When prices are high and production increases, new mines open and old ones are reopened. If a mine is located in a remote area, as is often the case, the communities around it depend on the mine for nearly all their income. Most local residents work either for the mine, for businesses that serve the mine, or for businesses that serve the people who work in the mine. As the mine goes, so goes the community. The following scenario is a typical one.

Both boom and bust are stressful in a mining town. Boom times usually bring an increase in population, a shortage of housing, a rise in rents and property values, and a shortage of public services. When immigrants come in large numbers, they bring problems to small towns. Everyday life for the permanent residents is disrupted, shops are more crowded, housing costs rise, and streets are blocked by construction. Unemployment and crime may also be problems if more immigrants arrive than are hired.

Boom times are not all bad, however, for nearly everyone has a job, property values increase, and business is good. The new money in town brings in new businesses, perhaps a second barber shop, a few gas stations, a discount department store, a bigger supermarket, a few restaurants, and several bars. Those lucky enough to get into business at the right time do very well and may amass small fortunes. Those who came in when the boom was already under way meet stiff competition and high costs but still manage to earn a living.

Then comes the bust. Maybe competition from cheaper imports is too rough, the higher grade ore is played out, or the world price may have fallen because of a recession. Maybe new materials are replacing the ore in a few critical industries. Or perhaps environmental requirements are making the mine less profitable than one in another state or another country. The actual cause doesn't really matter to those affected, because whatever the cause, it is beyond their control. At any rate, the mine is shut down, and perhaps 40 percent of the town's workforce is laid off with two weeks' notice and two months' severance pay. A few stay on for several months to help with removing the machinery that can be used elsewhere.

Some people leave town immediately, particularly those who had arrived most recently and hadn't established themselves yet. Unemployment compensation and savings keep the rest going for the better part of a year, but eventually that runs out, so most of them leave, too. Those with large debts go bankrupt. Many of the rest can't sell their houses for as much as they owe on the mortgage, and their mortgages are foreclosed.

Two years after the mine is closed, the town's population may have dropped by 50 percent. Before the boom, there was one barber shop, three gas stations, and one supermarket, all doing well. Now there are two barber shops, both having trouble making rent payments, one supermarket open and one closed, a closed department store, and six gas stations, only one of which is doing well. Most of the bars that opened during the boom are still there, but now they get more business during the day than at night.

Although the specific town just described is fictional, these things have happened in many towns in the United States and elsewhere, and more than once in most of them. Today, concern about the social impacts of mining is increasing, and many states have taken steps to lessen the blows. Severance taxes, charged to the mining companies when minerals are removed, are often used to pay for improvements in town services and infrastructure during growth times and for relocation or job training afterward. Mining companies are becoming more willing to contribute to these expenses in their attempts to maintain public goodwill. These changes will ease the ups and downs to some extent, but they will still occur and recur (Gulliford 1989).

(1) ensure that mining companies will be charged royalties for the minerals they extract from federal lands and (2) establish a federal program to minimize the environmental impacts of hard-rock mining after the mining operations cease. Finally, as part of the 1990 Clean Air Act Amendments, the mining and minerals processing industries are increasingly monitored for air emissions, especially lead compounds from smelters.

Conserving Minerals: Reuse, Recovery, Recycling

Recycling is the process whereby a material is recovered from the consumer product and then becomes a raw material in the production of a similar or different product. A significant amount of material can be recovered during the manufacture, use, and disposal of goods to decrease our need for raw ores (Table 13.4). Aluminum recycling is a good example. Aluminum cans that are returned to redemption centers are recycled, melted down, and used in the manufacture of new aluminum cans and other aluminum products (Fig. 13.10). In 1996, about one-third of

Table 13.4   Mineral Recycling

Mineral	Recycling as a percentage of apparent consumption, 1995
Aluminum	25
Antimony	99
Chromium	22
Cobalt	22
Copper	18
Iron ore	**
Lead	57
Magnesium	18
Mercury	65
Nickel	34
Molybdenum	3
Sulfur	22
Tantalum	22
Tin	17
Tungsten	13
Zinc	30

** *Insignificant*
Source: U.S. Geological Survey, 1996.

total aluminum production was from recycled aluminum. Because of its high price and availability, aluminum is consistently recycled and is often the target for scavengers. Nothing appears to be sacred. Aluminum siding and gutters have been stripped from New York City homes, swing sets from a Miami playground, and even cans from local recycling centers by vandals desperate for money.

The ease with which minerals can be recycled depends on several factors, including the technology of conversion to a desired product, the ease of accumulation of sufficient used material, and the relative costs of manufacture of a good from recycled as opposed to raw materials. This last factor is itself partly affected by differences in quality between products made from raw materials and those made from recycled materials. For most minerals, the cost of converting an ore to pure form is significantly greater than the cost of remanufacture from recycled material, not considering the cost of mining ore and the cost of accumulating recycled materials. This is true not only in monetary terms but also applies to energy use and environmental pollution. For example, manufacture of a given amount of aluminum from recycled scrap uses 90 to 95 percent less energy and generates 95 percent less pollution than refining aluminum from bauxite.

Accumulating sufficient material to recycle and maintain the purity of recyclable materials are major problems. These depend on the use and handling of materials. One of the biggest uses of lead, for example, is in storage batteries, such as those in automobiles. Old batteries are found at specific locations, primarily automobile junkyards and repair shops. The lead in them is valuable enough to warrant recycling, as is much of the lead used in other applications. As a result, in 1995, 60 percent of the U.S. lead consumption was from recycled materials. Titanium, on the other hand, is used primarily in dispersed forms. Over 95 percent of titanium used in the United States is for pigments in paints, and thus it winds up on the walls of houses, buildings, and so forth. It would be very difficult to collect used paint in sufficient quantities to recycle the titanium that it contains. Titanium recycling is therefore insignificant.

Figure 13.10   Recycling aluminum beverage cans saves both materials and large amounts of energy.

Over time, the changing use of metals in manufacturing also affects their recycling potential. Until the 1970s, the platinum group metals were recycled with efficiencies around 85 percent (Frosch and Gallopoulos 1989). However, in the mid-1970s the introduction of catalytic converters for automobiles to reduce exhaust emissions changed the recycling rates. Automotive use of platinum group metals now accounts for most of the permanent consumption of these metals. Although the industrial applications of the platinum group continue to recycle about 85 percent of the metals, poor recycling rates (less than 12%) characterize the automotive applications. The reason is quite simple. The poor recycling rates are a function of the limited means for collecting the discarded catalytic converters, which are found in scrap yards along with the discarded automobile. The technology for recycling is known, but the cost of locating, collecting, and empty-ing all the discarded converters and then transporting the platinum metals for recycling is too high for most recovery operations at current prices. If the price of platinum rises to more than $500 per ounce, then recycling of catalytic converters will become more pronounced.

Accumulation of material for recycling is easiest in industry, where large amounts of material tend to be found in a few locations. In many industrial processes, scrap is generated as part of the manufacturing process, and this is very easily recovered. For example, steel that does not meet specifications is recovered at the steel plant and is immediately returned to the production process as a raw material. This recycling of so-called new scrap is just a way of making the manufacturing process more efficient. Recycling of new scrap is not included in the data in Table 13.4.

Rechargeable batteries have increased in their use. These rechargeable batteries are made from cadmium (Cd) and nickel (Ni). Increasingly, Ni-Cd batteries are finding their way into municipal landfills because some consumers are not taking the time to recharge them. Cadmium, a hazardous substance according to the Environmental Protection Agency, must be diverted from the municipal waste stream and recycled separately (at a higher cost). While technically feasible, thus far there is not a large enough quantity of Ni-Cd batteries to make recycling practical for most consumers (Erickson 1991), although many states have recycling programs that will accept them.

CONCLUSION

Although we often think of minerals as nonrenewable resources, we are not going to run out of any of them. Variations in price are far too important in generating new supplies and in controlling demand to permit geologic considerations alone to determine use. Demand fluctuations occur primarily through substitution, but increased efficiency of use is also important. In the future, recycling, reuse, and recovery are likely to become increasingly important, as increasing demand raises prices and makes this source of materials economically more feasible. On the other hand, in many applications a shift has been made from mineral-based products to plastics. Many parts of new automobiles, for example, are now made of plastic rather than metals. The same is true for children's toys like trucks and cars. If that shift continues, then demand for some minerals may decline, reducing prices and recycling rates.

REFERENCES AND ADDITIONAL READING

Brobst, P. A., and W. P. Pratt eds. 1973. *United States Mineral Resources*. Washington, DC: U.S. Geological Survey. Professional Paper 820. Washington, DC: U.S. Geological Survey.

Chandler, W. U. 1983. *Materials Recycling: The Virtue of Necessity*. Worldwatch Paper no. 56. Washington, DC: Worldwatch Institute.

DeVore, C. 1981. Strategic minerals: a present danger. *Signal,* January, pp. 63–68.

Erickson, D. 1991. Cadmium charges. *Scientific American* (May): 122.

Frosch, R. A., and N. E. Gallopoulos. 1989. Strategies for Manufacturing. *Scientific American* 261: 144–152.

Goeller, H. E., and A. Zucker. 1984. Infinite resources: the ultimate strategy. *Science* 223: 456–462.

Gulliford, A. 1989. *Boomtown Blues: Colorado Oil Shale 1885–1985*. Boulder: University Press of Colorado.

Kinzer, S. 1997. Turks fight gold mine, saying prospect is poison. *New York Times*, April 16, p. A4.

Kotov, V., and E. Nikitina. 1996. Norilsk nickel: Russia wrestles with an old polluter. *Environment* 38 (9): 6–11, 32–37.

McKelvey, V. E. 1972. Mineral Resource Estimates and Public Policy. *Scientific American* 60: 32–40.

MacLeod, S. 1992. Diamonds aren't forever. *Time*, October 12, p. 73.

Schemo, D. J. 1996. Legally now, Venezuelans to mine fragile lands. *New York Times*, December 8, p. 6.

Sinclair, J. E., and R. Parker. 1983. *The Strategic Minerals War*. New York: Arlington House.

U.S. Bereau of the Census. 1997. *Statistical Abstract of the U.S.* Washington, DC: U.S. Government Printing Office.

U.S. Bureau of Mines. 1994. *Minerals Yearbook*. Washington, DC: U.S. Government Printing Office.

U.S. Congress, Office of Technology Assessment. 1979. *Materials and Energy from Municipal Waste*. Washington, DC: U.S. Government Printing Office.

U.S. Geological Survey. 1975. *Mineral Resource Perspectives*, 1975. USGS Professional Paper 940. Washington, DC: U.S. Geological Survey.

_____ . Office of Minerals Information. 1996. *Mineral Commodity Summaries*. Washington DC: ONLINE: USGS, *http://minerals.er.usgs/pubs/*

_____ . 1997. ONLINE: USGS, *http://minerals.er.usgs/pubs/mcs/base.gif*

For more information, consult our web page at ***http://www.wiley.com/college/cutter***

STUDY QUESTIONS

1. What are three reasons for the shifting boundary between reserves and other resources?

2. While we usually think of minerals such as ores as nonrenewable resources, a broader view of all resources of a given element would see this substance as a renewable resource, in which all occurrences of that element are potentially usable. What would it take to make a given mineral, such as lead, aluminum, or iron, a renewable resource?

3. Julian Simon maintains that price is the best measure of the scarcity of resources. The prices of many minerals fell significantly between 1980 and 1990. Does that mean that they became more plentiful?

CHAPTER 14

ENERGY RESOURCES

Of all demands placed on our world's natural resource base, the need for energy is perhaps the most far-reaching and basic. Energy provides heat for living and cooking, is used for lighting and refrigeration, and turns motors and wheels that power machines and move people and goods. Whether the energy is nuclear–generated electricity that lights an office building or wood burned in a cooking stove, everyone depends on it daily for physical health and economic prosperity.

Since the early 1970s, the world has experienced dramatic shifts in the availability and price of energy commodities, particularly petroleum. Because of supply disruptions such as embargoes and wars, temporary shortages of oil occurred repeatedly in the 1970s. This led to sharp increases in the prices of fuel oil, gasoline, chemicals, and other petroleum-derived products. During this period energy policy was a critical issue in many nations, and people came to view natural resources in a different way, seeing them as immediately exhaustible instead of indefinitely renewable. Since the early 1980s that situation has been dramatically reversed, at least on the surface, and we once again enjoy low energy prices. In the late 1990s, the real (inflation-adjusted) retail price of gasoline in the United States was lower than at any other time since World War II, and yet the underlying realities of a limited resource base and growing demand that precipitated the energy crises of the 1970s have not disappeared. Oil is an integral part of international politics and world economies.

Energy exists in many different forms and is used for many purposes. It includes the kinetic energy of a speeding train or of the wind, the radiant energy of the sun or of a warm building, and the stored energy of water in a reservoir above a hydroelectric plant or in fossil fuels. This chapter is concerned primarily with those forms of energy that are used to do work in the production of goods and services and that form the basis of our national and world economies. It will examine the complex nature of energy: where it comes from, how it is used, and how supplies and prices have varied in the last few decades.

ENERGY USE IN THE INDUSTRIAL AGE

Wood, Coal, and the Industrial Revolution

Intensive energy use is a feature of the industrial age which began in England and spread through northwestern Europe in the eighteenth century, North America and Japan (nineteenth century), and the rest of the world (twentieth century). Prior to the Industrial Revolution, the people of the world relied on renewable energy sources; primarily wood and charcoal but also dung, peat, and animal fats. But when modern steel-making developed, a new fuel was used, coal. Coal and steel use developed together—coal providing the energy source that made large-scale steel production possible, and steel providing the demand that led to the use of coal to power-drive steam engines and factories. In the 1870s in the United States, three-fourths of energy was derived from renewable sources, primarily wood and mechanical hydropower. Thirty years later coal produced three-quarters of U.S. energy (Fig. 14.1).

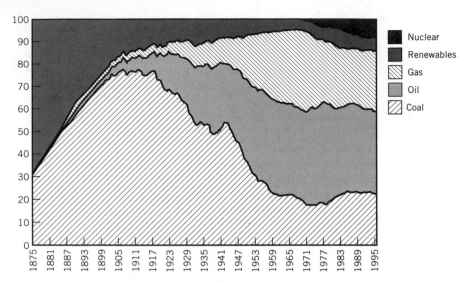

Figure 14.1   United States Energy production, by source. In the late 19th century wood and coal supplied almost all United States energy. Today, a more diverse mixture is used, including oil, gas, and nuclear power in addition to coal and wood. *Source:* Worldwatch Institute, 1996; United States Bureau of the Census, 1997.

In North America as in Europe, the development of coal also came at a time when wood supplies were dwindling. The areas surrounding rapidly growing cities could not possibly supply all the wood needed to heat homes and cook food in those cities. The exploitation of coal thus grew through a combination of dwindling supply of an alternative fuel and development of a new technology that could make use of it.

Oil and the Internal Combustion Engine

Another transition in energy use took place in the early twentieth century. This time there was no shortage of the existing energy supply, but rather the development of a new technology was the dominant factor. The new energy source was petroleum, and the technology that led the way was the internal combustion engine.

Although oil began to be developed in Europe and North America in the 1850s, relatively little was used. Oil was used mainly as a lubricant, with some used for lighting. In the 1860s and 1870s, however, the internal combustion engine was developed, and by the 1890s the first automobiles powered by this engine were in production. At first, automobiles were expensive and impractical, but by 1910 a large number of auto-

mobiles were in use, and society was adapting to this new form of transportation. Roads were improved for automobile use, gasoline stations opened, and repair services became more available. When the Ford Motor Company adopted mass-production techniques that reduced the price of the automobile, demand and production increased further.

As the use of oil increased, the petroleum industry itself grew and developed. Geologists explored for oil, drilled wells, and built refineries. The development of an infrastructure of refineries, pipelines, and distribution facilities reduced the cost of oil, encouraging its use. This helped make oil competitive with coal for other uses, such as home heating or electric energy generation, further hastening the transition from a coal- to an oil-based economy. Today oil is the largest single source of energy in the world, supplying about 40 percent of total energy use.

Energy Use in the Late Twentieth Century

World energy use expanded rapidly in the second half of the twentieth century. In 1950, world consumption of energy was about 100,000 *petajoules* (Table 14.1); by the mid-1990s, it was approaching 400,000 (Fig. 14.2). The average growth rate in this period was about 3 percent per year, faster than the population growth rate. This increase in energy use was driven by several factors, most importantly the expansion of the world industrial economy in the post–World War II boom. Petroleum was the major fuel supporting this growth, and the greatest increases in oil use occurred in the wealthy nations of west-

Table 14.1   Energy Equivalents

One petajoule (10^{15} joules) is the same as 0.0009478 quads (10^{15} British thermal units)
One quadrillion Btus (quad) equal:

50 million metric tons of coal

66 million metric tons of oven-dried hardwood

1 trillion cubic feet of dry natural gas

170 million barrels of crude oil

470 thousand barrels of crude oil per day for a year

293 billion kilowatt-hours of electricity converted to heat

27 days of petroleum imports to the United States

26 days of gasoline usage for American motor vehicles

ern Europe, North America, and east Asia. The automobile is at the center of this trend, but the growth was broad-based, including the residential and commercial sectors as well as industry and transport.

The growth has not been constant, however. Growth was most rapid in the 1950s and 1960s, and slowed significantly in three distinct episodes: 1973–1975; 1979–1982; and 1990–1993 (Fig. 14.2). The first two of these episodes were periods of rapid increases in oil prices precipitated by political events in the Middle East. The increases in oil prices came during (and were a partial cause of) a worldwide contraction in industrial production, which further inhibited growth in energy use.

In the early 1970s, rapid growth in oil use was causing an increase in demand for oil, much of which was derived from the Middle East. Oil production in countries like Saudi Arabia, Iraq, Iran, Libya, and the Persian Gulf states was largely controlled by European and North American oil companies which initally led and financed development of these resources. Nationalism was growing in the region, and many leaders in the area pressed for greater control of oil production and a greater share

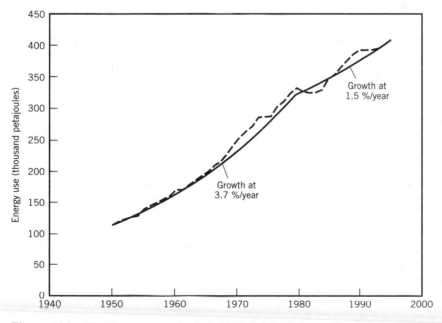

Figure 14.2   World energy production, 1950–1995. The rate of energy growth between 1950 and 1979 averaged 3.7% per year; from 1979 to 1995 the growth rate was only 1.5% per year. *Source:* World Resources Institute, 1996.

of the profits. In 1973 war broke out between Israel and its neighboring Arab countries, and Arab resentment of European and North American nations that were supportive of Israel increased further. For six months Arab oil-exporting nations refused to ship oil to Israel's supporters. Prices rose sharply on the world market, and consumption dropped in the United States.

A second energy crisis was precipitated by a revolution in Iran in 1979. The revolution caused another sharp, though temporary, increase in prices. But this time the world's industrial economies were more vulnerable. Many energy-intensive industries, especially the steel industry, were relatively inefficient, and there was excess productive capacity worldwide. When energy prices rose, the less efficient producers, especially those in older industrial regions such as the northeast United States and northern Europe, could not compete. Economic recession resulted, with a consequent decrease in energy use that lasted into the mid-1980s.

The last of the three episodes of low growth, the early 1990s, was a result of the economic collapse in eastern Europe that followed the breakup of the Soviet Union. That country and its Warsaw Pact allies in eastern Europe were heavy users of energy, especially coal, in their industrial sectors. Industrial production was controlled by the state with only limited regard for profitability. But when those economies collapsed in the early 1990s consumers could not afford to buy the industrial output of these countries, and factories shut down.

The decline of oil at the end of the twentieth century coincides with the rapid growth in use of electricity worldwide. As electric production and distribution networks expand, so does demand for electricity. Much of the growth in electric energy demand has been met by expansion of nuclear and coal-fired electric generation. As we look forward to the next few decades we can see trends that will increase our use of electricity (the growing interest in electric automobiles, for example) as well as the potential development of new energy supplies, such as photoelectric cells.

The history of energy use is thus one of shifting from one energy source to another. The shifts are driven by two main factors: the development of technology that can use a given energy source and the relative availability of one energy source over another. The history of recent trends in energy use has shown that technological developments and the social and economic changes that go with them are usually much more significant than the availability of natural energy resources in determining what fuel we use and how much.

Current energy consumption in the United States is dominated by the industrial (37%) and transportation (27%) sectors (Fig. 14.3). The preferred source of energy remains oil (primarily for transportation), followed by natural gas and coal. Regionally, nuclear sources are more dominant in the northeastern states (13% of total), whereas hydro sources are more pronounced in the west (12% of total). Fossil fuel use is fairly constant across all regions of the United States. Coal is the dominant fuel in the east north central, south north central, and mountain states.

ENERGY SOURCES

Oil and Natural Gas

Petroleum is the most important fuel in the world today, supplying about 40 percent of total commercial energy production. Most of the world's oil use is in the transport sector as fuel for internal combustion engines. This is especially true in the United States, where over 60 percent of oil use is in the form of gasoline and diesel fuel for automobiles and trucks and in aviation fuels. Industrial uses of oil are also important, mostly for heat production but also for petrochemicals. In the United States relatively little oil is used in electricity production, but elsewhere in the world this is an important use of oil.

Oil and natural gas are produced by the accumulation of organic matter in sedimentary rocks and the later alteration of that organic matter by the heat of burial in the earth's crust. Both oil and gas are composed of hydrocarbons, but they differ in their boiling temperatures. Oil is liquid in the ground, but gas is not. Oil and gas usually occur together, but sometimes they can become separated if gas migrates through a rock that is not permeable enough for oil to flow. *Crude oil* may contain natural gas in solution, and gas sometimes contains liquid petroleum. Because they coexist and are readily substitutable in most end uses, we discuss them together.

Sediments rich in organic matter are relatively

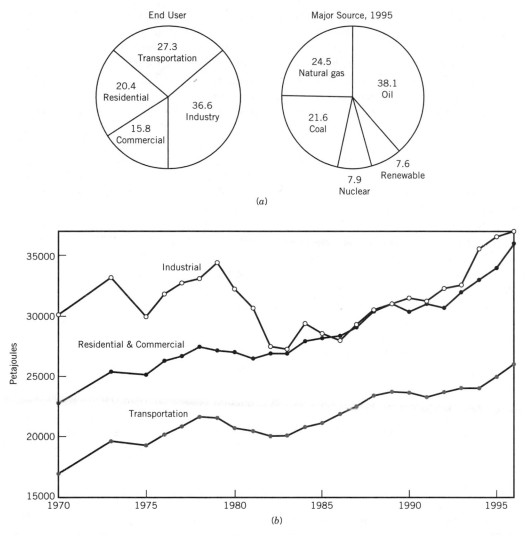

Figure 14.3 United States energy consumption, (*a*) use of energy by end-use and source, (*b*) trends from 1970–1996. Energy use in industry dropped dramatically in the mid-1980s as a consequence of increasing energy prices and economic recession. Use in transportation and residential and commercial sectors has stabilized with slight increases since the mid-1980s. Industry, however, remains the dominant user of energy in the United States.

common, but the geologic circumstances necessary to accumulate oil or gas in commercially useful quantities are not. For this to occur there must be a reservoir rock that is permeable enough for oil to flow through. Oil is less dense than water, and it is forced upward by density differences as well as pressures in the earth's crust. Another requirement is a trap, in which a reservoir rock is overlain by an impermeable rock that prevents the oil from escaping to the surface. Many different kinds of traps exist, and

exploration geologists usually look for such structures in their initial searches for oil. Accumulations of oil, or fields, vary considerably in size, with the number of fields inversely related to their size. There are very few giant fields. The largest known field is the Ghawar in Saudi Arabia (about 75 billion barrels). Oil also comes in many different forms, and the quality of crude oil depends on the mix of different hydrocarbons in the oil. Crude oil with a high proportion of high-boiling-point hydrocarbons is called heavy oil.

Tar and asphalt are major components of heavy oil. Light oil is rich in hydrocarbons with low boiling points, such as naphtha and kerosene. The proportion of various hydrocarbons affects both the ease of extraction and the price of the crude oil. Natural gas is made up of several different gases, including methane, propane, and butane.

Production and Consumption Oil-bearing formations are found all over the world, but the largest deposits are concentrated in a few areas. The 10 countries with the largest proven recoverable reserves are listed in Table 14.2. Most of the world's reserves are located in the Persian Gulf area, with Saudi Arabia, Iraq, Kuwait, Iran, and the United Arab Emirates holding over 60 percent of world reserves. This concentration of deposits of the world's primary energy source in a few countries has been a major source of world tension, with the United States particularly concerned because of its dependence on imported oil.

Global patterns of oil production and consumption have changed dramatically over the past several decades and have been the focus of many key economic and political issues. The United States was self-sufficient in oil for most of the first half of the twentieth century. There were shortages during World War I, and during World War II gasoline was rationed. Throughout this period, the real price of oil in the United States (adjusted for inflation) steadily declined, reaching a low in the late 1960s. By the mid–1950s, domestic oil began to get harder to find, and exploration in other regions of the world picked up. Domestic exploration, as measured by the number of wells drilled, peaked in 1956 and has not reached that level since, although by other measures exploration in 1981 was higher than ever before. American oil companies in the 1950s and 1960s placed more emphasis on exploration abroad, particularly in South America and the Middle East. Those areas held large untapped fields that could be developed more cheaply than the smaller fields in the United States. Even considering transportation costs, this oil was cheaper than domestic oil.

As a result of this exploitation of foreign oil, in the early 1970s the United States found itself a major importer of oil, with imports amounting to about 25 percent of consumption. Domestic oil production peaked in 1970, and natural gas production peaked in 1974. Domestic demand continued to climb, the difference being made up by imports. In 1981, 53 percent of our oil consumption was supplied by domestic production, with

Table 14.2   Known Recoverable Reserves of Fossil Fuels: Top 10 Nations

COAL: World total 1,031,610 million metric tons		OIL: World total 140,676 million metric tons		NATURAL GAS: World total 141,335 billion cubic meters	
State	*Percent of World Total*	*State*	*Percent of World Total*	*State*	*Percent of World Total*
United States	23	Saudi Arabia	25	Iran	15
China	11	Iraq	10	Russia	13
Australia	9	Kuwait	9	United Arab Emirates	4
India	7	Iran	9	Saudi Arabia	4
Germany	7	United Arab Emirates	9	United States	3
South Africa	5	Venezuela	7	Venezuela	3
Poland	4	Mexico	5	Algeria	3
Indonesia	3	Russia	5	Nigeria	2
Canada	1	Libya	4	Iraq	2
Turkey	1	United States	3	Canada	2
All others	29	All others	14	All others	50

Note: *Russia has substantial coal reserves, but accurate estimates of reserves are not available at this time.*
Source: World Resources Institute, 1996.

47 percent supplied by imports. Imports currently supply about 42 percent of the United States' consumption. However, the dramatic price increases that accompanied the oil shortages of the 1970s stimulated conservation, and by 1981 demand began to be reduced. This was partly a result of the cumulative effect of conservation measures such as reduction in size of automobiles, but it was also caused by the economic recession of 1981–1983. At the same time, domestic production was spurred by high prices, and supply increased. Similar trends occurred in other countries, and a worldwide surplus developed, with inventories at high levels and demand low. Oil prices peaked in 1981 and declined throughout the next two decades. The decline in oil prices in the 1980s and 1990s encouraged increasing consumption, and by the mid 1990s oil use in the United States had returned to mid–1970s levels.

Oil Futures   The oil shortages of the 1970s, like those of earlier years, generated much discussion about how much oil is available and how long it is likely to be before we run out. First, it should be recognized that, as with nonfuel minerals, we will never run out of oil. Rather, it will become so expensive that we will replace it with other sources, or we will reduce our demand for it. Nonetheless, it is important to ask just when oil and natural gas are going to become so hard to find and recover that the price must rise substantially, for at that time we will effectively cease to use these fuels for all but the most essential uses.

We can use two basic approaches to estimate how much oil we are likely to produce in the future: the geologic estimate and the performance-based estimate. The *geologic estimate* examines how much oil is in the ground in technically recoverable quantities, without regard to the larger economic forces affecting exploration and production. Most geologic estimates classify sedimentary basins with regard to petroleum-producing potential and use the well-known basins to extrapolate to the quantities likely to exist in poorly known areas. Thus, these are estimates of how much oil (or gas) is likely to be in an area, without regard to whether we have the desire or ability (other than technical ability) to get it out.

Geologic estimates have varied greatly over the years, generally increasing with time. In the 1940s, for example, ultimately recoverable oil resources were estimated at about 125 billion tons. Recent world estimates are generally in the range of 300 to 700 billion metric tons, with most of them clustering nearer the low end of that range. About 125 billion metric tons have already been used as of the mid-1990s. In 1993 the world's proved recoverable reserves of oil were 140 billion tons, or about 47 years' supply at 1993 consumption rates (World Resources Institute 1996; Worldwatch Institute 1996). If these numbers are correct, and if oil consumption were to continue to grow as expected in the next few decades, then we might exhaust these supplies by the third decade of the twenty-first century.

But such projections are based on many assumptions, not the least of which are the extrapolations of present conditions into the future. We know very well that conditions will change. Consumption rates will change, and new deposits will probably be found. Perhaps more importantly, both our use of oil and the amount we are willing to find and extract from the ground depend on our desire to have that oil, which is measured by its price.

Performance-based estimates of oil resources focus on the economic factors that drive oil production and consumption. They examine the pattern of exploration and production through time, considering all the economic forces that determine whether or not an oil company supplies oil and whether or not a consumer buys it. This technique was pioneered by M. K. Hubbert, who argued that for any stock resource there is a pattern of exponential growth in use of that resource, until the amount used begins to approach the approximate amount in the earth. Then production will level off and decline exponentially (Fig. 14.4). The decline is related as much to the fact that substitute commodities are found and adopted as it is to actual difficulty in obtaining supplies. Performance-based estimates have the advantage of being able to consider the true economic factors affecting oil production but have the disadvantage of being subject to questionable assumptions about future economic conditions. Most performance-based estimates of remaining oil suggest that world oil production will peak sometime in the second or third decade of the twenty-first century (World Resources Institute

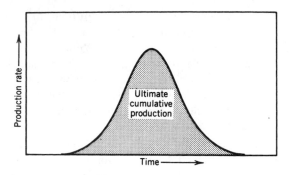

Production rate →

Time →

Ultimate cumulative production

Figure 14.4 Performance-based estimates of oil recoverability. In oil production, a pattern of exponential growth first occurs. Production levels off when the amount used approaches the amount naturally found in the earth. This is followed by an exponential decline in production and use. *Source*: Hubbert, 1969.

1996). In the United States, production peaked in 1970 and will probably dwindle to a small fraction of consumption by 2005–2010.

As we consider the future use of oil in comparison to other energy sources, we should also consider the environmental impacts of this activity. The most significant environmental concerns involve the transportation, refining, and burning of oil and natural gas. Because of the geographic locations of the major world producers and consumers, crude oil must be moved by ship (supertanker, tanker, or barge), pipeline, tank truck, or tank car. This is predominantly high seas traffic, with shipments of oil from the producing nations in the Middle East to European, Japanese, and North American markets. As a result of shipping these massive amounts so frequently, accidents are likely to happen—and they do. Pollution of the oceans from tanker accidents has both local and global impacts (see Chapter 9). Another environmental concern is the refining and burning of petroleum, which releases hydrocarbons and carbon dioxide to the atmosphere. This was discussed in Chapter 12.

Finally, a number of land-based problems are involved in petroleum production and natural gas storage. The withdrawal of both oil and natural gas has caused ground subsidence in such places as Long Beach, California, and Houston, Texas. Another problem with natural gas involves the transportation of *liquid natural gas (LNG)* by

tanker and its storage and support at land-based facilities. Large volumes of volatile gas are vulnerable to fires with potentially disastrous consequences. Fires have occurred but have been less devastating than feared. However, the possibility of monumental conflagrations causes concern over the location of LNG facilities near urban areas.

Coal

Coal is the most abundant fossil fuel in the world, with reserves far exceeding those of oil or natural gas. The United States is particularly well supplied with coal, with one-fourth of the world's reserves. Coal is also a dirty fuel, and the environmental impacts associated with its extraction and combustion are a matter of considerable concern.

Coal is the partially decomposed and consolidated remains of plants that were deposited in ancient swamps and lagoons. The original material was modified by heat and the weight of overlying materials from the original plant matter to a substance that is much harder, drier, and chemically different. The degree to which modification of coal has occurred varies greatly from one deposit to another, so that there are several different kinds, or ranks, of coal. The least modified form is *peat*. It has a very high moisture content and is being deposited in many areas today. In order, the remaining ranks of coal are *lignite, subbituminous, bituminous*, and finally *anthracite*, which is the most completely converted rank. Typical moisture contents vary from over 40 percent for lignite to less than 10 percent for anthracite. As moisture content is reduced and hydrogen is lost, the heat content per unit weight increases. In addition to rank, ash and sulfur contents are important to the value of coal deposits. Ash is derived primarily from mineral sediments deposited along with the plants. In some areas, ash content may be very high, but generally coal with ash greater than 15 percent is uneconomic. Sulfur accumulates in most sediments deposited in swampy conditions, and in coal sulfur contents typically vary from less than 1 percent to more than 3 percent.

Production and Consumption Unlike oil and natural gas, there is so much coal in the world that there is little concern about remaining resources. The largest deposits of coal are found in the United States, Russia, China, and central

Europe, though significant deposits also occur in South Africa, India, and elsewhere. Table 14.3 includes estimates of the ratio of reserves to production (R/P) for the top 20 coal-using countries. This ratio expresses the number of years a country's coal reserves would last at present rates of use. Nearly all the world's major coal users have abundant resources. Because of high transportation costs and the ease with which other fuels can be used, only those countries that have abundant coal are likely to use it extensively. Nonetheless, in those countries R/P ratios frequently are in hundreds of years, and the ratio for the world as a whole is over 200 years. Thus, there is plenty of coal to meet both United States and world demands for at least several decades, if not hundreds of years, even if we consider increasing per capita energy consumption and conversion from oil and natural gas to coal for some uses.

The United States has the largest share of coal reserves, with more than one-third of the world's proven recoverable reserves. Bituminous coal is the most abundant type of coal, and this is in the Appalachian Mountains in the East and in sections of the Midwest, particularly Illinois, Iowa, and Missouri (Fig. 14.5). Bituminous deposits are also found throughout the Rocky Mountains and in northern Alaska. Anthracite deposits are quite localized and are found in eastern Pennsylvania and in the Appalachian regions of West Virginia and Virginia. Subbituminous deposits are found throughout the Rocky Mountain region. Lignite deposits are found in North and South Dakota and Montana.

Table 14.3   The World's Top 20 Solid Fuel Users

Country	A Energy Production from Solid Fuels, 1993 (petajoules)	B Amount of Coal Required to Produce Amount of Energy in Column A (million metric tons)	C Proven Recoverable Coal Reserves (all types) (million metric tons)	D Reserves to to Production (R/P) Ratio (years)
China	24,045	748	114,500	153
United States	20,218	629	240,558	382
Russian Federation	6309	196	NA	NA
India	6141	191	69,947	366
Australia	4634	144	90,940	630
South Africa	4064	126	55,333	437
Poland, Republic of	3719	115	42,100	364
Germany	3675	114	67,300	588
Kazakhstan, Republic of	2809	87	NA	NA
Ukraine	2802	87	NA	NA
Korea, Democratic People's Republic of	2585	80	600	7
United Kingdom	1922	59	662	11
Canada	1571	48	8623	176
Czech Republic	1283	39	NA	NA
Indonesia	808	25	32,063	1274
Colombia	591	18	4539	247
Turkey	484	15	7148	474
Spain	427	13	1450	109
Romania	318	9	3117	315
Greece	315	9	3000	306
WORLD	91,748	2857	653,587	208

NA: Not Available.

Source: World Resources Institute, 1996.

China and the United States together account for about half the world's coal use; Europe is the other major coal-using region. Most of the world's coal is used for industrial purposes, especially electric generation. In China coal is not only the primary industrial fuel, but it is also widely used for space heating and cooking. In Europe and the United States little coal is used today for home heating, but it still is used in industry, primarily in producing iron and steel. In steel-making, coal is first converted to coke by driving off water and volatile matter through destructive distillation, and then it is burned in blast furnaces.

Since the energy crises of the 1970s, U.S. coal production has risen by about 30 percent of 1976 levels. In 1900, coal contributed about 70 percent of U.S. energy supplies, but today its contribution is much lower. In the last 30 years its contribution has varied from 40 percent in 1951 to a low of 17 percent in 1971. Today it contributes about 23 percent of total U.S. energy consumption and about 55 percent of U.S. electricity generation.

Extraction and Environmental Impacts

Coal is mined in three ways: underground; in surface strips; and with augurs. In the nineteenth and early twentieth centuries, most coal mining took place in the eastern United States, where most of the coal seams are in hilly areas and many are steeply inclined relative to the surface. In such situations most of the coal is well below the surface, and underground mining is necessary. *Underground mining* involves drilling, blasting, or otherwise excavating tunnels and chambers underground from which coal is removed and transported to the surface. Much of the coal must be left behind to support overlying

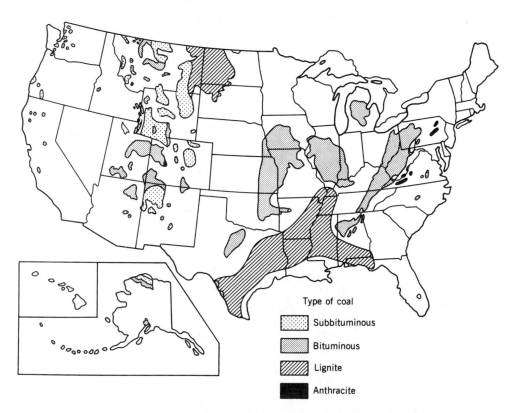

Figure 14.5 Coal resources in the United States. Anthracite deposits are found in eastern Pennsylvania and the Appalachian region of Virginia and West Virginia. Bituminous deposits are found throughout the United States, whereas lignite deposits are largely confined to the West. *Source:* Council on Environmental Quality, 1989.

rocks, and generally no more than 50 percent of the coal is removed. Underground mining is the most dangerous form of mining. Indeed, it is among the most dangerous occupations in the world. The greatest hazards are from explosions of methane gas, which is an important component of many coal deposits, and from rock bursts that result from removal of pressure on rocks deep underground.

Strip-mining or *surface mining* is conducted in areas where the coal is near the surface (Fig. 14.6). The *overburden*, or rock and soil overlying the coal, is first removed, and then the coal is removed. In areas of relatively flat terrain where the coal seams are horizontal, strip-mining can remove about 90 percent of the coal from a large area and is thus much more efficient than underground mining. In hilly areas, coal outcrops along hillsides are sometimes mined by stripping, leaving deeper coal unmined. Alternatively, coal in such areas may be mined by *auguring*, in which a large augur or drill bores into a coal seam, removing the coal in the process.

Until recently, most coal mined in the United States was mined underground in the East. In the last three decades, strip-mining has grown substantially, especially in the West. In 1974, surface mining surpassed underground mining, and as of

Figure 14.6   Area strip mining of coal in Missouri. The active face is along the left; areas to the right are being graded prior to reclamation.

1995 over 70 percent of U.S. coal was surface mined (Energy Information Administration 1996).

Coal mining and combustion are the most destructive methods in use today for obtaining energy. The environmental impacts are many and far-reaching. Underground mining has two major environmental effects; acid drainage and subsidence. *Acid drainage* results from air and water coming in contact with sulfur-bearing rocks and coal. The sulfur is oxidized to sulfuric acid, and groundwater flow carries this acid to streams. This is a particularly severe problem in mining regions of the Appalachians, where some streams have become too acidic to support fish life. Acidity of streams also affects the solution of metals in water, making it less suitable for human consumption. *Subsidence* is the sinking of the land as underground voids collapse. It results in structural damage to buildings overlying mined areas, and it is widespread in Pennsylvania and other underground mining areas.

Strip-mining is generally much more disruptive of the land than underground mining. Overburden must be removed, and so the soil and topography of the area underlain by coal are completely altered in the mining process. While the mine is in operation and until the land is reclaimed, the overburden is exposed to air and rain, resulting in accelerated runoff and oxidation of newly exposed rocks. Runoff from mined areas results in increased sediment loads of streams, oxidation of sulfur-rich rocks leads to the formation of sulfuric acid, and runoff water from these areas is usually very acidic. These problems are particularly severe in areas with steep slopes, where runoff and erosion are more rapid. In addition, steeply sloping spoils piles are sometimes prone to landsliding.

In 1977, Congress passed the Surface Mining Reclamation and Control Act, which requires reclamation on surface-mined lands. This includes removal of topsoil separately from lower overburden layers. When mining is completed, the overburden is replaced with topsoil above it, graded to its approximate original contour, and replanted with vegetation similar to that present before mining. The Act also places a tax on surface mining activities that is used to pay for reclamation of areas mined and abandoned before 1977.

Although mining impacts are locally significant, air pollution from coal combustion has much more far-reaching impacts. Concerns about acid deposition have increased demands for low-sulfur coal. Of U.S. coal reserves, about 20 percent is high-sulfur coal, 15 percent is medium-sulfur coal, and 65 percent is low-sulfur coal. Eastern coal is generally higher in sulfur than that west of the Mississippi River, which is unfortunate because the East is generally more susceptible to problems of acid precipitation than the West.

Carbon dioxide emissions, on the other hand, are not as controllable. CO_2 is produced as the end product of efficient combustion, and there is no known way to prevent this emission. As discussed in Chapter 12, coal produces proportionately more CO_2 than oil and natural gas, and if coal combustion is increased, then CO_2 emissions will increase. The nature of the environmental impact of those emissions is still open to question, but if we intend to prevent CO_2 buildup in the atmosphere, then the only alternative is to reduce coal combustion.

Other Fossil Fuels

In addition to oil, natural gas, and solid coal, vast deposits of potentially usable fossil fuels exist. The most significant of these fuels are tar sands and oil shale. These rocks can be mined, and burnable hydrocarbons extracted from them. Coal also can be converted to a gaseous form for easier transport and combustion. Fuels manufactured from these deposits are known as synthetic fuels, or *synfuels*. In some cases, the technology to convert these substances to usable fuels has been available for several decades, and in other cases it is yet to be commercially developed. As liquid petroleum resources dwindle, synfuels will likely attract more interest because they rely on raw materials that are much more plentiful than the oil they may replace.

Coal gasification or *liquefaction* means the conversion of coal to a gas or liquid that can be transported via pipeline and burned much as we burn conventional fuels today. Several different gasification techniques are available, but most involve the addition of hydrogen to the carbon in coal to make hydrocarbons. In some processes, the volatile hydrocarbons in coal are used as a source of hydrogen, and in others water (in the form of steam) is used. The most common gasification processes make gas that has a lower heat content than conventional fuels, though it can be further processed into high-quality gas and liquid fuels. Coal gasification is most easily carried out in above-ground facilities, but there is potential for development of below-ground, or *in situ*, technologies. The technology of coal gasification and liquefaction is fairly well known, but as yet, it is not economically competitive with conventional oil and gas.

Tar sands are deposits of sand that are high in heavy oil, or tar content. This tar is too viscous to be pumped from the ground as oil is, but if it is heated it will liquefy and can then be pumped and refined much as heavy crude oil is refined. In Alberta, Canada, extensive areas of tar sands near or at the surface are being commercially mined today. *Shale oil* is not true oil; rather, it is a waxy hydrocarbon called *kerogen* that is found in shale, a fine-textured sedimentary rock. Shale oil is extracted, or retorted, by first crushing and then heating the rock. This liquefies the kerogen, which seeps out of the rock and can then be piped away.

One of the most attractive aspects of synfuels is that the raw materials are available in vast quantities. At present rates of extraction, the United States has an ample supply of coal. Clearly, then, we could expand the use of coal for other purposes without jeopardizing its availability in the near future. In addition, if *in situ* methods of coal gasification or liquefaction prove to be economic, then deep deposits of coal could become exploitable. The largest U.S. deposits are in Colorado, Utah, and Wyoming.

Despite the vast amounts of fuel present in these deposits, it is unlikely that any of it will be exploited in the near future because of the environmental impacts of extraction. All the impacts associated with mining coal also apply to coal gasification—unless the conversion is made underground. If liquid or gaseous coal fuels are to replace oil, then our use of coal must increase, and so must the area affected by mining. The processing also requires large amounts of water, but water is scarce in many of our western coal regions. Gasified or liquefied coal probably would be cleaned of most sulfur in processing, and so sulfur emissions are not likely to be a major barrier to the use of these fuels. However, use of coal in any form, particularly one for which energy is lost in conversion, means that there will be substantial emissions of carbon dioxide.

Shale oil also has significant problems. First, to obtain a substantial amount of oil, large areas must be mined. If strip-mining is used, then all the problems associated with strip-mining of other minerals must be considered. Even with *in situ* retorting, about 25 percent of the rock's volume must be removed to make room for retorting. Second, retorting involves burning kerogen under conditions that are not conducive to clean combustion. This combustion produces emissions of hydrocarbons, carbon monoxide, and particulates. In the United States the areas where retorting would take place are areas of good air quality, and retorting would almost certainly cause some deterioration.

In addition to these environmental problems, economic conditions have not allowed exploitation of this resource. Commercial interest began during oil shortages in the 1920s, but to date there has been no successful commercial-scale extraction of synfuels in the United States. This is due to the relatively low price of conventional fuels, uncertainties about the extraction technology, and, more recently, environmental concerns. Most of the work in the area has been done either directly by the government or with major subsidies. When or whether extraction will become economic remains to be seen.

Nuclear Power

The first self-sustaining nuclear reaction took place in December 1942 at the University of Chicago. Although the first applications of nuclear energy were in weapons, atomic power was also used for peaceful purposes after World War II. Although the dichotomy between weapons applications and energy production still exists today, we will discuss only the commercial aspects of nuclear energy.

The first commercial use of nuclear power was to generate electricity in 1957 in Shippingport, Pennsylvania. Westinghouse Electric, in conjunction with the Atomic Energy Commission (now the Nuclear Regulatory Commission and Department of Energy), opened the first full-scale nuclear electrical power plant to be operated by a public utility. At 60 mW, the plant was small by today's standards. Nuclear generation of electricity has grown steadily since then, and in 1995 nuclear power supplied about 23 percent of U.S. electricity and 7 percent of total energy consumption (Energy Information Administration 1996). On a worldwide basis, nuclear energy production accounted for 7 percent of total commercial energy production in 1993 (World Resources Institute 1996).

Nuclear power is based on the *fission* process, in which the nuclei of heavy atoms of enriched uranium–235 (^{235}U) or plutonium–239 (^{239}Pu) (the latter a byproduct of the fission process) are split into lighter elements, thereby releasing energy in a chain reaction. The energy released is used to heat water into steam. The steam is then used to drive a turbine, which turns an electric generator.

Nuclear Fuel Cycle The nuclear fuel cycle consists of eight stages (Fig. 14.7). Unlike some of the more conventional fuel sources, which can be used with a minimum of processing, nuclear power requires several processing steps with transportation linkages between them. Uranium is the primary fuel for nuclear power plants. Most U.S. uranium resources are found in the Rocky Mountain states and are mined by both open-pit and underground techniques. Nearly two-thirds of the uranium is mined in New Mexico and Wyoming. Of the naturally occurring uranium, which is a mixture of the isotopes ^{235}U and ^{238}U, less than 1 percent, that is, only the ^{235}U, is highly fissionable. Thus, most of the uranium ore must be enriched or converted to make it sustain the fission process. Once mined, the uranium ore is milled to produce a purer concentrate called yellowcake. Yellowcake is about 85 percent natural uranium oxide (U_3O_8).

The third stage in the fuel cycle is the chemical purification and conversion of the yellowcake to uranium hexafluoride (UF_6). The conversion process prepares the uranium for enrichment, the next stage in the fuel cycle. At the enrichment plant the concentration of ^{235}U is increased from 0.7 percent to about 4 percent, to meet the requirements of the reactors. Once the UF_6 has been enriched, it is ready to be made into fuel rods. The UF_6 is converted into uranium dioxide (UO_2), which is then formed into small pellets and placed in alloy tubes. These tubes are then made into fuel rods and assembled into bundles, called fuel rod assemblies. The fuel rod assemblies are then shipped to individual reactors, where they are used to produce electricity.

Several different types of reactors are in use around the world. They differ in the medium used to extract heat from the reactor core and in the means for moderating the reaction. Most of the reactors in use in the United States are *light-water reactors* (Fig. 14.8), which means that ordinary water is used as the cooling agent. In some reactors, the water that circulates through the reactor vessel is used to generate steam directly, while in others pressurized water absorbs heat in the reactor, and this energy is transferred to the turbines via a separate loop that does not pass through the reactor itself. In a *high-temperature gas-cooled reactor*, helium gas is used as the coolant, transferring the heat from the core to the steam generator. *Heavy-water reactors* use water containing a higher than usual proportion of deuterium as the moderator of the fission process. Regular water passes through the core and carries heat to the secondary water/steam loop. Heavy-water reactors are not used in the United States, but they dominate the Canadian reactor program. Canada is also a large exporter of this technology and of the heavy water that is used in it. The reactor at Chernobyl, Ukraine, that exploded in 1986 was of a type that uses graphite to moderate the reaction.

One additional type of reactor bears mention because it is capable of creating more fissionable fuel than it uses. This is the *liquid metal fast-breeder reactor*, in which fissionable material is surrounded by nonfissionable material (^{238}U) in the core. Sodium is used as the moderating substance and heat exchanger. During the fission process, some of the nonfissionable material is converted to fissionable ^{239}Pu. The reactor produces more fuel than it consumes, hence the name breeder reactor. There are no breeder reactors in the United States, although they have been used in other countries for some time. Breeder reactors are a central feature of France's nuclear energy program, for example.

Spent fuel is removed from the reactor core and stored on site for several months to permit the levels of radioactivity to decline. Optimally, the spent fuel is then shipped to a reprocessing plant, where the unused portions of uranium and plutonium are separated from the fission wastes. The unused uranium is recycled back to the enrichment plant, and the unused plutonium is refabricated into new fuel pellets.

The last stage in the nuclear fuel cycle is disposal of the radioactive waste. *Low-level wastes* (only half of which are generated by nuclear power plants) are buried in metal or concrete containers. Since the start of the commercial reactor program, over 2 million cu ft (3 million m^3)

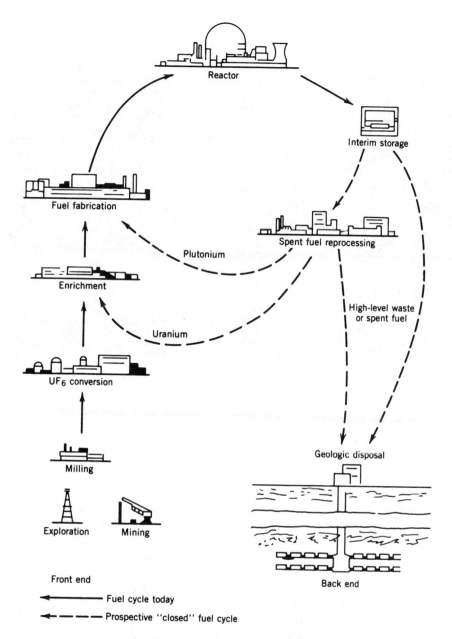

Figure 14.7 The nuclear fuel cycle. At each stage in the cycle, nuclear material is transported varying distances from mining regions to conversion and enrichment facilities, fabrication plants, and nuclear reactors. After use, spent fuel is reprocessed and/or disposed of. *Source:* Council on Environmental Quality, 1981.

of low-level waste have been buried. In 1993, for example, 800,000 cu ft of low-level waste were buried in two locations; Barnwell, South Carolina and Hanford, Washington. A permanent disposal facility for high-level waste is being developed at Yucca Mountain, Nevada. Currently, all high-level waste (28,000 metric tons in 1993) is stored in pools at the reactor sites. The repository project has been plagued with technical and management problems, however, and it is unlikely that a permanent high-level waste storage facility will be available in the United States

Figure 14.8   Power plant using a pressurized water reactor, Three Mile Island, Pennsylvania. The reactor experienced a loss-of-coolant accident in 1979.

before about 2010 (Flynn et al. 1997). Yet, estimates suggest that by 2003, these commercial reactors will produce an additional 48,000 metric tons of high-level waste.

The primary concern about the use of nuclear energy is the potential for human exposures to radioactivity, resulting in cancer, birth defects, and other health problems. Accidental releases of radioactivity occur at all stages in the fuel cycle, from the mining of uranium, which produces radon gas, to occupational exposures in fabricating fuel rods, to accidental releases at nuclear power plants. Releases of radioactivity can also occur as a result of sabotage and simple mishandling of materials. There is considerable debate on the effects of low levels of exposure to ionizing radiation.

There are also other environmental considerations at each stage in the fuel cycle. Land disturbance and radioactive mine tailings are the primary impacts of mining and milling. In the production of power, waste heat is produced, causing thermal pollution. This occurs with any type of steam-powered electricity plant. The most important environmental aspects of nuclear

power production involve the accidental release of airborne or water-borne radioactivity. For example, in the Chernobyl incident (Issue 14), radioactive fallout was spread over much of Europe, resulting in levels of contamination high enough to prevent the consumption of numerous food products produced in contaminated areas for at least several years following the accident (Gould 1991; Hohenemser 1996; Hohenemser et al. 1986; Hohenemser and Renn 1988). These safety issues cause great public concern about large-scale use of nuclear energy. The technology is hazardous, and the future extent of nuclear energy production will be a function of the risks that society is willing to tolerate in exchange for additional electric power.

Power Production Trends   Nuclear power is used only to generate electricity. In the United States, production of electricity using nuclear power increased substantially during the 1980s as plants under construction since the 1970s were completed and began operation. This growth in the United States nuclear industry ended in the

1980s, however, because nuclear power became much more expensive than other heat sources used to generate electricity and because the 1979 accident at Three Mile Island hindered public acceptance of nuclear power. The 1986 accident at Chernobyl (in the Ukraine) reconfirmed the public's fear about the safety of nuclear power plants. In 1995, there were 437 commercial nuclear units operating worldwide, 109 of these in the United States where they produced about 22 percent of our electricity. Improved capacity and performance at these U.S. plants account for the increases in net generation.

Because very few additional plants will be operating, United States generation capacity will not increase substantially in the next decade. Within the next 20 years, nearly half of the commercial nuclear power plants will reach the end of their operating licenses and be decommissioned, resulting in a decline in generating capacity. Worldwide nuclear capacity is expected to increase by about 5 percent in the next few years. It remains to be seen whether confidence in nuclear energy will be restored and growth will continue, or whether we already have reached the peak of nuclear energy generation. If nuclear energy is to become viable again, it will almost certainly require the development of new, safer technology that will restore public confidence in this energy source. Otherwise, the high costs of overcoming political opposition and meeting safety requirements will continue to make construction of nuclear plants prohibitively expensive.

In other parts of the world similar problems have arisen, though not everywhere. In much of western Europe, public concern about reactor safety increased dramatically after the Chernobyl incident (see Issue 14.1). In 1989, the British government acknowledged that its nuclear industry (which now generates about 25% of that nation's electricity) was not economic in comparison to conventional generation technology and abandoned plans for any additional power plants. France, however, which has had a very aggressive nuclear program since the 1950s, generates 75 percent of its electricity from 56 nuclear power reactors. France has remained firm in its commitment to this energy source.

Fuel availability is not a major deterrent to the future use of nuclear power. Public concern over safety, however, poses the biggest challenge. On the other hand, public concern over global climate change may force us to reconsider the nuclear option. Coal is the primary alternative to nuclear power in many U.S. regions. Nuclear energy is seen as relatively clean from an environmental perspective, and it offers the potential to increase electric generation capacity without contributing to global warming or acid rain, although long-term waste storage remains a problem. As we saw earlier, 40 percent of the energy demand in the United States is in the transportation sector, which cannot be supplied by nuclear sources at the current time.

Renewable Energy

Several renewable sources of energy are available today, and many more will probably become available in the future. *Renewable energy* is a term used to describe energy sources that are either continuously available, like heat and light from the sun, or those that are replaced relatively rapidly and therefore can only be temporarily depleted, like wood. Renewable energy sources are quite varied, such as radiant energy (the sun), chemical energy (biomass), potential energy (water stored in reservoirs), and kinetic energy (wind). Some, like wood fuel, have been used for thousands of years, while others are relatively recent developments (hydroelectric generation) or future options (ocean thermal energy conversion, or OTEC).

Although many different technologies are available for renewable energy sources, a few technologies are likely to be most important in the next few decades. Some of these will be produced in large, concentrated facilities (as most of our electricity is produced today) which we will call *centralized renewables*. In other cases, energy production will be in small facilities, like the photovoltaic cells that are used to power satellites, calculators, and remote communications facilities. These are called *decentralized renewables*.

Centralized renewables require large capital investments in single facilities, and most are used to generate electricity that is fed into the same grids that transport energy generated from fossil fuels or nuclear power. The primary centralized renewable energy sources in use today are hydroelectric generation, geothermal energy, tidal power, and biomass. The most promising technologies for future centralized renewable power include OTEC, low-temperature geothermal, and large-scale solar power facilities.

ISSUE 14.1:   THE LEGACY OF CHERNOBYL

Although nuclear energy is very useful and reported accidents are rare, the fear of another accident like the one at Chernobyl is one of the largest problems facing the nuclear industry. On April 26, 1986, a nuclear reactor at Chernobyl, near the Ukraine-Belarus border, became unstable and exploded. The explosion and resulting fire released nearly 200 times the amount of radiation released by the Hiroshima and Nagasaki bombs combined, and spread radioactive contaminants across Europe (Specter 1996). In the days immediately following, over 200,000 people were evacuated from areas exposed to the fallout (Stone 1996; Williams and Balter 1996). The ecological and medical impacts in the immediate area were enormous and long-lasting. The repercussions for the nuclear power industry were no less significant.

When the Soviet authorities finally acknowledged that the Chernobyl incident was major, they evacuated all the children in the immediate area, because young bodies are more vulnerable to the effects of fallout. It was too late for many. When they returned from their unexpected summer "vacation," many children were already ill with leukemia, thyroid cancer, and other radiation-induced diseases. The Soviet authorities paid a heavy price for their long-term policy of insisting that they could handle their own problems without help from the outside. In 1986 the Soviet government maintained that it could easily handle this local problem, that only 200 people had been contaminated, and that life and farming would soon return to normal. But the reality turned out to be much worse than the early official statements, and the Soviet government, and later the governments of Ukraine and Belarus, became much more open about the extent of the problem.

The effects of Chernobyl were felt internationally, and we still do not know the full impact of the drifting fallout on downwind areas in eastern Europe, the British Isles, and Scandinavia, where the Lapps' lives have been changed forever. Their reindeer, consuming contaminated lichens, are no longer permitted in livestock markets. In parts of Wales, England, and Scotland, heavy rainstorms occurring just as the cloud of fallout was passing overhead brought contamination to upland areas. For years following the accident, sheep from these areas had to be screened before being allowed on the market. Sheep pastured on contaminated hills were moved to uncontaminated areas for a period of several weeks to allow radiation levels to decline. These sheep were specially marked and are tested regularly until the levels reached are deemed safe for human consumption (Atherton and Atherton 1990).

With emergencies come technological breakthroughs, and it is now possible to detect irradiated areas from a helicopter equipped with radiation sensors. The maps resulting from this surveillance and from research on soils and runoff indicate that the cesium is becoming more environmentally active. The cesium is no longer simply lying on the vegetation but is weathering into the soil to be absorbed more efficiently by grass, the sheep's major food supply. The gradual loss of radiation in livestock in north Wales and other areas has leveled off and may begin to climb once more. North Wales farmers are unable to farm under these conditions; government compensation, where available, is no solace. Throughout the United Kingdom, 757 farms on 400,000 acres (160,000 ha) were affected by restrictions (Ghazi 1990).

Ten years after the accident, a vast region of southern Belarus and northern Ukraine is virtually uninhabitable. The area within a 30-km radius of the plant is officially closed to the public. Outside this are extensive areas in which no one is permitted to live or enter without a pass, and beyond these are zones in which residence is discouraged, health monitoring is required, and food production is prohibited. A thyroid epidemic is in progress among children in Belarus and Ukraine, with childhood thyroid cancer rates in Belarus increasing from fewer than 5 per year before the accident to over 80 by 1994 (Balter 1995). Those who inhabit the contaminated area fear more disease or another radioactive disaster. Fifteen of the 28 Chernobyl-type reactors in use in 1986 were still running in 1996, including two at Chernobyl. They have been modified to reduce the likelihood of another disaster, but many experts feel that the danger remains.

Decentralized renewables are energy sources that will be important for small facilities not connected to large-scale energy systems. The most significant of these is solar thermal energy for space or water heating. Other important decentralized energy sources for the future include photovoltaics and wind.

Hydroelectric Power From both economic and environmental considerations, hydroelectric power is the best source of electricity available to us today. It is generated by impounding water in a location where a substantial vertical drop is available, such as near a waterfall or in a steeply sloping and/or narrow portion of a river valley, and then passing the water through turbines that drive generators. Water power has been used for several centuries to drive various industrial facilities, but only in the last 100 or so years has it been used to generate electricity. In that time many large dams have been built, and in 1995 about 10 percent of United States electricity, or 4 percent of total United States energy consumption, was supplied by hydroelectric power. Worldwide, hydroelectric generation supplies less than 3 percent of total commercial energy production (Fig. 14.9).

Hydroelectric production is concentrated at the most desirable sites for this technology, specifically locations with large volumes of available water, narrow and deep valleys, and in some cases low population density. At these sites the cost of generating electricity is quite low in comparison to other methods. A rather large capital cost is involved in dam construction and land acquisition, but once this is paid for, the operating costs are extremely low. Most of the large dams in North America have been built either by governments or with large government subsidies, and this has contributed to the low cost of hydroelectric power in many areas. In the northwestern United States, for example, electricity prices are substantially lower than in the rest of the country because of the large contribution of hydroelectric power generated at federally built dams along the Columbia River and its tributaries.

Worldwide, there is considerable potential for increasing hydroelectric generation, especially in less-industrialized countries (Fig. 14.10). World hydroelectric-generating capacity has grown

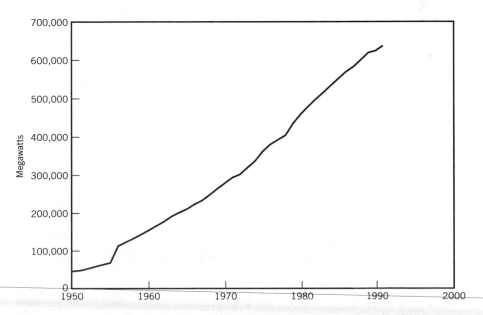

Figure 14.9 World hydroelectric generating capacity, 1950–1991. There has been a sharp increase in capacity during the last thirty years, a trend that shows no signs of slowing down. *Source:* Worldwatch Institute, 1996.

steadily since the 1950s at about 15,000 mW per year and will probably continue to grow for some time. The greatest potential for constructing new dams for hydroelectric generation is in the less-developed areas of the world, particularly in Asia, Africa, and South America, where many large rivers remain relatively unmanaged. The amount of untapped potential is vast; more than 15 times the current installed generating capacity. Tapping that potential, however, means overcoming substantial obstacles (see Issue 14.2).

There is relatively little potential for expansion of hydroelectric generation in the United States. Most of the best dam sites are already in use, and those that are not are generally not available because the river valleys have been committed to other uses, such as agriculture or wilderness preservation. There may be some opportunity for increasing power production at smaller dams, and there are a few examples of existing dams that were unused until recently, when higher energy prices made hydroelectric power generation on a small scale more feasible.

In New England, for example, hundreds of dams were constructed for hydroelectric power or industrial uses in the past but are no longer in use. In Canada, there is considerable potential for increased hydroelectric generation. Canada already exports substantial amounts of electricity to the United States, primarily from Quebec to New York. This trade is facilitated partly because the peak demand for electricity in Quebec occurs in winter, whereas the peak in most of the United States is in summer. Several additional dam sites are available in northern Quebec to increase this production, although capital costs, transmission distances, and opposition from native populations are significant barriers.

While hydroelectric generation is the cleanest source of electricity we have, it is not without its environmental problems. One of these is the loss of the land and aquatic habitat that is submerged when a reservoir is filled. The construction of dams and subsequent regulation of flow patterns may also have adverse effects on stream channels and aquatic life downstream. There have been

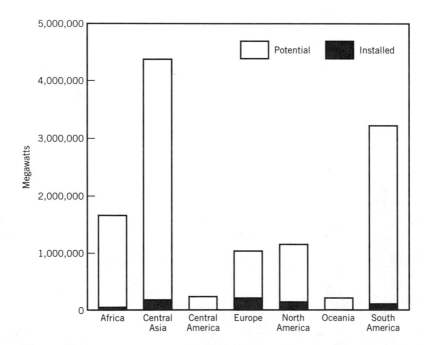

Figure 14.10 Potential and installed hydroelectric generating capacity. The potential for new hydroelectric development is vast, but political, economic, and environmental constraints will prevent most of this potential from being realized. *Source:* World Resources Institute, 1996.

problems of erosion in the Grand Canyon, for example, as a result of the construction of Glen Canyon Dam upstream. This led to an unprecedented experiment in the late 1990s where water was released from the dam to create flood conditions. In arid areas, such as the Colorado basin, reservoirs contribute to evaporative water losses by increasing water surface areas. Many valleys contain fertile agricultural land, and reservoir development has been a contributor to loss of agricultural land in the United States. There may also be effects on water quality as a result of impoundment, as nutrient-laden water stimulates algal blooms, leading to eutrophication. Despite these negatives, our existing hydroelectric facilities are important energy sources. Construction of new facilities, however, is a much more contentious issue, for they almost always entail the loss of some other valued resource.

Geothermal Energy *Geothermal energy* is derived from the internal heat of the earth. The core of the earth is hot, and this heat is convected and conducted outward toward the surface. In many parts of the earth's crust, sufficiently large amounts of heat are delivered to the surface to make the use of that heat feasible. Geothermal energy is used in many parts of the world today, for space and water heating, for industrial processing, and for electricity generation.

Three major types of geothermal resources are hydrothermal, geopressurized, and dry rock. Hydrothermal resources occur in locations where there is a source of heat relatively near the surface, and the overlying rocks are fractured enough to allow water to circulate. In addition, the water must be trapped in the ground to prevent heat from escaping rapidly to the surface. This results in the formation of hot springs and geysers. If this steam or hot water can be tapped, it can be used to generate electricity or heat buildings. Geopressurized resources are deeper pockets of water trapped in sedimentary formations in much the way as oil and gas are trapped. Hot dry rock is simply rock in areas of high heat flow but without large quantities of water contained in the rock. To tap this heat, the rocks must be fractured and wells drilled so that water can be injected into the rocks to draw the heat out. At present, geopressurized and hot dry rock resources are not in use.

Only one facility in the United States is currently generating electricity from geothermal energy—The Geysers, in California. It presently produces about 1000 mW at peak output, or about the same as a large conventional power plant. The output from this plant amounts to less than 0.2 percent of total U.S. electricity generation. One possibility for increased geothermal production is in the development of hot dry rock facilities. There are numerous areas of the United States, mostly in the West, where subsurface temperatures are particularly high. The economics of such ventures are still uncertain, however, so it is unlikely that geothermal energy will make large contributions to total electric generation in the near future.

Other Centralized Renewables In addition to hydroelectric and geothermal power, a few technologies offer limited potential for future development. One of these is the incineration of solid wastes. Heat from this burning can be used directly for industrial processes or for generating electricity. This process is often called *resource recovery*. At present several dozen resource recovery plants in the United States use solid waste as fuels, with most of these producing steam for industrial processes. In a few cases, wood or agricultural wastes are used for fuel, but in most plants municipal wastes are burned. The major incentive for burning solid waste at the present time is the high cost of disposal rather than the value of the steam produced, and the disposers pay to have the fuel burned rather than the plants buying fuel. In 1995, combustion of wood and municipal solid waste together with the production of alcohol from sugar and grain provided approximately 3 percent of the nation's energy needs, with alcohol being the largest part of this total (Energy Information Administration 1996).

Another centralized renewable energy source is *tidal power*. Tidal fluctuations produce strong currents in coastal embayments, and these currents can be harnessed to produce electricity. A large tidal range is required, and a dam must be constructed across the bay to create the hydraulic head necessary to drive turbines. Power can be generated only during a portion of the tidal cycle, and diurnal or semidiurnal tidal fluctuations do not always correspond to the fluctuations in demand. Thus, tidal power can be viewed only as a

ISSUE 14.2:   THE THREE GORGES DAM

As world population increases and demands on earth's water resources increase, the need for dams is certain to grow. Dams offer two important benefits that will be greatly needed in the coming decades: an increase in the amount of renewable water that is available for human use and the production of clean energy in the form of hydroelectricity. But dams are also expensive, and they fundamentally transform the landscapes in which they are placed, with immense impacts on humans and nature. They inevitably become the focus of controversy, and the Three Gorges Dam is no exception.

The Three Gorges Dam, currently under construction, is located in central China, more than 1600 km upstream from the river's mouth. The dam will be among the world's largest: about 185 m high, 1.9 km long, and impounding a lake 600 km long. The capacity of the reservoir will be 22 billion m^3, or about 24 times the mean annual discharge of the Yangtze at its mouth. Cost estimates range from about $20 to $75 billion. Completion is scheduled for 2009.

Like any big dam, the Three Gorges project has multiple benefits. In this case, the principal justification is flood control. The Yangtze has a long history of floods that cause vast damage to communities and farms along the river's floodplain. One of the most devastating recent floods occurred in 1954, killing 30,000 people and displacing 19 million. Following that flood, Mao Zedong vowed to proceed with the project that would lessen this flood risk. Forty years later construction finally began.

In addition to flood control, the Three Gorges Dam will generate 18,000 mW of electricity, boosting China's electric production by 10 percent. China's energy use is growing rapidly, and this added hydroelectric generation capacity could substitute for coal-generated electricity. The project also opens up possibilities for flow regulation that could be used to make more water available for irrigation and other uses, although to some extent this could conflict with the primary flood-control objective.

Opposition to the project focuses on its considerable negative environmental impacts and major engineering uncertainties. The greatest environmental impacts are associated with the loss of land along the Yangtze Valley. The area to be inundated includes 190 km^2 of farmland and the homes of roughly 1.2 million people, who will be relocated to other areas. The loss of agricultural land is very small in comparison with China's 950,000 km^2 of cropland. But the potential loss of cultural resources in the valley is large. The area to be flooded includes Shibaozhai, a tower of rock overlooking the river on which a pagoda was built in the eigthteenth

supplement to other sources of energy. At present, there is one large tidal power plant in operation in France and a smaller one in Nova Scotia.

Large-scale solar thermal and photovoltaic collectors, plants that harness wave energy, and large-scale wind powered generating facilities have also been proposed. There has been relatively little activity in these areas since the 1970s because of the low costs of conventional energy and the weak growth in demand for electricity. If prices rise significantly in the future, these methods may again be considered. Centralized renewable sources in general will probably continue to provide only small portions of our total energy supply, with only biomass (primarily municipal solid waste) and hydroelectric generation making a large contribution to total electricity generation. New power generation from all centralized renewable sources together will probably not contribute more than a small percentage of the total U.S. energy supply for a few decades.

Solar Energy   Among decentralized renewable energy sources, solar energy offers enormous potential for heating buildings and water, and thereby replacing more conventional energy sources such as fossil fuels and electricity. Solar energy is plentiful, though it is not uniformly available in space and time. The technology is reasonably well developed and is economically feasible in most of the United States. The major barrier to its use at present is capital costs.

century and a village that contains some of the best remaining examples of Ming Dynasty (1368–1644) structural art (Tyler 1996). And, of course, the lake will forever transform one of the most spectacular river valleys of the world from a natural-flowing stream into a reservoir, with unknown impacts on the river's biota.

Because the dam is by far the largest in China and among the largest in the world, the technical uncertainties are many. In projects of this scale, engineers simply don't have the experience on which to base their plans. One of the critical problems is sedimentation. The Yangtze carries an enormous load of sediment that would be deposited on the floor of the reservoir, diminishing its capacity. A much smaller dam in China, Sanmenxia, experiences a much higher sedimentation rate than that anticipated by its designers. As a result, the dam had to be modified and reservoir operation altered after just two years of operation (Leopold 1996). Even more important questions are those relating to the dam's flood-prevention potential. The Yangtze is fed by several major tributaries that enter the river downstream of the dam. Although the flow from the upstream portions of the Yangtze could be reduced, the flow from these tributaries would not be controlled by the dam. In addition, although the lake's volume is immense, most of this would already be filled with water at the beginning of a flood, and the amount of water that could be stored may be insufficient (Mufson 1996). These and other technical problems raise questions not only about the engineering feasibility of the project, but its financial aspects as well.

Like any major environmental issue, many of the debates are intertwined with other political differences. Domestically, opposition from academic and scientific circles has been strong, as have been the objections of those whose communities will be destroyed. In the late 1980s, internal opposition was sufficient to delay the project, but after the Tiananmen Square demonstrations in 1991, the government used the opportunity to forbid public opposition to the project and went ahead with construction of the dam. Internationally, strong opposition to the project has come from many points, and China has had a hard time borrowing money to pay for the dam. The World Bank, which includes environmental considerations in its policies, withheld its support for years. Despite pressure from some large engineering and construction-equipment manufacturers, in 1996 the U.S. Export-Import Bank also decided not to support it. As a result, virtually all the financing is coming from domestic Chinese sources, placing a considerable strain on that country's limited budgets for capital development.

Solar energy reaches the earth's surface in the form of radiant energy, and it is converted to heat when sunlight is absorbed on an exposed surface. The amount of radiant energy received varies with the time of day, season, weather conditions, and location on earth. For example, there is no sunlight at night, and during cloudy weather, sunlight is less intense, though it is still present. Seasonality influences the length of day, so that there are fewer hours of daylight in winter than in summer. Also, the angle of the sun changes during the year, reducing the intensity of solar radiation per unit of horizontal surface area in the winter. Because of these large fluctuations in solar energy availability, only a limited portion of the world can rely on solar energy as a single consistent source. In other regions, backup energy systems are required.

Solar energy is often discussed in terms of passive and active technologies. Passive solar heating and cooling involves neither mechanical devices nor the production and storage of electricity. *Passive solar power* employs proper design of structures, building materials that insulate or store energy, correct orientation of structures, and careful landscaping to provide heating and cooling. A house with many windows on the southern exposure allows for maximum sun during the winter. Planting deciduous trees on the south side of the house protects it from the hot summer sun's rays, yet allows the sunlight to penetrate during the winter months, when the trees have dropped their leaves. The use of adobe as a building material and the design of houses with shaded arcades and small windows, such as those of Spanish–style haciendas in the Southwest, are other examples of passive approaches to solar heating and cooling.

Active solar power uses mechanical devices to collect and store solar radiation for heating and cooling. The solar collector is the basic unit of a solar space heating system and can vary greatly in size and complexity. The simplest type of collector consists of a flat plate, painted black for maximum absorption, encased in an insulated, glass-covered box. The plate absorbs light, while the glass impedes energy loss, so that temperatures rise to about 200°F (93°C). This heat is then used to warm rooms and water as air moves across the black plate or water circulates through a pipe attached to the plate. Higher temperatures (up to 1000°F or 538°C) are obtained by concentrating the light with one or more curved mirrors, which rotate along with the sun's movement across the sky. Temperatures of up to 4000°F (2205°C) can be attained by focusing a bank of mirrors on a central point, such as a tower containing a water boiler for operating a steam turbine.

The amount of solar energy received by a collector varies with the time of day, season, and weather. These variations, as well as obstructions by trees and buildings, still allow for the use of solar energy for space heating. The heating and hot water needs of a one- or two-story building can be met by using available roof surfaces, southern walls, and other areas for the installation of collectors.

The use of solar collectors nationwide rose substantially in the late 1970s and early 1980s but slowed in the 1990s. Low-temperature collectors are used almost exclusively for swimming pool heating. Medium-temperature collectors are used both for space heating and cooling and for domestic water heating. Regionally, more collectors are in use in the western, high-sunshine states than in the East, but advocates maintain that solar collectors are capable of a quick return on investment even in the cloudiest of climates.

Among the more promising solar technologies for the future are *photovoltaic cells*—thin silicon wafers that convert sunlight directly to electricity. When first produced in the 1950s they were extremely expensive, but with the rapid growth in production technologies and concurrent increases in demand, the prices have fallen dramatically in the past decade. In 1982, the capital cost of purchasing solar cells was about $10 per peak watt, and by 1994 it had reached $4 per peak watt. These prices are still too expensive for large-scale generation, but there are many applications for these cells today, primarily in running small machines in remote locations where installing conventional electric service is expensive. Further price reductions may greatly expand the usefulness of photovoltaic cells (Fig. 14.11), and large-scale photovoltaic electricity production could become viable in the first decade of the twenty-first century.

One of the main challenges in solar energy technology is to develop storage devices for use at night, on cloudy days, and in cooler seasons. Fuel cells offer some promise of alleviating this problem. Fuel cells operate by passing electricity through a salty solution, splitting water into hydrogen and oxygen. These can later be recombined to produce electricity. One important advantage of fuel cells is their high efficiency, but at present they are too expensive for ordinary applications.

Although many reports claim that solar energy is the way of the future, obstacles will have to be overcome before it makes a truly significant contribution to our energy supplies. The most important economic barriers to residential heating and cooling are the high capital costs and relatively long payback period for an investment. This is particularly troublesome for retrofitting and less so for new installations. As a result of the slowdown in solar energy installation in the mid-1980s, substantial infrastructure in the form of manufacturers, dealers, and installers was lost (Rembert 1997). The economics of solar energy will have to improve substantially before there is another wave of installation of these systems.

Wind Power Windmills have been used worldwide since ancient times. We perhaps know them best in the United States as a symbol of the nineteenth-century farm, where wind energy was converted to mechanical energy to pump water from the farm well. Although windmills have largely been replaced with other pumping devices, the windmill is again feasible as a method of generating electricity. The industry is small but has considerable potential. Growth in this area was encouraged by a 1978 federal law requiring public

Figure 14.11   Photovoltaic cells generating electricity for lighting a road sign in New Mexico.

utilities to purchase electric power offered to them by small generating companies. The price is determined by the avoidance costs of producing equivalent amounts of energy by conventional sources.

The first utility company to incorporate windmill-generated power into its power grid was Southern California Edison Company in 1980. A privately financed 200-foot-tall wind turbine installed in the desert near Palm Springs, California, is capable of generating enough electricity for about a thousand homes. The blades are driven by reliable winds, which average 17 mph with gusts up to 40 mph. The amount of electricity generated by this turbine is equivalent to an annual saving of about 10,000 barrels of oil. Another example is the Wind Farm project operated by Pacific Gas & Electric in the Altamont Pass area in northern California. Each of the 407 windmills there turns out about 50 kW (Fig. 14.12).

In the late 1970s and early 1980s, the U.S. Department of Energy put millions of dollars into developing prototype wind machines that were rated from 200 to 2500 kW at peak power output. The largest of these has a blade span of 300 ft. Early 1980s projections estimated that wind energy would provide 2 to 4 percent of U.S. electricity by 2000, but lower oil prices in the middle and late 1980s slowed development of this and other alternative sources. In 1995 wind generation amounted to only 0.02 percent of total electric generation in the United States, and less than one percent of the world's electricity.

Wind power is recognized as the first renewable energy source since hydroelectricity to move beyond government sponsorship into control by traditional public utilities. Its application to large–scale electricity generation holds fewer uncertainties than other renewable sources. Wind power is also more easily integrated into existing utility power grids, which are necessary to provide backup power when wind velocities are low.

Energy Efficiency and Energy Conservation

One way to measure the efficiency of energy use is in strict physical terms: the amount of productive work accomplished for a given expenditure of energy or fuel, such as the number of miles a car will go on a gallon of gas. Modern automobiles are much more efficient than those made a generation ago, as a result of more precisely controlled engines, less weight, and improved aerodynamics.

Figure 14.12 A wind energy generating facility at Altamont Pass, California.

Similarly, fluorescent lights provide much more light per amount of electricity consumed than do incandescent lights, because they emit less heat. Many improvements in such physical energy efficiency have been achieved in recent years, and many more are possible. We will discuss some of these in more detail later in this chapter.

Another way to measure the efficiency of energy use is in terms of economic gain per unit of energy expended. Throughout much of recent U.S. history, energy has been plentiful enough that we did not consider the efficiency of energy use in most of our economic decisions. Today, however, we are very conscious of the contrasting patterns of energy use and efficiency between different nations and economic systems.

Traditional agricultural economies produce goods and services at a relatively low level, using virtually no energy except that provided by the sun through heat and photosynthesis. In contrast, mechanized agriculture uses large amounts of nonrenewable fossil fuel in every step of the production system from building the tractor to manufacturing fertilizer to fueling farm machinery. This system produces much more food per unit of human labor but much less per unit of energy input.

One indicator of energy efficiency is a comparison of per capita gross national product (GNP) with per capita energy consumption (Fig. 14.13). As a rule, the higher the GNP per capita, the higher the energy consumption, and vice versa. A nation with a higher income can spend more money on machines and raw materials to increase production and quality of life. This in turn leads to more energy consumption, which if expended in production, leads to more income. Industrialized nations consume much more energy per capita than less industrialized nations. The United States, for example, with about 5 percent of the world's population, consumes 25 percent of the world's energy, whereas China, with 21 percent of the world's population, consumes only 9 percent of the world's energy. Furthermore, there are great variations in energy efficiency among industrialized nations. Most of the Western European nations, for example, use less energy per unit of economic return than the United States. This is because energy prices have been much higher there for a long time, and Europeans have adjusted by driving smaller cars, driving shorter distances, heating buildings to lower temperatures, and so on. In contrast, Russia and other eastern European nations use large amounts of energy but have much lower incomes than their neighbors to the west.

Recent trends in the overall economic efficiency of energy use are illustrated in Fig. 14.14. For the world as a whole, average energy effi-

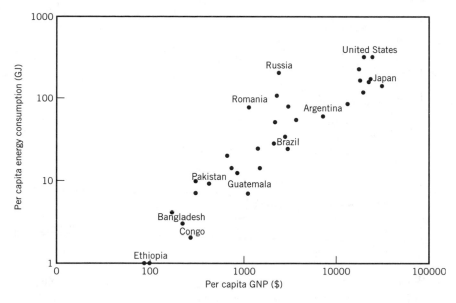

Figure 14.13 Per capita GNP and per capita energy consumption for selected countries, 1993. Countries that plot above and to the left of the trend are relatively inefficient; countries that plot on the lower right of the trend are more efficient. Note the logarithmic axes. *Source:* World Resources Institute, 1996.

ciency increased about 20 percent between 1970 and 1993. The greatest gains in efficiency occurred in the 1980s, spurred by increases in prices during the energy crises in the 1970s. At that time energy users at all levels, from government officials and corporate executives to individual consumers, realized that substantial savings were possible through energy conservation. Accordingly, a wide range of energy-saving technologies came into wider use. Also, during the 1980s production in energy-intensive heavy industries stagnated, while most of the economic growth took place in the service sector, which uses much less energy per unit of income generated. Some of the increase in energy efficiency seen in Figure 14.14 is a result of economic restructuring from the industrial sector to the service sector.

It is also clear that considerable differences in energy efficiency exist among nations. The world average is statistically dominated by trends in countries that generate the most income and use the most energy; the industrialized nations. In these economies, industry and transportation are the greatest consumers of energy.

Energy conservation has been the industrialized world's largest single source of "new energy" since the early 1980s. Conservation in this sense simply means using less or using what you have with more efficiency. As we have seen earlier in this chapter, total energy consumption in the United States peaked at 83,000 petajoules in 1979 and declined until 1988. It has since risen to nearly 99,000 petajoules in 1996. Total output was greater in 1996 than in 1979, so that the amount of economic activity per unit of energy was about 20 percent higher in 1996 than in 1979. Put another way, the amount of energy required to produce a dollar's worth of goods and services (adjusted for inflation) decreased about 18 percent between 1979 and 1996 in the United States.

Energy conservation developed gradually during this period. Initially, less fuel did less work; for example, people drove more slowly and reduced heat and light use. By the early to mid-1980s less fuel was used to do the same amount of work. This required minor design and investment decisions, not major overhaul of facilities or reorientation of an industry. Ideally, we would like to reach a condition in which less fuel is used to do more work. This would provide the greatest savings, yet it would require investment in applied research efforts in order to be effec-

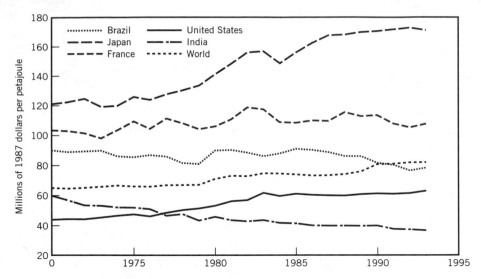

Figure 14.14 Economic efficiency of energy use for selected countries, 1970-1993. Economic efficiency is calculated as GNP per petajoule of commercial energy consumed. In industrialized nations efficiency has generally improved, but in some poorer industrializing nations energy efficiency has declined. *Source:* World Resources Institute, 1996.

tive. This applied research requires substantial technological innovations and usually takes at least several years to realize.

For example, in the mid-1970s consumers and auto manufacturers in the United States responded to higher gasoline prices by shifting from larger to smaller cars, smaller engines, and manual transmissions. Consumers also responded by driving less. Miles per vehicle decreased over 4 percent, and total motor fuel consumption dropped by 9 percent between 1978 and 1982. By the mid-1980s, most people were driving much more fuel-efficient cars. In 1976 the average fuel consumption by United States cars was 12.1 miles per gallon; by 1987 this had increased by 25 percent to 15.1 miles per gallon. In 1985 more people were driving more cars more miles per car but using less fuel than had been consumed in 1978.

But by the late 1980s gasoline prices were again low, and larger vehicles grew in popularity. In the 1980s the minivan replaced station wagons and sedans as the primary family vehicle. In the 1990s this was followed by a dramatic increase in the popularity of pickup trucks and four-wheel-drive sport utility vehicles. The greater height and lack of streamlining of these vehicles, as well as the added friction and weight of four-wheel drive, reduce fuel efficiency significantly, but low fuel

prices meant that this was not a concern. Families bought the larger models, while those who only needed smaller cars bought two-seaters instead of the small sedans that were popular in the early 1980s. In 1973, only about 10 percent of new light-duty vehicles sold in the United States were trucks, vans, or sport utility vehicles, compared to about 40 percent in 1996. As a result, the average fuel efficiency of household vehicles, which rose from about 13.1 mpg in 1975 to over 20.2 mpg in 1991, once again declined, reaching 19.3 mpg by 1996 (Wald 1996). And between 1970 and 1996 the average distance driven per person increased from just over 5000 to nearly 8000 miles.

The trends in less industrialized countries in the past few decades have been very different from those in the industrial world. To begin with, the less industrialized countries use vastly less energy per person and proportionately more traditional fuels (primarily wood and dung). The commercial fuels found in these countries tend to be used in older, less efficient machines and factories. In India, for example, per capita use of commercial energy is about one-thirtieth the level of the United States. Between 1970 and 1993 India's population increased by 62 percent, GNP increased by 150 percent (in constant dollars), and energy consumption went up by 310 percent. Thus, the economic efficiency of that energy use, in dollars of GNP per petajoule consumed, decreased by almost 40 percent. A similar trend is evident in Brazil in that same period, when population increased 63 percent, GNP increased 172 percent, and energy consumption increased 215 percent.

Why is energy efficiency decreasing in some poorer countries, but increasing in wealthy ones? The answer to this question differs from country to country, depending on the particular circumstances of economic growth and change. Probably the most common explanation is the growth of manufacturing in less developed countries. The economic restructuring in the wealthy countries that resulted in a shift from manufacturing to service industries also involved a transfer of manufacturing overseas, primarily to poorer countries with lower labor costs. The rapid growth of the maquiladora manufacturing centers just south of the Mexico-U.S. border is an excellent example. Consumer goods are manufactured in Mexico by U.S.-owned companies using low-cost labor, and the products are shipped north to be consumed in the United States. So the benefits of the energy used in manufacturing are still reaped in the United States, but statistically the energy consumption is recorded as having taken place in Mexico.

ENERGY FUTURES

As we consider the future of energy use in the world, it is clear that the range of possibilities is large. There is a high degree of substitutability between the various sources of energy, and a wide range of alternatives exist for aggregate energy supply and demand in the future. The choices for sources of energy and which to use for heating and which to use for electricity, are important policy decisions with far-reaching impacts. Let us consider some of the possibilities.

High-Energy Options

At the present time, most of the world is following an energy-intensive course. Economic growth is focused on industrial production of consumer goods, on international trade and the transport it requires, and on personal mobility (both on an everyday basis and in tourism). If we continue on such a course and include a greater portion of earth's growing population in economic develop-

ment, then large increases in total energy use are necessary. Where will this energy come from?

Fossil Fuels

One obvious possibility is continued and increased exploitation of fossil fuels. In the short term—the next 30 years or so—this would mean continued reliance on oil. The price of oil would have to rise somewhat to stimulate new exploration and development, but use would continue much as in the present. Coal would grow as the primary fuel for electricity generation, and long-distance trade in either coal or the electricity generated from it would grow. Increasing use of oil would lead to significant depletion of this resource, however, and so in the longer-term—30 to 60 years—significant development of synthetic fuels would be necessary. In such a world, the United States, with its vast deposits of coal and oil shale, would be fuel-rich and could conceivably become an energy exporter, as would other coal-rich nations.

Such a scenario would mean significant and continuing environmental impacts of energy use. A doubling of the CO_2 content of the atmosphere above pre-industrial levels would happen by the mid-twenty-first century, and in all likelihood global warming would continue or accelerate. Unless new technology for significantly reducing emissions of SO_x and NO_x from internal combustion engines, power plants, and other sources were developed, the extent of damage to forests and other ecosystems would expand accordingly. Finally, large areas would be subject to disruption by surface mining, some of them in areas that presently have relatively low levels of environmental impact.

Nuclear and Renewable Energy

Alternatively, a high-energy future is possible without heavy dependence on fossil fuels. Instead, we could increase our use of nuclear power and renewable energy, both centralized and decentralized. First, we would have to convert many activities that currently use fossil fuels to electricity or solar thermal power. Gasoline-powered automobiles would be replaced with electric ones. Freight-hauling with diesel-powered trucks would be limited, and further growth in long distance land-transport would focus on electric-powered railroads. Home heating in midlatitude climates, which today is accomplished mostly with oil and gas, would rely much more heavily on solar thermal systems.

This would require large increases in electric generation, not to mention replacing existing electric production from fossil fuels. Nuclear power could easily be expanded and could generate large amounts of electricity. Despite the low standing of nuclear power today, the major barriers to expansion of this technology are social and political, not technical. Public resistance is based more on fear and on the potential for accidents despite their rarity. If these fears could be overcome, then nuclear power would again have great promise.

Another major new source of electricity would be hydroelectric generation. As discussed earlier in this chapter, vast untapped hydroelectric power potential exists throughout the world. Hydroelectric power could make a much greater contribution to total energy production, without carbon emissions or radioactive waste. It would, however, require both a very large capital investment in capital-poor parts of the world and the loss of many ecosystems dependent on free-flowing rivers.

Finally, a significant investment would have to be made in installing solar energy systems in new homes and buildings, and retrofitting older structures to use solar energy instead of fossil fuels. Such an effort would also involve large investments in energy efficiency, such as increased insulation and heat storage systems.

A high-energy, low-fossil-fuel future would require both a commitment to developing nuclear and hydroelectric power and significant new investment in energy relatively soon. Such commitments are technically and economically feasible, but not necessarily realistic in the current social/political climate. It is not clear whether climate would change quickly enough to allow a conversion to such an energy system in the near future.

Low-Energy Options

It is not a foregone conclusion that the world will continue to increase the amount of commercially produced energy it uses in making and distributing goods and services. Many ways of reducing the amount of energy we use are available, and some of these also allow for continued economic growth and reduction of economic disparities between rich and poor.

Conservation-intensive   As discussed earlier, conservation of energy has been the largest single source of new energy in the United States since the 1970s. In 1993 we produced 43 percent more wealth per unit of energy consumed than in 1970. At 1970 economic efficiencies, the amount of wealth produced in the United States in 1993 would have required 119,000 petajoules instead of the 83,000 actually consumed. In these terms, conservation *produced* 36,000 petajoules in the United States in 1993, an amount greater than the energy consumption of 1.2 billion people in China; greater than the entire 1993 energy consumption of Africa and South America combined! Most of this increase in efficiency was achieved in a brief period during and immediately after the energy crises of the 1970s. Imagine the amount of energy efficiency improvement that would have occurred if gasoline prices had remained at their 1981–1982 levels (adjusted for inflation), instead of falling below 1972 prices in the early 1990s, as they did.

The increases in energy efficiency that occurred in the United States and some other countries were not entirely painless. They required new investments, and with the new investments came some social dislocations, such as the decline of the heavy-industrial sector and the communities that depended on it. It must also be remembered that much of the increase in economic energy efficiency was a consequence of economic restructuring, with a replacement of energy-intensive manufacturing with service industries that use less energy. We still consume manufactured goods and we still need energy to make them, but much of this energy consumption has been transferred overseas.

Nonetheless, many opportunities for energy conservation remain. Suppose the entire world had the economic energy efficiency of Japan. Based on 1993 data, the GNP of the world could be doubled, and we would still use only three-fourths of the energy used in that year. For those of us who live in the United States, this would involve some sacrifices, such as living in high-density cities, using public transport for most of our everyday trips, and using automobiles only occasionally. But imagine the benefits to human welfare if the GNP of the world were doubled and if most of that increase took place in the world's poorest countries!

Changes of this magnitude will not occur in the near future. To achieve them would require overcoming immense economic and political barriers and changes of life-style among the energy-guzzling countries of the world like the United States. But thinking about the possibilities should help us understand the enormous potential of reducing environmental damage without loss of wealth that is possible through energy conservation.

Low-growth Finally, we recognize that we could continue to use energy much as we do today, but simply use less (or stop increasing our use of energy). Without increases in efficiency, this would mean an end to economic growth in both the industrialized and less industrialized world. Such an alternative would be undesirable for a large portion of earth's human population. Unless significant changes in the way we use energy do take place in the next few decades, a low-growth scenario will be a necessity, particularly given the increase in world population expected during this time. A low-growth future would have at least some advantages for the earth's natural systems, to the extent that it would not lead to increased pollution, for example. But it can be argued that some of the worst environmental degradation is a consequence of poverty, rather than of wealth, as people clear forests for fuelwood or cause overgrazing in the desperate search for adequate food supplies.

Energy Policies for the Future

The scenarios described above represent extremes, and none of them is either entirely desirable or particularly likely. But all are physically possible. These scenarios demonstrate the great range of energy-use options that are available to us in the next few decades and our considerable choices with regard to future conditions. What policies can we pursue today to affect these future outcomes? How can governments, businesses, or individuals make such choices?

At the present time, most of the governments of the world are relying primarily on market forces to determine energy policy. In the United States, for example, the choice of fuels for generating electricity is made by private corporations, largely on the basis of cost. Environmental regulations somewhat alter these choices by favoring low-sulfur coal over high-sulfur coal, or increas-

ing the cost of nuclear power through stringent safety rules, but these have relatively minor impact. The fact remains that coal is still being used to generate most of our electricity, and the lack of new nuclear power plant construction is as much a function of flat demand as it is of the higher cost of that energy form. Similarly, larger, less fuel-efficient vehicles were much more popular in the mid-1990s than they were in the early-1980s because of a decade of low fuel prices. If the higher prices of the late 1970s and early 1980s had persisted, we would not be driving sport utility vehicles in such numbers as we are today.

Exceptions to these market-based policies do exist. In Europe, fuel taxes have long been used as a tool for altering energy-use choices by making motor fuels artificially expensive. This encourages people to drive more fuel-efficient vehicles (producing less pollution), drive less (reducing road congestion and construction costs), and take public transport (maintaining the viability of this mode of transport). For the most part, relatively short-term cost determines what fuel we use. We have even gone to war to maintain free trade in energy commodities, as when Iraq's invasion of Kuwait in 1991 threatened to change the balance of control over oil.

Some argue that the governments of the world's energy-consuming industrial nations should be taking more aggressive steps to reduce dependence on fossil fuels and speed the transition to renewable energy and energy conservation. Such steps could include investing in renewable energy technology such as photovoltaics, loosening restrictions on energy-saving or energy-producing innovations, increasing taxes on fossil fuels to encourage conservation, and providing tax incentives for development and installation of energy-conserving technologies. With the exception of increasing fuel taxes, all of these measures were used in the United States and in many other nations during the last two decades.

How should the lessons of these decades be interpreted? We can see that a small increase in the price of one energy commodity, oil, can stimulate enormous savings through conservation as well as moderate increases in supply. On the one hand, this can be interpreted as a demonstration of the power of the market and the flexibility of market economies. If the need arises in the future, these economies can respond again and shift to other energy sources relatively quickly. On the other hand, by demonstrating the possibilities of energy conservation and development of renewable technologies, we might argue that we are foolish not to take advantage of the opportunity of converting to renewable technology sooner, both avoiding future oil shortages and protecting the environment through reduction of pollution.

REFERENCES AND ADDITIONAL READING

Atherton, C., and D. Atherton. 1990. Disaster that fell with the rain on a bleak hill. *Guardian*, April 27, p. 25.

Balter, M. 1995. Chernobyl's thyroid cancer toll. *Science* 270: 1758-1759.

_____. 1996. Children become the first victims of fallout. *Science* 272: 357-360.

Brobst, P. A., and W. P. Pratt eds. 1973. *United States Mineral Resources*. U.S. Geological Survey. Professional Paper 820. Washington, DC: United States Geological Survey.

Burnett, W. M., and S. D. Ban. 1989. Changing prospects for natural gas in the United States. *Science* 244: 305– 310.

Committee on Nuclear and Alternative Energy Sources (CONAES). 1978. U.S. energy demand: Some low energy futures. *Science* 200: 142–152.

Commoner, B. 1977. *The Poverty of Power*. New York: Bantam Books.

Council on Environmental Quality. 1989. *Environmental Trends*. Washington, DC: U.S. Government Printing Office.

Energy Information Administration. 1989a. *Annual Energy Review, 1988*. Washington, DC: U.S. Government Printing Office.

_____. 1989b. *Commercial Nuclear Power 1989: Prospects for the United States and the World*. Washington, DC: Energy Information Administration.

_____. 1996. EIA web page. Table ES4. U.S. Coal Statistics, ONLINE: *http://www.ela.doe.gov*

_____. 1997. *Annual Energy Outlook 1997*. Washington, DC: U.S. Government Printing Office, US DOE/EIA-0380(97).

Feldman, D. L. 1995. Revisiting the energy crisis: how far have we come? *Environment* 37 (4): 16-20, 42-44.

Flavin, C., and A. B. Durning. 1988. *Building on Success: The Age of Energy Efficiency*. Worldwatch Paper no, 82. Washington, DC: Worldwatch Institute.

Flavin, C., and N. Lenssen. 1994. *Powering the Future: Blueprint for a Sustainable Electricity Industry*. Worldwatch Paper no, 119. Washington, DC: Worldwatch Institute.

Flynn, J., R. E. Kasperson, H. Kunreuther, and P. Slovic. 1997. Overcoming tunnel vision: redirecting the United States high-level nuclear waste program. *Environment* 39 (3): 6-11, 25-30.

Ghazi, P. 1990. Chernobyl fallout may affect British farmland for decades. *Sunday Observer*, April 29, p. 9.

Gibbons, J. H., P. D. Blair, and H. L. Gwin. 1989. Strategies for energy use. *Scientific American* 261 (3): 136-143.

Gould, P. 1991. *Fire in the Rain: The Democratic Consequences of Chernobyl*. Baltimore, MD: Johns Hopkins University Press.

Hall, C. S., and C. J. Cleveland. 1981. Petroleum drilling and production in the U.S., Yield per effort and net energy analysis. *Science* 211: 576-579.

Heiken, G., et al. 1981. Hot dry rock geothermal energy. *Scientific American* 69: 400–407.

Hohenemser, C., M. Deicher, A. Ernst, H. Hofsass, G. Linder, and E. Recknagel. 1986. Chernobyl: an early report. *Environment* 28(5): 6–13, 30–43.

Hohenemser, C., and O. Renn. 1988. Shifting public perceptions of nuclear risk: Chernobyl's other legacy. *Environment* 30 (3): 4–11, 40–45.

Hohenemser, C. 1996. Chernobyl: 10 years later. *Environment* 38 (3): 3.

Hubbard, H. M. 1989. Photovoltaics today and tomorrow. *Science* 244: 297–304.

Hubbert, M. K. 1969. Energy resources. In NAS, *Resources and Man*. San Francisco: W. H. Freeman, pp. 157– 242

Leopold, L. B. 1996. Sediment problems at Three Gorges Dam.
ONLINE: International Rivers Network: hyperlink *http://www.irn.org/im/programs/3g/leopold.html*.

Lovins, A. B. 1977. *Soft Energy Paths*. New York: Harper Colophon Books.

Mufson, S. 1996. Floods leave Beijing eager for new dam. *Washington Post*, August 6, 1996, p. A11.

Pasqualetti, M. J., and K. D. Pijawka, eds. 1984. *Nuclear Power: Assessing and Managing Hazardous Technology*. Boulder, CO: Westview Press.

Rembert, T. C. 1997. Electric currents. *E Magazine* 8(6): 28–35.

Sawyer, S. W. 1986. *Renewable Energy: Progress, Prospects*. Washington, DC: Association of American Geographers.

Shea, C. P. 1988. *Renewable Energy: Today's Contributions Tomorrow's Promise*. Worldwatch Paper no. 81. Washington, DC: Worldwatch Institute.

Specter, M. 1996. Ten years later, through fear, Chernobyl still kills in Belarus. *New York Times,* March 31, 1996, p. A1.

Stone, R., 1996. The explosions that shook the world. *Science* 272: 352–354.

Taylor, J. J. 1989. Improved and safer nuclear power. *Science* 244: 318–325.

Tyler, P. E. 1996. Chinese dam's inexorable future dooms rich past. *New York Times,* October 6, 1996, p. A1.

U.S. Bureau of the Census. 1997. *Statistical Abstract 1997*. Washington, DC: U.S. Government Printing Office.

U.S. Congress, Office of Technology Assessment. 1980a. *An Assessment of Oil Shale Technologies*. Vol. II: *A History and Analysis of the Federal Prototype Oil Shale Leasing Program*. Washington, DC: U.S. Government Printing Office, OTA-M-119.

———. 1980b. *World Petroleum Availability 1980–2000*. Washington, DC: United States Government Printing Office, OGA-TM-E-5.

U.S. Department of Energy. 1987. *Energy Security*. Washington, DC: U.S. Department of Energy.

Wald, Matthew. 1996. How America perpetuates its gas crisis. *New York Times*, May 5, p. D1.

Werner, C. 1990. Life in a land without birds. *Guardian*, April 27, p. 25.

Wilbanks, T. J. 1988. The impacts of energy development and use. In H. deBlij, ed. *Earth '88: Changing Geographic Perspectives*, pp. 96–114. Washington, DC: National Geographic Society.

Williams, N. and M. Balter. 1996. Chernobyl Research becomes international growth industry. *Science* 272: 355–356.

World Resources Institute, 1996. *World Resources 1996–97*. New York: Oxford University Press.

Worldwatch Institute. 1996. Worldwatch data diskette.

Yergin, D. 1991. *The Prize: The Epic Quest for Oil, Money, and Power*. New York: Simon and Schuster.

For more information, consult our web page at *http://www.wiley.com/college/cutter*

STUDY QUESTIONS

1. In the past, human energy use has focused for the most part on one fuel at a time: wood, then coal, then oil and gas. Today, we may be entering an era in which we use a diversity of fuels, with different fuels for different uses. How does this energy diversity affect overall energy efficiency? How does it affect energy security?

2. What would be the effect on energy use if the United States followed the lead of most other wealthy countries and instituted relatively high fuel taxes (to raise the price of gasoline to, say, $2 or $3 a gallon)? What would be the effect on the environment? Would such an action eliminate or reduce any environmental externalities?

3. In the history of oil prices between 1970 and 1990 we can see evidence of scarcity and evidence of plentiful supplies. Do oil prices accurately reflect the relative scarcity of oil in the world? What do you think the future of oil prices will be in the next decade? in the next 50 years?

4. Should the United States encourage the construction of dams for hydroelectric generation? Why or why not?

5. Are electric vehicles the answer to our energy problems in the next 50 years? Why or why not?

CHAPTER 15

THE TRANSITION TO A GLOBAL SUSTAINABLE SOCIETY

The history of economic growth and resource use since the Industrial Revolution, if not before, has been one of a direct relationship between development and environmental degradation. As technology has advanced, we have grown wealthier and we have demanded more goods, thereby using more resources and producing more pollution. This trend, in combination with population growth, has resulted in very rapid increases in raw material consumption and pollution output, with the consequences described in the preceding chapters.

In the late 1980s, an old word took on a new meaning in the debates about resource use, economic development, and the future. As we discussed in Chapter 3, at that time a new global awareness of the environment and human society emerged, and that awareness needed a word to focus debates. *Sustainability*, a well-established concept in renewable resources management in general and forestry in particular, began to be applied to the entire global environment and the human societies that rely on it and have profoundly altered it.

In this chapter we will explore the medium-term future of resource use: the next century or so. Our discussion begins with a look at some predictions of the future that have stimulated concern for sustainability. We then examine the different visions of sustainability being discussed today, indicating considerable divergence in how the concept is expressed. The final sections of the chapter describe some of the technologies that may help us move toward sus-tainability and suggest some social actions that may encourage their adoption.

LIMITS TO GROWTH?

Growth in population and resource use during the 1950s and 1960s was unprecedented, and many alarms were sounded about future disasters. Books with titles like *The Hungry Planet* (Borgstrom 1965), *Famine, 1975!* (Paddock and Paddock 1967) and *The Population Bomb* (Ehrlich 1968) were prominent in bookstores and academic discussions. Then in 1972, at the height of the environmental movement, an influential book entitled *Limits to Growth* was published (Meadows et al. 1972). This book reported on the results of a computer-based modeling study that extrapolated into the future then-recent trends in population growth and resource use. It concluded:

> If the present growth trends in world population, industrialization, pollution, food production, and resource depletion continue unchanged, the limits to growth on this planet will be reached sometime within the next 100 years. The most probable result will be a sudden and uncontrollable decline in both population and industrial capacity. (Meadows et al. 1972, p. 24)

The trends that were extrapolated to reach these conclusions were those of the 1950s and 1960s, an era of rapid growth in both population and resource use, with few if any checks on that growth. It was therefore impossible for the authors of *Limits to Growth* to see, for example, the energy and industrial crises that began in 1973, which profoundly changed the nature of economic growth and its relation to resource use. Instead, they saw only exponential growth in resource consumption and pollution output, inevitably leading to an "overshoot and collapse" outcome (Fig. 15.1).

A similar study, called *Global 2000*, was carried out by the U.S. government in the late 1970s (Council on Environmental Quality 1981). Like *Limits to Growth*, it was based on detailed global models, including such conditions as population growth, economic development, food production, environmental pollution, and energy use. And like *Limits to Growth*, it made projections of the future based on recent (1960s and 1970s) trends. *Global 2000* concluded:

> If present trends continue, the world in 2000 will be more crowded, more polluted, less stable ecologically, and more vulnerable to disruption than the world we live in now. Serious stresses involving population, resources, and environment are clearly visible ahead. Despite greater material output, the world's people will be poorer in many ways than they are today. (Council on Environmental Quality 1981)

Had *Global 2000* been published in the mid-1970s it would have had more impact on government policy. Instead, it emerged at the beginning of the Reagan administration when the prevailing views were less concerned about environmental conditions and much more focused on the ability of business to solve the world's problems. Many of the reactions to *Global 2000* were strongly critical, concentrating on the dangers inherent in extrapolating past trends into the future and highlighting occasional factual errors (Weinberg 1984). These criticisms were strengthened by the fact that in the 1970s two very significant changes in these trends occurred. Population growth and industrial resource use both began to slow considerably. In short, the doomsday predictions of the 1960s and 1970s that had been so convincing when they were first published weren't very credible a decade or two later.

Despite this reassessment and reaction to the concerns expressed in these studies, the basic fact of significant population growth and the desire

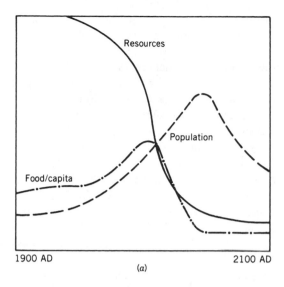

1900 AD   2100 AD
(a)

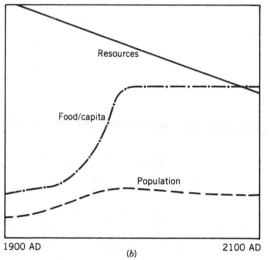

1900 AD   2100 AD
(b)

Figure 15.1 Results of the Limits to Growth model. (*a*) These curves were based on simple extrapolation of current (c. 1970) trends into the future. (*b*) These curves are based on early achievement of stability in population and resource use. *Source:* U.S. Congress, 1982.

for more economic growth in poorer countries still poses troubling questions for the future of the earth's environment and resources. And when the awareness of global environmental change, centered on issues such as climatic warming, ozone depletion, and deforestation, grew again in the late 1980s, the population/resources question once again came under discussion. The most significant document of this period is *Our Common Future,* also known as the Brundtland Report, prepared by the UN Commission on Environment and Development in 1987. One of the central arguments of *Our Common Future* is that economic development and environmental protection are not mutually exclusive. Instead, it is argued that economic development is necessary for good resource management. Unless people's basic needs are met and they have choices about how they will live, they will not have the opportunity to protect earth's resources for future generations. This idea is at the core of the movement for sustainable development.

WHAT IS SUSTAINABLE DEVELOPMENT?

In the late 1980s the terms *sustainability* and *sustainable development* entered widespread use in the context of earth's natural resource future. These terms mean many things to many people, and a definition of sustainability is a continuing problem. The central issue is: What is to be sustained? The problem is not a simple one, so it is important that we define our concept of sustainability.

Environmental Versus Economic Sustainability

If there are indeed real limits to growth, and if we are approaching them in the foreseeable future, then now is the time to change the way we use resources. One solution could be to reduce economic growth or halt it altogether. Many people believe that we have become addicted to economic growth, and so we demand growth for growth's sake. This is certainly true of our financial markets, where a company that doesn't grow is much less valuable than one that grows steadily.

But demanding an end to economic growth has three basic problems. One is population growth. As we learned in Chapter 5, the world's human population is almost certain to reach 10 billion sometime in the twenty-first century. Simply maintaining current standards of living would require economic growth equal to population growth. A second problem is that much of the world has a standard of living that many observers regard as undesirable, if not unacceptably low. Improving the standard of living in the developing world means increasing industrial and

agricultural output to provide food, housing, safe water and energy supplies, and consumer goods for large numbers of people. Finally, from the standpoint of political and social action, few people are likely to be willing to support a no-growth policy. Many people have desires or expectations of a better life for their children than for themselves, or at least the prospect of future improvement. To abandon that hope would be difficult.

In Chapter 1, in the context of environmental ethics, we described two different views of natural resources: a human-centered view and a nature-centered one. These two views illustrate the problems in setting priorities for sustainability. One way to approach the problem is to distinguish between environmental sustainability, economic sustainability, and social sustainability (Goodland and Daly 1994).

Environmental sustainability means maintaining the physical condition of the environment, especially those aspects of natural systems on which we depend for our health and welfare but also including other living things. This means not only maintaining the restorative capacity of renewable resources, but also limiting our output of waste so as not to exceed the capacity of the environment to absorb and reprocess it. The primary objectives of environmental sustainability are to maintain ecosystem integrity, carrying capacity, and biodiversity.

Economic sustainability means maintaining sufficient capital to support human needs indefinitely by providing the basis of production. This capital may include human-made capital such as machines, natural capital (forests), and social and human capital (the ability of workers and societies to organize themselves in productive ways). Its objectives are continued economic growth, equity, and efficiency.

Some authors also distinguish a third type, social sustainability, which means using resources in ways that increase social justice and social equity, while decreasing social disruptions. It requires direct community involvement in resource management decisions, as well as a significant commitment to restructuring social relations (Goodland and Daly 1994; Serageldin 1993).

Some would argue that the capacity of the earth's ecological systems to support life—human and otherwise—with a reasonable quality of life should be sustained. Others take sustainable development to mean continuing economic development and economic growth. Still others would consider maintaining and improving the health and well-being of the human population to be most important.

A Working Definition of Sustainability

The sustainability idea implies a much longer time-frame than what used in most day-to-day resource-use decisions. We recognize that we have an obligation not only to those living today, but also to future generations hundreds or even thousands of years hence. We must use resources in such a way as to leave for future inhabitants the same or better opportunities as we enjoy, rather than depending on future technological innovations or migration to other planets as a means to support future populations. In the words of the Brundtland Report, sustainable development means "development that meets the needs and aspirations of the present without compromising the ability of future generations to meet their own needs" (World Commission on Environment and Development 1987). For the purposes of this book, however, we need a working definition, and one that is more specific than that provided by the Brundtland Report.

We recognize that achieving sustainability is carried out by societies rather than by individuals, and thus defining goals should be left to political processes. Whether one takes an environmental, economic, or social perspective, it seems clear that the world faces several fundamental problems today. Foremost among these are large disparities in wealth between rich and poor, with many of the world's people suffering unacceptably poor conditions of health and welfare; and severe and increasing stresses on the world's natural resource base. Either of these situations could be improved by making changes in resource-use systems that increase the environmental efficiency of resource use. By this we mean *increasing the amount of material wealth generated per amount of natural resource degradation.* At the present time, we believe that our economic, social, and resource-use systems require much improvement, both in increasing wealth (especially for the poor of the world) and decreasing resource degradation (especially in industrial societies responsible for the majority of resource use). Thus, we can describe actions that

move *toward* sustainability without specifying in detail the ultimate goals of sustainability.

How Does Sustainability Work?

Increasing the environmental efficiency of resource use means breaking the link between economic wealth and environmental degradation. We already know that this link is not universal. In Chapter 14, for example, we saw that increases in energy prices in the 1970s were followed by a period of economic growth without increased energy use. In Chapter 10 you read that discharges of biochemical oxygen demand (BOD) and other important pollutants to rivers declined in the 1970s and 1980s, while Chapter 11 described the significant decrease in sulfur oxide emissions during the same period. Although these environmental improvements were not without an economic price tag, we were able to bear such costs without suffering a decrease in our standard of living. At the same time, we have not been able to significantly reduce either our output of CO_2, or our consumption of forest products. One reason for the lack of improvement in these areas is the economic costs that would be incurred.

Nonetheless, the possibility exists that we can decouple environmental degradation and economic activity (Fig. 15.2). Such a decoupling will be necessary to improve the standards of living of developing countries without overwhelming the earth's capacity to support a growing population. Realizing this change is at the heart of the transition to a sustainable society.

Data on sulfur dioxide concentrations in cities provide an interesting illustration of the problem (Fig. 15.3). In general, cities in poor countries have lower concentrations of SO_2 than cities in countries of intermediate levels of wealth, while cities in very wealthy countries have the lowest SO_2 levels. The disparity is due to the poor countries' relatively light use of fossil fuel. Cities in newly industrializing countries use substantial amounts of fossil fuel but without effective emission controls. The wealthiest cities can afford pollution controls.

Does this mean that the poorest cities will have to endure a period of high pollution before they can afford to control emissions? Not necessarily. Note in Figure 15.3 that SO_2 levels de-

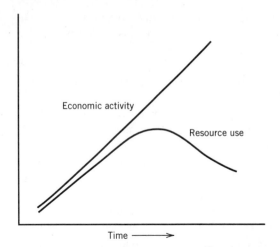

Figure 15.2 Decoupling of economic activity and resource use. In the past, increasing wealth has always meant increasing use of natural resources and pollution output. Can we effectively separate the two and continue to grow economically while improving the environment?
Source: Redrawn from World Bank, 1992.

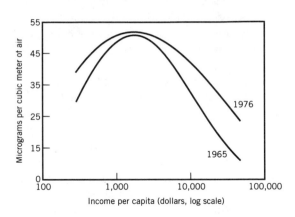

Figure 15.3 Urban sulfur dioxide concentrations in relation to GDP per capita.
Source: Redrawn from World Bank, 1992.

clined between 1976 and 1985, the period of rapid energy prices, in cities of all wealth levels. The declines were larger in cities in wealthy nations, which were installing pollution controls at this time, but reductions also occurred in the poorest nations. In other words, you don't have to be wealthy to reduce pollution.

Thus, an alternative to stopping growth altogether is to change the nature of economic growth. Most of our present resource-use systems are destructive and inefficient, and waste products are poorly managed. Thermal electric energy production is an obvious example. When coal is used to make electricity, less than 40 percent of the heat is actually converted, and the rest is discharged to the environment as waste. At the same time, we burn other fuels, or perhaps even use electricity, to heat buildings. If we could use the waste heat from electricity generation to heat buildings, we could use much less coal without losing either electricity or warm spaces to work and sleep.

Some of the decrease in SO$_2$ emissions seen in Figure 15.3 resulted from energy conservation through reduction of waste. Some resulted from emissions controls, which forced changes in the way fuel is burned. Another part of the decrease may have come from replacing fossil fuels with renewable energy such as hydroelectric power. A

significant part came from changing the types of things we do to generate income: decline in the industrial sector and growth in the service sector.

In the following paragraphs, we will describe four kinds of changes in resource use that will lead to sustainability: waste recycling; waste reduction; design for reuse and recycling; and changing the resource-use structure. These changes are feasible today, and many are already occuring. We believe, however, that these and other changes must be implemented much more rapidly if significant progress is to be made in the next few decades.

Waste Recycling

To achieve sustainability without continually switching from one set of resources to another requires that all resource use be renewable and that the stocks from which those renewable resources are drawn are maintained at constant, if not improving, quality. *Recycling* is the process whereby a material is recovered from the consumer product and then becomes a new material in the production of a similar or different product.

Recent efforts to improve recycling have been widespread, especially in areas that are facing difficulty in disposing of wastes. In the United States, these efforts initially took the form of encouraging waste-generators to collect materials for recycling rather than disposing of them. This is sometimes called supply-side recycling. Among the early efforts were laws enacted in the 1970s requiring that a deposit be collected on the sale of beverages in bottles or cans. Part of the impetus for bottle-deposit laws came from a problem of roadside litter. The consumer gets his or her deposit back when the container is returned to the point of sale. The deposit is merely a behavioral incentive to get the consumer to save and return the container.

When the landfill crisis struck in the United States in the mid-1980s, a new reason for recycling emerged; saving precious space in landfills. A variety of programs were instituted in communities large and small; some were voluntary and some were mandatory, but nearly all encouraged consumers to separate materials into different types to facilitate recycling. The programs were very successful in generating recyclable material—large amounts of paper, plastic, aluminum, and other materials were collected (Fig. 15.4). But problems quickly emerged. The supply of recyclable material was suddenly much greater than the amount that could be absorbed as raw materials. Without adequate outlets for used paper, stocks accumulated at collection points, creating nuisances and sometimes fire hazards.

The problem was particularly acute for municipalities that had instituted mandatory recycling. They made substantial investments in recycling equipment and bore the cost of collecting recyclable materials. They had planned to recoup these expenses through the sale of these materials. But the rapid increase in the supply of recyclables drove down the prices of these materials, which cut revenues for recycling programs (Fig. 15.5). Most recycling programs ran at substantial deficits, and often the deficits were so large that it became cheaper to dispose of these materials in landfills than to recycle them, even with landfill space at a premium.

One result of this problem was a shift in recycling policy toward so-called demand-side programs. These programs were intended to increase the demand for recyclable materials, usually by encouraging or requiring manufacturers to increase their use of recycled materials. Germany has been a leader in this area, in part because of its high landfill costs. In 1991, Germany enacted a

Figure 15.4 Recycling programs instituted in response to the landfill crisis in the 1980s dramatically increased supplies of recycled material, in many cases beyond the ability of processors to use the material. Nonetheless, the vast majority of solid waste generated in the U.S. is still deposited in landfills.

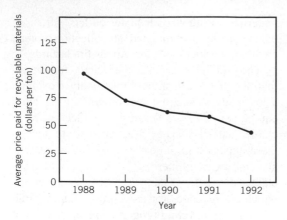

Figure 15.5 Effects of supply-side recycling programs on the price of recyclable materials.
Source: Waste Management of North America, 1992.

program that required manufacturers to take full responsibility for their packaging. By 1995, 80 percent of glass, steel, aluminum, card, paper, plastic, and composite material were to be collected, and of this 80 to 90 percent was to be recycled (Boerner and Chilton 1994). In response, a consortium of about 600 manufacturers developed a system for joint collection and recycling of materials. Packages produced by member companies bore a green dot, indicating that they were eligible to be collected and processed by the consortium.

Mandatory recycling programs tend to be expensive. The increased costs are of two types. First, collecting and processing recyclable materials is often more expensive than disposing of these materials in landfills. In the case of the German green dot program, the cost of collection and processing materials in 1994 was about double the cost of collecting and disposing other household waste. Second, the quality of recycled materials is often lower than that of virgin materials. In some cases this difference in quality is not important, but in other cases it can be significant, prohibiting the use of recycled materials. Even if recycled materials are acceptable, they may be more expensive to use than virgin materials because of added processing necessary to remove impurities. These higher costs, of course, are passed on to the consumer.

Although these costs may be high in the short run, if the law stays in place and if companies

work hard to adapt, they can modify their products and packaging in ways that will reduce these costs, perhaps to levels below the cost of using virgin materials. The high costs of processing waste materials can be a powerful incentive to reduce material requirements and waste generation. But such reductions may mean complete redesign of packaging and sometimes of the products themselves. Following redesign, new manufacturing, handling, and retailing facilities must be developed, and consumers have to learn to accept the new products. Shifting toward sustainability in materials use is not a simple matter.

The paper industry provides an example of the shift toward increased recycling in the long run. Paper recycling seems relatively simple—just substitute used paper for trees in the pulping process and make old paper into new paper. But it isn't that easy. Like most recycling situations, the biggest problems result from recycled materials that aren't clean or uniform. Used newspapers, for example, include inks, coatings on papers, metal staples, plastic wrappers, and miscellaneous materials mixed with the paper fibers used to make the original paper. As a result, these materials must go through special processing to remove unacceptable substances before they can be used to make new paper.

In the short run, these problems have limited the amount of paper that could be recycled, contributing to the problems with recycling programs. The situation was aggravated by relatively low paper prices, which made it difficult for paper companies to invest in new plants. But the price of paper rose substantially in the early 1990s, and by the mid-1990s several companies had installed new facilities capable of processing larger quantities of recycled paper. This resulted in a significant rise in the volume of paper recycled, as well as an increase in the price of used paper. The paper industry hopes to reuse or recycle half of all paper produced in the United States by the year 2000 (Kane 1996).

Waste Reduction

As discussed in Chapter 10, pollution control can be approached in two fundamentally different ways. One is to remove pollutants from the waste stream just before it is discharged to the environment; a sewage-treatment plant is a good example. This is known as end-of-pipe pollution control. The other approach is to not generate waste materials in the first place. This is known as waste reduction. Much progress has been made in this area in recent years, spear-headed by industrial concerns and done largely on a voluntary basis. Among the leaders in waste reduction in the United States are chemical companies that were major emitters of pollutants (Dow, duPont, and 3M, for example), but they were joined by a large range of manufacturing concerns anxious to reap the benefits of a cleaner way of doing business.

What are the benefits of waste reduction to a manufacturing company that would lead it to reduce pollution voluntarily? There are many benefits, though not all of them are directly economic. Let us consider a few.

- **Customer demand** Consumers of manufactured goods, at both the retail and wholesale level, are concerned to buy "environmentally friendly" products. If two products are side-by-side in the supermarket and one appears to have been produced with less pollution or has been produced by a company with a good environmental reputation, the consumer will be more likely to pick that product. This applies not only to individual decisions, but also to purchases by institutions and other manufacturers. Environmentally conscious firms prefer to buy clean products, so they can tell their consumers that the products they sell are made with clean materials. Students and faculty ask universities to buy recycled paper. Publishers demand recycled paper so that they can say their books are printed on recycled stock. Usually, this means that the environmentally friendly product can command a higher price, though perhaps not very much higher.
- **Reduced waste disposal costs** It is expensive to dispose of wastes. Tightening environmental regulations have greatly increased costs for manufacturers' waste disposal. Costs are especially high for toxic and hazardous substances, which must be taken by specially licensed waste-handling companies, which in turn have high costs associated with special equipment, employee training, and liability insurance. If wastes are disposed of in air or in water, a permit is usually needed. This kind of disposal requires that the polluter meet special conditions in addition to going through the costs of obtaining a permit. But even if the wastes are ordinary materials that can be taken to a landfill, the costs there have increased dramatically in recent years.

- **Reduced liability exposure** Many companies produce toxic or hazardous wastes as part of their manufacturing processes. In the past these wastes were often disposed of in the most convenient and inexpensive manner available, such as in landfills. When the Comprehensive Environmental Response, Compensation, and Liability Act (Superfund) took force in 1980, companies were suddenly made liable for wastes they had previously disposed of. If those wastes were found to be creating a hazard, then they had to be cleaned up. Often a company thought it was disposing of wastes properly, only to learn later that it had created a major contamination problem (Cutter 1993). Even if a company produced very little waste, if it was among the parties that had deposited wastes in a given site it could be held responsible for a share of the cleanup costs. These costs grew rapidly in the 1980s, sometimes running into billions of dollars for a single site.

A manufacturing company could therefore be held liable for substantial cleanup costs associated with past waste disposal. Furthermore, if a company purchased another company, it also purchased that company's potential liabilities. In many cases, companies didn't even know what wastes they might be held responsible for, let alone the potential costs they might be asked to bear. This presents a major risk for the company.

How can such risks be avoided? One way, as we have said, is to not generate the wastes in the first place. If we don't use or create toxic materials in manufacturing, then there can't be a disposal problem. Eliminating the use of potentially hazardous materials also eliminates the possibility that practices believed to be safe today will later be found to be dangerous.
- **Reduced material costs** In some cases, finding ways to manufacture a product using nonpolluting materials also means reducing the costs of inputs to a process. This may be especially true for hazardous substances, which may be more expensive to manufacture and handle than safer substances. Manufacturing processes that create less pollution do not always cost less, but cost savings are realized surprisingly often.
- **Enhanced public relations** Businesses need to forge good relations with the communities in which they are located. Government officials and agencies, from the national government down to the municipality, have regulatory authority over many business activities. Usually, decisions made under this authority involve a significant amount of discretion on the part of the decision makers. It helps if these decision makers have a positive attitude toward a company and its practices.

For example, suppose a manufacturer wants to expand its facilities at an existing plant and this expansion involves a zoning change, a building permit, an emissions permit, or some other approval from the local government. Suppose also that the company has a history of being secretive about its operations, or perhaps it experienced a chemical spill or significant industrial accident recently. The authorities responsible for approving the expansion plans may look very carefully at the proposal and may attach difficult conditions to their approval to protect the safety of the community. On the other hand, if the manufacturer has a good reputation for operating a clean facility, for handling its wastes properly, or not using significant amounts of hazardous materials, the local authorities are likely to be much more willing to approve the proposed expansion with a minimum of red tape.

- **Employee morale and loyalty** Good relations with one's employees are just as important as good relations with government regulators. Good employee morale is fundamental to a smooth-running organization. Employees are likely to feel better about working for a company that has a good environmental reputation than for one that is a known polluter. Recruitment of new employees is made easier for the same reasons. In addition, employees not only work for the company, but they usually live in the same community and thus are exposed to its emissions. For employees, the environmental impacts of their work are even more important than they are for other members of the community.

Design for Reuse and Recycling

Perhaps the greatest barrier to recycling is the mixture of materials found in waste. Separating different materials from each other is expensive, time-consuming, and difficult to mechanize. Asking consumers to separate glass from paper from plastic is one thing. But if different materials are joined together in a single object, as in drink boxes or foil-covered wraps, they become nearly impossible to recycle. What can be done to make materials more recyclable?

Fortunately, there are many opportunities to make recycling easier. Consider the changes in manufacturing practices described in the previous section. Nearly all of them brought changes in the way products are manufactured, distributed, sold, used, and disposed of. Such changes occur routinely as part of the process of developing new products, more efficient manufacturing techniques, and marketing strategies. These changes in product design and manufacturing are opportunities to move toward sustainability, if we choose to take them.

Automobiles are an excellent example. Autos are a source of much environmental degradation, because of their manufacture, use, and disposal. They are also complex machines containing a wide variety of materials including metals (primarily steel and aluminum), glass and fiberglass, rubber, oils and other petroleum products, and a wide array of plastics. A typical auto consists of about 70 percent ferrous metals (iron, steel), 5 percent nonferrous metals (copper, aluminum, zinc, magnesium), and about 25 percent non-metal materials. These materials are mixed together, attached to each other, and not easy to separate. Yet nearly all of them are reusable or recyclable in some way.

Most of the world's automobiles are at least partially recycled when their useful lives end. Valuable parts from newer wrecked vehicles and some older vehicles are removed and sold as spare parts at auto-salvage yards. Easily removed and valuable components such as tires and batteries are removed, and fluids are drained. The vehicle is then flattened and shipped to a shredding facility, where it is cut up into many small pieces. The iron and steel are magnetically separated, and the remaining material (fabric, rubber, glass, etc.) is disposed of in landfills. About 44 percent of the ferrous metals in a typical family vehicle made in the United States consist of recycled iron and steel. Relatively little of the nonferrous content of such vehicles is recycled (Steel Recycling Institute 1996).

Recognizing the need to improve automobile recycling, in the mid-1980s the BMW Company of Germany embarked on a program to design and produce automobiles that would be much more easily recycled than those presently produced (Management Institute for Environment and Business n.d.). The plastic content of automobiles is increasing, and most of this plastic is nonrecyclable. In Germany nonrecyclable parts of automobiles make up about 1 to 2 percent of municipal solid waste. With demands for recycling increasing, BMW hoped get a headstart in responding to the problem and gain a competitive advantage over other companies that would be forced by government regulations to adopt recycling requirements later. BMW continues to conduct research and development activities and is sharing its knowledge through partnerships with other companies.

One way in which industries can improve material recycling is to develop closer coordination among companies involved in different parts of the material cycle. Waste from one operation can be a raw material for another, if the material is handled properly and costs are kept to a minimum. For example, industrial parks might be developed in which a group of companies that use related materials locate near each other, sharing waste-handling facilities and exchanging materials between them. Plans are being developed for such facilities in several U.S. cities.

Clearly, there is much potential for movement toward sustainability in manufacturing and waste handling. But long lead times are needed for activities such as the complete redesign of an automobile with recycling in mind, or the coordination of independent companies in a single industrial park.

Changing Consumption Patterns

Changes in industrial practices designed to improve recycling and reduce waste could be significant factors in moving toward sustainability. But some would argue that these are only superficial changes and that real progress would require major changes in the kinds of goods we use and how we lead our day-to-day lives. This is a difficult challenge, especially for societies like the United States which has a long history of mass consumption. But opportunities exist to change consumer habits, both in wealthy industrial societies and in the developing world. Some of these opportunities involve sophisticated technology that is probably accessible only to consumers in wealthy countries, while others are relatively inexpensive and use simple, low-cost technology.

From the standpoint of environmental impact, among the most damaging activities of industrial societies are those involving energy use, especially combustion of fossil fuels. Together, the United States and the European Union emit about 9 billion metric tons of CO_2 per year, or 35 percent of total world emissions. On a per capita basis, the United States emits about 4 times the world average and 22 times India's level. A significant improvement in energy efficiency would

reduce not only these emissions, but also the hydrocarbons, nitrogen oxides, and other pollutants produced at the same time.

In Chapter 14 we discussed technology that could help automobiles or houses expend less energy. But what would it take for people to use less? One way might be for them to travel less, for transportation is the largest single user of energy in the United States.

Much of this travel consists of commuting to and from work. Efforts are being made to encourage commuters to car-pool or use public transit, but thus far these measures have not substantially reduced the use of individual automobiles for commuting. In the meantime, continued inexpensive fuel has encouraged the development of housing in remote suburban and rural areas far from urban workplaces. The rapid development of communications technology in recent years has made the virtual office possible, and increasing numbers of people are working at sites remote from their employers' physical offices.

Another way in which computer technology can improve energy efficiency is through use of "smart machines." Computers can be used to automatically monitor the environmental conditions and performance of machines as well as to regulate those machines to improve their efficiency. For example, much of the improvement in automobile performance and emission reductions since the mid-1980s has been achieved using computers to control ignition timing and fuel mixtures in engines. Modern office buildings are equipped with sensors that monitor temperature, humidity, and ventilation, automatically controlling the flow of heat and fresh air to maintain comfortable conditions without excessive energy use. Tiny computer chips are being studied for possible use in micro-flaps that can actively respond to small variations in air movement and control the air flow across the surface of an airplane, reducing drag and improving fuel efficiency.

Technology such as computerized buildings could be commonplace fairly soon in wealthy countries, but it will probably be too costly for most people in developing countries. And yet most of the economic growth taking place in the world is in relatively poor countries. Does this mean that new, environmentally friendly technology will not be available? Or should we view the rapid economic growth taking place in China, Latin America, and other developing areas as an opportunity to develop in ways that will be more sustainable?

The bicycle is an example of inexpensive technology that provides effective transportation without appreciable environmental impacts. It is a sustainable transport solution that can be used in poor as well as rich countries. In cities and suburban areas, where travel distances are generally less than a few miles, bicycles provide free transport that is often faster than motorized transport. In some countries, bicycles are a vital part of the transport system. In Denmark, for example, one in five journeys is made by bicycle. In the Netherlands, two-thirds of children ride to school on bicycles (*The Economist* 1995). In addition to being emission-free, bicycles take up much less space when parked.

Unfortunately, however, bicycles don't mix well with either pedestrian or motorized traffic. Safety is an issue here: on a per-mile basis, serious injuries are 20 times more likely on bikes than in cars. This means that roadways need to be designed in ways that will keep bikes separate from other traffic. In some cases, separate bicycle lanes can be designated on streets, while in other cases entire separate roadways must be constructed. Such designated bicycle routes are common in Denmark and the Netherlands, where they clearly have a positive effect.

Energy use is not the only area in which inexpensive sustainable technologies are readily available, but it provides a good illustration of the potential. Many existing sustainable technologies are labor-intensive in comparison to their counterparts in industrialized countries. When cultural attitudes include a bias against labor-intensive activities, it will be difficult to encourage them. But if the exercise and involvement of riding a bicycle instead of a bus, walking instead of driving, or donning a sweater instead of turning up the thermostat can be seen as desirable ways to live, then these approaches offer enormous potential in improving the efficiency of resource use.

TIPPING THE BALANCE

If the technologies that will lead to sustainability are either available today or can be created in a decade or two, why aren't we moving more rapidly to develop and adopt them? If relatively minor changes in how consumers use resources will have a significant positive impact on environmental quality at relatively low cost, why aren't we making these changes today?

Individual Action

The answer is that individually and collectively we lack the desire or the motivation to change. It is too easy to continue doing things the way we do. Gasoline is cheap, and we can afford to use as much as we want. Life in the suburbs or in the country is more desirable than life in the city, the land is available, and roads will take us to work quickly even if it is many miles away. Products come in packages designed to entice us to buy, and we have no convenient way of disposing of these packages except in the landfill.

Changing these habits requires a conscious decision to do so, and the decision has to come from the grass roots. On an individual basis, we have to decide that we are willing to pay slightly more for environmentally friendly products than for conventional products. We have to decide to do a little extra work to recycle our waste or to use less energy. These desires must be conveyed to the product designers, the manufacturing engineers, and the advertising agencies so that the companies that produce and sell commodities realize that making them in ways that conserve resources is good not only for business, but for society as well. And our government leaders—politicians and administrative staff—need to understand that the people want change and that they want government to play an active role in that change.

To a considerable extent, grass-roots support for environmental protection and conservation already exists. Numerous public opinion polls show that the environment is a major concern. People want government and business leaders to do more, not less. When the Republican Party embarked on a major campaign in 1995 to scale back environmental protection and transfer control of natural resources to private interests, there was a groundswell of public opposition to these changes, which forced them to withdraw or scale back their initiatives. In much of Europe, public opinion in favor of environmental protection is even stronger than in the United States, leading the European Union to adopt strict controls on many forms of pollution and to argue strenuously for significant reductions in CO_2 emissions. In South Korea, a 1996 government-funded poll found that 85 percent of those surveyed felt that pollution was getting worse every year and that the environment was more important than economic development. Nearly three-quarters of them indicated that they would support increased taxes on water and fees for mass transit to help control water and air pollution.

One way this public opinion is translated into action is through increased demand for environmentally friendly products, and corporations are responding to this demand. Major consumer products companies, for example, are producing more goods using recycled materials, and they are labeling these goods prominently to that effect. This movement extends to a wide range of industries. For example, motels and hotels are installing recycling bins in rooms and are offering options to extend towel and linen use beyond a day. Furniture made with wood from forests certified as "sustainably managed" is growing in popularity, as are products made from 'simulated' tropical woods. Although relatively few consumers are willing to pay large premiums for these products, simple attention to the difference can be enough to encourage businesses to act sustainably in pursuit of competitive advantage in the marketplace.

Corporate Action

Consumers' willingness to reward responsible businesses with higher prices and customer loyalty is just one factor motivating a change in corporate behavior. The realization that waste reduction can improve profits, discussed earlier, is another. In addition, a few industries are beginning to realize that excessive resource use and environmental damage affects them directly.

The insurance industry is an interesting example of an industry that is directly affected by environmental problems. In the late 1980s and early 1990s, several large storms struck Europe and North America, most notably Hurricane Andrew which devastated parts of south Florida in 1992. Economic losses from weather-related disasters rose substantially in this period. From 1990 to 1995, these losses worldwide averaged about 0.11 percent of gross world product; the average for the period 1960 to 1989 was less than 0.02 percent (Flavin 1994; Worldwatch Institute

1996). This increase came at a time when there was also growing concern about global warming and much speculation that at least some of these disasters might be associated with climate change. If global warming caused a rise in sea level, then the frequency of disasters like Hurricane Andrew could be expected to increase.

An increase in the number and severity of hurricanes could be a real problem for the insurance agency, which bases its premiums on the historic occurrences of such storms. Such concerns were at the forefront when insurance interests began to lobby in favor of actions to reduce CO_2 emissions.

Tourism is another important economic activity that depends on maintaining environmental quality. Most tourism focuses on outdoor activities, especially in coastal areas. Beach resorts have been critical to economic development in many tropical countries, especially in the Caribbean but also in the Indian Ocean and the Pacific. In many such countries, tourism is the major source of foreign exchange in addition to providing employment for large numbers of workers. Development of these resorts brings population growth and prosperity to the surrounding regions, but this same growth also puts pressure on resources in the coastal zone. Often the coastal waters are the only available place to dispose of sewage. At the same time, good water quality is obviously critical for attracting bathers to the beach. The tourist industry thus has a powerful influence on environmental policy in these areas.

Perhaps the greatest incentive for companies to change their behavior comes from the financial industry—large banks and financiers, and occasionally the stock market itself. Bankers in particular are careful to see that the collateral that secures their loans is worthy. But pollution can become a big financial risk if, for example, a company can be required to clean up its wastes. Concern about this risk has been an important factor forcing companies to reduce pollution and to adopt environmental auditing procedures that will verify compliance with environmental laws. At the same time, businesses, creditors, and insurers have been lobbying hard for government-imposed limits on this liability.

Although we can point to many examples of improved business performance with regard to natural resources, many problems remain. The simple fact is that in many situations it is still more profitable to exploit resources quickly or dispose of wastes carelessly without regard for the environmental quality or future resource needs. For example, Shell Oil has been heavily criticized by environmentalists for pollution associated with its operations in Nigeria. Although some U.S. paper manufacturers have been proactive in controlling pollution in advance of new regulations, others have staunchly resisted pressure to reduce waste discharges. Timber companies continue to argue for unrestricted logging of old-growth forests in the tropics and the midlatitudes. Without the *genuine* support of the majority of businesses (as opposed to support from the marketing and public relations departments only), progress toward sustainability will be limited.

Government Action

What can governments do to help and encourage individuals and businesses in the drive to sustainability? Fortunately, many things can be done, provided they have the political incentives to act. Opportunities abound in three major areas: considering the full economic consequences of resource-use decisions; enforcing stiff penalties for illegal resource degradation; and using the powers of taxing and spending to promote sustainability rather than waste.

Natural Resource Accounting   Perhaps the most fundamental requirement in measuring sustainability and in moving toward it is improved environmental accounting. As we discussed in Chapter 2, environmental degradation can be considered a result of externalities. Externalities are transfers of commodities such as air pollution without the consent of all parties involved—specifically, those who bear the consequences of pollution without gaining directly from the activities that generated it. If the receivers of these wastes were compensated for this service, then those who generate the pollution would probably pollute less. Similarly, if those who exploit natural resources were required to pay the full social costs of this exploitation, then they would probably use resources more carefully.

What do we mean by improved environmental accounting? It means considering the value of all the resources we use to produce wealth, and not just the money earned from the sale of goods and services. For example, if you wanted to evaluate your own economic performance in a given year, you would consider changes in the amount of money you have in the bank as well as your income. Suppose you began the year with $10,000 in the bank. You invest $5000 of this in a business. During the year the business generates $25,000 in net income, and at the end of the year the initial $5000 investment has depreciated to zero. You spend $22,000 of your income on living expenses, put $3000 in the bank, and end the year with $8000 in the bank. The total amount of money you earned in the year would thus be $23,000: the $25,000 net business income minus the $2000 net drawdown of capital in the bank.

At present when economists calculate the net income of a country—its gross national product (GNP)—they include changes in the amount of capital stored in bank accounts, but they do not include changes in supplies of *natural capital*. Natural capital includes the value of standing trees in the forest, oil in rocks, or fertility of the soil. Conventional calculations of GNP do not include the value of social capital; the education, health, and skills of a country's residents. And yet, if we clear-cut a forest and sell the timber, that is equivalent to spending money saved in the bank—money (or forests) that could be used to generate income in future years.

Economists argue that if we include such depletion of natural capital in GNP calculations, we will find that we are not generating as much wealth as we might think, because we are depleting natural capital faster than it is renewed. For example, Daly and Cobb (1989) calculated an index of sustainable economic welfare (ISEW) that attempts to include environmental values in GNP calculations. Although the conventionally calculated GNP of the United States rose more than 50 percent between about 1970 and 1985, the ISEW remained relatively unchanged. If we were more aware of dwindling stocks of natural capital, we would be more likely to take action to protect them.

Mandated Environmental Responsibility
Earlier in this chapter, we described the move away from government-mandated environmental protection toward private-sector initiatives, a movement that gained momentum in the early 1990s. Businesses voluntarily have been taking responsibility for improving their environmental performance by reducing waste and use of haz-

ardous chemicals, increasing recycling, and opening dialogues on environmental issues with the communities in which they operate.

These initiatives are motivated by several factors, some of which relate directly to the cost of doing business and some of which are intended to avoid liabilities and confrontations that have resulted from government regulations. To the extent that this improved business behavior is a response to government pressure, we may wish to maintain that pressure.

In what ways has government pressure led to voluntary change in business practices with regard to resources? One significant force has been the assignment of financial responsibility for environmental cleanup to parties contributing to pollution. The Superfund law is an excellent example. It allowed all parties contributing to certain major toxic pollution problems, such as toxic waste landfills, to be charged with the costs of cleaning up that waste. Because the costs of such cleanups can be enormous, businesses have sought to reduce the generation of hazardous wastes simply to avoid the possibility of being held responsible for a future cleanup. Similarly, accidental releases of toxic substances within or outside a manufacturing facility can easily bring expensive lawsuits. To reduce the possibility of litigation, many companies have instituted programs of periodic environmental audits to ensure that they are in compliance with the law and are handling hazardous materials safely.

Legislation such as the Superfund law and damage suits filed by parties exposed to pollutants have at times created very large penalties for polluters. Some argue that these penalties or cleanup costs are sometimes excessive; for example, restoring polluted land to a near-clean condition can cost much more than the value of the land after it has been cleaned. Corporations and insurance companies that provide businesses with liability coverage have pressured government to pass laws limiting corporate liability in such cases.

The annual publication of the Toxic Release Inventory (TRI) is another government program that has been effective in encouraging businesses to reduce pollution. When the lists of emissions are published, newspaper headlines immediately announce who are the biggest polluters in town. Few corporations want to look like the dirty kids on the block, and whether or not the bad public-

ity associated with the TRI is truly deserved, it helps to show businesses the value of reducing their emissions.

The TRI has been criticized on many grounds, including its tendency to add amounts of different pollutants together, like apples and oranges, without full regard for their differences. Similarly, the costs of cleaning up toxic wastes and the penalties imposed in civil lawsuits are sometimes excessive. But the fear of bearing such costs has provided a powerful incentive for businesses to reduce pollution. Requiring continued public accountability for corporate behavior can be important in maintaining and strengthening the growing record of good corporate citizenship.

Using the Power of Government   Governments are organizations set up by groups of people for the purpose of doing things that they cannot do as individuals. Despite widespread cynicism (at least in the United States) about the ability of government to accomplish meaningful goals and despite the popularity of criticizing excessive government regulation, governments can do many positive things to encourage responsible resource use.

One of these things is to use the necessary act of collecting taxes to promote sustainability. Most governments use tax policy routinely as a means of achieving various social ends, such as taxing the wealthy at higher rates than the poor so as to redistribute income more evenly. Perhaps the most effective way taxes can be used to improve the environment is through increasing the costs of resource degradation. If individuals are held responsible for at least some of the social/environmental costs of their activities, then the environmental externalities can be reduced.

For example, driving an automobile benefits the individual while generating many social and environmental costs. It discharges pollutants to the air, increases congestion on roads, and helps wear down the roads themselves. It also helps deplete future supplies of petroleum, increasing future costs of that fuel. Most countries charge taxes for operating motor vehicles, usually in the form of license fees and fuel taxes.

In most European countries, for example, taxes are assessed for both licensing an automobile and for purchasing fuel. European fuel costs in the mid-1990s were typically $1 to $1.50 per liter ($4 to $6 per gallon). As a result, people buy more fuel-efficient cars, drive less, and take public transit more than they would otherwise. But in the United States, these taxes are very low, and fuel costs much less: about $0.35 per liter ($1.33 per gallon) in the mid-1990s. As a result people in the United States drive more frequently and greater distances in less efficient cars, and we emit two to three times as much CO_2 per person as a typical European.

Not only does the United States fail to charge individual polluters such as automobile drivers for the social costs of their actions, but in many cases its tax system actually encourages inefficient behavior. For example, sport utility vehicles are heavier and less fuel-efficient than conventional sedans; and some of them are classed as trucks. Trucks are subject to less-stringent efficiency rules than autos, and some taxes are lower on trucks than on autos.

Governments encourage wasteful practices in other ways, often through subsidies. In Chapter 10 we saw how government subsidies on water in the western United States encouraged use of this water to grow low-value crops such as hay, instead of conserving the water for other uses. The U.S. Forest Service subsidizes timber harvesting on its lands through road construction and other activities, sometimes even to the point of spending more money to encourage logging than it earns in the sale of the timber. Such subsidies are common in many countries (Fig. 15.6).

Instead of using government funds to encourage waste, they could be used to encourage the development of new sustainable technologies. For example, photoelectric cells offer much promise for reducing demand for fossil-generated electricity. That potential is not yet realized because the cost of electricity that is generated using photoelectric cells is still relatively high in comparison to other sources. Their high cost, in turn, is in part caused by the small numbers of cells produced and the lack of economies of scale in manufacturing.

What is needed is for someone to make a large initial investment in photoelectric cells, perhaps in the form of a commitment to buy a given number of cells. This would prime the pump and would begin the positive feedback of more demand, more production, lower unit costs, more purchases, and so forth. In 1996, plans were announced to build a 10-mw photovoltaic power plant in Nevada, and a 50-mw plant in Rajastan, India. In both cases, the plants will be made possible in part by long-term government commitments to purchase the power generated. Although these plants are small in comparison to modern, conventional electric-generating plants, they are significant because they will increase the production of photovoltaic cells, leading to reductions in prices.

LOOKING FORWARD

In this chapter we have seen that sustainability, or at least significant progress toward sustainability, is technically and economically feasible. The technology necessary to substantially improve efficiency of resource use is either available today or could be developed within a decade or two. The resources on which we currently depend and which are being depleted can be replaced. We don't need to feed two-thirds of our grain to livestock as is done in the United States—diets with much less meat can provide all the nutrition we need, and we would probably be much healthier if we changed our diets. We don't need to cut old-growth forests to provide an adequate timber supply—we can make excellent products with smaller trees produced with intensive forest management, often at a lower cost than cutting forests in rugged mountains. We don't need to drive automobiles that get 19 miles to the gallon to get to work—autos with twice that efficiency are readily available and usually cost less.

The drive to sustainability is limited most by a cultural factor: the will to change. Personal habits such as a diet rich in meat or the enjoyment of driving a fast car, the social traditions of communities that are dependent on cutting trees in a remote area, and the self-interests of businesses and their shareholders demanding short-term profits are inertial forces. They keep us from changing in ways that we know we should, and they perpetuate the unsustainable practices that are occurring around the world today.

The recent history of the environmental movement has shown that when and where public sentiment for environmental protection and resource conservation is strong, our governmental, corporate, and individual behaviors respond. Maintaining that commitment is the best, and perhaps the only, way for human resource-use systems to become truly sustainable.

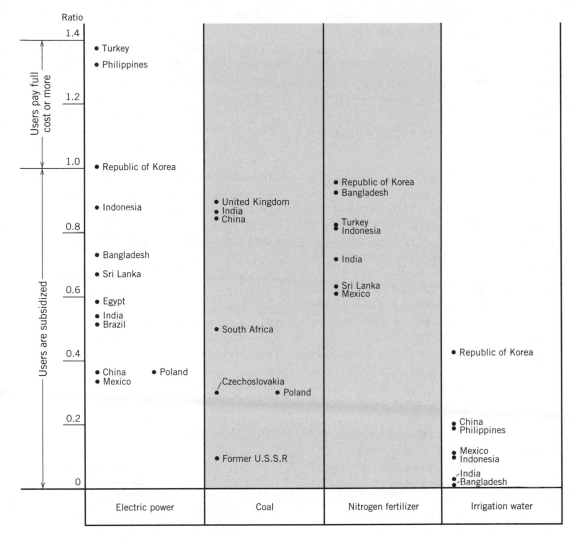

Figure 15.6   Ratio of price to production cost, selected energy, and agricultural inputs.
Source: World Bank, 1992, Fig. 3.2.

REFERENCES AND ADDITIONAL READING

Abramowitz, J. 1997. Valuing nature's services. In L.R. Brown, ed. *State of the World, 1997*. New York: W. W. Norton.

Boerner, C., and K. Chilton. 1994. False economy: the folly of demand-side recycling. *Environment* 36:1:6–15; 32.

Borgstrom, G. 1965. *The Hungry Planet: The Modern World at the Edge of Famine*. New York: Collier Books.

Costanza, R., and H. E. Daly. 1992. Natural capital and sustainable development. *Conservation Biology* 6: 37–46.

Costanza, R., R. d'Arge, R. de Groot, S. Farber, M. Grasso, B. Hannon, K. Limburg, S. Naeem, R. O'Neill, J. Paruelo, R. Raskin, P. Sutton, and M. van den Belt. 1997. The value of the world's ecosystem services and natural capital. *Nature* 387(6630): 253–260.

Council on Environmental Quality. 1981. *The Global 2000 Report to the President*. New York: Viking Penguin.

Cutter, S. L. 1993. *Living with Risk*. London: Edward Arnold.

Daly, H. E, and J. B. Cobb. 1989. *For the Common Good: Redirecting the Economy Toward Community, the Environment, and a Sustainable Future*. Beacon Press, Boston.

Economist, The. 1995. More puff, less smoke. *The Economist* September 2, 1995, p. 53.

Ehrlich, P. 1968. *The Population Bomb.* New York: Ballantine Books.

Flavin, Christopher. 1994. Storm warnings: Climate change hits the insurance industry. *WorldWatch,* December, pp. 10–20.

Frosch, R. A. 1995. Industrial ecology: adapting technology for a sustainable world. *Environment* 37 (10): 16–24, 34–37.

Goodland, R., and H. Daly. 1994. Environmental sustainability: universal and non-negotiable. Paper presented to Ecological Society of America, Knoxville, TN, August 1994.

Kane, Hal. 1996. Shifting to sustainable industries. in L.R. Brown et al., *State of the World 1996.* New York: W. W. Norton, pp. 152–167.

Management Institute for Environment and Business. n.d.. Bayerische Motoren Werke, AG: A proactive approach to vehicle recycling. Management Institute for Environment and Business.

Meadows, D. H., et al. 1972. *The Limits to Growth.* New York: Universe Books.

Nash, J. and J. Ehrenfeld. 1996. Code green: business adopts voluntary environmental standards. *Environment* 38 (1): 16–20, 36–45.

Paddock, W. and P. Paddock, 1967. *Famine 1975!* Boston: Little, Brown.

President's Council on Sustainable Development, 1996. *Sustainable America: A New Consensus for Prosperity, Opportunity, and a Healthy Environment for the Future.* Washington, DC: U.S. Government Printing Office.

Serageldin, I. 1993. Making development sustainable. *Finance and Development* 30, no. 4: 6–10.

Steel Recycling Institute. 1996. *Recycling Scrapped Automobiles.*
ONLINE: *http://www.recycle-steel.org/Auto.html.*

U.S. Congress, Office of Technology Assessment. 1982. *Global Models, World Futures and Public Policy: A Critique.* Washington, DC: Superintendent of Documents.

Waste Management of North America. 1992. *Recycling in the '90s: A Shared Responsibility.* Oak Brook, Il: Waste Management of North America.

Weinberg, A. M. 1984. Review of The Resourceful Earth. *Environment* 26:7, 25–27.

World Bank. 1992. *World Development Report 1992: Development and the Environment.* New York: Oxford University Press.

_____. 1995. *Monitoring Environmental Progress: A Report on Work in Progress.* Washington, DC: Environment Department, World Bank.

World Commission on Environment and Development 1987. *Our Common Future.* Oxford: Oxford University Press.

Worldwatch Institute. 1996. WorldWatch data diskette.

Young, J. E. 1995. The sudden new strength of recycling. *WorldWatch,* July/August 1995. pp. 20–25.

Young, J. E. and A. Sachs. 1994. *The Next Efficiency Revolution: Creating a Sustainable Materials Economy.* Worldwatch Paper no. 121. Washington, DC: Worldwatch Institute.

For more information, check our web site at *http://www.wiley.com/college/cutter*

STUDY QUESTIONS

1. Do you think global models are better than science fiction or crystal balls in predicting the future?
2. What are the most important resource issues in your region? How do these compare to national issues? global issues?
3. What can you do to address the local environmental issues facing your community? What can you do to stimulate others to take action as well?
4. How are resource issues different today than when your grandparents were your age? How might they differ when you become a grandparent?
5. Is sustainablity achievable in your lifetime? Why or why not?

Epilogue

Throughout the writing of this book, we have attempted to present a balanced analysis of environmental and resource issues. If parts are not completely balanced, at least we have undertaken to touch on the diversity of opinions. Here, we diverge from this textbook style and present an epilogue containing our own personal views about the conservation of natural resources. Unlike the rest of the book which was written with compromises required by joint authorship, these statements represent our less objective sides. After all, resource use and development is a matter of opinion as much as a matter of fact.

PUTTING THE ENVIRONMENT
IN PERSPECTIVE

William H. Renwick

Why should we worry about the environment? Presumably, our ultimate goal is to better the human condition through proper management of environmental resources. But as we stated in the introduction to this book, resources are created and defined by both human and environmental factors. In order to improve the human material condition, it is necessary to consider both the physical characteristics of natural resources and the ways in which we convert these raw materials into food, clothing, shelter, and the various other physical requirements of a comfortable existence.

It is my view that although certain aspects of the natural environment are very important to the ultimate well-being of human beings, the social or cultural aspects of our resource-use systems are much more critical in determining the quality of life. These social/cultural aspects include the creation and selection of various technologies for converting the raw materials of natural resources into things usable by humans, and the social and economic systems used to allocate and distribute resources and goods to people. I believe this because in my interpretation most of the major cases of large-scale human suffering can be attributable primarily (if not entirely) to human causes, and because hardships caused by the many environmental problems we have discussed are minor, even trivial, by comparison.

To someone who has just finished reading this book, or to a dedicated environmentalist, this idea may seem heretical, but a few examples will help illustrate the point. First, most major modern and historical episodes of widespread death or suffering are directly attributable to aggression by one group against another, either explicit in the case of most wars or indirect in the case of the eradication of native populations in the New World. There have been periods of severe population reduction by nonhuman agents, most notably the plagues in Europe in the Middle Ages. The causes of these tragedies were certainly complex and included environmental factors such as fluctuations in host animal populations. But few modern diseases cause human suffering on the scale caused by direct human action. The occurrences of famine in some poor countries are essentially attributable to economic/political causes. Yes, famines occur as a result of crop failures that are triggered by unfavorable weather and similar causes, and yes, rapidly rising populations have strapped the ability of the environment to supply us with food and water. But virtually all experts on food problems agree that if domestic and international political and economic conditions were different, these famines would not occur. Some would argue that more agricultural technology must be transferred from rich nations to poor ones, whereas others argue that the colonial status of the poor nations, today or in the past, is the cause of their economic problems. But few would argue that the physical limits of the environment's productivity have been reached.

The other side of the issue is to consider the severity of the natural resource problems facing us today. As examples I will mention urban/industrial pollution and soil erosion. Pollution today is certainly a problem, and we regret the fouling of water and air that is most acute in major urban areas. But in most of the industrialized world, this pollution has been going on for a long time—150 years or more. The major problem of water pollution, the contamination of potable water supplies with disease-causing organisms, has been all but solved by a combination of effluent treatment and chlorination. The most visible and acute forms of air pollution that caused severe health problems in past decades have also been much reduced. We are concerned about toxic substances in water and air, but at present we have little evidence that health problems from these sources will be significant in comparison to those caused by poor diet, smoking, or other individual habits. With regard to soil erosion, many areas of the world have experienced erosion at high rates for decades or even centuries. When economic conditions have allowed substituting other inputs to agriculture such as fertilizers and improved seeds, yields have increased dramatically, obscuring any effect of soil erosion on production.

Human-induced climatic change presents an interesting case. Predictions made in the late 1990s included a wide range of possible dire consequences, including a rise in sea level, droughts, and floods, with associated death and destruction, crop failures, and so forth. Some argue that radical reductions in CO_2 output are necessary to avert these tragedies, and they accordingly propose various measures to stop tropical deforestation, lessen automobile use, reduce combustion of fossil fuels by electric power plants, and so on. If we assume that these measures could actually stabilize CO_2 emissions at something near current levels, then global warming would be greatly slowed but not stopped. Would that not be a good thing?

Consider the social, economic, and political upheavals this would involve. Unless we build many new nuclear power plants, use of electricity would have to be seriously curtailed, with major adverse economic effects, including cost increases, unemployment, and possibly chronic recession. People in poor countries would be prohibited from increasing agricultural production by opening up new lands, thus limiting their options to increase intensive cultivation of existing lands and so slowing any improvement in diet. Economic development that involved greater use of fossil fuels by poor countries would have to be prevented, or such use by rich nations would have to be seriously reduced. Given the political realities of the world today, and the tendency for voters and politicians alike to be much more concerned about self-interest and short-term rather than long-term problems, measures such as these are very unlikely.

On the other hand, what if the greenhouse warming is allowed to take place and the predictions prove true? Sea-level rise will be a problem in rich countries but not an insurmountable one. We have the capability to build dikes a few meters high around coastal areas and pump water out of lowlands—the Dutch provide a good model for this. It would be a more difficult problem in poor countries. Bangladesh, much of which is within a few meters of sea level, would probably suffer the most. Agricultural problems caused by unfavorable weather might arise, but the history of farming over the past few decades makes it quite clear that farmers regularly adjust to market stresses and changes in policy that are much more dramatic than any weather fluctuations that are likely to occur as a result of global warming. Again the rich countries have the capital and technology to deal with the problem, and poorer nations would probably suffer more. So what is the real problem—climate change or poverty?

Having raised these issues, it is important to recognize that some environmental problems require considerable attention. Air and water pollution are becoming worse in much of the world, especially in poor countries. The extent of the problem in eastern Europe has recently become known in the west, and perhaps we will also begin to think about the situation in the more densely populated parts of the developing world. Land degradation by soil erosion and depletion of nutrients also continues to stress the food production system. Finally, even though I do not think we should concentrate our efforts on global warming in itself, curtailing fossil fuel use and tropical deforestation would certainly significantly improve air quality and preserve species.

Even though the many problems discussed in this book are environmental in scope, their solutions are political and economic. Given sufficient capital, poor land can be made to produce high yields, clean water can be made available, and energy can be supplied or conserved without causing a significant decline in standard of living. This has clearly been demonstrated in the wealthy nations. What is needed in the developing world are the economic resources and political power to make the necessary investments and return the proceeds of those investments to the land and people who need it most. Only when the economic and political changes that would make this possible come about will real progress be made in solving environmental problems.

WHEN YOU'RE 64

Susan L. Cutter

More than 25 years ago, Ernest Callenbach wrote *Ecotopia*, which described the newly seceded nation-state (formerly western California, Oregon, and Washington) of the same name. The novel, which is set in 1999, is narrated by a reporter from the United States who was sent to observe the new society. Weaned from a petroleum-based economy, Ecotopians have a healthy respect for nature, use bicycles as the primary form of transportation, and rely on decentralized renewables as their energy source. Around the same time, Edward Abbey penned *The Monkey Wrench Gang*, a novel about eco-terrorists who sabotaged the development of the Southwest by destroying billboards, disabling heavy machinery, and generally wreaking havoc in their efforts to keep the desert unspoiled.

Popular fiction has always mirrored societal concerns. Closely related to science fiction, environmental fiction is based on the environmental sciences and uses current environmental issues as the basis for stories. As environmental concerns became more pervasive in the last three decades, so did the number of fiction works focusing on the conservation of natural resources. Ecosystem disruption was a prevalent theme in the 1970s (*Cachalot* by Alan Dean Foster, 1980; *The Green Brain* by Frank Herbert, 1966; *The Milagro Beanfield War* by John Nichols, 1974; *Heartland* by David Hagberg, 1983; and *The Portent* by Marilyn Harris, 1981). By the 1980s, much of the environmental fiction had a decidedly postnuclear war theme (*Nature's End* by Whitley Strieber and James Kunetka, 1986; *O-Zone* by Paul Theroux, 1986, *The Shore of Women* by Pamela Sargent, 1987; and *Terra!* by Stefano Benni, 1985). By the 1990s, recurring themes included biodiversity (*Fertile Ground* by Charles Wilson, 1996), and post-greenhouse futures (*Earth* by David Brin, 1990; *Heavy Weather* by Bruce Sterling, 1994; and *Ocean Black* by Hank Bostrum, 1995).

Environmental fiction gives us a glimpse of what the future may bring based on current trends. But what might we anticipate for the future, say the year 2064? Here is one scenario.

By 2020, most of the world's nation-states were no longer in existence. Instead, regional alliances such as the European Community and the Americas dominated the international arena. During this time as well, the disparities between wealthy and poorer nations widened. In 2025, the ultimate disaster occurred: the world monetary system collapsed, and people no longer could use paper money or make wireless transfers into their accounts. All goods and services were transacted through a bartering system. The economic collapse led to the leveling of income disparities worldwide. Bioregions became the organizing unit for societies. The differences between the haves and have nots now was not income but technology.

The Global Environmental Facility (GEF; established in the early 1990s as part of the Earth Summit) operated as the major decision-making body for the world. As such, it had enormous power and control over the bioregions in terms of trade and bartering. It did not, however, have complete control over communications and computer technology. As part of their long-range planning toward sustainability, the GEF supported major exploratory efforts to other planets and galaxies to search for new life and new opportunities for human habitation. To many scholars of ancient earth, this was reminiscent of the "manifest destiny" policy four centuries earlier.

As these intergalactic explorations were taking place during the 2050s and 2060s), new warning signs were heard on Earth about the need to preserve the resources of other worlds. These voices were not coming from the bioregionalists but rather the technologists. It seems that the underground cybersurfers (or *digerati* as they were also known) had made contact with other life forms 20 years earlier. They had banded together to form a pro-environmental group called Earth Second!! dedicated to maintaining sustainability on all planets, not just Earth. The transboundary movement of people or pollution, or the extraction of resources from one planet to support another, was strictly forbidden. The Earth Seconders, led by a former GEF commander, Kirk Spock Picard, were extremely effective in communicating their message of living within limits—so much so that the GEF was disbanded in 2063 and the United Federation of Planets was established with Picard as its first leader a year later.

Despite advances in biotechnology, I won't be here to see this outcome. However, I have left my cyberaccount open. I look forward to hearing from you.

GLOSSARY

Absolute scarcity A condition when there is not enough of a resource in existence to satisfy demand for it.

Acid mine drainage Water leaving a surface or underground mine enriched in acid, usually surfuric acid.

Acid deposition The accumulation of acids, either in precipitation or through dry dustfall, on the land surface.

Active solar power Solar energy gathered by a device that collects this energy and mechanically distributes it to where it is needed.

Advection inversion A temperature inversion caused by warm air passing over a cool surface.

Age structure The relative proportions of a population in different age classes.

Agribusiness Large-scale, organized production of food, farm machinery, and supplies as well as the storage, sale, and distribution of farm commodities, for profit.

Agricultural runoff Water leaving areas of agricultural land use, usually enriched in nutrients, sediment, and agricultural chemicals.

Ambient air quality The chemical characteristics of air as it exists in the environment; measures pollutant concentrations in the air.

Amenity resource A resource valued for nonmonetary characteristics, such as its beauty or uniqueness.

Amenity value The nonmonetary, intangible value of a good or service.

Anadromous fish Fish that breed in fresh water but spend most of their adult lives in salt water. Examples are salmon and striped bass.

Animal unit month The amount of forage needed to support a certain number of grazing animals for one month.

Anoxic Water without dissolved oxygen.

Anthracite The highest rank of coal, most modified from its original plant form.

Anthropogenic Of human origin, such as carbon dioxide emitted by fossil fuel combustion.

Aquiclude An impermeable layer that confines an aquifer, preventing the water in it from moving upward or downward into adjacent strata. Shale and some igneous rocks often form aquicludes.

Aquifer A geologic unit containing groundwater; an underground reservoir made up of porous material capable of holding substantial quantities of water.

Arable land Land that is capable of being cultivated and supporting agricultural production.

Arroyo A deep, steep-sided gully found in semiarid areas, particularly in the southwestern United States.

Augur mining A coal-mining technique using a screw that extracts coal as it is drilled into a deposit.

Baby boom A period from 1945 to the mid-1960s in which the average fertility rate in the United States was over 3 children per woman.

Benefit-cost analysis A process of quantitatively evaluating all the positive and negative aspects of a particular action in order to reach a rational decision regarding that action.

Bioaccumulation The tendency for a pollutant to accumulate in the tissues of plants or animals.

Biochemical decay Breakdown of pollutants in water through the action of bacteria.

Biochemical oxygen demand (BOD) The amount of oxygen used in oxidation of substances in a given water sample. Measured in milligrams per liter over a specific time period.

Biocide Willful destruction of living things.

Biogeochemical cycle The movement of a particular material through an ecosystem over long periods of time.

Biological diversity The range or number of species or subspecies found in a particular area.

Biomagnification An increase in the concentration of a pollutant as it is passed up the food chain, caused by a tendency for animals to accumulate the pollutant in their tissues.

Biomass The total amount of living or formerly living matter in a given area, measured as dry weight.

Biomass harvesting A forest harvest technique in which whole trees are chipped and used as fuel.

Biome A major ecological region within which plant and animal communities are similar in general characteristics and in their relations to the physical environment.

Bioregion A geographic area defined by ecological characteristics. A bioregion includes an area of relatively homogeneous ecological characteristics, or a specific assemblage of ecological communities. It is similar to a biome but may refer to a smaller area with more specific characteristics.

Biosphere The worldwide system within which all life functions; composed of smaller systems including the atmosphere, hydrosphere, and lithosphere.

Biosphere resources Resources associated with living organisms.

Biotic potential The maximum rate of population growth resulting if all females in a population breed as often as possible and all individuals survive past their reproductive periods.

Birth rate The number of babies born per year per 1000 population.

Bituminous coal A rank of coal below anthracite, characterized by a high degree of conversion from the original plant matter and a high heat content per unit weight.

Boreal forest A biome dominated by coniferous forests and found in relatively high altitudes or latitudes, almost exclusively in the Northern Hemisphere.

British thermal unit (Btu) The amount of energy required to raise the temperature of one pound of water one degree Fahrenheit at or near 39.2°F.

Bubble approach An approach to air pollution emissions control that allows a plant to consider emissions from several sources as combined emissions from the plant.

Bureau of Land Management (BLM) The U.S. Bureau of Land Management, located in the Department of the Interior, established in 1946 to administer federal lands not reserved for military, park, national forest, or other special uses.

Carcinogen A substance that causes cancer.

Carrying capacity The maximum number of organisms in one species that can be supported in a particular environmental setting.

Cartel A consortium of producers of a single product who agree to limit production to keep the price of the product high.

Catadromous fish Fish that breed in salt water but live most of their adult lives in fresh water. The American eel is an example.

Centralized energy An energy conversion technology in which the key conversion (such as combustion of coal to create electricity) is made at a large scale at a single site (such as a power plant).

Chaparral A subtropical drought-resistant and fire-prone shrubby vegetation associated with Mediterranean-type climates.

Chlorofluorocarbons (CFCs) A group of substances that are compounds of chlorine, fluorine, and carbon. They are widely used in refrigeration and many industrial processes, and contribute to deterioration of stratospheric ozone.

Clean Air Act The name given to a series of air-quality improvement laws and their amendments passed in the United States beginning in 1963.

Clean Water Act The name given to a series of water-quality improvement laws and their amendments passed in the United States beginning in 1964.

Clear-cutting A forest harvest technique in which all trees in a particular area are cut, regardless of species or size.

Coal gasification A chemical process converting coal to a gas that can then be used in place of natural gas.

Cohort A group of individuals of similar age.

Coliform bacteria Bacteria of the species *Escherichia coli*, commonly occurring in the digestive tracts of animals; used as an indicator of the potential for disease-causing organisms in water.

Common property resource Resource such as air, oceans, or sunshine that is in theory owned by everyone but in practice utilized by a few. The question of regulation arises to prevent or lessen resource abuse.

Community A collection of organisms occupying a specific geographic area.

Concentration In the context of air or water quality, the amount of a substance per unit (weight or volume) of air or water.

Conservation The wise use or careful management of resources to attain the maximum possible social benefits from them.

Conservation tillage An agricultural system using tillage techniques designed to reduce soil erosion and overland flow. Most conservation tillage techniques involve less manipulation of the soil than conventional techniques, leaving more plant matter on the soil surface.

Consumer theory of value An approach to valuing commodities based on how much a consumer is willing to pay for them.

Consumptive use or Consumption Water use that results in water being evaporated rather than returned to surface water or groundwater after use.

Contingent valuation method A method for determining the value of a resource by asking how much they would be willing to pay for it under certain circumstances.

Continental shelf Area of the seafloor averaging less than 650 ft (200 m) deep, which generally was exposed at times of lower sea level in the past.

Contour plowing A soil conservation technique involving plowing parallel to the contour, across a slope rather than up and down it.

Cost-effectiveness analysis An analysis of all the costs involved in taking a specified action to determine the most efficient way to carry out the chosen action.

Cost theory of value An approach to valuing commodities based on the cost of production.

Crisis management A form of decision making that is a seat-of-the-pants response to the issue of the moment with no consideration of longer-term effects.

Criteria pollutants Air pollutants, including carbon monoxide, hydrocarbons, lead, oxidants, particulates, nitrogen oxides, and sulfur oxides, for which maximum permissible concentrations in ambient air are established.

Critical mineral A mineral necessary for defense of the United States and available partly in America or partly from friendly nations.

Criticality A term used to describe environmental regions that are so degraded that economic activity and human habitation are impossible in the short term.

Crop rotation A soil conservation technique involving changing crops grown on a given parcel of land from year to year. Crop rotations may include fallow periods.

Cropland Land in which crops are regularly planted and harvested. It includes land in fallow or pasture as part of a regular rotation system.

Crown fire An intense forest fire that consumes the tops of trees as well as lower strata of vegetation.

Crude oil Unrefined petroleum as it is extracted from the ground; it is liquid at normal ambient temperatures.

Death rate The number of deaths per year per 1000 population.

Decentralized energy source An energy conversion system characterized by numerous small-scale facilities located at or near the end-use site. Photovoltaic cells are an example.

Decreaser A plant species in a range community that declines in importance as a result of grazing pressure. Usually, decreasers are the most palatable to the grazing animals.

Deep ocean Ocean areas seaward of the continental shelf.

Deforestation Any process of replacement of forest vegetation with other types.

Demographic transition The process by which a human population goes through a growth pattern, including an early phase of high birth and death rates, an intermediate phase of high birth rates but low death rates, and a later phase of low birth and death rates.

Desalination Artificial removal of salt from water, such as by distillation or reverse osmosis.

Desert A biome characterized by plants and animals adapted to extreme moisture scarcity.

Desertification A process of land becoming more desertlike as a result of human-induced devegetation and related soil deterioration, sometimes aggravated by drought.

Dilution In water quality, a reduction in pollutant concentration caused by mixing with water with a lower concentration of the substance.

Dissolved oxygen Oxygen found in dissolved form in water.

Dissolved solids Substances normally solid at ambient temperatures but dissolved into ionic form in water.

Diversification The trend in many large corporations toward ownership of a wide array of companies producing unrelated goods and services.

Domesticate A species that has been bred for specific characteristics that humans value, thereby rendering the species dependent on humans for its continued survival.

Doubling time The length of time needed for a population to double in size. It is a function of the growth rate.

Drainage basin An area bounded by drainage divides and defined with respect to a point along a stream. All the runoff generated within the area must pass the point along the stream; runoff generated outside the basin will not pass that point.

Drip irrigation An irrigation method involving small pipes placed at the base of plants delivering water slowly to the plant roots.

Drought A period of time with unusually low precipitation.

Dry farming Agricultural production in climatically marginal lands without the use of irrigation.

Dry rock geothermal energy A method of extracting heat from the earth by pumping water through hot rocks.

Earth Summit The popular name given to the 1992 UN Conference on Environment and Development held in Rio de Janiero.

Ecology The study of the interrelationships between living organisms and the living and nonliving components and processes that make up their environment.

Ecosystem The collection of all living organisms in a geographic area together with all living and nonliving things they interact with.

Ecotone A transitional zone between two adjacent ecosystems.

Ecotourism Tourism focused on appreciation of nature rather than on built environments.

El Niño/La Niña A transient, periodic warming of the equatorial eastern Pacific Ocean, associated with fisheries depletion and large-scale climatic fluctuations.

Emissions trading A procedure in air-quality regulation by which one polluter can acquire permission to discharge pollutants formerly discharged by another discharger that has ceased emitting pollutants.

Endangered species A species in imminent danger of extinction.

Energy budget An accounting of all energy inputs and outputs for a system.

Energy conservation Using energy resources in such a way as to minimize energy consumption in relation to benefits gained.

Energy efficiency The amount of utility, either work performed or income generated, gained per unit of an energy resource.

Environmental cognition The mental process of making sense of the world that each of us inhabits.

Environmental ethics A philosophical position regarding the relation between humans and nature.

Environmental lapse rate The average rate at which temperature declines with increasing altitude in the troposphere.

Environmental refugee A person fleeing a natural or human-caused environmental disaster.

Environmental resistance Factors such as food supply, weather, disease, and predators that keep a population below its biotic potential.

Equity Fairness in the use and allocation of resources.

Erosion Removal of soil by running water or wind.

Erosivity The ability of rainfall to cause erosion. Erosivity is a function of rainfall intensity and drop size.

Estuary A semi–enclosed water body, open to the sea, in which seawater is significantly diluted by fresh water from the land.

Euphotic zone The upper portion of the sea, in which sunlight is intense enough to allow plant growth.

Eutrophication The process by which lakes become increasingly nutrient-rich and shallow. It is a natural process that is accelerated by water pollution.

Evapotranspiration The process by which liquid water is conveyed to the atmosphere as water vapor, including water use by plants.

Exclusive economic zone A zone of the oceans over which a particular nation has claims or exclusive control of certain economic activities, such as fishing.

Exploitation Use of a resource at the maximum profitable short-term rate, without regard for long-term resource quality or availability.

Externality A non-market exchange, in which at least one party to the exchange is not compensated and may have little choice in the exchange.

Extinction The process by which a species ceases to exist.

Farmland Land that is part of farm units, including cropland, pasture, small woodlots, and areas used for small farm roads and buildings.

Federal Land Policy and Management Act (FLPMA) Passed in 1976 this law consolidated diverse regulations of public land management and strengthened the power of the BLM to manage public lands.

Feedback An information transmission that produces a circular flow of data in a system.

Fertility rate   The average number of children that women in a given population bear in their reproductive years.

Fertilizer   A substance added to the soil to improve plant growth. The most commonly used fertilizers are those containing large amounts of nitrogen, potassium, and phosphorus.

Fire frequency   The average number of fires per unit time at a given location.

First law of thermodynamics   The law of conservation of energy, which states that energy is neither created nor destroyed, but merely transformed from one state to another or converted to or from matter.

Fission   A process of splitting heavy atoms of uranium or plutonium into lighter elements, thereby releasing energy.

Fixed costs   Costs of operating a business that do not vary with the rate of output of goods and services.

Flood irrigation   A means of irrigation whereby entire fields are occasionally inundated.

Flow resource   A resource that is simultaneously used and replaced. Perpetual and renewable resources are flow resources.

Food chain   A linear path that food energy takes in passing from producer to consumers to decomposers in an ecosystem.

Food security   The condition of having both physical and economic access to the basic food that people need to function normally.

Food web   A complex, interlocking set of pathways that food energy takes in passing from producer to consumers to decomposers in an ecosystem.

Furrow irrigation   A type of irrigation in which water is allowed to flow along the furrows (troughs) between rows of crops.

Fusion   The combination of two hydrogen atoms to create a helium atom, yielding energy.

Gaia hypothesis   A view of earth history that emphasizes the earth's tendency to maintain a balance or equilibrium of natural systems.

GAP analysis   The use of remote sensing and GIS techniques to identify holes or gaps in land ownership for species protection.

General circulation model   A computerized representation of the earth's atmospheric and oceanic circulation system used to simulate weather and climate.

General Systems Theory   A way of looking at the world or any part of it as an interacting set of parts.

Generational equity   The fairness doctrine applied to subsequent generations so they receive the environment in the same or better condition than the generation before them.

Genetic damage   Damage to individual cell tissues resulting in changes that are passed along to offspring in chromosomes.

Geographic Information System (GIS)   A computer database and data-manipulation system designed to use geographically organized data.

Geologic estimate of resource   An estimate of the amount of a mineral resource in the earth based on information about the concentration and distribution of that mineral in rocks, without regard for the economics of extraction.

Geothermal energy   Energy extracted from heat contained in rocks near the earth's surface.

Geopressurized resource   A geothermal resource in which hot groundwater is pressurized by natural forces.

Grassland   A biome dominated by grasses. Most grasslands have semiarid climates.

Green Revolution   A variety of agricultural systems developed for application in developing countries, involving the introduction of improved seed varieties, fertilizers, and irrigation systems.

Greenhouse effect   The tendency of the atmosphere to be transparent to shortwave solar radiation but opaque to longwave terrestrial radiation, leading to a warming of the atmosphere.

Greenhouse gases   Substances that are transparent to shortwave (solar) radiation but absorb longwave (terrestrial) radiation and thus contribute to warming of the atmosphere. Carbon dioxide, ozone, chlorofluorocarbons, methane, and water vapor are important greenhouse gases.

Ground fire   A forest fire that only burns at ground level, consuming litter and downed trees but not live standing trees.

Groundwater mining.   See *Overdraft*.

Groundwater   Water below the ground surface, derived from the percolation of rainfall and seepage from surface water.

Guest worker   A person allowed in a country on a temporary basis in order to increase the available labor force in that country.

Gully   A steep-walled stream channel incised in the soil by accelerated erosion.

Gyres   A circular flow pattern in the ocean.

Habitat Land that provides living space and sustenance for plants and animals.

Halocline A marked change in salinity at a particular depth in the ocean or an estuary; it signals the boundary between two layers of water.

Hardwoods Trees with particularly dense wood; primarily broad-leafed trees.

Heavy-water reactor A nuclear fission reactor using deuterium-enriched water to moderate the fission reaction.

High seas Areas of the oceans beyond the legal control of any nation.

High-temperature gas-cooled reactor A nuclear fission reactor using helium gas to transfer heat from the core to a steam generator.

Homestead Act A law passed in 1862 providing 160 acres of federal land free to settlers.

Homocentric A view of nature that only considers human, rather than plant or animal, needs.

Homosphere The lower portion of the earth's atmosphere, characterized by relatively uniform gaseous composition. Consists of the troposphere, the stratosphere, and the mesosphere.

Horizon A layer in the soil with distinctive textural, mineralogical, chemical, or structural characteristics.

Hydroelectric power Electricity generated by passage of runoff-derived water through a turbine, usually at a dam.

Hydrothermal mineralization A process of concentration of metallic ores caused by high-temperature geochemical processes in underground waters.

Illegal immigrant A person who enters and lives in a country in violation of that country's laws.

Incommensurables Effects of a given action that can, with some effort, be given monetary value.

Increaser A range plant species that is present in a range ecosystem prior to grazing and that increases in numbers or coverage as a result of grazing.

Incrementalism A type of decision-making strategy that reacts to short-term imperfections in existing policies rather than establishing long-term future goals. Decisions are made on a sequential basis and do not radically depart from existing policy.

Infiltration capacity The maximum rate at which a soil can absorb water.

Inorganic Describes a chemical substance that does not contain carbon.

Input Energy, matter, or information entering a system.

In-stream uses Uses of water that do not require it to be removed from a stream or lake. They include such things as shipping, swimming, and waste disposal.

Intangible A good, service, or effect of an action that cannot be assigned monetary value.

Integrated pest management A pest control technique that relies on combinations of crop rotation, biological controls, and pesticides.

Interbasin transfer A movement of water from one drainage basin to another, such as from the east side of the Rocky Mountains into the west-flowing Colorado River.

Internal waters Waters under the exclusive control of a coastal nation, including bays, estuaries, and rivers.

International Whaling Commission (IWC) An organization set up under the International Convention for the Regulation of Whaling in 1946, to regulate the whaling industry.

Invader A range plant species not present in a given area before grazing but entering the area as a result of the ecological changes caused by grazing.

Irrigation The artificial application of water to a crop or pasture beyond that supplied by direct precipitation.

Kerogen A waxy hydrocarbon found in oil shale.

Labor theory of value An approach to valuing commodities based on the amount of human labor required to produce them.

Land Capability Classification System A scheme used by the U.S. Natural Resource Conservation Service for assessing and classifying the productivity of land units.

Landfill A land-based disposal method, in which waste is deposited in layers and covered with earth.

Law of entropy The second law of thermodynamics. Entropy is a measure of disorder in a system.

Law of the Sea Treaty A treaty establishing jurisdiction over marine resources in coastal and deep-sea areas.

Leachate Water seeping from the bottom of a layer of ground and containing substances derived from that layer. Usually applied to landfills and other contamination sources.

Light-water reactor A type of nuclear power plant that uses ordinary water as the cooling medium.

Lignite   A rank of coal characterized by a relatively low degree of modification of plant matter.

Limits to Growth   A world model developed in the 1970s by a group called the Club of Rome; it predicted resource scarcity if world population and resource use growth continued.

Liquefaction   Conversion of coal into a liquid hydrocarbon that can be transported by pipeline and burned as a liquid.

Liquid-metal fast-breeder reactor   A nuclear fission reactor moderated and cooled by liquid sodium, and used to convert nonfissionable material such as uranium–238 to fissionable material such as plutonium–289.

Liquid natural gas (LNG)   Natural gaseous hydrocarbons that are pressurized and cooled in order to be stored and/or transported in liquid form.

Malthus   British economist who wrote (1798) that populations increase geometrically while food supplies increase arithmetically.

Materials balance principle   An approach to production systems that focuses on accounting and balancing inputs and outputs.

Maximum sustainable yield   The largest average harvest of a species that can be indefinitely sustained under existing environmental conditions.

Mesosphere   Layer of the atmosphere between 30 and 50 mi (50 and 80 km) in altitude, characterized by decreasing temperatures with increasing altitude.

Migration   The movement of people from one area to another in response to warfare, environmental degradation or perceived better opportunities.

Mined-land reclamation   The return of land disturbed by mining to a more productive condition, usually a use similar to that existing before mining took place.

Minimum tillage   A soil and water conservation technique that leaves the crop residue or stubble on the surface rather than plowing it under to minimize the number of times a field is tilled. Weeds are controlled by herbicides.

Mining Act   An act passed in 1872 providing free access to minerals on federal lands.

Mixed cropping   An agricultural system in which several different crops are grown in close proximity, in a rotation system, or both.

Mobile sources   Sources of air pollution that move, such as automobiles, boats, trains, and aircraft.

Monoculture   An agricultural system in which a single crop is grown repeatedly over a large area.

Monopoly   Control of access to a good or service by a single entity.

Montreal Protocol   An agreement signed in Montreal in 1987 in which signatory nations consented to limit production and consumption of ozone-damaging chemicals.

Multinational corporation   A business entity that operates in many nations and is not wholly subject to the laws of any one nation.

Multiple use   The use of lands for as many different purposes as possible in order to gain maximum benefit from them.

Multiple Use Sustained Yield Act   A law passed in 1960 establishing the principles of multiple use and sustained yield as guidelines for management of the national forests.

Municipal solid waste   Mixed solid waste derived primarily from residential and commercial sources.

National Forest Management Act   An act, passed in 1976, establishing operating principles and administrative divisions for the U.S. Forest Service.

National sovereignty   The right of individual nations to look after their own interests first and foremost and to manage resources within their territorial borders any way they see fit.

Natural capital   The stock of natural resources that provide or can be used to make benefical things.

Natural gas   Gaseous hydrocarbons extracted from subterranean reservoirs that hold gas at normal ambient temperatures.

Natural increase   In demography, the net change in population without regard to migration. It is the birth rate less the death rate, and it can be positive or negative.

Natural resource   Something that is useful to humans and exists independent of human activity.

Natural resource accounting   The inclusion of the full and often hidden costs of damages to natural resources in traditional benefit/cost analysis.

Neo-Malthusianism   Modern advocates of Thomas Malthus's ideas; those who advocate birth control to avert overpopulation and who see overpopulation as ultimately leading to widespread malnourishment and famine.

NEPA   The National Environmental Policy Act, signed on January 1, 1970, which established nationwide environmental goals for the United States and provided for the preparation of Environmental Impact Statements (EIS) to ensure compliance with those goals.

Net primary production   The net amount of biomass created by plants in an ecosystem once the respiration by those plants is deducted.

Neutral stuff   Something that exists but at present meets no known human material or non-material needs.

Nonpoint source   A pollution source that is diffuse, such as urban runoff.

Nonrenewable or stock resources   Resources that exist in finite quantity and are not replaced in nature.

Off-stream use   Use of water that requires that it be removed or withdrawn from surface or groundwater.

Oil   Hydrocarbons found in the earth, liquid at normal ambient temperatures.

Oligopolistic competition   A process in which a small group controls access to a good or service by agreeing on a single price or by restricting access to these commodities.

Oligotrophic   Describes lakes that are relatively deep and nutrient poor; opposite of eutrophic.

Organic   Refers to substances containing carbon.

Output   Energy, matter, or information leaving a system.

Overburden   Rock and soil that lie above coal or other mineral deposits and that must be removed to strip-mine the coal.

Overdraft or groundwater mining   Withdrawal of groundwater in excess of the replacement rate over a long period of time.

Overgrazing   Grazing by a number of animals exceeding the carrying capacity of a given parcel of land.

Overland flow   Water flowing on the soil surface and unchannelized, usually derived from precipitation that has not infiltrated.

Oxidants   A group of air pollutants that are strong oxidizing agents. Ozone and peroxyacetylnitrate are among the more important oxidants.

Ozone hole   A semi–permanent depletion in stratospheric ozone concentration over a polar region. Most prominent over the South Pole.

Parent material   The mineral matter from which soil is formed.

Particulate matter   In reference to air quality, solid or liquid particles with diameters from 0.03 to 100 microns.

Passive solar power   The collection of solar energy as heat at the end-use site, without any mechanical redistribution or storage of the energy.

Pastoral nomad   A person who herds animals, and has no permanent place of residence.

Pastoralist   A person whose livelihood is based on grazing animals.

Pasture   In U.S. terminology, land on which the natural vegetation is not grass, but which is used primarily for grazing.

Peat   The accumulated remains of plants, found in swampy or cool, humid areas. It is the initial material from which coal may be formed; may be dried and used for fuel.

Performance-based resource estimate   An estimate of the quantity of a mineral deposit available in the earth based primarily on the ability of prevailing technology to extract the mineral under existing and probable future economic conditions.

Permafrost   Ground below 32°F (0°C) all year round.

Permeability   A measure of the rate at which water will flow into or through soil or rocks.

Perpetual resources   Resources that exist in continual supply, no matter how much they are used. Solar energy is an example.

Pesticide   A general term used to refer to a chemical used to control harmful organisms such as insects, fungi, rodents, worms, and bacteria. Insecticides, fungicides, and rodenticides are kinds of pesticides.

Petajoule   A unit of energy equal to 10^{15} [ten to the 15], or 1,000,000,000,000,000 joules, or 947,800,000,000 British thermal units.

Photosynthesis   The formation of carbohydrates from carbon dioxide and water, utilizing light as energy.

Photovoltaic cell   A semiconductor-based device used to convert sunlight directly to electricity.

Placer deposit   A deposit of a mineral formed by a concentration of heavy minerals in flowing water, such as by a stream or waves.

Point source   A pollution source that has a precise, identifiable location, such as a pipe or smokestack.

Polluter pays principle, or **residuals tax**   A means of shifting the cost of pollution from the community to the polluter, usually in the form of a tax.

Pollution   Human additions of undesirable substances to the environment.

Pollution prevention   The elimination of potential pollutants at their source such as in a manufacturing process, rather than at the point of discharge to the environment (end-of-pipe) or later.

Pollution Standards Index (PSI) An index of air quality that is a combined measure of the health effects of several pollutants. It ranges from 0 (healthy) to 500 (extremely unhealthy).

Population dynamics The study of the rapidity and causes of population change.

Population pyramid A graphic representation of the number or portion of males and females in each of several age categories in a population.

Potential evapotranspiration The amount of water that could be evaporated or transpired if it were available.

Potential resource A portion of the natural or human environment that is not today considered of value, but that one day may gain value as a result of technological, cognitive, or economic developments.

Preservation The nonuse of resources; limited resource development for the purpose of saving resources for the future.

Primary standards Air pollution standards designed to protect human health.

Primary treatment Sewage treatment consisting of removal of solids by sedimentation, flocculation, screening, or similar methods.

Principle of limiting factors Whatever factor (nutrient, water, sunlight, etc.) is in shortest supply will limit the growth and development of an organism or a community.

Prior appropriation A doctrine of water ownership in which the first productive user of water establishes the right to the water indefinitely; the primary water-ownership doctrine in the western United States.

Privatization The transfer of government-owned resources, such as national forests, to private ownership or management.

Procedural Equity A situation in which there is a differential application of environmental regulations, laws, or treaties such that some areas bear more pollution burdens than others.

Production theory of value An approach to valuing commodities based on the inputs of some critical commodity needed to make it.

Proxy value A price applied to a commodity that has no established market value.

Quad A measure of energy use, equal to one quadrillion (1,000,000,000,000,000) British thermal units.

Radiation inversion A temperature inversion caused by radiational cooling of air close to the ground.

Radioactivity The emission of particles by the decay of atoms of certain substances.

Railroad Acts A series of acts passed in the United States in the 1850s and 1860s granting large amounts of land to railroad companies as a subsidy to railway construction and stimulant to settlement of western lands.

Range condition As defined by the U.S. Forest Service, an estimate of the degree to which the present vegetation and ground cover depart from that which is presumed to be the natural potential (or climax) for the site.

Rangeland Land that provides or is capable of providing forage for grazing animals.

Recycling Reprocessing of a used product for reuse in a similar or different form.

Relative scarcity Short supply of a resource in one or more areas due to inadequate or disrupted distribution.

Renewable energy Energy resources that are produced naturally as fast as they are consumed, such as solar, wind, and hydroelectric power.

Renewable resource A resource that can be depleted but will be replenished by natural processes. Forests and fisheries are examples.

Replacement cost The cost of replacing a resource that is used.

Replacement level The number of births that will replace a population at the same size, without reduction or rise; also called Zero Population Growth.

Reserve In the context of mineral resources, a deposit of known location and quality that is economically extractable at the present time.

Residual Waste products of production. Air pollution is an example of residuals from manufacturing.

Residual tax A tax on production based on the amount of waste produced.

Residuals management An approach to production of goods and services that includes accounting of waste products associated with both production and consumption phases.

Resource Something that is useful to humans.

Resource recovery Separation of waste into recyclable components such as metal, glass, and heat from incineration.

Respiration Oxidation of food that releases oxygen, water, and energy, which are dissipated in the biosphere.

Reuse Repeated use of a product without reprocessing or remanufacture.

Rill A small channel created by soil erosion and small enough to be obliterated by plowing.

Riparian areas Lands adjacent to and subject to flooding by streams.

Riparian rights A doctrine of water ownership in which those whose land adjoins a stream have the right to use the water in the stream. It is the primary water-ownership doctrine in the eastern United States.

Ruminant One of a group of grazing animals including cattle, bison, sheep, goat, which have digestive systems particularly adapted to grasses.

Sahel A semiarid east-west swath across Africa, environmentally transitional between the Sahara Desert (to the north) and equatorial rainforests (to the south), in which recent desertification and drought have been particularly severe.

Salinity The concentration of mineral salts in water. The average salinity of the oceans is about 35 parts per thousand.

Saltwater intrusion Movement of salt water into aquifers formerly occupied by fresh water as a result of groundwater withdrawal in coastal areas.

Satisficing A decision-making strategy that seeks a course of action that is good enough but not necessarily perfect. A few alternatives are compared, and the best course of action is chosen from this limited range of options.

Savanna Tropical or subtropical semiarid grassland with scattered trees.

Secondary standard An air-quality standard designed to protect human welfare (property, vegetation, etc.) as opposed to health.

Secondary treatment Sewage treatment that removes organic matter and nutrients by biological decomposition using such methods as trickling filters, aeration, and activated sludge.

Sedentarization Permanent settlement of once-nomadic people.

Sedimentation Deposition of solid particles by settling in a water body.

Selective cutting A timber-harvesting technique in which only trees of specified size or species are taken, leaving other trees.

Separate impacts Effects of a system's activity that can be measured separately.

Shadow price An artificial monetary value applied to those resources for which a simple price tag is not easy to calculate, for example, wilderness, habitat.

Shale oil see also *kerogen*. A petroleum-like substance found in high concentrations in some shale rocks.

Shelterwood cutting A two-phase timber-harvesting technique in which not all trees are taken in the first phase so that some trees may provide shelter for young seedlings; when these are established, the remaining older trees are cut.

Smog A term used to describe air pollution.

Social cost The cost of producing a good or service, plus its cost to humans in terms of pollution and other negative socio–environmental effects.

Social equity Situations in which there are different pollution burdens or access to resources based on race, ethnicity, age, or gender.

Softwoods Timber species with relatively low-density wood; primarily needle-leaf trees.

Soil A porous layer of mineral and organic matter at the earth's surface, formed as a result of the action of chemical and biological processes on rocks over a period of time.

Soil erodibility A measure of the inherent susceptibility of a soil to erosion, without regard to topography, vegetation cover, management, or weather conditions.

Soil fertility The ability of a soil to support plant growth through providing water, nutrients, and a growth medium.

Soil structure The way in which individual soil particles form aggregates, particularly the shapes and arrangement of such aggregates; especially important to soil hydrologic characteristics.

Soil texture The mix of different sizes of particles in a soil.

Solid waste Refuse materials composed primarily of solids at normal ambient temperatures.

Somatic damage Nonhereditary damage to individual cell tissues from radiation.

Species A group of organisms with similar genetic and morphologic characteristics that are capable of interbreeding.

Spent fuel Nuclear material that is no longer capable of sustaining the fission process.

Sprinkler irrigation Irrigation by pumping water under pressure through nozzles and spraying it over the land.

Stakeholders Individuals or groups who have a vested interest in a particular issue or policy or could be adversely affected.

Stationary source A pollution source that does not move, such as a smokestack.

Steady state When a system has inputs that equal outputs.

Stock resource See *Nonrenewable or stock resources.*

Stockpiling Amassing amounts of some substance well beyond present needs in anticipation of a shortage of that substance.

Strategic mineral A mineral necessary for defense purposes for which the United States is totally dependent on foreign sources.

Stratification A layering of a water body caused by differences in water density. It is commonly caused by temperature or salinity differences.

Stratified estuary An arm of the sea in which fresh water from the land overlies denser salt water.

Stratosphere Layer of the atmosphere between 3 and 30 mi (5 and 50 km) in altitude, characterized by increasing temperature with altitude.

Stress management A decision-making strategy that is reactive in nature. Once a resource issue becomes critical, then policy is determined to cope with the immediate problem without any consideration of long-term implications of such a policy.

Strip cropping A soil conservation technique in which parallel strips of land are planted in different crops.

Strip-mining or surface mining Extraction of a mineral from the ground by excavation at the ground surface.

Stubble mulch A soil covering composed of the unused stalks of crop plants.

Subbituminous coal A rank of coal intermediate between lignite and bituminous coal.

Subeconomic resource A resource that at present is unavailable for use because of the high cost of extraction.

Subsidence inversion A temperature inversion caused by differential warming of a sinking air mass. Upper portions of the mass are warmed more than lower portions, causing the inversion.

Subsidence Sinking of the land surface caused by removal of water, oil, or minerals from beneath the surface.

Substitutability The degree to which one material can be substituted for another in end uses.

Sulfur content The amount of sulfur found in coal. Combustion of coal with a high sulfur content results in emissions of sulfur oxides, which contribute to acid precipitation.

Surface fire A moderate-intensity forest fire in which low-level vegetation, such as shrubs, is consumed along with some of the surfaces (bark) of trees, but the crowns of trees are not consumed and trees survive.

Surface water Water and ice found in rivers, lakes, swamps, and other above-ground water bodies.

Suspended particulates In reference to air quality, solid or liquid particles with diameters from 0.03 to 100 microns.

Sustainability Economic growth with environmental responsibility; economic activity that could be carried on indefinitely without resource depletion.

Sustainable agriculture An agricultural system that is dependent solely on renewable resources and that maintains the soil in such a condition so that it will continue to be productive indefinitely.

Sustained yield Management of renewable resources conducted in such a way as to allow a constant rate of harvest indefinitely.

Synergistic impacts Effects of a system's activity that are different from the individual effects of component parts of the system.

Synfuel A contraction of synthetic fuel; liquid or gaseous fossil fuel manufactured from other fuels that are less useful as found in nature.

System An entity consisting of a set of parts that work together to form a whole. The human body, a transportation network, and the earth are all systems.

Tailings Solid waste products derived from mineral extraction or refinement.

Tar sand Sandy deposits containing heavy oil or tar. The sand must be heated to extract the oil.

Taylor Grazing Act An act passed in 1934 closing most United States public lands to homesteading and establishing controls on grazing use of federal lands.

Temperate forest A biome characterized primarily by deciduous broad-leaved trees.

Temperature inversion A condition in the atmosphere in which warm air overlies cool air. Inversions restrict vertical air circulation.

Terracing A soil and water conservation technique consisting of ridges on the contour, or level areas constructed on a slope.

Territorial sea A band of open ocean adjacent to the coast, over which the coastal nation has control. It is generally either 3 or 12 nautical miles (5.6 or 22 km) wide.

Tertiary treatment Any of a wide range of advanced sewage treatment processes aimed at removing substances not eliminated by primary or secondary treatment.

Thermal pollution Heat added by humans to a water body or to the air.

Thermocline A zone in a water body in which temperature declines rapidly with increasing depth. Vertical water circulation is limited by the presence of a thermocline.

Threatened species A species that is not endangered but has a rapidly declining population.

Throughput tax, or **disposal charge** A fee paid by a producer on materials that go into the production of polluting products. The fee reflects the social cost of the pollution.

Tidal power Energy generated by using tidal water-level differences to drive a turbine

Timber Culture Act An act passed in 1873 providing free access to timber on federal lands.

Toxic substance A substance that causes disease or death when organisms are exposed to it in very low quantities.

Total dissolved solids The total amount of dissolved solid matter found in a sample of water.

Transboundary pollution Transport of pollutants (particularly air pollutants) across national or state boundaries.

Trophic level One of the steps in a food chain.

Tropical rainforest A biome composed primarily of evergreen broad-leaved trees growing in tropical areas of high rainfall throughout most of the year.

Troposphere The lowest layer of the atmosphere, below about 9 mi (15 km) in altitude, characterized by decreasing temperature with increasing altitude.

Tundra A biome found in arctic and subarctic regions consisting of a dense growth of lichens, mosses, and herbs.

Underground mining A mineral extraction technique consisting of subsurface excavation with minimal disturbance of the ground surface.

Unidentified resource A mineral resource assumed to be present within known geologic districts, but not yet specifically located or characterized in detail.

Universal Soil Loss Equation A statistical technique developed by the U.S. Department of Agriculture for predicting the average erosion rate by rainfall under a variety of climatic, soil, topographic, and management conditions.

Upwelling An upward movement of seawater that usually occurs near the margins of oceans.

Uranium An element, two isotopes of which (^{235}U and ^{238}U) are important in atomic energy production.

Urban runoff Runoff derived from urban areas, usually containing relatively high concentrations of pollutants; also called urban stormwater.

Variable costs Costs of production that vary with the rate of output.

Visual blight Modification of a landscape that is visually undesirable.

Wastewater reclamation Any process in which wastewater is put to use, such as for cooling or irrigation, with or without treatment.

Water harvesting Any of several techniques for increasing the amount of runoff derived from a land area.

Water-holding capacity The ability of the soil to retain or store water.

Water table The upper limit of groundwater or of the saturated zone.

Weathering The breakdown of rocks into smaller particles or new chemical substances as a result of exposure to water and air at the earth's surface.

Willingness to pay A method of determining the proxy value of a resource by asking how much users of that resource would be willing to pay to use or not use it.

Windbreak A line of trees or shrubs planted perpendicular to the prevailing winds, designed to reduce wind velocities and thus reduce wind erosion.

Withdrawal The removal of water from surface water or groundwater.

Zero population growth A term applied to the fertility rate needed to attain a stable population over a long period of time.

Zoning A system of land-use management in which land is classified according to permitted uses.

INDEX